# TAMLA MOTOWN

*The Stories Behind The UK Singles*

First published in Great Britain in 2009 by Cherry Red Books (a division of Cherry Red Records Ltd.), 3a Long Island House, Warple Way, London W3 ORG.

Copyright Terry Wilson © 2009

ISBN: 1 978-1-901447-31-6

Design: Dave Johnson

# TAMLA MOTOWN

## *The Stories Behind The UK Singles*

### *Terry Wilson*

CHERRY RED BOOKS

# CONTENTS

*"Motown is the greatest event that ever happened in the history of music."*
**Smokey Robinson**

# PREFACE

Within the considerable volume of literature devoted to the music scene of the 1960s and 70s, the story of Motown, the most important and influential label of the era by a mile, has been underplayed. Partly this has to do with the significance accorded to various musical genres by scholars well versed in the movements and styles both reflected in and by 'serious' artists during this key era. Predominantly focussing on white acts whose music is comparatively easy to interpret as highbrow, the intellectual elite have canonised fairly marginal bands such as Love and The Velvet Underground while paying disproportionately little attention to what is seen as the unsophisticated, happy-go-lucky style of Motown soul. By way of example, *NME's* respected *Book Of Rock* with its potted biography of hundreds of acts well-known and not-so-well-known (and which was used as a standard point of reference for this book) carries a mere 65 lines on Motown, fewer than specific acts such as Credence Clearwater Revival, Rod Stewart or Family, and no individual entry at all for The Supremes, whose dozen US number 1s has been bettered only by Elvis and The Beatles. (The volume's coverage is, incidentally, entirely typical.) Possibly Motown is not deemed to fall in within the definition of 'rock'; yet if this is the reason for the omission, then what can account for the inclusion of profiles of Roberta Flack, Gilbert O'Sullivan, Hot Chocolate, Dolly Parton and many others?

In the face of what amounts to arbitrary selectivity, David Morse has argued persuasively against the prevailing values of musical criticism, indicating that its bias results from a view of rock shaped by an elitist product of a narrowly defined culture. Proposing that the distinction between 'serious' and 'non-serious' music is in the ear of the listener, he contends that the terms themselves remove the critic's obligation to explain why 'serious' is necessarily interchangeable with 'good', and the reverse argument is made by implication: "Why shouldn't we praise a record that is good for dancing not simply as good *dance* music but as good music?".[1]

The fact is Motown's legacy, with its unparalleled roster of acts, glittering catalogue of hit singles and inestimable knock-on throughout modern music, is every bit as articulate, as artistically influential, and as socially and politically significant as the *œuvre* of The Beatles or Bob Dylan, with a broadly cohesive body of work which is, to all intents and purposes, a popular style in its own right: It's just that critics routinely fail to acknowledge the fact. Moreover Motown's far-reaching innovations such as pioneering pop videos (see [502]) and use of 8-track recording[2], which pushed the wider industry forward, have tended to go largely unacknowledged and are seldom commented upon. Few have attempted to fully document all of this, notable exceptions being Nelson George and Sharon Davis, whose respective accounts can both stake some claim to being the definitive narrative on Motown. Others have also pitched in contributions from a number of perspectives, yet none thus far have succeeded in conveying all of the salient points in Motown's history, or placing it in the context of the music of the day.

Motown's volume of recorded output, taken in its entirety, is of incalculable importance to the development of post-war popular music. Many of the stylistic developments which Motown gave rise to have seeped so totally into the culture of pop and soul that to imagine the field without their input is impossible. Their influence on the emergent Beatles, Rolling Stones and Who alone has fundamentally altered the soundscape of the 1960s, which in the perspective of modern music is tantamount to affecting everything to have come in its wake. And that is to say nothing of the social and political waves made by the breakthrough of several esteemed black performers into the popular mainstream, standing equally alongside their white contemporaries. As Tom Schultheiss succinctly observed in 1988, Motown's impact went beyond the boundaries of music itself, "Motown can't be viewed simply as a record company; it assumes the role of catalyst for social change. It becomes a shaper of race relations, of human relationships, as much as it is a business. The simple fact is you can't preserve your prejudices for very long when you're laughing *with* someone of another skin colour, any more than you can hate and sing along with Smokey at the same time".[3]

Nevertheless, some will no doubt question why a study such as this, intent on 'documenting' Motown needs to exist at all. When all is said and done, music—especially soul music—is experienced full-body by the listener, something which no amount of words could hope to accurately define. Yet it is within human scope to be moved by any act of artistic creation and to seek further understanding; given the significance of Motown on Western culture and popular art during the last half-century, the label deserves full documentation and readers will no doubt find this book useful in drawing attention to specific areas in which the company's recorded work is exceptional. In the end, Motown is nothing without the records it released, or, to quote the company's publicity machine, 'It's what's in the groove that counts'. The central purpose of the work is an examination and evaluation of the *music* of Motown, the songs which have thrilled generations, and the hits which separately and collectively defined the enigmatic Motown Sound.

The narrative attempts to deconstruct its subject via the UK singles. The Tamla Motown label was international but never existed in America, where the company was based. For the home market, Berry Gordy set up a series of labels of varying stature, but in Britain it fell to existing big companies to retail Motown until March 1965, whereupon Tamla Motown was launched. Everything to come out from then onwards appeared on the new label, excepting a period in the early-1970s when the UK also started issuing certain Motown-sourced singles on Rare Earth and Mo-West respectively (see Appendix 3). (For Berry Gordy, American sales accounted for around half of his total global revenue, most of the rest coming from Europe. Given that US profits were spread across numerous imprints, the international 50% makes Tamla Motown easily his biggest brand name.)

Because of the potentially confusing terminology, the terms Tamla, Motown and Tamla Motown, all too often considered freely interchangeable in Britain, are used advisedly in this volume. 'Tamla Motown' refers always to the UK label and its parent UK-based organisation and 'Tamla' specifically to the American label of that name. The term 'Motown' however has three generally accepted applications which are worth defining: 1. The Motown Corporation itself; 2. The US Motown record label; 3. The blue UK label used from the end of 1976 onwards (which is often identified here for the sake of clarity as Motown-UK or Motown-EMI).

Motown began its operations in America in 1959, and from then until March 1965 a number of recordings which have gone down in legend were released in the UK under license to various British labels including London American, Fontana, Oriole American and Stateside. Because Tamla Motown was in existence only between 1965 and 1976, the scope of this work is very much delimited in time. The early singles are examined briefly in turn due to their importance in the development of the label, but those released on Motown-EMI after 1976 are excluded. The same applies to the Mo-West/Rare Earth singles mentioned above, which although in a general sense Motown product are by definition beyond the bounds of the study.

It could be argued that the cut-off years 1965 and 1976 are arbitrary points of reference, and to some extent this is true. Yet tackling *everything* Motown ever released would multiply this volume several times and risk meaninglessness, besides becoming too unwieldy a project for this author (the US tally runs towards 2,000 standard singles). In fact, virtually all the key hits to emerge from Motown in America appeared on Tamla Motown at some point, lending some credence to the notion that the label was effectively acting as a filter for less notable releases and specialising in the best the company had to offer. The point is of course contentious, and the UK singles discography includes nothing by Carolyn Crawford, Frances Nero, The Monitors, Linda Griner, Hattie Littles and other artists which the connoisseur may be appalled to see spurned. On the other hand, US readers will recognise many of the entries here as amongst the best-loved and most famous Motown titles, a robust sample of the company's total output and an engaging catalogue of recordings made during the (variously defined) 'Golden Era'.

Within the pages which follow, frequent mention is made of musical influences which have contributed to this or that composition or recording. In so doing there is an unstated acknowledgement that no musical creation exists within a vacuum. What I am attempting to convey is the development of music via the way successive ideas become infused into those who hear them. Influences from other artists of the day can often be traced through Motown's singles, and in drawing a developmental link between, for example, The Rolling Stones' "Sympathy For The Devil" and David Ruffin's "My Whole World Ended (The Moment You Left Me)", no suggestion of plagiarism is made—nor is such implied in the apparent reverse influence from "It's The Same Old Song" through to "Under My Thumb". Rather, there is a recognition that, in those days, popular recording artists would as a matter of course listen to one another with keen interest and take on board particularly striking ideas which they would consciously utilise as elements in their subsequent work. Funk Brother Hank Cosby for example observed of Norman Whitfield that, "He would bring me three different records and say, 'I want four bars of this, four bars of that, followed by these four bars from the other one'. He put his things together from pieces of other people's songs".[4] Stevie Wonder meantime, and his regular 1960s writing partners Sylvia Moy and Hank Cosby, elevated the method to a craft, scarcely any of their period works failing to announce loudly and clearly where their ingredients were inspired.

Many such hits were derived wilfully from earlier works by the same writers, specific melodic, structural and arrangement techniques openly re-worked in an attempt to revive winning formulae, lending to the widely perceived homogeny of the label's product. Virtually all of the leading writers attempted to deconstruct and re-assemble their own work, a prime example in this respect being the HDH team, David Morse's analysis of their technique finding that they, "Ruthlessly cannibalise old songs for spare parts; verbal phrases, thematic ideas, musical figures, accompaniments, even saxophone solos are shuffled together and reworked from disc to disc; every song is a collage".[5]

This method of writing is itself not unusual. Classical composers for example have frequently written pieces around specific musical phrases, or perhaps deconstructed a figure and re-assembled its components to make something new. However in the light of these observations, it is worth mentioning the tendency of popular music critics to over-intellectualise their subjects. Perhaps the most famous example of this failing is William Mann's suggestion in late-1963 that Lennon—McCartney incorporated Aeolian cadences into "Not A Second Time" in respect of Mahler's *Das Lied Von Der Erde*, when in fact they were either discovered by chance, or more probably, 'nicked' from doo-wop records, the primary point of reference most likely Smokey Robinson. (Lennon on the Aeolian cadence: "I have no idea what they are. They sound like exotic birds".) This incident, which has gone down in popular legend, has served to alert more knowledgeable critics to this essentially self-referential fault and yet did not stop Steve Lodder from remarking in his excellent study that Stevie Wonder's vision for his 1976 *Songs In The Key Of Life* was all-encompassing "like a Mahler symphony" (p98) when in truth the grand album's concept was merely an extension of Wonder's approach as developed on his previous three albums, this time running to a self-indulgent double set, which was transparent in its calculation to present him as above and beyond the plane of worldly existence.

In the case of Motown writers, musical inspiration would generally come from immediate surroundings—remarks made in conversation, chord changes overheard on the radio, some or other new dance craze—which could readily find a home in a new or developing composition. Despite the fact that several staff writers took an interest in classical music (a shot of Brian Holland reproduced in Nelson George's *Where Did Our Love Go* shows him seated with an LP of Bach pieces at his left elbow[6]) it is a perilous business to suggest the infusion of complex musicological ideas into Motown recordings, in the main constructed by untrained personnel. A notable exception to this would be Motown's string arrangers, particularly Paul Riser but others too, who clearly worked from an awareness of classical techniques, albeit slaved in practise to the pre-constructed form of each new song-in-progress.

Motown's philosophy from day one was to generate commercial clout with crowd-pleasing singles and with this in mind, with due acknowledgement of influential historical figures such as Ray Charles, Nat King Cole, Sam Cooke, The Coasters, The Drifters and so on, Motown's main point of reference was little outside of the recent top 40 and/or what fellow Motown writers were coming up with. While the development of soul and later funk in the 1960s undoubtedly affected what they were doing, one looks more in the direction of The Beatles than, for example, James Brown when contextualising the singles output. (This is clearly illustrated in the listing of non-Motown compositions released as singles by Tamla Motown, as listed in the section 'Facts & Feats'. Material by Lennon—McCartney, Neil Diamond, Phil Spector, Burt Bacharach etc. appears, but nothing by, for example, Otis Redding. There is one exception: Wilson Pickett's "Don't Knock My Love" [953].)

There is a case for arguing that Motown's most popular tracks were not 'soul' singles but pop music which happened to be performed by black personnel. Yet while there are obviously exceptions to this, in the context of the 1960s an outfit such as HDH should be seen as popular writers rather than specifically 'soul' writers; when Motown stars normally supplied by HDH performed white-sourced tracks such as The Four Tops' "If I Were A Carpenter", the level of objective soul in the recording is no less apparent than in Motown originals such as "Something About You", and compared to HDH originals such as "You Keep Me Hangin' On" [585], is arguably higher. The distinctive element of 'soul' lies in the qualities of the performance, as much as in the raw material.

On the matter of The Beatles, it should be acknowledged that the format of the book is based on the groundbreaking study *Revolution In The Head* by the late Ian MacDonald, a work of great influence in modern musical criticism. Following his lead, every entry in this volume is numbered for ease of cross-reference. Rather than introduce a system starting at [001], the decision was made to use the original TMG catalogue numbers as reference points. Thus, the first full entry in this book, TMG 501 is referenced throughout as [501], the last, TMG 1040 as [1040] and use of square brackets specifically indicates song entries in the main text of the book—all TMG numbers used after the Tamla Motown label was effectively wound up in 1976 are written in full. In other cases, the occasional use of the suffix a or b (as in [688b]) denotes, specifically, one or other side of the single in question, and the suffix n directs the reader to a footnote.

In addition to the main sequence, the 72 UK releases prior to the creation of the Tamla Motown label are also numbered. In these cases the prefix E is used to denote 'early', the separate numbering system running from [E01] upwards. This is mainly to help cross-referencing later on, and these entries are not fully annotated in the same way that the Tamla Motown singles are. A similar parallel system exists for releases on Tamla Motown in the years after 1976 (there being 119 so far), which are referenced with L signifying 'late', running from [L001] upwards.

Besides a discussion of the music itself, the scope of a study such as MacDonald's does not square with my own. Dealing with the story of a single band is comparatively straight-forward, with a handful of personalities to consider, and a fairly narrow focus of events. Motown by contrast is a huge subject, taking in the lives and activities of dozens of regular musicians, a clutch of world-class songwriters, producers and arrangers, and a wide roster of recording acts (The Miracles alone released almost twice as many recordings as The Beatles). Furthermore, by the time Tamla Motown issued their first 45, the involved personnel had been up and running for years, precluding a complete developmental study, and while this volume has no biographical pretensions the career of a figure such as Marvin Gaye reveals itself via his releases which are used as an opportunity to convey significant events in his current life and development.

For reasons obvious to those familiar with Tamla Motown's legacy, singles are focussed on exclusively. During the era under examination, Motown's studio albums were, virtually without exception, patchy affairs containing a smattering of in-house covers and an obligatory single or three, padded out with any amount of 'filler' usually including hits popularised by other artists. In truth, Motown was never an album label, the sheer volume of recordings in schedule at any given time effectively prohibiting sustained work on long-players, especially given Motown's predominant reliance on its one core studio band until 1972. Some are creditable though: The Isley Brothers' *This Old Heart Of Mine*, The Four Tops' *Still Waters* and The Miracles' *Make It Happen* are examples of LPs which, despite adhering to the company formula, are well worth repeated plays. Yet excepting perhaps self-directed and critically acclaimed album projects by Marvin Gaye, Stevie Wonder and (as producer) Norman Whitfield in the early-1970s, the LP format remained a side issue for Tamla Motown, making the 45, on which effort and creativity was at a peak, the natural focus of study, at least for the first two thirds of the era. Towards the middle of the 1970s Motown slipped into the wider industry convention of embarking on album projects from which singles were subsequently pinpointed and lifted in a turn-around of policy, although the bulk of these continued to be padded to some or other extent with cover material.

Those well-versed in Motown lore will have come across each of the singles under discussion, but few will own copies of them all. For most lay readers, many will be obscure and their documentation may prompt some investment in some of the lesser-known gems in the catalogue. In the main, Tamla Motown singles are not hard to locate, yet the scarcer ones command startlingly high prices on original 45. In part, this has helped fuel the label's re-issue policy whereby a good number of the little-known releases have appeared on CD, and often at reasonable prices. Others are more easily found via second hand copies of their concurrent albums or the substantial number of artist-specific compilations which have been put out on vinyl and CD over the years (the vinyl *Anthology* sets being largely comprehensive for each artist in this respect). Those seeking to track down a copy of each recording should also check out internet auction houses to locate the more difficult ones.

Because of the book's inherent nature, UK releases and chart activity take precedence in the discussion. UK releases in the main trailed those in America, many of which might not have appeared in Britain were they to fail the acid commerciality test at home, although from about 1972 the UK schedules attained significant independence. The corresponding US edition of each single is given, although it should not be assumed that both sides of each 45 necessarily always match, and the term 'equivalent' is used to indicate a parallel, though not necessarily identical American issue. The UK and US chart data is also given, taken from the most widely accepted listings in each country (*Record Retailer* and *Billboard* respectively). The pop chart is taken as standard for the US discussion, but *Billboard* also published a tandem R & B chart, and for the sake of interest, this data is also provided in each header block.[7] In all cases this is limited to a top 40, partly for the sake of relevance, and partly due to the availability of data. Placings outside of the 40 are always given as null, although the singles in question might well have charted lower.

Recording dates have not yet been fully published for all titles. Motown has latterly taken to supplementing retrospective CD releases with good quality sleeve notes which have pinned down the sessions to many tracks, although a substantial number remain unknown at the time of writing. Motown's standard practise was to record backing tracks in stages, generally dubbing the vocal on towards the end of the process. Because of this most tracks were not recorded on a single date, and I have opted to cite the final session for each A-side where known, rather than list an incomprehensible series of dates. (The discussion following each title will bring out any further points of interest in this respect.) Mention is due here to Keith Hughes whose industrious ongoing research into such matters has been consulted and is available via his *Don't Forget The Motor City* website, constructed for the net by Ritchie Hardin, and periodically updated as the work progresses.

Similar issues arise in the collation of release dates for singles. Although the American chronology has been exactly established and published numerous times, the UK one has not until now. Because of these restrictions, US dates have been sourced from available databases, Don Waller's listings used as standard, but UK release schedules have been taken directly from Tamla Motown demo labels, which state the planned release day in the small print. I should emphasise that these constitute *intended* dates and in practice do not necessarily reflect the actual day a given single was put into shop racks, a matter which will never be completely ascertained. (Similarly the stated play time of each track is primarily lifted from demo record labels and most of the half thousand or so have not been audio-checked by the author. In many cases, there are multiple edits and mixes of tracks circulating on vinyl and CD, and so these may not marry absolutely with the contents of any individual's collection, but are given for interest.[8])

So far as personnel is concerned, it will be noted that several acts had line-up changes during the period under review. In consequence I have elected to indicate the membership each time a group single was released. The listed individuals were those formally part of the act when the recording was made, not at the point of release, and it is sometimes the case that not all of them feature on the recording itself. The purpose is to guide readers through changes in time rather than state who can be heard on the track, details of which will be given in the discussion. Tamla Motown frequently released recordings out of sequence, and so line-up changes may at first seem inconsistent, until the recording chronology is taken account of. (For example the Temptations' early seventies sequence [741]; [749]; [773]; [783] appears to show Eddie Kendricks coming and going where in fact he left after [741], but [773] was released belatedly.)

And finally, a note on the names used for Motown's acts: Numerous groups had more than one official name during their time with Motown, The Miracles, The Supremes and Martha & The Vandellas for example all having their billing amended in 1967 to enhance the profile of their lead singers. In the case of The Spinners, *two* alternative group names were used to clarify the fact that they were Motown's band and not a UK folk ensemble who also used 'Spinners' and, confusingly to the uninitiated, Rita Wright became known as Syreeta during her time at Motown. Later on, acts such as these, as well as The Jackson 5, had re-issues appear with the act billed differently to that of the original release. Throughout the central section of this book, each single is credited as per the original record label. However in the indices, all group names are regularised and do not necessarily conform to the actual billing on individual releases. This should be self-apparent, and is intended to help delineate the careers and discographies of the acts in question.

[1] Morse, p51

[2] Motown's studios were not the first to use 8-track equipment, but were the first in this respect to have success in the pop world.

[3] Extracted from his foreword to *Heat Wave* (David Bianco).

[4] His comments appear in *Mojo* August 2001, p58

[5] p68

[6] The photograph also captures Holland with a copy of Richie Havens' *Something Else Again*, with its classical Indian title track. This detail dates the shot to the spring of 1968 at the earliest. Interestingly, Lamont Dozier's first solo album for ABC was the immodestly titled *Black Bach* (1974).

[7] The R & B chart has changed in scope and identity over the years, and is widely referred to informally as the soul chart. Some refer to it as the 'black' chart, giving rise to the inaccurate phrase 'white' chart for pop.

[8] To further confuse the issue, several demos have the play times intentionally understated, anything pushing above the three minute mark before about 1968 deemed risky in terms of getting DJs to play it. By claiming 2:58 or 2:59 for a disc which spun longer, Tamla Motown not only encouraged radio stations to select their records, but also achieved longer air time (and hence publicity).

# CHAPTER ONE

# RATS AND ROACHES, TALENT AND LOVE

## The Story to 1965

Of America's great cities, the one nestling on the northern banks of the Detroit River, Michigan, as it flows into Lake St. Clair, was famous for one thing in particular: motor cars. The city's industrial base was built on manufacturing, Henry Ford having set up shop there in 1903. Ford was of course a pioneer of the production-line ethos, which enabled high turnout of product by 'scientific' specialisation within the workforce. By 1915, a million Ford motors were in existence; 12 years later the 15 millionth rolled out; in 1937 the company had notched up 25 million.

Just up the road from Ford, the Olds Motor Works, opened in 1899 on Jefferson Avenue East, was leading the industrialisation of the sector. Cadillacs and Buicks followed, and by 1909, the lot were under the umbrella of General Motors. Dynamic Detroit, once famed mainly for its fur trade, was becoming the industrial centre of the western world, its round-the-clock mass-production facilities attracting migrant workers from far and wide—but especially from the South—and especially black Americans from the farming communities.

By the time America became involved in World War II, Detroit's burgeoning black population was pressing towards a quarter of a million. Feeding the factories day and night, this sizable influx of people necessitated a rapid growth in the city's infrastructure and housing. The solution was the quick development of early ghettos such as the area to Detroit's eastern side which became known in ironic terms as Paradise Valley. Depressingly bleak, these areas were filled with black workers' families who crowded together under the suspicious scrutiny of the older white population, as if thieves who arrived in the night to 'steal' opportunity. In truth, life for the migrants was fairly miserable, impoverished industrialised workers living amidst the American dream against a backdrop of segregation in which they were fundamentally and unavoidably marginalised from the rest of the city.

Whenever the poor are brought together under difficult circumstances, there is always a human spirit which arises from somewhere deep within, most often expressed through song. Here, black Detroiters had brought with them a knowledge of the blues, picked up on the southern reservations and carried north, leading to the establishment in the 1930s of urbanised black music, a new and unpredictable development. Rhythmic and primitive, Detroit's jazz-blues became the central focus of recreational life for many, clubs and bars springing up and of offering escape from the hard realities of the working day. And into the mix was thrown one Berry Gordy Jr., born in 1929 into an ambitious migrant family from Georgia.

Gordy's formative years taught him many lessons which would shape his future success. First and foremost, he learned to be a fighter—literally so, since from his early teens he harboured ambitions to become a professional boxer and showed some talent in the sport. But his schooling was effectively abandoned and he ended up conscripted into the army, at one point serving in Korea. By his mid-20s he was yet to find his station in life, married to Thelma Coleman but working for his father's construction firm. Uninterested in the physical toil which the authoritarian Pops forced upon him, Gordy developed a passion for jazz, frequenting Detroit's night clubs where an electrifying set of local musicians were gaining formidable reputations.

Sufficiently hooked, Gordy quit his day job, emptied out [
borrowed heavily from his father, and set up his first business re
discs from his 3-D Record Mart. Alas, the venture suffered as s(
from the skewed perspective of its proprietor who made the card]
of thinking everyone else shared his interests and tastes. The truth was, much
of the local black population cared comparatively little for jazz, preferring
instead the directly unsophisticated strains of bluesmen such as John Lee
Hooker. After two years' struggle, Gordy was forced to shut up shop,
penniless to the point that in the spring of 1955, he found himself working on
Ford's production line.

For someone with an active mind, life offers lessons wherever one looks.
For Gordy, he observed the practical, reductionist approach to manufacturing
with which Ford was synonymous. The production line system, while
stultifying for the component worker, was an object lesson in efficiency.
Through division of labour, turnover is maximised, and individual
specialisation at each stage adds up to reliable, high-quality production.
Unaware at the time of the value of this notion, Gordy took his place on the
conveyor belt, spending his time fixing chrome trim to automobile panels,
morning through to evening, hundreds of times over, the task so
unstimulating that his mind would roam back to his first love in life: music.

During his long hours at Ford, Gordy took to writing songs in his head.
With no instrumentation to hand, he would compose lyrics and melody
together, devising hooks and romantic phrases which he could cobble into
something resembling a composition. Via his sisters Gwen and Anna, Gordy
had come to meet several local musicians whom he would seek to impress
with claims of being a professional songwriter. From this, the seed was
planted which led to his responding to an appeal by local manager Al Green
for new material for his client Jackie Wilson, an old sparring partner of
Gordy's. After a while Gordy was in possession of a tape recorder and had his
own demos available.

The subsequent union between Gordy and Jackie Wilson led to some
significant early success, his co-compositions "To Be Loved" (after which
Gordy named his 1994 autobiography), "Lonely Teardrops", "Reet Petite",
"That's Why (I Love You So)", "I'll Be Satisfied" and other hits ensuing. As
a writer, Gordy had arrived, his vocation for the first time becoming defined.

During one audition with Wilson's manager Nat Tarnopol in 1957, an
unknown 17-year-old turned up with his backing group, hawking his own
compositions. Rejected, the teenager was surprised to be accosted by
Gordy outside the office and promptly given a lesson in how to hone a
song into viable shape. Thus, Gordy had made friends with, and
commenced an embryonic working relationship with one Smokey
Robinson. One of Robinson's early tracks, the monstrous eight minute
"Got A Job" was accordingly trimmed down and became his first proper
recording, with backing group The Miracles, leased by Gordy to New
York's End Records in 1958.

For Gordy, the aim of his involvement remained the establishment of
himself as a professional songwriter. Harbouring no ambition to run a
record label, it was with mild interest that in 1959, he observed sister Gwen

set up her own Anna imprint with then lover Billy Davis. (Distributed by Chicago's Chess Records, Anna would prove to be a fertile recruiting ground for Motown, attracting figures such as Lamont Dozier, David Ruffin, The Spinners, Barrett Strong and others.) Following her initiative, and aware of several talented and unsigned individuals on the Detroit circuit, Gordy organised rehearsals at Claudette Robinson's house late in the year, further sessions soon ensuing which among other things brought Marv Johnson into the fold.

Still with no fixed plans in place, Berry Gordy began tentatively putting what became Motown together, one of his first moves setting up Jobete, a music publishing house merging the names of his three children. The Rayber Service soon followed, making freelance demo recordings for local acts, and attracting several new faces including Brian Holland, with Berry Gordy by now establishing himself at the nucleus of a small musical empire. Financially though, Gordy was doing less well than he felt his work deserved, and it was from these experiences that it dawned on Gordy where the real money lay: not merely with writing, but with *selling* music; and not retail, for pennies, but wholesale, as the owner of the recordings themselves.

Accordingly, Gordy took the plunge and followed his sister in setting up his own label, borrowing $800 from his family to cover the costs of his first planned release, Marv Johnson's "Come To Me" [E01], a gamble which might have broken the label before it had started. As luck would have it, the track sold healthily and Gordy, and the new Tamla label which hosted the recording, was modestly off the ground.

Tamla issued a half-dozen 45s in the first half of 1959, the key release being Barrett Strong's "Money (That's What I Want)" [E02]. Unflagging in self-belief, Gordy simultaneously began searching for a business premises, finding a white-painted house on West Grand Boulevard in the summer of 1959, which would soon become the focal point of his operations, christened hopefully, if somewhat prematurely as, 'Hitsville'.

Hitsville was a residential building not best suited to housing a record company. It benefited from a photographic studio at the rear, which would be converted into a recording facility, and the upstairs bedrooms were earmarked for offices, but there was work to be done. Thus, several members of the Gordy clan, musical colleagues and hangers on rolled up their sleeves and in the spirit of mucking in, made 2648 West Grand Boulevard their collective head quarters. Motown though would outgrow its somewhat makeshift residence in no time, ongoing success necessitating expansion outwards, which Gordy managed by buying up several neighbouring houses. In 1961, Jobete moved into 2646 while 2650 to 2654 were bought in January 1962 for ordinary clerical offices, including Gordy's own (which was destroyed by fire in 1971).

By 1964 the 'Snakepit' recording studio, working day and night, was also buckling under, and when Gordy purchased rival Golden World studios on Davison Avenue, a few miles away, Motown had a second facility, giving rise to the 'Studio A' tag for the original and Studio B for Davison Avenue.

Throughout the 1960s, Motown continued to colonise further properties on West Grand Boulevard, 2656 for Motown Finance in 1965, followed by

2657 (opposite) for Artist Development, 2670 to 2672 for Internatic
Management (ITM) Limited and 2662 to 2668 for Sales and Marke
1966. By the end of that year, Motown was in possession of 11 bi
the street, with Hitsville at the approximate geographical centre. Y
piecemeal expansion proved inadequate and in 1967 Gordy inevitably merged
all the administrative and peripheral operations into one building, situated on
the Fisher Freeway, leaving just Hitsville on the street where it had all begun.

The Snakepit recording studio (so named because of the dozens of cables
laying about the floor) was the heart of Motown, operating almost
continuously for some years. The facility was shut down only for routine
maintenance for a couple of hours each morning, otherwise being alive with
recording sessions continuously throughout the 1960s. In the early part of the
decade, technology was primitive by modern standards and the company's
engineers were a crucial element in Hitsville's recording sessions. Head of
Technical Engineering was Mike McLean, who ran the engineering shop in
the building's basement, and oversaw the development of a number of pieces
of equipment, which Motown engineers would design specifically to meet
certain needs as they arose.

The industry standard at that stage was two- or three-track recording,
which necessitated an essentially live ensemble performance requiring all
performers to get their parts right simultaneously. Each track would be used
to record a certain group of instruments or voices at once, the three channels
then blended together to create a finished master. Hitsville was home to an
antiquated 1939 Western Electric console, which had two tracks but was
adapted to accommodate a third. Motown opted to have the rhythm section
(drums, bass, guitar and keyboards) laid down on one of the available tracks
first, the rest of the arrangement coming in subsequently on tracks two and
three.

Scope for 'dropping in' and 'punching in' (techniques whereby repairs
can be made to original recorded tracks) was minimal. Because all the
instruments were recorded together, none could be individually repeated, so
any mistakes would require the whole group to start over, considerably
delaying the process were the band not on form. Needless to say, many
minor technical errors were let through (for example an accidentally
extended bar in [571]), although the inherent lack of clarity in the very early
recordings often manages to mask this, even on today's digitised
reproductions. Furthermore, none of the individual instruments could be
mixed independently—for example the guitar could not be made louder in
relation to the drums (although equalisation was possible on the track as a
whole, so that boosting the treble would help bring guitars out). During
early recordings, the guitarists would play through the studio's 200 watt
McIntosh amplifier, which was adapted in-house to feature five volume
controls and VU meters, so that each musician could set his own level in
readiness before recording commenced.

After the rhythm track, Motown would record brass and strings on track
two, together with any other instruments required to fill out and 'sweeten'
the sound. Together with track one, the 'backing track' was thus complete,
and it fell finally to the vocalists to record their parts, often completely

independently of the session musicians (whose track they would be listening to through headphones). The three tracks would then be mixed together, generating the master—usually in mono during the first part of the decade. Here, a degree of balancing could be done, with vocals for instance increased in prominence as required although it was common for mixes to be rejected over and over, subtle adjustments being required until Gordy was satisfied.

In contrast to genearal mixing practice, Motown sought to bring the music 'up', with the vocals submerged in the arrangement. Gordy's view was that it was the backing rhythms which gave popular music its true excitement and appeal, and so the musical forces were the most vital elements. In reducing the prominence of the vocals, it was necessary to emphasise their clarity so that the words being sang would not be lost, and so Motown began playing with reverb on the backing music and using compression on the vocals, further refining the company's studio sound.

Since everything had do be done in the tiny Snakepit, there was little opportunity for producers to develop sound textures until much later on. The rapid turnover meant that there was no time to dwell, the studio operating at what today appears break-neck speed, turning out recording after recording for years. Even major singles were produced against a relentlessly ticking clock, "It's The Same Old Song" [528] for example made from scratch in a day; "Baby Love" [E56] done in two takes. It is little wonder given the conditions that Motown focussed so heavily on singles over albums; this was more than just business ideology, as scope for recording full original sets by act after act was all but impossible.

To help ease the workload, Gordy began to look elsewhere for facilities to make technical adjustments to recordings, since all such work done at Hitsville would completely tie up the studio. He initially had some usable facilities installed in his office, but when Studio B was acquired this became the main site for mixing and overdubbing. Studio B was designed to be used almost entirely with direct injection of instruments to mixing desk (i.e. not via microphones), which was in keeping with the company's technical trends generally.

Technical considerations apart, the Snakepit was, by all accounts, a ramshackle place in the early-1960s. For one thing, there was no proper ventilation, which not only made the assembled musicians uncomfortable, but actually affected the performance of their instruments—Earl Van Dyke singling out Marvin Gaye's "Try It Baby" [E50] as a release racked with tuning problems caused by temperature and humidity. Because of the essentially live nature of 1960s recording, the ambience of the room was an important factor in determining a studio's individual sound, and indeed, Motown's recognisable recording style has been attributed by some to the physical features of the Snakepit. Diana Ross has talked of the 'magical' quality of the place, believing that the unique effects to come out of the studio were the result of the way the sound bounced around the walls and stairwell. Opening or closing windows was said to change the 'mood', and a hole in the wall was even used to reflect the vocals back to the microphones in an unusual way. (Ross claims that she was occasionally recorded in the bathroom to create an echo effect.)

The continual demands on Studio A meant that the facility remained under constant strain for some years, the occasional fire breaking out because of the relentless over-use of heat-generating valve equipment, thus paralysing Motown's production line entirely. Breakdowns were not infrequent, and with modifications and additions to the rigs being made all the time, days could be unexpectedly lost tinkering with technical faults. Motown benefited as much as any studio of the day by the ingenuity of its staff, chief recording engineer Lawrence T. Horn able to further Motown's recording techniques by developing a novel system in which he used multiple tapes. He was thereby able to start separating out the initial rhythm track instruments by recording them in parts onto all three blank tracks. The key was devising a system for subsequently blending them together and putting them back onto track one of a new tape, leaving two tracks available for the other overdubs. The same process would go into the recording of strings, horns, etc. which eventually arrived on tracks two and three. In this way, all components could be better manipulated before the entire thing was placed on another new tape, vocals added, and the whole copied again.

This helped Motown greatly improve the separation and equalisation in their recordings, marked by a distinct advance in clarity by the introduction, in 1964, of a fore-runner to 8-track facilities. For one thing it enabled the vocal to be processed better as it could now be split at the first stage onto two separate duplicated channels, allowing for compression and reverb to be added separately, the two vocals being recombined to make for an exciting and clearly audible new track with an advanced quality of sound. But inevitably, Gordy opted to scrap Hitsville's antiquated recording equipment completely by the end of 1964, and replace it with a more modern studio set-up. Mike McLean was charged with re-wiring the studio in readiness for a state-of-the-art 8-track console, something he managed within a single week. At the time, 8-track machines weren't available commercially, so McLean and his staff were forced to design and construct one themselves, together with a suitable 8-track mixer, which was hooked to a single pair of stereo speakers. Each channel had an innovative 'pan pot', which enabled it to be positioned in the stereo spectrum, which gave rise to new possibilities for stereo recording and instrument positioning in an era when mono recording was standard. Once mastered, a confident producer could incorporate such techniques in the final mix, for example to impressive effect on "You Keep Me Hanging On" [585] (although singles throughout the 1960s consisted of alternative mono mixes).

Motown, in contrast to other studios dealing in soul music, was keenly interested in production standards. Multi-tracking was cutting edge not just for the idiom, but for popular music generally. Although 8-track dates back to 1958 it was not fully exploited until The Beach Boys created *Pet Sounds* in 1966. Motown was two years ahead of the game: The Beatles' *Sgt. Pepper's Lonely Hearts Club Band*, widely seen as the single greatest breakthrough in studio technique, was done entirely on 4-track equipment as late as 1967.

Instruments could be recorded in true isolation from one another, which crucially permitted the bass to be recorded on its own via a direct feed into the mixing desk. Part of the appeal of bassist James Jamerson's unique style,

's graduation from upright to electric bass in the early part of the
ınovation of his own which initially met with scepticism from
ıually importantly, it enabled saxophones, violins, tambourines
..o be mixed independently, vastly opening the scope for Motown
ριoducers such as the Holland—Dozier—Holland team for their ground-
breaking work with The Four Tops and The Supremes in 1966-67. By then of
course, the sound scope for Hitsville had improved beyond all recognition,
technical staff fully up to speed with the new technology. Of all the period
producers, it is perhaps Ashford & Simpson's work which best exemplifies
the range of better facilities, tending to be beautifully EQ-ed and especially
cleanly presented. (Towards the end of the 1960s, Motown upgraded again,
opting for an unheard of 16-track console. The 16-track machine was
commercially available from Ampex—the MM1000 model.)

Innovation was the word of the day, and Motown's recordings to 1967
show liberal use of new engineering and production ideas. The cross-the-
floor stomping which commences "Where Did Our Love Go" [E51] is a clear
example, the incorporation of sounds spooled backwards on "Motoring"
[502b] another. The recording studio would use every and any trick to
generate interesting effects, from slapping plywood together to shaking metal
chains. One notable production touch was obtained by slapping open hands
onto a wooden seat [579], which not only impressed Motown's contemporary
studios but also set a minor standard for HDH's ever-developing sound.

Given the often chancy circumstances surrounding recording dates and
the unremitting urgency with which tracks would have to be made, Berry
Gordy began from the outset to absorb the efficient production-line theory
into the organisation's operations. Compartmentalising the elements was the
trick, Motown employing writers on its books to come up with material, a
studio band to lay down the backing tracks, and vocalists to add the finishing
touches. Often the staff in these essentially independent roles would not cross
paths, although in a large number of cases the songwriter would co-ordinate
the others from the production chair.

However Gordy clearly viewed the creative process as a business process,
treating arrangers for example as if they were back at Ford, sticking chrome
onto vehicle shells. Advised by businessman Ralph Seltzer, Gordy was in
danger of taking the production-line approach to absurd lengths: Brian
Holland and Lamont Dozier, so central to Motown's early growth, were
issued with clocking-in cards and instructed to attend Hitsville daily from
9:00 until 5:00. Eddie Holland defied Gordy by refusing to collude in such
schemes, and by the time the Holland—Dozier—Holland (HDH) team were
collaborating regularly it was normal for them to work into the night, Gordy
conceding the point only on condition that they scored a first number 1 hit.
Nonetheless, the conveyor belt rumbled on, an increasing flow of product
coming out of Hitsville year on year.

The core component of Motown's corporate sound was the sole ever-
present element, the studio band. So far as recording session went, Motown
opted to maintain a select inner circle referred to loosely as The Funk
Brothers, most of whom came from jazz backgrounds and had been pulled
from Detroit's performing musical community. Aware of the band's crucial

contribution, Motown would actively scout for talented musicians. Mickey Stevenson would trawl the club circuit talent spotting, and was largely responsible for bringing the Funk Brothers together.

Working in close proximity, The Funks were forced to focus their playing tightly, generating a functional rapport despite a fairly basic approach to recording and performance. The earliest grouping to work with Berry Gordy was essentially The Joe Hunter Band, who were known through Detroit's club scene. The line-up included Hunter himself on piano, plus bassist James Jamerson, a virtuoso musician with a dazzling fluidity to his playing, executed entirely by the plucking of his right index finger (hence one of his many nicknames, The Hook). Jamerson made the Fender Precision his regular bass around 1962, refusing to change his strings for the rest of the decade unless they physically broke (which was rare), in the belief that their accumulated grime lent some intangible 'soul' to his recordings, but ignoring that fact that on several sessions he had wandered out of tune with the band. As the decade wore on Jamerson's reputation would grow to the point where he was seriously touted as the best in the business.

Close to Jamerson was drummer Benny Benjamin, an Alabama native with a CV including work with musical giants such as Charlie Parker, Ray Charles, Muddy Waters and Chuck Berry. Benjamin started out playing a Rogers kit, Hank Cosby purchasing a superior Gretsch set-up for the Snakepit, the drummer frequently stealing component parts to pawn for pocket money! Guitarists Eddie Willis on Fender Stratocaster/Gibson Firebird, Robert White with his Gibson L5 and Joe Messina on Fender Telecaster consolidated the core group and The Funks were essentially in place by the end of 1960.

According to Martha Reeves (p106), there were in excess of 100 musicians on Motown's books by around 1963. Most of the extra personnel were employed for touring bands, Motown's exclusively vocal stars by-and-large not having individual groups behind them. Inevitably, as Motown's workload increased several new faces were absorbed into the studio set-up, drummers Richard 'Pistol' Allen and Uriel Jones joining the fold as deputies to Benjamin, percussionists Eddie 'Bongo' Brown and Jack Ashford also becoming integral parts of the team. Pianists Johnny Griffith and Earl Van Dyke were also recruited, the latter assuming the role of band leader from the departing Choker Campbell. By 1967 Motown's continuing expansion saw the studio group swell yet further with significant figures such as Dennis Coffey and Golden World refugee Bob Babbitt arriving on the scene—but few others were able to penetrate the Snakepit during the 1960s.

Wary of the group's collective clout, Berry Gordy forestalled any thoughts of superstardom which any of The Funks might have harboured by keeping them more or less continuously out of sight in Hitsville's studio, uncredited on their recordings, their names generally unknown. They did get an album out in 1963 in the guise of The Twistin' Kings, and, behind Earl Van Dyke, they received billing as The Soul Brothers, but in the main they remained firmly hidden from the public eye, reliant on Motown's modest fees—perhaps $5 for a day's work. Although under exclusive contract to Motown, many moonlighted, defying Gordy's attempts to keep them under wraps. While he may have secretly approved their extra curricular appearance on old pal Jackie

our Love Keeps Lifting Me) Higher And Higher", there was no
r excursions to arch-rivals Golden World to cut tracks such as
"Stop Her On Sight (SOS)". (Conforming so closely to the
ormula, this and other period tracks were quietly re-issued as
otown originals once Gordy had acquired the label's back-catalogue later in
the decade [905].) Such was Gordy's concern, he sought to employ Johnny
Griffith as his mole, to report on any nefarious activities, the cheeky
keyboard man demanding a stack of cash and a new car for the job—which he
had no intention of actually doing.[1]

Given the relentless workload, The Funk Brothers would often assemble
down in the Snakepit with no idea of what the coming day had in store.
Typically, writers and producers would turn up with loose ideas, and The
Funks would develop their sketches into defined riffs and chord runs,
crafting the key musical elements of countless hit songs off-the-cuff. Lamont
Dozier's method was to write out a basic chord sheet which included
important lines of instrumentation but left space for the band to jam them
into shape. In practise, writing became to some extent a partnership between
composers and musicians, neither of whom could have created the songs
entirely independently. An incisive bass run or guitar lick for example would
be picked up by the producer and embraced as the core of a developing song.
As technology progressed, skilled arrangers such as Paul Riser began to
come to the fore, scoring classical instrumentation against the group's
backing, string sections added in where early raw brass arrangements would
have been relied on for colouration.

Certainly there is a case for calling The Funk Brothers the key to the
Motown Sound. The group appeared on just about every hit single until well
into the 1970s, prompting Uriel Jones to comment some years after the event,
"People always say it was everything but the musicians. They'd say it was the
artists, the producers, the way the building was constructed, the wood on the
floor, or maybe even the food. But I'd like to see them take some barbecue
ribs or hamburgers and throw them down in the studio and shut the door and
count off 'one, two, three, four' and get a hit out of it. The formula was the
musicians".[2] Despite this, Gordy resolutely refused them the recognition their
work warranted. According to accepted accounts, when Hitsville eventually
shut up shop, the regular band were not even forewarned, turning up for
work as usual to find a sign on the door informing them that the studio was
henceforth closed, the love of the 'family' apparently unrequited.

A key collaborator with the band on whatever material happened to be in
progress was the producer. For Motown, the jobs of songwriter and producer
generally went hand-in-hand, most hit singles created with at least one of the
song's composers also behind the desk. Thus, key writers such as HDH,
Smokey Robinson, Frank Wilson, Norman Whitfield, Ashford & Simpson
and so on would bring a basic track into the studio, tighten up the backing
track in tandem with the group before supervising the addition of all
subsequent processes including overdubs, the addition of vocals and
eventually mixing and EQ-ing to the point where a master could be cut.
Freedom to see this process through stage-by-stage gave the writer-producers
the facility to create their individual sounds, each realising their initial

conceptions without undue interference.

Largely untutored as producers, methods were idiosyncratic and some Motowners such as Norman Whitfield adopted an intensive hands-on approach in which he would have each miniscule step pre-planned so he could see his songs were developed just so. Others had a more remote technique, avoiding the studio floor and working from behind the mixing desk, which allowed The Funk Brothers greater individual input to their respective parts. The key task for a producer is to translate concepts into actual arrangements and develop abstract ideas into finished takes. Motown's principal writers usually worked in twos and threes within established, long-term partnerships, although most would cross-collaborate from time to time. Although The Funk Brothers were omnipresent, so far as the writers were concerned, they tended to be assigned specific acts by Gordy, for whom they would have particular responsibility, usually only until the hits dried up. Thus, they became very much a part of the act in question, Ashford & Simpson for example being virtual partners with Marvin Gaye and Tammi Terrell during the duo's time together.

Coincident with the rise of Motown, events in popular music generally were running apace, the emergence first of Bob Dylan, and almost immediately afterwards The Beatles giving rise to performers able for the first time to self-compose whole albums of original material. Motown's compartmentalised structure precluded this from their performing roster, the only notable exception being Smokey Robinson, who penned a substantial amount of material for The Miracles. Other capable writers such as Marvin Gaye and Stevie Wonder were regarded suspiciously by Gordy, and it was not until the early-1970s that they were able to fully explore the art of self-composing. In this respect, Gordy can be seen as old-school, hailing from an era when professional personnel wrote remotely for performers with whom they often had little personal connection. While Motown's close-knit structure determined that most staff were operating on similar wavelengths, the system nonetheless kept writers and performers largely segregated, except where record production necessitated direct collaboration.

In general terms, Motown's writers would compose in a straight-forward manner, usually in the first person. Frequently lyrics would be constructed hypothetically (such as "How Sweet It Is To Be Loved By You" [571], built on an imaginary scenario) but equally drawing on immediate surroundings. Smokey Robinson and Lamont Dozier in particular would repeatedly commence songs from phrases overheard on the radio or in conversation, [631] for example prompted by a slip of the tongue while out shopping, [510] from a spontaneous remark, [501] from a exclamation to an angry girlfriend and so on; inspiration was drawn from all around, including earlier song titles and riffs, not to mention the work of Motown's external peers.

The mechanics of song writing are always peculiar to the writer in question, Motown's leaders until 1967 being HDH and Robinson. HDH would approach the task methodically, their composite creations consisting of successive component parts locked together in infinite combinations. Characteristic of their greatest work is the incorporation of snappy phrasing in discrete sections, a result of their writing method in which Dozier and

---

Eddie Holland would work in direct collaboration, taking turns at throwing in riffs and lines of text. Usually driven by pre-conceived melody or chord structure, the process was essentially additive, lyrics sequenced in pieces until the requisite number of bars were meaningfully filled. Thus their work displays a stop-start quality, frequently cadencing and hypnotically circulating, for example in [E51], "Baby, baby [break] Baby don't leave me [break] Please don't leave me [break] All by myself [break]" and so on. HDH's classic output was effectively a microcosm of the assembly line, a 'factory within a factory'

Robinson on the other hand was essentially a solo writer who would make a point of collaborating with one of more of his group to avoid falling into routine. Robinson's effusive writing and performing were, in truth, extensions of his optimistic character, reflected in the playful way in which he pulls and pushes rhythms, phrasing and metre, and the joyful nature of his lyrics, with their intricate games and verbal contradictions, and their general talkativeness. "Tears Of A Clown" [745] for example contains essentially a single protracted sentence throughout its first verse and chorus, with scarcely a gap for breath, its grief-stricken theme overwhelmed by Robinson's sheer enthusiasm. In contrast to HDH, Robinson was a narrator, several of his major hits containing elegantly constructed chronicles of love's many faces, conceived on a grand scale and viewed as whole melodic and conceptual dramas. (Those who have seen his live performances will concur that Robinson the performer can scarcely stop smiling through his sets, his natural love of his craft seeping from every pore.)

Such observations are of course only part of the picture. Motown had many composers on its books, all of whom had different ideas about writing, Norman Whitfield in particular taking Motown into previously unexplored territory from 1968 onwards [707]. Seen as a whole, it is interesting to observe that as the 1960s gave way to the 1970s, Motown's songs generally expanded in length while simultaneously *slowing down*. (Tamla Motown singles, studiously kept within the 3:00 timeframe until 1968 broke that particular barrier for the first time with [650], pushing beyond 4:00 the following year. By 1973 more than half of releases were beyond 3:00, Tamla Motown by then having smashed even the 6:00 mark.) Partly there was an element of self-indulgence on the part of established writers, who in common with many non-Motown artists of the day, developed worrying tendencies towards self-mythologisation, attempting grandiose contemporary 'works' exemplified by Whitfield's own tellingly titled *Masterpiece*, The Temptations' 1973 album on which the producer was pictured larger than the group members. Indeed it was Whitfield and Strong above all others who expanded the scale of the 45, their creations accounting for most of Tamla Motown's longest singles.

But for much of the 60s, Gordy, through a combination of enforced anonymity and a public policy that no-one was indispensable, was able to keep control over his back-room staff. Autocratic to the point of paranoia, Gordy sought direct control over all operations within his empire, all personnel on his payroll, working from premises he owned, their music published and controlled by his companies. Every significant decision made was Gordy's own and, where the job was simply too large for one man to manage, he employed family members, various brothers and sisters responsible for personnel, management, public promotions and so on.[3] While this meant that Gordy could claim almost unqualified credit for the company's business success, his control of recording artists, most of whom regarded themselves as stars on their own terms, caused chronic tension within Motown's ranks.

Gordy had his star turns 'groomed' by Maxine Powell, taught how to behave and tutored in the rules of good etiquette. Motown booked gigs, looked after finances and generally ran groups and singers as any other corporation would administer its departments. Particularly in terms of remuneration, Gordy's monolithic stance in which not even sales figures were declared caused a festering resentment which became more pressing as time went on. Many notable acts left on bad terms, lawsuits coming in routinely from former Motown darlings such as Brenda Holloway, Gladys Knight, Martha Reeves, Mary Wilson and others. David Ruffin was legally blocked from departing in 1969, while HDH sued and were counter-sued with astronomical figures of unknown reliability floated.

Of course Gordy's system of total management determined that whenever one of his stars upped and left, they took with them nothing—no management structure, no backing band and no material to record. Consequently, the only acts to fly the nest successfully were those who were established before coming to Motown—most notably The Isley Brothers and Gladys Knight & The Pips. The only exception in this respect was The Jackson 5, who managed to resume their career to great effect, albeit without their group's name and less one member. (The career of Michael Jackson thereafter needs no recounting here.)

The prevalent picture of Motown as exploitative is, however not fully representative. The fact was, many of their stars had inflated expectations of how much money they were due and how much of their success was due to personal eminence. The other side of the coin is that Motown shielded many of its artists from exploitation by external agents and unscrupulous management, which could be every bit as monopolistic. A case in point is Florence Ballard, who left Motown with a £75,000 golden handshake in 1967, only to be bankrupted within a year via the ruthless business in which she was working. To Motown's credit it should be remembered that the company would frequently come to the rescue of errant employees in financial difficulties or in need of assistance. In the case of Stevie Wonder, Gordy set up a trust fund to handle the youngster's finances which was released once he turned 21, setting him up financially for the rest of his life. Moreover Motown can be seen as providing innumerable new opportunities not just for those involved directly, by breaking down social barriers and leading the emancipation of black musicians and performers across the board.

Much of the rumbling discontent doubtless stemmed from the highly competitive internal structure in which rival singers, writers and producers would not only fight for material and studio time, but frequently find themselves deprived of credit for their labours. Songwriters were in continual dispute with Motown over the apportioning of names to copyrights, on supposedly inaccurate documentation for tracks such as [E01], [E61b], [623],

[638], [682] and numerous others. In an incendiary 2001 interview in which she claimed credit for several Motown bass lines (see [515]), Carol Kaye implied that established Motown writers, aiming to secure ongoing work with given acts, would even resort to buying up promising material in order to see their names in the brackets.

Gordy of course would claim a royalty on anything attributed to his contracted bank of writers. Via his Jobete/Stein & Van Stock publishing concerns (and in the UK Belinda/Carlin), Gordy owned almost every original Motown number, with the added power of personal veto on what was released and by whom. His only regular concession in this respect was to Quality Control, the final stage of any production line, and the process by which Motown filtered wheat from chaff. Nominally run by Billy-Jean Brown, a former journalist and tape librarian, the process would involve the gathering of several writers, producers and performers to listen to and vote on current tracks in the frame for release. With competition keen, arguments could sometimes be fierce, the regular Friday morning meetings make-or-break for producers and artists alike.

Gordy ran the Quality Control system tightly. Tracks would be graded and scored according to the appeal of the title, lyrical content, arrangement touches and so on, Gordy sometimes commissioning new mixes or takes with different studio staff for comparison before passing final judgement. Songwriters and producers sometimes only learned after the event that Gordy had requested an edit or re-working of their material, to frequent and not unreasonable chagrin. So crucial did Gordy view the process that he would make audio recordings of the meetings and take notes on who voted which way. Those seen to be consistently getting it wrong would cease to be invited back. But no matter how minutely Gordy analysed recordings, he never forgot the valuable lesson learned in his ill-fated 3-D Record Mart, which taught him that the only opinion which truly mattered was that of the public. Accordingly, he made it a policy to invite groups of local black teenagers into Hitsville to ask them what they thought of this or that recording before it was approved.

Under the circumstances, Quality Control did a superb job, but nonetheless made some howling errors of judgement: Massive UK hits such as "I Heard It Through The Grapevine" [686], "The Tears Of A Clown" [745] and "I'm Still Waiting" [781] were all rejected or overlooked. At other times, Quality Control decisions gave rise to major disputes with figures such as Norman Whitfield, and were eventually proved wrong. Gordy also resisted Marvin Gaye's enormous *What's Going On* album, perhaps the biggest singular misjudgement of his career.

Ultimately, Quality Control's purpose was to second-guess the mood of the public, a notoriously difficult task hampered by rapid changes in tastes during the 1960s. Motown was developing a new brand of black music, popular in style and aimed to appeal equally to white audiences. This was something distinct from what had come in the 1940s and 50s, where formative figures such as Ray Charles, Nat King Cole, Sam Cooke and The Drifters had remained a largely 'alternative' strand in the pop charts, where their successes bucked a trend. Motown by contrast had the clear policy of pursuing commercial success in terms of singles, to the point where Berry Gordy instructed Quality Control that they were only to release tracks good enough to become top 10 hits—and for his biggest attraction The Supremes, only potential number 1s. His successes piled up as time went on: Motown topped the Billboard singles listing for the first time in 1961 [E05], repeating the feat in 1963 [E26] before scoring four number 1s in 1964, the year the British supposedly invaded the US charts ([E42]; [E51]; [E56]; [E65]). In the same period Motown claimed 12 R & B chart-toppers, proof that their records were being favourably received by listeners from all walks.

Motown's early publicity strategy was somewhat labour-intensive, gruelling tours such as the 1962 Motown Revue taking in town after town, week after week until artists and crew alike were on the point of exhaustion. Living and eating in the tour bus there was little chance for real rest as the entourage moved from state to state, perpetually running against the clock. Clearly this was not the way forward, Motown's goal in terms of marketing lying with radio and the desired public exposure for new releases.

Radio stations would be naturally reluctant to play numerous cuts from the same label, wanting not only to steer clear of charges of Payola (backhanders given by certain companies) but also avoid perceived sameness in their play lists. Gordy again learned the hard way, experiencing resistance to some very early releases on his inaugural Tamla label, and consequently created a range of other imprints, beginning in 1960 with the soon-to-be-flagship Motown label. Gordy arrived the following year, and VIP and Soul in 1964. Others came too, but most were comparatively peripheral with the exceptions of Rare Earth and Mo-West, both of which arrived around the start of the 1970s.[4]

Each of these American labels had a closed roster of acts, loosely sounding like each other. Motown was at the commercial cutting edge, home to The Supremes and Four Tops and later The Jackson 5. Tamla stuck with early names Smokey Robinson, Marvin Gaye and Stevie Wonder, while Gordy handled groups such as The Contours, Martha & The Vandellas and The Temptations. When the Soul label arrived it was aimed squarely at the black market and attracted some of Motown's less poppy acts including Junior Walker & The All Stars, Gladys Knight & The Pips and Jimmy Ruffin. Between them, Gordy's 'big four' labels continued pumping out product until late-1981 when Motown finally elected, UK-style, to consolidate acts on a single 'Motown' imprint.

With the Soul label as the exception to the rule, Motown's white-black 'crossover' policy was not accepted warmly in all quarters. The issue for many black listeners was not merely a matter of sound emanating from loudspeakers; it was a question of Motown's fundame'       ' basis assimilating with white tastes on the perceived assumpt had more legitimacy. In truth, Gordy's strategy in this r on a purely financial pursuit, the need to appeal to w market) a necessary step on his way to personal wealth such as The Supremes and The Temptations were put and tuxedos and booked onto the cabaret circuit. N selected including Rodgers & Hart numbers, Disney

**32**

western songs traditionally associated with white vocalists.

The name of the game was acceptance, a major part of which centred on personal etiquette and grooming, to facilitate his black artists' appeal to (supposedly better mannered) whites. Central to the strategy was the charm school which tutored Motown's working-class artists on how to conduct themselves, which mannerisms to use and how and when to speak. Maxine Powell, head of a modelling school for blacks, was responsible for socially 'refining' Motown's stars.

In truth there was an unavoidable contradiction inherent in what Motown were doing. Gordy was essentially the musical equivalent of Henry Ford, a model capitalist pursuing personal wealth—but at a juncture when the anti-materialist youth who were buying the records were rejecting the social values of their forefathers. Throughout the 1960s, youngsters, and in Detroit black youngsters especially, were confronting the establishment with increasing resolve, the wider civil rights movement calling the model of American society to account. Gordy, a working class black man was by instinct conservative, his loyalties torn between his own class, and the competitive market system, criticism of mainstream American values generally causing him a certain unease.

However In the face of racial confrontations, which in 1967 came right to their door (see [614]), several Motown artists were by then beginning to consider their political positions more carefully. Artistically Motown tended to play safe, but by 1965, social tensions were permeating much of American and British popular music and as time went on, Motown began to let through more pointed material: Stevie Wonder's reading of "Blowing In The Wind" [570] was viewed as comparatively ambiguous in the hands of a schoolboy in 1966, although by the time "Does Your Mama Know About Me" [654] was released two years later Gordy was beginning to recognise that the times were a-changing, and that it was now widely acceptable, even necessary, to express political comment through the medium of records. By the turn of the 1970s both Marvin Gaye and Stevie Wonder were becoming outspoken on the race issue while Gordy himself launched Black Forum in 1970 specifically to do what he had previously avoided: taking sides. Barrett Strong's lyrics for The Temptations and others going into the new decade further radicalised Motown to the point where they were seriously engaging the counter-culture's anti-war, anti-materialistic, pro-integrationist element and in some instances offering a lead—for example providing an impetus to mass demonstrators with Edwin Starr's anti-Vietnam chant "War" [754]. In truth though, Motown remained non-committal at heart and often hedged its bets; in the UK, Tamla Motown released "War" within weeks of Martha Reeves' "Forget Me Not" [762], the latter widely perceived as a veiled romanticism of American militarism.

Racism predictably reared its head more frequently in America's southern states. Most Motown artists from the early 1960s can recall incidents where they encountered open prejudice while on the road. From time to time the ▓▓▓ue tour bus would pull into a restaurant for something to eat, only to be ▓▓▓ith a curt refusal from white proprietors. Mary Wells has recounted an ▓▓▓ New Orleans where she was drinking from a water fountain only to become aware that she was being watched by a number of people. Initially assuming she had been recognised by fans, she was dismayed to spot a 'whites only' sign hanging next to the font.

On several occasions events were considerably more alarming. On the 1962 Revue, Miracle Bobby Rogers made the mistake of attempting to use a gas station bathroom in Mississippi, resulting in Motown's entire entourage being chased out of town by maniacs wielding shotguns. Martha Reeves and Otis Williams have also spoken of shooting incidents, one of which occurred in Kentucky, following the racist beating of the Four Tops' valet who required hospital treatment. The next night the tour bus was fired at while being loaded up, several singers and musicians diving for their very lives.[5]

Volatile though the situation was, Gordy initially toed the line and exercised a degree of self-censorship by consenting to keep black faces off the covers of several Motown long-players in the knowledge that some record stores would otherwise refuse outright to handle them. A good number had quirky cartoons substituted, although matters reached absurd levels in 1966 when The Isley Brothers' *This Old Heart Of Mine*, made entirely by black artists, carried a cover shot of two white lovers sitting on the beach.

It was well-known that black artists were hampered in the commercial arena by the difficulties they had in obtaining wide exposure. Historically, artists such as Elvis and Pat Boone had kept black originals out of public view by absorbing their styles and repackaging them as 'safe' white music. In Britain in the first half of the 1960s the trend was similar, several of the emergent beat groups scoring hits with songs originally recorded by black Americans, including from the outset, Motown acts. Probably the first were Faron's Flamingos whose cover of "Do You Love Me" [E10] was released on Motown's UK licensee Oriole in 1963, and followed up with a version of another Contours track, "Shake Sherry" [E15]. Meantime The Beatles were arriving on the scene hawking renditions of early Motown numbers such as "Money" [E02], their love of black American music well documented.

Once Motown was in business on its own terms, Gordy sourced a European outlet with a London-based company, the most suitable of the day being Decca-controlled London American which carried numerous US artists and was at its peak around the turn of the 1960s. Created for this very purpose, the label (and its associated London imprint) handled acts of the calibre of The Everly Brothers, Little Richard, Duane Eddy, Del Shannon, Bobby Darin and—shortly—releases from Phil Spector's family of groups including The Crystals and The Ronettes. Approached by Gordy in early 1959, London American wasted no time in issuing Motown's first US single "Come To Me", although their failure to follow up for almost a year reveals how little they rated Motown's output at the time. The truth was, London American were too big, and Motown too small, for the partnership to bear fruit, their two-year arrangement resulting in precious little by way of releases. Running through the initial batch of UK singles, only three acts would see material issued during the ensuing period, a modest beginning which would require more than one shift in labels to put right.

The following documentation deals in brief with each of the 72 Motown releases issued in the UK prior to the creation of the Tamla Motown label itself in 1965.

## London American

[E01] **Marv Johnson**: Come To Me / Whisper
*London American HLT 8856 (May 1959)*
Widely recognised as the first authentic release under the auspices of Berry Gordy's fledgling company, "Come To Me" was co-written by Gordy and Marv Johnson and recorded at United Sound Studios on Detroit's Second Avenue. Released locally as Tamla 101 in January 1959, the single drew attention from United Artists, who purchased the recording and gave it a national distribution, watching it enter the top 40 pop and climb to 6 on *Billboard's* R & B charts. Quick to recognise potential, United Artists set about acquiring Johnson's contract from Gordy and with continuing input from his former boss, the vocalist enjoyed numerous commercial hits over the succeeding two years including the transatlantic top-tenner, "You Got What It Takes". (Covered by Showaddywaddy in 1977, the mid-tempo R & B stomp stopped one place short of the UK number 1 spot.)

Usually regarded as part of Motown's early discography, Johnson had six further UK singles put out on London American, although none should rightly be seen as authentic Motown releases.[6] "Come To Me" stands as his only such single, until Berry Gordy re-signed an out-of-contract Johnson in 1965 (see [525]). The UK edition has the distinction of being the only Motown recording also to be released on 78 in Britain.

[E02] **Barrett Strong**: Money (That's What I Want) / Oh I Apologise
*London American HLU 9088 (Mar 1960)*
Under the London American licence, Motown had released nothing in 1959 bar Marv Johnson's first single, with Paul Gayten's New York recording of "The Hunch", which appeared in December, having originated only on the Anna label in America and not therefore qualifying as a Motown track. However six months after making the Billboard top 30 via an Anna label re-pressing, Barrett Strong's second Motown single, "Money (That's What I Want)", was issued in Britain.

"Money" may have gone unnoticed in 1960 in terms of sales, but the recording galvanised a small section of UK American music fans, including a 19-year-old John Lennon. The Beatles, hailing from Liverpool, were knowledgeable on certain strands of American music some years before they permeated British consciousness, pre-Motown discs brought into the docks by merchant seamen to a large extent determining The Beatles' formative style while they were still flogging sets in Liverpool and Hamburg dive bars. (Liverpool's Mardi Gras Club on Mount Pleasant opened in 1957, spinning imported R & B singles in an embryonic form of the later influential Northern Soul venues.)

Absorbed into The Beatles' repertoire, "Money" became one of the group's most raucous live hits, and was included in their unsuccessful audition set for Decca in 1962 before being recorded formally the following year. Opinion is sharply divided as to which version is better, Ian MacDonald for example championing The Beatles[7], Spencer Leigh tipping the nod to Strong's original.[8] Whatever the case, The Beatles' recording made the song famous, and arch rivals The Rolling Stones also picked up on it, "Money" becoming the only Motown song to be covered by both acts.[9]

"Money (That's What I Want)" was eventually released on Tamla Motown in 1988 [L077]: See Chapter 6. See also [586].

### [E03] **The Miracles**: Shop Around / Who's Loving You
*London American HLU 9276 (Feb 1961)*

The best part of another year went by before Motown's third UK release saw light of day, which like its two predecessors was part-penned by Berry Gordy, this time with co-writer Smokey Robinson. "Shop Around" was originally conceived for Barrett Strong as a follow-up to "Money" [E02], Gordy persuading Robinson that his group was better suited to the task. First released in September 1960, the Miracles' fourth US single was withdrawn shortly after going on sale, Gordy fancying a tighter and more rounded production of the track. In the end, "Shop Around" went to number 2 in the States, and topped the R & B charts for two months in early 1961, under the designation 'The Miracles featuring Bill "Smokey" Robinson'.

### [E04] **The Miracles**: Ain't It Baby / The Only One I Love
*London American HLU 9366 (Jun 1961)*

An up-tempo follow-up to "Shop Around" [E03] from the same Gordy—Robinson set-up, "Ain't It Baby" was released in America with its predecessor still riding high. Making relatively little impression, the single has been overlooked down the years despite earning UK release as the last of Motown's quartet under contract to London American. (By comparison, Motown had released more than two dozen American singles by now, all on the Tamla imprint.)

Powerful though London Records were, they clearly viewed the product of Detroit as a minor concern and opted to push only four releases in two years before the plug was pulled. During this period Motown had begun to establish solid sales in America, and there was no reason why the UK scene—still at that point dominated by American records—should not reflect this. Bowing out of their agreement with London, Motown instead drew up contracts with rival company Philips whose Fontana label, formerly a French independent, had been acquired in 1958. Utilised like London American specifically to push US recordings, Fontana had boasted on its roster acts such as Johnny Mathis, Dave Brubeck and Marty Robbins and had sufficient clout to be able to promote Motown's records to greater effect, although the union was to be extremely short-lived.

# Fontana
### [E05] **The Marvelettes**: Please Mr. Postman / So Long Baby
*Fontana H 355 (Nov 1961)*

Motown's first American chart-topper, "Please Mr. Postman" was recorded by The Marvelettes, a local teen quartet loosely fronted by Gladys Horton.

Offered as a potential hit by William Garrett, the bluesy first draft was worked on by Marvelette Georgia Dobbins before being further refined by Robert Bateman and Brian Holland (and possibly also Freddie Gorman). Taped in summer 1961, the track was probably the first to be recorded on Mike McLean's newly built three-track console.

Carrying an infectious vocal from Horton, "Please Mr. Postman" has become one of Motown's defining ventures in the high-school style, enlivened with chirpy teenage innocence, and featuring a young Marvin Gaye at the drummer's stool. Considered by Dave Godin (founder of the British Tamla Motown Appreciation Society) to be Motown's greatest single recording, "Please Mr. Postman" holds an affectionate place in the Motown story, and has been famously covered by The Beatles and The Carpenters. "Please Mr. Postman" was released on Tamla Motown in 1988 [L083] and again in 2004 [L112]: See Chapter 6.

### [E06] **The Miracles**: What's So Good About Goodbye / I've Been Good To You
*Fontana H 384 (Feb 1962)*
Penned alone by Smokey Robinson, "What's So Good About Goodbye" was a recent American single, Motown's UK agencies having passed up two of The Miracles' prior releases. Lyrically inspired by a gag overheard on a TV show, the track was supposedly recorded in Chicago and was only a modest hit at home, going largely unnoticed in the UK despite its inventive narrative showing evidence of 'Robinson's blossoming songwriting genius'.[10]

### [E07] **The Marvelettes**: Twistin' Postman / I Want A Guy
*Fontana H 387 (Mar 1962)*
With "Please Mr. Postman" [E05] having landed atop the American charts in December, Motown were keen to cash in, resulting in this embarrassingly unsubtle effort by Bateman and Holland together with Mickey Stevenson. Duly recorded by The Marvelettes and released at the tail-end of 1961, the track limped to 34 in America before being released in the UK in March.

### [E08] **Eddie Holland**: Jamie / Take A Chance On Me
*Fontana H 387 (Mar 1962)*
Berry Gordy's American operation had so far seen all recordings of note appear on his Tamla label. However with significant revenue having been earned from "Money (That's What I Want)" [E02] he was able in 1960 to re-invest and properly launch the American Motown imprint, having toyed with the name for some time. (Early Miracles demos appeared on an embryonic version of the label as early as September 1959.)

"Jamie" was written by Barrett Strong who intended to record the vocal himself. Holland though got hold of the tapes first and cut *his* version with the Detroit Symphony Strings wedged into the studio for the first time, the experimental score slightly out of kilter. The track became the first notable release on the Motown label (as Motown 1021) making number 30 pop and number 6 R & B, and although the single failed in a British market still largely unaware of the Motown stable, Holland would, within a couple of years, be a leading figure in developing the company's distinctive sound as a world-class writer-producer.

## Oriole American

Despite backing from the powerful Philips organisation, Fontana failed to establish Motown in the UK market and were quickly dropped. Instead, Motown approached London-based Oriole, a small independent label administered by CBS. (Oriole were well-known for their joint venture with the Woolworth retailer, who issued material on their Embassy imprint.) Oriole, with their quintessentially British flavour and comparatively small operation seemed a promising option for Motown, an American company who needed the backing of an organisation willing to devote time and effort to pushing its product in Britain. Although small, Oriole American knew the UK market, and supplied with suitably commercial stream of recordings, stood a chance of breaking some of Gordy's key acts. Accordingly, after a seven month break, Oriole American launched its first trio of Motown singles in September 1962.

[E09] **Mary Wells**: You Beat Me To The Punch / Old Love (Let's Try It Again)
*Oriole American CBA 1762 (Sep 1962)*
"You Beat Me To The Punch" was another Smokey Robinson number, this time recorded by Mary Wells, a talented singer-songwriter with one American top 10 hit already to her credit ("The One Who Really Loves You", number 8 in summer 1962). This new single emulated its predecessor by going top 10, but excelled it in becoming number 1 R & B. As usual, British record-buyers remained indifferent.

[E10] **The Contours**: Do You Love Me / Move Mr. Man
*Oriole American CBA 1763 (Sep 1962)*
Now enjoying success with his Motown label [E08], Berry Gordy was ready to further expand his horizons with the launch of Gordy, the eponymous imprint which began life in early-1962. Gordy's fourth American single was The Contours' third, the Berry Gordy-composed "Do You Love Me" (supposedly intended for The Temptations) released at the end of June, 26 days after it was recorded.

Regarded as a minor novelty act, The Contours would probably not have been signed to Motown were it not for the enthusiasm of Gordy's old friend Jackie Wilson. Rebellious and boisterous, The Contours' stage act drew hysterics from audiences, the quirky style of Berry Gordy's "Do You Love Me" suiting their group persona ('Watch me, now'), and putting the act firmly on the map with a number 3 showing nationally, and the coveted number 1 spot on the R & B charts. Although not a hit in the UK, the number was covered by Faron's Flamingos, as probably the first Motown song released by a British group, and then by Brian Poole And The Tremeloes, who placed the number atop the UK charts, displacing "She Loves You", in October 1963.

The Contours' original reached a new audience in the late 1980s when featured in the film Dirty Dancing, when it also climbed back up the US charts. "Do You Love Me" was released on Tamla Motown in 1974 [899] and again (twice) in 1988 [L077] (see Chapter 6 for details of the two editions).

[E11] **The Marvelettes**: Beechwood 4-5789 / Someday, Some Way
*Oriole American CBA 1764 (Sep 1962)*
Having passed up the group's "Playboy", Oriole American released this
May recording which by now had gone top 20 pop at home. Sung by
Gladys Horton, the track maintains the group's up-beat style but switches
subject matter little, being a sideways step from postal communication to
telephone calls.

[E12] **Mike & The Modifiers**: I Found Myself A Brand New Baby / It's Too Bad
*Oriole American CBA 1775 (Oct 1962)*
Detroit local Mike Valvano joined Motown as a teenager, his group's only
release seeing light of day in August 1962 on the new Gordy label. Little is
known for certain about the short-lived white act, despite the fact that Valvano
remained with Motown until the late-1970s, working in various capacities and
occasionally lending his hand to songwriting and recording (although none of
his own studio efforts were released). The group were apparently renowned
during their 15 minutes of fame, for *ad libbing* songs in response to audience
calls. The UK edition of "I Found Myself A Brand New Baby" is one of the
scarcest UK Motown releases, and at the time of writing commands a
catalogue value of several hundred pounds. The track was co-written by
Valvano and Clarence Paul, who also produced.

[E13] **The Miracles**: You Really Got A Hold On Me / Happy Landing
*Oriole American CBA 1795 (Jan 1963)*
Smokey Robinson's "You Really Got A Hold On Me" was not a hit in the
UK, but at home went top 10 pop and reached the summit of the R & B chart
in February, knocking' "Two Lovers" [E14] from pole position. An early
example of its author's romantic balladeering style, the song was penned in
New York, Robinson—Motown's vice president—there on business.
Retiring to his hotel room at a loose end, Robinson was attempting
something in the style of Sam Cooke's "Bring It On Home To Me", coming
up with a standard doo-wop cycle and thoughtfully emotive lyrics including
a trademark contradictory couplet for its opening. Made shortly after his
return, Robinson produced the recording himself, a move which further
consolidated his standing with the luxury of a uniquely autonomous position
within the company.

   Double-tracked by Bobby Rogers, the harmony vocal appealed to Lennon
and McCartney, and became the first Motown number covered by The Beatles
(their 18 July recording preceding that of "Money" [E02], made on the same
day). Courtesy of this reading, the song has achieved a global fame where it
may otherwise have slipped into obscurity, most of The Miracles' period pieces
being generally unknown today except by those with specialist interest.

[E14] **Mary Wells**: Two Lovers / Operator
*Oriole American CBA 1796 (Jan 1963)*
A second successive Robinson composition, "Two Lovers" was a chart-
topping R & B hit for Mary Wells, the singer's second in three months. Then
viewed as one of Motown's key assets, Wells was at this early juncture on a

career peak, the album *The One Who Really Loves You* Motown's best-selling long-player at the time, and her singles regularly scoring with record-buyers. UK audiences were still largely unaware of her, and the Oriole American pressing of "Two Lovers" did not appear on the *Record Retailer* chart. Tamla Motown, though, remembered it in 1972 and exhumed the track for the B-side to [820]. Taken literally the song title is misleading, Robinson's characteristically intelligent text instead portraying two conflicting sides of the same man whose personality is troublingly split.

### [E15] **The Contours**: Shake Sherry / You Better Get In Line
*Oriole American CBA 1799 (Feb 1963)*
The follow-up to "Do You Love Me" [E10], The Contours' new single was an abject flop compared to its predecessor. Written and produced by Berry Gordy, "Shake Sherry" was a 'hellfire rocker'[11] but failed to engage the public and is now forgotten.

### [E16] **Marvin Gaye**: Stubborn Kind Of Fellow / It Hurt Me Too
*Oriole American CBA 1803 (Feb 1963)*
Motown's maverick superstar Marvin Gaye was born Marvin Pentz Gay Jr, and brought up by a disciplinarian Christian minister who reportedly beat him daily. Made to sing in church, Gay developed his musical instincts by also taking up various instruments before fleeing home in his teens to join the US Air Force. Following his discharge, Gay joined The Moonglows as a vocalist behind Harvey Fuqua, travelling to Detroit for an engagement during which he was 'discovered' by Berry Gordy. Thus recruited, the multi-instrumentalist made himself useful at Hitsville as an all-round session man and after a few false starts, scored a first solo hit with "Stubborn Kind of Fellow" which went top 10 R & B.
   A real team effort, the track has its genesis in a Marvin Gaye/Mickey Stevenson piano jam, with Berry Gordy pitching in to help round the number off and an early incarnation of Martha & The Vandellas present on backing duties. Although not a hit in the UK, this first transatlantic release for Gaye marks his arrival in impressively assured style. From here on his stature would grow with each successive release. (Gaye consolidated his place in the Motown family, by marrying Gordy's sister Anna later in the year.)

### [E17] **Eddie Holland**: If It's Love (It's Alright) / It's Not Too Late
*Oriole American CBA 1808 (Mar 1963)*
Part-written and co-produced by his brother and future partner Brian, Eddie Holland's second UK single was the fifth of 11 issued by him in America. Lifted from his self-titled debut LP, the track was not intended as a single and sold few copies on either side of the Atlantic. Holland was by now beginning to think in terms of his writing career, no further albums ensuing.

### [E18] **The Valadiers**: I Found A Girl / You'll Be Sorry Someday
*Oriole American CBA 1809 (Mar 1963)*
Like Mike & The Modifiers, The Valadiers were an obscure white group, formed in Detroit and signed to Motown's Miracle subsidiary which existed

---

for most of 1961. Only 12 singles ever appeared on Miracle, one of them, The Valadiers' "Greetings (This Is Uncle Sam)" appearing in October of that year. By the time of their third American release "I Found A Girl", written by Clarence Paul and group member Marty Coleman, they had been transferred to Gordy. As with their previous two releases the single made no impression and the act was forgotten about, latter-day UK aficionados seeing to it that CBA 1809 is the top-priced UK Motown single on the collectors' circuit.

### [E19] **Martha & The Vandellas**: I'll Have To Let Him Go / My Baby Won't Come Back
*Oriole American CBA 1814 (Mar 1963)*

One of Motown's major discoveries, Martha & The Vandellas arrived in Gordy's lap almost by accident, their lead singer one of a number of teenagers taken to hanging around Hitsville in the hopes of picking up the odd titbit. Taking up singing under the name Martha LaVaille, Reeves was noticed by William Stevenson and invited to audition. Turning up unexpectedly at nine the next morning, she found a distracted Stevenson rushed off his feet and ended up answering the phones in his office. Thus she was given a job as a secretary, enabling her to develop contacts within Motown, Hitsville's producers often turning to office staff as stand-in backing singers and musicians.

Making regular appearances behind Marvin Gaye, Reeves was eventually spotted and The Vandellas, Rosalind Holmes (Ashford) and Annette 'Betty' Kelly, came together as her group, initially under the name The Vells, as whom they released their first recordings. (The three had previously recorded a few songs together for Chess.) The group's new name was supposedly derived from Van Dyke Street and the singer Della Reese, although the fact that another Motown singer had used the name for an earlier group throws this explanation into doubt.

"I'll Have To Let Him Go" was their first release as Martha & The Vandellas, put out on Gordy in the States. Penned by Mickey Stevenson and recorded on 1 August 1962, the single made little impression at the time but marks another key arrival on Motown's roster which was becoming steadily stronger as the months progressed.

### [E20] **The Marvelettes**: Locking Up My Heart / Forever
*Oriole American CBA 1817 (Apr 1963)*

"Locking Up My Heart" was a modest R & B hit in America and failed to chart in the UK, but has a place in UK popular musical history courtesy of the credited composing team: Holland—Dozier—Holland. Detroit locals all, HDH had come to Motown independently from one another, all fancying their chances as singers before gradually settling into back-room duties. (Eddie Holland even had two UK singles released, [E08] and [E17], the second just a month previously.) Teaming up as a trio for the first time in late 1962, this January recording was one of the first fruits of their collective labours. Wanda Young and Gladys Horton trade lead vocals on the track which ousted the popular ballad "Forever" and stands as a prototype of the soon to be famous HDH sound.

**[E21] Martha & The Vandellas**: Come And Get These Memories / Jealous Lover
*Oriole American CBA 1819 (Apr 1963)*
A second UK release for Martha & The Vandellas within a month, "Come And Get These Memories" had been released in America in February and dented the top 30 pop chart. Hastily prepared for the UK, this new track, also from HDH, reputedly prompted Berry Gordy to declare *'That's* the Motown sound'[12] and certainly the track's laid back melody and stomping 4/4 rhythm point the way ahead. At this stage, before the emergence of The Supremes, Martha & The Vandellas were set to become the company's most important female act, the partnership with HDH promising an exciting future.

**[E22] Mary Wells**: Laughing Boy / Two Wrongs Don't Make A Right
*Oriole American CBA 1829 (May 1963)*
Wells' third UK single was her seventh in the US, again supplied by Smokey Robinson and recorded the previous autumn. Not as successful as her recent releases the single was overlooked and slipped into obscurity despite making the R & B top 10. The UK remained indifferent, The Beatles (who topped the UK charts for the first time on May 2) stealing most of the public's attention.

**[E23] The Contours**: Don't Let Her Be Your Baby / It Must Be Love
*Oriole American CBA 1831 (May 1963)*
After the success of "Do You Love Me" [E10], Gordy continued to personally supply The Contours with new material. The failure of this latest effort caused him to lose much of his interest, the group already looking like a spent force.

**[E24] Marvin Gaye**: Pride And Joy / One Of These Days
*Oriole American CBA 1846 (Jul 1963)*
Recorded in the spring of 1963, "Pride And Joy" was Gaye's second UK single, penned by the singer with Norman Whitfield and Mickey Stevenson, the lyric of which concerns Gaye's new wife Anna Gordy. Primitive in form, with a walking bass from James Jamerson and backing vocals from Martha & The Vandellas, the track has a definite groove and hoisted Gaye into the national top 10 for the first time, and number 2 R & B. As ever, the recording was overlooked in the UK, where "Hitch Hike", his first American top 30 hit early in the year, had failed to appear at all.

**[E25] Mary Wells**: Your Old Standby / What Love Has Joined Together
*Oriole American CBA 1847 (Jul 1963)*
Regarded as a minor recording for Wells, "Your Old Standby" followed "Laughing Boy" in leaving her fans widely unimpressed (although it cracked the top 10 R & B). Somewhat up-tempo and from the normally reliable pen of Smokey Robinson, with input from Janie Bradford, the single's lukewarm reception marked a distinct decline in fortunes for the singer, who had recently headlined Motown's American Revue tours.

**[E26] Little Stevie Wonder**: Fingertips (II) / Fingertips (I)
*Oriole American CBA 1853 (Aug 1963)*
Supposedly brought to Motown by Miracle Ronnie White, Steveland Morris

was presented to Berry Gordy as an impoverished child genius, the 11-year-old having been rendered blind by an oxygen overdose just after his birth. A dubious Gordy took Wonder into the Snakepit to 'audition' and was dazzled by his multi-instrumental talents, Wonder shifting effortlessly about keyboards, brass and even drums. Taking on such a protégé was a tantalising move, his tender age and visual handicap no barrier for Berry Gordy who saw the marketing potential in the youthful performer from the outset. Playful of character and inclined to the odd impression or practical joke, Wonder was welcomed into Motown's circle and was taken under the wing of The Funk Brothers and his fellow recording artists.

Re-christened 'Little Stevie Wonder', he was sent out on the road, "Fingertips" a stage recording made at the Regal Theatre in Chicago, a feral R & B stomp onto which his pre-pubescent *ad libbed* vocals play second-fiddle to his wildly excited harmonica soloing. (At one point he playfully breaks into a section of "Merrily We Roll Along.") Roughly performed, with confusion amongst the band members at one point causing a breakdown, the recording was too lengthy for straight release on 45, Gordy opting to split it across two sides and gamble on Motown's most speculative single to date. His faith in Wonder was rewarded: "Fingertips" became Motown's second American number 1 (after [E05]) on August 10. (Preferring the second part of the track, American tastes determined that the UK release unusually carried Part 2 on the A-side.) Cashing in, Gordy packaged up some more recordings from the same gig, and released *Recorded Live!—The 12 Year Old Genius* to enthusiastic effect, the album lodging itself at the top of the *Billboard* charts for a week, Motown's first such success. At one point Wonder sat proudly at the summit of the LP, pop and R & B charts simultaneously, a remarkable success for a blind 13-year-old—and the stuff of which legends are born.

The Oriole pressing by contrast sold few copies in 1963, although it was clear that a major new talent had turned up. "Fingertips (II)" was exhumed for release on Tamla Motown 17 years later, as TMG 966 [L031b], and again in 1988 [L093] (see Chapter 6).

[E27] **The Miracles**: Mickey's Monkey / Whatever Makes You Happy
*Oriole American CBA 1863 (Sep 1963)*
Supplied by HDH, "Mickey's Monkey" was claimed by Smokey Robinson before it was finished, the singer overhearing Dozier and Brian Holland working on the song in one of Motown's 'writing rooms'. The curious 'mock-live' recording, likened in style to Bo Diddley[13], lies out of character for both the group and its composers, rough-and-ready and inspiring a number of stage moves for The Miracles. Surprisingly successful, "Mickey's Monkey" was the group's biggest pop hit since "Shop Around" [E03], leading to further collaborations with HDH over the ensuing months [E35]. The track was one of a number remade *sans* vocals under the guise of Choker Campbell's Big Band in 1965 [517].

## TIMELINE – 1959 to September 1963

### 1959

| | |
|---|---|
| Jan | Motown's first single, on Tamla label, Marv Johnson: "Come To Me" / "Whisper" (US) |
| Jan | Wade Jones: "I Can't Concentrate" / "Insane", on Rayber. Only release on label |
| Mar | Primettes: "Tears Of Sorrow" / "Pretty Baby" on Lu-Pine. Group will develop into Supremes |
| May | Marv Johnson: "Come To Me" / "Whisper" (UK) on London American label |
| Aug 2 | Gordy family acquire 2648 West Grand Boulevard, subsequently fitted out for offices and recording studio and named 'Hitsville USA' |

### 1960

| | |
|---|---|
| - | Most of Funk Brothers are in place by year-end |
| Jan | Hitsville opens for business |
| Jun | Barrett Strong: "Money (That's What I Want)" / "Oh I Apologise" (UK) |
| Dec 31 | Miracles: "Shop Around" enters US top 40 (peak 2; Motown's first million-seller) |

### 1961

| | |
|---|---|
| Jan 15 | Supremes officially sign with Motown (as Primettes) |
| Feb 15 | Jackie Wilson shot and seriously wounded by lover Juanita Jones |
| Mar 9 | Supremes' first single: "I Want A Guy" / "Never Again" (US) |
| Apr 18 | Jobete Publishing move into 2644-2646 West Grand Boulevard, next door to Hitsville |
| May 25 | Marvin Gaye's first single: "Let Your Conscience Be Your Guide" / "Never Let You Go" (US) |
| Jul 24 | Temptations' first single (on Miracle label): "Oh, Mother Of Mine" / "Romance Without Finance" (US) |
| Sep 7 | First release on Motown label, Satintones: "My Beloved" / "Sugar Daddy" (US) |
| Nov | Fontana take over UK issues from London American (only four will ever appear) |
| Nov | Marvelettes: "Please Mr. Postman" / "So Long Baby" (UK) |
| Dec 11 | Marvelettes: "Please Mr. Postman" number 1 in US (one week) |

### 1962

| | |
|---|---|
| Jan 23 | Gordy buys 2650 West Grand Boulevard, used for his personal office. Also buys 2652-2654 for admin office |
| Mar 16 | US Gordy label launched |
| July | Smokey Robinson appointed Vice President |
| Autumn | Holland—Dozier—Holland team come together for first time |
| Sep | Oriole take over distribution of UK releases from Fontana |
| Sep | Contours: "Do You Love Me" / "Move Mr. Man" (UK) |
| Oct 1 | Martha & The Vandellas' first single (under name The Vells), "You'll Never Cherish A Love So True" / "There He Is (At My Door)" (US) |
| Nov-Dec | First Motown Revue tour travels US east coast from Boston to Florida, with dozens of performers and band of musicians |
| Dec | Motown takes Christmas residency at Apollo Theater |

### 1963

| | |
|---|---|
| - | Choker Campbell quits Funk Brothers after failing to secure own releases. |
| Jan | Miracles: "You Really Got A Hold On Me" / "Happy Landing" (UK) |
| Feb 15 | Marvelettes: "Locking Up My Heart" released (US), first release from HDH |
| Summer | Gordy acquires Harvey and Tri-Phi labels, part-owned by sister Gwen. Gains control of several artists' contracts including Junior Walker & The All Stars |
| Summer | Motown opens New York office, run by Raynoma Gordy and her brother Mike Ossman |
| Jul | First UK album, *Do You Love Me* by Contours, on Oriole |
| Aug 10 | Little Stevie Wonder: "Fingertips Part 2" number 1 in US (three weeks) |
| Aug 24 | Little Stevie Wonder: *Recorded Live—The 12 Year Old Genius* number 1 album in US (one week) |
| Aug 28 | Martin Luther King delivers 'Dream' speech before 200,000 in Washington DC. The text is later released on vinyl by Motown |

## Stateside

Despite having released 19 singles on Motown's behalf, Oriole American's distribution arrangement was terminated in late 1963, the label having put nothing into the UK charts. Once again, Berry Gordy was in search of a suitable UK imprint having shed three different licensees already. By contrast, progress in America had been steady since 1959. Motown had managed to get 24 records into the US top 40, half of which had gone top 10. By September 1963 the company's growing portfolio included The Miracles, Mary Wells, Marvin Gaye, Martha & The Vandellas and Stevie Wonder, with several other promising acts on the periphery. Smokey Robinson and the HDH team were in business as writers, and the signs were that Motown, given the right backing, was capable of making parallel breakthroughs in Britain.

What might have happened next, had The Beatles not appeared and turned the UK market on its head can only be speculated on. "She Loves You" entered the UK charts at the end of August 1963, and was still number one come December. Group manager Brian Epstein also controlled several other acts including Gerry & The Pacemakers, Cilla Black and Billy J Kramer & The Dakotas, who during 1963-64 dominated the UK scene. Between April 1963 and July 1964, Epstein's acts scored an overwhelming 14 number 1s in the UK, leading to the inevitable export of the phenomenon to America. During the same period, the term Beatlemania was coined, and for the time being it seemed, Motown's discovery in Britain would have to wait.

Meanwhile there was the issue of a change in distributor, Motown sending Barney Ales and Gordy's sister Esther over for a series of meetings in several countries, including the UK. The outcome of their negotiations was a promising deal with EMI, the company behind Epstein and The Beatles' releases. EMI's choice imprint, Stateside, was only recently established with releases from several acts including future Motowners Chuck Jackson, The Isley Brothers and Jerry Butler, as well as certain star names from the Sceptre/Wand group including The Shirelles and Dionne Warwick. For Motown the move was portentous, Britain's hottest record company now handling affairs for America's most up-and-coming stable of young artists. In Stateside, Motown had found the key—the final distribution licence required to establish the company before Tamla Motown could stand on its own.

[E28] **Martha & The Vandellas**: Heat Wave / A Love Like Yours (Don't Come Knocking Every Day)
*Stateside SS 228 (Oct 1963)*
One of Martha Reeves' best-loved tracks, and possibly the earliest masterpiece from HDH (Professor Brian Ward: "An impossibly joyous rush of sound"), for many "Heat Wave" signals the start of Motown's rise to pre-eminence. Inspired by a television weather forecast during a sweltering Detroit summer, the track was recorded on June 20 and released 20 days later, making number 4 pop and number 1 R & B (knocking "Fingertips" [E26] from its perch). In Britain it missed the sunny spell and was not a hit, although it has retained a consistent popularity which saw it issued on Tamla Motown in 1980 (TMG 1176 [L015]—see Chapter 6). The initial title of the track was "Heat Wave", which on the 1980 re-issue became "Heatwave" (all one word). It has also appeared elsewhere as

both "(Love Is Like A) Heat Wave", and, short of the brackets, "Love Is Like A Heat Wave", as which it appeared on the US Yesteryear label in the 1970s. It seems possible that such fumbled amendments were made in an attempt to avoid confusion with the Irving Berlin number "Heat Wave".

### [E29] **Little Stevie Wonder**: Workout Stevie, Workout / Monkey Talk
*Stateside SS 238 (Nov 1963)*

The follow-up to Wonder's first successful single was fast coming, recorded and released while its predecessor was still high in the charts. Yet while it did moderate business in America riding the coat-tails of [E26], this rather inconsequential 'freight train blues' written by Clarence Paul and Hank Cosby failed to engage Britain. Wonder's basic harmonica solos, set against gospel backing vocals were likened by Bill Dahl to 'a mouse on speed'[14], an apt description of the adolescent's ineffectual if frantic improvisation.

### [E30] **Mary Wells**: You Lost The Sweetest Boy / What's Easy For Two (Is So Hard For One)
*Stateside SS 242 (Nov 1963)*

Bobbing its way up to number 22 pop and number 10 R & B, "You Lost The Sweetest Boy" was challenged in America by its B-side, "What's Easy For Two (Is So Hard For One)", which landed seven places short in the pop listings but bettered it R & B. With little to choose between the titles in terms of sales, Stateside UK opted for the former, written by HDH and recorded around the time of "Heat Wave" [E28].

"You Lost The Sweetest Boy" carries the team's trademark crotchet pulse, Wells taking to the task with enthusiasm and recovering from a run of relatively uninspired releases provided by Smokey Robinson. The track is regarded fondly by Wells' admirers, earning a welcome re-run as the flip to [820] in 1972.

### [E31] **Marvin Gaye**: Can I Get A Witness / I'm Crazy 'Bout My Baby
*Stateside SS 243 (Nov 1963)*

Penned by HDH, Marvin Gaye's new single was another product of the team's prolific summer of 1963, where their talents were suddenly in high demand. Built from blues chords with a rolling piano providing rhythmic anchoring, the track was recorded with various backing vocalists in attendance, supposedly including members of both The Supremes and The Miracles. Ostensibly about affairs of the heart, the 'witness' theme suggests a religious subtext, lines such as 'I *believe*' and the generally gospel-tinged arrangement hinting at something pious until the re-appearance of the line "The way love's supposed to be", re-cycled from "Heat Wave" [E28], breaks the spell. (Reeves' "Heat Wave" was recorded on 20 Jun 1963, the current track 27 days later.)

### [E32] **Martha & The Vandellas**: Quicksand / Darling, I Hum Our Song
*Stateside SS 250 (Jan 1964)*

Borrowing extravagantly from "Heat Wave" [E28] in form and mood, the rhythmically parallel "Quicksand" is softer in execution if colder in sentiment, and represents a hat trick of successive 45s from the HDH camp. Admired by its lead vocalist (who considered the release too hurried), "Quicksand" cracked the US top 10, backed with "Darling, I Hum Our Song", one of the team's earliest copyrights, first recorded by Eddie Holland in October 1962. This UK release sank without trace but was resurrected for the benefit of 'Northern' fans in 1969, as an appealing B-side to [684], Tamla Motown's full release of "Dancing In The Street" [E54].

### [E33] **The Marvelettes**: As Long As I Know He's Mine / Little Girl Blue
*Stateside SS 251 (Jan 1964)*
After the disappointing returns from "Locking Up My Heart" [E20], The Marvelettes had spent much of 1963 searching for direction. At one point entering the studio to record HDH's Phil Spector-esque "Too Hurt To Cry, Too Much In Love To Say Goodbye", diverted from their regular discography with the adoption of the pseudonym The Darnells[15], they bounced back in the autumn with the Smokey Robinson-penned "As Long As I Know He's Mine", returning to the upper reaches of Billboard's R & B listing. Double-tracked by Gladys Horton, this poppy number was released in the UK the following January and began a professional association with Robinson which would span much of the remainder of the 1960s (up to and including [659]).

### [E34] **The Supremes**: When The Lovelight Starts Shining Thru His Eyes / Standing At The Crossroads Of Love
*Stateside SS 257 (Jan 1964)*
Viewed with scorn by several stable-mates, The Supremes had released six flops in America during 1961-63[16], rival recording stars referring to them mockingly as the 'no-hit Supremes'. The group had arrived at Motown as The Primettes, a quartet featuring their soon-to-be-famous Ross/Wilson/Ballard line-up plus Betty McGlown. Rejected by Gordy primarily on the grounds that they were too young, The Primettes took to hanging around Hitsville, occasionally participating in recording sessions [E31] until in January 1961 they were finally signed. By then the group had lost McGlown, finding a temporary replacement in Barbara Martin before settling into their familiar three-piece set up, re-christened The Supremes by Flo Ballard.

From 1961 through to the end of 1963, The Supremes released half a dozen singles on the US Tamla and Motown labels respectively, the most successful of which, "A Breath Taking Guy", had reached a modest number 75. The follow-up, "When The Lovelight Starts Shining Thru His Eyes", quietly marked the arrival of the group, denting the US top 30 and peaking at number 2 R & B. Another product of the HDH team, the single is an energetic stomp with a sing-along chorus (supposedly aided by the presence of The Four Tops), unspectacular in articulation but sufficiently buoyant to catch the ear of the American public. Along with the US-only "Run, Run, Run" (Motown 1054), the group's milestone UK debut precedes their spectacular impact which began in earnest with "Where Did Our Love Go" [E51] later in the year, an air of hungry anticipation palpable in this bristling October 1963 recording.

**[E35] The Miracles**: I Gotta Dance To Keep From Crying / Such Is Love, Such Is Life
*Stateside SS 263 (Feb 1964)*
Recorded on September 18, the follow up to "Mickey's Monkey" [E27] was aimed uncompromisingly at dance-floor audiences. Penned like its predecessor by HDH, the single poses the question of why Robinson, provider of a significant quantity of contemporary material for his colleagues ([E22]; [E25]; [E33]; [E37]; [E38] etc.) was unable to come up with a viable track of his own. Ultimately something of a disappointment, this variation of "You Lost The Sweetest Boy" [E30] failed to sell and Robinson accordingly took the initiative for the group's next release [E39].

**[E36] Martha & The Vandellas**: Live Wire / Old Love (Let's Try It Again)
*Stateside SS 272 (Mar 1964)*
A pleasing stomp from HDH, possibly over-accelerated, "Live Wire" has the same snappy twin syllables in its title as the group's previous two singles [E28] and [E32], suggesting formulaic writing. It also bears a substantial likeness to "Heat Wave", particularly in the ascending piano figures, giving it a sense of re-hash, which detracts from an otherwise exciting and excited recording, The Funk Brothers' break-neck performance salvaging the recording. Made a week before Christmas, the track's appeal quickly fizzled out and it unexpectedly flopped. Tamla Motown utilised the number as the flip to "Nowhere To Run" when it was reissued in 1969 [694].

**[E37] The Marvelettes**: He's A Good Guy, Yes He Is / Goddess Of Love
*Stateside SS 273 (Mar 1964)*
The Marvelettes' second single of 1964 came from the reliable pen of Smokey Robinson, following up "As Long As I Know He's Mine" [E33] with a mid-tempo 'high-school' whimsy, curiously arranged in the style of HDH. Sung by Gladys Horton, the number made little impression and has been forgotten over the years.

**[E38] The Temptations**: The Way You Do The Things You Do / Just Let Me Know
*Stateside SS 278 (Apr 1964)*
Formed in 1961, The Temptations evolved from earlier groups The Distants, whose members included Otis Williams and Melvin Franklin, and The Primes, a Birmingham outfit which boasted Eddie Kendricks and Paul Williams. The familiar Temptations line-up was complete in 1963 when David Ruffin joined to replace early fifth member Al Bryant, booted out after a violent backstage incident with Paul Williams, the new quintet together for "The Way You Do The Things You Do", their first UK single but seventh in America.

Recorded with Kendricks on lead, the track has a seductive lilt beneath its playfully silly lyric, which carried it to the top of the R & B charts, sealing a working relationship with composer Smokey Robinson which would endure for a further two years and establish The Temptations as one of Motown's prime male groups. Generally recognised as their breakthrough release, the single's impact after several years' hard work represented such a triumph for the group that David Ruffin broke down and sobbed when he saw it listed at number 11 in the US pop charts.[17]

[E39] **The Miracles**: (You Can't Let The Boy Overpower) The Man In You /
Heartbreak Road
*Stateside SS 282 (Apr 1964)*
A curious text from Robinson, "(You Can't Let The Boy Overpower) The
Man In You" portrays the singer's father as moral guardian, reminding him of
his responsibilities in love and life. Rather ungainly in form and title, the track
plods through its verbose verses, Robinson's lead snappily rhythmic if
melodically ambiguous. Robinson revived it for Chuck Jackson in 1968 [651].

[E40] **Marvin Gaye**: You're A Wonderful One / When I'm Alone I Cry
*Stateside SS 284 (Apr 1964)*
Marvin Gaye's fourth British release sustained his collaboration with HDH
[E31], who along with Smokey Robinson, had accounted for 11 consecutive
UK A-sides stretching over the five months since [E30]. Seemingly
impenetrable, the dominance of Robinson and HDH would persist for several
years, these early foundation singles establishing Motown's emergent back-
room aristocracy and working arrangements which to a large extent would
come to define the company's style and sound.

Unusually commencing with an electric guitar riff, "You're A Wonderful
One" is a straightforward piece of R & B, not venturing beyond the standard
design. More 'authentic' than "Can I Get A Witness" [E31], usually referred
to as its direct model, it out-performed its forerunner on the US pop charts by
breaking into the top 20. Backing vocals are again from The Supremes.

[E41] **Little Stevie Wonder**: Castles In The Sand / Thank You (For Loving Me
All The Way)
*Stateside SS 285 (Apr 1964)*
Wonder's most melodic single to date, "Castles In The Sand" was the product
of early West Coast excursions for the filming of *Muscle Beach Party* and
*Bikini Beach*, a couple of William Asher movie vehicles for Frankie Avalon in
which Wonder played himself. A spin-off from Wonder's involvement was the
current track, vaguely tapping into the surf music style then popular, and
notable for the inclusion of ocean and seagull sound effects, a production detail
advanced for its day. The recording shows Wonder maturing, his voice fuller
and deeper than on previous releases and although not a hit, kept his profile
high enough that, around now, The Rolling Stones were booked to support
him on tour.

[E42] **Mary Wells**: My Guy / Oh Little Boy (What Did you Do To Me—)
Stateside SS 288 (May 1964) (UK charts: 5)
After 41 failed attempts, Motown finally landed a single in the UK top 40 with
what became Mary Wells' final release. Recorded on March 3, "My Guy" was
issued just ten days later in America and promptly topped *Billboard's* pop
charts, interrupting four months during which The Beatles monopolised pole
position. Crashing into the UK listings on May 21, the single edged its way
into the top 10, eventually peaking at 5 and causing ripples of excitement back
in Detroit.

Supplied by Smokey Robinson, the song is an uncomplicated statement of loyalty in love, supposedly taped at Hitsville but, according to Carol Kaye, recorded West Coast (see [515]). Lightly rendered, with a carefree rise-and-fall melodicism, the track's popularity was considerable, for the moment making Wells Motown's biggest act. Convinced that she could cut it alone, the 21-year-old walked out and accepted a half-million dollar contract with Twentieth Century Fox in September. Her career rapidly slumped and she would only score a few modest hits before several further unsuccessful label changes proved that it was the Motown machine which was making the major hits—not the star vocalists.

Wells' signature tune, "My Guy" was issued by Tamla Motown in 1972 [820], and again as TMG 1100 in the 1980s [L019] (see Chapter 6).

### [E43] **The Contours**: Can You Do It / I'll Stand By You
*Stateside SS 299 (May 1964)*
Built from the same three chords as "Do You Love Me" [E10] (raised by one semitone), and ushered in with a similar spoken passage, "Can You Do It" is a lame re-write of the former hit, almost two years too late to cash in, despite Billy Gordon's optimistic opening "1964, and we gonna dance some more". Recorded on January 24, the track was supposedly co-written by Berry Gordy's former wife Thelma, although post-compositional donation of copyright seems more likely, presumably for family financial reasons. (Current Monitor and future Temptation Richard Street share the credit and produce.) The track peaked at a modest 16 R & B.

### [E44] **Martha & The Vandellas**: In My Lonely Room / A Tear For The Girl
*Stateside SS 305 (Jun 1964)*
Ending the sequence of double-barrelled titles, Martha Reeves' latest single was recorded after the resignation of pregnant group member Annette Sterling and the recruitment of Velvelette Betty Kelly—although none of the Vandellas are present, backing duties falling to Motown session group The Andantes (see [507n]). Supplied by HDH, and out-of-step with the group's previous releases, "In My Lonely Room" is a melodically buoyant tune, the poignancy of which led Reeves to break into tears during the recording. Atypically light despite its baritone sax break, the track failed to sell, causing a temporary disassociation with HDH.

### [E45] **Brenda Holloway**: Every Little Bit Hurts / Land Of A Thousand Boys
*Stateside SS 307 (Jun 1964)*
An admirer of Mary Wells, Holloway was, according to her own accounts, spotted by Gordy performing "My Guy" [E42]. However the fact that the hit single was released just 13 days prior to Holloway's debut in the US throws this sequence of events into question, Holloway possibly confusing [E42] with one of Wells' earlier hits. Since Gordy initially refused to employ her as she had yet to graduate suggests that the singer, born in June 1946 and by now approaching 18, was likely approached before [E42] was recorded (Mar 3).

"Every Little Bit Hurts" was written by The Four Preps' Ed Cobb, who notably also penned "Tainted Love" (see [910]), and was recorded in Hollywood at Armin Steiner's. Sceptical over the song's 3/4 time signature,

Berry Gordy was reluctant to see it released, the sheer perfection of the recording winning him over. The US edition scaled the R & B charts, settling at 3, and made top 20 pop, leading to its summer UK release. The track remains popular amongst those in the know, for example featuring in 2004 on the UK soundtrack to *No Angels*, a Channel 4 drama which aired several vintage Motown recordings to a mass audience, to most of whom it was new.

### [E46] **Mary Wells & Marvin Gaye**: Once Upon A Time / What's The Matter With You Baby?
*Stateside SS 316 (Jul 1964)*

Marvin Gaye's first notable duet was recorded in April 1963 with Clarence Paul in the producer's chair. Copyrighted to Clarence Paul—Dave Hamilton—William 'Mickey' Stevenson—Barney Ales, this 'old time' ballad drifts casually through its three brief verses with a hint of cha-cha, Gaye and Wells harmonising rather than taking turns at the mike. Rather inconsequential, and weakened by a light-weight xylophone instrumental passage, the track had a moderately warm reception going high on the R & B listing but being out-performed by its flip-side in the US pop charts. The UK edition crept into the top 50, a second success after the recent "My Guy" [E42], and notably bills Wells ahead of Gaye, her profile much the higher at this point.

The union promised much but delivered little, the two recording an album's worth of material in dribs and drabs through 1963, hastily completed with sessions on October 19 and 20. Issued as *Together*, Wells had ironically signed contracts with Twentieth Century Fox by the time the UK pressing appeared and was touring with The Beatles, believing she could prosper outside of Motown's family. Wells' parting left Berry Gordy aggrieved but resolute, seeing to it that Gaye's embryonic career as half of a duo would continue uninterrupted, his first works with Kim Weston following almost immediately [E62].

### [E47] **The Temptations**: I'll Be In Trouble / The Girl's Alright With Me
*Stateside SS 319 (Jul 1964)*

The Temptations' second British single was supplied like its predecessor [E38] by the prolific Smokey Robinson. Recorded on March 25, the track was rush-released in America but waited until July for its Stateside debut. Neither territory showed much interest, the track slipping by discreetly during the nine month lull between [E38] and the landmark "My Girl" [E67].

### [E48] **Stevie Wonder**: Hey Harmonica Man / This Little Girl
*Stateside SS 323 (Aug 1964)*

Sourced from outside of Motown's main bank of writers, "Hey Harmonica Man" was composed by Marty Cooper and Lou Josie, the latter known for his country-style guitar playing (often categorised as rockabilly). Having recorded a number of sides in the late 1950s, Josie was by now concentrating more on writing than performing, teaming up with Cooper around 1963 and coming up with the current title in early 1964. A perfect vehicle for Wonder stylistically, the track was requisitioned by Motown and published by Jobete,

Wonder's recording produced by Hal Davis and Marc Gordon and released in America on May Day. With Wonder's feverish harmonica pushed high in the mix, the vocals are almost incidental, carried mainly by backing voices, and set against a sparse but kicking rhythm track.

Wonder reached the age of 14 on May 13, and reflecting his increasing maturity, Motown dropped the tag 'Little' on his record labels in time for the would-be incongruously titled "Hey Harmonica Man". The single was a notable R & B hit in the States but predictably failed in the UK.

**[E49] The Miracles**: I Like It Like That / You're So Fine And Sweet
*Stateside SS 324 (Aug 1964)*
Co-written by Robinson and Marv Tarplin, "I Like It Like That" commences with the latter's guitar phrasing before slipping into a lilting slow dance, boosted through its central sections by some unusually brassy trumpet breaks. Recorded in-studio with The Miracles providing their own audience effects, the track was made on the last day of April before being re-done on May 12 and released in the weeks which followed.

**[E50] Marvin Gaye**: Try It Baby / If My Heart Could Sing
*Stateside SS 326 (Aug 1964)*
Fresh from his ill-fated union with Mary Wells [E46], Marvin Gaye kept his place in Stateside's release schedules with "Try It Baby". Written by Berry Gordy, the track was recorded in January with The Temptations on backing vocals, and given its stellar cast ought to have packed more of a punch than it did. Somewhat insipid, if prettily done, hindsight shows the release to be an interim project at a time when Motown were about to step up their general standards, Gaye like numerous Motown stars on the verge of a significant breakthrough [E60]. (According to Gerald Posner (p139), Gordy wrote the song for Diana Ross [501].)

**[E51] The Supremes**: Where Did Our Love Go / He Means The World To Me
*Stateside SS 327 (Aug 1964) (UK charts: 3)*
With half a century of UK singles under its belt, Motown finally burst on the scene in September as The Supremes' second release flew into the top 3. Curiously the song was offered around and rejected by more than one act before being dumped on a less-than-enthusiastic Diana Ross for an April session, at which the full lyric had yet to be finalised. (The group were too distrustful of the track to muster enough enthusiasm for the intended backing vocal sections, Lamont Dozier instead throwing in the casual but now famous "Baby, baby" refrain on the spur of the moment.)

The end result was a hypnotically rhythmic pop song with a circulating pattern in which verses and chorus are as one, its commercial viability self-apparent. Yet despite this it sat in the can for a further two months before the American release of June 17, after which it eased its way up the charts to become Motown's fourth US number 1. The UK release almost emulated it, but despite not quite making number 1, the single's success marked a turning point on three fronts. Firstly, it put the patent HDH crotchet sound firmly on the map, the most significant recording in their canon to date largely defining how they would approach writing and production for the rest of their careers. Secondly, it put The Supremes at the top of Motown's agenda, the group emerging from nowhere to dominate Berry Gordy's future plans, with Diana Ross his principal obsession throughout the remainder of their professional union. And lastly, it marked the true arrival of Motown in the UK, threatening to open the floodgates on a musical style which was already becoming massive at home.

In the years since its original Stateside release, "Where Did Our Love Go" has become recognised as a Motown classic and remains one of the company's most famous recordings. Tamla Motown issued a full edition in 1974 [925] and another 30 years later [L104] (see Chapter 6).

### [E52] **The Marvelettes**: You're My Remedy / A Little Bit Of Sympathy, A Little Bit Of Love
*Stateside SS 334 (Sep 1964)*
In the shade of [E51], Smokey Robinson's new composition for The Marvelettes made no impact, the group watching on as The Supremes hit with a song they had previously turned down. Sung by Wanda Young, this preferred track was made in March and released in the States in June without breaking into the top 40. (Its peak position R & B was a modest 16.) Yet despite its unspectacular returns, it was duly offered to British audiences who largely ignored it.

### [E53] **Four Tops**[18]: Baby I Need Your Loving / Call On Me
*Stateside SS 336 (Sep 1964)*
Released with [E51] high in the UK charts, Motown-UK marked another major development in September with a first release for The Four Tops. The group had already been performing together for some ten years, having recorded for Chess in 1956, before being brought to Motown by Berry Gordy's old writing partner Roquel Davis who happened to be group-member Lawrence Payton's cousin. Initially unsure what to do with them, Motown diverted the group onto the minor Workshop Jazz label for a brief while before their historic pairing with HDH.

In fact, HDH had been drawn towards the group from the moment they arrived, although Berry Gordy appears to have personally paved the way for their first collaboration. Duly sanctioned, Brian Holland initiated the professional partnership, calling the group into Hitsville straight after a night gig on May 7 to record vocals for a track which had been sitting on the shelf for about a month. According to legend the group arrived at around 2:00am, with "Baby I Need Your Loving" ready and waiting for their vocal overdubs. The resultant take glows with the intimacy of the moment, Studio A's valve equipment giving the group's close harmonies a warm swell which makes the track's gentle sway as compelling today as when it was first recorded in the still of a Detroit night.

Issued in America in July, the single missed the national top 10 by a place, and crept up to 4 in the R & B listing. Providing the group with an inaugural British outing, the track fared less well in 1964, but is fondly remembered as one of The Four Tops' definitive pieces. "Baby I Need Your Loving" was eventually released on Tamla Motown as a B-side in 1970 (see [732b]) and as an A-side as late as 1982 [L044] (see Chapter 6).

**[E54] Martha & The Vandellas**: Dancing In The Street / There He Is (At My Door)
*Stateside SS 345 (Sep 1964) (UK charts: 28)*
Martha Reeves' signature song, "Dancing In The Street" was written in 1964 and was probably intended for Marvin Gaye, who was involved to some uncertain extent in its composition. Thanks to its pounding drive, accentuated by the fact that the song is carried largely on a single chord, the song won instant approval from all quarters of the audience. Recorded by Reeves on 29 June, it rapidly rose to number 2 in the US, and on release in Britain became Motown's fourth top 40 chart entry, peaking at 28.

The composition has since topped the UK charts in the hands of Mick Jagger & David Bowie, and in the course of four decades the original has come to be regarded as one of Motown's classic recordings. Tamla Motown have pressed it on 7-inch four times: See [684] (1969); [L011] (1976); [L015b] (1980) and [L101] (2004). Full details of the recording can be found in Chapter 3, under [684].

**[E55] The Temptations**: Why You Wanna Make Me Blue / Baby, Baby I Need You
*Stateside SS 348 (Oct 1964)*
This new Temptations 45 made little splash in 1964, but in an era when Motown were making substantial breakthroughs on several fronts, is notable for the names in the brackets. A very early collaboration by Eddie Holland and Norman Whitfield, the track marks the start of a run of successful compositions for the pair over the ensuing three years which came into full bloom with The Temptations' own [565] two years later. (Meantime, Whitfield's itching enthusiasm to write for The Temptations had to wait until Smokey Robinson's hits for the group dried up—see [557].) The Eddie Kendricks-led "Why You Wanna Make Me Blue" was recorded on 6 July and released in the US as "Girl (Why You Wanna Make Me Blue)".

**[E56] The Supremes**: Baby Love / Ask Any Girl
*Stateside SS 350 (Oct 1964) (UK charts: 1)*
Slow to latch on to what Motown were doing Stateside, the UK public couldn't miss The Supremes' explosive new single, and on the heels of "Where Did Our Love Go" [E51], it became a commercial monster. From the opening foot stomps from Mike Valvano [E12], "Baby Love" is a captivating recording, made on 13 August unashamedly in the vein of the group's last single, but like "Where Did Our Love Go" found The Supremes reluctant to record it. Yet come autumn, it was atop the charts on both sides of the Atlantic and whatever artistic reservations The Supremes expressed at the time, set the style for the rest of their professional lives.

"Baby Love" captures the thrill of its time like no other Motown recording, bursting forth with a classic HDH bounce and defining where the company was at in 1964. This major UK breakthrough made The Supremes famous, and in confirming that Motown was commercially viable in Europe, was instrumental in the creation of Tamla Motown itself. "Baby Love", like the recent [E53] and [E54] is a defining moment for the group in question, as Motown's gathering momentum made the company look as if it was about to take the world by storm. By fortunate timing the single appeared just as The Supremes were embarking on their first UK engagements, met on arrival by an entourage of fans and courting the British media over a two-week stay.

The recording was belatedly released on Tamla Motown in 1974 where it came back into the top 20: See [915]. Subsequently it has re-appeared as [L004] (1976) and [L104] (2004): see Chapter 6.

### [E57] **The Miracles**: That's What Love Is Made Of / Would I Love You
*Stateside SS 353 (Nov 1964)*
Copyrighted to Robinson—Rogers—Moore, "That's What Love Is Made Of" relies heavily on guitarist Marv Tarplin's see-sawing foundation for its musical substance. Built on much the same template as the earlier "The Way You Do The Things You Do" [E38], the track is, by Robinson's standards lightweight, and features a child-like lyric, a variation on the nursery rhyme *What Are Little Girls Made Of?* Despite its superfluity the track still cracked the R & B top 10 in America following its summer release there.

### [E58] **Earl Van Dyke**: Soul Stomp / Hot 'n' Tot
*Stateside SS 357 (Nov 1964)*
Motown's house-band The Funk Brothers were led by keyboard-man Earl Van Dyke, who had joined the fold in 1962. Already in his thirties and with a jazz background, Van Dyke fancied he could become a star act in his own right, the first hint at which was the release of this instrumental, supposedly co-written by an unlikely alliance of Berry Gordy's ex-wife Thelma, Richard Street and Billy Gordon (see also [E43]). The stomping band was recorded at Hitsville on July 6, and the resultant track released in America on the new Soul label, created by Gordy as an outlet for raw-edged material aiming purely at black audiences. Soul began life in March 1964 and within two years was Gordy's most important label outside of the 'big three' (see [509]).

### [E59] **Kim Weston**: A Little More Love / Go Ahead And Laugh
*Stateside SS 359 (Nov 1964)*
Brought to Motown as part of a gospel outfit, Weston's group The Wright Specials were signed to Berry Gordy's tiny Divinity label, where they released two low-key singles in 1962-63. Standing out as a potential star, she was quickly extracted from the group and signed as a solo artist, her debut single for Tamla the first recording of "It Should Have Been Me" [660], unreleased in the UK. Her British debut was in fact her fifth American solo release, "A Little More Love" a beautifully classy 'old-time' ballad which heralded not only her arrival but also that of lyricist Sylvia Moy, who co-wrote the song with Mickey Stevenson. The writers' professional relationship would last several years and spawn numerous hits, including Weston's follow-up [511]. The US edition was withdrawn after going on sale, making the contemporary UK pressing of this non-album track of particular worth to Motown collectors.

[E60] **Marvin Gaye**: How Sweet It Is (To Be Loved By You) / Forever
*Stateside SS 360 (Nov 1964)*
Marvin Gaye's third release of 1964, "How Sweet It Is" was created by Holland—Dozier—Holland after Eddie Holland had picked up on a phrase heard on television and formulated the chorus ready for recording on 24 July. (The track was taped hurriedly, Gaye reading from lyric sheets on the studio floor.) The paring of Gaye and HDH was a curious one, but had some potential, as evinced by one or two later hits such as "Your Unchanging Love" [618]. In truth though, the writers' unabashed commitment to commercial pop was irreconcilable with Gaye's 'serious' artistic aspirations, "How Sweet It Is" the singular moment at which the two world-views came into harmonious balance.

Greatly admired by Gaye, the track was a significant hit in America, taking him into the top 10 pop for only the second time [E24]. In the UK the recording just broke into the top 50, Gaye's second and Motown's sixth single to make the listings, although it would fall to Junior Walker to take the number further, with a much rockier rendition almost two years later [571]. Gaye's own version resurfaced on Tamla Motown in 1985 [L071] (see Chapter 6).

[E61] **The Velvelettes**: Needle In A Haystack / Should I Tell Them?
*Stateside SS 361 (Nov 1964)*
By the start of 1964, Berry Gordy had established three major US labels in Tamla, Motown and Gordy, and during the course of the year added two more notable imprints in Soul [E58] and, of relevance here, VIP. This latest addition to the roster got off to a slow start but in September released its first classic in the shape of "Needle In A Haystack", recorded by debutantes The Velvelettes. The group arrived at Motown in 1963 and were initially rejected before Mickey Stevenson gave them his support, and they were eventually signed to the fledgling label. "Needle In A Haystack" was recorded in July and became a modest R & B hit on release in September. The corresponding UK edition emerged late in 1964 to no effect, although down the years it has earned a following. The track was re-issued by Tamla Motown twice in the main run ([595b] and [806]) and twice more since ([L052] and [L107]: see Chapter 6).

[E62] **Marvin Gaye & Kim Weston**: What Good Am I Without You / I Want You 'Round
*Stateside SS 363 (Dec 1964)*
Marvin Gaye's first duet since his short-lived union with Mary Wells [E46] paired two singers both of whom had solo singles released a month earlier ([E59] and [E60]). This particular combination was, according to most accounts, engineered by Weston's long-term partner Mickey Stevenson in an effort to up her standing. Well-suited personalities, Gaye and Weston had a professional 'spark' but this failed to show in their recording of "What Good Am I Without You", a steadily plodding run-down of rhetorical questions at which each singer takes turns.

The track is copyrighted to Stevenson and the little-noted Alphonso Higdon, and was recorded on September 11 1964 to dip into the lower end of the R & B top 40. The session was followed by further recordings for a scheduled LP which never emerged, the duet not resurfacing for over two years [590].

### [E63] **The Marvelettes**: Too Many Fish In The Sea / A Need For Love
*Stateside SS 369 (Jan 1965)*

"Too Many Fish In The Sea" was another product of the new Whitfield—Holland team [E55], providing The Marvelettes with an eighth UK single. Recorded in September with Gladys Horton on lead and released in America the following month, this up-tempo rocker predictably fared well on the R & B charts and also made 25 nationally. (It is interesting with hindsight to hear each group-member take a momentary lead vocal for the rotating line 'short ones, tall ones, fine ones, kind ones', a precursor of Whitfield's later strategy for The Temptations, starting with [707].) The UK edition faltered as had the group's previous seven, although once Tamla Motown was up and running the group continued to see a high quantity of UK releases, one of which [609] charted.

### [E64] **Four Tops**: Without The One You Love / Love Has Gone
*Stateside SS 371 (Jan 1965)*

An effort by HDH to recapture the magic of "Baby I Need Your Loving" [E53], "Without The One You Love" has a similar musical progression but is sped up, masking the family relationship of the two numbers. Nonetheless, the opening line virtually reprises the famous chorus of its predecessor, introducing the track as a continuation of themes. Edging here towards the group sound which would make The Four Tops famous in the UK in 1965-66, the single is an easy-going recording completed on 2 October 1964. Given its poppy credentials, it achieved disappointing sales, but was noted by Motown nonetheless and resurrected for an extremely belated duet with The Supremes in 1972 [815].

### [E65] **The Supremes**: Come See About Me / Always In My Heart
*Stateside SS 376 (Jan 1965) (UK charts: 27)*

This HDH original, regarded as a classic in America, was poorly received in the UK despite having reached number 1 at home over Christmas, the middle in a run of five such successes for The Supremes with consecutive releases. Given that the group's earlier UK hits [E51] and [E56] had been such notable triumphs, the lowly number 27 placing came as an anti-climax, partly explained by the song's recent appearance on the group's inaugural UK album *Meet The Supremes*.[19] Buried on the LP, "Come See About Me" was only selected for 45 as a result of a competing cover version from Nella Dodds for the Wand label, which had been produced as a virtual copy of the original, and spurred Berry Gordy to strike a pre-emptive counter-blow.

Noted for its pioneering drum fade-in, a minor studio experiment which resonated with Motown's spirit of adventure at the time, the track predicted several similarly futuristic intros in the succeeding few years (not least that of its follow-up [501]). The release was unfortunately dwarfed by the group's other period singles but has nonetheless re-appeared on Tamla Motown a couple of times: as [L062b] (1985) and [L074b] (1986).

**[E66] The Miracles**: Come On Do The Jerk / Baby Don't You Go
*Stateside SS 377 (Jan 1965)*
The Miracles' new single (their tenth in the UK) was written off the back of Chicago hit 'The Jerk', which in turn homaged a flourishing dance craze. According to Bobby Rogers, the song was composed on the road and custom-made for stage performances, the group currently in California on touring duty.[20] It was properly recorded in LA on 4 November 1964, one of Motown's earliest West Coast products, with locally based Brenda Holloway [E45] present on backing vocals.

Smokey Robinson has put its failure to break through down to its being overshadowed by the enduring "Mickey's Monkey" [E27], which 'just would not die', describing "Come On Do The Jerk" as the 'follow-up' release.[21] Robinson though is confusing the chronology, there being several Miracles singles (not to mention a year and a half) separating the recordings. While his view might say something of its reception by live audiences, it fails to fully explain why national audiences were not sufficiently impressed to put the track into the top 40. A Tamla Motown pressing has since emerged: [696b].

**[E67] The Temptations**: My Girl / Talkin' 'Bout Nobody But My Baby
*Stateside SS 378 (Jan 1965)*
With The Miracles' disappointing "Come On Do The Jerk" [E66] in the air at the time, it is curious to say the least that Smokey Robinson, ambitious as he was for his own group, passed this major hit across to The Temptations, also tutoring them through the vocal parts and producing the session on which they claimed it as their own. Robinson has stated that the song was custom made for vocalist David Ruffin, which is surprising given that at that stage, he was not considered lead singer in the group. (Ruffin himself has gone on record as saying the song was written for his daughter, while Robinson's wife Claudette has said it was for her.[22])

Whatever was going through Robinson's mind when "My Girl" was being constructed, this cleverly conceived update of "My Guy" [E42] proves him at his most fertile, able to toss off an enduring soul classic with no pressing inspiration besides his own sense of fun in playing with song titles. (The two tracks, male and female counterparts of each other both topped the US charts, separated by only ten months.) Tamla Motown have issued the track as a B-side: See [688] for further details.

**[E68] The Contours**: Can You Jerk Like Me / That Day When She Needed Me
*Stateside SS 381 (Jan 1965)*
Celebrating the same dance step as had given rise to "Come On Do The Jerk" [E66], released just four days earlier in America, this new single by the raucous Contours almost did not appear. Following a dispute with Berry Gordy, the group effectively resigned from Motown, Billy Gordon agreeing behind the backs of the others to stay, and Gordy recruiting a new set of Contours to back him, much to the annoyance of his absent colleagues. Original member Sylvester Potts was brought back in nine months later and, thus re-formed, the group stayed on the books for several more years, with further line-up changes occurring from time to time.

"Can You Jerk Like Me" steamrollers along in the group's patent style, their fifth UK single so far. Recorded on 21 October 1964, the track went into the R & B top 20 and was re-pressed on Tamla Motown in 1974 [886b].

[E69] **Martha & The Vandellas**: Wild One / Dancing Slow
*Stateside SS 383 (Jan 1965)*
Coincidentally recorded just as The Shangri Las' "Leader Of The Pack" was being released[23], Martha & The Vandellas' new single was inspired by the classic 1953 biker movie *The Wild One*, directed by László Benedek and starring Marlon Brando as gang-leader Johnny Stabler. Johnny's leather attire and generally lawless behaviour created an iconic 1950s screen image, paving the way for figures such as James Dean and Elvis Presley in the following years, and to be honest, was an odd point of reference for Motown.

Nonetheless inspired, Mickey Stevenson and Ivy Jo Hunter came up with this mid-tempo stomper, carrying an appropriate lyric about defiant love for a misunderstood 'rebel'. "Wild One" though appeals not for its words but for the uncompromising slam of its percussion, anticipating "Nowhere To Run" [502] and thrilling dance audiences. It peaked highest on *Billboard's* R & B listings, going to number 11 over Christmas.

[E70] **Carolyn Crawford**: When Someone's Good To You / My Heart
*Stateside SS 384 (Feb 1965)*
Fondly remembered, Carolyn Crawford was brought to Motown as a 14-year-old, having won a Detroit talent contest on which Berry Gordy happened to be one of the judges. Recognising him, Crawford elected to sing Mary Wells' "Laughing Boy" [E22], Gordy's ears pricking up when she threw in an extra, *ad libbed* verse, suggesting she might be a songwriter-in-the-making. As it transpired, Crawford did not do a great deal at Motown, releasing just three US singles, "My Smile Is Just A Frown Turned Upside Down" the second, and best-known. Its follow-up, "When Someone's Good To You" was her only UK release although she did get another track on Tamla Motown's first EP in March (see Appendix 1). This debut UK single was written and produced by Berry Gordy, recorded on 22 July 1964 and released at home in November. A slowly pounding tale of woe, the track was not a hit, but its obscurity has added to the mystique surrounding Crawford's Motown recordings, copies of this Stateside pressing changing hands today for hundreds of pounds. Several years on the singer would join Motown's latter-day rivals Philadelphia International.

[E71] **The Velvelettes**: He Was Really Sayin' Somethin' / Throw A Farewell Kiss
*Stateside SS 387 (Feb 1965)*
The Velvelettes' second single has, like its predecessor [E61], come to be seen as something of a classic, "He Was Really Sayin' Somethin'" supplied by the same writing team (with additional input from Eddie Holland). High-school fun, this playful number was the first of the pre-Tamla Motown catalogue to be re-issued on the new label (as [595]), paired up with the group's earlier release. In fact, history has tied [E61] and [E71] together so intimately that they are considered almost a bipartite work, Tamla Motown's re-issue policy

from the late 1970s onwards resulting in their being issued together several more times, including [L052] (1983) and [L107] (2004), as well as the blue label Motown-UK pressing TMG 1124 (1978).

This first-ever UK pressing didn't chart, but the American equivalent on VIP made a creditable 21 in the R & B listings.

**[E72] Tony Martin**: Talking To Your Picture / Our Rhapsody
*Stateside SS 394 (Mar 1965)*

Bringing the curtain down on the Stateside-Motown arrangement, this final single was one of the most unlikely, Tony Martin (christened Alvin Morris) a 42-year-old actor-turned-singer based in LA. Recruited for no obvious reason, Martin recorded this single under direction of producers Hal Davis and Marc Gordon, both sides written by Billy Page. Not surprisingly a flop, the single was nonetheless followed up in October, Tamla Motown also taking a punt on the ageing vocalist to no avail [537].

# Developing The Brand

After 45 outings, Stateside abdicated its Motown licence, going out unspectacularly. However Tony Martin's final release was atypical, the rest of the company's talent coming up with the goods consistently by the start of 1965, and despite wallowing in the shadows of the beat-group explosion which had come to characterise most of the music stacking up in the UK charts, Motown was managing to gain some ground. Still viewed with an element of suspicion, this American brand had established a hardcore, almost underground following in Britain. In 1963, Dave Godin had started up the Tamla-Motown Appreciation Society (TMAS) with the very real ambition of promoting the music to such an extent that it was *bound* to be accepted. Within a year or so, TMAS counted its membership in the couple of hundreds, issuing a regular magazine and organising welcoming committees for visiting Motown acts.

During the Stateside era, Motown had finally made some commercial in-roads in the UK, Mary Wells the first to go top 10 during 1964 [E42], quickly followed by The Supremes [E51] and then Martha & The Vandellas [E54]. Come November, The Supremes sat for the first time at the summit of the UK listings with "Baby Love" [E56], the first American group to get there in two-and-a-half years.

Partly the success was down to the absorption of Motown by certain elements of the new mod scene. Played in tightly packed clubs to revellers hyped on amphetamine, Motown's driving rhythms held their own against some of the more energetic beat music, drawing British acts towards the Motown sound, which many would happily name-drop in interviews. The Rolling Stones openly borrowed from Motown and black American music generally (see note [9] below), but the key factor in terms of getting Motown into the minds of British youth came through liberal endorsement from The Beatles.

Lennon and McCartney knew of Motown long before visiting America for the first time in 1964, and had absorbed black styles into their live repertoire several years earlier (eg the pre-Motown Isley Brothers' "Twist And Shout", picked up during 1962). During the group's first year under contract to EMI, manager Brian Epstein had approached Berry Gordy to negotiate a rate for three Motown covers scheduled for inclusion on the Beatles' second LP. Approved and duly recorded, Lennon sang lead on all of the tracks, [E02], [E05] and [E13], songs hitherto largely unknown in Britain but consequently bought and listened to by the million. In terms of influence on the group's style, Motown's was one of the most pervasive, and yet one of the least documented, and in turn The Beatles channelled it through to their own unsuspecting public and, significantly, to their British peers.[24]

In terms of Lennon and McCartney's songwriting craft, Smokey Robinson in particular was a formative figure in some of their best early work, Lennon's absorption of his American counterpart expressed through numbers such as "No Reply", "Not A Second Time", "All I've Gotta Do" etc. with their doleful, winding melodicism and climactic middle-8s. That said, the less prolific George Harrison was Robinson's biggest fan in the group, claiming the harmony on their recording of "You Really Got A Hold On Me" [E13] above McCartney, while his partner's later melody to (Lennon's) "In My Life" was 'Miracles inspired'. A bassist with an exceptionally sharp ear for melody, McCartney has not surprisingly singled out James Jamerson as a prime influence, despite the fact that the latter's anonymity meant that McCartney (supposedly) did not even know Jamerson's name throughout the 1960s. McCartney's writing too showed evidence of Motown influence for several years, bouncing off the label's period sound in 1965 with "Eight Days A Week", soon followed by the Four Tops-esque "You Won't See Me" and the HDH-style "Got To Get You Into My Life".

More generally, Motown's cutting edge recording practises and studio technique, in which multi-track recording was developed, seeped into The Beatles' minds, the sheer volume obtained in Detroit dwarfing UK studios of the day and prompting Lennon to question why EMI couldn't achieve the same results. (Discussing the issue with The Four Tops' Lawrence Payton, he enquired whether Motown's drummers beat their kits with "a bloody tree".) The problem boiled down to technological advance, the signal-volume of a given record limited by the size of the groove, but in pushing EMI and their producer George Martin for development in this respect, The Beatles dragged much of the UK record industry up by its bootlaces.

One of the first Motown stars to cross the Atlantic was Mary Wells, prestigiously booked in 1964 to tour with The Beatles, who promoted her enthusiastically. Following the group's triumphant return from America later that year, The Beatles deliberately began plugging Motown, for whom their respect and professional interest was flourishing. McCartney, who had heard "Baby I Need Your Loving" [E53], made a point of recommending it repeatedly to the UK press, while Harrison, quizzed on his musical tastes informed DJ Tony Hall that he was listening specifically to "Mary Wells, The Miracles and Marvin Gaye". The following year, The Beatles were again vocal in support of the 1965 UK Motown Revue, and sought out Brenda Holloway to join them for their summer tour of America before including an off-hand sketch of "It's The Same Old Song" [528] on their Christmas fan-club record.

Appreciated back at Hitsville, The Beatles' advocacy drew warm tribute from Berry Gordy who was prompted to state, "We are very honoured The Beatles should have said what they did. They're creating the same kind of music as we are and we're part of the same stream", a quote pulled by the *Sunday Times* under the telling headline 'Nod From Beatles Puts Detroit Sound On Map'.[25]

In truth, by the turn of 1965, all the elements were in place for Motown's assault on the UK. Major acts to have broken through over the previous 18 months included the company's primary groups The Supremes, The Temptations and The Four Tops, and essentially the label's biggest names were now all in place. The problem as Berry Gordy saw it was merely one of marketing strategy, and appreciative of the loyalty of his UK fan-base, Gordy invited Dave Godin to Detroit to mull over the issue. Gordy was looking for Godin to pinpoint which artists and recordings should be especially promoted in Britain, The Supremes an obvious first choice. Godin though was thinking on a grander scale and saw that Motown could fire on all fronts if the public could be taught to recognise a new release simply by the company brand, and would therefore know what to expect from each upcoming act. The upshot of Godin's analysis was that Motown needed its own UK label. In contrast to the US where several imprints were in use, Britain required just one, readily identifiable and separate from the rest of the field. Previous releases on Stateside had included the phrase 'A Tamla-Motown Production' in the small print (from where TMAS derived their name), and this 'badge' was the one selected for the UK.

Gordy proposed the idea to current distributors EMI, who unusually consented to give Tamla Motown its own individual outlet. (This landmark decision represents the first time Motown had its own label outside of the USA, and was mirrored by the simultaneous creation of Tamla Motown globally.) The UK label was created using EMI's standard black design template, featuring the large '45' insignia, as used on the Stateside releases (and on other EMI labels such as Parlophone, His Master's Voice and (later) Columbia). The only amendment was the inclusion of the new Tamla Motown emblem, neatly inscribed and boxed, at the top. Avoiding the stigma of releasing a record numbered 001, the Tamla Motown numbers were to commence at 501[26], the prefix TMG derived from the initials of Gordy's three largest US labels.[27] Sleeves were designed and printed up in bright orange, Tamla Motown ready to go by March. EMI staff were assigned responsibility for the new project, Rex Oldfield and Colin Hadley joining A & R man Derek Everett in a largely self-contained London office whose job it was to accept viable cuts sent over from Detroit and present them to the British public. (Motown even recorded a special greetings record for UK fan-club members to which virtually all of the label's biggest stars contributed.[28])

## March 1965: 'A Triumph of Communication'

Launch date for Tamla Motown UK was set for Friday March 19, 1965. On that day, some 18 records were issued, six each of singles, EPs and LPs.[29] Meantime, Motown had sent six acts to Europe for a Revue tour, arriving in the UK on March 18. The entourage was greeted at Heathrow by a crowd of enthusiastic TMAS members before being whisked to the BBC television studios to tape a *Ready Steady Go!* special hosted by Dusty Springfield. (Aired on April 21 as *The Sound Of Motown*, this recording, since made available commercially, offers a fascinating insight into where Motown were at in the spring of 1965, stage choreography often primitive but engaging and involved personnel who were clean cut, tutored and immaculately attired.)

Thereafter it was off on a hectic 24 day UK tour, including 21 live dates. Commencing on March 20 at the Astoria in Finsbury Park, the Revue snaked across Britain taking in the major towns and cities. Bristol, Birmingham, Manchester, Leeds, up to Glasgow on April 1 followed by Newcastle and Liverpool before ending up in Portsmouth on April 12.[30] Dave Godin had fore-warned Gordy that it might be too soon for such an ambitious stunt, and it is true that the shows themselves met with varying levels of enthusiasm, and press coverage was mixed. Many of the venues were not filled, and the March 26 engagement in Kingston Upon Thames was so poorly subscribed that the promoter ended up giving a reported 1000 tickets away in a vain effort to fill seats. Featured on the tour were The Earl Van Dyke Sextet, acting as the Revue's backing band.[31] While glad of the rare chance of public exposure, some of the musicians became thoroughly fed-up with the schedule and miserable English weather, and caused a near catastrophic split with Gordy over remuneration for their *Ready Steady Go!* performance for which they had not received their dues for what turned out to be a live show. (They had expected to be miming.) Having eventually wrung a $52.50 fee from Gordy, they were then asked to give the payment back, and so two hours before the Liverpool gig on April 4 was due to commence, the band announced that they were on strike, forcing Gordy to pledge additional payments or deal with the prospect of the Revue closing down.

Despite the air of despondency in the camp, the tour pressed on and saw the gruelling program through before heading off to mainland Europe for further dates. The full line-up, besides Van Dyke's band, included Stevie Wonder, The Supremes, The Miracles, The Temptations and Martha & The Vandellas. Launching Tamla Motown, the inaugural singles [501] to [506] included one by each of these acts, the famous TMG series commencing with the pre-eminent Supremes, whose "Stop! In The Name Of Love" [501] was already climbing the American top 40 on its way to becoming their fourth straight number 1 there.

Motown and EMI had done all they could. The stars were on the road, the BBC put them into people's living rooms and the record company even printed a special feature in *Record Mail* (EMI's self-published paper) promoting the launch. Berry Gordy was quoted as saying, "The fact that our Tamla Motown label will be introduced in England by EMI this month is truly a milestone for us here. It represents a triumph of communication".[32] All he could do now was sit back and see how Tamla Motown would fare, 4,000 miles across the ocean.

## 1963

| | |
|---|---|
| Oct | UK releases licensed to Stateside, EMI imprint founded July |
| Oct | Martha & Vandellas: "Heat Wave" / "A Love Like Yours" (UK) |
| Oct 12 | Brian Poole & The Tremeloes' cover of "Do You Love Me" tops the UK charts for 3 weeks—first Motown composition to achieve the feat |
| Autumn | Soul music further popularised in US by Sam Cooke, Impressions, Rufus Thomas etc. |

## 1964

| | |
|---|---|
| Jan 23 | First release on VIP label, Serenaders: "If Your Heart Says Yes" / "I'll Cry Tomorrow" (US) |
| Early | Marv Johnson and Kim Weston visit UK for live dates |
| Feb 1 | Beatles top US singles chart for first time, marking start of so-called British Invasion. |
| Mar 23 | First release on Soul label, Shorty Long: "Devil With The Blue Dress" / "Wind It Up" (US) |
| May 16 | Mary Wells: "My Guy" number 1 in US (two weeks) |
| May 21 | Mary Wells: "My Guy" enters UK top 50 (peak 5); Motown's first UK top 10 hit |
| Jul 10 | Four Tops' first single: "Baby I Need Your Loving" / "Call On Me" (US) |
| Jul 30 | Mary Wells & Marvin Gaye: "Once Upon A Time" enters UK top 50 (peak 50) |
| August | Existing recording console at Hitsville replaced with custom-built 8-track machine |
| Aug 22 | Supremes: "Where Did Our Love Go" number 1 in US (two weeks) |
| Sep 3 | Supremes: "Where Did Our Love Go" enters UK top 50 (peak 3) |
| Sep 12 | Nine days of performances at Fox Theater, New York commence, by Supremes, Temptations, Contours, Martha & Vandellas, Marvin Gaye, Miracles and others |
| Sep | Four Tops: "Baby I Need Your Loving" / "Call On Me" (UK) |
| Sep | Mary Wells leaves Motown |
| Oct 7 | Supremes leave America for first UK tour. Meet Beatles on Oct 15 |
| Oct 29 | Martha & Vandellas: "Dancing In The Street" enters UK top 50 (peak 28) |
| Oct 31 | Supremes: "Baby Love" number 1 in US (four weeks) |
| Nov | Velvelettes: "Needle In A Haystack" / "Should I Tell Them?" (UK) |
| Nov 19 | Supremes: "Baby Love" UK number 1 (two weeks); Motown's first UK chart-topper; Motown tops UK and US singles charts simultaneously for nine days |
| Nov 20 | Marvin Gaye appears on UK TV Ready, Steady, Go! |
| Dec | Miracles on UK TV Ready, Steady, Go! |
| Dec 10 | Nobel Peace Prize awarded to Martin Luther King |
| Dec 10 | Sam Cooke shot and killed by owners of motel where he was staying |
| Dec 10 | Marvin Gaye: "How Sweet It Is (To Be Loved By You)" enters UK top 50 (peak 49) |
| Dec 19 | Supremes: "Come See About Me" number 1 in US (two weeks) |
| Dec 25 | Marvin Gaye, Marvelettes, Miracles, Supremes, Stevie Wonder perform in Motown Revue at Fox Theater, New York |
| Dec 27 | Supremes perform "Come See About Me" (currently US number 1) on Ed Sullivan Show |

## 1965

| | |
|---|---|
| Jan 21 | Supremes: "Come See About Me" enters UK top 50 (peak 27) |
| Feb | Velvelettes: "He Was Really Sayin' Somethin'" / "Throw A Farewell Kiss" (UK) |
| Feb 21 | Malcolm X shot and killed in New York. (By unfortunate coincidence, Junior Walker's "Shotgun" was hitting in America at the time) |
| Mar 4 | Motown Acquire 2656 West Grand Boulevard for finance dept. |
| Mar 6 | Temptations: "My Girl" number 1 in US (one week) |
| Mar 12 | Motown Revue comes to Europe for series of dates through to mid-April |
| Mar 18 | Temptations: "My Girl" enters UK top 50 (peak 43) |
| Mar 18 | Sounds Of Motown recorded London, televised special hosted by Dusty Springfield. Acts appearing include Supremes, Miracles, Stevie Wonder, Temptations, Martha & Vandellas |
| Mar 19 | Tamla Motown launched in UK |

[1] The camaraderie amongst The Funk Brothers was undisputed, and often expressed itself in humorous ways. Following an incident when he fell asleep at his kit mid-gig, Benny Benjamin earned himself a nickname when, waking with a start, he cried out 'Papa Zita, Papa Zita'. His drumming associates Pistol Allen and Uriel Jones would jokingly greet each other, "Hi Piss", "Hi Urine", and when white guitarist Joe Messina joined the fold, taking his place between Robert White and Eddie Willis, the three were dubbed The Oreo Cookie Section, a reference to the black biscuit with white centre filling.

[2] His words appear in The Funks' 2002 documentary *Standing In The Shadows Of Motown*.

[3] Berry was the second-youngest of eight siblings, all of whom had influence. In terms of formal company positions, sister Esther was appointed Senior Vice President, and Loucye (d.1965) was Vice President and director of Jobete. Robert Gordy also held senior status with Jobete, while Fuller became a company executive and Gwen a Motown producer. George contributed his songwriting skills, and Anna also worked in the business, her own early label instrumental in the creation of Motown. (Anna and Gwen married Marvin Gaye and Harvey Fuqua respectively.)

[4] There were 19 in total prior to the close of 1976, and several others in which Motown had an interest without directly controlling. The Motown-owned ones, and their first releases are as follows: Tamla (Jan 1959); Motown (Sep 1960); Miracle (Jan 1961); Gordy (Mar 1962); Workshop Jazz (May 1962); Mel-o-dy (Jun 1962); Divinity (Jul 1962); VIP (Jan 1964); Soul (Mar 1964); Rare Earth (Jun 1969); Weed (Nov 1969); Black Forum (Oct 1970); Mo-West (Jun 1971); Ecology (Mar 1971); Natural Resources (May 1972); Yesteryear (Nov 1972); Melodyland (Oct 1974); Prodigal (Oct 1975); Hitsville (May 1976). Fewer than half of these fed material to Tamla Motown.

[5] Accounts of such incidents can be found in Williams p103, Abbott p170, Dahl p22-3, Taraborrelli (1989) p202-3, and across the literature generally.

[6] These are nevertheless included in the discographies of Davis (1988) and Abbott. Although in the loosest sense Motown product, the recordings were not issued by Motown in America, and the UK London American editions make no mention of the company. The discs in question are "You Got What It Takes" / "Don't Leave Me" (Dec 1959); "I Love The Way You Love" / "Let Me Love You" (Apr 1960); "All The Love I've Got" / "Ain't Gonna Be That Way" (Jul 1960); "You've Got To Move Two Mountains" / "I Need You" (Sep 1960); "Happy Days" / "Baby Baby" (Jan 1961); and "Merry-Go-Round" / "Tell Me That You Love Me" (Mar 1961). Of similar status is Paul Gayten's "The Hunch" / "Hot Cross Buns" (Nov 1959). See [E02].

[7] MacDonald 1994: "The Beatles' version… comprehensively demolishes Barrett Strong's 1959 recording".

[8] Quoted in Abbott, p139: "Taken up by [The Beatles], Barrett Strong's original remains the best".

[9] The Beatles recorded two other early Motown numbers in 1963 ("Please Mr. Postman" and "You Really Got A Hold On Me"), The Rolling Stones another three in 1964-65 ("Hitch Hike", "Can I Get A Witness" and "My Girl"), after touring with Stevie Wonder [E41]. Much later The Stones would also release renditions of [547], [565], [690a] and [773], and widely bootlegged versions of [E28], [545], [722] and [846]. (They also recorded the non-Motown compositions [532] and [600].)

[10] Bill Dahl, in Abbott, p73.

[11] Dahl p225

[12] According to Esther Gordy, cited in Abbott, p169.

[13] Dahl p131

[14] p198

[15] The track reached the UK market on the Stateside EP *Chartmakers No. 3*. See Appendix 1.

[16] "I Want A Guy" / "Never Again" (Tamla 54038); "Buttered Popcorn" / "Who's Lovin'

You" (Tamla 54045); "Your Heart Belongs To Me" / "He's Seventeen" (Motown 1027); "Let Me Go The Right Way" / "Time Changes Things" (Motown 1034); "My Heart Can't Take It No More" / "You Bring Back Memories" (Motown 1040); "A Breath Taking Guy" / "The Man With The Rock And Roll Banjo Band" (Motown 1044). Another release under the group name Primettes pre-dates these, "Tears Of Sorrow" / "Pretty Baby", released on the unrelated LuPine label in 1960.

[17] According to Otis Williams, p74.

[18] The group were billed as 'Four Tops' on their records, although they are universally spoken of as 'The Four Tops'. There are one or two exceptions to this convention on the Tamla Motown output, such as [710] and [752].

[19] Recorded as far back as July 13, the track was issued on *Where Did Our Love Go* in America, a different album called *Meet The Supremes* having been released there in 1962. The UK edition of the latter title cannibalised both sets for its contents.

[20] As quoted in Abbott, p77.

[21] *ibid*

[22] The Ruffin claim is noted in Taraborrelli (1986) p33. Claudette Robinson's comments can be found in the notes to *The Complete Motown Singles Vol. 4*.

[23] In her autobiography (p119), Reeves implies that the song was written in the aftermath of "Leader Of The Pack", as if by direct influence. However "Leader" entered the US top 40 on October 24, almost two months after "Wild One" was begun and five days after it was completed.

[24] Stories have circulated that while The Beatles were seeking an American label they approached Motown who turned them down. It is hard to see how such an arrangement might have worked, the group self-reliant and based in London.

[25] See Hirshey p185. The semi-serious 'Stamp Out The Beatles" campaign, organised by some of the smaller Detroit promoters in the 1960s had nothing to do with Motown. However McCartney would have won few friends when, asked by a reporter what he thought about it, retorted that The Beatles had a campaign of their own, "To stamp out Detroit". A bizarre sequel to this occurred in 1969 when rumours emanated from Detroit that McCartney had died three years earlier, evidence of which could be found in a series of 'clues' embedded in The Beatles' record sleeves and lyrics.

[26] Demo copies of TMG 499 which have circulated (The Isley Brothers: "Why When Love Is Gone" / "My Love Is Your Love") are fakes, there being no such catalogue number (and indeed the group were not signed to Motown when the TMG series commenced).

[27] An alternative theory holds that TMG means 'Tamla Motown Great Britain'. This is supported by Tamla Motown singles released in certain parts of the world such as Nigeria where the prefix is TMN, and South Africa where TMS is used. However it does not account for the use of TMG in other European countries such as Denmark, Portugal and the Republic of Ireland. (Interestingly, Greece has GTM.) In each case the scheme is presumably devised by the local distributor rather than Motown itself, but does not always appear logical, Australian singles for example prefixed TMO, Swedish releases TMK, and Argentina's TMS. (When Motown merged its cataloguing systems for American releases in December 1981, the only three active labels remaining were Tamla, Motown and Gordy, the new single and album sequences becoming known, somewhat confusingly, as the 'TMG Consolidated' Series.)

[28] The contents of this legendary and scarce disc were eventually transferred to CD and issued as an extra on *A Cellarful Of Motown! Volume 2*.

[29] The EPs are detailed in Appendix 1. The LPs were: *A Collection of 16 Big Tamla Motown Hits* (Various Artists); *With Love (From Us To You)* (The Supremes); *I Like It Like That* (The Miracles); *How Sweet It Is* (Marvin Gaye); *Heatwave* (Martha & The Vandellas); *My Baby Just Cares For Me* (Mary Wells).

[30] The full itinerary is as follows: March 20: Astoria, Finsbury Park; March 21:

Hammersmith Odeon; March 23: Colston Hall, Bristol; March 24: Capitol Theatre, Cardiff; March 25: Birmingham Odeon; March 26: ABC, Kingston; March 27: Winter Gardens, Bournemouth; March 28: Leicester Odeon; March 30: Manchester Odeon; March 31: Leeds Odeon; April 1: Glasgow Odeon; April 2: ABC, Stockton; April 3: Newcastle City Hall; April 4: Liverpool Empire; April 6: ABC, Luton; April 7: ABC, Chester; April 8: City Hall, Sheffield; April 9: ABC, Wigan; April 10: Wolverhampton Gaumont; April 11: Ipswich Gaumont; April 12: Guild Hall, Portsmouth. The Revue proceeded to also visit France, Holland and Germany.

[31] The sextet comprised pianist Van Dyke, plus Robert White (guitar), Tony Newton (bass), Jack Ashford (vibes), Eli Fontaine (sax) and Bob Cousar (drums). Uriel Jones joined the band for the European dates, Cousar switching to trombone to accommodate him. Motown's drive to keep its central musicians in the studio from 1964 onwards accounts for the absence of most of the other key Funk Brothers. Recordings from the tour survive—see [532].

[32] Quoted in *Record Mail* March 1965 (Vol. 8 no.3), p 8. Gordy accompanied the Revue tour, bringing his parents and three of his four children (one-year-old Kennedy, who recorded for Motown in the mid 1980s under the name Rockwell, staying in Detroit). They met The Beatles during their time in London, a photographic memento of which can be found in Gordy, after p240.

# CHAPTER TWO

# A GOLDEN ERA

## *1965 to 1967*

**TMG 501**
**THE SUPREMES**
**Stop! In The Name Of Love** (2:51)
(Holland—Dozier—Holland)
Produced by Brian Holland/Lamont Dozier
Recording completed: 11 Jan 1965
**Released**: 19 Mar 1965
**B-side**: I'm In Love Again
**Position in Record Retailer Top 40**: 7
**Equivalent US Release**: Motown 1074 (8 Feb 1965)
**Position in Billboard Top 40 Pop**: 1
**Position in Billboard Top 40 R & B**: 2

Diana Ross / Florence Ballard / Mary Wilson

Conceived lyrically by Lamont Dozier, "Stop! In The Name Of Love" derives from a phrase spontaneously blurted out as a jokey attempt to defuse a row with his girlfriend.[1] Realising its poignancy, Dozier jotted down what became the song's title and took it to Brian Holland, who chanced to be running through a new chord sequence at Hitsville's piano. Dozier applied the phrase to the chords, and the chorus was thereby virtually ready, Dozier using it as a springboard for the track's harrowing monologue. Worked into shape and presented to Motown as a ruminative ballad, the song was incongruous with The Supremes' popular style and in the end was arranged up-beat, the jingling kinetic achieved with a xylophone, which holds a single notes for long passages, and a trademark 'baby, baby' [E51].

Committed to tape by Diana Ross—a woman—the text becomes all the more moving, the singer's heart-breaking appeals to her unfaithful lover a vain plea for mercy; that the central character knows what is being played out before her merely delineates her sense of despair, the title-phrase a solitary prayer from a girl afraid of the consequences of confrontation ('Think it over'). Overwhelming though is the glorious joy of the 4/4 rhythm, *de rigueur* for the team, which although highly infectious, obscures the minutely observed torment of the narrative—better read as poetry (which is more poignantly captured in Kim Weston's reading, unheard until 1998).

Perspective makes it impossible not to view the single as the third leg of a trilogy begun in the second half of 1964 with "Where Did Our Love Go" [E51] and followed by "Baby Love" [E56]. Although the sequence was interrupted with the comparatively unspectacular "Come See About Me" [E65], the continuation of production and compositional principals is writ large, all three sharing a powerful circulating chord sequence. Although minor, "Stop! In The Name Of Love" has most to do musically with "Baby Love", built on a descending bass run quoted overtly in the six step fall of the chorus vocal.

As a formulaic exercise the single could not fail, and duly topped the American charts. A more cautious Britain took it to number 7, but nevertheless the track has become one of Motown's key recordings, receiving a Grammy nomination in 1966. Taken on the road by the group, the song became a wild crowd-pleaser, buttressed by the Melvin Franklin-derived traffic-cop gesture which became a standard device whenever the song was performed or mimed.[2] For Gordy, the continuation of the group's hit status was a triumph for reasons personal as well as professional. By now divorced from Raynoma, and quietly remarried, he had at the same time become Diana Ross' lover, and one way or another the success of Ross was becoming so intensely important to him that he would never let go of his dream of her as the world's biggest star.

The opening rush of "Stop! In The Name Of Love", a daring touch obtained from James Gittens' electric organ, marks the arrival of Tamla Motown with an ominous stir. Resembling the sound of a studio tape machine operated from pause, and followed immediately by the song's first syllable blazing out like the throw of a spotlight, the effect symbolises the start of the show: A curtain-up not just for this track, but for the Tamla Motown catalogue itself.[3]

[1] Dozier has given several different versions of the incident over the years.

[2] In the context of Detroit's industrial heritage, the subtle, and probably inadvertent association with motor vehicles matches that of "Nowhere To Run" [502].

[3] The effect can be heard in a much milder form at the start of Marvin Gaye & Kim Weston's earlier "I Want You 'Round" [E62b]. This opening was not the original conception for "Stop! In The Name Of Love" as shown in the early version included on the group's eponymous 2000 box set.

**TMG 502**
**MARTHA & THE VANDELLAS**
**Nowhere To Run** (2:48)
(Holland—Dozier—Holland)
Produced by Brian Holland/Lamont Dozier
Recording completed: 21 Oct 1964
**Released**: 19 Mar 1965
**B-side**: Motoring
**Position in Record Retailer Top 40**: 26
**Equivalent US Release**: Gordy 7039 (5 Feb 1965)
**Position in Billboard Top 40 Pop**: 8
**Position in Billboard Top 40 R & B**: 5

---

Martha Reeves / Rosalind Ashford / Betty Kelly

---

Recorded as an instrumental during 1964 but shelved due to other commitments, "Nowhere To Run" was completed to order, Motown growing impatient for new product from Martha Reeves. Released on the same day as [501], the track gave its writer-producers a prestigious back-to-back schedule, and a chance to break Reeves in Britain. To some extent they succeeded, although the song's lowly chart placing paled compared to its top 10 status in America.

The finest record Reeves ever cut, the track's tense excitement is underscored by a driving 'one chord' foundation, as used previously for "Dancing In The Street" [E54]. The recording's crashing energy derives largely from the constant agitation of a tambourine, echoed by the shimmer of a car tow-chain, brought to the studio by Brian Holland in an effort to repeat the startling effect heard on the earlier track (see [684]), which he managed to outdo. Thanks to the availability of extra recording tracks on Motown's recently installed console, the chain effect was taped individually and positioned in the mix during the final stages, the whole thing bathed in luxurious echo and buttressed from below by the addition of a brass section.

The song's lyric explores the woman's plight, driven mad by an unhealthy fixation on a lover destined to wound her and with whom she knows she ought not to be, a *tour de force* which holds its own against [501], showcasing HDH's exceptional ability to write from the female perspective. Yet where the need expressed in The Supremes' single is essentially passive, Reeves' performance is genuinely burning, the singer fighting a nervous exhaustion caused by unforgiving touring commitments, her vocal pulling unsettlingly towards the minor third throughout.[1] The intense arrangement creates a raging anthem whose pent-up mania squarely fits the obsessive state of its first person, a deep, unrelenting paranoia expressed through half-hallucinatory visions glimpsed in the bathroom mirror, and obsessive thoughts running around the head as she wakes up; there's even a hint of damnation in the quasi-apocalyptical lines adapted from the gospel "Rock My Soul".[2] Tumultuous in every way, the recording succinctly illustrates the tension between Motown's two principal girl groups, Reeves claiming a maturity and weight in her recorded output, while simultaneously observing The Supremes comprehensively outsell anyone else on the label.

In one of Motown's most under-recognised moves, the group shot a promotional film for the single near the end of 1964 at the behest of presenter Murray The K, in which they mimed their vocals in the local Ford assembly plant. Surrounded by humming machines and with numerous operatives in shot, the this footage was made during a normal working day at Ford, and survives today. Staking its claim as the first pop video, "Nowhere To Run" pre-dates both Unit 4 Plus 2's location clip for "Concrete And Clay" and Bob Dylan's famous promotional film for "Subterranean Homesick Blues" by six months, a not inconsiderable coup for Motown which deserves wider acknowledgement. (The quintessentially Detroit-centric backdrop is reflected not only by the use of automobile accessories in the song's backing track, but also the choice of B-side, "Motoring" a Kim Weston number given over to Reeves in the late summer of 1964.)

Capturing vintage performances from James Jamerson and Benny Benjamin whose virtuosity have earned the track a place amongst Motown's most exhilarating creations, Martha & The Vandellas would never again reach the levels of excitement attained on this recording, which they would often attempt to reproduce as a sensational climax to their live performances. Tamla Motown re-issued the track in 1969 [694] and in 1988 it was included in the soundtrack to *Good Morning Vietnam* leading to re-release on licence to the A&M label (coupled with James Brown's "I Got You (I Feel Good)") which dipped into the lower-reaches of the UK charts.

[1] Compare with the perfect 3rd/7th emphasis apparent in the melody of "Dancing In The Street" [E54], altogether less urgently fearful.

[2] The traditional hymn includes the lines, "Too high, can't get over it; Too wide, can't get round it". See also [741].

**TMG 503**
**THE MIRACLES**
**Ooo Baby Baby** (2:57)
(Robinson—Moore)
Produced by William "Smokey" Robinson
Recording completed: 1 Feb 1965
**Release Date**: 19 Mar 1965
**B-side**: All That's Good
**Position in Record Retailer Top 40**: -
**Equivalent US Release**: Tamla 54113 (5 Mar 1965)
**Position in Billboard Top 40 Pop**: 16
**Position in Billboard Top 40 R & B**: 4

Smokey Robinson / Bobby Rogers / Claudette Rogers Robinson /
Warren 'Pete' Moore / Ronnie White

Performing live through 1964, The Miracles would end their shows with a rousing medley of material, original and non-original, usually culminating in a rendition of the doo-wop classic "Please Say You Want Me", a 1955 hit for short-lived Harlem group The Schoolboys. Carried away with the multiplicitous harmonies, The Miracles would sometimes sustain the song though *ad libbed* verses, buoying their audiences to a triumphant close. From such sketches, "Ooo Baby Baby" was formed, Robinson weaving intricately phrased and elegantly composed lines about the plainly simplistic chorus, which reveal an honest vulnerability. Proudly described by the writer as his 'national anthem', the occurrence of the song's title-phrase in the lyrics to the recent "Where Did Our Love Go" [E51] is coincidental.

In terms of its doo-wop origins, The Miracles' track is less archetypal than The Schoolboys', and but for the references to weeping, has surprisingly little in common. Offering a soothing antidote to HDH's energetic contemporary creations, "Ooo Baby Baby" is a relaxed ballad, bathed in warm harmonies, and occupying an intangible space above the clouds, floating dreamily across the sky. Part of its appeal lies in the gently swooning time structure which masks its straight 4/4 pattern with a counterpoint drum in 12/8, giving the recording a waltz-like flavour further teased by Robinson's typically playful phrasing. Considered principally a composer, Robinson's angelic tenor is the single most convincing ingredient in the track, one of his most sweetly delivered and happily florid contributions.[1]

In its tranquillity, "Ooo Baby Baby" lacked commercialism, and made no impact in a UK market preoccupied with beat groups. Despite this, its unmistakeable appeal has seen it grow in reputation through the decades, becoming one of The Miracles' most popular numbers in concert and selected for a cover version in 1969 [748b]. (The original was included in RCA's 1983 retrospective singles series as TMG 980 [L046]—see Chapter 6.)

Thirty two years after its release, "Ooo Baby Baby" was chosen for an emotional reunion performance for The Miracles, along with its famous follow-up "The Tracks Of My Tears" [522], at the Rhythm and Blues Foundation Pioneer Awards. Since then it has found further fame though inclusion in the 2001 movie *Bridget Jones' Diary 2* (along with a smattering of other Tamla Motown singles) leading to its inclusion on the soundtrack album and a group greatest hits CD named in the song's honour.

[1] Professor Brian Ward remarks on an "Utterly transcendent moment [at 2:09] when Robinson pauses an extra nanosecond between one 'baby' and the next" (Abbott p57).


**TMG 504**
**THE TEMPTATIONS**
**It's Growing** (2:57)
(Robinson—Moore)
Produced by William "Smokey" Robinson
Recording completed: 6 Mar 1965
**Release Date**: 19 Mar 1965
**B-side**: What Love Has Joined Together
**Position in Record Retailer Top 40**: -
**Equivalent US Release**: Gordy 7040 (18 Mar 1965)
**Position in Billboard Top 40 Pop**: 18
**Position in Billboard Top 40 R & B**: 3

---

Otis Williams / Melvin Franklin / Paul Williams / Eddie Kendricks / David Ruffin

---

In the weeks leading up to the launch of Tamla Motown, Smokey Robinson had prepared "My Girl" [E67] for The Temptations, as part of his ongoing battle with Norman Whitfield for control of the group's recording affairs. To Robinson's delight, the track became Motown's first US number 1 for a male group, and in Britain became only the eighth Motown recording to break into the top 50. Robinson's reward was a chance to record an album of his own material for the group, which included the current track amongst its 12 titles.

In truth, "It's Growing" is a re-working of "My Girl", probably purpose-built as a follow-up single, Robinson working in collaboration with Miracle Warren Moore. (The two numbers share a gently descending vocal melody underpinned by an *ostinato* which serves to nail down the home key.) Introduced with Earl Van Dyke's playful tinkling on a toy piano, "It's Growing" may lack the swell and harmonic seduction which makes its prototype so appealing but the comparison misses the point; thrifty with its chord changes and classically delivered by David Ruffin, "It's Growing" has its own hidden treasures, especially in the lyric of its much admired opening lines which usher in a sequence of delightful and quintessentially Robinson-esque metaphors.

---

Yet despite wearing a smile, the track remains a somewhat tense piece musically which liberates itself from formal constraint in what might be termed the chorus, which, being held off by a double-length first verse comes in one-third of the way through the song but thereafter resists a re-transition to the verse. (When a brief verse two finally does arrive, the lyrical charm is markedly lower, suggesting its authors laboured the extra section for structural effect). The expertise of Robinson-the-producer comes to the fore in the 'middle-8', effectively an instrumental break, in which all elements fuse, the group recording a second unison vocal track of wordless falsetto harmonies, shimmering with echoed percussion (claves?) which builds up to the word 'Stop!' —at which point the tension is defused by a momentary pause and immediate shift in key.[1]

Deserving a better reception amongst the public, "It's Growing" is regarded by critics as one of the gems of Robinson's song book, David Morse arguing that its sincerity and vitality effectively trivialises other popular music.[2] An exaggeration perhaps, but an indication of the extent to which "It's Growing" is admired by Motown aficionados.

[1] In terms of the effective 'stop', see also [501], recorded 4 days earlier.

[2] p61

**TMG 505**
**STEVIE WONDER**
**Kiss Me Baby** (2:10)
(Wonder—Paul)
Produced by Clarence Paul
Recording completed: 14 Aug 1964
**Release Date**: 19 Mar 1965
**B-side**: Tears In Vain
**Position in Record Retailer Top 40**: -
**Equivalent US Release**: Tamla 54114 (26 Mar 1965)
**Position in Billboard Top 40 Pop**: -
**Position in Billboard Top 40 R & B**: -

A fairly unimaginative attempt to cash in on the recent US top 30 success of "Hey, Harmonica Man" [E48], "Kiss Me Baby" consists of a similar 12-bar-blues in G, for which Wonder claims part copyright. Although fluent with the lead harmonica, Wonder sticks to a narrow register short on bent notes and generally unsurprising in articulation. The single has an air of pointlessness about it, as if its writers were not sufficiently bothered about the recording to finish it by supplying a lyric: But for an *ad libbed* fade, the only vocalising heard in the two minute session is the pronouncement of the song's title, which despite its thrift apparently warranted backing vocals.[1] (Presumably the phrase was a homage to Ray Charles' early-1950s track of the same name. The Four Aims—later The Four Tops—recorded yet another number with this title some years before joining Motown.)

Not featured on a contemporary studio album, "Kiss Me Baby" has been overlooked by Motown's re-promotion sub-industry but for its inclusion on 1987's *The Essential Stevie Wonder*, one of a number of early cuts by the emerging star which never achieved widespread exposure.

[1] Rick Taylor refers to Wonder's period singles somewhat disparagingly, as "Little more than harmonica instrumentals interrupted by occasional whoops and hollers" (p6). "Fingertips" [E26] was in a similarly lyric-less state when Wonder recorded it live, making up the words as he went.

## TMG 506
## EARL VAN DYKE & THE SOUL BROTHERS
**All For You** (2:55)
(Stevenson—Cosby—Hunter)
Produced by William "Mickey" Stevenson
Recording completed: 16 Feb 1965
**Release Date**: 19 Mar 1965
**B-side**: Too Many Fish In The Sea
**Position in Record Retailer Top 40**: -
**Equivalent US Release**: Soul 35009 (Scheduled but not issued)

The resignation of leader Choker Campbell from The Funk Brothers in 1963 (see [517]) allowed Earl Van Dyke to assume pole position, and like his predecessor Van Dyke harboured serious pretensions to individual stardom. An understandably worried Gordy managed to keep his employee's aspirations in check by arguing that no specific artist's contract existed for Van Dyke to permit releases under his name. Thus, the recording of "Monkey Talk" [E29b], which Van Dyke had earmarked for his first hit single was instead referred to Little Stevie Wonder (who had played harmonica on the session) and employed as a B-side, leaving the musician in stasis.

A persistent Van Dyke eventually wrung capitulation from Gordy, who co-produced "Soul Stomp" [E58] in the summer of 1964, granting release on both sides of the Atlantic. Mickey Stevenson meantime was discussing the idea that Van Dyke should dub some Hammond organ leads over the finalised backing tapes of some of Motown's better-known hits. The idea captured Van Dyke's imagination and in late January 1965, the two repaired to Hitsville and constructed what became *Earl Van Dyke Plays That Motown Sound*, dubbing lead tracks over vocal-less masters of numbers such as "How Sweet It Is (To Be Loved By You)" [E60], "Come See About Me" [E65], and "Money (That's What I Want)" [E02].

By now fearing that his band-leader might follow Campbell out the door, Gordy professed support for the project and saw the album through on the proviso that The Funk Brothers alter their name on record to better reflect Motown's corporate image. Uncertain as to how he should then proceed, Gordy had a performing outfit billed as "The Earl Van Dyke Sextet" booked in for the European Revue tour in early 1965 (see Chapter 1), thereby keeping them a safe distance from his key home market.

The predictable consequence of the group's exposure, which included billing in the *Ready Steady Go!* special, was the issue of a trailer-single, and

"All For You", a discarded and previously unheard Marvin Gaye track then known by the name "Make No Mistake", was requisitioned for the job. Gordy, still uneasy over the project, made an eleventh-hour block on it in the States, although in the light of the group's favourable concert receptions eventually sanctioned it, and a follow-up in "I Can't Help Myself" / "How Sweet It Is (To Be Loved By You)" [814].

Because of the inherently speculative nature of "All For You", it was, in truth, never going to be anything more than a curiosity. That is not to say it lacks quality; Van Dyke's keyboards are proficiently done, and the track (which shares some of the feel of "Needle In A Haystack" [E61]) carries a definite lilt, with a throaty guitar solo towards the end—probably Robert White, but sounding more like Joe Messina. Ultimately though it comes across as a self-indulgent exercise piece, not helped by the pronounced dating which the quintessentially 1960s organ imparts. In the UK, "All For You" turned out to be Motown's second successive instrumental release, a dubious strategy for a new label keen to exploit its commercial potential.

**TMG 507**
**FOUR TOPS**
**Ask The Lonely** (2:27)
(Stevenson—Hunter)
Produced by William "Mickey" Stevenson/Ivy Jo Hunter
Recording completed: 12 Aug 1964
**Release Date**: 26 Mar 1965
**B-side**: Where Did You Go?
**Position in Record Retailer Top 40**: -
**Equivalent US Release**: Motown 1073 (5 Jan 1965)
**Position in Billboard Top 40 Pop**: 24
**Position in Billboard Top 40 R & B**: 9

---

Levi Stubbs / Lawrence Payton / Abdul 'Duke' Fakir / Renaldo 'Obie' Benson

---

In its first calendar month, Tamla Motown unleashed seven 45s on the UK market, all from different acts. Two of these, both by female ensembles, entered the charts and earned classic status [501]; [502], but the others were as quickly forgotten. The last of the slew, a week behind the first six, was The Four Tops' new single, which had been pulled from their self-named January album in America to become their second top 40 hit, and, if raw potential were any predictor of success, must have been considered a serious contender for Great Britain.

Unusually commencing with an upwards gear shift the supertonic (possibly inspired by the similar device in the obscure 1961 Tamla single, "Poor Sam Jones" by Mickey Woods), the song proceeds to jockey up to Ebm repeatedly as if looking for a possible escape, but always collapses back to the home key of C#, seemingly resigned to the isolated fate of the lyric and held down by James Jamerson's 'one-note bass' (anticipating [705]). With female backing parts from The Andantes[1] and stuttering chorus triplets, Mickey

Stevenson and Ivy Hunter capture something of the effect subsequently heard in "Stop! In The Name Of Love" [501], but, lacking HDH's bold melodicism and shattering percussion, miss the commercial mark by some way. Opting instead for a classical romanticism, the style is (not surprisingly) more redolent of "Baby I Need Your Loving" [E53], with its swish strings and Levi Stubbs' calmly mature purring; the lyric even indicts 'the young and foolish', in a 'father-knows-better' tone which, having lead the group for over a decade already, he assumes convincingly. Stubbs' true vocal eminence however had yet to be discovered and would require the nuances Brian Holland and Lamont Dozier in the production seat to be fully exploited. (It is perhaps significant that Hunter's lyric to "Ask The Lonely" was completed just minutes before the vocal was committed to tape.)

1 The company's resident female backing outfit, consisting of Louvain Demps, Jackie Hicks, Marlene Barrow and Pat Lewis. The group's name refers to sheet music tempo dynamics, *andante* indicating a medium speed.

## TMG 508
## BRENDA HOLLOWAY
**When I'm Gone** (2:05)
(Robinson)
Produced by William "Smokey" Robinson
Recording completed: 12 Jan 1965
**Release Date**: 2 Apr 1965
**B-side**: I've Been Good To You
**Position in Record Retailer Top 40**: -
**Equivalent US Release**: Tamla 54111 (9 Feb 1965)
**Position in Billboard Top 40 Pop**: 25
**Position in Billboard Top 40 R & B**: 12

Written by Smokey Robinson for Mary Wells, "When I'm Gone" shares a similar nonchalant strut to her recent chart-topping "My Guy" [E42] which, in 1964 had briefly made her Motown's premier female soloist. In the interim, staggered by her own success and seduced by the prospect of global stardom, Wells unceremoniously decamped for 20th Century in a vain attempt to further her career with a national label, leaving "When I'm Gone" to gather dust.[1]

Not wishing to let a good song go to waste, Smokey Robinson found an alternative outlet for the track through Brenda Holloway, a Hollywood-based teenager whose first Motown single, "Every Little Bit Hurts" [E45] had gone top 20 the year before (and was possibly Motown's first West Coast recording). Whereas Holloway's few 1964 releases had been overseen by Hal Davis and Marc Gordon without direct input from Hitsville, Gordy determined that, if she were to be given the chance to become a big name, she would have to be fully engaged by the company structure, which meant her being flown to Detroit in January 1965 to record the vocal.

If being thrown into a snowdrift by Motown's 'welcoming' committee wasn't sufficient to ring alarm bells, the fact that she was enlisted only because the abandoned backing track needed a new singer should have warned Holloway not to expect too much support from Motown. As a generally absentee artist, she would forever be treated as a minor concern, something which would cause great distress in the years that followed.

The finger-popping "When I'm Gone" carries an unusually biting lyric, patronising in its rhetoric, challenging the unfaithful male character to consider whether capable of surviving on his own ('Whose shoulder are you gonna cry on?'). Featuring a succession of upwards key steps through its verses, the 'chorus' denies climax, tumbling down a diatonic run and landing back on the calmly emotionless verses, as Holloway makes a dispassionate spectacle of her despised lover. In this respect the track is the antithesis of Mary Wells' "My Guy" [E42] and an interesting project for her, had she stuck around, its bare-faced scepticism jettisoning the former's slushy devotion.

[1] Wells had already committed her vocal to tape when she signed her new contract, and although unreleased as a single, it saw light of day on the 1966 album Vintage Stock.

## TMG 509
## JUNIOR WALKER & THE ALL STARS
**Shotgun** (2:54)
(DeWalt)
Produced by Berry Gordy Jr./Lawrence Horn
Recording completed: 15 Dec 1964
**Release Date**: 2 Apr 1965
**B-side**: Hot Cha
**Position in Record Retailer Top 40**: -
**Equivalent US Release**: Soul 35008 (14 Jan 1965)
**Position in Billboard Top 40 Pop**: 4
**Position in Billboard Top 40 R & B**: 1

Jr Walker / Willie Woods / Vic Thomas / James Graves

Developments in black-American music in 1964-65 saw the rise in prominence of New York's Atlantic Records as well as Stax-Volt in Memphis (which had close ties with Atlantic through the 1960s), offering a supposedly 'authentic' counterpoint to Motown's mass-marketed sleekness. Conscious of the trend and in direct response, Gordy activated his Soul subsidiary, aiming to provide an outlet for a more gritty, less white-oriented brand of music. The new imprint's individual identity was to be shaped by a number of contemporary signings including Shorty Long, Jimmy Ruffin and Gladys Knight, who were strategically diverted away from his existing big three American labels.[1]

Junior Walker—born Autry DeWalt—has been credited with single-handedly bringing the saxophone back into the world of R & B after some years of unpopularity. Signed to the Harvey label in 1962 with two fellow band-members, he found his contract exchanged two years later when Motown swallowed up Harvey and Tri-Phi. Saxophone-leading aside, Walker's sound was novel for Motown in that he favoured 'dirty' recording, revelling in the taping of material in a slapdash 'live' style before studio staff and assembled musicians (his nearest comparable stable mate in this respect being the harmonica-chuffing Stevie Wonder). The opposing face to Smokey Robinson's polish, he gave the label a street-wise, fundamentally 'black' edge, appealing to a section of the dance market which some of his Motown peers would never do, and thereby proved conceptually perfect for the Soul label.

Pre-formed before arriving at Motown, The All Stars were a self-sufficient performing group as opposed to glorified backing vocalists, made up of Willie Woods on electric guitar, Vic Thomas on keyboards and James Graves on drums. The inspiration of a minor dance craze in 1964, "Shotgun" began with just a title, presented to an amused Berry Gordy ignorant of the song's dance-oriented meaning, who sanctioned a proper recording.

Reluctant to take the microphone, Walker had invited Former Jumping Jacks member Fred Paton to sing on the track, but his failure to appear compelled Walker to perform a part-gibberish guide vocal himself. Roughly jammed with swirling Hammond punctuation and obsessive, aggressive 7th chords the number needed little by way of production (but for a gun effect grafted onto the beginning[2]), taped live with Lawrence Horn at the controls and a stumped but impressed Gordy at his side.

Refusing to shift key, the ensuing recording has an obstinate drive with "the kick of a bull and the greasy feel of a pig's feet dinner" [3], the demanding drum groove requiring the expertise of Benny Benjamin on the session.[4] Retaining the spontaneous if improvisatory vocal, the track's main musical feature comes via Walker's rasping, bluesy Selmer Mark 6 saxophone, which pushes the pressure up to boiling point. Blasting its way up the American charts, "Shotgun" was the Soul label's first success, although it predictably proved too *outré* for British audiences. Not the most accomplished number in his back-catalogue—nor indeed his best known—Walker nevertheless selected it for his brief spotlight appearance on the TV tribute show *Motown 25*, showing his own affection for it some 18 years down-the-line.

[1] Motown, Tamla and Gordy. Two earlier Soul singles were released in the UK, [E58] and [512].

[2] Actually a processed piece of studio noise: Eddie Willis kicking his guitar amp. Brian Ward makes note of several striking Motown intros including this gunshot effect, evidence of the company's calculated drive to catch radio-listeners' ears (Abbott p51).

[3] George, p130.

[4] It is widely assumed that the Funks provide further instrumentation here, their superior talents required when The All Stars failed to hit the spot. See [712].

**TMG 510**
**MARVIN GAYE**
**I'll Be Doggone** (2:52)
(Robinson—Moore—Tarplin)
Produced by William "Smokey" Robinson
Recording completed: 29 Jan 1965

**Release Date**: 9 Apr 1965
**B-side**: You've Been A Long Time Coming
**Position in Record Retailer Top 40**: -
**Equivalent US Release**: Tamla 54112 (26 Feb 1965)
**Position in Billboard Top 40 Pop**: 8
**Position in Billboard Top 40 R & B**: 1

Of all the major stars to record for Motown, the most troublesome was Marvin Gaye, the would-be suave crooner whom Berry Gordy found almost impossible to market. Having been with Motown since early 1961, Gaye strove always to steer clear of the label's commercial sound, preferring instead to record material of a romantic, balladeering nature tending more towards Nat King Cole than to his Motown peers. Unfortunately for Gaye, the formula, which culminated in his misjudged *Hello Broadway* album of 1964, never worked, and despite his enduring potential, an exasperated Berry Gordy was ready to turn his back on Gaye by year-end.

The unexpected consequence of this was less direct supervision and hence increased access for Gaye to Motown's family of writers and producers. The first major fruits of his ensuing studio collaborations was the December 1964 breakthrough, "How Sweet It Is (To Be Loved By You)" [E60], written and produced by the HDH team. Taking him into the US top 10 and UK top 50 for the first time, the track was impossible to follow up due to HDH's prohibitive workload, despite being one of his most accomplished recordings to date. Instead, Smokey Robinson stepped forward to offer Gaye his recent composition "I'll Be Doggone", recorded in January 1965 with its architect producing.

The song itself originated with its central opening riff, devised by Miracles guitarist Marv Tarplin[1] and sounding highly suggestive of the similar figure in the group's very early "Shop Around" [E03]. Despite its resemblance, Robinson was, by his own testimony, electrified by what he heard, the phrase "I'll Be Doggone" suggesting itself to him instantly, which he retained as the basis of the lyric. As with much riff-based material, the resultant song moves around little, dependant on the recurring tonic cadences for its limited available chords and immutable harmonic grounding. (In the recording, the riff is taken up by bass and guitar, an additional lead guitar sticking to bi-tonal chops though the verses.)

Hyping Gaye for the session, Robinson wrung a vintage performance from the singer, full of zeal and genuine feel for the material. With its stop-time structure, heavy riffing and authoritative vocal, the song deservedly took a harder-edged Gaye back to the US top 10. Endeared to Robinson (who would subsequently refer to him as 'Dad'), Gaye had, it seemed, found his best and most dedicated producer yet, the combination giving rise to three further singles during the ensuing year or so [539], [552], [563], before the formula burnt itself out and Gaye resumed his partnership with HDH.

[1] A standard writing method for The Miracles ([522], [539], [598] etc.). Robinson: "[Tarplin's] music has always inspired me to write. He used to give me tapes of his music and I would fool around with them until I got an idea" (quoted by Bill Dahl in Abbott p79). Tarplin probably used various guitars over the years but is most identified with his Gibson Les Paul.

**TMG 511**
**KIM WESTON**
**I'm Still Loving You** (2:27)
(Hunter—Moy—Stevenson)
Produced by William "Mickey" Stevenson/Ivy Jo Hunter
Recording completed: 9 Dec 1964
**Release Date:** Apr 1965
**B-side:** Just Loving You
**Position in Record Retailer Top 40:** -
**Equivalent US Release:** Tamla 54110 (29 Jan 1965)
**Position in Billboard Top 40 Pop:** -
**Position in Billboard Top 40 R & B:** -

By the time Detroit-born Kim Weston's first Tamla Motown single came out, she had already missed her chance for global stardom, having lost out on "Dancing In The Street" [E54] before Martha & The Vandellas immortalised it and themselves. (Her original 1963 recording of "It Should Have Been Me" [660]; [1013] might have offered a similar opportunity, but for the fact that American DJs preferred to spin its flip-side.)[1] With the departure of Mary Wells at the start of the year, another chance presented itself, Motown ready to locate a replacement female solo star with only Weston and Brenda Holloway serious contenders for the premier crown.

Written and produced by the prolific Hunter—Stevenson team, with input from Sylvia Moy, this brassy affair begins with the exclamatory minor chorus introduced abruptly, before moving to the major verse via a gauche diatonic staircase. This stepping device owes a debt to Burt Bacharach, the same run having featured in "Reach Out For Me", a hit in the hands of Dionne Warwick in late-1964, shortly before "I'm Still Loving You" was taped (see also [579]). With rich instrumentation including an underlying oscillation on cello (G though G# to A and back), which gives the song's verses a puckish *chutzpah* (and reminds one of Monty Norman's 1962 James Bond theme[2]), the track out-shines Holloway's current rival number [508] in intensity of glare, if not in allure.

Although by 1965 Weston had already toured the UK with Gerry & The Pacemakers, she was still largely unknown there, the consequence of which was that "I'm Still Loving You" barely sold, and is today reckoned to be one of the three or four rarest, and hence most valuable 45s on the label. For Mickey Stevenson, the track's failure marked the end of his artistic control over his future wife's recordings [538].

[1] The distinction between A- and B-sides was less certain in America, where the labels had no such indication. A-sides were referred to as 'top-' sides or 'plug-' sides and it was not uncommon for top-sides to lose relative favour and become regarded as flip-sides, as was the case here. (In this book, the identification of American A- and B-sides conforms to the order in which they are stated in recognised discographies such as that published in Waller, 1985.)

[2] The same figure can be heard in Bobby Hebb's "Sunny" (1966), a number subsequently covered by The Four Tops, Stevie Wonder and (unreleased) Marvin Gaye. The earlier "Sweet Thing" [514] employs essentially the same foundation device, the intervals widened into a diatonic run based on that of "My Guy" [E42].

**TMG 512**
**SHORTY LONG**
**Out To Get You** (2:15)
(Long—Stevenson)
Produced by William "Mickey" Stevenson
Recording completed: 20 Mar 1964
**Release Date:** Apr 1965
**B-side:** It's A Crying Shame
**Position in Record Retailer Top 40:** -
**Equivalent US Release:** Soul 35005 (24 Aug 1964)
**Position in Billboard Top 40 Pop:** -
**Position in Billboard Top 40 R & B:** -

In acquiring the Tri-Phi label in 1964, part-owned by his sister, Berry Gordy gained a clutch of artists' contracts, some of whom he recorded for Motown. Alabama-born Frederick Earl "Shorty" Long was signed to Soul along with fellow refugee Junior Walker [509], his slow-blues "Devil With The Blue Dress On" (co-written with Mickey Stevenson) the label's first release.

"Out To Get You" was the American B-side to his follow-up, "It's A Crying Shame", and gave the 25-year-old multi-instrumentalist an inaugural British outing. Too rough-and-ready for the progressive popular charts of its time, this piano-led 12-bar busk failed by its own quirkiness, and the five-feet-tall singer would have a year-long wait for his next opportunity. Meanwhile Long's piano playing led to a natural camaraderie with Earl Van Dyke which endeared him to the Motown fraternity, and he was used by Motown as MC for their Revue tours.


**TMG 513**
**THE HIT PACK**
**Never Say No To Your Baby** (2:29)
(Staunton—Walker)
Produced by Robert Staunton/Robert Walker
Recording completed: 11 Feb 1964
**Release Date:** May 1965
**B-side:** Let's Dance
**Position in Record Retailer Top 40:** -
**Equivalent US Release:** Soul 35010 (24 Mar 1965)
**Position in Billboard Top 40 Pop:** -
**Position in Billboard Top 40 R & B:** -

Little has been documented The Hit Pack, whose uncertain Motown sessions apparently amount only to the two tracks presented here, plus one unreleased recording, "Didn't I", made a few weeks later. With no albums or live performances to their credit, "Never Say No To Your Baby" appears to be effectively a one-off, the favoured explanation being that The Hit Pack was a front for Motown's session musicians [506]. Lead vocalist here is also unclear, the singer in question sounding unlike anyone then recording for the label.

---

If the notion that The Hit Pack were the Funk Brothers in disguise is pervasive, the details of the recording tell a different story. The track stands in contrast to Motown's contemporary releases, and indeed to the label's style generally, performed in a mode more akin to that of some of the white British groups such as Manfred Mann and The Animals, recently invading the American charts (especially in the latter's "House Of The Rising Sun", a US number 1 the previous autumn). Furthermore, although the overall feel of the production is Motown-esque, direct design from the Snakepit's master musicians seems unlikely, with the vocal mixed too large and the instrumentation too stilted and underplayed to be a showpiece for the group.

Conversely, with its close-ratio chord cycle, the song harks back to "Hit The Road Jack", a Ray Charles hit to which The Funk Brothers would certainly have been happy to pay homage. Similar could be said of the single's B-side, "Let's Dance" a deep, grooving slice of R & B with an elaborated walking bass line which the Funks would have revelled in. Coupled with the fact that the single appeared on the relatively exclusive Soul label, as had [506], the finger does in fact point back to the same source, although Nick Brown refers to them as 'an obscure white group', which makes some sense.[1] Whatever the case, Motown's lack of documentation has left tracks such as this shrouded in mystery, and with the passing of the years, the truth behind the outfit's real identity will probably never be definitively known. Composers Robert Staunton and Robert Walker were a Motown writing team who also came up with "Tell Me Your Story" for Brenda Holloway, but never had a major hit to their name, eventually quitting the company with complaints that they were constantly in the shadow of Gordy's 'favoured' writers. They were behind both sides of this release as well as "Didn't I".

[1] His research appeared in Record Collector in the mid-1990s, and is reproduced in Abbott. See p215.

**TMG 514**
**THE SPINNERS**
**Sweet Thing** (2:40)
(Stevenson—Hunter)
Produced by William "Mickey" Stevenson
Recording completed: 25 Apr 1964
**Release Date**: May 1965
**B-side**: How Can I?
**Position in Record Retailer Top 40**: -
**Equivalent US Release**: Motown 1067 (9 Oct 1964)
**Position in Billboard Top 40 Pop**: -
**Position in Billboard Top 40 R & B**: -

Henry Fambrough / Bobbie Smith / Billy Henderson / Pervis Jackson / Chico Edwards

Contracted to Tri-Phi around 1960, The Spinners[1] scored the label's only notable hit, "That's What Little Girls Are Made For", although with an impressive stage act, they were always considered more of a live draw than a recording outfit. (Their arrival at Motown simultaneously with choreographer Cholly Atkins seemed portentous, the latter taking responsibility for stage-managing and grooming many of Motown's biggest acts for the live circuit.) Signed by Gordy in 1963, the group were accordingly employed to open the show on many of Motown's subsequent concert tours, their routine enlivened by humorous imitations of their peers including an absurd 'Brown Beatles' parody. In consequence, they were kept on the stage circuit and their Motown recordings are sparse, with just three singles released in the 1960s—all included on the same 1966 album.

Borrowing the implied diatonic rising and falling foundation from "My Guy" [E42], The Spinners' inaugural Tamla Motown single was an upbeat, fluent affair, drawing as much on the musical environment of its day as [513], and irresistibly seductive. Leaning more towards pop than R & B, "Sweet Thing" is a catchy track, light in tone and carefree in style, eschewing the dramatic import of Motown's more potent offerings. Yet to compound the group's troubles, this rare studio recording betrays an uncharacteristic lack of attention from its producer, the rhythmic patterning of James Jamerson's complex bass line over-ambitious and stuttering against the free-flowing vocals, with further uncertainty in the piano timing. How much blame can be apportioned to The Funk Brothers themselves is debatable, understandably revelling in their apparent freedom here; Mickey Stevenson must shoulder responsibility for not reining them in. Possibly he was working against the clock, Motown's vicious productivity schedule putting studio time at a premium for the company's less fashionable acts.

Peculiarities aside, "Sweet Thing" had the necessary components to be a hit single, with a heavily reverbed vocal, brassy flare and drop-in piano adornments including a *glissando* at the start and a sly cascade through the scale late on. Sadly overlooked in its day, the song has dated less favourably than most of the label's 1965 output and, but for the crotchet hand-claps, lacks the trademark Motown flavour. Nonetheless it is fondly cherished by Northern Soul fans as an artefact from an era when Motown were chucking out such quality recordings with abandon.

[1] The act's name in the States. To avoid a clash with a contemporary Liverpool folk outfit, Tamla Motown swiftly re-named them The Detroit Spinners, and later The Motown Spinners [755]. Re-pressings of [514] exist with the act credited as The Detroit Spinners.

**TMG 515**
**FOUR TOPS**
**I Can't Help Myself** (2:43)
(Holland—Dozier—Holland)
Produced by Brian Holland/Lamont Dozier
Recording completed: 9 Apr 1965
**Release Date**: 7 May 1965
**B-side**: Sad Souvenirs
**Position in Record Retailer Top 40**: 23

**Equivalent US Release**: Motown 1076 (23 Apr 1965)
**Position in Billboard Top 40 Pop**: 1
**Position in Billboard Top 40 R & B**: 1

Levi Stubbs / Lawrence Payton / Abdul 'Duke' Fakir / Renaldo 'Obie' Benson

Since the success of "Baby I Need Your Loving" [E53] HDH had been busy elsewhere and having had nothing to do with The Four Tops' previous release [507], risked jeopardising their association with the outfit. Realising the scale of the potential loss, they rallied to the cause and set about constructing a fail-safe hit, aware that disinterest from the record-buying public could result in the loss of future franchise to write and produce for the group.

The track was begun by Dozier, who earmarked the Tops for the developing piece early-on, collaring Duke Fakir in the audience of a Temptations concert in the early spring and taking him home to play the song through. Beginning as a somewhat dark, emotionally tormented ballad the song examines the intensity of paranoid feelings in the vein of "Nowhere To Run" [502], the narrator referring to himself as a 'fool in love', getting 'all choked up' at the sight of his lover. Over-ponderous for the pop charts, HDH worked the number into something more buoyant, wallpapering over the track's burden with the light, vernacular "Sugar Pie, Honey Bunch" refrain, derived from a stock greeting of Dozier's grandfather to visitors to his wife's home beauty shop.

Production-wise, the recipe already successfully established with The Supremes was drawn on, embracing the flagrant commerciality of tracks such as "Where Did Our Love Go" [E51] with shattering tambourine, elated strings and an irresistible pulsating beat. But especially prominent is the ceaselessly riffing bass guitar, in effect the lead instrument, and the cause of significant controversy in the years since its recording. At least three people have laid claim to the figure including of course James Jamerson, who is generally regarded as the player in question, and Lamont Dozier who asserts that he devised the riff in his head.[1] Most contentious of all though is the account given by Los Angeles session musician Carol Kaye, who claims to have recorded the track at Armin Steiner's studio in Hollywood, along with numerous 1960s Motown hits.[2] She specifically claims to have written the riff, provided with just the first bar, and states that Mike Terry's saxophone break was dubbed on later in Detroit. Dozier though has stated elsewhere that HDH would generally not record without Jamerson, a ringing endorsement of his ability but also a compelling reason to suppose "I Can't Help Myself" was indeed taped at Hitsville. (Duke Fakir states the song was done by the group 'in two takes'[3], although he doesn't specify how long the backing was already in the can, which by Motown's normal practice it would have been, if only by a matter of hours.) In any event, the finished recording set the musical and production standard for The Four Tops which would henceforth become their stock-in-trade.

"I Can't Help Myself" also follows the harmonics and chord structure of "Where Did Our Love Go" [E51] (C/G/Dm/G/F), subtly varying the progression by moving straight from Dm to F, sweetly fainting through the

G on its way back around. But for a more perceptible verse/chorus structure than its parent, it sticks with the basic pattern continuously, the only deviation coming in the form of a re-energising eight-bar sustain on the tonic C towards the end. Recorded with confident stereo separation, the concurrent album illustrates a qualitative step up for Hitsville's engineering staff, lending the group's records additional clout in terms of ear-catching dynamism, a match for anything then emerging on either side of the Atlantic.[4]

Determined to push the track, Tamla Motown issued it as the group's second UK 45 in ten weeks, despite [507] having flopped entirely. Simultaneously released in America, it topped the charts there, shunting from top-spot The Supremes' latest offering [516], and putting the rising Four Tops more firmly on the map.[5] Over the subsequent two-and-a-half years, the two groups would stand shoulder-to-shoulder as Motown's flagship acts, HDH's standing on the world stage consequently rivalling the best contemporary writers on the scene.

[1] Dozier's comments in Waller, p152 suggest he had no instrument to hand, 'rolling' his fingers to lock the rhythm. He draws attention to the figure's subsequent deployment on tracks such as Los Bravos' "Black Is Black", a major hit on both sides of the Atlantic in 1966. A later (and possibly more pertinent) example would be Billy Ocean's "Love Really Hurts Without You" (1976).

[2] [E42]; [557]; [579]; [601]; [613]; [635; [677], etc. These titles are specifically cited in the interview published in Abbott, p93-100. Whatever the veracity of Kaye's version of events, it is true that a good many 1960s Motown tracks were recorded in LA, the precise number of which is unknown, but likely included a good proportion of The Supremes' material from 1967 onwards. The claims would matter less were it not for the fact that the contested bass figures include some of Motown's most celebrated, hitherto ascribed invariably to Detroit-based Jamerson—Kaye's comments causing Jamerson's supporters to respond vociferously with sworn affidavits and statements which have served to all but conclusively rebut her assertions.

[3] Quoted in Davis 1988, p52.

[4] Tamla Motown issued all its singles in mono until late in the decade [715] and references in this book to stereo imaging on the 1960s singles should be read with this caveat. Rather than making a stereo master and simply combining the channels for mono, Motown, in common with many studios in the 60s, did entirely separate mixes for the two formats, which consequently differed in detail—sometimes considerably so.

[5] The feat of achieving back-to-back chart-toppers was remarkable at the height of the 'British Invasion'; at one point in May, UK acts held nine of the top 10 placings in the States.

**TMG 516**
**THE SUPREMES**
**Back In My Arms Again** (2:50)
(Holland—Dozier—Holland)
Produced by Brian Holland/Lamont Dozier
Recording completed: 24 Feb 1964
**Release Date**: May 1965
**B-side**: Whisper You Love Me Boy
**Position in Record Retailer Top 40**: 40

**Equivalent US Release**: Motown 1075 (15 Apr 1965)
**Position in Billboard Top 40 Pop**: 1
**Position in Billboard Top 40 R & B**: 1

---

Diana Ross / Florence Ballard / Mary Wilson

---

Finalised with the addition of The Supremes' vocals on 24 February 1964, "Back In My Arms Again" (originally "Back In *His* Arms Again") was released by Tamla Motown with "Stop! In The Name Of Love" [501] still in the UK top 40. That it came and went without overtaking its predecessor in the listings came as a bitter disappointment to the label, its commercial failure especially difficult to grasp in the wake of its chart-topping success at home. Perhaps doomed by the two-note chorus' lack of harmonic interest, "Back In My Arms Again" is short of the melodic clout of the group's prior UK hits, probably not designed as a potential single. Nevertheless, the song has a definite charm, running through its 'horizontal' verses with a natural propulsion—one of The Supremes' most authentic stabs at the girl-group idiom.

Hindsight lends the contumelious lyric added inference, particularly in verse three where Ross explicitly derides her two fellow Supremes ('How can Mary tell me what to do'/'And Flo', she don't know'). That neither complained over the line indicates that at this stage, relations within the group were more congenial than is often portrayed. "Back In My Arms Again" marked the onset of lean 16 months for group in Britain, after such a promising beginning. The group's fortunes could hardly have stood in greater contrast to their American success; "Back In My Arms Again" rounded off a run of five number 1 singles with successive releases, with another to follow before 1965 was out [543].

## TMG 517
## CHOKER CAMPBELL'S BIG BAND
**Mickey's Monkey** (2:00)
(Holland—Dozier—Holland)
Produced by Clarence Paul
Recording completed: 8 Jan 1964
**Release Date**: Jun 1965
**B-side**: Pride And Joy
**Position in Record Retailer Top 40**: -
**No Equivalent US Release**

Pivotal in the departure of Choker Campbell from Hitsville's inner circle in 1963 was the company's refusal to issue his live album *Shades Of Time*, recorded at the Graystone Ballroom, a dance and concert venue in Detroit which Motown had acquired to promote its acts. *De facto* leader of The Funk Brothers and virtuoso saxophonist, Campbell had ambitions to become a known figure in his own right rather than remaining a faceless session man, and saw such ventures as an obvious career path. Berry Gordy had different views, jealously guarding his premier musicians and keeping them safely hidden away in the Snakepit, unaccredited and unknown to the outside world, under the real threat that his key band members would be permanently poached by bigger companies—or at the very least earn sufficient leverage to demand bigger pay-outs from him.

Conceding to reality, Campbell quit the studio set up, but remained front-man of Motown's touring band, an outfit formally segregated from the central group of Funk Brothers. Yet despite the apparent severance, Gordy permitted Campbell to record a clutch of instrumentals which, in March 1965, was released under the title *Hits Of The Sixties*, a 12-track album covering Motown's more famous hit singles. Amongst the selections, "Mickey's Monkey" was an interpretation of a 1963 Miracles track [E27] which had made the US top 10. Perhaps attempting to capitalise on the curiosity recently aroused by Earl Van Dyke [506], Tamla Motown issued the track as a single in June, the only 45 to appear under Campbell's name in America or the UK.

A dance-floor stomper, "Mickey's Monkey" pitches instruments against each other, the group revelling in its two-chord swing which allows room for some high-flying solos including trumpets, sax and a sprightly flute. Two minutes of unadulterated fun, the track is a fascinating insight into Motown's early live sound, which unlike Van Dyke's overdubbed tracks, features a high-throttle performance from a group ensemble in full swing.

## TMG 518
## THE MARVELETTES
**I'll Keep Holding On** (2:27)
(Hunter—Stevenson)
Produced by Ivy Jo Hunter/William "Mickey" Stevenson
Recording completed: April 21 1965
**Release Date**: 11 Jun 1965
**B-side**: No Time For Tears
**Position in Record Retailer Top 40**: -
**Equivalent US Release**: Tamla 54116 (11 May 1965)
**Position in Billboard Top 40 Pop**: 34
**Position in Billboard Top 40 R & B**: 11

Gladys Horton / Wanda Young / Katherine Anderson

Still best-known for their very early hit "Please Mr. Postman" [E05], The Marvelettes were by now virtually unrecognisable from 1961 when they had made their breakthrough as a five-piece. Reduced to three, and with Wanda Young having assumed lead status from Gladys Horton, they soldiered on under direction from Motown's emerging aristocracy, having worked with Smokey Robinson, HDH, and here, Ivy Hunter and Mickey Stevenson.

Completed on April 21, "I'll Keep Holding On" is one of the group's most futuristic recordings, hard-driving and bitingly misanthropic, couched in the style of Martha & The Vandellas. An unnerving statement of intent, the lyric amounts to a terrifying vow from a blind obsessive determined to ensnare the object of her desire. Caught in her sneering sights, the unwitting victim is being scrutinised from a strategic distance, mocked for his innocent conversations with his friends, while being circled by a stalker threatening to teach him the ultimate lesson ('You better plan to make your final stand'). One of Hunter and Stevenson's triumphs, the track is classic Tamla Motown, pushed to excited levels by a modulating chord run into the chorus, the production glimmering with reverb-soaked tambourine, competing with "Nowhere To Run" [502] for consideration as the label's most seductively sleazy production of the era.

According to legend, the producers prepared the backing tracks as usual on Hitsville's 3-track console, before opting for a remake to take advantage of the newer 8-track machine. As a consequence, the vocal dubs were set back and the group were on tour when called on, the tapes being flown to New York where The Marvelettes were engaged at The Apollo Theatre in Manhattan (formerly a whites-only venue but subsequently famous for breaking a number of black stars).[1] The backing vocals can therefore be attributed to the group, and not to the ubiquitous session vocalists The Andantes, known to perform anonymously on many of Motown's hit recordings of the 1960s.

Despite its obvious intensity, surprisingly little has been said of the track, which sold disappointingly on both sides of the Atlantic. Later popular on the Northern Soul club circuit, the song has gained a latter-day reputation among soul aficionados for its sheer dancability and fearsome spirit, and has thankfully been made readily available once again courtesy of Motown's CD repackaging policy.

[1] Appropriately enough, the song's working title was "Wait".


## TMG 519
## BRENDA HOLLOWAY
**Operator** (2:55)
(Robinson)
Produced by William "Smokey" Robinson
Recording completed: 28 Jan 1965
**Release Date**: Jun 1965
**B-side**: I'll Be Available
**Position in Record Retailer Top 40**: -
**Equivalent US Release**: Tamla 54115 (14 May 1965)
**Position in Billboard Top 40 Pop**: -
**Position in Billboard Top 40 R & B**: 36

Written three years earlier, "Operator" finds Smokey Robinson referencing The Marvelettes, its thinly chanted backing vocals distinctly resembling those of "Please Mr. Postman" [E05]. Originally deployed on a Mary Wells B-side, the track was revived for relative newcomer Brenda Holloway, following the tactic employed on [508]. Inconsequential in 1965, the superficially pretty and pleasantly catchy song had little market penetration and was quickly forgotten. (The Marvelettes, on whose style the arrangement is based, had graduated from songs about letters to songs about telephone calls in 1962 with "Beechwood 4-5789" [E11], and had by now completely moved on [518].)

Holloway meanwhile was preparing to accompany The Beatles on their second US tour in August, an 11-show stint which brought her a level of public exposure which must have raised ripples of jealousy throughout Motown, and which led to a flurry of requests for personal appearances. Holloway later described the experience as, "The most fantastic, beautiful, educational, historic event of my life".[1]

[1] Quoted in Whithall, p112

## TMG 520
## JUNIOR WALKER & THE ALL STARS
**Do The Boomerang** (2:20)
(Cosby—DeWalt—Woods)
Produced by William "Mickey" Stevenson
Recording completed: 30 Mar 1965
**Release Date**: 2 Jul 1965
**B-side**: Tune Up
**Position in Record Retailer Top 40**: -
**Equivalent US Release**: Soul 35012 (13 May 1965)
**Position in Billboard Top 40 Pop**: 36
**Position in Billboard Top 40 R & B**: 10

| Jr Walker / Willie Woods / Vic Thomas / James Graves |
| --- |

Mainly recorded on March 24, with "Shotgun" [509] climbing the US charts, "Do The Boomerang" is a thinly veiled re-hash of Walker's first hit, devised during touring duty in Cleveland and name-dropping another obscure dance fad. Essentially the same song slowed to a more sedate plod and dropped by a semitone, it is unclear who took which role in assembling the number, and claiming a stake in the copyright. The recording suffers from sloppy synchronisation, the ensemble's timing suspect throughout, the performance slapdash and half-hearted, implying that it may not have been the tight Funk Brothers on the track [509]. (All of which leaves the title of its B-side seeming somewhat ironic.)

## TMG 521
## THE VELVELETTES
**Lonely Lonely Girl Am I** (2:11)
(Whitfield—Holland—Kendricks)
Produced by Norman Whitfield
Recording completed: 12 Apr 1965
**Release Date**: 9 Jul 1965
**B-side**: I'm The Exception To The Rule
**Position in Record Retailer Top 40**: -

**Equivalent US Release:** VIP 25017 (7 May 1965)
**Position in Billboard Top 40 Pop**: -
**Position in Billboard Top 40 R & B**: -

---

Carolyn Gill / Sandra Tilley / Annette McMillan

---

Having already released their two most famous tracks [E61]; [E71], this archetypal girl group from Michigan were beginning a period of terminal decline by the time "Lonely Lonely Girl Am I" appeared. Having all formed stable personal relationships by now, the group had started to disintegrate by 1965, when, as a re-jigged three piece, this, their final 'new' Tamla Motown single was recorded.

Appearing just a year after the group had beaten The Supremes into second place in Motown's internal Battle of the Stars competition at the Graystone Ballroom, the single, an up-beat number with a progressive quality compared with their earlier tracks, showed no sign that the group were falling apart. Whitfield's production here is more ambitious than on earlier releases, with heavy emphasis on string and horn sections, members of the Detroit Symphony Orchestra called into the Snakepit for the session.

Written mainly by Eddie Kendricks, the track was initially gender-reversed for Jimmy Ruffin, whose version did not surface until in 1968 [664b] leaving the composition ripe for a remake, The Velvelettes' nailing their vocals against a new backing track in April 1965. (Recorded by Ruffin in October 1964, the cheeky use of a recent HDH title [E44] is apparent in its first line.) The dejected tale of a jilted woman hoping in vain for a redeeming call from her ex, the track eschews self-pity with its stirring beats and acute guitar chops and was later picked up by the Northern Soul circuit.


**TMG 522**
**THE MIRACLES**
**The Tracks Of My Tears** (2:48)
(Robinson—Moore—Tarplin)
Produced by William "Smokey" Robinson
Recording completed: 19 May 1965
**Release Date**: Jul 1965
**B-side**: Fork In The Road
**Position in Record Retailer Top 40**: -
**Equivalent US Release:** Tamla 54118 (23 Jun 1965)
**Position in Billboard Top 40 Pop**: 16
**Position in Billboard Top 40 R & B**: 2

---

Smokey Robinson / Bobby Rogers / Claudette Rogers Robinson /
Warren 'Pete' Moore / Ronnie White

---

Widely regarded as The Miracles' first masterpiece, "The Tracks Of My Tears" deals with the tension caused by keeping emotional upset disguised behind jollity. Though cogent, the track was pieced together from disparate sources, Marv Tarplin and Warren Moore's opening section formed first, and offered as the basis of a song to Smokey Robinson. (They supposedly found it through playing around with "The Banana Boat Song", an old Harry Belafonte hit.) Thrown by what he termed its 'odd musical progression', Robinson developed the melody in the style of "It's Growing" [504], commencing with the same rising triplet before gently falling down through the scale. Attaching a complementary chorus, he bridged between the two sections with a juddering four bars of 3/4 ('My smile is my make up...'), probably suggested by the jumpy chords of another recent composition, "Ooo Baby Baby" [503]. However he struggled to come up with a suitable chorus lyric for over a fortnight, experiencing a succession of inspirational flashes which provided him with the finished lines piece-by-piece. Deciding that it was 'easy to trace' *something*, the song's title phrase was the last thing arrived at, concluding the text with uncanny perfection. As it transpires, Robinson's stanza contains arguably his finest lines, a confessional plea explicit in its acknowledgement of counterfeit cheer while reaching out for some recognition, and hence alleviation, of his suffering.

In the song's chorus, Robinson characteristically finds delight in paying with the time structures, giving his lines a dotted crotchet beat which throws them out of synch with the backing, *stretching* lines such as "Take a good *look at my face*" in the manner found for example of [503] ("What a price to pay"). The timing is further compounded by the placing of the brass section, which lands one beat ahead of the backing instruments; whether this musical jesting fits the mood of the piece is another matter.

Ultimately, the track is an outstanding production feat for Robinson, his handiwork positively glowing with perfect EQ-ing and a sparkle which, alongside "My Girl" [E67], earned him accolades as a first-rate soul producer. (The only musical blemish comes in the mildly fumbled instrumental prelude, played live on two guitars.) British songwriter Billy Bragg names the song as his favourite ever single, "Because of the heartfelt lyrics, the sublime vocal performance and the monumental counter-melody played by the horns in the chorus".[1] Yet despite its appeal and Claudette Robinson's softly girlish backing vocal, Britain remained unimpressed for some four years, whereupon the song was re-released and finally entered the top 10 [696].

[1] Quoted in Roberts, p192. Pete Townshend meanwhile was so inspired with Robinson's delivery of the word 'Substitute' that he wrote The Who's fourth single around it.

**TMG 523**
**THE DETROIT SPINNERS**
**I'll Always Love You** (2:44)
(Stevenson—Hunter)
Produced by William "Mickey" Stevenson/Ivy Jo Hunter
Recording completed: 28 Apr 1965

**Release Date**: 27 Aug 1965[1]
**B-side**: Tomorrow May Never Come
**Position in Record Retailer Top 40**: -
**Equivalent US Release**: Motown 1078 (4 Jun 1965)
**Position in Billboard Top 40 Pop**: 35
**Position in Billboard Top 40 R & B**: 8

---

Henry Fambrough / Bobbie Smith / Billy Henderson / Pervis Jackson / Chico Edwards

The Spinners' second Tamla Motown release in two months, [514] revived a backing vocal idea from the Four Tops' "Baby I Need Your Loving" [E53], the main riff employed here as the basis of the verse's melody. Carrying a compassionate child's-eye lyric about a departing lover, this rather inconsequential creation is redeemed by its arrangement. Airily delivered by lead-singer Bobbie Smith, flanked by a wealthy bank of backing vocals, the track features a bold compound-time bridge into its chorus, with high-flying dramatic punch. As with "Lonely Lonely Girl Am I" [521], the relatively obscure single was later warmly adopted by Britain's affectionate Northern Soul circuit.

[1] Initially scheduled for release as The Spinners, the record was to have appeared on 30 July. The release was put back to allow for the label credits to be amended. See [514n].


**TMG 524**
**MARVIN GAYE**
**Pretty Little Baby** (2:35)
(Paul—Gaye—Hamilton)
Produced by Clarence Paul
Recording completed: 22 Dec 1964
**Release Date**: 13 Aug 1965
**B-side**: Now That You've Won Me
**Position in Record Retailer Top 40**: -
**Equivalent US Release**: Tamla 54117 (18 Jun 1965)
**Position in Billboard Top 40 Pop**: 25
**Position in Billboard Top 40 R & B**: 16

As written by Clarence Paul and guitarist David Hamilton, "Pretty Little Baby" was originally intended for Stevie Wonder and went by the name "Purple Snowflakes". (It was presumably envisaged as a wintry sequel to the 1963 recording "Purple Raindrops" [545b].) However Marvin Gaye got hold of it and supplied a new lyric, recording the track himself a few days before Christmas 1964, its seasonal sleigh bells providing a suitably festive backdrop.

'Pretty Little Baby" represents a radical switch in style from his previous effort "I'll Be Doggone" [510], Gaye veering into melancholy as if lost for musical identity, and pushing down towards the bottom of his register. Neatly arranged with a sprightly tinkling piano introduction, the song aims at

---

something reflectively tender, Gaye pleading for his girlfriend to stay with him, yet with its thumping snare at the end of each bar shows conflicting focus, the track only truly coming to life in the *faux* cha-cha bridge into the chorus.

## TMG 525
## MARV JOHNSON
**Why Do You Want To Let Me Go?** (2:57)
(Gordy)
Produced by Berry Gordy
Recording completed: 29 May 1964
**Release Date**: Aug 1965
**B-side**: I'm Not A Plaything
**Position in Record Retailer Top 40**: -
**Equivalent US Release**: Gordy 7042 (28 May 1965)
**Position in Billboard Top 40 Pop**: -
**Position in Billboard Top 40 R & B**: -

Motown's first-ever single is generally recognised as "Come to Me", a 1959 recording by local singer Marv Johnson, released on Tamla in the US and London American in the UK [E01]. The singer swiftly snapped up by United Artists, Johnson subsequently enjoyed a succession of hits under Berry Gordy's direction until he fell off UA's books in the spring of 1964. Observing steady progress through the years, Gordy was not slow to sign him back, and in the summer Johnson returned to the fold, immediately recording "Why Do You Want To Let Me Go?", an early Gordy number originally recorded by Eddie Holland in 1960.

An uneventful, down-tempo time-capsule, archetypal for its age and possibly inspired by Neil Sedaka's early hit singles, the track is lifted by an effervescent miniature sax solo. Five years too late for the mass market, the single inevitably flopped, Johnson deciding thereafter to abandon his recording career in favour of songwriting. His planned album thereby shelved, a number of completed tracks were retained by Motown providing for an unexpected resurgence of interest in Johnson three years later [680].

Collectors of Tamla Motown rarities will note that [525] is one of a handful of releases not to have been distributed in promotional form, indicative of and perhaps precipitating the lack of interest in the single. It would have been better flipped for its attractive B-side, co-written by Johnson with Janie Bradford.

## TMG 526
## THE TEMPTATIONS
**Since I Lost My Baby** (2:49)
(Robinson—Moore)
Produced by William "Smokey" Robinson
Recording completed: 12 May 1965
**Release Date**: 20 Aug 1965

---

**B-side**: You've Got To Earn It
**Position in Record Retailer Top 40**: -
**Equivalent US Release**: Gordy 7043 (1 Jun 1965)
**Position in Billboard Top 40 Pop**: 17
**Position in Billboard Top 40 R & B**: 4

---

Otis Williams / Melvin Franklin / Paul Williams / Eddie Kendricks / David Ruffin

With its lazy chord patterns and studied deployment of the group's various vocal pitchings (most obviously Melvin Franklin's resounding bass interjections in verse one), The Temptations' summer single appears, like "It's Growing" [504], to have been distilled from "My Girl" [E67]. Repeating the latter's semitone drop into the chorus, "Since I Lost My Baby" carries a similar general aspect including an opening verse dealing with meteorology as metaphor for human emotion.[1]

Making the most of Robinson's natural melodic expressivity, the song's available scales are exploited in a soaring, swooping soundscape of melodic drama, particularly in the soul-stirring chorus, swelling blissfully before finding a gratified resolution on the song's tonic. The unrelinquished chorus theme then remains to overwhelm a middle-8 sustained for a grandiose 54 seconds, and brought to an exquisite peak by David Ruffin's liberating spot-falsetto ('won't you *please* help me find her') breaking the tension like a knife slicing through stretched rubber.

If "Since I Lost My Baby" has a specific inspiration however, it is likely spun off Bob Dylan's contemporary acoustic material, its step-by-step structure reminiscent of such tracks as "The Times They Are A-Changin'". While the experience of hearing a 1965 Dylan spitting vocals into his microphone against rough-tuned guitar is light years away from The Temptations' smoothly flowing stage choreography, the musical analogies are here in evidence. That Robinson kept a keen eye on Dylan was obvious (see [540]), the compositional technique on show here allowing (at least in theory) spaces for a musical 'answer' to each verbal phrase, in contrast to its author's usual effusive narratives. Indeed, Dylan may also have come to mind when David Ruffin recorded his authoritative part, as indicated in the Dylan-esque 'whoa' in the middle of each chorus, the vocal track as a whole characterised by a hoarseness simultaneously implying both gutsy courage and an injured sense of injustice, mirroring Dylan's own incisive period style.

Fumbling its way up the American hit parade, "Since I Lost My Baby" deserved a better reception than it got, the latest in a succession of scandalously underrated Motown recordings of the era never re-issued in Britain. (An American re-release saw it coupled with "It's Growing" [504] in 1972.) With his successful reading of "My Girl" entering the UK charts around now, David Ruffin's friend Otis Redding made further mileage from a subsequent cover of the track.

[1] The paradoxical pessimism of "The sun is cold/And the new day seems old" consciously reverses the earlier track's "When it's cold outside/I got the month of May".

---

**TMG 527**
**THE SUPREMES**
**Nothing But Heartaches** (2:41)
(Holland—Dozier—Holland)
Produced by Brian Holland/Lamont Dozier
Recording completed: 17 May 1965
**Release Date**: 27 Aug 1965
**B-side**: He Holds His Own
**Position in Record Retailer Top 40**: -
**Equivalent US Release**: Motown 1080 (16 Jul 1965)
**Position in Billboard Top 40 Pop**: 11
**Position in Billboard Top 40 R & B**: 6

---

Diana Ross / Florence Ballard / Mary Wilson

---

Recorded the day after The Supremes taped two miniature tracks for a Coca-Cola commercial, "Nothing But Heartaches" was included on the impressive, all-HDH *More Hits*. In Britain however, releases were running as usual behind schedule, the group's status undermined by dubious projects including a concurrent album-length tribute to Sam Cooke (who was shot dead in December 1964). Consequently, interest in The Supremes was waning, *More Hits* being delayed in the UK until December.

Mixing the dramatic descending chords of "Baby Love" [E56] with the chugging brassed-up verses of "Back In My Arms Again" [516], the track amounts to a workmanlike assemblage which has become their least-celebrated of the 1960s. Failing to chart in the UK and reaching a miserable number 11 at home, "Nothing But Heartaches" represents a low-point of The Supremes' career, interrupting a succession of US chart-toppers by the group.

With The Supremes appearing on the cover of *Ebony* in June, shortly before taping a contribution to CBS Television's show about Lyndon B. Johnson's 'War on Poverty', there were signs that they were joining the groundswell of racial radicalism which was underscoring much of the American music scene of the 1960s. As race riots ripped through LA in August, the group were booked into the Flamingo for a series of shows amid rumours that Diana Ross was preparing to leave The Supremes for a solo career, "Nothing But Heartaches" constituting an apt commentary on the group's current affairs. (As indeed did the track's provisional title, "I Just Can't Break Away".)

**TMG 528**
**FOUR TOPS**
**It's The Same Old Song** (2:42)
(Holland—Dozier—Holland)
Produced by Brian Holland/Lamont Dozier
Recording completed: 7 Jul 1965
**Release Date**: 27 Aug 1965
**B-side**: Your Love Is Amazing
**Position in Record Retailer Top 40**: 34

---

**Equivalent US Release**: Motown 1081 (9 Jul 1965)
**Position in Billboard Top 40 Pop**: 5
**Position in Billboard Top 40 R & B**: 2

Levi Stubbs / Lawrence Payton / Abdul 'Duke' Fakir / Renaldo 'Obie' Benson

Written, recorded and pressed in a single 24-hour span, The Four Tops' follow up to "I Can't Help Myself" [515] represents the most overt example of Motown's production-line ethic in the history of the company. The need to prepare a single instantaneously was a consequence of record distributors' policy of automatically ordering singles by any group having scored a recent hit: rival label Columbia, for whom The Four Tops had recorded a few tracks prior to joining Motown, unearthed an earlier single and re-released it[1], timing things such that the automatic orders would ensure they could nick a hit. Realising that Columbia would effectively deprive his company of imminent sales, Berry Gordy immediately halted work at Hitsville and called in HDH and the group to get a single of his own prepared, to see off Columbia's skulduggery.

Chief engineer Lawrence Horn was instructed to set up the studio at around 3:00pm, when HDH convened to begin writing the lyric to a backing track in the can since May. Half an hour later an embryonic version of the song was ready. With The Four Tops in the Snakepit awaiting their cue, the number was fine-tuned by the writers and with the clock ticking by, a first attempt made at around 5:00. Following a passable take, more vocals were added and a preliminary mix done, leaving the rest of the evening for further overdubs and re-mixing. When Gordy and his crew were finally happy, an initial batch of 300 promotional copies were immediately cut in-house[2], and by the following afternoon, one-and-a-half thousand had been pressed and were on their way to DJs across the United States. The next day, commercial copies were made available to the public.

The derivation of the song has been the subject of much comment, generally being interpreted as a bare-faced re-write of "I Can't Help Myself" [515]. This widespread misunderstanding is largely accounted for by its apparently double-edged title, leading many to suppose that HDH were publicly revealing a private truth. The evidence for the prosecution includes the fact that "It's The Same Old Song", even ignoring its title, holds a similar musical arrangement, with an accentuated bass riff and tambourine accents on the 2nd and 4th beats, differing structurally from its supposed model only inasmuch as the first chord of the chorus is an implied C6 as against a C major, thanks to the bass run landing on A.

But in fact, the song is but the latest instalment of a sequence of developing numbers, with "I Can't Help Myself" drawing extensively on "Where Did Our Love Go" [E51] (whose references to bee stings recur here). Moreover, "It's The Same Old Song" shares with [E51] a sax break and a wholly despondent mood absent from [515], indicating that if the song did have an archetype, it was more likely The Supremes' former hit. In truth, the song is a composite of pre-existing forms, illustrative of a derivative method not outside HDH's usual *modus operandi*. According to David Morse, HDH would routinely deconstruct and re-assemble using a stock of discrete pre-existing building blocks to fabricate new forms[3]—an accurate analysis of the team's method, and of Motown's more generally. HDH have consistently denied a derivative connection between [515] and the present single although, interviewed for the BBC's *The Producers* in 2007, Brian Holland confusingly claimed that the song's genesis was a doodle on "I Can't Help Myself", with the chords running in reverse. In any case it must have amused them when, within months, UK Motown admirers The Beatles ("You Won't See Me") and The Rolling Stones ("Under My Thumb") borrowed musical ideas from the track. (The same old song indeed!)

Despite the staggering achievement of creating a pop hit from nothing but a canned instrumental within a day, many of the involved personnel were dissatisfied with the quality of the work, which by the standards of its era displays a dull murkiness. (The promo copies contained an even rougher mix than the commercial version.) But whatever the technical shortcoming, imperceptible to most listeners, that the company was able to assemble its premier writing team and a leading male group at virtually no notice is testimony to the way in which Berry Gordy kept rein on his employees. Equally, the song's top 5 placing in America illustrates the extraordinary talent at Gordy's disposal, all parties involved displaying a prodigious commitment to their art under the most pressurised and unexpected circumstances.

[1] The single in question was "Ain't That Love" / "Lonely Summer" first issued in 1961.

[2] Motown had installed their own cutting machine in the basement of one of their West Grand Boulevard properties in 1963, to assist in vetting recordings by pressing them to disc for Quality Control sessions.

[3] p68

**TMG 529**
**JUNIOR WALKER & THE ALL STARS**
**Shake And Fingerpop** (2:43)
(DeWalt—Woods—Horn)
Produced by Berry Gordy Jr/Lawrence T Horn
Recording completed: 15 Apr 1965
**Release Date**: 3 Sep 1965
**B-side**: Cleo's Back
**Position in Record Retailer Top 40**: -
**Equivalent US Release**: Soul 35013 (8 Jul 1965)
**Position in Billboard Top 40 Pop**: 29
**Position in Billboard Top 40 R & B**: 7

Jr Walker / Willie Woods / Vic Thomas / James Graves

If Junior Walker's second single [520] was a copy of his first [509], "Shake And Fingerpop" found him straying little from the formula, relying again on a single-chord dance track punctuated by saxophone solos. Though this cautious treading of safe ground should come as no surprise given direct input from Berry Gordy, the recording stands far more focussed than its predecessor, with a formal lyric and a delineated bass riff, doubled by Willie Woods' guitar (assuming it to be him on the session, and not a Funk Brother).

As if to legitimise the transitory craze which inspired "Do The Boomerang" [520], the track quotes the earlier song's title in the lyric. Recapitulations were, it seems very much the order of the day for Walker; the B-side here is a belated sequel to a 1962 recording from his Harvey years, itself being re-worked for his contemporary album and about to be issued as a single [550].


**TMG 530**
**MARTHA & THE VANDELLAS**
**You've Been In Love Too Long** (2:57)
(Hunter—Paul—Stevenson)
Produced by Ivy Jo Hunter/Clarence Paul/William "Mickey" Stevenson
Recording completed: 13 Jun 1965
**Release Date**: 10 Sep 1965
**B-side**: Love (Makes Me Do Foolish Things)
**Position in Record Retailer Top 40**: -
**Equivalent US Release**: Gordy 7045 (26 Jul 1965)
**Position in Billboard Top 40 Pop**: 36
**Position in Billboard Top 40 R & B**: 25

---

Martha Reeves / Rosalind Ashford / Betty Kelly

---

Released six months after the sensational "Nowhere To Run" [502], Martha Reeves' new single was put together by Hunter—Stevenson, thereby establishing them as her principal writers with this Stevie Wonder cast-off. Hewn from the same block as [502] but slowed to a strut, "You've Been In Love Too Long" inevitably missed some of the excitement manifest in its predecessor, and yet, built on a wilfully plodding rhythm, maintained the group's style as previously defined by HDH. Blocked out with rasping brass and drop-in piano trembles, this solid piece of R & B holds its ground defiantly, vocals filled out with The Andantes joining The Vandellas for extra bulk.

By mid 1965, Reeves and her group had permanently lost status to The Supremes, to whom HDH were now devoting much of their time and energy. Intensifying the rivalry between Reeves and Ross, Motown's pecking-order mentality was exacerbated by the back-stage fights and devious one-upmanship in which the two women became embroiled. (Reeves details some of this in her autobiography, including an incident in which The Supremes deliberately went out on stage in exactly the same dresses as The Vandellas, forcing the latter group into a last-minute change, Ross proceeding to report a justifiably incensed Reeves to Berry Gordy, certain of where his loyalties would lie.)


**TMG 531**
**THE CONTOURS**
**First I Look At The Purse** (2:58)
(Robinson—Rogers)

Produced by William "Smokey" Robinson
Recording completed: 11 Mar 1965
**Release Date**: 17 Sep 1965
**B-side**: Searching For A Girl
**Position in Record Retailer Top 40**: -
**Equivalent US Release**: Gordy 7044 (23 Jun 1965)
**Position in Billboard Top 40 Pop**: -
**Position in Billboard Top 40 R & B**: 12

---

Billy Gordon / Gerald Green / Council Gay

---

Offering a humorous counterpoint to Smokey Robinson's sentimental contemporary ballads, The Contours' new single at first appears to be an appearance-discounting advocacy of true love before being spun around devilishly into an avowal of brazen gold-digging. Oddly commencing with a disembodied female catechism[1] and rejecting a litany of superficial physical traits, the listener is initially confused over the meaning of the faintly grotesque imagery until the song's punch line arrives complete with an ironic guitar-based gag.

Playing up to the theme of "Money (That's What I Want)" [E02], Robinson and Rogers devised the track on the way home from Virginia in the rear of a station wagon. (The track supposedly began as a variation of Eddie Holland's 1963 miss "Leaving Here".) Posing the question of what a man looks for in a woman, Rogers ventured the song's title phrase by way of a joke, the humour suggesting suitability for The Contours, whose quirky and over-excited stage act had earned them a reputation as something of a comedy combo. The song was accordingly offered for Billy Gordon's idiosyncratic enunciation (first heard on the group's surprise 1962 hit "Do You Love Me" [E10]), as an unpretentious piano-lead R & B ditty. The song succeeds in its sassy impertinence, ample proof that Motown weren't always interested in sensitive songs about human love affairs.

[1] Hank Cosby's wife Patricia, and not as is often assumed, the track's co-writer Bobby Rogers.


**TMG 532**
**STEVIE WONDER**
**High Heel Sneakers** (2:58)
(Higginbotham)
Produced by Robert Gordy/Clarence Paul
Recording completed: 13 Apr 1965
**Release Date**: 24 Sep 1965
**B-side**: Music Talk
**Position in Record Retailer Top 40**: -
**Equivalent US Release**: Tamla 54119 (2 Aug 1965)
**Position in Billboard Top 40 Pop**: -
**Position in Billboard Top 40 R & B**: 30

---

Of Motown's A-list artists, Stevie Wonder above all has shown a predilection for performing material sourced from without since the start of his career [E48], including in his Tamla Motown output singles written by the two most important external composing outfits of the 1960s ([570]; [772]). Here, he tackles a contemporary hit for Ohio-born Robert Higginbotham, aka Tommy Tucker with essentially a 'beat' interpretation of the lumbering original.

Showcasing the song at the Olympia Theatre in Paris as part of the European Revue to launch Tamla Motown, his live rendition captured here makes up with ferment what it lacks in finesse, maintaining his reputation for sensationalistic stage presentation. (The US edition includes a spoken intro from Wonder, edited off the UK release.) Further recordings from the night can be heard on the ensuing live album, released in America during the second half of 1965.

## TMG 533
## BILLY ECKSTINE
**Had You Been Around** (2:45)
(Jacques—Miller—Vandenberg—Yuffy)
Produced by William "Mickey" Stevenson
**Release Date**: 1 Oct 1965
**B-side**: Down To Earth
**Position in Record Retailer Top 40**: -
**Equivalent US Release**: Motown 1077 (17 May 1965)
**Position in Billboard Top 40 Pop**: -
**Position in Billboard Top 40 R & B**: -

1965 was a key period for Motown in its push to become a global brand. Besides launching Tamla Motown, Gordy also sought to expand the company's portfolio by taking on a number of established acts, with varying degrees of success. While signings such as The Isley Brothers and Gladys Knight & The Pips bore obvious dividends, and the recapture of Marv Johnson settled a historical anomaly, the recruitment of such figures as Tony Martin [537] and Barbara McNair [544] seemed less sure-footed. Falling into line with the latter acts was 51-year-old Billy Eckstine, an influential jazz baritone famous for his work in the 1940s and 50s. A minor inspiration to Berry Gordy, he was known directly to Motown via his live shows with a young Four Tops, eventually arriving at the label for a brief stay towards the end of 1965.

This, his only UK single, is an in-house construction tastefully pitched in the manner of Eckstine's 1940s slow-jazz numbers. With period harmonic movements and the requisite brass band arrangements, the track works as an exercise in style, albeit an obsolete one. (The Vandenberg credit is a pen-name used by the song's producer.)

Recording over an album's worth of material for Motown, Eckstine enjoyed further releases in the USA where "Down To Earth" had been better received (the UK single effectively swapping the sides). Thankfully Tamla

Motown decided that one release was enough for its fan-base to stomach, despite also putting out long-players by the crooner in February 1966 and April 1967.

**TMG 534**
**DORSEY BURNETTE**
**Jimmy Brown** (2:46)
(Burnette—Osborne)
Produced by Dorsey Burnette
**Release Date**: 1 Oct 1965
**B-side**: Everybody's Angel
**Position in Record Retailer Top 40**: -
**Equivalent US Release**: Mel-o-dy 116 (24 Jun 1964)
**Position in Billboard Top 40 Pop**: -
**Position in Billboard Top 40 R & B**: -

If recent outings by Tamla Motown had confused a hardcore fan-base with their novel diversity, Dorsey Burnette's only single for the label, issued alongside [533], was at best a mystifying diversion. Burnette, a minor sensation in pre-Elvis Memphis, had become well-known for his songwriting collaborations with his brothers, which spawned hit singles for both Dorsey and Johnny (the latter also hitting with his own, highly successful "You're Sixteen"). Joining Motown in 1964 as a reasonably hot prospect, Dorsey Burnette was assigned to the obscure Mel-o-dy imprint, a side project which had become a specialist outlet for folk/country releases. "Jimmy Brown", his second US single, saw light of day in June 1964, less than a year before the label folded.

The jocular ballad of a country musician inventing instruments from odd materials found lying about, the track falls outside of Motown's patent style and has been forgotten over the years. Although probably apropos of nothing, the name Jimmy Brown was possibly inspired by trumpeter husband of popular 1950s New York R & B singer Ruth. (An alternative possibility is the borrowing from Mac Wiseman's "Jimmy Brown The Newsboy", released on Dot in 1959, Dorsey's label at the time.) Published by Jobete, the track is contemporary, but input from Motown staff is uncertain, Burnette writing and producing for himself in collaboration with Joe Osborn (mis-spelled on the label), regular bassist for Rick Nelson. Why Tamla Motown opted for this belated UK outing is unknown.

**TMG 535**
**THE MARVELETTES**
**Danger Heartbreak Dead Ahead** (2:22)
(Stevenson—Paul—Hunter)
Produced by Clarence Paul/Ivy Jo Hunter
Recording completed: 2 Jun 1965
**Release Date**: 8 Oct 1965

**B-side**: Your Cheating Ways
**Position in Record Retailer Top 40**: -
**Equivalent US Release**: Tamla 54120 (23 Jul 1965)
**Position in Billboard Top 40 Pop**: -
**Position in Billboard Top 40 R & B**: 11

---

Gladys Horton / Wanda Young / Katherine Anderson

---

Recalling Jaye P. Morgan's 1955 hit, "Danger! Heartbreak Ahead", this new Marvelettes single was a straight-forward dance number from the same team which had provided the HDH-esque "You've Been In Love Too Long" [530] for Martha & The Vandellas the previous month. (In fact the song was initially written for them as "He Turned His Back On Me".) Sharing numerous thematic and musical elements with [530], including a skewing whole-tone plunge in the chorus, the connection is self-evident although the device equally resembles the similar figure in The Velvelettes' current American single "A Bird In The Hand (Is Worth Two In The Bush)".

Carrying an unceremonious key step after the second chorus, a little over half way through, the song suddenly comes alive with liberating brass riffing and backing vocals carrying the energised momentum through to the song's close. That the whole track was not produced in this vein is a pity; it could have been a worthy rival to the group's previous single [518]. Its bipartite nature notwithstanding, "Danger Heartbreak Dead Ahead" is one of The Marvelettes' most incisive tracks, characteristic of the group's mid-decade style and warranting more attention than it got.


**TMG 536**
**THE LEWIS SISTERS**
**You Need Me** (2:48)
(Gordy)
Produced by Berry Gordy
Recording completed: 9 Aug 1965
**Release Date**: 15 Oct 1965
**B-side**: Moonlight On The Beach
**Position in Record Retailer Top 40**: -
**Equivalent US Release**: VIP 25024 (31 Aug 1965)
**Position in Billboard Top 40 Pop**: -
**Position in Billboard Top 40 R & B**: -

---

Helen Lewis / Kay Lewis

---

Originally recorded by Brenda Holloway, "You Need Me" was a Berry Gordy composition with a surprisingly angular melody-line ranging over more than an octave in just three steps. With Holloway's version indefinitely suspended, the song was picked up by her West Coast associates Helen and Kay Lewis, two white teachers employed by Motown as backing vocalists and songwriters [576], who recorded their contributions at Hitsville.

---

With an archetypal female 'beat' arrangement complete with brass riffs and a subtle harmonica track, "You Need Me" was the second and final release for 'The Singing Schoolteachers', assigned to Motown's VIP subsidiary. The single effectively ended Gordy's interest in the outfit, which, according to Carol Kaye, he indulged in order to keep his LA musicians on the production line, blind to the fact that their recordings were being requisitioned for overdubs back in Detroit, The Lewis Sisters' original vocals being scrapped.[1]

[1] She refers to sessions where their mikes were not even plugged in, the studio group unaware that they were in fact making backing tracks for Motown's star names. Kaye describes the duo's singing as 'terrible' (Abbott p97).


**TMG 537**
**TONY MARTIN**
**The Bigger Your Heart Is (The Harder You Fall)** (2:42)
(Miller—O'Malley)
Produced by Hal Davis/Marc Gordon
**Release Date**: 22 Oct 1965
**B-side**: The Two Of Us
**Position in Record Retailer Top 40**: -
**Equivalent US Release**: Motown 1082 (16 Aug 1965)
**Position in Billboard Top 40 Pop**: -
**Position in Billboard Top 40 R & B**: -


Briefly in the spotlight in 1956 with a couple of top 10 hits, Tony Martin was considered worth a gamble by Berry Gordy who brought him to Motown in the second half of 1964. Old news by then, his first 45 for the label was also released in the UK as the final single under licence to Stateside [E72], and was comprehensively ignored. Described by Nelson George as a "washed-up MOR crooner"[1], Tony Martin was as uncharacteristic a signing for Motown as Billy Eckstine [533] or Dorsey Burnette [534], the current single the latest in a sequence of autumn releases which left the label's UK fans scratching their heads, and falsely implying that Motown were running dry.

Recorded West Coast, "The Bigger Your Heart Is" showcases Martin's vocal *timbre*, but with a badly dated arrangement and some poorly judged bass vocals, is devoid of any mitigating qualities.

[1] p139


**TMG 538**
**KIM WESTON**
**Take Me In Your Arms (Rock Me A Little While)** (2:55)
(Holland—Dozier—Holland)
Produced by Brian Holland/Lamont Dozier
Recording completed: 25 Jun 1965
**Release Date**: 29 Oct 1965

**B-side**: Don't Compare Me With Her
**Position in Record Retailer Top 40**: -
**Equivalent US Release**: Gordy 7046 (2 Sep 1965)
**Position in Billboard Top 40 Pop**: -
**Position in Billboard Top 40 R & B**: 4

Having failed to supply Kim Weston with a hit single [511], Mickey Stevenson found a predictably dissatisfied Berry Gordy ready to wrench her from his artistic control, despite (or perhaps because of) the couple having recently married. Switching Weston from Tamla to Gordy in America, a re-invigoration of the singer's career was being attempted through a pairing with HDH, who elected to supply a suitably gospel-tinged number to a serious performer sceptical of the team's commercial bent. Accordingly, HDH dug out a backing track made on 10 September 1964 for The Vandellas[1], and called Weston to Hitsville to dub on a vocal. She later claimed her contribution was done within two hours of her arrival, leaving her little time to learn her way around the lyric; she need not have worried though, the ensuing track rapidly became her most popular. Succinctly yet enthusiastically delivered by Weston, the track has a loose swing to it, undisciplined and more 'black' than Motown's generally recognised style.

With its pulsating floor toms, "Take Me In Your Arms" is a sensual affair, built on a single driving chord with a chorus cribbed from the verses of "Where Did Our Love Go" [E51], released in the summer of 1964 before the current backing track was recorded. (Compare the melodic and lyric similarities of the phrase "Take me in your arms..." with the latter's "You came into my heart...".) David Morse refers to the song as the link between [E51] and "You Can't Hurry Love" [575] (p85). However with the wistful Fm bridge (where the vocal sticks to the root note of the relative major) moving to a resolute Eb, it links more directly to "You Keep Me Hangin' On" [585], whose verses it almost exactly anticipates.

Much-admired since its release, the track has attracted attention from outfits such as The Doobie Brothers, who outscored Weston by taking it into the US top 20, as well as in-house covers on numerous occasions (see [652]; [851b]). In the wake of the single's release, Motown attempted to cash in by scheduling both an EP and album entitled *Take Me In Your Arms*. While the EP struggled to sell, the LP failed to appear at all.

[1] A version with Eddie Holland's guide vocal can be heard on *A Cellarful Of Motown!* Volume 2 (2005).


**TMG 539**
**MARVIN GAYE**
**Ain't That Peculiar** (2:50)
(Moore—Robinson—Rogers—Tarplin)
Produced by William "Smokey" Robinson
Recording completed: 12 May 1965
**Release Date**: 5 Nov 1965

**B-side**: She's Got To Be Real
**Position in Record Retailer Top 40**: -
**Equivalent US Release**: Tamla 54122 (14 Sep 1965)
**Position in Billboard Top 40 Pop**: 8
**Position in Billboard Top 40 R & B**: 1

In the interim since "Pretty Little Baby" [524], Marvin Gaye had experienced one of the private tribulations which were to dog him throughout his life. Wanting a child with wife Anna, Berry Gordy's daughter, he was troubled to learn that she was unable to conceive. The extraordinary solution, apparently mutually agreed, was for Gaye to impregnate Berry's granddaughter, 15-year-old Denise, in a potentially scandalous move which could not be publicly admitted. Yet the sudden appearance of a baby would obviously have to be accounted for somehow, and Anna was forced to wear padding around her waist to feign pregnancy, while in public the couple put on an artificial face of matrimonial normality. Born on November 12, Marvin Pentz Gaye III was fully adopted by Anna and Marvin with the blessing of all concerned, and the true facts behind his conception and birth remained buried until into the late-1970s.[1]

Returning to his musical career amidst such chaos, Gaye embarked on the recording of his new single in May, with an ironically suitable title. (Whether Robinson and his group were fully aware of Gaye's troubles is uncertain, although Warren Moore has stated that the lyrics they provided for 'Dad' were frequently intended to reflect his domestic life.[2]) The first in a run of three Tamla Motown singles written by various combinations of Miracles, "Ain't That Peculiar" is an uneventful 4/4 vamp with a trademark "Doggone" dropped in for good measure. As with "I'll Be Doggone" [510], the song was developed from a quasi-organic flash of inspiration, Robinson coming out with the song's title in unpremeditated response to a new Marv Tarplin guitar riff, the counterpoised bass lick added in-studio by arranger Willie Shorter.

The typically thoughtful song with its finely honed conflicting juxtapositions sufficiently impressed an American Christmas market wooed by the stomping percussion to become Gaye's third top ten hit in a year, despite his performance betraying a noticeable lack of enthusiasm, his mind no doubt elsewhere.

[1] For a fuller account see Turner, p88-91.

[2] He is quoted in Dahl, p73: "A lot of those lyrics are based on the relationship we saw with him and his wife".

**TMG 540**
**THE MIRACLES**
**My Girl Has Gone** (2:51)
(Robinson—Tarplin—Moore—White)
Produced by William "Smokey" Robinson
Recording completed: 10 Aug 1965

**Release Date**: 12 Nov 1965
**B-side**: Since You Won My Heart
**Position in Record Retailer Top 40**: -
**Equivalent US Release**: Tamla 54123 (22 Sep 1965)
**Position in Billboard Top 40 Pop**: 14
**Position in Billboard Top 40 R & B**: 3

---

Smokey Robinson / Bobby Rogers / Claudette Rogers Robinson /
Warren 'Pete' Moore / Ronnie White

---

Beginning with an atypical acoustic guitar figure, "My Girl Has Gone" tips a nod to the folk-rock movement whose popularity peaked in 1965, its influence heard across the popular music spectrum. Simultaneous with the meshing of folk-based styles with rock and roll, soul music was becoming a defined genre in its own right, mainly via Motown but also thanks to a succession of notable releases from pioneers including James Brown, Wilson Pickett and Fontella Bass, reaching out to widespread audiences for the first time. While there is little to connect the developing soul idiom with folk's derivative rock sub-category—apart from a common interest in emotive expressivity—many of Motown's recording artists were admirers of the genre's figurehead Bob Dylan, whose early recordings influenced a number of the label's singles one way or another ([570], [598], [601] etc).

For his part, Dylan virtually ignored soul until picking up the style in the mid-1970s[1], leaving the impression that he thought little of it. In fact he was as capable of being affected by its key movers as anyone, attending a 1967 Otis Redding show four nights running, and commencing his first novel with an evocative eulogy to Aretha Franklin. While his backing group covered material by HDH in their own right[2], Dylan had little to say publicly about Motown but singled out Smokey Robinson as a pre-eminent lyricist at a 1965 press conference.[3]

In the context of the largely unspoken respect between Dylan and Robinson, it is plausible to read Tarplin's softly picked prelude to "My Girl Has Gone" as a veiled acknowledgement. Although the decision to commence with solo guitar was a staple technique of Robinson's (witness for example [522] or his production of [E67]), the acoustic touch was a departure whose finger could but point at one inspiration. If this is the case, the group's tribute is terse, the song quickly abandoning guitar for a typecast Motown arrangement built largely on a two-chord undulation. With rich chorus vocals and an effective (though slightly mechanical) performance from Benny Benjamin, the track is an adequate addition to the group's repertoire, if anaemic against their previous single [522]. "My Girl Has Gone" emerged contemporaneously with the album which contained it, alongside the group's previous two A-sides.

[1] Dylan's absorption of soul, while little-acknowledged, is self-evident on his 'comeback' albums, especially Blood On The Tracks (1975) whose gentle, bass-high arrangements reflect the idiom in contrast to his generally provocative and hard-edged 1960s work. Even Dylan's idiosyncratic vocal *timbres* are rounded off.

[2] Dylan was backed by The Band from 1965, their presence on his recordings and stage performances causing outcry amongst his folk-oriented followers. During the infamous

---

1965-66 tour which took in Detroit, The Band hooked up with Mickey Stevenson who invited them back to Hitsville. Rumours have since circulated that he produced unreleased sessions for them.

[3] The comment was made in San Francisco on December 3. Dylan was asked to name some poets he admired, Robinson's name surprisingly cropping up in the list. Taking note, Motown's Director of Public Relations Al Abrams started the myth that Dylan had in fact called Smokey Robinson the greatest American wordsmith of his generation, a fallacy which has been widely repeated. Interviewed by *Rolling Stone* in 1969, Dylan was asked about the alleged earlier remark, which he proceeded to 'withdraw' ironically, invoking the deceased French symbolist Arthur Rimbaud (1854-1891) instead of Robinson.

## TMG 541
## THE TEMPTATIONS
**My Baby** (2:57)
(Robinson—Moore—Rogers)
Produced by William "Smokey" Robinson
Recording completed: 24 Aug 1965
**Release Date**: 19 Nov 1965
**B-side**: Don't Look Back
**Position in Record Retailer Top 40**: -
**Equivalent US Release**: Gordy 7047 (30 Sep 1965)
**Position in Billboard Top 40 Pop**: 13
**Position in Billboard Top 40 R & B**: 4

---

Otis Williams / Melvin Franklin / Paul Williams / Eddie Kendricks / David Ruffin

---

Mining the seminal "My Girl" [E67] yet again for inspiration (see also [504] and [526], both of which feature alongside this track on a 1966 Tamla Motown EP), Robinson risked his formula for The Temptations becoming sterile through sheer predictability, something presumably not lost on a watchful Norman Whitfield. Yet whereas the group's new single draws on "My Girl" to the extent that it shares a vocal fanning and major 7th foundation, for rhythmic and tonal ideas it looks more towards "My Girl"'s companion piece, "My Guy" [E42], and can be rightly seen as an androgynous fusion of the two former hits—title included.

As an exercise in toughening up the group's image, the release of "My Baby" serves to introduce a refreshingly energetic approach, pulling away from high-school doo-wop in favour of 'authentic' R & B, and preparing the ground for the triumphantly frenzied "Get Ready" [557]. Taken as a stepping stone in the group's career, "My Baby" (recorded during the same session as [526][1]) comes over as relatively expendable, although the articulate focus from James Jamerson illustrates a subtle upping of his role within the studio group's set up, also anticipating things to come.

The recording was the last Temptations single to carry a lead vocal from Paul Williams.

[1] Harold Keith Taylor, p3. The author engineered the session in question, which also yielded the current B-side.

---

**TMG 542**
**FOUR TOPS**
**Something About You** (2:48)
(Holland—Dozier—Holland)
Produced by Brian Holland/Lamont Dozier
Recording completed: 28 Jul 1965
**Release Date**: 26 Nov 1965
**B-side**: Darling I Hum Our Song
**Position in Record Retailer Top 40**: -
**Equivalent US Release**: Motown 1084 (21 Oct 1965)
**Position in Billboard Top 40 Pop**: 19
**Position in Billboard Top 40 R & B**: 9

---

Levi Stubbs / Lawrence Payton / Abdul 'Duke' Fakir / Renaldo 'Obie' Benson

---

A further investigation of single-chord songwriting, "Something About You" holds its Bb steady during its four verses, running a classic Chuck Berry riff throughout—indicative that this section was written on guitar. The track departs from potential cliché though with a surprise 'backwards' chorus (stepping directly to G#), which picks up the three-note riff of the verse for its melodic movement.

"Something About You" is a primitive number dealing with obsessive infatuation, reflecting the entrenched rise-and-fall of the song's construction, as suggested by its early title "Backslider". As with [541], the number has the qualities of a stylistic work-out, absolved partly by Levi Stubbs' rousing vocals against The Andantes' support. Carrying a frankly bizarre sax solo from Mike Terry, the single is a reliable though not outstanding development of HDH's drive to bring The Four Tops into line with The Supremes [528], and is in fact as close as the group came to emulating their stablemates' sound.

**TMG 543**
**THE SUPREMES**
**I Hear A Symphony** (2:41)
(Holland—Dozier—Holland)
Produced by Brian Holland/Lamont Dozier
Recording completed: 29 Sep 1965
**Release Date**: 26 Nov 1965
**B-side**: Who Could Ever Doubt My Love
**Position in Record Retailer Top 40**: 39
**Equivalent US Release**: Motown 1083 (6 Oct 1965)
**Position in Billboard Top 40 Pop**: 1
**Position in Billboard Top 40 R & B**: 2

---

Diana Ross / Florence Ballard / Mary Wilson

---

In assessing HDH's 1966 œuvre, Funk Brother Johnny Griffith referred to a "classical period", with particular reference to their dramatic Four Tops triptych beginning with "Reach Out I'll Be There" [579]. Some months ahead of this, the team's flowering interest in classical music and the arrangement possibilities it suggests was evinced by the symphonic allusions of this, The Supremes' sixth US number 1. (The first draft had it as "I Hear A Rhapsody".) Commenced by Lamont Dozier from a concept suggested by the stock employment of incidental music in movie love scenes, the song was fleshed out side-by-side at the piano with Brian Holland, with one of their most credulous lyrics, idealistic and fancifully romantic, and in consequence, one of their thinnest creations.

Recorded with guide vocal on September 22 under Holland's direction, the track was waiting for the group's contribution when Berry Gordy happened to hear it in the early hours. Promptly ordering that it be completed immediately, the exasperated producer found himself telephoning his brother at 3:00am to round-off the lyric, do some fine-tuning and make arrangements for The Supremes, 'resting' between tours, to come to Hitsville later that day.[1] While the resultant track betrays none of the time pressures which the similarly hurried "It's The Same Old Song" [528] had, Diana Ross' unrehearsed vocal is markedly out of tune in places, suggesting that a jaded Brian Holland simply couldn't muster the requisite energy to hype her for *another* take.

Representing a reversal in approach for The Supremes, "I Hear A Symphony" is a gushing love song set to a despondent, downwards moving structure. (It links to the group's earlier singles by the "Baby, baby" refrain of "Where Did Our Love Go" [E51], which also carries an analogous saxophone solo.) Kicking off with a bass guitar "heart beat", the song quickly expresses the 14 seconds of its only verse before running through a succession of chorus figures, sustaining interest via a sequence of semitonal step-ups which elevate the C major key through to its eventual home of Eb.

Issued almost immediately, the single was aired on television within days amid speculation that Diana Ross was about to leave The Supremes. (There is evidence that her departure was being planned for some point within the next 12 months [597].) Much loved by the group, "I Hear A Symphony" became a huge hit in the states, giving rise to a similarly hasty album of the same name, and was shortly covered more convincingly and to high acclaim by The Isley Brothers [572b], complete with Chopin-esque piano figures.

[1] Gordy's disregard of others' need for sleep is not without precedent; back in 1960 he decided to re-record The Miracles' "Shop Around" [E03] deep in the night, assembling a groggy group and session band at no notice for a 4:00am session.

## TIMELINE – March to December 1965

Tamla Motown release 43 singles, 20 albums and 9 EPs
Tamla Motown place 6 singles in the UK top 40. 1 makes top 10
Soul music expands fan-base further courtesy of James Brown, Fontella Bass, Wilson Pickett etc.

| | |
|---|---|
| **Mar 25** | Supremes: "Stop! In The Name Of Love" (Tamla Motown's first release) enters UK top 50 (peak 7) |
| **Mar 26** | Diana Ross is 21 |
| **Mar 27** | Supremes: "Stop! In The Name Of Love" is US number 1 (two weeks) |
| **Apr 21** | *Sounds Of Motown* first aired on BBC TV |
| **Jun 12** | Supremes: "Back In My Arms Again" number 1 in US (one week) |
| **Jun 19** | Four Tops: "I Can't Help Myself" number 1 in US (two weeks), toppling Supremes |
| **Jul 25** | Supremes open prestigious booking at New York's Copa |
| **Summer** | Funk Brother James Gittens killed in car crash |
| **Aug 11-15** | Race riots in Watts, LA |
| **Aug** | Brenda Holloway tours US with Beatles |
| **Sep 30** | Supremes embark on nine-day European tour |
| **Oct 7** | Supremes perform in Manchester for *Top Of The Pops* |
| **Oct 8** | Supremes perform in London for *Ready, Steady, Go!* |
| **Autumn** | Tamla Motown bucks popular taste, beginning period marked by releases from lesser-regarded acts including Billy Eckstine, Dorsey Burnette, Lewis Sisters, Tony Martin |
| **Nov 12** | Marvin Gaye's son is born to Berry Gordy's 15-year-old niece Denise |
| **Nov 20** | Supremes: "I Hear A Symphony" number 1 in US (two weeks) |
| **Nov 29** | Motown Revue goes to Paris, featuring Supremes, Miracles, Martha & Vandellas, Stevie Wonder |
| **Dec** | Gordy appoints Brian Holland Vice-President of Motown |

**TMG 544**
**BARBARA McNAIR**
**You're Gonna Love My Baby** (2:57)
(McNair—Miller—Perkinson)
Produced by Berry Gordy
Recording completed: 4 Nov 1965
**Release Date**: 7 Jan 1966
**B-side**: The Touch Of Time
**Position in Record Retailer Top 40**: -
**Equivalent US Release**: Motown 1087 (15 Nov 1965)
**Position in Billboard Top 40 Pop**: -
**Position in Billboard Top 40 R & B**: -

Having taken a December break from singles releases (which was to become normal practise), Tamla Motown's first offering of 1966 continued the label's interest in Motown's recent crop of imported 'names'. Chicago-born McNair was known for her cabaret work and had a string of recordings on various labels behind her when she joined Motown in late-1965, debuting with "You're Gonna Love My Baby".

Popular amongst soul fans, the single failed to engage the public with its corny mock-drama arrangement, Gordy's big 'Phil Spector' production somewhat overdone. That said, the song has a certain swing in its verse, rising into a forceful chorus and anticipating The Rolling Stones' "Out Of Time", recorded later in the year. (The flip-side backing vocalists included The Supremes, with a jealous Diana Ross particularly prominent.)

For McNair's part, she remained at Motown into 1968, by then pushing away from singing towards television and film acting (for which she became better known). Along the way she recorded the celebrated "Baby A Go-Go" and three long-players including an unreleased album of Smokey Robinson tracks.

**TMG 545**
**STEVIE WONDER**
**Uptight (Everything's Alright)** (2:53)
(Cosby—Moy—Wonder)
Produced by Henry "Hank" Cosby/William "Mickey" Stevenson
Recording completed: 15 Oct 1965
**Release Date**: 14 Jan 1966
**B-side**: Purple Raindrops
**Position in Record Retailer Top 40**: 14¹
**Equivalent US Release**: Tamla 54124 (22 Nov 1965)
**Position in Billboard Top 40 Pop**: 3
**Position in Billboard Top 40 R & B**: 1

Running out of fresh ideas in 1965, Stevie Wonder's development from harmonica-tooting kid to fledgling artist was earnestly begun in 1966, with a series of recordings aimed to salvage a youthful career which was looking like a fast-dying public fad. Recognising the long-term weaknesses associated with directionless live jams, Gordy had the child singer teamed with a new staff writing set up of Henry "Hank" Cosby and lyricist Sylvia Moy, and arranger Paul Riser, beginning a fruitful partnership which would endure throughout the rest of the decade. (The decision not to use a harmonica on the track, settled after discussion with his musical guardian Clarence Paul, was taken in consideration of the track's aesthetic, but clearly flags Wonder's stylistic development.)

One of the charms of "Uptight" is the irregular structural patterning used as an expressive format heedless of the 'correct' musical sequences. Accordingly, the choruses pop up unexpectedly and with no contrasting middle-8 the track is potently inexorable, constantly surprising the unwary listener.[2] In part, the track's perpetual recapitulation stems from the process by which it evolved. Begun by Cosby as a horn-driven instrumental inspired by The Rolling Stones' summer hit "(I Can't Get No) Satisfaction", the saxophone riffs roughly resemble Keith Richard's guitar licks.[3] Devoid of lyrics bar the word 'uptight', a Wonder colloquialism which in its time and place meant outstanding and positive, the backing track was given to Moy who returned a couple of weeks later with the completed text, which she fed to Wonder during the recording session from the control booth, via a set of headphones. (Notwithstanding, Wonder would later claim this as 'his' first composition, early copies carrying the co-credit S. Judkins, Wonder's real name.)

Lyrically somewhat vague, the song as a whole is a pugnacious portrayal of a rich girl courted by 'poor man's son', but with allusions to their separation 'across the tracks' hints at a racial divide besides a difference in social class, although the point is lost when Wonder stops dealing with the conflict of backgrounds for a digression into his devotion for the girl. The strength of "Uptight" though lies not in its lyrical 'message' (if indeed it has one) but its excitement as a performance, bristling with Benny Benjamin's snare crashes at the end of each chorus line[4] set against Joe Messina's sharply stabbing Telecaster. Prominent too is the newly liberated bass of James Jamerson, his agitated running riffs (played low on the fret-board) galvanising the studio group and sparking Wonder's impromptu "a-ha-ha-ha-ha" towards the end.[5] In "Uptight", The Funk Brothers show that when rising to the challenge they could rock as hard as any group then recording.

[1] The current single was Tamla Motown's first top 40 hit not penned by HDH.

[2] Essentially consisting of a sustained blur between verse and chorus, the sequence consists of: 1.A 12-bar intro followed by an eight-bar chorus; 2. Six lines of verse with a further two sung to the chorus tune; 3.A full eight-bar chorus followed by a recapitulation of the instrumental intro; 4.A four-line verse and a two-line half-verse (the latter also sung as a chorus) which is repeated; 5.Choruses to fade. (Listeners observing their CD player's clock will notice that the tempo subtly shifts throughout, proof of live, unregulated recording.)

[3] Stevie Wonder had toured with The Stones in America in 1964. The two acts would resume live collaboration in 1972, their stage shows culminating in a medley of "Satisfaction" and "Uptight" (see [841]).

[4] Which Steve Lodder considers more likely to be Wonder himself at the kit (p39).

[5] For a technical analysis of Jamerson's recorded track (including score) see Slutsky, p93.

**TMG 546**
**THE MARVELETTES**
**Don't Mess With Bill** (2:50)
(Robinson)
Produced by William "Smokey" Robinson
Recording completed: 20 Jul 1965
**Release Date**: 28 Jan 1966
**B-side**: Anything You Wanna Do
**Position in Record Retailer Top 40**: -
**Equivalent US Release**: Tamla 54126 (26 Nov 1965)
**Position in Billboard Top 40 Pop**: 7
**Position in Billboard Top 40 R & B**: 3

---

Gladys Horton / Wanda Young / Katherine Anderson

---

Recorded over the summer, "Don't Mess With Bill" saw Smokey Robinson taking an interest in the struggling Marvelettes still technically under control of the Hunter—Stevenson team. Following the commercial failure of "Danger Heartbreak Dead Ahead" [535], his efforts were rewarded with this recent track's approval for release as a new-year single in the UK, although duplication problems arose in the process and the final Tamla Motown 'mix' consists of just one channel of the original stereo take (available on album) sent to both for mono reproduction.[1]

"Don't Mess With Bill" is an unusually sedate and crawling number, custom-written for Wanda Young, who turns in a studied Ross-style performance. Ostensibly an innocent high-school number, the song comes shaded with a faintly threatening subtext in which extra-connubial partners of both protagonists are acknowledged, but warned to stay away. The narrator even lists a few of her lovers by name, before staking her paradoxically uncompromising claim to her regular boyfriend, as if blind to the double standards being applied.

Its title suggestive of a cryptic comment on the group's production set-up, Robinson denied the song was pointed at William "Mickey" Stevenson, claiming the name 'Bill' just rang well[2]; in fact it may equally have been suggested by Billy Gordon for whom Georgeanna Tillman had recently left the group. As an exercise for its writer, the track was an interesting project, its top 10 placing (the group's first in four years) temporarily capturing The Marvelettes for him, consolidating Smokey Robinson as Motown's most versatile single songwriter.

[1] I am indebted to members of the Soulful Detroit internet forum for this information. See references for web address.
[2] Robinson p129. Few Motown tracks cite actual names although the earlier "Mickey's Monkey" [517] (written by HDH) had similar connotations to this track.

**TMG 547**
**THE MIRACLES**
**Going To A Go-Go** (2:48)
(Moore—Robinson—Rogers—Johnson)[1]

---

Produced by William "Smokey" Robinson
Recording completed: 18 Aug 1965
**Release Date**: 4 Feb 1966
**B-side**: Choosy Beggar
**Position in Record Retailer Top 40**: -
**Equivalent US Release**: Tamla 54127 (6 Dec 1965)
**Position in Billboard Top 40 Pop**: 11
**Position in Billboard Top 40 R & B**: 2

---

Smokey Robinson / Bobby Rogers / Claudette Rogers Robinson /
Warren 'Pete' Moore / Ronnie White

---

In common with numerous artists of the mid-1960s, Robinson and his group took an interest in building songs from single chords, a technique explored by a variety of Motown's writers the previous year ([E54]; [502]; [509]; [520] and so on). "Going To A Go-Go" features a discordant guitar modulation to F, but with the shift unacknowledged in Jamerson's bass line, the G major foundation holds throughout, its crabbed melody clustering around the tonic.

Conceived as a dance track, the song refers to a proto-disco phenomenon celebrated at club events across America, and its associated sociological meaning, which Motown writers referenced numerous times. With The Miracles playing venues such as California's Whiskey-A-Go-Go in 1965, the need to develop a suitable dance repertoire was apparent after their recent ventures into sentimentality which risked restricting the group's appeal, Robinson's calculated response incorporating a jokey play on the word 'go' in its title. Galloping along convincingly, the track became a defining genre-piece for the group, after which the contemporary album was named.[2]

[1] The label credits are incorrect, co-writer Marv Tarplin presumably being confused with Marv Johnson.

[2] The group's following album *Away We A Go Go* also made reference to the phenomenon, as did the pending *Supremes A Go-Go*. Stevie Wonder meanwhile recorded "Love A Go-Go" for his Uptight album and the unreleased "At The Go-Go", and in a 1964 interview explained: "At the moment everything in the US is 'a go-go.' It's the new word. It means anything that involves some sort of action or movement. If someone thinks a record is good they might say, 'It's a go-go record'." (Quoted in Haskins, p45). Other Northern Soul recordings to reference the phenomenon include The Four Larks' "Grooving at the Go-Go" and The Detroit Sound's "Jumping at the Go-Go". In the UK, a group calling themselves the Go-Gos were signed to Motown's old distributor, Oriole. (In the 1980s the term was revived for a minor funk movement which grew out of Washington DC, while "Going To A Go-Go" was eventually covered by Motown admirers The Rolling Stones.)

**TMG 548**

**THE SUPREMES**
**My World Is Empty Without You** (2:33)
(Holland—Dozier—Holland)
Produced by Brian Holland/Lamont Dozier
Recording completed: 2 Dec 1965
**Release Date**: 11 Feb 1966

---

**B-side**: Everything Is Good About You
**Position in Record Retailer Top 40**: -
**Equivalent US Release**: Motown 1089 (29 Dec 1965)
**Position in Billboard Top 40 Pop**: 5
**Position in Billboard Top 40 R & B**: 10

---

## Diana Ross / Florence Ballard / Mary Wilson

---

Privately admitting the importance of HDH to Motown in the middle years of the 1960s, Berry Gordy sought to appease Eddie Holland's grumbling over the team's remuneration by appointing him Co-Vice President in December 1965. (Holland had assumed the position of financial spokesman for the team from the start of their professional association.) Considered virtually indispensable to the company—inasmuch as anyone was—HDH were less prolific than Smokey Robinson, but more reliably successful, handling affairs for Motown's two biggest groups and lining up a sequence of major hit singles which their colleagues could only envy.

"My World Is Empty Without You" shows HDH returning to the complexities of the pain felt in a dissolving relationship, after the comparatively frivolous "I Hear A Symphony" [543].[1] Not a hit in Britain, the song has tended to be overlooked as part of the lull in popular appeal between "Stop! In The Name Of Love" [501] and "You Can't Hurry Love" [575] but in truth, despite its deficiency of sales, is one of the team's most penetrating numbers. With an acutely perceptive lyric portraying the desolation experienced when one's love is lost and the external world appears as a series of insurmountable trials, the lyrical content is reflected by an expressive melody in wide steps, depicting the restless torment but repeatedly collapsing spent (by shifting to the relative minor) for the chorus. (The metaphor for sorrow is the unresolved conflict between rationalised solution and pessimistic defeat.) "My World Is Empty" is, from a creative perspective, one of HDH's most tightly wrought creations, as searingly guileless as anything they ever composed.

Sadly, the song's impact is cancelled out by the obligatory 'pop' mode in which The Supremes' version is set, arranged for radio play in the same manner as [501] before it, contorting its wistful beauty into a soul-less rush. Dozier and Eddie Holland's writing method, which generally consisted of the piecemeal construction of songs from discrete units, had an ease of dismantling and reassembly as required, and frequently alterations in structure and arrangement could be accommodated at the behest of production director Brian Holland if certain preliminary ideas proved unviable. The facility was not lost on perfectionist Berry Gordy who often, as here, insisted on last-minute changes which sometimes caused ill-feeling amongst his writer-producers. (For a more authentic idea of the song's initial conception see Lamont Dozier's *Reflections Of* CD, which despite its digitised production shows Dozier at home in the track's piano-led pensiveness.)

Caught between the composition's melancholy and the studio-band's exuberance, the production ends up lacking the free flow of the group's period recordings, its organ-heavy backing track clogging the soundscape.

---

sources state that Flo Ballard missed the vocal recording in
:r, Andante Marlene Barrow seamlessly standing in for her,
;h this is contradicted by the details of the studio log.) The track
was included on *I Hear A Symphony*, recorded over two days in
November 1965, along with some dubiously chosen covers such as
"Unchained Melody" and "Yesterday", highlighting Motown's problems
in finding time and material to devote to full studio sets. (The Supremes
had three albums abandoned for various reasons during the preceding
year.) By the time the LP was released in Britain, the group were already
trailering their follow-up single [560].

[1] Eddie Holland's lyrics were likely penned after the recording of "Darling Baby" [551b]
(also by HDH and originally intended for The Supremes), which contains towards the
close, the line 'This world is empty without you'. The Elgins' vocal for "Darling Baby" was
recorded on October 20, eight days before "My World Is Empty" was commenced and six
weeks before Diana Ross' vocal was recorded.

## TMG 549
## MARTHA & THE VANDELLAS
**My Baby Loves Me** (2:58)
(Moy—Hunter—Stevenson)
Produced by William "Mickey" Stevenson/Ivy Jo Hunter
Recording completed: 23 Aug 1965
**Release Date**: Feb 1966
**B-side**: Never Leave Your Baby's Side
**Position in Record Retailer Top 40**: -
**Equivalent US Release**: Gordy 7048 (4 Jan 1966)
**Position in Billboard Top 40 Pop**: 22
**Position in Billboard Top 40 R & B**: 3

---

Martha Reeves / Rosalind Ashford / Betty Kelly

---

Confidently mature against the pop-oriented Supremes, Martha & The
Vandellas were undergoing a process of reluctant re-definition in the face of
their rivals' overwhelming sales figures. Leaning towards high-school pop,
"My Baby Loves Me" was constructed largely by Mickey Stevenson for wife
Kim Weston, but was snatched away after an argument and given to Reeves,
following the precedent set by "Dancing In The Street" [E54]. The switch
worked well, the group's sound guided here towards the mass-market, casually
rocking through a succession of sentimental lyrical phrases, although Reeves—
who rates the song as one of her two finest recordings—admired its 'jazzy'
qualities, a genre she aspired to.

Sharing harmonic ideas with "My Guy" [E42], the track finds its writers
attempting something in the vein of Smokey Robinson; the rhyming of 'cute'
and 'substitute' in verse 2 had already been heard in "The Tracks Of My
Tears" [522]. Suffused with lush strings and weighing in at an extravagant
near-three-minutes, the effect is persuasive and romantic, Reeves'
commitment real, psychologically aiming her words at William, a former

fiancé who had betrayed her by marrying someone else in 1958. For reasons unknown The Vandellas did not attend the session, their vocal duties performed instead by The Four Tops and The Andantes. A minor beauty from the group.

**TMG 550**
**JUNIOR WALKER & THE ALL STARS**
**Cleo's Mood** (2:38)
(DeWalt—Woods—Fuqua)
Produced by Harvey Fuqua
**Release Date**: 18 Feb 1966
**B-side**: Baby, You Know You Ain't Right
**Position in Record Retailer Top 40**: -
**Equivalent US Release**: Soul 35017 (23 Dec 1965)
**Position in Billboard Top 40 Pop**: -
**Position in Billboard Top 40 R & B**: 14

---
Jr Walker / Willie Woods / Vic Thomas / James Graves
---

Following the purchase of Harvey Fuqua's collapsed labels in 1964 [509], Berry Gordy acquired rights to a stack of old recordings which, via Motown's far-reaching publicity machine, offered the opportunity for repackaging and the chance to bag some 'free' hits. Having already primed the British public to some extent [529b], Tamla Motown's only dip into the archives for a release on 45 yielded "Cleo's Mood", a 1962 recording written by Walker and Fuqua with the group guitarist Willie Woods, originally put out in the States as Harvey 117.

Consisting of an instrumental 12-bar-blues, "Cleo's Mood" is a surprisingly jazzy track, running five times around with a solo organ from Vic Thomas in one of the later verses. The rest of the 2:38 is dominated by Walker's saxophone, soulfully delivered with none of the rough-and-ready 'grit' for which he subsequently became known. Prequelling the style explored by Stax house-band Booker T & The MGs in the early 1960s (including "Green Onions" with which it was recorded contemporarily), the track was ripe for a second airing, and offers an insight into the group's sound before Berry Gordy adopted and re-styled them. (The Motown release was exactly as per the Harvey original, but EQ-ed again for a cleaner sound.)

**TMG 551**
**THE ELGINS**
**Put Yourself In My Place** (2:25)
(Holland—Dozier—Holland)
Produced by Brian Holland/Lamont Dozier
Recording completed: 28 Sep 1965
**Release Date**: 25 Feb 1966
**B-side**: Darling Baby

**Position in Record Retailer Top 40**: -
**Equivalent US Release**: VIP 25029 (31 Dec 1965)
**Position in Billboard Top 40 Pop**: -
**Position in Billboard Top 40 R & B**: 4

---

Saundra Mallett Edwards / Cleo 'Duke' Miller / Johnny Dawson / Robert Fleming

Almost embarrassing in its disclosure of private grief, "Put Yourself In My Place" was not designed for A-side exposure. Initially written as "My Darling It's You" for The Supremes, whose first two renditions were scrapped [575b], the track was diverted to The Elgins[1], a four-piece signed to Motown as The Downbeats in 1962 since when they had released nothing. (Early pressings of the US edition still carry the group's old name.)

Written by HDH with input from Johnny Thornton[2], cousin of the Holland brothers, the song comes across as an 'old time' ballad, simplistically shifting through its novel chord progression with every bar. The dispirited number commences with a tinkling piano which persists throughout the track, which, rather than clashing with the mood of the composition lends a lullaby air, but with the morose suggestion of rain falling—one of HDH's ventures into the use of illustrative sound effects.

Dealing with the predicament faced by a discarded lover, intensely dejected and pleading for pity, the track contrasts sharply with the team's steadfastly joyful arrangements which tended to mask the potency of their lyrics [548]. Possibly The Elgins were offered the song by an HDH team safe in the knowledge that they would have a far bigger say in how the recording was approached, the group having no pre-determined style to adhere to nor market-place clout to justify authoritarian tinkering from Berry Gordy. The resulting arrangement can thereby be seen as a generally faithful representation of how the song was conceived.

Regarded today as a minor classic, "Put Yourself In My Place" carries an English charm which Tamla Motown would flog relentlessly until they eventually wrung a hit from it, the most stubborn attempt to sell a song in the label's history ([575b]; [591b]; [642]; [708]; [787]). Released in the USA with the sides switched, the single was only marketed in the Detroit area, despite which it still made number 4 on the R & B chart, an indication perhaps of how central the city was to the movement.

[1] The group's name had been used previously by a number of different acts including an early incarnation of The Temptations.

[2] Thornton appears on the copyright but on neither the UK nor US record labels.

**TMG 552**
**MARVIN GAYE**
**One More Heartache** (2:39)
(Robinson—Moore—White—Tarplin—Rogers)
Produced by William "Smokey" Robinson
Recording completed: 9 Dec 1965

---

**118**

**Release Date**: 11 Mar 1966
**B-side**: When I Had Your Love
**Position in Record Retailer Top 40**: -
**Equivalent US Release**: Tamla 54129 (31 Jan 1966)
**Position in Billboard Top 40 Pop**: 29
**Position in Billboard Top 40 R & B**: 4

Criticism that Tamla Motown singles were too samey was being levelled in 1966 as one of the reasons for the label's failure to dominate in the UK, in contrast to the enormous impact currently being enjoyed in America. This though is paradoxical, US audiences being no more immune to repetition than British ones, and while it is true that formularised writing was employed by Motown as a further formula in itself, an open appraisal of the eight singles [544] though to [552] shows a range of styles as divergent as any popular group of the era (with the obvious exception of The Beatles).

The Miracles-penned "One More Heartache" is built on a bluesy musical foundation similar to "Cleo's Mood" [550], with a typical Motown arrangement including off-beat drums and an archetypal sax break. The track deals with the narrator's inability to withstand further emotional knock-backs, already at the end of his tether from an unstated series of let-downs, but liberal use of clichéd simile leaves the number rather insipid and uninspiring.

Tweaking it into shape in a series of sessions towards the end of 1965, an enthusiastic Robinson incorporated a falsetto backing spectrum, and overlaid the whole with a cuttingly EQ-ed electric guitar riff in a moderately successful effort to provide some zing. If use of an acoustic guitar in "My Girl Has Gone" [540] had referenced folk-rock, here the inspiration tended towards the quasi-'Indian' guitar sounds being expressed by the era's biggest groups.[1] Straddling the gap between the developing rock scene with its interest in exploring textural sound innovation and the recognisable Motown characteristic, the track, if only at surface level, dares to venture into progressive territories which sadly were not pursued and developed.

[1] Recent examples including The Beatles' "Ticket To Ride", The Byrds' "Mr. Tambourine Man", The Kinks' "Tired Of Waiting For You", The Rolling Stones' "Get Off Of My Cloud", and so on. The 'eastern' theme continued on the B-side, "When I Had Your Love" containing a recurrent 'Chinese' figure, played high on piano keyboard.

**TMG 553**
**FOUR TOPS**
**Shake Me, Wake Me (When It's Over)** (2:41)
(Holland—Dozier—Holland)
Produced by Brian Holland/Lamont Dozier
Recording completed: 6 Jan 1966
**Release Date**: 18 Mar 1966
**B-side**: Just As Long As You Need Me
**Position in Record Retailer Top 40**: -
**Equivalent US Release**: Motown 1090 (2 Feb 1966)

**Position in Billboard Top 40 Pop**: 18
**Position in Billboard Top 40 R & B**: 5

---

Levi Stubbs / Lawrence Payton / Abdul 'Duke' Fakir / Renaldo 'Obie' Benson

---

Tossing and turning through the torment of a restless sleep, "Shake Me, Wake Me" Is the most disturbed number in The Four Tops' singles discography. A paranoid portrayal of the singer's worst nightmares finds Levis Stubbs in a cold sweat, the terrifying truth of his lover's unfaithfulness overheard through the bedroom wall, a cruelly taunting semi-hallucination experienced as reality. (The track's working title was "Without My Baby".)

Groping in the dark for an inaccessible expressive feel, HDH succeed in finding and relaying the confusion between dream and reality which remains insoluble. The key transitional recording between the group's early and late-60s style, the song has the principal musical foundation of tracks such as "I Can't Help Myself" [515] and "Something About You" [542], but with the allusory-illusory qualities of more ephemeral material such as "7-Rooms Of Gloom" [612] and "Yesterday's Dreams" [665], suggesting a break with straight-forward relationship issues for The Four Tops. (How much of this is down to marijuana intake is open to speculation, but the sensual aspects of HDH's 1966-67 material, in common with much popular music of the day, illustrates an interest in quality of experience itself, wholly absent from their more rationalised earlier work.)

**TMG 554**
**KIM WESTON**
**Helpless** (2:35)
(Holland—Dozier—Holland)
Produced by Brian Holland/Lamont Dozier
Recording completed: 22 Dec 1965
**Release Date**: 18 Mar 1966
**B-side**: A Love Like Yours (Don't Come Knockin' Every Day)
**Position in Record Retailer Top 40**: -
**Equivalent US Release**: Gordy 7050 (14 Feb 1965)
**Position in Billboard Top 40 Pop**: -
**Position in Billboard Top 40 R & B**: 13

A track written for The Four Tops' current album *On Top*, "Helpless" carries a classic HDH chord cycle, with a stock Motown arrangement and obligatory sax solo. Popular at soul 'all-nighters' for its pronounced bounce, the track steers close to surface-level pop, patiently building by the introduction of a new instrument in every bar, and with a typically absorbing vocal track. Essentially the counter-feminist lyric depicts a woman incapable of survival without her man, but has a hint of slapdash about it, especially in the multi-rhyming chorus with the use of 'abusion' (i.e. abuse) opposite 'confusion'. (Ironically it was released on Valentine's Day in America.)

Having not done it justice, HDH would salvage the track's stronger points for a more accomplished reworking later in the year [583]. For Weston, the single marked the end of her solo work, only her more famous collaboration with Marvin Gaye [590] following before her departure for MGM.

## TMG 555
## THE ISLEY BROTHERS
**This Old Heart Of Mine (Is Weak For You)** (2:44)
(Holland—Dozier—Holland)[1]
Produced by Brian Holland/Lamont Dozier
Recording completed: 1 Dec 1965
**Release Date**: 25 Mar 1966
**B-side**: There's No Love Left
**Position in Record Retailer Top 40**: -
**Equivalent US Release**: Tamla 54128 (28 Jan 1966)
**Position in Billboard Top 40 Pop**: 12
**Position in Billboard Top 40 R & B**: 6

---

Ronald Isley / Rudolph Isley / O'Kelly Isley

---

Arriving ready-formed at Motown's door, Cincinnati family outfit The Isley Brothers came with two big hits already under their belt in "Shout" and "Twist And Shout". Convinced by their own hype, the brothers had left the Wand label in the early-1960s to set up T-Neck, a dubiously thought-out venture in self-management which failed to consolidate the act and was eventually wound up.

With no precedent to base his strategy on, Berry Gordy's first priority was to remould the act via a strong, formula-friendly opening hit, the obvious move being a pairing with his most fruitful writer-producers. As luck would have it, HDH happened to have a particularly attractive track ready under the working title "Don't Throw My Love Away", waiting for The Four Tops then away on touring duty.[2] Given to The Isley Brothers, the backing track required Ronald to stretch his register to a barely attainable high C, a task his numerous technical faults betray as arduous.[3]

Described by Lamont Dozier as an anthem to a relationship he was unable to relinquish, the story-line revolves around the plight of an unappreciated suitor, with an unabashed chorus statement pronouncing genuine love. Swamped by an elated arrangement, the sentiment is in no way despondent however, rushing impatiently into the second bridge (borrowed from "Back In My Arms Again" [516]), as if eager for self expression. (Also typical of HDH's recycling policy, the recurrent 'oohs' recall the similar device on tracks such as "Baby Love" [E56].)

Production-wise, "This Old Heart Of Mine" is an outstanding example of Brian Holland's precepts, introducing and overlaying instruments in systematic steps, culminating in a richly joyful unison chorus. Dominant throughout are Gordon Staples' Detroit Symphony Strings, whose ascending score is mixed especially prominently so as to act as the lead instrumental idea, in this context a sort of precursor to the development of soul music in the 1970s (for example in the Philadelphia scene: as illustration, compare with the string sections on Harold Melvin's "The Love I Lost" from 1973). Giving a sense of weightless euphoria, the soaring arrangement provides melodic form otherwise absent in the horizontal vocal lines, although not entirely independently; the main violin shapes are based on the chorus phrase, and draw too on James Jamerson's bass patterns, tracked also by piano and violin, and therefore fundamental to the song.

Striking gold with their first release, The Isley Brothers marked their arrival at Tamla Motown with one of the label's most exultant anthems, a timeless piece of popular music which has never dimmed in the public's affections. Re-pressed in 1968 (with the same catalogue number), it claimed a deserved top 10 place, seven years before Rod Stewart took his rendition into the upper reaches of the charts.[4]

[1] Sylvia Moy is co-credited on the track, although her name is missing from the labels.

[2] Conversely, Ronald Isley has claimed The Supremes were offered it first, and the sleeve notes in *The Complete Motown Singles Vol. 6* state that it was intended for Kim Weston. Nonetheless it seems The Isley Brothers were not in mind at the outset.

[3] Interviewed in 2005, Chris Clark commented that Motown routinely cut backing tracks at a pitch intentionally high, forcing vocalists to stretch themselves to the limits (Record Collector 313, p66).

[4] In 1989, Stewart released a re-recording of the track featuring Ronald Isley. He also had hits with "The Motown Song" with The Temptations in 1991 and a cover of "It Takes Two" [590] (with Tina Turner), as well as a cover of "I Wish It Would Rain" [641] as part of The Faces.


**TMG 556**
**BRENDA HOLLOWAY**
**Together 'Til The End Of Time** (2:57)
(Wilson)
Produced by Hal Davis/Marc Gordon
**Release Date**: 25 Mar 1966
**B-side**: Sad Song
**Position in Record Retailer Top 40**: -
**Equivalent US Release**: Tamla 54125 (11 Jan 1966)
**Position in Billboard Top 40 Pop**: -
**Position in Billboard Top 40 R & B**: -

By the start of 1966, Brenda Holloway had lost her main sponsor in Smokey Robinson, his attention elsewhere. Leaving her isolated in LA, Motown had created for themselves something of an outsider, difficult to direct musically, and thought by some listeners to be a white singer. Viewed as an uninspiring sideline for Motown's Detroit-based writer-producers, she would be passed around for the next 12 months before throwing in the towel completely.

"Together 'Til The End Of Time" is a nostalgic ballad written by Frank Wilson, with an aesthetic perfection and softly agile movement unmatched by Motown at that point. (The bridge into the chorus (0:32 to 0:46) visits every natural major chord bar A, present in its minor form.) Recorded at IPG Studios in Los Angeles, the track is a cool, sentimental affair contrasting with most contemporary Detroit product, soft chimes and a wistful concertina taking care of the middle-8. Pricking up ears back at Hitsville, "Together 'Till The End Of Time" was another step in the establishment of Motown-LA.

**TMG 557**
**THE TEMPTATIONS**
**Get Ready** (2:37)
(Robinson)
Produced by William "Smokey" Robinson
Recording completed: 29 Dec 1965
**Release Date**: 1 Apr 1966
**B-side**: Fading Away
**Position in Record Retailer Top 40**: -
**Equivalent US Release**: Gordy 7049 (7 Feb 1966)
**Position in Billboard Top 40 Pop**: 29
**Position in Billboard Top 40 R & B**: 1

---

Otis Williams / Melvin Franklin / Paul Williams / Eddie Kendricks / David Ruffin

---

Described by Smokey Robinson as his most direct song, the galloping verses of "Get Ready" are unflaggingly forward-hurtling, climaxing in a chorus in which the vocals splay out like the sun's rays emerging from behind a cloud. Coupled in subsequent stage performances by The Temptations' allegorical sweeping open of the arms from behind their custom four-header microphone stand, the effect was ascendant and exhilarating.[1]

Musically, the track has an extreme bottom end even for Tamla Motown. Jamerson's bass[2] is tracked by deep horns, which, with Benny Benjamin's drums (subsequently overdubbed by Richard 'Pistol' Allen) account for much of the musicianship audible on the track, with the notable addition of Kasuku Mafie's thrilling one-note saxophone wail flying though the air; entering before the bar, the section in question is the most stimulated passage on the record, at whose conclusion the string section, mixed so low that it is barely audible in the rest of the track, is finally allowed to flourish. (The chugging brass riffs may borrow from Burt Bacharach's "This Empty Place" (1963), later covered by Stephanie Mills [1020a].)

Lead vocal here is temporarily restored to Eddie Kendricks, his thinly angelic voice brought into relief by the big bass of the production, with Melvin Franklin's deep tones adding guts and colour. All told, the recording is a triumphant piece of R & B, its 'fe-fi-fo-fum' lyrics adding to the general sense of spontaneous joy, and pulling off the process of 'toughening' The Temptations with flying colours [541]. (In point of fact, the engineered move from the soft-hearted romance of track such as "It's Growing" [504] to the unbridled sexuality of "Get Ready" represents the start of a shift in spirit for the group away from fanciful idealism into physical reality, which would advance yet further three years later in the materialist-escapist "Cloud Nine" [707].)

---

One of the best-admired Tamla Motown singles today, "Get Ready" went virtually unnoticed in the UK in 1966, not charting until re-issued in the latter part of the decade [688]. Although Robinson confessed reservations over the track, the group were justifiably happy with the resulting cut, which won more approval from black audiences than white, topping the R & B charts. Ironically, its failure to cross over caused a split between Robinson and Gordy which resulted in The Temptations being wrenched from his control after two years of honing their sound and image. Instead, an eagerly awaiting Norman Whitfield finally won control of the group, a move which would have long-term consequences for Motown as a whole [565].

[1] The 'four-header' was created in 1968 by David Ruffin and became a group trademark.

[2] Claimed by Carol Kaye and the LA session group. The bass foundation is based on "We Call It Fun", an obscure 1965 American single by The Headliners (VIP 25026). A sad event occurred towards the end of Jamerson's life when he was booked to play bass on a disco remake of the track with Smokey Robinson, but to the latter's shock he was scarcely able to play the basic notes. (The track was issued as a solo Robinson single in 1979, as TMG 1152.)


## TMG 558
## STEVIE WONDER
**Nothing's Too Good For My Baby** (2:39)
(Moy—Cosby—Stevenson)
Produced by Henry "Hank" Cosby/William "Mickey" Stevenson
Recording completed: 14 Feb 1966
**Release Date**: 29 Apr 1966
**B-side**: With A Child's Heart
**Position in Record Retailer Top 40**: -
**Equivalent US Release**: Tamla 54130 (24 Mar 1966)
**Position in Billboard Top 40 Pop**: 20
**Position in Billboard Top 40 R & B**: 4

Having successfully brought Stevie Wonder to the centre-ground courtesy of "Uptight" [545], the writing team in question reconvened for the creation of a follow-up. By relying on the same tonic-centric pitching underpinned by a two-chord jockey also heard in the former hit, the team incorporate the main elements of [545] even to the extent of re-using the phrase 'pearl of a girl' in the first verse.

"Nothing's Too Good For My Baby" works though via its sheer animation, Benny Benjamin's battering end-of-the-line rolls explosive, especially in the high-energy middle-8. Culminating in a trademark "ah-hah-hah-hah", the song stands on its own merits, reinforcing Wonder's new approach despite the family resemblance to [545] lessening its import.


## TMG 559
## JUNIOR WALKER & THE ALL STARS
**(I'm A) Road Runner** (2:47)
(Holland—Dozier—Holland)
Produced by Brian Holland/Lamont Dozier

Recording completed: 8 Apr 1965
**Release Date**: 6 May 1966
**B-side**: Shoot Your Shot
**Position in Record Retailer Top 40**: -
**Equivalent US Release**: Soul 35015 (21 Mar 1966)
**Position in Billboard Top 40 Pop**: 20
**Position in Billboard Top 40 R & B**: 4

---

Jr Walker / Willie Woods / Vic Thomas / James Graves

---

If lifting singles from studio albums is utterly unremarkable these days, in the 1960s the practice was generally frowned upon; indeed for UK artists, many notable albums had no trailer-singles lifted at all, the practise being considered underhand. So far as Junior Walker & The All Stars were concerned however, their *Shotgun* album was being hawked to death, this being their fifth straight single from the set.[1]

"(I'm A) Road Runner" was custom-made by an enthused HDH shortly after the group's arrival at Motown. Wanting to get a take down at the earliest opportunity, the two producers collared Walker at Hitsville only to find him sax-less, and had to bide their time until he returned from a brief tour. Trouping into the Snakepit on 25 March 1965, a live take was made in a party atmosphere whose crackling vibes are tangible on the recording, Walker audibly hyped from his concert dates and joined in the studio by several Funk Brothers.

How much inspiration the lyric owes to Bo Diddley's "Road Runner" of 1960 is not known, although the fact that the earlier song starts out, "I'm a road runner, honey" suggests a link. But while Diddley's text is burdened with a selfish undercurrent, HDH's is openly joyous: kicking in with a lyrical repudiation of "Money (That's What I Want)" (which Walker also recorded in 1965 [586]), the song launches into a happy-go-lucky declaration of personal liberty, HDH's portrayal of freedom from constraint mirroring the happy indiscipline of Walker's patent presentation. Recorded straight, the track was slowed down to find the key of Walker's sax, then re-adjusted for the final mix, thereby giving the production extra impact. Needing, like Stevie Wonder [545], to up their game if they were to make a sustained commercial impact, the group's year-old recording was issued to a warm reception from dance enthusiasts, becoming their best-known track, but like [557] only charting in the UK on re-release in 1969 [691].

[1] Walker was by no means alone, The Miracles for example putting out four UK singles from *Going To A Go-Go* during 1965-66.

**TMG 560**
**THE SUPREMES**
**Love Is Like An Itching In My Heart** (2:53)
(Holland—Dozier—Holland)
Produced by Brian Holland/Lamont Dozier

---

Recording completed: 12 Oct 1965
**Release Date**: 13 May 1966
**B-side**: He's All I Got
**Position in Record Retailer Top 40**: -
**Equivalent US Release**: Motown 1094 (8 Apr 1966)
**Position in Billboard Top 40 Pop**: 9
**Position in Billboard Top 40 R & B**: 7

---

Diana Ross / Florence Ballard / Mary Wilson

Sounding tough against The Supremes' recent hits, "Love Is Like An Itching In My Heart" was largely laid down on June 24 the previous year and finds the group in unfamiliar territory ('rocking and a-reeling'), comprehensively overpowered by The Funk Brothers' raucous backing track. Opting to release the single immediately after the penetrating "My World Is Empty Without You" [548], Motown unintentionally contributed to its luke-warm reception, British audiences in particular preferring at this stage the group's 'baby, baby' style. The track was, in any case, ill-suited to exposure as an A-side, HDH's uncertainty over it exposed by the off-hand deployment of a kazoo on the stereo album mix, and the fact that the fade-out arrives prematurely, in order to conceal an error caused by a fault in Ross' headphones which she broke off singing to complain about.

Possibly material such as this would have been better directed to Martha Reeves, Diana Ross' sweetly innocent vocals entirely unsuited to the task despite her valiant effort to inject some grit via a calculated growl in the chorus. (The track may be seen as a prosaic reworking of Reeves' third UK single, in which the experience of being enamoured was described as 'like a heat wave' [E28].) The truth is that by now Ross was being viewed by Berry Gordy as the key figure in the group. From here on, many Supremes tracks would feature her alone, with Ballard and Wilson taking advantage of their precious time off, their roles being taken by session singers.

**TMG 561**
**TAMMI TERRELL**
**Come On And See Me** (2:22)
(Bristol—Fuqua)
Produced by Harvey Fuqua/Johnny Bristol
Recording completed: 26 Jan 1966
**Release Date**: 20 May 1966
**B-side**: Baby, Don'tcha Worry
**Position in Record Retailer Top 40**: -
**Equivalent US Release**: Motown 1095 (7 Apr 1966)
**Position in Billboard Top 40 Pop**: -
**Position in Billboard Top 40 R & B**: 25

With the exception of Gladys Knight [576], the last of Motown's great divas to arrive was Thomasina Montgomery, a 20-year-old from Philadelphia who, like The Isley Brothers, came via the Scepter/Wand stable. Universally known by her stage-name, Tammi Terrell was a tough youngster with a tempestuous relationship with James Brown, and a separate marriage and almost immediate divorce already behind her. Diminutive in stature and with an appealing, youthful face, she was moulded into a sexually alluring 'girl-next-door' caricature, a simplistic (if misleading) image for Motown to promote. 'Discovered' by Harvey Fuqua in 1965 (on-board following Motown's purchase of his business), the producer and his new partner Johnny Bristol launched Terrell with "I Can't Believe You Love Me" in November (unreleased in Britain), "Come On And See Me" her follow-up and only UK solo release.

Jauntily popularist, the track oozes commercial appeal, its warm C# major 7ths offering a relaxed sheen which never needs to exerts itself. Shuffling impatiently through steps, the song always rests back on its charming verses until the chorus is eventually revealed as an elated plateau more than half way through the song. Festooned with tinkling bells and clean brass riffs, the single had "hit" written all over it, Terrell's excitement audible in the intonation of her heavily reverbed vocal in the song's fade. In its unassuming way, one of Motown's finest singles. Marvin Gaye later dubbed sections onto the track, which consequently re-appeared as an album duet in 1968.

**TMG 562**
**THE MARVELETTES**
**You're The One** (2:47)
(Robinson)
Produced by William "Smokey" Robinson
Recording completed: 11 Jan 1966
**Release Date**: 27 May 1966
**B-side**: Paper Boy
**Position in Record Retailer Top 40**: -
**Equivalent US Release**: Tamla 54131 (4 Apr 1966)
**Position in Billboard Top 40 Pop**: -
**Position in Billboard Top 40 R & B**: 20

Gladys Horton / Wanda Young / Katherine Anderson

Prominently underscored by Earl Van Dyke's Hammond organ, the Marvelettes' new single was essentially a remake of "Don't Mess With Bill" [546], with its two-chord see-sawing and stealthy melodic crawl, but a more orthodox love theme to its lyric. Pitched in C, the vocal demands a falsetto high A from Wanda Young, taking her to the limit of her range.

An exercise in syncopation, the track features some neat bass triplets from James Jamerson, and a casually swaggering mood which has endeared the song to the group's fans, and as the second in a run of three Marvelettes A-sides from Smokey Robinson, helped consolidate the group's transitory new style. (The B-side stood in stark contrast, "Paper Boy" a previously unreleased recording from 1963, sung by Gladys Horton, which finds yet another angle on the group's then famous 'postman' theme [E05]; [E07].)

**TMG 563**
**MARVIN GAYE**
**Take This Heart Of Mine** (2:51)
(Robinson—Moore—Tarplin)
Produced by William "Smokey" Robinson/Warren Moore
Recording completed: 24 Mar 1966
**Release Date**: 10 Jun 1966
**B-side**: Need Your Lovin' (Want You Back)
**Position in Record Retailer Top 40**: -
**Equivalent US Release**: Tamla 54132 (2 May 1966)
**Position in Billboard Top 40 Pop**: -
**Position in Billboard Top 40 R & B**: 16

Inspired by, and taking its opening cue from the chorus riff in "Going To A Go-Go" [547] (and probably deliberately adapting the title from [555], recorded shortly before "Take This Heart Of Mine" was written), Marvin Gaye's new single was his last supplied by Smokey Robinson, and represents an attempt to bring some light-hearted relief to a singer entering a period of acute self-doubt—something not evident in his vocal contribution, which is both committed and animated.

Recorded with a quick-stepping backing, the song conveys a jocular point of view, with its jokey *ritardando* and a rare solo-spot for James Jamerson in the second chorus, coupled with a quirky lyric in which the singer prescribes his love as the cure for his girl's lonely woes. Ultimately a piece of fun, the song was never going to sustain Gaye's recording career, but did serve to keep him in the public eye during a time of personal uncertainty [539], his gathering depression effectively masked.

**TMG 564**
**THE CONTOURS**
**Determination** (2:39)
(Robinson)
Produced by Ivy Jo Hunter
Recording completed: 27 Jan 1966
**Release Date**: 10 Jun 1966
**B-side**: Just A Little Misunderstanding
**Position in Record Retailer Top 40**: -
**Equivalent US Release**: Gordy 7052 (18 Apr 1966)
**Position in Billboard Top 40 Pop**: -
**Position in Billboard Top 40 R & B**: 18

Joe Stubbs / Gerald Green / Council Gay / Sylvester Potts

Released as the equivalent A-side in America, "Just A Little Misunderstanding" was a progressive number part-written by the emergent Stevie Wonder, which represented a venturous diversion for The Contours. That it wasn't a hit may have played a part in Tamla Motown's preference for "Determination", a Miracles number from 1961 sung here by temporary recruit Joe Stubbs, brother of Levi.

After the cheeky "First I Look At The Purse" [531], the song constitutes something of a return to roots for The Contours, this straight-forward dance groove reminiscent of "Shotgun" [509] in its verses. However, "Determination" features distinctive congas throughout, Eddie 'Bongo' Brown the player in question, The Funk Brothers' resident comic and former valet to Marvin Gaye. Interestingly, "Determination" was interpreted as carrying a political subtext, presumably via its vague implication of interracial love, although the theme—if intentional—is obscure. The track was revived nine years later by The Commodores [944b].

**TMG 565**
**THE TEMPTATIONS**
**Ain't Too Proud To Beg** (2:32)
(Whitfield—Holland)
Produced by Norman Whitfield
Recording completed: 11 Jan 1966
**Release Date**: 17 Jun 1966
**B-side**: You'll Lose A Precious Love
**Position in Record Retailer Top 40**: 21
**Equivalent US Release**: Gordy 7054 (3 May 1966)
**Position in Billboard Top 40 Pop**: 13
**Position in Billboard Top 40 R & B**: 1

Otis Williams / Melvin Franklin / Paul Williams / Eddie Kendricks / David Ruffin

Seizing a chance to produce The Temptations, Norman Whitfield rose to the occasion by reinstalling David Ruffin as lead singer, and eliciting a famously husky performance which has become the current track's trademark. Pitched almost beyond reach, Ruffin threw everything he had into the take, pouring with sweat on the studio floor while Whitfield and Otis Williams goaded him from the sanctuary of the control booth. Ranging around the melody's profile with fervour and a fraught disregard for formal technique ('If I have to *sleep* on your doorstep'), Ruffin's vocal provides an air of wild indiscipline in what was to become one of the group's best loved recordings. Simultaneously tough and vulnerable, the song's title was a late re-think of the preliminary, over-sensitive "Please Don't Leave Me Girl", the theme reworked by Eddie Holland from the text of "Baby I Need Your Loving" [E53], which includes in its second verse, the embryo of the current composition.

Stylistically more 'Whitfield' than 'Holland', the track pans out across a flattened landscape, vocals dropping to the tonic repeatedly. The production ethos itself is also quintessentially Whitfield-esque, "Ain't Too Proud To Beg" a vivid and sharp creation, spaciously laid out with each individual instrument mixed to cut through; particularly effective are the deep, sustained C natural brass notes held long and low against Ruffin's pleading verses, without which the track would be sterile in its emptiness. With bass guitar sent high against a grooving rhythm, Jamerson's contribution is similarly well considered, strategically dropping off in the verse but bouncing jocularly through the choruses where, reminded of Wilson Pickett's 1965 hit "In The Midnight Hour", he adopts a similar riff. (As with The Temptations' previous single, the instrumental break consists of a sax solo in which the instrument holds more or less a single note throughout the seven bars.)

When the recording was presented to Quality Control early in 1966 directly against "Get Ready" [557], Whitfield and the group were stunned to find it rejected, hectoring Berry Gordy for a release until he eventually conceded that, if [557] flopped, it would be put out as their next 45. Since its predecessor only just scraped into the top 30 pop, Whitfield and the group had their way, "Beauty Is Only Skin Deep" out-selling Robinson's recording and securing for the group a new writer-producer. An instant favourite in Britain, the track became The Temptations' biggest UK hit to date, consolidating Whitfield's role as *de facto* musical director of the group, and subsequently attracting a cover from The Rolling Stones.


**TMG 566**
**THE ISLEY BROTHERS**
**Take Some Time Out For Love** (2:26)
(Kemp—Gordy)
Produced by Robert Gordy
Recording completed: 17 Mar 1966
**Release Date**: 24 Jun 1966
**B-side**: Who Could Ever Doubt My Love
**Position in Record Retailer Top 40**: -
**Equivalent US Release**: Tamla 54133 (29 Apr 1966)
**Position in Billboard Top 40 Pop**: -
**Position in Billboard Top 40 R & B**: -

---

Ronald Isley / Rudolph Isley / O'Kelly Isley

---

Seemingly based on their old hit "Twist And Shout", the verses to "Take Some Time Out for Love" employ the same standard F—Bb—C ascent, and some forced falsetto shrieks. Attempting to liven things up with a relentless tambourine, Holland and Dozier did their best with an unremarkable template, which inevitably comes over disappointingly drab after the mesmerising impact of the group's previous single [555]. (The track was co-written by Berry Gordy's brother Robert, recently installed as head of Motown's publishing arm Jobete and known for his early recordings which included an early Tamla single under the pseudonym Bob Kayle, answering Jimmy Dean's "Big Bad John" with "Small Sad Sam".)


**TMG 567**
**MARTHA & THE VANDELLAS**
**What Am I Going To Do Without Your Love** (2:57)
(Moy—Stevenson)
Produced by William "Mickey" Stevenson/Ivy Jo Hunter

---

Recording completed: 28 Mar 1966
**Release Date**: 24 Jun 1966
**B-side**: Go Ahead And Laugh
**Position in Record Retailer Top 40**: -
**Equivalent US Release**: Gordy 7053 (19 May 1966)
**Position in Billboard Top 40 Pop**: -
**Position in Billboard Top 40 R & B**: -

---

Martha Reeves / Rosalind Ashford / Betty Kelly

---

Continuing the jazzy undercurrent present in "My Baby Loves Me" [549] of which Martha Reeves fully approved, this summer release breezes through its three minutes as if in blind denial of the scenario being painted, never finding true resolution and persistently held in check by a stuttering percussion track. Despite its surface-level charm, the song is really the most despondent of the group's singles to date, the tortured predicament in which the singer finds herself alone and stranded delineated with some appropriately emotive strings. Musically, the high-register bass used in the novel introduction and, in the song's chorus, 'walking' through the scale, indicates that James Jamerson was attempting something less guttural than his usual pounding style.

The first of three successive group singles to end up on *Watchout!*, the track was largely overlooked in Britain, where its parent album would be held-off for another 12 months. Little-documented, "What Am I Going To Do Without Your Love" warrants only a passing mention in Reeves' autobiography, as do the other tracks of the era, a transitional phase between the blistering "Nowhere To Run" [502] and the resurgent "Jimmy Mack" [599].


**TMG 568**
**FOUR TOPS**
**Loving You Is Sweeter Than Ever** (2:46)
(Hunter—Wonder)
Produced by Ivy Jo Hunter
Recording completed: 14 Apr 1966
**Release Date**: 24 Jul 1966
**B-side**: I Like Everything About You
**Position in Record Retailer Top 40**: 21
**Equivalent US Release**: Motown 1096 (9 May 1966)
**Position in Billboard Top 40 Pop**: -
**Position in Billboard Top 40 R & B**: 12

---

Levi Stubbs / Lawrence Payton / Abdul 'Duke' Fakir / Renaldo 'Obie' Benson

---

Interrupting HDH's sequence of singles for The Four Tops, "Loving You Is Sweeter Than Ever" obscures the developmental link between the increasingly ponderous "Shake Me, Wake Me" [553] and "Reach Out" [579]. In truth, the single represents something of a stop-gap, released during the seven month interim to maintain the group's place in the market. Co-written by Stevie

Wonder, the song—his most successful composing credit to date—says more about *his* personal development than that of The Four Tops (see also [564]).

Commencing with a disembodied drum pattern by Pistol Allen[1], the track quickly stabilises into a drawn-out love song, relying almost entirely on the note of E gliding across the chord sequence. This, despite a dramatic plunge from C to an overemphasised C7 in the first lines which finds resolution to G via a reconciling F major. (The chorus, when it arrives, merely perpetuates the four chord cycle, fenced off from the verses by an oscillation between F and the root C.)

In terms of production, the track had unusually close attention, Quality Control requisitioning the recording and making significant alterations. An appalled Ivy Hunter later claimed this and other similar instances as examples of Motown's management pressing for an identifiably homogenous brand sound, claiming their re-mixing efforts 'destroyed' the original recording[2], and certainly the guitar and piano tracks end up mixed so closely that they effectively merge into a hazily indistinct middle ground, to say nothing of the rasping distortion evident in the backing instrumentation. The song's viability though comes from its massive percussion, the perpetual 4/4 tambourine successfully faking excitement, together with a dominant electric guitar for colouration. (The bass track on the recording is mixed unusually low for Motown.)

The first in a run of seven Tamla Motown singles by male artists, the track's failure may have seemed ominous, Berry Gordy unaware that the group were on the brink of their biggest ever hit.

[1] A minor gimmick for HDH and their colleagues, already employed on the group's "It's The Same Old Song" [528]. Other instances include [555], [559], [564], [565] etc. In the documentary *Standing In The Shadows Of Motown*, Allen gives a vocal demonstration of how to recognise the trademark rolls of Motown's three principal drummers.

[2] Quoted in Edmonds, p110. Co-writer Stevie Wonder had recorded the unmistakably loaded "I Gave Up Quality For Quantity" with Smokey Robinson in January 1965.

**TMG 569**
**THE MIRACLES**
**Whole Lot Of Shakin' In My Heart (Since I Met You Girl)** (2:47)
(Wilson)
Produced by Frank Wilson
Recording completed: 11 May 1966
**Release Date**: 8 Jul 1966
**B-side**: Oh Be My Love
**Position in Record Retailer Top 40**: -
**Equivalent US Release**: Tamla 54134 (27 May 1966)
**Position in Billboard Top 40 Pop**: -
**Position in Billboard Top 40 R & B**: 20

Smokey Robinson / Bobby Rogers / Claudette Rogers Robinson / Warren 'Pete' Moore / Ronnie White

LA writer-producer Frank Wilson's second Tamla Motown A-side [556] has all the hallmarks of a West Coast production, with its brightly resonating brass, disciplined punch and air of careful pre-planning. (Compare with the loose group performance on The Miracles' previous single [547].) However it was in fact made at Hitsville, a backing track recorded on April 19, prepared under the provisional title, "How Many Times Must I Tell You". A solid piece of R & B, the track remodels The Miracles, a hitherto self-determining outfit largely performing their own material as a standardised performing act under direction of an external musical director.

Could it be that Robinson was simply overworked and running out of fresh material? That Norman Whitfield had claimed The Temptations from under his nose [565] and Wilson himself had inherited Brenda Holloway earlier in the year [556] suggests as much: thus far Robinson had been involved in the composition of some 18 Tamla Motown A-sides, two ahead of his nearest competitors HDH, but from here-on he would be far less prolific, his rivals dominating Motown's output for the rest of 1966—including The Miracles' next single [584].

"Whole Lot Of Shaking" comes over as a contrived recording, its every move carefully premeditated. That said, the track as a whole is pleasingly up-beat, calculated for the dance-floor and sufficiently dynamic to warrant release. Slightly out of his idiom, Robinson salvages the recording with his typically buoyant vocal, skimming over the more constraining passages (in particular the extended melisma commencing at 2:13) with just enough verve to disguise the fact that, on this single, his hands were unusually tied.

## TMG 570
## STEVIE WONDER
**Blowin' In The Wind** (2:58)
(Dylan)
Produced by Clarence Paul
Recording completed: 15 Jan 1966
**Release Date**: 5 Aug 1966
**B-side**: Ain't That Asking For Trouble
**Position in Record Retailer Top 40**: 36
**Equivalent US Release**: Tamla 54136 (28 Jun 1966)
**Position in Billboard Top 40 Pop**: 9
**Position in Billboard Top 40 R & B**: 1

Tamla Motown's first release for a month was this radical recording, by far the most politically charged single on the label thus far, with a preaching oratory which signposts Wonder's professional maturity and follows his 16th birthday in May. Picked up after the 1963 hit version by Peter, Paul & Mary and incorporated into his stage repertoire, the song enraptured live audiences and grabbed the attention of his producer Clarence Paul, who set about getting a formal recording on tape before lobbying Berry Gordy for an official release. (Paul also participates in the performance, contributing the deep, unruffled backing vocals, his presence stemming from early rehearsals in which he sang ahead of Wonder to teach him the lyric. The recording is sometimes billed somewhat generously as a duet.[1])

Dylan's civil rights anthem was included on his first self-composed album *Freewheelin'* in 1963 and in the context of his contemporary work, was clearly striking a blow against racial oppression. Activist and theoretician Rev. James Lawson famously stated that, "At the heart of racism is the idea that a man is not a man", and this theme was picked up by the movement in the 1960s and used as a slogan, for example inspiring the widespread "I am a man" banners at the 1968 sanitation workers' strike in Memphis [654]. Thus, the opening lines of "Blowin' In The Wind" are Dylan's uncompromising question to white society at large, directly challenging the illogicality of denying human beings their due status, and exposing the ultimate futility of needless division.

Aware of Bob Dylan's enormous popularity yet wary of alienating a white market, Motown cut the most pointed lines from the original[2]—although for time constraints alone it was necessary to lose *some* of the track. What remains is a dispassionately philosophical text, rhetorical and questioning but crucially without committing to any specific political agenda. In essence the listener is invited to consider the self-enlightened stance, from which any individual conclusions may be drawn. (Wonder was perhaps wisely denied a Dylan-esque harmonica solo.)

Officially sanctioned, this uncharacteristically non-danceable single arrived without warning in an America long-polarised by racial hostilities. With the civil rights struggle flaring up repeatedly in 1966, matters reached a crisis point when black student and figurehead James Meredith was shot and almost killed by a sniper during a one-man freedom march, on the same day that Republican Ronald Reagan was nominated as candidate for the governorship of California. Taking up Meredith's cause, other prominent figures gathered to finish the march which consequently turned into a mass demonstration, Meredith recovering sufficiently to re-join the protest at its finale. Soon after, similar gatherings took place across America, with major conflagrations ensuing in Chicago, Cleveland and New York at the end of July.

For the main, Motown distanced itself from the gathering turmoil, although behind the corporate façade both Gordy and Stevie Wonder were active in the movement for racial equality. (As a youth, Wonder had attended a 1963 fund-raiser for Martin Luther King's famous march on Washington of which Gordy showed his private approval by releasing King's speeches on LP, and even using his 'I Have A Dream' oration as the flip-side to a 1963 Liz Lands single (Gordy 7023). 20 years later, King's speeches were utilised again, deployed as the flip to Wonder's campaign song "Happy Birthday" on a UK 12-inch (TMGT 1326).)

With the backdrop of race tensions flavouring the black gospel overtones of the recording (apparent also on Sam Cooke's prior version) Motown's take on "Blowin' In The Wind" is more sweeping in its implied meaning than the original, a fascinating union of America's two biggest musical innovators of the decade[3] (see also [540]). As with The Byrds' ground-breaking interpretation of "Mr. Tambourine Man" a year earlier, Wonder propels an acoustic Dylan number into territories unreached by its author, a considerable coup for a teenager still defining his style. Enthused by the single's favourable reception, Wonder released his own recording of "Mr. Tambourine Man" in November, again with input from Clarence Paul.

[1] Sharon Davis makes the surprising claim that Levi Stubbs performs additional backing vocals on the track (2006a, p49).
[2] From the missing second verse: 'How many deaths will it take till he knows/That too many people have died'.
[3] Dylan appeared alongside Wonder in 1984 to present an award at the Grammy ceremonies. A year later they recorded together as part of USA For Africa, a 1985 Band Aid spin-off which also featured Smokey Robinson, Diana Ross, Lionel Richie and numerous members of the Jackson family. (The track, "We Are The World", was co-written by Michael Jackson and Lionel Richie.)

## TMG 571
## JUNIOR WALKER & THE ALL STARS
**How Sweet It Is (To Be Loved By You)** (2:58)
(Holland—Dozier—Holland)
Produced by Johnny Bristol/Harvey Fuqua
Recording completed: 23 May 1966
**Release Date**: 12 Aug 1966
**B-side**: Nothing But Soul
**Position in Record Retailer Top 40**: 22
**Equivalent US Release**: Soul 35024 (8 Jul 1966)
**Position in Billboard Top 40 Pop**: 18
**Position in Billboard Top 40 R & B**: 3

Jr Walker / Willie Woods / Vic Thomas / Billy Nicks

Written in 1964 for Marvin Gaye, "How Sweet It Is" had provided the singer with a US top 10 hit, and even scraped into the British top 50 [E60]. As with a number of HDH tracks, Lamont Dozier discovered the title phrase by chance but elaborated the text from an actual situation, imagining the woman he was then chasing to be already devoted to him and crafting the song as a teasing move to woo her. Gaye's biggest hit to date also became one of his personal favourites, and was admired by a number of Motown artists.

The first cover version of note was Junior Walker's, the backing for which was taped at Hitsville on 27 April 1966 in a relaxed manner, with The All Stars' new drummer Billy 'Sticks' Nicks in place of James Graves, who resigned early in the year. The indiscipline of the session is evinced by James Jamerson's fluff at 1:11, in which he forgets to modulate back to the F#, causing All Stars' guitarist Willie Woods to accommodate an extra beat by way of recovery—an irregularity which would prompt most producers to begin the take afresh. Nonetheless it was allowed through for Walker's May vocal session, apparently recorded with the Snakepit full of personnel, various hangers-on inside the studio and joining in. Hushing everyone in preparation for a proper attempt, engineer Lawrence Horn played back the preliminary version which delighted Walker who instructed Horn to re-cut a master take in the same informal manner. Thus the ensuing recording has the feel of a party performance, some of the assembled revellers taking low mikes—one in particular (Johnny Bristol?) hyping and echoing Walker.[1] (The singer has since claimed that the party chatter was overdubbed later, which seems unlikely for the naturalness of the effect, and the fact that the studio log shows the vocals were recorded on the last day's work for the track. Perhaps he is confusing it with "Money" [586].)

Rhythmically potent and gutsy in the manner of Walker's earlier recordings, the single became his first UK hit, outselling Gaye's original and extending the song's fame. Of numerous subsequent cover versions (including one by Earl Van Dyke [814b]), James Taylor's was the most notable, climbing to number 5 on the US charts in 1975, the highest placing the song managed in any guise.

[1] Bristol was not shy of making his presence actively felt, his timely interjections and encouragement also audible on [721].

**TMG 572**
**THE ISLEY BROTHERS**
**I Guess I'll Always Love You** (2:38)
(Holland—Dozier—Holland)
Produced by Brian Holland/Lamont Dozier
Recording completed: 12 Apr 1966
**Release Date**: 19 Aug 1966
**B-side**: I Hear A Symphony
**Position in Record Retailer Top 40**: -
**Equivalent US Release**: Tamla 54135 (17 Jun 1966)
**Position in Billboard Top 40 Pop**: -
**Position in Billboard Top 40 R & B**: 31

Ronald Isley / Rudolph Isley / O'Kelly Isley

The Isley Brothers' third UK single in five months was a return to form after the disappointment of "Take Some Time Out For Love" [566], penned by an irrepressible HDH about to consolidate their position as unrivalled leaders of Motown's backroom staff. Returning to an early hit in Martha Reeves' 1963 recording "Heat Wave" [E28], HDH updated the number after the style of "This Old Heart Of Mine" [555], seeking to replicate the infectious orchestration although here, the classical strings are mixed almost out of sight.[1]

Salvaged from "Heat Wave" is the stepwise ascent into the chorus which, with the song's key transposed from Eb to C, shifts through Dm/Em/F/G (compare the bridge passage in question at 0:35 with the lines 'Has high blood pressure got a hold on me/Or is this the way love's supposed to be?' from the original). In addition, besides the obligatory sax break from Mike Terry, the songs share a 4/4 piano figure and a repetitively crashing tambourine, each swapping places in terms of their occurrence on the crotchet beats. Undoubtedly, the connection between the two songs suggested the pitching of Ronald Isley's falsetto at the top-end of his register, sounding distinctly female as compared to his performance on [555].

Enjoying the positivity which The Isley Brothers seemed to embody, HDH wrote the song around a blissfully happy love affair in contrast to much of the their troubled concurrent material for The Four Tops—although it is notable that Ronald Isley dwells "in the shadows" of his past, anticipating The Four Tops' next-but-one single [601]. Ever-conscious of including ear-catching incident, HDH fashioned the track to incorporate not two or four, but *three* lines of text in each verse, an irregularity slyly echoed by the triple key steps of the song's coda which promise an unfulfilled elevation.

Short of a true contrasting section, the chorus carries the same chord progression as the verses, complete with a recapitulation of the "Heat Wave"-inspired bridge ('You got the love I need'), a compositional trick seen elsewhere on numerous Motown recordings (eg [515]; [568]). Its catchy melody proved to be its biggest draw for other Motown artists, notably The Supremes who covered it in 1967 [632b]. (The Isley Brothers utilised a Supremes song as their B-side here, the cross-pollination of the two acts a recurrent theme.)

A perennial favourite amongst the group's fans, "I Guess I'll Always Love You" featured on their accomplished first Tamla Motown album in October (issued in the States in June), and returned to the charts two-and-a-half years after its initial release [683].

¹ The song's title, though hackneyed, may draw on that of [523].

**TMG 573**
**SHORTY LONG**
**Function At The Junction** (2:48)
(Long—Holland)
Produced by Brian Holland/Lamont Dozier
Recording completed: 24 Feb 1966
**Release Date**: 26 Aug 1966
**B-side**: Call On Me
**Position in Record Retailer Top 40**: -
**Equivalent US Release**: Soul 35021 (17 Mar 1966)
**Position in Billboard Top 40 Pop**: -
**Position in Billboard Top 40 R & B**: -

The follow-up to Long's "Out To Get You" [512] was over a year in coming. Aimed at the discotheque market (the 'function' in question being a dance party), the track is essentially a rather plodding Long instrumental with little harmonic dynamism. The main point of interest comes via Eddie Holland's quirky lyric, which depicts a number of amusing-sounding would-be revellers and a smattering of contemporary Western cultural icons (Long Tall Sally, 007, Minnesota Fats, etc.) alongside a litany of semi-fictional foodstuffs, borrowing a style from tracks such as the Chicago-based Five Du Tones' 1963 hit, "Shake A Tail Feather" (latterly famous for Ray Charles' rendition in the 1980 film *Blues Brothers*).

Unremarkable, the single was a commercial failure. US promotional copies were manufactured in red—one of the earliest instances of coloured vinyl being used commercially. (Backing vocals were supplied by newcomers The Originals [592].)

**TMG 574**
**MARVIN GAYE**
**Little Darling (I Need You)** (2:43)
(Holland—Dozier—Holland)
Produced by Brian Holland/Lamont Dozier
Recording completed: 6 May 1965
**Release Date**: 2 Sep 1966
**B-side**: Hey Diddle Diddle
**Position in Record Retailer Top 40**: -
**Equivalent US Release**: Tamla 54138 (26 Jul 1966)
**Position in Billboard Top 40 Pop**: -
**Position in Billboard Top 40 R & B**: 10

With Smokey Robinson stepping off the accelerator in 1966 [569], Marvin Gaye fell back on an old HDH number which started life as "I'm Willing To Pay The Price", and became the team's first A-side for the singer since the launch of Tamla Motown (and, incidentally, Gaye's last solo UK 45 for a year [618]). Recorded instrumentally in the spring of 1965 with a string section, the backing was stripped down for the UK single in an effort to provide a more straight-forward effect behind an assured structure which shifts rapidly and repeatedly through its four chords, resting only on a sustained G prior to the chorus.

Revealing a lack of confidence from those involved, the re-mix merely highlighted the startlingly piercing backing vocals, which negate the relaxation implied in Gaye's smooth lead, taped on May 6, which he initially appreciated for its melodicism. Ultimately no more than a fill-in release, the single's poor returns demanded a reappraisal from Gordy, who set about rekindling Gaye's career as a duet performer.

**TMG 575**
**THE SUPREMES**
**You Can't Hurry Love** (2:49)
(Holland—Dozier—Holland)
Produced by Brian Holland/Lamont Dozier
Recording completed: 5 Jul 1966
**Release Date**: 2 Sep 1966
**B-side**: Put Yourself In My Place
**Position in Record Retailer Top 40**: 3
**Equivalent US Release**: Motown 1097 (25 Jul 1966)
**Position in Billboard Top 40 Pop**: 1
**Position in Billboard Top 40 R & B**: 1

Diana Ross / Florence Ballard / Mary Wilson

Worked almost into the ground by Berry Gordy, The Supremes were, by mid-1966, reaching the point of exhaustion. Relentlessly touring or on standby to tour, they were effectively living out of suitcases, meeting their recording obligations back in Detroit during so-called days off, and snatching few moments for genuine relaxation. The strain of life as a Supreme was exemplified by the current song, debuted live on July 24 and in American record shops the following morning. By the time the UK release came about, the group were battling through a three-week tour of East Asia, Flo Ballard struggling the most to keep up, turning to an alcohol fix for support—a perilous indulgence which would worsen to dependency over the following 12 months [616], in tandem with a relationship with Berry Gordy's chauffeur Tommy Chapman which irritated her employer. (Mary Wilson meantime was dating Duke Fakir for The Four Tops.)

Put together by HDH from the bones of the part-written, gospel-flavoured "This Is Where I Came In", the track is a case-study in simplicity, the vocal line consisting almost exclusively of single syllables which shift note with every word such that its vertical momentum is its main feature, the obvious exception being the relatively 'flat' bridge ('How many heartaches must I stand...'), presumably conceived independently. Yet its basic nature merely highlights its effusion, allowing a doubling up of the elements, with repeated use of double choruses and middle-16s rather than 8s. (Running over time, an additional section was excised from the final take (at 1:56), the intact recording having since also surfaced.)

The bouncy arrangement is notable for a Robert White's particularly prominent guitar track running tightly against Earl Van Dyke's jangling piano. Yet of all the song's reductive components, its stomping three-bar introduction is perhaps the most note-worthy, pulled from James Jamerson's pulsating, uncharacteristic bar-long bass notes. Evidence of HDH and Motown's interest in deploying striking openings, it establishes a trademark hook which HDH would continue to utilise in the ensuing year, on tracks such as [582].[1] For her vocal part, Diana Ross pulled out all the stops in pushing her patent nasal style, something she would later recall with some embarrassment, but which gave the recording its quintessential Supremes-esque edge. (One of the most irresistible Motown creations, the track even warranted an Italian language take from Ross.)

The Supremes' eleventh UK single finally returned Motown's flagship act to the upper-reaches of the charts after a depressing succession of commercial flops. In doing so, it also marked the commencement of Tamla Motown as a force in the UK market, at a time when American music was clawing its way back into favour after three years of British domination. Thus, "You Can't Hurry Love" is a pivotal release, the point at which Tamla Motown's 'Golden Years' truly arrived. (Since [501] launched Tamla Motown 18 months previously, only one other single [545] had managed to crack the UK top 20. By the end of 1966, a further six would make it, with 12 to follow in 1967.)

During the 1980s the song belatedly became recognised as a classic, inspiring numerous imitations and eventually making the top of the UK charts.[2]

---

[1] Jamerson's famous bass figure for "You Can't Hurry Love" became an archetype during the 1980s, spawning numerous imitations including Philadelphia duo Hall and Oats' 1982 hit "Maneater", Billy Joel's "Tell Her About It" from 1983 and erstwhile colleague Stevie Wonder's 1985 single "Part Time Lover". Equally notable was a re-working of the song's intro by The Jam for "A Town Called Malice" in 1982. (The group's front-man Paul Weller was a Motown devotee, and in their time The Jam also released covers of "Heat Wave" [E28], "Back In My Arms Again" [516], and "War" [754]. Weller went on to craft a soulful post-Jam number with the hook line 'You're the best thing that ever happened to me' after a late Gladys Knight hit and teamed up with Jimmy Ruffin in 1984 to record "Soul Deep" as part of his 'Council Collective' project.)

[2] In January 1983, courtesy of Phil Collins, reflecting much of the contemporary interest in the bass patterning. Like Paul Weller, Collins was a major fan and besides covering this track collaborated with Brian Holland and Lamont Dozier for The Four Tops' 1988 comeback hit, "Loco In Acapulco". He also released a single with the borrowed title "I Wish It Would Rain" [641].

## TMG 576
## GLADYS KNIGHT & THE PIPS
**Just Walk In My Shoes** (2:35)
(Miller—Masters)
Produced by Harvey Fuqua/Johnny Bristol
Recording completed: 25 Apr 1966
**Release Date**: 16 Sep 1966
**B-side**: Stepping Closer To Your Heart
**Position in Record Retailer Top 40**: -
**Equivalent US Release**: Soul 35023 (7 Jun 1966)
**Position in Billboard Top 40 Pop**: -
**Position in Billboard Top 40 R & B**: -

Gladys Knight / Merald 'Bubba' Knight / Edward Patten / William Guest

Like Motown's other big 'imported' group The Isley Brothers [555], Gladys Knight & The Pips were a family outfit of some years standing when they came to Motown in 1966. Hailing from Atlanta, Georgia, Gladys and brother Merald (aka Bubba), plus cousins William Guest and Edward Patten had come together in 1952 to perform at Merald's birthday party. With a couple of personnel shuffles they settled into the eventual group line-up, and toured with big names such as Sam Cooke and future Berry Gordy associate Jackie Wilson. Suffering with their stage act after some years in the commercial wilderness, the group had fortuitously teamed up with choreographer Cholly Atkins who successfully approached Motown to get them a contract. The group themselves were uncertain of Motown, holding an internal ballot to decide whether to sign up, Gladys Knight being outvoted by her group three to one.

Recorded in April 1966, their first Motown single "Just Walk In My Shoes" ran at an extravagant three-minutes-plus, and was edited down and re-mixed for release. (Different versions have since surfaced, the original Soul 45 running at 2:25, the subsequent UK releases at 2:35 and others in circulation at 2:49. Modern CD versions of the latter currently on the market featuring audible splices at 1:38 and 2:40—the second outside the time-frame of the first edit.)

Written by The Lewis Sisters under their married names [536], and sharing a similar harmonic movement to "Ain't That Peculiar" [539], the track is a dispirited portrait of a deserted lover left to face the world alone. Using its chord shifts sparingly, the song alternates between a dour F major and a resolute Bb, endlessly switching between the four-bar phrases as if pacing to-and-fro, as the tormented narrator is doing psychologically. Notable for its use of the kazoo (?) in the opening section (see also [560]), the track while futuristic fails to provide any emotional resolution and consequently leaves behind an unhappy sense of defeat despite its pronounced marching rhythm. Lacking the commercialism of [575], it failed to chart, a watchful Diana Ross no doubt savouring a comprehensive victory over the most substantial threat to her supremacy ever to arrive at Motown.

**TMG 577**
**JIMMY RUFFIN**
**What Becomes Of The Brokenhearted** (2:57)
(Dean—Riser—Weatherspoon)
Produced by William "Mickey" Stevenson/William Weatherspoon
Recording completed: 23 Feb 1966
**Release Date**: 30 Sep 1966
**B-side**: Baby I've Got It
**Position in Record Retailer Top 40**: 8
**Equivalent US Release**: Soul 35022 (3 Jun 1966)
**Position in Billboard Top 40 Pop**: 7
**Position in Billboard Top 40 R & B**: 6

With its depiction of the wandering visionary contemplating the hardships of those around him, "What Becomes Of The Brokenhearted" is the most compassionate thing Motown ever released, and one of the most solemn statements to carry the label's name. Coming in the wake of The Beatles' "Eleanor Rigby", with its remarkable portrayal of loneliness, the track was considered viable for release as a single despite its atypical realism and the fact that Ruffin, brother of Temptation David, was a largely unknown gamble.

The singer had been on Motown's periphery for years, having already turned down a chance to sing for the Temptations in his brother's stead. (His first Motown release was as far back as January 1961, "Don't Feel Sorry For Me" appearing on the small Miracle label.) Homeless within the Motown institution, Ruffin, the company's potential answer to Sam Cooke, was transferred to the Soul imprint whereupon he overheard writer James Dean running through a recent unfinished composition intended for The Spinners, provisionally titled "Crying In The Night". Realising that *he* could pull off a definitive version, Ruffin pleaded with Motown's top-brass for a crack at it. The result, after protracted deliberation, one of Motown's most popular and enduring ballads (although the move cost Ruffin first refusal on [578], which went to his brother's group instead).[1]

The appeal of "What Becomes Of The Brokenhearted" comes largely from The Funk Brothers' foundation track, a 'horizontal' drone which pulls the song out like the lonely road being travelled. Fundamental to this is Jamerson's whole-bar, funereal solemnity in which he animates so little that his valid, though almost discordant sustained Fs cut through hypnotically, especially noticeable in the song's transition from introduction, where the implied F major resolves into the unexpected light of a Bb major.[2] (Here, the original conception was a spoken introduction from Ruffin, recorded but wiped after second thoughts, leaving eight vacant bars. The original mix has subsequently been restored and made available commercially, and indeed Diana Ross' 1969 rendition also incorporated the spoken section.)

Melodically the track is uninventive, its modal rises and falls conservative. Notably, the writers failed to supply a chorus line, resorting instead to a straight-forward reiteration of the verse's melody, raised by a tone to C major and thereby adding to the overall sense of timeless and immoveable ponderousness. (The word 'broken' falls in the same place in verse 1 as the corresponding 'brokenhearted' in the choruses.)

Using a deceptive game in which the 4/4 rhythm sounds like a 3/4 waltz, the track has a weight defying the boost of a high string section (mixed discreetly) and some studied backing vocals from The Originals, including a falsetto coda. Graphically emotive, the song seeks some sort of redemption only in the (supposedly) *ad libbed* closing lines, in which Ruffin, focussing back on himself, resolves to find a lifeline from the universal despair of the foregoing. (Here, a key change is deemed unnecessary, the abandonment of formal melody sufficient to fool listeners into thinking they are getting more than they actually are.)

Instantly popular, Ruffin found himself required for a Motown Revue with acts such as The Supremes, later claiming that he was removed from the tour for winning too big a reception with the audiences [604]. Taken aback by the scale of his success, Ruffin did not warm to life as a touring attraction which partly explains his failure to capitalise on the extraordinary impact of "Brokenhearted". Four decades after its release, the song is his signature tune, and has become a standard, attracting numerous covers and a spot in an Ian Mune film named after it.

[1] Between the initial sessions and Ruffin's final vocal (his second attempt), The Isley Brothers also had a crack at it, recording a version on Christmas Day 1965, listed under the title "Smile", presumably ironically.

[2] The intro is based on that of "You Can Cry On My Shoulder", a 1965 Brenda Holloway recording written by Berry Gordy and released as a single in America (Tamla 54121). The track also contains the line, "A man ain't supposed to cry" which resurfaced on [629].

**TMG 578**
**THE TEMPTATIONS**
**Beauty Is Only Skin Deep** (2:21)
(Whitfield—Holland)
Produced by Norman Whitfield
Recording completed: 11 May 1966
**Release Date**: 30 Sep 1966
**B-side**: You're Not An Ordinary Girl
**Position in Record Retailer Top 40**: 18
**Equivalent US Release**: Gordy 7055 (4 Aug 1966)
**Position in Billboard Top 40 Pop**: 3
**Position in Billboard Top 40 R & B**: 1

Otis Williams / Melvin Franklin / Paul Williams / Eddie Kendricks / David Ruffin

Emboldened by the success of [565], his first Temptations single in two years [E55], Norman Whitfield's follow-up was the song rejected by Jimmy Ruffin [577] which itself dates back to April 1964. Recorded in readiness for the group's vocals, the backing tape ended up going to The Miracles, whose version failed to see the light of day until later in 1966. Its delay was surprising on the face of it, the track pulled off with a brilliant contribution from The Funk Brothers, whose performance constitutes the first time group musicianship was allowed to overshadow a regular vocal on a Tamla Motown single. Jamerson's bass playing in the verses is of such high profile that it dominates the arrangement, which significantly includes two drummers (Richard 'Pistol' Allen and Uriel Jones [557]) as well as congas from Eddie 'Bongo' Brown, in a foretaste of Whitfield's later complex percussion-led style [707]. With belated vocal overdubs from The Temptations, the track falsely appears as derivative, the repertoire of tricks heard on the later [565] present here also.

"Beauty Is Only Skin Deep" departs from the sense of self-depreciation apparent in [565] with its air of hopeful generosity. Accepting his partner warts-and-all, the narrator is almost churlish ('A pretty face you may not possess') in stressing the value of personality over aesthetics, a gimmick guaranteed to score points with the female audience. Received with great approval, the track kick-started the group's commercial renaissance, although its disproportionate popularity belies its creative shortcomings. Most difficult to understand is Motown's Quality Control passing David Ruffin's vocal track, whose sharp peaks are at moments unstable and embarrassingly out of tune.[1]

Lacking a timely album outlet, the song was inserted into The Temptations' premature *Greatest Hits* in America, in time for Christmas 1966. A live version then appeared on LP early the following year, by which time The Miracles' version had also finally surfaced. A commercial success it may have been, but as a style definition it proved too mechanical in its formulation, forcing a change of direction for their next hit [587].

[1] In particular the mis-hit falsettos at 0:19 and 0:42. He recovers form in the second-half of the track.

**TMG 579**
**FOUR TOPS**
**Reach Out I'll Be There** (2:58)
(Holland—Dozier—Holland)
Produced by Brian Holland/Lamont Dozier
Recording completed: 27 Jul 1966
**Release Date**: 7 Oct 1966
**B-side**: Until You Love Someone
**Position in Record Retailer Top 40**: 1
**Equivalent US Release**: Motown 1098 (18 Aug 1966)
**Position in Billboard Top 40 Pop**: 1
**Position in Billboard Top 40 R & B**: 1

---

Levi Stubbs / Lawrence Payton / Abdul 'Duke' Fakir / Renaldo 'Obie' Benson

---

The years 1965 to 1967 were marked by an unprecedented expansion of popular music's scope, both in terms of technical innovation and artistic development which, in the process, practically defined the future of pop and rock. 1966 alone had seen the release of The Beatles' proto-psychedelic *Revolver*, while in America The Beach Boys had come up with the studio-constructed *Pet Sounds*, and with the concurrent emergence of 'rock' groups such as Cream, The Jimi Hendrix Experience and The Velvet Underground, popular music was at an excitingly unpredictable juncture whose next progression could, apparently, come from anywhere.

More apparent with hindsight, soul music was moving in parallel with the developing 'rock' idiom, pushing its own boundaries and capturing the attention of UK listeners. In May, Percy Sledge released "When A Man Loves A Woman", and other key figures such as Wilson Pickett and Otis Redding were popularising the Muscle Shoals sound.[1] And while James Brown enjoyed his biggest UK hit with "It's A Man's Man's Man's World" in June, prompting his first British visit, Tamla Motown stood poised to take full advantage of the developing public tastes, its roster of artists as impressive as the rest of the field combined.

Of all the key Motown recordings of the era, "Reach Out I'll Be There" stands as the greatest single achievement, a transatlantic number 1 and the label's biggest-ever seller in the UK.[2] Drawn up by Brian Holland and Lamont Dozier side-by-side at a piano, the narrative followed a discussion about what women really want from their partners, treading the same ground as their earlier "Call On Me" [E53b], each writer adding in sections and lines and together borrowing an opening from "Ask The Lonely" [507]. (By design HDH ended up with five lines of dialogue in each verse rather than the orthodox four [572], a subtly crafted ploy to sustain listener interest.)

Yet despite the resonance of several back-catalogue HDH numbers, the most omnipresent influence is Burt Bacharach and Hal David's 1964 hit "Reach Out For Me" (see also [511]), the chorus of which provides the verse's chords. The extent to which direct reference was made is unknown, but particular elements suggest that HDH were taking a keen interest in the track, whose title phrase appears in the lyric along with the adornment, 'Darling reach out', both tracks commencing with the words 'When you'. Furthermore, Hal David's text includes 'Don't worry, reach out for me' which surfaces here as 'You don't have to worry', and also incorporates 'Feel that you have a reason for living', which in the hands of HDH becomes 'Feel that you can't go on' (with later recording "Standing In The Shadows Of Love" [589] utilising 'Taken away my reason for living').

Striving to push The Four Tops to their limit, HDH devoted an exceptional two hours to the recording, something hitherto unheard of at Hitsville. ("I Can't Help Myself" [515] had been recorded in just two takes, while their follow-up "It's The Same Old Song" [528] was made at break-neck speed. See also [589].) Brian Holland and his colleagues' attention to detail is evident from the start, the track activated by 13-year-old Danya Hartwick's flute[3], equalised to translucence and hectored by a percussive flapping in triple time. The production effect here, introduced after four and a half seconds, puzzled producers elsewhere who could not pin down the instrument used, until Berry

Gordy eventually revealed it to be nothing more exotic than the tapping of hands on a wooden chair.[4]

Yet the most pervasive quality in the spacey recording is the urgent passion of Levi Stubbs' lead vocal. Initially hesitant about the song (he suggested one of the other group members take it on instead), he resigned to give it his best shot. Seemingly unable to contain his self-hyped frenzy, the double-tacked 'Hah!' behind the opening few words of verse 1 is duplicated with increased pressure during James Jamerson's agitated pre-chorus bass wallows. (Jamerson's wide-ranging playing here is the cement which binds the track. Simultaneously jocular and obsessive, the lines showcase his developing dynamism which would characterise his work over the subsequent four years.)[5]

Taken as a whole, the musical ideas present on the track mark the genesis of HDH's 'classical period', characterised by a tendency towards complexity of arrangement, dramatic incident (such as the pregnant pause prior to the onset of the chorus proper) and unexpected tempo changes. Milked for the rest of their time at Motown, the precepts established here (described by some as the *real* wall of sound) set fresh dramatic standards for The Four Tops which, reprocessed, would spawn a further two monumental singles in the ensuing months [589]; [601]. Topping the US chart on October 15, "Reach Out" made the number 1 spot in Britain 12 days later, and nearly two years after the Supremes had first achieved the feat on Motown's behalf [E56]. The group's biggest success by far, the song became the title track of a semi-compilation 1967 album and has been covered innumerable times including in-house efforts such as [781b] and [807].

Touring relentlessly, The Four Tops arrived in London towards the end of 1966 to rapturous receptions, performing "Reach Out" at The Saville Theatre and provoking a wild and emphatic audience response. Visibly overwhelmed by the outpouring of emotion from the group's hardcore UK fans, Stubbs led the group back for another British tour early in the new year (see [589]).

[1] Along with Booker T & The MGs, The Muscle Shoals Band were Atlantic/Stax's equivalent to The Funk Brothers, a studio ensemble who performed on a substantial number of hits by these and other artists including Etta James, Sam & Dave and Aretha Franklin. The Muscle Shoals facility was located in Alabama, and both Memphis-based Stax and New York's Atlantic artists would use the studio. Stax's main premises was dubbed Soulsville, a clear reference to Hitsville, pointedly highlighting the perceived 'authenticity' of their brand of soul which came as a considerable challenge to Motown's populist style (see [509]).

[2] As it is now known. Motown refused to disclose its actual sales until into the 1980s by which time "I Heard It Through The Grapevine" [686] and "The Tears Of A Clown" [745] had been released and out-sold the current single. Due to Gordy's policy—presumably an attempt to avoid taxation—Motown never received awards for American sales either and so opted to manufacture their own 'gold' records to award to artists, several of which were subsequently put on show in the Woodward Avenue building [614] (Dahl, p34). When one Motown star attempted to actually play one, it transpired that it was an entirely different single which had been spray-painted!

[3] She had to be carried into the studio for the session by James Jamerson and Joe Messina, due to a recently broken leg.

of 'Where Did Our Love Go' [E51].

⁵ In the interview published in Abbott 2001 (p76), Carol Kaye's comments on the recording amount to a rewriting of history. Claiming to have played the bass figure, she goes as far as to state that arranger Gene Page wrote out the lines for her, implying that Jamerson may have actually composed them although his recording was not the one finally used.

**TMG 580**
**THE VELVELETTES**
**These Things Will Keep Me Loving You** (2:25)
(Fuqua—Bristol—Moy)
Produced by Harvey Fuqua/Johnny Bristol
Recording completed: 11 May 1966
**Release Date**: 21 Oct 1966
**B-side**: Since You've Been Loving Me
**Position in Record Retailer Top 40**: -
**Equivalent US Release**: Soul 35025 (25 Aug 1966)
**Position in Billboard Top 40 Pop**: -
**Position in Billboard Top 40 R & B**: -

---

Carolyn Gill / Mildred Gill / Norma Barbee / Bertha Barbee / Sandra Tilley /
Annette McMillan

---

Under contract to Motown until 1969, The Velvelettes' recording dates had by now dried up, despite their counting two classics amongst their five singles [595], which were re-issued while the group was still, in theory, available. In the face of effectively abandoning the act, Motown bizarrely exhumed this 1964 recording, featuring a group line-up of Carolyn and Mildred Gill and Norma and Bertha Barbee, and dubbed on contributions from current Velvelettes Sandra Tilley and Annette McMillan.

Commencing with a round of finger-clicking, this easy Supremes-esque song sets out its stall early on. Appealing mainly to the pop market, the decision by Berry Gordy to release it on his black-oriented Soul label merely adds to its curiosity (the group's American releases formerly appeared on VIP). Possibly Gordy was planning to engineer a re-invention of the group at that stage, but whatever the logic, "These Things" was the last single the group had out. None cracked the US top 40.

**TMG 581**
**BRENDA HOLLOWAY**
**Hurt A Little Everyday** (2:50)
(Cosby—Moy—Stevenson)
Produced by William "Mickey" Stevenson/Henry "Hank" Cosby
Recording completed: 20 May 1965
**Release Date**: 4 Nov 1966
**B-side**: Where Were You?

**Position in Record Retailer Top 40**: -
**Equivalent US Release**: Tamla 54137 (25 Aug 1966)
**Position in Billboard Top 40 Pop**: -
**Position in Billboard Top 40 R & B**: -

Providing a string of hits for Dionne Warwick and others throughout the 1960s, Burt Bacharach was the most prominent classically-minded songwriter of his generation, working primarily from New York's Brill Building and specialising in attractive and disciplined, yet dramatic ballads, many of which have become standards.[1] Bacharach and his lyricist Hal David were known to have cut some tracks in Detroit, the suggestion being that they were in the city to surreptitiously 'borrow' Motown's Funk Brothers. A popular figure amongst Motown's writers and production staff, Bacharach's influence is more apparent in "Hurt A Little Everyday" than almost any other in-house Tamla Motown single.

Recorded in Detroit for Kim Weston, West Coast-based Holloway dubbed her vocals onto the backing track in the knowledge that, as with "When I'm Gone" [508], she was getting someone else's cast-offs. Suffering a perceived lack of interest from Motown's hierarchy, Holloway's sense of marginalisation was reaching crisis-point by the end of 1966. (The extent to which she was justified is perhaps evident in that early pressings of [581] carelessly credit the song to Brenda *Holiday*.)

Given its genesis, it is unlikely that "Hurt A Little Everyday" was an attempt to re-work her earlier hit "Every Little Bit Hurts" [E45] (written by Ed Cobb), although the coincidence of the titles is striking, and both are set to a 3/4 backing. In fact, "Hurt A Little Everyday" has its own distinct style, and with its spoken introduction foreshadows later material by Diana Ross [751], and is therefore, in its small way, a noteworthy development, if a commercial nonentity.

[1] The Brill Building was originally a clothing store on 1619 Broadway, rented out to music publishers during The Depression. Much of the music to emerge there was in fact made in nearby offices at 1650 and 1697 Broadway, but the Brill Building is remembered as the focal point of the stable of New York writers which also included Gerry Goffin & Carole King [1010], Neil Sedaka & Howard Greenfield, Barry Mann & Cynthia Weil [945], Jeff Barry & Ellie Greenwich [777] and Jerry Leiber & Mike Stoller. (Other figures such as Phil Spector [777]; [945] and Van McCoy [609] were also on the scene.) As with Motown, the emergent new artists of the 1960s showed genuine respect to the heritage of the Brill Building with the singular exception of a dismissive Bob Dylan.

New York rivals Atlantic had healthy ties with the local Brill Building, purchasing Leiber—Stoller's Spark record label in 1955. Leiber—Stoller provided several Atlantic acts with hits from the late-1950s including Ruth Brown ("Lucky Lips"), The Coasters ("Poison Ivy"; "Yakety Yak"), Ben E. King ("Stand By Me"), The Drifters ("On Broadway") etc. Other Brill-sourced hits for Atlantic include King's "Spanish Harlem", The Drifters' "Up On The Roof" and "Saturday Night At The Movies", plus Aretha Franklin's version of "(You Make Me Feel Like) A Natural Woman".

Motown installed an office in the Brill Building for a short while, under management of Gordy's estranged wife Raynoma who, absurdly starved of funding, pressed and sold several thousand illicit copies of "My Guy" [E42] in an attempt to raise some cash.

More than enough Bacharach—David covers were recorded by Motown's major groups to fill a themed compilation CD in 2002 and Stephanie Mills recorded an album with them in the mid-1970s [1020a]. See also [801]; [844].


## TMG 582
## MARTHA & THE VANDELLAS
**I'm Ready For Love** (2:52)
(Holland—Dozier—Holland)
Produced by Brian Holland/Lamont Dozier
Recording completed: 15 Sep 1966
**Release Date**: 11 Nov 1966
**B-side**: He Doesn't Love Her Anymore
**Position in Record Retailer Top 40**: 29
**Equivalent US Release**: Gordy 7056 (6 Oct 1966)
**Position in Billboard Top 40 Pop**: 9
**Position in Billboard Top 40 R & B**: 2

---

Martha Reeves / Rosalind Ashford / Betty Kelly

---

Finished in late-1966 with an eye on the forthcoming *Watchout!* album, "I'm Ready For Love" sees Martha & The Vandellas again credited alongside their favoured writer-producers after a period of some uncertainty under the musical stewardship of Mickey Stevenson. Behind the scenes, the true sequence of events paints a less than rosy picture: HDH, unwilling to throw new material in the group's direction, merely hoicked Martha Reeves' group into Hitsville to add some overdubs to a remake of an unreleased 1964 recording.[1]

Notable for the bass-pulse introduction borrowed from "You Can't Hurry Love" [575], the merriment quickly pales, the weaving flute behind Martha Reeves' fragile vocal failing to provide sufficient charm to lift the song's sense of superficiality. Light where "Nowhere To Run" [502] had been merciless, the track's brief pause prior to the third verse merely collapsed its momentum and four bars were unsubtly jettisoned in the single edit, the splice audible at 1:49.[2] Despite only surface-level nicety, the track was a hit in the US and, as an effort in getting the group back into public affection, has to be judged a success.

[1] Some sources state that the recording was made in LA.

[2] In the notes which accompany *The Complete Motown* Singles Vol. 6, Reeves is quoted admiring the spliced section, evidence that the edit was made against her will.


## TMG 583
## THE ELGINS
**Heaven Must Have Sent You** (2:36)
(Holland—Dozier—Holland)
Produced by Brian Holland/Lamont Dozier
Recording completed: 2 Jun 1966
**Release Date**: 18 Nov 1966

**B-side**: Stay In My Lonely Arms
**Position in Record Retailer Top 40**: -
**Equivalent US Release**: VIP 25037 (25 Aug 1966)
**Position in Billboard Top 40 Pop**: -
**Position in Billboard Top 40 R & B**: 9

---

Saundra Mallett Edwards / Cleo 'Duke' Miller / Johnny Dawson / Robert Fleming

---

Another venture in recycling by HDH resulted in The Elgins' second single, based on stylistic components from "Little Darling (I Need You)" [574] and a buoyant see-sawing foundation first heard in "Helpless" [554]. Fortunately, timing meant that HDH were bang-in-form, their thanks-giving lyric to devoted love breezing away the forlorn introspection of The Elgins' debut "Put Yourself In My Place" [551]. (Despite which the track's original conception shows the team dwelling in melancholy, working with the makeshift title "So Many Years Of Tears".)

Blithely unsophisticated, "Heaven Must Have Sent You" eschews the formal convention of choruses in favour of an endless double-bar doo-wop run in C. Effortless vocals from Saundra Mallett Edwards provide a soulful veneer for an unadulterated piece of pop which should have been a smash hit. Why wasn't it? Popularly considered the most mystifying chart failure in Motown's canon, "Heaven Must Have Sent You" was originally viewed as a throwaway but picked up by club crowds to earn a reputation as a classic of the genre. Largely ignored by the mainstream in its day, a lack of sales effectively blocked further investment in The Elgins who were consequently allowed to slip out of the reckoning, afforded just one further single [615]. "Heaven Must Have Sent You" eventually made number 3 in the UK as a re-issue [771], leading to a rare US re-release (VIP 25065).

**TMG 584**
**THE MIRACLES**
**(Come 'Round Here) I'm The One You Need** (2:33)
(Holland—Dozier—Holland)
Produced by Brian Holland/Lamont Dozier
Recording completed: 21 Sep 1966
**Release Date**: 18 Nov 1966
**B-side**: Save Me
**Position in Record Retailer Top 40**: -
**Equivalent US Release**: Tamla 54140 (19 Oct 1966)
**Position in Billboard Top 40 Pop**: 17
**Position in Billboard Top 40 R & B**: 4

---

Smokey Robinson / Bobby Rogers / Claudette Rogers Robinson /
Warren 'Pete' Moore / Ronnie White

---

Assembled by HDH from a clutch of incomplete sections, "(Come 'Round Here) I'm The One You Need" is almost schizophrenic in its lurches from sunny openness to dark obsession, encapsulating the widest range of moods in its two-and-a-half minutes of any contemporary Motown track. Introduced with a deceptive quasi-classical overture, in fact plucked from the song's middle-8, this complex creation was intended for the melodramatic Levi Stubbs, assembled with The Four Tops specifically in mind before being nicked by Smokey Robinson. In adopting a spoken style in the song's bridges, Robinson paradoxically sounds more like Bob Dylan than on any of his previous recordings, the cross-influence unmistakable, yet the section in question is a clear derivative of Robinson's earlier "Choosy Beggar", indicating that if HDH were planning to give the song to The Four Tops, it may have had some late amendments, which if true would warrant mention of Robinson in the credits.

Certainly one can *hear* The Four Tops performing the song; that Robinson-the-vocalist was able to effect such an adept presentation testifies to his interpretive skills, "Come 'Round Here" with its unpredictable accusations and arrogations alien territory for the romanticist, reverse title and all (Robinson-the-composer would have tended towards the more generously spirited '*You're* the one *I* need').


**TMG 585**
**THE SUPREMES**
**You Keep Me Hangin' On** (2:45)
(Holland—Dozier—Holland)
Produced by Brian Holland/Lamont Dozier
Recording completed: 1 Aug 1966
**Release Date**: 25 Nov 1966
**B-side**: Remove This Doubt
**Position in Record Retailer Top 40**: 8
**Equivalent US Release**: Motown 1101 (12 Oct 1966)
**Position in Billboard Top 40 Pop**: 1
**Position in Billboard Top 40 R & B**: 1

---

Diana Ross / Florence Ballard / Mary Wilson

---

The fourth successive Tamla Motown single written by HDH was the team's eighteenth release of 1966, accounting for almost a half of the label's 45s that year. That their writing and production was in demand from virtually all of Motown's major acts evinces the view held by Dave Godin that, in the middle years of the 1960s, 'Holland-Dozier-Holland *were* Motown'.[1]

Conscious of the expansive scope which the growing 'rock' genre offered in 1966, HDH set about pushing The Supremes' sound more towards the white-oriented rock market than on any of their previous productions. In drawing swooping guitar panning and sharpened sound effects into their idiosyncratic 'soul', HDH can be seen in this context as the true pioneers of psychedelia within the genre, some years ahead of Norman Whitfield; yet the effect is mere dressing. From HDH's perspective, "You Keep Me Hangin' On" probably began as a variation of "Stop! In The

Name Of Love" [501], with which it shares a one-note descending step in its opening vocal bars.

The song is unusual in the horizontal pull of its melody line which barely ever emerges from a constrained manœuvring between two whole tone intervals. Like [501], lyrically centred on actual comments made to Dozier by a girlfriend, the composition repudiates the victim-centric sentiment of its predecessor through sheer intolerance (the track's working title was "The Payback") and thus foreshadows HDH's post-Motown work with Laura Lee (see [831]).

The song's famous seven-second introduction amounts to a telegraphed distress call created by Robert White's[2] urgent 'one-note staccato', anticipating the distraught content of the lyrics (and in this interpretation putting an unexpected slant on the telephonic phrase 'hanging on'). Organ-backed and swiped uncompromisingly left-right with each bar, its audible flying between the channels on stereo pressings suggests that it was panned 'live' during the mixing stage, before being left to rest on the left hand speaker where it raises its head in each of the choruses. (Clashing against it in the right channel is the same jockeying, triplet-rapping 'chair drum' effect heard in "Reach Out" [579].)

Beneath the electrical surface, a syncopated tambourine provides shimmer and brightens the soundtrack in which bass and percussion are mixed into a murky shade, masking the creative range of Jamerson's picking. Musically there is little to guide the listener, the track devoid of audible chords and relying on Jamerson's choice of notes against the vocal line to imply a structure, without which the track would effectively be a drone in the then influential Indian classical tradition.

Of similar interest are the provocatively prominent backing vocals, showing a rare passion and taking centre-stage for one of the choruses after Ross' defeated spoken pronouncement at 1:30 (very like those heard on the recent "Hurt A Little Everyday" [581] and "Come 'Round Here (I'm The One You Need)" [584]). With Ross' double-tracked lead out of synch in the final sections, "You Keep Me Hangin' On" has none of the polished show-biz trappings with which the group's live act is associated, being a sharp and defiantly insistent remonstration from a woman spurned. Completed in an earlier form on the same day as "You Can't Hurry Love" [575] which was preferred by Quality Control (to Brian Holland's annoyance), the single had to sit in wait for release, before arriving to spend a fortnight at the summit in America, the group's eighth chart-topper there. This adventurous recording attracted attention from numerous white outfits, most notably New York heavy-rockers Vanilla Fudge, who pruned down their own seven-and-a-half-minute version splattered with dramatic effects and exotic instrumentation, and took the song back into the American top 10. (Brian Holland reckons this his favourite cover of all of HDH's compositions.) Other notable versions include a modest 1969 soul hit by Wilson Pickett and, 17 years later an uninspired reading from Kim Wilde which went to number 2 in the UK.

---

[1] *Record Collector* issue 267, p57. Besides The Supremes and The Four Tops, HDH had provided singles during the year for Martha & The Vandellas, Marvin Gaye, The Miracles, The Isley Brothers and Junior Walker & The All Stars. Additionally, Eddie Holland worked

extensively with Norman Whitfield on The Temptations' 1966 recordings.

[2] The track features three electric guitars, recorded relatively 'clean'. Besides White, Eddie Willis tracks the main riff with Joe Messina in the background.


**TMG 586**
**JUNIOR WALKER & THE ALL STARS**
**Money (That's What I Want) Part I** (2:05)
(Bradford—Gordy)
Produced by Berry Gordy Jr./Lawrence Horn
Recording completed: 10 Jun 1966
**Release Date**: 2 Dec 1966
**B-side**: Money (That's What I Want) Part 2
**Position in Record Retailer Top 40**: -
**Equivalent US Release**: Soul 35026 (27 Oct 1966)
**Position in Billboard Top 40 Pop**: -
**Position in Billboard Top 40 R & B**: 35

---

Jr Walker / Willie Woods / Vic Thomas / James Graves

---

Eavesdropping on a Barrett Strong jam a few days after the opening of Hitsville at 2648 West Grand Boulevard back in 1959, Berry Gordy chanced on an embryonic version of "Money", then an instrumental 12-bar, and seeing its potential spent the next couple of days fashioning the arrangement and staunchly materialistic lyric with songwriter and office receptionist Janie Bradford. Although Gordy later played down the uncompromising eulogy to avarice, complaining that it had been over-analysed (in an interview in 1990, he claimed that the ostensibly personal statement was conceived as a sort of jokey counterpoint to the ubiquitous love song[1]), the text was nevertheless inspired by his own financial hardship at a time when his business empire was still a mere dream.

Released by Strong in August of that year [E02], the track was given a national distribution courtesy of the bigger Anna imprint and fought its way up to 23 on the *Billboard* chart, eventually notching up sales estimated to be in excess of one million. Appropriately, "Money" heralded a turning point for Gordy and brought in sufficient capital for him to expand his business, helped in 1963 by a more acclaimed rendition by The Beatles.

Re-recorded in an extended form on 27 February 1965, new-boy Junior Walker was presumably intent on currying favour with his sceptical new boss, the improvisatory recording never intended for release as a single (if at all). Left in the vaults for 16 months, the song was rescued for inclusion on *Road Runner* (simultaneously with another album version by The Supremes), and 'livened up' with some mock studio noise, giving it the same party feel as "How Sweet It Is" [571], which had charted higher than expected.

In the six years since Strong's original hit, Motown had expanded to occupy a market position unparalleled in the industry (three-quarters of its 1966 singles made the US charts). With Ewart Abner poached from Vee Jay to act as director of Motown's artist management arm (ITMI) and with over 100 acts on the books, it is little wonder that Gordy, and Motown generally, had cause to reflect on the song which started it all and which, whatever his public protestations, remained his private manifesto.

With little impact in the idealistic 1960s, the song made commercial headway via another cover version in August 1979, New Wave group The Flying Lizards taking a wilfully emotionless adaptation to number 5, a radical if apt treatment given society's shift in values at a time when Margaret Thatcher was beginning her 11-year reign as Prime Minister. Detractors who seek to characterise Motown's product as over-produced and excessively sentimental would do well to listen to Walker's 1965 version, as rough-hewn as R & B comes.

¹ Interview in *Rolling Stone* issue 585, reproduced in Abbott, p31.

**TMG 587**
**THE TEMPTATIONS**
**(I Know) I'm Losing You** (2:26)
(Whitfield—Holland—Grant)
Produced by Norman Whitfield
Recording completed: 16 Sep 1966
**Release Date**: 9 Dec 1966
**B-side**: Little Miss Sweetness
**Position in Record Retailer Top 40**: 19
**Equivalent US Release**: Gordy 7057 (2 Nov 1966)
**Position in Billboard Top 40 Pop**: 8
**Position in Billboard Top 40 R & B**: 1

Otis Williams / Melvin Franklin / Paul Williams / Eddie Kendricks / David Ruffin

Drawing inspiration from George Clinton's recent "(I Wanna) Testify", "(I Know) I'm Losing You" was commenced by Cornelius Grant and bassist Bill Upchurch, their studio jam fortuitously overheard by Norman Whitfield. His interest immediate, Whitfield took the basic riff (which forms the song's introduction) to his writing partner, who crafted the sharply articulate and wrought verses from thin-air. (The title phrase "I Don't Wanna Lose You" was vetoed in favour of its eventual name due to its recent employment elsewhere.) Recorded with exceptionally weighty sonics, Grant's creeping guitar intro is suffused with disquiet, the ominous thrum of bass adding to the tension, mounting before a word has been said. (This most electrifying opening amongst Tamla Motown's singles is flawed by background noise, the mark of a dirty vocal track.)

"(I Know) I'm Losing You" stands as one of Tamla Motown's most extreme records, not just for the anguished dread of the lyric, but for the suffocating arrangement. Produced bass-heavy with Earl Van Dyke's low piano pushed against deep, pressurised brass saturated in reverb, the ensuing sound seems distanced from the material world, utilising a single chord for most of the song. Yet the finest moments come during the instrumental break, an aggressive tussle between trumpet and trombone, who swap terse phrases to depict the head-on clash looming for the song's two main characters.

David Ruffin's subsequent vocal overdub brilliantly conveys his despair, caught in the helpless torment of 'knowing' his woman is being unfaithful to him. Tripping over the choruses, Ruffin is barely capable of expressing himself, so overwhelmed by the unmistakable signs which his ruthlessly obsessive detective work have lain before him. He can see the terrible truth in the look on her face, sense it in her touch, and whichever way he stacks it the agony of realisation is unavoidable. Penetrating and intuitive, his assertion near the end, that he can 'feel it in his bones' sends a deathly shiver down the spine, implying that the central character may literally be unable to live without his lover.

Proposed as The Temptations' next single by its justifiably ecstatic producer, a startled Berry Gordy, unnerved by the unprecedented sound palette on show refused its release, causing a near-catastrophic rift between the two men. For a while, Whitfield insisted he would make no further records for Motown unless the song came out, and for a period it looked as if the usually resolute Gordy would lose one of his most creative producers. In the end, a nervous Gordy conceded, Tamla Motown sensing a shift in direction for the group and rejecting the American B-side in favour of Smokey Robinson's "Little Miss Sweetness", a number more typical of The Temptations' established sound but with enough of a sensual depth to hold its own against the A-side. Gordy needn't have troubled himself: "I'm Losing You" went top 10 at home and top 20 in Britain, seen with hindsight as one of Motown's consummate recordings.

**TMG 588**
**STEVIE WONDER**
**A Place In The Sun** (2:59)
(Miller—Wells)
Produced by Clarence Paul
Recording completed: 27 Jul 1966
**Release Date**: 9 Dec 1966
**B-side**: Sylvia
**Position in Record Retailer Top 40**: 20
**Equivalent US Release**: Tamla 54139 (24 Oct 1966)
**Position in Billboard Top 40 Pop**: 9
**Position in Billboard Top 40 R & B**: 3

1966 had been key for Tamla Motown, finally making a consistent mark in the UK charts, with half of its releases since the summer going top 40. Sadly, their final single of the year was this childish composition supplied to Stevie Wonder, his musical directors blotting his discography with this twee piece of whimsy masquerading as an oblique 'protest' number in the wake of "Blowin' In The Wind" [570], mainly courtesy of the lines in verse 1 pertaining to running towards dreams and reaching for freedom. Notable for the fact that James Jamerson plays his favoured upright bass on the recording, the track was quickly followed-up in America by a novelty Christmas single, which flopped. Some US promo editions of "A Place In The Sun" appeared as red vinyl, early examples of non-black discs. (The B-side is not, as has been suggested, specifically about Sylvia Moy. Copyrighted to Moy—Cosby—Wonder, the deliberate use of her Christian name was a prank devised by Cosby and played out by Wonder as an in-joke.)

## TIMELINE - 1966

Tamla Motown release 45 singles, 19 albums and 8 EPs
Tamla Motown place 13 singles in the UK top 40. 4 make top 10 and 1 reaches number 1
James Jamerson's bass work becomes noticeably more complex and animated, indicating developing style
Motown opens further facilities in LA and New York

| | |
|---|---|
| **Jan** | Stevie Wonder: "Uptight" first notable composition from Cosby—Moy team |
| **Jan** | Tamla Motown is best-selling US label in UK |
| **Jan 12** | Motown's Artists Development office moves into 2657 West Grand Boulevard, opposite Hitsville |
| **Mar** | Martha & Vandellas tour UK |
| **Mar 25** | First release for new signings Isley Brothers |
| **Apr** | HDH attend BMI ceremony and receive eight awards |
| **Jun** | Norman Whitfield assumes control of Temptations from Smokey Robinson |
| **Jun** | Motown open further New York offices, managed by Shelly Berger |
| **Jul** | Race riots in various US cities |
| **Jul 5** | Motown purchase 2670-2672 West Grand Boulevard as base for ITMI department (International Talent Management Incorporated) |
| **Jul 11** | Motown purchase 2662-2668 West Grand Boulevard for sales and marketing HQ |
| **Sep 3** | Supremes begin 20-day tour South East Asia |
| **Sep 8** | Supremes: "You Can't Hurry Love" enters UK top 50 (peak 3). Success marks start of Tamla Motown as commercial force in UK |
| **Sep 10** | Supremes: "You Can't Hurry Love" number 1 in US (two weeks) |
| **Sep 16** | Gladys Knight & Pips release first single for Tamla Motown |
| **Sep** | Four Tops play London's Saville Theatre |
| **Sep** | Gordy begins purchase of Golden World company. Over next two years secures properties, master tapes and contracts of performers including Edwin Starr. Golden World's Davison Avenue studio will become Motown's Studio B |
| **Oct 15** | Four Tops: "Reach Out I'll Be There" number 1 in US (two weeks) |
| **Oct 22** | Supremes: *Supremes A Go-Go* number 1 album in US (two weeks) |
| **Oct 27** | Jimmy Ruffin: "What Becomes Of The Brokenhearted" enters UK top 50 (peak 8) |
| **Oct 27** | Four Tops: "Reach Out I'll Be There" UK number 1 (three weeks) |
| **Nov 19** | Supremes: "You Keep Me Hangin' On" number 1 in US (two weeks) |
| **Dec 1** | Supremes: "You Keep Me Hangin' On" enters UK top 50 (peak 8) |
| **Dec** | Motown Revue at Fox Theater includes Martha & Vandellas, Jimmy Ruffin, Chris Clark, Stevie Wonder, Temptations, Gladys Knight & Pips |

**TMG 589**
**FOUR TOPS**
**Standing In The Shadows Of Love** (2:36)
(Holland—Dozier—Holland)
Produced by Brian Holland/Lamont Dozier
Recording completed: 6 Nov 1966
**Release Date**: 6 Jan 1967
**B-side**: Since You've Been Gone
**Position in Record Retailer Top 40**: 6
**Equivalent US Release**: Motown 1102 (28 Nov 1966)
**Position in Billboard Top 40 Pop**: 6
**Position in Billboard Top 40 R & B**: 2

---

Levi Stubbs / Lawrence Payton / Abdul 'Duke' Fakir / Renaldo 'Obie' Benson

---

Before embarking on their end-of-year tour which took in London [579], it was imperative The Four Tops get a follow-up to "Reach Out" in the can in order to catch the Christmas market. Instructed by Berry Gordy at virtually no notice, HDH called the group in while the new track was still in preparation, the team finalising the lyrics to the embryonic "My Search Has Ended" on the studio floor while The Four Tops waited patiently at their microphones, with no opportunity to properly rehearse the song.

Thanks to its revised title, the track is popularly thought to derive from the 1963 Supremes throwaway, "Standing At The Crossroads Of Love" [E34b], but is in fact distilled from another Supremes number, re-using essentially the same chorus chords as the seminal "Stop! In The Name Of Love" [501][1], no direct musical connection linking "Crossroads" and "Shadows". Raising the key by a semitone to the unusual Bbm, the master was probably speeded up post-mix from the same original Am, a studio trick which 'tightens' recordings and which numerous current releases in rare keys such as [561]; [602] indicate as common practice for Hitsville's producers. Carrying throughout a sense outraged injustice—grist to the mill for Levi Stubbs—"Standing In The Shadows Of Love" casts an indignant rhetoric ('What did I do to cause all this grief/Now what'd I say to make you want to leave?'), Stubbs' pitching extraordinarily intense, unconstrained by the formalised melody and carrying a direct, speech-like quality as if he were standing face-to-face with his lost love, demanding explanations. (The vocals were recorded at Golden World, on Davison Avenue in the first Motown session to take place there: see [630].)

The dense production arrangement is based on that of "Reach Out" [579], featuring prominent bongos, yet more 'chair drum', and a four-beat tambourine, but remains distinctive for James Jamerson's definitive bass playing. Inspired from his knowledge of Eastern music, Jamerson infused what he called a spiritual, 'Arabic' feel[2], his scales drawing on those heard via local musicians amongst Detroit's high immigrant population.

Continuing their love affair with British audiences, The Four Tops appeared at the Royal Albert Hall in London on January 28, watched by 14,000 fans, before embarking on a tour of the UK's major cities. Earning rave

---

reviews and on the back of their chart-topping "Reach Out I'll Be There" [579], the group's new single missed the Christmas boom in Britain but caught its moment perfectly, matching its earlier number 6 placing in America. (*The Four Tops Live!* was astutely released in Britain in February 1967, charting for an amazing 67 weeks.)

[1] The unobvious similarity of the titles exposes the derivation, just two words being substituted from The Supremes' original. The phrase perhaps finds its amended form via The Rolling Stones' "Have You Seen Your Mother, Baby, Standing In The Shadow", a top 10 hit in August 1966.

[2] Quoted in George, p110.

## TMG 590
## MARVIN GAYE & KIM WESTON
**It Takes Two** (2:57)
(Moy—Stevenson)
Produced by William "Mickey" Stevenson/Henry "Hank" Cosby
Recording completed: 2 Mar 1966
**Release Date**: 13 Jan 1967
**B-side**: It's Got To Be A Miracle (This Thing Called Love)
**Position in Record Retailer Top 40**: 16
**Equivalent US Release**: Tamla 54141 (2 Dec 1966)
**Position in Billboard Top 40 Pop**: 14
**Position in Billboard Top 40 R & B**: 4

Finding a niche for Marvin Gaye was a perennial issue for Motown [510] which Berry Gordy sought to resolve numerous times by pairing him up with female counterparts. Teamed with Mary Wells in 1964 for "Once Upon A Time" [E46] (on which Gaye was billed second), he was left stranded by her prompt departure, and their part-made album was temporarily continued with VIP singer Oma Heard[1] in Wells' shoes before being abandoned altogether. A 'full time' replacement was found in Kim Weston, their first release, "What Good Am I Without You?" [E62] coming at the close of the year, followed by the completion of an album which was similarly pulled by Motown at the eleventh hour.[2]

In the ensuing two years repeated attempts were made to rekindle the partnership, but with no recordings seeing the light of day both singers continued pursuing their respective solo careers. Yet with Weston's faltering, her husband Mickey Stevenson stepped in and, appealing to Motown on Weston's behalf, salvaged a year-old track for immediate release. (Often portrayed as something of a tormentor, Stevenson is alleged to have viewed Kim Weston as his personal route to wealth, pushing her career for his own gain; yet this interpretation doesn't sit comfortably with the fact that he enjoyed a much higher profile then she within the Motown corporation, with a far greater degree of professional success in his own right than he would ever have had via her singing.)

As it transpired, Stevenson's efforts in getting the single out were futile in the long-term, Weston seeing nothing further released, her future as half of this double act about to be severed by the arrival on the scene of Tammi Terrell [611]. Within a year, Stevenson, by now Director of A & R, lobbied for a share in Motown's stock, and unsuccessful, tendered his resignation. Heading for a lucrative contract with MGM, he took Weston with him, although she never found her spiritual home, moving from label to label and even recording for Motown's rivals Stax at one point. (A few years after their Motown departure the couple were divorced.)

"It Takes Two" is a simplistic affair, written around one chord and relieved by an ascent in the (very brief) choruses. With its orchestrated slow-time intro and 'big' strings and brass, the recording is attractively punchy, Weston leading Gaye through the alternating vocal lines, an unsophisticated yet imaginative rundown of the numerous ways in which being in a partnership is preferable to being single. A minor hit in 1967, the song underwent a curious revival of interest in the late-1980s. With Weston's return to recording with the MotorCity label, after some years in retirement, a remake was done with Marvin Gaye's brother Frankie. Soon after, a slew of covers of this catchy number charted in the UK, none too inspiring: a rap version in 1988; a semi-comedy reading by British DJs Liz Kershaw and Bruno Brookes in 1989; and finally Rod Stewart and Tina Turner's cover the following year (see [555n]).

[1] She is incorrectly listed as Oma Page on her duets with Gaye, the name belonging to another, unconnected Motown singer. Heard also recorded under her married name Oma Drake.

[2] Some of the shelved tracks with both Wells and Weston were included on the 1990 *Marvin Gaye Collection*. There are also rumours that Dusty Springfield taped a number of tracks with Gaye, but contractual difficulties blocked their release.


**TMG 591**
**CHRIS CLARK**
**Love's Gone Bad** (2:21)
(Holland—Dozier—Holland)
Produced by Brian Holland/Lamont Dozier
Recording completed: 24 Jun 1966
**Release Date**: 20 Jan 1967
**B-side**: Put Yourself In My Place
**Position in Record Retailer Top 40**: -
**Equivalent US Release**: VIP 25038 (14 Jul 1966)
**Position in Billboard Top 40 Pop**: -
**Position in Billboard Top 40 R & B**: -

Six-foot Californian blonde Chris Clark was hardly a typical candidate for Motown stardom. Previously going by the name Connie Clark, she was snapped up at 17 by Hal Davis, who recorded some demos with her, but after two years of office work Clark was forced to personally petition Berry Gordy for some releases. Requesting an immediate, unrehearsed acappella performance in his office, Motown's president was suitably impressed and drew up a contract, subsequently producing a debut single in December 1965, an assembly of curious Motown personnel watching from the control room. (Besides talent but she had an important thing in her favour: she was to become one of Gordy's lovers. According to Mary Wilson, on tour he would see to it that he took hotel rooms between Clark's and Diana Ross'[1], presumably so that he would have easy access to both, but also perhaps to keep them apart.)

The follow-up "Love's Gone Bad" was her first UK release, given its despondent title a surprisingly up-beat number from the HDH team, as a re-think of the first draft "Serve Yourself A Cup Of Happiness". Relying principally on a chuffing Hammond Organ for its musical palette, the track utilises the same syncopated rhythm as "Wild Thing", a 1966 hit for UK outfit The Troggs shortly before "Love's Gone Bad" was recorded. Taping her vocal under instruction to 'go mad' towards the end, a self-conscious Clark broke into the lyrics of "In The Midnight Hour", causing an irritated Brian Holland to halt the recording and reprimand the singer.

Although not a massive seller, the release brought forth public appearances which famously shocked Motown fans imagining Clark to be black. They subsequently referred to her as 'The White Negress', an affectionate nickname also bestowed on Motown champion and diva Dusty Springfield.[2] Others were not so accepting; early on, Clark was regularly booed at the Fox Theater and the Apollo.

[1] 1986, p179.

[2] Springfield had hosted the Sounds of Motown television special edition of Ready Steady Go! in the spring of 1965 which included a live performance with Martha & The Vandellas. Her recorded œuvre includes versions of "You Really Got A Hold On Me" [E13], "Can I Get A Witness?" [E31], "When The Lovelight Starts Shining Through His Eyes" [E34], "Needle In A Haystack" [E61], "A Love Like Yours (Don't Come Knocking Every Day)" [554b], "I Can't Give Back The Love I Feel For You" [643] and "Ain't No Sun Since You've Been Gone" [818b]. (She also recorded an unreleased cover of "Ben" [834].) See also [590n].

## TMG 592
## THE ORIGINALS
**Goodnight Irene** (2:50)
(Leadbetter—Lomax)
Produced by Clarence Paul
Recording completed: 5 Nov 1966
**Release Date**: 27 Jan 1967
**B-side**: Need Your Lovin' (Want You Back)
**Position in Record Retailer Top 40**: -
**Equivalent US Release**: Soul 35029 (27 Dec 1966)
**Position in Billboard Top 40 Pop**: -
**Position in Billboard Top 40 R & B**: -

---

Freddie Gorman / Walter Gaines / C P Spencer / Henry "Hank" Dixon

---

A second successive Tamla Motown debut marked the arrival of The Originals, a four-piece including one Freddie Gorman, a known figure who previously sang in a variety of outfits with members such as Lamont Dozier and David Ruffin, and co-wrote numerous early Motown tracks with Brian Holland including "I Want A Guy" [E07b] and "Please Mr. Postman" [E05] (as it happens, Gorman's own day job). Signed to Ric Tic as a solo artist in 1965, he was pulled into The Originals by fellow members Walter Gaines and Henry Dixon, along with C P Spencer.

Assigned to Motown's Soul label, the group opened their account with this, an old Lead Belly number produced by Clarence Paul. "Goodnight Irene" (also known as "Irene, Goodnight") is a traditional number which Lead Belly formalised with John Lomax. Subsequently recorded by The Weavers and Frank Sinatra (amongst many others, including Motown's early prospect Paul Gayten (see [E02])), the track was something of a standard but unsure of the group's studio savvy, Clarence Paul recruited former Contour Joe Stubbs [564] as anonymous lead vocalist. Yet despite his efforts, the track has little to commend it, constituting a forced stomp shoehorned into 'the Motown sound'. Betrayed by its compromising style, the single flopped and The Originals were largely ignored by Motown for the next two years, having to settle for anonymous backing vocal duties for Motown's male soloists such as Jimmy Ruffin [577], [593], [603], Edwin Starr [672], David Ruffin [689] and Stevie Wonder [679], [717].


**TMG 593**
**JIMMY RUFFIN**
**I've Passed This Way Before** (2:46)
(Dean—Weatherspoon)
Produced by James Dean/William Weatherspoon
Recording completed: 8 Oct 1966
**Release Date**: 3 Feb 1967
**B-side**: Tomorrow's Tears
**Position in Record Retailer Top 40**: 29
**Equivalent US Release**: Soul 35027 (15 Nov 1966)
**Position in Billboard Top 40 Pop**: 17
**Position in Billboard Top 40 R & B**: 10


David Morse has criticised Jimmy Ruffin's ballads for their emphasised chorus phrases, arguing that Ruffin's delivery is too unsubtle, constituting 'the nadir of the Motown formula'.[1] This however is harsh if taken as comment on the singer: Jimmy Ruffin, like all Motown artists of the day, was under direction of his writer-producers and, although he did not have the vocal faculty of a Levi Stubbs or a Smokey Robinson, recorded at least one classic single [577] and was entitled to maintain a patent style which set him apart from the field.

Following-up a smash hit is an onerous task, with public expectation invariably overblown. With the spotlight suddenly on Ruffin, his writer-producers were under unrealistic pressure to repeat the success of [577], an impossible challenge at which "I've Passed This Way Before" was a creditable attempt. Although it shares thematic elements with Ruffin's first single, including lonely journeys, and inevitably the phrase 'brokenhearted' at the end of the final verse, musically it is a breath of fresh air, pulling out of the dolour of [577] with measured brio. Looking towards Motown's centre ground, the track incorporates an attention-getting triplet bounce borrowed from [516], plus spoken sections currently in vogue, which Ruffin performs somewhat half-heartedly expecting them not to make the final cut, following the corresponding emasculation of [577]. Indeed the vocal as a whole is carelessly done and badly pitched in places, suggesting a provisional run through which was not initially intended for public consumption. (The original stereo mix omits various elements present in mono, including backing vocals and horns.)

[1] p92


## TMG 594
## THE MARVELETTES
**The Hunter Gets Captured By The Game** (2:47)
(Robinson)
Produced by William "Smokey" Robinson
Recording completed: 17 Sep 1966
**Release Date**: 10 Feb 1967
**B-side**: I Think I Can Change
**Position in Record Retailer Top 40**: -
**Equivalent US Release**: Tamla 54143 (27 Dec 1966)
**Position in Billboard Top 40 Pop**: 13
**Position in Billboard Top 40 R & B**: 2

---

Gladys Horton / Wanda Young / Katherine Anderson

---

Given that the similarly macabre sounding [546] was widely interpreted as a dig at William Stevenson, the current ungainly title appears to contain a cryptic reference to his writing partner Ivy Hunter, Robinson probably aiming to provoke further (mis-)interpretation and at the same time have a private chuckle. Extrapolating the predatory implications of [518], this new song concerns an entrapment which backfires, the female protagonist embroiled in her own web of dissimulation.

Most remarkable is Robinson's creatively picturesque chord progression, starting out with a plunging leap from an open Dmaj7 to a guarded Bb, before skulking through the shadows of Gm—F#7—Em run, padding through its creeping rhythm with the stealth of a stalking lioness. Containing too, a jazzy five-chord dash from a low Em to a tottering Bm, the sequence perfectly depicts the act of entrapment, one of Robinson's most cunningly devised musical sequences.

Featuring a rare cadenced ending, unorthodox 'thin' arrangement and with an uncomfortable stepping riff on keyboard (?) doubling James Jamerson's bass[1], the track makes no attempt to match Motown's contemporary popularist output, standing purely on its own artistic worth. Described by its author as 'funky'[2], the recording was disapproved by Motown's management and would have been shelved were it not for Robinson's personal resolve to have it released. Although not a big hit, the track has attracted interest since 1967, covered numerous times including an effort by Blondie in 1982 and another by Massive Attack for the film *Batman Forever* (1995).

[1] He particularly liked his 'walking' run here. See interview in *Bass Player*, Spring 1990.
[2] p144


## TMG 595
## THE VELVELETTES
**He Was Really Saying Somethin'** (2:30) **[E71]**
(Whitfield—Stevenson—Holland)
Produced by Norman Whitfield
Recording completed: 7 Dec 1964
**Release Date**: 17 Feb 1967
**B-side**: Needle In A Haystack [E61]
**Position in Record Retailer Top 40**: -
**Equivalent US Release**: VIP 25013 (28 Dec 1964)
**Position in Billboard Top 40 Pop**: -
**Position in Billboard Top 40 R & B**: 21

---

Carolyn Gill / Mildred Gill / Bertha Barbee / Norma Barbee

---

Virtually ignoring The Velvelettes as an ongoing concern [580], Tamla Motown kept the group's profile up by repeated re-use of old material. In this case, the group's first two singles, originally released on Stateside in Britain, were paired up and released in the hope that interest in the label would be sufficient to hoist them up the UK charts. (The relatively primitive nature of the recording is exposed by noise during the piano intro, after approximately one second.)

Based on a popular street phrase of the day, "He Was Really Saying Somethin'"[1] is a classic slice of high-school *kitsch*, a faithfully observed foray into the genre complete with "Bop bop suki-doo wop" refrain. As one would expect the track is lyrically naïve to the point of chaste, the girl courted by an open-shirted suitor who sees her home while winning her over to a second rendezvous (though, 'ladylike it may not be').

Bolstered by the presence of The Andantes on the recording, the track is a bristling example of early Motown, described by Velvelette Cal Gill as "Dynamite".[2] Faring better on the US soul charts and selling more heavily around Detroit, the original single never made a significant impact nationally, and in the UK is better known via British trio Bananarama, who teamed up with Fun Boy Three to take a 1982 cover to number 5 (see also [782]).

[1] The Tamla Motown edition added a 'g' to the title's original Sayin'.
[2] *Record Collector* issue 308, March 2005


## TMG 596
## JUNIOR WALKER & THE ALL STARS
**Pucker Up Buttercup** (2:57)

---

(Fuqua—Bristol—Coggins)
Produced by Harvey Fuqua/Johnny Bristol
Recording completed: 27 Apr 1966
**Release Date**: 17 Feb 1967
**B-side**: Any Way You Wanta
**Position in Record Retailer Top 40**: -
**Equivalent US Release**: Soul 35030 (17 Jan 1967)
**Position in Billboard Top 40 Pop**: 31
**Position in Billboard Top 40 R & B**: 11

---

Jr Walker / Willie Woods / Vic Thomas / James Graves[1]

---

This 'absolutely savage dance raver'[2] was lifted as the fourth A-side from *Road Runner* (released six months earlier in the US but held off in Britain until December 1966), 11 weeks after its predecessor [586]. "Pucker Up" is a well-produced, straight piece of R & B, the first amongst Walker's singles to carry an authentic blues chord structure (bar "Money" [586] which, as an old cover, has little relevance to his career development). As rough-and-ready as Stevie Wonder's comparable "High Heel Sneakers" [532], the track, written with input from ex-Moonglow and associate of Harvey Fuqua, Danny Coggins, was probably inspired by James Brown's "Papa's Got A Brand New Bag" a US top-tenner shortly before "Buttercup" was recorded.

[1] By the time the backing track was made, Graves had left the group. However Billy Nicks had yet to join [571], a temporary stand-in found for the session on 30 March 1966 in the shape of Ted Irby.

[2] Bill Dahl, in *Goldmine*. Reproduced in Abbott p124.


**TMG 597**
**THE SUPREMES**
**Love Is Here And Now You're Gone** (2:35)
(Holland—Dozier—Holland)
Produced by Brian Holland/Lamont Dozier
Recording completed: 21 Sep 1966
**Release Date**: 24 Feb 1967
**B-side**: There's No Stopping Us Now
**Position in Record Retailer Top 40**: 17
**Equivalent US Release**: Motown 1103 (11 Jan 1967)
**Position in Billboard Top 40 Pop**: 1
**Position in Billboard Top 40 R & B**: 1

---

Diana Ross / Florence Ballard / Mary Wilson

---

Coming as an anticlimax after the group's previous two singles, "Love Is Here" chokes with a cacophony of high frequencies. Employing a wiry harpsichord together with treble-heavy orchestration dubbed on under Holland and Dozier's supervision at the LA studios, Gene Page's arrangement quickly becomes grating. An attempt by HDH to create a vividly dramatised vignette, in the style explored by The Rolling Stones in 1965-66 ("Lady Jane",

"As Tears Go By", etc.), the track is obviously contrived and lacks naturalness, Jamerson's over-elaborate acoustic bass for once failing to supply effective counter-balance (if indeed he is the player on the session).

Poorly performed by Diana Ross, whose over-stressed intonation merely sounds insincere (and almost fails at 2:02), the track is further marred by some of the most blatantly bored backing vocals on any Motown record. Conceived as a gimmick to make Ross more sultry, the spoken sections here verge on comical, and on the stereo mix available on CD, include a sloppily engineered drop-in at 1:24, a trace of the original vocal still audible. A relative failure in the UK, loyal American fans dragged it to the top for a week before The Beatles' new single deposed it. Neither Diana Ross nor Mary Wilson mention the track in their respective autobiographies, something which, coupled with the weak studio performance, hints at the group's jeopardy; Gordy had reputedly offered Ross the option to quit at the end of 1966, while simultaneously weighing up Barbara Randolph as a possible replacement for Flo Ballard [616].

## TMG 598
## SMOKEY ROBINSON & THE MIRACLES
### The Love I Saw In You Was Just A Mirage (2:59)
(Robinson—Tarplin)
Produced by William "Smokey" Robinson/Warren Moore
Recording completed: 28 Dec 1966
**Release Date**: 10 Mar 1967
**B-side**: Swept For You Baby
**Position in Record Retailer Top 40**: -
**Equivalent US Release**: Tamla 54145 (27 Jan 1967)
**Position in Billboard Top 40 Pop**: 20
**Position in Billboard Top 40 R & B**: 10

---

Smokey Robinson / Bobby Rogers / Claudette Rogers Robinson /
Warren 'Pete' Moore / Ronnie White

---

Yet more references to Bob Dylan [540] appear here in Marv Tarplin's plucked intro, doubled by mandolin and strongly suggestive of the famous opening of The Byrds' "Mr. Tambourine Man" (June 1965), the most important cover from Dylan's extensive songbook. Played in G, Tarplin's riff was probably written on the guitar's three bass strings, and likely formed from a doodle around Roger McGuinn's original figure, from which Robinson developed the song's structure. As with "Mr. Tambourine Man", the resultant verses rely heavily on a two-chord exchange, swapping between G and C¹, a casual Robinson uncharacteristically short on musical inspiration.

Conversely, his much-admired lyric, 'the zenith' of 'Robinson's penchant for imaginative metaphors'², shows genuine sagacity, concerning the shattering realisation that the girl of the singer's desires had been toying with him all along. Picturesque and eloquent, Robinson's verses make much of the apparent illusory aspect of his predicament, portraying common-or-garden insincerity on her part as a clandestine complex of trickery and deceit, a self-defensive attitude prevalent amongst the spurned, and possibly sourced from true experience (although Robinson had been with Claudette for nine years, marrying her in 1959).

Issued in January 1967, the track carried full credit to Smokey Robinson in the group's name, a move aimed to capitalise on his pre-eminence and symbolic of Motown's recurrent drive to make individual stars out of its group's leading lights ([616]; [621]; [797], etc.). Subsequently included on *Make It Happen*, the track shared album space with "The Tears Of A Clown" [745], which when eventually recognised and issued as a single in America was backed with "Promise Me" before a re-mixed version of "The Love I Saw In You Was Just A Mirage" was substituted (Tamla 54199).

[1] In the Harmonised Major scale, we are referring to I-IV. Dylan's original is in F, The Byrds transposing to D to accommodate their complex vocal arrangement—much harder to play than in Tarplin's G. The riff also bears comparison with that of "My Girl" [E67], pitched in C but also playable on the guitar's bass strings, and used by Robinson as an endless source of inspiration during the mid-1960s.

[2] Bill Dahl. See Abbott p79.


## TMG 599
## MARTHA & THE VANDELLAS
**Jimmy Mack** (2:47)
(Holland—Dozier—Holland)
Produced by Brian Holland/Lamont Dozier
Recording completed: 17 Jan 1967
**Release Date**: 17 Mar 1967
**B-side**: Third Finger, Left Hand
**Position in Record Retailer Top 40**: 21
**Equivalent US Release**: Gordy 7058 (3 Feb 1967)
**Position in Billboard Top 40 Pop**: 10
**Position in Billboard Top 40 R & B**: 1

---

Martha Reeves / Rosalind Ashford / Betty Kelly

---

An early critic of Berry Gordy's remuneration policy, Martha Reeves found herself intermittently at loggerheads with Motown in 1967, unhappy about the company's attitude towards her once powerful group, by now in their eighth different incarnation. Informing Berry Gordy one day that she considered him incapable of running Motown properly, she found herself increasingly isolated and starved of top material. In fact the extent of her estrangement from the heart of Motown is revealed by her claim that "Jimmy Mack" was prepared for release without her knowledge, which if true vindicates her position somewhat.

"Jimmy Mack" was, like [582], an old track, first made on 18 June 1964 and mixed for release as a single in July, only to be usurped by the undoubtedly superior "Dancing In The Street" [E54] and shelved. (Dave Godin remembered hearing it during his first trip to Detroit in the 'early summer' of that year.[1]) Lamont Dozier claims to have found the central character's name at a BMI awards ceremony in 1963, the 'real' Jimmy in fact Ronnie Mack, who had won a posthumous award for The Chiffons' "He's So Fine", his emotional mother there to collect it on his behalf.[2] In this light the track's subject matter, a female's yearning for her missing lover, seems oblique if written around the events Dozier observed, the thrust of the final lyric implying to Reeves an association with the Vietnam war: With 'Jimmy Mack' away, the narrator finds herself drawn towards another man, pleading rhetorically for Jimmy to return home and save her from her own temptation, in this context, a wholly 'unpatriotic' scenario for an American pop song.

Guaranteed to provoke a backlash if seen as such, "Jimmy Mack" was probably begun with no such connotations in mind. Nonetheless, the 1964 recording was shelved until its belated inclusion of the group's *Watchout!* at the tail end of 1966. At once noticed by Berry Gordy, "Jimmy Mack" was prepared for single, HDH returning to the original tapes to find an alternative take which was mixed for release. Brightened up and 'modernised' with the inclusion of stomping feet on sheets of cardboard on 17 January, the appearance of this alternative version falsely implies that the single version was a recent remake.[3]

Released as race riots were erupting in various American cities, "Jimmy Mack" is, like "Dancing In The Street" [684], rather insinuating, linked by time and place with civil unrest. In Britain where the atmosphere was cooler, "Jimmy Mack" slipped in and out of the top 30 almost unnoticed, not making any significant impact. Re-pressed and re-distributed on 1 May 1970 on the back of a couple of successful re-issues [684], [694], fans returned it to the charts for a prolonged stay, in total amassing some five months in the listings without ever entering the top 20.[4]

The intervening period was one in which the group consolidated its UK following, re-recording a number of early numbers for a compilation album, but the single's continued popularity saw it again re-pressed in 1972, its popular appeal helped by HDH's B-side, itself of minor cult status. This time the sides were swapped for radio play, "Third Finger, Left Hand" a mid-1964 cut sent out to DJs for a 're-release' on 9 Jun 1972.

The song celebrates the wedding of its central character, and specifically the 'placing' of the 'wedding band', a naïvely antiquated notion in the aftermath of the sexually liberating 1960s [677]. The song may well have taken its cue from the world of movies (see also [E69]), its title corresponding to the Robert Z. Leonard film of 1940, in which black actor Ernest Whitman was depicted as educated, intelligent and ultimately successful, in contrast to the general screen portrayal of black people in its day. The theme of the song however has nothing further to do with the movie, being purely an exclamation of delight at the fact that the couple are in the process of tying the knot.

The release was never going to be a hit, making the re-promotion of the disc somewhat difficult to comprehend. The label's other flipped singles ([690b], [692b] and [783b]) had been planned to pick up on current interest in their B-sides; this recording pre-dated even the Tamla Motown label and was best left as a B-side.

[1] Abbott, p22.

[2] Quoted in Davis 1988, p191. (Davis erroneously dates the event to 1966.)

[3] It is possible to verify that the two versions are entirely separate takes since the

single, made on Hitsville's 8-track console, runs at almost the same tempo as the other but pitches just over a semitone lower. The stereo album version was later released in the UK on October's British *Motown Chartbusters*. (This compilation album also features the unedited version of [582] rather than the single version.) This LP was the first in a series of about a dozen, initially coming out as year-end anthologies of the label's biggest recent hits, and overlapping with the *Big Hits* compilations which continued to appear, based on similar lines. The first of the *Chartbusters* collections covered singles released between August 1966 and June 1967 (comprising [570]; [571]; [577]; [582]; [585]; [587]; [589]; [590]; [597]; [599]; [603]; [604]; [607]; [609]; [612]; [613]). Later volumes milked Tamla Motown's re-issues to bolster their contents.

[4] Reeves claims that the song's fame gave rise to the semi-offensive rappers' term Mack Daddy (Reeves, p141), although in fact the phrase dates back to the 1950s.

## TMG 600
## SHORTY LONG
**Chantilly Lace** (2:30)
(Richardson)
Produced by Clarence Paul
Recording completed: 10 Nov 1966
**Release Date**: 17 Mar 1967
**B-side**: Your Love Is Amazing
**Position in Record Retailer Top 40**: -
**Equivalent US Release**: Soul 35031 (26 Jan 1967)
**Position in Billboard Top 40 Pop**: -
**Position in Billboard Top 40 R & B**: -

Tamla Motown's landmark 100th single belongs to Shorty Long, his third 45 and one of the label's more curious releases. A self-composed hit for Texas-born Jiles Perry Richardson (aka The Big Bopper) in 1958, the song was his only success before his death less than a year later at the age of 28, in the same plane crash which claimed Buddy Holly and Ritchie Valens.

Long's version slows the song to a swagger, the archetypal Funk Brothers performance locating it firmly within Motown's mainstream despite its novel (for them) pace. Ultimately too flat for the dance market and too staid for the hit parade, the track, while competently executed, goes nowhere. (It was omitted from Long's *Essential Collection* CD in 2000.) The flip-side, a Four Tops album track from HDH, would have made a better choice—possibly it was stylistically too similar to [599] to be considered viable.

## TMG 601
## FOUR TOPS
**Bernadette** (2:57)
(Holland—Dozier—Holland)
Produced by Brian Holland/Lamont Dozier
Recording completed: 25 Jan 1967
**Release Date**: 23 Mar 1967[1]
**B-side**: I Got A Feeling
**Position in Record Retailer Top 40**: 8

**Equivalent US Release**: Motown 1104 (16 Feb 1967)
**Position in Billboard Top 40 Pop**: 4
**Position in Billboard Top 40 R & B**: 3

Levi Stubbs / Lawrence Payton / Abdul 'Duke' Fakir / Renaldo 'Obie' Benson

The opening of Motown's LA studios in June 1966, whist ostensibly providing for greater turnover, altered the dynamics between The Funk Brothers and Motown (i.e. Berry Gordy) for good. Believing themselves irreplaceable, the band worked as normal through the late 1960s, confident that Gordy would never consider dispensing with their services, so sure were they that he recognised their virtuosity as the bedrock of Motown's success. For his part, Gordy never lost sight of the fact that Motown was his *business*, and in expanding out of Detroit, he knew he was weakening the collective clout of his employees, and reserving an option on replacing them altogether, should the need ever arise.

As regards the recording of "Bernadette" in early-1967, opinion is sharply divided as to whether it is in fact LA product. Although it is possible that the track was part-made in Detroit with additional overdubs in LA (as was the contemporary [597]), the issue of the octave-ranging bass line, one of Motown's most admired, is particularly thorny. Carol Kaye has strenuously claimed the performance as her own, recalling a session directed by Gene Page in which she and the band fluffed the first couple of takes.[2] Unsurprisingly, Jamerson's supporters have rallied to his cause, drummer James Gadson recalling discussing the session with him, details of which Jamerson specifically remembered.[3] Unravelling the truth with Jamerson not around to make his case is difficult, hampered by the fact that, where employed, Motown's other bass players were instructed to imitate Jamerson to the extent that the figures they came up with would often be virtual steals from his catalogue, while engineers elsewhere would strive to supply the necessary EQ-ing to simulate the exact bass sound acquired at Hitsville. Some critics claim to be able to differentiate between Kaye and Jamerson on the basis that the former used a plectrum, whereas Jamerson played all his lines with just his index finger, but pulling such detail aurally from tracks such as "Bernadette", with its swelteringly dense arrangement, is fraught with difficulty, especially as points of reference—his other contemporaneous lines—must by the same token be of uncertain status.

"Bernadette" is structured from the same descending chord sequence as "Standing In The Shadows Of Love" [589], transposed from Am to Ebm (probably to assist Levi Stubbs with the vocal line). Sharing the same 'Arabic' qualities which occurred to Jamerson previously, the melodic rises and falls of the chorus constitute a style-exercise unmistakably Eastern in flavour.[4] In the afore-mentioned discussion with James Gadson, Jamerson stated that when recording his bass parts, he was 'dreaming that I was in the desert riding a camel', which while appropriate as an application to absorb the song's mood, is for Jamerson a flight of fancy. (He has cited inspirations from his everyday surroundings for other bass lines including the sound of car engines, the sway of flowers in the breeze and, on one Temptations number, the rhythm of an overweight woman's backside as she walked.) Suitably inspired, the bass line has an irrepressible energy, loaded with double and triple notes where singles would do, Jamerson unable to restrain himself and pitching in one of his most admired contributions.

The subject of the song, the enigmatic *femme fatale* is in fact a composite character based on a number of real Bernadettes known through prior relationships to all three of the HDH team. Imbued with personal meaning for each of them, the uncommon use of a specific name in the chorus was agreed at the behest of Brian Holland, main architect of the track's arrangement. Most of the remaining lyric was his brother's, taking direct quotes from a telephone conversation with a troubled girlfriend (see also [501], prompted via a similar process).

Commencing with an oppressive thumping of bass shivering with tambourine, this pressured and feverish number stands comparison with both "Reach Out I'll Be There" [579] and "Standing In The Shadows Of Love" [589] (usually regarded together as a trilogy). Yet while the three tracks share a wide-frequency layering thanks to their musical arrangements, "Bernadette" has little else to do with [589], borrowing just the flute feel (shifted here to the French horn), confined to a brief middle-8. Otherwise, it stands intensely paranoid against "Reach Out's" ungrudging generosity, relaying the plight of a man racked with jealousy and cut off from his closest friends through imagined designs they may have on his Bernadette. Paradoxically accusing them of being out of control, it is Stubbs, unable to live without his lover, who is beyond rationality, lost in a whirl of hysteria and on the verge of collapse. (Crashing back with increased fervour after a tension-filled pause for breath, he can be heard at the song's very close breaking down with an imploring 'My darling!'.)

Widely regarded as superlative, Stubbs' singing on "Bernadette" becomes thinner and more frantic as things progress, his accentuation and diction famously likened by Phil Spector to that of Bob Dylan. Soaring through the song with emergency, his performance verges on a gutsy roar, developed beyond recognition from the controlled suaveness of "Ask The Lonely" [507] just two years previous. Greatly admired by Berry Gordy, Stubbs' recording convinced him that the singer, 'Could interpret and deliver the meaning of a song better than anybody'[5], his virtuosity here supported by a bank of angelic, wordless backing vocals.[6] With both The Four Tops and HDH reaching the height of their achievements, Gordy's faith in the team may have known no bounds at the start of 1967, but unknown to him this would be their last truly great collaboration.

[1] Demo copies have the date stated erroneously as 23 Feb.

[2] See Abbott, p92-100. Kaye claims that she recognised the bass line as hers when the track was broadcast over the radio, citing a brief mistake which was let through. (She is not specific as to where this occurs. Although loosely improvised in places, there is no technical error audible to this listener, except possibly an unintentional missing octave leap in the final chorus at 2:26.)

[3] Slutsky, p39.

[4] The Arabic scale, which works against a drone, is not fully viable in the Western modal system. A 'true' Arabic melody against Eb would have no C# as sung here, yet the more valid D would sound discordant with the harmonics of Western pop music.

[5] Gordy, p223. He continued, "He made Bernadette live. I wanted to meet her myself."
[6] Heard in isolation on the BBC's *The Producers* (2007), the backing vocals have a disturbingly ethereal quality. Andante Louvain Demps [507n] likens them to Gregorian chanting.

## TMG 602
## STEVIE WONDER
**Travelin' Man** (2:53)
(Miller—Wells)
Produced by Clarence Paul
Recording completed: 10 Jan 1967
**Release Date**: 31 Mar 1967
**B-side**: Hey Love
**Position in Record Retailer Top 40**: -
**Equivalent US Release**: Tamla 54147 (9 Feb 1967)
**Position in Billboard Top 40 Pop**: 32
**Position in Billboard Top 40 R & B**: 31 [B-side reached 9]

After a year-or-so of inconsistency, this jocular non-album track represents the most melodic single yet released by Wonder. A variation of the southern lullaby "Hush Little Baby" (possibly unintentional), it carries an air of drowsy contentment with Wonder's reflective vocals at odds with the theme of the text, which, like the animated "(I'm A) Road Runner" [559], deals with the lifestyle of a drifter.

Yet the essence of [559] is liberation through self-determination, contrasting sharply with Wonder's portrait of the wanderer here as aimless, isolated and ultimately desolate. Pitched in a similarly encumbered mood and tempo to The Beatles' "Nowhere Man", a big US hit a year earlier, the track utilises much the same phrase patterning in its verses, the same repertoire of chords (allowing for the transposition to G#), and a comparable title, leading to inevitable comparisons. (In fact another likely inspiration would been Jerry Fuller's unwanted composition of the same name for Sam Cooke, which Ricky Nelson picked up and took to number 1 in 1961.)

Featuring some busy bass from James Jamerson, the track is neatly constructed and was undeserving of the disregard with which it was met. (With a number of Wonder's singles containing cryptic cross-references (e.g. "Nothing's Too Good For My Baby" [558] pulling a quote from "Uptight" [545]), the phrase 'old, worn-out heart' can be read as an apt contortion of 'Poor, restless heart' from his previous 45 [588], written by the same team.) In America "Hey Love" won over dance audiences and out-performed its A-side in the R & B charts.

## TMG 603
## JIMMY RUFFIN
**Gonna Give Her All The Love I've Got** (2:39)
(Strong—Whitfield)

Produced by Norman Whitfield
Recording completed: 22 Aug 1966
**Release Date**: 14 Apr 1967
**B-side**: World So Wide, Nowhere To Hide (From Your Heart)
**Position in Record Retailer Top 40**: 26
**Equivalent US Release**: Soul 35032 (23 Feb 1967)
**Position in Billboard Top 40 Pop**: 29
**Position in Billboard Top 40 R & B**: 14

Built largely on a single chord, the empty, bass-dependent verses of Jimmy
Ruffin's third UK single leave his scoped vocals dangerously exposed,
revealing a shaky falsetto at 1:02, another forced at 2:08 (for which he can be
heard drawing breath) and some superfluous decorations in the choruses,
which occasionally clash with The Originals' backing singing. Further
technical imperfection can be heard on James Jamerson's enterprising bass
which sustains the note of C through much of the song, including the 16-bar
intro in which his Fender is tuned fractionally sharp.

Putting these flaws aside, "Gonna Give Her All The Love I Got" is a
buoyant article, brought to a rousing climax in its swervingly orchestrated
chorus sections. The carefree tale of a just-released jailbird looking forward
to returning to his former love after years of lonely incarceration (to 'hug
her, kiss her, squeeze her...'), the song says nothing of the central
character's history, focussing exclusively on the joy of liberty. (Finding
Ruffin in Sam Cooke territory, the song's sparse arrangement is
reminiscent of "Chain Gang" (1960), with its similar portrayal of a
prisoner missing his woman, and whose 'ooh-aahs' Ruffin makes takes a
half-hearted stab at.)[1]

Effectively marking the arrival of the Barrett Strong—Norman Whitfield
team, the track warrants a significant footnote in Tamla Motown's history.
Requiring a more committed co-writer than Eddie Holland, over-worked
within the HDH setup, Whitfield had at last found his key collaborator,
back in the fold after some years working for Chicago-based Vee Jay. By the
end of 1967 the duo would be firmly at the forefront of Motown's future
reckoning.

[1] The Supremes had recorded a version of "Chain Gang" for *We Remember Sam Cooke*
(April 1965), also included on the 1966 UK EP *Shake* (see Appendix 1).


**TMG 604**
**GLADYS KNIGHT & THE PIPS**
**Take Me In Your Arms And Love Me** (2:56)
(Strong—Penzabene—Grant)
Produced by Norman Whitfield
Recording completed: 21 Jan 1967
**Release Date**: 28 Apr 1967
**B-side**: Do You Love Me Just A Little, Honey
**Position in Record Retailer Top 40**: 13

**Equivalent US Release**: Soul 35033 (16 Mar 1967)
**Position in Billboard Top 40 Pop**: -
**Position in Billboard Top 40 R & B**: -

Gladys Knight / Merald 'Bubba' Knight / Edward Patten / William Guest

Pulled from tour with The Supremes for upstaging them, Gladys Knight found herself joining the rumble of discontent being heard from a number of Motown's stars in 1967 [599]. Perceiving career-blocking favouritism from Gordy, various staff were becoming sufficiently restless that a meeting to discuss matters was convened at Knight's home in the spring of 1967, attended by Marvin Gaye and Martha Reeves amongst others.

An outsider, Knight was confident that she and her self-reliant group could survive the ultimate sanction of being sacked by Gordy and was more willing to push her luck than some of her colleagues, dependent as they were on Motown for future employment (among them too, her frustrated producer Norman Whitfield). In the end, 'the malcontents' achieved little, rumours that Gordy was onto them sufficient to stymie the threatened rebellion, against the backdrop of hardship in Detroit which would face anyone pushed out and—as was Gordy's wont—blacklisted.

Good timing ensured that "Take Me In Your Arms And Love Me" became Gladys Knight & The Pips' first UK hit, bubbling around the lower end of the top 40 for some three and a half months. The bulk of the lyric and title, recalling HDH's earlier "Take Me In Your Arms (Rock Me A Little While)" [538], was seemingly supplied by Roger Penzabene (in collaborations with Cornelius Grant), reflecting the turmoil of his personal life in 1967. His marriage in disarray, he formulated the central theme in which the singer implores her lover to embrace her by way of initiating a lasting reconciliation (the overtly sexual nature of which was masked behind the well-worn euphemism, 'love me').

Although Knight's vocals are reliably soulful, something is lost via the arrangement, Whitfield's production uncharacteristically suffused with gimmicky harpsichord doodles, and an instrumental break in which strings doggedly reproduce the vocal melody.[1] Short of choruses, the song's title phrase at the end of each double line provides the hook, "Take Me In Your Arms" carrying an immediacy which won favour with British audiences, which was consolidated towards the end of the year when the group performed the song at the Saville Theatre to a rapturous response. Given the success of this and the imminent "I Heard It Through The Grapevine" [629], the shared malcontent of Knight and Whitfield developed into a professional bond which would endure for the next three years to their mutual advantage.

[1] Those playing this and [603] back to back will notice the similarity of the introductions, both commencing with the same G bass note overlaid with a high riff, again carelessly out of tune here. Jamerson famously refused to re-string his bass guitar, only replacing individual stings on the rare occasions that they broke, but must have corrected his tuning before and during every recording session.

**TMG 605**

**THE CONTOURS**

**It's So Hard Being A Loser** (2:37)
(Dean—Weatherspoon—McMullen)
Produced by William Weatherspoon/James Dean
Recording completed: 14 Dec 1966
**Release Date**: 5 May 1967
**B-side**: Your Love Grows More Precious Every Day
**Position in Record Retailer Top 40**: -
**Equivalent US Release**: Gordy 7059 (9 Mar 1967)
**Position in Billboard Top 40 Pop**: -
**Position in Billboard Top 40 R & B**: 35

---

Dennis Edwards / Gerald Green / Council Gay / Sylvester Potts

---

The Contours' third and final Tamla Motown single (re-issues aside) illustrates a belated attempt to pull the group into the commercial arena currently occupied by Motown's primary male artists. The track's self-sorry lyric steers towards the recent ballads of Jimmy Ruffin, for whom it was initially intended, but with an effete chorus which guts the track of real feeling. (Lead singer here is recent recruit and future Temptation Dennis Edwards [707], backed by The Andantes.)

A pleasant single in the popular context, "It's So Hard Being A Loser" hints at where The Contours' development might have been leading, had Berry Gordy retained interest in the group which had provided him with one of his earliest successes [E10]. (The group's forthcoming album, only their second, was scrapped before release.)


**TMG 606**

**THE ISLEY BROTHERS**

**Got To Have You Back** (2:45)
(Hunter—Ware—Bowden)
Produced by Ivy Jo Hunter
Recording completed: 9 Jan 1967
**Release Date**: 12 May 1967
**B-side**: Just Ain't Enough Love
**Position in Record Retailer Top 40**: -
**Equivalent US Release**: Tamla 54146 (30 Mar 1967)
**Position in Billboard Top 40 Pop**: -
**Position in Billboard Top 40 R & B**: -

---

Ronald Isley / Rudolph Isley / O'Kelly Isley

---

Freelancer Leon Ware had been on the periphery of Motown for some years, having formerly sung with The Romeos, alongside Lamont Dozier and his collaborator here, future Original Ty Hunter. A rudimentary composition built mainly on a chord shuffle around C#, the track is notable for its proto-psychedelic arrangement, the most unusual sound yet employed on an Isley Brothers production.

More deliberately 'Indian' than Tamla Motown's prior venture into the idiom [552], "Got To Have You Back" engages a prominent sitar-like lead guitar, mixed hard-right in stereo and overdriven to resonate over the studio ensemble; the lead guitar was probably taped live with the rest of the band, James Jamerson playfully tracking the riff on bass at 1:26. Competing with the sitar-guitar effect is a particularly acute harpsichord, confusingly also placed on the right channel and indicating that the keyboard instrument may have been a temporary fixture at Hitsville, explaining its presence on a number of contemporary numbers such as [597] and [604]. (In which case, the tense arrangement on [597] owes its bulk to Detroit's arrangers.)

Unfortunately, the effort expended in dressing up a solid soul stomp with flavour-of-the-month effects backfired, merely detracting from the central quality of The Isley Brothers' raw recording. Coupled up with an old Eddie Holland number, the single was released in Britain in May but ignored by the general public.


**TMG 607**
**THE SUPREMES**
**The Happening** (2:50)
(Holland—Dozier—Holland—DeVol)
Produced by Brian Holland/Lamont Dozier
Recording completed: 8 Mar 1967
**Release Date**: 5 May 1967
**B-side**: All I Know About You
**Position in Record Retailer Top 40**: 6
**Equivalent US Release**: Motown 1107 (20 Mar 1967)
**Position in Billboard Top 40 Pop**: 1
**Position in Billboard Top 40 R & B**: 12

---

Diana Ross / Florence Ballard / Mary Wilson

---

The widespread youthful idealism of 1966-67, focussed by the flowering hippie movement, brought with it a number of cutting-edge avant-garde arts events, known in the parlance of the day as 'happenings'. Ranging from impromptu concerts to audience-participation events, the underlying purpose was to challenge to the quality of one's awareness, the term 'happening' as plainly descriptive and (theoretically) non-predictive as the self-defining 'be-in', the blossoming youth movement's overlapping LSD-inspired social-inclusion events.

Pinning down the key clash between young and old in the 1960s, the hip emphasis on the quality of the here-and-now was irreconcilable with the previous generation's credence that gratification be deferred and one's excessive impulses curbed. Rooted in the triumph of science over mysticism, the underlying philosophical shift of the 1960s was a widespread resignation to the view that life itself was largely the product of blind mechanical-biological determinism. Effectively erasing God from the reckoning, and with it, any conceivable notion of an afterlife, the exercise of denial in return for some future pay-off became seen as a pointless scam, the suspicion being that the old were plotting at the expense of the young.[1]

The backlash to this paradigm shift from the conservative powers of the day was determined on both sides of the Atlantic. The irreconcilability of the two world-views was brought home to Detroit on April 30, when a peaceful hippie gathering in the city was forcibly terminated by a police-led riot, followed within days by the arrest in Britain of three Rolling Stones. On May 21, a mass rally against the Vietnam war was staged in London, ignored by an indifferent government bent instead on persecuting countercultural figures such as John Hopkins, jailed on June 1 (the day *Sgt. Pepper* was released), two days before race riots erupted in Boston.

Impossible to translate into the material world of commerce, the concept of 'happenings'—which belonged to their participants—was inevitably hijacked and applied to business ventures in an attempt to package and sell them to young audiences. *The Happening* was a briefly popular Hollywood movie starring Anthony Quinn and Faye Dunaway, concerning a bungled kidnapping and scored by Frank DeVol, a renowned Hollywood movie composer-conductor whose contemporary work included the theme to *The Dirty Dozen*. Commissioned to provide a title track for the film, HDH borrowed from DeVol to construct the current song which consequently carries one of their most unorthodox chord sequences: starting plainly with a run through G/C/D/G the song unexpectedly lurches to Bb, pulling up through Eb to an assertive G#, which is finally released on an ambiguous D major, ready to go back around again (Ian MacDonald: 'Almost pure Broadway').[2] Commencing with an instrumental section written as the song's middle-16[3], the recurring collision between adjacent verses necessitates forced truncation or, where unavoidable, an overlapping of lines in order that everything be packed into the limited space.

Correspondingly inventive, the lyrics veer between the orthodox love scenarios of old and something altogether more ambiguous and ephemeral, an undercurrent of perceptive confusion clouding the issue, probably descended in part from John Lennon's recent "Strawberry Fields Forever" in which a similar sense of uncertainty between reality and illusion is present. The line referring to 'pretty balloon' however pays more direct homage to the child's perspective of the psychedelic scene, and specifically anticipates The Fifth Dimension's contemporary hit "Up Up And Away".[4] Yet the song may have been finished to deadline, as betrayed by some of the lazy rhymes. (Compare the casual slant of "woke up" and "walked up" in the first verse with the more typically emboldened rhyming of 'sure', 'secure' and 'detour' in the second. Some speculate that DeVol may have been largely responsible for the lyric, which would mean his compositional input ultimately dwarfs that of HDH.)

According to accepted accounts, the backing track for "The Happening" was recorded in LA on March 2, the tapes shipped back to Detroit where an unimpressed Berry Gordy insisted The Funk Brothers re-record it. Some sources however claim that only Jamerson was required at Hitsville to re-do the bass, although standard practice would have been to leave the vocal overdub session until last. Whatever the case, the musicianship on "The

Happening" is exceptional, the bass parts of particular merit, and the ensemble style-exercise jazzy and polished. Cleverly produced, the understated flutes track the lead vocals except in the contrasting sections where they switch their attentions to the backing singers, vying for supremacy with bass and brass in the brilliantly atmospheric second 'middle-16', the track's most penetrating passage.[5]

Issued as a stand-alone single to coincide with the film premiere, "The Happening" topped the American charts, peaking at a respectable number 6 in the UK. The final Supremes single with Florence Ballard present, hindsight gives an altogether different angle on the text of the song, so uncannily do the contradictory and inconclusive lyrics fit her story. Significantly, in the interval between the US and UK releases, Ballard was suspended from the group's stage act prior to a performance at the Hollywood Bowl. Her stand-in was Cindy Birdsong—see [616].

[1] Coincidentally, the Darwinian view of the origins of life had been taken its inevitable step to include human beings by T. H. Huxley, grandfather of 1960s LSD guru Aldous.

[2] 2003, p187. A possible inspiration was the track 'My Favourite Things' from the then massively commercial *Sound Of Music* soundtrack, a number included in the group's American Christmas album of 1965 which contains a similarly inelegant chord run.

[3] The structure of the song is vague. There is no defined chorus, the 'hook' occurring at the close of each verse. Two different 'middle-8s' can be identified, the first of which ('One day you're up...') takes the place of the usual chorus, the other (ranging across 16 bars) consisting of the intro's recapitulation ('And then it happened ...').

[4] The Fifth Dimension were managed by Motown's Marc Gordon (see for example [537]) and played support to The Supremes in April 1967. "Up Up And Away" was written by Jimmy Webb and covered in turn by The Supremes later in the year.

[5] An early version, included in the box set The Supremes (2000) features superfluous lead vocals across this instrumental section, wisely excised during work on the track.

## TMG 608
## BRENDA HOLLOWAY
**Just Look What You've Done** (2:53)
(Wilson—Taylor)
Produced by Frank Wilson
Recording completed: 29 Dec 1966
**Release Date**: 19 May 1967
**B-side**: Starting The Hurt All Over Again
**Position in Record Retailer Top 40**: -
**Equivalent US Release**: Tamla 54148 (9 Mar 1967)
**Position in Billboard Top 40 Pop**: -
**Position in Billboard Top 40 R & B**: 21

Why "Just Look What You've Done" missed out as a hit single is puzzling, carrying as it does an irresistible pulsing rhythm and an adventurous, catchy melody which rises boldly to an unexpected G during the song's chorus. Buoyantly moulded, the single deals with its doleful theme with good cheer, eschewing the underlying anxiety of the similarly pitched "What Am I Going To Do Without Your Love" [567].

With Motown electing to close its administrative centre at Los Angeles in 1966, Frank Wilson was now permanently based in Detroit, collaborating here with Richard Dean Taylor, a white Canadian tutored by Brian Holland. The track must have been regarded as a potential monster, its commerciality coupled with Holloway's sensual image the right ingredients for a smash hit. Yet Holloway, with no regular writer-producer to help shape her career, was consistently discounted by Motown's Detroit-centric establishment, finding a number of songs earmarked for her snatched away by others before she could record them, in the interests of production-line maximisation. Clearly frustrated by her lack of sales, Holloway was on the point of walking away for good.

**TMG 609**
**THE MARVELETTES**
**When You're Young And In Love** (2:38)
(McCoy)
Produced by James Dean/William Weatherspoon
Recording completed: 27 Oct 1966
**Release Date**: 19 May 1967
**B-side**: The Day You Take One (You Have To Take The Other)
**Position in Record Retailer Top 40**: 13
**Equivalent US Release**: Tamla 54150 (6 Apr 1967)
**Position in Billboard Top 40 Pop**: 23
**Position in Billboard Top 40 R & B**: 9

Gladys Horton / Wanda Young / Katherine Anderson

Penned in 1962 by Leiber & Stoller's 18-year-old protégée Van McCoy, "When You're Young And In Love" has a novel chord structure which makes a joyous feature of its liberating key changes, giving the illusion of ceaseless ascent. (In fact, the verses are constructed from basic doo-wop chords, an initial run in C followed by the same progression in Eb.) First recorded in 1964 by Ruby & The Romantics, the track was picked up by Motown for The Marvelettes, considered by Gordy to have been led incautiously out of their territory by Smokey Robinson with [594].

Prefixed by a somewhat overblown Gershwin-esque 'classical' introduction[1], backed up with a 15-second drum-roll, the song proper arrives as a carefree release, the reassuring bass guitar and high-flying violins defusing the implied tension of its prelude. Ultimately a bit of fun, the track got The Marvelettes into the UK top 40 at the fourteenth attempt (!), finally reflecting their popular appeal in America, where they had already enjoyed a string of hits.

Putting "When You're Young And In Love" on the map, The Marvelettes' definitive version spawned numerous further covers over the years including a top 10 acappella version in 1984 for The Flying Pickets.

[1] Probably based on the overture to "Live Wire" [E36]. Compare also with the similarly dramatic prelude to Gloria Gaynor's 1979 hit "I Will Survive", co-written by former Motowner Freddie Perren.

**TMG 610**
**THE TEMPTATIONS**
**All I Need** (2:59)
(Wilson—Holland—Taylor)
Produced by Frank Wilson
Recording completed: 15 Feb 1967
**Release Date**: 26 May 1967
**B-side**: Sorry Is A Sorry Word
**Position in Record Retailer Top 40**: -
**Equivalent US Release**: Gordy 7061 (13 Apr 1967)
**Position in Billboard Top 40 Pop**: 8
**Position in Billboard Top 40 R & B**: 2

---

Otis Williams / Melvin Franklin / Paul Williams / Eddie Kendricks / David Ruffin

Oddly leading *New Musical Express* to complain that The Temptations' material was becoming formulaic[1], "All I Need" is in fact quite unlike their recent singles, strong on propulsive melody and lightly melancholic in contrast to the intensity of "Get Ready" [557] and "(I Know) I'm Losing You" [587] and the musical discontinuations of "Ain't Too Proud To Beg" [565] and "Beauty Is Only Skin Deep" [578]. Sketched out in instrumental form, "All I Need" was a Frank Wilson creation relying on the same triplet-bouncing foundation as "You Can't Hurry Love" [575]. Shown to partner Eddie Holland and his brother's student R. Dean Taylor [608], the track was swiftly polished off as one of the groups' most mercurial and uncertain to date.

With its tortured sequence of unresolved chords and lucid representation of the pain of experienced by a remorseful adulterer ('tears of guilt running down my face'), the track is a balancing counterpoint to [587], implying that, in situations of personal betrayal, everyone involved eventually loses.

[1] Review excerpted in Morse p31:"Absolutely typical of the Tamla [sic] output... The Temptations would do well in future to vary their style a bit". More likely, *NME* were merely intent on unimaginatively continuing the current swell of anti-Motown opinion in the music press, perversely leading their criticism back on itself.

**TMG 611**
**MARVIN GAYE & TAMMI TERRELL**
**Ain't No Mountain High Enough** (2:28)
(Ashford—Simpson)
Produced by Harvey Fuqua/Johnny Bristol
Recording completed: 29 Jan 1967
**Release Date**: 2 Jun 1967
**B-side**: Give A Little Love
**Position in Record Retailer Top 40**: -
**Equivalent US Release**: Tamla 54149 (20 Apr 1967)
**Position in Billboard Top 40 Pop**: 19
**Position in Billboard Top 40 R & B**: 3

Having made a minor name for themselves in the mid-1960s, primarily through some novel compositions for Ray Charles, Nickolas Ashford and Valerie Simpson were speculatively approached by Motown and signed to Jobete in 1966. One of their first products was "Ain't No Mountain High Enough" drawing inspiration from Phil Spector's "River Deep, Mountain High", recorded by Ike and Tina Turner earlier in the year (and which The Supremes & Four Tops would subsequently cover [777]). Attracting interest from the Fuqua—Bristol team, the song was accordingly acquisitioned and offered to Tammi Terrell, who recorded her spontaneous-sounding vocal early in the new year (at one point she turns from the mike to read from a lyric sheet, causing a minor drop out at 0:18).

Elsewhere, Berry Gordy was contemplating his unsettled fellow Marvin Gaye, whose recently promised move into duets had been thwarted for a second time, by the loss of Kim Weston [590]. Remarking around the turn of the year that "Ain't No Mountain High Enough" might suit Gaye, Billie-Jean Brown planted an idea in Gordy's mind; experiencing a flash of historic insight, he realised that Terrell's track would be the perfect vehicle to revive Gaye's duetting career, and duly arranged for him to dub some vocals onto the master on January 29, wiping some of Terrell's original lines.[1] The consequent collage, sparkling and seamless, radiates an unadulterated joy through its 2:28 like nothing recorded previously, standing proud amongst Motown's finest-ever creations. Commencing with a premonitory, rattling introduction, the track gradually unfurls in stages, vibes and bells glistening, before the chorus gloriously arrives, bursting with exhilaration and shimmering with tambourine, at once elated and dazzling.

In truth, the strength of the track lies in the coming together of its constituents, uncannily fusing some first-class musicianship and inspired production which belie its piecemeal development. And yet deconstruction is difficult; clearly Ashford & Simpson deserve a good deal of credit along with the track's producers, but so too does Berry Gordy, whose spark of genius took the recording to its new dimension. As for The Funk Brothers, James Jamerson's bubbling bass, replete with characteristic triplets was reckoned by him his best ever, prompting *Rolling Stone* to describe his contribution as 'explosive', adding that no other contemporary player could have devised the lines.[2] And that is to say nothing of the song's two chief performers, whose electrifying sexual chemistry underpins the recording, and was missed by few who heard it, despite the fact that neither Gaye nor Terrell ever admitted a relationship beyond the platonic.

With its religious metaphors and sweeping devotion working exquisitely for a minister's son, "Ain't No Mountain High Enough" was Marvin Gaye's renaissance piece, revelatory and forward-looking, setting a benchmark for a performing partnership which would salvage his career. Why it performed only modestly in the commercial arena is unclear, particularly given its exposure via a 1967 Coca-Cola television advert. It is perhaps unfortunate that Diana Ross' version [751], in which she disregards the melody in favour of a spoken lyric, has become the better-known; Gaye and Terrell's original brings Motown's diverse strengths together for a brief, unique moment in which it is more than mere cliché to say that the whole is greater than the sum of its parts.

[1] In an interview cited in Turner (p95) Johnny Bristol strongly implies that the two vocals were taped together live, recalling the assembled studio staff jumping up and down with delight at the result. While this idea suits the naturalness of the recording, especially in Gaye's spontaneous falsetto "ooh" during the middle-8, it contradicts the accepted version of events, and in any case is incongruous with the existence of Terrell's original solo recording. Versions have circulated with different vocal overdubs, suggesting that Gaye might have read the whole song, sections being mixed in and out subsequently.

[2] Jamerson's fluttering clusters in the chorus generate melodic ideas not otherwise present in the song, constituting a counterpoint musically independent of the track's chord structure and making sense on its own terms. The interview transcribed in 1990 for *Bass Player* records Jamerson's comments: "Probably my best melodic performance... I should have written a pop tune off that melody. I could have retired to Jamaica."

## TMG 612
## FOUR TOPS
### 7-Rooms Of Gloom (2:31)
(Holland—Dozier—Holland)
Produced by Brian Holland/Lamont Dozier
Recording completed: 23 Jan 1967
**Release Date**: 9 Jun 1967
**B-side**: I'll Turn To Stone
**Position in Record Retailer Top 40**: 12
**Equivalent US Release**: Motown 1110 (4 May 1967)
**Position in Billboard Top 40 Pop**: 14
**Position in Billboard Top 40 R & B**: 10

Levi Stubbs / Lawrence Payton / Abdul 'Duke' Fakir / Renaldo 'Obie' Benson

With *Sergeant Pepper's Lonely Hearts Club Band* sending what Ian MacDonald called a 'psychic shiver'[1] through the western world in June 1967, popular music appeared to be concerned primarily with optimistic ideals embodied by the so-called Summer of Love. Principally of more significance to white audiences than black, the tangible buzz in the air nonetheless crossed over, the mid-month Monterey Pop Festival attracting enthusiastic receptions for black performers including Jimi Hendrix and Otis Redding (the latter making one of his last appearances before his untimely death in December).

Amid the sunshine and flowers, The Four Tops' new offering was an encumbered affair which, perhaps due to its timing, became their first single in a year not to make the top 10. The dramatic narrative tells of an abandoned man isolated in a house which, metamorphosed by his grief, becomes a hollow, empty cage, the non-sequential line 'Turn this darkness into light' hinting at something allegorical and invoking the 'shadows' of his love affair [589]. Fading away unresolved, the track is pregnant with misery, Stubbs' vocals so imbued with emotion that he is almost raging at the microphone through three verses of unremitting torment.

Realising that the song was not as commercial as the group's recent singles, HDH put some effort into the arrangement in an attempt to provide some lift. Starting out with a miniaturised statement of the track's central theme from electric guitar and harpsichord, the verse proper arrives with drums and percussion, followed by Jamerson's bass, inventively panned across the stereo spectrum (although the mono single loses this detail). Yet the effects were cosmetic, "7-Rooms Of Gloom" a marked disappointment after "Bernadette" [601] despite the additional, unacknowledged input of the emergent R. Dean Taylor.[2]

Worthy of note, the flip-side was written a year previously for The Supremes, The Four Tops recording an unreleased version before taking it into their live act. (A rendition appeared on the early 1967 album, *Live!*) This, their second studio attempt, would subsequently gain release as an A-side, five years down the line [829].

[1] MacDonald, 1994

[2] Quoted in Davis 1988, p59, Taylor complains, "They [HDH] used to pay me cash for whatever I wrote and left my name off." He cites [589], [597] and [623] as similar examples.


**TMG 613**
**STEVIE WONDER**
**I Was Made To Love Her** (2:37)
(Cosby—Hardaway—Moy—Wonder)
Produced by Henry "Hank" Cosby
Recording completed: 31 Mar 1967
**Release Date**: 30 Jun 1967
**B-side**: Hold Me
**Position in Record Retailer Top 40**: 5
**Equivalent US Release**: Tamla 54151 (18 May 1967)
**Position in Billboard Top 40 Pop**: 2
**Position in Billboard Top 40 R & B**: 1

Supposedly written in ten minutes, Stevie Wonder's eighth Tamla Motown single was his first to enter the UK top 10, the lyric inspired by one of his former girlfriends [679b] and co-credited to his mother, former gospel singer Lula Hardaway (*née* Morris, *née* Judkins) in return for her supplying numerous staff with food during session work. As with a number of his earlier recordings (notably [545]), the track confidently ignores writing convention by avoiding structural norms, built from a sequence of four-bar 'verses' (the lyrics to some suggesting refrains, in that they cite the song's title) bisected by one brief contrasting section. Hypnotically cycling, the structure creates its relentless excitement from virtually nothing, the quadruple-bar repeats (according to Hank Cosby) pioneering and anticipating the discothèque boom of the 1970s.

Lyrically, the song repeats the rich-girl/poor-boy theme of [545], but with more novelty, idiosyncratically invoking chickens, magnolia trees and pigtails, and a choice use of the vernacular 'boo-hoo'. Tucked amongst the high-velocity excitement are a number of inside jokes which the writing team frequently play with for their own amusement, including a direct quote from Moy's own "My Baby Loves Me" [549], and another mention of Wonder himself at the fade.

Lyrical interest excepted, it would be folly not to acknowledge the recording's single most ear-catching ingredient: its astonishing, wide-ranging bass playing, taking in two octaves and displaying an articulacy remarkable even for Motown. The complete bass figure starts out with two bars of formalised riff (tracked in places by other instrumentation), which was probably provided by the song's composers and breaks free into some agitated improvisation around the octave-dropped riff notes for a further bar, followed by a rapid walk down to the note of Eb, rounding up on ascending triads through the keys C#, Eb and home to F. Dazzling in its casually delivered dexterity, Stevie Wonder was prompted to remark that Jamerson's playing "Made a certain fabric of my life visual"[1], the naturalness with which bass and vocals work together here illustrative of an artistic affinity between the two.

Notwithstanding, many claim that the track was recorded in LA, Kingsley Abbott claiming it 'well acknowledged', and throwing up questions as to who the featured musicians actually were.[2] Carol Kaye has accordingly claimed the bass line[3] (see also [515]), which if true would bring into doubt the similar sounding figures on some of Wonder's subsequent singles (especially [679] and [717]).

A composite group performance with discreetly mixed guitar, the song benefits from Wonder's inventive use of keyboards in the shape of celeste and Wurlitzer electric piano, a colourful tambourine and some high bells which add to its inherent sense of riotous fun. Conversely, the drumming (which consists mainly of a time-keeping bashing of the snare) is uncharacteristically light, suggesting in the context of Kaye's claims that it was not Benny Benjamin's handiwork.

At 17 years old, Wonder's rising popularity demanded some UK dates and in 1967 he appeared before elated crowds at Streatham's Locarno ballroom, a venue becoming renowned for its soul nights, and also attracting Edwin Starr amongst its headliners. For Wonder, 1967 was a pivotal year in which, after the disappointing "A Place In The Sun" [588] and 'Travelin' Man" [602], his career could have gone either way. As it transpired, "I Was Made To Love Her", with its innovative keyboard, laid the foundation stone for his work into the 1970s, remaining one of his best-loved track to this day.

[1] Quoted in Abbott, p91

[2] Ibid p92

[3] Although many Jamerson fans rubbish Kaye's claims, it is fair to say that she also has her supporters. Her comments on this track include the following from her interview in Abbott, which prove that she has at least studied the recorded line for its anatomical detail: "I particularly remember one, as it was the first time I was asked to play a lot of notes especially... This was the track for 'I Was Made To Love Her'... [I] had the first riff line written out, and only the first bar of the piece. Then the Db and Eb triads were written in that one bar, but I played them slightly different as I inched up the neck for the final riff in F". She continued, "I mentioned [to Wonder in 1988] 'I Was Made To Love Her' and he said, 'Yes, you cut that and quite a few others I did also'".

**TMG 614**
**SMOKEY ROBINSON & THE MIRACLES**
**More Love** (2:47)
(Robinson)
Produced by William "Smokey" Robinson
Recording completed: 26 Apr 1967
**Release Date**: 7 Jul 1967
**B-side**: Swept For You Baby [598b]¹
**Position in Record Retailer Top 40**: -
**Equivalent US Release**: Tamla 54152 (26 May 1967)
**Position in Billboard Top 40 Pop**: 23
**Position in Billboard Top 40 R & B**: 5

---

Smokey Robinson / Bobby Rogers / Claudette Rogers Robinson /
Warren 'Pete' Moore / Ronnie White

---

Countering the romantic view of 1967's summer as one in which universal love was the overriding value, the period was in truth marked by a steepening of tension between the establishment and the new generation [607]. That two incompatible world-views came to collide at the same time as mass pressure for racial equality is no coincidence; the movement for black emancipation was a central part of the widespread drive for social justice, the perceived threat to the conservative powers provoking a disproportionate clamping down on any signs of civil unrest.

In fact the stark cleavage between theatre and reality was vividly delineated in a series of violent incidents throughout the year, which Smokey Robinson & The Miracles experienced at first hand on May 20 when hundreds rioted following a concert in San Diego. In early July race riots ensued in Newark, where four days of mayhem suggested a less than all-inclusive relationship between black youth and the authorities. Eight days after 'order was restored', a Los Angeles love-in was staged simultaneously with the outbreak of race riots in Detroit, sharply delineating the era's ideological disparities and the gulf of experience separating the affluent (mainly white) youth from the ghettoised poor.²

The city's notorious 'Tac Squads' (police hit-squads who spent much of their time scouring black neighbourhoods, stop-searching youths, hunting down petty crime and raiding bars) helped turn the place into one of America's hot-beds of racial tension. At a rally in July, H. Rap Brown stated that if "Motown" [i.e. Detroit] didn't come around, then carnage would ensue and as if to wilfully light the touch paper, police raided a black gentleman's club on Detroit's 12th Street on July 23, drawing an angry crowd of youngsters who forced them to flee before going on the rampage and attacking white-owned establishments. After five days of mayhem, the military were sent in to put an end to things, but left a bloody trail behind them, with 43 black people slaughtered and another 1,200 injured (besides which an incredible 7,000 were arrested).

Sitting in the middle of the carnage was Hitsville, focal point of Berry Gordy's empire, at which accusing fingers were pointed from black protesters interpreting Motown's crossover policy as a pandering concession to white power. On the night the riots began, Martha & The Vandellas were performing at the local Fox Theater, where they were pulled off stage, hurrying to their respective homes amid sirens and gunshots. An appalled Marvin Gaye meantime was at his home watching events unfold on television, disbelieving of the carnage which would leave a deep enough impression to affect his outlook for years to come [802]. At the same moment, down at Studio A The Funk Brothers were emerging from a late-night session to the unexpected sight of burning buildings, prompting a number of them to run for their safety, while fearful Motown staff hurried around Motown's complex on West Grand Boulevard clutching precious documents and master tapes.

In the aftermath of what became known as America's worst-ever race riot, Smokey Robinson recorded the heartfelt "I Care About Detroit", released as a promotional single in an effort to calm tensions. Black society however was by-and-large in no mood for forgiveness, a festering tension permeating the Detroit air long after the disturbances had dissipated [667] and the police guard at Hitsville was stood down. Berry Gordy reports receiving abusive phone calls and bomb threats from former rioters, and in due course decided that, in the interests of self-protection, he would relocate his central offices uptown to the 10-storey Donovan Building at 2547 Woodward Avenue, a move which marked the beginning-of-the-end for the eight-year-old Hitsville set up.

Bang in the middle of these troubles, Tamla Motown put out the current single in the UK, its title a seeming approbation of the prevailing popular ideology. In fact "More Love" was written months earlier with no such connections in mind. A devotional mitigation of the pain then being endured by his wife Claudette, following the death of her new-born twins in 1966 and a shattering sequence of miscarriages, Smokey Robinson's moving text was a personal gift to her, a genuine love song with which he would open his shows for the next decade. The track contains, in its nonchalant rhyming of 'act' and 'fact' a timeless example of the elegant simplicity of its writer's lyricism, lines fashioned from the directness of every day speech, yet with a rare level of emotional potency.

Sympathetically recorded by Motown's West Coast group, despite a frenetic drum track (and a jarring edit at the key change (1:49)), "More Love" is an alluring number swaying in a waft of warmly reassuring major 7ths. Following her heartbreaking apologies for what she saw as her own personal failures, the track palpably eases Claudette's distress, a profound and gentle statement of love, sending out a universal message of hope to anyone in similar circumstances.

---

[1] The UK single was re-pressed almost immediately with the alternative B-side, "Come Spy With Me", making the first pressing a rare and valuable collectors' piece.

[2] With The Beatles atop the UK and American charts that summer with the utopian nursery rhyme "All You Need Is Love", UK folkie Leon Rosselson was prompted to pen a bitingly scornful response pointing out the futility of proclaiming unrequited love for social institutions founded on violence and coercion ("Flower Power = Bread", 1968).

---

**TMG 615**
**THE ELGINS**
**It's Been A Long Long Time** (2:50)
(Fuqua—The Five Quails)
Produced by Harvey Fuqua/Johnny Bristol
Recording completed: 10 Apr 1967
**Release Date**: 21 Jul 1967
**B-side**: I Understand My Man
**Position in Record Retailer Top 40**: -
**Equivalent US Release**: VIP 25043 (8 Jun 1967)
**Position in Billboard Top 40 Pop**: -
**Position in Billboard Top 40 R & B**: 35

---

Saundra Mallett Edwards / Cleo 'Duke' Miller / Johnny Dawson / Robert Fleming

---

This archetypal doo-wop number has been recorded by numerous artists over the years including, in 1961, The Five Quails, Harvey Fuqua's old group—although he did not participate in the original recording. Why he chose to revive the number for The Elgins is unclear—possibly the track held personal significance for him. In any case, it was put out as a surprise choice, the last of the group's three Tamla Motown singles, and the weakest by some distance. (Their 1966 album was held off until September 1968 in Britain, finally appearing during a protracted campaign of re-issues of their first two 45s.)

**TMG 616**
**DIANA ROSS & THE SUPREMES**
**Reflections** (2:50)
(Holland—Dozier—Holland)
Produced by Brian Holland/Lamont Dozier
Recording completed: 9 May 1967
**Release Date**: 25 Aug 1967
**B-side**: Going Down For The Third Time
**Position in Record Retailer Top 40**: 5
**Equivalent US Release**: Motown 1111 (24 Jul 1967)
**Position in Billboard Top 40 Pop**: 2
**Position in Billboard Top 40 R & B**: 4

---

Diana Ross / Florence Ballard / Mary Wilson

---

Behind the scenes, the political balance within The Supremes reached a watershed in mid-1967, prompting the direct intervention of Berry Gordy. Central to the crisis facing the outfit was the mounting tension between Florence Ballard and the other two, centred on her descent into petty alcoholism and a slapdash attitude towards her work caused by sheer burn-out. (According to Ross, a depressed and lethargic Ballard had gained so much weight that she couldn't wear her stage outfits in 1967.)

Ominously for Ballard, the group elected to recruit an understudy, at first auditioning Velvelette Norma Barbee before settling on Cindy Birdsong, formerly of Patti LaBelle's Blue Belles. Instantly accepted by the others and discreetly inserted into the stage act [607], Birdsong seemed a viable prospect and consequently a formal switch in personnel was hatched behind Ballard's back, the stunned singer told as much at a meeting on July 26. Due to contractual detail, Ballard had no deal as an individual performer and was immediately out of work, although not without a mitigating pay-off amounting to $75,000. Attempting a solo career was an option—indeed she shortly signed to ABC, but the prospect of solo stardom was beyond her, a series of disappointing failures ensuing and leaving her bankrupt within the year.

Sympathy for Ballard was intensified by an apparent admission of side-taking by Gordy, who opted for a minor re-launch of his primary group with the promotion of Diana Ross to star billing, despite vociferous protests from Mary Wilson. In truth, beyond the political level, Gordy was motivated by his keen business sense, aware that with 'Diana Ross & The Supremes', he now potentially had *two* big-name acts at his disposal, the first public admission that Ross was being earmarked for a solo career. Thus, Berry Gordy had dealt with the first major fracture to beset one of his primary groups, and had, it seems, emerged victoriously.

With the dust still settling, the group's 'business as usual' summer release was "Reflections", a studio-experimental response to the adventurous psychedelic pop currently in vogue. The basic track laid down in LA[1], the masters were sent back to Hitsville for the addition of vocals and Jamerson's bass line, the uncontrollable activity of which makes little sense in terms of the track's harmonic structure, and yet somehow works against the song's contemplative chord changes. (Jamerson was said to be hurt by the perceived snub, viewing the use of Motown's LA band as a criticism of The Funk Brothers *per se* which may explain the extra animation on display here, as if he had a point to make.)

More significantly, effort was spent on the inventive overdubs, HDH revelling in the rare studio time available. Aiming at something boldly up-to-date, the team made innovative use of a signal generator designed by Russ Terrana for acoustically testing the studio space for resonances, which was recorded onto a tape loop and dropped conventionally into the mix with the addition of delay effects. Commencing with a rapidly recurring electronic bleep followed by an ethereal rush of sound which wanders back-and-forth across the speakers on the stereo mix, the production is at once extraordinary and mesmeric.[2] The stereo panning reminiscent of "You Keep Me Hangin' On" [585], HDH place the double-tracked tambourine, both slapped and shaken, to the left, the metallic cycling of which evokes a spinning wheel and gives a sense of forward momentum, with some archetypal 'flapping' percussion taking the place of an orthodox drum track. With snippets of cello, accordion and lazy keyboards dropped in the gaps, the result is as sensuously rhythmic as anything from the era, a period-piece which melds Motown's patent brand with the LSD-charged atmosphere of its day in a manner hitherto only hinted at. (That the single appeared in mono is to the production's cost.)

Cramming such enterprise into the 7-inch format necessitated a truncation evident in the splicing out of a second middle-8, unsubtle edits audible at 2:29 and 2:39, with the original cadenced ending removed. A hit on both sides of the Atlantic, the single was kept from the top in America by "All You Need Is Love", but is just as much a defining sound for 1967 as the Beatles' anthem, and a peak moment in The Supremes' unsettled career.

[1] It was recorded on the same day as "The Happening" [607].

[2] HDH's evaluation of such invention was dismissive, routinely referring implicitly to the overdubs in "Reflections" as 'ear candy', although modesty may have played its part. Speculation over the technology used has resulted in a widespread misconception that a Theremin was employed, a novelty gadget famously used in 1966 by The Beach Boys on "Good Vibrations", and concurrently in the soundtrack to William Beaudine's *Billy The Kid Vs Dracula*. Others claim that a Moog synthesiser was used, despite the fact that the instrument ('invented' in 1963) was still in development, Robert Moog not making it commercially available until 1968. Both the Theremin and the Moog work on the same basic principal as Terrana's invention, which was not in fact conceived as a musical instrument.

## TMG 617
## JIMMY RUFFIN
**Don't You Miss Me A Little Bit Baby** (2:58)
(Whitfield—Penzabene—Strong)
Produced by Norman Whitfield
Recording completed: 16 May 1967
**Release Date**: 18 Aug 1967
**B-side**: I Want Her Love
**Position in Record Retailer Top 40**: -
**Equivalent US Release**: Soul 35035 (29 Jun 1967)
**Position in Billboard Top 40 Pop**: -
**Position in Billboard Top 40 R & B**: 27

Despite looking backwards to [604b], "Don't You Miss Me" has a futuristic flavour, cleanly mixed and EQ-ed for crisp separation of instruments which make full use of the scope afforded by Hitsville's stereo facility, again lost to some extent by the mono press for 45. Built mainly from a two-chord modulation in whole bars, the chief harmonic interest derives from a bridge in which the expected G is supplanted by an irascible Bb, Ruffin's smooth composure lurching into accusatory wrath before coming back to rest in a chorus passage based on the same tranquil chord foundation as its verse.

No less viable than his previous release [603], the track was probably hampered by its failure to appear on a contemporary album. In any respect, it became Jimmy Ruffin's first flop, indicating that his appeal had temporarily waned, and ushering in a barren nine months during which the song was passed around Norman Whitfield's favoured acts before resurfacing on Ruffin's 1969 album *Ruff 'N' Ready*. Used as a B-side for later re-issues [911], this generally unappreciated track was incorrectly cited on a 1972 US single in the 'Yesteryear' series (see [853]) by the insertion of a confusingly unnecessary 'Just' in the song's title.

**TMG 618**
**MARVIN GAYE**
**Your Unchanging Love** (2:58)
(Holland—Dozier—Holland)
Produced by Brian Holland/Lamont Dozier
Recording completed: 29 Jan 1965
**Release Date**: 25 Aug 1967
**B-side**: I'll Take Good Care Of You
**Position in Record Retailer Top 40**: -
**Equivalent US Release**: Tamla 54153 (12 Jun 1967)
**Position in Billboard Top 40 Pop**: 33
**Position in Billboard Top 40 R & B**: 7

With Gaye's "I Heard It Through The Grapevine" [686] safely in the can, producer Norman Whitfield was stunned to learn that Quality Control had vetoed the single, which later became Tamla Motown's all-time top seller, on the grounds of uncommerciality. Up against it was a January 1965 recording plucked from *Moods Of Marvin Gaye*, a romantic, mid-tempo ballad which a conservative Berry Gordy determined would make a safer bet for Gaye's first solo single in a year, thus ensuring that the definitive recording of "Grapevine" would remain unheard for another 12 months.

Consciously moulded from Gaye's 1964 hit "How Sweet It Is (To Be Loved By You)" [E60], the current track sounds badly dated against his recent duet [611] and flies in the face of Motown's current singles which confidently push ahead in terms of production, arrangement and recording technique. Why Quality Control considered a pointless fifth lift from the album appropriate is unclear, but the move represents a clear misjudgement of public mood. That it struggled to 33 in the States illustrates the pace at which musical tastes were developing in 1966-67, a process which the normally astute Berry Gordy for once seemed blind to.

**TMG 619**
**GLADYS KNIGHT & THE PIPS**
**Everybody Needs Love** (2:58)
(Holland—Whitfield)
Produced by Norman Whitfield
Recording completed: 2 May 1966
**Release Date**: 1 Sep 1967
**B-side**: Since I've Lost You
**Position in Record Retailer Top 40**: -
**Equivalent US Release**: Soul 35034 (12 Jun 1967)
**Position in Billboard Top 40 Pop**: 39
**Position in Billboard Top 40 R & B**: 3

Gladys Knight / Merald 'Bubba' Knight / Edward Patten / William Guest

A second successive 'oldie' from Tamla Motown consisted of Gladys Knight & The Pips' contemporary recording of a 1965 Temptations track, which due to its timing, came out in the UK with their own rendition of "I Heard It Through The Grapevine" also now available. Used as the title track of Knight's first Motown album, "Everybody Needs Love" shares the same two-chord basis as the Whitfield-produced "Don't You Miss Me A Little Bit Baby" [617], a whole tone lower and delivered in a sultry manner not heard on the group's two prior releases. Possibly this relaxed love song was selected for its implied universality, another in a chain of allusions to the 'Summer of Love' *zeitgeist* which Motown was apparently referencing from a discreet distance.

Issued in advance to DJs through September, promo copies also featured a cover of Marvin Gaye's "Stepping Closer To Your Heart" (previously used as [576b]), before the album track "Since I've Lost You" was substituted, thereby making demo copies especially highly sought-after by collectors.


**TMG 620**
**THE TEMPTATIONS**
**You're My Everything** (2:59)
(Whitfield—Penzabene—Grant)
Produced by Norman Whitfield
Recording completed: 15 Feb 1967
**Release Date**: 1 Sep 1967
**B-side**: I've Been Good To You
**Position in Record Retailer Top 40**: 26
**Equivalent US Release**: Gordy 7063 (13 Jun 1967)
**Position in Billboard Top 40 Pop**: 6
**Position in Billboard Top 40 R & B**: 3

---

Otis Williams / Melvin Franklin / Paul Williams / Eddie Kendricks / David Ruffin

---

The most free-flowing Temptations single to date, "You're My Everything" finds its co-composers on Smokey Robinson turf, the lyric summoning sunshine and the natural seasons to convey the manner in which the singer's love-object has brightened his life [E67]. Begun by Cornelius Grant as a romantic showcase for Eddie Kendricks, the lyric was developed with Roger Penzabene as "Love Is Wonderful", before being offered to the group's musical director Norman Whitfield. With its radiantly cheerful character, the recording was embraced by its producer, aiming to grab an assured commercial hit after having had no input on the group's previous single [610].

While putting the debonair Kendricks up-front was merely a case of appeasing the group's female following, the move irked self-appointed leader David Ruffin, who besides seeing himself as the defining sound of The Temptations, was becoming increasingly disgruntled by Motown's denying him veto on finished mixes and track selections. Stealing a few lines in verse three mitigated his irritation to some extent, but more pointedly opened up the possibility of The Temptations having more than one lead singer at once, an old gambit for the group which Whitfield contemplated at length over the following year, in tandem with his absorption of the emergent funk idiom signalled by the summer release of James Brown's "Cold Sweat" and Wilson Pickett's "Funky Broadway" [707].

This light, summery pop song climbed to number 6 on the US charts, satisfying its producer and suggesting to Ruffin that he was not indispensable after all.

## TMG 621
## MARTHA REEVES & THE VANDELLAS
**Love Bug Leave My Heart Alone** (2:10)
(Morris—Moy)
Produced by Richard Morris
Recording completed: 10 Apr 1967
**Release Date**: 8 Sep 1967
**B-side**: One Way Out
**Position in Record Retailer Top 40**: -
**Equivalent US Release**: Gordy 7062 (3 Aug 1967)
**Position in Billboard Top 40 Pop**: 25
**Position in Billboard Top 40 R & B**: 14

---

Martha Reeves / Rosalind Ashford / Betty Kelly

---

With Motown's contemporary policy of pushing its vocal leaders to prominence, Martha Reeves was in line for star-treatment on the heels of Smokey Robinson [598] and Diana Ross [616], in this case, by the formal addition of her surname to the group's billing—without her countenance. In a strange parallel with The Supremes' internal affairs, the move coincided with Betty Kelly's sacking, her friendship with Reeves under pressure for some time until the situation rapidly deteriorated when both elected to start relationships with members of their touring band The Kinfolks. The sticking-plaster solution was Kelly's replacement by Reeves' reluctant sister Lois; yet while Motown were attempting to boost Reeves' profile, the singer was undergoing private turmoil which would unravel much of her hard-won stature, centred in the main on her ill-considered decision to marry another man enigmatically referred to simply as 'Wiley' in her autobiography, whom she had bumped into on tour in 1966. Having tied the knot, an emotionally unstable Reeves promptly fled to England for some concert dates, leaving Wiley to install himself and several relatives into her Detroit home. Shortly thereafter, her fragile state of mind was exposed during a live engagement at the Twenty Grand in mid-1967 during which she broke down on stage (her anguish exposed for all to hear on the album *Martha & The Vandellas Live!*). Shortly thereafter, Reeves appeared to come to her senses and had her marriage annulled, but found further strife shortly afterwards when someone 'spiked' her with LSD, leaving her hospitalised and severely depressed.

As if in anticipation of these events, former Golden World staff writer Richard Morris [630] provided Reeves with the uncannily appropriate "Love Bug Leave My Heart Alone" ('I don't want to love a guy who truly don't love me') which, despite its aggravated tone and dense, stifled arrangement, is deceptively bright in outlook. Turning the phrase 'love bug' away from its common meaning in favour of a half-joking play on the American slang for insect, the lyric evokes the calming rural phenomena of warm spring breezes and butterflies on the wing, and a number of gentle word-plays ('the ever changing sun that warms my heart and leaves') not to mention an opening line adapted from "Dancing In The Street" [E54].

With a melody-line in the verses resembling that of "Loving You Is Sweeter Than Ever" [568], "Love Bug" is the most substantial thing the group released since "You've Been In Love Too Long" [530]. Not a big seller, the track nevertheless heralds a new writing combination which would provide the group with another single in January 1968 [636].


**TMG 622**
**BRENDA HOLLOWAY**
**You've Made Me So Very Happy** (2:54)
(Gordy—Wilson—Holloway—Holloway)
Produced by Berry Gordy Jr.
**Release Date**: 22 Sep 1967
**B-side**: I've Got To End It
**Position in Record Retailer Top 40**: -
**Equivalent US Release**: Tamla 54155 (17 Aug 1967)
**Position in Billboard Top 40 Pop**: 39
**Position in Billboard Top 40 R & B**: 40


With a number of recording artists aggravated by an apparent withholding of revenue coupled with an inherent favouritism for commercially proven names [604], Brenda Holloway was feeling the pinch more than most at Motown, having never established a successful partnership with any of the company's principal writer-producers. This, her final Tamla Motown release, was self-penned with sister Patrice during a lull between business meetings in Las Vegas, Holloway resolving to come up with something positive to lift her from the doldrums which had been intensified recently when her partner left her.[1]

Presented with up-beat lyrics, Holloway demo-ed the song to Frank Wilson who helped lick it into shape by supplying an atmospheric drop-out chorus, before Berry Gordy got his hands on it and insisted it be recorded at a more moderate 'mellow' tempo, which caused a fractious exchange of views with the singer, who ruminated on the matter before penning a heartfelt letter to Gordy in which she calmly bemoaned the lack of support, measured against some of the company's other acts.[2] Yet belying this tense backdrop, the resultant production is coolly sophisticated, delivered in Holloway's brooding, breathy style and held in check by a focussed precision bass line revealing its West Coast origins. More attention might have sharpened it further: somehow amid the re-arranging and overdubbing, the track elements ended up marginally off-pitch, the orchestral sections fractionally sharp by comparison to the band and garish against with Holloway's reflective vocals.

"You've Made Me So Very Happy" remains an elegant construction with a carefully-thought-out structure, which was deserving of a major hit. Inevitably, in the wake of Holloway's reading failing, the number was picked up by Blood Sweat And Tears in 1969, who took it to number 2 in America, just as Holloway was plotting litigation against Gordy and the Motown Corporation which had failed to make her a star [700]. According to Holloway, their version more faithfully reflects her original conception[3], and there is some evidence to suggest that in this respect, Frank Wilson was on her side.

[1] According to her comments in Whithall, p111. David Cole claims it was written 'With Tina Turner in mind' (Abbott, p161).
[2] The full text of her letter is reproduced in George, p155-7.
[3] See comments in Dahl, p251.

## TMG 623
### FOUR TOPS
**You Keep Running Away** (2:48)
(Holland—Dozier—Holland)
Produced by Brian Holland/Lamont Dozier
Recording completed: 29 Jun 1967
**Release Date**: 6 Oct 1967
**B-side**: If You Don't Want My Love
**Position in Record Retailer Top 40**: 26
**Equivalent US Release**: Motown 1113 (29 Aug 1967)
**Position in Billboard Top 40 Pop**: 19
**Position in Billboard Top 40 R & B**: 7

---

Levi Stubbs / Lawrence Payton / Abdul 'Duke' Fakir / Renaldo 'Obie' Benson

---

An attempt to revive fortunes for The Four Tops with a patent 'big' arrangement after the doubtful "7-Rooms Of Gloom" [612], HDH's new offering, a stand-alone 45, benefited from one of the most tightly limited brass arrangements on any Motown record. Bolstered by Levi Stubbs' masterly performance, the song tells of how the central character's confidence lies shaken by a lover who cannot commit to staying with him, a suitably torturous scenario to prod the singer into the anguished corners in which he thrives.

Utilising essentially the same chord progression as "If I Were A Carpenter" [647], a cover version at this point still buried on *Reach Out*, the track's all-engulfing production raises the basic template yet fails to mask the fact that, while proficiently composed, "You Keep Running Away" is no "Bernadette". In truth, HDH were to some extent easing their standards, their best work suddenly and quite noticeably behind them.

Significantly, the flip-side (also by HDH) dates to 1964, the previously unreleased archive track used for want of a contemporary recording, the group's writer-producers withdrawing their industrious good-will in an effort to goad Berry Gordy into giving them the better deal which their commercial success warranted.

## TMG 624
### CHRIS CLARK
**From Head To Toe** (2:42)
(William "Smokey" Robinson)

---

Produced by Warren Moore
Recording completed: 11 Nov 1966
**Release Date**: 13 Oct 1967
**B-side**: Beginning Of The End
**Position in Record Retailer Top 40**: -
**Equivalent US Release**: Motown 1114 (7 Sep 1967)
**Position in Billboard Top 40 Pop**: -
**Position in Billboard Top 40 R & B**:

A second release for Berry Gordy's white protégé, "From Head To Toe" was a Smokey Robinson original from 1965's *Going To A Go-Go*. Apparently selected for her by fellow Miracle Warren Moore and recorded for Clark's summer album, this quirky number was a poor choice of single, caught as it is uncomfortably between authentic soul and minor comedy. The opening percussion effect wittily derived from the tapping keys of a typewriter references Clark's former secretarial duties at Hitsville, yet the song lacks identity, her vocal track veering from happy high-school kitsch to gospel-tinged rapture, as if unclear on the disposition of the piece—which she openly disliked.

Built on a playful four-step ascending walk on bass guitar, Moore's sparse arrangement relies principally on a basic percussion track plus a close-tracking electric guitar (presumably Moore himself) which lack sufficient strength to provide body to the recording. (It features a George Harrison-esque 'Indian' riff in the song's choruses.) Adding brassy overdubs, a Levi Stubbs-style "Ha!" and a valiant series of key shifts towards the finish, Moore attempted to bring some clout to the song which in spite of him remains one of the slightest singles Tamla Motown released. (The US edition came out on Motown, Clark having been moved from the VIP label during the year.)


**TMG 625**
**MARVIN GAYE & TAMMI TERRELL**
**Your Precious Love** (2:59)
(Ashford—Simpson)
Produced by Harvey Fuqua/Johnny Bristol
Recording completed: 23 Mar 1967
**Release Date**: 20 Oct 1967
**B-side**: Hold Me Oh My Darling
**Position in Record Retailer Top 40**: -
**Equivalent US Release**: Tamla 54156 (22 Aug 1967)
**Position in Billboard Top 40 Pop**: 5
**Position in Billboard Top 40 R & B**: 2

Unlike "Ain't No Mountain High Enough" [611] with its piecemeal construction, "Your Precious Love" was conceived as a duet, giving the first true glimpse of Ashford & Simpson's composing prowess for the two singers. As a couple with a romantic interest themselves, they were perfectly placed to write for Gaye and Terrell, bringing the fine balance of gender perspective to proceedings. As intended, vocals were recorded live on March 23, the two side-by-side at the mike for the first time, and in consequence the electrical spark between the two performers, which its fore-runner hinted at, is tangible.

"Your Precious Love" is both relaxed and suave, the song built from a doo-wop run in Bb complete with finger-clicks panned to the extremities, bathed in 1950s-style reverb, and authentic period backing vocals. Terrell positively thrives in the soft glow of the arrangement, her contribution an extemporised delight of prime facility. Yet the song's gently rocking allure bursts into full bloom in the chorus, elevated by a powerful tone-and-a-half rise, in which the two harmonise what should naturally have been the track's title, had it not already been utilised elsewhere [583].[1] (The correspondence was a pity, leaving the song's consequent name clashing with Gaye's recent solo release [618].)

Relaxed at the mike, Terrell's habit of turning her head during recording [611] caused a drop-out at 2:29 which Billie-Jean Brown later commented resulted in at least 40 re-mixes in a vain effort to repair[2]; Gaye by contrast almost loses his self-discipline completely at 2:06. Vocal idiosyncrasy apart, Fuqua and Bristol's production plays up the song's classy sophistication with a calculated precision in an enjoyable session. Transcribing Jamerson's rise-and-fall bass line for Joe Messina, the guitar and bass lock in impeccable unison in the style of [624], although the track ends up somewhat unimaginatively mixed for stereo, with both vocals tending to the left channel and instrumentation mainly right.

With a gushing lyric, the track repudiates the sentiment of "Standing In The Shadows Of Love" [589], whose Bacharach-David-inspired 'You've taken away all my reasons for living' is explicitly turned around and re-stated in the positive. Yet if the first authentic collaboration between the singers promised a bright future for the act, warning signs were in evidence, Terrell suffering from bouts of increasingly worrying headaches which were ascribed by more than one within her inner-circle to the stress of her ongoing relationship with moody Temptation David Ruffin.

Released in America in August, "Your Precious Love" went top five, paving the way for its UK release two months later, which coincided with a performance at the Hampton-Sydney College in Virginia on October 14, during which Terrell collapsed into a bewildered Gaye's arms. The first solid indication of her subsequently diagnosed brain tumour, news of Terrell's illness sent ripples of gossip around Motown, with accusing glances aimed at her lover.[3]

[1] Gaye had also recorded a track entitled "Heaven Sent You I Know" with Kim Weston, released at the tail-end of 1966 as an album cut.

[2] Waller p62

[3] A rumour circulated that Ruffin, who had supposedly once pushed her down a flight of stairs, had caused the brain injury by striking Terrell with a hammer. According to Ron Taylor, friend of both Terrell and Martha Reeves, a hammer incident did take place, but it was some time prior to David Ruffin's involvement with her (Reeves, p157).

**TMG 626**
**STEVIE WONDER**
**I'm Wondering** (2:53)
(Cosby—Wonder—Moy)

Produced by Henry "Hank" Cosby
Recording completed: 16 Aug 1967
**Release Date**: 13 Oct 1967
**B-side**: Every Time I See You I Go Wild
**Position in Record Retailer Top 40**: 22
**Equivalent US Release**: Tamla 54157 (14 Sep 1967)
**Position in Billboard Top 40 Pop**: 12
**Position in Billboard Top 40 R & B**: 4

If HDH were keen on cobbling songs together from old sources, Cosby—Wonder—Moy would out-score them in this respect through 1967 with their extravagant borrowing of elements. Thematically this new track, with its provocative jealousy of 'Jimmy', appears a purpose-made counterpart to "Jimmy Mack" [599], viewed from the perspective of one of the characters in Reeves' tale. The tempting suitor—the absent 'Jimmy'—is portrayed as having left his loyal lover and gone away, leaving Wonder, who co-composed the lyric with Sylvia Moy, to try his every trick to draw the girl of his desires into his own arms.

In fact, the record references not just [599] but a number of sources: the title possibly derives from the early "Wondering", written by the singer in collaboration with Clarence Paul (on *The Jazz Soul Of Little Stevie Wonder*, 1962) and its opening melismatic '*Well...*' is cribbed from "Bye Bye Baby", a very early Mary Wells single which made the R & B top 10 in 1960. (It unintentionally resembles James Jamerson's triplets in "I Can't Help Myself" [515].) The song also steals a glance at Sandie Shaw's April number 1, "Puppet On A String" in verse 3, and comparison should be made between the quick-fire stacking up of 'insecure', 'sure' and 'endure' towards the song's close with verse 2 of "The Happening" [607], which deploys similar rhymes in a comparable manner.

Recorded with an air of youthful exuberance, credit is due to arranger Paul Riser, a frequent collaborator with Cosby and whose unsung contributions to a high number of Motown recordings warrant more attention than they generally get. Using some unusually angular string figures to animate the choruses, the track strides forward confidently, supported by James Jamerson's very fast and busy bass. But with its shaker-laden intro and big snare sound, it is the rhythm and percussion which drive the recording, which features an effect like the tapping of fingers on a tambourine, heard on the far-right channel in stereo pressings (which seems to be exactly what it is, the percussion unexpectedly subsiding at 2:38 to be replaced by orthodox shaking of the instrument for the song's final 13 seconds).

When all is said and done, Wonder nonetheless claims the song as his own with an obligatory harmonica solo and double-tracked vocal in the final chorus, to say nothing of the embedding once again of his surname, this time in the song's title. With his former mentor Clarence Paul having left the fold on the back of the Mickey Stevenson/Kim Weston departure [590], "I'm Wondering" marks a new beginning for the teenaged singer, his next two singles following the style established here and bouncing off the track lyrically as effective sequel pieces.

**TMG 627**
**THE SPINNERS**
**For All We Know** (2:54)
(Lewis—Coots[1])
Produced by Ivy Jo Hunter
Recording completed: 7 Mar 1967
**Release Date**: 27 Oct 1967
**B-side**: I'll Always Love You [523]
**Position in Record Retailer Top 40**: -
**Equivalent US Release**: Motown 1109 (11 May 1967)
**Position in Billboard Top 40 Pop**: -
**Position in Billboard Top 40 R & B**: -

Henry Fambrough / Bobbie Smith / Billy Henderson / Pervis Jackson / Chico Edwards

Written by Sam Lewis and J. Fred Coots in the early 1930s, "For All We Know" became a standard, covered by numerous vocalists including Nat King Cole (1943), Nina Simone (1957), and Dinah Washington (1962). Picked up by The Spinners, the ensuing Motown recording was sufficiently compelling to warrant release on 45, the studio band's performance solid and effusive, completed with lustrous flutes and falsetto backing vocals from the group.

Motown though neglected to push the single, nullifying any chance The Spinners might have had in the commercial arena. Indeed the company sanctioned few releases by them, and here, their previous single [523] was lamely utilised as the B-side. Having supposedly dropped the use of 'Detroit' in the group's name [514], their album *The Original Spinners* was confusingly re-named *The Detroit Spinners* for the UK market, and rounded up both sides of each of their three singles to date amongst its dozen titles.

[1] Some releases of the track elsewhere have Coots mis-spelled as Coutts.


**TMG 628**
**BARBARA RANDOLPH**
**I Got A Feeling** (2:58)
(Holland—Dozier—Holland)
Produced by Hal Davis
Recording completed: 17 Aug 1967
**Release Date**: 3 Nov 1967
**B-side**: You Got Me Hurting All Over
**Position in Record Retailer Top 40**: -
**Equivalent US Release**: Soul 35038 (14 Sep 1967)
**Position in Billboard Top 40 Pop**: -
**Position in Billboard Top 40 R & B**: -

Little-noted vocalist Barbara Randolph, daughter of actress Lillian, had sung briefly with The Platters in 1964-65 and was called into Hitsville with an eye on replacing on the then fragile Florence Ballard in The Supremes. Eventually finding herself surplus to requirements, Randolph brought with her enough talent to warrant the opportunity of some solo recording dates, this thrilling HDH composition, recently used as a Four Tops B-side [601], rightly remade for her. Randolph's version of "I Got A Feeling" slows the Four Tops' impatient original but nonetheless flies off the turntable, with its gripping minim-rhythm hand claps and jazzy, oscillating brass interjections, Hal Davis' studio savvy tangibly elevating HDH's raw composition in the LA production.

The basis of the number is the skeleton of "Heaven Must Have Sent You" [583] (itself drawing largely on [554]), whose chord-progression with its 'missing' chorus is repeated here, built upon a full-scale descending bass foundation disguised by an octave rise not present in The Four Tops' original. Further touches typically import ingredients from other tracks in the HDH catalogue—the double-use of 'feeling' in the opening line suggesting the pattern of 'baby, baby' in "Where Did Our Love Go" [E51], a point picked up by Davis with the phrasing echoed in the trumpet figure, which in turn includes an end-of-line quotation from "I Can't Help Myself" [515].

Deploying a relentless clapping track also reproduced from the Supremes' 1964 hit, the song's joyful exuberance colours the exhilarating backing vocals, whose playful "Rockin' and a-reel*innn*" provoke audible hysterics. HDH's outpouring of enthusiasm is also evinced in the track's third verse, an excited rush of superlatives—earth-quaking, soul-shaking, ever-loving, breathtaking, electrifying, satisfying—which say as much about the happy energy of the song itself as the character depicted.[1] In the end an irresistibly infectious dance track, the number has seeped into Northern Soul legend, compelling Tamla Motown to re-issue it on more than one occasion.[2]

Given the undeniable triumph of the recording, "I Got A Feeling" should have put Randolph firmly on the map, yet as it panned out, became her only UK single. In America, a second 45 went out in 1968 (a cover of Marvin Gaye's "Can I Get A Witness" [E31] utilising the same B-side), coinciding with Randolph's pairing up with Gaye in his live act, in place of an ailing Tammi Terrell. Nothing further was heard from Randolph, bar some shelved 1969 recordings which were finally put out on CD three-decades-or-so late, adding to the sense that "I Got A Feeling" is one of Motown's mysterious gems, of inestimable worth to those 'in the know' and a source of eternal joy to listeners of all generations. The only pity is that it fades too soon.

[1] The lines in question also hark back to early days, drawing on the original, less than snappy title of The Supremes' fifth US single (supplied by Smokey Robinson): "A Breath Taking, First Sight Soul Searching, One Night Love Making, Next Day Heartbreaking Guy" (rapidly shortened to the more practical "A Breath Taking Guy").

[2] Besides [788], the song was issued again in 1979 as TMG 1133 [L013] (see Chapter 6).

**TMG 629**

**GLADYS KNIGHT & THE PIPS**
**I Heard It Through The Grapevine** (2:52)
(Whitfield—Strong)

Produced by Norman Whitfield
Recording completed: 17 Jun 1967
**Release Date**: 10 Nov 1967
**B-side**: It's Time To Go Now
**Position in Record Retailer Top 40**: -
**Equivalent US Release**: Soul 35039 (28 Sep 1967)
**Position in Billboard Top 40 Pop**: 2
**Position in Billboard Top 40 R & B**: 1

---

Gladys Knight / Merald 'Bubba' Knight / Edward Patten / William Guest

---

Something of a white elephant in 1967, "I Heard It Through The Grapevine", which sold over a million copies twice, would likely have been buried altogether had it not been for its producer's self-believing perseverance. Turned down by The Isley Brothers the previous year and then recorded (unissued) by The Miracles, The Temptations' would-be definitive rendition was hijacked and overdubbed at the eleventh hour by Marvin Gaye [686], but also canned before Gladys Knight & The Pips were offered the song in May 1967. (The group's lead singer was reportedly peeved at being given an unwanted hand-me-down, but was nonetheless impressed with its potential.)[1]

Taking home an instrumental demo, Knight and the group spent the better-part of a month rehearsing the song's vocals and developing its nuances. As a result a specific homage to Aretha Franklin appears at 2:05, a paraphrase of her current American number 1 "Respect".[2] Collaring Whitfield in his office and performing the song live against the original backing tape, an excited group were hurried into studio A on the spot (evicting a working Smokey Robinson) in order to nail the song once and for all.

Supposedly the first collaboration of the Whitfield—Strong partnership, the lyric commenced with just its title phrase, Strong having thought it up while walking through Chicago, realising it had likely never been incorporated into song before, although his use of 'through' rather than 'on' the grapevine is idiosyncratic. (It has since been suggested that the lyric concerns an actual event involving Berry Gordy.) Taking it to Hitsville, Strong developed a basic musical foundation on piano, striking the chords of his old hit "Money" [E02], which he used as a basic template. Recognising his speciality lie in lyrics rather than music, Strong took what he had to Whitfield, who filled out the arrangement, in which little from "Money" ended up, aside from the common basic blues progression. (A trace of "Money" could be heard in the two-chord shuffling in the song's chorus (major, in Knight's rendition), as exposed by the briefly prominent piano break prior to the instrumental passage. If anything, the chorus would appear to be based on that of "Whole Lot Of Shakin' In My Heart" [569] whose chords are almost identical, and whose key of Ebm had resurfaced in Gaye's prior version.)

Musically "Grapevine" is cautious with its movement, jostling in an agitated shuffle between adjacent chords, succinctly—if accidentally—depicting the song's guarded insinuation without fully committing itself; lyrically, the dilemma is plain enough, the central character catching wind of

---

her partner's intent to leave for a former lover. Something learned via idle gossip, the rumours render the narrator nervously unsure of their accuracy, prodding at the guilty party for explicit confession ('I just can't help being confused—if it's true, please baby won't you tell me').

Recorded in June, Knight's vocal was a significant capture for the Soul label [509], as authentically 'black' as the current singles emerging from Atlantic/Stax, and a robust match for Franklin. Mixed right for stereo against backing vocals on the left, Knight's performance is impassioned and emotive, one of her best takes to-date and enlivened with improvisation and free-play around the track's foundation. At times forceful, Knight makes effective use of repetition in the gospel tradition, giving additional emphases to certain words and phrases, positively hammering them home. Eschewing the shady solemnity of Gaye's version, Norman Whitfield's backing track is also a loose affair, 'African' in its innovative use of war drums and hi-hats together in the opening[3], before rasping piano along with backing vocals and stabbing guitar, add to the track's sense of goading accusation, as if braced for a fight.

Rush-released after "Everybody Needs Love" [619], the single was not publicised by Motown (see Knight, p182), but despite their apparent indifference a thrilled and defiant Norman Whitfield watched it climb to number two in the US (held off the top by The Monkees' new single). Vindicated in his championing of the song, Whitfield scored a noted victory over Berry Gordy, which besides winning him extra kudos, also put Gladys Knight's Motown career on track for the first time since her arrival. (The UK public was less impressed, failing to lift the song into the charts at all.)

[1] Knight complains in her autobiography that Marvin Gaye recorded their hit (p183-4). Although accepted wisdom holds that Knight has confused the song's chronology, it is intriguing that Gaye himself concurs with Knight (as quoted in Abbott p109), and Smokey Robinson relays the same sequence of events in his memoirs (p49). Possibly these insiders were not privy to the full facts, uncovered by subsequent research.

[2] Smokey Robinson states that the backing arrangement was inspired by Franklin (p149), probably drawing Knight's attention to "Respect".

[3] According to Slutsky (p56), Benny Benjamin was so weakened by his long-term addiction to heroin that on the session, he was unable to muster the strength to play his full kit.

**TMG 630**
**EDWIN STARR**
**I Want My Baby Back** (2:37)
(Kendricks—Whitfield—Grant)
Produced by Norman Whitfield
Recording completed: 9 Aug 1967
**Release Date**: 17 Nov 1967
**B-side**: Gonna Keep On Trying Till I Win Your Love
**Position in Record Retailer Top 40**: -
**Equivalent US Release**: Gordy 7066 (5 Oct 1967)
**Position in Billboard Top 40 Pop**: -
**Position in Billboard Top 40 R & B**: -

Continuing the expansionist policy which had seen him take over Harvey and Tri-Phi in 1964 [509], Berry Gordy took the decision in September 1966 to begin acquiring neighbouring labels Ric Tic and Wingate, outlets controlled by Ed Wingate's Golden World company.[1] From 1964 onwards, Wingate's small empire had grown in reputation, offering some local competition to Motown, helped by The Funk Brothers' frequent weekend moonlighting which included anonymous work on two of Golden World's biggest hits—"Agent Double O Soul" [790] and "Stop Her On Sight (SOS)" [905], both by Edwin Starr.

Significantly, the protracted two-year deal included a reputed $1m bid for Golden World's recording facility on Davison Avenue, a studio renowned for capturing high-quality string sounds, which was further upgraded by Gordy with a state-of-the-art 8-track machine equivalent to that installed at Hitsville as early as 1964. Dubbed DAF (Davison Avenue Facility), the premises became better known as Studio B, a local back-up to Studio A. used mainly for orchestral and vocal overdubbing[2], Motown's other recently constructed set-up at Woodward Avenue [614] also now available for mixing work.

Buying up Golden World, Gordy gained ownership of the contracts of numerous performing acts including The San Remo Strings, J. J. Barnes, and The Fantastic Four besides the company's stock of master tapes. While re-issuing tracks from the back-catalogue was a viable option (he secured rights to the recordings in late-1968—see [678]), in the case of Nashville-born Charles Edward Hatcher, better known as Edwin Starr, it made sense to continue actively pushing him as a recording artist.

Returning from a UK tour late in 1966, Starr, unaware of Gordy's interest in Golden World, was surprised to learn that Motown now owned his contract. His belated first recording session for his new employers yielded both sides of this single, "I Want My Baby Back", a stomping 8-bar vamp in Eb, selected as the 'plug' side. Swingingly delivered and carrying a chugging 'train' sax in its instrumental break, the track was aimed squarely at the dance-floor, accounting for its failure to make the national charts. Strong enough to gain Gordy's sanction—at this stage he was still personally approving everything released, despite spending an increasing amount of his time at his Sunset Boulevard offices in LA—the single effectively embedded Starr in Motown's 'family', leading the way for further releases over the ensuing seven years.

[1] The purchase also secured the much smaller Stephanye and Maltese labels.
[2] The first Motown session there was on 19 October 1966, for the vocals on [589].


**TMG 631**
**SMOKEY ROBINSON & THE MIRACLES**
**I Second That Emotion** (2:39)
(Robinson—Cleveland)
Produced by William "Smokey" Robinson/Alfred Cleveland
Recording completed: 22 Sep 1967
**Release Date**: 24 Nov 1967
**B-side**: You Must Be Love
**Position in Record Retailer Top 40**: 27
**Equivalent US Release**: Tamla 54159 (12 Oct 1967)

**Position in Billboard Top 40 Pop**: 4
**Position in Billboard Top 40 R & B**: I

---

Smokey Robinson / Bobby Rogers / Claudette Rogers Robinson /
Warren 'Pete' Moore / Ronnie White

---

Ever-alert for inspirational ideas, Smokey Robinson was provided with the genesis of the current track while out Christmas shopping in 1966 with Motown songwriter Al Cleveland. Striking up a conversation with a sales assistant over some jewellery Robinson was purchasing for Claudette, Cleveland sought to remark "I'll second that motion" but in mispronouncing the final word, inadvertently supplied his friend with the title of a new song. Jotted down on a napkin, the evocative phrase was taken back to Hitsville where the two fleshed out a full text, finding the double rhyme of 'notion' and 'devotion'.

Their creative juices in full flow, the two writers devised three verses espousing meaningful love over a transitory fling. Yet the full version was deemed too indulgent by Berry Gordy, who, weighing up the song's aesthetic, ordered that the track be trimmed down by the removal of a full verse, leaving Robinson disappointed but conceding the point. Recorded in D major, Marv Tarplin's guitar licks high up the fret-board of his Gibson Les Paul lend the lazily soulful recording an element of focus it might have otherwise lacked, flourishing towards the song's close. An instant favourite amongst Miracles fans, the track was performed on the group's inaugural *Ed Sullivan Show* appearance in the new year, as part of a medley of their hits, and duly became The Miracles' first American top 10 hit since 1963 [E27].

**TMG 632**
**DIANA ROSS & THE SUPREMES**
**In And Out Of Love** (2:37)
(Holland—Dozier—Holland)
Produced by Brian Holland/Lamont Dozier
Recording completed: 7 Jul 1967
**Release Date**: 24 Nov 1967
**B-side**: I Guess I'll Always Love You
**Position in Record Retailer Top 40**: 13
**Equivalent US Release**: Motown 1116 (25 Oct 1967)
**Position in Billboard Top 40 Pop**: 9
**Position in Billboard Top 40 R & B**: 16

---

Diana Ross / Florence Ballard / Mary Wilson

---

Recorded in a series of sessions between April and July, The Supremes' new single, aimed at the Christmas market[1], was the latest in a succession of exploratory HDH tracks which pushed the group further from Motown's patent brand of soul than any other major outfit. (Each of their previous four releases fall into the same generalised style-category as this single, lending some credence to David Morse's view that The Supremes are the least typical group on the label, despite also being—via their unmatched sales and popularity—the most representative.)[2]

With its wide-stepping bass foundation, "In And Out Of Love" is an ungainly number concerned with love's repeated failure, with an obstinately ascending melody tackled by an expressive Ross, who peaks towards the song's finish. Yet despite the 'beat' arrangement provided mainly by a driving crotchet snare, the song is tense and difficult to fathom, missing the easy appeal of "Reflections" [616].

Performed on the *Ed Sullivan Show* on November 19, the single accordingly failed to engage the public, just scraping into the US top 10. Its pairing up with "I Guess I'll Always Love You", sourced from the earlier *The Supremes Sing Holland—Dozier—Holland*, is indicative of HDH's withholding of new material (see [623]), and continues the practise of swapping B-sides with The Isley Brothers [572] whose musical backing track was re-deployed here for The Supremes' over-dubbed vocals.

[1] The track's working title "Summer Good, Summer Bad" suggests it may have been earmarked for earlier release. The backing track was laid down on April 20, overdubs taking place mid-June, before the recording was completed and mixed in July. Some sources state that the vocals were laid down in LA along with the group's previous two singles, [607] and [616] yet the issued version seems to feature subsequent overdubs from The Andantes.

[2] p65

**TMG 633**
**THE TEMPTATIONS**
**(Loneliness Made Me Realise) It's You That I Need** (2:36)
(Whitfield—Holland)
Produced by Norman Whitfield
Recording completed: 21 Jan 1967
**Release Date**: 1 Dec 1967
**B-side**: I Want A Love I Can See
**Position in Record Retailer Top 40**: -
**Equivalent US Release**: Gordy 7065 (26 Sep 1967)
**Position in Billboard Top 40 Pop**: 14
**Position in Billboard Top 40 R & B**: 3

Otis Williams / Melvin Franklin / Paul Williams / Eddie Kendricks / David Ruffin

In a revealing interview a few days before his death in 1991, David Ruffin observed that numerous Temptations songs contain implicit references to God, describing them in this context as 'gospel'.[1] Citing the current track, Ruffin argues that the substitution of 'The Lord' for the 'You' of the song's title would reveal its true spiritual message, claiming that the standard love scenario was a contortion necessitated by 'marketing reasons'.

While Ruffin's comments throw a surprising light on the group's repertoire, there is no particular reason to suppose Whitfield and Holland had anything religious in mind when penning "(Loneliness Made Me Realise) It's You That I Need". (Indeed they commence with a quotation from "Lonely Lonely Girl Am I" [521].) The thrust of the lyric is a broken relationship, the male singer relaying his restless nights spent longing for his lost love to return. Soft-treading in the doo-wop tradition, the track features the triple-tapping percussion touch of numerous contemporary HDH hits in its first verse, laboriously brought to bear by Eddie Holland, and accompanied by an effect resembling the tapping of a drumstick on the lip of a milk bottle. In the end a somewhat stolid matter, the composition was possibly inspired by Ben E King's "Stand By Me", whose general arrangement and chord sequence it echoes. (The song was recently covered in a hit rendition by Motown associate Spyder Turner, with vocal impressions of David Ruffin, Smokey Robinson and Chuck Jackson.)

[1] Reproduced in Abbott, p137.

## TMG 634
## FOUR TOPS
**Walk Away Renee** (2:42)
(Brown—Calilli—Sarsone)
Produced by Brian Holland/Lamont Dozier
Recording completed: 4 Jan 1967
**Release Date**: 8 Dec 1967
**B-side**: Mame
**Position in Record Retailer Top 40**: 3
**Equivalent US Release**: Motown 1119 (18 Jan 1968)
**Position in Billboard Top 40 Pop**: 14
**Position in Billboard Top 40 R & B**: 15

Levi Stubbs / Lawrence Payton / Abdul 'Duke' Fakir / Renaldo 'Obie' Benson

Popularly thought to have stockpiled hundreds of Motown originals courtesy of his over-demanding Quality Control rejections, Berry Gordy was in fact in continual need of new product, to the point where old tracks would often have to be patched up and issued for want of new recordings—something also evinced by the reliance on cover versions in many of the company's long-players. (His primary outlet The Supremes had gone head to head with *Sgt. Pepper* over the summer with the non-original *The Supremes Sing Rogers & Hart*, following precedents such as *We Remember Sam Cooke* and *The Supremes Sing Country & Western & Pop*.)[1]

So far as The Four Tops were concerned, they had released just three studio albums to date, July's *Reach Out* the strongest yet, containing four of their previous five singles but nevertheless padded out with a range of covers including two Monkees songs. Held off until November in the UK, *Reach Out* also contained a recording of "Walk Away Renee", originally a 1966 American top 10 hit for New York group West Banke. With nothing forthcoming from the normally reliable HDH team, Motown were without a Christmas single for The Four Tops, Tamla Motown opting to pluck the track from the group's album by way of contingency.

Liberally backed by a repeatedly crescendoing brass section, The Four Tops' version, despite its melancholy subject matter, packs a punch by making the most of the whole-octave-confined melodic progression. Something of an experiment, Tamla Motown were delighted to see the single rise to the upper-ends of the UK charts and become their biggest hit of the year, something observed with curiosity in Detroit, where a US release was hastily prepared and also did reasonable business.[2]

[1] Their albums were in danger of becoming acutely embarrassing by the end of 1967, recent scheduled releases including a set of Disney songs, and some recycling in the form of two greatest hits collections and a live set, all of which were aborted.

[2] Davis (1988, p52) claims that the single was chosen 'Because Gordy wanted to push [The Four Tops] out of the teeny-bopper market', a notion incongruous with the order of events, and indeed the group's sophisticated recordings over the previous two years.

**TMG 635**
**MARVIN GAYE & TAMMI TERRELL**
**If I Could Build My Whole World Around You** (2:21)
(Fuqua—Bristol—Bullock)
Produced by Harvey Fuqua/Johnny Bristol
Recording completed: 21 Mar 1967
**Release Date**: 29 Dec 1967
**B-side**: If This World Were Mine
**Position in Record Retailer Top 40**: -
**Equivalent US Release**: Tamla 54161 (14 Nov 1967)
**Position in Billboard Top 40 Pop**: 10
**Position in Billboard Top 40 R & B**: 2

Its title probably cribbed from the lyrics to "You're My Everything" [620][1], Marvin Gaye and Tammi Terrell's third single was, after their two dramatic Ashford—Simpson-penned duets, something of an anticlimax, pulled like [634] from a summer album. Chirpily straight-forward with its vocal scatting, the song bobs across its F# tonic without exerting itself, espousing the idealism of the world each would create for the other's eternal happiness. Reaching a conclusion of sorts in its third verse, Gaye and Terrell finally come together and share the daydream before the track peters away into its fadeout.

Popular amongst soul listeners, mainly for James Jamerson's archetypal bouncing bass, both sides of the American edition made the R & B top 40, the A-side kept from pole position only by "I Second That Emotion" [631].

[1] If the track's title is thus derived, it is in keeping with similar 'coincidences' shaping the names of the duo's other 1967 singles ([611] from [777], and [625] in view of [583]).

## TIMELINE – 1967

Tamla Motown release 47 singles, 19 albums and 2 EPs
Tamla Motown place 19 singles in the UK top 40. 6 make top 10
George Clinton's Parliaments and James Brown signal development of funk
Aretha Franklin is most popular non-Motown soul star

| | |
|---|---|
| **Jan** | Four Tops begin triumphant UK tour at Royal Albert Hall, London |
| **Jan 12** | Four Tops: "Standing In The Shadows Of Love" enters UK top 50 (peak 6) |
| **Feb 11** | *Four Tops Live!* Enters UK album chart where it will stay for well over a year |
| **Feb** | Marvin Gaye's "I Heard It Through The Grapevine" completed but rejected by Quality Control |
| **Spring** | Meeting of unsettled Motown personnel held at Gladys Knight's house |
| **Mar** | Smokey Robinson given specific billing on releases by Miracles |
| **Mar 11** | Supremes: "Love Is Here And Now You're Gone" number 1 in US (one week) |
| **Mar 30** | Four Tops: "Bernadette" enters UK top 50 (peak 8) |
| **Apr 30** | Detroit love-in. Police attack participants and riots ensue |
| **Apr** | First releases from Whitfield—Strong team |
| **May** | Ewart Abner appointed director of ITMI |
| **May** | Jobete receive 14 awards at BMI ceremony |
| **May 11** | Supremes: "The Happening" enters UK top 50 (peak 6) |
| **May 11** | Supremes open two-week residency at Copa in New York |
| **May 13** | Supremes: "The Happening" number 1 in US (one week) |
| **Jun** | First releases from Ashford—Simpson team |
| **Jun** | Rumours that Ross and Gordy had secretly married. Motown offices inundated with 'wedding' gifts |
| **Summer** | Brenda Holloway refuses to re-sign when contract expires |
| **Jul 23-27** | Race riots in Detroit, forcibly quelled leaving 43 dead |
| **Jul 26** | Florence Ballard sacked from Supremes and replaced by Cindy Birdsong. Berry Gordy appoints Diana Ross as group's official leader |
| **Jul 26** | Stevie Wonder: "I Was Made To Love Her" enters UK top 50 (peak 5) |
| **Aug 30** | Supremes: "Reflections" enters UK top 50 (peak 5) |
| **Sep** | Supremes tour Japan |
| **Oct 14** | Tammi Terrell collapses on stage. Later diagnosed with brain tumour |
| **Oct 21** | First of 12 *British Motown Chartbusters* albums enters UK album chart |
| **Oct 28** | Supremes: *Greatest Hits* number 1 album in US (five weeks) |
| **Autumn** | HDH on 'go-slow' |
| **Dec 4** | Motown issue internal memo stating that Eddie Holland has stepped down as head of A & R |
| **Dec 10** | Otis Redding dies in plane crash |
| **Dec 13** | Four Tops: "Walk Away Renee" enters UK top 50 (peak 3) |
| **Dec 23-Jan 1** | Motortown Revue residency at Fox Theater, includes Stevie Wonder, Miracles, Marvelettes, Contours, Chris Clark, Gladys Knight & Pips, Bobby Taylor & Vancouvers |

# Summary of era [501] to [635]

The rise-and-fall of Motown spans around three decades, but a large constituency would concur that the period 1965 to 1967 was the label's 'Golden Era', an age in which the talents of Motown's early stars and writers came into a glorious bloom. Across-the-board, popular music was developing apace, the key shift centred on the emergence of music written and performed by non-trained, generally working class individuals and groups. Bringing a level of direct communication which never existed beforehand, the autonomy of artists such as The Rolling Stones, The Beatles and Bob Dylan served to liberate the art from its 'professional' constraints, allowing scope for expression which found its ultimate form in the arrival of rock music, with the development of acts such as Cream, The Who, Frank Zappa, Lou Reed and so on. Yet the creative ripples were spreading in all directions including folk, jazz and classical, and in particular to this study, American soul music.

Within the context of its age, Motown was exemplary of the do-it-yourself ethos and simultaneously anachronistic: Motown, while self-contained, was a microcosm of the 1950s structures, writers fenced off from performers in separate rooms and composing tunes with no intention of delivering them to the general public themselves. (There is a notable exception: Smokey Robinson.) At the forefront of Motown's factory system were HDH, the team accounting for a succession of major American hits through the mid-1960s whose only serious competition, at least as defined by the commercial climate, was Lennon—McCartney. During the period 1964 to 1967, HDH were responsible for a dozen American number 1s, all recorded by The Supremes and The Four Tops. (During this run, The Supremes scored a historic run of five number 1s with successive releases.)

Motown's flagship group, The Supremes almost single-handedly rebutted the 'British Invasion' of 1964. Carrying the US flag in the face of prolonged onslaught, the group's constant presence in the upper-reaches of the singles chart bucked a historically significant trend, and in this respect, Britain itself was slow to catch on. Tamla Motown scored no significant hits in the UK after its first batch of releases, until "You Can't Hurry Love" [575] entered the top 40 on 8 September 1966, after which the floodgates were at least loosened.

During the ensuing year, Tamla Motown became a global brand, marketed successfully throughout the western world. Crucial to its irresistible appeal was the label's characteristic sound. More than just a company name, Motown established itself as a *style*, a way of recording music which for most defines the essential fusion of soul with pop (or, to view it from another angle, merges black music with white music; rhythm with melody; feel with form; body with mind). In part, Motown's impact resulted from its studio method, where multi-tracking was significantly advanced in comparison with the rest of the world of soul music.

During these years, Motown's sound was not homogenous as is widely considered by the casual listener. Hitsville progressed as the years ticked by, developing from the basic piano and sax foundation of tracks such as "Where Did Our Love Go" [E51] to the densely-layered complexity of "Reach Out, I'll Be There" [579] with an apparently seamless progression. In 1965, Motown's central sound was percussion-led, bass and sax pushed high and strings and brass low. As time went on, percussion sank and strings rose, which with backing vocals becoming steadily more crafted and integrated into the whole, smoothed Motown's rough edges and gave the music a lubricated, forward-driving ethic which was as sophisticated as it was seductive.

In the middle years of this pivotal decade, the process was gradually cultivated, saxes rounded off and sometimes supplanted by smoothly-limited trumpets, rasping bass DI-ed and cleaned up, vocals EQ-ed, drums pushed back and piano chops replaced by electric guitars, sometimes with effects. These refinements, helped by the post-recording manipulation which Motown's technology afforded, fine-tuned the sound-image and ironed out unnecessary abrasions.

Nevertheless, Motown's period recordings tend to define the generally acknowledged 'Motown Sound'. In discussing the subject in his 2002 autobiography, Dennis Coffey (who was at this stage an outsider), interprets the distinctiveness of these records in terms of the studio band, paying particular attention to Benny Benjamin and the generally underrated guitar section, to which he would later become integral (p108-110). Ben Edmonds by contrast takes a less pragmatic view, ascribing the spirit of the music as inherent to Detroit itself (p263). In fact there is something of both explanations in the equation, the third and decisive element being the fabric of the studio. Central to the industry-standard recording process in those days was the 'live' set-up, where bands would record as team units, all instruments firing at once. Because of this method, studio ambience and the particular placing of instruments and microphones profoundly affected the dimensions of any studio's sound. Motown's Snakepit settled with age, the drum-kit taking root and the piano embedding itself into the essential area of the studio floor which remained undisturbed throughout the decade. Regardless of who happened to be working with The Funk Brothers, the room itself had a unique, intangible quality which reverberated through its key recordings as surely as Levi Stubbs' or James Jamerson's idiosyncratic styles have echoed down the years.

In seeking to define Motown's sound, it is too easy to see Berry Gordy's "Rats and Roaches" comment[1] as diplomatically evasive but in fact, he was probably unconscious of the real elements embedded in the music which was generated by a few songwriting teams on similar wavelengths in competition with one other. In the period 1965-67, Motown writers began to depart from regularised chord cycles and take on adventurous animation and unexpected forms. In common with the expanding horizons of popular music more generally, especially that of Bob Dylan and Lennon—McCartney, lyrics began dealing with deeper philosophical issues and taking on a more intelligent and expressive form which pushed the 'meaning' of the records into hitherto unexplored areas. This process is exemplified by the era's leaders HDH, whose themes while rarely lazy or hackneyed, shifted from the relationship narratives of [501], [502], [515], [516], [528] and so on, to the ambitious ephemerality of a track such as "Bernadette" [601] with its implied terrors ('I need you to live') or "Reflections" [616], with its professed unreality and detachment from events ('As I peer through the window of lost time, looking over my yesterdays'.) Primarily considered a musical phenomenon, Motown's lyrical content has been undervalued by critics overwhelmed by the style's emphasis on rhythmic and harmonic ideals when in fact, many Motown tracks exhibit extraordinarily expressive depth and emotion in their texts. (Smokey Robinson and the HDH team in particular show great lyrical ability which deserves better understanding and acknowledgement.)

This period of artistic growth was mirrored by the emergence of Tamla Motown from an obscure label with just a couple of hits under its belt by mid-1966, to part of the pop mainstream by the end of 1967. UK record-buyers were slowly won over and central to this was the role of broadcasters in drawing attention not just to Motown tracks, but to soul music more generally. Broadcasting in the UK tended to be monopolised by the BBC, notoriously conservative and with their own perception of what constituted suitable material. In-line with the simmering tension between the old-guard and the explosion in youth culture which was to define the 1960s, the BBC faced competition from 'pirate' stations broadcasting from outside of the UK's jurisdiction (famously, from ships anchored at sea), and therefore without official control over their play-lists. Stations such as Radio Caroline, Radio Luxembourg and Radio London were picked up by large numbers of teenaged listeners in the early 1960s and were pivotal in exposing strands of popular music rarely heard over the UK airwaves.

Without a BBC rival channel, these stations became part of the sub-culture of youth rebellion, the music thus broadcast feeding an 'in-crowd' of those in-the-know. American soul music tended to be plugged especially heavily by the pirate stations, with disc jockeys such as Tony Blackburn influential in their unabashed support for Tamla Motown and other US-sourced labels. Gradually gathering momentum, the growing popularity of black-American music began to be reflected in the British charts, James Brown scoring his first top 20 hit in the summer of 1966 ("It's A Man's Man's Man's World"), a year in which Wilson Pickett scored three top 40 hits and Otis Redding another four (all for Atlantic). Marking the breakthrough too of Tamla Motown, this era, though widely remembered almost exclusively for the emergence of psychedelia and rock music, was equally significant for the breakthrough of soul music, and with it black acts, into the popular consciousness. The most pervasive view of 1967 was that it constituted a 'summer of love', commemorated in tracks such as Scott McKenzie's "San Francisco (Be Sure To Wear Some Flowers In Your Hair)" and The Beatles' "All You Need Is Love"; however history shows that this is only half the story, June 1967 marking the arrival in the UK top 10 of Aretha Franklin with her outraged and outrageous "Respect", the 'blackest' recording to break as high thus far.

Realising that this was a movement over which they had no control, the UK government took steps during 1967 to rein in the wildly unregulated pirate stations. Passing the Marine Broadcasting Offences Act in August, Prime Minister Harold Wilson's administration effectively extended their sphere of authority out into international waters, a dramatic move which spelled the end of almost all of the pirates. Hand-in-hand came the creation of the BBC's counter-offensive, Radio 1 broadcasting for the first time on September 30, Tony Blackburn poached to host the first show.

Through these processes, and the continuing high quality of material shipped over from Detroit, the period 1965-67 marked the triumphant first successes for Tamla Motown, whose place in the panorama of 1960s music was eternally secured via the foregoing 135 singles. And yet the music world was in a state of continuing instability, 1967 a year of reassessment on several fronts and notable for Bob Dylan's semi-retirement, The Beatles' withdrawal from view (only to unleash the profound *Sgt Pepper's Lonely Hearts Club Band* in June), and the consolidation of acts such as The Jimi Hendrix Experience, Cream and The Velvet Underground. Motown was flying through these turbulent times at full-pace, but come year-end several restless staff were resisting the company's dictatorial stance. Against their drive to push forward, Berry Gordy was trying to keep his personnel on the rails, a battle which by his very engagement he was bound to lose. HDH in particular were defying his unquestioned authority, a turbulent period lying ahead in which Motown would need to dig deep to avoid premature dissolution.

¹ Gordy's actual definition was "A combination of rats, roaches, talent, guts, force and love".

# CHAPTER THREE

# TENSION IN THE AIR

## *1968 and 1969*

**TMG 636**
**MARTHA REEVES & THE VANDELLAS**
**Honey Chile** (2:56)
(Morris—Moy)
Produced by Richard Morris
Recording completed: 27 Sep 1967
**Release Date**: 5 Jan 1968
**B-side**: Show Me The Way
**Position in Record Retailer Top 40**: 30
**Equivalent US Release**: Gordy 7067 (31 Oct 1967)
**Position in Billboard Top 40 Pop**: 11
**Position in Billboard Top 40 R & B**: 5

---

Martha Reeves / Rosalind Ashford / Betty Kelly

---

Motown had experienced ups and downs in 1967, on the one hand consolidating their place in the UK and American markets with a succession of big hits and the acquisition of new artists such as Edwin Starr, on the other suffering their share of misfortune and rebellion which had caused significant rifts behind the scenes. Moving into 1968, the signs were mixed, an uncertain period laying ahead for a company heavily reliant on its unsettled Detroit staff. Prominent amongst the wayward was Martha Reeves, a cause for concern to Berry Gordy throughout the year, for reasons both personal and professional [599]; [621].

Recorded around the time of her ill-fated marriage some months beforehand, her January single acknowledges the arrival on the recording scene of serious competition in the form of Aretha Franklin [629], who had earned herself a record-breaking four gold singles in 1967. Meeting backstage at the Apollo during the previous summer, Reeves was warned off covering Franklin's songs by a humourless diva apparently in the mood for confrontation.[1]

Borrowing from Franklin's recent hits, "Honey Chile" was a custom-built 'southern' number from the Morris—Moy team[2] whose punchy 'powerhouse' arrangement was set in direct collision with Stax's Muscle Shoals Band. With Motown on their mettle, The Funk Brothers had a point to prove, which they managed with genuine enthusiasm, Reeves' blazing, octave-wide vocals completing the picture.

Playing up to her Alabama roots, the track makes extravagant use of country imagery, lyrically unrefined and sketching out the life and love of a teenaged farm-girl brought up by her grandmother. Anticipating 1968's emerging trend towards unpretentiousness—a reaction to the psychedelic artifice of 1967 best exemplified by 'back to basics' albums such as Bob Dylan's *John Wesley Harding*, and The Band's *Music From Big Pink*—the narrative is, behind its unsubtle arrangement, quaintly touching, despite the punch of its rhymes.

A comparatively minor hit in Britain and America, the track was a surprise choice by The Grateful Dead, who, with a considerable amount of alteration, covered it in 1973. The song's country tone may also have inspired Dolly Parton's 1981 chart-topper "9 To 5" which has near identical verses.

<sup>1</sup> Nonetheless, Reeves' *Ridin' High* of May 1968, which contained "Honey Chile", also included a version of "I Say A Little Prayer".

<sup>2</sup> The first of their compositions for Reeves. Released out of sequence, it sheds light on the bucolic flavour of [621].

**TMG 637**
**JUNIOR WALKER & THE ALL STARS**
**Come See About Me** (2:57)
(Holland—Dozier—Holland)
Produced by Brian Holland/Lamont Dozier
Recording completed: 21 Jul 1967
**Release Date**: 5 Jan 1968
**B-side**: Sweet Soul
**Position in Record Retailer Top 40**: -
**Equivalent US Release**: Soul 35041 (7 Nov 1967)
**Position in Billboard Top 40 Pop**: 24
**Position in Billboard Top 40 R & B**: 8

---

Jr Walker / Willie Woods / Vic Thomas / Billy Nicks

---

For Junior Walker 1967 was a difficult year, only February's "Pucker Up Buttercup" [596] seeing light of day, and the group learning that their former drummer James Graves had been killed in a car accident, not long after his departure from the group [571]. His woes compounded by a lack of quality material to record, Walker had been forced to make do with covers of songs already popularised by his stable mates, [571] and [586] preceding the present recording, an interpretation of The Supremes' third American chart-topper from December 1964 [E65].

Starting with the same fade-in gimmick as The Supremes' attractive original (ground-breaking in 1964) during which some very faint vocal scatting is audible, Walker's version has more swing but is less regimented, dropping the disciplined metronome percussion in favour of a punchy snare. Counterbalanced by a bubbling bass line, possibly from James Jamerson[1], the track is one of Walker's most appealing, rounding off the rough edges of his 1965-66 work. Cleanly done by Holland and Dozier (who had also produced The Supremes' recording), the track was an astute selection for the singer and a rare late work from HDH for an artist not generally identified with them [559].

<sup>1</sup> In its range and general tone, reminiscent of the bass track on "Ain't Too Proud To Beg" [565].

**TMG 638**
**CHRIS CLARK**
**I Want To Go Back There Again** (2:39)
(Gordy)
Produced by Berry Gordy

---

Recording completed: 4 Feb 1967
**Release Date**: 12 Jan 1968
**B-side**: I Love You
**Position in Record Retailer Top 40**: -
**Equivalent US Release**: VIP 25041 (23 Feb 1967)
**Position in Billboard Top 40 Pop**: -
**Position in Billboard Top 40 R & B**: -

Chris Clark's last Tamla Motown single is the best of her three, ostensibly supplied and produced by a close Berry Gordy. Clark though has different recollections, claiming that she co-wrote the song, but was content to be omitted from the credits, recognising that next to Gordy she was 'in the learning process'.[1]

Built from discrete elements depicting different angles on a poignant desolation, the lyric's insoluble predicament is turned over in the mind of a woman whose beautiful love affair has passed away. With an anxiously impatient verse and choked chorus, the track steers through a tangle of emotions, fond nostalgia brusquely ousted by the hot-tempered suspicion that a deceptive game was being played all along, the male character for whom she is yearning contorted into a rogue by her mind's inability to integrate the loss.

Recorded with trembling piano and harpsichord and stabbing electric guitars dominant, the track, on which The Lewis Sisters [536] provide backing vocals, was made around the start of 1967, the American release falling between "Love's Gone Bad" [591] and "From Head To Toe" [624] almost a year earlier, and made its UK debut in support of her upcoming *Soul Sounds* album—also by now long-available in the States, but about to be re-released there in stereo.

Clark's recording career effectively coming to a close, a further American release on the Weed label surprisingly appeared at the end of 1969, the only disc put out on Gordy's provocatively named subsidiary, mysteriously titled *CC Rides Again* and featuring a baffling cover shot of the singer riding a donkey. Most Motown fans recognised the 'CC' in question, who remained with the company through the 1970s in the Film and Television department [848]. A personal favourite of Berry Gordy, "I Want To Go Back There Again" was subsequently recorded by Thelma Houston in 1971 (released as an American single as Mo-West 5008) and again by Charlene in 1983 (Motown 1663).

[1] Cited in Davis 1988, p43. Gordy also acknowledged the track's co-authorship in his autobiography, describing it as one of many collaborations between the two (p243).


**TMG 639**
**THE MARVELETTES**
**My Baby Must Be A Magician** (2:31)
(Robinson)
Produced by William "Smokey" Robinson
Recording completed: 11 Sep 1967
**Release Date**: 19 Jan 1968
**B-side**: I Need Someone
**Position in Record Retailer Top 40**: -

**Equivalent US Release:** Tamla 54158 (21 Nov 1967)
**Position in Billboard Top 40 Pop**: 17
**Position in Billboard Top 40 R & B**: 8

---

Ann Bogan / Wanda Young / Katherine Anderson

---

Supplied by Smokey Robinson, this playfully unorthodox number began with something of a joke chorus line, which inspired its eventual comedic arrangement [531]. Sending itself up with a deep-bass curtain-raiser from Temptation Melvin Franklin, the light-hearted approach clearly rubbed off on The Funk Brothers who turn in a larkish performance mainly thanks to James Jamerson wandering unpredictably around his fret board, and a haywire guitar warble warranting a good belly-laugh.

Perhaps misjudged, the effects detract from the composition which, despite its slapstick elements, is effectively atmospheric with an eerily dropping chord foundation, fluently delivered by Wanda Young, Robinson's favoured lead vocalist for the group. (Former lead Gladys Horton had recently resigned from the act due to pregnancy, her place taken by Ann Bogan, an old associate of Harvey Fuqua.) The song managed a surprising top 20 placing in the US.

**TMG 640**
**MARVIN GAYE**
**You** (2:25)
(Bowen—Hunter—Goga)
Produced by Ivy Jo Hunter
Recording completed: 11 Sep 1967
**Release Date**: 26 Jan 1968
**B-side**: Change What You Can
**Position in Record Retailer Top 40**: -
**Equivalent US Release:** Tamla 54160 (21 Dec 1967)
**Position in Billboard Top 40 Pop**: 34
**Position in Billboard Top 40 R & B**: 7

If Berry Gordy's account is anything to go by, his influence over Marvin Gaye's musical suppliers amounts to a conspiratorial master plan which culminated in the present song.[1] How much direct input Gordy actually had is debatable, many of Gaye's former hits the work of self-contained writer-producers at least two of which [510]; [539] were born of the spontaneous inspiration of Smokey Robinson, and many containing self-referential titles belying the assertion. And if "You" was guided by anything, it was certainly not a vision of the crooning love which Gordy invokes; "You" is a loaded affair, 'heavier' in arrangement than his previous singles, and conveying a guarded paranoia strongly suggesting a 'forbidden' inter-racial relationship.

Commencing with an apparition of his lover seen in the mirror (probably referencing the similar vision in "Nowhere To Run" [502] and suggesting a restless night), the track is densely arranged, its impenetrable canopy providing the screen behind which the secret lovers skulk. The foundation of

---

the production is likely developed from "You Keep Running Away" [623] (with which it is contemporary), whose rhythmic patterns are repeated here, including an opening whole bar afforded only the key word 'You'.

Switched from the major to a more penetrating D minor, Gaye's song makes more of its rhythm track, replete with bongos, which Bill Dahl sees as illustrative of 'the soul idiom's increasing emphasis on funky rhythm patterns at the expense of intricate melodic lines'.[2] While this is partly true, the melody's reliance on the minor 5th effectively precluding a carefree ranging, the song is progressive along the lines established by Norman Whitfield over the preceding 12 months [686] and does not explicitly aim at the soul arena *per se*. In fact, the track is a notable stepping stone in Gaye's developing late style, its lyrical depth echoed by his contemporary material recorded for *In The Groove* which tends towards reflective, essentially pessimistic themes and includes the resigned B-side to the current single, which Gaye co-wrote.

The truth was the singer, ever restless, was by now developing an unhealthy reliance on cocaine, more freely available in Detroit through 1967, and which he would imbibe through rubbing small quantities onto his gums. Affecting in his period output, the drug's long-term inducement of edginess and anxiety meant the emotionally unstable singer was playing with fire, compounding his personal unrest and further alienating himself from Berry Gordy, something in which the maverick in him privately revelled. That he lacked the enterprise to leave Motown altogether and take responsibility for his art speaks of his listlessness and lack of motivation at the time. (Gaye was well-known for his love of lounging in bed or repairing to the golf course when in truth, his career was in need of some reinvigoration.)

[1] p236. Claiming to have deliberately steered Gaye's material, Gordy stated, "Marvin was a sex symbol from the start. That gave me the idea to encourage the writers to create 'You' type songs where he could sing directly to women… He even recorded a song just called 'You'."
[2] Abbott p109

**TMG 641**
**THE TEMPTATIONS**
**I Wish It Would Rain** (2:51)
(Whitfield—Strong—Penzabene)
Produced by Norman Whitfield
Recording completed: 14 Sep 1967
**Release Date**: 2 Feb 1968
**B-side**: I Truly Truly Believe
**Position in Record Retailer Top 40**: -
**Equivalent US Release**: Gordy 7068 (21 Dec 1967)
**Position in Billboard Top 40 Pop**: 4
**Position in Billboard Top 40 R & B**: 1

Otis Williams / Melvin Franklin / Paul Williams / Eddie Kendricks / David Ruffin

Modelled on Carole King's "Crying In The Rain", a track popularised in the 1962 hit version by The Everly Brothers, "I Wish It Would Rain" speaks of the misery felt when yearning for the return of a lost love, and using inclemency as a literal mask for one's tears. Yet the resemblance between the two songs might be obscure, were it not for the fact that Barrett Strong elected to utilise essentially the same melodic pattern of King's title phrase in the piano track, set in its home key of Bb major, as against the original's minor pitching. (The phrase 'A man ain't supposed to cry' is similarly recycled, having already appeared in Whitfield and Strong's "I Heard It Through The Grapevine" [686].)

Nonetheless, the emotion heard in the narrative is authentic. Penned by Roger Penzabene, the tale is true, his wife having left him shortly beforehand (see [604]), his despair apparent in the fact that, during the recording session, he was said to be continually sobbing. Unable to endure, Penzabene took his own life days after the track was recorded, the Temptations hearing the sad news in New Jersey during a fittingly protracted downpour.

In seeking to summon a sense of the elements, Whitfield mixed in some seagull and ocean sound effects, earning praise out of proportion to the resulting production's merits, the track becoming one of the group's more admired. (Spawning a 1973 cover version from The Faces which made number 8 in the UK, "I Wish It Would Rain" also attracted several in-house versions such as [674]; [868b].) Dennis Coffey has claimed the guitar track[1], which if true would date his involvement with Motown to the late summer of 1967, some months prior to that generally cited [707].

[1] Coffey, p216


## TMG 642
## THE ELGINS
**Put Yourself In My Place** (2:25)
**Re-issue of [551]**
**Release Date**: 9 Feb 1968
**Position in Record Retailer Top 40**: -

---

Saundra Mallett Edwards / Cleo 'Duke' Miller / Johnny Dawson / Robert Fleming

---

Before normal service terminated towards the end of 1976, Tamla Motown re-used prior A-sides 37 times, the first such venture a re-appearance of The Elgins' inaugural single. With the group having gone their separate ways in 1967, their VIP album *Darling Baby* was seen as a rich fund by Tamla Motown, who planned a belated 1968 UK issue of the 12-track set, which included each of their three 45s as well as covers of "In The Midnight Hour" and "When A Man Loves A Woman". This single was its appetiser, released to little effect seven months before the album, and carrying the original B-side.


## TMG 643
## RITA WRIGHT
**I Can't Give Back The Love I Feel For You** (2:38)
(Ashford—Simpson—Holland)
Produced by Brian Holland/Lamont Dozier

---

Recording completed: 17 May 1967
**Release Date**: 16 Feb 1968
**B-side**: Something On My Mind
**Position in Record Retailer Top 40**: -
**Equivalent US Release**: Gordy 7064 (11 Jan 1968)
**Position in Billboard Top 40 Pop**: -
**Position in Billboard Top 40 R & B**: -

Contracted via Brian Holland in 1966 following an impressive audition, would-be ballet dancer Syreeta Wright had served her Motown apprenticeship (as had a number of her female colleagues) with secretarial duties and occasional backing singing. Finding herself consistently thwarted, Wright resorted to badgering Holland for a recording date, until he eventually capitulated and agreed to provide her with a potential single.

Not willing to offer any new compositions [623], Holland took Wright into Studio A at the tail-end of 1967 to work on a track written by Ashford & Simpson. Lying in wait for a female vocal, the keyboard-heavy backing tapes were requisitioned by Holland, the emergent number revealed as one of Tamla Motown's most delicately poised (witness the adroitly restrained bass notes at 0:04, 0:19, 1:06 etc, expertly contrasting with the rapid-pulsing playing in the bridges).

"I Can't Give Back The Love I Feel For You" finds the central character confessing her willingness to surrender any material thing to the lover who no longer needs her, while unable to relinquish the love itself which still lives inside. Wright's vocal explores the contrasting passion and reflection of the track's main sections neatly, her sharp, precise reading lending an air of emotional detachment which her isolation naturally conjures. The joy of the recording though shines through its alluring choruses, in which instruments and orchestral score move around the sophisticated vocals, at the service of Wright's classily aloof horizontality. (The recording succeeds despite being book-ended by a discordant opening trumpet blast and questionable key change at the close.)

With input from some of Motown's stellar writer-producers and a decent publicity campaign, there was every reason to expect this compelling single which stands as one of Motown's most pleasing popular ballads of the era would become a hit, justifying the Anglicisation of Wright's first name for the mass-market. However it failed miserably on both sides of the Atlantic, and Wright was forgotten, until teaming up with Stevie Wonder in 1970 [744].


**TMG 644**
**SHORTY LONG**
**Night Fo' Last (Vocal)** (2:28)
(Paul—Long)
Produced by Brian Holland/Lamont Dozier
Recording completed: 15 Sep 1967
**Release Date**: 23 Feb 1968

**B-side**: Night Fo' Last (Instrumental)
**Position in Record Retailer Top 40**: -
**Equivalent US Release**: Soul 35040 (11 Jan 1968)
**Position in Billboard Top 40 Pop**: -
**Position in Billboard Top 40 R & B**: -

A return towards Long's familiar style after the anomalous "Chantilly Lace" [600], "Night Fo' Last" is essentially "Function At The Junction" [573] part two, something acknowledged in the track's prelude. Performed in a more relaxed manner showcasing Long's gravelly vocal, the single is his most appealing to date, carrying more of Motown's patent sound than his previous A-sides and yet retaining a raw edge. With characters including Dr. Feelgood, Skinny Minnie, Betty Boo and a crowd of screaming hippies, this light-hearted stomp won approval from dance audiences despite flopping commercially. (The phrase 'shake your tail feather', while deployable in any number of period recordings, reveals the original inspiration of Long's [573].)

Notably, the single has an instrumental rendition on its flip, taking a cue from the world of reggae where the inclusion of 'versions' is standard practice. With lead Hammond keyboards from Long, the recording further emphasises his rising profile, an album and hit single pending [663].


**TMG 645**
**GLADYS KNIGHT & THE PIPS**
**The End Of Our Road** (2:19)
(Penzabene—Strong—Whitfield)
Produced by Norman Whitfield
Recording completed: 14 Dec 1967
**Release Date**: 1 Mar 1968
**B-side**: Don't Let Her Take Your Love From Me
**Position in Record Retailer Top 40**: -
**Equivalent US Release**: Soul 35042 (25 Jan 1968)
**Position in Billboard Top 40 Pop**: 15
**Position in Billboard Top 40 R & B**: 5

---

Gladys Knight / Merald 'Bubba' Knight / Edward Patten / William Guest

---

With a candid, autobiographical lyric from Roger Penzabene, "The End Of Our Road" lays out the background events which led to his suicide [641]. From the opening 'It's all over', through the acknowledgement of his wife 'Running around with every guy in town', and the telling line 'I just broke up running out of tears', his text admits the despair present in [641], his madness palpable and the references to reckless driving hinting at his imminent death.

Translated into a recording by Whitfield and Strong, the pain expressed is obscured, the follow-up to Gladys Knight's "I Heard It Through The Grapevine" [629] treading a similar path and sharing the key of C major. Built from a standardised blues sequence powered along by Knight's passionate vocal and underpinned by a pointed, stabbing guitar, the song packs a punch equal to [629] but lacks originality and harmonic interest, accounting for its stalling at number 15 in the US charts.

## TMG 646
## EDWIN STARR
**I Am The Man For You Baby** (2:33)
(Dean—Weatherspoon—Bowden)
Produced by James Dean/William Weatherspoon
Recording completed: 17 Jan 1968
**Release Date**: 16 Feb 1968
**B-side**: My Weakness Is You
**Position in Record Retailer Top 40**: -
**Equivalent US Release**: Gordy 7071 (21 Mar 1968)
**Position in Billboard Top 40 Pop**: -
**Position in Billboard Top 40 R & B**: -

A step-up after Starr's inaugural Tamla Motown release [630], "I Am The Man For You Baby" carries a bold opening figure which promises a venture into the pop vein, before rooting itself in a gutsy riff, bass and guitar in tight unison. Drawing on the newly developing funk idiom (see [620]), this passage is amongst Motown's most progressive from the era, lending the track a rugged solidity, brought into relief by the wilful airiness of the chorus arrangement (presumably derived independently: funk music tends to evolve from a foundation riff, often spontaneously arrived at in-studio, and used as a necessarily constrained framework for the other instruments).

Attractive if inconsequential, the track passed the general public by, Gordy's most promising acquisition from Ric Tic not recovering his commercial edge until later in the year [672].

## TMG 647
## FOUR TOPS
**If I Were A Carpenter** (2:47)
(Hardin)
Produced by Brian Holland/Lamont Dozier
Recording completed: 26 Oct 1966
**Release Date**: 8 Mar 1968
**B-side**: Your Love Is Wonderful
**Position in Record Retailer Top 40**: 7
**Equivalent US Release**: Motown 1124 (11 Apr 1968)
**Position in Billboard Top 40 Pop**: 20
**Position in Billboard Top 40 R & B**: 17

Levi Stubbs / Lawrence Payton / Abdul 'Duke' Fakir / Renaldo 'Obie' Benson

A second successive cover for The Four Tops, "If I Were A Carpenter" was sourced from the same album as its predecessor [634], a sixth title from the set to appear on 45, during an era when album sales generally were surpassing those of singles for the first time. Penned by New York-based singer Tim Hardin (and successfully covered by future Motowner Bobby Darin in 1966), "If I Were A Carpenter" masks its folk origins with a soulful veneer, Levi Stubbs handling the solo vocal against falsetto backing singers mixed into a semi-incoherent recess, which for long periods hold their 'harmonies' via a single sustained chord. A song musing the legitimacy of the central relationship, it poses its rhetorical question in the context of social (and financial) status.

Catchily rendered, the 17-month-old track took the group back into the top 10, thereby serving to keep them in the public eye. (In truth, The Four Tops were at a standstill as a recording outfit, nothing new appearing between October 1967 [623] and August 1968 [665].) A less enthusiastic American public hoisted it to number 20 in May, their least successful showing in three years.

## TMG 648
## SMOKEY ROBINSON & THE MIRACLES
**If You Can Want** (2:26)
(Robinson)
Produced by William "Smokey" Robinson[1]
Recording completed: 19 Jan 1968
**Release Date**: 15 Mar 1968
**B-side**: When The Words From Your Heart Get Caught Up In Your Throat
**Position in Record Retailer Top 40**: -
**Equivalent US Release**: Tamla 54162 (8 Feb 1968)
**Position in Billboard Top 40 Pop**: 11
**Position in Billboard Top 40 R & B**: 3

---

Smokey Robinson / Bobby Rogers / Claudette Rogers Robinson / Warren 'Pete' Moore / Ronnie White

---

In view of his colleagues' recent exploration of more extensive sound palettes—in particular, recent outings from of Marvin Gaye and The Temptations—"If You Can Want" shows Smokey Robinson aiming at something more intense and 'hip' than his recent singles, aware that he was losing ground on his rivals. Using essentially the same chords as "More Love" [614], "If You Can Want" drops the vocal line onto the tonic (pitched a third sharp), toughening the basic template and presenting a more robust foundation. In fleshing out the production with agitated percussion and riffing brass, Robinson exploits the *depth* of the arrangement, relying on a leaden bass trumpet for support. (The arrangement is probably inspired by Archie Bell & The Drells' "Tighten Up", then a popular B-side but about to become a major hit single in its own right, on the Atlantic imprint.)

Apparently reviving the benevolent spirit of "Reach Out I'll Be There" [579], the track was developed under the working title "When You Want Me I'll Be There", based on its chorus lyric, but in fact pointing equally to The Beatles' (earlier) "Any Time At All" (and, in keeping with the ongoing chain of cross-references, can be seen as a forerunner to The Spinners' 1972 cut for Atlantic, "I'll Be Around"). One of the most jumbled texts in its author's catalogue, the lyric's curiously convoluted logic defies direct derivation, "If You Can Want" revealing him in uneasy mood, his natural articulacy for once floundering in confusion.

[1] The label gives the producer erroneously as '"Smokey" Cleveland'.

## TMG 649
## JIMMY RUFFIN
**I'll Say Forever My Love** (2:57)
(Dean—Weatherspoon—Bowden)
Produced by James Dean/William Weatherspoon
Recording completed: 17 Oct 1967
**Release Date**: 22 Mar 1968
**B-side**: Everybody Needs Love
**Position in Record Retailer Top 40**: -
**Equivalent US Release**: Soul 35043 (13 Feb 1968)
**Position in Billboard Top 40 Pop**: -
**Position in Billboard Top 40 R & B**: -

Written and produced by the same team as "I Am The Man For You Baby" [646], Jimmy Ruffin's fifth British single carries a characteristically emphatic chorus line, which overshadows the relatively uninspired verses. Concerning the singer's attempts to convince a lover of his devotion in the face of doubts expressed by others, the track is a pleading affair, whose musical form fails to match the thrust of the lyric despite its large bass and classical orchestration.

Missing the top 40 in Britain and America, "I'll Say Forever My Love" seemed to indicate that Ruffin's appeal was waning, after considerable initial promise. This however does not anticipate his continued popularity on the UK Northern Soul scene, this single one of several by Ruffin which would gain a second wind around the turn of the decade [740].

## TMG 650
## DIANA ROSS & THE SUPREMES
**Forever Came Today** (3:13)
(Holland—Dozier—Holland)
Produced by Brian Holland/Lamont Dozier
Recording completed: 23 Jan 1968
**Release Date**: 5 Apr 1968
**B-side**: Time Changes Everything
**Position in Record Retailer Top 40**: 28
**Equivalent US Release**: Motown 1122 (29 Feb 1968)

**Position in Billboard Top 40 Pop**: 28
**Position in Billboard Top 40 R & B**: 17

---

### Diana Ross / Florence Ballard / Mary Wilson

Working relentlessly into 1968, The Supremes had come through a troubled period with a business-as-usual presentation which successfully concealed the political wranglings of the previous summer, much of the outside world unaware of the group's change in personnel. Visiting the UK at the start of the year, The Supremes were booked for a fortnight's stint at the Talk Of The Town, a venue in the heart of London's artsy quarters off the Charing Cross Road. Opening the series of performances before stellar guests including Paul McCartney, Cliff Richard and Shirley Bassey, the sell-out shows were afforded universal acclaim by the British press, and were widely regarded as an unmitigated triumph. Footage from the two-week residency was broadcast by the BBC in a one-hour special on February 3 and the tapes quickly packaged into a live album[1] (the group's first recorded output from the UK) released with their *Greatest Hits* collection already sitting at the summit of the British charts.

And yet with the group's popularity as high as ever, there were problems of immense magnitude behind the scenes. Informed that HDH were 'on some sort of strike' at the end of 1967, it was becoming increasingly apparent that an impasse had arisen which threatened to fracture Motown completely, with Gordy to some extent caught unawares by his self-imposed isolation at Sunset Boulevard. (HDH, still at this stage open to negotiation, were said to be unable to make contact with him.) Faced with the pending loss not just of his foremost writing outfit but also in the Holland brothers his head of A & R and Quality Control respectively, Berry Gordy had to contemplate the prospect of continuing without them, the alternative amounting to an impossibly humbling submission.

Characteristically resolving to press ahead regardless, Gordy sought to capitalise on The Supremes' crest of popularity by plucking the current title from the vaults. The backing track recorded in LA for The Miracles on 20 April 1967, "Forever Came Today" was, like "In And Out Of Love" [632] before it, an HDH number which served to fill a gap in their release schedules, implying to the record-buying public that, down at Hitsville, all was well. Sitting in the can with no suitable release to accommodate it, the song was a strong leftover ripe for airing, which The Supremes overdubbed in January 1968, and which, according to Mary Wilson, features only Diana Ross from the group.[2]

Carrying a wistful opening verse, "Forever Came Today" is the most evocative of the group's singles to date, which HDH were particularly pleased with.[3] Tellingly, the track clocks in at 3:13, the first Tamla Motown 45 to over-run three minutes, during which it manoeuvres evasively around its inventive chord changes, as if deliberately avoiding coming to a conclusion, only returning to a trademark crotchet beat in the choruses. Given its expressive strength and credentials as a bona-fide HDH recording, the song's moderate returns dumbfounded Gordy, its lowly 28 placing in the US the group's poorest in more than four years. Convinced of its merit, Gordy would re-work structural elements of the song later in the year for a single calculated to re-launch The Supremes with a vengeance [677].

[1] See [722n]

[2] Wilson 1986, p267-8

[3] Brian Holland: "It was like a miracle song to me. At that moment of fulfilment, as a producer and writer, I thought it was an awesome piece of product." (Quoted in liner notes to The Supremes, a 5-CD box set released in 2000.)

**TMG 651**
**CHUCK JACKSON**
**Girls, Girls, Girls** (2:41)
(Robinson—Cleveland)
Produced by William "Smokey" Robinson/Alfred Cleveland
Recording completed: 11 Oct 1967
**Release Date**: 11 Apr 1968
**B-side**: (You Can't Let The Boy Overpower) The Man In You
**Position in Record Retailer Top 40**: -
**Equivalent US Release**: Motown 1118 (1 Feb 1968)
**Position in Billboard Top 40 Pop**: -
**Position in Billboard Top 40 R & B**: -

With a couple of hits for the Wand label under his belt and a firmly established reputation for quality soul, New Yorker Chuck Jackson's arrival at Motown in September 1967 promised great things. A friend of the Gordy family for some years, Jackson was known also to Smokey Robinson who took care of the newcomer's affairs, putting a whole album together with him, consisting largely of choice numbers from the Jobete catalogue, over a six-month span. Of the titles recorded, "(You Can't Let The Boy Overpower) The Man In You", a cover of the Miracles' single from 1964 [E39], was amongst the strongest, and was duly selected by Robinson as Jackson's first American Motown single in February 1968. Yet his deep baritone *timbre* coupled with Robinson's punchy arrangement showed questionable judgement, the song's public failure provoking criticism of Motown's production-line ethic, Jackson's modified style seen to "consist largely of empty mannerisms, delivered with a good deal of energy but without much conviction".[1]

Two months later, the single was optimistically flipped for a UK release, despite its title clashing with an old Coasters song recently taken into the UK charts by The Fourmost. "Girls, Girls, Girls" is a solidly rocking number, showing a melodic resemblance in its choruses to Robinson's "(Come 'Round Here) I'm The One You Need" [584]. Ending up somewhat austerely constrained, Jackson's recording leans more toward cabaret than Motown's brand sound, the singer not surprisingly continuing to focus primarily on his live act, a succession of powerful performances at Detroit's Twenty Grand club drawing considerable local attention. A follow-up single would be two years coming [729].

[1] Morse, p93

**TMG 652**
**THE ISLEY BROTHERS**
**Take Me In Your Arms (Rock Me A Little While)** (2:39)
(Holland—Dozier—Holland)
Produced by Brian Holland/Lamont Dozier
Recording completed: 20 Jan 1968
**Release Date:** 19 Apr 1968
**B-side:** Why When The Love Is Gone
**Position in Record Retailer Top 40:** -
**Equivalent US Release:** Tamla 54164 (14 Mar 1968)
**Position in Billboard Top 40 Pop:** -
**Position in Billboard Top 40 R & B:** 22

---

Ronald Isley / Rudolph Isley / O'Kelly Isley

---

As a strategy aimed to keep revenue within Hitsville, Motown acts would be instructed to regularly cover material by their stable-mates where originals were in short supply, ensuring that albums were often bulked out with Jobete-owned compositions. While this was standard practice, the re-use of singles tracks as A-sides was less common in the UK, but nevertheless occurred on 18 occasions.[1] Although most of these were legitimately recorded as part of the artist in question's career development, a few were essentially marketing gimmicks dreamt up by Motown's management. The first such instance in the UK was the current single, formerly recorded and released by Kim Weston [538], but previously earmarked for Martha Reeves & The Vandellas.

Using the Vandellas' original unused backing track from 10 September 1964, The Isley Brothers' release eschews bright tambourine for bongos, and a low-level Hammond organ stands in for the jangling piano, providing darker shading than anything on the recording prepared for Weston. Yet pitched in the same key and tempo, the differences are ultimately slight, there being little to justify this release but for a requirement for product in the absence of contemporary HDH material.

[1] Of Motown's writer-producers, only Norman Whitfield showed sustained interest in reinterpreting his own hits. See 'Facts & Feats' section for specific instances.

**TMG 653**
**STEVIE WONDER**
**Shoo-Be-Doo-Be-Doo-Da-Day** (2:44)
(Cosby—Moy—Wonder)
Produced by Henry "Hank" Cosby
Recording completed: 2 Feb 1968
**Release Date:** 26 Apr 1968
**B-side:** Why Don't You Lead Me To Love
**Position in Record Retailer Top 40:** -
**Equivalent US Release:** Tamla 54165 (19 Mar 1968)
**Position in Billboard Top 40 Pop:** 9
**Position in Billboard Top 40 R & B:** 1

---

Viewed as a sequel to "I'm Wondering" [626], this strutting parade under the nose of his love rival reveals Wonder in taunting mood, predicting the day when 'she' will come into his arms. Celebrating the perceived failures of his adversary, Wonder pokes a finger in the face, almost gloating over the upset his love-desire is enduring, the rejoicing dance of the song's wordless refrain amounting to an arrogantly triumphant sneer.[1]

Recorded with the same mode-defining kinetic as his recent singles [613]; [626], the track has an energetic spring, built from syncopated guitar and Wonder's clavinet keyboard, mixed imaginatively by Hank Cosby against a foundation bass riff from James Jamerson. Drawing on his similar figure in the introduction to "Reach Out I'll Be There [579], Jamerson's tightly focussed contribution achieves greater animation than in the contemporary "I Am The Man For You Baby" [646], his most comprehensive absorption of the funk technique to date. Made tensely atmospheric with lofty violins and deep cello riffs (eg at 1:09, probably inspired by George Martin's scores for The Beatles in 1967, in particular "I Am The Walrus"), the production is consummate, sadly underrated against Wonder's period 45s.

[1] The title draws on the doo-wop tradition, recalling titles such as "Shoo Doo Be Doo", a 1954 Moonglows track. The "Shoo Be Doo" refrain also worked its way into the high-school idiom, a subtle variation appearing in "He Was Really Saying Somethin'" [595]. Wonder however was naturally inclined towards vocal scatting, including non-lyrical outbursts in several of his hits ([545]; [558]; [613]; [690b] and so on).

## TMG 654
## BOBBY TAYLOR & THE VANCOUVERS
**Does Your Mama Know About Me** (2:51)
(Chong—Baird)
Produced by Berry Gordy
Recording completed: 12 Dec 1967
**Release Date**: 3 May 1968
**B-side**: Fading Away
**Position in Record Retailer Top 40**: -
**Equivalent US Release**: Gordy 7069 (27 Feb 1968)
**Position in Billboard Top 40 Pop**: 29
**Position in Billboard Top 40 R & B**: 5

---

Bobby Taylor / Wes Henderson / Tommy Chong / Eddie Patterson / Robbie King / Ted Lewis

---

By turn of historical events, Motown's most manifest discourse on inter-racial relationships arrived at a historically defining moment coincident on both sides of the Atlantic. Having delivered his famous 'I've Been to the Mountaintop' speech in front of striking sanitation workers on April 3 1968, Martin Luther King was gunned down in Memphis the following day. The loss of America's leading civil rights advocate in such a brutal and unnecessary way sent a shockwave across the land, which erupted into violence following his funeral a week later[1], putting additional pressure on outgoing president

Lyndon Johnson who swiftly sanctioned the Civil Rights Act, undermining institutionalised racism in areas of housing and employment.

In Britain the situation was scarcely less volatile, Wolverhampton MP Enoch Powell addressing a meeting in Birmingham on April 20 with his infamous 'Rivers of Blood' prophesy, predicting widespread racial violence if the country maintained its then current immigration policy. Advocating repatriation of immigrant communities, Powell was sacked by his party the following day, but not before strikes had broken out amongst supporters and opposition within British industry, against a backdrop of rising tension which saw the early emergence of the neo-Nazi National Front.

Meanwhile in France, students were simultaneously beginning occupation of campus buildings in a series of protests which inspired sympathy action throughout French society. By the end of May France was at a virtual standstill, workers on mass strike and riots breaking out repeatedly, the De Gaulle government forced to dissolve the National Assembly and call immediate general elections.

Such is the epochal spring of 1968 remembered by social historians.

Amid the fighting and mayhem, Tamla Motown issued the present single, a gently calming anthem originally written as a poem by group member Thomas Chong.[2] With its telling racial subtext, "Does Your Mama Know About Me" is one of Motown's most poignant recordings of the era, lucidly delineating the personal fears experienced by a black boy entering into a relationship with a white girl, unfolding the inevitable prejudice both will encounter: will the girl's father 'think the usual way', and does her mother 'know just *what* I am'?

Set to music by record producer Tom Baird, the melodic style echoes that of Burt Bacharach with much of the feel of "Don't Make Me Over" (1963), whose pointed 'Accept me for what I am' refrain resembles Chong's 'Accept me as a man' to the extent that direct inspiration is likely. Taken to Golden World for recording by Berry Gordy, the number's lullaby arrangement is extravagant, the cinematic string sections integral to its melodic progression and evocative of the novel-esque lyric in which the chief characters are outlined against society's harshly judgemental backdrop.

Bobby Taylor was a New Yorker, whose group included guitarist Chong (Chinese-Canadian) and—uniquely for Motown—both black and white members in Eddie Patterson (guitars), Wes Henderson (bass), Robbie King (organ) and Ted Lewis (drums). Discovered by The Supremes in 1967, the group released only one single in the UK (as against three in the US), Taylor making an additional mark on Motown's history by spotting The Jackson 5— something widely and incorrectly attributed to Diana Ross [724]. "Does Your Mama Know About Me" remains their best-known recording, capturing a point in time with uncanny pertinence.

[1] Berry Gordy hastily arranged a benefit concert in Atlanta on request of King's widow Coretta, cancelling several dates in order to free-up Stevie Wonder, The Temptations, The Supremes and Gladys Knight & The Pips.

[2] Who subsequently formed the Cheech & Chong duo with Richard Marin, progressing from stand-up to 'rock-comedy', scoring a handful of hits in the early 1970s.

**TMG 655**
**MARVIN GAYE & TAMMI TERRELL**
**Ain't Nothing Like The Real Thing** (2:14)
(Ashford—Simpson)
Produced by Nickolas Ashford/Valerie Simpson
Recording completed: 6 Oct 1967
**Release Date**: 10 May 1968
**B-side**: Little Ole Boy, Little Ole Girl
**Position in Record Retailer Top 40**: 34
**Equivalent US Release**: Tamla 54163 (28 Mar 1968)
**Position in Billboard Top 40 Pop**: 8
**Position in Billboard Top 40 R & B**: 1

Gaye and Terrell's fourth UK release was an autumn recording with Ashford & Simpson from the *You're All I Need* project, and represents a recovery of singles form after the workmanlike "If I Could Build My Whole World Around You" [635]. Arranged primarily by Valerie Simpson, her time-stop stumble into verse 1 (omitted from the commencement of verse 2) caused synchronisation problems in the studio, the respected producer's challenging charts prompting Joe Messina to express fear of her sessions.[1] For Gaye's part, he was said to be sceptical of the producers' craft, Gaye & Terrell's previous duets having been produced by Harvey Fuqua & Johnny Bristol, requesting each team make their own version. Subsequently referred to Quality Control for a decision, Ashford & Simpson won the day, consolidating their role as musical directors for the pair.

Commencing on a snare shuffle, clipped bass and Gaye's falsetto 'ooh' usher the song in classically, the clarity of the stepping flute lending an air of weightlessness. Drifting on a breeze of violins, the recording obviates the hard-work behind its construction and the chronic woes experienced real-life by both vocalists, Terrell especially fighting emotional and health issues with all the grit of the street-wise fighter which, beneath her public face, she was. Portrayed by Brenda Holloway as an aggressor towards the unsettled Gaye[2], the demure singer was capable of holding her own in Motown's keenly competitive structure, reflected in her taking the lead in the present song, dominating the melody against Gaye's subservient harmonising.

Neatly balanced and dissected by its middle-8, "Ain't Nothing Like The Real Thing" is a suave concern, taking the act into the UK charts for the first of five occasions, and gaining top 10 status at home. Five years later it was picked up by The Jackson 5 and put out as a UK B-side [865b].

[1] Slutsky, p38

[2] Marsh, p143. The observation by her friend provides a new angle on Terrell's part in her violent relationship with David Ruffin [625n].

**TMG 656**
**R. DEAN TAYLOR**
**Gotta See Jane** (2:59)
(Holland—Miller—Taylor)
Produced by R. Dean Taylor

Recording completed: 7 Nov 1967
**Release Date**: 17 May 1968
**B-side**: Don't Fool Around
**Position in Record Retailer Top 40**: 17
**Equivalent US Release**: VIP 25045 (9 Apr 1968)
**Position in Billboard Top 40 Pop**: -
**Position in Billboard Top 40 R & B**: -

Courted by Berry Gordy through 1968, R. Dean Taylor was being drawn into Motown's 'inner circle', reflected here in a first UK release, despite that his two previous American singles included the subsequently lauded "There's A Ghost In My House" [896]. In truth, Taylor's primary trade was as performer, although his coaching by the now truant Brian Holland had set him in good stead for production and writing assignments, and naturally saw him behind the controls for his own recordings.

With a greater degree of artistic freedom than most of his fellow recording artists, Taylor was able to hone his idiosyncratic sound largely untrammelled, his creative use of stereo panning in the present track's intro (absent from the mono single mix) conveying the passage of a speeding car, doubtless the inspiration of his erstwhile tutors [616]. With substantially reverbed vocals, dramatic 'police siren' cello and a smattering of sound effects, Taylor's depiction of the central character's flight is vividly captured, the inclusion of some onomatopœic rain against the windscreen adding to its sense of time and place.

Interesting though the result is, "Gotta See Jane" remains oddly unappealing. Released in Britain in the early summer of 1968, the track made it into the top 20, but was not followed up for nearly two years [763], by which time Taylor's apparent niche had been found with his diversion to the newly-formed Rare Earth label [742]. "Gotta See Jane" was granted a second UK release in the aftermath of the belated success of "There's A Ghost In My House", in late-1974 [918], but was met with indifference second time around.


**TMG 657**
**MARTHA REEVES & THE VANDELLAS**
**I Promise To Wait My Love** (2:05)
(Johnson—Gordy—Story—Brown)
Produced by Henry "Hank" Cosby/Billie-Jean Brown
Recording completed: 18 Jan 1968
**Release Date**: 24 May 1968
**B-side**: Forget Me Not
**Position in Record Retailer Top 40**: -
**Equivalent US Release**: Gordy 7070 (4 Apr 1968)
**Position in Billboard Top 40 Pop**: -
**Position in Billboard Top 40 R & B**: 36

---

Martha Reeves / Rosalind Ashford / Lois Reeves

---

This largely straight piece of 12-bar, despite showing influence of Archie Bell & The Drells' "Tighten Up" (see also [648]), comes over as a fairly overt bid to

---

draw the group—and Reeves in particular—further towards the trail-blazing sound of Aretha Franklin [636], who had scored her sixth American top 10 hit in a year in March. While the style emulation is authentic enough, credit here is due to Hank Cosby's production skills, the track itself something of a writer's experiment, pieced together by Quality Controller Billy-Jean Brown along with Allen 'Bo' Story and (supposedly) a couple of Berry Gordy's relatives.

Early in 1968, Betty Kelly was fired from the group after falling out with Reeves, a replacement located in the latter's kid sister Lois, although none of the Vandellas appear here. With Brown vocalising instead, as well as co-producing, Reeves' view that the company were failing her group by providing sub-standard material [599] was apparently evinced, Reeves nonetheless happy to see the recording through on this occasion.[1] While the sincerity of her ostensibly generous spirit is debatable, it strangely resonates with the song's unconvincing narrative in which the central character is loyally awaiting the return of her lover, currently off on some extra-marital jaunt, admitting as much through gritted teeth.

Although the track was soon forgotten, the 'un-hip' flip-side was drawing attention, and became a single in its own right in 1971 [762].

[1] Quoted in Dahl (p110), Reeves viewed the track as a 'gift', and felt 'blessed to have it'.


**TMG 658**
**THE TEMPTATIONS**
**I Could Never Love Another (After Loving You)** (3:15)
(Whitfield—Strong—Penzabene)
Produced by Norman Whitfield
Recording completed: 19 Feb 1968
**Release Date**: 31 May 1968
**B-side**: Gonna Give Her All The Love I've Got
**Position in Record Retailer Top 40**: -
**Equivalent US Release**: Gordy 7072 (18 Apr 1968)
**Position in Billboard Top 40 Pop**: 13
**Position in Billboard Top 40 R & B**: 1

---

Otis Williams / Melvin Franklin / Paul Williams / Eddie Kendricks / David Ruffin

---

Pitched in the same style as Jimmy Ruffin's "Gonna Give Her All The Love I Got" [603], "I Could Never Love Another" shares the same C major chord throughout most of its verse, only leaning on the crutch of F for interest in its choruses. That the two songs have a common basis is undoubtedly the result of Whitfield and Strong revisiting their earlier work; but in the intervening 12 months, the writing partners had grown in confidence, this new production showing a boldness lacking in Ruffin's earlier recording.

After the initial bass notes (referencing the opening moments of the group's early "My Girl" [E67]), the first chord is introduced one note at a time, courtesy of a triple-layered violin sawing against a pattering percussive—possibly a variation of the 'chair drum' technique of HDH [579]. David Ruffin contributes an assured vocal, his precision falsetto at 0:15 leagues ahead technically of the similar attempt in "Ain't Too Proud To Beg" [565]. Of numerous further cross-references available, Ruffin's complaint that his girl's farewell has 'taken away my reason for living' is cribbed from "Standing In The Shadows Of Love" [589] (to say nothing of its prior redeployment by Ashford & Simpson in "Your Precious Love" [625]). The track's main technical flaw comes in a clumsy collision of its final verse, edited and cross-faded with the chorus at 3:09, calculated to bring the track to an unnecessarily hasty conclusion but creating an unpleasant clash which mars the track.


**TMG 659**
**THE MARVELETTES**
**Here I Am Baby** (2:46)
(Robinson)
Produced by William "Smokey" Robinson
Recording completed: 21 Mar 1968
**Release Date**: 7 Jun 1968
**B-side**: Keep Off, No Trespassing
**Position in Record Retailer Top 40**: -
**Equivalent US Release**: Tamla 54166 (2 May 1968)
**Position in Billboard Top 40 Pop**: -
**Position in Billboard Top 40 R & B**: 14

---

Ann Bogan / Wanda Young / Katherine Anderson

---

The most novel series of recordings made at Motown during the 1960s were Smokey Robinson's compositions for The Marvelettes, which since the end of 1965 had displayed a playful disregard for commercialism in favour of quirky humour. What this meant in terms of the group's projected fan-base is unclear, most of the singles from "Don't Mess With Bill" [546] onwards flopping entirely, such that by the end of 1968 they were on the verge of dissolution.

The present composition was in fact designed for Barbara McNair, released as a US single and title track for her first album late in 1966. Remade for The Marvelettes, the song features a jarringly angular repeating riff which breaks the spell of the otherwise smoothly soulful group performance. Probably 'written' as an improvisation on bass, the run locks onto the major triad, a creative technique from which countless jazz tunes were evolved, and which thereby found its way into similar swathe of soul, funk and R & B.[1]

With its hypnotically repetitive patterns and bold Hammond chords, the track shows The Funks in Booker T territory, their gently grooving foundation[2] providing a suitably sensual arena for Wanda Young's close-miked, breathy lead vocal. (The track justifies the title of its contemporary parent album, *Sophisticated Soul*, released in America in August, but held off until January 1969 in the UK.)

---

[1] The run, heard for example as the basis of Glenn Miller's "In The Mood", can also be identified in countless other places including the underlying pattern of Smokey Robinson's "My Girl Has Gone" [540], the ascending xylophone introduction to "If I Were A Carpenter" [647], the imminent "A Little Bit For Sandy" [670] and the opening

phrase of Stevie Wonder's "Sir Duke" (1976). What makes it significant here is the tracking of xylophone with guitar and bass, giving the pattern a bulky prominence which becomes the song's main hook.

[2] A noticeable technical flaw comes in the fluffed timing on the 'blues' guitar run at 0:33—0:37, the 'live' studio set-up at this stage still precluding separation of instrumental tracks which would have facilitated a spot-repair.

**TMG 660**
**GLADYS KNIGHT & THE PIPS**
**It Should Have Been Me** (2:59)
(Whitfield—Stevenson)
Produced by Norman Whitfield
Recording completed: 16 May 1968
**Release Date**: 14 Jun 1968
**B-side**: You Don't Love Me No More
**Position in Record Retailer Top 40**: -
**Equivalent US Release**: Soul 35045 (16 May 1968)
**Position in Billboard Top 40 Pop**: 40
**Position in Billboard Top 40 R & B**: 9

---

Gladys Knight / Merald 'Bubba' Knight / Edward Patten / William Guest

---

A second consecutive Tamla Motown release to consist of a contemporary re-working, the pained "It Should Have Been Me" was a cover of an early Whitfield—Stevenson number originally donated to Kim Weston and issued in 1963 (Tamla 54076), and considered to be Whitfield's first composition for Motown. (The song shares its title with an early Ray Charles number.) While Weston's original with its abrupt vocal was forthrightly tearful, Knight's remake, which slows the tempo to a despondent drag, is more true to the composition's original mood.

Suitably Gospel-tinged, the narrative takes place inside a church where the singer's true love is marrying another woman, the minister's routine invitation of objections eliciting the indignant/defeatist outburst of the song's chorus. Yet while we learn little of the male character, his sly smile as he walks the aisle insinuates that he has ongoing interests in *both* women, implying that the desperate loyalty of the singer, unable to 'hold her peace' is either misjudged or wantonly submissive—perhaps both.

Modernised by Norman Whitfield, the track is starkly set, its classic doo-wop chord sequence held in place mainly by a wandering bass guitar and tense string section. (Borrowing an opening guitar idea from his own "(I Know) I'm Losing You" [587], the arrangement also thereby owes a distant debt to Cornelius Grant.)

**TMG 661**
**SMOKEY ROBINSON & THE MIRACLES**
**Yester Love** (2:16)
(Robinson—Cleveland)

Produced by William "Smokey" Robinson[1]
Recording completed: 4 Jan 1968
**Release Date**: 21 Jun 1968
**B-side**: Much Better Off
**Position in Record Retailer Top 40**: -
**Equivalent US Release**: Tamla 54167 (13 May 1968)
**Position in Billboard Top 40 Pop**: 31
**Position in Billboard Top 40 R & B**: 9

---

Smokey Robinson / Bobby Rogers / Claudette Rogers Robinson /
Warren 'Pete' Moore / Ronnie White

---

Like the emergence of the sun after a storm, "Yester Love" follows the morose [660] with a lightness of touch belying the lyric's bleakness. Yet the incongruity of theme and style merely show the track's emotional burden to be the result of Robinson's conflicting moods in 1967-68 which, owing to the complications of his marriage to Claudette, had driven him into the arms of a Playboy Bunny Girl whom he had met in Michigan. Still in love with his wife, Robinson was nonetheless seduced by the idea of continuing his illicit affair, keeping his mistress Kandi out of sight of Claudette without terminating either relationship.

For Claudette's part, the likelihood is that she knew of the affair, but was resolved to keep the marriage intact through thick and thin. Yearning for a baby [614], she and Robinson had been persuaded by fertility specialist Dr. Throckmorton that their only course of action would be a surrogate pregnancy, the technology for which was still in its early infancy. Able to conceive successfully but not carry for the full nine months, a fertilised egg was transplanted from Claudette into the womb of a second woman, the risky process duly resulting in a successful birth, on August 16 1968, of a healthy boy. After the requisite legal adoption, the Robinsons named their son Berry William Borope, the first two names deriving from Gordy's and Robinson's own, the unique third invented as tribute to Miracles *Bo*bby Rogers, *Ro*n White and Warren "*Pe*te" Moore.[2]

Released in America a month ahead of the Tamla Motown edition, and three months prior to Berry's birth, "Yester Love", with its disparate sections, reflects the looming contradictions in its composer's emotional life. Ostensibly laying out the regret of a lost love, the lyric seems ominous, its opening line apparently predicting the end of his marriage. Yet the theme is tangled, Robinson resorting to a definition of terms in the unusually pragmatic middle-8, his veiled explanation coming via an apologetic assertion that he still loves his wife. (This section, with its laboured rhymes, probably derives from the similar metrical passages in "The Tracks Of My Tears" [522].)[3] One assumes that *she* has left *him*; yet his cheery observation before the first verse is out that 'tomorrow might bring me one better' implies liberation from constraint, as if her departure were a secret victory.

In terms of musical inspiration, "Yester Love" appears to owe a debt to Stevie Wonder, whose presence can be sensed in the song's musical/harmonic progression borrowed from "Loving You Is Sweeter Than Ever" [568]. The most overt cross-reference though comes via the opening three-chord-trick, an

---

assertive step from Bb through C to a resolving D major—a near direct steal from Wonder's "I Was Made To Love Her" [613], while it also contains lyrical references to "Yester baby" and "Yester kisses", probably inspired by the earlier (but as yet unreleased) "Yester-me, Yester-you, Yesterday" [717]. (Note also the reciprocal influence in Wonder's "Signed, Sealed, Delivered, I'm Yours" [744], borrowing from Robinson's "Here I Am Baby" [659].)

Liberally decorated with 'country' lead guitar, the track like [659] shows Robinson and his group falling back on riffs and musical patterning as the basis of their more recent numbers—indicating that they were composed from the music upwards, probably from group jams. Whether this represents a calculated stylistic measure or is simply the result of Robinson losing his edge is not clear, although in terms of productivity the lead Miracle was back in business, this his fifth Tamla Motown A-side of 1968 after two years of comparative inactivity [569].

[1] Although the disc credits only Robinson, other sources list this as a co-production with Al Cleveland.

[2] Robinson adopts a quintessentially Motown-esque use of the portmanteau: Gordy's publishing company was named in contraction of Joy, Berry and Terry, three of his grandchildren; The Rayber Voices derive from Berry and wife Raynoma; The Vandellas a reduction of Van Dyke and Della Reese; Even Motown itself merges Motor with Town.

[3] Specifically, the appropriate "My smile is my makeup/I wear since my break-up".


**TMG 662**
**DIANA ROSS & THE SUPREMES**
**Some Things You Never Get Used To** (2:23)
(Ashford—Simpson)
Produced by Nickolas Ashford/Valerie Simpson
Recording completed: 7 May 1968
**Release Date**: 28 Jun 1968
**B-side**: You've Been So Wonderful To Me
**Position in Record Retailer Top 40**: 34
**Equivalent US Release**: Motown 1126 (21 May 1968)
**Position in Billboard Top 40 Pop**: 30
**Position in Billboard Top 40 R & B**: -

---

Diana Ross / Cindy Birdsong / Mary Wilson

---

By the autumn of 1968 it had become alarmingly clear that The Supremes had lost their way, with "Forever Came Today" [650] failing to crack the top 20 in America and Berry Gordy faced with the task of revitalising his primary act. Their already incomprehensible album strategy reached a new low in August with the release of *Diana Ross And The Supremes Sing And Perform 'Funny Girl'*, a cynical cash-in on the Barbara Streisand movie with which Motown had no involvement, the long-player shifting an embarrassingly paltry 76,000 copies.[1]

Running into the summer, the group's scheduled release was their recording of Bacharach—David's "What The World Needs Now Is Love"

[801], a pleasantly positive title lifted from *Reflections* and allocated the US catalogue number Motown 1125. However the single was pulled at the eleventh hour in favour of Ashford & Simpson's "Some Things You Never Get Used To", probably pre-constructed without The Supremes in mind, and already, like [643], recorded in-wait for a vocal track. Featuring only Ross (backed by the track's producers), the move was significant, forecasting events 18 months down the line [721], yet the failure of this, the first non-HDH Supremes single since 1963, made Ross' pairing with Ashford & Simpson a false dawn (it attained a lower placing in America than any of the previous 16). Not surprisingly suspicions were raised that Berry Gordy's commitment to the group extended little further than his personal interest in Ross, a story circulating once again around now that the two were on the brink of marriage, her solo performances on tracks such as this fuelling the flames for those 'in the know'—not least the other Supremes.[2]

"Some Things You Never Get Used To" is an unpretentious soft-rocker, pitched minor, and climaxing in a 'shouted' chorus, its only surprise coming via an attention-getting jolt into the C# of its middle-8. Neatly mixed in its producers' usual manner, compressed brass and redolent vocals enhance the listening experience in an optimistic attempt to make the most of an unspectacular basic track blotted by the a clumsy tambourine drop-in/out for the instrumental passage. (Unable to find a musical route back to the verse, the song merely comes to a halt before kicking-off again regardless.)

[1] Taraborrelli 1989, p199. The author speaks highly of the recordings while acknowledging their failure to engage fans and critics.

[2] In view of the fact that [616], [632] and [650] were laid down before the sacking of Flo Ballard (see [616]), her replacement Cindy Birdsong had yet to feature on a UK single by the group.

## TMG 663
## SHORTY LONG
### Here Comes The Judge (2:33)
(Brown—De Passe—Long)
Produced by Shorty Long/B. J.
Recording completed: 24 Apr 1968
**Release Date**: 5 Jul 1968
**B-side**: Sing What You Wanna
**Position in Record Retailer Top 40**: 30
**Equivalent US Release**: Soul 35044 (7 May 1968)
**Position in Billboard Top 40 Pop**: 8
**Position in Billboard Top 40 R & B**: 4

"Here Comes The Judge" was pieced together by Shorty Long together with quality controller Billie-Jean Brown [657] (the 'B. J.' in the producer credits) and Suzanne de Passe, recently brought in to Motown and soon to be appointed Creative Vice-President. The singer's fifth UK single shows him at play, the song's in-joke developed from recurring gag in *Rowan & Martin's*

*Laugh-In*, a madcap sketch show which ran for several years and in its time, attracted numerous show-biz guests. One of these was Sammy Davis Jr. whose on-screen character inspired the lyric, and who was invited to the session to supply the intermittently heard voice of the judge[1], refereeing the comic courtroom of fudge-eating, hat-wearing rabble and absurdly passing sentence on a lad charged with inability to dance.

The spectacle was ludicrous enough to prompt James Jamerson to dismiss the track as 'shit', the final take having the loose quality of a studio improvisation, but with some bite provided by Dennis Coffey's two-note guitar track. However the song won over American audiences with its irreverent swagger, despite the challenge of more than half-a-dozen contemporary versions including one by comedian Pigmeat Markham, which matched Long's number 4 R & B showing but couldn't compete in the pop listings.[2] In truth, despite knocking this particular song, Jamerson called Long "one of the funkiest guys at Motown", citing his own inspired performances on Long's concurrent album as some of his finest.[3] The album in question, named after this track, emerged in August in America (December in UK), enhancing Long's reputation with its impressive variety of humour and incisive musicianship (including earlier singles [573] and [644]).

Moving into 1969, the omens were good for Long, his late recordings including an impressive cover of "A Whiter Shade Of Pale" as well as the moving "I Had A Dream", described by David Morse as having 'a sombre, apocalyptic intensity, a brooding, trance-like solemnity that is positively disturbing'[4], eventually emerging on the suitably titled *The Prime Of Shorty Long*. Tragically, Long would not live to see it released; out fishing in Detroit on Sunday 29 June 1969, Long's boat capsized and he was drowned, aged just 29. Attending the funeral on July 2, an emotional Stevie Wonder laid his harmonica on Long's coffin, a poignant gesture for the singer whose brief legacy won him the respect of his peers and, courtesy of a retrospective CD collection in 2000, lives on in its modest way.

[1] Leading to a brief Motown contract for Davis which saw a US-only album issued in May 1970 followed by the setting up of the ill-fated Ecology label in 1971, co-owned by him and Berry Gordy.

[2] Pigmeat Markham's interest is explained by the fact that he is thought to have invented the basis of the original sketch as far back as the 1930s.

[3] Interview published in *Bass Player* magazine, Spring 1990.

[4] p95. The track was released as a US-only single in February 1969.

**TMG 664**
**JIMMY RUFFIN**
**Don't Let Him Take Your Love From Me** (2:41)
(Whitfield—Strong)
Produced by Norman Whitfield
Recording completed: 14 May 1968
**Release Date**: 19 Jul 1968
**B-side**: Lonely Lonely Man Am I

**Position in Record Retailer Top 40**: -
**Equivalent US Release**: Soul 35046 (20 Jun 1968)
**Position in Billboard Top 40 Pop**: -
**Position in Billboard Top 40 R & B**: -

Containing the most freely moving melody of Ruffin's half-dozen singles to date, "Don't Let Him Take Your Love From Me" was originally given to Gladys Knight & The Pips [645b]. Recorded in an 'easy' style, the single was a candidate for pop success, the chirpy appeal for faithfulness in love 'pushed' by a piercing brass chart which matches the song's air of contented superfluity. Its lukewarm reception though was mainly the result of Motown's diminishing expectations, the vocalist now regarded as something of a one-hit wonder. Like its A-side, the single's flip was a gender-switched cover from Whitfield's back-catalogue [521], evincing a woeful lack of interest in Ruffin who would end up complaining publicly about the predicament, his UK following regarded as anomalous in Detroit and prompting his eventual emigration [753]. The resurgence of interest in Britain would however be another year coming [703].

**TMG 665**
**FOUR TOPS**
**Yesterday's Dreams** (2:55)
(Hunter—Bullock—Goya—Sawyer)
Produced by Ivy Jo Hunter
Recording completed: 13 Jun 1968
**Release Date**: 16 Aug 1968
**B-side**: For Once In My Life
**Position in Record Retailer Top 40**: 23
**Equivalent US Release**: Motown 1127 (27 Jun 1968)
**Position in Billboard Top 40 Pop**: -
**Position in Billboard Top 40 R & B**: 31

Levi Stubbs / Lawrence Payton / Abdul 'Duke' Fakir / Renaldo 'Obie' Benson

Providing new impetus for The Four Tops after a fallow period, "Yesterday's Dreams" marks the start of the group's post-HDH era, a new team of writers coming together for the task, including Pam Sawyer, a white British woman who would go on to have a major hand in [677]. Considered by many to be the most mournful track in the group's discography, this lachrymose 3/4 ballad to a lost love finds Stubbs lamenting his plight with none of the defiance present in "Standing In The Shadows Of Love" [589] and a lack of the grit for which the group were famous.

The song bobs through its verses with an optimistic triplet bass, which bridges from the introduction into the first chorus with a riff borrowed from "Don't Mess With Bill" [546]. But sadly the song's emotive arrangement, tinkling with lullaby bells and crooning vocals, defeats the adeptness of Ivy Hunter's production, with drums, bass, strings, electric guitar and tearfully discordant piano all sent across the spectrum in the stereo mix. While

American audiences were having none of it, the song's *kitsch* sentimentality struck a chord in the UK where the song went top 30 and earned its place at the top of the group's next album.

For a flip-side, "For Once In My Life" was selected, a track about to be made famous by Stevie Wonder [679]. While the Tops' reading marries conceptually with its A-side, it is ultimately as fatigued, and weighs heavily on the ear.


**TMG 666**
**STEVIE WONDER**
**You Met Your Match** (2:42)
(Hunter—Wonder—Hardaway)
Produced by Don Hunter
Recording completed: 18 May 1968
**Release Date**: 23 Aug 1968
**B-side**: My Girl
**Position in Record Retailer Top 40**: -
**Equivalent US Release**: Tamla 54168 (25 Jun 1968)
**Position in Billboard Top 40 Pop**: 35
**Position in Billboard Top 40 R & B**: 2

Having established himself in 1967-68 with a series of up-tempo rockers, Stevie Wonder had turned 18 in May and enjoyed the success of his first *Greatest Hits* package, the UK edition of the summer taking him into the album charts for the first of several times. Riding high on his flourishing fortune, Wonder set about expanding his horizons with an album of harmonica solos set against largely self-made backing tracks in a foretaste of his 1970s musical autonomy. Released in America on Gordy under the pseudonym Eivets Rednow, the record was an amusing enterprise, the deviously cheeky Wonder revelling in the occasional comments coincidentally thrown his way by fans failing to see through his thinly veiled alter-ego.

"You Met Your Match" continues where "Shoo-Be-Doo-Be-Doo-Da-Day" [653] had left off, Wonder switching his aggravated attention to his woman, hounding her over Jimmy (and Freddy!) with a snarlingly defiant admission of having 'taken care of' Cindy and Suzie. What makes "You Met Your Match" unnerving is the implication of violence prickling beneath its raving surface, Wonder's menacing 'wait until I get you home' and brazen admission of calculated cruelty delivered in the context of the triumphant assertion of the song's title, held off until the very end when he positively relishes his expected victory.

Matching the tension of the saga with a funky arrangement and a captivatingly apoplectic vocal from Wonder [690a], the recording is his most clamorous since "Uptight" [545], deserving of a more generous reception. The track was coupled-up here with Wonder's version of "My Girl" [E67], a rendition which departs little from the original and is Tamla Motown's third successive 'hand-me-down' flip-side.

**TMG 667**
**JUNIOR WALKER & THE ALL STARS**
Hip City (Part 2) (2:57)
(DeWalt—Bradford)
Produced by Lawrence Horn
Recording completed: 14 Jul 1968
**Release Date**: 9 Sep 1968
**B-side**: Hip City (Part 1)
**Position in Record Retailer Top 40**: -
**Equivalent US Release**: Soul 35048 (23 Jul 1968)
**Position in Billboard Top 40 Pop**: 31
**Position in Billboard Top 40 R & B**: 7

---

Jr Walker / Willie Woods / Vic Thomas / Billy Nicks

---

It is tempting to interpret the title of Junior Walker's tenth Tamla Motown single as a tribute to his home Detroit, a city still feeling the aftershock of the 1967 riots which had torn communities in two and caused concern for Gordy's own safety [614]. Shifting the centre of his power base from West Grand Boulevard to the Donovan Building had been a precautionary move which coincided with Gordy's purchase of a new luxury dwelling, a three-storey mansion on Boston Boulevard with marbled floors, swimming pool and personal cinema.[1] By now recognised as the richest black man in America, Gordy advertised his success with an elaborate showiness capped by the hanging of his portrait in the guise of Napoleon, in the building's lobby. Wealthy enough to give his former home on Outer Drive to his sister Anna and her husband Marvin Gaye, Gordy nonetheless felt insecure in his opulent new palace, isolated from reality and caught between his class-conscious and race-conscious roots, and his acquired status as king of all he surveyed.

But where did he stand in the eyes of Detroit's citizens? Was he a champion of black communities, representative of their struggle for emancipation; or was he part of the enemy 'system', pursuing the privileged 'white' dream in the midst of so much poverty?

The tension in the air was scarcely eased in August 1968, with a new round of race riots in the Watts district of LA, three years after the most notorious conflicts [527], and just nine weeks after the assassination locally of Robert Kennedy. The situation had hardly calmed down when further uprisings occurred in Chicago, television cameras capturing Mayor Daley's police forces running amok at an anti-war demonstration, beating and injuring hundreds of pacifists.

Fearing that he was becoming a legitimate target, Berry Gordy was left to ponder the very real prospect of another flare-up in Detroit, and the distinct possibility that this time, his family, his business empire and Gordy Manor itself might not escape unscathed. If being walled up in a mausoleum was not his ideal, the answer could only be to flee altogether, to abandon Detroit and the neighbourhood which had been his own, and make his life elsewhere. With this in mind, Gordy found a new house in California, a property in Hollywood Hills which he purchased from comedian Tommy

---

Smothers. Moving home for a second time in the autumn of 1968, Gordy began the process which would culminate in the shift west for Motown itself, a monumental undertaking which would not come to full completion for four years [814].

Pressing on for now in the 'Hip City', Junior Walker's new release was a lengthy 'live' jam, firmed up lyrically with assistance from Janie Bradford, who was apparently called into Hitsville while recording was already underway, and who subsequently delighted in taking a slice of the action for relatively little effort. Recorded sketchily with background noise (dubbed on subsequently) and borrowing the melodic shape of the saxophone riff from "Uptight" [545], the track continues in the extemporised style of "Shotgun" [509], Walker's patent rough-house approach continuing to furrow a groove wilder than any of his stablemates. Spread over two sides, the recording could have come from no other Motown artist. In America, Pt 2 was plugged as the hit cut, making a respectable 31 nationally.

[1] Some photographs of the mansion are reproduced in Benjaminson, p100-1.


**TMG 668**
**MARVIN GAYE & TAMMI TERRELL**
**You're All I Need To Get By** (2:38)
(Ashford—Simpson)
Produced by Nickolas Ashford/Valerie Simpson
Recording completed: 29 May 1968
**Release Date**: 13 Sep 1968
**B-side**: Two Can Have A Party
**Position in Record Retailer Top 40**: 19
**Equivalent US Release**: Tamla 54169 (9 Jul 1968)
**Position in Billboard Top 40 Pop**: 7
**Position in Billboard Top 40 R & B**: 1

Recorded in stages over a six-week spell in the spring of 1968, "You're All I Need To Get By" is the defining moment for Gaye and Terrell, referred to by Nelson George as "a landmark, as good as anything else created by Motown"[1], and certainly from the moment the bass and vocals emerge in the song's introduction it is apparent that here, Ashford & Simpson have created a highlight amongst Tamla Motown's late-1960s catalogue. In their masterful lyric, the profundity of mutual devotion is eternal and immutable, Gaye's towering vows mirrored in Terrell's passionate dedication, the text all-encompassing wherein the two transcend physical love for something deeper and more divine.

One of the finest technical products to come out of Hitsville, the arrangement commences with a four bar introduction with high-pitched bells and ethereal backing vocals (Ashford & Simpson themselves) consisting of the title phrase sung in a chromatic stepwise run from the 5th (E) down to the 3rd (C#), the whole underpinned by an ominously thrumming root A on bass. That done, the figure goes around again, with the added presence of Marvin

Gaye's vocal striding across shifting chords as if single-mindedly in pursuit of love, and then again with Terrell taking centre stage. Against high-held strings, the two central characters are thus introduced, the song proceeding to shake itself loose in the following eight bars which swell and grow to the point of exquisite urgency, climaxing in the thrill of the harmonised chorus, as if the two were finally consummating their union. Gaye's whispered 'Tammi, listen' at the onset of verse two draws Terrell into his sanctified inner space, in which he confides his deepest adoration, his spontaneous 'I know you can' retort to her pledge to 'inspire a little higher' sealing their love with unbridled conviction.

Its importance understated against some of the less crafted and more direct contemporary Tamla Motown releases, the track still sounds arrestingly inventive today, and despite making little splash on release, dwelt in the UK top 50 until into February 1969, easily the longest stay of any of Gaye's hits including "I Heard It Through The Grapevine" [686], but without ever climbing higher than 19. It did its real business in America, going top 10 pop and rightly topping the R & B charts from late August into October. Tracks like this and "Ain't No Mountain High Enough" [611] constitute the pinnacle of duetting in soul music and are the yardstick by which other such collaborations must be assessed.

¹ p137

## TMG 669
## MARTHA REEVES & THE VANDELLAS
**I Can't Dance To That Music You're Playing** (2:37)
(Richards—Dean)
Produced by Deke Richards
Recording completed: 2 Jul 1968
**Release Date**: 20 Sep 1968
**B-side**: I Tried
**Position in Record Retailer Top 40**: -
**Equivalent US Release**: Gordy 7075 (25 Jul 1968)
**Position in Billboard Top 40 Pop**: -
**Position in Billboard Top 40 R & B**: 24

---

Martha Reeves / Rosalind Ashford / Lois Reeves

---

Having fallen in love with her touring band's guitarist David Walker, Martha Reeves' unstable emotions seemed to be on a relatively even keel through mid-1968, but problems would surface during sessions for the current track. A lively tale involving a musician found being unfaithful to his woman, the metaphorical dance of the lyric was, in Reeves' eyes, her own relationship spelled out with disastrous consequences. (That the track's energy stems mainly from a subtle wah-wah guitar possibly brought matters home to her.) In the spirit of professionalism, Reeves commenced the basic track with Deke Richards on 29 May, which contains a sublime moment where her vocals fuse with the sax break at 1:35 in an immaculately seamless cross-fade for which the producer deserves credit.[1]

Finding herself increasing uncomfortable with the lyric, Reeves ended up asking for some last-minute amendments, to be met with flat refusal by Richards. With both parties quickly backing into their respective corners, the situation became insoluble, Reeves walking out of the session in the belief that "I Can't Dance" would never see light of day. Richards however was anticipating a hit single, and in attempting some edits on the raw tape ended up losing part of Reeves' vocal, the solution to which was found in the hiring of Rita Wright and The Andantes to complete the vocal track in Reeves' absence, the song subsequently appearing as a *bona-fide* Vandellas single. The result is decidedly unpalatable, Wright's chorus (which Reeves compared to Diana Ross) clashing with the verses, an understandably livid Reeves left to ruminate on her position in a company willing to treat her with such contemptible disregard.

Sadly, this single would mark the effective end of Reeves' time in the limelight. The singer was becoming worryingly hooked on sleeping pills, and heading for a breakdown from which her career would never fully recover [694].

[1] Whether by direct influence or not, the technique was revived more extravagantly by Pink Floyd in 1977, in the 10 minute-plus "Sheep" (from Animals). The ticking clocks between tracks on the group's Dark Side Of The Moon also has a Motown precedent: [770].

## TMG 670
## PAUL PETERSEN
## A Little Bit For Sandy (2:33)
(Taylor)
Produced by R. Dean Taylor
Recording completed: 27 Jun 1968
**Release Date**: 27 Sep 1968
**B-side**: Your Love's Got Me Burning Alive
**Position in Record Retailer Top 40**: -
**Equivalent US Release**: Motown 1129 (8 Aug 1968)
**Position in Billboard Top 40 Pop**: -
**Position in Billboard Top 40 R & B**: -

Best-known for his appearances on the *Donna Reed Show* sitcom between 1958 and 1966 (in which he played Reed's son Jeff Stone), California-born Petersen had already released a handful of singles including the US top 10 "My Dad" in 1962. (Released on Pye in the UK, none of his releases were hits.) The white child-star turned 21 in 1966, coincident with his signing to Motown via the company's West Coast offices, though quite what Motown thought they could do with Petersen is not clear; initially under direction of Frank Wilson, his first release was "Don't Let It Happen To Us" (May 1967), now remembered more for its B-side, the first airing of "Chained", a future hit for

Marvin Gaye [676]. 15 months passed before Petersen was offered a follow-up, the reins on his sessions having been passed to R. Dean Taylor for "A Little Bit For Sandy". (The backing track was made in Motown's LA studios, the vocals dubbed on back in Detroit. Wilson was behind the single's B-side however.)

Starting with the re-appearance of the familiar riff recently heard on "Here I Am Baby" [659], but feebly rendered on Hammond organ and tracked with steel guitar, the arrangement slips into *faux* country, off-beat hand claps and some wince-inducing rhymes ('I just happened to be handy... for Sandy') suggesting perhaps an eye on Petersen's comedic background. Whatever the rationale, the single is as oddly out-of-place in Tamla Motown's discography as "Jimmy Brown" [534], and marked the end of the label's interest in him.


## TMG 671
## THE TEMPTATIONS
Why Did You Leave Me Darling (2:13)
(Dean—Lussier)[1]
Produced by Norman Whitfield
Recording completed: 25 Apr 1967
**Release Date**: 4 Oct 1968
**B-side**: How Can I Forget
**Position in Record Retailer Top 40**: -
**No Equivalent US Release**

---

Otis Williams / Melvin Franklin / Paul Williams / Eddie Kendricks / David Ruffin

---

Trademark voice of The Temptations, the sometimes volatile David Ruffin had watched with keen interest as Berry Gordy conferred special attention on some of his group's lead singers in 1967 [598]; [616]; [621]. Feeling that he warranted similar treatment, Ruffin had tactically distanced himself from the rest of the group by mid-1968, requesting specific billing on their releases, hiring his own limousines and adopting an aloof air of authority by which he would frequently elect not to show up for rehearsals, and most disastrously of all, live engagements. Matters came to a head in June, when he was voted out of the group (ie sacked), sending his psyche in two directions at once: The toppled leader who needed the band behind him for his very survival; and the liberated artist with a possibility of the solo stardom which he had yearned for all along (see [689]).

"Why Did You Leave Me Darling" was to be Ruffin's swansong release— oddly so, since "Cloud Nine" [707] was ready for release simultaneously in America, the present track being entirely overlooked there and begging the question of why it was selected at all for the UK. Pitched minor, the song shifts to the relative major for the unsubtle choruses, in the generally pronounced style of Jimmy Ruffin, complete with brassy 'marching' trumpets and walking bass line. Norman Whitfield's production however incorporates a brief energising pause prior to the chorus (presumably written separately), recalling the similar device used in the group's "(I Know) I'm Losing You" [587].

---

In the end little more than a creditable album track, "Why Did You Leave Me Darling" is flippant beside "I Wish It Would Rain" [641] and unadventurous next to "Cloud Nine" [707], the group's single-in-waiting, the coming winter's interregnum imposed to make room for some re-asserting collaborations with The Supremes [685].

[1] Debbie Dean was a Motown staffer who began as a recording artist (Motown's first white signing) and later wrote frequently with Deke Richards [669]. Dennis Lussier is Richards working under a pseudonym.

## TMG 672
## EDWIN STARR
**25 Miles** (2:59)
(Fuqua—Bristol—Starr)[1]
Produced by Harvey Fuqua/Johnny Bristol
Recording completed: 26 Jul 1968
**Release Date**: 27 Sep 1968
**B-side**: Mighty Good Lovin'
**Position in Record Retailer Top 40**: 36
**Equivalent US Release**: Gordy 7083 (2 Jan 1969)
**Position in Billboard Top 40 Pop**: 6
**Position in Billboard Top 40 R & B**: 6

Purpose-written in 1963 as a number to close his live shows, Starr had failed in his attempts to get a studio version of "25 Miles" down and might never have done so had he not opted to air the song on the television show, *20 Grand Live*. Provoking a rush of enquiries from the public, the performance convinced Barney Ales that it had commercial potential and should be released as soon as possible, and so Starr convened at Hitsville with Johnny Bristol, Harvey Fuqua and members of The Spinners, to work out a proper chart.

Delighting in the spontaneity of the track which positively celebrates his mammoth trek to the home of his woman, the assembled staff threw in some appropriate foot stomping, and some choice colloquialisms in Starr's count-down vocal. It was worth the five year wait—"25 Miles" became his first top 10 hit in America and his first crack of the top 40 in Britain, putting him firmly in the reckoning and prompting Motown to line up some collaborations with Blinky Williams [720].

[1] Wilson Pickett's "Mojo Mama" bears such a likeness to "25 Miles" that Jerry Wexler and Bert Berns have since been added to the writer credits.

## TMG 673
## SMOKEY ROBINSON & THE MIRACLES
**Special Occasion** (2:17)
(Robinson—Cleveland)
Produced by William "Smokey" Robinson/Al Cleveland

Recording completed: 5 Jun 1968
**Release Date**: 18 Oct 1968
**B-side**: Give Her Up
**Position in Record Retailer Top 40**: -
**Equivalent US Release**: Tamla 54172 (30 Jul 1968)
**Position in Billboard Top 40 Pop**: 26
**Position in Billboard Top 40 R & B**: 4

---

Smokey Robinson / Bobby Rogers / Claudette Rogers Robinson /
Warren 'Pete' Moore / Ronnie White

---

The title track of the group's concurrent album, "Special Occasion" has been overlooked in the group's repertoire, despite finding its chief author in preferred territory where his lyrical eloquence blossoms through relaxed sentiment. Essentially dealing with the excitement still felt from the regular touches of his lover, each one a cherished moment, the track is as unencumbered as "Yester Love" [661] is acutely charged, as if Robinson had found momentary resolution to his personal complications. The track shares similar mock-military fanfares to "Why Did You Leave Me Darling" [671] whose parent album was released ahead of *Special Occasion*. In its unassuming way, one of Robinson's most accomplished throwaways.

**TMG 674**
**GLADYS KNIGHT & THE PIPS**
**I Wish It Would Rain** (2:51)
(Whitfield—Strong—Penzabene)
Produced by Norman Whitfield
Recording completed: 20 Jun 1968
**Release Date**: 25 Oct 1968
**B-side**: It's Summer
**Position in Record Retailer Top 40**: -
**Equivalent US Release**: Soul 35047 (8 Aug 1968)
**Position in Billboard Top 40 Pop**: -
**Position in Billboard Top 40 R & B**: 15

---

Gladys Knight / Merald 'Bubba' Knight / Edward Patten / William Guest

---

Striving not only for artistic excellence but also to maximise his personal stature, Norman Whitfield would make as much as possible from his compositions, frequently passing them around his favoured acts looking for repeat hit singles. Especially noteworthy are the recurrent titles swapped between The Temptations and Gladys Knight & The Pips, who would share five amongst their Tamla Motown singles, the current track however the only example of a mutual A-side.[1]

Just eight months after The Temptations' reading [641] had appeared, Knight's rendition materialised, pitched in the same Bb and running at identical tempo. A fairly uninventive cover which lacks the original's sound effects, Knight's version sticks so close that the utilisation of the same basic backing tracks in the early stages seems possible, although the key instrumentation such as the piano is new to the mix. The main differentiating factor, the lead vocal, is genuinely heart-felt, the two recordings fairly scoring about equally—although The Temptations, having got their hands on the track first, claimed the lion's share of unit sales.

[1] Three more Temptations releases were picked up by Knight for use as B-sides: [587] as [813b]; [620] as [844b]; [707] as [903b]. Only one was swapped in the opposite direction, the flip to the current single which surfaced in September 1970 as [749b] and then again as an A-side a year later [783].

## TMG 675
## FOUR TOPS
**I'm In A Different World** (2:54)
(Holland—Dozier—Holland)
Produced by R. Dean Taylor/Brian Holland/Lamont Dozier
Recording completed: 16 Apr 1968
**Release Date**: 1 Nov 1968
**B-side**: Remember When
**Position in Record Retailer Top 40**: 27
**Equivalent US Release**: Motown 1132 (19 Sep 1968)
**Position in Billboard Top 40 Pop**: -
**Position in Billboard Top 40 R & B**: 23

---

Levi Stubbs / Lawrence Payton / Abdul 'Duke' Fakir / Renaldo 'Obie' Benson

---

The stand-off between Berry Gordy and HDH [650] had reached stalemate by the middle of 1968, Motown ploughing on without them and finding alternative writer-producers for the groups HDH once catered especially for. For their part, Dozier and the Holland brothers waited guardedly to see if Gordy would cave in, but as time went by it became increasingly clear that an amicable outcome would never be found, the two parties not even communicating with one another by the middle of the year. Under agreement with Motown, HDH were viewed by Gordy as legally obligated to him, their withdrawal of labour tantamount to breach of contract. Once he got wind that Capitol Records had approached the team, he initiated action against HDH in the form of a $4million lawsuit filed on 29 August which succeeded in barring HDH from offering their creative services elsewhere, at least until the case had been settled.

According to his autobiographical accounts, Gordy took the step primarily to provoke them into returning to work[1] but whether this was his true logic at the time is debatable. Although his contractual argument was on-the-face-of-it sound, and his potential loss of revenue justification enough for his actions, he must have known that the step would cause an irreversible fracture in relations, preventing the very resolution he claimed to have been seeking. The response from HDH nonetheless surprised him: they countersued for some $22million, alleging long-term discrepancies in Motown's remuneration and requesting the company be put into receivership, besides affirming that no written contract between them and Gordy had existed since mid-1967, precluding the alleged breach.

In the event, there could be no reconciliation, The Four Tops' new single their last HDH recording, marking the end of an era for The Four Tops and Motown and indeed popular music as a whole. The track was custom-made for Levi Stubbs, the narrow vocal range allowing him to dwell in the characteristic rasping range of his high tenor. The central concept revealed through the lyric is that of the 'lovelight' [E34] which transports the main character from the despondency of the real world into a blissful interior space, his lover relieving the lifelong gloom which has tormented him. Bracketing the track with 'dream/illusion' numbers such as "Shake Me, Wake Me" [553] and "Yesterday's Dreams" [665], David Morse locates the song amongst the group's reflective recordings.[2] However the fact that the track is pitched in the present, redeeming love fully at hand, gives it an optimism missing from the earlier singles.

Interviewed by BBC DJ Richard Allinson in 2004, Lamont Dozier named "I'm In A Different World" his favourite track from his own back-catalogue, a surprising choice which expresses the creative high HDH were on when affairs with their employers conspired to turn sour. Despite the underlying positivity of the song, "I'm In A Different World" failed to sell when put out as a September single in America, subsequently limping to number 27 in the UK, an ignominious end for one of the most electrifying musical unions of the 1960s.

[1] p262-3
[2] p79


## TMG 676
## MARVIN GAYE
**Chained** (2:35)
(Wilson)
Produced by Frank Wilson
Recording completed: 20 Jun 1968
**Release Date**: 8 Nov 1968
**B-side**: At Last (I Found A Love)
**Position in Record Retailer Top 40**: -
**Equivalent US Release**: Tamla 54170 (20 Aug 1968)
**Position in Billboard Top 40 Pop**: 32
**Position in Billboard Top 40 R & B**: 8

Frank Wilson's "Chained" was originally given to new-boy Paul Petersen [670] in 1967, since when Barbara Randolph had also had a crack at it. And although numerous other Motown artists would tackle the song, the definitive reading belongs to Gaye, the evasive chords matching his recent weighty style exactly, the June vocal dubbed onto a backing track put together between February and May.

Stomping through its four verses, the song's minor key progresses edgily, Gaye's precarious mind-set eliciting more than one penetrating moment as he admits to trembling at the prospect of losing his love. In this scenario, the chains are emotional rather than worldly, evoking the similar sentiment in Goffin—King's "Chains" (a hit for The Cookies in 1962). The fact that Gaye may have read personal meaning into the text is suggested by an interview by biographer David Ritz in which the subject of his marriage to Anna surfaced, "I felt chained. I saw no way out. I couldn't control the cheating—mine or Anna's".[1]

Produced with enough kick to earn release as a single, Gaye's performance on "Chained" won praise from his producer but made little impact in terms of national sales, its main success coming via the R & B market. Backing vocals are by The Originals.

[1] Ritz, p162

## TMG 677
## DIANA ROSS & THE SUPREMES
**Love Child** (2:55)
(Sawyer—Taylor—Wilson—Richards)
Produced by The Clan
Recording completed: 20 Sep 1968
**Release Date**: 8 Nov 1968
**B-side**: Will This Be The Day
**Position in Record Retailer Top 40**: 15
**Equivalent US Release**: Motown 1135 (30 Sep 1968)
**Position in Billboard Top 40 Pop**: 1
**Position in Billboard Top 40 R & B**: 2

---

Diana Ross / Cindy Birdsong / Mary Wilson

---

Facing up to the possibly insurmountable problem which the departure of HDH had left, Berry Gordy realised that something decisive was required to turn around the fortunes of The Supremes, suffering at the tail-end of a lean 12 months. Unwilling to admit defeat, Gordy determined to create a single for them which would reinstate them as the label's leading force, while at the same time sending a defiant message across the legal divide to HDH. But how to do it? In truth Gordy was stumped, his prolonged absences from Detroit [667] distancing him from the mood of the camp. Having retreated to LA, Gordy wasted little time in finding a residence for Diana Ross, who within weeks had set up home a stone's throw from his mansion. What this meant for The Supremes was at this stage not certain, although it was becoming increasingly clear that Ross was being disengaged from the group, the prospect that The Supremes phenomenon might be approaching its demise starkly apparent.

So far as the task to hand was concerned—getting The Supremes back to number 1—the group's failure in the hands of accomplished writer-producers such as Ashford & Simpson [662] suggested the issue ran deeper than Gordy first thought. The solution, born of his obstinate determination to succeed, amounted to the imprisonment of several Motown staffers, summoned to Detroit's Pontchartrain Hotel on the evening of Friday September 13. Throwing together a clutch of songwriters with little or no experience in collaboration seemed on the surface a hiding to nothing, but Gordy informed them that they *had* to come up with something or remain incarcerated at the hotel indefinitely. Forced to interact, the awkward congregation of Frank Wilson, Hank Cosby, Deke Richards, R. Dean Taylor and lyricist Pam Sawyer promptly set about raiding the hotel bar, drinking until well into Saturday morning, which while on one level a flagrant waste of time, served to break some ice amongst the understandably uptight company.

Getting down to serious work the following day, the group set up a couple of guitars with portable amplifiers and began tentatively jamming, hitting on the chords to The Ventures' "Walk Don't Run" which formed "Love Child's" eventual chorus.[1] With the title-words expressed, probably by Sawyer, a second section which would become the verse was also formulated, clearly taking its melodic cue from the opening lines of "Forever Came Today" [650]. By the end of Saturday, the track's key elements were therefore in place, Sawyer attentively noting down lyrical phrases as the musician-writers worked on sequencing the song's developing elements. Come Sunday afternoon, the structure was essentially worked out, the bridge to chorus ('This love we're contemplating...') dropped in during a final tweaking session at Gordy's house where the song's running order was decided.

Given the unusual circumstances behind its composition, that "Love Child" works as a composite is surprising, its 48 hours in-the-making producing three distinct and independently conceived musical passages. Partly this was the natural consequence of the method, in which too many writers were pitching in to make for an 'organic' composition. Yet the resultant work moves expressively through its sections, the track's energy ebbing and flowing with the mood of Sawyer's narrative.

Repairing to Hitsville on the Tuesday, Paul Riser sketched an arrangement which incorporated a stunningly atmospheric opening, incorporating a reverse glissando in a likely reference to "Stop! In The Name Of Love" [501], its descending fall like the slamming of a door suggesting the closure of the HDH years with a vengeance. With The Funk Brothers briefed on the significance of the September 17 session, all parties were galvanised into producing one of Motown's key recordings, made in artificial circumstances and recorded against the clock, but nonetheless carrying all the propulsive vitality of anything in The Supremes' back-catalogue.[2]

The final part of the session was reserved for the dubbing of Ross' vocals, supported by The Andantes in place of Mary Wilson and Cindy Birdsong [662]. (At this stage the track had an additional verse, which Ross duly recorded. It was cut from the release, but surfaced in 2004 on a group retrospective CD.) Given that she had at most a day to learn the lyric, Ross' performance is assured and robust, her enunciation of the song's tougher lines convincing. The track's theme, the resistance of unmarried pregnancy and its social and financial reverberation, while apparently composed *ad-hoc*, reflects one of the key social issues of the 1960s. Part of the value-shift from deference to authority to self-determination which characterises the main philosophical move of the decade, The Pill had been approved by the Food and Drug Administration in 1960 and legalised in the UK the following year, and by 1965 become the most commonly used contraceptive in America, its widespread use putting the issue of control of fertility firmly on the political agenda. The matter was not so much one of family planning strategy as of a changing morality: for the first time in history, women were becoming at liberty to experience sex not just for the sake of dutiful reproduction but as a recreational activity free from associated risks. Alarming to the conservative order, the prospect of The Pill's social ramifications became a central battle ground between old and young, the unstoppable tide of sexual freedom inevitably winning out in the face of oppressively reactionary government, the victory the most frequently cited social change of the 1960s.

In the context of "Love Child" however, the focus emerges not as a debate over sexual liberation, but as observation on class and race. When Sawyer's lyric talks of starting out in 'a worn, torn dress that somebody threw out', she speaks of the experience of growing up in Detroit's slums.[3] And although the song's character loves her man, she staunchly refuses to risk pregnancy with a child destined to be 'born in poverty', her denial of natural instinct circumscribed by the pressures of survival in the ghetto. Arriving in the wake of racially acute tracks such as "Does Your Mama Know About Me" [654], the infusion of elements from 'black power pop' is conspicuous, the movement having started to gather momentum in mid-1967 in the wake of Aretha Franklin's "Respect", reaching a landmark as James Brown's "Say It Loud, I'm Black And Proud" entered the R & B chart over the weekend in which "Love Child" was written.

For The Supremes, the move from songs about affairs of the heart to the grittier aspects of adult relationships demanded a re-think of image, lyrics concerning slum-dwelling incongruous with the silk gowns and sparkling jewellery which were previously the group's standard stage-wear. The obvious solution was to dress The Supremes in street attire, provocative afros replacing luxurious wigs, leather coats and jeans modelled in photographs of the group shot in tenement alleyways. Thus re-presented for the *Love Child* album (which also included a recording of [654]), the image transformation was revolutionary for an act previously groomed to immaculacy for white acceptance, the visual impact equivalent in import to the profound change in lyrical subject matter.

Motown had never previously approved its main acts becoming involved in socio-political matters, keeping tight rein on interviews and press-releases. Here though, the underlying issues were becoming pressing, particularly at a time when record-buyers *expected* established artists to not only hold opinions relevant to the younger generation but take a lead in expressing them. Spearheaded by the folk-rock movement, the politicisation of serious popular performers became pervasive between 1963 and 1968, even the hitherto apolitical Beatles speaking out in September (Lennon's "Revolution", recorded between May and July, a direct communication with the increasingly militant New Left).

For The Supremes, words continued to be chosen carefully but matters

inevitably erupted on occasions on which racism reared its
Taraborrelli recounts an incident in 1968 when Ross was r
public).[4] Booked to appear at London's prestigious J
Performance before several members of the Royal Family *
was appalled to see The Black and White Minstrels sharing
not to perform at all unless the act was removed. Eventuaity
irked singer seized her chance to speak out during the group's perform..
"Somewhere", a number from *West Side Story* arranged to incorporate a
spoken eulogy to Martin Luther King written by Maurice King. Elaborating,
Ross stepped forward appealing for unity between peoples of all backgrounds,
declaring society "Free at last" as tears streamed down her face. While it is easy
to see this public display as empty by virtue of its choreography, the emotion
was real, Ross' voice charged with genuine emotion. The subsequent television
broadcast of the event tactfully edited the sequence out following press
outrage in the days immediately following the show.[5]

Released in America ahead of events, "Love Child" was debuted on the *Ed
Sullivan Show* on September 30, an appearance which compelled a livid
Wilson and Birdsong to lip-synch the backing vocals which they of course
had not originally sung. "Love Child" climbed slowly to the top of the
national charts, arriving there on the last day of November, and providing for
Gordy arguably his greatest single personal victory; he wouldn't have
objected to the fact that it was eventually toppled from the summit by "I
Heard It Through The Grapevine" [686]—he had *proved* that success would
be his with or without HDH, his accomplishment here dramatic and
triumphant, against all odds.

[1] These chords—a descent from Am to E via G and F—have been used innumerable
times in popular music, being readily identifiable as the basis of "Standing In The Shadows
Of Love" [589] and The Supremes' own "Stop! In The Name Of Love" [501] (which
alters the sequence only by resisting the final fall to E). Naturally appealing to guitarists,
the descending bar-chord run has been used for example in The Kinks' "Dead End
Street" and in 1981 when The Stray Cats turned it into a riff, claiming it as their own
with "Stray Cat Strut".

[2] Carol Kaye's claim to the bass line is certainly false. That it is played in the same style as
"Bernadette" [601] and "I Was Made To Love Her" [613]—both of which she also
claims—undermines her case considerably, pointing persuasively back to James Jamerson
as originally thought.

[3] Although Sawyer was British—and white—she writes here from acquired perspective.

[4] Taraborrelli (1989) p202-3

[5] Ironically, Gordy's decision to mask the production team on "Love Child" beneath the
corporate front "The Clan" sparked suggestions that he was obliquely referencing the Ku
Klux Klan.

**TMG 678**
**THE FANTASTIC FOUR**
**I Love You Madly** (3:03)
(Hanks—Garrett)
Produced by Mike Hanks
**Release Date**: 22 Nov 1968

e: I Love You Madly (Instrumental)
**ition in Record Retailer Top 40**: -
**quivalent US Release**: Soul 35052 (24 Sep 1968)
**Position in Billboard Top 40 Pop**: -
**Position in Billboard Top 40 R & B**: 12

---

James Epps / Joe Pruitt / Ralph Pruitt / William Hunter

---

Sourced from the back-catalogues of the numerous Detroit labels Berry Gordy acquired in the mid-1960s, a clutch of recordings were revived for Tamla Motown, the current former Ric Tic title the second to be picked up.[1] The group's final release for the label, "I Love You Madly" was already high in the R & B listings when Motown claimed it and had it re-pressed on Soul to peak at 12 in the US.

Recorded at Detroit's Magic City Studios on 4-track, the production was overdubbed and mixed at United Sound on 5840 Second Avenue, its cleanly EQ-ed production strongly reminiscent of The Temptations' contemporary sound. Written by William Garrett and Mike Hanks, conscious imitation seems possible even down to "Sweet" James Epps' lead vocal style, closely conforming to that of David Ruffin. (The crafted balance of the recording founders on the unintentionally funny spoken section, similarly suggestive of Melvin Franklin's deep tones.)

Initially pleased to acquire Ric Tic's most successful act, Motown released a further trio of singles by the group in America plus a compilation of early tracks before losing interest in them. Entering semi-retirement in 1970, the group experienced a minor revival in the mid to late 1970s when signed to Eastbound Records with a new line-up.

[1] Already released was the Harvey-owned [550]. See 'Facts & Feats' section for more details.

## TMG 679
## STEVIE WONDER
**For Once In My Life** (2:49)
(Miller—Murden)
Produced by Henry "Hank" Cosby
Recording completed: 9 Sep 1968
**Release Date**: 29 Nov 1968
**B-side**: Angie Girl[1]
**Position in Record Retailer Top 40**: 3
**Equivalent US Release**: Tamla 54174 (15 Oct 1968)
**Position in Billboard Top 40 Pop**: 2
**Position in Billboard Top 40 R & B**: 2

Having put all of Motown's in-house compositions under control of his publishing arm Jobete, Berry Gordy had collected substantial royalties for broadcast and public performances of compositions throughout the 1960s.

Gordy realised though that the 'Motown' tag applied to the this key revenue-generator risked pigeon-holing certain tracks in his portfolio and accordingly expanded his interests by setting up Stein & Van Stock as early as 1964, deliberately named to sound "classy and Jewish".[2] Calculated to act as handler for compositions which he considered potential standards of the future, one of Stein & Van Stock's first successes was "For Once In My Life", shortly to become Motown's most-covered song and taken up by mainstream performers such as Tony Bennett, Frank Sinatra, Perry Como and Andy Williams.

Penned in 1965 by Ron Miller and Orlando Murden, the track's inspiration lies with an Elgie Stover number entitled "Once In A Lifetime" (for which Miller paid the composer compensation to the tune of $200[3]) and was initially donated to Chess artist Jean DuShon whose version made little impact. So far as Motown were concerned, the track was quickly recorded by Barbara McNair, The Four Tops [665b], The Temptations and later, numerous other acts including Gladys Knight & The Pips [876b]. (The Supremes also recorded it twice during the 1960s, neither rendition seeing the light-of-day.) The definitive reading though is Wonder's, the composition accelerated and brought to life by an enterprisingly energetic arrangement from producer Hank Cosby which included three electric guitars. (Having Cajoled Wonder into tackling the song, Cosby found himself on the receiving end of Ron Miller's fury when he heard the recording's irreverent treatment of his soon-to-be-famous composition, a factor which may have contributed to its sitting in the can for almost a year.)

The appeal of the recording stems from its inventive arrangement, Steve Lodder making mention of the descending orchestral semitones which create a succession of new chords on their way down.[4] Commencing with staccato electric guitar (reminiscent of the introduction to "You Keep Me Hangin' On" [585]), the recording is replete with incident including sprightly piccolo, honky-tonk piano from Earl Van Dyke and backing vocals from The Originals. Notable too is the flying harmonica solo from Wonder, which although short on bent notes is his most articulate to date, angular and piercing and pushing the harp to its extreme upper limit at 2:00. But the most admired musicianship on the recording is Jamerson's, his fingers flying around the fret-board freely locating notes which compile an entirely original foundation track which Gene Page describes as "a concerto for bass".[5] That the single fades prematurely is presumably down to radio-play consideration, but at 2:49 the track could happily have endured through another chorus line or two.

Stevie Wonder's biggest hit to date in the UK, "For Once In My Life" almost topped every chart for which it was eligible, only Motown's contemporary product holding it off in America (see [680]). Disappointingly, Wonder's contemporary album was a set of Christmas carols, the long-player named in honour of this track not materialising until the following February.

---

[1] The single's B-side, composed by Wonder with Cosby and Moy, concerns Angie Satterwhite, Wonder's first real girlfriend who inspired a number of his late-1960s compositions including "I Was Made To Love Her" [613].

[2] Gordy p227. Motown writers adopted pseudonyms for Stein & Van Stock copyrights, for

example Gordy and his brother Robert using the names Martin & Kay for Bobby Breen's "You're Just Like You" (1964). Mickey Stevenson adopted the flamboyant moniker Avery Brandenberg on tracks such as [533].

[3] Edmonds p45. However, Taraborrelli (1989) claims the track as written "In honour of [Miller's] daughter on the day she was born". The notion undoubtedly fits the lyric and anticipates Wonder's own "Isn't She Lovely", composed in exactly these circumstances several years later.

[4] p50

[5] Quoted in Slutsky, p184.

## TMG 680
## MARV JOHNSON
**I'll Pick A Rose For My Rose** (2:34)
(Dean—Weatherspoon—Johnson)
Produced by James Dean/William Weatherspoon
Recording completed: 15 Feb 1968
**Release Date**: 6 Dec 1968
**B-side**: You Got The Love I Love
**Position in Record Retailer Top 40**: 10
**Equivalent US Release**: Gordy 7077 (3 Oct 1968)
**Position in Billboard Top 40 Pop**: -
**Position in Billboard Top 40 R & B**: -

Well past three years since his previous UK single, Marv Johnson's career had been in limbo too long for him to continue recording for a living, the singer resolving to move back-office and concentrate on songwriting. Paradoxically, Johnson was the subject of a revival in fortunes just as his withdrawal from the public eye was underway, Motown retrieving an archived 1966 recording for release on both sides of the Atlantic. And with growing interest from the UK's Northern Soul crowds (see [683]), "I'll Pick A Rose For My Rose" was lifted into the top 10, Johnson taken aback by this unforeseen turn of events.

One of Motown's less widely appreciated hits, the track deals with the hopeful tale of a man travelling to a reunion with his childhood sweetheart, confident that their love will blossom like the rose he holds for her. Yet the class mismatch between them (and its associated hint of a racial divide) underpins their history, the girl's parents having ensured the separation 'years ago' by sending Rose off, out of harm's way.

To his credit, Johnson adorns the melody with some attractive melismas. Appealing too is the brass chart, sadly reduced to the point of virtual inaudibility in a mix exploiting the possibilities of stereo placing. Cheerily bouncing along, the track is ultimately light, James Jamerson's over-active bass failing to mask the simplicity of the composition on which Johnson is credited as co-writer. Shrill backing voices on a dirty vocal track fail to lift the song from its elementary diatonic progression, the final assemblage further spoiled by some crude editing (eg at 1:37). Giving rise to a cash-in album of the same name (not issued in America), the success of the single induced Johnson to embark on a 1969 tour of the UK, his retirement from performing temporarily on hold.

Despite its failure at home, Motown was, at this juncture defying the widely held view that the company was heading for a major fall. Motown's chart dominance in America towards the end of 1968 was an unmitigated coup which comprehensively silenced the doubters. For the entire duration of December, Motown records occupied the top three places in the *Billboard* charts with [686], [677] and [679], which were joined by [685] and [707] in the top 10 before the month was out. (With back-to-back number 1s holding top-slot continuously between November 30 and February 1, the feat constitutes the biggest ever monopoly of the upper-reaches of the US chart, with the exception of The Beatles' 'invasion' of February-April 1964.) As Berry Gordy observed several years later, "And we'd done it without HDH. The verdict was in: We would survive".[1]

And this, in the face of some serious competition during 1968 from several hits for Philadelphia-based acts such as The Intruders, The Delfonics, Cliff Nobles & Co and Archie Bell & The Drells [648], anticipating the rise of Philadelphia soul in the early 1970s [890]. Simultaneously with this threat was the emergence of San Francisco quartet Sly & The Family Stone, whose arrival would affect Motown's future style in a manner not fully grasped at the start of the year [707]. For now though, Gordy was free to bask in the glory of his achievements, the new down-town Donovan Building a monument to his business success, his pampered Hollywood lifestyle evidence that he had achieved all he possibly could on a personal level. From his perspective at the close of 1968, he stood invincible, master of his own destiny, with his Motown empire famous throughout the world and seemingly nothing standing between him and yet further expansion into television [709] and eventually, his true ambition, motion pictures [848].[2]

[1] Gordy p277. The *Billboard* table of December 28 is reprinted in Benjaminson, p76-7. Dion's original recording of [734] appears in the top 10 alongside the five Motown singles.

[2] The significance of Motown's involvement in the movie business, while generally underplayed, is evinced by the monument erected outside 2648 West Grand Boulevard, a plaque briefly summarising the company's achievements which includes seven lines of text about music, with a further six about television and film.

## TIMELINE – 1968

Tamla Motown release 45 singles and 28 albums
Tamla Motown place 14 singles in the UK top 40. 4 make top 10
Nationally, album sales exceed those of singles for first time ever
Rumours continue to circulate that Diana Ross and Berry Gordy are secretly married
Philadelphia Soul gathers momentum, courtesy Archie Bell & Drells, Intruders, Delfonics etc.
Sly & Family Stone arrive on scene

| | |
|---|---|
| **Jan 22** | Supremes begin series of appearances at London's Talk Of The Town. Performances recorded, subsequently released on LP |
| **Feb** | Temptations, Stevie Wonder, Martha & Vandellas tour Far East |
| **Feb 10** | Four Tops: *Greatest Hits* tops UK album chart (one week), toppling *Sgt. Pepper* |
| **Feb 17** | Supremes: *Greatest Hits* tops UK album chart (three weeks), toppling Four Tops |
| **Mar** | Motown opens offices at Donovan Building on Detroit's Woodward Avenue |
| **Spring** | HDH 'go-slow' becomes effective strike |
| **Mar 13** | Four Tops: "If I Were A Carpenter" enters UK top 50 (peak 7) |
| **Apr 4** | Assassination of Martin Luther King. Riots in numerous US cities follow funeral on April 11. Numerous Motown acts stage benefit concert in Atlanta |
| **Jun** | Supremes release "Some Things You Never Get Used To", their first post-HDH A-side |
| **Jun** | David Ruffin leaves Temptations. Replaced by Dennis Edwards |
| **Aug 12** | Race riots in Watts, LA |
| **Aug 16** | Smokey Robinson's son born, after wife Claudette had suffered several miscarriages. Baby is named Berry |
| **Aug** | Motown sue HDH for breach of contract |
| **Autumn** | Isley Brothers leave Motown |
| **Oct 23** | Isley Brothers: "This Old Heart Of Mine" re-enters UK top 50 (peak 3) (originally released 1966) |
| **Nov 17** | Supremes play Royal Command Performance, London. Object to appearing on same bill as Black & White Minstrels. Ross makes impromptu speech on racial harmony |
| **Nov** | Tamla Motown issue final Four Tops single with HDH credits |
| **Nov 30** | Supremes: "Love Child" number 1 in US (two weeks). Single marks change in subject matter (and dress style) for Supremes |
| **Dec** | Motown enjoy most successful period ever in US singles chart with major hits from Gaye; Supremes; Wonder; Temptations; etc |
| **Dec 9** | Supremes and Temptations appear on US TV special, *TCB* |
| **Dec 14** | Marvin Gaye: "I Heard It Through The Grapevine" number 1 in US (seven weeks), toppling Supremes. Motown hold top three places in US chart for further four weeks |
| **Dec 18** | Stevie Wonder: "For Once In My Life" enters UK top 50 (peak 3) |

**TMG 681**
**MARVIN GAYE & TAMMI TERRELL**
**You Ain't Livin' Til You're Lovin'** (2:27)
(Ashford—Simpson)
Produced by Nickolas Ashford/Valerie Simpson
Recording completed: 7 Mar 1968
**Release Date**: 3 Jan 1969
**B-side**: Oh How I'd Miss You
**Position in Record Retailer Top 40**: 21
**Equivalent US Release**: Tamla 54173 (24 Sep 1968)
**Position in Billboard Top 40 Pop**: -
**Position in Billboard Top 40 R & B**: -

Lifted from *You're All I Need*, "You Ain't Livin' Til You're Lovin'" was issued in America in September as the B-side to "Keep On Lovin' Me Honey". Yet the single's failure to chart caused Tamla Motown to try a different ploy, dispensing with the American A-side and elevating the current track in its place, coupled with a song taken from the year-old *United*. As generally limp as "I'll Pick A Rose For My Rose" [680], the release smacked of a conveyor-belt attitude by the label, there being little to commend the single after the majesty of "You're All I Need To Get By" [668]. With its hushed introduction, awkward title and over-stressed choruses, the track lacks savvy yet somehow managed a top 30 placing in the UK at a time when Tamla Motown was enjoying a commercial revival.

**TMG 682**
**JUNIOR WALKER & THE ALL STARS**
**Home Cookin'** (2:57)
(Moy—Cosby—Willis)
Produced by Henry "Hank" Cosby
Recording completed: 19 Nov 1968
**Release Date**: 10 Jan 1969
**B-side**: Mutiny
**Position in Record Retailer Top 40**: -
**Equivalent US Release**: Soul 35055 (23 Dec 1968)
**Position in Billboard Top 40 Pop**: -
**Position in Billboard Top 40 R & B**: 19

| Jr Walker / Willie Woods / Vic Thomas / Billy Nicks |
| --- |

The backing track laid down on 24 November 1967, "Home Cooking" was over a year old by the time it appeared as Tamla Motown's second single of 1969, starting a run of three oldies. Ostensibly Hank Cosby's work, written in partnership with Melvin Moy (brother of Sylvia: see [762]), the track was, according to Jack Ashford composed entirely by guitarist Eddie Willis in 1966.[1] Whatever the truth, "Home Cookin'" barely deviates from the group's established style, consisting of another 'dirty' R & B jam in Ab, with the added interest of a subversive B major chord in place of the expected step to the orthodox Eb. Playing up to the unusual chord movement, Jamerson (on upright bass) plays liberally with passing notes, lazily finding his open D strings to sustain the bass line, enjoying the dissonant effect where Eb would have been more natural, his thudding bass disguising the frequencies.[2]

[1] Ashford p78-9. See introduction for comments on writer disputes.
[2] See interview in *Bass Player*.


**TMG 683**
**THE ISLEY BROTHERS**
**I Guess I'll Always Love You** (2:46)
**Re-issue of [572]**
**Release Date**: 10 Jan 1969
**New B-side**: It's Out Of The Question
**Position in Record Retailer Top 40**: 11

Ronald Isley / Rudolph Isley / O'Kelly Isley

While Motown-Detroit were celebrating considerable contemporary success [680], Stateside executives watched with a mixture of curiosity and amusement as several old Motown recordings which had been relative failures in the UK began re-selling. One, "This Old Heart Of Mine" [555], was re-distributed to DJs and put back on sale on 11 October 1968, peaking at number 3 in the charts and hanging around its lower-reaches until well into February 1969.[1] With interest in The Isley Brothers thereby rekindled, Tamla Motown opted to repeat the trick, pulling from the vaults another single which had made little impression on first release. This time a full-scale re-issue was granted with an alternative B-side selected from *Soul On The Rocks* (1967) and a new catalogue number assigned. Again the single sold well, missing out on a top 10 placing by one notch.

The reasons for this overdue success were two-fold: Firstly, Tamla Motown had yet to break-through in Britain when tracks such as this first came out. Since autumn 1966 however, the label's popularity had escalated considerably, promising a degree of automatic interest from DJs and record-buyers who may not have taken too much notice three years earlier. Secondly, feeding into and from this process, the 'Northern Soul' phenomenon was rising, fuelled by fanatical pockets of fans in several of the UK's medium-to-large towns.

Centred on the club scene, most of which would host extravaganzas and 'all-nighters' with live appearances by well-known soul performers, the movement has its genesis in the mid-1960s, with venues such as the Twisted Wheel in Manchester, which opened in 1963 as an underground café before embracing soul music by 1965. Around then the celebrated Blackpool Mecca started up, going on to attract DJ Ian Levine[2], and equally significantly the Golden Torch in Stoke-On-Trent opened its doors, having started as a Mod club before converting to soul around 1967. (These venues were later challenged for supremacy by the Wigan Casio—see [853].)

Well acknowledged by 1969, the movement was characterised by a passionate interest in American soul music, extra kudos being earned by revellers hip to lesser known gems and obscure B-sides, in principal the rarer the cut the better. While Motown was undoubtedly at the core of the phenomenon, some aficionados baulked at its commercial edge and wide sales, arguing that it didn't even qualify as soul, although tracks such as "I Guess I'll Always Love You" were so infectiously danceable that they won over club-goers anyway.

Supplying the crowds with their favourite dance-floor hits on 7-inch, Tamla Motown, having thus far re-issued only one of its 182 UK singles [642], went to town in 1969 with eight during the first half of the year[3], and adopted the on-going policy of utilising admired 'Northern' hits as flip-sides on re-issues and originals alike (for example [705b]). While this recognition of the label's recent legacy was welcome, it had the effect of backing up the release schedules, "Cloud Nine" [707] in particular having to wait until August for its UK release, despite having gone top 10 in America before Christmas. Thus Tamla Motown was caught working on two conflicting fronts, pioneering advance held in check by retrospective policy perilously close to conservative nostalgia.

[1] In the intervening period, The Impressions had recorded and released "Can't Satisfy" which borrowed so heavily from "This Old Heart Of Mine" that Curtis Mayfield was forced to give the copyright to Motown. (The track was not a hit in the UK.)

[2] Levine is well-known for creating MotorCity Records in the 1980s, recruiting to the fold a slew of former Motowners including Mary Wells, Syreeta, Edwin Starr, Martha Reeves, G C Cameron and others for contemporary sessions which frequently consisted of remakes of their former hits. Levine's policy of adopting 1980s production standards alienated some soul fans, but the label holds an affectionate place in the hearts of many Motown followers. A MotorCity discography is available in Bartlette, further background information in Davis 2006b (p176-186).

[3] [683]; [688]; [691]; [694]; [696]; [699]; [700]; [703], not to mention old recordings making their debut on Tamla Motown, [684]; [686]; [693].

## TMG 684
## MARTHA REEVES & THE VANDELLAS
**Dancing In The Street** (2:37) **[E54]**
(Stevenson—Gaye)
Produced by William "Mickey" Stevenson/Ivy Jo Hunter
Recording completed: 29 Jun 1964
**Release Date**: 3 Jan 1969
**B-side**: Quicksand [E32]
**Position in Record Retailer Top 40**: 4
**Equivalent US Release**: Gordy 7033 (31 Jul 1964)
**Position in Billboard Top 40 Pop**: 2
**Position in Billboard Top 40 R & B**: 8

---

Martha Reeves / Rosalind Ashford / Betty Kelly

---

Referred to by insiders as 'our national anthem', "Dancing In The Street" is one of Motown's best-known products, the pertinent lyrics to which have provided the title for several albums and books, including Reeves' 1994 autobiography. The track itself dates to 1964, penned at home by Mickey Stevenson, inspired by the sight of black and white children playing together in the road under the spray of a burst water hydrant. With Ivy Hunter and Marvin Gaye present when the track was being formed, input from each is likely, the latter taking disproportionate credit for his offhand comment that the song sounded like 'dancing in the street', for which he aggressively bargained a 25 percent royalty.[1] Further uncertainty as to who contributed what surrounds Reeves' repeated claim that she effectively wrote the melody, rejecting the original draft as pitched below her register—which if true, makes her co-composer.[2]

The fact is, "Dancing In The Street" was not conceived with Reeves in mind at all. The original demo carried a vocal by Gaye and was in the male range, indicating that he had an eye on the song himself. The backing track was recorded on May 22 with little advance planning, Gaye handling piano duties, Joe Messina on his trusty Telecaster, and Jamerson on his upright bass. Benny Benjamin was not present, drums handled here by touring-band member Fred Waites, his contribution overshadowed by the presence on the studio floor of Ivy Hunter, who in a moment of inspiration hauled some car tyre chains into the studio for a sensational crashing percussion, achieved by repeatedly slamming them against a piece of wood, until his hands were bleeding. The massiveness thus achieved was a landmark for Motown's studios, and was repeated to yet greater effect on the group's classic "Nowhere To Run" [502].

The track was initially offered to Kim Weston who turned it down, although she subsequently expressed surprise at the idea, claiming not to have known that she had first refusal.[3] In any case, once Reeves started work on the song the issue was quickly settled, her dropping the vocal from the fifth to the third putting the finishing touches in, Stevenson coaching her through the June session on which all three composers turned up to contribute backing vocals. (Another of the backing vocalists present that day was Betty Kelly, who subsequently became a fully-fledged Vandella.) Ripping into the song, Reeves completed a full run-through only to learn that Stevenson had neglected to operate the tape, securing the finished vocal at the second attempt.

Built largely from a sustained E7 chord, the song's pulsating verses drive forwards relentlessly, the huge percussion rivalling anything HDH had done at that stage. Issued on Gordy in America at the height of summer 1964 it caused a minor sensation, peaking at number 2 and even making the UK top 30 on Stateside. The fact is though, "Dancing In The Street" has, behind its happy-go-lucky persona, a rather subversive subtext, widely interpreted as a call to arms for America's black population, following a marked steepening of tensions. Notorious police chief Bull Connor had recently created outcry in Birmingham, Alabama when he broadcast a speech on how to stop the racial equality movement, advocating—and subsequently deploying—dogs and fire hoses as a method to drive protesters off the streets. Arrested there in the spring of 1963 for participating in a sit-in protest, Martin Luther King composed his *Letter From A Birmingham Jail* in a police cell, before emerging to make his triumphant "I Have A Dream" speech in Washington.[4] Meantime, Bob Dylan was leading the way in documenting the widespread racial unrest through the medium of music, receiving acclaim on the protest circuit for his (as yet unrecorded) "The Death Of Emmett Till" which relayed the story of the brutal slaying and mutilation some years earlier of a black 14-year-old holidaying in Mississippi, and his "Only A Pawn In Their Game", which recounted the racist slaughter of civil rights leader Medgar Evers on 12 June 1963. Released the following spring, Dylan's *The Times Are A-Changin'*, while not exactly putting the subject into the pop charts, galvanised American youth, making the imminent arrival of "Dancing In The Street" all the more pointed and open to interpretation by a radicalised populace.

Analysed more than any other Motown recording, several individuals including poet and activist LeRoi Jones have interpreted the lyric as an encouragement to riot, something Martha Reeves has taken pains to deny.[5] Yet so pervasive was the view that, following the Detroit riots of July 1967 [614], the track was widely suspended from radio play, the group's travelling entourage subsequently confronted by lynch mobs mistaking them for protesters after the manner of the Freedom Riders, who would transport themselves across America in Greyhound busses to orchestrate civil unrest.

The lyrics to "Dancing In The Street" take a tour around many of America's major cities, some of which were clearly associated with the civil rights struggle[6], and included America's four largest urban black populations—New York, Chicago, Philadelphia and Detroit itself. Several of the named locations had been the scene of open rioting during the decade including the Harlem area of New York July 18 1964 and Philadelphia on August 28, a week before "Dancing In The Street" entered the *Billboard* top 40.

Yet a contrasting analysis can be had from the fact that several of the localities are also acknowledged centres of black music, leading back to a literal translation of the song's 'dancing' title. Fundamental to the excursion is a homage to the roots of soul, the Chicago blues school which included Buddy Guy, Muddy Waters, Elmore James, Howlin' Wolf and many others, responsible to a great extent for the development of what became R & B through the 1940s and 50s. Of more immediate interest to Motown, Chicago was a focal point of the embryonic soul idiom, where several leading figures emerged including Sam Cooke, Curtis Mayfield & The Impressions, the Vee Jay label, and the Chess Records roster which at one time included Harvey Fuqua's Moonglows, of whom Marvin Gaye became a member in 1959.

New Orleans on the other hand had spawned Jelly Roll Morton (the claimed 'inventor' of jazz), and became a centre for artists such as Roy Brown, Fats Domino, and later Little Richard, Allen Toussaint and others. New York meanwhile, besides being home to the Brill Building (see [581n]), was where Atlantic Records were based, whose portfolio included The Drifters, Ray Charles, The Coasters, Solomon Burke and so on. And by the time "Dancing In The Street" was re-issued in 1969, Philadelphia had also put itself on the map [680] and would go on to seriously rival Motown as leader in the field by 1973.[7]

Whichever reading is preferred, by curious coincidence the 1969 re-issue arrived just as ant-racist demonstrations in London had deteriorated into riots with police, the new year threatening a continuation of the civil unrest of 1968 [654]. Re-released during a particularly chilly winter, the song's opening gambit that 'Summer's here and the time is right' puts a question mark over its timing, which would have been more effective in the idealistic sunshine of 1967. Historically associated with the social tensions of its day, the track could never seriously be described as Motown's equivalent to "All You Need Is Love", although as an anthem which captures the mood of the moment, it is without equal in its field.

This new edition coupled the song with another former Stateside single, its ascendancy to number 4 leading to a UK album of the same name. In the decades since, "Dancing In The Street" has gradually come to be seen as a standard, notably covered as part of the Live Aid project by Mick Jagger and David Bowie, whose rendition (with lyrical amendments to reflect the international focus of the event) topped the UK singles chart for a month. While the debate over its true message remains unresolved, there is no questioning the humanitarian and political issues which Live Aid sought to address, the black-white dichotomy of third world poverty acutely brought into focus by the predominantly white concerts staged on 13 July 1985.

[1] The track is copyrighted to Stevenson—Gaye—Hunter although the credits shown here are as stated on the UK single release. If Gaye did indeed make such comment it casts doubt on the song's supposed inspiration, the sight of children frolicking outdoors.

[2] See for example Reeves p104: "They said 'OK Martha, give it your treatment,' and I came up with the melody."

[3] See her interview in Whithall, p102.

[4] A recording of which was released by Motown on more than one occasion—see [570].

[5] This re-issue appeared a few months after The Rolling Stones released "Street Fighting Man", which includes the line 'Summer's here and the time is right for fighting in the street'. However a widely repeated quote has Reeves commenting, "I never called anyone to riot. All I wanted was a little gravy for all of us". This should be qualified by the fact that Reeves had no hand in the text, and was not present when the song was written. Indeed the fact that her family were actually in want in the midst of an affluent society is itself damning enough.

[6] In order, Chicago (IL), New Orleans (LA), New York City (NY), Philadelphia (PA), Baltimore (MD), [Washington] DC, Motor City [Detroit] (MI) and Los Angeles (CA).

[7] No mention is made in the song of Memphis where Sun Records had started, discovering one Elvis Presley in 1954, and where the Stax-Volt labels also arose. Possibly the competition in 1964 was a little too fierce for comfort.

**TMG 685**
**DIANA ROSS & THE SUPREMES & THE TEMPTATIONS**
I'm Gonna Make You Love Me (3:07)
(Gamble—Ross)
Produced by Frank Wilson/Nickolas Ashford
Recording completed: 4 Sep 1968
**Release Date**: 24 Jan 1969
**B-side**: A Place In The Sun

**Position in Record Retailer Top 40**: 3
**Equivalent US Release**: Motown 1137 (21 Nov 1968)
**Position in Billboard Top 40 Pop**: 2
**Position in Billboard Top 40 R & B**: 2

Diana Ross / Cindy Birdsong / Mary Wilson / Otis Williams / Melvin Franklin /
Paul Williams / Eddie Kendricks / Dennis Edwards

With The Supremes' career having slumped during 1968, Berry Gordy was open to ideas on how to recover their standing, before forcing the issue with "Love Child" [677]. Prior to this, he hit upon the idea of pairing the group with The Temptations, the acts having appeared together for a series of live engagements in late September 1967 leading to a joint booking on *The Ed Sullivan Show*, aired in November of that year. With both groups in the process of redefining themselves through 1968, studio dates were sporadic, but the two acts nonetheless cobbled sufficient material together for *Diana Ross and the Supremes Join the Temptations*, eventually released in late-1968 (held off in the UK, like the current single, until the new year).

The track pencilled in as the first release from the set was "The Impossible Dream", a title plucked from the 1965 Broadway adaptation of *Don Quixote, Man Of La Mancha*. Switched at the last minute, "I'm Gonna Make You Love Me" was a safer bet, a number proposed to producer Frank Wilson by Suzanne de Passe. Another cover version, the song originated with the Philadelphia-based Gamble—Ross team (see [890]) having been recorded previously by Dee Dee Warwick and again by Madeline Bell in a rendition which went top 30 US pop shortly before the current single appeared.[1]

The recording details on "I'm Gonna Make You Love Me" show the track to be a somewhat half-hearted effort, Diana Ross recording her vocal sections in LA under Frank Wilson's guidance, before Nickolas Ashford overdubbed The Temptations' contribution separately in Detroit, Eddie Kendricks handling lead duties. Compared with Ross, Kendricks comes through as the more relaxed, Ross' intentionally huffy lines commencing with a "Look y'here", previously heard on "Some Things You Never Get Used To" [662]. (The grammatical flaw in the song's chorus goes unnoticed, the Americanised 'Yes I will' sounding natural in relation to 'I'm gonna'.)

Running to 3:07, the track is one of the most lengthy Tamla Motown singles to date, partly due to its indulgent 20-second introduction, apparently based on the (similarly lengthy) opening passage on "What Becomes Of The Brokenhearted" [577]. These flattened bars notwithstanding, James Jamerson's work on "I'm Gonna Make You Love Me" continues his high-animation of 1967-68, the bass line cited by Allen Slutsky as one which caused producers and musicians elsewhere to 'shake their heads in awe'.[2] In reality, the unlikely success of the song stems from its producers' expertise in presentation, the seamless marriage of two independent vocal tracks glossed with some deep sustained brass and inventive orchestration (vaguely pitched in the style of Western film music). The result was a massive commercial success, which had it come six months earlier—which better organisation would have ensured—would undoubtedly have affected the careers of the two groups: Both "Love Child" [677] and "Cloud Nine" [707] may quite possibly never have been recorded.

¹ The idea of a link with "I Was Made To Love Her" [613], as suggested by the two titles, is false. Note should be made however of Stevie Wonder's "I Wanna Make Her Love Me" (1968), probably an 'answer' to the present track. It will be noted that another Stevie Wonder track [588] appears as the flip-side here, as well as on [730].

² p56


## TMG 686
## MARVIN GAYE
### I Heard It Through The Grapevine (2:59)
(Whitfield—Strong)
Produced by Norman Whitfield
Recording completed: 10 Apr 1967
**Release Date**: 7 Feb 1969
**B-side**: Need Somebody
**Position in Record Retailer Top 40**: 1
**Equivalent US Release**: Tamla 54176 (30 Nov 1968)
**Position in Billboard Top 40 Pop**: 1
**Position in Billboard Top 40 R & B**: 1

A fifth successive 'oldie' from Tamla Motown, Gaye's "I Heard It Through The Grapevine" dates to 1967 [629], its failure to appear sooner mystifying with hindsight: the single rapidly became the label's biggest seller of the 1960s, the evergreen recording going on to appear on more Tamla Motown re-issues than any other.¹ But while the track has gradually been accorded legendary status, its appearance on 45 owes as much to chance as to its undoubted weight as a piece of musical production. The early-1967 backing track was constructed with The Temptations in mind, Gaye contributing his famous vocals in a session on April 10, the track then remaining unreleased for over a year before being employed as an album-filler. Even then, it was selected as a measure to shut Norman Whitfield up, the producer having aggressively and unrelentingly hectored Berry Gordy over the recording.²

Responsibility for the track's extraordinary delay rests solely with Berry Gordy, who at a Quality Control meeting in mid-1967 overruled a favourable majority view and insisted that "Your Unchanging Love" [618] be Gaye's next single. Remembering events 27 years later, Berry Gordy claimed to have preferred "Grapevine" to that released in its stead³, a mystifying admission perhaps coloured by the wisdom of hindsight. Daringly advanced for its day and out-of-keeping with Gaye's romantic image, the track may have worried Gordy although its sheer sonic impact might have been enough to allow the notoriously conservative boss to go out on a limb. As it was, Whitfield and Gladys Knight & The Pips cashed in [629], while Gaye's career struggled on.

The backing track is notable for its sedate tempo, Whitfield having opted for a more penetrating sound than initially conceived. The sessions ran over four dates in February 1967, the band ensemble recorded live, as evinced by the rattling wires on Benny Benjamin's snare drum, clearly audible in the introduction, vibrating in resonance with Johnny Griffith's calmly concentrated electric piano. Cut across by electric guitar (Eddie Willis and Joe Messina), with Jack Ashford's taunting, provocative tambourine, the 20-second introduction is amongst Motown's most memorable, the mesmerising effect of which gives flight to the song proper, Gaye letting rip against Jamerson's upright bass.[4] Far more cutting than Knight's undisciplined version, the musical track here tells the story of the narrative by itself, the rattling presence of percussion lurking in its doorways and gossiping female backing section giving the impression of a crowd of onlookers snooping gratuitously on Gaye's crushed pride.

The lyrical measures, caught like the central character's frantic mind between authoritative demands and impotent resignation, brought out one of Gaye's most agonised vocals, his lines variously whispering, soaring and growling. According to Ben Edmonds, Whitfield was largely responsible for Gaye's remarkable pitching, the backing track just beyond his natural reach, so that the single-minded producer 'pushed and pushed and then pushed some more to get it; the producer and singer reportedly almost came to blows during the vocal session'.[5] Others have speculated that the lyrics stuck a personal chord with Gaye in early 1967 such that he didn't need to fake his anxiety, although the resultant vocal stands as the most mesmerising within Gaye's extensive discography. Little wonder that Norman Whitfield never lost faith in the immediate power of the recording made in turbulent circumstances, and in the end hard-fought-for.

Gaye's definitive reading of "I Heard It Through The Grapevine" slipped out almost unnoticed in August 1968, the fourth track on side 1 of *In The Groove*, sequenced immediately after his previous single [676], and appeared simultaneously with another version on The Miracles' *Special Occasion*. (Typically, both albums were running late in the UK, emerging side by side in January 1969.) Yet the track's electrifying intensity guaranteed attention, and on hearing *In The Groove*, Chicago DJ Phil Jones took the unusual step of spinning the album cut, provoking a veritable stir amongst his listeners. With the track's reputation rapidly spreading it became clear that Motown had a potential hit on their hands and by November, Berry Gordy relented and authorised the single's release in America. "I Heard It Through The Grapevine" knocked "Love Child" [677] from the number 1 slot, staying at the top for seven weeks over Christmas 1968, easily the longest stint of any Motown release.

Put out in the UK in early February, the track inevitably topped the listings, surprisingly only the second Tamla Motown single to achieve the feat during the decade [579]. Becoming in the process Gaye's first UK top 40 hit, "Grapevine" succeeded where Knight's version had failed, leading Motown to re-press and re-name *In The Groove* after the song, which critic Dave Marsh considers the finest single ever released.

[1] Five to date: [923] (1974); [L005] (1976); [L056] (1983); [L073] (1986) and [L108] (2004)—as well as further 12-inch and blue label pressings. See Chapter 6 and Appendix 1 and 2 for further details.

[2] See Edmonds, p31. Some report that Whitfield so annoyed Gordy that he actually jeopardised his position within Motown.

[3] Gordy p273

[4] A technical analysis of Jamerson's work here can be found in Rubin.

[5] p30

## TMG 687
## SMOKEY ROBINSON & THE MIRACLES
**Baby, Baby Don't Cry** (3:29)
(Cleveland—Johnson—Robinson)
Produced by William "Smokey" Robinson/Warren Moore/Terry Johnson
Recording completed: 31 Oct 1968
**Release Date**: 21 Feb 1969
**B-side**: Your Mother's Only Daughter
**Position in Record Retailer Top 40**: -
**Equivalent US Release**: Tamla 54178 (12 Dec 1968)
**Position in Billboard Top 40 Pop**: 8
**Position in Billboard Top 40 R & B**: 3

| Smokey Robinson / Bobby Rogers / Claudette Rogers Robinson / Warren 'Pete' Moore / Ronnie White |
| --- |

Continuing in the vein of his recent soothing balladry, Smokey Robinson's first single of 1969 concerns the singer's patient devotion for a woman abandoned by the man she has loved. Declaring him 'out of his mind' for leaving her, Robinson assures the woman that 'Love is here, standing by'. Recorded in alleviating mood with soft-focussed vocals and tender keyboards despite the fact that bass and guitars are badly out of tune, the track casts a yearning glance towards "More Love" [614], although the lyric scenario is clearly written from a hypothetical perspective. (The contrasting middle-8 essentially re-works the verses of "You" [640], temporarily breaking the spell.)

Co-produced by Robinson with Warren Moore, the gentle sentimentality of the recording speaks nothing of the growing unease between the two old friends, grievances over their financial disparity clouding their relationship.[1] Weighing up his options, Robinson resolved in early-1969 to leave The Miracles, yet his sense of solidarity compelled him to stay put for now, in the knowledge that his departure would undoubtedly cost his colleagues in terms of sales and royalties. Another three years would pass before Robinson jumped ship [811], before which the group would score by far their biggest and most lucrative hit [745].

[1] Robinson (p169) apportions blame to Moore's wife for 'poisoning his mind'.

## TMG 688
## THE TEMPTATIONS
**Get Ready** (2:37)
**Re-issue of [557]**

**Release Date**: 28 Feb 1969
**New B-side**: My Girl [E67]
**Position in Record Retailer Top 40**: 10

---

Otis Williams / Melvin Franklin / Paul Williams / Eddie Kendricks / David Ruffin

---

A second 'double-header' on Tamla Motown after [684], the re-appearance of "Get Ready" in February contributed further to the delay of "Cloud Nine" [707]. As with the label's other recent re-issues, the single comfortably out-sold its original incarnation, justifiably making the UK top 10 with the group's "I'm Gonna Make You Love Me" [685] also high in the listings. But while The Temptations' volcanic 1966 single deserved its revived success, its pairing with "My Girl" was a considerable added attraction for record-buyers, the track previously available on single only via its Stateside edition early in 1965, which few had acquired.

Conceived as an audacious 'reply' to his own "My Guy" [E42], "My Girl" was written by Smokey Robinson with Ron White's involvement calculated to help Robinson resist the danger of habitual, formulaic writing. Carrying some of its author's most charming lyrical couplets, the song was not originally intended for The Miracles, Robinson stating since that he had David Ruffin in mind all along, reckoning correctly that a tender love song delivered in Ruffin's rough-textured style would be a hit with female listeners.[1] On catching The Temptations at the Twenty Grand, Robinson collared him to say a song was ready and waiting for the group's vocals, which would represent Ruffin's fist lead slot. Coaching The Temptations during backstage intervals at The Apollo over the following weeks[2], Robinson was satisfied that they were up-to-the-job, taking them into Hitsville on 21 December, 1964.

Taped on Studio A's limited three-track console, Robinson was forced to bounce down the vocals several times[3], achieving a complexity of sound remarkable for its day. In a Quality Control meeting, Norman Whitfield, himself looking at The Temptations as a potential vehicle, had the task of recommending the inevitable smash hit to Berry Gordy, reluctantly helping secure the outfit for his rival, until the current A-side marked the end of Robinson's control over the group (see [565]).

Still recognised as The Temptations' definitive recording, "My Girl" has retained its popularity throughout four decades, released as a Tamla Motown A-side in 1986 and again, under licence to Epic, in 1992 when it made number 2 in the UK. (The recording was ranked the label's all-time number one in a 1997 poll of Motown and MotorCity Fan Club members.) On first-release the pattern was similar, the 1964 American edition becoming Motown's first chart-topper by a male group (to Robinson's surprise and delight), and going on to attract numerous covers including [666b], [863b], and noted interpretations by The Rolling Stones and Otis Redding respectively.

Yet despite its high status, the recording has a sad footnote: Guitarist Robert White, the man behind the song's famous ascending introduction, was sitting in a café during the 1980s when the opening bars came over the jukebox. Surprised and excited, White began to relay his involvement in the recording to the waiter, but suddenly realised that he would merely come over as some sort of crank and declined to finish his tale, an event highlighting the appalling way The Funk Brothers were kept out of the limelight. White died unknown in the early 1990s, his famous lead riff which inspired the similar pattern on The Beatles' "Day Tripper" known to millions who sadly have never heard his name.

[1] The Miracles eventually released a radically different version of the song on *Time Out*, Jan 1970.

[2] A photograph of one such session appears in George, opposite p76.

[3] A process whereby two or more recorded tracks are blended together onto a spare, leaving the original tracks available for re-use with additional material. Motown staff sometimes referred to the technique as 'ping-ponging'.

## TMG 689
## DAVID RUFFIN
**My Whole World Ended (The Moment You Left Me)** (3.28)
(Fuqua—Bristol—Sawyer—Roach)
Produced by Harvey Fuqua/Johnny Bristol
Recording completed: 26 Nov 1968
**Release Date**: 21 Mar 1969
**B-side**: I Got To Find Myself A Brand New Baby
**Position in Record Retailer Top 40**: -
**Equivalent US Release**: Motown 1140 (20 Jan 1969)
**Position in Billboard Top 40 Pop**: 9
**Position in Billboard Top 40 R & B**: 2

With his departure from The Temptations somewhat acrimonious [671], David Ruffin was, at the start of 1969, at an uncertain juncture. Ostensibly removed from the act for failing to appear at a gig in Cleveland, Ruffin's psyche was precariously volatile and his life in a state of contradiction, his self-opinion inflated by the success he had had with his former group, yet his career lying in tatters and quite possibly irredeemably so. Declaring The Temptations finished without him, Ruffin set about turning his back on Motown, signing a new management deal with C. B. Atkins and preparing psychologically for a clean break. Gordy though had other ideas and, holding Ruffin to the content of his 1966 contract, successfully sued the troubled singer, thereby blocking his departure. Uncertain of where this would leave him, Gordy sought to keep Ruffin onside by signing him individually to the American Motown label, an arrangement to which Ruffin was receptive, embarking on his solo career instead from the continued sanctuary of the corporation with which he had achieved virtually all of his success to date.

Ruffin though was unable to fully accept his split from the group, and for a while in 1968 he took to showing up at their live engagements, and when the mood took him, attempting to clamber on stage and re-join the act, The Temptations having to book extra security staff to keep him at bay. Making a start on his solo career was to be the turning point, and to this end Johnny Bristol provided a new song, albeit penned with Ruffin in mind before it emerged that he was no longer a Temptation.

"My Whole World Ended" commences with a 'classical' prelude [584]; [609]; [693], the ironic title of which could not have gone unnoticed by the other group members, and whose flute sections cheekily reference those on Ruffin's last single with The Temptations [671].[1] Backed by The Originals, Ruffin handles the song with his trademark vigour, the number built from a descending three chord figure widely used in pop, and present in such numbers as "You Keep Running Away" [623] and "If I Were A Carpenter" [647]. However before Ruffin taped the track, The Rolling Stones released *Beggars Banquet* (December 1968), the opening track of which, "Sympathy For The Devil", shares the same fundamental pattern.[2] Using the Stones' arrangement as inspiration, the track travels from C through Bb and F (prior to its classic Motown key change at 2:13), transposed from the original's E major. Relying largely on shakers for percussive effect, the debt is obvious and is emphasised by the crazed flurries on the chorus flute, based on Keith Richards' similarly entangled lead guitar figures in "Sympathy For The Devil", and in the song's length which sets a new longevity record at 3:28. (Jokingly, Fuqua and Bristol also allowed The Originals' backing vocalists a falsetto "ooh-ooh" at 3:15 in direct acknowledgement of "Sympathy".)[3]

Scoring a notable success in America, David Ruffin had made a promising start as a solo star. Unbeknown to him at the time though, it would be almost seven years before he again appeared in the charts on either side of the Atlantic [1017].

[1] The backing track was compiled with a view to having The Temptations record the song, prior to Ruffin's departure.

[2] The album also includes The Stones' "Street Fighting Man", with its hard-edged reference to [684].

[3] Interestingly, the lyric includes the unusually (for Motown) violent image of a gun held to the head in its first verse, possibly picking up on the menace implicit in the Rolling Stones' song (compare Junior Walker's harmless "Shotgun" [509] from 1965). Performed by The Stones in December 1969 at the infamous Altamont festival, "Sympathy For The Devil" was twice interrupted by riotous Hell's Angels whose interpretation of 'security' for the event consisted of randomly beating sections of the audience, including Meredith Hunter, a black teenager brutally stabbed and beaten to death in front of the band.

**TMG 690**
**STEVIE WONDER**
**I Don't Know Why (I Love You)** (2:40)
(Hunter—Hardaway—Wonder—Riser)
Produced by Don Hunter/Stevie Wonder
Recording completed: 20 Dec 1968
**Release Date**: 14 Mar 1969
**B-side**: My Cherie Amour
**Position in Record Retailer Top 40**: 14 / 4

**Equivalent US Release:** Tamla 54180 (28 Jan 1969)
**Position in Billboard Top 40 Pop**: 39 / 4
**Position in Billboard Top 40 R & B**: 16 / 4

Extrapolating the orchestration patterns on "Shoo-Be-Doo-Be-Doo-Da-Day" [653], this new composition appears to have evolved from numerous sources, the title itself suggesting that of "I Don't Know Why (But I Do)", a 1961 hit for Clarence "Frog Man" Henry which contains the full title of Wonder's song in its refrain. Commencing with an unassumingly despondent 'Three Blind Mice' clavinet figure, "I Don't Know Why" bursts into life with a vocal pitched surprisingly on the 5th, Wonder's voice prickling against the dingy backing. The track proceeds through eight segmented sections, instrumentation increasing in density with each run-through[1], suffocation building with unexpected chord shapes reinforcing the tension of the lyrical theme, which concerns the torture of a humiliated lover reduced to begging for some reciprocation.

Undeniably the electrifying effect of the recording comes mainly from 19-year-old Wonder's wild vocals, constituting the most ferocious amongst Motown's recordings. Gradually losing control, he is by the final verse shrieking and gasping for breath, the track's repeating 8-bar verses, which in their musical structure also encompass the hook line, driving home the lyric's obsessive anxiety. (According to Steve Lodder, Wonder developed his breathing technique in imitation of a Baptist minister who used similar effects to stir his followers. In the light of this, the vocal on "I Don't Know Why" was to some extent pre-fabricated, although the sheer hysterics with which Wonder delivers his lines belie any feigning.)[2]

In view of time-pressures on the Hitsville studio, there was frequently little time for full-scale rehearsals and an opportunity to learn tracks by heart and, in recording "I Don't Know Why", Wonder entered the studio without full knowledge of the lyric. Normal practise under such circumstances was for vocalists to sight-read on the studio floor, but Wonder unable to do so frequently relied on a colleague (usually Clarence Paul) to guide him through from the control booth via an extra headphone feed, with Wonder at the live mike. According to witnesses, Don Hunter did exactly this with the present track, which makes Wonder's vocals here all the more remarkable.[3]

Put out as a single in early 1969, the recording proved too raw-edged for popular approval, stalling at a modest number 14 in Britain, and returning similarly disappointing sales in America. However, shortly arriving in the UK for some live dates with South Carolina girl-group The Flirtations (with one of whom he was romantically connected), Wonder and his entourage were surprised by the enthusiastic reception accorded to the single's B-side, the ensuing public clamour forcing Tamla Motown to relent and re-promote the single with the sides switched. (The single was re-launched on 27 Jun 1969.)

According to James Haskins, "My Cherie Amour" had been written in 1966 in half-an-hour[4] as "Oh My Marcia", a homage to a dancer with whom Wonder had become involved, and was taken into the studio the following year before being amended at the last-minute, probably at the behest of Hank

Cosby. (The vocals were recorded on 15 January 1967, two months after the backing track.) An unusually romantic creation, the track opens with flute, bass and Robert White's Gibson electric (and with a degree of tape hiss) on one of Stevie Wonder's most memorable riffs, its French-tinged charm and coyly manœuvring chords offering a lightness of touch which lifted the gloom from its A-side.

Considered by Wonder to be his best track to date, "My Cherie Amour", like "I Heard It Through The Grapevine" [686], rebutted Berry Gordy's early scepticism, the UK re-pressing extending the residency of [690] to six months in the charts, a degree of success which Wonder never bettered. It eventually climbed back up to number 4, the American edition similarly well-received, scoring exactly the same placing on both the pop and R & B charts.

[1] The additive nature of the recording is analysable as follows: (a) 10-second intro (fuzz-toned electric guitar, with plucked bass on the third above); (b) 21-second verse (conventionally played bass and drums, mainly snare, and 2nd guitar, probably Robert White's); (c) 21-second verse (with drums switching to tom toms and 2nd guitar mixed louder); (d) 20-second verse (with harder drum sound and strings and brass mixed low); (e) 40-second double verse (2nd guitar up front and strings mixed larger and increasingly prominent brass towards end); (f) 20-second verse (with brass pushed fully up, and loss of 2nd guitar); (g) 20-second verse (with 2nd guitar re-introduced); (h) 14-second fade out. Oddly, section (e) is book-ended by two distinct 'clicks' which sound like digital edits, but since they appear on the original (analogue) 45, can't be. (These can be heard on CD at 1:12 and 1:52 respectively.) Yet neither do they sound like tape drop-outs, although they do cut right across the soundscape. It is possible that these indicate edits in the finished mix, but since the brass is clearly mixed over the supposed join at the start of (f), even this seems unlikely.

[2] Lodder, p46. Sharon Davis (2006a, p51) states that the vocal track on "I Was Made To Love Her" [613] was deliberately modelled on the minister's style.

[3] See also [545] and Sylvia Moy's comments in Davis (2006a, p47). On the 2005 CD A Cellarful Of Motown! Vol. 2, there is an audible 'ghost' on the track "I Gave Up Quality For Quantity", which is probably Clarence Paul's guide vocal leaking from Wonder's headphones.

[4] p49

**TMG 691**
**JUNIOR WALKER & THE ALL STARS**
**(I'm A) Road Runner** (2:45)
**Re-issue of [559]**
**Release Date**: 21 Mar 1969
**New B-side**: Shotgun [509]
**Position in Record Retailer Top 40**: 12

Jr Walker / Willie Woods / Vic Thomas / James Graves

Another 'double-header' custom-made for the Northern Soul market paired up Walker's two most successful singles of 1965-66, earning him a belated debut appearance in the UK top 20. Thus far the formula was holding up, each of Tamla Motown's classic pairings scoring notably on the UK charts. Yet as with the previous re-release [688], the single's appearance had the adverse effect of delaying Walker's innovative new recording until October, "What Does It Take (To Win Your Love)" [712] making the American top 10 while [691] was doing its business in Britain.


**TMG 692**
**EDWIN STARR**
**Way Over There** (2:42)
(Robinson)
Produced by Norman Whitfield
Recording completed: 12 Sep 1967
**Release Date**: 28 Mar 1969
**B-side**: If My Heart Could Tell The Story
**Position in Record Retailer Top 40**: -
**Equivalent US Release**: Gordy 7078 (26 Oct 1968)
**Position in Billboard Top 40 Pop**: -
**Position in Billboard Top 40 R & B**: -

Smokey Robinson's 1961 two-chord track "Way Over There" was inspired by The Isley Brothers' "Shout", as recorded by the group in 1959, six years before they joined Motown. Yet the biblical imagery of deep rivers, steep mountains and non-insurmountable barriers to be conquered anticipates both Phil Spector's "River Deep, Mountain High" of 1966 [777] as well as Motown's own "Ain't No Mountain High Enough" [611]. An accomplished reading with exuberant vocals and a crotchet-stomping snare from Benny Benjamin, Starr's recording was made two years earlier, and was lifted from *Soul Master* in America prior to "25 Miles" [672], providing the singer with an obvious follow-up release for the enthusiastic UK market, which comprehensively flopped.

However over the summer, Tamla Motown elected to re-promote the single as with [690], noting interest in its B-side and flipping it for re-launch on 13 June 1969. "If My Heart Could Tell The Story" was even earlier than "Way Over There", and penned by Dean—Weatherspoon, was initially assigned to The Monitors, but overdubbed with Starr's vocals in April 1967. Offered as a 'new' A-side the track failed to lift [692] into the UK charts, but was to be included on the singer's later *25 Miles* album.

Given its lack-lustre sales, "Way Over There" / "If My Heart Could Tell The Story" was to be Starr's last UK single for almost a year [725], popularity on the Northern Soul scene insufficient to persuade Tamla Motown that he had commercial viability. Touring Britain in 1969, Starr was presented to the Northern circuit as if he had been a Motown recording artist all along, few realising that as recently as 1966 he was recording for Golden World [630].


**TMG 693**
**THE ISLEY BROTHERS**
**Behind A Painted Smile** (2:45)
(Hunter—Verdi)

Produced by Ivy Jo Hunter
Recording completed: 2 May 1967
**Release Date**: 3 Apr 1969
**B-side**: One Too Many Heartaches
**Position in Record Retailer Top 40**: 5
**Equivalent US Release**: Tamla 54175 (5 Nov 1968)
**Position in Billboard Top 40 Pop**: -
**Position in Billboard Top 40 R & B**: -

---

Ronald Isley / Rudolph Isley / O'Kelly Isley

---

Continuing to mine their back-catalogue in early-1969, Tamla Motown followed their American counterparts in dusting down the current track, originally included on the 1967 set *Soul On The Rocks*. But whereas "Behind A Painted Smile" had appeared as the B-side of Tamla 54175 (to the non-charting "All Because I Love You"), in Britain it was accorded A-side status, and with the group's popularity on a high following the re-issued "This Old Heart Of Mine" [555] and "I Guess I'll Always Love You" [683], this effortless piece of pop slipped into the top 5.

Introduced with another 'classical' miniature for flute and piano (derived from the melodic shape at the verse-endings), the track asserts itself via a heavily fuzz-toned electric guitar figure, revealing the substantial emotional burden behind its sunny façade, which by accident rather than design exactly mirrors the thrust of the lyric. Here, the 'painted' smile is a mask hiding the tears of the main character, probably suggested by Smokey Robinson's similarly dejected "The Tracks Of My Tears" [522] in which the singer's 'smile is my makeup'. The connection though came as a late amendment to the original "Behind A *Faded* Smile", under which name the track was copyrighted, and which gives a sense of futility to the text, not apparent in the resolve of the finished article. In fact, the lyric is far from defeatist, Ronald Isley defiant ('I don't need your sympathy') and drawing strength for an ambitious falsetto middle-8. (The original single also concludes with an aggressively choleric battering on Benjamin's tom toms, a brief outburst shorn from many subsequently released editions.)

The group's third major UK hit in a few months, "Behind A Painted Smile" arrived too late to salvage The Isley Brothers' fortunes with Motown, appearing just as the group, who had signed with CBS in late-1968, were re-launching their own T-Neck label. About to score a significant hit in the shape of "It's Your Thing" which topped the R & B charts before month-end[1], the group's UK releases would emerge on the Major-Minor label. Tamla Motown nonetheless issued an album entitled *Behind A Painted Smile* in September, a compilation containing the bulk of *Soul On The Rock*, padded with a clutch of additional recordings already in the public sphere.

---

[1] Motown claimed the song was written on their time, and consequently sued the group. Although Motown won the case, The Isley Brothers successfully appealed the decision.

---

**TMG 694**
**MARTHA REEVES & THE VANDELLAS**
**Nowhere To Run** (2:48)
**Re-issue of [502]**
**Release Date**: 28 Mar 1969
**New B-side**: Live Wire [E36]
**Position in Record Retailer Top 40**: -

---

Martha Reeves / Rosalind Ashford / Betty Kelly

---

By the end of the 1960s, Martha Reeves was in poor psychological health following the escalation of numerous personal issues which had left her isolated and broken. Learning that Motown's management arm ITMI was being wound up, it dawned on Reeves that she had seen precious little of the revenue her recordings and live shows had generated over the last few years, setting her at loggerheads with the company (see also [599]). Alarmed at her precarious financial situation, Reeves was further traumatised by a number of physical beatings dished out by the men in her life, one of which involved the father of her unborn child.[1] Experiencing a series of nervous breakdowns over the next two years, Reeves was effectively entering forced retirement, the group thereby splitting up and releasing nothing more until their brief re-emergence in 1971 [794].

Riding the crest of "Dancing In The Street" [684] early in 1969, the current pairing was released in the UK, coupling the appropriately traumatic "Nowhere To Run" [502] with a respected 'Northern' B-side, originally put out on Stateside in March 1964. The single stalled at 42, but could nevertheless be counted a success, leading to a re-appearance of [599] in the charts, which peaked at 21 in the middle of the outfit's three-year hiatus.

[1] Reeves recounts events in her autobiography, p165-73.

**TMG 695**
**DIANA ROSS & THE SUPREMES**
**I'm Living In Shame** (2:57)
(Sawyer—Taylor—Wilson—Cosby—Gordy)
Produced by The Clan
Recording completed: 30 Dec 1968
**Release Date**: 18 Apr 1969
**B-side**: I'm So Glad I Got Somebody (Like You Around)
**Position in Record Retailer Top 40**: 14
**Equivalent US Release**: Motown 1139 (6 Jan 1969)
**Position in Billboard Top 40 Pop**: 10
**Position in Billboard Top 40 R & B**: 8

---

Diana Ross / Cindy Birdsong / Mary Wilson

---

The bedrock of the Motown sound, no matter how defined, was the studio-band's backline, the virtuoso James Jamerson on bass and his close friend and colleague Benny Benjamin on drums. Benjamin though had developed a heroin dependency during the late 1960s which had affected his ability to perform [629n], and in early 1969 took its eventual toll, Benjamin suffering a stroke which left him bed-ridden and hospitalised. Expecting him to pull through, his friends and fellow musicians rallied around but on April 20, news reached a stunned Hitsville that Benjamin had died. The Funk Brothers, ensconced in Studio A working on Stevie Wonder's "You Can't Judge A Book By Its Cover" [892b] were shaken, Jamerson particularly hard-hit, his own self-destructive tendencies coming into sobering relief. For the first time in the best part of a decade, Hitsville shut-up shop for the day as a mark of respect to the much-loved and irreplaceable drummer.[1]

Arranged by Paul Riser, the appropriately grief-stricken "I'm Living In Shame" was recorded the previous Boxing Day and appeared in Britain just as news of Benjamin's passing came through. Concerning the embarrassment experienced by an upwardly-mobile young woman whose mother shared none of her sophistication, the tale is a somewhat distasteful account of personal disownership, the main character fearing the negative judgement of others would reflect adversely on her. In a clever twist, the scenario spins full-circle when it transpires that her estranged mother has died alone while continuing a life-long burden of domestic toil, transferring her shame from mother to self as long-overdue realisation of her ignominious behaviour finally registers.

Widely misinterpreted, the subtext was popularly read as "I'm living in sin", Sharon Davis for example claiming that 'the lyrics dealt with the social stigma attached to unmarried couples living together'.[2] In truth the song, while consciously composed as a follow-up to the political comment in "Love Child" [677] (by the same clutch of writers), drew inspiration from Douglas Sirk's 1959 film *Imitation Of Life*, concerning the desire of a young black servant girl to pass herself off as white, thereby breaking the chains of poverty by rejecting her mother, and indeed her race, to embark on a new life as a light-skinned woman. (If the purpose of the song was to comment on racial inequality, the point becomes lost in the generally objectionable character's collusion with those 'better' than her own family.[3])

Recorded in Detroit, the track shimmers with rapid notes, tinkling bells and a bass riff resembling that on "Love Child", in whose general style it is predictably arranged. 'Thin' for Motown, the track was nevertheless a hit with the UK public, going one place higher than "Love Child". Included on *Let The Sunshine In*, "I'm Living In Shame" would be the group's final custom-made single prior to the departure of Diana Ross [721].

[1] In a touching gesture, his colleague Jack Ashford placed a tambourine bell in Benjamin's coffin, over which the two had shared a joke during the session for "Going To A Go-Go" [547] in 1965.

[2] Davis, 2000, p52.

[3] The track was initially named "The Eyes Of Love", which throws a more compassionate slant on the theme, and switched to "I Live In Sin" before the final title was agreed.

**TMG 696**
**SMOKEY ROBINSON & THE MIRACLES**
The Tracks Of My Tears (2:48)
Re-issue of [522]
Release Date: 25 Apr 1969
New B-side: Come On Do The Jerk [E66]
Position in Record Retailer Top 40: 9

---

Smokey Robinson / Bobby Rogers / Claudette Rogers Robinson /
Warren 'Pete' Moore / Ronnie White

---

Tamla Motown's fifth re-issue in four months, "The Tracks Of My Tears" was coupled with an obscure early number pitched at the Northern Soul dance market. In this case, "Come On Do The Jerk" was selected, having originally emerged as an early-1965 offering on Stateside. Once again the single was a success on the charts, and like [694] marked the onset of a prolonged spell for the group in question, during which only aged recordings were released on 45, a cluster of US selections overlooked entirely in Britain.


**TMG 697**
**MARVIN GAYE & TAMMI TERRELL**
Good Lovin' Ain't Easy To Come By (2:27)
(Ashford—Simpson)
Produced by Nickolas Ashford/Valerie Simpson
Recording completed: 21 Nov 1968
Release Date: 9 May 1969
B-side: Satisfied Feeling
Position in Record Retailer Top 40: 26
Equivalent US Release: Tamla 54179 (14 Jan 1969)
Position in Billboard Top 40 Pop: 30
Position in Billboard Top 40 R & B: 11

With the severity of Tammi Terrell's illness still unclear, Motown had prematurely announced at the end of 1968 that she would be returning to normal duties 'shortly after Christmas'.[1] The truth though was to prove somewhat different to Motown's optimistic prognosis, Terrell losing weight alarmingly to the point that she was so weak that she required a wheelchair. Battling on, she was seen on numerous occasions recording at Hitsville from her seat, embarking on the *Easy* album with Gaye, filled with resolve to fight her illness. With the solo set *Irresistible* issued in January 1969, there were signs that her career was getting back on course but, when *Easy* appeared in September, many listeners noted several vocal tracks sounding subtly unlike her earlier recorded performances, the general supposition being that producer Valerie Simpson was substituted in order to see the project to completion.

The notion has been fuelled by various comments over the years, Johnny Bristol for example claiming at one point that he could hear Simpson on the album, although he was not explicit as to which tracks she supposedly sings. Gaye too is on record as admitting the scam, his comments to David Ritz amounting to an open admission.[2] Simpson on the other hand has consistently denied involvement, admitting only to standing in for Terrell on occasions when Gaye was recording his own sections and required a female guide vocal, and insisting that Terrell handles all the parts ascribed to her on the finished LP.

As things stand, the jury is still out. Although those who believe that Terrell was substituted argue that there is an identifiable difference in texture between the two women's voices, this should be countered by the fact that she was unwell, and particularly if seated while recording, would quite possibly not sound like her old self. (A compromise theory holds that *both* singers were recorded, Motown's final mix based on whichever was the most effective at the time, the true identification of the singer in question remaining ultimately unknowable.)

Pulled from the sessions ahead of schedule, "Good Lovin' Ain't Easy To Come By" dates to well-before Christmas, and shares with "You're All I Need To Get By" [668] a briefly hypnotic introduction in which Jamerson's bass holds a single pulsating note against a similarly sustained violin section. Breaking from the Eb chord into a seductive Cm7, the warming chorus offers the track's main interest, the generally tuneless verses an efficient exercise in connecting the song's hooks. (The track probably gave rise to the album's eventual title.)

[1] The front-page piece in Soul newspaper of 2 December (reproduced in Morse, p63) reports, under the headline "Tammi Terrell Alive, But Can She Return?", false rumours that she was already dead, as well as commenting on exploratory brain surgery for which her head had been shaved [and from which her tumour was diagnosed].

[2] "Tammi didn't do most of that last album with me. She wasn't able to sing then" (Ritz, p157).


**TMG 698**
**FOUR TOPS**
**What Is A Man** (2:34)
(Bristol—McNeil)
Produced by Johnny Bristol
Recording completed: 20 Jan 1969
**Release Date**: 23 May 1969
**B-side**: Don't Bring Back These Memories
**Position in Record Retailer Top 40**: 16
**Equivalent US Release**: Motown 1147 (10 Apr 1969)
**Position in Billboard Top 40 Pop**: -
**Position in Billboard Top 40 R & B**: -

---

Levi Stubbs / Lawrence Payton / Abdul 'Duke' Fakir / Renaldo 'Obie' Benson

---

Lacking a re-launch equivalent to The Supremes' "Love Child" [677] The Four Tops continued in uncertain circumstances, Motown unable to secure a productive writer-producer team for the outfit who had lost their momentum almost entirely in 1968. Desperate for a career-reviving hit single, the group

---

recorded the current track in January, the purpose of which remains an enigma.

Included on the concurrent *Four Tops Now!* (delayed until September in the UK) it was presumably seen as little more than an album-filler. Doris McNeil was a minor staff writer who teamed up here with Johnny Bristol to devise a frankly bizarre track with no relevance to the group's established mode. With self-doubt running through the text, "What Is A Man" shows Levi Stubbs uncharacteristically feeble of character, his efforts in showing backbone in the song's verses quashed by the softly tumbling group chorus. The song's structure, like its general disposition is ill-defined, there being no contrasting section and no hook-line, predictably resulting in one of the group's biggest flops to date, American audiences showing no interest at all.

**TMG 699**
**THE TEMPTATIONS**
**Ain't To Proud To Beg** (2:32)
**Re-issue of [565]**
**Release Date**: May 1969
**New B-side**: Fading Away [557b]
**Position in Record Retailer Top 40**: -

---

Otis Williams / Melvin Franklin / Paul Williams / Eddie Kendricks / David Ruffin

With "Get Ready" [688] having recently gone top 10, Tamla Motown wasted little time in preparing a follow-up, the group's third release since the new year overloading the public to some extent, and contributing to its failure. Interestingly the track, which marked the arrival of Norman Whitfield as the group's musical director, was coupled with "Fading Away", previously seen as the B-side to "Get Ready" in its first incarnation [557].

**TMG 700**
**BRENDA HOLLOWAY**
**Just Look What You've Done** (2:48)
**Re-issue of [608]**
**Release Date**: 6 Jun 1969
**New B-side**: You've Made Me So Very Happy [622]
**Position in Record Retailer Top 40**: -

Repeatedly relying on catalogue recordings, Tamla Motown opted for back-to-back re-issues with [699] and [700], the latter a pairing of Brenda Holloway's last two A-sides. While the re-appearance of "Just Look What You've Done" was calculated for Northern Soul buffs, the choice of B-side was inspired by a recent version of the song by Blood Sweat And Tears which had almost topped the American charts in March, and had since gone top 40 in Britain. A particularly strong 'double-header', the single nonetheless sold few copies and like each of Holloway's previous 45s, did not chart. (The Stateside-era "Every Little Bit Hurts" [E45] may have made a better choice for the flip-side.)

Disgruntled with her employers for some years (see [622]), Holloway had reunited with Smokey Robinson for some 1968 sessions, but unable to contain her frustration, ended up rowing and walking out, resolving never to work for Motown again. Uninterested, Berry Gordy allowed her to remain in self-imposed isolation until her contract expired, donating her backing tracks to other Motown stars. Meantime, Tamla Motown issued her only album *The Artistry Of Brenda Holloway*, but pressed so few copies—probably no more than a few hundred—that the project appeared little more than tokenism.

At the last minute Gordy and Robinson attempted to coax Holloway into accepting a new deal but seeing no point in the idea, she refused, Motown publicly explaining her resignation as the need for her to answer a call from God.[1] In a less-than-forgiving frame of mind, Holloway responded by suing Berry Gordy for access to her financial records. From a professional angle, she then took revenge by recording for HDH, the first American single on their Music Merchant subsidiary appearing in February 1972 as Holloway's "Let Love Grow" (see [745n]; [831]).

[1] Most likely a sarcastic reference to her relationship with a Christian preacher, whom she married in 1970.

## TMG 701
## THE MARVELETTES
**Reachin' For Something I Can't Have** (2:44)
(Weatherspoon—Dean—Weatherspoon)
Produced by James Dean
Recording completed: 14 Sep 1967
**Release Date**: 20 Jun 1969
**B-side**: Destination: Anywhere
**Position in Record Retailer Top 40**: -
**No Equivalent US Release**

---
Ann Bogan / Wanda Young / Katherine Anderson
---

Recorded for *Sophisticated Soul*, a creditable set which also included "You're The One" [562], "My Baby Must Be A Magician" [639] and "Here I Am Baby" [659], "Reachin' For Something I Can't Have" was selected as the group's most straight-forward single in two years, a clomping Wanda Young-led number written with input somewhere along the line from William Weatherspoon's father Cato.[1] Set in Motown's classic late-60s 'Northern' style, this easy song deals with unrequited love, the poor boy of the singer's desire impervious to her 'up-town' advances.

Conceived as an album cut, an imperfect drop-in was let through at 0:22, before Tamla Motown recognised its upbeat appeal and issued it as a single in the summer. The group's American label Tamla was working on a different agenda and having already released "Destination: Anywhere" as an A-side the previous September, resisted "Reachin' For Something I Can't Have" altogether.

Another outfit defeated by the relentless passage of the 1960s, The

Marvelettes—who had provided Motown with their first pop number 1 almost a decade earlier [E05]—were winding up affairs, "Reachin' For Something I Can't Have" their final UK release. The group's subsequent *The Return of the Marvelettes* was a half-hearted attempt to maintain Wanda Young's standing by teaming her with the anonymous Andantes, the trailer-single "Marionette" released in America in mid-1970.

¹ It has long been suspected that several Motown copyrights were 'given' to family members by the true writers, similar cases including [E43], [551], [613], [666] etc.


**TMG 702**
**THE ORIGINALS**
**Green Grow The Lilacs** (2:45)
(Miller)
Produced by Ron Miller/Tom Baird
Recording completed: 14 Jan 1969
**Release Date**: 27 Jun 1969
**B-side**: You're The One
**Position in Record Retailer Top 40**: -
**Equivalent US Release**: Soul 35061 (6 May 1969)
**Position in Billboard Top 40 Pop**: -
**Position in Billboard Top 40 R & B**: -

---

Freddie Gorman / Walter Gaines / C P Spencer / Henry "Hank" Dixon

---

After two-and-a-half years of performing backing vocals for other artists' recordings [592], The Originals were accorded a second full release, the florid "Green Grow The Lilacs" penned by Ron Miller and clearly regarded as a potential standard: Published by Stein & Van Stock [679], the track was rapidly sent around Motown's acts, the current version the third of four readings released in 1969 alone.¹

Inspired by the title of a Celtic folk-song popular in 19th century Texas (and widely thought to have provided the Mexican 'Gringo' as a mistake for 'Green Grow'), the number is a feather-light drift on a summer breeze, gratifyingly peaceable in the idyll of the open country. Taking pains over the session, Miller produced the track immaculately, the group harmonies meandering about Tom Baird's strings and brass, bathing in the warmth of its sunshine.

Dismissed by Ben Edmonds as 'A lovely piece of pop fluff'², the track was given the thumbs-up by Quality Control, delaying the appearance of "Baby I'm For Real" [733] by four months in the States, and nine in the UK. Excited about the prospect of a major hit, Motown had the group hurry through sessions for an album of the same name, their miscalculation over [733] deflating in that "Green Grow The Lilacs", inappropriately released on Soul in America, was shunned by DJs and public alike. Rapidly forgotten, the number was overlooked in the group's *Essential Collection* (2002), despite being one of just five A-sides released by The Originals for Tamla Motown.

## TMG 703
## JIMMY RUFFIN
**I've Passed This Way Before** (2:46)
**Re-issue of [593]**
**Release Date**: 4 Jul 1969
**Position in Record Retailer Top 40**: 33

The last of Tamla Motown's re-issues for the time being, "I've Passed This Way Before" retained its original flip-side, and fell just four places short of its 1967 chart-placing. Filling the 19-month gap between "Don't Let Him Take Your Love From Me" [664] and "Farewell Is A Lonely Sound" [726], this new edition was Ruffin's only single of 1969.

## TMG 704
## DIANA ROSS & THE SUPREMES
**No Matter What Sign You Are** (2:38)
(Gordy—Cosby)
Produced by Berry Gordy Jr./Henry "Hank" Cosby
Recording completed: 22 Apr 1969
**Release Date**: 11 Jul 1969
**B-side**: The Young Folks
**Position in Record Retailer Top 40**: 37
**Equivalent US Release**: Motown 1148 (9 May 1969)
**Position in Billboard Top 40 Pop**: 31
**Position in Billboard Top 40 R & B**: 17

---
Diana Ross / Cindy Birdsong / Mary Wilson
---

Opening on Broadway in April 1968, the stage musical *Hair* famously caused sensation for its graphic promotion of nudity and sexuality, a deliberate confrontation to the conservative order of the day. Guaranteed to provoke out-cry, *Hair* was celebrated by American and British youth as an affront to the repressive 'system', although the legal processes ended up powerless to prevent the show from running for a further four years, until dwindling public interest forced its closure. Apart from a highly successful soundtrack compilation which topped the US album charts for 13 weeks, the main spin-off was the hit single "Aquarius" / "Let The Sunshine In", as recorded by the Fifth Dimension [607n], which picked up the then-current penchant for astrology, one of the staple interests of the hippie movement.

Tapping into the mood, The Supremes lifted from the depression of "I'm Living In Shame" [695] with the present track, clearly inspired by "Aquarius" and making much of name-dropping zodiac signs for a lyric. Iridescent with sitars, "No Matter What Sign You Are" dabbles with its subject cackhandedly, cosmic destiny in the pairing of the two central figures hinted at but simultaneously repudiated, the sitar playing along in the chromatic scale rather than Indian, with an intermittently squealing Diana Ross clumsily proclaiming 'Your water sign just lit my fire'.[1]

Continuing the theme, the group set about recording *Let The Sunshine In* (including a facsimile of the Fifth Dimension's earlier hit as the opener to side 2), housed in a multi-coloured, mock-Alfons Mucha jacket designed by Dean O. Torrence and accidentally retrospective in style. (Here at least the astrological 'message' was dropped, The Supremes spared the fate which would befall old rivals Martha & The Vandellas in 1971, their studio set *Black Magic* [843] ridiculously defining each group member according to star sign on the reverse.)

Described a little unfairly by Mary Wilson, who was not employed on the recording, as 'Among the worst things ever released under The Supremes' name'[2], "No Matter What Sign You Are" marks the inevitable demise of the act billed as Diana Ross & The Supremes, the press already speculating on who the lead singer's replacement might be, and fanning the flames of rumour which drew additional attention to the group, who had sold out the Latin Casino in Cherry Hill, New Jersey for a fortnight in June.

[1] Speaking of Motown's numerous attempts to appeal to hippiedom, Chris Clark explained that they were attempting to exploit the psychedelic market but 'none of us knew exactly what it was about' (*Record Collector* 313 p66). More evocative working titles for the track included "Don't Destroy Me" and "The Paper Said Rain".

[2] 1986, p225


**TMG 705**
**MARVIN GAYE**
**Too Busy Thinking About My Baby** (2:57)
(Whitfield—Bradford—Strong)
Produced by Norman Whitfield
Recording completed: 15 Mar 1969
**Release Date**: 18 Jul 1969
**B-side**: Wherever I Lay My Hat
**Position in Record Retailer Top 40**: 5
**Equivalent US Release**: Tamla 54181 (2 Apr 1969)
**Position in Billboard Top 40 Pop**: 4
**Position in Billboard Top 40 R & B**: 1

Probably based on the lyrics of Sam Cooke's 1960 hit "Wonderful World" in which schooling is rendered impossible by the singer's obsession with his love object, Gaye's new single dates back to 1964, originally supplied by Norman Whitfield to Jimmy Ruffin with two different sets of lyrics.[1] Recorded by Ruffin and then by The Temptations, the track sat dormant for five years before Whitfield revived it for a reunion with Gaye in order to follow up "I Heard It Through The Grapevine" [686]. Relying mainly on bass and percussion, "Too Busy Thinking About My Baby" is an unassuming affair, brought to life by a glistening orchestral sweep into the chorus. Jamerson's foundation track here is a remarkable piece of minimalism consisting almost entirely of the song's C# root, dragging itself lethargically up to Eb on occasion only to collapse back down obstinately each time. (The one-note bass design has a model: [603].)

Released in the UK in July, the single was well-received, assisted by interest in the B-side, a Northern 'floor-filler' which, like its A-side was several years old by the time [705] appeared. "Wherever I Lay My Hat" was recorded by Gaye in September 1962, and copyrighted to Gaye and Whitfield. Pitched in Bb, the number clocks in at under 150 seconds, its self-depreciating sentiment off-set by a quasi-reggae arrangement and infectious melody line. Available in Britain only on the Stateside album *Marvin Gaye* (1964), its appearance on 45 was welcomed by DJs, the recording having been spun throughout the decade from cumbersome LPs. The track achieved belated fame in 1983 courtesy of British vocalist Paul Young who picked the song for his first hit single and took it to the summit of the British charts six months after Phil Collins had done likewise with "You Can't Hurry Love" [575].

With the Gaye—Whitfield partnership thus cemented, the two pieced together *MPG* early in the year which, besides the present single also spawned "That's The Way Love Is" [718]. The relationship between the two though was far from easy [686], the tough, former pool shark Norman Whitfield renowned for treating his collaborators as instruments to be manipulated and moulded to fit his preconceived ideas as to how they should perform. Not one to toe the line, Gaye was by instinct rebellious to authority, and when the mood took him would decamp for various periods of time to consider what he would like to do next. Yet despite winding one another up, the two retained a professional respect, Gaye begrudgingly conceding that his adversary was 'good for him'.

Diana Ross recalls in her autobiography (p147-8) Gaye being particularly troubled during this era, especially depressed by Tammi Terrell's illness [697]. Sitting next to him at a piano, she recounts Gaye's compositional draft of a contemporary song concerning his desire to kill himself, although none of this sentiment is evident in the aged "Too Busy Thinking About My Baby". Whitfield by contrast was in his prime, celebrating success on several fronts through 1969. Interviewed by Paul Zollo in the early 1980s Whitfield remembered "Too Busy Thinking About My Baby" fondly, citing the track, which had almost slipped by unnoticed, as a surprise candidate for his favourite amongst his own compositions, noting that it had sold 'a quiet 2 million'.[2]

[1] The alternative version is entitled "I Know How To Love Her", Eddie Kendricks supplying the text. The song is also known to have gone by the name "Stop Leading Me On".

[2] See Abbott, p148.

**TMG 706**
**THE HONEST MEN**
**Cherie** (2:59)
(Leander—Mills)
Produced by Basart
**Release Date**: 1 Aug 1969

**B-side**: Baby
**Position in Record Retailer Top 40**: -
**Equivalent US Release**: VIP 25047 (23 Apr 1969)
**Position in Billboard Top 40 Pop**: -
**Position in Billboard Top 40 R & B**: -

Little has been documented of Dutch group The Honest Men, one of several minor white acts to appear in Motown's VIP label discography. Produced by Fred Neil under the banner of the Basart company, the track is an irritatingly twee piece of pop, the decision to issue in the UK one of Tamla Motown's most mystifying.

The Honest Men never worked with Motown, their 1967 recording "Cherie" licensed by the company in an attempt to pick up on the developing Dutch pop scene. In this respect, Motown were ahead of the competition, the Shocking Blue quartet becoming the first Netherlands group to top the US singles charts later in the year. (Motown later also recruited Dutch outfit The Cats, assigning them to the Rare Earth label.)


**TMG 707**
**THE TEMPTATIONS**
**Cloud Nine** (3:25)
(Whitfield—Strong)
Produced by Norman Whitfield
Recording completed: 2 Oct 1968
**Release Date**: 15 Aug 1969
**B-side**: Why Did She Have To Leave Me (Why Did She Have To Go)
**Position in Record Retailer Top 40**: 15
**Equivalent US Release**: Gordy 7081 (25 Oct 1968)
**Position in Billboard Top 40 Pop**: 6
**Position in Billboard Top 40 R & B**: 2

---

Otis Williams / Melvin Franklin / Paul Williams / Eddie Kendricks / Dennis Edwards

---

Having parted ways with David Ruffin [671], The Temptations wasted little time in finding a replacement vocalist, former Contour Dennis Edwards having caught the group's eye some years earlier and been pencilled in prior to Ruffin's dismissal. Endowed with a similar range and with a rasping edge to his singing voice, Edwards was performing in small-time group The Firebirds before receiving his call in July 1968 and debuting with The Temptations at the Los Angeles Forum (the group having handled the first half of the set as a four-piece).

Moving into the second part of 1968, The Temptations were one of several major Motown acts stuck for a new direction. In the context of soul music generally, Motown was at that stage risking stagnation, progressive new sounds pushing back the boundaries throughout the previous six months, Motown slow to catch on. Figures such as James Brown, Curtis Mayfield and George Clinton were working on different fronts in the development of what later came to be known as the 'blaxploitation' field. Having moved to Detroit with a view to signing for Motown, Clinton ended up signed by Gordy as a writer-producer, local rival label Revilot snapping up his proto-psychedelic "(I Wanna) Testify" to score a major hit in July of that year, right under Motown's nose.[1] Mayfield's group The Impressions meantime had released the rhythmically 'heavy' "We're A Winner" in 1968, and would shortly introduce the subject of slavery in their lyrics, "This Is My Country" going top 10 R & B just as Mayfield set up his own Curtom record label. Simultaneously, claimed 'inventor' of funk James Brown was preparing to unleash "Say It Loud, (I'm Black And I'm Proud)" in mid 1968 [677], which appeared on the R & B listings on the day the backing tapes for "Cloud Nine" were being made at Hitsville.

The key development of 1968 however was the arrival of Sly & The Family Stone, an experimental San Francisco family act who consciously set about bringing psychedelic rock and R & B together, "Dance To The Music" released in March and causing a ripple of excitement through the world of soul. Rotating vocal duties, the group's idiomatic 'acid-funk' as presented on September's *Dance To The Music* album opened up new horizons, its spaced-out disposition crossing over to white listeners on a level which Motown as yet had barely yet hinted at.[2]

Grabbing the attention of numerous Detroit-based performers, Sly Stone's new sounds filtered through to The Temptations, Otis Williams commending "Dance To The Music" to Norman Whitfield over the summer, the group's producer initially expressing the noncommittal view that it was 'nothing but a passing fancy'.[3] Something was playing on Whitfield's mind however, his itch to make a track equally progressive causing him to dwell on the concept of a Motown recording deeper, and without the customary 4/4 backbeat. Stopping in on a producer's workshop session at Golden World, an informal gathering of Motown's wider circle of session men where songs could be played through and developed, Whitfield was taken by recent recruit Dennis Coffey's use of the wah-wah pedal on a run-through of the track, its deployment in soul music a novel innovation. (Coffey had arrived at the workshop at James Jamerson's request, the bassist responsible for organising the sessions and finding at the last-minute that Eddie Willis was unavailable.) A few days later, Coffey was recalled for a proper rehearsal in Studio A, Whitfield announcing to the core group that something new and different was to be attempted, and commencing a formalisation of the earlier session jam into what became "Cloud Nine".

Making use of Hitsville's new Ampex tape machines, Whitfield set about coaching The Funk Brothers through an extemporaneous session in which he directed each musician as the sound concepts began to unfold. "Cloud Nine" thus began life with Uriel Jones playing a percussive cymbal, the rhythm track taking shape with the addition of Eddie Brown's congas, James Jamerson pitching in with a pulsating bass rhythm. Developing the groove as a unit, the studio-band proved equal to Whitfield's challenge, Coffey earning a place amongst Motown's elite inner circle with penetrating wah-wah from his Gibson Firebird (the same instrument as used by Eddie Willis).

The atmospheric, white-smoke-filled backing track thus secured, Barrett Strong's suitably audacious lyrics were supplied to The Temptations for recording on the October 1 session. Taking Sly Stone's cue, a justifiably excited

Whitfield separated out The Temptations' individual voices, having the group members trade sections against Dennis Edwards' dominant, gravelly lead passages. (In parts, Edwards audibly stands off the mike, allowing for maximum power.) Paul Williams and Eddie Kendricks thus took the opportunity to display their widely contrasting pitching and technique against the hypnotic drone of the backing rhythms. A consummate production firing on all cylinders, the final mix of "Cloud Nine" captured precisely what the producer was aiming at: something fearlessly innovative, new not just to Motown but to soul music *perse*, an integrated landscape of sound in which elements fuse and dissipate like the formulation and dissolution of clouds drifting across the sky.[4]

On the face of it, the lyrical content of the track is a clear espousal of altered states, the poverty-stricken, ghettoised narrator describing the depressing hardships of life in the real world, 'needing something to ease his troubled mind'. Analysing society at large as a self-centred battle for survival, the escape of 'Cloud Nine' transports one 'higher' to a place where reality is suspended and 'every man is free'. (The inclusion of the chanted phrase "up, up and away" may have been borrowed from The Fifth Dimension's hit of the same name; see [607].) Yet despite the clarity of the message, lyricist Barrett Strong denies any suggestion that the lyric references drug-use, and in this respect surprising support comes in the shape of both Dennis Edwards and Otis Williams, the latter commenting, "We were talking about just a state of mind... but [fans] thought we were talking about drugs, and we weren't".[5]

Hearing the tapes, Berry Gordy was in no doubt as to the true subtext, immediately taken by the feel of the track but insisting on a re-think of the lyric. Already at loggerheads with Whitfield over the then-dormant "I Heard It Through The Grapevine" [686], Gordy had another battle on his hands, Whitfield cajoling him and eventually convincing him that the track was innocuous. Conceding to Quality Control's vote, Gordy allowed the single out and watched it climb up the American charts alongside [686]. The UK edition had to wait another ten months while Tamla Motown cleared their decks of stockpiled recordings, becoming their fortieth top 20 hit. With 16 of Tamla Motown's 27 singles released thus far in 1969 consisting of compositions a year or more old (eight of which were straight re-issues—see [683n]), "Cloud Nine" came over as refreshingly new, released in the wake of the July moon landings, which while illustrating a spectacular triumph over nature, also threw into relief the very social and economic problems with which earth-bound humanity was facing.

Revolutionary in its scope, "Cloud Nine" was Motown's sharpest piece of social coverage to date, and in its musical objectives opened dramatic new possibilities for both Norman Whitfield and The Temptations. Marking the commencement of the group's protracted psychedelic era, it effectively terminated their first-phase work. Arriving at this historically decisive moment, Dennis Edwards' involvement in The Temptations points to a radical future and as David Morse points out, 'The Temptations led by David Ruffin and The Temptations led by Dennis Edwards sound so utterly different that it seems logical to discuss them as if they were separate groups'.[6]

[1] Clinton's backing outfit The Parliaments, rechristened simply Parliament, later signed to HDH's Invictus label. See [745n]; [831].

[2] The outfit would take matters further through 1969, with tracks such as "Everyday People" and "I Want To Take You Higher". One of very few black acts to appear at the Woodstock Festival in mid August, Sly & The Family Stone's performance of "I Want To Take You Higher" constituted 'transcendence: a music capable of addressing the body and soul at once, dissolving sexual, social and racial barriers' (MacDonald, 1994, p299).

[3] The exchange is recounted in Williams, p138-9.

[4] Whitfield carelessly let through a vocal error at 2:12.

[5] See Dahl, p37 (Strong and Edwards) and ibid p170 (Williams).

[6] p59

## TMG 708
## THE ISLEY BROTHERS
**Put Yourself In My Place** (2:38)
(Holland—Dozier—Holland)
Produced by Brian Holland/Lamont Dozier[1]
Recording completed: 17 Mar 1966
**Release Date**: 8 Aug 1969
**B-side**: Little Miss Sweetness
**Position in Record Retailer Top 40**: 13
**No Equivalent US Release**

---

Ronald Isley / Rudolph Isley / O'Kelly Isley

---

Having twice released The Elgins' "Put Yourself In My Place" without success [551]; [642], Tamla Motown opted to exploit The Isley Brothers' recent popularity by putting their 1966 recording of the song out as a single, and duly scored a fourth successive top 20 hit for the group. Originally made for *This Old Heart Of Mine*, The Isley Brothers' version employs The Elgins' backing track, the group merely dubbing on a new set of vocals. The original though is comfortably the better effort, Saundra Mallett Edwards displaying a level of feel for the song missing from Ronald Isley's reading.

The B-side is another in-house cover (see [587b]) taken from the group's follow-up album *Soul On The Rocks* (1967).

[1] The label credit omits Johnny Thornton.

## TMG 709
## DIANA ROSS & THE SUPREMES & THE TEMPTATIONS
**I Second That Emotion** (2:28)
(Robinson—Cleveland)
Produced by Frank Wilson
Recording completed: 6 Sep 1968
**Release Date**: 5 Sep 1969
**B-side**: The Way You Do The Things You Do

**Position in Record Retailer Top 40**: 18
**No Equivalent US Release**

---

Diana Ross / Cindy Birdsong / Mary Wilson / Otis Williams / Melvin Franklin /
Paul Williams / Eddie Kendricks / Dennis Edwards

---

With *Diana Ross & The Supremes Join The Temptations* in preparation during 1968, Berry Gordy was keen to promote his new pairing, accepting an offer from NBC for a television spectacular featuring the two acts on the back of their joint appearance on *The Ed Sullivan Show*. (Gordy was happy to nurture his cordial professional relationship with NBC, developing productively since The Supremes had appeared on a episode of *Tarzan*, aired on 12 January 1968.) Taped over ten days, *Taking Care Of Business* (*TCB*) was unleashed on the American public as a one-hour Christmas special on 9 December 1968 to impressive reviews, and represented a major coup for the Motown empire and a first real breakthrough into broadcasting.

With a supporting album and single in the American shops, there was little real need for a specific tie-in, although that did not stop Motown from milking the show's success first with a rush-released soundtrack LP, put out in the UK as late as July 1969, despite the fact that *TCB* had been entirely ignored by British television networks. Meanwhile, Motown had released a follow-up to "I'm Gonna Make You Love Me" [685] in America, in the shape of "I'll Try Something New", a relative flop issued in February 1969. By September they also had *Together*, another collaborative album out, and were deliberating over "Stubborn Kind Of Fellow" [E16] as a third single before opting for a cover of The Band's "The Weight". Running behind schedule, Tamla Motown were still promoting *TCB* and *Diana Ross & The Supremes Join The Temptations* (from which the current single is lifted), *Together* not appearing until the following February—confusingly so since by then Diana Ross, who had top billing, was no longer a Supreme.

"I Second That Emotion" was a standard album-filler, a version of The Miracles' 1967 single [631] which had not been a major UK hit. Backed with another in-house cover from The Temptations' early repertoire [E38], the single constitutes an uninspired recycling job, but is salvaged by its genuinely buoyant production. Sharpened a semitone from The Miracles' original, the track extrapolates on its first draft, emphasised by uplifting strings and a far more extravagant use of backing vocals (as might be anticipated from the fact that eight singers were vying for a share of 2:28). Dominated by Ross this time (unlike [685] where Eddie Kendricks had assumed lead status), the recording outsold The Miracles' 1967 version.

**TMG 710**
**THE FOUR TOPS**
**Do What You Gotta Do** (2:43)
(Webb)
Produced by Frank Wilson/Lawrence Payton/Wade Marcus

---

**288**                    *Tamla Motown - The stories behind the UK singles*

Recording completed: 18 Jan 1969
**Release Date**: 12 Sep 1969
**B-side**: Can't Seem To Get You Out Of My Mind
**Position in Record Retailer Top 40**: 11
**No Equivalent US Release**

---

Levi Stubbs / Lawrence Payton / Abdul 'Duke' Fakir / Renaldo 'Obie' Benson

---

Following the dismal "What Is A Man" [698], this UK-only single, while by no means vintage Four Tops, was a pleasing enough venture in the group's recent, more reflective style, dealing with the recurrent theme of relationship breakdown. Their biggest chart-hit in a year-and-a-half, "Do What You Gotta Do" was composed by Jimmy Webb, an established figure drafted in to write for Jobete. (In fact The Four Tops had also taped Webb's "MacArthur Park" in November 1968, a popular recording which appeared on 45 in America during the summer of 1971.)

Brief in its component sections and edited down for single, "Do What You Gotta Do" is effectively telescoped by the deployment of a symmetrical arrangement consisting of verse 1/verse 2/verse 2/verse 1. Lacking a formal middle-8, contrast arrives in the repeat of verse 2, Lawrence Payton taking a rare lead vocal, his high register sounding angelic against Stubbs' grainy texture. While the idea of rotating lead vocals was hardly new, it was likely in this case directly suggested by The Temptations' new approach [707], but must also be seen in the context of Payton's involvement in production duties, suggesting the idea may in fact have been his own.

Clearly defined, with resonant reverberated brass, "Do What You Gotta Do" is one of the group's most specious recordings, its uneventful repetitiveness successfully shaded by expert arranging from Wade Marcus and some neat EQ-ing. Locking bass and drums together the heavy handed chops in the chorus offer counterpoint and provide moments of rousing emotion in an otherwise passive text, the song's rapid bass triplets becoming freer as the number progresses.[1]

[1] The track was probably recorded West Coast, the bass most likely not Jamerson's.

**TMG 711**
**DAVID RUFFIN**
**I've Lost Everything I've Ever Loved** (2:55)
(Kemp—Bristol)
Produced by Johnny Bristol
Recording completed: 8 Mar 1969
**Release Date**: 26 Sep 1969
**B-side**: We'll Have A Good Thing Going On
**Position in Record Retailer Top 40**: -
**Equivalent US Release**: Motown 1149 (20 Jun 1969)
**Position in Billboard Top 40 Pop**: -
**Position in Billboard Top 40 R & B**: 11

---

In the shadow of The Temptations' dazzling new single [707] David Ruffin's second solo effort pales, being an unspectacular mid-tempo number with a particularly despondent lyric involving multiple personal losses and emotional upheavals. Unfortunately, the track's exuberant, up-beat arrangement lends a sense of black comedy to the unrelenting bad luck depicted. Bolstered by an extraordinarily passionate lead vocal, possibly stylistically inspired by that of "I Don't Know Why (I Love You)" [690a], the song shares the same whole-note drop at the start of its chorus as "I Am The Man For You Baby" [646], and ultimately lacks identity.

For Ruffin, this would be his last UK single for half a decade [936], his extensive interim recordings which included a set of duets with brother Jimmy ignored by Tamla Motown, and his attempts to assemble a new band under the name The Fellas coming to nought. Ruffin was jailed in the new decade for tax evasion, shortly after the death of partner Tammi Terrell, lending the current title a prophetic quality unintended by its authors.

**TMG 712**
**JUNIOR WALKER & THE ALL STARS**
**What Does It Take (To Win Your Love)** (2:58)
(Bristol—Fuqua—Bullock)
Produced by Harvey Fuqua/Johnny Bristol
Recording completed: 30 Jan 1968
**Release Date**: 10 Oct 1969
**B-side**: Brainwasher
**Position in Record Retailer Top 40**: 13
**Equivalent US Release**: Soul 35062 (25 Apr 1969)
**Position in Billboard Top 40 Pop**: 4
**Position in Billboard Top 40 R & B**: 1

---

Jr Walker / Willie Woods / Vic Thomas / Billy Nicks

---

Written during 1967, "What Does It Take (To Win Your Love)" was earmarked for Junior Walker from the outset. The saxophonist though was unimpressed by the number, a lilting ballad pitched against his patent roughneck style and the project was apparently forgotten. Johnny Bristol's mind was set though and almost a year later he caught Walker off-guard during sessions for "Hip City" [667][1] and won agreement to give the track a shot on pain of continued nagging.

Bearing resemblance in its melodic form to the title phrase of "Come On And See Me" [561], the composition is a terse article with just two six-line verses punctuated with Walker's infectiously sailing sax patterns cruising over a modulated Gm—Fmaj7 foundation. Buoyantly performed, Jamerson's bass[2] bounces around 5th intervals, relentless tambourine brightening the despondency apparent in Walker's vocals, loosely tracked by Johnny Bristol.

Suavely discharged, the recording, which has featured on innumerable compilations since its release, was given a cool reception by Motown, Berry Gordy said to have disliked it. Surprise was therefore expressed when the track conquered the American charts, going number 1 R & B in July (toppling "Too Busy Thinking About My Baby" [705]). Waiting until "(I'm A) Road Runner" [691] was out of the way, the UK edition emerged late in the year, backed like its US counterpart with the older "Brainwasher", dug from the Harvey label archives [509]. Embarking on a UK tour in 1969, Walker found his popularity on a high, the single's impact cementing his professional bond with Johnny Bristol, although co-producer Harvey Fuqua, Walker's former boss, was about to depart for RCA.

[1] At least, this is the track recalled by Walker in 1990 (see Abbott, p124). The recording dates though appear not to bear him out, "Hip City" made in its entirety in June and July 1968, after "What Does It Take" was finished. Either Walker is confusing sessions, or there is more history to "Hip City" than known.

[2] Here, The Funk Brothers handle musical duties, Walker's backing band from now on dispensed with so far as studio sessions were concerned.


## TMG 713
## MARV JOHNSON
**I Miss You Baby (How I Miss You)** (2:46)
(Paul—Broadnax)
Produced by William "Mickey" Stevenson/Ivy Jo Hunter/Clarence Paul[1]
Recording completed: 1 Oct 1965
**Release Date**: 10 Oct 1969
**B-side**: Bad Girl
**Position in Record Retailer Top 40**: 25
**Equivalent US Release**: Gordy 7051 (4 Mar 1966)
**Position in Billboard Top 40 Pop**: -
**Position in Billboard Top 40 R & B**: 39

Of similar vintage to "I'll Pick A Rose For My Rose" [680], Marv Johnson's third Tamla Motown single was a 1966 recording originally overlooked in the UK. Put out in the wake of the top 10 placing of its predecessor, the pounding rhythm of "I Miss You Baby (How I Miss You)" proved sufficient to lift it into the charts, further delaying Johnson's retirement from performing.

   With no American Motown album release to his credit, Tamla Motown took the initiative, cobbling some archive recordings together for August's *I'll Pick A Rose For My Rose*, which contained both sides of this single.

[1] No production credits are given on the label.


## TMG 714
## GLADYS KNIGHT & THE PIPS
**The Nitty Gritty** (2:59)
(Chase)
Produced by Norman Whitfield
Recording completed: 23 Apr 1969
**Release Date**: 24 Oct 1969

**B-side**: Got Myself A Good Man
**Position in Record Retailer Top 40**: -
**Equivalent US Release**: Soul 35063 (26 May 1969)
**Position in Billboard Top 40 Pop**: 19
**Position in Billboard Top 40 R & B**: 2

---

Gladys Knight / Merald 'Bubba' Knight / Edward Patten / William Guest

---

Used as the title track of Gladys Knight & The Pips' fourth Motown studio album, "The Nitty Gritty" was a 1963 hit for West Indian singer Shirley Ellis, penned by Lincoln Chase, better known for his subsequent "Clapping Song". Incorporated into the repertoire of several Motown groups (including The Velvelettes whose February 1964 live version has been released on CD in recent years), the song was in the frame for a studio recording for some time, The Supremes taking first shot before the current rendition was taped.

Popular legend has it that the nitty gritty is slang for the debris to be found on the deck of slave ships (nits and grit), although this is probably erroneous, not only because the theory makes no sense in view of the term's meaning (the practical details of something), but due to the fact that there is no record of the phrase being used before the 1950s. Moreover Chase's text, which consists of a sequence of rhythmic mottos with no coherent meaning, defies interpretation along historical/political lines, making the notion redundant as an exposition on the number.

Pitched in a vaguely funky style, Norman Whitfield's production revolves mainly around a mechanically shaken tambourine against Dennis Coffey's electric guitar (ludicrously distorted at 1:54) and James Jamerson's bass which reflects the track's dearth of chords by resting on a single note for much of it [705]. A blot on the group's discography, the single is their weakest since joining Motown in 1966.


**TMG 715**
**MARVIN GAYE & TAMMI TERRELL**
The Onion Song (2:55)
(Ashford—Simpson)
Produced by Nickolas Ashford/Valerie Simpson
Recording completed: 17 Mar 1969
**Release Date**: 31 Oct 1969
**B-side**: I Can't Believe You Love Me
**Position in Record Retailer Top 40**: 9
**Equivalent US Release**: Tamla 54192 (20 Mar 1970)
**Position in Billboard Top 40 Pop**: -
**Position in Billboard Top 40 R & B**: 18


Employing identical intro and outro passages as technical 'book-ends' (with a rare cadenced conclusion), the curiously named "Onion Song" contains some archetypal Motown orchestration arranged by Paul Riser, and a passionate vocal track in which Gaye and his partner implore humanity to 'do their share' and spread the message that 'love is the answer'. Anticipating The O'Jays' "Love Train" by three-and-a-half years, this evangelical call to distribute enlightened philosophy founders on a succession of unconvincing declarations in which the onion is a tear-inducing symbol for the world's problems. The naïve solution of knocking on doors and remaining 'headstrong', proposed for rich and poor alike, entirely lacks any insight as to the cause-and-effect of the social problems being vaguely referenced and offers little: blurring the central culinary metaphor, the 'spices' of pain and fear can apparently be overcome only by the planting of 'love seeds'.

Few listeners though were troubled by any such detail, the infectious push of the production making this one of Gaye and Terrell's more potent singles. Whether Terrell is in fact on the track is in dispute [697], this being one of the more hotly debated titles from *Easy*. In his informed study, Ben Edmonds not only claims Valerie Simpson handles the female section but goes on to describe Gaye's submission to the plan, in order to assist Terrell's family financially at a time when the seriousness of her illness was all too apparent.[1]

[715] has the distinction of being Tamla Motown's first stereo single release[2] and was issued in a promotional picture sleeve, another first. As a result of these added attractions it spent three months on chart, and became the duo's only top-tenner. Interested in its potential, Motown followed suit by granting a US release on March 20, coincidentally the day that Tammi Terrell was buried on a depressingly bleak Philadelphia afternoon [734].

[1] p25. David Ritz concurs, specifically citing "The Onion Song" (p158). No such issues hang over the single's B-side however, "I Can't Believe You Love Me" an early Terrell solo recording overdubbed with Gaye's vocals by Harvey Fuqua, in the manner of "Ain't No Mountain High Enough" [611].

[2] UK singles stated the matrix number in print on the left of the labels. Stereo recordings show the prefix YTMG as opposed to TMG. The switch to stereo was not initially adopted universally by Tamla Motown, and was gradually phased in over the ensuing years.

## TMG 716
## THE TEMPTATIONS
**Runaway Child, Running Wild** (4:30)
(Whitfield—Strong)
Produced by Norman Whitfield
Recording completed: 31 Dec 68
**Release Date**: 24 Oct 1969
**B-side**: I Need Your Lovin'
**Position in Record Retailer Top 40**: -
**Equivalent US Release**: Gordy 7084 (30 Jan 1969)
**Position in Billboard Top 40 Pop**: 6
**Position in Billboard Top 40 R & B**: 1

---

Otis Williams / Melvin Franklin / Paul Williams / Eddie Kendricks /
Dennis Edwards

---

Since his departure from The Temptations, David Ruffin's singles releases suggest covert messages being thrown the group's way, "My Whole World

Ended (The Moment You Left Me)" [689] being followed by "I've Lost Everything I Ever Loved" [711]. Although most likely inadvertent, the group's earlier "Runaway Child" also hints at a swipe in Ruffin's direction, the track recorded while the wayward singer was embroiled in a failed attempt to flee Motown. If this is the case, several lines in the text are fairly barbed, the scornful portrayal of the character as an unruly kid accentuated by lines such as 'Going nowhere fast/You're on your own at last'. (See also [800].)

Recorded in the immediate aftermath of "Cloud Nine" [707], the track is a second venture in the group's new-phase psychedelia. A fundamental breakthrough for Whitfield, [707] suggested the ambience of "Runaway Child" which again showcases the group's distinctive range of individual vocals, close-miked and EQ-ed to emphasise their textual contrast. Extravagantly mixed, this new track incorporates two electric guitars, fuzzed and wah-wahed and sent to different channels. Its sound-world further abstracted with a disjointed electronic crescendo and distant cries of the lost kid, "Runaway Child" was a ruffled creation, somewhat accusatory in tone and with edgy vocal blusters in its unsettling introduction. Self-indulgent where [707] had been objective, the finalised track clocked in at almost five minutes, necessitating a trimming down for release on 7-inch (although at 4:30 it remains comfortably the longest Tamla Motown single to date). Nonetheless America was spell-bound, hoisting it to the top of the R & B charts, its much later UK release by contrast making virtually no impact.

**TMG 717**
**STEVIE WONDER**
**Yester-me, Yester-you, Yesterday** (2:57)
(Miller—Wells)
Produced by Harvey Fuqua/Johnny Bristol
Recording completed: 24 Jan 1967
**Release Date**: 7 Nov 1969
**B-side**: I'd Be A Fool Right Now
**Position in Record Retailer Top 40**: 2
**Equivalent US Release**: Tamla 54188 (30 Sep 1969)
**Position in Billboard Top 40 Pop**: 7
**Position in Billboard Top 40 R & B**: 5

Born in May 1950, Stevie Wonder had been a junior throughout the 1960s, compelled to receive formal education despite his fame. Forced by the Board Of Education to stay in school until he was 19 (to compensate for his absences due to performing commitments), he was tutored by Ted Hull until graduating from the Michigan School For The Blind in June 1969. Interested in pursuing his musical interests, Wonder was at this point publicly speculating on enrolling for formal musical education at university, although the extent to which this was ever seriously considered is debatable, Wonder continuing recording and performing throughout the year and talking even at this early point of acquiring a synthesiser to further his progressive interests at Motown.

In the face of this, the company's choice of singles material was notably conservative, "Yester-me, Yester-you, Yesterday" his third successive oldie after "For Once In My Life" [679] and "My Cherie Amour" [690b]. Recorded in 1967 in the wake of Chris Clark's first attempt at it, this pleasantly affable ballad was made for *I Was Made To Love Her* under direct instruction from Berry Gordy, but left off the set for reasons unknown. Contemporary with [690b] and sharing its general lightness, the recording was romantically arranged by Paul Riser, with Jamerson's ever-dependable bass bubbling under the instrumentation, sharpened with acute electric guitar.

Calculatedly released towards year-end the track justified the move commercially by becoming Wonder's biggest UK hit to date, pointing optimistically towards the 19-year-old's future despite its vintage.

## TMG 718
## MARVIN GAYE
**That's The Way Love Is** (3:15)
(Whitfield—Strong)
Produced by Norman Whitfield
Recording completed: 12 Dec 1968
**Release Date**: 14 Nov 1969
**B-side**: Gonna Keep On Trying Till I Win Your Love
**Position in Record Retailer Top 40**: -
**Equivalent US Release**: Tamla 54185 (4 Aug 1969)
**Position in Billboard Top 40 Pop**: 7
**Position in Billboard Top 40 R & B**: 2

Norman Whitfield's fifth A-side in as many months, "That's The Way Love Is" rounded off a year in which he had become the undisputed leader of Motown's backroom staff. Continuing Tamla Motown's ongoing policy of issuing aged numbers, this recording was finalised a full year beforehand; dating back to 1967, the track had been a failed American single for The Isley Brothers, Whitfield producing this and another interim version by Gladys Knight & The Pips before he had Marvin Gaye attempt it in December 1968.

With "I Heard It Through The Grapevine" [686] causing a stir at the time, it is little surprise that Whitfield's arrangement, set in the same Ebm, amounts to a fair imitation of the earlier number, incorporating a rattlesnake introduction and wordless opening vocal. But as first conceived, the two compositions had little in common, the present song a resigned shrug of the shoulders in the face of emotional heartbreak, carrying none of the pregnant hysteria of its predecessor. Indeed Whitfield and Gaye seem to have gone to some effort to re-mould the song in the image of "Grapevine", effectively re-writing the melody so that it is almost unrecognisable beside The Isley Brothers' original.

Released after "Too Busy Thinking About My Baby" [705], the track, pulled from *MPG*, was a questionable choice for a single, sounding like a pale imitation of his earlier hit. In fact Gaye's recording duties were becoming so thin on the ground by the end of the year that Motown were forced to name his next album after the track and include it in the listing for the second time in half a year. Gaye would release just one more single in the next 18 months [734].

## TMG 719
## THE ISLEY BROTHERS
Take Some Time Out For Love (2:26)
Re-issue of [566]
Release Date: 7 Nov 1969
Position in Record Retailer Top 40: -

---

Ronald Isley / Rudolph Isley / O'Kelly Isley

---

Ironically, The Isley Brothers were one of Tamla Motown's hottest properties in 1969, scoring three top 20 hits despite the fact that they had left Motown before the start of the year. This, their second re-issue after [683], re-ran the group's early follow-up to "This Old Heart Of Mine" [555]. "Take Some Time Out For Love" did not chart second time around, and would be the last product of Tamla Motown's revived interest in the group until four years and a string of non-Motown hits later [877]. It's a pity Berry Gordy had not put more effort into retaining them.

## TMG 720
## BLINKY & EDWIN STARR
Oh How Happy (2:39)
(Hatcher)
Produced by Frank Wilson/Billie-Jean Brown
Recording completed: 1 May 1969
Release Date: NOT RELEASED Demo copies exist dated 2 Jan 1970 (see [748])
B-side: Ooo Baby Baby
Equivalent US Release: Gordy 7090 (20 Jul 1969)
Position in Billboard Top 40 Pop: -
Position in Billboard Top 40 R & B: -

This aggravatingly simplistic composition with few lyrics save its endlessly repeated title was the work of Starr himself, written in his pre-Motown days for soul group Shades Of Blue. Devised as an effort to persuade the local Impact label (which Berry Gordy subsequently purchased) to release something by a white group, "Oh How Happy" succeeded and reached number 12 nationally in the summer of 1966. Two years later, Starr's own recording surfaced on *Soul Master*, by which time he was himself a Motown artist with a clutch of unsuccessful releases to his name.

LA-based Sondra 'Blinky' Williams meantime had been a promising prospect for both Vee Jay and Atlantic, neither of whom made her a star, before she signed with Motown in late 1968. With these two dormant talents on the books, it fell to Billie-Jean Brown to suggest a pairing up, an effort to break both in the style of Marvin Gaye & Tammi Terrell. Placed in the hands of Frank Wilson, "Oh How Happy" was selected for a first release, the track radically re-worked and put out as a 45, widely and erroneously claimed to have been a hit. (In fact it did not enter the top 40 of any chart for which it was eligible.) Nonetheless, Motown had enough belief in the partnership to invest in an album project, *Just We Two* appearing in September 1969 (January 1970 in Britain).

Summed up by Sharon Davis as 'enjoyable but bland'[1], the single was scheduled for UK release on the second day of 1970 before being shelved.[2] The reasons for this are not entirely clear, although the same fate would befall almost everything Blinky recorded for Motown. [720] was pressed only as a demo, although a high number appear to be in circulation suggesting perhaps a technical mix-up during the pre-distribution stage. In any case the single was not to be, the recording re-scheduled for release in August 1970 [748]. For Blinky's part, she was transferred to Mo-West [799] before making a famed appearance in *Lady Sings The Blues* [848]. Starr meanwhile was on the brink of solo success [754], putting paid to the partnership for good.

[1] 1988, p70

[2] In the TMG sequence, four singles were aborted before going on sale, the others being [786]; [867]; [885].


## TMG 721
## DIANA ROSS & THE SUPREMES
**Someday We'll Be Together** (3:14)
(Beaver—Bristol—Johnson)[1]
Produced by Johnny Bristol
Recording completed: 13 Jun 1969
**Release Date**: 14 Nov 1969
**B-side**: He's My Sunny Boy
**Position in Record Retailer Top 40**: 13
**Equivalent US Release**: Motown 1156 (14 Oct 1969)
**Position in Billboard Top 40 Pop**: 1
**Position in Billboard Top 40 R & B**: 1

---
Diana Ross / Cindy Birdsong / Mary Wilson
---

With the sunshine optimism of the mid-1960s having clouded during 1968 [654], there was a mood in the air at the close of this historic decade which suggested matters had turned decisively for the worse. The changing tides were plainly delineated on December 6 when The Rolling Stones' free concert at Altamont near San Francisco, conceived in the communal spirit of America's West Coast hippies, rapidly degenerated into an uncontrollable exercise in mob violence by a sect of Hell's Angels. Naïvely hired as stewards for the event, the Angels set about delivering random beatings to members of the audience, one of whom was murdered right in front of the stage (see [689n]). Truly the sun was setting on the idyllic 1960s.

For Motown, the changing tides of 1968-69 had seen several fundamental upheavals which had pointed to a brave new future, flagship act The Supremes by now on the point of disintegration. The same week as Altamont, Supreme Cindy Birdsong was attacked in her Los Angeles home by a knifeman, and held hostage in a speeding car for nearly an hour during which she was badly cut, before breaking free and running for her life. Coming in the wake of Charles Manson's murder of Sharon Tate, just four months earlier and in the vicinity of Birdsong's home, the general mood following this latest attack was, to say the least, edgy.[2] For her part, Mary Wilson had also relocated to LA, but was suffering flagging health, her hair falling out in clumps and an ongoing relationship with singing star Tom Jones bringing her more stress than happiness.

Of course for anyone in the know at the time, it was obvious that Diana Ross was waiting to leave the group, the matter of finding a suitably epic parting gesture the only detail outstanding. Officially announced in November, Ross' departure was to be marked by a series of Las Vegas concerts, the group's new single already out in America and clearly bidding her goodbye. Choice of track for this milestone release was, appropriately, Berry Gordy's. "Someday We'll Be Together" dates to 1961, written by a team which included both members of Jackey (Beavers)[3] & Johnny (Bristol). Recorded by them for Tri-Phi in quasi-Caribbean mode [705b], Bristol elected to remake the number in 1969, initially approaching Junior Walker who turned it down. Referring the matter to Gordy for advice, Bristol was directed to The Supremes instead, a sharp piece of judgement from Gordy and an option Bristol readily seized. As it turned out, only Diana Ross from the group would feature on the recording, backing vocals being handled by Maxine and Julia Waters.[4] (In fact, similar arrangements had been made for almost all of the group's 45s since the loss of HDH, The Supremes becoming little more than a brand name in 1968-69 so far as singles were concerned.)

Despite substantial evidence that the backing track was recorded at Hitsville, there are several who dispute the notion including Kingsley Abbott, who refers to it as "well acknowledged as being LA cut".[5] Against Abbott is Earl Van Dyke's recollection of the session at which Detroit-based James Jamerson was present. Experimenting with the use of a fretless instrument, a frustrated Jamerson completed the recording before hurling the guitar down and cursing its poor action (the pitching of his instrument can be heard to wander minutely in the opening bars). Dennis Coffey also claims to be on the track[6] and is adamant that it was Detroit product, these 'eye-witness' accounts effectively closing the argument.

As for Ross' vocal, while adequately executed, the most-remarked-upon aspect is the repeated interjection of Johnny Bristol (eg at 0:36, "You tell 'em"). With Ross flagging towards the end of the session, Bristol sought to gee her up by giving her some direction as she sang, entering a second recording booth with mike and headphones and providing intermittent guidance and encouragement. Playing back the whole thing from the desk, Berry Gordy (who was in attendance) was impressed by the effect and suggested it be mixed for release as it stood.

"Someday We'll Be Together" was the obvious choice for the group's final TV appearance with Ross, mimed on the *Ed Sullivan Show* on December 21. Effectively starting their three week farewell engagement, this date showed The Supremes in dejected mood, their subsequent live appearances dogged by a degree of bitterness during which Ross was being touted as a future solo star, the group itself uncertain as to where they would go from here (if anywhere). The last night of the concert series came around on 14 January 1970 at Las Vegas' Frontier Hotel, a sadness permeating events, culminating in the performance of this last single before a tearful finale in which Berry Gordy took to the stage—as did one Jean Terrell [735].[7] And from that point, Diana Ross & The Supremes were no more.

An emotive tale of unrequited love, "Someday We'll Be Together" is a somewhat melodramatic number, whose touching sense of loss made it the perfect expression of lament for a group who had embodied Motown's Golden Age and now faced the very real possibility of permanent demise, despite a new lead singer and single lined up for release [735]. No Motown recording has so succinctly caught its point in history, capturing the hearts of American audiences more acutely than in inherently sceptical Great Britain.

Characterised as a depressing historical period by Don Waller[8], the 1960s passed here with a tangible regret. Citing segregation and anti-drug laws as examples of the decade's oppressive reality, Waller compares the materialistic 1980s favourably. This analysis misses what the era was about, namely the rise in a spiritual liberation from such constraints. On 13 December 1969, Segregation was finally ended in America's south, five days before the UK abolished its death penalty. By March 1970, reports would appear of American police intervening to protect black children from attacks by whites, the political and social turnaround unmistakable. Mirroring a sense of growing empowerment in the late 1960s, black music had risen immeasurably in prominence, in parallel with a people's movement which was now capable of proudly pronouncing its aims and beliefs. (Motown launched its political Black Forum label in 1970, issuing speeches by Martin Luther King and future leader of the Black Panthers, Elaine Brown.)

Berry Gordy has since recounted with pride the broadcast of "Someday We'll Be Together" at a service for a Chicago Black Panther leader murdered in his bed, and so poignant is the track that it was also played at the funeral of former Supreme Florence Ballard in 1976. Seven years later it was the anthem used to close *Motown 25*, several luminaries from Motown's glorious past joining in the emotive chorus. Echoing through the years, the song's hint of a golden future arising in the face of reluctant farewells has found many deeply touching interpretations, and appropriately ends Tamla Motown's 1960s discography, closing a chapter on the label's biggest act.

---

[1] One of several inaccuracies on Tamla Motown labels, the composition should be credited to Beavers—Bristol—Fuqua.

[2] In addition to this there was cause for Motown to be on their guard following a shooting at Hitsville in February, leading to rumours that Motown was in the grips of organised criminals.

[3] His name is mis-spelled as Beaver on the UK single.

[4] Over time further claims of involvement on backing duty have materialised from other Motown recording stars, as well as Clydie King and Sherlie Matthews, members of The Blackberries (see [751n]).

[5] p92

[6] p215

[7] The concert was released as the double album *Farewell* during 1970.

[8] p16

## TIMELINE – 1969

Tamla Motown release 40 singles and 39 albums
Tamla Motown place 26 singles in the UK top 40. 10 make top 10 and 1 reaches number 1
Motown expand LA base with opening of several new offices
Numerous UK live appearances by Stevie Wonder, Junior Walker & All Stars, Marv Johnson,
Edwin Starr etc. who perform in Northern Soul venues such as Manchester's Twisted Wheel
and Stoke-On-Trent's Golden Torch

| | |
|---|---|
| Jan 15 | Martha & Vandellas: "Dancing In The Street" enters UK top 50 (peak 4) |
| Jan 22 | Marv Johnson: "I'll Pick A Rose For My Rose" enters UK top 50 (peak 10) |
| Jan 29 | Diana Ross & Supremes & Temptations: "I'm Gonna Make You Love Me" enters UK top 50 (peak 3) |
| Feb 8 | Diana Ross & Supremes & Temptations: *TCB* number 1 album in US (one week) |
| Feb 15 | *Diana Ross & The Supremes Join The Temptations* tops UK album chart (four weeks) |
| Spring | Martha Reeves withdraws from public view after breakdown |
| Spring | Tamla Motown re-issue numerous singles as Northern Soul market booms |
| Mar 5 | Temptations: "Get Ready" enters UK top 50 as re-issue (peak 10) |
| Mar 26 | Marvin Gaye: "I Heard It Through The Grapevine" UK number 1 (three weeks) |
| Apr 2 | Marvin Gaye is 30 |
| Apr | Various Motown artists appear in string of concerts marking anniversary of Martin Luther King's assassination |
| Apr 16 | Isley Brothers: "Behind A Painted Smile" enters UK top 50 (peak 5) |
| Apr 20 | Funk Brother drummer Benny Benjamin dies form long-term substance misuse. Studio A closes for day |
| May 7 | Miracles: "Tracks Of My Tears" enters UK top 50 as re-issue (peak 9) |
| Jun 29 | Shorty Long drowns in accident |
| Jul 16 | Stevie Wonder: "My Cherie Amour" enters UK top 50 (peak 4) as re-promotion of TMG 690, initially released with "I Don't Know Why (I Love You)" as 'hit' side (number 14, Mar 1969) |
| Jul 23 | Marvin Gaye: "Too Busy Thinking About My Baby" enters UK top 50 (peak 5) |
| Summer | Marvelettes disband |
| Aug 15 | Temptations' "Cloud Nine" (US, Oct 1968) signifies new direction for group and consolidates Norman Whitfield as Motown's most creative producer. Guitarist Dennis Coffey becomes integral Funk Brother |
| Aug | Rare Earth label starts up in US, run from LA offices |
| Oct 18 | Temptations: "I Can't Get Next To You" number 1 in US (two weeks) |
| Nov 14 | Tamla Motown's final single of 1960s, "Someday We'll Be Together", which also marks end of Diana Ross' recording career in Supremes |
| Nov 15 | Marvin Gaye & Tammi Terrell: "The Onion Song" enters UK top 50 (peak 9) |
| Nov 15 | Stevie Wonder: "Yester-Me Yester-You Yesterday" enters UK top 50 (peak 2) |
| Nov 28 | Berry Gordy is 40 |
| Dec 13 | Segregation abolished in southern US |
| Dec 27 | Supremes: "Someday We'll Be Together" number 1 in US (one week) |
| Dec 28 | Mayor of Detroit declares today 'Temptations Day' |

# Summary of era [636] to [721]

Having made the historic breakthrough into the pop mainstream by 1967, Tamla Motown found their American parent company at a turning point come the start of 1968. Instability amongst their leading acts and writers was causing a pervasive tension which can be heard beneath their period recordings. While developments over the last two years of the decade hardly constituted a crisis (indeed Motown's US chart-domination at the end of 1968 was a peak achievement [680]), Motown was a different animal by the start of 1970.

Central to the changes in the air was the loss or collapse of an alarmingly high number of the company's established acts. While long-time groups such as The Isley Brothers drifted away to pastures new, some, such as The Marvelettes, were terminated entirely, seen as surplus to requirements by the start of a new decade. For others, the period was shrouded in uncertainty as to what the future would hold, Martha Reeves falling silent as her group began to crumble and she suffered a personal depression, and Tammi Terrell disengaging from the industry entirely in the face of her crippling illness. Others too would fall one way or another, and the flight of HDH during 1968 was felt by the major groups once reliant on them for product. And while Motown's conveyor belt rolled on defiantly, everyone within the company was stunned at the unexpected loss of Benny Benjamin in 1969 which fractured The Funk Brothers' bedrock rhythm section.

Yet it would be misleading to see the years 1968-69 as purely ones of dissolution. Along with these losses came signs of regeneration with behind-the-scenes adjustments to most of Motown's big acts with production standards and musical philosophy having been approached afresh. Foremost amongst the re-invented were The Temptations, tuxedos and bow-ties cast aside as Smokey Robinson's favourite old group effectively ceased to exist. Gone too was their distinctive lead vocalist David Ruffin to embark on a solo career, and in was a brand of dense, multi-layered 'psychedelic' soul, the act transformed into street-wise, politically aware avatars of a new Motown Sound. Conceived almost completely by Norman Whitfield, this enterprising shift in style constituted a cutting-edge for the label, as the tailored 'crossover' appeal of the mid-1960s was supplanted by an adventurous and outspoken sonic realm which the group themselves could not have conceived.

Likewise, shifts were afoot for The Supremes, considered Berry Gordy's priority through 1968 and 1969 purely for the fact that they were fronted by Diana Ross. Gordy assembled committees to work on new material for the group, the resultant "Love Child" [677] a milestone in his management career. With it came what was effectively another new act, Diana Ross & The Supremes now seen as distinct from the old Supremes, re-dressed in casuals and re-branded for the black working classes. No longer much interested in recording the group at Hitsville, LA-based Gordy succeeded in converting them first into a launch-pad for Ross, and then splitting them entirely, two-thirds of the classic line-up gone by 1970.

As for The Four Tops, new angles were sought for them too, albeit without their defining a stable new style. Nonetheless, Berry Gordy's employment of another panel of writers for the new-phase "Yesterday's Dreams" [665] heralded the onset of a more mellow group sound which contrasted with the intensity of their late-HDH work. Similar processes were underway for Junior Walker, who after successfully recording with Johnny Bristol, re-emerged with an altogether different studio sound, The All Stars no longer to be employed on his recordings as his style was engineered towards the gentler pop mode. And coincident with this process was the further development of Ashford & Simpson, who sought to improve Motown's patent sound in their own way, upping production standards with their immaculate techniques and, like Whitfield, taking advantage of Motown's improved recording facilities. Between them Whitfield and Ashford & Simpson largely shaped what would become the patent sound of Motown in the early 1970s, working variously on futuristic sonic invention and cleanly gliding balladry.

In short, for most of what formed the backbone of Motown's roster, the period 1968-69 saw the decline of the old order, and the emergence of a bank of re-formed acts poised to spearhead the company's recovery. It should be noted that this calculated rising from potential disaster was not something which happened of its own accord. Norman Whitfield's work perhaps excepted, much of it was strategy on Berry Gordy's part, his tactical moves rescuing a series of precarious situations. Not only did he dare to re-brand his most successful artists, he also followed industry trends with more concerted emphasis on the album format, Tamla Motown enjoying particularly high successes in Britain with The Four Tops' *Reach Out*, which spent more than half of 1968 on the UK charts. Tamla Motown also blazed a commercial trail all-its-own with some highly successful collections, The Four Tops' *Greatest Hits* topping the UK listings only to be deposed by The Supremes' own such retrospective, and *British Motown Chartbusters* spending most of 1968 in the listings with a peak position of 2. 1969 continued to exploit this new arena, the chart-topping *Diana Ross & The Supremes Join The Temptations* followed by the similarly successful *Chartbusters Volume 3*.

Although most of the main UK album successes constituted assemblages of hits rather that studio sets, Tamla Motown was learning to exploit the material available through effective marketing. Fuelling the success of collections such as the *Chartbusters* series was the UK-centric Northern Soul boom, which gave the label an agenda of its own, as American product began to be issued somewhat more sparingly and the British scene more generously indulged. There is no mistaking the fact that, in this way, Tamla Motown's priorities were irrevocably split in 1969 as a succession of re-releases outsold contemporary product coming over from Detroit. From here on the label would be forever swinging between two poles, unsure whether to press forward with new material or look backwards to its rich catalogue, as the general intensity of the music of the 1960s began to dissipate.

Unknown as 1969 drew to a close, Motown had another decisive move up its sleeve, with the launching of a kid group known as The Jackson 5. About to be unleashed on the UK, this outfit would further split the label's following, as purists baulked at the blatant commercialisation of Motown, younger listeners simply accepting the group for what they were. As 1969 concluded with the last of the old Supremes' singles, 1970 would begin a new phase entirely, with The Jackson 5's debut release "I Want You Back" [724] already on its way to the top of the US singles chart. From here, the goalposts had unmistakeably shifted and Motown headed into the 1970s with a revitalised zeal, and new ideas on how records should be made.

# CHAPTER FOUR

# NEW WAYS

## *1970 to 1972*

**TMG 722**
**THE TEMPTATIONS**
**I Can't Get Next To You** (2:53)
(Whitfield—Strong)
Produced by Norman Whitfield
Recording completed: 3 Jul 1969
**Release Date**: 2 Jan 1970
**B-side**: Running Away (Ain't Gonna Help You)
**Position in Record Retailer Top 40**: 13
**Equivalent US Release**: Gordy 7093 (30 Jul 1969)
**Position in Billboard Top 40 Pop**: 1
**Position in Billboard Top 40 R & B**: 1

---

Otis Williams / Melvin Franklin / Paul Williams / Eddie Kendricks / Dennis Edwards

On a high from "Cloud Nine" [707] through 1969, Norman Whitfield had recorded an album of the same name for US-release in February, a ten-track follow-up ready come late summer in the shape of *Puzzle People*. Released there as a trailer-single in July, "I Can't Get Next To You" topped soul and pop charts, thereby comfortably outdoing its predecessor and offering a tantalizing prospect for Tamla Motown once 1969's backlogs were cleared.[1]

Introduced with sound-effects, the group supposedly interrupting a party to unveil their new song, the track shows them having fun, honky-tonk piano and falsetto "oohs" lending to the celebratory mood. Yet the production in this respect clashes with Barrett Strong's ultimately defeatist text, the lament of a man capable of every manner of supernatural feat, but unable to win the heart of his woman.[2] Extracting the middle-8 of "Cloud Nine", with its round-the-table vocal arrangement, the recording makes a feature of the group's sequential contributions, establishing the technique as standard henceforth. Yet while the gimmick succeeds here due to its sheer sonic impact, the lyric is clearly pitched from the perspective of an individual, suggesting that Whitfield was in this instance concentrating more on playing with studio techniques than on sensitively interpreting his partner's contribution.[3]

Arriving in London for the first time in January 1970, the group's appearance at the Talk Of The Town was warmly received and recorded for subsequent release on LP.[4] Their popularity reaching fresh heights in Britain, "I Can't Get Next To You" was released on the first working day of the new decade and made number 13 in the charts, their biggest success thus far bar the recent re-issue of "Get Ready" [688].

[1] The UK schedules omitted the group's "Don't Let The Joneses Get You Down" released to little effect in America ahead of the current track, as Gordy 7086.

[2] The line 'I can sail a ship on dry land' is borrowed from Frank Wilson's earlier "If You Will Let Me, I Know I Can" [726b]; [845]. So perfectly does the line encapsulate the overall theme of "I Can't Get Next To You" that it may well have inspired the entire cong.

[3] Employed on numerous Temptations numbers, the vocal trading sometimes comes across as absurd, for example on the group's cover of "Hey Jude", sequenced immediately after "I Can't Get Next To You" on *Puzzle People*.

---

4 The album was the middle one of three recorded at the London venue and issued by Tamla Motown, each entitled *Live! At The Talk Of The Town*. The Supremes' set appeared in early 1968 (see [650]), The Temptations' in April 1970, and Stevie Wonder's in October 1970 (see [744]).

## TMG 723
## THE CONTOURS
**Just A Little Misunderstanding** (2:39)
(Broadnax—Paul—Wonder)
Produced by Clarence Paul/William "Mickey" Stevenson
Recording completed: 10 Mar 1966
**Release Date**: 9 Jan 1970
**B-side**: First I Look At The Purse [531]
**Position in Record Retailer Top 40**: 31
**Equivalent US Release**: Gordy 7052 (18 Apr 1966)
**Position in Billboard Top 40 Pop**: -
**Position in Billboard Top 40 R & B**: 18

Joe Stubbs / Gerald Green / Council Gay / Sylvester Potts

Released in America in 1966, "Just A Little Misunderstanding" had almost been passed by in the UK, relegated initially to the B-side of "Determination" [564]. Northern Soul fans were hungry for the track however, leading Tamla Motown to resurrect it here, coupled with a re-run of "First I Look At The Purse" [531] which saw it break into the UK top 40. (Evidence of its popularity can be found via the Motown and Motor City Fan Club poll of 1997, in which the recording came in at a surprise number 2 behind "My Girl" [E67].)[1]

Recorded with temporary group-member Joe Stubbs handling lead vocals, "Just A Little Misunderstanding" is an archetypal Motown dance tune, crashing snare drum holding regular time against James Jamerson's boundlessly animated bass line. Yet its joyful enthusiasm didn't translate into sales, and by 1968 the group who had never once managed to repeat the success of "Do You Love Me" [E10] had thrown in the towel. This belated edition of "Just A Little Misunderstanding" represents their only incursion into the UK charts.

1 The full list of 100 titles is reproduced in Abbott, p250.

## TMG 724
## THE JACKSON 5
**I Want You Back** (2:44)
(The Corporation)
Produced by The Corporation
**Release Date**: 16 Jan 1970
**B-side**: Who's Loving You
**Position in Record Retailer Top 40**: 2
**Equivalent US Release**: Motown 1157 (7 Oct 1969)

**Position in Billboard Top 40 Pop**: I
**Position in Billboard Top 40 R & B**: I

---

Jackie Jackson / Tito Jackson / Jermaine Jackson / Marlon Jackson /Michael Jackson

Pushed into performing by a disciplinarian father, the quintet of siblings who would become The Jackson 5 were already well-known on the live circuit before Michael, youngest of the lot, had reached puberty. In fact Gladys Knight got wind of them long before they arrived at Motown and had recommended them in vain to her manager, although they were shortly snapped up by the Atco-controlled Steeltown label for whom they cut a couple of singles. At this stage, it was not entirely clear what, if anything, the group had to offer. Hailing from Indiana, the brothers ranged between ages ten and 17, pushing an act consisting largely of Michael's James Brown-style dance-moves against covers including a liberal sprinkling of Motown titles. Until now they had spent much of their short career travelling from state to state under the name Ripples & Waves Plus Michael, hoping for professional openings, ending up in a talent contest in Chicago where they happened to come up against Bobby Taylor & The Vancouvers [654].[1] At that point father and group manager Joe Jackson was claiming to have an option on signing with Atlantic, but Taylor knew there was something out of the ordinary here and took them back to Detroit.

Difficult to understand with hindsight, Berry Gordy initially showed no interest in the group. Besides performing, Taylor was employed as a group manager and producer and thanks to his position he was able to see that they signed contracts, yet without interest from Gordy he could take the act no further. In the end, Suzanne de Passe took the matter up and arranged for an audition in front of Gordy in a small rehearsal room in Motown's Woodward Avenue building, footage of which survives. By his own account, the unprepared Gordy was mesmerised by what he eventually saw.

If Gordy was to push the act, he would need an angle. Surveying the US pop charts through 1968, there was clearly an emerging market for bubblegum, several big hits arriving in the shape of "Green Tambourine" (The Lemon Pipers); "Yummy Yummy Yummy" (Ohio Express); "Young Girl" (The Union Gap); "Simon Says" (1910 Fruitgum Co.) and so on—and so Gordy elected to do something he had not done with his previous child star Little Stevie Wonder and package them specifically for the youth market. In this respect, Gordy and the group's stand-in manager de Passe were prepared to pull out all the stops, using every PR trick at their disposal. The group were shown artists' impressions of themselves in various get-ups in order to work on how to dress and present themselves, while the usual grooming process was undertaken and costumes designed. According to Michael Jackson's account, the brothers were formally 'tested' to make sure they had appropriate answers ready for the press, checked for correct grammar and manners and generally adjusted, coached and primed in anticipation of their first large-scale public exposure, which also necessitated the trimming back of their potentially 'political' afros.[2]

Equally, Gordy spent an extraordinary amount of effort sourcing their debut Motown single, taking a personal responsibility beyond anything he had done before—including his lavish attentions to Diana Ross. For the moment

The Jackson 5 were given a selection of Jobete numbers to record, Gordy unclear on exactly where the group's first hit would come from. Ultimately the solution came via his former collaborator in The Clan [677], Deke Richards who had spent a substantial amount of 1969 working on a track entitled "I Wanna Be Free", with fellow writers Alphonzo 'Fonce' Mizell and Freddie Perren. Custom-built for Gladys Knight, the backing track was duly recorded and played to Gordy, who in one of his clearest moments recognised it as the key for his new group and requested it be given the 'Frankie Lymon treatment'.[3] (The writer-producers, including Gordy, began to think of themselves as a team engaged on a high-level project, dubbing their small club The Corporation, which suited Gordy's desire for anonymity as a measure to prevent his individual staff from rising in public profile as HDH had.)

With Frankie Lymon cited as a point of reference, The Corporation were able to focus on remaking the backing track for Michael Jackson's lead vocals. The accepted version of events holds that the musicianship on "I Want You Back" was recorded in LA. Deke Richards already had an embryonic West Coast equivalent of the Funks in place by mid-1969, consisting of guitarists Louie Shelton, Don Peake and David T. Walker, drummer Gene Pello and Clarence McDonald on keyboards (replaced early on by Joe Sample). Handling bass was Ron Brown, and the musician very much in the frame for the prominent lines on "I Want You Back", Wilton Felder, formerly with The Jazz Crusaders alongside Sample. Keeping the ensemble together with regular salary payments, Richards went further by kitting out the LA studios at Dave Hassinger's "Sound Factory" in imitation of the Snakepit, even installing a false floor from reclaimed timber to boost the resonance of the drum kit, as per the Detroit facility. Though not readily apparent at the time, Richards' work in this respect was instrumental in the closure of Hitsville and the disbanding of The Funk Brothers within a couple of years [814].[4]

Getting the group's vocals recorded was as-ever the final stage in the process. An unprecedented amount of time was spent in getting an immaculate take down, the group working into the early hours in search of perfection. By the time they had finished, Motown had expended something like $10,000 on the recording, three or four times the typical cost of making a hit single.[5] Yet Gordy was not finished, agonising over the track's every millisecond and making innumerable fine adjustments in an obsessive effort to achieve flawlessness; Jackson later claimed quite believably that more time and effort was invested in "I Want You Back" than the rest of its parent album combined.[6]

Creating a mystique around the group, Motown went to painstaking lengths to mould a public image of the brothers as superstars-in-waiting, a strategy which worked spectacularly well. The group's name itself was defined by Gordy and Richards, opting to utilise a numeral rather than the word 'Five'. Most significantly, the group's early discovery by Gladys Knight and then Bobby Taylor was airbrushed out, Diana Ross effectively hired to promote the act. Thus, history has recorded Ross as the key figure in the story, a myth reinforced by the naming of the group's debut album as *Diana Ross Presents The Jackson 5*, on which she penned liner notes extravagantly embellishing her own involvement. Further dubious moves surrounded the clearly pre-scripted utterances of the group members, Michael Jackson on-record as having declared a desire for "peace for the world" at age 5, a ridiculous notion which smacks of calculated myth-making.[7] Due as much to the falsity of the group's public persona as to anything emerging from their studio work, "I Want You Back" did more to alienate hard-core soul fans than anything Motown had put out thus far.

Nevertheless, the impact of the single on release was spectacular. Coupled with the Detroit-recorded "Who's Loving You", a 1960 Smokey Robinson number first recorded by The Miracles, the single was hailed as a major breakthrough from the start. Don Waller, writing in the *Los Angeles Times* called it the best pop record of all-time, a sentiment echoed by Paul Gambaccini and numerous commentators since. Certainly, whatever one's personal musical tastes, in the context of the pop charts, the song is extremely engaging. Commencing with a swooping *glissando*, a last-minute addition by Richards, the song brims with multiple hooks and riffs, the chorus featuring a descending bass line during the first half and an enterprising exploration of the fret-board in the second, which gives the illusion of chords shifting with each word sung. (In fact the chorus recycles the verse, the octave-plunging bass figure playing tricks on the listener.) Carrying all of the key HDH tricks, with incessantly drilling backbeat and electric guitar holding a single chopping chord, its commercial success was beyond doubt, the record duly topping soul and pop charts in America, and sealing the arrival of The Jackson 5 with a vengeance.

Hawked around America by Diana Ross, who would introduce them on stage and television, the group became something of an overnight phenomenon. If their first appearance on the national networks mustered a stir on the Ross-presented *Hollywood Palace*, their subsequent arrival on the *Ed Sullivan Show* on December 14 caused a sensation, "I Want You Back" climbing the charts week-on-week for two months before nestling at the very top a fortnight after the UK release.

The appearance of this single, above any other, was a decisive move in the history of Motown. By mid 1970 Gordy could boast a major new act on his books, and a writing and production unit in The Corporation as hot as anything Motown ever had, including HDH. The LA studio arrangement was legitimised, the West Coast studio-band settling into place, just as a new decade was stretching out ahead. In this context, the piano *gliss* which opens this exuberant creation appears to be more than just a device for commencing a record; under Berry Gordy's guidance, it speaks of a more generalised fresh start, a symbolic sweeping of the left hand, brushing aside Motown's recent troubles and landing unmistakably on a firm new dawn.

[1] Taraborrelli however states the concert was at Gilroy Stadium in Gary, Indiana. He dates it to September 27, 1968 (1986, p64).

[2] p63

[3] Taraborrelli (1994) p51. Lymon was a teenage star during the 1950s, his biggest hit "Why Do Fools Fall In Love". He died a year before "I Want You Back" was recorded, aged 25.

4 Some dispute the notion that the backing was made entirely by the LA band. According to Slutsky (p60), West Coast bassist Ron Brown claims Jamerson flew out to dub on his own bass part, while an alternative version states that Jamerson and Dennis Coffey overdubbed sections back in Detroit. Bassist Bob Babbitt, a frequent session man for Golden World through the 60s who was by now becoming a regular at Hitsville, has

further confused matters by claiming that he plays bass on the recording (ibid), although recollections are doubtless blurred by the existence of a contemporary Detroit-recorded version, vocalised by David Ruffin, which was buried in Motown's vaults and forgotten until surfacing on CD in 1998 on *David—The Unreleased Album* (see [936n]).

[5] According to Deke Richards, quoted in Taraborrelli (1994) p53.

[6] p65

[7] Cited in Dineen, p7. This would have been prior to his arrival at Motown and 'recalled' subsequently.


## TMG 725
## EDWIN STARR
**Time** (2:56)
(Brucato)[1]
Produced by Edwin Starr
Recording completed: 28 Nov 1969
**Release Date**: 23 Jan 1970
**B-side**: Running Back And Forth
**Position in Record Retailer Top 40**: -
**Equivalent US Release**: Gordy 7097 (20 Jan 1970)
**Position in Billboard Top 40 Pop**: -
**Position in Billboard Top 40 R & B**: 39

After the comparatively disappointing collaborations with Blinky Williams [720], Edwin Starr rediscovered his form with this, his fifth solo Tamla Motown single. Self-produced (and arranged by Wade Marcus), "Time" shows marked influence from Norman Whitfield, with whom the singer was presently working ([692]; [754]). Using essentially the same metrical scheme as "I Can't Get Next To You" [722], the track is Starr's 'heaviest' to date, skirting around the global issues of war and peace which would dominate his output over the following 12 months ([754]; [764]).[2] Showing an enterprising advance in scope and impact, the single is Starr's pivotal release, paving the way for his definitive "War" later in the year.

[1] The label credit is erroneous, "Time" copyrighted to Starr and Richard 'Popcorn' Wylie. The mistake was rectified for the re-issue [1028]. (Charles 'Chuck' Brucato was a member of Rustix, a New York group signed to Motown's Rare Earth label in 1969 [742], but was apparently uninvolved here.)

[2] Starr's concurrent album was entitled War And Peace (inexplicably held off in the UK until January 1971).


## TMG 726
## JIMMY RUFFIN
**Farewell Is A Lonely Sound** (2:56)
(Dean—Weatherspoon—Goga)
Produced by James Dean/William Weatherspoon
Recording completed: 30 Mar 1967
**Release Date**: 6 Feb 1970
**B-side**: If You Will Let Me, I Know I Can

**Position in Record Retailer Top 40**: 8
**Equivalent US Release**: Soul 35060 (7 Oct 1969)
**Position in Billboard Top 40 Pop**: -
**Position in Billboard Top 40 R & B**: -

Eschewing his patent 'power chorus' style for a more reflective mode, "Farewell Is A Lonely Sound" finds Ruffin returning to his roots, this ruminative ballad pointing back to "What Becomes Of The Brokenhearted" [577]. Penned by the same Dean—Weatherspoon team (with Jack Goga), the track is early, plucked from the *Ruff 'N' Ready* album of a year previous, the recording itself pre-dating even this, resembling in form and melody his 1967 release "I've Passed This Way Before" [593] (recently re-issued [703]), although the debt to "Brokenhearted" is most palpable.

"Farewell Is A Lonely Sound" accounts the rationalised process of reluctantly abandoning a lover, the thoughtfully analytical lyric admitting the emotional distress as the departing person jumps on a train. Too closely observed, the tears and pitiable waving goodbye are overblown, the lyric's *schmaltz* somewhat sickly. The track wins however with its musical foundations, Paul Riser's suitably treble-heavy arrangement tugging against the song's ceaseless chord cycle, which like [577] refuses to deviate for its chorus. The sequence here, G#/Cm/Fm/C# has a circulating quality suggestive of doo-wop, James Jamerson's rich triplets succinctly capturing the song's underlying nostalgia.

Ignored in America, the track made its breakthrough in Britain, equalling Ruffin's previous best chart placing and opening a period where his popularity amongst UK soul fans would culminate in his emigration [753].

## TMG 727
## JUNIOR WALKER & THE ALL STARS
**These Eyes** (3:20)
(Cummings—Bachman)
Produced by Johnny Bristol
Recording completed: 13 Jun 1969 (?)
**Release Date**: 13 Feb 1970
**B-side**: Got To Find A Way To Get Maria Back
**Position in Record Retailer Top 40**: -
**Equivalent US Release**: Soul 35067 (2 Oct 1969)
**Position in Billboard Top 40 Pop**: 16
**Position in Billboard Top 40 R & B**: 3

Jr Walker / Willie Woods / Vic Thomas / Billy Nicks

During sessions for *Gotta Hold On To This Feeling* (re-released as *What Does It Take To Win Your Love* in respect of the commercial success of [712]), Walker and his producer adopted the standard Motown practise of padding out the set with covers of recent hits. In this case, "These Eyes" was selected, a top 10 single in the spring of 1969 for rock band The Guess Who (which started a rise to pre-eminence culminating later in 1970 when they became the first act from Canada to top the *Billboard* pop charts).

Deploying the same relaxed mood as [712], the track, which features Walker's most technically accomplished vocal to date, was an obvious candidate for release on single and was duly lifted for a modest American hit at the tail-end of 1969. The UK edition of the new year slipped by largely unnoticed, and one wonders why the LP's title track, simultaneously heading to 21 in the US, was overlooked. (It eventually re-surfaced as [894] in 1974.)

**TMG 728**
**GLADYS KNIGHT & THE PIPS**
**Didn't You Know (You'd Have To Cry Sometime)** (3:15)
(Ashford—Simpson)
Produced by Nickolas Ashford/Valerie Simpson
Recording completed: 20 Dec 1968
**Release Date**: 27 Feb 1970
**B-side**: Keep An Eye
**Position in Record Retailer Top 40**: -
**Equivalent US Release**: Soul 35057 (13 Feb 1969)
**Position in Billboard Top 40 Pop**: -
**Position in Billboard Top 40 R & B**: 11

---

Gladys Knight / Merald 'Bubba' Knight / Edward Patten / William Guest

---

Symptomatic of a changing emphasis in the first half of 1970, [728] was a third successive ballad for Tamla Motown, and signposts the direction the label was heading in. Each of the titles was released on the Soul imprint in America, originally conceived to provide Motown with an outlet for uncompromising R & B [509]. Yet the label was becoming obsolete by 1970, only Knight and Junior Walker—both of whom had mellowed beyond recognition—keeping it afloat between 1970 and its protracted demise of 1976-78.

Carried by the full force of Knight's husky vocals, the track is performed in a gospel style out-of-phase with Ashford & Simpson's clinical production. 'Quiet' in mood, tempo and impact, the bare bones of "Didn't You Know" are at odds with Knight's designs and perhaps lacking *raison d'être*, the single flopped. (It began life as "Love Has Another Side", a particularly sensitive title exposing its tender qualities.) Originally taped for US release as early as February 1969, the track was initially overlooked by Tamla Motown until its inclusion on December's *Nitty Gritty* brought about capitulation.

**TMG 729**
**CHUCK JACKSON**
**Honey Come Back** (3:15)
(Webb)
Produced by Frank Wilson
Recording completed: 22 Nov 1969
**Release Date**: 6 Mar 1970

---

**B-side**: What Am I Going To Do Without You?
**Position in Record Retailer Top 40**: -
**Equivalent US Release**: Motown 1152 (8 Aug 1969)
**Position in Billboard Top 40 Pop**: -
**Position in Billboard Top 40 R & B**: -

Widely viewed as squandered at Motown, Chuck Jackson's second and last UK single came after a futile switch to the VIP label at home, which effectively closed this particular chapter of his career. Partly the problem stemmed from the company's promotions strategy; Jackson's material was strong enough, but made no impact, the long-term consequence of which was that the singer, once a bright prospect, was now almost lost from public view. Moving to ABC after two further years of stalemate, the rueful singer summarised his decision to sign with Motown as "One of the worst mistakes I ever made in my life."[1]

Jimmy Webb's "Honey Come Back" is a mournful petition to a lost lover, embroiled in a relationship with another man, whose suggested wealth seen through the eyes of the main character indicates a rural setting, the woman leaving for 'the bright lights'. Stirring with its robust chord changes and authoritatively read by Jackson, the track deserved to break through but lying outside of Motown's standard style-range failed, leaving Glenn Campbell to cash in and take a rendition to number 4 on the UK chart in May.

[1] Quoted in George, p158.


## TMG 730
## DIANA ROSS & THE SUPREMES & THE TEMPTATIONS
**Why (Must We Fall In Love)** (2:59)
(Richards—Matthews)
Produced by Frank Wilson
Recording completed: 24 Mar 1969
**Release Date**: 13 Mar 1970
**B-side**: Uptight (Everything's Alright)
**Position in Record Retailer Top 40**: 31
**No Equivalent US Release**

---

Diana Ross / Cindy Birdsong / Mary Wilson / Otis Williams / Melvin Franklin / Paul Williams / Eddie Kendricks / Dennis Edwards

---

A laborious third collaborative album for these two acts, both of whom had better things to do elsewhere, rounded off a year in which the union had been marketed to death. A second television special had been aired in the US in November, unfortunately titled *GIT On Broadway* [Getting It All Together], in which a selection of Broadway standards was performed (the soundtrack becoming an unbearable *fourth* LP).

*Together* was a studio set made during early-1969, with Ross retaining top-billing on the trailer-single despite her having left The Supremes by now. Part-penned by Deke Richards, fresh from his success with "Love Child" [677], it is no surprise to find elements of The Supremes' earlier track surfacing here, most notably the opening melody which conforms generally to the corresponding section 'Started my life/in an old, cold, run down tenement slum', major as against minor.

Having prepared a master for release, Frank Wilson was instructed to make last-minute amendments to the closing section, which required the dropping in of an earlier mix. Annoyed to find the required tape wiped, Wilson had to utilise an inferior alternative mix, leaving a rather murky conclusion to the stereo edition of the last joint release by the two groups.


**TMG 731**
**STEVIE WONDER**
**Never Had A Dream Come True** (2:59)
(Moy—Wonder—Cosby)
Produced by Henry "Hank" Cosby
Recording completed: 11 Aug 1969
**Release Date**: 20 Mar 1970
**B-side**: Somebody Knows, Somebody Cares
**Position in Record Retailer Top 40**: 6
**Equivalent US Release**: Tamla 54191 (13 Jan 1970)
**Position in Billboard Top 40 Pop**: 26
**Position in Billboard Top 40 R & B**: 11

With a recurring tendency towards whimsicality [588]; [690b], Stevie Wonder's first release of 1970 was a love song to no-one in particular, the object of his desires apparently a fantasy created in his imagination. (So addicted is he to his vision, it seems he lives his life in this half-world, to the point where his own parents disown him.) Written and recorded in 1967 (with some more recent overdubs), the track was canned for three years, a proposed American outing in 1969 scrapped, and it was finally released at home one week before this Tamla Motown edition in the new year. Kept at surface-level niceness by Cosby and Paul Riser's romantic lilt, the track fails to assert itself despite choppy guitar stabs and some of Jamerson's trademark triplets which seek in vain to provide some much-needed energy.


**TMG 732**
**FOUR TOPS**
**I Can't Help Myself** (2:43)
**Re-issue of [515]**
**Release Date**: Mar 1970
**New B-side**: Baby I Need Your Loving [E53]
**Position in Record Retailer Top 40**: 10

Levi Stubbs / Lawrence Payton / Abdul 'Duke' Fakir / Renaldo 'Obie' Benson

Opting to celebrate their tenth anniversary in 1970 for reasons unknown (Motown began operations in 1959), Gordy had several acts lined up to play

UK dates early in the year. The Four Tops were sent over in March, who while avoiding concert venues, taped a series of television performances. Hosting a press conference in London, proceedings were unexpectedly interrupted by police, who made a bee-line for Levi Stubbs and promptly arrested him on suspicion of possession of cocaine. Although acquitted (he was fined for carrying a small amount of ammunition on his person), the event marred an otherwise productive week, The Four Tops making numerous appearances before the UK media.

Timed to coincide with the extra publicity, Tamla Motown pulled two of the group's earlier singles for release as the first re-issue of 1970. "I Can't Help Myself" [515] had been a UK hit five years previously, while "Baby I Need Your Loving" was making its first appearance on the label, the original having appeared on Stateside [E53] as the group's debut. Ever-popular, the coupling scaled the UK charts, putting The Four Tops in the top 10 for the first time in two years [647].

## TMG 733
## THE ORIGINALS
**Baby I'm For Real** (3:00)
(Gaye—Gaye)
Produced by Richard Morris
Recording completed: 3 Jan 1969
**Release Date**: 26 Mar 1970
**B-side**: The Moment Of Truth
**Position in Record Retailer Top 40**: -
**Equivalent US Release**: Soul 35066 (12 Aug 1969)
**Position in Billboard Top 40 Pop**: 14
**Position in Billboard Top 40 R & B**: 1

---

Freddie Gorman / Walter Gaines / C P Spencer / Henry "Hank" Dixon

---

Written in 1969 by Marvin Gaye and wife Anna at their home on Outer Drive [667], "Baby I'm For Real" was developed from the earlier "The Bells", which currently lay dormant.[1] Custom-made for The Originals, Gaye demoed the track on his home piano, coaching the group through the vocal exchanges, swapping between their individual textures in the manner recently explored by Norman Whitfield [722].[2] Vocal rotations aside, the track has little else to do with Whitfield's contemporary work, waltzing through its doo-wop verses with lullaby bells and warm, Moonglow-esque backing vocals.

Ushered in with a Four Seasons-style falsetto [819] and confidently at ease with beautiful major 7ths and Eli Fontaine's relaxed saxophone, the track has a mesmeric quality due to the assured scope of its production, a breakthrough for Gaye personally who would begin to develop his interest in *making* records during the 1970s [775]. (Gaye co-produced the track but, since he was not contracted as a producer, could not be credited on the single.)

Motown though was still busy packaging The Originals' debut album *Green Grow The Lilacs* [702], and was reluctant to simultaneously release a

**316**                    *Tamla Motown - The stories behind the UK singles*

non-album title, the compromise being a late addition of "Baby I'm For Real" to the set, the effect of which was substantial radio play and a profound reception in Detroit. With [702] having stalled, Motown were forced to recant and issue the track as a single in America, whereupon it predictably scaled the charts. Embarrassing for the company, *Green Grow The Lilacs* had to be re-packaged as *Baby I'm For Real*, The Originals suddenly in demand and booked for a series of engagements with Bobby Taylor (now performing as a solo artist).[3]

For The Originals, "Baby I'm For Real" is their defining moment, and had Tammi Terrell's illness not sent Gaye into a tail spin [734], may have heralded the start of a golden era for the group. Despite numerous attempts to repeat its success in America, a follow-up in the UK would be well over a year in coming.

[1] "The Bells" was eventually recorded by The Originals and had already been released in the US as Soul 35069, heading to number 4 R & B in advance of Britain's [733].

[2] All four take lead sections: Freddie Gorman—verse 1; Hank Dixon—verse 2; Walter Gaines—bridge; C P Spencer—'chorus'.

[3] Taylor had been offered "The Bells" ahead of The Originals, Berry Gordy (with whom Gaye was constantly at odds) resisting the recording on the grounds that the lyric was not up to par.


## TMG 734
## MARVIN GAYE
**Abraham, Martin And John** (4:30)
(Holler)
Produced by Norman Whitfield
Recording completed: 26 Aug 1969
**Release Date**: 17 Apr 1970
**B-side**: How Can I Forget
**Position in Record Retailer Top 40**: 9
**No Equivalent US Release**

Having taken a turn for the worse in 1970, Marvin Gaye's old partner Tammi Terrell was sent back to her home town of Philadelphia in perilous health. Having endured eight operations since being diagnosed with a brain tumour, she was to suffer paralysis and loss of memory, finally succumbing in Philadelphia's Graduate Hospital at 8:55am on March 16, aged 24.

In the years which followed, Gaye never opened up on the issue, opting instead to imply that there was more to the matter than is publicly acknowledged.[1] In truth, the moment of her death was a catalyst for Gaye, who hit a personal low in the preceding months and reached the point of bankruptcy, his mounting debts with the IRS resulting in bailiffs taking his car. Having spent much of the early part of 1970 away from home in LA, his personal relationships were dissolving as he slipped into a well of self-absorption, mirrored by a growing awareness of the social strife at large across America and the world. With his brother Frankie having returned after a traumatic three-year stint in Vietnam, Gaye began to muse on the human milieu, a hazardous process for an introspective depressive which threatened to spiral his psychology out of control.

Terrell's funeral was hastily arranged for March 20, when she was buried in pouring rain at the Jane Memorial Methodist Church before a mass of several thousand mourners which included Gaye and a swathe of Motown colleagues. Gaye appeared to those present to break down, streaming with tears and trying to talk to Terrell as she lay in her coffin, clearly unable to cope with the tragedy of her passing. So devastated was Gaye that he became a virtual recluse for some time thereafter, refusing to record and, but for one or two particular occasions, not returning to concert performance for four years.

Angry over the debacle of Valerie Simpson's secret substitution on several recent recordings attributed to Terrell [697], his disgust must have been amplified by Motown's inadvertent scheduling of the US edition of "The Onion Song" [715] for the morning of the funeral. Not one to take such things quietly, Gaye at one point declared he was walking out on the music industry completely, mooting his desire to become a professional footballer. (How serious he was is debatable, but he was determined enough to undertake physical training in readiness.) Meantime, Tamla Motown were not about to let the popular singer's lack of product impact on release schedules and prepared the current single for UK release without his explicit consent.

Written by Dick Holler, "Abraham, Martin And John" was a hit in 1968 for guitarist and singer Dion, which had nestled in the US top 10 alongside five Motown singles in December 1968 [680]. Continuing Smokey Robinson's vague interest in the folk-rock movement, the track had been noted and recorded by The Miracles in April 1969, and taken back into the US top 40 (Tamla 54184), prompting Marvin Gaye to tackle a version which surfaced on *That's The Way Love Is*.

Recorded in intimate mood in a light-dimmed Snakepit on 26 August 1971, Gaye's commitment to the lyric was real, emotively running down the song's four heroes, Abraham Lincoln, Martin Luther King, John F. Kennedy and Robert Kennedy.[2] In the eyes of the American public, all stood for political liberalism, personal freedom and the rights of the individual to self-determination—and all were eventually assassinated. It is however the inclusion of King alongside some giants of American government which makes the track's sentiment particularly pointed in the context of the drive for racial equality; that King and John F. Kennedy were contemporary adversaries is not mentioned in the superficial analysis in which both simply 'freed a lot of people'.[3]

Slick in production, some copies of the recording commence with an ominous blues lick on electric guitar, edited off the UK single. Another in the sequence of reflective ballads for Tamla Motown, the track won over audiences and became Gaye's last top 10 single for Tamla Motown. It was subsequently picked up for a (very different) cover courtesy of Tom Clay [801].

[1] Hirshey for example (p219) notes Gaye "saying only that there was a great deal behind Tammi Terrell's death that the public did not know".

[2] Dion's recording was made shortly after Robert Kennedy's assassination of June 1968. Since he does not appear in the song's title, and his inclusion in the lyric is confined to a peripheral final verse (as 'Bobby'), it seems likely he was included at the last-minute.

[3] More acute due to its timing in the context of Tammi Terrell's death was the impact of

the line, "It seems the good die young". Similarly, the single's Stax-influenced B-side could be misconstrued by its title, although it was nothing to do with Terrell, having been first recorded by The Temptations [671b], and then by Gaye in August 1969.


**TMG 735**
**THE SUPREMES**
**Up The Ladder To The Roof** (2:58)
(DiMirco—Wilson)
Produced by Frank Wilson
Recording completed: 30 Jan 1970
**Release Date**: 24 Apr 1970
**B-side**: Bill, When Are You Coming Home
**Position in Record Retailer Top 40**: 6
**Equivalent US Release**: Motown 1162 (16 Feb 1970)
**Position in Billboard Top 40 Pop**: 10
**Position in Billboard Top 40 R & B**: 5

| Jean Terrell / Cindy Birdsong / Mary Wilson |
| --- |

With two-thirds of The Supremes' famous line-up of 1964-67 having departed, the group's challenge going into 1970 was to re-establish itself in the face of several fans resolving to 'support' Diana Ross from here-on. Ross' replacement was already publicly known, Jean Terrell[1] having made a cameo appearance at the 'farewell' concert of January 14 [721]. Terrell had come to Motown in 1969, signed as a solo artist in June and at Berry Gordy's behest, lined up to replace Ross later in the year. Typically though, events behind the scenes were somewhat barbed and, finding Terrell far less cooperative than Ross had been, Gordy attempted to do an about-face and instead draft in Rita Wright, causing a dispute with Wilson and Birdsong which culminated in Gordy's declaration that he wanted nothing more to do with The Supremes.[2] (So shocking is the claim, made within weeks of Ross leaving, that the possibility is raised that Gordy privately wanted to wind the act up at this point, stating his intent to abandon them at the first real excuse.)

As it was, Wilson and Birdsong stuck to their guns and, in a rare personal defeat for Gordy, succeeded in making Jean Terrell a full-time Supreme as planned. Where they stood without their employer's direct backing was less certain, however. The Supremes were staring obsolescence in the face, as exemplified by *Time* magazine's contemporary observation that by now, "you have to memorise their wigs to remember which is which".[3] Yet the other side of the coin was that without the all-pervasive presence of Ross, the singers could re-establish an internal democracy and, no longer suffering the ignominy of being billed on records they had nothing to do with, could develop an inter-personal studio chemistry again.

The first product of the new-look act was "Up The Ladder To The Roof", a track penned by New York soul performer Vince DiMirco, recently discovered by Frank Wilson. Written on guitar, presumably composed with an ear on The Drifters' 1962 hit, "Up On The Roof", the track needed some re-working from Wilson, who with arranger David Van DePitte shaped the composition into something lying intriguingly between their more sophisticated recordings of 1967-69 and the classic HDH era, complete with wah-wah and triplet jockeying percussion last heard to such effect in The Four Tops' "Standing In The Shadows Of Love" [589]. Recorded on the second day of January, the track was re-done in its final form on the 30th, after Ross had finally waved goodbye.

Poetic in its romanticism, the song, while probably conceived as a love ballad, has been interpreted as a call for racial unity, revolving around the lines 'And we shall let expression sing/Hear freedom's virtues ringing', and 'Come on and sing about love and understanding' and suggesting that the journey to the roof represents a metaphor for higher thinking. As a whole though, the lyric resists such a reading, being a message from one person to another, rather than to society at large. Forcefully recorded by the group, Terrell's first Supremes performance rings out, particularly at the culmination of the middle-8 (2:28), in which her vocals soar skywards, as the lyric implores. Birdsong and Wilson pitch in with individual backing lines, and for the first time in several years, The Supremes are a *group* again, "Up The Ladder To The Roof" described by David Morse as "their most electrifying disc in years".[4]

Giving The Supremes back their patent crotchet pulses, any thoughts that the group might not survive without Ross were assuaged as the single climbed the charts on both sides of the Atlantic. An unmitigated success on all fronts, the hit must have left a few wondering whether time would show that it was in fact Ross, and not her old group, who was cut adrift. (It would be some months until she could boast a hit of similar proportions [751].) For The Supremes, the release was triumphant, marking the start of their most consistently successful period in Britain—a fact which, on one level, ought to have troubled Gordy considerably.

[1] Despite the unlikely coincidence of their names, Jean is no relation to Tammi, whose true surname was Montgomery.

[2] See Wilson, p238 and Taraborrelli (1989) p238.

[3] Quoted in Benjaminson, p84.

[4] p71. He continues, "Superb mastering made the record positively explode against the limits of its dynamic range."

**TMG 736**
**FOUR TOPS**
**It's All In The Game** (2:49)
(Dawes—Sigman)
Produced by Frank Wilson
Recording completed: 28 Oct 1969
**Release Date**: 15 May 1970
**B-side**: Love Is The Answer

**Position in Record Retailer Top 40**: 5
**Equivalent US Release**: Motown 1164 (21 Mar 1970)
**Position in Billboard Top 40 Pop**: 24
**Position in Billboard Top 40 R & B**: 6

---

Levi Stubbs / Lawrence Payton / Abdul 'Duke' Fakir / Renaldo 'Obie' Benson

---

Started as far back as 1912 by Nobel Prize-winner Charles Dawes (US Vice-President from 1925 until 1929), "It's All In The Game" was initially an instrumental known simply as "Melody In A Major". Lyrics were added by Carl Sigman in 1951, curiously pitched from the perspective of a third-party outsider ('you had words with him'). Successfully recorded in recent years by both Tommy Edwards and Cliff Richard, whose respective versions made number 1 and 2 in Britain, the song was an interesting selection for release as a Four Tops single and proved an astute piece of judgement, charting high again in the UK and becoming the group's first top 40 hit in America since "If I Were A Carpenter" [647] some two years previously. (During this era, the group had been lost for direction, few singles appearing and nothing at all being lifted from *Soul Spin* (November 1969).)

Arranged by Jerry Long & Jimmy Roach under direction of Frank Wilson, "It's All In The Game" is the group's most tranquil hit to date, Levi Stubbs' progressively fervent vocals ranging through the octave-wide melody against a calm backing, whose indistinct chords rely mainly on the bass foundation for definition. Recorded in late 1969 for *Still Waters Run Deep,* the track can be seen as part of a move by Wilson to re-create the group, appealing for its passive, accepting stance in which a relationship is of no real consequence, it success merely a strategy-dependent pastime. The producer was here aiming at something remote and transcendent, parallel to the group's contemporary material such as "Still Water (Love)" [752] and their ambitious interpretation of "Reflections" [616].

Notably, the cover of *Still Waters* credits the producer and arrangers, one of the earliest instances of public acknowledgement of Motown's staff. Along with the impact of "Up The Ladder To The Roof" [735], the album, touted as the group's best to date, represents a major accomplishment for Wilson, now handling both of what were HDH's principal acts. This UK edition was issued with "I Can't Help Myself" [732] still in top 40, exploiting public interest in The Four Tops, currently engaged on a major UK tour and enjoying back-to-back top 10 hits once again.

---

**TMG 737**
**MARV JOHNSON**
**So Glad You Chose Me** (2:25)
(Dean—Weatherspoon—Bowden)
Producer unaccredited
Recording completed: 18 Aug 1968
**Release Date**: 15 May 1970

---

**B-side**: I'm Not A Plaything [525b]
**Position in Record Retailer Top 40**: -
**No Equivalent US Release**

Recorded for his only studio album, Marv Johnson's final UK single followed up two successful releases ([680]; [713]) but showed little imagination, running methodically through its 2:25. Selected for its obvious appeal to Northern Soul enthusiasts, the song stomps along pleasantly, hinting at distant derivation from Sam Cooke's "Wonderful World", a hit single in 1960. The highlight of the recording is James Jamerson's energetic bass patterning, throwing triplets around liberally, and giving the track a tangible lift. (For a flip-side, Tamla Motown plucked the vintage [525b].)

Never released on any format in America, "So Glad You Chose Me" was a minor excursion for Tamla Motown, released during 'Motown Month', self-declared and promoted with UK visits by Johnson and other acts. ('Motown Month' was ostensibly part of the 10th anniversary 'celebrations' [732].) At this point, things were looking rosy for Tamla Motown, with several hit singles arriving and a 3-year extension of EMI's distribution contract agreed. Back in Detroit however, clouds were gathering and Vice-President Barney Ales was forced to circulate a memo, on April 10, categorically denying rumours that Motown was intending to move out of the city.[1]

For Johnson's part, while still enjoying popularity in Britain, the time was coming to retire from performing [680] as he headed into a sales executive role with Motown. He returned to the stage in 1987 but collapsed and died while performing in May 1993.

[1] The full text is given in Edmonds, p246, and includes the sentence, "Motown Record Corporation is *not* moving to the West Coast." [Emphasis in original]

**TMG 738**
**THE JACKSON 5**
**A B C** (2:38)
(The Corporation)
Produced by The Corporation
**Release Date**: 8 May 1970
**B-side**: The Young Folks
**Position in Record Retailer Top 40**: 8
**Equivalent US Release**: Motown 1163 (13 May 1970)
**Position in Billboard Top 40 Pop**: 1
**Position in Billboard Top 40 R & B**: 1

Jackie Jackson / Tito Jackson / Jermaine Jackson / Marlon Jackson / Michael Jackson

In the spring of 1970, The Jackson 5 were in much the same position The Supremes had found themselves a year earlier, after the success of "Love Child" [677]. With a major hit single having been painstakingly assembled under Gordy's direction, all eyes were on the group, the pertinent question of whether they could follow-up about to be answered: That their new single topped the US charts in April, knocking "Let It Be" from its perch, emphatically silenced any doubters. Yet despite its commercial success, the song is irritatingly juvenile, deliberately aimed at the youth market beneath the level of bubblegum.[1]

The track was written at Fonce Mizell and Freddie Perren's apartment, and begun by Deke Richards on electric piano. Deliberately adopting HDH's recycling strategy, Richards began with the chorus figure to "I Want You Back" [724], assembling the absurdly simplistic lyric with his co-writers by throwing in meaningless phrases in a bare-faced attempt to fashion a pop hit. On hearing the result, Gordy requested the lyric be rearranged as "1, 2, 3, as easy as A. B. C." before hearing back a demo and conceding that the original structure was better. However there remains uncertainty over the recording of the finished track, Dennis Coffey insisting that he participated in the session in Detroit, Freddie Perren claiming it as an LA creation.[2]

Seen as a style exercise, "A B C" is a genuinely buoyant track built on the foundation of a single major chord, and in light of its artistic aims (or lack thereof), must be counted a success. Simplistic by its very nature, the composition carries a chorus which simply dances about its five diatonic notes *ad infinitum*, ranging up and down with contrived effervescence. As a group performance, "A B C" finds the Jackson brothers taking turns at lead vocal, with many mistaking the word 'teacher' for 'Tito' at 1:06. Although Michael Jackson names the track as one of his favourites in his 1988 autobiography, it shows him at his least mature, distinctly lightweight even by his own early-1970s standards. (Due to its appeal to children, the song was instrumental in defining the group's market, leading to an animated Jackson 5 television show in 1971, appropriately financed by ABC Television.)

The UK edition came with a promotional picture sleeve.

[1] The UK charts were clogged with infantile pap in 1969-71, for example "Sugar Sugar" (The Archies), "Knock Knock Who's There" (Mary Hopkin), "All Kinds Of Everything" (Dana), "Chirpy Chirpy Cheep Cheep" (Middle Of The Road), "Grandad" (Clive Dunn), "Knock Three Times" (Dawn) and so on. Unfortunately the prominence of the Jackson 5 merely fuelled the process, concurrently giving rise to the grotesque Osmonds family group who dominated the British charts by 1973 [769]. (13 years on, "A B C" inspired the similarly ghastly number 1 "Candy Girl" by New Edition, featuring a 14-year-old Bobby Brown on lead vocals.)

[2] Slutsky (p60) runs down competing claims of involvement from various quarters.

**TMG 739**
**KIKI DEE**
**The Day Will Come Between Sunday And Monday** (2:30)
(Sawyer—Hinton)
Produced by Clay McMurray
Recording completed: 8 Dec 1969
**Release Date**: 22 May 1970
**B-side**: My Whole World Ended (The Moment You Left Me)

**Position in Record Retailer Top 40**: -
**Equivalent US Release**: Tamla 54193 (17 Jun 1970)
**Position in Billboard Top 40 Pop**: -
**Position in Billboard Top 40 R & B**: -

Recorded in Motown's established 'cool' style for female soloists ([544]; [561]; [622]; [638]; [643]), "The Day Will Come" is a robustly brassy affair, punching through its choruses with resolute spirit. Produced by Norman Whitfield's student Clay McMurray, the track is somewhat obscurely couched, the point of the lyric that the day the singer relinquishes her devotion will never arrive. Dee delivers the text with vigour, against David Van DePitte and Jerry Long's tight arrangement. (The introductory bars are reminiscent of those on "Bernadette" [601], though that is where the similarity ends.)

Dee was a Brit born in Bradford, recording for Fontana through the 1960s and was noticed through her work with Dusty Springfield. Approached by Motown in 1969 she was signed to Tamla, recording an album's worth of material toward year-end. *Great Expectations* was followed by a switch to Rare Earth (see [742]), but the ensuing *Love Makes The World Go Round* failed to sell, Dee moving away. During her stint at Motown she hooked up with manager John Reid, who arranged for her to duet with another of his clients, Elton John in 1976; thus she is today principally known for the staggeringly successful transatlantic number 1 "Don't Go Breaking My Heart".

**TMG 740**
**JIMMY RUFFIN**
**I'll Say Forever My Love** (2:57)
**Re-issue of [649]**
**Release Date**: 29 May 1970
**Position in Record Retailer Top 40**: 7

Following the re-issue of "I've Passed This Way Before" [593] as [703], Ruffin was allocated a second re-run courtesy of "I'll Say Forever My Love", originally a miss in early 1968. Retaining its original B-side, the single appeared in support of his UK tour, marking 'Motown Month' and the label's anniversary [737]. This time around the track entranced his growing fan-base and was hoisted into the top 10, polling higher than anything previously.

**TMG 741**
**THE TEMPTATIONS**
**Psychedelic Shack** (3:53)
(Whitfield—Strong)
Produced by Norman Whitfield
Recording completed: 6 Dec 1969
**Release Date**: 5 Jun 1970
**B-side**: That's The Way Love Is

**Position in Record Retailer Top 40**: 33
**Equivalent US Release**: Gordy 7096 (29 Dec 1969)
**Position in Billboard Top 40 Pop**: 7
**Position in Billboard Top 40 R & B**: 2

---

Otis Williams / Melvin Franklin / Paul Williams / Eddie Kendricks / Dennis Edwards

Instalment number four of The Temptations' new-wave output, "Psychedelic Shack" conforms to the established formula but, thanks to the vitality of its arrangement, packs a punch lacking in its more sensual predecessors. The group's most overt espousal of drug-taking life-styles to date, the song's title refers to low-key clubs frequented by hippies and counter-culturals in the late-1960s and early-1970s, where the developing rock and underground music could be absorbed in the context of general usage of psychedelics.

Whether in selecting this as a subject Barrett Strong was acknowledging his interest in this particular sub-culture, or merely employing the imagery in a calculated attempt to appeal to a specific audience is debatable, but clearly the theme appealed to his co-conspirator Norman Whitfield, who made sure the point was not lost. Arranging an extravagant 8-minute-plus version for its associated LP, Whitfield recalled the 'interrupted party' effects grafted onto the start of "I Can't Get Next To You" [722], and sampled the earlier track to create an extrapolated prelude here (one of the earliest uses of sampling in popular music). The enhanced intro includes the sound of someone knocking at a creaking door, to be welcomed by revellers within, who promptly call for hush in order to spin the ensuing recording. (In this context, "Psychedelic Shack" is being heard by the party-goers, so is an 'underground' creation.)

Using the various group-members as soloists, the dramatic and rapid switches in *timbre* lend proceedings a sense of multi-culturalism. Although predictable in light of the group's recent singles, the technique maintains Whitfield's experimental style but breaks down with Melvin Franklin's comical bass tones during the section "So high you can't get over it/So low you can't get under it" in which one can almost hear him grinning. (This part of the lyric diverts from the song's theme to quote from the traditional hymn "Rock My Soul In The Bosom Of Abraham", which George Clinton's The Parliaments [707] would employ as the starting point of "One Nation Under A Groove" in 1978. It also points back at HDH's "Nowhere To Run" [502].)

"Psychedelic Shack", not properly re-worked for single, merely starts to drift away after 3:35 as the faders are pushed down. American listeners were entranced; UK fans took little interest in the single.

**TMG 742**
**RARE EARTH**
**Get Ready** (2:46)
(Robinson)

---

Produced by Rare Earth
Recording completed: 17 Jul 1969
**Release Date**: 5 Jun 1970
**B-side**: Magic Key
**Position in Record Retailer Top 40**: -
**Equivalent US Release**: Rare Earth 5012 (18 Feb 1970)
**Position in Billboard Top 40 Pop**: 4
**Position in Billboard Top 40 R & B**: 20

---

Gil Bridges / Pete Rivera / Rod Richards / John Parrish / Kenny James

---

After several minor attempts to break into the rock market, Motown went the whole hog in 1969, launching the Rare Earth label in America. Although ostensibly out of step with their public, Motown were in fact following a course set by long-time rivals Atlantic, who had diversified into what could loosely be termed white rock by signing British group Led Zeppelin in 1969 with spectacular success. That same year they also brought on board Yes and Crosby, Stills & Nash, providing the company with new direction, particularly via serious ingression into the album market.

Conceptually, Rare Earth was to be Motown's equivalent, aiming at the 'underground' scene (as explicitly proclaimed in press shots). Launched in a blaze of publicity in mid-1969, Rare Earth was headed up by Joe Summers and Al DiNoble as a self-contained entity under the Motown umbrella and, in terms of acts at its disposal, could have achieved great things: Having handled releases by The Pretty Things and The Easybeats, the label also recruited future superstar Meatloaf, and could add established Motowners such as the Rare Earth group and R. Dean Taylor to its roster, as well as Kiki Dee in 1971. Taken more seriously, Rare Earth could have been one of Gordy's most successful projects of the 1970s.

The label was named after the group, who had established a reputation for explosive live performances in and around Detroit before being introduced to Motown and recording their first material during 1969. Essentially an effort to capture their live act on tape, the sessions resulted in the *Get Ready* album, released in the States in September. Lifted from the set was the title track, a former Temptations hit ([557]; [688]), which in its original form ran to an absurdly indulgent 21:30 and accounted for the entire second side of the LP. Self-produced, the thundering rendition has the qualities of a genuinely live performance (although the crowd noises heard at the beginning were artificially grafted on), the obvious constraints of the 45 format necessitating a dramatic truncation, paring the recording down to a sensible 2:46 at the expense of its massive impact. Nonetheless, this loosely swinging run-through had its admirers and did impressive business in the States, reputedly selling upwards of a million units.

The track would be their only release on Tamla Motown, the group transferred to the UK arm of the label which carried their name in time for September's "The Seed" (see Appendix 2). Numerous personnel changes ensued before they moved on to the Prodigal imprint in 1977, which Motown had by then acquired.

---

**TMG 743**
**DIANA ROSS**
**Reach Out And Touch (Somebody's Hand)** (2:59)
(Ashford—Simpson)
Produced by Nickolas Ashford/Valerie Simpson
**Release Date**: 19 Jun 1970
**B-side**: Dark Side Of The World
**Position in Record Retailer Top 40**: 33
**Equivalent US Release**: Motown 1165 (6 Apr 1970)
**Position in Billboard Top 40 Pop**: 20
**Position in Billboard Top 40 R & B**: 7

Commencing her career as a soloist, pains were taken over the best way to launch Diana Ross, and in particular which song would be appropriate for her debut release. For a while, Laura Nyro's "Time And Love" was in the frame, but the backing tracks were eventually given to The Supremes who employed them on *Touch* (May 1971).[1] Proffered instead was Ashford & Simpson's "Reach Out And Touch", a suitably anthemic number which drew complaints from Berry Gordy over its 3/4 time signature, out of step with Ross' established style. (Gordy was instinctively opposed to waltzes, only "Every Little Bit Hurts" [E45] truly standing out in Motown's back-catalogue.) In the end it was Ross herself who won Gordy over, reading an anti-drugs subtext in the lyrics and resolving to send a message of hope to the young people she had recently encountered during a nostalgic trip through the Brewster Projects of Detroit. (Although utopian, there is nothing in the lyric which specifically references drug-use, Ross probably reading from her own current perspective.)

Stepping through its chord changes with assured classicism, "Reach Out And Touch" shows the influence of Burt Bacharach in its melodic shapes, particularly in the transition from chorus to verse, which hangs on an open Em in the style of "What The World Needs Now Is Love" (itself recorded by Ross & The Supremes in 1968 for *Reflections* and soon to be picked up by Tom Clay [801]). In fact, if the track has a direct inspiration, its overarching theme of 'making the world a better place' suggests Bacharach—David's earlier call for global unity although the song's title points equally towards the same team's "Reach Out For Me", which in turn helped HDH develop "Reach Out I'll Be There" [579].

Concerned over whether the single would succeed, Barney Ales sent a specially pressed copy to Motown's distributors incorporating a spoken message over the song, imploring them to push "Reach Out And Touch". But with its modest chart performance, the jury was still out on Ross at this stage, Motown uncertain on how to market her, the contemporary album featuring a cover-shot of the singer as a boy, sitting barefoot in T-shirt and shorts on a piece of cloth sacking. (The more familiar image of Ross as cabaret star featured on the reverse.) The photograph, suggestive of a hungry refugee was conceived as a joke, and a poor one at that given the millionairess' move around now into a $350,000 mansion in Beverly Hills. Nonetheless, in the context of Ross' pronouncements on the 'message' behind "Reach Out And

Touch", the cover struck a chord and remains one of the most memorable images from her solo career.

Although not the major hit Ross was hoping for, "Reach Out And Touch" was to become a spectacular winner with live audiences, its sweeping exhilaration amplified by Ross' pleas that the crowd turn to each other and literally put its words into action.

[1] The fact that material was so freely interchangeable illustrates the extent to which The Supremes were in Ross' shadow. Had she contributed a vocal to "Time And Love", it could conceivably been issued as Diana Ross & The Supremes without input from the others, were the political climate favourable, in the manner of most of their post-1967 singles. In fact, Ross had been operating largely as a soloist within the act since HDH departed, and to some extent even beforehand.

**TMG 744**
**STEVIE WONDER**
**Signed, Sealed, Delivered, I'm Yours** (2:45)
(Wonder—Garrett—Wright—Hardaway)
Produced by Stevie Wonder
Recording completed: 26 Aug 1969
**Release Date**: 26 Jun 1970
**B-side**: I'm More Than Happy (I'm Satisfied)
**Position in Record Retailer Top 40**: 15
**Equivalent US Release**: Tamla 54196 (3 Jun 1970)
**Position in Billboard Top 40 Pop**: 3
**Position in Billboard Top 40 R & B**: 1

Stevie Wonder's summer single is notable in terms of his career development not so much for the recording itself as the names in the brackets. Rita Wright had been largely cast-aside by Motown after "I Can't Give Back The Love I Feel For You" [643], but thanks to her lyric-writing talents, had endeared herself to Wonder and after one or two false starts, came up with "Signed, Sealed, Delivered, I'm Yours". (Given the track's recurrent hook "Here I Am Baby", derivation from [659] seems likely, The Marvelettes' recording broadly contemporary with Wright's earlier single.) So successful was the number that Wright became a permanent fixture, collaborating on the album whose name the single gave rise to, as well as much of Wonder's material over the ensuing couple of years (see also [755]; [779]; [798]). (Co-conspirator Lee Garrett was a friend who would collaborate further [755], the blind singer finding a natural rapport with Wonder. He is also known for his 1976 hit "You're My Everything"—self-composed and not in fact a cover of [620].)

"Signed, Sealed, Delivered, I'm Yours" commences with an 'Indian' run down the scale of $F^1$, played by Eddie Willis on electric sitar, held in check by a high F drone. After one run-through, the bass enters, positioned centrally and following the general tone of the playing on [704], which Paul Riser also arranged, the microscopic stutter into the triplet figure (eg at 0:10) indicating that it was the same musician[2] whose rising and falling throughout provides the track's main impetus.

Performed somewhat roughshod, the track suffers from minute synchronisation problems, the backing vocals (which include Rita Wright and future Supreme Lynda Lawrence, plus Lawrence's sister Sundray Tucker) ragged and at times out of tune. The performance though thumps home, and in his first attempt at self-production, Wonder prepared a provisional mix for Berry Gordy, who was said to be so knocked out that he called Wonder and instructed him to submit the preliminary version as a final take.

The significance of the single's success was apparent in Wonder's move to the producer's role on his subsequent album. Edging towards potential autonomy in the same way that Marvin Gaye was [733], Wonder was preparing in earnest for his future, which at this stage did not necessarily entail a commitment to Motown. Meantime he continued expanding his musical interests, discovering Deniece Williams, recruiting her into his vocal backing group Wonderlove along with Wright, taking them on a UK tour in June which included a booking at the Talk Of The Town (see [722n]). (Wonder and Wright announced their engagement in London on June 18, marrying on September 14.)

"Signed, Sealed, Delivered, I'm Yours", although not a major hit in the UK, has retained a perennial appeal, and when boy-band Blue picked it up in 2003, Wonder participated in a remake which achieved greater chart success than the original had, albeit in an era when singles sales were substantially lower.

[1] Not quite: the passing D is unnatural. (See also [704].)

[2] Jack Ashford (p99) names the player as Bob Babbitt. Jamerson was not employed on the album, Michael Henderson being called on instead for the bulk of the project.

## TMG 745
## SMOKEY ROBINSON & THE MIRACLES
**The Tears Of A Clown** (2:56)
(Cosby—Robinson—Wonder)
Produced by Henry "Hank" Cosby/Smokey Robinson
Recording completed: 9 Nov 1966 [re-mix dates unknown]
**Release Date**: 17 Jul 1970
**B-side**: You Must Be Love [631b]
**Position in Record Retailer Top 40**: 1
**Equivalent US Release**: Tamla 54199 (24 Sep 1970)
**Position in Billboard Top 40 Pop**: 1
**Position in Billboard Top 40 R & B**: 1

Smokey Robinson / Bobby Rogers / Claudette Rogers Robinson / Warren 'Pete' Moore / Ronnie White

Possibly the most fruitful day of Smokey Robinson's life was in December 1966 when "I Second That Emotion" [631] was conceived and written. The result of a Christmas shopping trip, Robinson must have considered his day's work complete when he turned up to Motown's Christmas party that night, only to be taken aside by Stevie Wonder and given a demo of an instrumental put together by Wonder with Hank Cosby. With Sylvia Moy for some reason not asked to provide a lyric, the tape was 'donated' to Robinson that evening, as were several contemporary pieces.[1]

Robinson's first impression of Wonder's riffs was the suggestion of circuses, which brought to mind Ruggiero Leoncavallo's 19th Century opera *Pagliacci*, the tragic (supposedly true) tale of the spurned lover Canio, who despite his personal torment, is forced to adopt a happy persona on stage. The central paradox of one providing happiness to others being himself unloved played on Robinson's mind (his lyrical themes are, after all, characterised by such contradictions), and from this seed grew the song's text. Suitably inspired, Robinson's lyric is one of his finest, making a worthy companion piece to his earlier 'tears' song [522]. Emotionally less burdened, the lyrical games are sharp and enchanting, such that the *faux*-rhyme 'Really I'm sad/I'm sadder than sad' passes unobtrusively. On the whole, the elastic phrasing makes for a piece of poetry imaginative in reason and acutely locked into the songs rhythmic form without hesitating for a moment, as the narrative runs down the various angles on hiding one's pain.

Musically, Wonder's typical derivative method is apparent, the verse melody closely resembling the backing vocal on "Baby I Need Your Loving" [E53][2], while the general lack of harmonic change is also telling. The track itself, while famous for the opening hook, is primarily driven by James Jamerson's clustered bass triplets which hurry the verses along with enthusiasm, belying the gruelling recording process itself which entailed upwards of 40 takes to get the backing nailed. The arrangement's most inspired moment however is the momentary pause on the word 'than', just as the chorus line seems to be reaching a climax, and in its self-deflating way, the song lands back to earth, beaten like its central character's spirit just as the tears arrive.

Thus completed, the recording was used to close The Miracles' impressive August 1967 album *Make It Happen* (Feb 1968 in Britain).[3] That it languished there is surprising not just for the fact that a normally alert Berry Gordy completely missed it, but because of the extraordinary care Robinson had taken over the recording. Tucked away on the LP the track was largely overlooked until an astute Tamla Motown employee finally picked up on it in 1970 and pressed for a full release. Correctly judging the mood of the day, Tamla Motown issued the song on the heels of the re-issue of "The Tracks Of My Tears" [696], with "You Must Be Love" pulled from the same album for a flip-side. (The single was quickly withdrawn however, re-appearing with Ashford & Simpson's new "Who's Gonna Take The Blame" in its place, in an echo of the fate which befell the group's earlier [614].)

The single's staggering popularity in Britain saw it become Tamla Motown's fourth-best-selling 45 ever, and led to a re-release of *Make It Happen*, re-named after the track. The single began its impressive six-week climb of the British singles chart on August 1, finally nestling at the summit on September 12.[4] As the song's reputation spread, it repeated the feat in a number of European countries before Berry Gordy finally capitulated and issued it in America where it also went to number 1 over Christmas. Never shy of flogging a hit, Motown proceeded to re-use the song on The Miracles'

US album *One Dozen Roses*, while Tamla Motown re-issued the single in 1976 whereupon it re-entered the top 40 as TMG 1048 (see Chapter 6), just before The Miracles departed Motown for Columbia Records. (The track was taken into the UK top 10 again in 1979 courtesy of Birmingham ska band The Beat.)

"The Tears Of A Clown" constitutes the pinnacle of Robinson's career, one of the biggest hits he would ever enjoy and the jewel in the crown of his 4,000 or so compositions.

[1] The Miracles recorded a series of tracks in 1967 co-written by Wonder: "Can You Love A Poor Boy", "My Love Is Your Love (Forever)", "After You Put Back The Pieces (I'll Still Have A Broken Heart)" and "The Tears Of A Clown" finding their way onto vinyl.

[2] The melodic "oohs" of the earlier track predict the shape of "If I appear to be carefree".

[3] Several different takes of the song are in circulation, the mono edition of the LP for example featuring an entirely different version to the familiar stereo single.

[4] It was deposed by one of the year's biggest hits in Freda Payne's "Band Of Gold", released on Invictus. The label was one of two launched at the end of the 1960s by HDH, a succession of hits over a four-year span appearing on Invictus and Hot Wax for artists such as Chairmen of the Board, Freda Payne, 100% Proof Aged In Soul, The Flaming Ember and The Honey Cone. Several Invictus and Hot Wax recordings were made in studios on Grand River Avenue, and HDH employed various Funk Brothers for illicit sessions. ("Band Of Gold" for example featured Dennis Coffey on guitar (Coffey, p83).) At this stage, it looked as if Invictus and Hot Wax might be poised to challenge Motown's dominance in the pop-soul field, as in 1970 the labels charted nine singles in the US. The following year they scored seven more including a number 1 courtesy of The Honey Cone's "Want Ads" but thereafter interest began to wane, only Chairmen Of The Board sustaining any real following, predominantly in the UK. Lamont Dozier departed in 1973 to pursue a solo singing career, leaving the Holland brothers to struggle on until towards the end of the decade when, after the addition of a third label in Music Merchant, the Invictus brand was wound up. See also [831].

## TMG 746
## THE JACKSON 5
**The Love You Save** (2:42)
(The Corporation)
Produced by The Corporation
**Release Date**: 24 Jul 1970
**B-side**: I Found That Girl
**Position in Record Retailer Top 40**: 7
**Equivalent US Release**: Motown 1166 (13 May 1970)
**Position in Billboard Top 40 Pop**: 1
**Position in Billboard Top 40 R & B**: 1

Jackie Jackson / Tito Jackson / Jermaine Jackson / Marlon Jackson / Michael Jackson

Written, produced and arranged by The Corporation, "The Love You Save" was the second single from *ABC*, essentially a variation on the group's debut [724]. Commencing with a terse "Stop!", the single nods at "Stop! In The Name Of Love" [501], once regarded as part of a succession of childish 'baby' recordings by The Supremes. The Jackson 5's contemporary singles far outdo anything The Supremes recorded in this respect, "The Love You Save", like "A B C" [738] referencing going off to school in the lyric. As artistically barren as its predecessor [738], the track's triumph in becoming a third US chart topper in as many attempts for the group justified its release to Motown. As with The Jackson 5's previous single, it knocked a Beatles classic from the top and come late summer, Motown were claiming with pride that the act had shifted a staggering 10 million units in nine months.


**TMG 747**
**THE SUPREMES**
**Everybody's Got The Right To Love** (2:38)
(Stallman)
Produced by Frank Wilson
**Release Date**: 31 Jul 1970
**B-side**: But I Love You More
**Position in Record Retailer Top 40**: -
**Equivalent US Release**: Motown 1167 (25 Jun 1970)
**Position in Billboard Top 40 Pop**: 21
**Position in Billboard Top 40 R & B**: 11

---

Jean Terrell / Cindy Birdsong / Mary Wilson

---

Following the impact of "Up The Ladder To The Roof" [735], The Supremes' sedate follow-up came as something of a disappointment. Lifted from their first post-Ross studio set *Right On*, the track is an airy bounce through 2:38, with an appealing descending bass figure and a confident, yet sweetly rendered lead from Jean Terrell. Written by freelancer Lou Stallman, the track asserts the need to find a partner without ever losing its cool composure.


**TMG 748**
**BLINKY & EDWIN STARR**
**Oh How Happy** (2:39)
**Re-issue of [720]**
**Release Date**: 21 Aug 1970
**Position in Record Retailer Top 40**: -

After the aborted attempt to release "Oh How Happy" at the end of 1969 [720], Tamla Motown succeeded in getting the single out during a particularly lean August. Coupled with the classic "Ooo Baby Baby" [503], the single trailed the UK issue of *Just We Two*, the only other thing released by the duo, by some seven months.

Blinky continued to record for Motown as a solo artist, issuing some six US singles on Motown, Soul and Mo-West before parting ways. Starr meantime was on the point of breakthrough, with "War" [754] already in the US charts, "Oh How Happy" slipping by unnoticed as little more than a marketing exercise.

TMG 749
THE TEMPTATIONS
**Ball Of Confusion (That's What The World Is Today)** (4:04)
(Whitfield—Strong)
Produced by Norman Whitfield
Recording completed: 14 Apr 1970
**Release Date**: 4 Sep 1970
**B-side**: It's Summer
**Position in Record Retailer Top 40**: 7
**Equivalent US Release**: Gordy 7099 (7 May 1970)
**Position in Billboard Top 40 Pop**: 3
**Position in Billboard Top 40 R & B**: 2

---

Otis Williams / Melvin Franklin / Paul Williams / Dennis Edwards / Eddie Kendricks

---

One of Norman Whitfield's most ruthlessly driving creations, "Ball Of Confusion" was described by Otis Williams as "funkier than an unwashed armpit"[1], and was built on a bass line 'discovered' by Norman Whitfield via "American Woman", an album recording by Canadian rock outfit The Guess Who which would shortly be plucked for a single and top the US charts (toppling "A B C" [738]). And with Dennis Coffey's overlaid wah-wah and two drum-kits fighting it out, the soundscape is as dynamic as any of the group's 'psychedelic' singles, hypnotically coiling around its C bass foundation, a trance-like quality emphasised by the mono mix presented here in which all instrumentation is compressed into a mercurial stream of sound. Unfortunately, interest in the quality of Whitfield's production technique has seen the recording re-mixed for stereo with wide panning, and drums sent to opposite channels, which has spoiled the core effect (although the over-arching drift of Coffey's guitar during the track's introduction remains effective).

Supplied by Strong, the lyric commences with the line 'People moving out, people moving in/Why? Because of the colour of their skin', a prelude for what is to follow: a chain of dispassionately observed social and political senselessness from which the narrator remains detached. Capturing the sense of unreality which both narcotics and psychedelics (including cannabis) give rise to, the theme threatens to be another espousal of drug culture [741], before the comment 'The sale of pills are at an all time high' makes this too a symptom of social decay. Remote and non-participatory, the point-of-view resonates with the values of the 1960s pacifist/hippie ideology in which the spectacle of society, consisting largely of organised insanity, is surveyed from without with incomprehension (while, indifferent to the widespread destruction, 'the band played on').

Nonetheless, the text is anything but passive, Strong focusing on several issues of the day including sarcastic inferences of political corruption, support for native American societies and an approving nod to the anti-Vietnam War movement in the final verse. (The lyric is encapsulated by the line, sung in unison, 'Round and around and around we go/Where the world's headed, nobody knows.') Keeping it relevant, Strong also speaks of the direct experience of life for America's young in the fall-out of the epochal 1960s, recalling by name Barry McGuire's 1965 number 1 protest song "Eve Of Destruction" and "The Beatles' New Record"[2] besides a mention of mod clothing and hippies fleeing urban decay for a rural return to nature.

The lyric itself, besides its industrious scope, finds Strong deploying words not only for textual meaning, but for their rhythmic impact (in its way a precursor of rap). The most adroit group member Dennis Edwards handles the trickier lines, which Otis Williams compares to Bob Dylan's "Subterranean Homesick Blues".[3] (Other vocal turns are taken by Melvin Franklin, Paul Williams and Eddie Kendricks, Otis Williams sitting out.) Ultimately one of The Temptations' most successful period-pieces, "Ball Of Confusion" was left off the group's contemporary albums, and has attracted numerous covers including efforts from Tina Turner, and courtesy of Norman Whitfield, both The Undisputed Truth and Edwin Starr. This original remains the definitive reading, precisely located in time and place and concisely capturing the mood of the day.

[1] *Record Collector* 327 p67

[2] The Beatles had by now split up, their final American single "The Long And Winding Road" released simultaneously with "Ball Of Confusion" and helping keep it from the top of the charts.

[3] p148. Williams also mentions in his 2006 *Record Collector* interview that the 'turnaround' in the track was based on Harry Belafonte's "Matilda, Matilda" (1953), although the connection is lost on this particular reader. Possibly Williams is getting confused—he also wrongly ascribes Bob Babbitt's bass line to James Jamerson.

## TMG 750
## JUNIOR WALKER & THE ALL STARS
**Do You See My Love (For You Growing)** (3:14)
(Bristol—Beavers)
Produced by Johnny Bristol
**Release Date**: 25 Sep 1970
**B-side**: Groove And Move
**Position in Record Retailer Top 40**: -
**Equivalent US Release**: Soul 35073 (17 Jun 1970)
**Position in Billboard Top 40 Pop**: 32
**Position in Billboard Top 40 R & B**: 3

---

Jr Walker / Willie Woods / Vic Thomas / Billy Nicks

---

This robust slab of popular soul was to be Walker's twelfth and final American top 40 single. Like "Someday We'll Be Together" [721], the track was an early Tri-Phi release as recorded by Johnny & Jackey, and was revived by Bristol for Walker. A hopeful confession of blossoming affection, the lyric implores the singer's love object to recognise his increasing devotion at a decisive point in their early relationship. Somewhat inane in the reverberating echo of "Ball Of Confusion" [749], the track works on an entirely different plane, its happy production persuasive and infectious, bouncing along optimistically, with Walker's impassioned vocal contribution deserving of a bigger hit. It would be two years before he was afforded another UK outing [824].

**TMG 751**
**DIANA ROSS**
**Ain't No Mountain High Enough** (3:15)
(Ashford—Simpson)
Produced by Nickolas Ashford/Valerie Simpson
**Release Date:** Aug 1970
**B-side:** Can't Wait Until Tomorrow
**Position in Record Retailer Top 40:** 6
**Equivalent US Release:** Motown 1169 (16 Jul 1970)
**Position in Billboard Top 40 Pop:** 1
**Position in Billboard Top 40 R & B:** 1

Diana Ross' self-titled debut album had been commenced with producer Bones Howe but passed over to Ashford & Simpson half-complete, an uncertain Motown organisation nervous about the work in progress. As it happened, the LP which finally appeared over the summer contained less than 50 percent new material and was not a major hit, meeting only modest interest. Closing side one was an ambitious six-minute-plus interpretation of "Ain't No Mountain High Enough", an Ashford—Simpson title first recorded by Marvin Gaye & Tammi Terrell [611] and subsequently also covered by Ross with The Supremes and The Temptations in 1968.

Its inclusion would have been less controversial had it not been programmed next-but-one after a version of "You're All I Need To Get By" [668], another sacred text for Tammi Terrell's fans. Equally irreverent was Ashford & Simpson's treatment of the song, completely re-writing the verses and creating what amounts to a new track. Disassembling the original, the producers reconstructed the number in novel sequence, throwing in several brand-new sections and replacing the melody with dramatic spoken passages harking back to the technique deployed on several earlier Supremes cuts (including "You Keep Me Hangin' On" [585] and "Love Is Here And Now You're Gone" [597]).

Arranged by Paul Riser, the recording is nonetheless utterly mesmerising, benefiting from a dense bank of backing vocals from Billie Rae Calvin and Brenda Joyce Evans, members of the newly signed Delicates (whom Norman Whitfield would shortly re-form into The Undisputed Truth [776]) plus Ashford & Simpson themselves. With its emphasis on grandiose impact, the track is something of a *magnum opus*, but lacking simple directness left Berry Gordy unmoved. Certainly its scope is beyond the normal focus of the top 40, yet in the wake of Simon & Garfunkel's similarly monumental "Bridge Over Troubled Water", its creators badgered Gordy successfully for a release.

Editing the track down to three-and-a-half minutes was a pre-requisite, achieved with numerous painstakingly worked-out and technically proficient splices.[1] Retaining its engaging power, the single features a moment of sublime inventiveness from James Jamerson, who in resisting the chord change at 0:33 (and subsequent corresponding passages) and sustaining his G#, provided the verses with an exquisite poise few bassists have had the lucidity to find.[2]

All concerned were equally delighted and relieved by the single's climbing to the summit of the US charts on September 19. (Its arrival at number 1 deposed "War" [754].) Just as it did so, Ross began a first solo tour[3], proving herself in the face of widespread scepticism that she would succeed without The Supremes. (At this late stage, still fearing the worst, Berry Gordy bribed Las Vegas locals with $20 bills to ensure a full-house for the opening gig, which Ross commenced with the words 'Welcome to the "Let's See If Diana Ross Can Make It Alone" show'.) That the tour was a roaring success, and "Ain't No Mountain High Enough" was nominated for a Grammy, silenced any doubters; Ross the solo star had arrived and was here to stay.

[1] The intro itself comes in on an edit, the only noticeable subsequent join at 0:51, effective in substantially pruning the opening verses.

[2] His top string is badly out of tune again. See also [604].

[3] She was supported by The Blackberries, a vocal outfit latterly filling the role of The Andantes. The group was composed of Sherlie Matthews, Clydie King and Venetta Fields, who are rumoured to have already appeared on "Someday We'll Be Together" [721] and later received billing on "What The World Needs Now" [801].


**TMG 752**
**THE FOUR TOPS**
**Still Water (Love)** (2:58)
(Robinson—Wilson)
Produced by Frank Wilson
Recording completed: 9 Jan 1970
**Release Date**: 18 Sep 1970[1]
**B-side**: Still Water (Peace)
**Position in Record Retailer Top 40**: 10
**Equivalent US Release**: Motown 1170 (6 Aug 1970)
**Position in Billboard Top 40 Pop**: 11
**Position in Billboard Top 40 R & B**: 4

---

Levi Stubbs / Lawrence Payton / Abdul 'Duke' Fakir / Renaldo 'Obie' Benson

---

This new single was begun by Frank Wilson, spurred by *In-A-Gadda-Da-Vida*, a 1968 album by San Diego rock group Iron Butterfly (widely held to be the America's first Heavy Metal outfit). Musing a similar concept-work for The Four Tops, Wilson made a start on the backing track for "Still Water", playing what he had to Smokey Robinson who offered to contribute a lyric for the song's verses, which were duly polished off over the space of a couple of days. Recorded in the same softly reflective vein as "It's All In The Game" [736], the track's original inspiration becomes lost. "Still Water" is a mood piece over two movements, its aura of transcendence flagging the group's new sound, as unveiled on the consequent *Still Waters Run Deep* set with its rippled cover shot, kaleidoscopic wash of sounds and sharp production.

Thus steered by Wilson, The Four Tops were finally in the process of re-creation, abandoning the populist styles of the HDH years for something more spiritually meaningful. Attempting to account for this in a contemporary *NME* interview, the group put their new direction down to a mellowing stemming from a nine-month break from touring duty, failing to publicly admit that it was largely their writer-producers who remained behind their career development.[2]

Employed on a rare Four Tops session, Dennis Coffey contributes the gently swinging incidental lead guitars opposite James Jamerson's rocking triplets, providing a languid serenity—the 'still water' in which Levi Stubbs is engulfed. Arranged by Jerry Long and Jimmy Roach, the track has The Delicates on backing duties [751], and for its producer constitutes a notable step forward, pointing the way for Marvin Gaye whose work would carry a similarly laid back flavour in the ensuing couple of years [775].

[1] The record was released on the day Jimi Hendrix died.

[2] See Davis (1988) p91. "Still Water" was recorded prior to their 1970 UK visits ([732]; [736]).

## TMG 753
## JIMMY RUFFIN
### It's Wonderful (To Be Loved By You) (2:45)
(Dean—Weatherspoon)
Produced by James Dean/William Weatherspoon
Recording completed: 30 Jan 1968
**Release Date**: 2 Oct 1970
**B-side**: Maria (You Were The Only One)
**Position in Record Retailer Top 40**: 6
**No Equivalent US Release**

Like Edwin Starr [725], Jimmy Ruffin was at a personal crossroads going into the 1970s, Motown having run out of promotional steam with a questionable pairing of the Ruffin brothers, most notable for their curious cut of Leiber & Stoller's "Stand By Me", issued at home as Soul 35076 in September but unreleased in Britain. Instead, Tamla Motown dipped into the early-1969 set *Ruff 'N' Ready*, plucking out "It's Wonderful (To Be Loved By You)", which justified their independent choice by becoming one of the label's biggest hits of 1970. The fact that Berry Gordy did not request a US equivalent issue is surprising; asked to comment on why his contemporary recordings were not translating into American hits, Ruffin summed up the reason in an instant: "Because they weren't promoted".[1]

The simple sentiments expressed in "It's Wonderful (To Be Loved By You)" disguise a certain unease in the composition, suggested by a move to the minor for the revelatory answer to the song's opening conundrum. Reminiscent of the unpredictable mood changes in "(Come Round Here) I'm The One You Need" [584], the dive from sunny contentment to something uncomfortably apprehensive sharpens the focus on what would otherwise be a somewhat characterless piece. Outside of this expressive chord switch, the track sustains Ruffin's established style, most of his successful hits to date having been provided by the same Dean—Weatherspoon team. With the end of an era looming, Ruffin was about to complete his final album but knew where his true public following was located. By now planning a permanent move to London, which he completed before the end of 1970, the singer effectively terminated his Motown career by jumping before he was pushed.

[1] Quoted in Dahl, p300.


## TMG 754
## EDWIN STARR
**War** (3:22)
(Whitfield—Strong)
Produced by Norman Whitfield
**Release Date**: 9 Oct 1970
**B-side**: He Who Picks A Rose
**Position in Record Retailer Top 40**: 3
**Equivalent US Release**: Gordy 7101 (8 Jun 1970)
**Position in Billboard Top 40 Pop**: 1
**Position in Billboard Top 40 R & B**: 3

The culmination of Barrett Strong's political radicalisation as revealed in his increasingly pertinent recent lyrics, "War" was written for The Temptations and recorded by them in January for *Psychedelic Shack*. Motown's most open political statement, "War" leaves no doubt as to its author's views, hammering home its argument that war equals nothing but death and destruction with a torrent of nightmare images including bereaved mothers, physical disabilities[1] and gleeful undertakers. Taken as abstract, the argument is irrefutable but, in the context of America 1970, positions were considerably less clear-cut, the recent campus-based protests of New Left students confronting a conservative mainstream determined to assert its authority. Looking towards Europe for their impetus, the student revolts of the late 1960s accommodated a strong anti-Vietnam War thread within a more generalised protest movement which for a while appeared to seriously threaten the security of the American government. Massing at the end of April 1970, student radicals at Ohio State University began a campaign of direct action which on May 4 provoked a police riot in which four students were shot dead. The following day the US military elected to invade Cambodia, causing international outcry while Ohio students staged open revolt by publicly burning their draft cards.

Against this backdrop, *Psychedelic Shack* was enthusiastically received, thousands of students and anti-war protesters besieging Motown with letters demanding "War" be released on single. Yet fearing a backlash, Berry Gordy would not risk The Temptations' reputation on such an outspoken venture, leading Norman Whitfield to resolve the issue by commissioning a blockbusting new recording, convinced that a major hit was there for the taking. Assembling The Funk Brothers in Studio A, a blistering backing track was swiftly prepared in readiness for the vocal, at that point earmarked for Whitfield's protégées Rare Earth.

A sheer experience in sound, the musical track packs an ominous thump in its bottom-heavy arrangement, Bob Babbitt on bass guitar, cut through with searing, angular fuzz-toned lead courtesy of Dennis Coffey. Extraordinary even by Whitfield's standards, "War" is the epitome of 'psychedelic soul', fusing Motown's popular style with acid-rock in one sweeping moment, a prolonged sensation from its opening drum-roll to its clomping cavalry drums in the final chorus. (The Delicates again feature as backing vocalists [751].) Yet to Whitfield's disbelief Rare Earth were unimpressed and, wanting to record their own originals, passed up a commercial monster, leaving the door open for Edwin Starr to cash in.

Starr though had his own agenda and was prepared to stand his ground to get the vocal done *his* way. Rising to the occasion, Starr's contribution is a screaming tumult of outrage, easily his most technically advanced to date and influenced by James Brown, particularly in the (supposedly) off-mike *ad libs*, "Huh!", "Look out!", "Good God, y'all!" etc. which have immortalised his performance. Thoroughly disgusted by the subject at hand, Starr verges at times on the hysterical, growling and falsettoing, his rasping cries capturing the full force of Strong's emphatic lyric.[2]

Unleashed on America on June 8, a month after the Ohio killings and 11 days after Maoist students had rioted in Paris, the track's timing was impeccable, the electrifying impact of the single broadcast across the US airwaves seeing it to the top of the charts on August 29. Released in Britain in October, it almost repeated the feat, but more important than its chart placing, the song struck a deep chord across the Atlantic, adopted as an anthem by the international anti-Vietnam lobby and rivalling John Lennon's "Give Peace A Chance" as the era's definitive protest chant. Motown followed it up with the first releases on their Black Forum subsidiary[3] while Starr himself, having found his form as a political artist, recorded *Involved* and a follow-up single in the shape of "Stop The War Now" [764].

The strength of the track is not its historical associations however, but its universal truth. Etched into the consciousness of its generation, the song has an eternal message, and has been famously covered by The Jam [575n], Frankie Goes To Hollywood and Bruce Springsteen (a follow up to his pointed "Born In The USA"). Edwin Starr revisited it for a less notable re-recording in 1993, returning to the lower reaches of the British charts in association with Shadow (from the television show *The Gladiators*), but the significance of its basic philosophy remains undimmed by the passing of time.

---

[1] The shattering experiences of several Vietnam veterans, injured in conflict but then rejected by the society they were supposedly fighting for, was instrumental in bringing about wholesale improvements in the rights of disabled people in America. During the 1960s, the issue was seen as a development of the wider civil rights movement, leading to national legislation in the early 1970s through the Rehabilitation Act.

[2] Within the text, the phrase "Blows my mind" re-appears after its inclusion in "I Can't Get Next To You" [722].

[3] Martin Luther King's *Why I Oppose The War In Vietnam* was the first. Equally relevant, *Guess Who's Coming Home* was released on the label 16 months later, credited to 'Black Fighting Men Recorded Live In Vietnam'.

**TMG 755**
**THE MOTOWN SPINNERS**
**It's A Shame** (2:57)
(Wonder—Garrett—Wright)
Produced by Stevie Wonder
**Release Date:** Oct 1970
**B-side:** Sweet Thing [514]
**Position in Record Retailer Top 40:** 20
**Equivalent US Release:** VIP 25057 (11 Jun 1970)
**Position in Billboard Top 40 Pop:** 14
**Position in Billboard Top 40 R & B:** 4

---

G C Cameron / Henry Fambrough / Bobbie Smith / Billy Henderson / Pervis Jackson

---

The Spinners' first UK 45 in three years, "It's A Shame" resulted from the close friendship through 1969 of lead singer G C Cameron and Stevie Wonder. Written with Syreeta and Lee Garrett [744], the backing track was made under Wonder's direction (on which he plays numerous instruments), standing in as producer which, despite his blindness, he pulled off competently, spurring him to further such work for Motown peers including Syreeta ([912]; [926]; [933]; [954]), G C Cameron, Smokey Robinson and Jermaine Jackson, as well as his own recordings from [744] onwards.

According to Dennis Coffey, who plays guitar on "It's A Shame", Wonder the producer was pedantic to the point of obsession, having pre-conceived ideas for every musical detail. His account of sessions for the current track indicates that Wonder's insistence on perfection eventually led to both Pistol Allen and Uriel Jones surrendering duties to Wonder, who turned in his own drum-track thereby setting a precedent for a Motown producer by proving that he was not entirely reliant on The Funk Brothers.[1] Having captured what he wanted, the backing track was played to Cameron late one night and vocals recorded the following morning.

Thematically, "It's A Shame" revolves around the regret of a man whose lover is apparently not much interested in him. While he sits by the phone waiting fruitlessly for her call, she is out in the sun enjoying herself, the suggestion being that she is 'messing around' with someone else. Endlessly going over the same ground, the track's obsessive concentration on the scenario depicts the vain hours spent on standby, while the brooding singer shuffles the predicament in his restless mind. In Cameron's hands however the track is brought out of its dejection with a gripping vocal performance whose falsetto through the middle-8 has become its trademark. 'Up' too is the arrangement, the sharp guitar prelude one of Tamla Motown's most memorable. Riffing in two lines, a strummed part by Robert White against Coffey's upper melody, the lick looks back to tracks such as "My Girl" [E67] but equally points the way ahead, influential on the soul styles of the 1970s.[2]

For reasons unclear, Motown showed little interest in the track and it took almost a year of pressure from its creators to get it out in the States. Its commercial success guaranteed a UK outing, scheduled as [755] with

"Together We Can Make Sweet Music" [766] on its flip-side, in line with the American edition. However at the last minute the B-side was switched for the group's 1965 'Northern' release, leaving [766] in wait as a follow-up. A second alteration took place with the group's billing on the revised labels switched to The Motown Spinners, although the reason why Detroit Spinners was discontinued remain vague. Sadly this high-point of their recording career was reached just as the group began preparing to leave Motown.

¹ Coffey's comments can be found in his autobiography, p91-2.

² Compare for example the intro to Philadelphia International's "The Love I Lost" from 1973 (see [890])


## TMG 756
## GLADYS KNIGHT & THE PIPS
**Friendship Train** (3:30)
(Whitfield—Strong)
Produced by Norman Whitfield
Recording completed: 30 Sep 1969
**Release Date**: 23 Oct 1970
**B-side**: You Need Love Like I Do (Don't You)
**Position in Record Retailer Top 40**: -
**Equivalent US Release**: Soul 35068 (6 Oct 1969)
**Position in Billboard Top 40 Pop**: 17
**Position in Billboard Top 40 R & B**: 2

---

Gladys Knight / Merald 'Bubba' Knight / Edward Patten / William Guest

---

Not included on a contemporary studio album, "Friendship Train" suggests its authors were to some degree going through the motions, the year-old recording pre-dating the song's appearance on The Temptations' recent *Psychedelic Shack*. Throwing lyrical ideas about loosely, Barrett Strong's would-be profundity is undermined by some jokey elements including the "Toot Toot" of a train whistle and the pointless name-dropping of "Eve Of Destruction" (which had also re-surfaced in "Ball Of Confusion" [749]). Set against a drab, 'heavy' arrangement these games trivialise the song's utopian message in which the train is a symbol of spiritual progress 'for sisters and brothers' (which is to suggest that the song is in fact a call for black unity as much as for humanity more broadly).

These sentiments, plus the refrain "Shake a hand, make a friend" lent themselves to live performances in which the group would encourage audience members to interact with one another, while The Pips went through an absurd choreographed steam train dance on stage. Notable for the (poorly edited) exchange of vocal duties at 1:52, the track is the group's most comprehensive attempt at the patent Whitfield style to date, and in its subject matter, like "The Onion Song" [715], anticipates The O'Jays' "Love Train" by three years (see [890]).

---

**TMG 757**
**STEVIE WONDER**
**Heaven Help Us All** (3:07)
(Miller)
Produced by Ron Miller/Tom Baird
**Release Date**: 30 Oct 1970
**B-side**: I Gotta Have A Song
**Position in Record Retailer Top 40**: 29
**Equivalent US Release**: Tamla 54200 (29 Sep 1970)
**Position in Billboard Top 40 Pop**: 9
**Position in Billboard Top 40 R & B**: 2

A second track plucked from the *Signed, Sealed And Delivered* sessions [744], Stevie Wonder's new single was written by Ron Miller, who had been supplying him intermittently for several years. (This would be the last such instance.) A gentle prayer for the welfare of humankind, the track's themes suggested a gospel arrangement, which Miller and Tom Baird managed with rowdy backing vocals and an enthused, breathy vocal from Wonder who rounds off with the fervour of a church minister addressing his congregation[1]. Ultimately missing the popular target, the track stumbled in the UK although American soul music fans embraced it warmly.

[1] See [690] for an explanation of the spiritual inspiration to Wonder's singing style.

**TMG 758**
**THE JACKSON 5**
**I'll Be There** (3:35)
(Gordy—West—Hutch—Davis)
Produced by Hal Davis
**Release Date**: 13 Nov 1970
**B-side**: One More Chance
**Position in Record Retailer Top 40**: 4
**Equivalent US Release**: Motown 1171 (28 Aug 1970)
**Position in Billboard Top 40 Pop**: 1
**Position in Billboard Top 40 R & B**: 1

Jackie Jackson / Tito Jackson / Jermaine Jackson / Marlon Jackson / Michael Jackson

Through 1970 it was becoming clear to Motown's Detroit staff that the company was increasingly looking west to its growing LA base. If Gordy's April memo denying any imminent move [737n] reassured a few doubters, the fact that from time-to-time pieces of equipment would go missing from Hitsville inflamed the situation, Motown physically shifting its operations away bit by bit, right under the noses of The Funk Brothers. Berry Gordy continued spending much of his time in California, by now embroiled in a lengthy project to get Diana Ross onto the big screen [848], and, with his latest hot property The Jackson 5 also settled there, it seemed there was little to draw him back across the 2,000-mile gulf.

For the group's part, they had moved together into 'Fort Knox', a mansion set in expansive grounds, with high-security fencing and facilities including swimming pools and sports pitches. A virtual prison, the house would be the group's head quarters for the rest of their time at Motown, a sanctuary from the clamour of the media who by this stage were monitoring the brothers' every move, their superstardom reaching unprecedented levels. Playing to the Los Angeles Forum in July, the group's audience reached levels of near hysteria which at one point involved mass trampling as fans tried to rush the stage. With a record-breaking crowd of over 18,000, the situation rapidly became alarming, the group forced to flee before the set was over.

Lining up a new single was a commercial priority for Motown, and, with The Corporation having nothing in waiting, responsibility passed to LA-based Hal Davis who worked on this new number with arranger Bob West, piecing together a backing track and formulating the song's title. This done, Davis made a late-night call to newcomer Willie Hutch [862], who had previously worked with former Motowner Mickey Stevenson at the latter's Venture Records, and asked if he could supply a lyric. Rising to the challenge, Hutch came up with the remainder of "I'll Be There", which seems to have started life as a polemic on racial unity, its opening lines retaining a trace of the first draft. However in re-working the text and toning down the 'message', Hutch chanced upon a chorus which reminded him of The Four Tops' "Reach Out I'll Be There" [579], which he used as a springboard to finalise the lyric, and jokingly ran off the song's fifth line ('I'll *reach out* my hand for you').

Although this connection is scarcely noticeable in the finished track, it was not lost on Berry Gordy who had Michael Jackson pronounce (at 3:02), 'Just look over your shoulders honey', a mildly fluffed imitation of Levi Stubbs' earlier interjection.[1] If the underlying approach for the group's singles to date was modelled on the early style of The Supremes, Gordy would have seen this as more than idle play: Gordy is here referencing Motown's illustrious past, and embedding The Jackson 5 in the tradition of his most successful male stars of the 1960s, from the heart of the Detroit era which was now seeming so remote. (Although glancing backwards, Gordy's attention was on the future, his old stalwarts The Four Tops at this point amongst the many being left behind in the drive to modernise.)

Diverting the group from its established sound, "I'll Be There" is a serious ballad which might have better-suited the deeper tones of the more mature Jermaine. However with on-the-spot coaching from Suzy Ikeda, Michael pulls off a performance which is both controlled and poignant, his faint tremolo precisely right and justifying Berry Gordy's faith in the 11-year-old.[2] As was frequently done at Motown, the backing track was wilfully cut high so as to push Michael's register to the limit, resulting in what Willie Hutch later described as 'a really angelic sound, so flawless'.[3] (Jermaine managed to have his moment in the spotlight, handling solo passages in the middle-8s.)

Yet despite its obvious quality, Berry Gordy remained unsure of the track for no clear reason. Certainly it was a positive departure for The Jackson 5, and with its polished allure and gently uplifting melodic structure, could hardly fail. Hitting the top on October 17, it sat at the summit of both American charts for a further five weeks, shifting in excess of three million units and giving the act an unprecedented fourth chart-topper with as many releases. (UK audiences were less convinced but still hoisted it to an impressive number 4.)

1970 had been an historic year for The Jackson 5, who at this point could do no wrong. Embarking on further live dates through the autumn, the group were followed by a trail of pandemonium with hysterical fans screaming and fainting wherever they appeared, recalling the height of Beatlemania six years earlier. Come Christmas, the group were needing a well-earned rest, Motown taking advantage of their popularity with an album of Christmas carols and a trailer-single in "Santa Claus Is Coming To Town" which broke their impressive record by failing to make the top 40. The UK equivalent would take two further years to materialise: see [837]. "I'll Be There" remains a Jackson 5 favourite, the brothers reuniting for a moving live rendition at the *Motown 25* spectacular in 1983.

[1] Jackson inadvertently pluralizes 'shoulder'. The group's *Third Album* of September, which contains "I'll Be There", also includes a song entitled "Reach In".

[2] Michael turned 12 on August 29, the day after the American release.

[3] Taraborrelli (1994) p72.


## TMG 759
## EARL VAN DYKE
**6 By 6** (2:22)
(Nixon—Riser)
Produced by Henry "Hank" Cosby
Recording completed: 3 Aug 1966
**Release Date**: 20 Nov 1970
**B-side**: All For You [506]
**Position in Record Retailer Top 40**: -
**Equivalent US Release**: Soul 35028 (21 Dec 1966)
**Position in Billboard Top 40 Pop**: -
**Position in Billboard Top 40 R & B**: -

Tamla Motown's last single of a year in which they had put a best-ever tally of 26 records in the UK top 40, was a return to roots, "6 By 6" an old recording put out in America four years earlier. Since its first release under the name Earl Van Dyke & The Motown Brass, the pianist had released little but resumed recording under his own name with a 1969 cover of "Runaway Child, Running Wild" (Soul 35059) and was about to release a new mock-live set called *The Earl Of Funk*.

These contemporary efforts never surfaced in the UK, the choice of single here aimed at Northern Soul crowds, as evinced by the choice of B-side [506]. "6 By 6" is a Hammond-and-brass-led instrumental stomp in Am, built from a close-ratio chord cycle recalling Bobby Hebb's then recent "Sunny" (See also [511]) and so-called because of its requirement of six standard group members (ie Funk Brothers) and a brass sextet (it was first noted as "Six Plus Six"). An interesting heirloom in 1970, the track was never destined for chart success, but was greeted with delight on the club circuit. (Years later a vocal was written, and "6 By 6" was re-recorded by Van Dyke for Ian Levine's MotorCity label [683n].)

## TIMELINE – 1970

Tamla Motown release 38 singles and 44 albums. First time album releases have outnumbered singles, reflecting general shift in market forces

Tamla Motown have most successful year on UK chart, placing 17 singles in top 10 and 26 in top 40, both all-time best tallies. One single reaches number 1

| | |
|---|---|
| Jan | Temptations appear in UK for first time at Talk of the Town, London |
| Jan 14 | Supremes stage 'farewell' concert in Nevada, last time Diana Ross will appear with them. Performance subsequently appears on LP. Ross is replaced in act by Jean Terrell |
| Jan 31 | Jackson 5: "I Want You Back " enters UK top 50 (peak 2) |
| Jan 31 | Jackson 5: "I Want You Back" number 1 in US (one week). Their next three will repeat the feat. Motown will claim group sold 10 million units in nine months |
| Feb 14 | *Motown Chartbusters Volume 3* tops UK album chart (one week) |
| Feb 28 | Jimmy Ruffin: "Farewell Is A Lonely Sound" enters UK top 50 (peak 8) |
| Mar | Levi Stubbs arrested during press conference and charged with possession of cocaine and ammunition |
| Mar 16 | Tammi Terrell dies in hospital in Philadelphia. Funeral takes place Mar 20. Marvin Gaye visibly devastated and never resumes old-style recording |
| Mar 19 | Stevie Wonder opens at New York's Copa |
| Mar 21 | Four Tops: "I Can't Help Myself" enters UK top 50 as re-issue (peak 10) |
| Mar 28 | Stevie Wonder: "Never Had A Dream Come True" enters UK top 50 (peak 6) |
| Apr 25 | Jackson 5: "A B C" number 1 in US (two weeks) |
| May | Four Tops tour UK |
| May 1 | Thousands of Jackson 5 fans threaten rampage at Philadelphia International Airport where group due to land |
| May 2 | Supremes: "Up The Ladder To The Roof" enters UK top 50 (peak 6) first post-Ross single |
| May 7 | Diana Ross performs first solo set at Frontier Hotel, LA |
| May 9 | Marvin Gaye: "Abraham Martin & John" enters UK top 50 (peak 9) |
| May 16 | Jackson 5: "A B C " enters UK top 50 (peak 8) |
| May 30 | Four Tops: "It's All In The Game" enters UK top 50 (peak 5) |
| Summer | Motown celebrate 10th anniversary with *Motown Story* box set |
| Jun 19 | Diana Ross' first solo release on Tamla Motown |
| Jun 27 | Jackson 5: "The Love You Save" number 1 in US (two weeks) |
| Jul 4 | Jimmy Ruffin: "I'll Say Forever My Love" enters UK top 50 (peak 7) |
| Aug 1 | Jackson 5: "The Love You Save" enters UK top 50 (peak 7) |
| Aug 29 | Edwin Starr: "War" number 1 in US (three weeks). Motown begin period in which their singles are top of US chart for 91 of next 119 days |
| Summer | Supremes tour UK |
| Sep 12 | Diana Ross: "Ain't No Mountain High Enough" enters UK top 50 (peak 6) |
| Sep 12 | Miracles: "Tears Of A Clown" UK number 1 (one week). Toppled by "Band Of Gold", on HDH's Invictus label |
| Sep 14 | Stevie Wonder marries Syreeta. Wonder suffers nosebleed which delays ceremony |
| Sep 18 | Jimi Hendrix dies from effects of drug overdose |
| Sep 19 | Diana Ross: "Ain't No Mountain High Enough" number 1 in US (three weeks), toppling Edwin Starr |
| Sep 19 | Temptations: "Ball Of Confusion" enters UK top 50 (peak 7) |
| Oct | Motown launch Black Forum label in US. Eight political LPs released before label wound up early 1973 |
| Oct 3 | Four Tops: "Still Water (Love)" enters UK top 50 (peak 10) |
| Oct 17 | Jimmy Ruffin: "It's Wonderful (To Be Loved By You)" enters UK top 50 (peak 6) |
| Oct 17 | Jackson 5: "I'll Be There" number 1 in US (five weeks) |
| Oct 24 | Edwin Starr: "War" enters UK top 50 (peak 3) |
| Nov | CBS television refuse to broadcast "Stoned Love" |
| Oct 31 | *Motown Chartbusters Volume 4* tops UK album chart (one week) |
| Nov 10 | Martha Reeves gives birth to Eric Jermal Graham |
| Nov 21 | Jackson 5: "I'll Be There " enters UK top 50 (peak 4) |
| Nov 30 | Supremes and Four Tops perform at Royal Albert Hall |
| Dec 12 | Miracles: "The Tears Of A Clown" number 1 in US (two weeks). Motown's seventh US chart-topper in 1970, their highest tally in any one year |

**TMG 760**
**THE SUPREMES**
**Stoned Love** (2:49)
(Wilson—Samoht)
Produced by Frank Wilson
**Release Date**: 8 Jan 1971
**B-side**: Shine On Me
**Position in Record Retailer Top 40**: 3
**Equivalent US Release**: Motown 1172 (15 Oct 1970)
**Position in Billboard Top 40 Pop**: 7
**Position in Billboard Top 40 R & B**: 1

---

Jean Terrell / Cindy Birdsong / Mary Wilson

---

Having released nothing through December, Tamla Motown resumed business with this, The Supremes' finest post-Ross release. Penned by budding writer Kinney Thomas[1], the track was brought to Motown by Frank Wilson, who discovered Thomas via Detroit radio and arranged a meeting. (Thomas supposedly demoed "Stoned Love" on a guitar with four broken strings.) Brushed up by Wilson and recorded in early 1970 with an ornate baroque prelude, the single was edited down to commence with its title phrase, followed by a momentum-gathering percussion ushering in verse 1 with no undue fuss. On the back of "Up The Ladder To The Roof" [735], Frank Wilson was clearly attempting to consolidate the group's re-emergence with another regression to the trademark crotchet beats of the early 1960s, most likely looking to "Come See About Me" [E65] for inspiration. (Besides sharing a similar 'fade-in' device, the elegant build into the chorus plus the track's general horizontality of motion unmistakably invoke HDH's 1964 number.) In terms of the track's chord changes, the attractive I-III relationship between verse and middle-8 recalls Smokey Robinson's "Special Occasion" [673].

The production ethic however is distinctly non-conservative, heavily fuzzed guitar providing a contemporary electrical veneer and textual mass. Probably recorded in LA (with the group's vocals in New York), the bass line too is unusual for Motown, pragmatic and impatiently beating, the polar opposite of James Jamerson's freely adventurous lines in "Reflections" [616], suggesting he did not play the session. However the backing track is elevated from its earthiness by David Van DePitte's articulate orchestral arrangement, high-flying strings offering beguiling uplift and a level of atmospheric 'high', the aural equivalent of a cannabis rush.

Given its broadly trippy aura, it is surprising that such little controversy surrounded the single's release, particularly given its boldly straight-forward title. A step beyond the veiled implications of "Cloud Nine" [707], "Stoned Love" spells matters out, equating the state of drug-induced euphoria with a sense of universal adoration which goes as far as to suggest that being high offers salvation for the human race. How it got past Quality Control is anybody's guess, but equally puzzling was the acceptance it met from the mainstream media. While some US radio stations were unsure of the song, and

CBS refused to air a live version on their *Merv Griffin Show*, the reception was generally positive and in the UK it was let through without apparent concern, 40 months after the BBC had banned The Beatles' harmless "With A Little Help From My Friends" for its mention of getting high.

None of which is to imply that the establishment's attitude towards drug-use was softening: In Britain from 1967 police sergeant Norman Pilcher made a personal crusade of 'busting' high-profile rock figures for drugs-use which included Rolling Stones Mick Jagger and Keith Richards (who were sentenced to jail terms), Donovan, and both John Lennon and George Harrison in separate incidents. In America the backdrop was broadly similar. Having declared the start of his 'War on Drugs' in 1969, President Nixon called for the screening of popular music lyrics for supposed inducement in 1970, leading MCA to drop 18 artists from their books, followed by the Federal Communications Commission telegramming radio stations with threats of stripping them of their broadcast licences if they played music seen to advocate drug use. Meantime, the Illinois Crime Commission was preparing a list of tracks for publication, identifying them as including drugs references, pinpointing such potentially subversive children's favourites as Peter, Paul and Mary's "Puff The Magic Dragon" and The Beatles' "Yellow Submarine".

The matter was more than just political reaction however and in 1970 substance misuse was having a serious effect on popular music and some of the principal artists on the scene. The death of Jimi Hendrix from a drugs overdose on September 18 was followed 16 days later by that of Janis Joplin in LA. Jim Morrison was simultaneously making his final appearances with The Doors prior to his demise in 1971, thought to be caused by heroin or cocaine overdose, and in general the innocence of the 1960s 'pot' and flower-power culture was giving way to something altogether darker and more insidious.

Cantering up the American charts at the end of 1970, "Stoned Love" offers an optimistic counterpoint to the gloom in the air, preceding its arrival in Britain where it scored higher than any Supremes single bar "Baby Love" [E56]. Alongside it came the group's acclaimed *New Ways But Love Stays*, conceived by Wilson as a 'concept' piece to sit alongside The Four Tops' *Still Waters Run Deep* [752]. In truth the set contains Motown's usual array of covers and a selection of current singles, the inclusion of a version of "Together We Can Make Such Sweet Music" [766] segueing into "Stoned Love" one of the group's more effective openers. Pencilled in as *Stoned Love*, the LP title was switched in reference to the group's current style, but the album sold disappointingly despite the attraction of this, its strongest track, and nothing further was lifted from the set.

---

[1] Thomas was cryptically billed as Yennik Samoht, his name spelled backwards in the style of Eivets Rednow [666].


**TMG 761**
**SMOKEY ROBINSON & THE MIRACLES**
**(Come 'Round Here) I'm The One You Need** (2:33)
**Re-issue of [584]**

**Release Date**: 15 Jan 1971
**New B-side**: We Can Make It We Can
**Position in Record Retailer Top 40**: 13

---

Smokey Robinson / Bobby Rogers / Claudette Rogers Robinson /
Warren 'Pete' Moore / Ronnie White

---

With The Miracles having scored two major hits in 1969 and 1970 with old recordings ([696] and [745]), Tamla Motown opted to give the group another retrospective in 1971. Confessing surprise at the favourable public response to these catalogue titles, Robinson hinted in contemporary interviews that his uncertainty over the future direction for his group was thereby resolved, because "it's given me a good idea of what people want".[1] In truth though, Robinson was still looking for a way out of The Miracles, and was resolved to bringing in a replacement, his mind now set on retiring from performance with daughter Tamla born on Dec 15 [811]. The fact that The Miracles' career was at a high presented him with a dilemma, split between duty to family and loyalty to his group.

The partner track here, "We Can Make It We Can", is an Ashford & Simpson number lifted from the group's 1969 album *Four In Blue*.

[1] Davis (1988) p94.


**TMG 762**
**MARTHA REEVES & THE VANDELLAS**
**Forget Me Not** (2:45)
(Morris—Moy)
Produced by Norman Whitfield[1]
Recording completed: 16 Jan 1968
**Release Date**: 22 Jan 1971
**B-side**: I Gotta Let You Go
**Position in Record Retailer Top 40**: -
**Equivalent US Release**: Gordy 7070 (4 Apr 1968)
**Position in Billboard Top 40 Pop**: -
**Position in Billboard Top 40 R & B**: -

---

Martha Reeves / Lois Reeves / Sandra Tilley

---

In business again after a period of ill-health, Martha Reeves bounced back to recording activity with the late-1968 line-up of sister Lois and former Velvelette Sandra Tilley (drafted in to replace the recently sacked Rosalind Ashford) for their first full sessions. The results were released in the form of *Sugar 'N' Spice* and *Natural Resources*, two long-players which slipped out quietly in 1969 and 1970 respectively. Ready to go back on the road, the group were booked for a UK tour in support of Stevie Wonder, but with no US hits of late to draw on Tamla Motown were forced to fathom a suitable new single. Despite *Natural Resources* having appeared in late 1970, the album's contents were completely overlooked in favour of an old B-side (from [657]) penned by the Morris—Moy team and puzzlingly selected for its perceived popularity. (It is the last of four successive re-releases for Martha Reeves & The Vandellas covering the period since the debacle of "I Can't Dance To That Music You're Playing" [669].)

An eyebrow-raising counterpoint to Edwin Starr's comprehensive denunciation of military aggression [754], "Forget Me Not" concerns the departure of a soldier sailing off to battle, and was inspired by the recruitment of Moy's brother Melvin into the US Navy. A romantic song for parted lovers clinging to one another's hearts across the ocean and set to the sound of cavalry charges, the track's context during the bloody Vietnam War makes its sentimentality flatly inane against a conflict which took millions of lives, and resulted in almost a quarter-of-a-million US military killed or injured. A more realistic selection would have been the group's (unsuccessful) US single from February 1970, "I Should Be Proud". Written by Hank Cosby, Pam Sawyer and Joe Hinton, the track recounts the death of a loved one missing in action, and is touted as Motown's first 'protest' song, ahead of "War". (It was also included on *Natural Resources*.) Whatever the logic, "Forget Me Not" was issued in the UK with its slushy spoken section edited out.[2] Record buyers were nonplussed.

[1] The production credit is erroneous, "Forget Me Not" the work of Richard Morris. Tamla Motown corrected their mistake for the re-issues [L049] and [L085].

[2] 'Each night I will pray for peace on earth/Goodwill to all men/And my little heart will say these tender words/Time and time again.'


## TMG 763
## R. DEAN TAYLOR
**Indiana Wants Me** (3:05)
(Taylor)
Produced by R. Dean Taylor
Recording completed: 4 Dec 1969
**Release Date**: 5 Feb 1971
**B-side**: Love's Your Name
**Position in Record Retailer Top 40**: 2
**Equivalent US Release**: Rare Earth 5013 (10 Apr 1970)
**Position in Billboard Top 40 Pop**: 5
**Position in Billboard Top 40 R & B**: -

The long-awaited follow up to "Gotta See Jane" [656], "Indiana Wants Me" surfaced in America almost a year earlier than in the UK, on the Rare Earth label, Taylor having been switched from VIP. But with the UK branch not yet operational (see [786]), the recording was put out on Tamla Motown, and almost made the summit of the singles chart.

Staying for a while in a Detroit hotel, Taylor woke one night to the sound of gunshots and police sirens, and in a heightened state of awareness, mentally absorbed the sounds emanating from the street into the sketch of a new song. Incorporating the police megaphone into the scenario, Taylor crafted a narrative in which the central character is on the run, having shot a man for being disrespectful to his wife, and in the final verse is surrounded and writes his farewell letter just as the fatal bullets start to fly. (Taylor claims to have written the entire track in less than half-an-hour.)

As remarkable as the tortured narrative, is the studio recording in which sound effects are used liberally to convey the intensity of the scene. Conceived by its writer before recording began, Taylor had an active hand in building the sound stage, the full track recorded in sessions between Studios A and B with Don Gooch playing the cop. Commencing ahead of the backing with the wail of a police siren, the effects are reported to have startled car drivers, leading Rare Earth to issue a more radio-friendly mix. Engaging with the array of studio techniques on show, including a double-tracked chorus vocal, the single's commercial success perhaps outweighs its strength as a composition, although its parallel ascendancy in America shows Taylor's enterprising judgement to be spot on.


**TMG 764**
**EDWIN STARR**
**Stop The War Now** (3:25)
(Whitfield—Strong)
Produced by Norman Whitfield
**Release Date:** Jan 1971
**B-side:** Gonna Keep On Trying Till I Win Your Love [630b]
**Position in Record Retailer Top 40:** 33
**Equivalent US Release:** Gordy 7104 (19 Nov 1970)
**Position in Billboard Top 40 Pop:** 26
**Position in Billboard Top 40 R & B:** 5


Keen to take advantage of the ripples which "War" [754] had caused, Whitfield and Strong wasted no time in concocting "Stop The War Now", a brazen cash-in perpetuating the political theme. Essentially the same song with an alternative slogan, audiences saw through its tactical undercurrent and took comparatively little interest.[1] Cheekily borrowing John Lennon's famous pacifist slogan at 1:18, 2:02 and 2:46, the song's sense of futile rehash found even Starr himself dismissing it as needless[2], although his performance on the recording is as highly animated as on [754], including a sustained falsetto at 3:06. Notable too is the presence of lead guitarist Wah-Wah Watson (Melvin Franklin), a young Detroiter drafted in by Norman Whitfield, who would become a regular on the producer's sessions. Both the US and UK editions were coupled with the older "Gonna Keep On Trying Till I Win Your Love", originally the flip to Starr's Motown debut [630].

[1] As cash-ins go, the release was no less unsubtle than a number of Motown precedents, obvious examples being Barrett Strong's "Money (That's What I Want")" [E02] / "Money And Me", The Marvelettes' "Please Mr. Postman" [E05] / "Twistin' Postman" [E07], Junior Walker's "Shot Gun" [509] / "Shoot Your Shot" [559b], The Supremes' "Love Child" [677] / "I'm Living In Shame" [695] etc.

[2] See Dahl p313.

**TMG 765**
**GLADYS KNIGHT & THE PIPS**
**If I Were Your Woman** (2:59)
(Ware—Sawyer—McMurray)
Produced by Clay McMurray
**Release Date:** Jan 1971
**B-side:** The Tracks Of My Tears
**Position in Record Retailer Top 40:** -
**Equivalent US Release:** Soul 35078 (29 Oct 1970)
**Position in Billboard Top 40 Pop:** 9
**Position in Billboard Top 40 R & B:** 1

---

Gladys Knight / Merald 'Bubba' Knight / Edward Patten / William Guest

---

Having worked through the ranks, Norman Whitfield's assistant Clay McMurray took charge of Gladys Knight & The Pips in 1970, writing and producing "If I Were Your Woman", following his success on Kiki Dee's "The Day Will Come Between Sunday And Monday" [739]. Working with Pam Sawyer, the two were boosted here by input from Gloria Jones [910], under the pseudonym Laverne Ware. (As a result, Sawyer and Jones began writing together as a matter of course, although McMurray showed little interest in their subsequent collaborations.)

"If I Were Your Woman", despite the strong female presence, is a somewhat vague piece, in which the singer confesses unflinching love for the man of her desires, who in reality is with someone else. Considered pro-feminist for the toughness of its opening lines[1], the track troubled Knight, who saw no relevance of the defiant devotion to her own views on life and love, nor for that matter to her singing career to date. Equally uncomfortable are the backing vocals, which in being performed by male singers required an unfortunate gender swap ('If *you* were *my* woman'), leaving Knight trading passionate sentiments with her own family members.

Going through with the session regardless, Knight pitched in with a competent vocal, satisfied that the track would surface as an album cut at some point. McMurray though had other ideas and proposed the song as a single to Quality Control, who voted it down on the basis that it clashed with the group's established formula. Pressing the point, the producer convinced Berry Gordy that in fact, "If I Were Your Woman" was a potential hit, citing "Letter Full Of Tears" as an example of a successful 'slow' number for the outfit.[2] Gordy was eventually convinced and decided to back the release, breaking the news personally to a less-than-enthusiastic singer who struggled in vain to change his mind again.

McMurray's initial judgement proved correct, the track rising to the top of the R & B listings on 23 January, backed with the classic "The Tracks Of My Tears" from the two-year-old *Silk 'N Soul*. Boosted by their biggest success since "I Heard It Through The Grapevine" [629], Gladys Knight & The Pips had the honour of appearing on the final *Ed Sullivan Show* in the spring. The UK release meantime was generally overlooked.

---

¹ 'If I were your woman/And you were my man/You'd have no other woman/You'd be weak as a lamb.' The woman is overpowering her man rather than vice-versa.

² "Letter Full Of Tears" was released before the group signed to Motown, a 1961 hit on the Fury label.


**TMG 766**
**THE MOTOWN SPINNERS**
**Together We Can Make Such Sweet Music** (3:04)
(Colman—Drapkin)
Produced by Clay McMurray
**Release Date**: 5 Mar 1971
**B-side**: Truly Yours
**Position in Record Retailer Top 40**: -
**Equivalent US Release**: VIP 25057 (11 Jun 1970)
**Position in Billboard Top 40 Pop**: 14
**Position in Billboard Top 40 R & B**: -

G C Cameron / Henry Fambrough / Bobbie Smith / Billy Henderson / Pervis Jackson

The Spinners' final Tamla Motown single, "Together We Can Make Such Sweet Music" is a pleasantly melodic soft-soul tune, with an attractive chorus line which casually rises and falls through its G major scale. The track was penned by Martin Colman and Richard Drapkin, the latter a writer of some years' standing whose back-catalogue includes "Devil In Her Heart", famously recorded by The Beatles on the same day they covered "Money" [E02] and "You Really Got A Hold On Me" [E13].

Originally issued in America together with "It's A Shame" [755], the tracks were separated for the UK market, each paired up with Northern Soul oldies, in this case a recording which had been a modest American hit in 1966 (as Motown 1093). Giving its producer back-to-back releases, the track was dubbed with extra strings, including an incompetently executed and poorly EQ-ed cello solo, but failed in the UK, despite pointing the way to the group's subsequently highly successful 1970s style.

The Spinners would leave Motown late in 1971 once their contract had expired, joining old rivals Atlantic (see [871]), although G C Cameron had by then signed to Motown as a solo performer [1033]. Meantime Tamla Motown continued their new-found interest in the act, including a group recording on a contemporary flexi-disc, plugging the current *Second Time Around* album (see Appendix 1.) Sadly, a case of too little too late.


**TMG 767**
**JIMMY RUFFIN**
**Let's Say Goodbye Tomorrow** (3:04)
(Dean—Weatherspoon)
Produced by James Dean/William Weatherspoon
Recording completed: 28 Jan 1969

**Release Date**: 19 Mar 1971
**B-side**: Living In A World I Created For Myself
**Position in Record Retailer Top 40**: -
**No Equivalent US Release**

Ruffin's fourth release in just over a year, "Let's Say Goodbye Tomorrow" is an unobtrusive pop song in the singer's established vein, the strong chorus dominating the lazily tuneless verses. Recorded for *The Groove Governor*, the track was likely not intended as a single, the UK-only release coupled with the US B-side to "Maria (You Were The Only One)" [753b]. Ruffin, by now living in London [753], might have expected his loyal UK fans to lift it into the charts.

**TMG 768**
**DIANA ROSS**
**Remember Me** (3:09)
(Ashford—Simpson)
Produced by Nickolas Ashford/Valerie Simpson
**Release Date**: 26 Mar 1971
**B-side**: How About You
**Position in Record Retailer Top 40**: 7
**Equivalent US Release**: Motown 1176 (8 Dec 1970)
**Position in Billboard Top 40 Pop**: 16
**Position in Billboard Top 40 R & B**: 10

Having been closely courted by Berry Gordy through the 1960s, it was felt by many that the marriage of Diana Ross and her boss/lover was an eventual inevitability, rumours flying intermittently for several years. Living in LA, just up the road from one another, Ross and Gordy remained intimate through 1970, and it has since been claimed that Gordy had already proposed on two occasions and been turned down both times. The likelihood is that Gordy, already married twice and with children and several current lovers to contend with, was too risky a prospect for Ross, who also had love interest outside of this particular relationship. During 1969 she had met rich socialite Bob Ellis[1] in Beverley Hills and started a low-key romance, a development which apparently put Gordy's nose considerably out of joint.

Matters took a fateful turn at the start of 1971 when it emerged that Ross was pregnant with Gordy's child [781], marriage by this stage a remote prospect. Yet living life in the public gaze, the unhitched Ross had to do *something* to mitigate a potential scandal, and the world outside her inner circle was stunned by the surprise wedding to the generally unknown Ellis, a brief ceremony held in LA on January 20 1971.[2] The couple announced 'they' were pregnant a fortnight later, events effectively precluding any Ross—Gordy union for good.

During the winter, Motown had released Ross' new single as a stand-alone issue, entirely ignoring 1970's *Everything Is Everything*, a lack-lustre collection of 11 tracks made under the direction of Deke Richards and Hal Davis, which had sold poorly. (It did however contain a cut subsequently recognised as a classic [781].) "Remember Me" was a safer bet, written by the reliable Ashford & Simpson team, and arranged in vintage Motown style by aul Riser. (The rapid orchestral swoop at 1:43 is taken directly from the opening moments of "Love Child" [677].)

The track was originally conceived as a vehicle for Valerie Simpson, who was making embryonic moves to launch herself as a singer. (Her debut album *Exposed* would be released by Motown in May.) Inspired by Simpson's delivery of the number, Ross cut her version in late in 1970, with close-miked, breathy vocal affording volume for the grand crescendo which blossoms at the close of each chorus. These passages, building line-on-line are a technical *tour de force* for Ashford & Simpson, making an exquisite peak from virtually nothing, the melody uneventful and shifting little, with the choruses draping themselves around a single supporting note. In fact the charm of "Remember Me" stems largely from its horizontal character, the underlying tension constantly threatening to break its shackles, only to fall back onto its bass root A every time as if exhausted from the passion of the foregoing.

Whether by accident or not, the narrative here mirrors Ross' position at the time, the lyric bravely waving goodbye to a former lover, imploring him to focus on the good times. (The line 'inspire you a little higher' is reworked from "You're All I Need To Get By" [668], which Ross had also recorded in 1970.) Although not conceived as a farewell to Berry Gordy, the track could have been especially selected as a personal message, and it is doubtful that the poignancy of lines such as 'I won't forget it, I have no regrets' and 'Remember me when you drink the wine/Of sweet success and I gave you my best' was lost on him—or for that matter her—at the time.

Tinged with sadness, the song's touching sense of courage in the face of heartbreak won approval from UK fans, the single making the top 10 in the spring and remaining on chart for 3 months.

[1] His real name was Silberstein.

[2] None of Ross' friends were there. Gordy also did not attend, but had he done so he would have heard Ellis' marriage vow not to become Ross' manager.


**TMG 769**
**THE JACKSON 5**
**Mama's Pearl** (3:09)
(The Corporation)
Produced by The Corporation
**Release Date**: 2 Apr 1971
**B-side**: Darling Dear[1]
**Position in Record Retailer Top 40**: 25
**Equivalent US Release**: Motown 1177 (7 Jan 1971)
**Position in Billboard Top 40 Pop**: 2
**Position in Billboard Top 40 R & B**: 2

---

Jackie Jackson / Tito Jackson / Jermaine Jackson / Marlon Jackson / Michael Jackson

The Jackson 5's most tasteless exercise in kiddie-pop to date, "Mama's Pearl" predictably attempts to repeat the success of "I Want You Back" [724], borrowing specific elements including a diatonic descent on bass during the chorus and a semi-spoken bridge section culminating in 'That's what you need' (at 2:01), almost directly quoting the earlier hit. Enthusiastically delivered by Michael (with star spots for both Jermaine and Jackie), the song lacks any real purpose, merely recycling a formula which was already looking tired. America was more convinced than the UK, where the release capsized at 25 (despite appearing in a promotional picture sleeve).

Meantime, Berry Gordy had turned down "One Bad Apple", a song submitted to Motown by (unrelated) songwriter George Jackson. Subsequently offered to Utah five-piece The Osmonds, who carried off a creditable imitation of The Jackson 5, the song went to the top of the US charts in February, marking the arrival of serious competition and leaving Gordy kicking himself for missing a hit.[2]

[1] The B-side features a highly animated bass from James Jamerson, one of several instances of his performing on period Jackson 5 cuts. The backing track was recorded at Hitsville with the standard Funk Brothers line-up during the summer of 1970.

[2] While The Osmonds and The Jackson 5 would share a fierce rivalry, by 1975 group member Alan Osmond would be pitching in for Motown, writing and producing "High Tide" for Mo-West act The Allens. (Released as MW 3029: See Appendix 3.)

**TMG 770**
**FOUR TOPS**
**Just Seven Numbers (Can Straighten Out My Life)** (2:57)
(Sawyer—Jones)
Produced by Frank Wilson
Recording completed: 30 Jul 1970
**Release Date**: 8 Apr 1971
**B-side**: I Wish I Were Your Mirror
**Position in Record Retailer Top 40**: 36
**Equivalent US Release**: Motown 1175 (28 Dec 1970)
**Position in Billboard Top 40 Pop**: 40
**Position in Billboard Top 40 R & B**: 9

---

Levi Stubbs / Lawrence Payton / Abdul 'Duke' Fakir / Renaldo 'Obie' Benson

---

Maintaining The Four Tops' move towards more reflective recording, signposted by "Still Water (Love)" [752], this new single is the group's slowest to date, plodding lamentably through its three minutes of lost love. With unusually pragmatic subject matter for The Four Tops, "Just Seven Numbers" refers to the singer's yearning to make contact with his former girlfriend, pride alone preventing him from calling. Having spelled out his predicament, Stubbs comes to life with characteristic fury ('You haven't been fair to me'), providing some defiant contrast in what is, otherwise, something of a tear-jerker.

Provided by Sawyer—Jones (see [765]) and recorded mid-1970, the track's ascending structure resembles that of "You're All I Need To Get By" [668], but in firming up the sequence into defined chords, carries a surprisingly bold shift from its opening G to an A major, where minor is more commonly employed. Endlessly turning through the cycle in which the verses simultaneously function as choruses, an airy detour to Am eventually arrives ('If I only knew') with tangible atmosphere, but is passed-over too briefly. Instead, much of the producer's attention seems to have been focussed on infusing the Tops' contemporary material with superfluous sound effects, including here a 1960s telephone dial dubbed over its extended coda.

Meanwhile, The Four Tops' *Changing Times* was in preparation, emerging in September 1970 in America (March 1971 in the UK) and including several examples of Frank Wilson's production strategy for the group, including a *Sgt. Pepper*-like opening of a brass band in the park, mixed into chiming clocks, whose ticking oddly rears its head during the gaps between tracks. Idiosyncrasies aside, the production quality on display is exemplary, cleanly mixed with real depth, which makes the fact that "Just Seven Numbers" was the only lift somewhat surprising.[1] (The track was in effect the centrepiece of the album, evocatively reprising part-way through the closing title, a cover of "The Long And Winding Road".)

In truth, despite the group's more adventurous 1970s releases, they were clearly failing to recapture the vitality of their HDH years, and as with their old rivals The Supremes, were finding Motown less interested in them than was the case a few years earlier. Concentrating more on album projects, the group had recorded *Soul Spin* in 1969 which had no trailer singles and although the *Still Waters* project spawned two [736]; [752], both *Changing Times* and the 1972 follow-up *Nature Planned It* carried just one each, as their time at Motown began winding slowly to a sad conclusion [823].

[1] In the US, the album's title track was also issued on 45 (as Motown 1185), but didn't crack the *Billboard* top 40.


**TMG 771**
**THE ELGINS**
**Heaven Must Have Sent You** (2:36)
**Re-issue of [583]**
**Release Date**: 23 Apr 1971
**Position in Record Retailer Top 40**: 3
**Equivalent US Release**: VIP 54202 (9 Sep 1971)
**Position in Billboard Top 40 Pop**: -
**Position in Billboard Top 40 R & B**: -

---

Saundra Mallett Edwards / Cleo 'Duke' Miller / Johnny Dawson / Robert Fleming

---

With Motown drifting west in the early 1970s and setting up new imprints, the old VIP label was being laid to rest, a clutch of singles during 1971 closing this particular outlet, which was one of Motown's most important outside of the 'big three'. The Spinners were by now leaving [766], Chuck Jackson out of contract and R. Dean Taylor recording for Rare Earth, gutting VIP of its central roster and *raison d'être*.

Meantime in Britain, The Elgins' 1966 single was brushed off for a re-run, which saw it climb high into the UK top 10 as it ought to have done first time around. Enthused by its success, the group were spurred to re-form, speculation rising that they might re-sign to Motown and resume a recording career. The notion was bolstered by Motown's rare decision to re-release the track in America as one of VIP's final outings, although it fared less well and attention on The Elgins inevitably began to fade again.

Despite the scant success the group had, their theme-song has continued to be popular, eventually entering the American top 20 in 1979 courtesy of latter-day Motowner Bonnie Pointer (formerly of The Pointer Sisters), helped by one of James Jamerson's best performances of his final years. (The UK equivalent emerged as TMG 1134.)

**TMG 772**
**STEVIE WONDER**
**We Can Work It Out** (2:53)
(Lennon—McCartney)
Produced by Stevie Wonder
Recording completed: 15 Jun 1969
**Release Date**: 30 Apr 1971
**B-side**: Don't Wonder Why
**Position in Record Retailer Top 40**: 27
**Equivalent US Release**: Tamla 54202 (18 Feb 1971)
**Position in Billboard Top 40 Pop**: 13
**Position in Billboard Top 40 R & B**: 3

According to bassist Bob Babbitt, "We Can Work It Out" was his first recording session at Motown.[1] If true, this would date the track to around 1966, which, while generally acceptable in terms of the song's vintage, would mean that it had laid unreleased for some five years. Dennis Coffey however has also claimed involvement[2], and since his work for Motown began in earnest towards the close of the decade, his account accords with the established recording dates. Most likely, the solution is that Wonder recorded an embryonic version in 1966 which was never issued, Babbitt perhaps confusing the sequence of events in view of Wonder's other 'big' cover [570], recorded at precisely the correct time.

In fact, with allowance for Coffey's presence, "We Can Work It Out" is almost entirely Wonder's own work, the musician handling several instruments himself as well as producing the track. His development in this respect may owe a debt to Paul McCartney who became the first major pop artist to self-record an album on which he handled all instrumental duties (*McCartney*, April 1970), which would account too for Wonder's choice of material here. Mainly written by McCartney, the track was recorded by The Beatles in 1965 during an era when the group was fully absorbing black American music, naming their concurrent album *Rubber Soul* in veiled admission of the fact. The affinity between Motown and The Beatles which blossomed in 1964-65 (see Chapter 1) had never truly dimmed in the years since, the group for example busking "The Tracks Of My Tears" [522] and "You Really Got A Hold On Me" [E13] during sessions in 1969, both long-available on bootlegs.[3]

For Motown's part, The Supremes had released a tribute album *A Bit of Liverpool* (re-titled in Britain as *With Love (From Us To You)*) in 1964, which included five Lennon—McCartney numbers amongst its titles, since when most Motown acts had also made versions of Beatles material at some point, McCartney's compositions generally winning more favour than his partner's.[4] But undoubtedly the most successful of these is the present track, an exuberant 'party' version of the sombre original in which Wonder ignores the sentiment of the lyric, revelling instead in a groove which he accentuates via metrical alterations which dispense with The Beatles' pensive suspensions and tonal contrasts, for example by locking vocals into a regularised rhythm during the chorus. Wonder's double-tracked vocal is similarly punchy, while neither fully synchronised nor formally harmonised, and includes several moments of accomplished falsettoing, particularly in his self-made backing passages. Assuming Wonder to have played bass rather than Babbitt or Jamerson, he also deserves credit for the animated octave bubbles and emphatic end-of-line stops, while his high-flying and unusually studied harmonica solo fizzes against fuzz-toned clavinet and Coffey's electric guitar work, excitement the track's overarching feature.

Touring the UK in early 1971, Wonder was noticeably expanding his horizons, his stage activity contrasting with the conservative sets from support act Martha Reeves & The Vandellas [762], in which he employed synthesisers and keyboards extravagantly and, according to Jim Stewart, who attended the show, at one point took to singing into the microphone through a piece of tubing to affect his vocal *timbre*.[5] A month after "We Can Work It Out" was released, Wonder celebrated his 21st birthday, a coming-of-age which coincided with a period of self-transition important for his reassessment of his position within Motown. Supremely sure of his abilities, Wonder had effectively forced Berry Gordy to allow him substantial compositional responsibility, early fruits of which had been the *Signed Sealed And Delivered* album, which would culminate in his break with Motown's production-line system over the ensuing year [798]. In this context, this largely autonomous single marks a watershed for Wonder, breaking from his early career and pointing confidently towards the rest of the 1970s.

[1] He makes the claim in the DVD edition of the *Standing In The Shadows Of Motown* documentary.

[2] p216

[3] These Miracles numbers were probably selected by Harrison, whose love of Smokey Robinson is well-noted (see [949n]). For McCartney's part, he returned Wonder's compliment here by including the Braille message 'We love ya baby' on the cover of his 1973 album Red Rose Speedway. In the early 1980s the two collaborated on the tracks "What's That You're Doing" and "Ebony And Ivory", for McCartney's *Tug Of War*, the latter a major hit single. (McCartney followed these duets by writing and recording three songs with Michael Jackson.)

[4] These include for example, The Four Tops: "Eleanor Rigby", "The Fool On The Hill" and "Michelle"; The Temptations: "Hey Jude"; Marvin Gaye: "Yesterday"; Smokey Robinson: "And I Love Her" and so on. A number of these were collected and issued under the title *Motown Meets The Beatles* in 2001.

[5] See Abbott, p232.

**TMG 773**
**THE TEMPTATIONS**
**Just My Imagination (Running Away With Me)** (3:39)
(Whitfield—Strong)
Produced by Norman Whitfield
Recording completed: 3 Dec 1970
**Release Date**: 14 May 1971
**B-side**: You Make Your Own Heaven And Hell Right Here On Earth
**Position in Record Retailer Top 40**: 8
**Equivalent US Release**: Gordy 7105 (14 Jan 1971)
**Position in Billboard Top 40 Pop**: 1
**Position in Billboard Top 40 R & B**: 1

Otis Williams / Melvin Franklin / Paul Williams / Eddie Kendricks / Dennis Edwards

Arguably The Temptations' most enduring recording, "Just My Imagination" was knowingly crafted as a return to the group's "My Girl" [E67] period sound. In the half-decade since Norman Whitfield had taken control of the act's studio career, The Temptations' development had seen them metamorphosed from a polished team of immaculately-suited vocalists to social commentators in street wear, their recordings from 1968-onwards amounting to a re-creation of the act. And while their collaborations with the producer were often gripping, and at their best startlingly innovative, there remained amongst the group a yearning for a return to simpler times.

Conceding to Eddie Kendricks in particular, "Just My Imagination" was a 1968-vintage composition, which Whitfield offered up towards the end of 1970, and recorded in an intimate night session at Hitsville, Kendricks' atmospheric lead vocal captured at around dawn on December 4. A semi-hallucinatory account of unrequited love in which the central female is unaware of her secret admirer, "Just My Imagination" shares the airiness of Smokey Robinson's "My Girl" [E67], and perhaps borrows also from the middle-8 of the composer's contemporary "Yester Love" [661], whose 'Yester is the prefix that we fix to things that have gone by' is echoed here in the meter and pitching of the song's first verse.

Elated at the resultant track, The Temptations considered it more-or-less complete before Whitfield mixed in Jerry Long's orchestral overdubs, which took the track's romantic melancholy up several notches. The finished article, which Otis Williams acknowledges left the group 'knocked-out'[1], glides and moves mysteriously around its lulling fantasy, at times pensive and yet relentlessly calm, as if the narrator knows he is trapped in a harmless daydream. (The production as a whole is rightly acknowledged alongside "Papa Was A Rolling Stone" [839] as Whitfield's outstanding triumph with The Temptations.)

Released straight after Christmas in America, the single floated effortlessly to the top of every chart it could reach, marking a spectacular return to form. Yet once more, the public success concealed tension behind the scenes which almost dissolved the group in 1971. No sooner had "Just My Imagination" surfaced than lead singer Eddie Kendricks exited the group, apparently by mutual consent, and following a disastrous series of personal disputes with his colleagues which came to a head on stage at the Copa in December 1970. (His departure was officially announced in March 1971, prior to the UK release.) Wasting no time, the group road-tested Ricky Owens as a potential replacement before recruiting Damon Harris full time. And so the show went on, but more worrying yet was the condition of the other solo vocalist on "Just My Imagination", Paul Williams, whose personal life was taking a nose-dive due to an over-indulgence in drink and drugs which left him at times unable to fulfil his obligations as a full-time Temptation. His position would become untenable in the ensuing months [783].

Kendricks' last success with the group, "Just My Imagination" has gone down as one of Motown's all-time great ballads. Its popularity saw it re-released on Tamla Motown on October 10 1975 (with the same catalogue number), and it also attracted a noted cover from The Rolling Stones (*Some Girls*, 1978). And yet despite its success, the track proved to be a mere digression for The Temptations as, come 1972 they were back on the psychedelic war-path as if nothing had happened [800], lending to the impression that "Just My Imagination" had been a dream all along.

' p150


## TMG 774
## SMOKEY ROBINSON & THE MIRACLES
**I Don't Blame You At All** (2:57)
(Robinson)
Produced by William "Smokey" Robinson/Terry Johnson
Recording completed: 15 Jan 1971
**Release Date**: May 1971
**B-side**: That Girl
**Position in Record Retailer Top 40**: 11
**Equivalent US Release**: Tamla 54205 (30 Mar 1971)
**Position in Billboard Top 40 Pop**: 18
**Position in Billboard Top 40 R & B**: 7

---

Smokey Robinson / Bobby Rogers / Claudette Rogers Robinson /
Warren 'Pete' Moore / Ronnie White

---

After three successive oldies, Tamla Motown put The Miracles' releases back on course with [774], a 1971 recording lifted from *One Dozen Roses* (on which "The Tears Of A Clown" [745] inevitably resurfaced). However for UK fans, the release proved a false dawn, becoming Smokey Robinson's last single with the group before his departure in 1972 [811]. As Motown's Vice-President and Berry Gordy's closest confederate, Robinson was under pressure to follow his boss to LA, as it became increasingly apparent that Gordy was not coming back to Detroit. Initially dismissive of the idea, Robinson brooded during 1971 and by Christmas was still unconvinced, despite having by then wrapped up his recording career with The Miracles with just a swansong album, *Flying High Together*, left to complete.

"I Don't Blame You At All" is an unattractive number, stepping through its octave-wide-angled chorus determinedly. The track was co-penned with Terry Johnson, a former member of Chicago doo-wop group The Flamingos, whom Robinson had recruited for Motown in 1964 (see also [687]).


**TMG 775**
**MARVIN GAYE**
**What's Going On** (3:40)
(Cleveland—Benson—Gaye)
Produced by Marvin Gaye
Recording completed: 10 Jul 1970
**Release Date**: 28 May 1971
**B-side**: God Is Love
**Position in Record Retailer Top 40**: -
**Equivalent US Release**: Tamla 54201 (21 Jan 1971)
**Position in Billboard Top 40 Pop**: 2
**Position in Billboard Top 40 R & B**: 1

In the decades since "What's Going On" was first released, the recording, which Berry Gordy initially declared the worst he'd ever heard, has acquired a shroud of saintliness which has seen it lauded as the greatest black recording ever made, held up as the starting-point of 1970s soul itself, and was even once cited by Nelson Mandela as a spiritual crutch during his years of imprisonment. Much of the mystique surrounding the song has been the result of myth-making historical revisionism, Gordy himself stating "I loved what he had said. There was no way I was going to try and hold him back"[1], 24 years after blocking its release. Ben Edmonds meantime has hailed it as Motown's first true social commentary, dismissing in the process the company's album releases by Martin Luther King and others as 'more talk than action'.[2]

Yet how much of this is warranted? Commentators quick to deify the song routinely fail to acknowledge that, while credited as co-writer, Gaye's input into the lyric of "What's Going On" was probably negligible, the track penned in the main by Renaldo Benson of the Four Tops and staffer Al Cleveland. Benson has since claimed that he gave Gaye a co-writing credit as inducement to record the track, which was designed for The Originals[3] (see also [684]). Partly the misinterpretation stems from the perspective of hindsight which has given lines such as 'Brother, brother, brother, there's far too many of you dying' and 'Father, father, we don't need to escalate' a resonance with Gaye's private life in which his brother Frankie was traumatised from army duty [734] and his tempestuous relationship with Marvin Snr. led to his eventual murder. Coupled with the fact that, in the aftermath of Tammi Terrell's death Gaye was beginning to take an interest in matters both political and spiritual, the scenario is seductive but at-odds with the course of events in which "What's Going On" was repeatedly refused by Gaye, who eventually submitted to Obie Benson's pestering and dispatched the track in a hasty session on July 10.

How seriously Gaye took the song in 1970 is debatable. While the marijuana-filled atmosphere of the Snakepit lent proceedings a spacey, sensual quality which reverberates through the music, the fact that Gaye allowed two of his footballing associates [734] Mel Farr and Lem Barney to participate in the vocals suggests that he considered the session a throwaway. Indeed legend has it that a stoned James Jamerson played the bass part lying on his back, to say nothing of the fact that Gaye couldn't decide which of two lead vocals he preferred, in the end opting to chuck both into the mix, giving the song a ragged edge.

And yet it is precisely this sense of relaxed communality which allows the *soul* of "What's Going On" to filter through. (Gaye subsequent attempted a more formal vocal take with proper backing parts, but abandoned it on the realisation that the first version carried more feel.) In this context the key product of the session was the establishment of Gaye the producer, his self-supervision convincing him in a flash that he was not reliant on Motown and could direct and record his own material better by himself without Berry Gordy's authoritarian interference. (A parallel development was underway for Stevie Wonder at this point. See [755].)

Taking the completed tapes to Gordy with a sense of self-vindication, Gaye was stung by the hostility they received, his vengeful boss ready to shoot him down in flames. At once refusing to release the track, Gordy had halted Gaye's career development in its tracks, leading to a six-month stand-off during which Gaye recorded nothing further. At length, a resigned Gordy conceded the matter and, convinced that "What's Going On" would flop, sanctioned its release in the new year.

In some ways, "What's Going On" is a muddled creation. Caught between enlightenment and mystification, the lyric is tellingly non-committal, mentioning key social issues such as industrial conflict without any real purpose. (This tension is reflected in the fact that Obie Benson's question mark in the song's title was removed, leaving uncertainty as to whether Gaye is asking or telling us what's going on.) Nevertheless, in an America still feeling the shock of the civil unrest of the 1960s, the song's puzzling analysis rang a chord, and it rapidly began an ascent of the American charts, something Berry Gordy observed with mixed feelings. The single ended up spending five weeks atop the R&B listings, and was held off the summit of the pop chart only by "Just My Imagination" [773]. (Britain was largely uninterested, failing to take the single into the charts at all when released half a year later.)

Having slowly been recognised as Gaye's signature song, "What's Going On" was poignantly performed at the *Motown 25* special in 1983 and has since been reissued several times (see Chapter 6). The single most important track in his canon, "What's Going On" lends itself to interpretation, listeners able to project into the inconclusive lyrics any number of philosophical positions, something which has enabled the recording, while saying so little, to mean so much to more than one generation of listeners.

[1] p302
[2] p216
[3] Ritz, p193; Turner, p119.

**TMG 776**
**THE UNDISPUTED TRUTH**
Save My Love For A Rainy Day (3:30)
(Penzabene—Whitfield)
Produced by Norman Whitfield
**Release Date:** 4 Jun 1971
**B-side:** Since I've Lost You
**Position in Record Retailer Top 40:** -
**Equivalent US Release:** Gordy 7106 (2 Feb 1971)
**Position in Billboard Top 40 Pop:** -
**Position in Billboard Top 40 R & B:** -

---
Joe Harris / Billie Calvin / Brenda Evans
---

With Norman Whitfield's rise to pre-eminence in 1969-70, the producer was at his creative peak and actively scouting around Motown for artists to record his material. With his principle group The Temptations working at full capacity, Whitfield sought to manufacture his own act in 1971, bringing together two of his favoured female session vocalists, Billie Rae Calvin and Brenda Joyce Evans (who had featured on [751] and [754]) with local singer Joe Harris, launching the outfit with a back-to-back re-working of two earlier numbers.

"Save My Love For A Rainy Day" is archetypal Whitfield, pulling horizontally through its single-chord foundation, which The Temptations had first attempted on *With a Lot O' Soul* (1967). (The widely covered B-side is even older, dating to 1964.) Released without a splash in 1971, the single was a tentative start for a manufactured outfit who would strike gold in America with their follow-up [789]. Some UK editions of [776] sneaked out of EMI's pressing plant on Parlophone labels, making a novel curio for collectors.


**TMG 777**
**THE SUPREMES & FOUR TOPS**
River Deep, Mountain High (3:05)
(Spector—Barry—Greenwich)
Produced by Nickolas Ashford/Valerie Simpson
**Release Date:** 11 Jun 1971
**B-side:** It's Got To Be A Miracle (This Thing Called Love)
**Position in Record Retailer Top 40:** 11
**Equivalent US Release:** Motown 1173 (5 Nov 1970)
**Position in Billboard Top 40 Pop:** 14
**Position in Billboard Top 40 R & B:** 7

---
Jean Terrell / Cindy Birdsong / Mary Wilson / Levi Stubbs / Lawrence Payton /
Abdul 'Duke' Fakir / Renaldo 'Obie' Benson
---

Having milked The Supremes' temporary union with The Temptations to exhaustion in 1969-70, Motown were at it again in 1970, teaming up their premier female outfit with their most successful male group. Conceived as an

---

exercise to keep The Supremes' momentum up, the project shows Motown lacking faith in a remodelled outfit who had, by now, confirmed their ongoing commercial potential with a modest run of hit singles. This collaborative exercise was pursued through 1970, September's *The Magnificent 7* (UK: May 1971) pre-dating the appearance of the double act at London's Royal Albert Hall on November 30.

The first lift from the set, which comprised an odd smattering of oldies gathered from far-and-wide, was "River Deep, Mountain High", an old Brill Building classic [581n] immortalised via Ike and Tina Turner's 1966 reading.[1] Motown's remake expends little effort in trying to out-do the original, Motown's house-band locking effortlessly to the rhythm, with an unusually workmanlike Jean Terrell and Levi Stubbs taking a verse each. A flat-out album filler, the track's selection as the launch-pad for this group duo was mystifying, although interest in the respective acts saw it dragged laboriously into the top 20.

[1] The US release on Philles was not a significant hit. Its creator Phil Spector was thereby convinced that there was an industry-wide campaign against him, which provoked a four year 'retirement'.

**TMG 778**
**THE JACKSON 5**
**Never Can Say Goodbye** (2:56)
(Davis)
Produced by Hal Davis
**Release Date**: 2 Jul 1971
**B-side**: She's Good
**Position in Record Retailer Top 40**: 33
**Equivalent US Release**: Motown 1179 (16 Mar 1971)
**Position in Billboard Top 40 Pop**: 2
**Position in Billboard Top 40 R & B**: 1

Jackie Jackson / Tito Jackson / Jermaine Jackson / Marlon Jackson / Michael Jackson

Following the disappointing returns for "Mama's Pearl" [769], The Jackson 5's least successful release so far, Motown sought to re-direct the group with this, their most 'mature' single to date. Written by actor Clifton Davis, the song was an emotional catharsis for him, which he donated reluctantly, wishing he could have recorded it himself. Pricking up ears from the moment it was presented, the song was an obvious hit which The Supremes tried unsuccessfully to bag ahead of The Jackson 5.

Forced by Michael, the lyric's emotive intensity ill-suited a 12-year-old's style, not helped by the song's D pitching which pushed his thin tones to their upper limit. The result is oddly two-dimensional, Jackson at that point unable to comprehend the tangle of insoluble love in the lyric, at one point turning to Davis to enquire innocently what the word 'anguish' meant. Yet so persuasive is the raw material, with its alluring major 7ths and beguiling melody-line which ebbs and flows (down-beat where the singer is reflective, keyed-up where the torturous moments are admitted) that it rapidly became a standard. Within weeks of its American release of March, the number was picked up for a hit cover by Isaac Hayes, Gloria Gaynor following suit and a sprinkling of Motown acts recording their own versions.

With Hayes' rendition already in the US top 40, Tamla Motown sought to head-off the competition by releasing "Never Can Say Goodbye" as a UK summer single. What the group's British fans made of it is reflected in its poor chart showing, the group's second successive flop, and last chart entry for over a year [833]. Why their fan-base was losing interest so quickly—a mere 18 months after "I Want You Back" [724] had made such an impact—is puzzling all the same. Loyal beyond measure in the US, their home following remained strong at this stage, although it too would start to wobble under pressure from The Osmonds, who in various combinations scored a succession of major hits from early 1971.[1]

[1] See [769]. Their arrival in the UK would wait until 1972, whereupon they seriously undermined The Jackson 5's novelty within the pop arena.

**TMG 779**
**STEVIE WONDER**
**Never Dreamed You'd Leave In Summer** (2:53)
(Wonder—Wright)
Produced by Stevie Wonder
**Release Date**: 9 Jul 1971
**B-side**: If You Really Love Me
**Position in Record Retailer Top 40**: -
**Equivalent US Release**: Tamla 54202 (18 Feb 1971)
**Position in Billboard Top 40 Pop**: -
**Position in Billboard Top 40 R & B**: -

Following the musical liberation begun with "We Can Work It Out" [772], Wonder's career development turned a decisive corner in 1971, following his 21st birthday in May. While the products of his graduation from Motown's artistic control still lay ahead of him, there is no missing the direction he was heading in with *Where I'm Coming From*, his final work under his 1966 contract which he knowingly allowed to expire without re-signing. *Where I'm Coming From* was largely Wonder's own, Motown's involvement restricted to studio-arranging Wonder—Wright's nine new compositions, Wonder himself producing the set.

Sessions for this new album were protracted despite its creator moving for the first time towards the 'concept' scale, and as a result the album remains somewhat disjointed, its piecemeal recording generating a cross-section of styles. If there is a common thread, it is Wonder's gathering political radicalisation, the album hinting at social and military protest in its cover and lyrics, which in a rare move for Motown were published in full on the reverse.

"Never Dreamed You'd Leave In Summer" was released ahead of the set in the US, as the flip-side to [772] in February. In the UK it was held back until

July and issued as Wonder's 19th Tamla Motown single, as a direct trailer to the LP. In truth, the track selection in this respect was misjudged, the single lacking a commercial edge which, coupled with poor radio play, saw it collapse without trace. (Its B-side, [798], was a more obvious choice.)

Notwithstanding the song's lack of success, "Never Dreamed You'd Leave In Summer" remains one of Wonder's most poignant pieces. Delicately pitched, the track runs plaintively around its recurring lead motif which hugs closely to the keyboard-written melody line, with a yearning chord-change in the third line of the verse (edging up from the relaxed C/Fmaj7 axis to a distressing Dm). Mirroring the wistful harmonic, Wright's lyric tugs at the soul with its portrayal of loss, spoken from the depths of isolation without mustering the strength to mourn its broken heart.

Arranged with input from Paul Riser, the final touches involved the dubbing of subtle orchestration whose sadly winding oboe is the most effective single moment. It remains a pity that this miniaturised painting of lonely grief, with its classical framing, garnered such meagre attention in its day. Proof in any case, that Wonder was rapidly growing up.


**TMG 780**
**THE VELVELETTES**
**These Things Will Keep Me Loving You** (2:25)
**Re-issue of [580]**
**Release Date**: 16 Jul 1971
**Position in Record Retailer Top 40**: 34

---

Carolyn Gill / Sandra Tilley / Annette McMillan

---

The career development of Diana Ross in 1970-71 had an inadvertent benefit for some of her Motown colleagues, as the material provided for her from the Jobete catalogue drew attention to several old tracks. One of them was "These Things Will Keep Me Loving You", which Ross covered for her eponymous debut album while the original recording remained largely unknown in the UK, having never charted.

"These Things Will Keep Me Loving You" had been The Velvelettes' last single on both sides of the Atlantic in 1966 and yet despite a dearth of releases, the group had remained on Motown's books through the second half of the decade with a variety of line-ups before original member Carolyn Gill married future Temptation Richard Street [783] in 1969, at which point the group called it a day. It is a matter of historical curiosity that this re-issue was the group's most successful UK release, bettering two classics in the shape of [E61] and [E71] by entering the UK top 40.


**TMG 781**
**DIANA ROSS**
**I'm Still Waiting** (3:35)
(Richards)

Produced by Deke Richards/Hal Davis
**Release Date**: 23 Jul 1971
**B-side**: Reach Out I'll Be There
**Position in Record Retailer Top 40**: 1
**Equivalent US Release**: Motown 1192 (13 Oct 1971)
**Position in Billboard Top 40 Pop**: -
**Position in Billboard Top 40 R & B**: 40

Heavily pregnant with Berry Gordy's daughter, Diana Ross had gone into temporary hibernation in mid 1971, her recording career on hold and plans afoot to break into movies [848]. Ross gave birth to her first daughter Rhonda Suzanne by Caesarean section on 14 August, with her new album, *Surrender* just out in America, and keeping her career on schedule. With her previous album *Everything Is Everything* more or less overlooked, and a period of inactivity looming, fortune smiled when UK disc jockey and Motown fan Tony Blackburn[1] discovered "I'm Still Waiting" tucked within side 1 and began spinning it on national radio in a campaign to have it released as a belated single. Observing the resultant public clamour, Tamla Motown scheduled it for July 23, shifting the proposed single "Reach Out I'll Be There"—already released in America—to the flip-side. The strategy worked, "I'm Still Waiting" racing up the UK charts for a month-long stay at number 1, and becoming one of the label's all-time best sellers.

Penned by Deke Richards, the track was probably inspired by The Beatles' "Long And Winding Road" which had topped the US charts in mid 1970, and which Ross had covered under Richards' guidance on the concurrent *Everything Is Everything*. (The two songs feature a similar descending opening run and upturn at the start of the vocal line.) Built on a purely diatonic melody, "I'm Still Waiting" ranges dourly across six notes, cadencing repeatedly, until released by the high-poised bridge ('Little girl...'), pitched horizontally a fifth above the tonic.

But the track's strong point is its novel lyric which twists the hackneyed infatuation/break-up theme by recounting the tale of a girl whose innocent playground sweetheart is snatched from her by a family move. Promising her that some day her true love will arrive and replace him, he leaves unaware that now grown, she remains unable to relinquish the love she once felt, rejecting latter-day lovers in the face of advice from all quarters and imploring him to return. While intensely sentimental, Richards' text is genuinely tender, Gene Page's string arrangement aptly wistful, and thereby more sympathetic to the composition than had been Richard Hewson's parallel work on The Beatles' earlier recording.

So immense was the single's impact in Britain that it was shoe-horned onto the start of the forthcoming *Surrender* as an extra track, with the set rechristened after the song (which thereby appears on successive studio albums by Ross). It has since been re-issued as TMG 1041 when it charted again, and was re-mixed in 1990 on Motown's blue label, making the UK top 50 for a third time (see Appendix 2). (The 1971 B-side was also popular and resurfaced on the 1978 LP *Ross*.)

The success of "I'm Still Waiting", more than any other single recording, accounts for Motown's 1970s fixation with the 'big ballad' style, and consequently the company's late reputation for slick production on an over-grand scale. Motown's technically advanced, LA-centric operation had none of the pressures of Detroit's single-studio set-up, musicians and producers no longer working with a sense of urgency, Motown's product from here on entering a steady and irreversible decline in excitement levels.

¹ He had provided sleeve notes to 1968's *British Motown Chartbusters Volume 2*.


**TMG 782**
**THE SUPREMES**
**Nathan Jones** (2:58)
(Caston—Wakefield)
Produced by Frank Wilson
**Release Date**: 13 Aug 1971
**B-side**: Happy (Is A Bumpy Road)
**Position in Record Retailer Top 40**: 5
**Equivalent US Release**: Motown 1182 (15 Apr 1971)
**Position in Billboard Top 40 Pop**: 16
**Position in Billboard Top 40 R & B**: 8

| Jean Terrell / Cindy Birdsong / Mary Wilson |
| --- |

"Nathan Jones" was composed by staff writers Kenny Wakefield and Leonard Caston, and recorded in orthodox vein as part of the ongoing *Touch* sessions. The bare bones of the song are a standard F blues structure which bubbles mysteriously through the chorus sections courtesy of an evasive Cm. Sung by Jean Terrell, the vocal is tracked throughout by a 'harmony' which adds a sense of extra-dimensionalism around a narrative on absent love (reminiscent of the theme of "Jimmy Mack" [599], which also names the boy in question), beefed up with jazzy brass in verse 2.

Stockpiled amongst the group's pending album cuts, a tape of "Nathan Jones" was plucked out by Russ Terrana who had recently developed a phasing technique which he wished to show to Frank Wilson. Intending to use the effect elsewhere, the accidental result of its deployment on the randomly selected "Nathan Jones" impressed both men to such an extent that producer Wilson elected to retain it in the final mix.¹ Thus "Nathan Jones" continued The Supremes' recent emphasis on 60s-style beats accentuated with modern studio sounds [760], which provide an indefinably spacey sheen (particularly prominent in the *outro*) and which caught the ear of UK pop listeners. (Why Tamla Motown opted for a mono mix as a single release is unclear.)

Somewhat daringly, the track was released more-or-less head-to-head with Diana Ross' "I'm Still Waiting" [781], and entered the charts on the day Ross' ballad hit top-spot. An impressive top 5 placing justified the adventurous studio mix, and ushered in The Supremes' UK tour in which they appeared at the Royal Albert Hall (see [777]). *Touch* meantime had surfaced but was met with a cool reception despite The Supremes enjoying a period of success in the singles listings.

A late footnote for "Nathan Jones" was its reappearance in 1988 as recorded by Bananarama. Having racked up 18 UK hit singles, the group were on the verge of breaking the record for a British female outfit, selecting the track for their next release as an open acknowledgement of The Supremes, who held the overall UK chart record. The remake went to number 15.

<sup>1</sup> He is quoted by Dahl (p153) as mistakenly ascribing the effect to a synthesiser unit recently constructed by Motown employee Cal Harris.


**TMG 783**
**THE TEMPTATIONS**
**It's Summer** (2:58)
(Whitfield—Strong)
Produced by Norman Whitfield
Recording completed: 24 May 1971
**Release Date**: 27 Aug 1971
**B-side**: Ungena Za Ulimwengu (Unite The World)
**Position in Record Retailer Top 40**: -
**Equivalent US Release**: Gordy 7109 (24 Jun 1971)
**Position in Billboard Top 40 Pop**: -
**Position in Billboard Top 40 R & B**: 29

---

Otis Williams / Melvin Franklin / Paul Williams / Dennis Edwards

---

Originally recorded by Gladys Knight & The Pips for their *Nitty Gritty* album, "It's Summer" was conceived as a light-hearted idyll, and was put out early as the B-side to the conceptually opposite "I Wish It Would Rain" [674]. Letting it rest for over a year, Norman Whitfield then took the composition to The Temptations who laid down a take in early 1970 during sessions for *Psychedelic Shack*. This time the producer decorated the recording with songbirds and had Melvin Franklin 'narrate' proceedings, the resultant track ultimately slight if entertaining. This new version was also requisitioned for a flip-side, to that September's "Ball Of Confusion" [749], and offered a relaxing counterpoint to its intense A-side.

Since then, The Temptations had scored with the more gentle "Just My Imagination" [773] and, sniffing a potential hit, Whitfield fancied he could get *more* mileage from "It's Summer" and set about another remake. Taking The Temptations back into the studio on 24 May 1971, he arranged the track more formally, with Dennis Edwards handling vocals and Jerry Long providing orchestral arrangement. This time, the dreamy ballad was issued as an A-side at the height of the holiday season, but quite why it was considered worthy of such generous attention is puzzling; while pleasant enough, none of the existing renditions are particularly remarkable and the direct quote from George Gershwin's "Summertime" in its middle-8 hints unsubtly at its original inspiration.

The song's public reception was luke-warm, and the release proved a

---

failure, mitigated by the inclusion of the earlier US single "Ungena Za Ulimwengu" (Swahili for "Unite The World") as an attractive B-side. Recorded in August 1970, the track featured a group line-up which included Eddie Kendricks, the song having already been pulled from *Sky's The Limit* for a US single, earning dubious distinction as the group's first in six years to fall short of the US top 30 pop. Confusing in its arrangement, the track commences with a Kinks-style fuzz-guitar riff before sliding into a blues harmonica wail, Barrett Strong's most overt call for racial equality, the world united 'hand in hand, black and white', emerging from this curious introduction. (Reflecting the climate of the day, the major threat to this vision of global union comes after half a minute, Melvin Franklin posing the conundrum, 'Will the Russians push the button?')

In the context of its lyrics, the title's translation into an African language was entirely relevant, if a little difficult for record-buyers to swallow. The single's poor showing revealed the first substantial crack in the Temptations/Norman Whitfield union, after three turbulent years for the group but, despite this warning sign, attracted enough interest in the UK to usurp [783a]. After the manner of [690] and [692], Tamla Motown recognised their initial error and elected to re-distribute the single, with the B-side promoted as the 'hit' recording, for a new launch on 26 November 1971.

Between its recording and its release, original Temptation Paul Williams had succumbed to a drug and alcohol dependency which compounded his worsening health due to sickle cell anaemia. Eventually realising that his performing and recording career was suffering to the extent that the group itself was compromised, Williams departed the act during 1971, the third of the 'classic' line up to do so in as many years. Yet unlike his former band-mates David Ruffin and Eddie Kendricks, the prospect of a solo career seemed unlikely and as time would tell, Williams never recovered his health [866]. For The Temptations, a replacement was rapidly drafted in, former early colleague and Williams' understudy Richard Street selected and in the studio with the rest of the group before year-end. And so the show continued, The Temptations masking the fact that 60 percent of the original act was now absent even more successfully than had the similarly afflicted Supremes.

**TMG 784**
**JIMMY RUFFIN**
**On The Way Out (On The Way In)** (2:36)
(Dean—Weatherspoon)
Produced by James Dean/William Weatherspoon
Recording completed: 28 Aug 1969
**Release Date**: 20 Aug 1971
**B-side**: Honey Come Back
**Position in Record Retailer Top 40**: -
**No Equivalent US Release**

Jimmy Ruffin's final Tamla Motown single (barring re-issues) was another unremarkable recording in his usual style, lifted like its predecessor "Let's Say

Goodbye Tomorrow" [767] from *The Groove Governor*. (The single shows no producer credit, but is likely the work of James Dean and William Weatherspoon, who was on the verge of leaving Motown for a reunion with HDH in their Invictus corporation.) Even Ruffin's devoted British followers could take no more, and largely ignored this limping UK-only single, which was paired with another album track, his recording of the 1970 Chuck Jackson single "Honey Come Back" [729].

Ruffin's contract expired in 1971 and the UK-based singer entered a period of semi-retirement. He would re-emerge in 1974 after signing with Polydor, whereupon Tamla Motown unsurprisingly re-discovered an interest in the singer's back catalogue [911]; [922].

**TMG 785**
**THE FOUR TOPS**
**Simple Game** (2:49)
(Pinder)
Produced by Tony Clarke
Recording completed: 5 May 1970
**Release Date**: 10 Sep 1971
**B-side**: You Stole My Love
**Position in Record Retailer Top 40**: 3
**Equivalent US Release**: Motown 1196 (4 Jan 1972)
**Position in Billboard Top 40 Pop**: -
**Position in Billboard Top 40 R & B**: 34

---

Levi Stubbs / Lawrence Payton / Abdul 'Duke' Fakir / Renaldo 'Obie' Benson

---

On tour in the UK in the spring of 1970 [736], The Four Tops came off stage from one of their London engagements on May 4, to be accosted by Tony Clarke, producer of UK rock group The Moody Blues. (The US-based Four Tops reputedly did not know who he was.) Having heard the Tops' current single "It's All In The Game" [736], Clarke had taken it upon himself to foist a demo of the similarly philosophical "Simple Game" on the group, the number recently penned by The Moody Blues' keyboard player Mike Pinder. Knocked-out by what they heard, the Tops and their entourage arranged to visit Clarke the following day to make a recording of the song, for which Clarke had presumed to pre-record a backing track.

Convening at Wessex Studios in Highbury on the morning of May 5, The Four Tops found that the tapes, arranged by Art Greenslade, were in a fortunately suitable key at which Clarke's team had taken an educated guess. With members of The Moody Blues and British band Blue Mink in attendance, the vocal was duly polished off and the studio ensemble set about a couple of other tracks, including the B-side here, a Clarke composition, and the subsequently released "So Deep Within You" [850], before parting ways. Transferring a rough mix of "Simple Game" onto cassette for between-gig listening, The Four Tops resumed their UK tour, and the master tapes were shipped over to Motown for a final mix-down.

What emerged from the day's work was a powerhouse 'rock' ballad which was the group's most forceful single in several years. Despite sharing a perspective with [736] that life itself was merely a passively observed recreation, the urgency of the performance suggests that this conclusion, far from being defeatist, was a source of inspiration and that, by playing along, the world could find liberation from imagined constraint and hence achieve spiritual freedom. (In this sense, elements of the Buddhist 'awakening' are suggested, Pinder's lyric tapping into the then-widespread penchant for Eastern mysticism amongst Western youth, which has its origins in the 1960s counterculture and which was hanging-over in certain quarters until well into the 1970s when a generalised disillusionment took hold.)

"Simple Game" inexplicably sat in the can for over a year before Tamla Motown released it as a stand-alone single, most likely as a by-product of Tony Clarke's then recent work for the Rare Earth label. Its timing kept another cover, "MacArthur Park", off the British schedules, which following its poor showing Stateside was never picked up for UK release. "Simple Game" meantime became a major hit for the group, bettered in chart terms only by "Reach Out I'll Be There" [579], and was inevitably earmarked for a corresponding American edition in the new year.

## TMG 786
## R. DEAN TAYLOR
### Ain't It A Sad Thing
(Taylor)
Produced by R. Dean Taylor
**Release Date**: NOT RELEASED
**B-side**: Back Street
**Equivalent US Release**: Rare Earth 5023 (19 Jan 1971)
**Position in Billboard Top 40 Pop**: -
**Position in Billboard Top 40 R & B**: -

The US Rare Earth label, unlike Motown's other imprints, had a defined autonomy within the organisation (see [742]) which naturally lent to the suggestion that a UK branch could be established. Incredibly this took two years to organise, and when arrangements were eventually worked out, the label arrived in Britain. The development was significant: until now all UK Motown product had appeared on an exclusive imprint at any given time, but now there were two running in parallel, which raised the prospect of further labels being established, as was the case in America. (Indeed a second UK sub-division arrived in 1972 [828].)

In the period to mid-1971, only two American Rare Earth releases had been selected as Tamla Motown singles: [742] and [763].[1] A third was lined up in R. Dean Taylor's "Ain't It A Sad Thing", but with the label's British launch imminent, the single was requisitioned as the first outing for Rare Earth-UK, leaving TMG 786 vacant in the Tamla Motown sequence. (So late in the day did the switch come that Rare Earth pressings show a tell-tale 'TMG 786' stamped in the run-out groove.) Self-made by Taylor with David Van DePitte,

"Ain't It A Sad Thing" was a weak debut for the new British label, its country dance flavour and nonchalant whistled sections accentuating a sense of do-it-yourself casualness.

Rare Earth-UK was able to put out around 20 singles before being wound up in 1975, including a second from R. Dean Taylor and ten British recordings from a succession of obscure acts who never recorded for Motown in America. See Appendix 3 for details.

[1] The American label also released [656], which had already appeared on Tamla Motown in 1968.


## TMG 787
## THE ELGINS
**Put Yourself In My Place** (2:25)
**2nd Re-issue of [551]**
**Release Date**: 17 Sep 1971
**New B-side**: Little Miss Sweetness
**Position in Record Retailer Top 40**: 28

---

Saundra Mallett Edwards / Cleo 'Duke' Miller / Johnny Dawson / Robert Fleming

---

Having made a significant impact with the re-released "Heaven Must Have Sent You" [771], The Elgins had re-formed in 1971 and embarked on a UK tour, with Yvonne Allen drafted in to replace original singer Saundra Edwards, who was by now retired from performing. Modestly successful, the exposure this gained prompted Tamla Motown to tap into the group's catalogue once again, providing an unprecedented *third* release for "Put Yourself In My Place", which this time charted.

This new edition carried a replacement B-side, a version of "Little Miss Sweetness" which The Temptations had also recorded in 1966 [587b]. It would be the last single released by The Elgins, before a re-constituted group by the same name arrived at Ian Levine's MotorCity label in the late 1980s [683n]. Yvonne Allen fronted this late incarnation, Saundra Edwards by then also recording for the label as a soloist.


## TMG 788
## BARBARA RANDOLPH
**I Got A Feeling** (2:58)
**Re-issue of [628]**
**Release Date**: 24 Sep 1971
**Position in Record Retailer Top 40**: -

A week after [787] appeared, Tamla Motown delivered another re-issue in the shape of Barbara Randolph's much-underrated "I Got A Feeling", originally put out in 1967. Randolph had recorded little else, and in the intervening years had appeared on stage alongside Marvin Gaye, deputising for the then sick Tammi Terrell. Why

---

[787] was selected for re-release is unclear, the single once again flopping and Randolph, who was now recording elsewhere, remaining in obscurity.

In recent years Motown have unearthed several recordings by her which have surfaced on latter-day CD collections. The current title was released by Tamla Motown for a third time in 1979 [L013] (see Chapter 6), marking the re-birth of the label after some years of retirement.

## TMG 789
## THE UNDISPUTED TRUTH
**Smiling Faces Sometimes** (3:16)
(Whitfield—Strong)
Produced by Norman Whitfield
**Release Date**: 8 Oct 1971
**B-side**: You Got The Love I Need
**Position in Record Retailer Top 40**: -
**Equivalent US Release**: Gordy 7108 (13 May 1971)
**Position in Billboard Top 40 Pop**: 3
**Position in Billboard Top 40 R & B**: 2

---

Joe Harris / Billie Calvin / Brenda Evans

---

Recorded by The Temptations for *Sky's The Limit*,[1] "Smiling Faces Sometimes" was unleashed as a 12-minute-plus epic, shortly before The Undisputed Truth unveiled their own recording of the song, a wilfully 'down' version whose cloudy atmosphere conjures a sense of shady double-dealing and opaque intentions. Ostensibly about basic human mistrust (and arriving a few months before The O'Jays' "Backstabbers", which references "Smiling Faces Sometimes" in its closing lyrics) some interpreted the song's web of intrigue as an oblique comment on the dubious Nixon administration which was eventually found out through the Watergate scandal, exposing a plethora of illegal and deceitful activity throughout the early 1970s.

But while this reading accords with Barrett Strong's lyrical themes at the time, there is little specific in "Smiling Faces Sometimes" which fits the notion. Quoted in Dahl (p325) Strong implies that the lyric has more to do with personal life within the music industry, and his clever turn-around of the phrase 'a smile is just a frown turned upside down' at 1:19, from cheery pick-me-up to guarded warning references an early track from rival Smokey Robinson.[2]

So effective was Whitfield's production here, and lead singer Joe Harris' performance, that the recording captivated American audiences, and made The Undisputed Truth a minor sensation. Sadly they never recaptured this moment of sublime potency.

[1] Subsequently released on 45: [832].

[2] This casual musical quotation continues a stream of similar instances in Strong's recent texts, including "Give Peace A Chance" on [764] and "Summertime" on [783a].

**TMG 790**

**EDWIN STARR**

**Agent Double O Soul** (2:45)

(Starr—Sharpley)

Produced by William Sanders

**Release Date**: 15 Oct 1971

**B-side**: Back Street

**Position in Record Retailer Top 40**: -

**No Equivalent US Release**

*Originally released as Ric Tic RT-103 (Jul 1965)*

Interrupting a sequence of Whitfield—Strong creations which had entirely modernised Edwin Starr's sound, Tamla Motown elected to release this 1965 track which the singer had recorded while still under contract to Ric Tic (see [630]). In its day the recording had fared well on the US R & B charts, assisted by the clandestine presence of Motown's Funk Brothers during one of their legendary moonlight flits.

"Agent Double O Soul" was largely written by Starr himself (with help from Bill Sharpley), inspired by the current James Bond movie which he chanced to see three times during a break from touring in New York.[1] Subverting the phrase 'Agent 007', Starr took the raw composition to his band The Bill Doggett Combo but was fobbed off, prompting him to walk out and hook up instead with Ed Wingate. Thus, Starr and "Agent Double O Soul" arrived on the Detroit scene.

Six years later, with Gordy having purchased Ric Tic, Tamla Motown were able to pass-off the track as a Motown original, this first UK release playing up to the singer's Northern Soul following. It was followed soon afterwards by another exhumed oldie from the same archive (see [795]).

[1] This was most likely *Goldfinger*, which opened in the US in December 1964, "Agent Double O Soul" released between this and the follow-up *Thunderball*.


**TMG 791**

**RITA WRIGHT**

**I Can't Give Back The Love I Feel For You** (2:38)

**Re-issue of [643]**

**Release Date**: Oct 1971

**Position in Record Retailer Top 40**: -

Like "These Things Will Keep Me Loving You" [780], this latest re-issue (Tamla Motown's sixth of 1971) was prompted by a recent Diana Ross version, included on *Surrender* (about to be released in the UK as *I'm Still Waiting*— see [781]). In fact, her rendition had been made under the auspices of The Supremes, taped on July 28 1969 with the other group members in attendance, although it had been shelved for the duration of Ross' time with the outfit. With this belated release, and anticipation of renewed interest in the song, and with Syreeta currently in the media thanks to her marriage and musical collaborations with Stevie Wonder, the decision was made to dust down the original version and chance a new edition, with the 1968 B-side intact. The recording again made little impact but was welcomed by Northern fans who had missed it the first time around.

**TMG 792**
**DIANA ROSS**
**Surrender** (2:53)
(Ashford—Simpson)
Produced by Nickolas Ashford/Valerie Simpson
**Release Date**: 22 Oct 1971
**B-side**: I'm A Winner
**Position in Record Retailer Top 40**: 10
**Equivalent US Release**: Motown 1188 (29 Jul 1971)
**Position in Billboard Top 40 Pop**: 38
**Position in Billboard Top 40 R & B**: 16

1971 had been a major year in the career of Diana Ross, with three sizeable hits to her credit and her consequent establishment as a major contemporary recording star. In the wake of the spectacular "I'm Still Waiting" [781], the UK screening of *Diana!* on BBC television in September consolidated the singer's position as one of Motown's premier attractions, the hour-long show giving Ross an opportunity to display her character acting talents and also air several of her solo hits (including "Ain't No Mountain High Enough" [751] and "Remember Me" [768]). Providing a platform for The Jackson 5 and several guests including Bill Cosby to join in this wanton celebration of success, the show served to prime the public for Ross' big-screen debut in 1973 [848] which would further propel her beyond the sphere of mere Motown vocalist.

The concurrent single "Surrender" was provided by the reliable Ashford—Simpson team and recorded as the original title track of Ross' summer album *I'm Still Waiting*. Apparently constructed in two separate sections, "Surrender" commences with a crotchet snare over which a tunelessly quirky text pans out, before blooming into an "Ain't No Mountain High Enough" [751] style chorus, the two elements clumsily welded together with a stuttering chromatic bass run. And while the verses are ineffectual, it is the resounding chorus which salvages the recording, borrowing from [751] the same C/Bb/G descent, over which the lyric to "Ain't No Mountain High Enough" can be exactly sung.

But for some minor recordings with The Supremes & Four Tops, this blatant re-write would be the last product from the Ashford & Simpson team who had served Ross so well since her break into solo stardom, with Valerie Ashford by now recording in her own right [768]. Diana Ross had made it through this pivotal year and emerged victorious, undaunted by an uncertain period ahead in which she would need to find new writer-producers to sustain her singing career.

For a single, the track was paired with an aptly selected Supremes leftover [791] and, unusually, issued in both mono and stereo editions.

**TMG 793**
**THE SUPREMES & FOUR TOPS**
**You Gotta Have Love In Your Heart** (2:48)
(Zesses—Fekaris)
Produced by Clay McMurray
**Release Date**: 5 Nov 1971
**B-side**: I'm Glad About It
**Position in Record Retailer Top 40**: 25
**Equivalent US Release**: Motown 1181 (11 May 1971)
**Position in Billboard Top 40 Pop**: -
**Position in Billboard Top 40 R & B**: -

---

Jean Terrell / Cindy Birdsong / Mary Wilson / Levi Stubbs / Lawrence Payton / Abdul 'Duke' Fakir / Renaldo 'Obie' Benson

---

Following the lack-lustre *The Magnificent Seven*, this pairing of two premier vocal groups spawned a second album in November, *The Return Of...* heralding another 11 titles wrapped in a cover portraying the personnel ludicrously dressed as cowboys and -girls. This plodding trailer-single featured the lead-tracks from each side, "You Gotta Have Love In Your Heart" a mid-tempo sing-along built on a descending bass line. An unimpressive selection, it staggered to 25 in the charts and in the US reached a derisory 154, which Mary Wilson later described as 'an embarrassment for all of us'.[1]

[1] 1990, p56

**TMG 794**
**MARTHA REEVES & THE VANDELLAS**
**Bless You** (2:58)
(The Corporation)
Produced by The Corporation
**Release Date**: 12 Nov 1971
**B-side**: Hope I Don't Get My Heart Broke
**Position in Record Retailer Top 40**: 33
**Equivalent US Release**: Gordy 7110 (14 Sep 1971)
**Position in Billboard Top 40 Pop**: -
**Position in Billboard Top 40 R & B**: 29

---

Martha Reeves / Lois Reeves / Sandra Tilley

---

With an introductory guitar suggesting the electrifying opening to "I Want You Back" [724][1], "Bless You" appears to offer a bright new beginning for Martha Reeves, who had released no new singles in the UK in three years [669]. Supplied by The Corporation with direct interest from Berry Gordy, the final production, archetypal for the team, leans unmistakably towards their recent work with The Jackson 5 and yet this quasi-benediction also hints at the classic Supremes sound, arranged against an energetic hand-clapping and tambourine-shaking backing track complete with baritone sax break: in either context Berry Gordy's input is pervasive. (The percussion arrangement conspires to provide both a slow lolloping rhythm and an high-tempo energy simultaneously.)

Bang up-to-date and acting as a springboard for the forthcoming *Black Magic* the release is, on the face of it, indicative of re-birth, Reeves apparently reconciled with Gordy and her emotional troubles behind her. Yet this apparent positivity, welcomed by Motown's marketing machine, concealed an unresolved turbulence which would rapidly reach boiling point. Behind the scenes Reeves was continuing to struggle with the free availability of cocaine, fashionable in Hollywood, which got the better of her once too often when she collapsed in the street and suffered convulsions. Hospitalised, the troubled singer was in a perilous condition and following an altercation with medical staff ended up in a strait jacket, locked for days in a padded cell. According to her own account of the period[2], Reeves received few well-wishers.

This second personal crisis [694] convinced Berry Gordy that Reeves was beyond immediate help. On discharge, the singer visited Gordy at his office on Sunset Boulevard with her hospital wristband still on, and was ordered in no uncertain terms to 'go away and get well'. This latest event effectively spelled the end for Reeves and Motown, Gordy resolving to wash his hands of the group, Reeves later claiming that she stopped being paid royalties at this stage[3], a legal tussle inevitably ensuing [843]. In-the-can was much of *Black Magic*, which saw light of day in early 1972, with one US and no UK trailer-singles, thereby marking the permanent demise of the act.

[1] A version of "I Want You Back" was included on the group's follow-up single in America.
[2] p179-83
[3] As quoted in Marsh, p66.

## TMG 795
## THE SAN REMO STRINGS
**Festival Time** (2:31)
(Bratton—Bunton)
Producer unaccredited
**Release Date**: 26 Nov 1971
**B-side**: All Turned On
**Position in Record Retailer Top 40**: 39
**Equivalent US Release**: Gordy 7060 (6 Apr 1967)
**Position in Billboard Top 40 Pop**: -
**Position in Billboard Top 40 R & B**: -

Holidaying in northern Italy, Ric Tic proprietors Joanne Bratton (who co-wrote the present track) and Ed Wingate were struck by the picturesque resort of Sanremo, and while there noted the annual Festival of Italian Song, which had been hosted by the town each year since 1953. On their return they created a studio outfit which consisted of members of the Detroit Symphony Orchestra (at that stage led by Bob Wilson) recording alongside a standard band section (usually including various Funk Brothers), who they named after the town for no other reason than fond memory.

The first single released in the guise of the newly formed outfit (then going by the name The San Remo Golden Strings) was the pre-existing instrumental "Hungry For Love", already used as a Barbara Mercer flip-side, followed by an album of the same name. A couple more singles ensued over the next few months, one of which, a casually throbbing instrumental, was appropriately named "Festival Time", in further reference to their Italian sojourn.

Produced by the Solid Hitbound company, run by Lebaron Taylor and Don Davis and released by Ric Tic in April 1966, the track was noted as a potential hit, the label therefore electing to dub a vocal onto the basic track to create a more commercially viable soul dancer which was released as "To Win Your Heart", head-to-head with the original. Soon thereafter Berry Gordy's company takeover occurred [630] and he acquired both versions. Unusually opting for an instant re-issue, the original instrumental was favoured and put out on the Gordy label in April 1967. Some years elapsed before Tamla Motown elected to follow suit, this late-1971 edition their second from the Ric Tic archives in a matter of weeks [790]. (Laura Lee's vocal interpretation would duly follow [831].)


**TMG 796**
**MARVIN GAYE**
**Save The Children** (4:01)
(Cleveland—Gaye—Benson)
Produced by Marvin Gaye
Recording completed: 31 Mar 1971
**Release Date**: 26 Nov 1971
**B-side**: Little Darling (I Need You) [574]
**Position in Record Retailer Top 40**: -
**No Equivalent US Release**


There is no doubting the personal transformation undergone by Marvin Gaye since the close of 1969. This had seen his recording career effectively dry up, only "What's Going On" [775] revealing he had not retired completely. Away from the clamouring public, the singer was becoming a virtual recluse, absorbed in a private world of spiritual enlightenment in which he came to see personal success as trivial in the context of the historic destiny of humankind, something which began to invade his thought processes continuously. Few around him could miss this change in attitude, reflected in his dispensing with sharp suits and trappings of luxury in favour of a knowingly messianic modesty of appearance which if nothing else brought him closer to audience-level. And as if to prove that he lay beyond Gordy's control, he took to wearing a selection of woolly hats (probably to mask his developing baldness) and gave up shaving, sprouting a patchy beard through 1971.

Whether his career was still salvageable was impossible to say. Certainly he had lost a passion for performing, although with [775] he appeared to have *something* deep within which needed public expression, few aware at this stage what it was, least of all Gaye himself who began sessions which resulted in the *What's Going On* album unclear on what he wished to achieve. Fumbling his way through 10 days of self-guided recording split between Hitsville and Studio B, Gaye had started off without co-conspirators Al Cleveland and Obie Benson, aware that he had at most four weeks to get this new album finished, having already accepted a filming commission in LA in early April.[1]

Essentially making it up as he went, Gaye appears to have opened out the session to everyone and anyone present, uninterested in providing his musicians with formal instruction. Whether as an exercise in free organic expression or simply born of his legendary laziness, Gaye was by all accounts intermittently stoned on cannabis, seeming to care little about how the new material was being recorded, satisfied in his vague conception of doing something 'different' and letting chance dictate the rest. Fortunately he had a crack band available in The Funk Brothers, who revelled in the artistic freedom and helped develop the progressing tracks by throwing spontaneous ideas around, some of which Gaye picked up on and retained.[2]

More-or-less finished by March 26, Gaye entered Studio B over a three-day period to 'direct' the final vocals. Ben Edmonds' account of the sessions has the studio lights down, Gaye wandering around the floor with a hand-held microphone, creating mock advertisements for cannabis with his giggling cohorts between takes.[3] The singer was apparently continuously smoking joints which, while against Motown's direct instruction, put all concerned in sufficiently relaxed and creative mood to capture the vocal tracks in a suitably elevated state which comes through on the finished album.

As might have been expected given relations in the spring of 1971, Berry Gordy's initial reaction was dismissive. Unfamiliar with the proposed LP's contents, he was less than impressed on first hearing and arguing that Gaye's selling point was a sexual allure, informed him that the album was unsuitable for release. Gaye though had a key ally in his wife Anna, Gordy's sister, and as a result of her badgering Gordy's stance was reluctantly changed. Grudgingly approved and finally mixed in LA on May 6, *What's Going On* was released in haste 15 days later, housed in a cover depicting a close-up Gaye contemplating life in the snow and rain of his own back garden.

Causing low-level ripples in America, *What's Going On* was a top 10 album over the summer, welcomed by critics and fans alike, but was almost completely overlooked in the UK (where the release was delayed until September). At home, the set constituted a resounding success for its creator who, in defeating Gordy's insistence that it would fail, had taken another decisive step in breaking Motown's hold over him. But while the album was a big seller in 1971, its importance has since been talked up into the stratosphere, *What's Going On* today routinely cited as one of the greatest albums *ever*.

In truth, this procession of quasi-spiritual commentary, set against a generally changeless swill of percussion and strings, shows an emphasis on presentation over substance. Many of its 'political' stances show little depth of understanding and are at times trite. (Witness the current song, in which Gaye remarks 'Let's save all the children', as if such common concern were something extraordinary, or the line in its title track, 'War is not the answer' which while to-the-point, is hardly profound insight, or for that matter original.) Similarly, its gathering legend has found several inaccurate myths grow up around it including the erroneous and widely repeated claim that it was the last thing recorded at Hitsville, and that it was Motown's first album to feature printed lyrics or credit its backroom staff.[4]

More significantly, *What's Going On*'s latter-day hype has seen its artistic shortcomings routinely ignored or glossed over, Ben Edmonds for example calling the somewhat turgid album, "More than the black *Sgt Pepper*... it goes *Pet Sounds* one better... it is a pop symphony to God".[5] Given the directionless drift of the sessions, it must be clear that unlike *Sgt Pepper* and *Pet Sounds*, *What's Going On* came about with no clear artistic aim in mind, and yet biographer Steve Turner has paraphrased Gaye's claim that the LP "was an attempt to unlock areas of music that hadn't been unlocked before, to touch on new dimensions of sound that had previously been unimaginable."[6] Not bad for a week-and-a-half's work commenced in a frivolously unguided manner.

The first single released from the album in the UK (apart from the premature [775]) was "Save The Children", the fourth song on side 1. Perhaps taking its lyrical theme from Gaye's late fear of Biblical apocalypse, the text is a blank plea for inter-human consideration, which Gaye admitted used the subject of children solely as a focal point. Agreeing that the stance was poignant, the three writers involved each set about composing their own lyrics which, by process of comparison and piecemeal deletion, were amalgamated to the necessary length. The resultant lyrical collage includes several spoken sections, including a somewhat melodramatic introduction predicting a time when flowers will cease to grow, and declaring the world 'destined to die'.

The number was recorded in Studio A on the first day's work on the album (March 17) and characteristically floats aimlessly for about four minutes without elaborating on a solution to the world's problems. Usually cited as one of *What's Going On*'s key tracks, the single was passed over in America where "Mercy Mercy Me" [802] was preferred, and in the UK was paired with a conservative B-side, originally put out in 1966 [574]. Although it didn't chart, the song was revived in 1974 for a charity concert and film project at the behest of Rev. Jesse Jackson. See [917].

---

[1] The film was *Chrome And Hot Leather*, a poorly received biker movie directed by Lee Frost, whose Vietnam War subtext had relevance for Gaye.

[2] He is quoted in George (p177) as likening the process to 'building', "Like an artist paints a picture" (sic).

[3] p177-80

[4] Each of these claims is demonstrably false: Hitsville continued functioning for several years after the LP was completed, Norman Whitfield for example using it through 1973 and The Commodores' *Machine Gun* recorded there as late as 1974 [902]. So far as the sleeve details go, Stevie Wonder had already printed lyrics on the cover of *Where I'm Coming From* (April 1971), and producers and arrangers had been receiving cover billing since at least *Still Waters Run Deep* (March 1970). It was however the first time the individual musicians had been named.

[5] p218

[6] p132

---

## TIMELINE - 1971

Tamla Motown release 36 singles and 25 albums. (A further 4 singles and 4 albums are released in the UK on Rare Earth.)
Tamla Motown place 23 singles in the UK top 40. 9 make top 10 and 1 reaches number 1
Becomes apparent that Motown is gradually shifting operations to LA offices on 6255 Sunset Boulevard
Berry Gordy's private office at 2650 West Grand Boulevard burns to ground

| | |
|---|---|
| **Jan 16** | Supremes: "Stoned Love" enters UK top 50 (peak 3) |
| **Jan 20** | Diana Ross marries Robert Silberstein (also known as Bob Ellis) |
| **Feb** | Osmonds popular in US, white 'answer' to Jackson 5 |
| **Spring** | Stevie Wonder tours UK with Martha & Vandellas |
| **Mar 16** | *Why I Oppose The War In Vietnam*, recording of Martin Luther King speeches on Black Forum label, receives Grammy |
| **Apr 3** | Temptations: "Just My Imagination (Running Away With Me)" number 1 in US (two weeks) |
| **Apr 3** | Diana Ross: "Remember Me" enters UK top 50 (peak 7) |
| **Apr 3** | R. Dean Taylor: "Indiana Wants Me" enters UK top 50 (peak 2) |
| **Apr 17** | *Motown Chartbusters Volume 5* tops UK album chart (three weeks). Becomes third consecutive LP in series to reach top, and Tamla Motown's fifth and last |
| **Apr 18** | ABC broadcast *Diana!* special, recorded 5 Dec 1970 |
| **May 1** | Elgins: "Heaven Must Have Sent You" enters UK top 50 as re-issue (peak 3) |
| **May 13** | Stevie Wonder is 21. Uses coming-of-age as lever to renegotiate contract with Motown, gaining substantial control over own recordings. Wins improved royalty rate, and access to $1m trust fund |
| **May 22** | Temptations: "Just My Imagination (Running Away With Me)" enters UK top 50 (peak 8). Group's last single before Eddie Kendricks leaves to be replaced by Richard Street. Shortly afterwards Paul Williams leaves, replaced by Damon Harris |
| **Jun** | Mo-West launched in US |
| **Jun** | Stevie Wonder: *Where I'm Coming From* first album under new contract. Now runs own production company (Taurus) and publishing company (Black Bull). From now on, albums are central focus of career |
| **Summer** | Jackson 5 embark on tour which encompasses 100 US cities |
| **Summer** | Jimmy Ruffin's contract expires and is not renewed |
| **Aug 14** | Diana Ross' first daughter Rhonda Suzanne born, biologically fathered by Berry Gordy |
| **Aug 21** | Supremes: "Nathan Jones" enters UK top 50 (peak 5) |
| **Aug 21** | Diana Ross: "I'm Still Waiting" UK number 1 (four weeks) |
| **Sep** | Rare Earth label launched in UK |
| **Sep** | UK TV screening of *Diana!*, first shown in US Apr 18 |
| **Sep** | Marvin Gaye, *What's Going On* released (May 1971 in US). Fails to enter UK album chart |
| **Sep 11** | Cartoon series of Jackson 5 commences broadcasting on ABC |
| **Sep 19** | Temptations: "Ball Of Confusion" enters UK top 50 (peak 7) |
| **Sep 25** | Four Tops: "Simple Game" enters UK top 50 (peak 3) |
| **Oct** | Ashford & Simpson leave Motown |
| **Oct** | Michael Jackson signs solo contract and releases first solo single in US |
| **Oct 30** | Diana Ross: "Surrender" enters UK top 50 (peak 10) |
| **Nov** | Martha & Vandellas: "Bless You" / "Hope I Don't Get My Heart Broke". First new single for three years, following Reeves' breakdown in 1969 |
| **Dec 21** | Martha & Vandellas give last concert as group |

**382**                                          *Tamla Motown - The stories behind the UK singles*

**TMG 797**
**MICHAEL JACKSON**
**Got To Be There** (3:23)
(Willensky)
Produced by Hal Davis
**Release Date**: 14 Jan 1972
**B-side**: Maria (You Were The Only One)
**Position in Record Retailer Top 40**: 5
**Equivalent US Release**: Motown 1191 (7 Oct 1971)
**Position in Billboard Top 40 Pop**: 4
**Position in Billboard Top 40 R & B**: 4

On 3 January 1972, Berry Gordy finally settled his four-year-old dispute with HDH, drawing a line under a particularly unsavoury part of Motown's history which had cost all parties huge sums of money. Looking forward to 1972, one of his priorities for the year was the establishment of Michael Jackson as a solo star, something begun in America in the fall with the release of this, the teenager's first single. While Motown's history shows several of its prominent group members pulled out for such treatment, the impetus behind the move, aside from the financial incentive, was likely the similar multi-faceted recording and marketing available to rival act The Osmonds, who had made a solo star of Donny in May 1971 (and who had a child-star of their own, Little Jimmy, waiting in the wings). As with Donny Osmond, the plan hatched in July 1971 saw Michael Jackson undertake his own recordings while retaining a place in his group—a first for Motown.

The chosen vehicle for Jackson's launch was "Got To Be There", supplied by Motowner Elliot Willensky and carrying a boldly stepping melody line which Jackson handles with apparent ease. Arranged by Dave Blumberg with vocals directed by Willie Hutch, the overall production is full and assured, sweetly ushering in the arrival of a performer who would go on to become one of the all-time biggest stars of popular music.

The American edition of "Got To Be There" had already gone top 5 by the turn of 1972, this UK pressing (coupled with a version of [753b]) fortuitously repeating the feat at a time when the group's fortunes were taking a downturn. This historic recording has since been put out twice more by Tamla Motown (see Chapter 6).

**TMG 798**
**STEVIE WONDER**
**If You Really Love Me** (2:52)
(Wonder—Wright)
Produced by Stevie Wonder
**Release Date**: 7 Jan 1972
**B-side**: Think Of Me As Your Soldier
**Position in Record Retailer Top 40**: 20
**Equivalent US Release**: Tamla 54208 (Aug 1971)

This second lift from *Where I'm Coming From* signals the first of several prolonged interludes in Stevie Wonder's career, which (on the heels of [783b]) Tamla Motown sought to fill by re-issuing the singer's previous B-side [779]. Taking his time musing his future professional direction, Wonder was stalling on re-signing with Motown through the second-half of 1971, instead opting to set up home in a New York hotel from where, having received his $1 million 'coming-of-age' entitlement from his former employer, he rented studios in Greenwich Village and began work on some new material, well away from Berry Gordy and his former colleagues.[1]

Announcing at one point that he would never re-sign for Motown, Wonder set about organising his business affairs and created two autonomous companies, Taurus Productions and Black Bull Music, which would handle his production and publishing duties respectively. However, sensing that the star was on the loose, CBS began breathing down his neck and interest was emerging too from other sections of the industry, which prompted Wonder and his new legal representative Johannan Vigoda to contemplate sealing a deal to consolidate his future.

Realising that Wonder was now beyond his control, Berry Gordy had one last option open and, in a last-ditch effort to win him back, emerged with one of the most generous contract offers in the history of pop music. Gordy's concession was that if Wonder recorded and produced his own material at will from here-on, the company would act as free publicists and distributors, profits split down the line, 50/50. After six weeks of cogitation, negotiation and bargaining, all parties signed a 120-page document sealing the agreement, Stevie Wonder's third contract with Motown and one which now provided him with cherished artistic freedom—and a vast projected income to boot.

Though few realised it at the time, Wonder had in-effect flown Motown's nest. While the company continued promoting and pressing his records, Wonder's liberation meant that he was no longer under Berry Gordy's management and would never again be instructed to record covers of other people's work in order to fill out average albums. In this sense, 1971 was his coming-of-age in more ways than one and a turning-point not just for him but for Motown too—in that it set several precedents which would have long-term ramifications. Having similarly 'lost' Marvin Gaye in 1971 [796], this new situation smacked of a second defeat for Gordy which he was seeking to mitigate at the end of the year with the launch of Michael Jackson [797] and a new West Coast record label [799], events moving apace.

As if to celebrate the renewed partnership, Tamla Motown issued this buoyant new single in the first week of 1972, made by Wonder the previous year while exploring the studio potential of the synthesiser. Deploying an early RMI Electra-Piano, Wonder was able to capture a resounding bass sound, bolstering the orthodox track (very 'Jamerson' in style). Rhythmically playful, the song is as much the sound of liberation as anything Wonder had recorded, the happily circulating chorus figure drawing Syreeta along, with liberally sprinkled hand claps punctuating

David Van DePitte's jazzy brass arrangement. A moment of sublime musical confidence, "If You Really Love Me" is the real thing—Stevie Wonder basking publicly in his talents and showing Motown—and the world—how effortlessly it could be done. Little surprise that he could no longer be contained by Motown's authoritarian regime.

Six days after the single was released, Wonder was opening a UK tour in London, in which he showcased some of his new material, improvising with keyboards and synthesisers on stage with mixed results. The move didn't go down well, many concert-goers hoping instead for a standard selection of his old hits, but public approval was not top of Wonder's priorities for the moment. Pushing ahead with his new 'toys', this tentative development was opening the doors on his 'classic' period, well underway with his new album already in the can.

[1] The result was to be *Music Of My Mind*. See [827].

## TMG 799
## THELMA HOUSTON
**I Want To Go Back There Again** (2:35)
(Gordy)
Produced by Hal Davis
**Release Date**: 7 Jan 1972
**B-side**: Pick Of The Week
**Position in Record Retailer Top 40**: -
**Equivalent US Release**: Mo-West 5008 (2 Nov 1971)
**Position in Billboard Top 40 Pop**: -
**Position in Billboard Top 40 R & B**: -

With Motown's concentration on its LA operations increasing with time, a telling step was taken in mid-1971 with the creation of a new American label based on the West Coast. Unashamedly named Mo-West, the imprint's early roster included several acts already on Motown's books and moved sideways, as well as a cluster of new names which appeared to offer bright prospects.[1] Through 1972, US releases on Mo-West were sent over to the UK and transferred as normal to Tamla Motown, several seeing light of day thus, before a UK branch was also established (see [828]).

Thelma Houston was a Mississippi vocalist who had arrived in California in her childhood and was discovered by Dunhill in 1969, aged 26. (Her UK releases were licensed to Stateside.) With Dunhill she met and worked with Jimmy Webb, who was on his way to Motown at the turn of the decade. Houston followed him for a contract with the new Mo-West division, releasing her first single in November 1971, a cover of Chris Clark's "I Want To Go Back There Again" [638].

Hal Davis' production of this remake does its best to commercialise Berry Gordy's composition, rounding off the rough edges and dropping the tinkling piano in favour of electric keyboards and—significantly—heavily wah-wahed guitar. Input in this respect is from arranger James Carmichael, new on the scene and about to embark on several successful collaborations with various combinations of the Jackson family.[2] Davis and Carmichael succeed in getting down a confident version of the track, which was viewed as a hit-in-waiting, although arranging it in a popular vein undermined its key sense of forlorn regret and it flopped on release.

Houston's career subsequently faltered purely through lack of material. She released *Thelma Houston* in 1972 which spawned a trailer-single, but nothing else by her surfaced. When Mo-West was established in the UK, she was transferred from Tamla Motown but releases had dried up by the middle of the decade, Houston resuming her Motown career with a vengeance in 1977, with a version of Gamble—Huff's "Don't Leave Me This Way" which topped the US charts. Motown have since purchased and released her early Dunhill recordings.

[1] With VIP effectively now finished, the move restored Gordy's US portfolio to six major active labels: Mo-West, Rare Earth, Soul and the 'big three' of Tamla, Motown and Gordy.

[2] He also arranged [816]; [825]; [833]; [842]; [874]. Carmichael is credited as a key player in helping another new Mo-West act, The Commodores, rise to stardom later in the decade, from [902] onwards.

## TMG 800
## THE TEMPTATIONS
**Superstar (Remember How You Got Where You Are)** (2:52)
(Whitfield—Strong)
Produced by Norman Whitfield
Recording completed: 21 Sep 1971
**Release Date**: 28 Jan 1972
**B-side**: Gonna Keep On Trying Till I Win Your Love
**Position in Record Retailer Top 40**: 32
**Equivalent US Release**: Gordy 7111 (19 Oct 1971)
**Position in Billboard Top 40 Pop**: 18
**Position in Billboard Top 40 R & B**: 8

---

Otis Williams / Melvin Franklin / Richard Street / Dennis Edwards / Damon Harris

---

After Paul Williams' recent exit [783], and with Eddie Kendricks no longer around, The Temptations had drafted in two new members for their latest recording sessions, Richard Street joining the fold and 21-year-old Damon Harris settling into Kendricks' shoes after LA vocalist Ricky Owens had failed to hit the mark. The plan to recruit the inexperienced Harris initially divided the group but eventually finding agreement, the new-look band set about recording *Solid Rock*, a somewhat overblown album with several flabby extended tracks, seen by many as a low point for the Whitfield-Temptations alliance.

The set's biggest spin-off hit was "Superstar", which thanks to the re-promotion of [783b] was a second Temptations run-out in nine weeks. Burdened in mood, the lyric was widely seen as an attack on someone in particular, opinion divided as to who. One suggestion is that it concerns Sly Stone, another theory holding that Whitfield and Strong were having a dig at Berry Gordy. But the most pervasive and persuasive reading is that "Superstar", with its close-to-home warnings against over-inflated ego, concerns former Temptations Eddie Kendricks and/or David Ruffin, both of whom had at some point considered themselves 'above' the group and opted to pursue solo stardom.[1] In the context of The Temptations' personnel issues at the time, the notion seems likely, and is further in keeping with several other recent lyrics which appear to contain 'in-messages' (eg [716]).

Arranged entirely predictably, the track was Dennis Coffey's last work with the group, and includes standard vocal turns for each group member, and the call "Higher!" duplicated from "Cloud Nine" [707]. Over-indulgent, the original recording ran beyond the reasonable running time of a hit single, unimaginatively resolved with an undisguised edit at 1:55 before the fader is pushed down at 2:52. For the UK release of January 1972, the track was married with "Gonna Keep On Trying Till I Win Your Love", an old Eddie Kendricks lead from 1969 which had originally surfaced on *Cloud Nine*. (Written by Whitfield—Strong, the number had been rattling around for some years [630b]; [718b].)

[1] See [671] and [773]. This version is advocated by Otis Williams—see Williams p156 and his interview in *Record Collector* 327 (Sep 2006): "Yep, Norman [sic] wrote it with them in mind". David Ruffin himself presumably saw things differently; he recorded a version himself, released as a US single in 1975 (Motown 1336).


**TMG 801**
**TOM CLAY**
**What The World Needs Now Is Love – Abraham, Martin And John** (6:10)
(Bacharach—David—Holler)
Produced by Tom Clay
**Release Date**: 28 Jan 1972
**B-side**: The Victors
**Position in Record Retailer Top 40**: -
**Equivalent US Release**: Mo-West 5002 (22 Jun 1971)
**Position in Billboard Top 40 Pop**: 8
**Position in Billboard Top 40 R & B**: 32


By way of personal comment on America's political climate in the late 1960s, LA disc jockey Tom Clay constructed a collage of news reports and spoken recordings which he set to music and broadcast during his transmissions for KGBS Radio. Inspired by Dick Holler's "Abraham, Martin And John" [734], the central element of the piece is a series of three miniature collections of speeches and broadcasts soundtracking the song's subject matter. (The assassinations of President J. F. Kennedy on 22 November 1963 and Martin Luther King on 4 April 1968 are readily accommodated, the inclusion of the similar fate which befell Senator Robert

Kennedy on 5 June 1968 skipping over the lack of corresponding audio records for the 'Abraham' of the song's title.)

Bracketed by an interview with a young child ('What is segregation...') and various sounds of soldiers chanting and background gunfire, the track has no overall political purpose beyond dispassionate observation, although the anti-Vietnam War flavour is unmistakeable.[1] Mixed in-and-out of the sequence are sections of Bacharach—David's poignant "What The World Needs Now Is Love" (see [662]) as performed by The Burt Bacharach Orchestra, offering calm reflection on the destruction portrayed in the foregoing.

So effective was the sequence that KGBS listeners registered warm approval, and this was picked up by an alert Mo-West label scouting for new talent. Despite clocking in at twice the length of a typical hit single[2], the track was formally mixed at Mo-West by Gene Page with The Blackberries on vocals [751n] and afforded a full release in mid-1971. (A special pressing of 12,000 copies was prepared for mailing to KGBS listeners.) Surprisingly, this unorthodox 'spoken' recording scaled the US charts, lodging at number 8 in August, and enthused by its success, Mo-West arranged for a Tom Clay album to be assembled, *Whatever Happened To Love* ensuing.

The fact that the material incorporated into [801] had far less relevance to British listeners, who in any respect tended to be too sceptical to fall for such vague sentimentality, accounts for the UK edition of January 1972 being ignored. However it was re-issued by the UK branch of Mo-West in late 1973 (see Appendix 3).

[1] This is also the subject matter of the B-side.

[2] It is in fact the longest recording released on 45 by Tamla Motown thus far. It would be eclipsed by [839].

**TMG 802**
**MARVIN GAYE**
**Mercy Mercy Me (The Ecology)** (2:39)
(Gaye)
Produced by Marvin Gaye
Recording completed: 5 May 1971
**Release Date**: 11 Feb 1972
**B-side**: Sad Tomorrows
**Position in Record Retailer Top 40**: -
**Equivalent US Release**: Tamla 54207 (10 Jun 1971)
**Position in Billboard Top 40 Pop**: 4
**Position in Billboard Top 40 R & B**: 1

The success of Marvin Gaye's *What's Going On* recordings on the US singles chart, where three of the tracks had gone top 10, inspired Tamla Motown to release "Mercy Mercy Me" a little over two months after the UK edition of "Save The Children" [796] had sunk without trace. The recording, the strongest on the album, was written entirely by Gaye, its title possibly derived via his old school friend Don Covay who had recorded "Mercy Mercy" in 1964. The fact that the track is Gaye's own probably accounts for its particular potency, more tautly focussed than his contemporary material and kicking straight into verse one, a powerfully circulating four-chord run which goes around five times in a minute and a half.

The text is one of Gaye's more outreaching, the singer musing humanity's destructive tendencies, encapsulated by pollution of the natural environment, nuclear radiation and global over-population, all of which were the domain of a marginal 'radicalised' minority in 1971. So oblique were the issues at stake that several have claimed that Berry Gordy had to enquire as to what the word 'ecology' meant[1], although this apocryphal dig at his intelligence is negated by the fact that Gordy had already helped set up a record label called Ecology several months prior to the current track being recorded [663n].

Taking this apparently urgent 'message' song into sessions for *What's Going On* on 17 March 1971, the resultant track ended up recorded in the same lazily drifting vein as the rest of the LP. Gaye, though, was unhappy with it, and in a rarely decisive moment insisted on a remake, starting from scratch in Studio B two days later. Unusually impatient in delivery, Gaye tends to stumble over the crowded verses giving the impression of dropped beats, his double-tracked vocals finalised in a separate late session on May 5, although his sense of place fades again at 1:40, with a semi-whispered 'My Sweet Lord', quoting from George Harrison's first solo single, number 1 in America during January 1971. In the light of this quiet plea to God, Gaye's subsequent comment that "Mercy Mercy Me" is 'about Jesus' makes more sense than if taken as a purely abstract claim.[2]

All-done at this point, Gaye leaves the remainder of "Mercy Mercy Me" to The Funk Brothers, a wailing sax solo from a stoned 'Wild' Bill Moore flying headlong into a quasi-apocalyptic breakdown. (Much of the instrumental colour in the track is provided by a mysterious clomping effect obtained by Jack Ashford cupping an obscure wooden percussion instrument in his hand.) Taken to LA with the rest of the tapes for *What's Going On*, the track was overdubbed with Mellotron and mixed on May 6, ahead of the album's release on May 21.

An obvious single, "Mercy Mercy Me" was extracted almost immediately in America, where is made number 4 pop and number 1 R & B over the summer. Why "Save The Children" [796] was preferred in the UK is unclear, although "Mercy Mercy Me" did not chart when finally released in the new year.

[1] For example, Earl Van Dyke laughs, "Berry Gordy didn't understand the word 'ecology'. It had to be explained to him." (Cited in Turner, p131.)

[2] See Gaye's comments in Ritz, p199.

**TMG 803**
**FOUR TOPS**
**Bernadette** (2:57)
**Re-issue of [601]**
**Release Date**: 18 Feb 1972

---

**Additional track on B-side**: It's The Same Old Song [528]
**Position in Record Retailer Top 40**: 23

| Levi Stubbs / Lawrence Payton / Abdul 'Duke' Fakir / Renaldo 'Obie' Benson |
| --- |

Heading back to the UK in the spring of 1972 for some live dates, The Four Tops continued to woo their loyal British audiences, who had already put five of the group's singles into the top 40 in 1970-71. Interest in Northern Soul generally was showing no signs of flagging, signalled by this, a re-run of "Bernadette" which also went top 40 despite having been a big hit just five years earlier.

[803] was Tamla Motown's first 'maxi-single' on which an extra B-side was inserted.[1] In this case the attractive freebie was [528], a gem for collectors and DJs, many of whom had missed the chance to secure a copy on 7-inch seven years earlier.

[1] Seven more would follow in the ensuing year and a half: [820]; [822]; [824]; [837]; [853]; [857]; [870]; and another in 1975 [1009]. (One more surfaced as a retrospective Tamla Motown release in 1979 [L013]. See Chapter 6.)

**TMG 804**
**THE SUPREMES**
**Floy Joy** (2:34)
(Robinson)
Produced by William "Smokey" Robinson
**Release Date**: 25 Feb 1972
**B-side**: This Is The Story
**Position in Record Retailer Top 40**: 9
**Equivalent US Release**: Motown 1195 (14 Dec 1971)
**Position in Billboard Top 40 Pop**: 16
**Position in Billboard Top 40 R & B**: 5

| Jean Terrell / Cindy Birdsong / Mary Wilson |
| --- |

Having attempted to write hits for The Supremes in their early days (most notably coming up with "A Breath Taking Guy" in 1962), Smokey Robinson's association with the group ended with the explosive arrival of HDH in 1963, severing creative links for almost a decade. A reunion of these two early acts occurred in December 1968 with the recording of "The Composer", issued as a US-only single (Motown 1146) the following spring. Further opportunities to collaborate on a more concerted level arose following the group's ill-fated sessions for *Promises Kept*, assembled with a variety of writers and producers, and which was abandoned during 1971.[1] Aiming to get the group back on course, Robinson arrived with a clutch of new songs, some of which appear to have been deliberately written *à la* HDH.

The first thing to emerge from this interesting collaboration was "Floy Joy" (originally "Floyd Joy"), a bouncy hand-clapping piece of pop custom-made for Mary Wilson's vocal. In the end Wilson and Jean Terrell swap lines throughout this song, an arrangement which, under the dominant force of Diana Ross, would have been unimaginable, and there is little doubt that Robinson was highly enthused by this latest project, taking a keen interest in the group's vocal harmonies and coaching them minutely through the session on which he also takes responsibility for writing, producing and arranging.

It is possible to regard "Floy Joy" as a found time capsule; after the quasi-psychedelia of "Stoned Love" [760] and "Nathan Jones" [782], the song arrives like an old friend, starting on a fade-in [E65] and developing a relentless, pulsating beat akin to that of "Where Did Our Love Go" [E51]. Unashamedly harking back to 1964, the recording approximates how The Supremes might have sounded years earlier, had Robinson been able to develop his embryonic relationship with them during the 1960s.

[i] In 2006 Motown released *This Is The Story: The '70s Albums Vol I* which contained the full contents of *Promises Kept*. The 13 titles include versions of "Still Water (Love)" [752] and "If I Were Your Woman" [765], and covers of "Eleanor Rigby" and "It's Too Late". Frank Wilson is credited as executive producer.

## TMG 805
## GLADYS KNIGHT & THE PIPS
**Make Me The Woman That You Go Home To** (3:29)
(McMurray)
Produced by Clay McMurray
**Release Date**: 3 Mar 1972
**B-side**: I Don't Want To Do Wrong
**Position in Record Retailer Top 40**: -
**Equivalent US Release**: Soul 35091 (18 Nov 1971)
**Position in Billboard Top 40 Pop**: 27
**Position in Billboard Top 40 R & B**: 3

Gladys Knight / Merald 'Bubba' Knight / Edward Patten / William Guest

Written and produced by Clay McMurray, "Make Me The Woman That You Go Home To" is a morose overture to a hopeless love, written from the perspective of a mistress observing the man she loves routinely abandon her to play the field. Wanting his exclusive attentions, the text has the woman cooking and doing domestic chores for her double-timing boyfriend, offering this as evidence of her unrequited devotion, while tortured by the knowledge that he is out 'fooling around'. (McMurray has recently stated that the scenario comes from a real situation involving a close female friend.) Encapsulating the age-old disparity between male and female, the song portrays an all too common experience in which the female needs the commitment of a life partner, the male wanting only a physical lover.

With notable input from guitarist Robert White, probably half-conscious of The Rolling Stones' similarly despondent "Wild Horses" (a hit in mid 1971), the arrangement incorporates some compellingly pained backing vocals and pulls an extraordinarily powerful performance from Knight, whose emotion, if not personally authentic, is entirely convincing. The track was paired up with "I Don't Want To Do Wrong", a Pips original released as a US single almost a year earlier, but failed to register on the UK charts.

**TMG 806**
**VELVELETTES**
**Needle In A Haystack** (2:29) **[E61]**
(Stevenson—Whitfield)
Produced by Norman Whitfield
Recording completed: 17 Jul 1964
**Release Date**: 10 Mar 1972
**B-side**: I'm The Exception To The Rule [521b]
**Position in Record Retailer Top 40**: -
**Equivalent US Release**: VIP 25007 (3 Sep 1964)
**Position in Billboard Top 40 Pop**: -
**Position in Billboard Top 40 R & B**: 31

---

Carolyn Gill / Mildred Gill / Bertha Barbee / Norma Barbee

---

Originally released on Stateside in 1964, this debut Velvelettes recording had already been pressed once on Tamla Motown [595b], before being selected again here for A-side exposure. Raw in every respect, the single arrived like an old black-and-white photograph amongst a full-colour pop scene, which even its Northern Soul approval couldn't transcend. (It was issued on the back of "These Things Will Keep Me Loving You" [780], which had made the UK charts.)

The lyric by Mickey Stevenson, a root-and-branch denunciation of the male gender, was supplied to the inexperienced group in sketchy form, the singers filling it out themselves on the studio floor. Given its unremitting hostility to half of the human race, it seems likely that some of the more accusatory lines were derived by The Velvelettes themselves rather than their (male) songwriters, although the exact details have been lost to memory. Indeed, recollections vary from group-member to group-member, Bertha Barbee commenting in 1986 on the nerve-wracking July 1964 session, "I thought we did about 17 takes on 'Needles'. Mildred [Gill] thought it was about 13".[1] In any respect, a session requiring somewhere upwards of a dozen attempts was unheard of for Motown, the cost of which was being billed to the group themselves, which they learned mid-session and promptly addressed with a passable take.

Further uncertainty surrounds the personnel present on the day. While the studio-band line-up is known (James Jamerson on bass, Earl Van Dyke on keyboards and percussionist Eddie 'Bongo' Brown joined by Paul Riser on trombone), reliable sources have claimed that Mildred Gill was absent due to pregnancy, Carolyn Gill and Bertha and Norma Barbee recording as a three-piece. Yet if this is the case, there is no basis to Mildred's claim that the vocal took 13 takes—which Bertha apparently accepts at face value. The truth will likely never be pinned down precisely.

Musically, Whitfield's basic design makes much of just one chord, sustaining the central key for a prolonged duration, a strategy which

---

**392**          *Tamla Motown - The stories behind the UK singles*

effectively generates a droning feel ahead of its time. Borrowing an ear-catching opening from "Where Did Our Love Go" [E51], the final work is bubbling and energised, one of Motown's key successes in the 'girl-group' style which has since been recognised as a classic in the field.

The Velvelettes' first release was appropriately also their last on Tamla Motown (barring some retrospective re-issues: see Chapter 6), and was coupled with an unexpected B-side, lifted from [521]. A further coincidence was the pregnancy of Mildred's sister Cal Gill at around the time of this new release, taking events almost full-circle for the act which was by now wound up. In the years since, the fondly remembered Velvelettes have reformed for brief spells, and more recently a fake group called The Velvellettes (with a litigation-dodging mis-spelling) have toured to the consternation of the remaining original group members.

[1] The interview was published in *Goldmine*, and reproduced in Abbott, p165.

**TMG 807**
**THE SAN REMO STRINGS**
**Reach Out I'll Be There** (2:52)
(Holland—Dozier—Holland)
Produced by Gil Askey/Larry Maxwell
Recording completed: 16 Dec 1967
**Release Date**: 24 Mar 1972
**B-side**: Hungry For Love
**Position in Record Retailer Top 40**: -
**No Equivalent US Release**

This instrumental act's second and last Tamla Motown 45 (see [795]) was, unlike its predecessor, a Motown original, in sound and feel a product of arranger Paul Riser. First-released on the US album *Swing* in 1968, the production is a world away from that on [795], despite the fact that the musicians are essentially the same, and former Golden World producer Gil Askey is involved.

This run-through of The Four Tops' classic [579] pounds along with James Jamerson replicating his original bass line, and a tambourine mixed left, shaking incessantly in a style later picked up in automated form by the disco boom. There is little else of note on what sounds like a vocal-less backing track, making [807] a somewhat futile release, essentially a collector's domain.

**TMG 808**
**THE TEMPTATIONS**
**Take A Look Around** (2:59)
(Whitfield—Strong)
Produced by Norman Whitfield
Recording completed: 4 Jan 1972
**Release Date**: Mar 1972
**B-side**: Smooth Sailing From Now On

**Position in Record Retailer Top 40**: 13
**Equivalent US Release**: Gordy 7115 (3 Feb 1972)
**Position in Billboard Top 40 Pop**: 30
**Position in Billboard Top 40 R & B**: 10

---

Otis Williams / Melvin Franklin / Richard Street / Dennis Edwards / Damon Harris

---

Attempting to eke a third hit from *Solid Rock* [738]; [800], *another* Temptations single arrived in March, "Take A Look Around" the album's opening number, recorded slow and intimate. Classically orchestrated by Paul Riser[1] with novel instrumentation including harpsichord and timpani, the sound-stage is stunning, Norman Whitfield driving the futuristic swirling prelude into a tightly delivered musical landscape with textured electric guitar *obligato* and ominous 'thunder clouds'. Few creations have been so light and yet so dark at the same time.

Featuring a lead vocal from Damon Harris, "Take A Look Around" at first appears as an effort to recreate "Just My Imagination" [773]. However the song's subject matter—another of Barrett Strong's gritty observations on society—pulls it into the realm of the group's 'psychedelic' canon, although unusually Strong is not focussed, throwing unrelated comments about, many of which are hackneyed. (The line 'think about the children' was probably suggested to him by [796]. Musically similar games are suggested, the chord sequence which closes the opening line, a triple-step through C#/Eb/F reminiscent of the inverted cadences in "I Was Made To Love Her" [613].)

The confusion of theme and sound registered little with the group's long-term fans who were tiring of this burdened and over-complex style. The track made a creditable 13 on the UK charts however.

[1] Wrongly credited to Tom Baird on the label. The error was corrected for [L032] in 1980.


**TMG 809**
**THE JACKSON 5**
**Sugar Daddy** (2:34)
(The Corporation)
Produced by The Corporation
**Release Date**: 30 Mar 1972
**B-side**: I'm So Happy
**Position in Record Retailer Top 40**: -
**Equivalent US Release**: Motown 1194 (23 Nov 1971)
**Position in Billboard Top 40 Pop**: 10
**Position in Billboard Top 40 R & B**: 3

---

Jackie Jackson / Tito Jackson / Jermaine Jackson / Marlon Jackson / Michael Jackson

---

One of the most ghastly records released under Tamla Motown's banner, "Sugar Daddy" was assembled by The Corporation, probably drawing on a very old Berry Gordy copyright by the same name recorded by The Satintones and listed as the first-ever single on the US Motown label, catalogue number 1000. (It was in fact released out-of-sequence in September 1961, missing the honour by some way). This grating new recording arrived as a non-album single in America shortly before its (optimistic) inclusion on the group's first *Greatest Hits* compilation.

Following "Maybe Tomorrow", a US-only release which had stalled at number 20, the single just made the top 10 but missed the chart entirely in the UK, its glaring failure marking The Corporation's resignation from the group's singles output. Meantime The Jackson 5 were being further flogged by Motown via *Goin' Back To Indiana*, a television film based on one of the group's 1970 recordings, in which they return to their home town for a concert. The project inevitably spawned a soundtrack album while in the UK, the original song found its way onto Tamla Motown's first promotional flexi-disc (see Appendix 1). As if to underline this period of intense marketing, both "Goin' Back To Indiana" and "Sugar Daddy" were licensed to Kellogg's, who 'issued' them as barely-playable cut-out records on boxes of Rice Krispies.

**TMG 810**
**EDWIN STARR**
**Funky Music Sho' Nuff Turns Me On** (2:59)
(Whitfield—Strong)
Produced by Norman Whitfield
**Release Date**: 7 Apr 1972
**B-side**: Cloud Nine
**Position in Record Retailer Top 40**: -
**Equivalent US Release**: Gordy 7107 (30 Mar 1971)
**Position in Billboard Top 40 Pop**: -
**Position in Billboard Top 40 R & B**: 6

Lifted from 1971's *Involved* (released in January 1972 in Britain) this new Whitfield—Strong number lived up to the promise of its title, strutting through its three minutes with a gutsy throb, tailor-made for the night-club scene. Meaningless beyond the context of its hedonistic dance groove, the track is pure 'feel', a radical creation in bodily sensation created by Whitfield and orchestration director Paul Riser. (The 'Turns me on' of the song's title is likely a *double entendre*, the 1960s phrase, referring to something which stimulates interest, having clear sexual overtones—more 'body' over 'mind'.)

On one level a somewhat hollow affair, the recording shows where Motown were heading as the 1970s progressed, the structural form of the 1960s, so integral to many of the company's early hits, in which phrases, bars and middle-8s were sweated over, increasingly subsiding under the influence of new and advanced electronic music which was elevating quality of sound above depth of expression. While this had the effect of placing a track such as "Funky Music Sho' Nuff Turns Me On" on a flat, unshifting plateau, it also gave rise to musical and psychic *experiences* which were hitherto unreachable, chemical stimulants and a predisposition to trance-like states amplifying the effect. Much of the club scene of the 1980s and 90s owes a direct debt to tracks such as this.

Pleased with the cut (on which The Delicates provide backing [751]), Whitfield repeatedly recorded it with his other Motown artists ([866b]; [913]). This first attempt however is definitive, and was coupled with a rendition of [707] from the same studio album. Given its form, it is no surprise that pop listeners showed little interest in Britain or America, while on the R & B chart the track scored highly.


**TMG 811**
**SMOKEY ROBINSON & THE MIRACLES**
**My Girl Has Gone** (2:51)
**Re-issue of [540]**
**Release Date**: 14 Apr 1972
**New B-side**: Crazy About The La La La
**Position in Record Retailer Top 40**: -

---

Smokey Robinson / Bobby Rogers / Claudette Rogers Robinson /
Warren 'Pete' Moore / Ronnie White

---

After years of agonising over retiring from The Miracles ([687]; [761]) Smokey Robinson finally elected to leave the act in 1972, announcing his intent at the start of the year. His final recordings with the group for *Flying High Together* went unreleased in Britain, 1972 spawning nothing new through Tamla Motown bar this re-issue of "My Girl Has Gone".

The choice was curious, there being plenty of contemporary tracks to choose from, to say nothing of the rest of Robinson's back-catalogue which had seen both [696] and [761] score well of late. Dating to the tail-end of 1965, "My Girl Has Gone" was not a UK hit in its day, nor on re-issue in 1972, when coupled with "Crazy About The La La La" from *One Dozen Roses* (1971).

His last public appearance with The Miracles took place on July 16 at the Carter Baron Amphitheatre in Washington, which, after the style of Diana Ross' departure from The Supremes, duly arrived as a live double album (*1957-1972 Live!*, issued by Tamla Motown in April 1973). Robinson was finally free from touring obligations, LA-bound and looking forward to a prolonged period of relaxation.


**TMG 812**
**DIANA ROSS**
**Doobedood'ndoobe, Doobedood'ndoobe, Doobedood'ndoo** (4:53)
(Richards)
Produced by Deke Richards
**Release Date**: 28 Apr 1972
**B-side**: Keep An Eye
**Position in Record Retailer Top 40**: 12
**No Equivalent US Release**

With Diana Ross' popularity on a high (The UK *Disc & Music Echo* had her polled 'World's Leading Female Singer' in February), Tamla Motown were keen to keep product flowing, despite the fact that Ross had no new recordings in the offing, filming of *Lady Sings The Blues* having commenced in December 1971 [848]. And so in an effort to repeat the commercial feat of "I'm Still Waiting" [781], the label elected to dip back into the ageing *Everything Is Everything* and pull out the current track, with its playfully obscure title rivalling that of [653]. (There was no contemporary release in America.)

This ungainly assemblage of sections shares a disjointedness with "Surrender" [792], which is even more pronounced here, giving the impression that it was thrown together with little consideration to holistic form or structure. Indeed several elements correspond to material heard elsewhere, adding to the sense that "Doobedood'ndoobe" is a collection of spare parts: the verse commences in a style and pitch directly reminiscent of "You've Made Me So Very Happy" [622], while the lyric comes in on the title of "Heaven Must Have Sent You" [583]. After shuddering into its first (meaningless) chorus the song then delves into a bridge seemingly derived from the similar sections in Edison Lighthouse's "Love Grows (Where My Rosemary Grows)", a hit in the spring of 1970. Unsurprisingly this creation did not match [781] in terms of sales, placed respectably in the top 20.

**TMG 813**
**GLADYS KNIGHT & THE PIPS**
**Just Walk In My Shoes** (2:22)
**Re-issue of [576]**
**Release Date**: 2 Jun 1972
**New B-side**: (I Know) I'm Losing You
**Position in Record Retailer Top 40**: 35

Gladys Knight / Merald 'Bubba' Knight / Edward Patten / William Guest

For reasons not entirely clear, this latest re-issue was held off its proposed April release until a busy June, whereupon it crawled into the lower-reaches of the top 40, the first time the group had managed to get there since 1967 [604]. A re-run of their first Tamla Motown release, this worthy rocker was edited to run a few seconds shorter than the original pressing, and was coupled with a classic B-side originally made for 1969's *Nitty Gritty*.

**TMG 814**
**EARL VAN DYKE & THE SOUL BROTHERS**
**I Can't Help Myself** (2:42)
(Holland—Dozier—Holland)
Produced by Brian Holland/Lamont Dozier
Recording completed: 24 Aug 1965
**Release Date**: 12 May 1972
**B-side**: How Sweet It Is (To Be Loved By You)

**Position in Record Retailer Top 40**: -
**Equivalent US Release**: Soul 35014 (30 Sep 1965)
**Position in Billboard Top 40 Pop**: -
**Position in Billboard Top 40 R & B**: -

Surviving in a ruthlessly competitive music industry as an independent is a task so arduous that few record companies have succeeded for more than a couple of years. Motown was the obvious exception, having by now held their ground for over a decade during which expansion was achieved extraordinarily rapidly. In the main this can not be attributed purely to marketing or financial muscle on Motown's part, but on Berry Gordy's astute perceptiveness in sussing-out what his audience wanted, sometimes before they even realised it themselves. Essentially working class, Gordy's mixture of street-wise savvy and determination to fight to the top gave him a winning edge. From the start his self-run Motown 'corporation' simply out-classed most of the supposed luminaries and 'artistes' of the late 1950s and early 1960s who looked instantly staid and old-fashioned by comparison to what was emerging from Hitsville. As time went on, Motown grew larger by throwing resources into sniffing out hit compositions, experimenting with recorded sounds, 'crossing over' to new sectors and picking up trends from elsewhere and absorbing them into their own uniquely exciting brand-style. And, of course, Gordy had an extraordinary amount of talent at his disposal in his studio band.

But the fact remained by the early 1970s that Motown was a small fish in a very large and unforgiving pond. By now there was a structural shift going on which few in the business were failing to notice, as the majors began to close ranks and centralise the industry to a greater extent than ever. Several artists in the R & B world were drifting to the big labels, James Brown notably secured by Polydor in 1971 and several high-profile Motown acts also being poached. Stevie Wonder was almost snapped up by CBS during the same year [798], The Four Tops were on their way to ABC-Dunhill [823], and both Ashford & Simpson and The Isley Brothers were about to migrate to Warners and Epic respectively. Greater ripples were felt in 1972 when it emerged that the struggling Stax label, independent since 1968 when parent company Atlantic was bought up by Warners, was itself being sold to CBS, who also controlled Philadelphia International and therefore a substantial amount of Motown's direct competition.

This fierce period of centralisation had its effect on Gordy who had been drifting west for several years with eyes on the glamour and fortunes available in Hollywood. Looking to keep expanding, he had psychologically abandoned the old Hitsville set-up, gradually congregating his star turns around him in LA, Diana Ross, Smokey Robinson, Marvin Gaye and The Jackson 5 all joining him to live and record there with eyes on even greater fame and success. And while The Funk Brothers stayed put in Detroit, much of Motown's infrastructure was drifting too, recording equipment, office furniture, personal belongings etc bit by bit going missing around them and fuelling the idea that the Hitsville operation was on the point of closure.

Motown sought to mitigate these potentially damaging rumours in April by circulating another written statement to the effect that no such closure plan was being hatched. Some believed the re-assurances, some did not, but then in June 1972 the ultimate calamity happened. The Funk Brothers and several associated personnel arrived one morning at Studio A to find the door bolted shut, a note pinned up reading, 'Today's session is cancelled and will be rescheduled'. The musicians realised at once what this meant, the manner of this almost unbelievable snub to the band who had been the backbone of The Motown Sound for over a decade intensifying the shock; why had they not been warned in advance? Later that day it emerged that Motown had made the news official, and the worst fears of The Funk Brothers were confirmed: Motown was effectively gone, a chapter in American musical history closed.[1]

While this scandalous move was being hatched, Tamla Motown was in the process of paying tribute to The Funk Brothers in Britain, having prepared for release their old recording of "I Can't Help Myself" by way of follow-up to similar recent projects including [759], [795] and [807]. The track was originally made in 1965, Van Dyke dubbing his piano lead over the Funks' backing track to [515] for an American single released that September (see [506]). The recording had missed the outfit's album *That Motown Sound* in 1965, but was partnered here with the set's "How Sweet It Is", in an appropriate, if unwitting tribute to the group who had created these famous recordings with the old HDH team an age ago, down in Hitsville's Snakepit.

So now, seven years on, the question was how these musicians would survive without Motown to provide employment. Many of them saw little option and at varying stages the bulk of the group headed west to hook up again with the company which had abandoned them. Earl Van Dyke and James Jamerson plotted a move together, which in turn brought both Robert White and Eddie 'Bongo' Brown along for the ride. Hank Cosby initially headed off to New York for a spell with CBS, before LA lured him and he too made the trek west, Dennis Coffey joining them in 1973.

However any thoughts that these musicians would be able to pick up where they left off were dashed almost at once. Motown provided little for The Funk Brothers, most of whom found the West Coast producers uninterested in employing them on sessions. A rapidly disillusioned Van Dyke headed back to Detroit in defeat less than a year later, while others struggled on, supporting each other where possible. In one telling incident recounted by Jack Ashford[2], who had moved out in 1975, he, Bongo Brown and James Jamerson appeared at the Motown studio on Romaine Street to be stopped at the gate by a security guard who singled out the world-renowned Jamerson and informed him that he hade been instructed to deny the bassist entry onto the premises. In a move of solidarity, the others refused to play that night. But the truth was clear to those brave enough to admit it: The Funk Brothers were simply no longer needed.

Other former performing stars found similar treatment. Many were simply left stranded by the move west, several letting their contracts run out and effectively entering forced retirement. Berry Gordy showed little concern for these human 'left overs', and was virtually unreachable on the other side of the country. Martha Reeves, once the darling of Motown and whose "Dancing In The Street" [E54] is the company's defining anthem, spent several months off-

and-on trying to get through to Motown's Detroit offices following her breakdown in 1971 [794] before a receptionist eventually picked up the phone, "Didn't you know? The company has moved to Los Angeles."[3]

[1] The exact point of closure has been the subject of some confusion, memories fallible and recollections of dates varying wildly. Martha Reeves for example states that Motown 'suddenly moved out of Detroit' in 1971 (p176), Jack Ashford claiming 'Motown/Hitsville shut down in Detroit in 1973' (p102). June 1972 is generally accepted as accurate.

[2] p117-8

[3] Reeves, p176.

## TMG 815
## THE SUPREMES & FOUR TOPS
**Without The One You Love** (3:26)
(Holland—Dozier—Holland)
Producer uncredited[1]
**Release Date**: 5 May 1972
**B-side**: Let's Make Love Now
**Position in Record Retailer Top 40**: -
**No Equivalent US Release**

Jean Terrell / Cindy Birdsong / Mary Wilson / Levi Stubbs / Lawrence Payton / Abdul 'Duke' Fakir / Renaldo 'Obie' Benson

A week after "Doobedood'ndoobe" [812] had emerged, with its first line recycling an old Tamla Motown hit, The Supremes & Four Tops' latest 45 arrived doing much the same—in this case quoting the chorus text from "Baby I Need Your Loving" [E53]. But unlike Diana Ross' release, this instance is explicable by the fact that the track was penned by HDH in 1964 in the direct wake of [E53], and recorded and released by The Four Tops for their eponymous 1965 album. Given HDH's predilection for dropping pre-written phrases into their contemporary work (a sort of fore-runner to musical sampling), the move is not entirely surprising and note should also be made of a 1962 Aretha Franklin recording which shares its title, and likely provided inspiration. In any case, "Without The One You Love" continues Tamla Motown's love-affair with the past, most of their 1972 output to date consisting either of old recordings or comparatively new tracks looking backwards for their inspiration.

Wanting to squeeze as much as they could from this star pairing, the label pushed aside the outfit's latest LP [793] and stepped back to 1971, dipping into *The Magnificent Seven* for this particular recording. Thrown onto the album as little more than a filler, the unusually troubling lyric of "Without The One You Love" verges on a suicide threat, the blasé treatment received for this remake ill-befitting its original purpose. Running at full throttle, and with an irrelevant bongo track hammering through, the number was never intended as a single, this inconsequential lift resulting in a non-hit which Tamla Motown's American counterparts didn't bother with.

## TMG 816
## MICHAEL JACKSON
**Rockin' Robin** (2:30)
(Thomas)
Produced by Mel Larson/Jerry Marcellino
**Release Date**: 12 May 1972
**B-side**: Love Is Here And Now You're Gone
**Position in Record Retailer Top 40**: 3
**Equivalent US Release**: Motown 1197 (17 Feb 1972)
**Position in Billboard Top 40 Pop**: 2
**Position in Billboard Top 40 R & B**: 2

Having launched Michael Jackson with the impressive "Got To Be There" [797], Motown followed-up with this dire ditty, a cover of an old Bobby Day song written by Leon René (who owned the LA-based Class label), under the working name Jimmie Thomas.[1] Unremarkably recorded, and featuring some unintentionally funny period wah-wah guitar, the track was paired with a remake of [597] and somehow managed to outdo Jackson's first hit on all charts.

[1] Unlike other versions of the song, Day's appeared as "Rock-in Robin".

## TMG 817
## MARVIN GAYE
**Inner City Blues (Make Me Wanna Holler)** (2:58)
(Nyx—Gaye)
Produced by Marvin Gaye
Recording completed: 5 May 1971
**Release Date**: 26 May 1972
**B-side**: Wholly Holy
**Position in Record Retailer Top 40**: -
**Equivalent US Release**: Tamla 54209 (10 Jun 1971)
**Position in Billboard Top 40 Pop**: 9
**Position in Billboard Top 40 R & B**: 1

Having received high acclaim for *What's Going On* in 1971, Marvin Gaye was in a state of self-centred satisfaction during 1972, guardedly enjoying the accolades bestowed on an 'artist' in full creative mode. (He was reputedly hurt that the album did not win a Grammy.) Convinced by his own hype, Gaye was settling into the role of Messiah figure, gradually talking himself and his album up to the point where, as interviewers frequently broached *What's Going On*, he would espouse any number of laudable claims, his recurrent thesis that the album came through divine intervention a perverse exercise in false modesty: "I was only the instrument in the album. All the inspiration came from God himself".[1] Meanwhile basking in his own glory, Gaye humbly accepted an award for 'The nation's most socially significant entertainer' from the National Association for the Advancement of Colored People', and agreed an invitation to host the Martin Luther King Birthday Commemoration in Atlanta in January 1972 (from which he eventually withdrew).

Between awards ceremonies and industry functions, Gaye was also re-launching his live career, agreeing to a rash of intermittent benefit concerts, although in his typically turbulent manner, he would cancel a high number of them. The period is best-remembered for the announcement in Washington DC of 'Marvin Gaye Day' on May 1, which after several changes of heart, he eventually arranged to attend. In the end stretching to a week of activity and events during which Gaye was presented with the key to the city, the centrepiece of the celebration was a gig at the John F Kennedy Centre for Performing Arts which met with waves or adulation from the assembled crowds. Gaye's appearance, in which tracks from *What's Going On* were openly worshipped by the throng confirmed his view that he was somehow 'above' the material world, preaching enlightenment to his 'followers' through the haze of a cocaine and marijuana 'high'. (His dual paranoia and inflated self-estimation in 1972 are exposed by his own analysis as to why he was apprehensive about appearing. In truth, the singer suffered stage-fright, but tellingly observed, "Until the last few minutes, I wasn't going to go. You see, I'd just turned thirty-three. That was the age Jesus died".)[2]

By this stage, feeling that his work was done, Gaye had already commenced recording follow-up material, releasing the new "You're The Man" in America in April. Conceived as the central theme of a movie soundtrack, this project like several others was dropped when Gaye simply lost interest in it. In the UK, the track was not released, Tamla Motown well behind schedule and still plundering *What's Going On* for singles, this fourth title released in a vain bid to wring a British hit from the album.

"Inner City Blues" began as a variation of an old Drifters' number, commandeered by Gaye after being initially developed (uncredited) by Elgie Stover. Using the basic rhythms as a canvas, Gaye and Motown's lift operator James Nyx began throwing phrases around, hinting at social and political issues randomly. Much of the resultant lyric is consequently disjointed, 'trigger happy policing' included mainly for its lyric ring, other lines inspired by current affairs, and a complaint about taxation dropped in as a private joke, Gaye and Nyx both being indebted to the IRS at the time. Left incomplete under the working title "The Tail End", the track was completed after Nyx stumbled on the title phrase in the Detroit press, Gaye's rejoinder 'Make me wanna holler' completing the piece.

As made for *What's Going On*, the track was cut on March 19, along with the remake of "Mercy Mercy Me" [802], Bob Babbitt providing bass guitar. (He subsequently dubbed a second bass onto the mix, sometimes wrongly interpreted as a Babbitt-Jamerson collaboration.) Ultimately something of a dirge, "Inner City Blues" was mixed for mono and edited for release on 45, impressing the devoted American market but, like the rest of Gaye's period releases, meeting no interest in the UK.

[1] Quoted in Davis, 1984 p63.
[2] Quoted in Ritz, p209.

## TMG 818
## THE UNDISPUTED TRUTH
**Superstar (Remember How You Got Where You Are)** (2:52)
(Whitfield—Strong)
Produced by Norman Whitfield
**Release Date**: 16 Jun 1972
**B-side**: Ain't No Sun Since You've Been Gone
**Position in Record Retailer Top 40**: -
**No Equivalent US Release**

Joe Harris / Billie Calvin / Brenda Evans

Forced to build much of their career from Temptations hand-me-downs [776]; [789], The Undisputed Truth had recorded their second Motown album *Face To Face With...* in 1971, which included in its seven titles only one original [897b]. The rest were predominantly Norman Whitfield re-works, including "Superstar", issued on 45 by The Temptations as recently as January [800], and a nine-minute-plus version of "What's Going On" [775].[1]

Illustrative of his vision for the group, Whitfield alters the texture of "Superstar" substantially for this new recording. Set at a rapidly marching pace, and punching through its treble-heavy mix with ringing cymbals and Dennis Coffey's fuzzed and frantically thrashing electric guitar, the track is brightly energetic where The Temptations' model had been 'dark' and hypnotising.

Not picked up in America, the release passed most people by, a somewhat inopportune choice and one which Tamla Motown would not follow-up for two years [897]. The travesty of the selection was that the Truth's original version of "Papa Was A Rollin' Stone" which they released contemporaneously in America (Gordy 7117), became lost and fell to The Temptations to immortalise [839], inevitably giving the false impression that their own initial rendition was just another cover version.

[1] The album is an early example of Motown crediting The Funk Brothers, all listed on the back with special mention of "Motown's one and only Eddie Brown".

## TMG 819
## FRANKIE VALLI & THE FOUR SEASONS
**You're A Song (That I Can't Sing)** (3:11)
(Gaudio—Gaudio)
Produced by Bob Gaudio

**Release Date**: 9 Jun 1972
**B-side**: Sun Country
**Position in Record Retailer Top 40**: -
**No Equivalent US Release**

Frankie Valli / Bob Gaudio / Nick Massi / Joey Long

The biggest pre-established act to sign to Motown, The Four Seasons were brought in towards the end of 1971 by Berry Gordy apparently for no other reason than that he liked them. The Four Seasons had come together in 1961, the quartet of American-Italians settling in New York on the coat-tails of the Brill Building set [581n]. Once there, keyboardist and future songwriter Bob Gaudio was recruited, and the act were signed to Chicago's Vee Jay label, quickly establishing a substantial following, breaking into the UK market with their twin hits, "Sherry" and "Big Girls Don't Cry", both distinguished by Frankie Valli's extraordinary falsetto.

As quintessentially East Coast as the Beach Boys were West Coast, The Four Seasons withstood the British Invasion by refusing to compromise their approach[1] but the 1960s were extraordinarily progressive and towards the end of the decade the popularity of the group's dated sound began to tail off, despite attempts to break into progressive rock. In 1970 they lost Tommy DeVito from the line-up, sparking a prolonged withdrawal for the act who looked as if they were finished.

Fortunes were revived in 1971 when The Four Seasons were unexpectedly approached by Berry Gordy, who happened to be on the look-out for talent to bolster his white-oriented Rare Earth and Mo-West portfolios ([742]; [799]). Promising to revive them with his personal support and studio time, Gordy's commitment proved hollow when he rapidly lost interest, pre-occupied during 1972 with Diana Ross' *Lady Sings The Blues* project [848].

Left largely to their own devices, and contracted to a peripheral label in Mo-West, the act struggled from day one, their first release *Chameleon* (which was widely praised in the music press) failing to sell.[2] A US trailer-single in "The Night" was then cancelled before going on sale, and "Walk On, Don't Look Back" issued instead, so that by mid 1972 the situation was looking woeful. In the UK, prospects for the group were slightly more favourable, Valli's own "You're Ready Now" (on the Philips label) having been picked up by Northern Soul crowds for a belated hit in January 1971, leading to a UK tour. Tamla Motown therefore saw fresh potential in the group and despite not releasing *Chameleon,* selected "You're A Song (That I Can't Sing)" for a hopeful debut single.

Having little or no appeal to dance crowds, this recording is archetypal California soul, sophisticatedly laid-back and borrowing its mood from West Coast rock. Whether this is the result of its being recorded in LA is debatable, but emerging at the precise time The Eagles were breaking, the crossover is tangible, something apparently abroad in the relaxed California air of 1972 as psychedelic rock began to give way to the gentler influence of country.

This pleasant diversion for Motown failed to consolidate The Four Seasons, who had an unstable period ahead. No other Tamla Motown singles would emerge, the act shifted sideways to the UK Mo-West imprint. (See Appendix 3 for their Mo-West singles.) The act strangely re-appeared on Tamla Motown in 1980, their Northern Soul hit "The Night" selected for a surprise re-issue with its Mo-West catalogue number intact [L020].

[1] Vee Jay owned the US rights to several early Beatles recordings, at one point assembling *The Beatles Vs The Four Seasons*, containing recordings by both acts.

[2] The LP contained two recordings billed as solo Frankie Valli tracks, which had been released on Mo-West ahead of anything by the group.


**TMG 820**
**MARY WELLS**
**My Guy** (2:45) **[E42]**
(Robinson)
Produced by William "Smokey" Robinson
Recording completed: 3 Mar 1964
**Release Date**: 23 Jun 1972
**B-side**: You Lost The Sweetest Boy [E30] / Two Lovers [E14]
**Position in Record Retailer Top 40**: 14
**Equivalent US Release**: Motown 1056 (13 Mar 1964)
**Position in Billboard Top 40 Pop**: 1
**Position in Billboard Top 40 R & B**: 1

Of the 45 Motown-sourced singles issued on Stateside between October 1963 and March 1965, six were re-released as Tamla Motown A-sides, "My Guy" quickly following "Needle In A Haystack" [806].[1] Originally put out in May 1964, "My Guy" was Motown's UK breakthrough, rising to 5 on the singles charts after going to the very top at home. The record's success in the face of the then-pervasive Beatles hysteria was a major achievement for the 21-year-old Wells, after two years recording for Motown under the artistic direction of Smokey Robinson. Several of her other early recordings had been pop successes at home, and she had, by the time [E42] appeared, been granted some five previous UK singles in an effort to break her, only The Marvelettes and The Miracles having racked up more.

This legendary track, made in the spring of 1964, was begun by Robinson, and after a hard day's work, jammed by the exhausted Funk Brothers into a tighter form. Musicians with a background in jazz, the group noticed a resemblance in the lazily rocking introduction to the jazz standard "Canadian Sunset", which Earl Van Dyke jokingly picked up on, adding in a section from "Beguine The Beguine". From such idle musings, the basis of the track's introduction was formulated, although these influences scarcely permeate the finished product.

Robinson's lyric, which deals with the indomitable strength of true love, is replete with its author's playful internal rhymes and jokey couplets, even slipping through a double-use of the word 'opinion' in the middle-8 which suggests Wells may have mis-read the lyric sheet (there being any number of preferable nouns available). Her performance on the track is strengthened by her recognition of its raw potential, which prompted her to rehearse it to-death in order to deliberately damage her vocal chords and thus give her recording an added husk—which stands in mature contrast to the light-hearted backing vocals ("tell me *more*").

Production-wise, "My Guy" is very much a product of its time, the feebleness of the brass push at 2:00 subject to the technological limitations of the day. This though matters little in the final estimation. The infectious charm of the track has nothing to do with hi-fidelity reproduction, and everything to do with the spirit in which it was made. A moment of unbridled joy, the song captures a time of optimistic innocence in Wells' life, which in winning over the public was pivotal in her leaving Motown altogether, with eyes on even bigger things (see [E42]).

Revived by Tamla Motown in 1972, this new edition of the song paired it with two other recordings for a 'maxi-single'. Both of its partner tracks had been UK A-sides early on, [E30] on Stateside and [E14] on Oriole American. Interestingly, both show the Motown studio playing with recording effects, "Two Lovers" incorporating sounds of running water, supposedly taped in Hitsville's bathroom and "You Lost The Sweetest Boy" featuring a pair of spoons! This three-track edition which delighted Wells' fans was her first and only Tamla Motown single before the label was wound up in 1976, and creditably made the top 20.

Over the years "My Guy" has retained its popularity, and Wells a place in the hearts of the label's fans. The song was covered in 1976 [1030] and Tamla Motown issued the original again in 1980 (see Chapter 6). A few years later, Wells contributed a live segment from the song to the *Motown 25* show, after which she continued to perform her old hits with other former Motown acts. Tragically, Wells died in 1992 aged just 49, following two years of cancer treatment which had left her more or less penniless, a tragic demise for one of Motown's pioneers and much-loved early stars.

[1] The full six consist of [595]; [684]; [806]; [820]; [915] and [925]. See also Statistics, Facts And Feats section.

**TMG 821**
**THE SUPREMES**
**Automatically Sunshine** (2:35)
(Robinson)
Produced by William "Smokey" Robinson
**Release Date**: 30 Jun 1972
**B-side**: Precious Little Things
**Position in Record Retailer Top 40**: 10
**Equivalent US Release**: Motown 1200 (11 Apr 1972)
**Position in Billboard Top 40 Pop**: 37
**Position in Billboard Top 40 R & B**: 21

Jean Terrell / Cindy Birdsong / Mary Wilson

The Supremes/Robinson collaborations which had given rise to [804] in February revealed their full scope in May with the unveiling of *Floy Joy*, an album's worth of recordings all of which have Robinson's name on the copyright. (The UK pressing had yet to appear, seeing release in September.) Highly regarded by all involved, the album allowed vocal spots for both Jean Terrell and Smokey's old friend Mary Wilson, who shares "Automatically Sunshine", the new single.

Based on a heliocentric metaphor, the track follows several precedents including that of *Let The Sunshine In*, the album on which Robinson and the group had first rekindled their working relationship (via the cut "The Composer"; see [804]), and his own [E67] with its famous opening declaration. Knowingly checking back over the 1960s for musical 'tone', the writer here revisits the HDH period, deliberately looking at revamping The Supremes' famous style and incorporating a tongue-in-cheek eight-beat drum pattern cribbed from "Where Did Our Love Go" [E51], much as he had done with the fade-in on [804]. Further evidence that Robinson was reworking the group's early hits soon arrives with a flourishing rush of Hammond organ, resembling the commencing moments of "Stop! In The Name Of Love" [501] so unmistakably that innocent coincidence seems all but impossible.

The song itself proves the case, built on a descending chord run exactly as per the sequence of HDH hits which include both "Standing In The Shadows Of Love" [589] and "Bernadette" [601] (transposed to Em for the sake of the female vocals). In this respect, Robinson is working HDH's productions exactly as the team once did themselves, deconstructing and re-assembling components to generate new forms and novel combinations. That he builds a *faux*-HDH hit in this manner is impressive, but is masked by a production ethic in which, rather than look backwards, Robinson employs a 'laid back' feel, most likely stemming from recent extra-Motown West Coast recordings (see [819]). If so, the song's 'flavour' may have been suggested by California-based groups such as The Turtles, whose 1960s hits "Elenore" and "Happy Together" carry a similarly mellow groove, the latter sharing once more the same falling chord run as "Automatically Sunshine".

With its catchy punch and bouncy, if somewhat laboured optimism, the track—since requisitioned for 'automatic' soap powder commercials—convinced the group's believers and scraped into the UK top 10. American fans were less impressed, the song failing disappointingly. If at one time the 'sunshine' of The Supremes' flamboyant group persona had seemed as natural as their next hit single, by the early 1970s, they were looking backwards so doggedly that hopes of forward development were becoming increasingly dashed after the initial flourish of post-Diana hits. The group were now entering a period of internal upheaval and would never score another top 10 hit.

**TMG 822**
**THE ORIGINALS**
**God Bless Whoever Sent You** (3:15)
(Sawyer—McMurray)
Produced by Clay McMurray
**Release Date**: 30 Jun 1972

**B-side**: I Like Your Style / Baby I'm For Real [733]
**Position in Record Retailer Top 40**: -
**Equivalent US Release**: Soul 35079 (18 Nov 1970)
**Position in Billboard Top 40 Pop**: -
**Position in Billboard Top 40 R & B**: 14

---

Freddie Gorman / Walter Gaines / C P Spencer / Henry "Hank" Dixon

---

Having released nothing on Tamla Motown since "Baby I'm For Real" [733] more than two years earlier, The Originals were booked for an extravagant UK tour, intended to try and break them in Britain. The 28-day stopover was due to commence on July 3, Tamla Motown electing to support it with this opportunistic release, three days prior to their arrival.

"God Bless Whoever Sent You" dates to 1970, recorded for the group's *Naturally Together*, a non-UK set which served to follow-up their successful *Green Grow The Lilacs*. Principally performed by Walter Gaines, the track features vocal rotations in the manner of The Temptations and is pitched in the slow and gentle mood of the group's previous singles. (Tamla Motown were plugging this style as 'sweet soul' in 1972.) Co-written by its producer, "God Bless Whoever Sent You" is built from a repeating run of bar-length chords against which the lyrics consist of a stream of clichéd declarations of love which quickly pales.

In the interim between its being recorded and released here, The Originals had struggled to maintain their appeal and underwent a recent line-up change with the departure of C P Spencer for a solo career. In his place came Ty Hunter, a formative group member who had been unable to pursue the project at its inception due to an existing contract with Chess. (Meantime he had become a member of Glass House, signed to Invictus. See [831].)

The additional titles on this 3-track maxi-single consist of "I Like Your Style", a modest R & B hit in America during 1970, and "Baby I'm For Real" [733], their biggest success and previous UK A-side. The group would have to wait until 1976 for another [1038].

**TMG 823**
**FOUR TOPS**
**Walk With Me, Talk With Me Darling** (2:35)
(Dean—Glover—McMurray)
Produced by Frank Wilson
**Release Date**: 14 Jul 1972
**B-side**: L. A. (My Town)
**Position in Record Retailer Top 40**: 32
**No Equivalent US Release**

---

Levi Stubbs / Lawrence Payton / Abdul 'Duke' Fakir / Renaldo 'Obie' Benson

---

The Four Tops' current album *Nature Planned It* had a generally cool reception in the summer of 1972, but for the last track on side 1, which, recalling the group's mid-1960s style was attracting attention from fans and DJs. Quick to latch-on to this, Tamla Motown released it as a single, comparing the process of discovery in their publicity material to that of "I'm Still Waiting" [781].[1]

Another mid-range stomp, similar in mode to the group's recent Supremes collaborations, particularly "You Gotta Have Love In Your Heart" [793], the emergent 45 had little to commend it besides its strong beat, and Levi Stubbs' ever-forceful vocals. The track's most effective element is James Jamerson's bass, reminiscent of his late-1960s style, bubbling with triplets and earning him particular mention on the concurrent album sleeve ('bass personified').

The sad reality was that The Four Tops' career at Motown had run aground. The group had not placed a single in the US top 10 since 1967 [601], and while loyalty in the UK had kept them afloat for several unspectacular years, the act never recovered the loss of HDH in 1968. Still based in Detroit and sensing that Motown had left them behind, the group began looking for deals elsewhere, the once unthinkable step of leaving Motown very suddenly imminent. By the end of 1972 it had emerged that their contract had been purchased by ABC, and come December they were in the US top 10 again with their new label Dunhill. (Their records were released on Probe in the UK.)

*Nature Planned It* would be their swan-song, Tamla Motown's release policy disguising this effectively with the subsequent appearance on 45 of several further recordings already in-the-can. Poignantly, the B-side selected here was "L. A. (My Town)", lifted from the 1970 album *Still Waters Run Deep* [752]. This subtle swipe at Motown by the UK arm seemed to anticipate the loss of the group, and with it, another chapter of Motown's glittering past was quietly closed, the loss of this golden group almost too much for fans to bear.

[1] Sound effects can be heard on the album, the noise of a woman taking a shower apparent on the intro to the current song, which can be faintly ascertained on the single mix, indicating the effect was embedded in the master.

**TMG 824**
**JUNIOR WALKER & THE ALL STARS**
**Walk In The Night** (2:50)
(Bristol—McLeod)
Produced by Johnny Bristol
**Release Date**: 21 Jul 1972
**B-side**: Right On Brothers And Sisters / Gotta Hold On To This Feeling
**Position in Record Retailer Top 40**: 16
**Equivalent US Release**: Soul 35095 (29 Feb 1972)
**Position in Billboard Top 40 Pop**: -
**Position in Billboard Top 40 R & B**: 10

---

Jr Walker / Willie Woods / Vic Thomas / Billy Nicks

---

Aware that Junior Walker & The All Stars had been waiting for almost two long years for a new release, Tamla Motown conceded to this maxi-single, aware that they had passed-over each of the group's last three US 45s (all of which they would subsequently concede to issue: [840]; [857]; [872]). As with The Four Tops [823], this policy of dipping into the archives for ostensibly new singles disguised the fact that, for several years, Tamla Motown were merely recycling the group's back-catalogue, no all-new 45 emerging from Walker again (bar his 'solo' effort [1027]).

As a basic composition, "Walk In The Night" was assembled by Walker's old sponsor Johnny Bristol, sitting side-by-side with new arrival Marilyn McLeod, the two exchanging musical phrases and ideas and gradually building the song's progression between them. (Bristol probably threw in the F#/Fm chorus, the vocalised chords suggesting inspiration from "Ain't No Mountain High Enough" [611], on which he had worked.) Conceived as an instrumental from the outset, Junior Walker was the natural choice to record it, and was duly offered the basic track on which his solemnly melodic sax solos take centre-stage.

Highly repetitive, and pleading for a lead vocal over the backing group, the song was arranged by H. B. Barnum and Willie Shorter as a shady jazz number, likened by Bill Dahl to 'a blaxploitation flick theme'.[1] Certainly the production has intense atmosphere, gliding through its alternately relaxed and tense backdrops as if cruising through the bright lights and dark alleyways of a down-town city district, its title evocative and wholly apt.

However as part of the *Moody Junior* album, a sleekly produced suite of recordings which pulled Walker's style further away from his famous 'rough-house' style, the single shows sedation setting in, the lack of vocal track perhaps significant in this respect. This UK release was coupled with "Right On Brothers And Sisters" from 1971 and "Gotta Hold On To This Feeling" from 1969, which would again be resurrected as an A-side in 1974 [894].

[1] p183

## TMG 825
## THE JACKSON 5
**Little Bitty Pretty One** (2:48)
(Byrd)
Produced by Mel Larson/Jerry Marcellino
**Release Date**: 8 Sep 1972
**B-side**: Maybe Tomorrow
**Position in Record Retailer Top 40**: -
**Equivalent US Release**: Motown 1199 (4 Apr 1972)
**Position in Billboard Top 40 Pop**: 13
**Position in Billboard Top 40 R & B**: 8

Jackie Jackson / Tito Jackson / Jermaine Jackson / Marlon Jackson / Michael Jackson

This new Jackson 5 single was a remake of an oldie, like "Rockin' Robin" [816] from Bobby Day's back-catalogue (and copyrighted by him, under his birth-name Robert Byrd), which fellow Indiana singer Thurston Harris had scored a hit with in 1957. (Clyde McPhatter also recorded a version in 1962 which made 25 on the pop charts but unusually failed to register on the R & B top 40.)[1]

Delayed, so as to avoid clashing with "Ain't No Sunshine" [826], this frivolous single floundered and might have fared better had it been flipped for the American hit B-side, originally written by Deke Richards for Sammy Davis Jr [663]. The group were unmistakably now in decline, the marriage of Tito and secret lover Dolores Martes on June 17 offering signs that the childhood Jacksons were inevitably growing up.

[1] McPhatter died from a heart attack on 13 June 1972, aged 39. He had spent much of his later years living in the UK.

## TMG 826
## MICHAEL JACKSON
**Ain't No Sunshine** (4:09)
(Withers)
Produced by Hal Davis
**Release Date**: 28 Jul 1972
**B-side**: I Wanna Be Where You Are
**Position in Record Retailer Top 40**: 8
**No Equivalent US Release**

Demonstrating beyond doubt the extent to which Motown and its contemporary labels had changed the face of popular music, the US charts were stacked with recordings by black artists during the spring and summer of 1972. At one point in May, all of the top 8 were by black acts, Roberta Flack, Al Green, The Stylistics, Aretha Franklin, The Chi-Lites and The Staple Singers all scoring major hits in a chart which also included [825] and Jackson Browne's original version of "Doctor My Eyes" [842]. Another group making their mark were The O'Jays, back in business over the summer on the Philadelphia International label [890], with "Back Stabbers" pointing the way ahead for American soul and mainstream black pop.

Also new on the scene was Bill Withers, who had arrived the previous summer with his soulful "Ain't No Sunshine" and was about to follow-up with "Lean On Me". Withers' debut hit was produced by another key figure in black music, Booker T— and, ever alert for strong material, Motown covered the song in January, both The Temptations and Michael Jackson having a stab at it. With Bill Withers' original not having been a UK hit, Tamla Motown lifted it from Jackson's debut album *Got To Be There*, and scored an opportunist top 10 hit. The song's title recalls "Ain't No Sun Since You've Been Gone", a Jobete original which had been passed around Motown for several years, and in its sunshine theme links to [821].

Arranged under the direction of respected composer Eddy Manson, the track maintains Jackson's general style, despite his youthful voice sounding anaemic beside Withers', although he takes flight in the extended closing choruses. Filling the gap between the abhorrent "Rockin' Robin" [816] and his biggest solo hit "Ben" [834], this pleasing filler captured the composition for Jackson, many UK listeners assuming it to be a Motown original.

**TMG 827**
**STEVIE WONDER**
**Superwoman** (3:29)
(Wonder)
Produced by Stevie Wonder
**Release Date**: 1 Sep 1972
**B-side**: Seems So Long
**Position in Record Retailer Top 40**: -
**Equivalent US Release**: Tamla 54216 (May 1972)
**Position in Billboard Top 40 Pop**: 33
**Position in Billboard Top 40 R & B**: 13

Recording independently of Motown for the first time [798], Stevie Wonder had ensconced himself in the late Jimi Hendrix's Electric Lady studios in New York and began work on some new compositions. Wonder found two collaborators in Robert Margouleff and Malcolm Cecil, a pair of synthesiser wizards who had constructed their own super-instrument in 1970 by adding-on and wiring into a basic Moog, their monstrous creation christened Tonto (The Original New Timbral Orchestra). Having previously recorded an album of synth tracks for Embryo, they realised that this new music, while futuristic, would remain marginal if presented purely on its own terms and so made themselves and Tonto available to mainstream recording artists, which is how Stevie Wonder crossed paths with them in 1971.

Installing the lumbering Tonto at Electric Lady, the team pushed against its limitations, the contraption continuing to grow as the sessions progressed. This process necessitated more and more add-on modules which Steve Lodder analyses as consisting at one stage of 'Moog, plus four Oberheim SEMs, two ARP 2066s, a cornucopia of EMS and Serge modules and several sequencers, including an adapted EMS 256'.[1] The apparatus was at one stage about nine feet long, arranged in an arc around its operators, who were forced to run from end-to-end as they worked. The three toiled predominantly by night over several months, gradually building a generous portfolio of new work which would revolutionise Wonder's career.

Besides the aesthetic, the attraction of Tonto (and synthesisers generally) lie in their facilitating full control of recorded instrumentation. Due to their capacity for piecemeal tracking (which at this stage of technology required Margouleff and Cecil's expertise in programming the equipment), songs could be built up layer-on-layer, enabling Wonder to play everything just as he heard it without the unwanted nuances of session musicians (see [755]). Furthermore, they provided a high degree of sound control, Wonder able to switch effortlessly from 'instrument' to 'instrument', playing with arrangements and voicings with the touch of a button, allowing for the 'accidental' discovery of effective arrangements by trial and error.

According to the sleeve notes of the emergent *Music Of My Mind*, Wonder played all instrumentation on the sessions himself (bar the guitar solo on the present track and one other trombone passage), claiming all synthesiser work as his own, as well as handling various keyboards, harmonica and a conventional drum-kit. And what was released here was only a small selection of the music generated in these semi-secret sessions, Wonder's boundless energy transferring onto his collaborators who between them assembled several hundred other part-made tracks at a total estimated cost of a quarter of a million dollars.

The first single, "Superwoman" records Wonder's break-up with Syreeta. The album version stretched to a full eight minutes, consisting in truth of two independently conceived tracks which were meshed together courtesy of an eerie instrumental passage on Tonto commencing at 3:04. The second part is Wonder's emotion laid bare, as he insinuatingly enquires, 'Where were you when I needed you last summer?', and openly declares his love at an end. (The couple would separate by year-end [841].) However, an eight-minute epic was clearly not viable on 7-inch and in its released edit, it was the first half of "Superwoman" which made the cut.[2] This opening three minutes shows Wonder on the offensive, laying accusations about the place and generally pouring scorn on his subject. Assuming it too is about Syreeta, it shows a different side to his personality, short on patience and, in its final summing up, condemning her 'filthy head' under his breath.

Given its catty tone and sarcastic title, the track was an unusual selection for a single, but one which, disguised by the free-flowing lightness of its melody, raised surprisingly few eyebrows even from within Motown (for whom Syreeta remained contracted as a writer-performer). Dropping beats for fun, Wonder's musical soundscape is as blithely unencumbered as anything in his discography, its thoughtful structure perhaps proving itself above the level of the hit parade (see also [779]). Following mediocre sales in America[3], the UK edition failed to scale the top 40, a rare failure for an artist growing in stature with each successive release. Similarly, *Music Of My Mind,* which received high acclaim on release, was not initially embraced by music fans, taking several years to earn its reputation as a Wonder milestone and finding its place through the prism of hindsight as the point at which the artist found his true potential.

[1] p75. In a contemporary interview (cited in Davis 1988, p125) Wonder remarked that he was currently working with a VS04 synth.

[2] The extended guitar solo by Buzzy Feiten (spelled Feiton on the LP cover) is located in the second section, therefore not featuring on the 7-inch.

[3] The Tamla pressing billed the track as "Superwoman (Where Were You When I Needed You?)".

**TMG 828**
**SISTERS LOVE**
**Mr. Fix-it Man** (2:59)
(Hutch—Wakefield)
Produced by Willie Hutch
**Release Date**: 8 Sep 1972
**B-side**: You've Got To Make Your Choice
**Position in Record Retailer Top 40**: -

**Equivalent US Release**: Mo-West 5014 (9 Mar 1972)
**Position in Billboard Top 40 Pop**: -
**Position in Billboard Top 40 R & B**: -

| Vermettya Boyster / Lillie Fort / Gwen Berry / Jeannie Long |
| --- |

Having launched Mo-West as an American imprint in 1971 (see [799]), Motown had assembled a promising roster of new signings and existing names, their UK output channelled through Tamla Motown. However in October the UK operation launched Mo-West in Britain as it had done with Rare Earth [786], and the current single by new signings Sisters Love would be the last of the American releases transferred, as the UK arm took over. Yet problems beset the new label within months when it emerged that the American branch was being wound up and had dropped much of its roster, hottest property The Commodores joining several acts moved sideways to the main Motown label. For a while it was touch-and-go whether the UK label would be viable without a stream of material to release, but in due course it found its feet and ran for several years (see Appendix 3).

Sisters Love had started out as a quartet of backing vocalists for Ray Charles who got into the habit of calling each other 'sister'. Having emerged in their own right around 1970, they were signed to A & M, supposedly as the company's first black artists[1], and enjoyed a minor hit in 1971 with "Are You Lonely", in collaboration with writer Gene Chandler. Their arrival at Motown (after some personnel changes) offered the act their big chance to break-through, Kenny Wakefield and Willie Hutch's "Mr. Fix-it Man" released on Mo-West in March.

The Tamla Motown edition duly emerged in September, this jocular funk creation sung by Gwen Berry holding a chord of D major through almost its entire length. That it wasn't a hit mattered relatively little at this stage, the group arriving in the UK in November in support of The Jackson 5 [833], and mesmerising crowds with their explosive stage presence. The UK press were apparently so keen to get coverage of the act that a special show was hastily convened for the media, and it seemed as if the group would be a major success.

If the cancellation of their US follow-up in October didn't ring alarm bells it should have; more than half of Mo-West's US releases from here on would be scrapped before release, Sisters Love seeing just one more single out, their proposed album shelved. The UK situation was much the same, [1002] creeping out first on Mo-West then as a late Tamla Motown issue, but the dissolution of Mo-West in America really spelled the end of the act who had promised so much.

[1] Sonny Charles & The Checkmates, Ltd probably predated them.

**TMG 829**
**FOUR TOPS**
**I'll Turn To Stone** (2:33)
(Holland—Dozier—Holland—Taylor)
Produced by Brian Holland/Lamont Dozier
Recording completed: 6 Aug 1966
**Release Date**: 15 Sep 1972

**B-side**: Love Feels Like Fire
**Position in Record Retailer Top 40**: -
**Equivalent US Release**: Motown 1110 (4 May 1967)
**Position in Billboard Top 40 Pop**: -
**Position in Billboard Top 40 R & B**: -

---

Levi Stubbs / Lawrence Payton / Abdul 'Duke' Fakir / Renaldo 'Obie' Benson

---

Originally recorded in 1967, "I'll Turn To Stone" was relegated to B-side status [612] and forgotten until British mixed-race group The Foundations released their hit single "Build Me Up Buttercup" at the close of 1968. Recognising the near-identical melody and chord progressions in Tony Macaulay's composition (not to mention the opening 'ooh' cribbed from "Baby Love" [E56] and the title steal from [596]), Motown initiated lengthy legal action, thereby bringing overdue public exposure to the Four Tops' song.[1]

Never shy of an opportune cash-in, Tamla Motown issued the track as an A-side in September 1972, coupled with another HDH number from the group's earlier *Second Album*. "I'll Turn To Stone" is a mid-tempo track originating from the fertile *Reach Out* sessions, and in materialising here as a single, takes the LP's count to seven.[2] Carried by its infectious bounce, classic-HDH in mood and form, the song had every chance of being a UK hit in 1967. The elevation of the downbeat "7-Rooms Of Gloom" is probably explicable in terms of "I'll Turn To Stone" being arranged in a manner markedly dated even for its time, with piano and baritone sax holding the centre ground.

[1] Ironically, the copyright issue reared its head again after Abba's 1974 number 1 "Waterloo" drew inevitable comparisons with "Build Me Up Buttercup", the chorus again built on the same basic template.

[2] See also [579]; [589]; [601]; [612]; [634]; [647].


**TMG 830**
**GLADYS KNIGHT & THE PIPS**
**Help Me Make It Through The Night** (3:50)
(Kristofferson)
Produced by Johnny Bristol
**Release Date**: 20 Oct 1972
**B-side**: If You're Gonna Leave (Just Leave)
**Position in Record Retailer Top 40**: 11
**Equivalent US Release**: Soul 35094 (6 Mar 1972)
**Position in Billboard Top 40 Pop**: 33
**Position in Billboard Top 40 R & B**: 13

---

Gladys Knight / Merald 'Bubba' Knight / Edward Patten / William Guest

---

Prior to Tamla Motown's poaching of "Ain't No Sunshine" [826], Motown flagged the tactic in America by issuing their own hit cover, Gladys Knight & The Pips' version of "Help Me Make It Through The Night" following successful renditions by several acts. Written by Kris Kristofferson and first-recorded by him, the track concerned a man longing for his absent lover. Picked up by country singer Sammi Smith, the lyric was gender-changed such that it read as an invitation to bed, causing minor controversy and helping hoist it to number 8 pop in 1971.

Further successful recordings in the soul vein followed by both Joe Simon and O. C. Smith (following up his cover of "Baby I Need Your Loving" [E53]), although as with [826], the song remained largely unknown in the UK. This Tamla Motown release therefore drew considerable attention, going to number 11 and earning on-its-way an estimation as the definitive reading. Similar in several ways to [826], "Help Me Make It Through The Night" has a spoken introduction (edited off some re-issues) and is of similar tempo and despondent mood, the two hits in quick succession saddling Tamla Motown with a reputation for bloated ballads which would never be fully shaken off.

This simplistic understanding though does not account for Knight's authority, her powerful solo vocal penetrating the sparse, bass-dependent arrangement and H. B. Barnum's slowly swaying orchestration. (The percussion track is incongruously suggestive of military marching drums.) With its intimacy and emotional need, Knight's reading could have been made for late-night FM radio, and set for her a style which she would draw on throughout the rest of her career. Coinciding with the release, Gladys Knight & The Pips arrived in the UK for a brief tour which took in the London Palladium on November 5.


**TMG 831**
**LAURA LEE**
**To Win Your Heart** (2:30)
(Bunten—Bratton)
Produced by Ed Wingate
**Release Date**: 29 Sep 1972
**B-side**: So Will I
**Position in Record Retailer Top 40**: -
**No Equivalent US Release**
*Originally released as Ric Tic RT-111 (Mar 1966)*

Since 1969, Tamla Motown had warmly embraced its UK Northern Soul following, leading to several issues of old material from the Ric Tic vaults. Having released "I Love You Madly" [678] shortly after acquiring the rights, Tamla Motown also unearthed "Agent Double O Soul" [790] and "Festival Time" [795] during 1971-72, the latter a swinging instrumental recorded in 1966. Shortly after the recording was first-released, its writers Ed Wingate and Joanne Bratton chanced upon Laura Lee, a local club singer with an explosive vocal capacity, who was promptly brought to Ric Tic, her remit the recording of vocals over the existing instrumental.

Fearing that her voice would fail against the powerful musical arrangement, and suspicious of the key which took her to the bottom end of her register, a well-rehearsed Lee nonetheless managed an accomplished take at the second attempt. In pulling off this update, Lee and her producer Ed Wingate propelled the basic track into a storming dance number, the arrival of the lyric providing earthy relief and allowing the backing strings and rhythms to soar.

Deserving of a hit, this intensely drilling number was her only release for Ric Tic, the unsigned Lee drifting off to Chess for a run of R & B hits before landing up at Hot Wax, HDH's label set up in 1969 as the start of their Invictus company (see [745n]). There, she enjoyed a successful spell with several pro-feminist numbers including "Women's Love Rights", "Wedlock Is A Padlock" and the outrageous "Rip Off" in 1972. Although she never recorded directly for Motown, Lee was one of several artists to cross between company catalogues. In their time HDH recruited both Levi Stubbs' brother Joe [592] (as part of the group 100 Proof Aged In Soul) and former Motown star Brenda Holloway (see [700]). They also signed Glass House, which included future Supreme Scherrie Payne [884] and Ty Hunter, latterly of The Originals [822], plus long-time Detroit performer Popcorn Wylie [932].

Pulled out of oblivion by Tamla Motown less than a year after "Festival Time" had primed the club circuit, the thrilling "To Win Your Heart" shows why, in the mid 1960s, Ed Wingate's Golden World/Ric Tic labels were considered serious rivals to Motown's local dominance.

## TMG 832
## THE TEMPTATIONS
**Smiling Faces Sometimes** (3:37)
(Whitfield—Strong)
Produced by Norman Whitfield
**Release Date**: 13 Oct 1972
**B-side**: Mother Nature
**Position in Record Retailer Top 40**: -
**No Equivalent US Release**

Otis Williams / Melvin Franklin / Paul Williams / Eddie Kendricks / Dennis Edwards

As recorded for *Sky's The Limit* in 1971, the epic "Smiling Faces Sometimes" was the album's centrepiece, stretching over 12-and-a-half minutes of modulating bass rhythms and dotted instrumentation which, with its unchanging monotony, becomes rather stultifying. Whether the group's fans preferred such weighty masterworks was a matter for debate, but there is no doubting Norman Whitfield's commitment to his art which saw him and co-writer Barrett Strong pictured at work on the LP cover.

Having already released "Just My Imagination" [773] and "Ungena Za Ulimwengu" [783b] from the album, Tamla Motown unexpectedly dipped back again for an edited version of this track, trimmed to an acceptable three-and-a-half minutes. As sung by Eddie Kendricks, The Temptations' version is dispassionate compared to The Undisputed Truth's [789], and yet filled with a sense of mysterious half-light and premonitory caution which its clouded bass patterning intensifies graphically. Better-suited to the 7-inch format, the overweight recording comes into sharper focus, attesting to the principle that less is sometimes more.

**TMG 833**
**THE JACKSON 5**
**Lookin' Through The Windows** (3:33)
(Davis)
Produced by Hal Davis
**Release Date**: 27 Oct 1972
**B-side**: Love Song
**Position in Record Retailer Top 40**: 9
**Equivalent US Release**: Motown 1205 (23 Jun 1972)
**Position in Billboard Top 40 Pop**: 16
**Position in Billboard Top 40 R & B**: 5

Jackie Jackson / Tito Jackson / Jermaine Jackson / Marlon Jackson / Michael Jackson

The title track to The Jackson 5's most recent album (delayed in the UK to accommodate their *Greatest Hits* of August), "Looking Through The Windows" was the group's most attractive single in a disappointing year in which sales had slumped. By their own standards the fall-off was alarming although "Looking Through The Windows", their weakest seller to date, still shifted over half-a-million.

Written by Clifton Davis and arranged by James Carmichael, the base track makes a feature of its juddering rhythm sections which at 1:42 reference "I Can't Help Myself" [515]. More significantly, the omnipresent riffs and sharp guitar stabs borrow from Isaac Hayes' classic funk hit "Theme From Shaft", number 1 in late 1971. (Compare the opening moments of "Looking Through The Windows" with the closing section of Hayes' recording.)

Pulling off one of his most articulate vocals to date, Michael Jackson found frustration in John Bahler's strictly mapped template, wanting instead to do it 'his way'. Meeting resistance from his producer, Jackson promptly telephoned Berry Gordy, who arrived in person at the studio and overruled a disgruntled Hal Davis. The moment was a watershed, Jackson allowed greater freedom of input into his vocal contributions from here on.

With the record fresh in the shops (and promo copies circulating in a rare, full colour picture sleeve), the group was one of a number arriving in Europe in 1972 for a brief tour. (They brought along 11-year-old future member Randy to 'blood' him on stage.) Mayhem greeted the group during their UK dates, the brothers frequently mobbed and deafening screams permeating their performances, to the group's amazement. Propelled by the media attention, "Looking Through The Windows" became their first UK top 10 hit in five attempts.

**TMG 834**
**MICHAEL JACKSON**
**Ben** (2:42)
(Black—Scharf)
Produced by The Corporation
**Release Date**: 10 Nov 1972
**B-side**: You Can Cry On My Shoulder

**Position in Record Retailer Top 40**: 7
**Equivalent US Release**: Motown 1207 (12 Jul 1972)
**Position in Billboard Top 40 Pop**: 1
**Position in Billboard Top 40 R & B**: 5

Phil Karlson's sequel to the 1971 movie *Willard*, in which the central character seeks solace from a hostile world through his friendship with a couple of rats named Ben and Socrates, appeared in the summer of 1972. Picking up where *Willard* had ended, *Ben* turns its rodent star into a killer, leading a band of psychotic vermin on a rampage of gore resulting in their mass extermination. All of which would remain the province of cult horror buffs were it not for the peculiar fact that the wholesome Michael Jackson was invited to perform the movie's theme song, as supplied by Walter Scharf and lyricist Don Black.[1] (Whether the song was written expressly for the film is uncertain, although lines such as 'Ben, you're always running here and there' suggest that, at the very least it was shaped to fit.)

The more disturbing elements of the story were mirrored in subsequent interviews in which Michael Jackson admitted that he had kept rats of his own as a youngster, caged in his Beverly Hills home. Alarmed one night to witness them eating one another, Jackson placed the cage in the cold air of night, freezing them all to death.[2] This underlying flavour of macabre cruelty peeks from behind the curtains of "Ben", pitched in a plain lullaby mode, whose child's-eye view of friendship masks the sense of veiled abomination which shrouds the whole project.

Excited about seeing his name on the movie credits, Jackson claims to have gone to watch repeated screenings, delighting in the scale of his success. Released on vinyl, "Ben" became his first US number 1 despite being shunned by LA radio stations wise to its subject-matter. The song subsequently won a Golden Globe and was nominated for an Academy Award, accolades out of proportion to its value as a recording. In truth, "Ben" is willfully simplistic, its most compelling moment coming in an unexpected shift to the minor key (at 0:49) which throws the song deliberately off-balance. Jackson's change in ambience for the song's varied sections marks a solid contribution and one which consolidates "Ben" as one of his more popular ballads which, if taken purely at face value, is as compelling as his earlier "Got To Be There" [797]. (That no-one apparently read a homosexual subtext into a teenaged boy singing a love song to 'Ben' is indicative of the more innocent age in which the song was recorded.)

[1] According to J. Randy Taraborrelli (1986, p146) "Ben" was initially given to arch-rival Donny Osmond, Berry Gordy successfully prising it from his grip.

[2] See for example the 1977 *Rock Lives* interview by Timothy White.

**TMG 835**
**THE SUPREMES**
**Your Wonderful Sweet, Sweet Love** (2:59)
(Robinson)
Produced by William "Smokey" Robinson

---

**Release Date**: 3 Nov 1972
**B-side**: Love It Came To Me This Time
**Position in Record Retailer Top 40**: -
**Equivalent US Release**: Motown 1206 (11 Jul 1972)
**Position in Billboard Top 40 Pop**: -
**Position in Billboard Top 40 R & B**: 22

---

Jean Terrell / Cindy Birdsong / Mary Wilson

---

This disappointing failure in The Supremes' early-1970s catalogue was written in 1966, taking its lyrical cue from the chorus of "I'm Ready For Love" [582] and recorded by Kim Weston on October 27 of that year. Cast aside as not up to standard, Weston's recording was unreleased but its author was reminded of the number due to its HDH flavour, and brought it to sessions for *Floy Joy* where an updated version was duly knocked off by Jean Terrell.

The track, however, lacks substance with its uneventful rise-and-fall through a standard three-chord blues run, and, despite its propulsive rhythm aided by 'African' drums, was a dim prospect for a hit single.


**TMG 836**
**THE SUPREMES & FOUR TOPS**
**Reach Out And Touch (Somebody's Hand)** (4:20)
(Ashford—Simpson)
Produced by Nickolas Ashford/Valerie Simpson[1]
**Release Date**: 17 Nov 1972
**B-side**: Where Would I Be Without You Baby
**Position in Record Retailer Top 40**: -
**No Equivalent US Release**

---

Jean Terrell / Cindy Birdsong / Mary Wilson / Levi Stubbs / Lawrence Payton / Abdul 'Duke' Fakir / Renaldo 'Obie' Benson

---

Stretching the old *Magnificent Seven* album for yet another spin-off single, the release of "Reach Out And Touch" was a clear comment on the quality of these groups' most recent collaborations, The Supremes & Four Tops having by now released a *third* album together which was entirely ignored (*Dynamite*, April 1972). A pragmatic remake of [743], this version differs little from Ross' original (vocals aside) until 2:49, when a brand new section arrives offering an amiable antidote to the track's foregoing grandeur. Thereafter the groups give it their all, the closing sections up-tempo and shoe-horned into a lively 4/4. Ending on an energised high these re-thinks from Ashford & Simpson lift what would otherwise be a somewhat pointless exercise, which put The Supremes in the shops twice in 14 days.

[1] Production credits are not stated on the original UK single, but are given on the re-issue TMG 988.

**TMG 837**
**THE JACKSON 5**
**Santa Claus Is Coming To Town** (2:25)
(Coots—Gillespie)
Produced by Hal Davis
**Release Date**: 8 Dec 1972
**B-side**: Someday At Christmas / Christmas Won't Be The Same This Year
**Position in Record Retailer Top 40**: -
**Equivalent US Release**: Motown 1174 (25 Nov 1970)
**Position in Billboard Top 40 Pop**: -
**Position in Billboard Top 40 R & B**: -

Jackie Jackson / Tito Jackson / Jermaine Jackson / Marlon Jackson / Michael Jackson

Not generally considered part of the group's standard discography, this seasonal novelty record arrived in December as Michael Jackson's fourth vocal in as many months. Always interested in cashing-in on the Christmas market, Motown had put its artists on the road each December, starting with a residency at the Apollo in 1962 and stage shows most years since (see Timelines). Equally the company had put out an extravagant series of seasonal recordings, dating back to 1961 when The Twistin' Kings first did the honours.[1] In its wake came a slew of albums from The Miracles (*Christmas With The Miracles*, 1963), The Supremes (*Merry Christmas*, 1965), Stevie Wonder (*Someday At Christmas*, 1967), Various Artists (*Merry Christmas From Motown*, 1968), before the festive season of 1970 saw an unjustifiable four new albums in the record racks, from The Jackson 5 (*Christmas Album*), Various Artists (*Christmas Gift Wrap*), The Miracles (again!) (*The Season For Miracles*), and The Temptations (*Christmas Card*). (In addition to these long-players, several further associated 45s were issued over the years.)

In the UK, the viability of these records was lower, only three having ever been issued on Tamla Motown, one of which was *The Jackson 5 Christmas Album*, parent to the current single, two years earlier. Why "Santa Claus Is Coming To Town" was belatedly plucked for release is unclear, although the track appears to have been something of a Motown favourite: besides The Jackson 5, The Temptations, The Miracles and The Supremes had all recorded versions, the latter going to number 1 in Singapore in February 1966![2]

Although it didn't make the charts, the A-side of this maxi-single was included on a 1987 release on Motown's blue UK label, informally known as 'The Christmas EP' (see Appendix 2).

[1] "Xmas Twist" was released as Motown 1022.
[2] According to Taraborrelli 1986, p54.


**TMG 838**
**JERMAINE JACKSON**
**That's How Love Goes** (3:23)
(Bristol—Jones—Brown)
Produced by Johnny Bristol

**Release Date**: 15 Dec 1972
**B-side**: I Lost My Love In The Big City
**Position in Record Retailer Top 40**: -
**Equivalent US Release**: Motown 1201 (14 Jul 1972)
**Position in Billboard Top 40 Pop**: -
**Position in Billboard Top 40 R & B**: 23

Taking a lead from The Osmonds who had run solo careers for several group members in parallel with the ongoing collective, Berry Gordy launched another of the Jackson brothers as a solo artist in 1972, Jermaine recording an album of covers for release over the summer. (It didn't surface in the UK until after the new year.) Jermaine's graduation was in truth a fairly obvious move. He was lead singer until Michael emerged in 1967, and during their Motown tenure featured as a soloist on sections of hits such as "I'll Be There" [758] and "Mama's Pearl" [769], effectively making him the group's second-in-command.

This new single, a rare original from the sessions, was one of a rash of recent releases by various Jacksons which overwhelmed their UK fans.[1] Sitting comfortably in the territory between funk and pop, "That's How Love Goes" is a fast-grooving affair, the verses crowded with syllables which Jackson tackles with little melody but an adept sense of rhythm, in which his punchy vocal delivery is in effect another instrument, interlocking with drums and bass guitar (especially effective in his vocal elaborations and the end of each line).

While this gives the track an added dynamic, what he's actually singing about is lost, the lyric a sharply vindictive warning to a girl who has betrayed her lover, apparently with indifference. A verbal 'slap in the face', the line 'You're gonna have to be penalised' hints at retribution, belying the apparent indifference of its title and main hook. (That this mish-mash of styles and themes holds together as a whole is surprising.) Commencing Jermaine Jackson's singles catalogue, "That's How Love Goes" was an accomplished, if not outstanding start which failed to set the pop world alight. He would have some way to go to catch younger brother Michael who, by contrast, had gone top 10 with each of his first four UK solo singles.

[1] Tamla Motown had released no fewer than nine singles in 1972 featuring one or more of the group: [797]; [809]; [816]; [825]; [826]; [833]; [834]; [837]; [838], accounting for one-in-five of the label's output. The last four of these spanned just seven weeks.

**TIMELINE - 1972**

Tamla Motown release 42 singles and 24 albums. (A further 6 singles and 6 albums are released in the UK on Rare Earth and Mo-West.)
Tamla Motown place 17 singles in the UK top 40. 7 make top 10
Numerous Detroit musicians migrate to LA in hope of continued work with Motown
Four Tops, Supremes, Martha & Vandellas, Gladys Knight & Pips tour UK
Cindy Birdsong leaves Supremes, replaced by Lynda Lawrence
Philadelphia International label has first hits

| | |
|---|---|
| Jan | Michael Jackson releases first UK solo single "Got To Be There" / "Maria" |
| Jan 3 | Motown—HDH 1968 lawsuit settled |
| Feb | US VIP label winds up |
| Feb 12 | Michael Jackson: "Got To Be There" enters UK top 50 (peak 5) |
| Mar | Commodores release first Motown single in US |
| Mar 4 | Supremes: "Floy Joy" enters UK top 50 (peak 9) |
| Mar 9 | Temptations open at Copa in New York |
| Apr | In face of persistent rumours, Motown circulate statement that Detroit operations are not about to be "phased out" |
| May 1 | Marvin Gaye Day celebrated in Washington DC. Gaye appears at Kennedy Center to perform entire *What's Going On* album |
| May | Top 8 singles on US chart are by black artists |
| May | Martha Reeves' final Motown album, comprising previously rejected tracks |
| May 20 | Michael Jackson: "Rockin' Robin" enters UK top 50 (peak 3) |
| Jun | Hitsville building closes without prior notice, numerous staff instantly out-of-employment |
| Jun 13 | Clyde McPhatter dies of heart, liver and kidney diseases |
| Jun 17 | Tito Jackson marries Delores (Dee Dee) Martes after secretive romance |
| Jun-Jul | Stevie Wonder supports The Rolling Stones on their US tour |
| Jul 15 | Supremes: "Automatically Sunshine" enters UK top 50 (peak 10). Group's last significant hit in UK |
| Jul 16 | Smokey Robinson's last live show with Miracles, after which he officially resigns |
| Aug 19 | Michael Jackson: "Ain't No Sunshine" enters UK top 50 (peak 8) |
| Oct | *Lady Sings The Blues* opens in US cinemas |
| Oct | Mo-West label launched in UK (Jun 1971 in US) |
| Oct 7 | Spinners: "I'll Be Around" on Atlantic becomes first of 6 US top 10 hits after leaving Motown |
| Oct 14 | Michael Jackson: "Ben" number 1 in US (one week) |
| Oct 29 | Diana Ross' second daughter Tracee Joy born |
| Oct 30 | Jackson 5 appear in London for Royal Command Performance |
| Nov | Gladys Knight & Pips play UK dates. Shortly depart Motown for Buddah |
| Nov 11 | Jackson 5: "Lookin' Through The Windows" enters UK top 50 (peak 9). Group play first UK dates as part of European tour |
| Nov 18 | Four Tops' first post-Motown single "Keeper Of The Castle" enters UK top 40 |
| Nov 25 | Michael Jackson: "Ben" enters UK top 50 (peak 7) |
| Dec 2 | Temptations: "Papa Was A Rolling Stone" number 1 in US (one week) |
| Dec 15 | Jermaine Jackson's first solo release, simultaneously with Jackson 5 Christmas single |
| Dec 21 | Martha Reeves' final performance as Motown artist |

*Tamla Motown - The stories behind the UK singles* **423**

# Summary of era [722] to [838]

Come 1970, Motown had more or less turned its back on the classic studio sound they had cultivated in the years 1965-67. Most of their major artists had either wound up, or been transformed through one or other process into something almost unrecognisable. In some instances these changes were unavoidable, although it should be acknowledged that without moving with the times the company could easily have dwindled by the early 1970s as popular music elsewhere continued to evolve.

This bright new era is best summed-up by the dual forces of its two key finds, The Jackson 5 arriving for a UK debut at the start of 1970 and Diana Ross removed from The Supremes and set for solo stardom at the same point. In both cases the underlying principle was modernisation, of look, sound and style. And while The Jackson 5 were marketed to adolescents, Motown's reputation being forever affected, Ross was heading for the cabaret world and eyeing-up a career as a Hollywood actress which came to bear during 1972. In fact it seemed for a while as if she was intending to retire from recording, as she spent much of the year away from the studio, working on the *Lady Sings The Blues* [848], with Berry Gordy's full backing.

So enthusiastic was Gordy about this new venture that he took his eye off his main business, and through 1972 was conspicuous by his absence. Consequently the company began to show signs of cracking, as planning for the future was fatally neglected. Indeed in 1972 Gordy even considered selling out, seriously exploring the possibility of floating Motown on the Stock Exchange. Although ultimately he pulled back, the notion was revealing, Gordy looking at Motown as a means to further his designs on Hollywood, as the record company forged on largely without him. And of his existing acts, both Marvin Gaye and Stevie Wonder had extracted themselves from direct control and set about furrowing their own groove with a more or less parallel expansion into the album format.

What these processes meant was the gradual erosion of the established Motown sound, as a succession of producers began to redefine the company's recording ideals. Most obviously, Norman Whitfield's work with The Temptations and other acts developed an entire strand of music which had little in common with what was being recorded five years earlier. And in the process, The Temptations became virtually a new group, not only through their recordings but through personnel changes which saw the loss of both Eddie Kendricks and Paul Williams, with David Ruffin having departed shortly before the start of the decade. Diana Ross too was central to defining a new Motown sound with her sequence of poised and sleekly produced ballads which would constitute another distinct style which many of her colleagues would tap into.

And yet Motown, and the Tamla Motown label, nonetheless thrived through this era of re-definition, and continued to score well on the UK chart. The 'psychedelic' Temptations would place six singles in the UK top 40 in these three years, Diana Ross enjoying number 1s on both sides of the Atlantic, and The Supremes, even without her, earning a run of five top 10 singles in seven releases, a record of which HDH would have been proud. The re-constructed Supremes entered the decade under direction of Frank Wilson, and he would also lend his expertise to another popular act, The Four Tops enjoying their most consistent run of chart success which saw all of their releases during 1970 and 1971 charting, and four (including the re-issue [732]) going top 10. But unlike The Supremes, The Four Tops would not see the era through, jumping ship in 1972 and leaving Motown to ponder the loss of an act still competing at a high commercial level.

Others too would fall by the wayside, most notably Martha Reeves who would not survive the company's move to LA. Although Motown always had an inner circle of favoured artists who were afforded special attentions, never was the class divide so great as in 1970-72. This fact is underlined by the dearth of new talent emerging in these transitional years, only Ross and The Jackson 5 making any major impression. Caught-up in his Hollywood dream, Gordy failed to recognise that act after act was exiting while few were coming in to replace them. According to Peter Benjaminson, Motown had 100 acts on the books in 1966; by 1973 it was down to 51.[1] And of course the termination of Hitsville effectively shut out many more, as Gordy's hub simply closed up. Not troubling to advise his trusted musicians, and indeed not apparently caring if they continued to work for him, Gordy simply made the move west and reasoned that he no longer needed the extended Motown family. Cut adrift, The Funk Brothers would never again hold a central role in Motown's recording sessions, the glorious studio sound of the '1960s' truly coming to an end in mid-1972. Although Hitsville was still intermittently in use for a few more years, this single move was the most pivotal in the history of Motown. Not only did the company relinquish its core musicians, it tended to abandon the notion of a house band at all and began instead to employ session musicians the way any other label might.

And so this era is really summed up by the slow abandonment of Detroit as Motown increasingly looked west for its future. Centred on Sunset Boulevard, Motown's new facilities included a busy studio on Romaine Street, fitted out to a state-of-the-art spec by Guy Costa. With new musicians coming on the scene, the transformation of Motown was by now seriously underway, the rest of the 1970s stretching out ahead. Left behind was the Hitsville building, a small painted house, its basement converted an age ago into a ramshackle recording studio. While the winds blew down West Grand Boulevard, the ghosts of Motown's past could still be heard from this or that open window, from a passing automobile or a distant transistor radio. And The Donovan Building was in a similar state of quiet, the reduced staff and intermittent recording sessions testifying to the fact that Motown-Detroit was fast slipping into history. From here, there could be no return, and Hitsville would never again churn out hit after hit as it had done in the 1960s. Time, it seems, had simply moved on.

[1] p159

# CHAPTER FIVE

# LA, MY TOWN

## *1973 to 1976*

TMG 839
THE TEMPTATIONS
**Papa Was A Rollin' Stone (Vocal)** (6:54)
(Whitfield—Strong)
Produced by Norman Whitfield
Recording completed: 28 Jun 1972
**Release Date**: 5 Jan 1973
**B-side**: Papa Was A Rollin' Stone (Instrumental)
**Position in Record Retailer Top 40**: 14
**Equivalent US Release**: Gordy 7121 (28 Sep 1972)
**Position in Billboard Top 40 Pop**: 1
**Position in Billboard Top 40 R & B**: 5

Otis Williams / Melvin Franklin / Richard Street / Dennis Edwards / Damon Harris

Having settled in the sunshine of California, Berry Gordy had dragged most of his Motown empire with him, which is to say, the bits he wanted to keep. Gordy went into 1973 on the brink of conquering Hollywood [848] and set about a formal restructuring, creating a new business called Motown Industries in January, of which there were several sub-divisions including publishing, films, television and Motown Records. Having resigned as president of the pre-existing records arm in order to assume the position of Chairman of Motown Industries, Gordy appointed Ewart Abner in his place, his successor having served Motown in a senior capacity for six years [586]. One of Abner's first moves was to formally wind up the dying Mo-West label [828] and transfer its more promising acts to the Motown imprint, the Rare Earth label being similarly scrapped soon thereafter.

Yet in the face of this relentless march of progress, the ghost of Detroit still haunted Motown, as soundtracked by the present song, the abandoned buildings and unemployed musicians giving West Grand Boulevard an eerie feeling. Although some of the offices still functioned, and the studios were intermittently in use, the buzz had died and there was a sense of gloom in the air. Detroit itself had suffered immediate economic decline as a result of Motown's move, and local radio stations felt betrayed, some for a while ceasing to play Motown records.

Of those who refused the drift west, The Temptations and their musical director Norman Whitfield were the most prominent and significantly it was they, along with The Funk Brothers, who were most adventurously taking Motown's music into the mid 1970s. Detroit-based Whitfield had more or less created a group to serve his artistic needs in 1971 [776], The Undisputed Truth working as a springboard for recording projects and swapping a good deal of material back and forth with Whitfield's centrepiece The Temptations. And it was The Undisputed Truth who were first handed "Papa Was A Rollin' Stone", which Motown issued on 45 in America in May 1972 (Gordy 7117).

Feeling the song had more to offer than he had wrung from this prototype, Whitfield had a re-think and in June, went back into Hitsville and re-cut an extravagant version with The Temptations in mind, but without their specific knowledge. Had they been aware of what he was plotting, and the scale of the track in the making, there is little doubt that they would have attempted to block the project. Thoroughly fed-up with the direction their career had taken under Whitfield, The Temptations were against recording yet another album of futuristic soul and this had already caused some friction (mitigated in part by the appeasement of [773]).

Arranged by Paul Riser, this epic new creation ran to almost 12 minutes, and purely on its instrumental merits was a major accomplishment. Swirling and alternately intensifying and dropping out, this ocean of sound personifies the demons which troubled and pulled at the absent Papa during his debauched life. With Wah-Wah Watson's guitar phases intermittently rising up from the deep like a restless spirit, the family of mourners are haunted by the grim spectres of Papa's life materialising from the shadows around them. Underscoring this dark melodrama is Leroy Taylor's[1] obsessively driving bass (on which there are minute tuning discrepancies), which holds the same basic three notes for the entire track, morosely pulling every head back down each time they threaten to see the light. That such gripping intensity can be created is one thing; the fact that Norman Whitfield manages to sustain it over such a lengthy duration without any harmonic movement and without ever relenting, is extraordinary.

Dazzled by what he had come up with, Whitfield would not let The Temptations refuse the track. In the face of the group 'fighting tooth and nail not to record it'[2], and summoning all his skills in persuasion to get compliance, Whitfield must have been aware that the proposed *All Directions* might strain relations beyond breaking point. Conceding through gritted teeth, they recorded their vocal overdubs in a bad-tempered session in which Whitfield and the group clashed on the studio floor, the already volatile situation exacerbated by the song's seemingly pointed opening words, 'It was the third of September... that my daddy died'. It seems more than chance that Dennis Edwards, who ended up singing the line, had lost his own father on that precise date, the fact that The Undisputed Truth happened to record it first not refuting the suggestion that Barrett Strong had it calculated to stir some fire in Edwards' gut, rightly assuming he would eventually tackle it.[3]

The lyric portrays a family gathering in which they mourn the death of Papa, long-estranged and having left behind a crowd of unwanted children who barely knew him. Interrogating Mama, they seek in turn to extort the truth from her, as she deals the ugly facts in blows (despite not participating directly in the dialogue). Papa, they learn, was a womanising thief, a double-dealer who exploited all around him and refused to take a job. This disturbing narrative shows Strong at his most penetrative which, although profoundly concentrated, he insists was not based on true experience.[4]

In the can by the end of June, this troubled and troubling conception was programmed to sit on side 1 of *All Directions*. Accounting for two-thirds of the play time, it dominated the side and drew immediate fascination from all who heard it. On tour in the wake of its release, The Temptations were repeatedly dumfounded to overhear this disliked and colossal track emanating from radios and record players, the fact gradually dawning on them that they had unwittingly participated in the creation of a significant career milestone.

For Motown's marketing people the next step was apparent: "Papa Was A Rollin' Stone" had to be issued as a single.

The immediate problem faced was the song's extraordinary length. Trimming extended material down for 7-inch had been done before (eg [751]; [827]; [832]), but with this track, the task would be arduous due to the amount of musical incident on the recording, the reduction of which would compromise its impact. Seeking to retain all key sections, the introduction, which ran to almost four minutes, was truncated to a still extravagant two, and the main musical section in the centre was almost entirely excised. These measures, plus an early fade trimmed the basic track to almost seven minutes, outrageously lengthy by pop standards. What was left unused was sequenced into an "instrumental' version on the B-side (also credited to the group [931b]), and this masterpiece of editing and mixing was released in September to become The Temptations' third 'new-style' pop number 1 ([722]; [773]) after an appropriately lengthy three-month climb.

The Tamla Motown edition of January 1973 fared less well, but it hardly mattered. "Papa Was A Rollin' Stone" was a remarkable moment in the label's history which consolidated its place in legend by winning Motown's first Grammy in March for Group Best R & B Vocal Performance. To put the icing on the cake, the B-side also won a Grammy in the instrumental category which was awarded to Whitfield and Paul Riser, Whitfield and Strong picking up a third as writers. Unsurprisingly, there have been many further edited versions of this famous song over the years, usually designed to bring its length down further. In 1987, Motown even commissioned an entirely new mix (see Appendix 2) but none of these editions come close to the sheer sonic experience which is the original, and in particular the full album version. Tamla Motown have released the whole thing on 12-inch single more than once, and it remains the peak of Norman Whitfield's illustrious career, and by extension, arguably of The Temptations' as well.

[1] Frequently ascribed to Bob Babbitt. In fact Babbitt was unavailable for the session, duties passing to The Undisputed Truth's backing-group bassist.

[2] As recalled by Otis Williams (p157).

[3] The notion is supported by reports that Whitfield went out of his way to get Edwards to re-do the line over and over.

[4] See his comments in Dahl, p173. The lyric should be seen in the context of its likely inspiration: group associate Royce Moore, who encouraged David Ruffin to leave The Temptations, used to call the singer by the nickname Papa, putting a persuasive slant on the song's genesis. Strong may also have been mindful of his colleague Whitfield's [705b] when devising the line 'Wherever he lays his hat is his home'.


**TMG 840**
**JUNIOR WALKER & THE ALL STARS**
**Take Me Girl, I'm Ready** (2:59)
(Bristol—Ware—Sawyer)
Produced by Johnny Bristol
**Release Date**: 12 Jan 1973
**B-side**: I Don't Want To Do Wrong

**Position in Record Retailer Top 40**: 16
**Equivalent US Release**: Soul 35084 (8 Jul 1971)
**Position in Billboard Top 40 Pop**: -
**Position in Billboard Top 40 R & B**: 18

---

Jr Walker / Willie Woods / Vic Thomas / Billy Nicks

---

This affirmative single, with its easy-style sax passages, was issued in America in July 1971, taken from the then current *Rainbow Funk*. One of a run of US releases by Walker between "Do You See My Love (For You Growing)" [750] and "Walk In The Night" [824] not at first picked up in the UK, the release started the process of 'catching up', the album also newly available in the UK. This though came at a cost, Walker's group seeing nothing remotely current released in the UK again as their chart presence gradually faded, the positive disposition of "Take Me Girl I'm Ready" concealing what was transpiring.

Arranged casually by David Van DePitte, the track is as unchallenging to its listeners as [839] is disquieting, perfect material for the pop charts (to its singer's displeasure). In truth smoothly produced material such as this has more to do with Johnny Bristol than the unkempt Junior Walker, gliding freely through its descending choruses and major 7ths. Walker's contribution, apart from saxophone, consists of a full-throttle vocal which peaks at 2:37, dropping out in the choruses where the 'backing' parts assume a lead role. Lacking formal verses, the song consists of three hook sections linked by bridges, ushered in and out by instrumental passages, following the general principle set out in the catalytic "What Does It Take (To Win Your Love)" [712].

Unlike the US original, this Tamla Motown edition coupled the track with "I Don't Want To Do Wrong", composed by Gladys Knight & The Pips [805b].

**TMG 841**
**STEVIE WONDER**
**Superstition** (3:59)
(Wonder)
Produced by Stevie Wonder
**Release Date**: 19 Jan 1973
**B-side**: You've Got It Bad Girl
**Position in Record Retailer Top 40**: 11
**Equivalent US Release**: Tamla 54226 (24 Oct 1972)
**Position in Billboard Top 40 Pop**: 1
**Position in Billboard Top 40 R & B**: 1

In the spring of 1972, the self-managed Stevie Wonder was approached by Wartoke Concern, a promotions company handling The Rolling Stones' forthcoming US tour, and asked to join them on a proposed jaunt accounting for some 50 gigs. Recognising that he could obtain widespread exposure to an audience perhaps not quick to accept his contemporary work, Wonder accepted despite the fact that, in taking support position, he was humbling himself. (The two acts had toured together previously, Wonder taking top

---

billing in 1964 [E41].) Wonder quickly assembled a stage band, and a backing vocal section which he called Wonderlove[1], and headed off for an opening night in Vancouver.

The gruelling tour stretched through the whole of June and July, and on the way there were several low points as well as high. Sharing a mutual respect going back years, Wonder and the Stones were nonetheless very different in terms of lifestyle and musical aspirations. There were reports of several fraught moments in the camp, and at one point Wonder lost his drummer, causing the cancellation of one appearance which the Stones castigated him for publicly. In the end they parted amicably with a joint live rendition of "Uptight", in a medley with the song which it inspired in 1965, "(I Can't Get No) Satisfaction" (see [545]), at Madison Square Gardens on July 26.[2]

The tour had allowed Wonder to debut one of his new recordings, the as-yet unreleased "Superstition", which was itself shrouded in friction. During sessions for *Music Of My Mind*, Wonder had hooked up with Jeff Beck, a British rock guitarist and one-time member of The Yardbirds. Beck had met Wonder in England and been offered the new song "Maybe Your Baby", resulting in an invite to Electric Lady studios to work on it. Wonder, though, had a change of heart and withdrew the offer, instead recording a version himself which surfaced on *Talking Book*. Meantime, in idle jams at Electric Lady, Wonder and Beck chanced upon the basic groove of "Superstition". Verbally 'scatting' a melody, Wonder built the song from the rhythm up, devising its powerful riff on keyboard: played in Eb, the run is available via the black keys only, which is how it was recorded. However it seems plausible that Beck may have found it first, the riff readily performed on just two 'walking' frets of a standard guitar neck.

Duly rounded off, Wonder saw an opportunity to compensate Beck for the debacle of "Maybe Your Baby", and informed him that he could have what existed of "Superstition" for his upcoming *Beck, Bogert & Appice*. Produced by Margouleff and Cecil shortly thereafter, Beck's version was played back to Wonder who recognised its hit potential and at once regretted his momentary generosity. Reneging on his pledge once again, Wonder informed Beck that he wanted the song back, which understandably strained their friendship and resulted in Wonder offering up a *third* song, which Beck perhaps wisely declined.[3]

Wonder set about his own version of this famous track, which has become one of his most admired, with some sources stating that it was made in London at George Martin's AIR Studios.[4] Lyrically, Wonder aims at something allusive and throws around several ill omens including cracked mirrors and falling ladders, but any potential apprehension is lost by a vagueness of purpose and the generally agitated dance mode in which it is arranged, delivering its driving main riff on the lower notes of a clavinet, and not, as is sometimes stated, on a bass guitar. (In fact the bass sections, also on keyboard, pump at the groove without tracking the riff itself, lending a pounding depth while also providing interest-maintaining background activity.) Equally gripping are the jazzy brass sections, possibly suggested to Wonder by the similar parts in the chorus to "You Met Your Match" [666], itself built from the same musical principle as "Superstition".

Thrown into the mix for *Talking Book*, along with several other leftovers from *Music Of My Mind*, Wonder's recording appeared ahead of Beck's, on an album sequelling his previous set. *Talking Book* inhabits a similar world to its predecessor and, with the public knowing what to expect this time, was a major hit, showered with awards and sailing high in the US charts. By way of a supporting single, it was down to Wonder to elect a suitable candidate which he did in "Big Brother", which nestled on side 2. Motown, though, defied their contractual agreement in which Wonder had final say on his releases and overruled him, picking out "Superstition" as the strongest recording on the set. Aware that the move would further alienate collaborator Jeff Beck and prevent him from ever having a hit with it, Wonder attempted to block the release without success and watched the track scale the pop listings, his first such success since "Fingertips" [E26] a decade earlier. By the time the UK release emerged in January, Wonder had separated from Syreeta, forming a relationship with one of his professional aides named Coco. Pushing into 1973 at full speed, his career was continuing to ascend, thoughts already on his next project, the lauded *Innervisions*, which would emerge in the summer.

[1] Wonderlove had an ever-changing line-up, tending to be a group name used by whichever female backing vocalists Wonder happened to be working with. Over the years, Wonderlove's members included Syreeta, Supreme Lynda Lawrence, Minnie Riperton and Deniece Williams.

[2] There were plans to release a live album from the tour which never materialised.

[3] Beck and Wonder put the incident behind them, and the latter accepted an invitation in 1975 to assist with Beck's Blow By Blow.

[4] For example Davis 2006a, p87.


**TMG 842**
**THE JACKSON 5**
**Doctor My Eyes** (3:12)
(Browne)
Produced by Hal Davis
**Release Date**: 2 Feb 1973
**B-side**: My Little Baby
**Position in Record Retailer Top 40**: 9
**No Equivalent US Release**

---

Jackie Jackson / Tito Jackson / Jermaine Jackson / Marlon Jackson / Michael Jackson

---

Continuing to exploit The Jackson 5's *Lookin' Through The Windows* [825]; [833], Tamla Motown issued the group's third single in 21 weeks, a version of "Doctor My Eyes", a recent US hit for Jackson Browne. Noting that it had not been a success in the UK, and mindful of the similar trick pulled off with "Ain't No Sunshine" [826], the label squeezed this extra hit onto the group's discography, taking them into the UK top 10 for the sixth time. Played at a steady bounce, this over-estimated album-filler built from a descending bass run was not bothered with in America, where "Hallelujah Day" [856] was preferred.

---

**TMG 843**
**MARTHA REEVES**
**No One There** (3:32)
(Bristol—Goga—Minor—Green)
Produced by Johnny Bristol
**Release Date**: 9 Feb 1973
**B-side**: (I've Given You) The Best Years Of My Life
**Position in Record Retailer Top 40**: -
**No Equivalent US Release**

Having entered a period of uncertain separation from Motown [814], Martha Reeves' career was in disarray at the start of 1973. Aside from a tentative re-pressing of [599b] which had emerged quietly in June 1972, she had released nothing in a year, her previous album a Motown project over which she had grave reservations. Originally entitled *Black Lace*, the set was conceived for Diana Ross, who on hearing the material decided she wasn't interested. The discarded tapes, recorded in keys to suit Ross' higher pitching, were accordingly passed on to Reeves who, despite recognising what was afoot, characteristically threw her all into the album.

The final release under the revised title *Black Magic* appeared in early 1972 and was generally welcomed as an accomplished set (which included the earlier [794]). The jacket too was admired, a back-lit shot of the group in deep blue capturing them in a moody frame, sharpened by the photographer's having kept them waiting several hours before the shoot.

Meantime cut adrift by Motown's move to LA, Martha & The Vandellas had no more recording dates and were forced to continue playing live. Their final engagement came around on 21 December 1972 at the Cobo Hall in Detroit, an emotional farewell which the group realised would terminate their career together. Motown's only interest in Martha Reeves going into 1973 was the UK edition of "No One There" lifted from the year-old *Black Magic* and for no clear reason billed as a solo effort, possibly because Motown knew by now that The Vandellas would never record for them again. (A similar move was made on the proposed US single "I Won't Be The Fool I've Been Again", scheduled for early 1973 but scrapped.)

"No One There" is a wistfully hanging number whose air of despondency is intensified by its timing. Several of the lines (such as 'The future is hard to see when you're looking through a tear') resonate so unmistakably with the circumstances that it is hard not to read its release on single as a message in support of Reeves, sent back to Gordy by Tamla Motown. (This would not be the first time such a gesture had been implied: [814].)

Reeves' parting-shot was a lawsuit with Motown over royalties, but by all accounts it was she who would be out-of-pocket, having to buy herself out of her contract. Paying Gordy $200,000 for release to sign to MCA in 1973, she also abdicated the name Vandellas, ensuring there could be no revival of this legendary group. Under contract to MCA, she ironically ended up relocating to LA where she recorded an album with Richard Perry. Optimistic that her career would be revitalised, Reeves saw only a handful of releases over the next decade or so, and slowly she slipped out of public view and into musical history. Her Tamla Motown discography ensures that Martha, and her Vandellas live on.

## TMG 844
## GLADYS KNIGHT & THE PIPS
**The Look Of Love** (3:56)
(Bacharach—David)
Produced by Norman Whitfield
**Release Date**: 16 Feb 1973
**B-side**: You're My Everything
**Position in Record Retailer Top 40**: 21
**No Equivalent US Release**

---

Gladys Knight / Merald 'Bubba' Knight / Edward Patten / William Guest

---

Following the recent "Help Me Make It Through The Night" [830] with another external cover, Gladys Knight & The Pips' tenure at Motown was clearly winding down, like that of several of their stablemates. On the back of their recent UK tour [830] the label dug out "The Look Of Love", the old Bacharach—David number which the group had recorded in 1968 for *Silk 'N Soul*.

The track, one of its authors' most alluring, was first-recorded by Dusty Springfield for inclusion in the 1967 movie *Casino Royale*, but had not been a hit in the UK, prompting Tamla Motown to take a punt on it. To some extent they succeeded, despite its lowly chart placing the recording coming once more to define the song in UK terms. Knight's reading is relaxed and soulful, Norman Whitfield's swirling arrangement glistening with strings and carrying its counter-melody high above Jamerson's understated bass line.

Proficiently done, the recording had little real relevance to Knight's career in 1973, and come spring she would be out of contract and ready to move on [855]. Craftily, Buddah had already announced the group's signing to them, while they were still under contract to Motown, the shift by now inevitable.

## TMG 845
## EDDIE KENDRICKS
**If You Let Me** (3:16)
(Wilson)
Produced by Frank Wilson
**Release Date**: 23 Feb 1973
**B-side**: Just Memories
**Position in Record Retailer Top 40**: -
**Equivalent US Release**: Tamla 54222 (Aug 1972)
**Position in Billboard Top 40 Pop**: -
**Position in Billboard Top 40 R & B**: 17

Having negotiated a solo project in mid 1970 despite his continued involvement with The Temptations, the moody Eddie Kendricks was seen as a potential threat to the group's stability, Ewart Abner fearing that if he were successful on his own terms this could unsettle the band. Having plotted some recordings with Frank Wilson, Kendricks learned Abner had requested Wilson 'take him out of town'[1], the two consequently heading off for a tour which took in New York and Chicago, and during which Kendricks found his backing group, the Washington DC-based Young Senators.

Officially leaving The Temptations in early 1971 [773], Kendricks launched his solo career immediately, his first album *All By Myself* and an associated single appearing in America in April of that year, recorded with his new group. Largely ignored, Kendricks had no hits off the album, a second set following in *People... Hold On*. This LP, claimed by its producer to be 'a social statement to African-Americans'[2], was fundamentally tinged with the flavour of The Young Senators, deliberately aiming to catch their live sound on vinyl. Consequently several tracks are unlike Motown's period releases, the single "If You Let Me" featuring jazzy brass riffs, closely limited and reminiscent of the sound developed by several Atlantic-Stax artists as backed by Booker T & The MGs, such as Sam & Dave in "Hold On I'm Coming" [579n].

The track itself, penned by Wilson, dates to early 1969 and was first tackled by Jimmy Ruffin [726b], released with a slightly different title. Due to the sequence in which this and "I Can't Get Next To You" [722] appeared, it seems that the song's recurrent line 'I can sail a ship on dry land' is directly pulled from The Temptations' hit. In fact the reverse is true, although this does not stop "If You Let Me" from sounding, in the hands of Kendricks, as if the singer was goading his former colleagues, particularly given the song's title. In fact, "If You Let Me" is a neatly contained, attractive piece of soft soul which pleads for love, and might have been a hit, its fortunes hampered perhaps by Motown's reluctance to see Kendricks mount a commercial challenge to his former group.

[1] See Dahl, p269.
[2] See interview with Frank Wilson reproduced in the notes to *Eddie Kendricks: The Ultimate Collection* (Motown CD, 1998).

**TMG 846**
**MARVIN GAYE**
**Trouble Man** (3:50)
(Gaye)
Produced by Marvin Gaye
**Release Date**: 30 Mar 1973
**B-side**: Don't Mess With Mr. T
**Position in Record Retailer Top 40**: -
**Equivalent US Release**: Tamla 54228 (8 Dec 1972)
**Position in Billboard Top 40 Pop**: 7
**Position in Billboard Top 40 R & B**: 4

Marvin Gaye had married Anna Gordy in 1961, their union enduring for a dozen years despite her being 17 years his senior. Aged 50, her husband, still in his early 30s, was changing emotionally and spiritually to the point where he no longer showed interest in marital commitment and come 1973, was seeking dissolution and looking elsewhere for fulfilment [868], the couple having separated over the previous summer.

Working on his next project after *What's Going On*, Gaye had dabbled with an album project under the working title *You're The Man* but characteristically lost interest in it, only a US single of the same name emerging. Instead his attentions turned to *Trouble Man*, an uninspired Ivan Dixon blaxploitation flick for which he was invited to provide a soundtrack. Edging into the field in 1971-72, figures such as Isaac Hayes (*Shaft*) and Curtis Mayfield (*Superfly*) had created a funky, urbanised brand of soul which had defined the blaxploitation style. Gaye, however, was seeking to blaze a trail of his own, announcing ahead of work, "I'm going to do something that will revolutionise motion picture music. I'm starting with a totally new concept that won't even use conventional instruments. I think films need overhauling and I'm going to reconstruct and recreate a sound through another dimension that will bombard the senses."[1]

In the event, Gaye lacked the energy and interest to follow up this rash promise, his contribution to *Trouble Man* a set of instrumentals with just one vocal track: the current single, delivered in an airy falsetto. Uneventful and lethargic, the track was a meaningless keyboard-led vamp in Dm which, in the wake of his *What's Going On* album, was an undeserved top 10 hit in America. By the time this UK edition appeared, Gaye had forgotten about his revolutionising of film scores and was at work on his new album [868].

[1] Quoted in Davis (1984) p67. At around the same time Gaye claimed to have a symphony already composed 'four or five years ago', which was never revealed. (His interview with *Crawdaddy* in 1973, extracted in Ritz, p225-6, illustrates his state of mind in which he describes himself as an embryonic Beethoven and claims to have invented new musical scales, while also confessing a lack of inspiration since *What's Going On*, because 'there have really been no changes to write about'.)

## TMG 847
## THE SUPREMES
**Bad Weather** (2:59)
(Tucker—Wonder)
Produced by Taurus Productions
**Release Date**: 9 Mar 1973
**B-side**: It's So Hard For Me To Say Goodbye
**Position in Record Retailer Top 40**: 37
**Equivalent US Release**: Motown 1225 (22 Mar 1973)
**Position in Billboard Top 40 Pop**: -
**Position in Billboard Top 40 R & B**: -

Jean Terrell / Lynda Lawrence / Mary Wilson

A Supreme since the middle of 1967 [616], Cindy Birdsong had become pregnant in 1971, forcing her to contemplate retiring from the group who were continuing to tour relentlessly. In sessions for *Floy Joy*, an understudy had been found in Lynda Lawrence,[1] a vocalist with a professional association with Stevie Wonder [841n] who presumed to promise her a place in The Supremes. Not officially departing until 1973, it was already long apparent that Birdsong was no longer a part of the act, following the group's 1972 UK tour in which Lawrence had claimed her place on-stage, and so in their fourth incarnation since becoming famous, the group set about recording this stand-alone single, unusually released in the UK ahead of America.

Taking care of duties, Stevie Wonder supplied the track, co-written by Lawrence's brother Ira Tucker (Wonder's road manager), and most-likely derived from the 1968 Spinners track "Bad Bad Weather (Till You Come Home)", which had appeared as an American 45 (Motown 1136).[2] Originally looking to Lynda Lawrence to perform the song, group etiquette dictated that Jean Terrell handle lead duties on this punchy number, the most hard-edged single the group had released. (The track was recorded between live dates at Detroit's Elmwood Casino, the likelihood being that the vocal at least was taped at Motown's own studios which would be the final time The Supremes used the Detroit facility.)

Hanging with the density of brass instruments and blasting whistles, "Bad Weather" shuffles along with its bongo-laden percussion track, Wonder's production touch pulling the sound towards that of his own contemporary releases. Whether such a move was well-judged can be determined by the single's performance on release in which it flopped on both sides of the Atlantic. And despite having enjoyed the experience of working together, a proposed album project was duly shelved, The Supremes left smarting from the disappointment. Lacking direction for the rest of their careers the group would never recover their commercial standing, "Bad Weather" their last UK hit (barring the re-issued [915]).

[1] Lawrence appears in the group-shot on the cover of the LP.

[2] By accident or design, Tamla Motown were currently showing a fascination in tracks about weather: [821]; [826]; [847]; [852] etc.


**TMG 848a**
**MICHEL LEGRAND**
**Love Theme From "Lady Sings The Blues"** (2:51)
(Legrand)
Produced by Berry Gordy
**Release Date**: 16 Mar 1973
**Position in Record Retailer Top 40**: -
**Equivalent US Release**: Motown 1219 (30 Jan 1973)
**Position in Billboard Top 40 Pop**: -
**Position in Billboard Top 40 R & B**: -

Watching The Supremes perform in May 1969, film producer Jay Weston had recognised in Diana Ross a potential star for his planned move about blues singer Billie Holiday. Approaching Berry Gordy with an outline of what he was looking for, director Sidney Furie argued that Ross could excel in the role, a notion which, in the face of her inexperience, Gordy nevertheless took no time to become fully seduced by.[1] In fact, Ross was not without some acting talent which she had already proven in small-screen projects such as *Tarzan* in 1968 [709] and, later on, *Diana!* in which she had pulled off impressive character imitations of Charlie Chaplin and Harpo Marx [792]. Having dwelt on the project in the intervening couple of years, it was around the time of *Diana!* that Gordy again convened with Weston and Furie, and began firming up plans which included Motown funding the film's scripting.

Meantime, Berry Gordy's end of the deal involved the making of a soundtrack which was to be completed ahead of shooting. Scored by world-renowned composer Michel Legrand and conducted by Motown's Gil Askey [807], the orchestral suite was recorded at Mo-West and was accompanied by several orthodox vocal tracks, including covers of some of Billie Holiday's hits and a couple of recordings by Blinky Williams and Michelle Aller (the latter a version of "Had You Been Around" [533]).

Having waited on Terence McCloy's script, Gordy was unimpressed when it arrived, announcing that he would re-write it himself. Taking characteristic pains, Gordy called on Christine Clark[2] and Suzanne de Passe, who between them re-drafted several passages over a six-week spell; this caused delays. Shooting eventually commenced in December 1971, but work was continually interrupted by Gordy who increasingly sought to control the entire affair. He was taking over areas with which he technically had nothing to do, at one point causing ructions by having the entire wardrobe disposed of and replaced at Ross' request.

In the end it became clear that the film was costing too much and, in a shrewd move, Paramount cut their losses and sold Gordy the entire project which he continued to shoot at his own, not inconsiderable expense. Untutored in film production, Gordy simply applied his record-making philosophy to proceedings, making *ad-hoc* amendments to the dialogue and cutting different versions of scenes to inter-splice and overdub as if mixing an audio track. In the end, Gordy spent in the region of $3.6million, driven both by his obsessive desire to succeed and the impetus of making Diana Ross a Hollywood star.

Unveiling her to the world on 12 October 1972 with the film's New York premiere, *Lady Sings The Blues* met with generally positive reviews. Ross' movie debut was seen as a resounding success, although the film itself was criticised for its romantic portrayal of Holiday's tortured life. An abused child who grew up to become a prostitute and drug-user, Holiday's tale is in many ways tragic, her death at the age of 44 preceded by her shocking autobiography, on which the film script was based, by two years.

The UK premiere which Ross attended had to wait until 4 April, by which time she had already been nominated for an Academy Award (which ended up going to Liza Minnelli) and the soundtrack was readily available in the shops. The music stretched across two LPs, and was a major success in the US where it sold a third-of-a-million in a week and topped Billboard's album charts in April. The US trailer arrived with an especially designed label and was originally intended as a Mo-West issue (MW 5051) before the imprint was closed down. In the UK the album was considerably less well-received, but trailer-singles were nevertheless also arranged, [848] and [849] appearing on the same morning, both having been sent out in promotional picture sleeves.

"Love Theme From 'Lady Sings The Blues'"[3] is a romantic piano-led instrumental with some of the decorative passion of a Rachmaninov piece. Pitched in D major, the composition is built essentially atop a standard pop chord sequence, although its plaintive mood and delicate design suggest the minor. Credited like its B-side to its author, this instrumental ran to less than three minutes, and was a curious release selected purely for its import in promoting the double LP. More effective was Ross' own associated single [849] although that too failed to break in the UK where the whole *Lady Sings The Blues* phenomenon slipped by largely unnoticed.

The project, while on a professional level successful, had taken a good deal of Berry Gordy's time and money, at the expense of Motown's records division. Ultimately failing to establish his company in the world of movies, the venture was of dubious merit, Ross' excellent performances salvaging what would otherwise have been something of a miscalculation. Gordy was adamant in his convictions and would follow *Lady Sings The Blues* with *Mahogany* in 1975 [1010].[4]

[1] Ross was at one point considered for the 1967 movie *The Lost Man* opposite Sidney Poitier and in April 1969 it was announced that she would be starring in Walter Seltzer's *Darker Than Amber*. Neither came to fruition.

[2] Generally known as Chris Clark, the former Motown singer was now Vice-President of Motown's films division. Besides Clark, Gordy also roped in her old backing vocalists The Lewis Sisters, for an on-screen appearance.

[3] The track later had a lyric added by Smokey Robinson, and became known as "Happy", attracting versions by Robinson himself (see [949n]), Diana Ross, Michael Jackson [L054] and Bobby Darin.

[4] After *Mahogany*, Motown involved themselves in four more movies, *The Bingo Long Travelling All-Stars And Motor Kings*, *Almost Summer*, *Thank God It's Friday*, and *The Wiz*, which starred Ross and Michael Jackson.


**TMG 848b**
**GIL ASKEY**
**Any Happy Home** (1:18)
(Askey)
Produced by Gil Askey

The B-side to "Love Theme From 'Lady Sings The Blues'" was a brief, semi-comedy piece of film dialogue and music, ushered in with Jew's harp and going out with Ross in Holiday mode. Appearing on the soundtrack as "Country Tune", this curious piece is credited to Gil Askey, making it worthy of special mention. Askey had worked with The Supremes in the 1960s and handled musical arrangements for *Diana!*, making him the natural choice to direct recording of the *Lady Sings The Blues* soundtrack. This little item is his only credit on a Tamla Motown single, although he also released "Don't Explain" concurrently in America (Motown 1220), plucked from the same project.

**TMG 849**
**DIANA ROSS**
**Good Morning Heartache** (2:20)
(Higginbotham—Drake—Fisher)
Produced by Berry Gordy
**Release Date**: 16 Mar 1973
**B-side**: God Bless The Child
**Position in Record Retailer Top 40**: -
**Equivalent US Release**: Motown 1211 (18 Dec 1972)
**Position in Billboard Top 40 Pop**: 34
**Position in Billboard Top 40 R & B**: 20

"Good Morning Heartache" was one of Diana Ross' studies for *Lady Sings The Blues*. Recorded by Billie Holiday for her 1957 album *Solitude*, the track had already been made for Motown by Billy Eckstine and released in 1968. Musically orthodox, Ross delivers this slow blues in suitably disconsolate style, having extensively researched Holiday's life to the point where she was virtually living in character.

For Ross, pregnancy with her second daughter Tracee Joy (born 29 October 1972) had led to a year in which little was done in public between the filming and release of the movie. Consequently "Good Morning Heartache" was Diana Ross' first single in almost a year [812], and was the only part of her Tamla Motown *œuvre* not to make the UK top 40.

**TMG 850**
**FOUR TOPS**
**So Deep Within You** (3:07)
(Pinder)
Produced by Tony Clarke
**Release Date**: 23 Mar 1973
**B-side**: Happy (Is A Bumpy Road)
**Position in Record Retailer Top 40**: -
**No Equivalent US Release**

Levi Stubbs / Lawrence Payton / Abdul 'Duke' Fakir / Renaldo 'Obie' Benson

Originating from the same session as "Simple Game" [785], "So Deep Within You" was another Mike Pinder number, previously recorded by The Moody Blues for *On The Threshold Of A Dream* (1969). Arranged in a rock style, with fuzz-toned guitar solo and hammering tom toms, the backing track is outside The Four Tops' usual scope, and has the sense of being made for fun. That it was not released for three years, and did not feature on an album, suggests that it was viewed as a throwaway, but with the group having left Motown in 1972 [823], made a convenient 'new' single, squeezed onto 7-inch by a premature fade.

**TMG 851**
**JERMAINE JACKSON**
**Daddy's Home** (2:59)
(Shephard—Miller)
Produced by The Corporation
**Release Date**: 13 Apr 1973
**B-side**: Take Me In Your Arms (Rock Me A Little While)
**Position in Record Retailer Top 40**: -
**Equivalent US Release**: Motown 1216 (15 Nov 1972)
**Position in Billboard Top 40 Pop**: 9
**Position in Billboard Top 40 R & B**: 3

Pulled from his solo album *Jermaine*, this new single was a cover of an old doo-wop number made famous by Shep and the Limelites, a New York trio led by James Sheppard. Taken to number 2 in the US charts in 1961, the song was an 'answer' to "A Thousand Miles Away", made by Sheppard's former group The Heartbeats. Maintaining Motown's habit of promoting oldies by the Jackson family ([816]; [825]), the track arrived with a vintage Motown original on the flip [538]. The composition has since gained further fame via a Cliff Richard recording which took it to number 2 in 1981.[1]

[1] Richard also took a version of "You Keep Me Hangin' On" [585] into the top 20, in June 1974.

**TMG 852**
**STEVIE WONDER**
**You Are The Sunshine Of My Life** (2:45)
(Wonder)
Produced by Stevie Wonder
**Release Date**: 4 May 1973
**B-side**: Look Around
**Position in Record Retailer Top 40**: 7
**Equivalent US Release**: Tamla 54232 (12 Mar 1973)
**Position in Billboard Top 40 Pop**: 1
**Position in Billboard Top 40 R & B**: 3

Self-produced for *Talking Book*, "You Are The Sunshine Of My Life" was an earlier title, written as an overture to Syreeta shortly after she and Wonder had met. Considered for *Music Of My Mind* the track was held-off for almost a year, the decision to release it at that point belying the fact that by then, the couple were in the process of breaking up [827]; [841]. Given its strength as a mid-tempo pop song, the recording was an obvious lift, and duly scaled the US charts to become Wonder's second consecutive number 1.

In fact, "You Are The Sunshine Of My Life" has little depth behind its happy persona and, were it not for Wonder's contagious, high-spirited production, would weigh heavy. Frantic panning grabs the attention during the introduction which features an ascending run of one-and-a-half octaves in novel whole-tone steps, wearing its smile on its sleeve. With an evasive chord structure, the musical foundation is mainly substantiated by a surprisingly kinetic bass line, pushed by a celebratory backing in which chatter and laughter are audible, as if the number were being performed live at a party. (The single's intoxicating counter-melody carried through its brass chart was a late addition for the 45 mix.)

The lyric commences with a pair of guests, session man Jim Gilstrap and Wonderlove vocalist Gloria Barley, who introduce the theme with a twin declaration of love[1] and as if to emphasise its self-delight, Wonder again name-drops an old recording in the lyric, this time citing "Drown In My Own Tears", a Ray Charles number which Wonder had recorded in 1962.[2]

[1] Unaccredited at the time, they did not receive their due gold discs, Wonder giving Gilstrap his as a mark of appreciation.

[2] Giving Barrett Strong a run for his money, Wonder and his erstwhile colleague made a point of quoting at least one song in their early 1970s texts (*passim*).


**TMG 853**
**SMOKEY ROBINSON & THE MIRACLES**
**Going To A Go Go** (2:48)
**Re-issue of [547]**
**Release Date**: 27 Apr 1973
**New B-side**: Whole Lot Of Shaking In My Heart (Since I Met You Girl) [569] / Yester Love [661]
**Position in Record Retailer Top 40**: -

---

Smokey Robinson / Bobby Rogers / Claudette Rogers Robinson /
Warren 'Pete' Moore / Ronnie White

---

A central focus of the Northern Soul scene [683], the Wigan Casino opened its doors in 1973 and in due course would become the best-known of England's soul venues, attracting live appearances by Edwin Starr and Junior Walker. It also has a modest claim to Motown history on two counts, being the place where Frank Wilson's legendary "Do I Love You (Indeed I Do)" was first exposed to crowds of revellers (see Chapter 6 [L014]), and is the location which prompted journalist Dave Godin to coin the phrase Northern Soul in the first place.

The Casino was open until 1981, and helped push a selection of Tamla Motown oldies which the label continued to re-issue with pleasure. A sort of latter-day UK equivalent of the 'Go-Go' [547], the club scene kept many of these oldies alive during an era when they were being largely forgotten about elsewhere, the first such re-issue of 1973 this new pressing issued as a maxi-single with the rarer [569] and [661].

Having observed the phenomenon from afar without really understanding it, Motown's American offices finally capitulated in late 1972 launching their own Yesteryear label. This specialist re-issue imprint delivered many cherished oldies to US fans, and arrived on November 20 with a batch of 84 (!) singles, one of which was "Going To A Go-Go" (Y 414). Over the course of 15 years, Yesteryear issued a sum total of around 300 re-issues.

**TMG 854**
**THE TEMPTATIONS**
**Masterpiece (Vocal)** (5:30)
(Whitfield)
Produced by Norman Whitfield
**Release Date**: 19 Apr 1973
**B-side**: Masterpiece (Instr)
**Position in Record Retailer Top 40**: -
**Equivalent US Release**: Gordy 7126 (1 Feb 1973)
**Position in Billboard Top 40 Pop**: 7
**Position in Billboard Top 40 R & B**: 1

Otis Williams / Melvin Franklin / Richard Street / Dennis Edwards / Damon Harris

Following the tense sessions for "Papa Was A Rolling Stone" [839], over which Norman Whitfield was entirely vindicated, The Temptations were pushed into a similar album project, their musical director seeking to repeat his success. For this next set of recordings, however, he had lost his writing partner Barrett Strong, who by all accounts fancied a change in direction and simply quit Motown for Epic. This left Whitfield alone, and the producer elected henceforth to handle his own lyric duties, writing The Temptations' next album by himself.

Providing them with another collection of pre-made backing tracks, Whitfield had created a bloated 14-minute epic in "Masterpiece", "Papa Was A Rolling Stone" Part II. His estimation of the track, and of the forthcoming album generally is exposed by the immodest title which has no relevance to the material unless read as adjectival. However where "Papa" had been inspired—a moment of precise penetration—"Masterpiece" was wholly ground-out, deliberately attempting something much the same which, in the process, misses the very essence of its innovative fore-runner.

The full recording is built on another bass riff, a repeating three-note figure which Bob Babbitt, playing live, reiterates across around 420 bars, stretching the full 14 minutes. Worked above this foundation is an array of instrumentation (including a percussion effect based on Booker T & The MGs' "Soul Limbo"), and after approximately four minutes, a tripartite vocal section concerned with the strife of the ghetto, which is the heart of the track (and which was extracted to form the single edit). Thereafter, the song merely runs around and around for over seven more minutes and, although impressive for the quality of the sonics, ultimately becomes boring.

For a vocal group, the imposition of lengthy instrumental sections on 'their' albums was difficult to swallow. The fact was The Temptations wanted professional and artistic integrity more than they wanted ongoing glory while Whitfield, by contrast, was engaged in a Marvin Gaye-style programme of self mythologisation, as evinced in the sleeve of *Masterpiece*. No doubt his work, the cover depicts a full sized close-up of the producer with The Temptations themselves miniaturised above his head, the whole framed as if an exhibit in a museum.

On release, this trimmed edition of the title track did strong business in America, but failed in the UK. Much the same was true of the LP itself and, if Whitfield did not yet concede the point, he and The Temptations were no longer pulling together. There would be no further collaborations once the follow-up was done and dusted [887].


**TMG 855**
**GLADYS KNIGHT & THE PIPS**
**Neither One Of Us (Wants To Be The First To Say Goodbye)** (4:15)
(Weatherly)
Produced by Joe Porter
**Release Date**: 11 May 1973
**B-side**: Can't Give It Up No More
**Position in Record Retailer Top 40**: 31
**Equivalent US Release**: Soul 35098 (26 Dec 1972)
**Position in Billboard Top 40 Pop**: 2
**Position in Billboard Top 40 R & B**: 1

---

Gladys Knight / Merald 'Bubba' Knight / Edward Patten / William Guest

---

"Neither One Of Us" was supplied to Gladys Knight & The Pips by producer Joe Porter, who had recently discovered the recorded work of its composer Jim Weatherly and enthused about his talents. Weatherly was a Mississippi singer-songwriter, signed to RCA, who recorded the track himself, before Porter remade it in an evening session in LA. Due to fly back to Detroit, Gladys Knight & The Pips had the vocals half-completed when they left the studio, but during the ride to the airport, could not get the number out of their minds and realised it was going to be a major hit. Doing an about-turn, they went back to the studio to complete it, and secured for themselves a US number 2 single, equalling their previous biggest success [629]. This emotion-charged tragedy is delivered by Knight in what would become her patent slow, silky style, soaring through the melody despite a heavy heart, a mode of delivery which would largely define the rest of the group's career.

Released at the end of 1972, the single coincided with the expiry of their Motown contract, for which they attempted to bargain a better deal. Meeting little success, and with Motown withholding royalties apparently due to them, they began talking to Buddah, agreeing the switch just as "Neither One Of Us" was pushing its way towards the top of the charts.[1]

The move paid dividends for Gladys Knight & The Pips, Buddah according them professional respect and artistic freedom which was mirrored by Buddah smartly signing Jim Weatherly to write for the group on a semi-permanent basis. The ensuing hits far outstripped what they had achieved with Motown, "Midnight Train To Georgia" and "Best Thing That Ever Happened To Me" quickly following. Unjustifiably feeling robbed, Motown packaged *Neither*

---

*One Of Us* for release and, in the UK, Tamla Motown continued issuing recordings from the group for some time (including a re-issue of the present track [1009]). Inevitably Gladys Knight ended up suing Motown for royalties on these belated releases and also sought to stop her former label from exploiting her recordings in such a brazen manner [945].

[1] At around this pivotal time, Knight also divorced her husband James Newman.

**TMG 856**
**THE JACKSON 5**
**Hallelujah Day** (2:53)
(Perren—Yarian)
Produced by Freddie Perren/Fonce Mizell
**Release Date**: 25 May 1973
**B-side**: To Know
**Position in Record Retailer Top 40**: 20
**Equivalent US Release**: Motown 1224 (26 Feb 1973)
**Position in Billboard Top 40 Pop**: 28
**Position in Billboard Top 40 R & B**: 10

---

Jackie Jackson / Tito Jackson / Jermaine Jackson / Marlon Jackson / Michael Jackson

---

This uncomplicated and unashamed piece of pop fun was written by former Corporation member Freddie Perren and his wife Christine Yarian. Aimed as a celebration of life itself, the track not only name-drops "Dancing In The Street" [E54] but also implores listeners to 'Sing along with The Jackson 5', as if it were being performed on stage. Something of a flop, the release prompted the group's father Joe to take up the issue of their alarming slide with Ewart Abner, who resignedly suggested that perhaps their appeal had simply burned itself out.

**TMG 857**
**JUNIOR WALKER & THE ALL STARS**
**Way Back Home (Vocal)** (2:59)
(Felder—Bristol—Knight)
Produced by Johnny Bristol
**Release Date**: 1 Jun 1973
**B-side**: Way Back Home (Instrumental)[1]
**Position in Record Retailer Top 40**: 35
**Equivalent US Release**: Soul 35090 (4 Nov 1971)
**Position in Billboard Top 40 Pop**: -
**Position in Billboard Top 40 R & B**: 24

---

Jr Walker / Willie Woods / Vic Thomas / Billy Nicks

---

Another track from *Rainbow Funk* (1971), this latest release from Junior Walker originated with Texas instrumental group The Jazz Crusaders, who

had recorded it in 1970 for *Old Socks New Shoes, New Socks Old Shoes*.[2]
Written by group member Wilton Felder, "Way Back Home" lacked a lyric,
Johnny Bristol and Gladys Knight doing the honours, the latter having sought
for some years to assert her abilities in this respect, Bristol her main supporter.
The 'home' of the text is America's deep South, from where Bristol, Knight
and Walker all hail. The lyric begins with a cautionary image of black and
white separation, depicting its effect and threatening to develop into a
monologue on racism. However it is flipped around into a nostalgic
reminiscence about golden days of childhood, delighting in the sounds, smells
and feelings of growing up in the open country.

In keeping with its theme, David Van DePitte's arrangement makes much
of the trade-off between vocals and sax, which take turns in the style of the
blues. (Blues typically consists of a rapidly switching vocal/instrumental/
vocal/instrumental structure, originating from the difficulty of the untutored
musician playing and singing at once.) Carrying a variation of the standard
blues progression in C#, the song also plays up its gospel credentials, backing
vocals ringing out towards the end, in celebration of God's earth.

The track was edited for release on single across two sides, the 'vocal'
version subsequently inserted onto Walker's follow-up album, *Moody Junior*.

[1] 20,000 copies of the single were manufactured initially. It was then re-pressed with the
addition of an extra B-side: "Country Boy", a recording lifted from *Peace And Understanding
Is Hard To Find*, Walker's early 1973 LP.

[2] As The Crusaders, they were subsequently signed to Mo-West for a brief spell.

**TMG 858**
**FOUR TOPS**
**I Can't Quit Your Love** (3:37)
(Caston—Wakefield)
Produced by Frank Wilson
**Release Date**: 22 Jun 1973
**B-side**: I Am Your Man
**Position in Record Retailer Top 40**: -
**Equivalent US Release**: Motown 1198 (20 Apr 1972)
**Position in Billboard Top 40 Pop**: -
**Position in Billboard Top 40 R & B**: -

Levi Stubbs / Lawrence Payton / Abdul 'Duke' Fakir / Renaldo 'Obie' Benson

This rather belated release was lifted from *Nature Planned It*, the group's year-
old set which had closed their Motown discography [823]. An unspectacular
mid-tempo stomp notable for its wah-wah guitar, the track was written by
Caston—Wakefield [782] and originally sat on side 1 of the album. By now the
group had scored several hits for their new label, "I Can't Quit Your Love"
timed to coincide with *Shaft In Africa*, a blaxploitation movie for which The
Four Tops had recorded a soundtrack. This indirect cash-in would be the
group's last Tamla Motown single, bar a 1975 re-issue [1011].

**TMG 859**
**THE SUPREMES**
Tossin' And Turnin' (3:55)
(Lewis—Rene)
Produced by Jimmy Webb
**Release Date**: 8 Jun 1973
**B-side**: Oh Be My Love
**Position in Record Retailer Top 40**: -
**No Equivalent US Release**

---

Jean Terrell / Lynda Lawrence / Mary Wilson

---

After the collaborations with Stevie Wonder had failed to blossom [847], The Supremes had no immediate project to hand and, feeling that Motown were not fully backing them, began musing their position. Passionate about the group, Jean Terrell pushed hard to have producer Jimmy Webb brought in, the one-time Jobete songwriter [710]; [729] having now established himself elsewhere, thereby promising a higher profile album for the group. Thus, the curious pairing of The Supremes with a non-Motown producer was hatched, Webb arriving during the lengthy crossover between Lynda Lawrence's arrival and Cindy Birdsong's departure.

With Webb, who brought his own vocalists along to the sessions, the group recorded 11 tracks for the proposed *Beyond Myself* set, which would surface in late-1972 as *The Supremes Produced And Arranged By Jimmy Webb*, released in the UK in March 1973. In truth, Motown never supported the project and when the album was completed, they issued it in a drab sleeve depicting a close-up shot of a sunflower seed head. The sessions themselves were similarly uninspiring, spawning a handful of cover versions, one of which was "Tossin' And Turnin'".

This out-and-out rocker was originally a hit for Bobby Lewis, which although largely unknown in Britain was a major hit in America, where it topped the pop listings for 7 weeks in 1961, shifting three million copies in the process. Motown had of course taken note, The Marvelettes releasing a live version in 1963 before the track's surprise re-appearance here. Recorded in mock-bar-room style, with Wilson and Lawrence *ad libbing* noisily behind Jean Terrell's excited lead, the recording was tossed-off during the sessions with Webb himself pitching in on barrel-house piano. That it was selected from the available material as the group's next Tamla Motown single was an error of judgement unparalleled in The Supremes' discography.

**TMG 860**
**THE MARVELETTES**
Reachin' For Something I Can't Have (2:44)
Re-issue of [701]
**Release Date**: 7 Sep 1973

**New B-side**: Here I Am Baby [659]
**Position in Record Retailer Top 40**: -

---

Ann Bogan / Wanda Young / Katherine Anderson

---

The Marvelettes left Motown in 1971 (see [701]), their final single reprised here for an unexpected re-issue. The single was scheduled for release on 29 June, but a pressing error resulted in the proposed B-side, "I Need Someone" [639b] being inadvertently switched for its original A-side, "My Baby Must Be A Magician" [639]. Realising the mistake, Tamla Motown destroyed all copies (bar a tiny handful which escaped to collectors), and a re-think saw "Here I Am Baby" [659] released on the flip-side instead. The single was aimed again at Northern Soul crowds but, as a result of the mix-ups, didn't appear on the market until September 7.

**TMG 861**
**DIANA ROSS**
**Touch Me In The Morning** (3:51)
(Miller—Masser)
Produced by Mike Masser/Tom Baird
**Release Date**: 6 Jul 1973
**B-side**: Baby It's Love
**Position in Record Retailer Top 40**: 9
**Equivalent US Release**: Motown 1239 (3 May 1973)
**Position in Billboard Top 40 Pop**: 1
**Position in Billboard Top 40 R & B**: 5

For many the most moving track in Motown's catalogue, "Touch Me In The Morning" is a plea from a heartbroken lover, sung to a man she needs just as he is about to leave. Begging him not to depart in the night and to wait until morning, the lyric takes on the form of a dream, as if the two are sleeping side-by-side and flicking back through the pages of their love, reliving the joy of being alive together. In reality, and for reasons unstated, he is about to depart, her physical desire for him expressed in the phrase 'touch me' and the fact that she wants to spend this last night with him.

The track's genesis lies with its evocative title, Ron Miller developing it specifically for Diana Ross and using her as a model of a self-contained, modern woman able to express her sexual desires confidently. Miller has since explained the lyric in a manner which makes little overall sense, "Once it was the man who might give a woman the brush-off after a one-nighter telling her 'nothing good's gonna last forever'; now it could be the other way around."[1] Yet this only holds as an analysis of the thematic starting point, and the comments expressed in the first verse. These, though, are recalled from a time now passed: this isn't the culmination of a one-night-stand in which she pushes him aside, but the account of a genuine love which has died because the man no longer wants her—precisely in the fashion Miller repudiates. The rest of the tale is spun around to depict the female as victim, having to be strong as her man walks away from her. The discrepancy with Miller's

---

perspective probably stems from the fact that he commenced the track alone, and therefore had a pre-conception of its theme, while the full text may have been finalised with later input from Michael Masser, a classically trained composer brought to Motown to work on *Lady Sings The Blues* [848]. Primarily a musical writer, Masser may nonetheless have steered it from its initial line, particularly if, as the accounts imply, Miller had it incomplete when the music was underscored.

Played to Ross by Miller on piano, the singer expressed reservations about the song, Berry Gordy encouraging her with the promise that it would be a hit. The fact was, Ross was by now seeing herself primarily as a Hollywood actress, projects such as this not merely an inconvenience but a means by which she was being pulled away from what she saw as her true calling. It is telling that in her autobiography, published 20 years later, Ross says nothing of her period recordings, bridging between her recollections of *Lady Sings The Blues* and *Mahogany* with the single sentence, 'I continued to do concerts and release albums *between my films*'.[2]

In the end conceding to record it, Ross showed her displeasure by bickering several times over its key.[3] Yet despite her disinterest, Ross' contribution is keenly studied, and in its grand, double-tracked finale, sung entirely from the heart. Perfectly matching the light-and-shade of Tom Baird and Gene Page's arrangement, she is calm where the lyric is nonchalant, urgent in its more desperate moments, the audio experience of merely *listening* to the track equivalent to its running commentary. Whatever interest she may or may not have had in the number, Diana Ross was always a professional in the studio.

With an unusually florid and high-profile bass from Bob Babbitt, "Touch Me In The Morning" is one of Motown's defining ballads. Like "I'm Still Waiting" [781] before it, the recording has a timeless quality, perfectly encapsulating its mood in its every musical nuance, at once overwhelming in its desolation and ameliorating in its formal perfection. Unsurprisingly the track was a major hit, Ross' first single to go top 10 in both the UK and the US, where it topped the listings in August, despite the accidental use of the original cut with its prolonged play time, which was supposed to have been substituted by a specially prepared single edit. (The shorter version ended up on her LP also by mistake.)

On the heels of this release, Ross was booked to perform on a European tour which was to bring her to the UK as a solo artist for the first time.[4] It is nonetheless true that as a vocalist, Ross was easing off, this particular single paired with a 1970 recording from *Diana Ross*, and her current album, named in honour of this track, made in several disjointed sessions with a number of different producers.[5] And yet the album too went into the respective top 10s of Britain and America, an astonishing achievement and one of the paradoxes of Ross' career: at the precise point she wanted to walk away from singing, she was casually making records which were regarded in their day as amongst the finest being cut by Motown.

[1] See Taraborrelli, 1989 p280.
[2] p205 (my emphasis).

[3] Taraborrelli (1989 p281-2) states Miller and Ross clashed over whether it should be pitched in Ab or Bb. In fact the song is recorded in C#. (In 2007, p263 he has attempted to rectify this, giving the correct key ('Db') but claims Diana wanted it in Cb, there being no such key.) The elegant melody uses all—and only—the diatonic notes, if pitched in C, a piano's white keys, suggesting that it was composed that way.

[4] The UK leg opened on September 15 in Birmingham, followed by shows in London (Royal Albert Hall), Manchester and Liverpool.

[5] *Touch Me In The Morning* was recovered in part from her abandoned 1972 album *To The Baby* which was to celebrate her pregnancy with Tracee Joy via a selection of appropriately themed material. Tracks which survived include "Little Girl Blue"; "My Baby (My Baby My Own)" and "Brown Baby/Save the Children". Others recorded but shelved include "Young Mothers"; "The First Time Ever I Saw Your Face"; "Got To Be There"; "A Wonderful Guest" and "Turn Around".

## TMG 862
## WILLIE HUTCH
**Brother's Gonna Work It Out** (2:56)
(Hutch)
Produced by Willie Hutch
**Release Date**: 10 Aug 1973
**B-side**: I Choose You
**Position in Record Retailer Top 40**: -
**Equivalent US Release**: Motown 1222 (14 Feb 1973)
**Position in Billboard Top 40 Pop**: -
**Position in Billboard Top 40 R & B**: 18

With Motown diverting its attention into movies, several acts were simultaneously taking an interest in the developing blaxploitation genre [846]; [858], which tended to be soundtracked by an urban funk-driven style of music advanced for its time. Willie Hutch had arrived at Motown around 1970, supplying the lyric to "I'll Be There" [758] and working behind the scenes in the intervening years [828]. He was approached in 1972 to write and record a soundtrack for *The Mack*, the tale of an ex-convict turned pimp, with its famous 'Annual Players Ball' scene, his consequent recordings packaged and released by Motown.

Hutch's soundtrack plugs into the style confidently, this spin-off single featuring a funky, wah-wah guitar foundation, period saxophone passages and a gritty lyric calling for black advancement. Questioning how 'brothers and sisters' can unite in the face of 'pimps, the hustler, the pusher' in their own ranks, the position is one for which the blaxploitation school was criticised, with its stereotypical depiction of drugs and violence which tended to vulgarise the reality of ghetto life. Nonetheless, in recording in this vein, Hutch succeeds in conjuring the film's atmosphere, "Brother's Gonna Work It Out" also marking his debut in the R & B charts.

## TMG 863
## MICHAEL JACKSON
**Morning Glow** (3:36)
(Schwartz)

Produced by Bob Gaudio
**Release Date**: 27 Jul 1973
**B-side**: My Girl
**Position in Record Retailer Top 40**: -
**Equivalent US Release**: Motown 1218 (12 Apr 1973)
**Position in Billboard Top 40 Pop**: -
**Position in Billboard Top 40 R & B**: -

Spotlighting Motown's drive to appeal to a broad fan-base, the dark blaxploitation-themed [862] was immediately followed in the TMG sequence by this cheery Broadway spin-off, sourced from the musical *Pippin* (after the novel by Roger O. Hirson). Part-financed by Motown, the show was scored by Stephen Schwartz and tells the story of Pippin The Hunchback, on a journey of personal discovery which culminates in his almost being captured by the devil before one of the troupe, feigning to step out of character, saves him from certain death, the curtain falling on a dramatic false ending.

For his part, Schwartz had contributed several compositions which were recorded by the original stage cast and released as a US album in December 1972.[1] From the material, several Motown versions were duly made, most notably The Jackson 5's cover of "Corner Of The Sky", a US hit in late 1972, and The Supremes' "I Guess I'll Miss The Man" [884].

Michael Jackson tackled another, "Morning Glow" written for the scene where Pippin overcomes the tyrant Charles to assume the position of king. Produced by Bob Gaudio of The Four Seasons [819],[2] Jackson's rendition is proficiently done if unspectacular, the most interesting feature of this blithe pop number an effective *ritardando/accelerando* in the final verse. Released as a 45 in the UK, the track was paired with a remake of the classic [E67] (see also [666b]), recorded for *Ben*.

[1] One of the cast was Irene Ryan, an actress formerly famed for her role as Granny in *The Beverly Hillbillies*. She subsequently had "No Time At All" lifted as a US single, and is sometimes noted with surprise as the oldest signing Motown ever made!

[2] The Four Seasons were supposed to record "Corner Of The Sky" first, their repeated failure to convene for the session resulting in it going to The Jackson 5.

**TMG 864**
**GLADYS KNIGHT & THE PIPS**
**Take Me In Your Arms And Love Me** (2:56)
**Re-issue of [604]**
**Release Date**: 27 Jul 1973
**New B-side**: No One Could Love You More
**Position in Record Retailer Top 40**: -

Gladys Knight / Merald 'Bubba' Knight / Edward Patten / William Guest

With the group recording for Buddah, Motown sought to confront the competition with this single, timed to coincide with their first releases on their new label which included the June single "Where Peaceful Waters Flow". Not a hit in the UK, it was nonetheless a starting-point for Buddah, followed up by "Midnight Train To Georgia", which Motown might have bagged themselves had there been more foresight.

This Tamla Motown release coupled the early [604] with "No One Could Love You More" from *Standing Ovation* (1971), a celebrated Northern Soul track making its debut on 7-inch. Thanks to this pairing, [864] has become one of the most sought-after of Tamla Motown's 1970s singles and indeed of Knight's generally, catalogued on a par with the rare "Just Walk In My Shoes" [576]. It's a pity that clamour for the track in 1973 was insufficient to lift it into the UK charts.

## TMG 865
## THE JACKSON 5
**Skywriter** (3:10)
(Larson—Marcellino)
Produced by Mel Larson/Jerry Marcellino
**Release Date**: 24 Aug 1973
**B-side**: Ain't Nothing Like The Real Thing
**Position in Record Retailer Top 40**: 25
**No Equivalent US Release**

Jackie Jackson / Tito Jackson / Jermaine Jackson / Marlon Jackson / Michael Jackson

This latest Jackson 5 release, their seventh in 17 months, was a Mel Larson— Jerry Marcellino creation ([816]; [825]) made for the album of the same name. Lacking substance, the track is carried away by its surface instrumentation, a ceaseless crotchet beat underpinning an array of keyboard effects including mock-harpsichord, a hyperactive bass bubbling in octave jumps and a heavily fuzzed lead guitar. Featuring phased lead vocals [782] and closing with an unexpected cadence, the production is, if nothing else, full of ideas, its defining quality a get-up-and-go liveliness.

Pointing the way to the group's late sound, the track was re-issued in 1977 on Motown-EMI as TMG 1081 (see Appendix 2). This original Tamla Motown pressing paired the song with a version of [655], taken from the group's previous album, and which rivals Donny and Marie Osmond would later also cover. Promotional copies were issued in picture sleeves.

## TMG 866
## THE TEMPTATIONS
**Law Of The Land** (3:37)
(Whitfield)
Produced by Norman Whitfield
**Release Date**: 17 Aug 1973
**B-side**: Funky Music Sho' Nuff Turns Me On

Otis Williams / Melvin Franklin / Richard Street / Dennis Edwards / Damon Harris

Having exited The Temptations in 1971 suffering the ravages of alcoholism and substance misuse [783], Paul Williams had attempted to get his life back on-track by going into business with a make-up boutique in Detroit, a perilous venture into which he sank all available funds. Running aground in 1973, Williams was in debt to the tune of a reported $80,000 and sinking back into depression and for him its flip-side, an alcohol crutch. Williams had, of late, contemplated a return to recording, cutting the apparently confessional "I Feel Like Giving Up", which lay unreleased during a spell in which he was also expressing thoughts of suicide to those close to him. Finding no resolution to his troubles, a drunken Williams took a drive on August 17, parking up in the West Grand Boulevard area near to where the Hitsville building stood. Dressed just in swimming trunks on this hot summer day, he proceeded to shoot himself in the head, committing suicide at the age of just 34.[1]

The Temptations were in New York for the wedding of Damon Harris when news broke, learning of Williams' death straight after the ceremony. Flying back to Detroit, the group were in a state of shock, present and former Temptations coming together for a rare moment of unity at his funeral on August 24. David Ruffin paid tribute to his erstwhile colleague by singing "The Impossible Dream" at the service, one of Williams' personal favourites recorded by the group in the comparatively happy days of 1967. He was buried at Lincoln Memorial Park in Macomb County, some miles north-east of Detroit.

By twist of fate, the day Williams killed himself, Tamla Motown had scheduled release of "Law Of The Land", a second and final pull from *Masterpiece* [854]. Not put out in America[2], the single is known for its dance beat, a regularised tambourine-boosted percussion lifting an otherwise dour recording. Attacking the lyric, a cliché-laden piece of cod-philosophy from Whitfield whose upshot is acceptance of the inevitable, Dennis Edwards flies full throttle into an Edwin Starr-style rage [754], complete with off-mike exclamations. For want of some dynamic interest, the formula soon wears thin, another archetypal 1970s Whitfield piece based on a single repeating riff.

Its B-side is a live recording pulled from the earlier *All Directions*. A rendition of [810], it was supposedly taped at the 'Funky Monkey' although some have questioned whether the background revellers were dubbed onto an orthodox studio cut for effect.

[1] One of Motown's most persistent conspiracy theories holds that his death was not suicide and that he was in fact murdered, possibly by gangsters to whom he was indebted, and rumours have circulated that the gun was found in his 'wrong' hand. Close friend Otis Williams rejects the notion (Williams p164).

[2] From here on, the group's US and UK singles discographies would diverge considerably, only [931a] from their remaining Tamla Motown releases appearing as a US hit-side.

**TMG 867**
**MARTIN & FINLEY**
**It's Another Sunday** (3:26)
(Martin—Finley)
Produced by Bob Gaudio/James Carmichael
**Release Date**: NOT RELEASED Demo copies exist dated 28 Sep 1973
**B-side**: Best Friends
**Equivalent US Release**: Motown 1242 (29 May 1973)
**Position in Billboard Top 40 Pop**: -
**Position in Billboard Top 40 R & B**: -

---

Tony Martin Jr / Guy Finley

---

Signed to Mo-West in America, this duo consisted of two individuals with known and well-connected fathers. Guy Finley was the son of US television personality Larry, and was a personal friend of several stars including Liza Minnelli and Frank Sinatra. Tony Martin's father, his namesake, had himself recorded for Motown a decade earlier [E72]; [537], and was the channel by which this new act was signed. Their first album *Dazzle 'Em With Footwork*, was recorded with input from Beach Boy Brian Wilson and scheduled for Mo-West in America but scrapped when the label wound up. It eventually appeared on the Motown label in 1974, prior to which this non-album track was recorded.

A guitar-based 'soft rock' number, the song deals with the boredom of living life in a rut, imploring everyone to 'get up' and live their lives to the full. Co-produced by Bob Gaudio and James Carmichael, this curious piece was scheduled to appear in the UK on September 28 but never materialised. The act's tenure with Motown soon expired, Guy Finley having since built a career as a well-known philosopher and spiritual teacher, the seeds of which can be found in the lyric to this song.

**TMG 868**
**MARVIN GAYE**
**Let's Get It On** (3:58)
(Gaye—Townsend)
Produced by Marvin Gaye/Ed Townsend
Recording completed: 4 Apr 1973
**Release Date**: 7 Sep 1973
**B-side**: I Wish It Would Rain
**Position in Record Retailer Top 40**: 31
**Equivalent US Release**: Tamla 54234 (15 Jul 1973)
**Position in Billboard Top 40 Pop**: 1
**Position in Billboard Top 40 R & B**: 1

Settling into bachelor life [846], Gaye's mood in late-1972 was characterised by a sense of complacency in which he had achieved everything professionally and was content to pursue recreation with old friends and consider further recording at his leisure. Keen to get more product from him, Berry Gordy had cajoled Gaye for a year-and-a-half without anything substantial resulting, matters not taking a decisive turn until the latter hooked up with an old acquaintance, singer Ed Townsend. It so happened that Townsend had several new songs in the making, one of which was provisionally entitled "Let's Get On", which he demo-ed at Gaye's apartment in Culver City, to the south of Los Angeles.

Early in 1973, Gaye finally made the permanent move West, relocating to LA and taking much of his extended family with him. In no time he was in possession of several properties, and purchased a house on Outpost Drive with his estranged wife where his eight-year-old son Marvin Jr. could live (see [539]). Once there, Gaye was within touching distance of the new Motown hub, and took Townsend into Mo-West to work on new material including "Let's Get On" and some numbers which he'd had hanging around since the *What's Going On* sessions.

"Let's Get It On" was central to this phase of work, Townsend's conception a call to 'get on with life', but transformed in the hands of Gaye to something sensual, with the lyric gradually re-worked as matters progressed. The song's erotic potential was crystallised by the arrival in the studio of Townsend's friend Barbara Hunter, and in particular her beautiful 17-year-old daughter Janis, with whom Gaye immediately became obsessed. Despite his status as a married man—and the fact that Janis was still in school—they became lovers.

The arrival on the scene of Janis seemed to galvanise the normally listless Gaye, who threw himself into this new project as if to show his talents off to his new muse. Absorbing his current fixation into his work, much of the contemporary material for *Let's Get It On* took on an obvious sexual flavour, tracks such as the sledgehammer-subtle "You Sure Love To Ball" spelling matters out. But most significant was the sequel to "Let's Get It On", with which side 1 was book-ended, "Keep Getting It On" the result of an extended studio jam in which Gaye threw his lustful exhortations across the studio floor in Janis' direction.

The actual title track was recorded in sessions over March and April 1973, and in an early incarnation was chanced upon by Berry Gordy, at that point rekindling his interest in recording after having been immersed in *Lady Sings The Blues* for over a year [848]. Knocked out by the track, Gordy had the studio engineer run him off a copy which he retained for comparison with Gaye's finished work, ultimately convincing the singer that the earlier take was 'the one'. (This move was not without precedent. See for example [721]; [744].)

Gently rising and falling through its four-minutes or so, "Let's Get It On" could not have existed as a musical entity without *What's Going On*, in which the basic musical mood and style was defined. Relying on a gently pounding bass, the track is infused with a relaxed intimacy, captured in the seductively whispered title phrase. However Gaye's needs are more urgently expressed in his agonised growls during the verses which at times verge on the orgasmic, the track not merely a hypothetical love song but a means of actual seduction. Talking Janis into bed by equating emotion and fucking as if they were one-and-the-same, a concept which a teenaged girl might fall for, lines such as 'If you believe in love, let's get it on' and 'If the spirit move you, let me groove you' have only one intent in mind, and are sung to just one person.

Characteristically, Gaye's public musings on this new material were somewhat extravagant, veering from theories that the album was conceived as an honest examination of love-making's facets to claims that it was some sort of marital aid for impotent men.[1] Clearly not built on any such premise, this public expression of personal lust was nonetheless of significant import, paving the way for subsequent soul-erotica in the hands of artists such as Teddy Pendegrass and Barry White. Later in his career Gaye would attempt to sustain this version of himself, recording tracks such as "Sexual Healing" and incorporating into his stage act increasingly lewd gimmicks in an effort to keep upping the ante. (An embarrassing photograph of Gaye on-stage with his trousers around his ankles appears in Ritz, op. p233.)

Welcomed in America with unbounded enthusiasm *Let's Get It On* reportedly went gold on the day it was released, Motown taking out billboards boasting of its sales figures which even by their standards were phenomenal. It so happened that in the summer of 1973, Gaye's Motown contract would expire, the timing of this new album putting zeros on Motown's estimation of his value (Gaye had delivered just one standard studio album in nearly four years). The single when it appeared was similarly massive in America, but tended to be ignored in the UK. Hedging their bets in case of censorship Tamla and Tamla Motown respectively married "Let's Get It On" with a classic oldie, taken from his 1969 set, *That's The Way Love Is*. But for Gaye, such details were unimportant as he enjoyed a second monumental career success, and in his ongoing affair with Janis, had found someone with whom he could truly find himself again. The two married in October 1977.

[1] See his comments in Abbott, p111 and Davis 1988, p127.

## TMG 869
## STEVIE WONDER
**Higher Ground** (3:10)
(Wonder)
Produced by Stevie Wonder
**Release Date**: 28 Sep 1973
**B-side**: Too High
**Position in Record Retailer Top 40**: -
**Equivalent US Release**: Tamla 54235 (27 Jul 1973)
**Position in Billboard Top 40 Pop**: 4
**Position in Billboard Top 40 R & B**: 1

With *Talking Book* his biggest success to date, Stevie Wonder was on a creative and professional high through 1973, and eager to move on with his next project, provisionally entitled *Last Days Of Easter*. The biblical allusion is one which would be reflected in much of his emerging material, as Wonder continued to write about his personal spiritual quest, counterpoised by a critique of the contemporary political arena and therefore treading much the same ground as his erstwhile colleague Marvin Gaye two years earlier. In-the-end deciding that the Easter reference would distract listeners, he elected to call the forthcoming set *Innervisions*, hinting at what he wanted listeners to read: this was something profound, from the soul and aspiring to humanity's higher senses.

Recorded between the twin poles of Media Sound in New York and Record Plant in LA, the set was largely Wonder's own work again, entirely written by him and with a sprinkling of session musicians pitching in on some of the backing tracks. Wonder's main artistic collaborators were the reliable Cecil—Margouleff team [827], programmers of the synths on which the album is constructed, and assuming here the elevated role of Associate Producers. What emerged in *Innervisions* is held in popular estimation to be Wonder's best work, its nine tracks of a consistently high calibre and meshing together to make a coherent whole. The album was packaged for release with striking cover art across its gatefold sleeve, painted by Efram Wolff. Meeting instant acclaim, the LP was set to be another major success and became his biggest transatlantic hit to date.

At this point, Wonder's sense of achievement was clouded by a fear of doom in which he is said to have considered his own mortality as imminent (in a *Rolling Stone* interview in April he announced that he was going to die soon). And while being driven through South Carolina for a night gig on August 6, three days after *Innervisions* emerged, Wonder's disturbing premonitions were very nearly realised. Asleep in the passenger seat of a car being driven by his cousin John Harris, a truck they were tailing made an abrupt stop Harris ploughed into it and unbalanced its cargo of logs, one of which crashed through the windscreen of their car and struck Wonder on the front of the head. Rushed to hospital, Wonder was diagnosed with a fractured skull and contusion of the brain[1] and, with a grave prognosis, spent a week unconscious.

Few expected him to survive but, determined to get Wonder out of his coma and back to health, his road manager and assistant Ira Tucker had the insight to recognise that the singer's sole passion was music. He managed to make contact with him by singing one of his new tracks, "Higher Ground", at full volume in Wonder's ear. Somehow the idea worked and, to everyone's surprise and relief, Wonder began to respond, this momentary flash of inspiration rousing him from the depths. Eventually coming to, Wonder was still in a perilous state, but the signs were that he could make a recovery of sorts, no-one at that stage certain of what long-term damage might have been done. When Tucker had a clavinet brought into the hospital, Wonder showed that he had not lost his musical abilities nor faculty to play a keyboard, although the accident cruelly deprived the blind 23-year-old of his sense of smell, a valuable point of contact with the world around him.

Appropriately, the song which helped him emerge from this unconsciousness was the first single to be issued from *Innervisions*—"Higher Ground" a deep, funk-driven groove pitched in the general style of "Superstition" [841]. Entirely Wonder's own work, the track endlessly cycles on its basic riff, essentially an accelerated blues bass line, giving a sense of perpetual motion. Whether this suggested the lyrical theme is unclear, but

Wonder's text speaks from the perspective of the Hindu concept of reincarnation, with its implied circularity of existence, in which life simply 'goes around again'. Regretting his sinful former-self, and glad of the chance to make amends, Wonder is aspiring upwards, striving for a higher plane of being—a spiritual quest but also, in the context of his death premonition, suggestive of something darkly portentous.

Juxtaposed with this aura of spiritual ascent are portrayals of lying politicians, ultimately pointless wars and, interestingly, endlessly preaching preachers, suggesting that whatever religious process was underway in Wonder's psyche, it was not conversion to the western view of God and church. In the light of this, the Hindu theme makes more sense, Wonder speaking from the perspective of Moksha (enlightenment), or more likely, the Buddhist Satori.[2] (This reading also sheds light on his scrapping the album's working title, *Last Days Of Easter*, the nearest Christian equivalent of the rebirth concept.)

Wonder's recovery from injury was remarkable, with little outward sign that he had ever been so gravely hurt. Adding to his growing legend, he amazed everyone who knew him by appearing live on stage with Elton John on September 25, seven weeks after the accident. And this extraordinary period of Wonder's life took a further twist as he met Yolanda Simmons, brought in to work for his Black Bull Publishing concern [798] and with whom he first spoke while convalescing. Simmons would become his lover, and the couple would have two children together.

The following spring, at Wonder's 24th birthday party in LA, Ewart Abner personally presented him with a gold disc for "Higher Ground", closely following his scooping five Grammy Awards in March. From the brink of death, Wonder had bounced back and stood at his artistic zenith.

[1] Contusion (meaning essentially bruising) was the title given to one of the tracks on Wonder's 1976 album *Songs In The Key Of Life*.

[2] The difference between the Hindu and Buddhist concepts of reincarnation are that Hinduism holds the soul of the individual is reborn, in keeping with Wonder's theme here. Buddhists take a more general view of the principle, holding that the individual is lost but that the eternal cycle continues.

**TMG 870**
**J J BARNES**
**Real Humdinger** (2:35)
(Hamilton—Morris—Hamilton)
Produced by Al Kent/Richard Morris
**Release Date**: 14 Sep 1973
**B-side**: Please Let Me In / I Ain't Gonna Do It
**Position in Record Retailer Top 40**: -
**No Equivalent US Release**
*Originally released as Ric Tic RT-110 (Mar 1966)*

Jimmy Jay Barnes was a teenager when he released his first single in 1960, after which he switched labels and eventually ended up with Ric Tic in 1965. "Real

Humdinger" was his second single there, released the following year and making an impressive 18 R & B. Barnes did not survive the Motown buy-out [630], the fact that he was thought to have sounded much like Marvin Gaye hampering his chances.[1]

Motown of course had purchased his catalogue to-date, this very late re-issue extracted from the Ric Tic archives for the Northern Soul market. "Real Humdinger" is a mid-tempo dance number which features a pre-Motown Dennis Coffey on electric guitar. His stabbing action and a rolling bass line push the track along beneath the main piano, Barnes' vocals clear and fluid.

This maxi-single included the track's original B-side, plus the flip to his first Ric Tic release. Its timing coincided with an inevitable piece of repackaging from Tamla Motown, *Ric Tic Relics* emerging in August and including the three titles presented here plus [790], [790b], [795], [807b], [831] and [905] amongst its 16 tracks .

This belated single drew extra attention to Barnes on the Northern Soul circuit, and his career was accordingly revived with some new recordings on the UK Contempo label.

[1] This may account for the strained relations between Barnes and Gaye, outlined in Edmonds (p42-43).


## TMG 871
## THE DETROIT SPINNERS
**Together We Can Make Such Sweet Music** (3:04)
**Re-issue of [766]**
**Release Date**: 21 Sep 1973
**New B-side**: Bad Bad Weather (Till You Come Home)
**Position in Record Retailer Top 40**: -

G C Cameron / Henry Fambrough / Bobbie Smith / Billy Henderson / Pervis Jackson

As with the recent "Reachin' For Something I Can't Have" [860], Tamla Motown opted to revisit this formerly signed act by re-issuing their last single, released two-and-a-half years previously. (This is in fact the first time a single from the 1970s had been re-issued.) This new edition updated the act's name to 'Detroit Spinners' to take advantage of the group's recent high profile in this guise, signalled by their Atlantic single "Could It Be I'm Falling In Love", which had made number 11 in May.

The Detroit Spinners had the fortune on leaving Motown to work with Thom Bell of the Philadelphia International organisation (see [890]) and, in recruiting Phillippe Wynne to replace G C Cameron who had stayed behind [766], commenced 1973 on a clear ascent. A string of hits soon ensued on both sides of the Atlantic, making the group one of the arch-proponents of the Philadelphia style, and for many a defining force in popular soul during the mid 1970s.

Notably, this re-release was flagged by a rare American equivalent

(Motown 1235) issued in April 1973, courtesy of the fact that the group had by then placed both "Could It Be I'm Falling In Love" and "I'll Be Around" in the top 10 there. Cashing-in was par for the course for Tamla Motown, but again, in the light of what happened to Gladys Knight & The Pips in the years immediately following their departure, the company must have realised that major talent was slipping through their fingers.

This pressing dispensed with the original B-side in favour of "Bad Bad Weather", a US-only single from 1968.


## TMG 872
## JUNIOR WALKER & THE ALL STARS
**Holly Holy** (4:00)
(Diamond)
Produced by Johnny Bristol
**Release Date**: 21 Sep 1973
**B-side**: Peace And Understanding Is Hard To Find
**Position in Record Retailer Top 40**: -
**Equivalent US Release**: Soul 35081 (24 Nov 1970)
**Position in Billboard Top 40 Pop**: -
**Position in Billboard Top 40 R & B**: 33

---
Jr Walker / Willie Woods / Vic Thomas / Billy Nicks
---

Penned by New York singer-songwriter Neil Diamond, "Holly Holy" had been a number 6 pop hit in 1969 which did not chart in the UK (Diamond had yet to break through as a performer at that stage). A curious affair, the track's lyric is vague, Diamond seeming to focus most on playing with words, the subject of the song apparently a woman named Holly, who has 'holy eyes'.[1]

Recorded by Walker for *A Gas*, this remake plays up the lyric's spiritual dimensions, starting out with piano and gospel backing sections, and bringing forth an uncharacteristically sleek vocal. As it progresses, Walker hits form, letting rip against electric guitar and finding his sax at 2:49, oddly split across the stereo spectrum. A minor R & B hit in 1970, the track skipped by unnoticed in the UK.

[1] It is interesting to compare the title with Marvin Gaye's "Wholly Holy" [817b], direct influence likely.


## TMG 873
## EDDIE KENDRICKS
**Keep On Truckin' (Part 1)** (3:21)
(Wilson—Poree—Caston)
Produced by Frank Wilson/Leonard Caston
**Release Date**: 5 Oct 1973
**B-side**: Keep On Truckin' (Part 2)
**Position in Record Retailer Top 40**: 18

**Equivalent US Release:** Tamla 54238 (3 Aug 1973)
**Position in Billboard Top 40 Pop:** 1
**Position in Billboard Top 40 R & B:** 1

The most successful release of Eddie Kendricks' solo career, "Keep On Truckin'" is built from a synthesiser foundation with a hammering rhythm custom-made for the dance-floor. It also features an effective vibraphone solo part way through, retained for the single edit and drawing on the jazz tradition. Atop this musical foundation, Wilson and Caston back Kendricks' feather-light vocals, giving the track both earthy drive and a high-flying finesse.

Originally running to eight minutes, "Keep On Truckin'" has won dubious accolades as the first-ever disco recording, the phenomenon at that stage mainly centred on the New York club scene and drawing a sub-culture of hedonistic decadence characterised by drug-use and an open display of gay and straight promiscuity. Still marginal in 1973, the movement was gathering pace, *Rolling Stone* famously featuring a 'disco' article in 1973 from where the abbreviated word slipped into common usage. "Keep On Truckin'" has elements of the subsequently developed style, its main body a continuously looping, largely unchanging groove.

High on style and low on substance, "Keep On Truckin'" works on a purely physical level beneath rational consciousness, the lyrics mere style accessories, its title a tongue-in-cheek innuendo from Anita Poree, and its subject matter essentially non-existent. One wonders what Kendricks thought of the line, 'In old Temptations rain, I'm ducking', apparently an allusion to [641].


## TMG 874
## JERMAINE JACKSON
### The Bigger You Love (The Harder You Fall) (3:25)
(Larson—Marcellino)
Produced by Mel Larson/Jerry Marcellino
**Release Date:** 5 Oct 1973
**B-side:** I'm In A Different World
**Position in Record Retailer Top 40:** -
**No Equivalent US Release**

With a couple of solo singles under his belt, Jermaine Jackson recorded his second album early in 1973, *Come Into My Life* a prophetic title reflecting his blossoming relationship with Berry Gordy's only daughter Hazel, whom he had been discreetly dating. The couple announced on September 19 that they were to marry, the move promising to unite the Gordy and Jackson families in a manner which would establish once and for all the power axis within Motown. (Marvin Gaye, still legally wed to Anna Gordy was said to be miffed at the news.)

So far as his recording career went, Jackson's new album hit the shops in the UK just as the announcement was made, trailered by this single, apparently re-working a title from [537]. Larson and Marcellino's composition had first been unveiled in 1971 on The Supremes & Four Tops' *Dynamite* and was re-recorded here by Jackson under its composers' direction. Set in a mildly funky mode, Jackson's own bass guitar work provides much of the bulk on this inoffensive pop song, aimed at the hit parade and of no real consequence.

More pressing matters were at hand, the wedding of Jermaine and Hazel taking place in an opulent ceremony in Beverley Hills on December 15. Attracting considerable publicity, news leaked out that the wedding had cost hundreds of thousands of dollars, an embarrassed Berry Gordy shamed into compensating for this over-extravagance by donating an undisclosed sum to a local housing project for black families. A particular highlight of the day was Smokey Robinson's performance of "Wedding Song", which he had written especially for the occasion and later recorded for *A Quiet Storm* [949n].

Potentially now one of the most powerful recording artists on Motown's books, Jermaine Jackson's solo career nonetheless ground to a halt after the marriage, nothing further released from him for three years. Had it not been for the fact that The Jackson 5 elected to depart Motown without him in 1975 [1001], it is possible that he may never have resumed recording under his own name, which he did just as the Tamla Motown label was being abandoned (see [1040]).


**TMG 875**
**EDWIN STARR**
**You've Got My Soul On Fire** (3:29)
(Whitfield)
Produced by Norman Whitfield
**Release Date**: 12 Oct 1973
**B-side**: Love (The Lonely People's Prayer)
**Position in Record Retailer Top 40**: -
**Equivalent US Release**: Motown 1276 (21 Aug 1973)
**Position in Billboard Top 40 Pop**: -
**Position in Billboard Top 40 R & B**: 40

One of several stand-alone singles recorded by Starr in the early 1970s for the Gordy label, "You've Got My Soul On Fire" is a Norman Whitfield number made during 1973. Due to the absence of Barrett Strong [854], the number was entirely Whitfield's, the writer still largely Detroit-based, Edwin Starr having also refused the move west and therefore readily available for sessions such as this.

In fact, the track may have been written for The Temptations, their own version appearing almost simultaneously in America on *1990* [887]. Whether it was indeed conceived for them is debatable, the number essentially a love song phrased in the style of an angry tirade, atypical for either act in the context of their most successful 1970s material. Lyrics aside, the recording is of Whitfield's classic design, forging through its verses without shifting key, its bass anchoring giving flight to sensationalistic sounds including several effects-laden guitars.

---

Not a hit on first release, Tamla Motown re-issued the single on 8 April 1974, in the wake of the UK edition of The Temptations' *1990*. The move again failed to take it into the charts.


**TMG 876**
**GLADYS KNIGHT & THE PIPS**
**Daddy Could Swear, I Declare** (3:42)
(Bristol—Knight)
Produced by Johnny Bristol
**Release Date**: 28 Sep 1973
**B-side**: For Once In My Life
**Position in Record Retailer Top 40**: -
**Equivalent US Release**: Soul 35105 (9 Apr 1973)
**Position in Billboard Top 40 Pop**: 19
**Position in Billboard Top 40 R & B**: 2

---

Gladys Knight / Merald 'Bubba' Knight / Edward Patten / William Guest

---

Co-composed by Gladys Knight, this track was written around 1971, but objecting to its quirky lyric, Berry Gordy blocked its recording—which supports her later claim that Motown attempted to stop her from developing her writing skills.[1] With Gordy no longer on the scene, Knight managed to get a version done for *Neither One Of Us*, the group's final studio album, which therefore became their last Tamla Motown single which could reasonably be termed 'new'. In-the-event, this made four UK releases in 1974, a best-ever tally for the group indicating the degree to which Tamla Motown were milking their existing catalogue.

"Daddy Could Swear" is a light-hearted affair, whose middle verse takes the form of a letter recounting one particular incident which brought forth profanities from 'Daddy', a small foul-mouthed man with a tendency to cuss. Its inherent jocularity, though, is buried by its production, a dense bank of bass, guitar and brass with a galloping rhythmic underpinning. Essentially humourless, the manner of recording turns out a rocky number, contrasting with recent singles and closing Knight's Tamla Motown years with an up-beat yarn. (For a B-side Tamla Motown took the much-travelled "For Once In My Life" from the same LP [665b]; [679].)

[1] Some commentators claim that the track was co-written by Gladys and Bubba Knight (see [857]).


**TMG 877**
**THE ISLEY BROTHERS**
**Tell Me It's Just A Rumour Baby** (2:52)
(Fuqua—Bristol—Bullock)
Produced by Harvey Fuqua/Johnny Bristol
Recording completed: 31 Aug 1966

---

**Release Date**: 26 Oct 1973
**B-side**: Save Me From This Misery
**Position in Record Retailer Top 40**: -
**No Equivalent US Release**

---

Ronald Isley / Rudolph Isley / O'Kelly Isley

---

Standing out from Tamla Motown's recent releases, this rasping number from 1966 made its first appearance on 45 both for Northern fans, and to exploit the fact that the group had just enjoyed their first post-Motown top 20 hit ("That Lady", released in the UK on Epic). Initially released on *Soul On The Rocks*, "Tell Me It's Just A Rumour Baby" was written in the aftermath of The Four Tops' "Shake Me, Wake Me (When It's Over)" [553], on which the musical progression is clearly based. Slightly faster in tempo, the track is also pitched a semitone higher, possibly suggesting that the backing was speeded up for added punch before the vocals were added. Arriving on an unsteady Bb/G# foundation, the track differs from its model in that it accommodates a chord change for its chorus, although the vocals continue to be pitched against the Ab tonic of the verse.

Lyrically too the theme is similar. The original HDH text finds its narrator learning about his unfaithful lover through a bedroom wall, whereas this scenario has the truth materialising as a rumour—in this respect fore-shadowing "I Heard It Through The Grapevine" [629], at that stage yet to be recorded. With Ronald Isley's frantic vocals, the number captures its moment precisely, a vintage Motown stomper deserving of wider circulation in its day, but nonetheless thrilling club crowds in 1973.

**TMG 878**
**THE JACKSON 5**
**Get It Together** (2:47)
(Larson—Gordy—Davis—Fletcher—Marcellino)
Produced by Hal Davis
**Release Date**: 2 Nov 1973
**B-side**: Touch
**Position in Record Retailer Top 40**: -
**Equivalent US Release**: Motown 1277 (3 Aug 1973)
**Position in Billboard Top 40 Pop**: 28
**Position in Billboard Top 40 R & B**: 2

---

Jackie Jackson / Tito Jackson / Jermaine Jackson / Marlon Jackson / Michael Jackson

---

Seven years is an age in pop music, and the contrast in styles between [877] and [878], separated by such a span, represents an unbridgeable generational leap. These two recordings, released a week apart, illustrate more precisely than any other back-to-back Tamla Motown singles the extent to which Motown's heritage was buried as the company sought to progress through the 1970s with new acts and musicians and an entirely different production ethic.

---

Yet the gulf between this typical 1970s piece and the product of Motown's 'Golden Era' was not just in the manifest, but in the underlying mood or disposition in which compositions are set. Where "Tell Me It's Just A Rumour" expresses vulnerability through fear that the relationship is in jeopardy, and is therefore fundamentally caring, "Get It Together" is the very opposite, confronting the female participant and threatening her with abandonment if she doesn't toe the line. Although the male singer claims to love her, there is little emotion apparent in the text as she is taunted for being on her 'high horse' and being unable to keep his love. Here, there is no compassion implied and apparently no love lost.

Following Jermaine Jackson's imminent marriage to Berry Gordy's daughter [874], the re-appearance here of Motown's boss in the credits led some to assume that he was taking special care of the group. In fact, it stemmed more from Gordy's new-found enthusiasm after the *Lady Sings The Blues* period in which he had neglected music, free once more to pursue his first love. Available to involve himself in Motown product, he was gradually re-establishing himself in the studio [868] and looking to drive the company forward again after a period of restructuring and realignment.

"Get It Together" is produced in the progressive proto-disco mode [873], still referred to as 'funk' in 1973, dragging the group into the more adult world of dance clubs, and away from their child-friendly tradition (eg [738]; [746]; [769] etc.). Michael Jackson's voice too was starting to display a maturity as he grew. The emergence of the track looked as if it might reinvigorate the group's career after a period in the doldrums, but the reunion of Gordy and former colleague Hal Davis for this hit proved to be a one-off, there being no new Corporation formed as a result.

The associated album contained a selection of relatively uninspired covers, as the group showed themselves still stagnating.[1] Nonetheless, on the live circuit the group remained hot property, embarking on a sell-out tour of the Far East over the summer. The fact was, though, that in terms of record releases they were looking like yesterday's news, and would never chart another single in Britain.

[1] The album was called *Get It Together*, the initials GIT emblazoned across the front—an old joke first cracked by The Supremes & The Temptations [730].


**TMG 879**
**DIANA ROSS & MARVIN GAYE**
**You're A Special Part Of Me** (3:15)
(Wright—Johnson—Porter)
Produced by Berry Gordy
**Release Date**: 9 Nov 1973
**B-side**: I'm Falling In Love With You
**Position in Record Retailer Top 40**: -
**Equivalent US Release**: Motown 1280 (13 Sep 1973)
**Position in Billboard Top 40 Pop**: 12
**Position in Billboard Top 40 R & B**: 4

During 1972, Diana Ross was expecting her second daughter and was spending some time away from the recording studio pending release of *Lady Sings The Blues* [848]. Marvin Gaye meanwhile was in a slump following the failed *You're The Man* project [846], Berry Gordy still at that point hoping for a follow-up to *What's Going On*. Musing on these two big stars, who appeared to be marking time when they could be recording, Gordy hit upon the idea of pairing them up for some duets, a move fuelled solely by its potential financial pay-off.

Gordy though was out of touch and had misjudged Marvin Gaye who, having vowed after the death of Tammi Terrell that he would never record any more duets, had in any case shaken off Gordy's old image of the romantic crooner and reinvented himself as an artist working on his own terms. In this respect, the bringing together of Gaye, would-be spiritualist and political spokesman, with Ross, mother and wannabe movie star, was ill-conceived, the project largely doomed by its protagonists' artistic differences before it had begun.

The mismatch of personalities was apparent from the first session. Attempting to sing together on the studio floor, Gaye characteristically lit up a joint, Ross stomping off to the control room to complain to Berry Gordy that she was pregnant and didn't want to breathe in the smoke. Gordy obligingly buzzed through the intercom to Gaye, who merely smiled and told him he needed a smoke to be able to record. From that moment on it became apparent that the project would not ignite and, with Ross and Gaye barely communicating, vocals were taped separately, the two never in the studio at the same point.

In the end, this laborious project resulted in 18 mock-duets, although it seemed for a while that they would never be issued. However almost a year on, ten were mixed for masters and issued as *Diana And Marvin*, the billing of course putting Gordy's darling Ross first. Received coolly, the album contained six Jobete copyrights and a curious selection of cover versions, several of which were selected by Tamla Motown for release on 45. The first such lift, however, was an original composition, written by Greg Wright, Harold Johnson and Andrew Porter, three-fifths of the group The Devastating Affair who were signed to Mo-West before becoming Diana Ross' stage vocalists, appearing with her at London's Royal Albert Hall in September 1973 (see [861n]).[1]

A competent enough attempt at an impassioned love song, "You're A Special Part Of Me" lacks backbone in its array of lyrical platitudes, the circumstances of its recording precluding any enlivening spark between the two vocalists. The delay between recording and release merely served to underline the irrelevance of the project for its two participants, Gaye by now on the crest of *Let's Get It On* [868] and Ross already famed for her silver screen appearance and back to recording in her own right, with a recent US number 1 under her belt [861]. This footnote in the career of both would have been better left to gather dust, Tamla Motown refusing to let it die by releasing an entirely unwarranted four further singles from it over the following year and a half.

[1] The remainder of The Devastating Affair, its female section, consisted of Karin Patterson [950] and Olivia Foster. See also Appendix 3 for their Mo-West single of 1973.

**TMG 880**
**DIANA ROSS**
**All Of My Life** (3:05)
(Randall)
Produced by Michael Randall
**Release Date**: 30 Nov 1973
**B-side**: A Simple Thing Like Cry
**Position in Record Retailer Top 40**: 9
**No Equivalent US Release**

21 days after the disappointing unveiling of [879], Diana Ross was due another release in the form of this new single, a UK-only hit written by staff producer Michael Randall. Coming in on an elegant 'classical' prelude, "All Of My Life" is another in Diana Ross' sequence of 'power ballads' ([781]; [861]) which was becoming her patent style.

The track was most-likely not seen as single material when recorded for *Touch Me In The Morning*, and was not issued on 45 in America. However its stylistic resemblance to the currently popular Carpenters may have drawn particular attention to the song, which Tamla Motown pulled at the end of 1973, scoring a top 10 hit in the process.[1] Carrying a broadly ranging melody line, the composition's main interest comes via an unexpected shift from the major G to the relative minor for the second half of each chorus. Introducing a chromatic bass run, these sections offer contrast and prevent the song from becoming complacent.

The track was paired up with "A Simple Thing Like Cry", which like [861b] was an early album cut, evidence that even at this stage Tamla Motown were interested in plugging Ross' back-catalogue.

[1] The Carpenters, while having nothing substantial in common with Motown, nonetheless took "Please Mr. Postman" [E05] back to the top of the US charts in 1975. It peaked at 2 in the UK.


**TMG 881**
**STEVIE WONDER**
**Living For The City** (3:12)
(Wonder)
Produced by Stevie Wonder
**Release Date**: 30 Nov 1973
**B-side**: Visions
**Position in Record Retailer Top 40**: 15
**Equivalent US Release**: Tamla 54242 (1 Nov 1973)
**Position in Billboard Top 40 Pop**: 8
**Position in Billboard Top 40 R & B**: 1

The centrepiece of *Innervisions* [869], "Living For The City" was conceived as a seven-minute-plus epic, depicting the lives and trials of a black family from Mississippi. Poverty-stricken and working incessantly, the parents are portrayed as the modern-day equivalent of slaves, toiling for survival by day and night, and trying in the face of open hostility to provide for their children, in a place where '[employers] don't use coloured people'.[1] The children are also sketched out, the attractive young sister still in school, and the brother smart enough to realise that there is no future for him in his home town. Suffering endless unemployment, he heads up to New York to make his fortune.

In its original state, the song proceeds from here by following the lad on his quasi-adventure. Wonder includes a collage of sounds intended to capture the essence of the city's soundscape[2], and dialogue overdubbed by colleagues who happened to be around the studio when it was recorded, these moments capturing the point at which the boy arrives in New York and is promptly set up for a drugs bust and thrown in jail. (The famous line, 'Get in that cell, nigger' was spoken by a studio cleaner.) From this bridging section, the song's conclusion arrives, the lad incarcerated and the political system shown as redundant, with the key question of whether this state of affairs could ever be changed, left hanging. The decision to release this important piece on 45 however necessitated editing of the finished track, and so the single edition terminates before the main character's arrival in the city, thereby stripping it of its thematic goal. And yet despite losing this intensely relevant part, the 45 edit stands on its own terms, and remains an effective portrayal of life in the Deep South as experienced by many of the poor and, in particular, black inhabitants.

Starting out with a widely panned keyboard run reminiscent of the famous riff from "Satisfaction" (see [841]), what remains of the piece is entirely Wonder's own, fabricated from synthesiser tracks which, in conforming in their execution to standard rock instrumentation, do not advertise the fact. Indeed, the 'electric piano' of the song is articulated with an application possible with an orthodox keyboard, Wonder devising a graphically defeatist run down the scale for the end-of-chorus passages (at 1:08 and 2:28), in whole notes from F# to Bb, stabilising on the A to lock back in. Coiled around this is a steeply angular and fluid solo, the track's instrumental showpiece, in which Margouleff and Cecil's synthesisers enjoy centre-stage.

For a vocal, Margouleff strove to pull some grit from Wonder by goading him, deliberately switching off the studio tape while Wonder was in mid-flow. The ploy succeeded, with Wonder's contribution delivered with all the drive and disgust which the lyric demands, the producer here earning his salt albeit at Wonder's immediate expense. Subsequently released to acclaim, the track became a favourite of Wonder's fans and a number which, courtesy of its repeating riffs he would use to monumental effect in extravagant stage performances. According to John Rockwell, these live renditions 'surpassed anything Wonder has ever done on record'[3], which is not to discredit the studio version which, despite its enforced brevity on single, remains one of the most sharply delineated studies of Wonder's career, its audio qualities parallel to a miniature movie.

[1] Although subject to national law, Mississippi refused to ratify the Thirteenth Amendment which abolished slavery until 1995.

[2] This effective section, besides its function in progressing the narrative, also allows Wonder to communicate the essence of the urban environment for a person without sight, prompting him to distribute blindfolds to journalists for a bus ride through New York in promotion of *Innervisions*.

[3] *Rolling Stone* article reproduced in Abbott, p132.

## TIMELINE – 1973

Tamla Motown release 42 singles and 38 albums. (A further 13 singles and 8 albums are released in the UK on Rare Earth and Mo-West)
Tamla Motown place 17 singles in the UK top 40. 4 make top 10
UK branches of Rare Earth and Mo-West labels up profile with numerous releases from British acts
Wigan Casino opens
Soul music dominates US charts

| | |
|---|---|
| **Jan** | Berry Gordy resigns as president of Motown Records, as Motown Industries is formed, bringing several arms under one umbrella. Ewart Abner assumes position for Motown Records, Gordy becomes Chairman of Board and president of Motown Industries |
| **Jan 27** | Stevie Wonder: "Superstition" number 1 in US (one week) |
| **Feb 1** | Buddah announce signing of Gladys Knight & Pips |
| **Feb 17** | Jackson 5: "Doctor My Eyes" enters UK top 50 (peak 9) |
| **Mar 6** | Temptations win Grammy award for best R & B Single, "Papa Was A Rolling Stone" and two others. Motown's first Grammys except 1971 award for spoken-word Black Forum LP *Why I Oppose The War In Vietnam* |
| **Apr** | UK film premiere of *Lady Sings The Blues* |
| **Apr 7** | Diana Ross: *Lady Sings The Blues* number 1 album in US (two weeks) |
| **May 19** | Stevie Wonder: "You Are The Sunshine Of My Life" number 1 in US (one week) |
| **May 19** | Stevie Wonder: "You Are The Sunshine Of My Life" enters UK top 50 (peak 7) |
| **Summer** | Motown-EMI establish arm to recruit UK artists for Rare Earth/Mo-West |
| **Jun** | Ashford & Simpson sign to Warners |
| **Jul 14** | Diana Ross: "Touch Me In The Morning" enters UK top 50 (peak 9) |
| **Aug** | Marvin Gaye: "Let's Get It On" signals new, sensual direction for singer |
| **Aug 6** | Stevie Wonder narrowly escapes death in car accident which deprives him of sense of smell |
| **Aug 17** | Former Temptation Paul Williams commits suicide by gunshot |
| **Aug 18** | Diana Ross: "Touch Me In The Morning" number 1 in US (one week) |
| **Sep 8** | Marvin Gaye: "Let's Get It On" number 1 in US (two weeks) |
| **Sep 15** | Diana Ross plays first date of UK tour at Birmingham Odeon |
| **Nov 10** | Eddie Kendricks: "Keep On Truckin'" number 1 in US (two weeks), toppling Gladys Knight & Pips' "Midnight Train To Georgia" on Buddah |
| **Nov** | The Corporation cease working together, leaving Jackson 5 in limbo |
| **Dec 15** | Jermaine Jackson marries Berry Gordy's daughter Hazel |
| **Dec 29** | Motown singer Bobby Darin dies during surgery |

**TMG 882**
**MARVIN GAYE**
**Come Get To This** (2:40)
(Gaye)
Produced by Marvin Gaye
**Release Date**: 4 Jan 1974
**B-side**: Distant Lover
**Position in Record Retailer Top 40**: -
**Equivalent US Release**: Tamla 54241 (Oct 1973)
**Position in Billboard Top 40 Pop**: 21
**Position in Billboard Top 40 R & B**: 3

With nothing appearing during December, Tamla Motown went into 1974 with this new effort from Marvin Gaye, taken from *Let's Get It On*. Originally intended for The Originals [733], the track has a standard verse arrangement and drum-kit, unlike much of Gaye's contemporary work, and thereby comes over as an oldie although it was written comparatively recently, during sessions for *What's Going On*. Lacking a defined chorus, and with a title pulled half-stated from the end of verse one, the track has a sense of incompletion about it, and floats past tunelessly without ever reaching conclusions musical or lyrical. (Trying to keep the style contemporary, Gaye can be heard providing semi-orgasmic moans in the background.)

The release here coincided with Gaye's 'comeback' tour, his first date at Oakland Coliseum staged on the day the single was released. Affected by Gaye's current drive to present himself as a human sex-machine (co-incident with his moving in with Janis [868]), this tale of longing was contorted on-stage into a crude invitation to copulate, coupled with Gaye's suggestive thrusting forward of the hips. Released as a live album in the summer (see [923]), this gig and the tour generally was notable for the fact that his group included on bass guitar an anonymous James Jamerson, still struggling to find West Coast studio work.[1]

[1] The rest of the group included Ray Parker Jr. (guitar), Ernie Watts (sax) and Joe Sample (keyboards).


**TMG 883**
**SMOKEY ROBINSON**
**Just My Soul Responding** (5:00)
(Robinson—Tarplin)
Produced by William "Smokey" Robinson/Willie Hutch
**Release Date**: 11 Jan 1974
**B-side**: Sweet Harmony
**Position in Record Retailer Top 40**: 35
**Equivalent US Release**: Tamla 54246 (18 Apr 1974)
**Position in Billboard Top 40 Pop**: -
**Position in Billboard Top 40 R & B**: -

Having unilaterally decided he was no longer a Detroiter, Berry Gordy had cut adrift his Senior Vice-President, Smokey Robinson initially staying put with his family. However in the early part of the 1970s Robinson's professional drive, and Berry Gordy's pestering, resulted in Robinson moving with his family to LA and back to the heart of Motown. By now officially in retirement as a singer [811], Robinson managed to refrain from recording for less than a year when Marv Tarplin turned up with a tape of songs. Despite himself, Robinson felt the irresistible urge to explore the material and wound up back in the studio. Convincing himself that he was retired specifically from the stage and not the studio floor, this born entertainer duly made "Sweet Harmony" in tribute to The Miracles, released as a single in America in April 1973 (Tamla 54233), less than a year after he quit the group, thereby opening the door on a possible 'comeback'.

Keeping it low-key, Robinson—who at this stage could presumably have re-joined The Miracles had he been so disposed—refrained from playing live and hooked-up with Willie Hutch [862], the two producing between them *Smokey*, a first solo set. Released in June 1973 (November in the UK), the album included "Sweet Harmony" plus "Just My Soul Responding", both lifted here by Tamla Motown for his first release as a solo artist.

The recording—and its selection for 45—were uncharacteristic for Robinson. Drawing on Motown's age-old penchant for writing songs based on a single chord, the track holds its F major from start to finish, in contrast to its authors' usual irrepressible animation. But it is in the lyric where the track sets itself apart, Robinson's text a scathing spectacle of politics, discrimination and war split into three sections. Verse 1, introduced with a sarcastic rendition of "Happy Birthday To You" recounts the coming-of-age of a young lad who consequently finds himself packed off to fight in some war with which he has hitherto had nothing to do. This is followed by two verses dealing in turn with Native Americans living in degradation on reservations, and an exposé of black people surviving in the ghetto.

That Robinson opted to recommence recording with such material is in itself surprising, his grim portrayal of life in verses 2 and 3 raising fundamental questions about American society and the existence of those considered marginal within it. With its title a clever deflection of the weighty subject matter, this composition marks the start of a new chapter in Robinson's career, although any thoughts that he would become a 'spokesman for the people' were short-lived, Wonder and Gaye handling such responsibilities so far as Motown were concerned. Robinson here has said his piece, and intentionally or not, had picked up the recording bug again, his 'retirement' over almost before it had been noticed.

**TMG 884**
**THE SUPREMES**
**I Guess I'll Miss The Man** (2:40)
(Schwartz)
Produced by Sherlie Matthews/Deke Richards
**Release Date:** 11 Jan 1974

**B-side**: Over And Over
**Position in Record Retailer Top 40**: -
**Equivalent US Release**: Motown 1213 (15 Sep 1972)
**Position in Billboard Top 40 Pop**: -
**Position in Billboard Top 40 R & B**: -

---

Jean Terrell / Lynda Lawrence / Mary Wilson

---

The Supremes' union with Jimmy Webb had resulted in an album which although admired by many fans, was an unmitigated failure commercially [859]. Particularly hard-hit was Jean Terrell who had pushed the project forward and in doing so had gone out on a limb, leaving herself vulnerable to criticism from all involved. While relations with Motown were less than rosy in any case, the resultant loss of camaraderie with Mary Wilson caused a catastrophic rift within the ranks, culminating in Terrell resigning from The Supremes in late-1973.

The group's troubles though did not end there, Lynda Lawrence becoming pregnant and leaving original Supreme Mary Wilson unsure whether The Supremes could record for Motown again. While the group had weathered the storm of Diana Ross' departure and their subsequent struggle to re-establish themselves without Berry Gordy's backing, this latest turn of events appeared to mark the end of the road for Motown's most successful act. Wilson, though, was not about to accept defeat and began ringing around her industry contacts, scouting for replacement members in a desperate effort to keep the group alive.

Booked for some concert dates in January 1974, Wilson hastily recruited Cindy Birdsong back into the fold despite the fact that Lawrence had not yet departed officially, and on a tip-off from her old producer Lamont Dozier, put a call through to his girlfriend at the time, Scherrie Payne, a member of Invictus group The Glass House [831]. Successfully auditioning, Payne was hired as the group's third lead vocalist and with this new line-up The Supremes would at least be able to meet their touring commitments, suggestions that they were finished temporarily abated.

This new release was taken from the earlier Jimmy Webb album, an anomalous inclusion with which the writer-producer had nothing to do. In fact it had been included on the set as an afterthought to plug the *Pippin* musical [863] from which the number is sourced, Motown estimating that the remainder of the available material had few potential hits amongst it. If its inclusion was an annoyance to Webb, its subsequent release on 45 was an open affront, underlining Motown's attitude to the album and drawing a line under it for good.

Yet despite its likely political motives, and its benefit in publicising *Pippin*, "I Guess I'll Miss The Man" ultimately made its appearance on the top-side of [884] thanks to its quality. Written by Stephen Schwartz, the number is a reflective ballad capturing the moment when Pippin leaves his lover Catherine in his continuing personal quest, and as such is Catherine's song of lament. Acknowledging that Pippin in many ways fell short of the man of her dreams, Catherine nonetheless confesses love for him, a sentiment which echoes the real-life experiences of millions. Taken out of context of the musical, the lyric still stands, recorded here in an acoustic-orchestral mode accentuating its portrayal of personal grieving and intensifying Schwartz' elegantly expressive chord changes. It deserved better on release than it received.

Thus placed back on the market, The Supremes continued to appear in public as if nothing were amiss. Their public engagements continued uninterrupted and in February the new trio headed off to Mexico City, while back home their manager was scouting around alternative labels for a new deal. Motown simply had no desire to back The Supremes, denying the group any recording dates through the remainder of 1974, vaguely citing Payne's contract with Invictus as the stumbling block. Smokey Robinson at one stage agreed to record with them again [821] although this also came to nothing, and it would be a year and a half before they produced any new recordings [950], this once spectacularly successful act spluttering to a standstill as, all around them, the world simply moved on.

## TMG 885
## WILLIE HUTCH
**Tell Me Why Has Our Love Turned Cold**
(Hutch)
Produced by Willie Hutch
**Release Date: NOT RELEASED**
**B-side**: Mother's Theme (Mama)
**No Equivalent US Release**

Following up his soundtrack for *The Mack*, Willie Hutch recorded his first studio set for Motown, *Fully Exposed* released in Britain in January 1974. Made under the guidance of Norman Whitfield, the album included a cover of Hutch's co-composition "I'll Be There" [758] and credited Rose Royce on production duties, the act a recent creation of Whitfield's in the vein of The Undisputed Truth [776].[1]

Lining up a trailer-single, Tamla Motown pulled out "Tell Me Why Has Our Love Turned Cold" from the start of side 2, a funky number driven by Hutch's own wah-wah electric guitar. The release was accordingly assigned a catalogue number in the TMG sequence, but for reasons unclear was scrapped before any copies were manufactured. Thus, this gap in the sequence uniquely exists with no 45 to account for it.[2] Almost two years would pass before Tamla Motown afforded Hutch a new single [1008].

[1] The group were originally known as Total Concept Unlimited, and became stars on the producer's own label in the late 1970s. Both The Undisputed Truth and Willie Hutch were also eventually signed to Whitfield Records [1013].

[2] Of the four Tamla Motown singles which never made the shops, this and [786] were pulled prior to making the demo pressing stage, although the latter appeared on Rare Earth, with its TMG matrix number in the dead wax.

## TMG 886
## THE CONTOURS
**Baby Hit And Run** (3:01)
(Dean—Weatherspoon)
Produced by William "Mickey" Stevenson

**Release Date**: 8 Feb 1974
**B-side**: Can You Jerk Like Me [E68]
**Position in Record Retailer Top 40**: -
**No Equivalent US Release**

---

Dennis Edwards / Gerald Green / Council Gay / Sylvester Potts

---

Recorded circa 1965, this up-tempo dance track was attempted on three separate occasions, with vocals from sometime group members Joe Stubbs, Billy Gordon and, lastly, new recruit Dennis Edwards in 1967, as released here.[1] Scheduled as "Baby Don't Leave Me" the track was pencilled-in for *The Contours Sing It's So Hard Being A Loser*, just as Motown were losing interest in the group. The album never appeared, the track thereby being archived for seven years although why it was not pulled for a 1967 single anyway is a mystery, the recording several notches up in intensity from the group's contemporary "It's So Hard Being A Loser" [605]. Jokingly commencing with a couple of misleading bars pitched in the group's early style, the recording is robust in its dance groove, classic period Motown which may well have been a hit in its time. Pulled out of stasis and copyrighted in 1974, this Tamla Motown pressing debuted the number for the Northern Soul circuit where, coupled with the scarce [E68], it was greeted with elation. It has yet to appear on any format in the US.

[1] The Billy Gordon vocal has since been released on the CD, *A Cellarful Of Motown* (2002).

**TMG 887**
**THE TEMPTATIONS**
**I Need You** (3:05)
(Whitfield)
Produced by Norman Whitfield
**Release Date**: 22 Feb 1974
**B-side**: Hey Girl (I Like Your Style)
**Position in Record Retailer Top 40**: -
**Equivalent US Release**: Gordy 7136 (16 May 1974)
**Position in Billboard Top 40 Pop**: -
**Position in Billboard Top 40 R & B**: -

---

Otis Williams / Melvin Franklin / Richard Street / Dennis Edwards / Damon Harris

---

Knowing in his heart that it would be his last album with The Temptations, Norman Whitfield brought the group together for the *1990* sessions convinced that he could pull one more masterwork from them. Gathering as many of the remaining Funk Brothers as he could, Whitfield assembled a studio band with James Jamerson, Dennis Coffey, Eddie Willis, Jack Ashford, Earl Van Dyke and several other known session men (including future members of Rose Royce [885]), perhaps hoping that, behind the progressive surface of his contemporary compositions, something of the old magic would ignite in The Temptations.

One of the more curious products of this new spell of recording was "I

Need You", a 'psychedelic' number with a Latin twist which, in a rare lead for Richard Street, against a laid-back Brazilin groove, suggests the early 1960s style of Stan Getz and Astrud Gilberto. Out of their idiom, The Temptations and The Funk Brothers nevertheless pull an engaging performance together, crowned by a jazzy keyboard solo, probably from Van Dyke.[1] The lightness of the track gives Street's vocal some air on which to float, while the general Samba rhythms provide a sense of celebration which belies the unhappiness lurking behind the scenes.

Pressed and packaged, *1990* appeared around the turn of the year but Whitfield's decision to include a 13-minute-plus version of "Zoom" on side 2, leaving room for just one further title, did little to appease the group who had the added irritation of suspecting their fans were being short-changed. Once the album was wrapped up, the awkward situation was referred directly to Berry Gordy by Otis Williams, spokesman for the group, who announced that they would accept no further commissions from Whitfield. Part of the reason cited was their collective dislike of the material being produced but another was the fact that Whitfield, sensing his position of power, tended to treat them as work-horses from whom it was his job to squeeze endless takes.

Gordy, who knew Whitfield of old, understood Williams' point and, in having the matter out with the producer, made The Temptations' views clear. Whitfield countered that he had provided for them an immense amount of fame and wealth, which obviously came at the price of hard work, and insofar as the 1973 Grammys were concerned [839], few could argue with his analysis. However The Temptations were not in the mood for persuasion and so, in a somewhat acrimonious finale to their eight-year partnership, Whitfield and The Temptations parted company scarcely communicating with each other.

For the group's part, they were by this stage fancying writing their own material and seeking publishing rights to avoid future compositions falling into the hands of Jobete. At this juncture, relations with Gordy took a less cordial turn, the Motown boss observing another of his star acts trying to break loose of his direct control. Preparing for their future without Whitfield, The Temptations took the decision early in 1974 to move out to LA, Dennis Edwards leaving first, followed in stages by his colleagues. And so, one of the last outposts of the Detroit family finally succumbed to the drift West, leaving in their wake the memories of this last set of recordings in which several familiar old faces came together to make music again, as they had so many times before. There would be very few such occasions to come, as the slow demise of Hitsville reached its sad conclusion [902].

[1] His jazz background suggests as much. Other keyboardists on the sessions were Mark Davis and Victor Nyx.

**TMG 888**
**EDDIE KENDRICKS**
**Boogie Down** (3:30)
(Wilson—Caston—Poree)
Produced by Frank Wilson/Leonard Caston

**Release Date**: 8 Feb 1974
**B-side**: Eddie's Love
**Position in Record Retailer Top 40**: 39
**Equivalent US Release**: Tamla 54243 (6 Dec 1973)
**Position in Billboard Top 40 Pop**: 2
**Position in Billboard Top 40 R & B**: 1

Abbreviated from the jazz-blues phrase 'boogie-woogie', the word 'boogie' came into common usage in the early 1970s in connection with the mushrooming disco phenomenon [873], applied to virtually anything with a pronounced beat in the bass-end. Thus towards the latter part of the decade the word was thrown into dance hits indiscriminately, applied to several classics of the genre such as "Boogie Nights" (1977), "Blame It On The Boogie" (1978) and "Boogie Wonderland" (1979), Tamla Motown previewing the trend with the current track plus titles such as "The Boogie Man" [895] and "Boogie On Reggae Woman" [928].

The first example to surface, Eddie Kendricks' "Boogie Down" was a conscious effort to remake "Keep On Truckin'" [873], the track wilfully focussing on its bass rhythm to the expense of almost everything else, there being no meaningful harmonic progress nor purpose to the lyric. Originally running to seven minutes for the concurrent *Boogie Down* album, the single edit comes off as Kendricks' weakest to date, serving its function in a discotheque but failing to translate to the home stereo.


**TMG 889**
**JUNIOR WALKER & THE ALL STARS**
**Don't Blame The Children** (3:03)
(Bristol—McLeod—Ghant)
Produced by Johnny Bristol
**Release Date**: 1 Feb 1974
**B-side**: Soul Clappin'
**Position in Record Retailer Top 40**: -
**No Equivalent US Release**

---

Jr Walker / Willie Woods / Vic Thomas / Billy Nicks

---

Relying solely on old recordings to sustain Junior Walker's singles discography, Tamla Motown skipped over his 1973 set *Peace And Understanding Is Hard To Find* (which spawned three US singles), plucking from *Moody Junior* the present track, which they coupled with a contemporary recording on the flip. "Don't Blame The Children" shows evidence of having been constructed from external material, repeating the title of a 1967 Sammy Davis Jr track and borrowing a first line from Bob Dylan ("The Times They Are A-Changin'"). More significantly, though, the song's forceful G/B/C/A chord progression comes directly from Otis Redding's "Dock Of The Bay", a major posthumous hit in 1968 on the Volt label (released on Stax in the UK).

Built on Walker's standard sax-verse-sax-verse-sax skeleton, the track is an interesting defence of juvenile delinquency, its lyrical thrust that children become how they are as a result of society's forces, and therefore cannot be held responsible for their own anti-social behaviour. A point of view likely to provoke derision if stated explicitly today, it is nonetheless true on its level, the post-Freudian western world recognising that human beings are to a large extent a product of their environment, which for children means their upbringing. In quoting from the Bible ('They know not what they do'), it is unclear whether the text is intended as a lecture to the older generation or spoken from the perspective of a young people generally. If the latter, the word 'children' was likely to win few backers, most unruly teenagers defining themselves as young adults, the track therefore of no perceived relevance to them.

**TMG 890**
**DIANA ROSS & MARVIN GAYE**
**You Are Everything** (3:10)
(Bell—Creed)
Produced by Hal Davis
**Release Date**: 11 Mar 1974
**B-side**: Include Me In Your Life
**Position in Record Retailer Top 40**: 5
**No Equivalent US Release**

Through the 1960s, Motown's main competition in the field of popular soul came via New York's Atlantic stable, particularly in the years they were aligned with Stax-Volt. However, by the start of the 1970s, Atlantic had metamorphosed into a rock album-oriented concern (see [742]), Motown thereby without an immediate rival. On the scene came a new threat to Motown's pre-eminence. Philadelphia International was launched in 1971 under control of Kenny Gamble and Leon Huff, the latter a replacement for Thom Bell in Gamble's old group The Romeos. For his part, Bell stayed on the scene and established a career as a writer-producer, forging a productive partnership with Linda Creed under the Philadelphia International umbrella.

To a large extent, the label based its strategy on Motown's, building an in-house production line with staff writers and musicians, referred to collectively as MFSB (Mother Father Sister Brother), and an impressive roster of star acts. These included The O'Jays, Harold Melvin & The Blue Notes, Billy Paul, The Three Degrees, and ahead of the rest in commercial terms, The Stylistics.[1] Already signed to Avco Records, The Stylistics were not formally transferred to Philadelphia International, but were under the direction of Bell—Creed, who supplied the group with a succession of hit singles including "Stop, Look, Listen (To Your Heart)" [906], "Betcha By Golly, Wow", "I'm Stone In Love With You", "You Make Me Feel Brand New", and, as early as 1971, "You Are Everything", which was not a hit in the UK.

Picked up by Motown for Diana Ross and Marvin Gaye's duets album [879], Tamla Motown noted its relative obscurity in Britain and pulled it for release on single, following the successful strategy of tracks such as [826], [844] etc. Handled by Ross and Gaye, the recording is consequently held as definitive in the UK, one of Tamla Motown's great 1970s ballads which has been regularly extracted for compilation albums plus a couple of later re-issues [L007]; [L068] (see Chapter 6). The performance itself though is unremarkable, Ross handling the opening verse in her 'quiet' voice, Gaye attempting to inject some soul into proceedings in the second. Ultimately, this attempt to bond on record when the singers were performing separately founders on their underlying lack of empathy for one another, the polar opposite of the intangible vitality of Gaye's recordings with Tammi Terrell. Nevertheless, the UK market proved receptive, Tamla Motown embracing the competition by poaching the song for a top 10 hit.

[1] Philadelphia International also had an interest in several former Motown acts including The Spinners [871] and The Jacksons [1001].

## TMG 891
## THE MIRACLES
**Don't Let It End ('Til You Let It Begin)** (3:05)
(Perren—Yarian)
Produced by Freddie Perren/Fonce Mizell
**Release Date**: 18 Mar 1974[1]
**B-side**: I Wanna Be With You
**Position in Record Retailer Top 40**: -
**Equivalent US Release**: Tamla 54237 (Aug 1973)
**Position in Billboard Top 40 Pop**: -
**Position in Billboard Top 40 R & B**: 26

Billy Griffin / Bobby Rogers / Warren 'Pete' Moore / Ronnie White

The migration of Smokey Robinson to LA [883] had repercussions for his former group not only inasmuch as their main artistic force had been lost, but also in that he took with him another member in his wife Claudette, and soon-after Marv Tarplin, an informal collaborator with The Miracles whose guitar-work had formed the foundation of many of the group's hits. Seeing this coming, The Miracles had been scouting for a new lead singer since late-1971, Temptation Damon Harris recommending an old friend in Billy Griffin, who successfully auditioned in time for Robinson's farewell tour [811] where he was officially introduced to fans.

Significantly younger than the other Miracles, Griffin nonetheless slotted in and by the start of 1973 the group were recording again, although their album *Renaissance* did not appear in the UK until October. This single was their first shot at the British charts, supplied by Freddie Perren and his wife [856], and recorded in the soft-focus style of the Philadelphia school [890]. In particular recalling the sound of The Stylistics, the production makes the most of the group's close-harmony chorus sections, EQ-ed for maximum fluency against a sweetly orchestrated backdrop. Lead duties are handled in turn by the group, the arrangement accommodating a spoken section and some quaint woodwind lending to its air of relaxed tranquillity.

Although the single was not a hit, it nonetheless announced that The Miracles were still in business, and could stand on their own without Robinson's direct support. Motown rightly backed the group, a succession of albums ensuing over the following few years, which resulted in one major hit single [1015].

---

[1] Suggesting problems with pressing or distribution, Tamla Motown's only two releases in March, [890] and [891] both appeared on Mondays, rather than the standard Fridays.

**TMG 892**
**STEVIE WONDER**
**He's Misstra Know-It-All** (5:41)
(Wonder)
Produced by Stevie Wonder
**Release Date:** Apr 1974
**B-side:** You Can't Judge A Book By Its Cover
**Position in Record Retailer Top 40:** 10
**Equivalent US Release:** Tamla 54281 (22 Mar 1977)
**Position in Billboard Top 40 Pop:** -
**Position in Billboard Top 40 R & B:** -

Emerging from a period of personal upheaval in which he had almost lost his life [869], Stevie Wonder entered 1974 threatening to end his career while it was at its peak. Having resumed live performances in January, Wonder had arrived in the UK for some warmly received dates as part of a European excursion before returning to New York for a triumphant appearance at Madison Square Garden, where he was joined on-stage by Eddie Kendricks and Sly Stone. Earning hot reviews wherever he went, Wonder's pre-eminence was truly underlined in March when he was awarded a staggering five Grammys, one of which commemorated *Innervisions* as Album of the Year for 1973.

On the face of it, Stevie Wonder was on a personal high and yet the emotional fall-out of his accident had convinced him that such success carried no spiritual meaning, and he began convincing himself that the answer to life's mysteries lay outside the music industry. Divorcing Syreeta around now, Wonder rashly announced his intention to retire at a press conference on March 14, giving himself two years to raise money for charity through concert appearances, before a planned farewell gig pencilled in for late 1975. His avowed intent at this point was to move to Ghana to work with blind people, a laudable vocation which was quietly forgotten about over the ensuing 20 months as his life settled back to normality.

The extent to which he was serious is questionable, his words no doubt picked for maximum impact, at a time when he was being touted as an individual with higher callings than much of the human race. What is known is that, towards the tail-end of 1973, Wonder had found time in convalescence to begin preparing material for his next album, which would emerge before

---

year-end as *Fulfillingness' First Finale*, evidence that, at the very least, his plans at this point included more than mere benefit concerts.

Released in the wake of the Grammy Awards, "He's Misstra Know-It-All" is one of Stevie Wonder's best-loved tracks in the UK, although it was not a hit in America, overlooked in the release sequence until belatedly thrown onto the flip-side of "Sir Duke" in 1977. Its omission is surprising given Wonder's popularity at the time and the fact that the recording is one of his more melodic period pieces which would almost certainly have been a major hit if released in sequence, the UK and US singles otherwise appearing in direct parallel.

Yet not far beneath the song's easy-going façade, there lies something pointedly accusatory, the character which Wonder outlines an enigmatic composite of big business, street-wise conman and petty criminal whose exact target defies identification. There appears to be an element of resentment towards the music industry itself, glimpsed in lines such as, 'Any place he will play/His only concern is how much you'll pay' and 'Give a hand to the man... Check his sound out' and so on, and yet this reading fails to accommodate the song's overall slant against those who purport to know everything, while in reality interested only in procuring cash by means fair or foul. It is possible that this angle was prompted by Wonder's knowledge of the ruthless 'management' practices within the business, but the references to counterfeit money, if taken literally, imply that his real beef is with the fast-living, shady-dealing street dudes of New York, which the use of urban doggerel in the song's title tends to support.

Whatever its original message (if indeed it has one), "Misstra Know-It-All" works mainly for its musical strengths which show none of the rancour expressed in the words. Set to a sedate swing, the number catches Wonder working on conflicting fronts, mirroring his mindset in early 1974, on the one hand cursing the failures of society around him while also expressing a level of self-serenity which locates him somewhere outside of the struggle itself.

This engaging piece, running to the better part of six minutes, was paired by Tamla Motown with "You Can't Judge A Book By Its Cover", a 1969 recording which was in development at Hitsville on the day Benny Benjamin died [695]. Poignantly placed here, the song harkens back to a time five short years earlier when Detroit was the centre of Motown's operations and Wonder, still in school, was held at the heart of the family.

**TMG 893**
**DIANA ROSS**
**The Last Time I Saw Him** (2:45)
(Masser—Sawyer)
Produced by Michael Masser
**Release Date**: 8 Apr 1974
**B-side**: Everything Is Everything
**Position in Record Retailer Top 40**: 35
**Equivalent US Release**: Motown 1278 (6 Dec 1973)

**Position in Billboard Top 40 Pop**: 14
**Position in Billboard Top 40 R & B**: 15

The title track of Diana Ross' seventh solo album (coupled here with the counterpart from her second), "The Last Time I Saw Him" was edited down for release on 45, appearing in the US before Christmas. Little-noted, the album was an assemblage of ten generally unrelated tracks produced and arranged by numerous Motown personnel which did little to enhance Ross' standing.[1] (It would be her last studio set for over two years [1024].)

Made under Michael Masser's supervision, this trailer-single is the light-hearted tale of a girl waving her sweetheart goodbye as he boards a Greyhound bus with pockets full of her cash, promising he'll be back soon. Waiting in vain for his return, the female recounts her ceaseless pining for the man, her futile devotion provoking smiles from the knowing listener, particularly when mimicking his hollow pledge in the last chorus. Set in a mock-hillbilly mode with twanging banjos, this piece of wry fun clashed with Ross' established style, sailing over the heads of most of her fans.

In truth, material such as this was inappropriate for Motown's star attraction, wasting an opportunity to release something substantial at a time when her career was being undermined by intermittent and lifeless duets with Marvin Gaye. Notwithstanding, Motown elected to declare Diana Ross Month in May, marked by the inconsequential release of a first live album by the singer, recorded a year earlier at Caesar's Palace.

For reasons unclear, the single was put out on Monday 8th rather than Thursday 11th (the natural slot, Friday 12th, being a bank holiday in the UK).

[1] Despite which it was mixed in quadraphonic for a rare Japanese pressing.


**TMG 894**
**JUNIOR WALKER & THE ALL STARS**
**Gotta Hold On To This Feeling** (3:15)
(Bristol—Hinton—Sawyer)
Produced by Johnny Bristol
Recording completed: 28 Aug 1969
**Release Date**: 19 Apr 1974
**B-side**: I Ain't Going Nowhere
**Position in Record Retailer Top 40**: -
**Equivalent US Release**: Soul 35070 (29 Jan 1970)
**Position in Billboard Top 40 Pop**: 21
**Position in Billboard Top 40 R & B**: 2

---

Jr Walker / Willie Woods / Vic Thomas / Billy Nicks

---

Closing Junior Walker & The All Stars' Tamla Motown singles discography in ineffective style, this April release resurrected an old recording put out as a US single as long ago as 1970, already used in the UK as [824b]. Why Tamla Motown were pursuing such a policy is not clear, an otherwise unknown track diverted here to the B-side. Falsely suggesting that Walker had gone stale, the release continued the perplexing bypassing of *Peace And Understanding Is Hard To Find*, still available for pickings had Tamla Motown been so inclined.

Conforming to Walker's standard formula, the number is recorded on the mid-tempo sax-verse-sax-verse-sax structure also seen in the recent "Don't Blame The Children" [889], and indicative of its vintage. (The song was the title track to a 1969 album quickly re-issued as *What Does It Take To Win Your Love*—see [712].) That much of this material is largely tuneless contributed to its failure to sell, such sweetly recorded numbers let down by the fact that Walker, despite his best efforts, was not equipped to pull melodic detail from lines pitched high against a repeating backing riff. One can hear him come alive during the saxophone instrumentals, his true musical calling proving that he was primarily a *musician*, something the Motown conveyor belt never learned to accommodate.

As it transpired, the single appeared just as its producer Johnny Bristol's contract was up. Wanting to record his own material but unable to reach agreement, Bristol left Motown for a contract at MGM which spawned a run of R & B hits which, true to form, could have been Motown's had they invested in the talent already at their disposal. (One of his compositions, "Love Me For A Reason" was picked up by Motown rivals The Osmonds for a UK number 1 in August.)

**TMG 895**
**THE JACKSON 5**
**The Boogie Man** (2:58)
(Richards)
Produced by Deke Richards
**Release Date**: 26 Apr 1974
**B-side**: Don't Let The Sun Catch You Crying
**Position in Record Retailer Top 40**: -
**No Equivalent US Release**

---

Jackie Jackson / Tito Jackson / Jermaine Jackson / Marlon Jackson / Michael Jackson

---

Playing on the coincidence of the children's phantom 'Bogie Man' with the burgeoning language of disco [888], this Jackson 5 single penned by Deke Richards is caught between the gag of its central word play, and its adult theme in which 'playing around in the dark' is a metaphor for sleeping about. Unable to decide which pole to gravitate towards, Richards ended up opting for ironic cartoon-cinematic humour, introducing the song with a Warner Brothers-style musical device depicting the arrival of the spectre, whose ghoulish pals emerge from hiding in what stands for the instrumental break (at 1:50). Possibly inspired by contemporary television animations such as *Scooby Doo* and *The Mad, Mad, Mad Monsters* (the latter title of 1972 made by ABC, the company behind The Jackson 5's animated series [738]) the track is an interesting precursor to Michael Jackson's later

"Thriller" which took much the same theme and sense of humour to far more extravagant (and lucrative) lengths.

An odd choice, the single was released in the UK only, as the planned US edition was pulled. It appeared shortly after the low-key launch of group-member Jackie as a solo recording artist, his eponymous album generating no spin-off singles and falling into obscurity.

**TMG 896**
**R. DEAN TAYLOR**
**There's A Ghost In My House** (2:34)
(Holland—Dozier—Holland—Taylor)
Produced by Brian Holland/Lamont Dozier
Recording completed: 26 Oct 1966
**Release Date**: 3 May 1974
**B-side**: Let's Go Somewhere
**Position in Record Retailer Top 40**: 3
**Equivalent US Release**: VIP 25042 (30 Mar 1967)
**Position in Billboard Top 40 Pop**: -
**Position in Billboard Top 40 R & B**: -

The first tangible effect of the emergence of the Wigan Casino on Tamla Motown's release schedules [853], "There's A Ghost In My House" was 'discovered' by DJ Russ Winstanley sitting on side 1 of a recent budget album.[1] Recognising its potential, the Casino 'broke' the track in the UK, leading to increased sales for Taylor's album. Tamla Motown's marketing people quickly picked up on this by opting for a 7-inch edition which promptly rose to an impressive number 3. (The original US single of 1967 had bombed, the track having since appeared nowhere else.) Smartly judging their audience, the label paired it up with the similarly obscure "Let's Go Somewhere", a non-album title which had been Taylor's debut A-side for VIP in 1965.

Recorded soon thereafter, "There's A Ghost In My House" is co-credited to his tutors HDH, and in its prominent use of electric guitar, was advanced for its day. Probably this was a result of Taylor devising the descending riff alone, in which case HDH's input would have consisted of knocking the bare bones of the composition into shape. The team's presence is revealed in phrases such as 'shadows from the past', a recurrent lyric theme which blurs the distinction between reality and dream [589], and 'a love you took from me' which was later woven into the chorus of "Reflections" [616]. Its general theme too, of an empty house haunted by the 'gloom' of a lost love predicts "7-Rooms Of Gloom" [612], in this light a notable period-piece lending credibility to Taylor's claim to have co-written numerous classic hits generally considered the exclusive work of HDH (see [612n]).

In the three years since "Indiana Wants Me" [763] was released, Taylor had been switched to the Rare Earth label (see [786]), no UK hits resulting and leaving Taylor on the point of leaving Motown. Delighted Wigan Casino revellers freshly discovering this vintage recording managed to persuade him out of live retirement to perform at the venue which, coupled with this belated chart success, offered him the opportunity to reinvigorate his career (but not at Motown: see [909]).

[1] The LP had two titles on the front, *Gotta See Jane / Indiana Wants Me*. It was pressed in September 1973 on EMI's mid-priced Sounds Superb label, one of three such imprints used to re-issue Tamla Motown recordings in the 1970s (Starline and Music For Pleasure the other two). The discography in Davis (1988) lists all of these.


## TMG 897
## THE UNDISPUTED TRUTH
**Help Yourself** (3:13)
(Whitfield)
Produced by Norman Whitfield
**Release Date**: 17 May 1974
**B-side**: What It Is
**Position in Record Retailer Top 40**: -
**Equivalent US Release**: Gordy 7134 (14 Feb 1974)
**Position in Billboard Top 40 Pop**: -
**Position in Billboard Top 40 R & B**: 19

---
Joe Harris / Billie Calvin / Brenda Evans
---

Norman Whitfield's Undisputed Truth had recorded some four albums by mid 1974, *Down To Earth* the latest[1], yet to be released in the UK. Its opening track, "Help Yourself" was an out-and-out dance number, consisting of a tightly locked bass riff above which the group vocals kick and wrestle. Urgent with internal tension, the production is an underrated work, holding its intensity by effective deployment of its sparse instrumentation which includes exquisitely distorted electric guitar and a gripping clapping track. High on funk, the number was released for the contemporary dance market, but failed to cross over to the pop world. Unfortunately the keyboard sound, radical in its day, has dated badly.

[1] This set was recorded (or at least polished off) at Motown's Studio B and is probably the last major work carried out there. (The studio was in use to some extent until September.)


## TMG 898
## SMOKEY ROBINSON
**A Silent Partner In A Three Way Love Affair** (3:45)
(Robinson—Jones)
Produced by William "Smokey" Robinson/Willie Hutch
**Release Date**: 10 May 1974
**B-side**: Baby Come Close
**Position in Record Retailer Top 40**: -
**Equivalent US Release**: Tamla 54239 (Nov 1973)

**Position in Billboard Top 40 Pop**: -
**Position in Billboard Top 40 R & B**: -

Returning the solo Smokey Robinson to the single format, this new release was pulled from the same debut album as "Just My Soul Responding" [883] and sits in stark contrast to its predecessor in both style and purpose. Archetypal Robinson, the track hangs on its warm major 7th chord sequence, recounting the age-old dilemma of being in love with the woman of a best friend. In this scenario, Robinson is the 'silent' party, confessing his predicament in song while the two lovers remain oblivious to his amorous state.

Written with his half-sister Rose Ella Jones (who would become a frequent collaborator [1019]), the tale almost certainly comes from a hypothetical viewpoint, Robinson's private life, while by no means stable at this moment in time, negating suggestions that the track was self-referential. During 1974 Robinson had met and begun an affair with an 18-year-old admirer and would-be fan-club organiser named Meta, eventually falling in love with her and separating from his wife of 15 years (although the two were reconciled in 1975).

This single paired the track with "Baby Come Close", a Robinson—Tarplin number which proved the more popular in America, going 27 pop and 7 R & B at the start of the year. The respective performances of the two titles raise the question of why Tamla Motown programmed the single this way around, "Silent Partner" failing on both sides of the Atlantic.

**TMG 899**
**THE CONTOURS**
**Do You Love Me** (2:52) **[E10]**
(Gordy)
Produced by Berry Gordy Jr.
Recording completed: 3 Jun 1962
**Release Date**: 24 May 1974
**B-side**: Determination [564]
**Position in Record Retailer Top 40**: -
**Equivalent US Release**: Gordy 7005 (29 Jun 1962)
**Position in Billboard Top 40 Pop**: 3
**Position in Billboard Top 40 R & B**: 1

---

Billy Gordon / Billy Hoggs / Joe Billingslea / Sylvester Potts / Hubert Johnson /
Huey Davis

---

The classic "Do You Love Me" was written by Berry Gordy in the very early days, borrowing its basic structure from tracks such as "Twist And Shout", itself a variation on the ubiquitous "La Bamba". (The principal difference lies in the extension of the first F chord, shifting the changes back against the rhythm.) Like another of his hits, "Money" [E02], the track is semi-autobiographical, Gordy's inability to dance hampering his chances with women and prompting the lyric in which the discovery of inventive moves such as the Twist, the Mashed Potato, the Jerk, the Hully-gully and so on lead to an effusion of confident propositions.

During sessions for the track Berry Gordy had to deal with an unimpressed studio band, James Jamerson in particular goading his boss with a calculated over-elaboration highlighting the crude simplicity of the composition. Nevertheless, Benny Benjamin's drumming on the take is remarkably 'up' for Motown, which coupled with gimmicks including a novel premature fade meant whatever became of the track on release it certainly wouldn't slip by unnoticed, its raw excitement a match for anything on the market in 1962.

Originally considering The Temptations for the song, Gordy taped his own guide vocal which reminded him of Billy Gordon, lead singer of The Contours, who were duly brought in to complete the track. Joe Hunter regarded the group as a comedy turn and told them outright it would not be a hit, and yet Gordon's spoken introduction and blistering vocals elevated "Do You Love Me", the single released a few weeks after recording on the newly inaugurated Gordy label.

A major early success in America, the UK edition [E10] was overlooked, allowing Brian Poole And The Tremeloes to cash in and take it to number 1 in 1963, the first product of the Detroit production line to achieve the feat. In the intervening decade, however, The Contours had arrived on the Northern Soul scene [886] and, courtesy of recent interest, Tamla Motown finally made "Do You Love Me" available again, coupling the track with [564] and bringing both rarities back to 7-inch after several years of obscurity. (Its appearance here coincided with the group's first UK album in over a decade, *Baby Hit And Run* appearing on the budget Music For Pleasure label: See also [896n].) "Do You Love Me" is today regarded as a minor classic in Motown's canon, and has since been twice re-released on the label ([L077] and a special re-issue thereof).

**TMG 900**
**MICHAEL JACKSON**
**Music And Me** (2:36)
(Larson—Marcellino)
Produced by Mel Larson/Jerry Marcellino
**Release Date**: May 1974
**B-side**: Johnny Raven
**Position in Record Retailer Top 40**: -
**No Equivalent US Release**

Over a year old, Michael Jackson's third album *Music And Me* was his first not to make the top 40 in America or Britain. Lacking any new recordings from the maturing star, Tamla Motown released the title track as a single, Jackson's only 45 during 1974. A gentle love song to music itself, the opening lines, 'We've been together for such a long time/Don't care if all our songs rhyme' hints that it may have been conceived as a 'message' to Michael's brothers. Recorded in a softly acoustic mode, for which Jackson did the necessary guitar-clutching duties on the cover shoot, this tranquil number is marred by a poor drop-in on the vocal track at 2:04 which gives the impression that Jackson's pitching was faulty.

## TMG 901
## EDDIE KENDRICKS
**Son Of Sagittarius** (3:12)
(Wilson—Caston—Poree)
Produced by Frank Wilson/Leonard Caston
**Release Date**: 7 Jun 1974
**B-side**: Can't Help What I Am
**Position in Record Retailer Top 40**: -
**Equivalent US Release**: Tamla 54247 (16 Apr 1974)
**Position in Billboard Top 40 Pop**: 28
**Position in Billboard Top 40 R & B**: 5

Whenever the subject of astrology surfaces in Motown recordings, it does so with a sense of absurdity, precedents including The Supremes' "No Matter What Sign You Are" [704] and Martha Reeves' album *Black Magic* [843]. Aimed again at the disco set, Eddie Kendricks' new single follows suit, threatening to be a biographical piece from a singer born on December 17 but turning instead into a vaguely suggestive overture to women generally, mentioning in passing that he'll settle for Aries or Leo if needs be.

The track's opening line shows that its writers have done their homework, Sagittarius the ninth sign of the Zodiac, from the fire element. Those born under the sign are considered to be dominated by the hips and thighs, providing a vaguely appropriate context for the track's underlying eroticism.

## TMG 902
## THE COMMODORES
**Machine Gun** (2:45)
(Williams)
Produced by James Carmichael/The Commodores
**Release Date**: 21 Jun 1974
**B-side**: There's A Song In My Heart
**Position in Record Retailer Top 40**: 20
**Equivalent US Release**: Motown 1307 (23 Apr 1974)
**Position in Billboard Top 40 Pop**: 22
**Position in Billboard Top 40 R & B**: 7

Lionel Richie / Thomas McClary / Ronald LaPread / William King /
Walter Orange / Milan Williams

The last recordings made at Hitsville before the building was closed have never been precisely pinned down, although they are thought to date from early 1974. One of the candidates would be the sessions resulting in The Commodores' *Machine Gun* album, known to have been cut in Detroit and most likely at Studio A although, given that the group took care of its own instrumentation, no late incarnation of The Funk Brothers would have been required. (The Temptations' *1990* [887] may have been the last occasion on which anything resembling the old studio-band convened.)

The Commodores had arrived at Motown in 1971 after a brief spell with Atlantic, a solitary failed single seeping out before they fell out of favour. Acting on a tip-off from the group's stand-in manager Benny Ashburn, Motown's Creative Vice-President Suzanne de Passe travelled New York to watch them play the Turntable Club and, deciding they would make a useful addition to the company's roster, almost immediately had them booked as support act for The Jackson 5, aiming to bring them some national exposure.

Touring on the live circuit kept the group busy into 1972 when their recording career began in earnest, after they were teamed with James Carmichael, an arranger with Jackson 5 connections [799] who happened to have a precise empathy for the group's sound. Signed to Mo-West, The Commodores embarked on a course which within a few years would make them Motown's hottest property, the starting-point of which was "The Zoo (The Human Zoo)" issued in March 1972 but unreleased in the UK until November 1974 [924].

The group's big breakthrough came in the spring of 1974 when they laid down the present track, a driving instrumental devised by keyboard man Milan Williams on clavinet. Throwing what sounds like a barking dog into the mix, James Carmichael honed the basic number into a pulsating piece of 1970s electro-funk which the group dubbed "The Ram" and offered up as their fourth US single. Deeply impressed, de Passe took a copy to Berry Gordy, holidaying on the Caribbean island of St. Maarten, who warmed to the track despite its lack of vocals and, perceiving the staccato arrangement's resemblance to rapid gunfire, re-christened it for them. (These events make for an interesting sequel to the story behind "Shotgun" [509], almost a decade earlier.)

On release, "Machine Gun" suitably arrived with a bang, going top 10 R & B which led to an inaugural UK release which grazed the top 20. This now famous piece marked the arrival of the group from Alabama in its modest way, opening the door to a succession of UK singles which initially failed to follow suit, while in America they would become one of the biggest acts of the late-1970s.

**TMG 903**
**GLADYS KNIGHT & THE PIPS**
**Didn't You Know (You'd Have To Cry Sometime)** (3:15)
**Re-issue of [728]**
**Release Date**: 14 Jun 1974
**New B-side**: Cloud Nine
**Position in Record Retailer Top 40**: -

---

Gladys Knight / Merald 'Bubba' Knight / Edward Patten / William Guest

---

Continuing to mine Gladys Knight & The Pips' back-catalogue mercilessly [855], Tamla Motown prepared an *Anthology* album for release in March, a plushly packaged double set reviewing the group's Motown career.[1] Allied to the release was this trailer-single, a re-run of the comparatively recent [728], coupled with the group's version of the ever-popular "Cloud Nine" [707] (see also [810b]), which had originally surfaced alongside [728] on *Nitty Gritty* (1969). The single failed to make the charts in a lean year for the group in the UK. (They scored two US top-tenners in 1974 for Buddah.)

[1] The album marked the start of a series of *Anthology* albums for the company's major acts, most of which also spawned promotional EPs. See Appendix 1 for details.

**TMG 904**
**THE JACKSON 5**
**Dancing Machine** (2:29)
(Davis—Fletcher—Parks)
Produced by Hal Davis
**Release Date**: 7 Jun 1974
**B-side**: It's Too Late To Change The Time
**Position in Record Retailer Top 40**: -
**Equivalent US Release**: Motown 1286 (19 Feb 1974)
**Position in Billboard Top 40 Pop**: 2
**Position in Billboard Top 40 R & B**: 1

Jackie Jackson / Tito Jackson / Jermaine Jackson / Marlon Jackson / Michael Jackson

The tale of a coin-operated pseudo-female disco appliance, "Dancing Machine", title included, is another notable step in Motown's drive to expand into the contemporary club style. Pushing the boundary further than previous efforts such as "Keep On Truckin'" [873], "Get It Together" [878], "Boogie Down" [888] and "Machine Gun" [902], the recording relies mainly on closely time-regulated rhythms, an energetic and relentless bass and percussion kicking against funky electric guitar and brass riffs, highly charged but mixed low. Underpinned by a deeply resonating bass sax, the track is adventurously produced, including in its instrumental passage a recording of a discotheque bubble-making device.

With Michael Jackson's fast-deepening vocals in evidence, the rapid-fire lyric finds him on form, sufficiently excited that in performing the track on *Soul Train* in early 1974 he devised a custom dance move dubbed the Robot. Causing a minor sensation, the dance would become a Jackson trademark in the years which followed, giving "Dancing Machine" an underplayed role in his career development both in terms of its sound and its visual hook.

This UK edition followed the American success, timed to coincide with The Jackson 5's British tour in June. However, still provoking pandemonium amongst female fans, the group's arrival in the UK was hushed-up to avoid any potential repeat of the catastrophe at a David Cassidy concert in London during May where several hundred were injured and one teenaged girl killed in a stampede. Due to arrive at Heathrow on June 9, The Jackson 5's flight details were revealed to the press by their father Joe, causing the group's security staff to baulk and cancel the tour completely, thereby starving "Dancing Machine" of publicity, a paradoxical consequence of the group's popularity.[1]

**TMG 905**
**EDWIN STARR**
**Stop Her On Sight (SOS)** (2:08)
(Hatcher—Hamilton—Morris)
Producer uncredited[1]
**Release Date**: Jun 1974
**B-side**: Headline News
**Position in Record Retailer Top 40**: -
**No Equivalent US Release**
*Originally released as Ric Tic RT-109 (Feb 1966)*

Of all the Ric Tic recordings procured in the 1960s, the one most frequently mistaken for a Motown original is the present track, first put out in the UK on Polydor in 1966 when it scraped into the top 40. The song was originally written as "Sending Out Soul", but in perceiving its clash with the then recent "Agent Double O Soul" [790], Starr and Richard Morris changed the lyric.[2] The theme thereby arrived at suggested to Starr the notion of searching and, idly watching the TV show *20,000 Leagues Under The Sea*, he hit upon the Morse code distress signal which, translated to piano, makes for the song's introduction. (Since "Stop Her On Sight" was released in America in January 1966, it pre-dates the similar device in "You Keep Me Hangin' On" [585] and may even have suggested it to HDH.)

Sounding every bit like a product of Hitsville, the popular misconception stems from two factors, the first being the clandestine presence of The Funk Brothers on the session (see also [790]), who turn out a solidly rocking piece of R & B, with Dennis Coffey pitching in on electric guitar. The second is Motown's compliance in passing the hit off as their own, including it on innumerable compilation albums without further comment, for example on *Motown Chartbusters Volume 3*, which topped the UK album chart in early 1970 (see [599n]). By then, Polydor had already re-issued it whereupon it rose to number 11, making this Tamla Motown edition largely unnecessary, if pleasing for the label's fans.

[1] The Ric Tic pressing gives the producers as Al Kent/Richard Morris.

[2] A third permutation exists on a Ric Tic promo entitled "Scott's On Swingers", made for local DJ Scott Regan.

**TMG 906**
**DIANA ROSS & MARVIN GAYE**
**Stop, Look, Listen (To Your Heart)** (2:44)
(Bell—Creed)
Produced by Hal Davis

**Release Date**: 21 Jun 1974
**B-side**: Love Twins
**Position in Record Retailer Top 40**: 25
**No Equivalent US Release**

Fortunately for Tamla Motown, the Gaye—Ross collaborations which spawned the hit "You Are Everything" [890] also included a second Bell—Creed number, making it an automatic choice for the follow-up. "Stop Look And Listen To Your Heart" had been a minor hit for The Stylistics in 1971, released on Avco Embassy. This remake, running slightly faster than the original, adds little to the arrangement bar a laboured electric guitar solo which merely re-states the main melodic hook. Lacking the polish of Russell Thompkins' lead vocal, Ross and Gaye dispatch the track routinely, the latter's closing falsetto straining to match his partner's high Eb.

**TMG 907**
**THE REFLECTIONS**
**(Just Like) Romeo And Juliet** (2:10)
(Hamilton—Gorman)
Produced by Rob Reece
**Release Date**: 28 Jun 1974
**B-side**: Can't You Tell By The Look In My Eyes
**Position in Record Retailer Top 40**: -
**No Equivalent US Release**
*Originally released as Golden World GW9 (Mar 1964)*

Tony Micale / John Dean / Phil Castrodale / Dan Bennie / Ray Steinber

Following "Stop Her On Sight" [905] in June 1974, this latest resurrected track originated on a Golden World 45 ten years earlier, one of the first products of Ed Wingate's inaugural label. The UK edition had appeared alongside Motown's own exports on the Stateside label, this the only Golden World single to be picked up for re-release on Tamla Motown, who retained its original B-side.

Written by future Original Freddie Gorman and Bob Hamilton, with Gorman's brother Sonny Sanders arranging it for disc, the number was recorded at United Sound and shipped to RCA in Chicago for Tony Micale's lead vocals. Emerging as a hand-clapping plodder, the track had the distinction of going top 10 pop, forcing Berry Gordy to sit up and take notice of this local rival.

Continuing to record for Wingate's labels, The Reflections put out a further eight 45s for Golden World before Berry Gordy eventually bought the label and ended their tenure. The group moved to ABC but never recovered their form, this belated UK single, far too old-fashioned for mass appeal by the mid 1970s, noted purely by connoisseurs.

**TMG 908**
**STEVIE WONDER**
**Don't You Worry 'Bout A Thing** (3:40)
(Wonder)
Produced by Stevie Wonder
**Release Date**: 5 Jul 1974
**B-side**: Do Yourself A Favour
**Position in Record Retailer Top 40**: -
**Equivalent US Release**: Tamla 54245 (14 Mar 1974)
**Position in Billboard Top 40 Pop**: 16
**Position in Billboard Top 40 R & B**: 2

A third lift from *Innervisions* [881]; [892], "Don't You Worry 'Bout A Thing" draws on the South American musical tradition, utilising as its foundation a variation on the mambo (see also [887]). Partly this stems from chance, long-time bongo player Wonder well-versed in the instrument's traditional scope through the tutelage of several articulate Funk Brothers such as Eddie Brown, and partly the track's flavour comes from Wonder's New York sojourn [827] in which he assimilated the sounds of his immediate environment, inevitably working them into his contemporary material (notably [881]).[1]

Recruiting Yusuf Roahman and Sheila Wilkinson to handle the exotic percussion, Wonder presents the track as a Spanish bar-room skit, introducing it with mock chit-chat about having travelled the world ('I speak very, very, erm... fluent Spanish'). Shakers and bongos aside, the track has little specifically relating it to Latin music, utilising the American vernacular in its title and lines such as 'They say your style of life's a drag', dropping in a likely nod to Whitfield and Strong on the way ('fooled by smiling faces' [789]), making its flamboyant dressing a style-game probably devised post-composition.

Pleasingly up-beat, the track's selection was a mild gamble which came to nothing, UK fans who already owned the album by now failing to lift it into the charts.

[1] The Latin styles derive their rhythmic basis from African music, brought to South America via the slave trade. Styles from Cuba and Puerto Rico subsequently found their way to New York where they were adopted by local jazz bands.

**TMG 909**
**R. DEAN TAYLOR**
**Don't Fool Around** (2:31)
(Taylor—Holland)
Produced by Brian Holland/Lamont Dozier
Recording completed: 10 Jan 1964
**Release Date**: 28 Jun 1974
**B-side**: Poor Girl
**Position in Record Retailer Top 40**: -

**Equivalent US Release:** VIP 25042 (30 Mar 1967)
**Position in Billboard Top 40 Pop**: 16
**Position in Billboard Top 40 R & B**: 2

Keen to follow up "There's A Ghost In My House" [896], Tamla Motown unearthed an obscure R. Dean Taylor track for release, "Don't Fool Around" recorded on 10 January 1964 and, given its vintage, probably the first thing recorded by Taylor at Motown, or at least the earliest which has been made commercially available. Subsequently used as the B-side to "Gotta See Jane" [656], the song was a dubious selection here which didn't chart, its primitive rhythm section consisting mainly of a crotchet-battering tom tom and tambourine, set against a strummed electric guitar (played as if it were an acoustic). The general style and production of "Don't Fool Around" shows evidence that it was made prior to the revolutionary British Invasion of 1964, its shifting major barre chords conforming approximately to a standard blues run.

Now hitting on Polydor, Taylor was enjoying a high profile in the mid 1970s, boosting his popularity on the UK Northern Soul scene, at whom this single is directed. Taylor had created his own label in 1973, Jane Records—a short-lived venture which served to fill the lull between the closure of the Rare Earth label (see Appendix 3) and the signing of his Polydor contract—and, on July 20, Taylor was persuaded out of self-imposed retirement to play the Wigan Casino [853]. He surprised many including the club's owner Gerry Marshal by the fact that he was white—evidence of how poorly Taylor had been promoted even to hardcore fans.[1]

[1] Personal recollections of several Motown stars' appearances at the Casino can be found in the pages of Winstanley & Nowell.

**TMG 910**
**GLORIA JONES**
**Tin Can People** (2:30)
(Gardner—Jones)
Produced by Tom Buckley
**Release Date**: 26 Jul 1974
**B-side**: So Tired (Of The Way You're Treating Our Love Baby)
**Position in Record Retailer Top 40**: -
**No Equivalent US Release**

A former member of gospel group The Cojics, along with Frank Wilson and Blinky Williams, Gloria Jones had embarked on her recording career in the mid 1960s, one famous solo cut arriving in the form of "Tainted Love", released on the Champion label in 1965. Subsequently meeting up with Pam Sawyer, Jones came to Motown as half of a constructive Jobete writing partnership (see [765]; [920]) before recording in her own right, *Share My Love* appearing in 1973 as a largely self-composed set, from where this single is plucked.

"Tin Can People" is a tightly drilling funk number, featuring Willie Weeks on bass guitar, spread across just two-and-a-half minutes. The central metaphor, probably race-related, concerns the plight of those 'kicked around' by society, Jones contributing a double-tracked vocal contorted in form by her own screaming passion. A progressive choice of single by Tamla Motown, the track was pitched at the disco market, but was not picked up by the mainstream.

It did however catch the ear of Northern Soul followers, Jones popular at the Casino where one regular named Marc Almond came across "Tainted Love", later recording it himself for a number 1 hit. Electing to move permanently to the UK where Jones knew she would be in demand, she convened with Marc Bolan, becoming his keyboard player and girlfriend. By cruel fate, Jones happened to be driving Bolan through London in his Austin Mini when, on 16 September 1977, she span out of control and struck a tree. Bolan was killed in the accident.

## TMG 911
## JIMMY RUFFIN
**What Becomes Of The Brokenhearted** (2:57)
**Re-issue of [577]**
**Release Date**: 12 Jul 1974
**New B-side**: Don't You Miss Me A Little Bit Baby [617]
**Position in Record Retailer Top 40**: 4

Having parted company with Motown in 1971 [784], Jimmy Ruffin's career had been largely dormant until 1974 when, like R. Dean Taylor [909], he was signed to Polydor. Catching wind of a potential resurgence of interest, Tamla Motown dusted off Ruffin's classic "What Becomes Of The Brokenhearted", pairing it up with [617] for a 'double-header' which deservedly drew attention and went back into the UK top 10. (Its number 4 peak had been bettered only once by the label in more than two years [896].)

Given the single's success, Tamla Motown quickly prepared a follow-up [922], Motown in America also taking note and re-issuing "What Becomes Of The Brokenhearted" in January 1975 (Motown 1329). For the moment, this almost forgotten singer was back at the top of Tamla Motown's priorities, his back-catalogue ready to be pitched at his UK fan-base again, Ruffin well settled in Britain with a loyal local following.

## TMG 912
## SYREETA
**Spinnin' And Spinnin'** (3:32)
(Wonder—Wright)
Produced by Stevie Wonder
**Release Date**: 23 Aug 1974
**B-side**: Black Maybe
**Position in Record Retailer Top 40**: -
**No Equivalent US Release**

The artist formerly known as Rita Wright re-appeared on the scene in 1974 under her new name, after a spell recording for Mo-West which spawned the album *Syreeta* plus a UK trailer-single (see Appendix 3). Curiously, Syreeta's re-emergence owes a significant debt to her estranged husband Stevie Wonder who produced her comeback album which, as a continuation of their musical partnership [744], is less remarkable than the fact that they continued to collaborate for subsequent LPs, their short-lived marriage apparently not casting shadows over their ongoing friendship. *Stevie Wonder Presents Syreeta* underlines their unity in the studio, Wonder producing the set at the Record Plant in LA, and either writing or co-writing with Syreeta its entire content, in addition to which he contributes backing vocals, drums and synthesisers.

The lyrical content of much of the material lent itself to interpretation, several fans finding coded references to Wonder and Syreeta's break-up therein, something both have since glossed over, their mutual affection genuine.[1] "Spinnin' And Spinnin'" is one such title, a 3/4 waltz through a romantic let-down in which Syreeta dreams of having fun and enjoying love, while admitting that just a couple of compliments would be an improvement on her present state. (The final line, 'Wonder how much I'll see' can't help coming over as a subtle dig at her former husband, his name tagged on as if written on the envelope.)

Something of a fantasy piece, in which Syreeta pictures herself endlessly twirling through the air, the lyric suggested show music to Wonder who set it in an elegant 'Broadway' style, Paul Riser's romantic string arrangement swirling around the background like a stage design. Given the ubiquity of the style, it seems doubtful the track has a specific model although melodic and rhythmic resonances with "My Favourite Things" from *The Sound Of Music* are apparent.[2] This graceful thing might have been a hit but for the fact that Syreeta had spent too long in obscurity to have any sort of following. However the album would in due course offer a top 20 single in early 1975 [933], prompting Tamla Motown to have another go with "Spinnin' And Spinnin'" which was re-released with catalogue number unchanged on 27 March 1975.

[1] See for example their comments in Davis 2006a, p99-100. Some of the material included on Syreeta's two albums in fact originated from Wonder's abandoned Supremes project of 1973 [847]. (Although, see the possible subtext in [926].)

[2] Outside of this context, Wonder's choice of chords and melody suggest most closely Burt Bacharach, elements from the composer's back-catalogue detectable in Wonder's piece, for example the second line of the verse ('A man will shower me with expensive gifts') which echoes a melody line from "Do You Know The Way To San Jose?" ('LA is a great big freeway').


**TMG 913**
**YVONNE FAIR**
**Funky Music Sho' Nuff Turns Me On** (2:59)
(Whitfield—Strong)
Produced by Norman Whitfield

**Release Date**: 16 Aug 1974
**B-side**: Let Your Hair Down
**Position in Record Retailer Top 40**: -
**Equivalent US Release**: Motown 1306 (28 May 1974)
**Position in Billboard Top 40 Pop**: -
**Position in Billboard Top 40 R & B**: 32

Arriving at Motown as early as 1970 through a cordial relationship with Chuck Jackson (the two having toured together), Virginia vocalist Yvonne Fair was initially signed to the Soul label, before four years of stagnation punctuated only by an appearance in *Lady Sings The Blues*. In 1974 her career was revived with this gut-wrenching recording of Whitfield—Strong's "Funky Music" (see also [810]; [866b]), living up to its title more emphatically than previous versions. This Paul Riser-arranged recording starts out as a whisper before Fair arrives full throttle at 0:40, vocals seething and rasping line-on-line. Continually escalating in intensity the performance ends up lashing at the lyrics in an apoplectic rage, the verbal equivalent of thrash guitar. Too brutal for all but the most dedicated R & B fans, this miniature eruption of fire drew long-awaited attention from Motown, Fair following-up with an album and hit single in 1975 [1013].

**TMG 914**
**THE MIRACLES**
**Do It Baby** (2:55)
(Perren—Yarian)
Produced by Freddie Perren
**Release Date**: 16 Aug 1974
**B-side**: Wigs And Lashes
**Position in Record Retailer Top 40**: -
**Equivalent US Release**: Tamla 54248 (20 Jun 1974)
**Position in Billboard Top 40 Pop**: 13
**Position in Billboard Top 40 R & B**: 4

---

Billy Griffin / Bobby Rogers / Warren 'Pete' Moore / Ronnie White

---

More Stylistics influences are apparent in The Miracles' new single ([890]; [891]; [906]), a soft-focus harmony following the style of the group's first post-Robinson single, but set at a faster pace. From the same Perren—Yarian setup, "Do It Baby" is an atmospheric creation with an up-beat chorus, and on the way quotes an old San Remo Strings title [807b].

Featuring Dennis Coffey on one of his earliest LA sessions, pitching in with a semi-staccato rhythm track (the style of which he calls 'chicken pickin"[1]), the production sets the song somewhere between pure soul and the more rhythmic funk idiom, passing itself off simultaneously as both love song and dance track. Taking the group back into the American top 40 after a break of three-and-a-half years [774], the Tamla Motown edition was expected to do better, prompting a re-release of [914] on 25 October with further publicity (see also [912]). The ploy failed, "Do It Baby" not a hit in the UK at either attempt.

[1] Coffey, p147.


## TMG 915
## DIANA ROSS & THE SUPREMES
**Baby Love** (2:34) **[E56]**
(Holland—Dozier—Holland)
Produced by Brian Holland/Lamont Dozier
Recording completed: 13 Aug 1964
**Release Date**: 9 Aug 1974
**B-side**: Ask Any Girl [E56b]
**Position in Record Retailer Top 40**: 12
**Equivalent US Release**: Motown 1066 (17 Sep 1964)
**Position in Billboard Top 40 Pop**: 1
**Position in Billboard Top 40 R & B**: 1

---

Diana Ross / Florence Ballard / Mary Wilson

---

Motown's most successful recording outfit, The Supremes saw none of their Tamla Motown singles re-released on the label, although this new edition of [E56] re-ran an early Stateside hit, complete with its original flip. Along with [925], the single arrived during a spell of intensive re-issuing in a more general sense, almost a third of Tamla Motown's output during the year or so between "Baby Hit And Run" [886] and "When You're Young And In Love" [939] accounted for by 1960s recordings. This selection, as had been the case with "Didn't You Know (You'd Have To Cry Sometime)" [903], arrived in support of a group *Anthology* compilation, mirrored by a promotional EP (see Appendix 1), all contemporary records showing the group billed as Diana Ross &... an ironic consequence of her individual success during the decade since "Baby Love" was recorded.

What remained of The Supremes in 1974 was unclear, in the wake of several ill-fated attempts to push the group up Motown's agenda courtesy of ambitious projects with Smokey Robinson [804], Stevie Wonder [847] and Jimmy Webb [859]. The only original member still in the line-up, Mary Wilson had remained staunchly protective of the group's reputation through these unsettled years, deeply wounded by the meagre terms on offer when her Motown contract was due to expire in early 1974. Fearing the same fate as befell her former colleague Florence Ballard [1029], Wilson was not willing to re-sign, reluctantly putting The Supremes on the brink of obsolescence, the situation salvaged by Berry Gordy's late intervention and the offer of a 50 percent stake in the name 'Supremes' which she seized upon. Assuming the clause would secure her financially, Wilson had failed to grasp the gist of the deal in which she simply had a share in the sale-price of the group's identity in the unlikely event that Motown ever disposed of it.[1]

"Baby Love" arrived back in the charts in 1974 like a distant echo, recorded when Motown was young and fresh and still trying to break in the UK. Penned by HDH, the number was offered up as a sequel to "Where Did Our Love Go" [E51], sharing with its predecessor the 'baby' theme which had so irritated the group. This though was mere adornment, the composition itself a ponderous work whose lyric comes from personal experience, based on Dozier's first serious relationship. A tortured plea to an uncaring lover, the song's child-like simplicity lacks any sense of struggle, meeting its fate with a passive acceptance which, in Diana Ross' disinterested performance, becomes unexpectedly vital.

First recorded on 24 July 1964, the track was presented to Berry Gordy, only to receive robust criticism for its perceived lack of commercial potential, coming in sedate tempo and devoid of Motown's preferred 'gimmicks' at its start. Bravely accepting the rejection, HDH went back to the drawing board, devising a new introduction with trademark "ooh-ooh" and re-recorded the backing in an up-beat 'pop' mode with the coming third verse playfully allowed to dissolve into a sax break. Throwing their full creative energies into the project, HDH utilised Mike McLean's new 8-track console in what has gone down in legend as its first employment, the additional tracks used to futuristic success for Jamerson's upright bass, an auxiliary feed from Hitsville's lavatory (doubling as echo chamber) and a 'clapping' effect supplied by Mike Valvano crashing his boot onto two pieces of plywood held together with springs.[2]

Donated thus to The Supremes for the vocal on August 13, the finishing touches from Ross involved her deliberately cultivating an accentuated nasal sound, seemingly oblivious to the pain concealed beneath this happy façade. (A trace of Dozier's original lament is detectable in the heart-rending dip to Bb for the second chord of the chorus.[3]) The song, seemingly built on a succession of choruses and bridges without a defined verse, unsurprisingly followed "Where Did Our Love Go" to the top of the US charts and, uniquely for its time, repeated the feat in Britain, displacing Roy Orbison on 19 November. Generally regarded as the pinnacle of the early Supremes catalogue, "Baby Love" is by no means the group's most accomplished release but, with its classic period sound, propulsive beat and catchy hook line, remains one of HDH's key achievements and The Supremes' most successful single recording. This 1974 re-run notched up an impressive number 12, bridging the gap in the group's contemporary career and paving the way for the obvious [925] in November.

[1] Days after signing the contract, Wilson married long-term partner Pedro Ferrer.

[2] The less animated original version was finally released in 2006 as an extra on *Where Did Our Love Go: 40th Anniversary Edition*.

[3] The tension implied by this plunge is accentuated by Ross finding her high A just as Jamerson's bass picks out the harmonically adjacent Bb, clashing discord averted by the separation of several octaves.

**TMG 916**
**EDDIE KENDRICKS**
**Girl You Need A Change Of Mind (Part 1)** (3:20)
(Caston—Poree)
Produced by Frank Wilson/Leonard Caston

**Release Date**: 27 Sep 1974
**B-side**: Girl You Need A Change Of Mind (Part 2)
**Position in Record Retailer Top 40**: -
**Equivalent US Release**: Tamla 54230 (19 Feb 1973)
**Position in Billboard Top 40 Pop**: -
**Position in Billboard Top 40 R & B**: 13

Following the attractive "If You Let Me" [845], arguably Kendricks' most alluring solo release, Tamla Motown returned to the aged *People... Hold On* album in September to retrieve "Girl You Need A Change Of Mind", a seven-and-a-half minute slow-dancer retrospectively seen as pioneering in the disco vein. Famous for it extended coda, in which the funk groove is most pronounced, the track's emasculation for the 7-inch format worked to its detriment, only partially salvaged by the inclusion of 'Part 2' on the B-side.

Penned by Leonard Caston and Anita Poree, the track's provocative lyric is a slap-down for the growing Feminist movement, from the diminutive 'Girl' of its title to the generally lecturing nature of its content. Declaring himself an emancipator through his sheer sexual prowess in which 'love' is defined as 'true liberation', the very nature of the proposition in which women can find freedom only through relationships with men, far from stating the solution, emphasises the problem itself. Coupled with the crude spectacle of Kendricks 'filling your loving cup', the lyric's domineering slant on society's power structures (he is almost giving females *permission* to have a point of view) proves the gulf between old-style chauvinism and second-wave Feminism to be as wide as ever in some quarters, months ahead of John Lennon and Yoko Ono's furious antithesis, "Woman Is The Nigger Of The World". (All of which makes Anita Poree's input surprising, which is not to say that all women cleave to Feminism, but finding a female credit against a text in which the woman is 'cured' of her political views by a good seeing-to remains decidedly curious.)

Containing a healthy sprinkling of Motown in-references including a Marvin Gaye-esque mention of picket lines [775] and an Edwin Starr-style 'Huh!', expressing a level of disgust, the track was a flop commercially when released in America during 1973, although its number 13 showing on the R & B charts reflected its popularity on the dance-floor. (According to Bill Dahl, "Girl You Need A Change Of Mind" was top of Studio 54's play list.[1])

[1] See Dahl, p270. Studio 54 was a legendary New York night club central to the disco movement, although it did not open until 1977.

**TMG 917**
**DIANA ROSS**
**Love Me** (2:47)
(Baird—Zesses—Fekaris)
Produced by Tom Baird
**Release Date**: 13 Sep 1974

**B-side**: Save The Children
**Position in Record Retailer Top 40**: 38
**No Equivalent US Release**

A second lift from *The Last Time I Saw Him* [893], "Love Me" represents Diana Ross' 36th Tamla Motown single in all set-ups, a tally unbettered in the label's history. Not released in America, "Love Me" was preferred by Tamla Motown in the wake of the poor showing of Ross' summer release "Sleepin'", which in missing out on the US top 40 became the most abject failure of her solo career to date. "Love Me" just managed to chart in Britain, its easy Bacharach-esque choruses carrying the song neatly, if somewhat blandly in the final reckoning.

Lacking a hook, the single is ultimately forgettable and would be consigned to a footnote were it not for its selected B-side, a cover of Marvin Gaye's "Save The Children" [796], pulled from Ross' *Touch Me In The Morning* for its contemporary relevance. *Save The Children* was the title of 1974's annual Black Expo by Operation PUSH (People United to Save Humanity), an organisation sponsored by Gaye's friend the Reverend Jesse Jackson. Hosted in July, *Save The Children* took the form of a benefit concert for which several star names from the world of black entertainment volunteered their services, Gaye centre stage and supported by Motown colleagues The Jackson 5, The Temptations and The Supremes as well as former Motowners Gladys Knight & The Pips.[1] The concert was filmed, and a soundtrack album duly prepared by Motown and released on both sides of the Atlantic, although for reasons unclear The Supremes' contribution was deleted from both album and movie. Thus Diana Ross, who technically had nothing to do with the project, indirectly stole the group's thunder with this release, leaving former colleague Mary Wilson 'crushed'.[2]

[1] Knight cheekily performed "I Heard It Through The Grapevine" [629] in front of Gaye. Other stellar participants included Sammy Davis Jr., Roberta Flack, Quincy Jones, Curtis Mayfield, The O'Jays, Nancy Wilson, Bill Withers and several others. Save The Children was unrelated to the UK charity organisation of the same name.

[2] Wilson, 1990, p74.


**TMG 918**
**R. DEAN TAYLOR**
**Gotta See Jane** (3:05)
**Re-issue of [656]**
**Release Date**: 6 Sep 1974
**New B-side**: Candy Apple Red
**Position in Record Retailer Top 40**: -

With R. Dean Taylor experiencing a curiously belated comeback in 1974 (see [896]; [909]), Tamla Motown raided the archives again in September for this, a re-issue of [656], the singer's first UK single back in 1968. This time the ploy failed, "Gotta See Jane" not charting second time around.

Due to the re-release of the single's original flip-side, "Don't Fool Around", as a recent A-side [909], Tamla Motown were forced to do a switch, the replacement track a choice attraction of 1971 vintage, unreleased in the UK until the recent *Gotta See Jane / Indiana Wants Me* album (see [896]). It had originally emerged as a US-only 45 on Rare Earth, Taylor's penultimate release on the label and, as it so happened, his last on Tamla Motown.

## TMG 919
## THE UNDISPUTED TRUTH
**I'm A Fool For You** (3:04)
(Whitfield)
Produced by Norman Whitfield
**Release Date**: 20 Sep 1974
**B-side**: Mama I Got A Brand New Thing (Don't Say No)
**Position in Record Retailer Top 40**: -
**Equivalent US Release**: Gordy 7139 (25 Jun 1974)
**Position in Billboard Top 40 Pop**: -
**Position in Billboard Top 40 R & B**: 39

---

Joe Harris / Billie Calvin / Brenda Evans

---

A trailer for *Down To Earth*, The Undisputed Truth's second single of 1974 had been road-tested in America over the summer, and despite its mediocre sales was approved for the UK. One of Norman Whitfield's less distinguished works, "I'm A Fool For You" points the way to his post-Motown work with the group, its monotonously driving production pushing its base chord through with little dynamic interest. Made for dance crowds, the track also prequels Whitfield's later style with acts such as Rose Royce, with whom he would achieve considerable success later in the decade (see [1013]).

## TMG 920
## DIANA ROSS & MARVIN GAYE
**My Mistake (Was To Love You)** (2:55)
(Sawyer—Jones)
Produced by Hal Davis
**Release Date**: 11 Oct 1974
**B-side**: Just Say, Just Say
**Position in Record Retailer Top 40**: -
**Equivalent US Release**: Motown 1269 (17 Jan 1974)
**Position in Billboard Top 40 Pop**: 19
**Position in Billboard Top 40 R & B**: 15

Returning to *Diana & Marvin* for a fourth spin-off single, Tamla Motown plucked two tracks from the album's second side, the lead selection "My Mistake (Was To Love You)". Structurally and rhythmically similar to Gaye and Terrell's exquisite "Ain't No Mountain High Enough" [611] (recorded like the present track with its vocalists working separately from one another), which Ross also had a famous previous crack at [751], the song's lack of uplift is merely accentuated by the comparison.

Written by the Sawyer—Jones team [765], the track is an adequate album-filler, its release as an A-side unnecessarily taking the false partnership of Ross and Gaye to extraordinary lengths, with 80 percent of the album now raided for singles. ([953] would take the tally to 90 percent before the project was thankfully laid to rest.)


**TMG 921**
**STEVIE WONDER**
**You Haven't Done Nothin'** (3:20)
(Wonder)
Produced by Stevie Wonder
**Release Date**: 4 Oct 1974
**B-side**: Happier Than The Morning Sun
**Position in Record Retailer Top 40**: 30
**Equivalent US Release**: Tamla 54252 (23 Jul 1974)
**Position in Billboard Top 40 Pop**: 1
**Position in Billboard Top 40 R & B**: 1


On a career peak in 1974, Stevie Wonder had agreed to unveil a new album, his first substantial recording work since his accident [869], scheduled for release in July. Time though was against him, and having devoted much of his recent efforts to developing material for Syreeta [912] and some-time Wonderlove vocalist Minnie Riperton[1], Wonder was unable to cobble together sufficient material for the proposed double set. Instead, he assembled a clutch of new recordings, formally recorded in New York and Los Angeles with Margouleff and Cecil, and raided his stockpiles for suitable titles with which they were supplemented for a single album.[2]

The emergent work, tentatively entitled *Fulfilling Ness's First Finale*, ran to ten tracks and appeared in August with its title tweaked to avoid an inadvertent reference to a legendary Scottish monster. In the wake of the successful *Innervisions*, the album was received as a sequel, the notion fuelled by its cover art, reminiscent of the former set and incorporating images of Wonder's past life, including illustrations of an old Motor Town Revue bus, Wonder as teenaged harmonica player, and sketches of Wonder's post-Detroit album covers (including *Innervisions*). The imagery also includes several obvious musical references including gramophones, gold records and an ascending piano 'staircase', but more pointedly includes portraits of Martin Luther King and John F Kennedy (who had been joint subjects of [734]), juxtaposed with references to Africa, encapsulated by a herd of stampeding elephants. Just visible to the right is a depiction of Wonder's car accident, with a log smashing through an automobile windscreen.

Musically however, *Fulfillingness' First Finale* failed to live up to its adventurous packaging, noticeably falling short of its predecessor in the grooves, which Wonder's exceptional popularity uncritically excused. The album topped the American charts, went number 5 in Britain, won another slew of Grammys and spawned several hit singles, including the current track, a scathing attack on the redundant Nixon administration, booted from office in August following the disastrous Watergate scandal (see also [789]). Watergate had shaken faith in the American governmental system, revealing underhand political manœuvring and deception at the highest level, exposed only by information obtained from a party HQ break-in. Several prominent politicians fell from grace over a period of months, culminating in the resignation of President Nixon himself in early August.

Written prior to the full revelation of the affair, "You Haven't Done Nothing" is a scathing attack on the government of its day, so uncompromising in its level of invective that Wonder is almost embarrassed by it, taking the trouble to explain himself in verse 2 ('It's not too cool to be ridiculed/But you brought this upon yourself'). As a piece of political criticism the lyric is both incisive and naïve at once, throwing its vituperation in the face of government while revealing its supposed hammer-blow through the lame accusation of the song's title: the worst Wonder could accuse the deceitful President of was failure to make a difference. Nonetheless, the text reveals a level of disgust unmatched in his catalogue to date, the lines condemning the democratic process itself amongst his most devastating, describing himself, and by extension the electorate as, 'Much concerned but not involved with decisions that are made by you'.

Musically, "You Haven't Done Nothing" is all Wonder's own, bar a bass line contributed by Reggie McBride.[3] Heavily reliant on keyboard riffs, the musical backdrop is similar to that of "Superstition" [841], with its constantly drilling bottom end, contrasting with jeering 'brass' riffs, probably also played on keyboard. Matching the toughness of the song's theme, the overall effect was striking, the song attracting interest from the Jackson 5, who duly consented to appearing as backing vocalists.[4] (The track probably inspired Wild Cherry's 1976 hit "Play That Funky Music".)

Its release in the fall-out of Watergate made it all the more pertinent and an astute choice of single, which topped the US charts. (Its comparative irrelevance to Britain goes some way towards explaining its failure to cross the Atlantic, as had been the case with [801].) Effectively closing Wonder's second-phase work which began with *Music Of My Mind* [827], *Fulfillingness' First Finale* would not be followed-up for two years. But for a second album lift [928], Wonder's Tamla Motown catalogue was at its conclusion, the belated follow-up, *Songs In The Key Of Life*, not issued in the UK until after the label was retired. For the rest of 1974 and 1975, Wonder was happy to enjoy his time at the top of his professional tree, touring the US through the autumn and preparing for fatherhood, his partner Yolanda expecting a baby (see [928]).

[1] Both of whom guest on Wonder's new album.

[2] These include "Heaven Is 10 Zillion Light Years Away" from the *Talking Book* era, and "Boogie On Reggae Woman" [928], originally intended for *Innervisions*.

[3] McBride was an emerging Detroit session man, summoned to New York by Wonder. Album sessions also included a surprise spot for James Jamerson, the track "Too Shy To Say" earning him an accolade from Wonder in the sleeve notes: 'Your talent is unlimited, thank you'.

4 Wonder introduces them in the song. He later stated that he would have liked to have The Osmonds on the track as well, as a symbolic union of black and white (see Haskins, p124).


**TMG 922**
**JIMMY RUFFIN**
**Farewell Is A Lonely Sound** (2:56)
**Re-issue of [726]**
**Release Date**: 18 Oct 1974
**New B-side**: I Will Never Let You Get Away
**Position in Record Retailer Top 40**: 30

Keen to cash in on the top 10 placing of "What Becomes Of The Brokenhearted" [911], Tamla Motown hurried into another Jimmy Ruffin re-issue, "Farewell Is A Lonely Sound" coupled up with the choice rarity, "I Will Never Let You Get Away". Unreleased in its day, this B-side first surfaced on one of EMI's budget albums, the Music For Pleasure collection *I've Passed This Way Before* which had appeared in August (see [896n]).

Ruffin's late revival was meantime continuing apace, his branching into disco in 1974 resulting in the Polydor single "Tell Me What You Want" which charted within a fortnight of "Farewell Is A Lonely Sound", giving Ruffin two top 40 placings at once. Stateside, Chess Records picked up on the Polydor hit and had Ruffin sign, leading to a US edition and yet more interest in a singer held in high affection by soul fans. Tamla Motown were not yet done, and Ruffin would see another re-issue the following year [934].


**TMG 923**
**MARVIN GAYE**
**I Heard It Through The Grapevine** (2:59)
**Re-issue of [686]**
**Release Date**: 1 Nov 1974
**New B-side**: Chained [676]
**Position in Record Retailer Top 40**: -

Three weeks after Gaye appeared on "My Mistake (Was To Love You)" [920], he was back on Tamla Motown's schedules with this release, a second outing for his famous release of 1969. Strengthening the single's potential, "I Heard It Through The Grapevine" was paired with another former A-side, "Chained" [676] a late-1968 single which appeared immediately before "Grapevine" in his UK discography. Strong though this double-header was, it didn't crack the UK top 40, despite the enduring popularity of the A-side which is rightly considered one of Motown's peak achievements.

Shy of such re-issues, Motown-America avoided the track, opting instead for a live version of "Distant Lover" [882b] backed with "Trouble Man" [846], both titles plucked from *Marvin Gaye Live!*, recorded in January at the

McAfee Coliseum in Oakland, California. The album and spin-off single herald the re-emergence of Gaye as a live draw [882], his engagements during the year also including an appearance with Bob Marley in Jamaica, and an August tour which was one of the highest grossing in American history.

Marking time between albums, Gaye's use of cocaine was said to be increasing during the period, his sensibilities reined in to some extent by the fact that he was, like his colleague Stevie Wonder [921], consumed by the pregnancy of his partner Janis, who in September had given birth to a daughter, Nona Aisha. Unsurprisingly, his wife Anna began filing for divorce, paving the way for Gaye to marry Janis, which he finally did in 1977.

## TMG 924
## THE COMMODORES
**The Zoo (The Human Zoo)** (3:16)
(Sawyer—Jones)
Produced by Pam Sawyer/Gloria Jones
**Release Date**: 1 Nov 1974
**B-side**: I'm Looking For A Love
**Position in Record Retailer Top 40**: -
**Equivalent US Release**: Mo-West 5009 (16 Mar 1972)
**Position in Billboard Top 40 Pop**: -
**Position in Billboard Top 40 R & B**: -

Lionel Richie / Thomas McClary / Ronald LaPread / William King / Walter Orange / Milan Williams

Having introduced The Commodores to the UK via "Machine Gun" [902], Tamla Motown saw fit to issue "The Zoo", which had been the act's US debut single two-and-a-half years earlier on the Mo-West imprint, and which had since appeared on the *Machine Gun* album. Originally sung by drummer Walter "Clyde" Orange, the group's early lead vocalist, "The Zoo" had brought Lionel Richie to the fore for duetting duties, establishing him as the act's front-man both figuratively and literally, his desire to take centre-stage permanently relegating Orange.

"The Zoo" is a proto-disco recording which, given its vintage, is recognised as one of the genre's formative pieces. Commencing with an oddly discordant instrumental passage, the track relies on a ceaseless beat accentuated by all instruments crashing onto the crotchet foundation (including at its fade, an electric guitar pulse sounding like dripping water). Adventurous in 1972, Pam Sawyer and Gloria Jones' recording was, by 1974, still looking fresh and particularly contemporary, released in the UK amidst several new-wave dance singles which were beginning to signal the wider shift from old-school R & B to the disco boom.[1]

Though not a hit, "The Zoo" would feature in the 1978 disco movie *Thank God It's Friday*, in which The Commodores make a cameo, the movie starring Donna Summer as an ambitious singer in a Hollywood night club named after the song.

[1] In the UK charts in late 1974 were hits such as "Hang On In There Baby" (Johnny Bristol), "You're The First, The Last, My Everything" (Barry White), "Get Dancing" (Disco Tex & The Sex-O-Lettes), "Rock Your Baby" (George McCrae), and so on.

## TMG 925
## DIANA ROSS & THE SUPREMES
**Where Did Our Love Go** (2:32) **[E51]**
(Holland—Dozier—Holland)
Produced by Brian Holland/Lamont Dozier
Recording completed: 8 Apr 1964
**Release Date**: 15 Nov 1974
**B-side**: Nothing But Heartaches [527]
**Position in Record Retailer Top 40**: -
**Equivalent US Release**: Motown 1060 (17 Jun 1964)
**Position in Billboard Top 40 Pop**: 1
**Position in Billboard Top 40 R & B**: 1

---

Diana Ross / Florence Ballard / Mary Wilson

---

Begun by Lamont Dozier on piano, during a particularly harsh cold spell in Detroit, "Where Did Our Love Go" concerns its author's pained feelings over the end of a brief love affair, in which he found himself pondering how a seemingly strong bond could prove so transitory. Lyrically sparse, Dozier showed what he had to Brian Holland, who recognised its potential and began working out a structure and arrangement ahead of the text's completion, a basic chart devised with assistance from Hank Cosby. Earmarked at this stage for The Marvelettes, the song was cut in Gladys Horton's key of C, a backing track laid down with The Funk Brothers in the spring of 1964 in which the song's relentless pulse caused difficulties in timing and concentration.[1] (Jamerson's bass, while central to the timing along with Richard "Pistol" Allen's drums, is remarkably basic even for 1964.)

Aware of the need for mass appeal, HDH went out of their way to avoid any hint of melancholy in the arrangement, despite the lyrical content, and the track thus committed to tape oozes commerciality, its tonic chorus melody ranging effortlessly up and down, dancing across the home triad with abandon. Melodically, the track resembles "Heat Wave" [E28], which HDH had given to Martha Reeves and the Vandellas a year earlier, particularly in the melody of its title phrase which sticks closely to that of the line "Something inside" from the earlier number.

Excited by the result, Dozier and Brian Holland called The Marvelettes in for the session only to find a defiant Gladys Horton refusing to sing it on the grounds that it was too immature. While this level of non-co-operation was rare at Hitsville, HDH had little history with the group on which to draw, the act having been looked after recently by Smokey Robinson. Forced to back down, HDH put the track aside, before electing to record it with The Supremes, still at that point without a hit to their name.[2]

With the lyric by this stage still not complete, Eddie Holland slipped in a line developed from Cole Porter's "Night And Day"[3], and sketched out some complex backing vocal sections for Wilson and Ballard. And yet, to their chagrin, HDH were met with resistance once again, The Supremes protesting over the song's simplicity and Diana Ross quite reasonably unhappy about the pitching which took her towards the bottom of her register, causing a jealous Mary Wilson to stake a claim as lead singer with support from Eddie Holland. Out-voted, she ended up staying behind Ross, and with tension in the air Lamont Dozier resolved to get the job over with by abandoning the backing arrangements and instructing the group to sing the now famous 'baby, baby' sections instead, which lazily reiterate throughout, regardless of where the lead vocal goes. Causing yet further ill-feeling, an acceptable take was nonetheless secured on April 8, and the track pencilled in for release in June.

Touring America as support for Gene Pitney when the single broke, The Supremes found themselves cheered increasingly loudly as it climbed the US charts all the way to the top, in the end upstaging Pitney and seeing their name moved up the bill. On their triumphant return to Detroit they wisely renegotiated their Motown contract, finally getting the deal (and peerapproval) they wanted. The track's success would have ramifications for Motown itself, and is recognised today as one the definitive period recordings. Motown's first crossover hit, it was heard in places where the company's earlier records had not been, Brian Holland later referring to it as "Colourless music, the reason Motown changed from being a little R & B company into music for everyone". Seen in this light, the track stands as the most important single recording in Motown's history, laying the foundation stone for all that followed, and if, at the start of 1964, The Marvelettes still considered themselves Motown's premier girl-group, in turning down "Where Did Our Love Go" they allowed themselves to be comprehensively usurped by The Supremes who henceforth would dominate the company's market share.

Popular in the UK where it originally peaked at a lofty number 3, the track has proved a perennial favourite, taken back into top 10 in 1972 by Donnie Elbert and re-released here over a decade after it was recorded. Although it failed to emulate "Baby Love" [915] on the chart this time around, this first Tamla Motown pressing secures the single for collectors of the label and serves as a timely reminder of the Golden Age of Motown, fast becoming a distant memory.

[1] The track speeds up slightly as it proceeds, and Earl Van Dyke's piano wanders off the crotchet rhythm here and there (eg between 1:22 and 1:25).

[2] In a 2005 interview, Velvelette Cal Gill remarked that the song was also submitted for her group, observing that, "[HDH] offered the song to almost everybody on the label". (*Record Collector* No. 308, March 2005, p53)

[3] "Such a hungry, yearning, burning inside of me", recognisable in HDH's finished text. (Notable readings of Porter's composition were done by Fred Astaire, Frank Sinatra and Ella Fitzgerald.)


**TMG 926**
**SYREETA**
**I'm Goin' Left** (3:18)
(Wonder—Syreeta)
Produced by Stevie Wonder
**Release Date**: 1 Nov 1974

**B-side**: Heavy Day
**Position in Record Retailer Top 40**: -
**Equivalent US Release**: Motown 1317 (11 Jun 1974)
**Position in Billboard Top 40 Pop**: -
**Position in Billboard Top 40 R & B**: -

Pulled from Syreeta's summer album *Stevie Wonder Presents* [912], "I'm Going Left" was a collaborative effort between its singer and producer. Founded on a single chord throughout, in the style of several early Motown hits, the production ethic veers towards contemporary dance music, Reggie McBride's writhing bass-patterning driving relentlessly against Ollie Brown's hi-hat.

Lyrically, the track appears to have been conceived as a curious sequel to "Together We Can Make Such Sweet Music" [766], whose opening lines, "Why should you go to the left/Why should I go to the right" imply a parting of ways, which may have resonated with Wonder and Syreeta's relationship troubles. If true, the track openly acknowledges the couple's break-up, while incorporating the possibility of salvation ('Lead me to what is right').

Syreeta though has since claimed that the song is 'about politics'[1], which is difficult to accept as an overall theme. However the second and final verse lurches unexpectedly into social affairs and specifically, plans to redistribute wealth, suggesting that it may in fact be a fusion of two separately written numbers. In this context the unresolved left-right dichotomy of the song title indicates a level of non-commitment and even confusion about the contemporary political arena, thereby dissolving any incisiveness which the main text might have carried.

[1] See Davis, 1988 p130.


**TMG 927**
**THE JACKSON 5**
**The Life Of The Party** (2:32)
(Davis—Drayton—Smith)
Produced by Hal Davis
**Release Date**: 29 Nov 1974
**B-side**: Whatever You Got, I Want
**Position in Record Retailer Top 40**: -
**No Equivalent US Release**

Jackie Jackson / Tito Jackson / Jermaine Jackson / Marlon Jackson / Michael Jackson

Lifted from *Dancing Machine* [904], "The Life Of The Party" was a UK-only single which relegated the group's current American hit to its B-side. ("Whatever You Got, I Want" made an impressive number 3 R & B.) Another flop, the single failed to chart in the UK, despite its solid dance groove and the taut chord structure of its chorus.[1] Melodically void, the number lacks a commercial edge, but has more substance than the group's recent singles which had tended towards comedy-absurdity, and failed to impress the public.

A rather futile release, "The Life Of The Party" happened to coincide with Jackie Jackson's marriage to Enid Spann, which he appears to have entered into with little serious commitment (see his interview transcribed in Taraborrelli, 1994, p141). The wedding at the start of December made Jackie the third Jackson brother to marry, indicating that the child act was unavoidably outgrowing its public image and threatening self-obsolescence for Motown's biggest discovery of the decade.

[1] The close-ratio B/Bb/Ebm may have acted as a model for Stevie Wonder's later "Pastime Paradise", which adopts the run (transposed to G#).


**TMG 928**
**STEVIE WONDER**
**Boogie On Reggae Woman** (4:05)
(Wonder)
Produced by Stevie Wonder
**Release Date**: 13 Dec 1974[1]
**B-side**: Evil
**Position in Record Retailer Top 40**: 12
**Equivalent US Release**: Tamla 54254 (23 Oct 1974)
**Position in Billboard Top 40 Pop**: 3
**Position in Billboard Top 40 R & B**: 1

Knocked together during sessions for *Innervisions*, "Boogie On Reggae Woman" was initially shelved, but re-claimed a year later for *Fulfillingness' First Finale*, thanks mainly to the enthusiasm of Margouleff and Cecil. Essentially a 12-bar blues with embellishments, the number sits uncomfortably between styles, possibly intended as a fusion of the reggae and boogie of its title. Boogie though in this context refers to the contemporary disco scene, rather than the rootsy boogie-woogie style (see [888]), although the distinction is further confused by some barrel-house piano, played by Wonder and giving the otherwise contemporary arrangement an oddly old-fashioned flavour.

Wonder's initial decision to abandon the song illustrates that he may not have rated it, the lyric seemingly a throwaway with a lewd undercurrent and an unusual emphasis on visual stimuli. Yet whatever the import of the raw composition, Wonder and his collaborators recorded a take stretching to almost five minutes. Electing to release it on 45, Motown were forced to pare it down to a little over four, and released it in the UK just ten weeks after Wonder's previous single. Due to the fact that releases of successive TMG numbers began to fall out of chronology at this stage, [928] turned out to be Tamla Motown's last single of 1974; more significantly, it would also be Wonder's final release on the label, marking the end of a run of 29 spanning a decade. That it was a left-over made this relatively uninspiring selection something of an anti-climax for Wonder, its lodging at an inconsequential number 12 on the charts a disappointing conclusion for one of Tamla Motown's most consistent recording artists.

Notwithstanding, Wonder continued to enjoy a period of high popularity, releasing nothing for the next couple of years but meeting an endless succession of public engagements, including an attendance at the 1975 Grammys in March 1975, at which he emulated his historic success a year earlier by scooping five awards, one of which commemorated "Boogie On Reggae Woman" as Best Male R & B Vocal of 1974. Two months later, Wonder was Special Honoree at the Human Kindness Day in Washington DC, at which he performed in front of a 200,000 throng, and later in the year he hooked up with Bob Marley in Jamaica, performing live with The Wailers and reminding his audience that the reggae inflection of this last Tamla Motown single was more than idle fancy.

Mirroring this peak period in his professional life, Wonder's personal affairs were also stabilising and, in April 1975, Yolanda gave birth to a daughter who they named Aisha Zakiya. The family settled into a new home in Manhattan at around this point, and it seemed to the outside world that Wonder had fulfilled his every ambition, personal and professional.

Taking his time about recording new material, Wonder continued to consolidate his legal and contractual affairs over the ensuing year, recruiting Ewart Abner to act as his business consultant and working out the terms of his next contract, which was eventually sealed in early 1976. Thereafter he set about recording the extravagant *Songs In The Key Of Life*, without Margouleff and Cecil, and stretching for the first time to a double LP. Emerging in late 1976, the album and its associated singles just missed release on Tamla Motown, as the label was retired. Nonetheless, these period recordings won further acclaim for Wonder and are regarded by some as his best, albeit somewhat thinly spread across a double set. At the point of writing, Wonder remains an active Motown recording artist.

---

[1] Release dates in this volume are taken from the original demo copy labels. [928] gives the release date as 13.12.75, but since the single charted in January 1975, this must be a misprint for 1974, which places the disc in its correct chronological position. The error may have stemmed from an original schedule for the New Year, a notion strengthened by Tamla Motown's irregular sequencing around now and the fact that it came too close to [921] for comfort (see discussion above).

## TMG 929
## THE DYNAMIC SUPERIORS
**Shoe Shoe Shine** (3:25)
(Ashford—Simpson)
Produced by Nickolas Ashford/Valerie Simpson
**Release Date**: 17 Jan 1975
**B-side**: Release Me
**Position in Record Retailer Top 40**: -
**Equivalent US Release**: Motown 1324 (22 Aug 1974)
**Position in Billboard Top 40 Pop**: -
**Position in Billboard Top 40 R & B**: 16

---

George Wesley Peterback / Michael McCalpin / Tony Washington /
George Spann / Maurice Washington

---

Held-off until after Christmas, [929] marked the arrival of The Dynamic Superiors, a Washington DC vocal group brought to Motown by Ewart Abner after being spotted performing at the Black Music Association in Atlanta. Paired up with Ashford & Simpson, working here as freelancers[1], the group recorded an album's worth of material, the first sign of which was the current single. Pitched in the soft-focus sentimentality of The Stylistics, "Shoe Shoe Shine" is a pleasantly lilting ballad, Tony Washington's airy vocals sailing high above a dreamy arrangement with poised electric piano and casually gliding strings. Set at serene pace, the track proved a surprise R & B hit, riding the coat-tails of the Philadelphia set [890], but failed to break through in the pop arena. This encouraging debut was followed up with a second album project [1016], as the group settled into a productive three-year tenure.

[1] The label credit makes mention of Hopsack & Silk, Ashford & Simpson's own publishing company. (They would later create a record label of the same name.)

## TMG 930
## EDWIN STARR
**Who's Right Or Wrong** (3:19)
(Starr)
Produced by G C Cameron/Mark Davis
**Release Date**: 6 Dec 1974
**B-side**: Ain't It Hell Up In Harlem
**Position in Record Retailer Top 40**: -
**Equivalent US Release**: Motown 1326 (1 Oct 1974)
**Position in Billboard Top 40 Pop**: -
**Position in Billboard Top 40 R & B**: -

Continuing Motown's involvement in the blaxploitation movie genre [862], Edwin Starr accepted an invitation in 1973 to provide a soundtrack for *Hell Up In Harlem*, a Larry Cohen gangster flick for which James Brown was first approached. Grateful for the commission, Starr provided a set of recordings which Motown duly issued on LP, trailered in America by the title track which appeared as Motown 1284 in February 1974.

In the UK the single never emerged, the best part of a year passing before it surfaced on the B-side of the non-album "Who's Right Or Wrong", a Starr original co-produced by G C Cameron. This new track, which concludes Starr's Tamla Motown catalogue (bar a re-issue [1028]), continues in the vaguely psychedelic vein of his 1970s output from "War" [754] onwards, featuring jazzy brass and a tough lead vocal with substantial texture and characteristic high animation. Running down the end of Starr's contract, Motown failed to promote the single and "Who's Right Or Wrong" slipped by unnoticed, his seven years with the company quietly expiring.

Tamla Motown release 47 singles and 28 albums. (A further 18 singles are released in the UK on Rare Earth and Mo-West.)
Tamla Motown place 13 singles in the UK top 40. 3 make top 10
Wigan Casino becomes recognised as premier Northern Soul venue. R. Dean Taylor emerges from retirement to perform there
Rise of early disco music

| | |
|---|---|
| **Jan** | Smokey Robinson: "Just My Soul Responding" / "Sweet Harmony" first solo single |
| **Jan** | Jean Terrell and Lynda Lawrence leave Supremes. Consequently, Cindy Birdsong re-joins group, and Scherrie Payne also recruited |
| **Jan 5** | Diana Ross: "All Of My Life" enters UK top 50 (peak 9) |
| **Spring** | Diana Ross tops *NME* poll as top female performer |
| **Mar 2** | Stevie Wonder wins five Grammy awards |
| **Mar 23** | Diana Ross & Marvin Gaye: "You Are Everything" enters UK top 50 (peak 5) |
| **Mar 26** | Diana Ross is 30 |
| **Apr 13** | Stevie Wonder: "He's Misstra Know It All" enters UK top 50 (peak 10) |
| **Apr 22** | Mary Wilson successfully bargains for 50% of Supremes' group name |
| **May 7** | Mary Wilson marries Pedro Ferrer |
| **May 11** | R. Dean Taylor: "There's A Ghost In My House" enters UK top 50 (peak 3) |
| **Jun** | Tamla Motown begin period of frequent re-issues of old recordings |
| **Jun 9** | Jackson 5 fail to arrive for UK tour after news of flight leaked to press |
| **Jul** | First UK release for Commodores |
| **Jul 27** | Jimmy Ruffin: "What Becomes Of The Brokenhearted" enters UK top 50 as re-issue (peak 4) |
| **Aug** | Marvin Gaye tours US for first time since 1967 |
| **Sep 14** | Stevie Wonder: *Fulfillingness' First Finale* number 1 album in US (two weeks) Motown's sixth album to top American chart |
| **Nov 2** | Stevie Wonder: "You Haven't Done Nothin'" number 1 in US (one week) |
| **Nov** | Jackie becomes third Jackson brother to marry, wedding Enid Spann |
| **Dec** | Prodigal label commences in US |
| **Dec** | Stevie Wonder enters period of inactivity with no releases for two years |

**TMG 931a**
**THE TEMPTATIONS**
**Happy People** (3:29)
(Bowen—Baldwin—Richie)
Produced by Jeffrey Bowen/Berry Gordy
**Release Date**: 10 Jan 1975
**Position in Record Retailer Top 40**: -
**Equivalent US Release**: Gordy 7138 (21 Nov 1974)
**Position in Billboard Top 40 Pop**: 40
**Position in Billboard Top 40 R & B**: 1

---

Otis Williams / Melvin Franklin / Richard Street / Dennis Edwards / Damon Harris

---

Having parted company with Norman Whitfield, musical co-ordinator for around eight years, The Temptations embarked on their next album in Hollywood, with high-hopes that a new producer would afford them scope for greater artistic development. Berry Gordy, realising that The Temptations were in need of a new impetus, put Jeffrey Bowen in charge of the project following his successful stab at producing a version of "Glasshouse" which ended up on side 1 of the ensuing set. (Bowen's résumé included the group's 1967 album *In A Mellow Mood*, on which he had collaborated with Frank Wilson.[1]) In a sign of things to come, Berry Gordy took exception to the manner in which Damon Harris had approached the recording and instructed the rest of the group, on the spot, to fire him. Duly ejected, Harris would take no further part in the album sessions, not therefore participating in the current track.

The album proper was commenced at Gordy's home, with bad feeling already in the air, before being transferred to Motown's Hollywood studio. Friction would continue to ensue between the group and Bowen, which at one stage caused a fall-out so severe that Otis Williams suffered a consequent attack of nervous exhaustion, for which he was rushed to hospital.[2] Recognising that, far from offering a new beginning, the group's fortunes were in fact reaching new lows, the four-piece continued working on *A Song For You* which, in spite of the problematic circumstances, emerged in January 1975 as a rather strong set, following a period fashion for splitting the material between dance tracks (side 1) and ballads (side 2).

"Happy People", penned in collaboration with Lionel Richie, was initially conceived as a vehicle for The Commodores. However in preparing it for The Temptations, Bowen devised a bipartite conception of the track, recording separate vocal and instrumental versions which served to book-end side 1 of the album. A generally tuneless attempt at the disco style, "Happy People" follows Motown's mid 1970s development which was coming to characterise their post-Detroit sound, with instrumentation EQ-ed into a flat background sheen, which Bill Nelson's funky bass solo fails to transcend. The track's title masks the tension of its recording, pulled for a hopeful single with its instrumental counterpart of the flip. Pop markets took little notice, although the track held top position on the R & B charts for a solitary week in February.

---

¹ Bowen had spent part of the intervening period working at Invictus [745n], where he would have encountered the group The Glass House, which included future Supreme Scherrie Payne, and Ty Hunter. There is no apparent connection between the group and the song.

² This is recounted in his autobiography (p169).

**TMG 931b**
**THE TEMPTATIONS BAND**
**Happy People (Instrumental)** (2:54)
(Bowen—Baldwin—Richie)
Produced by Jeffrey Bowen/Berry Gordy

Although not released as a double A-side, [931b] is worthy of particular attention due to the fact that, like [848b], it is credited to an act otherwise absent from the Tamla Motown discography. The instrumental take of "Happy People", which concluded the dance section of its parent album, provided an opportunity to showcase the session musicians, who are, in effect, The Eddie Hazel Band, respectfully billed here as The Temptations Band. Hazel and his colleague Billy 'Bass' Nelson, were veterans of Funkadelic, who had also recorded for Invictus under the name Parliament and whose Motown connections stretched back several years.¹

Recorded with a dirty funk, lacking on the vocal version, this short instrumental outstrips its A-side for impact, featuring a star spot for Melvin 'Wah-Wah' Ragin and generally pushing Bill Nelson's bass into a gut-churning thump thanks to a deep, bottom-heavy mix. Rightly credited to the ensemble rather than The Temptations, [931b] is the second time a Tamla Motown single billed different acts on either side and was a rare example of a Motown studio group receiving open recognition. (The move set a precedent followed in 1976 [1023b].)

¹ Funkadelic's first album (1971) had included unaccredited input from Bob Babbitt, Ray Monette (of Rare Earth) and Earl Van Dyke.

**TMG 932**
**POPCORN WYLIE**
**Funky Rubber Band (Vocal)** (2:48)
(Wylie)
Produced by Ollie McLaughlin
**Release Date**: 7 Feb 1975
**B-side**: Funky Rubber Band (Instrumental)
**Position in Record Retailer Top 40**: -
**Equivalent US Release**: Soul 35087 (12 Aug 1971)
**Position in Billboard Top 40 Pop**: -
**Position in Billboard Top 40 R & B**: 40

Legendary in Detroit, Richard 'Popcorn' Wylie was a peripheral figure at Motown who had been on the scene virtually since the company's inception, working early on with future luminaries including Norman Whitfield and Lamont Dozier. Having cut several sides for Motown in 1960-61, under various names and including a cover of "Money (That's What I Want)" [E02], he was utilised as a stage band-leader and session pianist, credited with piano tracks on "Money" [E02] and "Please Mr. Postman" [E05], amongst others. Falling into dispute with Berry Gordy, Wylie left Motown for rivals Golden World, where he wrote and produced many singles, developing a productive relationship with The Reflections [907]. Working elsewhere as a freelancer through the 1960s, Wylie's output included recordings for the small Karen label, run by Detroiter Ollie McLaughlin, one of which was "Funky Rubber Band", made with McLaughlin and arranger Mike Terry.

Around 1969, Wylie crossed paths with Motown again, through his work with Edwin Starr (see [725]), and in 1971 Motown elected to purchase "Funky Rubber Band" and release it as a 45 in America, watching it scrape into the lower reaches of the R & B charts. Thus re-established, Wylie remained on the scene, signing to Invictus in 1973 just as the label was winding up, before following Lamont Dozier to ABC in 1974 and seeing a handful of new releases which, together with his 'Northern' credentials, prompted Tamla Motown to dust off "Funky Rubber Band" for a belated UK debut.

The deep groove of "Funky Rubber Band", pushing against its Eb foundation, made it a strong dance-floor contender in 1975, its pure funk groove a match for anything recorded at Motown. Packing a sizeable punch, Wylie's scratchy vocals, embellished with street vernacular and a choleric sneer, push the track's pervasive energy through the ceiling, earning him accolades from the UK Northern Soul scene despite sailing over the heads of the general public. Courtesy of this releases such as this, Wylie remained popular into the 1980s, continuing to crop up intermittently on Motown sessions (eg The Supremes' 1976 *High Energy*). Sharon Davis (1988, p223) recounts events in 1984 where this little-known Detroiter was afforded standing ovations at low-key UK gigs, overwhelmed by the depth of UK fans' knowledge and adoration of his music. He later recorded for MotorCity (see [683n]).

**TMG 933**
**SYREETA**
**Your Kiss Is Sweet** (3:53)
(Wonder—Wright)
Produced by Stevie Wonder
**Release Date**: 3 Jan 1975
**B-side**: How Many Days
**Position in Record Retailer Top 40**: 12
**No Equivalent US Release**

Lifted from *Stevie Wonder Presents Syreeta* [912] for a UK-only single, "Your Kiss Is Sweet" is a collaborative effort with Wonder which accidentally emerges as a variation on "Jack In The Box", a hit for Northern Irish vocalist Clodagh Rogers, which had been the UK entry to the 1971 Eurovision Song Contest. Treading similar ground musically, "Your Kiss Is Sweet" is just as infantile, unmitigated by Syreeta's efforts to provide vocal colouration or

Wonder's production which includes a banal, plonking piano track.

Appealing to the juvenile market, the single scored reasonably highly on the UK chart, vindicating Tamla Motown's track selection and providing Syreeta with her first British hit.[1] Coinciding with the release, the vocalist was booked for some concert appearances in London, where she was warmly welcomed. "Your Kiss Is Sweet" would be the last single lifted from *Stevie Wonder Presents*, although her next single [954] would continue the collaboration with her former husband.

[1] "Spinnin' And Spinnin'" [912] had scraped into the charts, reaching number 49 in September 1974.

TMG 934
**JIMMY RUFFIN**
**I've Passed This Way Before** (2:46)
**2nd Re-issue of [593]**
**Release Date**: 10 Jan 1975
**New B-side**: Sad And Lonesome Feeling
**Position in Record Retailer Top 40**: -

With Ruffin now hitting on Polydor, Tamla Motown were keen to run with recent policy of plundering his back-catalogue for re-issues (see also [911] and [922]). However they were short of ideas in 1975 and lamely elected an unnecessary third outing for "I've Passed This Way Before", which had already charted twice, as [593] and [703], and inevitably flopped this time. (Its new B-side, "Sad And Lonesome Feeling", was pulled from his 1969 album *Ruff 'N' Ready*.)

This would be his last single on Tamla Motown, Ruffin continuing to record elsewhere throughout the late-1970s, moving to RSO for collaborations with The Bee Gees which spawned the hit "Hold On To My Love" in 1980. He has since worked with both Heaven 17 and Paul Weller and has continued to be held in high regard within the industry and by Motown fans.

TMG 935
**THE COMMODORES**
**Superman** (2:39)
(Richie)
Produced by James Carmichael/The Commodores
**Release Date**: 21 Feb 1975
**B-side**: It Is As Good As You Make It
**Position in Record Retailer Top 40**: -
**No Equivalent US Release**

| Lionel Richie / Thomas McClary / Ronald LaPread / William King / Walter Orange / Milan Williams |
| --- |

A blazing funk-disco production, "Superman" coincided with the arrival in the UK of a swathe of major hits which pushed the genre to the fore of the contemporary pop world. (These included Gloria Gaynor's version of "Never Can Say Goodbye" [778], which marked her arrival on the scene and came within a whisker of topping the chart.) Penned by Lionel Richie, "Superman" is a tongue-in-cheek reference to the fictional superhero, picking up on his widespread presence in popular culture ahead of Christopher Reeve's 1978 big-screen re-creation.

Making humorous mention of Kryptonite and leaping over tall buildings, the song references elements of the comic-book hero's extraordinary abilities, metamorphosed into an assertion of personal power with a semi-comedic lyric which Richie can't resist sending-up in his mock-gruff vocal in the song's extended instrumental ('I'm rough and tough and big bad stuff'). Somewhere down the line, it may have been inspired as a counterpart to Stevie Wonder's "Superwoman" [827]. Pop listeners though were unamused by so much absurdity and the single, pulled from the end of *Machine Gun*, failed to register.

**TMG 936**
**DAVID RUFFIN**
**Take Me Clear From Here** (3:35)
(DiMirco)
Produced by Norman Whitfield
**Release Date**: 24 Jan 1975
**B-side**: Blood Donors Needed (Give All You Can)
**Position in Record Retailer Top 40**: -
**Equivalent US Release**: Motown 1332
(Scheduled but not issued)

An old Vincent DiMirco number [735] first-recorded by Edwin Starr in 1972, "Take Me Clear From Here" marked the long-awaited return of David Ruffin in the UK after a gap of more than half a decade [711]. (During the intervening period, he had continued to record albums such as *Feelin' Good* (1970), *David* (1971) and *David Ruffin* (1973).[1]) This new 45 appeared in support of the contemporary *Me 'N Rock 'N Roll Are Here To Stay* which, courtesy of producer Norman Whitfield, included curious re-workings of Temptations hits such as "Smiling Faces Sometimes" [832] and "Superstar (Remember How You Got Where You Are)" [800], which some have speculated was written with a glance in Ruffin's direction.

This single, which relies heavily on Paul Riser's sharply arranged orchestration for support and direction, is an uncluttered creation, Ruffin's voice breathing through the gaps between violin and electric guitar. Reflecting the 'laid-back' flavour of much of the 1970s music emanating from America's West Coast, the overall mood of the piece is calm, vocals pushed to the front above repeating chord modulations which rise and shift back down through the smooth falling bass of the song's end-of-verse hooks.

An attractive top-side, "Take Me Clear From Here" was a worthy selection by Tamla Motown which bucked the US schedules where the single was assigned a Motown catalogue number before being pulled.[2] This UK pressing came coupled with a track from *David Ruffin,* "Blood Donors Needed (Give All You Can)" a ghetto-based campaign song penned by Bobby Miller and published by Jobete.

[1] *I Am My Brother's Keeper* also appeared in 1970 in the US, recorded with Jimmy Ruffin. His second solo album *David* was recorded but unreleased until 1998, when it emerged on CD.

[2] In favour of "Superstar (Remember How You Got Where You Are)" (Motown 1336).

**TMG 937**
**THE ISLEY BROTHERS**
**This Old Heart Of Mine (Is Weak For You)** (2:44)
**Re-issue of [555]**
**Release Date**: 31 Jan 1975
**Position in Record Retailer Top 40**: -

---
Ronald Isley / Rudolph Isley / O'Kelly Isley
---

Since The Isley Brothers' last Tamla Motown release [877], the group had scored a significant UK hit for Epic with "Summer Breeze", which had gone top 20 in mid 1974. Returning to their stock of recordings, "This Old Heart Of Mine" was exhumed for a second time, the classic 1966 number having charted in 1968. This formal re-issue retained the original B-side but failed in the commercial sense.

Tamla Motown would release nothing further by the act, but the group would follow-up with another successful new recording for Epic in the form of "Harvest For The World", which took them back into the top 10 the following year. The celebrated group continued as a significant commercial force until the mid 1980s, when they wound-up their American T-Neck label. This though was not the end of the act, and with personnel changes their appeal has endured to date, with intermittent R & B hits keeping their legend alive. (They were inducted into the Rock And Roll Hall Of Fame in 1992.) "This Old Heart Of Mine" is the group's definitive Motown recording, and it is appropriate that it closes their main Tamla Motown discography. It has since been re-issued twice, as [L010] and [L099]: See Chapter 6.

**TMG 938**
**CASTON & MAJORS**
**Child Of Love** (3:16)
(Caston—Wakefield)
Produced by Leonard Caston
**Release Date**: 14 Feb 1975
**B-side**: No One Will Know
**Position in Record Retailer Top 40**: -
**No Equivalent US Release**

---
Leonard Caston / Carolyn Majors
---

Leonard Caston made his breakthrough as lead singer of The Radiants, a Chicago outfit signed to Chess Records in the early 1960s. Having made himself useful as a writer and session musician (including, famously, handling piano duties on Fontella Bass' classic "Rescue Me" (1965)), Caston eventually drifted away from Chess and hooked up with Motown, where he made his mark with a credit on "Nathan Jones" [782], leading to a recording project which culminated in the US Rare Earth album *Jesus Christ's Greatest Hits*, credited to The God Squad Featuring Leonard Caston.[1] However side projects such as this merely filled his time, Caston truly establishing himself in the Motown circle after teaming up with Frank Wilson, with whom he supplied several Eddie Kendricks hits, including the popular "Keep On Truckin'" [873] and several other notable releases (eg [888], [901] and [916]).

Meantime, Caston had been asked to salvage some recent recordings which had stalled due to problems behind the scenes and, in recruiting vocalist Carolyn Majors to assist on backing sections, commenced a working relationship which would blossom through 1974: the two gradually assembled their own, self-titled album, for which they employed several musicians including James Jamerson. The emergent LP comprised Caston originals, and given that he also arranged and produced the set, Carolyn Majors' credit as half of a double-act stemmed from her presence on vocals, which she shared with Syreeta.[2]

The album's opening track "Child Of Love" was co-written with Kathy Wakefield and recounts its quasi-spiritual callings against single pious G major, pitched in semi-gospel mode. While its musical credentials are viable, the lyrical theme with its biblical imagery and evangelical plot is uncomfortable, the decision to release it on single profoundly abstruse. That neither this, nor any of the act's subsequent recordings received similar treatment in their home country is telling, Caston & Majors an outfit in which Tamla Motown invested considerable faith without being rewarded with a hit.

[1] The album appeared in January 1972, Caston's interest in gospel lending to interpretations of tracks such as "My Sweet Lord", "Spirit In The Sky", "Amazing Grace", "Oh Happy Day" and several similar selections.

[2] The act's slightly generous billing perhaps reflected Leonard Caston's personal interest in her, the two later marrying.


**TMG 939**
**THE MARVELETTES**
**When You're Young And In Love** (2:38)
**Re-issue of [609]**
**Release Date**: 14 Feb 1975
**Position in Record Retailer Top 40**: -

---

Gladys Horton / Wanda Young / Katherine Anderson

---

Reminding UK fans of Motown's Golden Age, this re-issue of The Marvelettes' "When You're Young And In Love" stands in light relief against Motown's contemporary recordings, its sweetly innocent touch intangibly nostalgic. The last time The Marvelettes would appear on the label (bar retrospective re-issues—see Chapter 6), the single brings a close to their fondly remembered catalogue which produced just one UK hit, the first outing of the present track back in the spring of 1967. In the years since, Gladys Horton made several attempts to re-form the group, but none came to fruition until she finally teamed back up with Wanda Young in 1990 for *The Marvelettes*. The group's name has since been sold, resulting in the emergence of touring stage acts with none of the original members involved.


## TMG 940
## THE MIRACLES
**Where Are You Going To My Love** (3:16)
(Day—Goodison—Hiller—Leslie)
Produced by Joe Porter
**Release Date**: 28 Feb 1975
**B-side**: Up Again
**Position in Record Retailer Top 40**: -
**No Equivalent US Release**

Billy Griffin / Bobby Rogers / Warren 'Pete' Moore / Ronnie White

An easy piece of pop balladry, "Where Are You Going To My Love" was concocted by British writer Tony Hiller, in collaboration with his protégés Brotherhood Of Man, for a 1970 follow-up to their hit, "United We Stand".[1] A modest success, the track was generally forgotten until The Miracles took it up for their second post-Smokey Robinson album, *Do It Baby*, released in April 1974 in America, but held off until December in the UK. The title track had already emerged in the UK [914], this trailer-single selected as the next-best option ahead of several Motown originals. (The contemporary US selection was "Gemini", lifted from their following album *Don't Cha Love It*, already available in the States.)

"Where Are You Going To My Love", while adequately recorded, was ultimately too flimsy to register the group's fan-base passing over the February single in droves. That both this and "Gemini" failed must have caused alarm bells to ring, suggesting the group were suddenly foundering without their leader. But the precarious notion that they were a spent force commercially was about to be refuted by the spectacular "Love Machine" [1015].

[1] The group were little-known at this point, the Eurovision victory which made them stars not arriving until 1976.


## TMG 941
## DIANA ROSS
**Sorry Doesn't Always Make It Right** (3:19)
(Masser—Sawyer)
Produced by Michael Masser

**Release Date**: 21 Feb 1975
**B-side**: Together
**Position in Record Retailer Top 40**: 23
**Equivalent US Release**: Motown 1335 (11 Feb 1975)
**Position in Billboard Top 40 Pop**: -
**Position in Billboard Top 40 R & B**: -

As had been the case with the *Lady Sings The Blues* project [848], Diana Ross' involvement in the filming of the Berry Gordy-directed *Mahogany* put her recording career on the back-burner while she involved herself in shooting, beginning in November 1974 (see [1010] for further details). With no concurrent album to push, Ross' new single was a stand-alone recording, supplied by Michael Masser and Pam Sawyer.

A tale of woe recorded in country style, the song's point is confused, the sorrow of its slide guitar and harmonica passages nullified by the pretty veneer of a nonchalantly extemporised piano track. One of the most solemn vocals in her discography, which takes her towards the bottom end of her register, the performance ranks with Ross' inconsequential 1974 singles, released as a measure to keep her in the public eye during the lull before *Mahogany*. The track would later re-appear on *Ross* (1978).


**TMG 942**
**THE JACKSON 5**
**I Am Love (Part 1)** (5:30)
(Larson—Marcellino—Fenceton—Fancifer)
Produced by Jerry Marcellino/Mel Larson
**Release Date**: 7 Mar 1975
**B-side**: I Am Love (Part 2)
**Position in Record Retailer Top 40**: -
**Equivalent US Release**: Motown 1310 (23 Dec 1974)
**Position in Billboard Top 40 Pop**: 15
**Position in Billboard Top 40 R & B**: 5

Jackie Jackson / Tito Jackson / Jermaine Jackson / Marlon Jackson / Michael Jackson

The centrepiece of *Dancing Machine*, "I Am Love" kick-started the set with seven-and-a-half minutes of changeable soul-funk, the vocal unusually led by Jermaine, whose soft rendering in the opening verses is supplanted by Michael's sharper pitching in some of the faster sections. Ultimately, the song's restrained first few minutes give way to several leaps in style, announced with a dazzling (if slightly flubbed) fuzz-guitar solo from Tito[1] which subsides into a pacey discotheque-oriented second half.

Extravagant in conception and needle-time, "I Am Love" was too powerful to leave on LP, a 45 edit duly run off and, in the UK, split over two sides of a 7-inch disc. Although the track had lifted The Jackson 5 back into the US top 20 after an exceptionally lengthy climb through the lower reaches, the abbreviated UK counterpart failed, despite its appearance in the immediate wake of the group's first UK tour dates in more than two years. This would be their penultimate UK 45, one more album and single needing to go before the group flew the nest for good [1001].

[1] While leaning towards California rock styles, in tone and texture the passage resembles Ernie Isley's lead in The Isley Brothers' "Summer Breeze" which had hit in America in the early summer of 1974. (Ernie had joined his family's group in 1973.)

**TMG 943**
**THE UNDISPUTED TRUTH**
**Law Of The Land** (3:42)
(Whitfield)
Produced by Norman Whitfield
**Release Date**: 21 Mar 1975
**B-side**: Lil' Red Ridin' Hood
**Position in Record Retailer Top 40**: -
**Equivalent US Release**: Gordy 7130 (5 Jun 1973)
**Position in Billboard Top 40 Pop**: -
**Position in Billboard Top 40 R & B**: -

Joe Harris / Billie Calvin / Brenda Evans

19 March 1975 marked the tenth anniversary of the Tamla Motown label, a date which slipped past unacknowledged two days before The Undisputed Truth's sixth single appeared. The title track of the ageing *Law Of The Land* album, the single was a fourth cover version for the act (see also [776]; [789]; [818]), Tamla Motown's belated interest in it exposing a lack of confidence in the group, with the concurrent US release tucked-away on the B-side.

Originally recorded by Norman Whitfield's premier vehicle The Temptations in 1973 [866], this remake dated from soon thereafter, paling by comparison and failing to dent the US charts when released at the time.[1] Why Tamla Motown pulled it for the UK in 1975 is unclear, the group having several viable, more recent recordings available. Predictably the ill-conceived move resulted in another miss.

[1] The US edition carried a different mix to the UK.

**TMG 944**
**THE COMMODORES**
**I Feel Sanctified** (2:40)
(Bowen—Miller—The Commodores)
Produced by Jeffrey Bowen
**Release Date**: 27 Mar 1975
**B-side**: Determination
**Position in Record Retailer Top 40**: -
**Equivalent US Release**: Motown 1319 (1 Oct 1974)

**Position in Billboard Top 40 Pop**: -
**Position in Billboard Top 40 R & B**: 12

---

Lionel Richie / Thomas McClary / Ronald LaPread / William King /
Walter Orange / Milan Williams

---

Another lift from *Machine Gun*, "I Feel Sanctified" mirrored the group's US single of late 1974, pairing it with "Determination", released in America on 45 in 1973. Treading much the same path as the act's previous release "Superman" [935], the recording falls flat as a result of its reluctance to deviate from its driving E major riff, drawing-out the sound with little to retain listener interest. This though, is to evaluate the track on the basis of its aesthetic content. "I Feel Sanctified", like several contemporary Motown recordings, was not designed to be heard from the armchair, the club circuit receiving it in a different context to general audiences who would tend to encounter it over the strangulated tones of transistor radios.

## TMG 945
## GLADYS KNIGHT & THE PIPS
**You've Lost That Loving Feeling** (3:42)
(Mann—Weil—Spector)
Produced by Norman Whitfield
Recording completed: 20 Jun 1968
**Release Date**: 4 Apr 1975
**B-side**: This Child Needs Its Father
**Position in Record Retailer Top 40**: -
**No Equivalent US Release**

---

Gladys Knight / Merald 'Bubba' Knight / Edward Patten / William Guest

---

Mindful of the material which emerged from New York's Brill Building in the 1950s and 60s [581n], several Motown groups and producers had wilfully covered their hit singles, one of which was the standard "You've Lost That Loving Feeling". Commenced by Barry Mann with its perfectly poised and evocative opening line, the text was completed with his writing partner Cynthia Weil and, with input from Phil Spector, honed into one of the Brill Building's great period products. Donated to The Righteous Brothers and released on Spector's Philles label in 1964, the track became a major international hit, leading to a stack of cover versions which continue to appear with regularity.[1]

Motown acts ready to grab a piece of the action included The Miracles and Barbara McNair, Gladys Knight & The Pips joining in with this 1968 reading from *Silk 'N Soul*. Accelerated from The Righteous Brothers' version, Norman Whitfield's respectful production boosts the bass end, the melody-tracking string sections played down compared to the overblown original.

Raiding Knight's archives yet again, this late Tamla Motown pressing arrived days after she had initiated legal action against Motown and Jobete for damages and an accounting of royalties. The case also carried an appeal to halt Motown from releasing catalogue material which might interfere with the group's current releases on Buddah, alleging that they were in any case not getting their percentages. That Tamla Motown had further such releases in the pipeline ([955]; [1009]) showed Knight powerless to stop the practice, Motown continuing to exploit her fame which, given that they owned the recordings in question, they were entitled to do.

[1] The Righteous Brothers' original topped the UK charts in February 1965 on the London American label, and has since returned to the top 10 on two further occasions. Martha Reeves also released a recording of the song on 45 for Arista in 1976.


## TMG 946
## MICHAEL JACKSON
One Day In Your Life (4:15)
(Brown—Armand)
Produced by Sam Brown
Release Date: 25 Apr 1975
B-side: With A Child's Heart
Position in Record Retailer Top 40: -
Equivalent US Release: Motown 1512 (Mar 1981)
Position in Billboard Top 40 Pop: -
Position in Billboard Top 40 R & B: -

Following a considerable break, Michael Jackson resumed solo recording with *Forever, Michael*, a ten-track collection which marked his having turned 16 the previous August. While the album made little impression in its day it remains of historical significance, heralding the return of Brian and Eddie Holland to the Motown fold after seven years. Hired as freelancers, the brothers were no longer working with Lamont Dozier who, sniffing the demise of the Invictus empire in 1973, had decamped for a recording career at ABC, while his former label-mates wound down operations and returned to what they knew best.[1] Swallowing their pride, the Hollands teamed up with Jackson at Motown's Hollywood studios, contributing three titles to the work in progress, which they also produced.

Celebrating this forward-looking reunion, Motown marketed all three Holland—Holland numbers as US singles in early 1975, "We're Almost There" / "Take Me Back" (Motown 1341) followed by "Just A Little Bit Of You" (coupled with "Dear Michael") (Motown 1349), resulting in back-to-back R & B top-tenners. Tamla Motown might have followed suit were it not for the intervention of John Marshall, product manager at the London office, who took a shine to "One Day In Your Life", with its "Ben"-style elegance, poignant modulations and lulling impressionism.[2]

Written by Sam Brown III and Renee Armand, the track is tinged with nostalgia in contrast to "Ben's" contented façade, an effect accentuated by Brown's lushly romantic arrangement which plays up the track's tugging major 7ths. A late addition to Motown's canon of slow-tempo balladry begun in 1971 with "I'm Still Waiting" [781], the track contained all the necessary ingredients to dent the UK charts, its failure all the more disappointing for the fact that the comparatively exciting Holland—Holland recordings were eschewed.

John Marshall's judgement may have seemed questionable in 1975, but his sense of hit-potential was vindicated six years on when Tamla Motown re-mixed the number and released it as TMG 976 [L042], watching it finally top the UK listings on June 27.[3] It was helped in no small measure by Jackson's then intense popularity during the interval between *Off The Wall* and *Thriller*, which Motown-EMI had sought to exploit by releasing *One Day In Your Life* under cover of a 'lost' studio LP, the title track taken from the single. Timing alone however should not detract from the song's inherent appeal. "One Day In Your Life" is amongst Jackson's most memorable hits during this peak period, earning him a silver record and his first ever residency at the UK summit.

[1] Their renewed involvement with Motown in 1975-76 is flagged by subsequent singles such as [1006], [1012], [1027] and [1029].

[2] The number contains a sly reference to another of Jackson's power ballads, with the closing line, 'Just call my name and I'll be there' [758], itself a jokey hint to [579].

[3] It toppled Smokey Robinson's last pop smash, "Being With You" (TMG 1223) having sat at the top for a fortnight. See Chapter 6.


**TMG 947**
**EDDIE KENDRICKS**
**Shoeshine Boy** (3:15)
(Booker—Allen)
Produced by Frank Wilson/Leonard Caston
**Release Date**: 2 May 1975
**B-side**: Hooked On Your Love
**Position in Record Retailer Top 40**: -
**Equivalent US Release**: Tamla 54257 (13 Jan 1975)
**Position in Billboard Top 40 Pop**: 18
**Position in Billboard Top 40 R & B**: 1

Tamla Motown's second 'shoe shine' single in quick succession [929], Eddie Kendricks' new release was pulled from *For You*, a much-anticipated follow-up to *Boogie Down* [888], which lowered the pace with its relaxed feel. Received with a sense of anti-climax in late-1974, the only trailer-single lifted was the current track, penned by Harry Booker and Linda Allen (America preceded it with "One Tear" (Tamla 54255)).

Allen was a white songwriter from Washington known on the folk circuit, her partner here an aspiring writer-performer who composed the lyric from personal experience (he had worked as a shoe shiner in his youth). Raising eyebrows at Motown for its perceived slight on black people, the lyric found Eddie Kendricks sceptical about the track, Frank Wilson having to cajole him into recording it. Even then others had misgivings, the recording eventually rubber-stamped by Berry Gordy who recognised that shoe shiners are not from any exclusive racial group, the overriding thread that they are from poverty-stricken backgrounds. In sponsoring the release, Gordy here showed that his keen sense for hit material was not dimmed, the track resting at the top of the R & B charts for a week in April.

"Shoeshine Boy's" curious lyric makes little sense without its autobiographical context, the rhetorical question of what will become of the main character addressed through lines such as 'you'll reach the top' and 'you're a star', which cloud the issue. However seen as Booker's own rags-to-riches tale, the contrasting images of unrewarding labour interspersed with aspiring optimism fall into place, "Shoeshine Boy" revealed as an uplifting commentary on life's trials. UK record-buyers though were unmoved by such simple sentiments, the track failing to emulate its American success on release in May.


TMG 948
**THE TEMPTATIONS**
**Memories** (3:57)
(Baldwin—Bowen—Wakefield)
Produced by Jeffrey Bowen/Berry Gordy
**Release Date**: 9 May 1975
**B-side**: Ain't No Justice
**Position in Record Retailer Top 40**: -
**No Equivalent US Release**

---

Otis Williams / Melvin Franklin / Richard Street / Dennis Edwards / Damon Harris

---

The Temptations' 29th Tamla Motown A-side, "Memories" was retrieved from the 'slow' side of *A Song For You*, and edited down for a nostalgic farewell single.[1] Not that its poignancy in the group's history was apparent at the time, the outfit continuing to record for Motown though 1975 despite their recent personnel problems [931a], "Memories" viewed at that point as merely a latest release for a group with ongoing appeal.

Recorded in sessions for its parent album without input from the sacked Damon Harris, the track's images of falling stars and fantasy trains to the distant past, float across a dream-like mirage of lost love. Notable too is Donald Baldwin's evocative and wistful clarinet and Moog instrumental, one of the most effective musical passages in the group's singles *œuvre* which captures the song's stabbing grief in one acutely penetrating movement. Yet, pulling it from the soft-centred romanticism of the pervasive Philadelphia school [890], the track is shaded by James Carmichael's darkly dramatic score whose rapt tension and angular swerves resist any sense of resolution, playing out the restless anguish which wallows beneath its surface.

A worthy composite piece, producers, musicians and singers unite on "Memories" for one moment of clarity amidst The Temptations' troubled contemporary affairs, its choice as a UK-only single worth the risk of its failure in the market. Falling into dispute with Barney Ales over their choice of legal representative, The Temptations were entering a troubled period mitigated only by the recruitment of Glenn Leonard as Damon Harris' replacement, the release of ensuing albums such as *House Party*, *Wings of Love* and *The Temptations Do The Temptations* seeing out the Tamla Motown years with no further UK singles in the offing.

Likened by Tamla Motown's publicity people to "Just My Imagination" [773], "Memories" undoubtedly inspired the return-to-press of the group's former hit for re-promotion on 10 October 1975, the final time they would be represented on the label before its demise. Soon thereafter, the group began moves which would take them to old rivals Atlantic, three years of alienation from Motown ensuing before their welcome return in 1980. By then, time had overtaken the group and despite subsequent reunions with David Ruffin and Eddie Kendricks, the old magic was never to be recaptured, although they continued to score on the charts throughout the 1980s. The Temptations were inducted into the Rock And Roll Hall Of Fame in 1989, shortly before the premature deaths of both Ruffin and Kendricks, Melvin Franklin also passing away in 1995.

[1] The edit knocked two minutes off the play time by shuffling sections into a new sequence, two verses chopped out in the process.

## TMG 949
## SMOKEY ROBINSON
**Baby That's Backatcha** (3:36)
(Robinson)
Produced by William "Smokey" Robinson
**Release Date**: 30 May 1975
**B-side**: Just Passing Through
**Position in Record Retailer Top 40**: -
**Equivalent US Release**: Tamla 54258 (17 Feb 1975)
**Position in Billboard Top 40 Pop**: 26
**Position in Billboard Top 40 R & B**: 1

Pleased with the results of his first solo recordings [883], Smokey Robinson had recorded and released the follow-up *Pure Smokey* in 1974, Tamla Motown showing limited interest and refusing any trailer-singles.[1] Robinson though was musing a 'concept album' along the lines of Marvin Gaye's *What's Going On*, hitting on the image of a butterfly trapped in a hurricane which in turn suggested the idea of songs being carried on a gusting breeze. Firming up the basis of his next project, Robinson conceived a suite of songs connected with a continuous track of wind noises, which he attempted to shape into something grandiose, an album which in his words would be 'a killer'.[2]

The results of his scheme emerged in March 1975 (UK: June), as *A Quiet Storm*, a seven-track assemblage of titles, at least two of which pre-date his album concept.[3] The first evidence of this activity in the UK was the current single, pulled from side 1 of the LP, following its earlier success in the States. "Baby That's Backatcha" is a gently-flowing stream of music which bobs around the melody's E note without ever deviating meaningfully. As a drone, the song works on a semi-hypnotic level, its musical detail always subservient to the strand of its unchanging keys, pushing through three-and-a-half minutes of invariable ambience.

The song's rhythmic pulse hints at a direct re-phrasing of "More Love" [614], written in 1967 as an ameliorative to Robinson's wife. That the couple, who had separated in 1974 [898], were reunited early in the year suggests that he had the former track in mind when composing "Backatcha", its theme of reciprocated love apt if unsubtly phrased by Robinson's standards.

[1] In America, three 45s were lifted, as Tamla 54246; Tamla 54250; and Tamla 54251. All were R & B hits. The album title was borrowed by George Harrison in 1976 for the affectionate "Pure Smokey", included on his album *Thirty Three And A Third*. In the lyric Harrison fondly recalls The Beatles' version of "You Really Got A Hold On Me" [E13]. (See also [772n]).

[2] Robinson, p205

[3] The contents include "Wedding Song", written in 1973 for Jermaine Jackson [874], and "Happy (Love Theme From Lady Sings The Blues)" [848a].

TMG 950
**THE SUPREMES**
**He's My Man** (2:55)
(Wright—Patterson)
Produced by Greg Wright
**Release Date**: 15 Aug 1975
**B-side**: Give Out But Don't Give Up
**Position in Record Retailer Top 40**: -
**Equivalent US Release**: Motown 1358 (12 Jun 1975)
**Position in Billboard Top 40 Pop**: -
**Position in Billboard Top 40 R & B**: -

---

Cindy Birdsong / Scherrie Payne / Mary Wilson

---

Since The Supremes' 1972 sessions with Jimmy Webb [859], which had failed to revitalise the act, all had been quiet on the release front bar a couple of re-issues [915]; [925]. More than two years since their last studio album, The Supremes were emerging from a period of readjustment, stabilising into the new Birdsong—Payne—Wilson line-up despite intensifying personal pressures on the latter. Two months pregnant in September 1974, Wilson was on the receiving end of a beating from husband Pedro Ferrer which left her shaken and able to find escape only through gruelling tours which were becoming the group's sole *raison d'être*. Ferrer meantime had become The Supremes' manager, his trying relationship with Wilson soon spreading to a generalized conflict with the other group members, and Berry Gordy, all of whom were suspicious of his motives and capabilities. And yet somehow, through these rather depressing winter months, there were signs that fortunes were turning. In December, The Supremes at long last entered the studio to begin work on what became their self-titled album, and the following spring Wilson gave birth to daughter Turkessa (a variation on the Spanish word for turquoise).

With *The Supremes* ready for release (held back until July in Britain), the group had cause to be optimistic, going back on the road to promote the forthcoming set, and in particular, to plug the new line-up's inaugural single, "He's My Man", penned by Jobete writer Greg Wright and Karin Patterson, with whom he had formed part of the Mo-West group The Devastating Affair [879]. (Vocals on this new track were split between Scherrie Payne and Mary Wilson, probably at Ferrer's insistence, a move which consolidated the original Supreme's standing as leader—if not lead singer—of the group.[1]) Taking The Supremes into the ubiquitous disco arena, "He's My Man" is an unencumbered ditty whipped into shape by Wright's percussive patterning and Dave Blumberg's tightly contemporary arrangement. Vibrant with boundless excitement, the track makes up for its lack of depth with a sheen of wah-wah guitar licks and shakers which send the group hurtling into the second-half of the decade with no hint of regret; that the song, which passed-by the R & B listings with a paltry showing at 69, proceeded to top Billboard's newly inaugurated disco charts speaks of shifting musical trends, which made the group's vintage sound seem like a relic form the ancient past.

Troublingly, the UK release of May was placed on hold, and it seemed unclear for a while whether it would emerge at all. And yet oblivious to the impending problems to beset Tamla Motown, The Supremes went on a triumphant tour during which Wilson's old friend and partner Florence Ballard hooked up with the group, appearing on stage to emotional standing ovations.[2] Booked to play the UK in September, the group's popularity demanded Tamla Motown release "He's My Man" without further delay, and the label broke its two-month near-silence on August 15, releasing the single to a somewhat limp reception. Its poor sales though were of less import than the fact that The Supremes, Tamla Motown's all-time top act, were finally back in business, and looking forward to further recordings and releases which, they hoped, would re-establish them as a commercial force.

[1] The Ferrer-Wilson axis held sway in successfully resisting the first-choice cut, "It's All Been Said Before", which featured a solo Payne vocal. The single was scheduled in America as Motown 1350 but scrapped before release.

[2] Ballard had been back in the news early in the year, reports flying that she was penniless and dependent on welfare to support her children. The news shocked the group's fans and shamed both Diana Ross and Mary Wilson into coming to her aid. (Not that their assistance had any long-lasting effect: see [1029].)

**TMG 951**
**CASTON & MAJORS**
**Sing** (2:32)
(Caston)
Produced by Leonard Caston
**Release Date**: 6 Jun 1975

**B-side:** There's Fear
**Position in Record Retailer Top 40:** -
**No Equivalent US Release**

---

Leonard Caston / Carolyn Majors

---

Following the optimistic release of "Child Of Love" [938], Tamla Motown elected to lift a second track from Caston & Majors' eponymous long-player, "Satisfied Mind (Sing)" appearing with abbreviated title and half-a-minute shorn from its play time though the excision of verse 1. (The removal of this section, in which Leonard Caston takes centre-stage, leaves the single edit as more or less a Carolyn Majors solo. Why it was done is unclear; the full recording runs to a mere 3:25, shorter than many contemporary Tamla Motown A-sides.)

Written mainly on a rapid one-note pulse, "Sing" is an exhortation to religion, a washing powder commercial for inner cleanliness which can be achieved only through surrender to the Lord. The track concludes with a pious choir imploring the listener to sing to God, its disturbing collapse to an unresolved minor failing to provide spiritual elevation. The single came backed with another recording from the album's first side, "There's Fear", a somewhat unsettling number penned by Caston and Mattie Lynks which casts an ominous shadow across the LP.


**TMG 952**
**THE COMMODORES**
**Slippery When Wet** (2:58)
(McClary—Orange)
Produced by James Carmichael/The Commodores
**Release Date:** 13 Jun 1975
**B-side:** The Bump
**Position in Record Retailer Top 40:** -
**Equivalent US Release:** Motown 1338 (2 Apr 1975)
**Position in Billboard Top 40 Pop:** 19
**Position in Billboard Top 40 R & B:** 1

---

Lionel Richie / Thomas McClary / Ronald LaPread / William King /
Walter Orange / Milan Williams

---

More uncompromising funk from The Commodores, "Slippery When Wet" follows Stevie Wonder's "You Haven't Done Nothing'" [921], from which it takes its general rhythm, guitar foundation and vocal detail, in which Richie turns the end of several phrases upwards for a momentary squeal. With its thumping bass-end and taut brass riffing, the production by the group is consummate, percussion flying around gutsy vocals in an archetypal example of the period slow funk-dance genre. The single was the first to emerge from the group's second Motown album *Caught In The Act*, released in the UK in May, "Slippery When Wet" paired with another title from the set.

---

**TMG 953**
**DIANA ROSS & MARVIN GAYE**
Don't Knock My Love (2:13)
(Shapiro—Pickett)
Produced by Hal Davis
**Release Date**: 18 Jul 1975
**B-side**: I'm Falling In Love With You [879b]
**Position in Record Retailer Top 40**: -
**Equivalent US Release**: Motown 1296 (18 Jun 1974)
**Position in Billboard Top 40 Pop**: -
**Position in Billboard Top 40 R & B**: 25

Finally bringing the curtain down on Ross and Gaye's collaborative efforts of 1972 [879], one of the few as yet unused tracks from the album was extracted for a fifth trailer-single, backed with the already-poached [879b]. (This B-side was oddly repeated over the one title still unused as a single track, the Bob Gaudio-produced "Pledging My Love".) "Don't Knock My Love" is an annoyingly blaring cover of Wilson Pickett's 1971 Atlantic hit which had originally toppled "Want Ads", on HDH's Hot Wax label, from the top of the R & B charts. Written by Pickett and Brad Shapiro, the track's utilisation by Motown must have amused the singer, who as it turned out would end up recording for the company himself in the 1980s.

Diana Ross' opinion of the recording was revealed in 1990 when *The Marvin Gaye Collection* was released as a 4 CD box set: an alternative mix of "Don't Knock My Love" was included, on which Ross can be heard complaining, "This is the song I hate". It was also the first title attempted during the sessions, work on which led to the stand-off between the two singers which was never resolved (see [879]). The track was issued in June in America, but held-off in the UK until mid-July, after both [954] and [955] had already appeared. It failed to chart.


**TMG 954**
**SYREETA**
Harmour Love (3:28)
(Wonder)
Produced by Stevie Wonder
**Release Date**: 13 Jun 1975
**B-side**: What Love Has Joined Together
**Position in Record Retailer Top 40**: 32
**Equivalent US Release**: Motown 1353 (23 May 1975)
**Position in Billboard Top 40 Pop**: -
**Position in Billboard Top 40 R & B**: -

Syreeta's last single for Tamla Motown, "Harmour Love" was a non-album recording made with Stevie Wonder, the backing track probably prepared with a view to Wonder recording his own vocal. As such, it was something of a leftover, lyrically slight and awash with seashells and calypso grooves, the meaningless title possibly an inconsequential twist on 'harbour'. The production continues in the vein of Syreeta's recent twee pop ditties such as "Your Kiss Is Sweet" [933], irritatingly catchy and earning itself a top 40 placing in the UK, paired with a lift from *Syreeta*, a cover of an old Mary Wells number [E25b] written by Smokey Robinson and Bobby Rogers and since also recorded by The Temptations [504b].

"Harmour Love" would be Syreeta's last work with Stevie Wonder, closing this period of her career, although it would be resurrected for inclusion on her 1977 album *One To One*. By then Syreeta was married to Curtis Robertson and ready to embark on further recordings which hit their zenith in 1979 in collaboration with Billy Preston for the sensuous "With You I'm Born Again", a UK number 2 as TMG 1159. "Harmour Love" was included in the 2005 Phil Morrison film *Junebug*, prompting latter-day sales for *One To One* as a consequence of there being no soundtrack album available.


**TMG 955**
**GLADYS KNIGHT & THE PIPS**
**If I Were Your Woman** (2:59)
**Re-issue of [765]**
**Release Date**: 27 Jun 1975
**New B-side**: The Only Time You Love Me Is When You're Losing Me
**Position in Record Retailer Top 40**: -

---

Gladys Knight / Merald 'Bubba' Knight / Edward Patten / William Guest

---

Continuing to ruthlessly pillage their stockpiles of Gladys Knight & The Pips recordings which so irritated the group, "If I Were Your Woman" re-appeared on the heels of the group's Buddah hit, "The Way We Were". For the second time, the track failed to dent the UK charts, despite the interest of a new B-side, "The Only Time You Love Me Is When You're Losing Me" taken from *All I Need Is Time* (1973). Knight need not have worried unduly about the intrusion on her official release sequence, her ongoing success with Buddah continuing unabated in the late summer with "Best Thing That Ever Happened To Me", one of her biggest UK hits. This Tamla Motown cash-in slipped by almost unnoticed, marking the end of the main sequence of TMG numbers employed continuously since March 1965 as the Tamla Motown label entered a period of inactivity over the summer of 1975 (see below).

---

**INTERREGNUM**
For reasons which have never been fully accounted, Tamla Motown had a three-month hiatus in the summer of 1975 during which singles and albums stopped appearing (with the exception of the delayed [950] and [953]). While Berry Gordy was celebrating the birth of his eighth child and The Supremes were preparing to leave for South Africa, similar events were affecting the American release schedules, leading some to wonder where—if anywhere—Motown was now going. (In his autobiography, Berry Gordy makes no mention of these events,

confining his account of the period almost exclusively to the *Mahogany* project.)

In fact, Motown was losing its market share to such an extent that Ewart Abner, president of Motown Records [839], was in the process of resigning, to be replaced temporarily by Gordy, although Barney Ales was quickly brought back in and appointed with a specific remit to re-invigorate Motown's recordings and repertoire policy and review their promotional strategies. (Ales recently had success with his own Prodigal label, which Motown consequently subsumed, thereby acquiring Charlene and contracts for a clutch of minor recording artists including, bizarrely, former heavyweight boxing champion Joe Frazier.) In the UK, Tamla Motown announced it was to become independent of EMI as from September 1, accounting for the TMG sequence coming to an abrupt halt with [955] while the transition to a new distributor was organised. However the proposed deals fell through and Tamla Motown were forced to do a humbling about-face and re-sign with EMI for another year, releases thereafter getting back on track within days of the due date's passing.

When business resumed, it turned out that the Motown Record Corporation had ceased to exist, replaced by Motown International. In the UK, it became clear that the Mo-West label, always a side operation, was effectively being wound up, and the Tamla Motown singles started afresh with a catalogue sequence beginning TMG 1001, exactly 500 numbers ahead of the very first single on the label. So far as contemporary UK albums went, a similar process occurred, the abandonment of the old number sequence at STML 11293 in July (The Supremes' eponymous LP) followed in September with STML 12001 (Eddie Kendricks: *The Hit Man*).

The missing 45 catalogue positions in the singles run, TMG 956 to TMG 1000, were apparently to be left dormant but, ever aware of collector interest and the value of a well-timed re-issue, Tamla Motown created retrospective singles between 1980 and 1985 gradually back-filling the gap. All 'missing' numbers were eventually used, giving the unaware the false impression that releases were continuous through to TMG 1052, and these are detailed in Chapter 6.

---

**TMG 1001**
**THE JACKSON 5**
**Forever Came Today** (3:25)
(Holland—Dozier—Holland)
Produced by Hal Davis
**Release Date**: 5 Sep 1975
**B-side**: I Can't Quit Your Love
**Position in Record Retailer Top 40**: -
**Equivalent US Release**: Motown 1356 (10 Jun 1975)
**Position in Billboard Top 40 Pop**: -
**Position in Billboard Top 40 R & B**: 6

---

Jackie Jackson / Tito Jackson / Jermaine Jackson / Marlon Jackson / Michael Jackson

---

By the time Tamla Motown sorted out their licensing and distribution arrangements, the summer of 1975 was slipping past, releases having backed up

---

somewhat. On September 5, UK fans were finally treated to The Jackson 5's latest single, a cover of The Supremes' final HDH release from 1968 [650] which had remained comparatively unknown due to its unspectacular chart placing first time out.

As updates go, Hal Davis' production qualifies as a success in modernisation, ironing out the original's brooding twists with a sharply hammering percussion track, with the added excitement of trumpet fanfares and, discreetly mixed, the bubble machine as heard on "Dancing Machine" [904]. Pitched at the disco market, The Jackson 5's recording lacks meaning but offers elevation, pushing apace through its three and a half minutes with inventive animation. Full of ideas to maintain its momentum, the track fulfils Davis' intent, exploring the underlying dance groove in Holland—Dozier—Holland's original work, something they had taken pains to understate in 1967. The contrast in styles between the two versions reflects the shifting times, depth of expression giving way to a surface sensationalism as the hollow form of disco steadily replaced emotionally and politically purposeful 'soul' as the principal medium by which the young were finding something to dance to—without necessarily bothering to listen to it.

As it turned out, this glance back to Motown's Golden Era was the last single released by The Jackson 5. Through 1974 the group had found themselves increasingly disenchanted with Motown, frustrated over Berry Gordy's refusal to allow them a say in the material they were recording despite the group having ambitions to write for themselves. Coupled with declining sales, which had all-but seen them disappear off the radar, the group's father Joe was becoming restless in the face of Motown's plans to push the act along their established, and by now well-worn route. As late as July 1975, the company were pressing The Jackson 5 for more recording dates, a memorandum dispatched to Joe meeting with curt refusal. Part of the issue was the bulging stockpile of unreleased Jackson 5 material already in the vaults, reckoned by J Randy Taraborrelli to be almost 300 recordings.[1]

Instead, Joe was in talks with CBS, and in the throes of carrying out his long-standing threat to wrench the group from Motown for good. CBS recognised that the group had a deal of untapped potential and offered dazzling royalties and a substantial signing-on fee to lure the brothers, four of the five consenting to terms and signing contracts. The sticking point was Jermaine, whose marriage to Hazel Gordy [874] split his loyalties. If published accounts are anything to go by, Jermaine resolved quickly to stay put, resisting the group's move with determination and causing an irreparable split.[2] Quite how the situation would pan-out was initially unclear, but with Jermaine adamant and his brothers already contracted to CBS, a break-up was inevitable, the solution found by the full recruitment of Randy into the act (see [833]), as Jermaine's replacement, while his brother stayed on Motown's books as a solo artist.

Inevitably lawsuits flew as a result, and in early 1976 Motown sued for breach of contract. Claiming ownership of 'Jackson 5', Motown forced Epic to re-brand the act, which they achieved by marketing the brothers simply as The Jacksons (which, with some carefully designed lettering on their record sleeves, effectively masked the switch from a 5 to an S). At CBS the group were assigned to the Epic imprint, but as it transpired, their new label was initially no more keen on them writing for themselves than Motown had been and sought to team them up with Philadelphia hit makers Gamble—Huff [890].[3] Their first Epic album was almost entirely supplied by Gamble—Huff (with a couple of Jacksons originals thrown in) and included the period classic "Show You The Way To Go", which became their first UK number 1 in June 1977.

In due course the dust settled, and The Jacksons were able to go on to establish themselves as major movers in the pop-disco world with a succession of hits seeing them into the 1980s, and for Michael in particular to elevated superstardom. Their Tamla Motown discography accounts for 19 singles in under six years, the most released by any act on the label during the 1970s.

[1] He quotes figures of 469 songs recorded by mid 1975, only 174 of which had been released (1994, p169). Motown dug many of these out during the 1980s to cash in on Michael Jackson's massive popularity.

[2] The extent to which the brothers were still united is called into question by Marlon's marriage to 18-year-old Carol Parker in August 1975, arranged without prior announcement and without the apparent knowledge of his immediate family, who didn't learn of the union until several months later.

[3] The respected pair had been indicted on charges of payola over the summer.


**TMG 1002**
**SISTERS LOVE**
**I'm Learning To Trust My Man** (3:10)
(Sawyer—Ware)
Produced by Hal Davis
**Release Date**: 5 Sep 1975
**B-side**: Try It, You'll Like It
**Position in Record Retailer Top 40**: -
**No Equivalent US Release**

---

Vermettya Boyster / Lillie Fort / Gwen Berry / Jeannie Long

---

The UK Mo-West label had seen several releases through the first half of 1975, which over the summer had noticeably tailed off (see Appendix 3). The fact was that Mo-West was being wound-up, only a handful of singles released from there until the last, MW 3035, in July 1976. Aware that the label was falling into disuse, Tamla Motown began earmarking notable Mo-West material itself, requisitioning current track for a label-switching re-issue.

Although not a British recording, "I'm Learning To Trust My Man" was first released on Mo-West in September 1973 as a UK-only single (MW 3009) with no parent album. Arranged by Gene Page, the track is a knowingly frenetic creation, with an ungainly opening chant, but succeeds for its exceptional vocal track shared between the group, and in particular Vermettya Boyster's startling scream at the close. The reassuring account of a woman's growing faith in her lover, the track has a fundamentally positive slant and was affectionately regarded by Northern Soul crowds, accounting for this late re-issue. (The group had, by now, left Motown and gone into retirement.)

**TMG 1003**
**EDDIE KENDRICKS**
**If Anyone Can** (3:22)
(Caston—Wakefield)
Produced by Frank Wilson/Leonard Caston
**Release Date**: 12 Sep 1975
**B-side**: Get The Cream Of The Crop
**Position in Record Retailer Top 40**: -
**No Equivalent US Release**

With his album *For You* having made little impression, Tamla Motown wasted no time in releasing Eddie Kendricks' follow-up, *The Hit Man* a sixth studio set from the former Temptation. The first lift, "If Anyone Can" is a morose plod, animated by a James Jamerson bass line dancing with triplets and prodding the musical progression through its lumbering bars. The intent though was not lethargy, Kendrick's floating vocals flagrantly suggestive and demonstrating an attempt at something smoochy and throbbing. Its effectiveness though can be gleaned by the genital symbolism of Kendricks' 'mean machine' and 'magic wand', which in their crudeness border on comedy. In truth, this may be what Caston—Wakefield wanted, the track's exaggerated claims of prowess and its wide-eyed female backing vocals hinting at the tongue-in-cheek. (In this light, the track could be read as a parody of Marvin Gaye [868], although its context in Kendricks' period output resists such interpretation, "Son Of Sagittarius" [901] and "Girl You Need A Change Of Mind" [916] for example presenting the singer as sexual predator. If a joke were intended at all, it was probably in the form of self send-up.)

**TMG 1004**
**MAGIC DISCO MACHINE**
**Control Tower** (3:18)
(Daniels—McFaddin)
Produced by Frank Wilson
**Release Date**: 12 Sep 1975
**B-side**: Scratchin'
**Position in Record Retailer Top 40**: -
**Equivalent US Release**: Motown 1362 (29 Jul 1975)
**Position in Billboard Top 40 Pop**: -
**Position in Billboard Top 40 R & B**: -

The disco boom was, by 1975, gathering such momentum that it was threatening to conquer all in its path, current hits in the style including "Lady Marmalade" (Labelle), "Walking In Rhythm" (The Blackbyrds), "The Hustle" (Van McCoy), "Jive Talkin'" (The Bee Gees), "It Only Takes A Minute" (Tavares), "Hold Back The Night" (The Trammps), "You Sexy Thing" (Hot Chocolate) and so on. Motown of course was never shy of hopping on a bandwagon and, notwithstanding the drift towards disco revealed in several Tamla Motown singles over the previous few years (*passim*), went the whole hog in 1975 with the release of *Disc-O-Tech*, an album of dance tracks credited to The Magic Disco Machine.

The LP's contents in fact consisted of leftover backing tracks never assigned to acts for vocal overdubs. (In this respect a parallel may be drawn with the earlier work of Earl Van Dyke [506].) Originating from a variety of sources, and with a plethora of musicians left uncredited, the material was assembled and mixed by Russ Terrana in LA, the album's first title consisting of "Control Tower", a Frank Wilson-produced variant on "Get Ready" [557]. Co-written by future song writing star Terri McFaddin, the track is danceable if ultimately something of an experiment, its ceaseless grooves built for the contemporary club circuit.

Motown-UK followed up "Control Tower" in October with "Midnight Rhapsody" (TMG 1055), released just a fortnight after the last Tamla Motown single and billed as William Goldstein & The Magic Disco Machine. Goldstein was a new recruit to Motown, a serious composer whose television themes had caught Berry Gordy's ear. (Goldstein saw another of his recordings issued soon afterwards, "Razzle Dazzle" used as the B-side to Thelma Houston's "The Bingo Long Song" (TMG 1059), a support single for Motown's movie *The Bingo Long Travelling All-Stars And Motor Kings* which Goldstein had scored.)

Thus, the Magic Disco concept was perpetuated, and Motown continued to push their way onto the scene with albums such as *Discotech*, *Motown Discotech No. 2*, *Motown Magic Disco Machine No. 2*, *Motown Discotech No. 3* and *A Motown Special Disco Album*, all following over the next 18 months.

## TMG 1005
## CASTON & MAJORS
### I'll Keep My Light In My Window (3:41)
(McFadden—Caston)
Produced by Leonard Caston
**Release Date**: 26 Sep 1975
**B-side**: Say You Love Me True
**Position in Record Retailer Top 40**: -
**No Equivalent US Release**

Leonard Caston / Carolyn Majors

Written by Leonard Caston with newcomer Terri McFadden [1004], "I'll Keep My Light In My Window" was given to Diana Ross & Marvin Gaye for their collaborative album [879], although their reading didn't make the final cut.[1] Re-recorded by its co-writer, the track was lifted from *Caston & Majors* for a third and final UK single, which also marked the overall end of the duo's Motown discography.

A personal declaration of religious virtuosity, the text deals with a calling to 'help one's fellow man', unpalatably holier-than-thou with its self-sacrificial puritanism. In context, the light in the window is a symbol of Christian hope, signalling a welcoming hand to those in distress, whose worldly plight is apparently no cause for concern against the gift of salvation: the track is pitched in a complacent pop style, almost dancing about the pain of others, which brings forth the welcome opportunity to exercise dutiful redemption. Lapsing further into poor taste, the recording concludes with a ghostly evangelical choir, symbolic of the ascent to heaven—the reward awaiting the song's ecstatic proponent.

ᴵ It has since surfaced as an extra on the CD re-issue.

## TMG 1006
## MICHAEL JACKSON
**Just A Little Bit Of You** (3:08)
(Holland—Holland)
Produced by Brian Holland
**Release Date**: Oct 1975
**B-side**: Dear Michael
**Position in Record Retailer Top 40**: -
**Equivalent US Release**: Motown 1349 (29 Apr 1975)
**Position in Billboard Top 40 Pop**: 23
**Position in Billboard Top 40 R & B**: 4

After the failure of "One Day In Your Life" [946] to break through in 1975, Tamla Motown elected to follow its US counterpart's lead and issue one of the new Holland—Holland compositions as a single.ᴵ A bold piece with a strong melodic frame, "Just A Little Bit Of You" is a catchy number emboldened with brassy marching riffs, and in its sectioned structure shows glimpses of the HDH team's classic style. The track's main contrast arrives through its drop-out middle-8, a tension-filled pause-for-thought before the surface cheer kicks back in, a functional passage reminiscent of similar devices in tracks such as "I Can't Help Myself" [515] and "The Happening" [607].

Ultimately a piece of light fun, the single is devoid of depth but lifts the spirits. What it lacks, and what differentiates it from the writers' famous work, is a sense of exploration; there is no essence of adventure beneath what is a formulaic exercise in pop which progresses logically and regularly and is more reminiscent of HDH's Invictus-period style. (Possibly the Holland brothers were missing Lamont Dozier's creative spark.)

This hit-that-never-was would be Michael Jackson's final outing on Tamla Motown. On his way out the door along with his group [1001], Jackson would spend the next few years of his life consolidating his reputation before establishing himself as one of the major figures of post-war popular music, particularly through *Thriller*, a 1982 opus for Epic which would shift over 100 million, breaking every sales record in the book. His Motown catalogue, while variable, contains several significant cuts and in "One Day In Your Life" [946] a track which would become, courtesy of a 1981 re-issue [L042], his first UK number 1.

ᴵ The others, "Take Me Back" and "We're Almost There" would eventually also appear on 7-inch, released as TMG 976b [L042] and TMG 977 [L043] respectively in 1981. See Chapter 6 for details.

**TMG 1007**
**THE COMMODORES**
**Let's Do It Right** (3:36)
(Richie)
Produced by James Carmichael/The Commodores
**Release Date**: 10 Oct 1975
**B-side**: This Is Your Life
**Position in Record Retailer Top 40**: -
**No Equivalent US Release**

---

Lionel Richie / Thomas McClary / Ronald LaPread / William King /
Walter Orange / Milan Williams

---

The Commodores' first single since "The Zoo" [924] not to be built from a sequenced riff, "Let's Do It Right" finds the group in more reflective mood. Starting with a sensitive descending bass figure, instruments arrive in the mix from the wings, discreet elements exemplified by jazzy brass punctuations and Milan Williams' searing keyboard passage. A tightly wrought production, "Let's Do It Right" hints at an unexpressed tension beneath its mellowed surface, Lionel Richie's controlled low-register vocal sometimes seen as a nod to Sly Stone. (Lead duties are shared in parts with Walter 'Clyde' Orange.)

Pulled by Tamla Motown from *Caught In The Act*, the track was favoured over "This Is Your Life", the group's contemporary American miss. That it fared no better may not have come as a surprise, given the group's inability to penetrate the UK market at this stage, although this change in emphasis hinted at where The Commodores were headed artistically. In any case the group had by now completed their next album, the aptly titled *Moving On*, which would deliver an even gentler follow-up single at the turn of the year [1018].

**TMG 1008**
**WILLIE HUTCH**
**Love Power** (3:29)
(Hutch)
Produced by Willie Hutch
**Release Date**: 3 Oct 1975
**B-side**: Get Ready For The Get Down
**Position in Record Retailer Top 40**: -
**Equivalent US Release**: Motown 1360 (9 Jul 1975)
**Position in Billboard Top 40 Pop**: -
**Position in Billboard Top 40 R & B**: 8

Having made a notable impression with his blaxploitation theme "Brother's Gonna Work It Out" [862], Willie Hutch sought to revive his luck with a soundtrack to Jack Hill's *Foxy Brown* in 1974. However in the wake of the aborted "Tell Me Why Has Our Love Turned Cold" single [885], Tamla Motown lifted nothing from the set, waiting instead until the singer delivered *Ode To My Lady*, released in the UK in January 1976. The appetiser, "Love

Power" emerged in October, Hutch's second and final Tamla Motown single, which came backed with an earlier album track. Why the label shied away from his period singles is unclear; the US Motown organisation sanctioned seven prior to "Love Power" while Tamla Motown themselves had put out four albums to date, the pending *Ode To My Lady* his fifth in not much more than two years.

An R & B hit Stateside, "Love Power" is an attractive mid-tempo celebration of romance which, although cleaving to the minor, remains joyful throughout. Revelling in deep satisfaction, Hutch is exultant, his carefree self-production lifting heavenwards with stings and brass, through softly plateau-ed verses. Yet "Love Power" avoids sentimentality in its implied toughness, Hutch walking through the ghetto streets at night, high on the all-engulfing 'Love Power' which is the primal driving-force of the human spirit, felt 'down to the bones'. (He even pauses for a moment to reflect on what 'causes nations to fight'.)

Despite its appeal, the track failed in the UK and with a frustrating run through the mid 1970s Hutch opted to leave Motown under persuasion from Norman Whitfield, who was in the process of launching his own record label [1013]. No hits ensued however and in due course Hutch came back to Motown. Continuing to record through the 1980s and 1990s, Hutch passed away in September 2005, aged 60.


**TMG 1009**
**GLADYS KNIGHT & THE PIPS**
**Neither One Of Us (Wants To Be The First To Say Goodbye)** (4:15)
**Re-issue of [855]**
**Release Date**: 17 Oct 1975
**New B-side**: Everybody Needs Love [619] / I Wish It Would Rain [674]
**Position in Record Retailer Top 40**: -

---

Gladys Knight / Merald 'Bubba' Knight / Edward Patten / William Guest

---

Closing Gladys Knight's Tamla Motown discography, "Neither One Of Us (Wants To Be The First To Say Goodbye)" was a fourth re-issue in a little over two years and, as with its predecessors, the point was to profit from the group's ongoing series of hits for Buddah. Tamla Motown paired this smoothly dramatic ballad with a double B-side, making for the label's ninth maxi-single (see [803n]). The partner tracks here consist of a couple of former A-sides from 1967 [619] and 1968 [674], making for a release which almost amounts to an EP of hits. Strong though the contents undeniably were, [1009] would not chart, Buddah retaining the lion's share of the market and Tamla Motown seeing their opportunist efforts fail once again.


**TMG 1010**
**DIANA ROSS**
**Theme From Mahogany (Do You Know Where You're Going To)** (3:19)
(Masser—Goffin)
Produced by Michael Masser

---

**Release Date**: 24 Oct 1975
**B-side**: No One's Gonna Be A Fool Forever
**Position in Record Retailer Top 40**: 5
**Equivalent US Release**: Motown 1377 (24 Sep 1975)
**Position in Billboard Top 40 Pop**: 1
**Position in Billboard Top 40 R & B**: 14

Following the success achieved by Motown's first motion picture *Lady Sings The Blues* [848], Berry Gordy and Diana Ross had been besieged by offers from other film-makers, numerous scripts foisted on Motown's boss over the ensuing couple of years. Gordy though was a shrewd mover, and bided his time before committing to a follow-up, which fell into his lap when Motown Productions' Rob Cohen showed him a rough sketch of what would become *Mahogany*. This so impressed Gordy he was won over instantly, describing his decision as a 'no-brainer'.[1] The basic plot centres on the affairs of a fashion model who becomes highly successful and heads off to Rome for a glamour life with an unbalanced photographer, who views her as an objective commodity whom he dubs Mahogany. Eventually returning home to her old love interest in Chicago, via an extra relationship with a wealthy Italian, the moral of the story is the well-worn maxim that money and success do not in themselves bring happiness and are no substitute for love.

The potential for Gordy lay not in the story-line itself so much as the potential for Diana Ross to sparkle, the tale's romantic dimensions affording an on-screen reunion with Billy Dee Williams and, inasmuch as the central character is involved in the world of fashion, a chance for his starlet to be adorned in extravagant gowns and presented as the fantasy *femme fatale*. Massaging Mahogany's lines and scenes to fit around Ross, Cohen hit upon an idea to galvanise her (and ensure she would see the project through), offering her the chance to design the movie's costumes for which Ross was provided with a workshop by Paramount.

Filming got underway in November 1974, the Chicago scenes shot in the middle of a run-down slum district which brought with it dangers from the crime-ridden local environment, not least through the threat of off-set violence and a proliferation of drug abuse. Even within the ranks there was tension in the air, with director Tony Richardson, a well-to-do white Brit, unable to relate to his surroundings and making several pointed remarks which caused offence to the film's stars.[2] At-length, and in a repeat of events during *Lady Sings The Blues*, Berry Gordy removed Richardson from the project and took-over direction himself.

Matters scarcely improved however, Gordy having several personal issues to deal with during filming, including the pregnancy of his latest fiancée Nancy Leiviska (with his eighth child) coinciding with the pregnancy of his star Diana Ross. When filming inevitably shifted to Rome in January 1975, Gordy was hurried back to America by the imminent death of his mother who passed away at the end of the month and, before filming was through in February, Gordy had split from Leiviska.

So far as the soundtrack was concerned, Gordy had spent little time on sourcing material, the bulk of the music consisting of Michael Masser's incidental scores. However he had a theme tune in the frame courtesy of an old Masser song recently prepared in readiness for a vocal track from Thelma Houston, but requisitioned for *Mahogany* in early 1975. Chancing upon it before it was recorded, Masser's friend and Brill Building legend Gerry Goffin re-worked some of the song's lyrics to fit the general movie scenario, earning himself credit as co-composer.

"Do You Know Where You're Going To" was quickly prepared for release on single, two mixes competing for approval until at the last minute Michael Masser physically erased the one he didn't like, ensuring he had his way. A beguiling number with a classically manœuvring melodic profile, the song follows the power ballad style established for Ross with recordings such as "I'm Still Waiting" [781] and "Touch Me In The Morning" [861], both of which had been major commercial successes. Deceptively simple, the ranging melody visits every chromatic note, deftly shifting through its chord changes as the character Mahogany flits from relationship to relationship in search of happiness. And yet in spite of its appeal, the general public initially took no notice of the track, perceived as a flop in America and Britain.

*Mahogany* meantime was released towards the end of 1975 and comprehensively panned by critics, the soundtrack album which appeared alongside it similarly received. (Diana Ross' own views on the movie project are apparent from her autobiography, in which she dwells almost exclusively on her wardrobe design input.) And yet the film surprised a good many, including presumably Ross herself, when it began making a box-office stir, selling-out theatres in America and grossing over $7 million. And slowly, by word of mouth and prolonged public exposure, this elegant theme song began selling, gathering a momentum after the turn of the year which saw the American edition top the national charts for a week at the end of January 1976. The Tamla Motown issue, which had failed to register on chart in 1975 eventually broke into the top 40 the following April, easing its way to a creditable number 5 placing, Ross' biggest UK success bar "I'm Still Waiting" [781] despite the hindrance of unwanted competition from Ross' own "Love Hangover" [1024]. Its public acceptance slow in coming, "Do You Know Where You're Going To", which was nominated for an Academy Award in 1976, has gradually been accepted as one of the singer's definitive 1970s recordings, a contender for the strongest ballad amongst her singles discography.

[1] Gordy, p335

[2] Taraborrelli (1989, p309) makes reference to a perceived racist slight when Richardson referred to the actors as 'you people', causing a fractious exchange with Billy Dee Williams which also resulted in the word 'Sambo' being removed from the script.


**TMG 1011**
**FOUR TOPS**
**Walk Away Renee** (2:42)
**Re-issue of [634]**
**Release Date**: 17 Oct 1975

**New B-side:** You Keep Running Away [623]
**Position in Record Retailer Top 40:** -

---

Levi Stubbs / Lawrence Payton / Abdul 'Duke' Fakir / Renaldo 'Obie' Benson

---

The Four Tops' last Tamla Motown single re-ran the group's late-1967 success [634], paired up with the track which preceded it in their singles discography. This 1975 re-issue serves no real purpose, The Four Tops having failed to score a UK hit for two years now, and Tamla Motown having nothing to plug album-wise. Unsurprisingly the single did not chart, The Four Tops' career having reached an all-time popularity low.

The quartet, who had left Motown in 1972, were currently recording for ABC, who continued to put out one or two singles each year until the group's contract expired. Moving to the Casablanca label in 1981, The Four Tops suddenly re-discovered their touch, placing "When She Was My Girl" at number 3 in the UK (and, at home, at the top of the R & B charts), renewed interest resulting in a shift back to Motown in 1983. The group's line-up remained unchanged through the decades, original members Levi Stubbs, Abdul 'Duke' Fakir, Lawrence Payton and Obie Benson performing together for a total of 43 years until the death of Payton in 1997. The outfit continue to work as a performing band to date, although the passing of time has inevitably brought further changes to the line-up. The group retain a unique place in the hearts of UK soul fans, best-remembered for the HDH years during which they recorded their most enduring hits.

**TMG 1012**
**THE SUPREMES**
**Early Morning Love** (3:11)
(Beatty—Holland—Holland)
Produced by Brian Holland
**Release Date:** 7 Nov 1975
**B-side:** Where I Belong
**Position in Record Retailer Top 40:** -
**Equivalent US Release:** Motown 1391 (16 Mar 1976)
**Position in Billboard Top 40 Pop:** -
**Position in Billboard Top 40 R & B:** -

---

Cindy Birdsong / Scherrie Payne / Mary Wilson

---

After the release of *The Supremes* [950], the group went on the road, almost meeting catastrophe in London on September 5, while staying at the Hilton Hotel on Park Lane. Bombed by the IRA, then engaged on a campaign of similar attacks in the UK (including, the previous summer, a bomb-blast in the Houses of Parliament, and shortly afterwards, the notorious Birmingham Pub attack), the building suffered extensive damage and two people were killed, although none of The Supremes' entourage was hurt.

And they were out of the frying pan and into the fire when they landed in

South Africa for a controversial tour in the apartheid-riven country on September 30, against the advice of several friends and professional peers. Determining to make the tour politically fruitful, the group went out of their way to highlight the predicament faced by black South Africans, visiting the Soweto township and playing to the Teach Every African Child (TEACH) group in Johannesburg. Irritated meantime by the dismissive attitude of the local media, who complained that the apartheid regime was being breached, the group faced overt and covert segregation at concert venues and were forced to carry permits bestowing on them the status of 'honorary whites'. At length, they lost their tolerant resolve and, in speaking their minds to Durban's *Daily News*, Cindy Birdsong and Scherrie Payne precipitated The Supremes' ejection from the country, the situation aggravated by pressure from certain sections of the American black community opposed to the tour.

Meantime, Motown had been prevaricating over the group's singles releases, "Where Do I Go From Here" scheduled in America for the autumn, but pulled before going on sale. In Britain, Tamla Motown were ready to follow up "He's My Man" [950], and picked up on current interest in the album track "Early Morning Love", a number spun liberally by DJs through the summer. Undoubtedly part of its appeal to the label was the magic of the Holland brothers' names in the brackets[1]; after a gap of eight years during which both The Supremes and HDH suffered splits in their ranks, a reunion of sorts was trumpeted as seeming to offer a potentially bright future for both outfits.

The cut, on which Mary Wilson shares lead duties with Cindy Birdsong (as on [950]), has something of the mood of the Holland brothers' contemporary "Just A Little Bit Of You" [1006], with a calculated 'power chorus' and an endlessly recycling chord-run which scarcely deviates, except in a ruminative horizontal middle-8. The song chugs through its verses with calculated propulsion, effectively a device for linking the dominant chorus sections, a thinly veiled celebration of sex on awakening.

As might be expected given its style and target audience, the track's lyrical content is superficial, the casual rhyme of 'wake up' and 'make up' unimaginative and hackneyed (used previously, for example, in "I Say A Little Prayer"[2]). Released in the run-up to Christmas, the up-beat recording was ill-suited to the winter period, the traditional seasonal mood no doubt contributing to its flopping. In America, with "Where Do I Go From Here" permanently shelved, "Early Morning Love" was pulled for the flip to "I'm Gonna Let My Heart Do The Walking" [1029] the following May (as Motown 1391), otherwise slipping past with the minimum of fuss during a difficult period for the group.

[1] The song was co-written with Harold Beatty, drafted in semi-permanently to replace Lamont Dozier in the team.

[2] The lyric name-drops another Bacharach—David number, "The Look Of Love" [844].

**TMG 1013**
**YVONNE FAIR**
**It Should Have Been Me** (3:27)
(Whitfield—Stevenson)

Produced by Norman Whitfield
**Release Date**: 14 Nov 1975
**B-side**: You Can't Judge A Book By Its Cover
**Position in Record Retailer Top 40**: 5
**Equivalent US Release**: Motown 1384 (30 Jan 1976)
**Position in Billboard Top 40 Pop**: -
**Position in Billboard Top 40 R & B**: -

Following her cover of "Funky Music Sho' Nuff Turns Me On" [913] over a year previously, Yvonne Fair was granted a second UK release taken from her debut album, provocatively entitled *The Bitch Is Black*. Like its predecessor, the new single was a cover of an old Norman Whitfield track [660], which its author arranged and produced. Not originally a hit in the UK, the song was ripe for a re-run, Whitfield re-arranging it for Fair with a sparser backing track, built largely on a subtle wah-wah guitar and deeper classical strings. Slowed marginally (and dropped by a semitone), this re-make better emphasises the tortured theme of the lyric, Fair's growling, howling vocals standing out against a severely morose backdrop. Artistically accomplished, the recording was a risky selection for the pop charts, but vindicated Tamla Motown by nestling in the top 5 in the new year. Accordingly, a US release was also prepared which failed to emulate the UK single's success.

This would be Whitfield's final hit for Tamla Motown, as the producer set about following HDH's lead by launching his own record label, Whitfield Records. Taking both The Undisputed Truth and Willie Hutch with him, Whitfield would go on to form Rose Royce from members of Motown's 1970s backing group Total Concept Unlimited, the act scoring major hits in 1976-77 with "Car Wash", followed by "Wishing On A Star" and the UK number 2, "Love Don't Live Here Anymore". Junior Walker was also brought into the fold in 1979. Whitfield Records collapsed in the early 1980s, its chief returning to Motown and a reunion with The Temptations.


**TMG 1014**
**THE UNDISPUTED TRUTH**
**Higher Than High** (3:17)
(Whitfield)
Produced by Norman Whitfield
**Release Date**: 21 Nov 1975
**B-side**: Spaced Out
**Position in Record Retailer Top 40**: -
**Equivalent US Release**: Gordy 7145 (4 Aug 1975)
**Position in Billboard Top 40 Pop**: -
**Position in Billboard Top 40 R & B**: -

Joe Harris / Billie Calvin / Brenda Evans

If "Cloud Nine" [707] was considered daring for its implied references to being stoned, "Higher Than High" / "Spaced Out" dispensed with any obfuscation, stating its subject matter explicitly. ("Higher Than High" was the title track of the group's sixth and final Motown album, its B-side taken from the earlier *Cosmic Truth*.) Released back-to-back with "It Should Have Been Me", the single represented a late spell of interest in Norman Whitfield, despite the fact that "Higher Than High" failed to sell for Tamla Motown.

With its "chick-a boom-boom" backing vocals, the track comes in vaguely in the style of the early Jackson 5, but it rapidly becomes apparent that the recording is anything but fluffy. The production's overall sonic load, coupled with Joe Harris' dark vocals, is as extreme as anything in Whitfield's catalogue, with a gloomy diatonic plunge down the keys thrown in and a suffocating brass instrumental break. Other distinguishing elements can be heard, including the fundamental 'Higher!', recalling not only the similar motif in both "Cloud Nine" [707] and "Superstar (Remember How You Got Where You Are)" [800] but also, tellingly, Sly Stone's "I Want To Take You Higher" (1969) which may in fact have served as a working prototype.

Oppressive next to the glitz and glamour of the fashionable disco trend, the track is doomed by its time and place, Whitfield's admirable attempt to provide depth defeated by his own dark introspection. [1014] would be the last Tamla Motown single to bear his name, and a final outing for The Undisputed Truth, who would eventually score a UK hit outside the Motown stable with Whitfield's own label (see [1013]), "You + Me = Love" making a modest 43 during 1977.


**TMG 1015**
**THE MIRACLES**
**Love Machine (Part 1)** (2:55)
(Moore—Griffin)
Produced by Freddie Perren
**Release Date**: 21 Nov 1975
**B-side**: Love Machine (Part 2)
**Position in Record Retailer Top 40**: 3
**Equivalent US Release**: Tamla 54262 (19 Sep 1975)
**Position in Billboard Top 40 Pop**: 1
**Position in Billboard Top 40 R & B**: 5

---

Billy Griffin / Bobby Rogers / Warren 'Pete' Moore / Ronnie White

---

Comfortably Motown's most successful stab at disco, "Love Machine" emerged from The Miracles' concurrent *City Of Angels*, an ambitious attempt by the group to pay homage to the lifestyles of Los Angeles, the album's title referencing the city's nickname, derived from its literal translation from the Spanish.[1] Besides its famous recreational and pleasure facilities, the vast city of LA is also a focal-point of the American entertainment industry—of which Motown had been a significant part for some years and, in paying their respects here, The Miracles are effectively washing their hands of their past, openly embracing the new West Coast world which they envisaged would be their spiritual home from now on.[2] In this context the LP, and the current single, constitute a psychological milestone not just for the group, but also for Motown itself, the comparative bleakness of Detroit, struggling in the wake of the gasoline crisis of 1973 and the departure of Motown itself, receding into memory.

Consisting of a suite of ten supposedly interconnected tracks, the album aims to recount the adventures of a soon-to-be-famous boy named Michael who heads to the city to recapture his former lover Charlotte, who has fled to be with another man, Michael encountering the city's infamously hedonistic night-life on the way. According to group-members Pete Moore and Billy Griffin, the project was conceived in Hollywood and developed over the span of a year-and-a-half, during which they co-composed the album's entire contents.[3] As a whole, though, the material was somewhat disjointed, and the album's producer Freddie Perren ended up requesting his wife Christine Yarian pen a 'Libretto' for the sleeve, guiding the listener through the twists of the underlying story. (This 'classical' touch married conceptually with certain other elements of the project, including the leading 'Overture' [1023b].)

In any respect, the thread sometimes proceeds tenuously, and one track, "Ain't Nobody Straight In LA", deals openly with the city's gay community, and the consequent induction of Michael. Causing prickles of disquiet around Motown, this daring recording was wilfully masked by Yarian's annotation, where the implication is that the 'straight' of the title in fact refers to simple honesty rather than sexual orientation. (Yarian's claim that the central character is here being dressed for success and stardom falsely suggests that it was written around Michael Jackson's experiences [724], the coincidence of name unmistakeable.) That Motown had recently broached the subject through the one-off Gaiee project (see Appendix 3) may have been a factor in the track's being passed for release, Motown catching up with the times through openly gay stars such as Tony Washington of The Dynamic Superiors, who made no secret of his homosexuality in an era when public admission was beginning to be widely acceptable.

The album's key lift however was to be "Love Machine", a seven-minute opus which served as the lead-track to side 2. A somewhat hastily delivered dance groove for synthesiser, "Love Machine" contains a humorous lyric in which the technological metaphor is used liberally for analogous blowing of fuses and flowing currents, lending the track a light-heartedness which again belies Yarian's laborious analysis. In fact the lyric hints at game-playing by the writers, not only through its droll imagery but also via some classic Motown in-references including the line 'Earth-quaking, soul-shaking' borrowed from "I Got A Feeling" [628], and Bobby Rogers' deep grunting intro, echoing the similar device on "My Baby Must Be A Magician" [639]. (In fact the group appear to have sweated over the details of the song for a protracted period, having re-written it several times before settling on the final form.[4])

Extravagant and in all respects up-beat, the track made a natural choice of single, the only prohibiting factor its extended play time. Following precedents such as [873] and [916], Motown solved the matter by splitting it in two, which while compromising its impact nonetheless afforded a standard 7-inch release, which promptly asserted itself in the chart listings. (Aware of the club circuit's role in elevating tracks such as this into the public consciousness, a promotional 12-inch was also pressed in the States with the full album version, as this new format began to catch on there.) Climbing to number 3 on the UK charts, the hit was the group's biggest bar "The Tears Of A Clown" [745], and at home spent an impressive four-and-a-half months in the top 40, eventually nestling at the summit in March 1976. Easily The Miracles' biggest triumph without Smokey Robinson, "Love Machine" has become their defining late-period anthem, and in the UK was granted a 1988 re-issue [L084], credited to The Miracles Featuring Billy Griffin.

[1] LA was originally part of Mexico, its founder Felipe de Neve declaring it 'El Pueblo de Nuestra Señora la Reina de los Angeles de Porciúncula', which translates to 'The Village of Our Lady, Queen of the Angels of Porciúncula'.

[2] City Of Angels can be seen as an extrapolation of The Four Tops' "L.A. (My Town)" [823b]. It is interesting to compare the concept with Smokey Robinson's "I Care About Detroit" (see [614]) and Junior Walker's "Hip City" [667], both recorded in the Hitsville era.

[3] Davis (1988) p131. The Hollywood theme is presented in the LP's cover art, which features a self-aggrandising shot of what purports to be the group's star on Hollywood's Walk of Fame. (In fact the image is a mock-up.)

[4] Ibid

## TMG 1016
## THE DYNAMIC SUPERIORS
**Deception** (3:17)
(Ashford—Simpson)
Produced by Nickolas Ashford/Valerie Simpson
**Release Date**: 28 Nov 1975
**B-side**: One Nighter
**Position in Record Retailer Top 40**: -
**Equivalent US Release**: Motown 1365 (5 Sep 1975)
**Position in Billboard Top 40 Pop**: -
**Position in Billboard Top 40 R & B**: -

---

George Wesley Peterback / Michael McCalpin / Tony Washington / George Spann / Maurice Washington

---

After the recording of "Shoe Shoe Shine" [929], The Dynamic Superiors entered A & R's New York Studios with Ashford & Simpson to capture some further tracks for their second album *Pure Pleasure*, nine of which were written by the duo. (Not all of the set was new: "Ain't Nothing Like The Real Thing" [655] was given a dramatic overhaul, Paul Riser arranging, and [929] was thrown onto the UK Tamla Motown pressing as an extra.)

The album's opening track was requisitioned for the group's second 45, "Deception" a darkly accusatory number manœuvring between the opposing faces of truth and lies, insinuating a sinister 'smile underneath a smile'. Luring the innocent with lemonade and candies, the musical construct is as deceitful as its subject matter, the throbbing dance style and prettily diaphanous flutes further exercises in concealing the menace which stings beneath its surface. An engaging single, "Deception" was not picked up and proved to be the group's last Tamla Motown release. The Dynamic

Superiors continued recording for Motown until 1977 when they formally disbanded, coming back together for a spell in the mid 1990s at the behest of George Spann.

**TMG 1017**
**DAVID RUFFIN**
**Walk Away From Love** (3:18)
(Kipps)
Produced by Van McCoy
**Release Date**: 5 Dec 1975
**B-side**: Love Can Be Hazardous To Your Health
**Position in Record Retailer Top 40**: 10
**Equivalent US Release**: Motown 1376 (21 Oct 1975)
**Position in Billboard Top 40 Pop**: 9
**Position in Billboard Top 40 R & B**: 1

Confusion exists as to the true sequence of events which led to David Ruffin's recording of "Walk Away From Love", a gentle ballad penned by Charles Kipps Jr. Taken up by Van McCoy and recorded during 1975 for Washington group The Choice Four on RCA, the song was at some stage noticed by Ruffin, presumably in view of his impending collaborations with the producer. However Ruffin has stated that in rehearsals for the track, he was visited by Mick Jagger who requested a rendition of The Temptations' "Ain't Too Proud To Beg" [565], the singer demurring and suggesting that Jagger sing it himself.[1] According to Ruffin, the incident led to The Rolling Stones taping a cover of the track 'a few months later', which was duly released as an American 45 and charted in the top 20. However The Rolling Stones' version was started in 1973 and completed in May 1974, which would mean that if Ruffin's recollections are accurate, he was demoing "Walk Away From Love" during the spring at the very latest, long before The Choice Four's version had surfaced.

Whatever the true facts, Ruffin's collaborations with Van McCoy occurred at an opportune moment. McCoy's *Disco Baby* had appeared during 1975 on the Atco label, featuring the track "The Hustle" which became a surprise disco smash over the summer, placing McCoy firmly in the public gaze. Ruffin's decision to collaborate with him for some New York sessions at Media Sound could not therefore have been better timed, and the two emerged in October with a substantial album in the shape of *Who I Am*.

Filled with commercial potential, the set was ripe for pickings and the first lift was the current single, an easy-swinging pop track with a morose lyric concerning the insecure singer's intent to abandon his loved one. Warmly appreciated across the musical spectrum, the single duly became Ruffin's biggest hit, proudly topping the Billboard R & B charts, going one better than his other commercial success [689]. In the UK the story was similar, the Tamla Motown edition becoming Ruffin's first and only top 10 single. Placing him squarely in the pop mainstream after some moderate years, "Walk Away From Love" signalled a re-birth for the singer, and would be rapidly followed with another lift from *Who I Am* [1022].

[1] As recounted by Ruffin in Abbott, p138.

## TIMELINE – 1975

Tamla Motown release 42 singles and 27 albums. (A further 10 singles and 2 albums are released in the UK on Rare Earth and Mo-West.)
Tamla Motown place 7 singles in the UK top 40. 4 make top 10
Motown fails to put a single at top of US chart for first time since 1962. In UK, Tamla Motown has worst year commercially since 1965
Norman Whitfield leaves Motown
Brian and Eddie Holland recommence working for Motown, as freelancers

| | |
|---|---|
| **Jan 31** | Berry Gordy's mother Bertha dies from brain haemorrhage |
| **Feb** | Jackson 5 return to UK for concert appearances, the group's first since October 1972 |
| **Mar** | Gladys Knight & Pips sue Motown |
| **Mar 1** | Stevie Wonder wins five Grammy awards for the second year running |
| **Mar 6** | Jackson 5 embark on tour of Africa |
| **April 7** | Stevie Wonder's daughter Aisha Zakia born. Name is Swahili for 'strength and intelligence' |
| **May** | Human Kindness Day. Stevie Wonder performs at Washington Monument before 125,000 |
| **May 14** | Jackson 5 inform Berry Gordy of intent to leave Motown. Deal shortly struck with Epic. Jermaine refuses to sign and stays as solo artist |
| **Jun** | Tamla Motown terminate EMI contract with intent of re-launching as UK independent. Enter three months of commercial inactivity |
| **Jul** | Final single released on Rare Earth |
| **Aug** | Stevie Wonder agrees new $13m deal with Motown, up to 1982. Won't sign contracts until following spring |
| **Aug 16** | Marlon Jackson secretly marries Carol Parker. Does not inform family until Jan 1976 |
| **Sep 1** | Due date for Motown's independent distribution to commence. Passes without any new releases and Motown resume with EMI, releasing two new singles on Sep 5 |
| **Sep** | Supremes tour UK. Hilton Hotel bombed by IRA on Sep 5, Supremes inside but unhurt |
| **Sep 10** | Ewart Abner resigns as Motown Records' president to be replaced by Gordy and then Barney Ales |
| **Sep** | Jackie Wilson enters coma from which he never recovers |
| **Sep 30** | Supremes commence tour of South Africa. Are asked to leave country following outspoken comments on apartheid |
| **Nov 4** | Diana Ross' third daughter Chudney Lane born |
| **Dec** | Shooting during Smokey Robinson concert at Apollo Theater. 18-year-old man is killed |
| **Dec 19** | Stax Records is declared bankrupt and dissolved |

**TMG 1018**
**THE COMMODORES**
**Sweet Love** (3:26)
(Richie—Commodores)
Produced by James Carmichael/The Commodores
**Release Date**: 16 Jan 1976
**B-side**: Better Never Than Forever
**Position in Record Retailer Top 40**: -
**Equivalent US Release**: Motown 1381 (25 Nov 1975)
**Position in Billboard Top 40 Pop**: 5
**Position in Billboard Top 40 R & B**: 2

---

Lionel Richie / Thomas McClary / Ronald LaPread / William King / Walter Orange / Milan Williams

---

Entering its final year, Tamla Motown was in clear decline having released just seven top 40 singles through 1975, the label's worst tally since its first year of existence. Musical tastes had moved on and Motown, once pioneers in the field of popular soul, had been overtaken on several fronts and were forced to follow in the footsteps of others.

But it was not just Motown feeling the pressure, similar problems besetting old rivals Stax. Investigated in 1973 by the IRS, Stax had come under increased scrutiny when it emerged that the company was in financial difficulties and unable to pay several staff through 1974. In due course the label ran aground and many of its top artists drifted away, Isaac Hayes amongst several to bring legal proceedings against the company. Stax was eventually forced into involuntary bankruptcy in December 1975, closing an historic era in American music and offering stark warning to Motown as to what can happen when independent companies are allowed to slide.

Motown's hottest discovery of the 1970s were to spearhead their salvation, The Commodores poised to score a string of major hits in the latter part of the decade. In this context, "Sweet Love" can be seen as a key release, the group charting in the US top 10 for the first time with what was a clear shift to the popular centre-ground, as heralded by their previous single [1007].

"Sweet Love" was recorded for the group's late-1975 album *Movin' On*, in a version running to well-over six minutes. Trimmed for single, this soft-focussed production benefits from impressionistic close-harmonies by Richie and the group, and a sprinkling of sound effects inserted in largely self-produced sessions. Swaying through its underlying major 7ths, the track resembles in character J J Cale's "Magnolia", a popular title from his *Naturally* album (1971). Richie raises hackles only in the track's final verse, a plea to keep searching for the elusive love, a determined call to fulfil the promise of the song's tranquilising opening lines. Issued in the UK seven days ahead of Smokey Robinson's defining new single [1019], "Sweet Love" inadvertently walks away from Motown's past, opening the UK's 1976 discography in portentous style.

**TMG 1019**
**SMOKEY ROBINSON**
**Quiet Storm** (3:49)
(Jones—Robinson)
Produced by Willie Hutch
**Release Date**: 23 Jan 1976
**B-side**: Asleep On My Love
**Position in Record Retailer Top 40**: -
**Equivalent US Release**: Tamla 54265 (21 Nov 1975)
**Position in Billboard Top 40 Pop**: -
**Position in Billboard Top 40 R & B**: 25

Released in mid 1975, Smokey Robinson's *A Quiet Storm* had become his first solo hit on the US album charts, and spawned a successful spin-off single in "Baby That's Backatcha" [949]. The set's title track was also to some extent a declaration of artistic aims, Robinson having set about a collection with coolly understated intensity offering a relaxed surface shine. Welcomed by fans, *A Quiet Storm* had caused what its title predicted, giving rise to a late-night radio-friendly format and taken up as the title of a regular Washington broadcast by DJ Melvin Lindsey. (Appropriately enough, the title track to Robinson's album was the first disc spun on the show.) Still influential today, the musical mood is all-pervasive on night radio, characterised by "smooth, mellifluous, jazzy soul"[1]; Robinson's achievement in this respect amounts to the establishment of a sound-concept, 'Quiet Storm' a sub-genre within soul, and therefore within the more general style which is Motown's own.

Running to 7:47, the track's inevitable selection for 45 necessitated yet another editing job, a strategy which was becoming commonplace, this the third such exercise among Tamla Motown's last five releases ([1015]; [1018]). "Quiet Storm" was co-written with Robinson's sister [898], the lyric revolving around Robinson's ongoing affair with Meta and recorded during his separation from Claudette. (Robinson later referred to Meta as 'the quiet storm I felt blowing through my life'[2], indicating that the track might literally be a narrative on their relationship.)

Blown by the winds of his emotion, the centred tranquillity of "Quiet Storm", while inspired by his estrangement, was nonetheless indicative of a soul at rest. Robinson was, come 1976, finding his level, re-uniting with his wife and about to move into a new phase of his professional career, having over-immersed himself in the business side of Motown for some time. Ready to throw his energies back into his natural talents, Robinson signed new contracts as a recording artist in March, and focussed his personal life back on his family. (His forthcoming solo album was entitled *Smokey's Family Robinson*, the allusion to Johann David Wyss' novel disguising the fact that he was in fact publicly resolving his personal contradictions.)

One of Robinson's next projects was a failed musical with Willie Hutch. *Cotillion* was abandoned unfinished but, with this singular exception, he was to enjoy commercial success over the ensuing years, culminating in his biggest hit "Being With You" (TMG 1223, a UK chart-topper in 1981). Robinson also assembled a backing group by the name Quiet Storm, who in the early 1980s would record for Motown in their own right, evidence that this particular track, and the sound-world it opened up, was of long-range significance to the singer who, above all others, was a pillar of Motown's success both in the studio and behind the scenes. Robinson continues touring and performing at the time of writing, his boundless love of music undiminished by the passing of the years.

[1] Peter Doggett in *Record Collector* 266, October 2001, p64.

[2] p209


**TMG 1020**
**STEPHANIE MILLS**
**This Empty Place** (3:21)
(Bacharach—David)
Produced by Hal David/Burt Bacharach
**Release Date**: 20 Feb 1976
**B-side**: If You Can Learn How To Cry
**Position in Record Retailer Top 40**: -
**Equivalent US Release**: Motown 1382 (1 Dec 1975)
**Position in Billboard Top 40 Pop**: -
**Position in Billboard Top 40 R & B**: -

Having been influential on Motown from the outset [581]; [801]; [844], Burt Bacharach and Hal David came briefly into the fold in 1975, working on a debut album for Stephanie Mills, a New Yorker brought in by Jermaine Jackson after having toured with The Isley Brothers. Working closely with her writer-producers, Mills assembled ten recordings, eight new Bacharach—David numbers and two remakes. Of the pair of oldies, "Loneliness Remembers (What Happiness Forgets)" conforms generally to Dionne Warwick's 1970 original and sits comfortably with the rest of the collection; "This Empty Place" by contrast is an updated reinterpretation, agitated with a dominant percussion track which detracts from the elegant simplicity of Warwick's 1963 recording whose title refers to a mourning lover's empty arms.

Released in October 1975 as *For The First Time*, Mills' album made no significant impression, the US trailer-single "This Empty Place" failing to attract any further attention. Aware of the situation, Tamla Motown scheduled the track for [1020], coupling it with the album cut "I See You For The First Time" in line with the US edition, and a few demo copies were manufactured. Hesitant over the release, they then opted to press further copies with the new composition "If You Can Learn How To Cry" included as the B-side, which were distributed within the industry and correspond to the commercial pressings.

There is however some residual uncertainty about the structure of the release, which appears to be a standard single. However the second demo in circulation carries the telling A tag on both labels, indicating that it may have been intended as Tamla Motown's only standard double A side, or conversely that the decision on which side to plug remained open until the last minute. The partner track, "If You Can Learn How To Cry", is perhaps the more attractive cut, its mid-tempo melodicism marrying its composers' classic style with Motown's late penchant for soft soul, although it lacks the punchy impact of its eventual A-side.

For Mills' part, her career was in a state of slump almost before it had begun. Agreeing to appear in *The Wiz* was her only further involvement with Motown, who let this promising star escape. Mills would go on to score several hit singles elsewhere, most notably "Never Knew Love Like This Before", a transatlantic top-tenner in 1980 for 20th Century. She also enjoyed no fewer than five R & B number 1s in the 1980s, something Motown could only view from afar with envy; had they shown more commitment in 1976, they could have bagged this esteemed performer for themselves. As it is, her Bacharach—David-produced album, and this sole single, represent nothing more than a footnote in the history of Tamla Motown, slipping by unnoticed at a time when Motown could have sorely done with a success story to celebrate.

## TMG 1021
### EDDIE KENDRICKS
**He's A Friend** (3:22)
(Felder—Gray—Conway)
Produced by Norman Harris
**Release Date**: 6 Feb 1976
**B-side**: All Of My Love
**Position in Record Retailer Top 40**: -
**Equivalent US Release**: Tamla 54266 (16 Jan 1976)
**Position in Billboard Top 40 Pop**: 36
**Position in Billboard Top 40 R & B**: 2

Following a succession of disappointingly meagre album sales, Eddie Kendricks' solo career required a kick-start, a plan being hatched to send the singer to Philadelphia for his next project in an attempt to capture something of the positivity in the air. *He's A Friend* was the result, recorded in collaboration with Norman Harris, one of the star session men and producers from the Gamble—Huff stable and a founder-member of Philadelphia International's studio band MFSB (see [890]).

A half-disguised salutation to the Lord, the album's title track is a disco-flavoured gospel hymn penned by three of Philadelphia's regular staff, Allan Felder, Bruce Gray and T G Conway. (Felder also arranged the vocals on the recording.) Punching exultantly through its energetic verses, "He's A Friend" is vigorous where "If Anyone Can" [1003] had been downcast, the recording pushing its way up the US R & B charts through March and April and confirming Kendricks' view that the move to Philadelphia was worthwhile. Released to indifference in the UK, the single failed to register, Kendricks unable to score a sizeable hit for Tamla Motown.

## TMG 1022
### DAVID RUFFIN
**Heavy Love** (3:14)
(McCoy—Cobb)

Produced by Van McCoy
**Release Date**: 19 Mar 1976
**B-side**: Rock 'n' Roll (Are Here To Stay)
**Position in Record Retailer Top 40**: -
**Equivalent US Release**: Motown 1388 (6 Feb 1976)
**Position in Billboard Top 40 Pop**: -
**Position in Billboard Top 40 R & B**: 8

Occupying back-to-back catalogue numbers with his former band-mate, David Ruffin's new single was a second lift from *Who I Am* [1017] aimed to capitalise on his recent high-profile. Stemming from the same New York sessions as "Walk Away From Love", "Heavy Love" was co-authored by its prestigious producer in collaboration with regular partner Joe Cobb. Coincident with [1021], the track has an unmistakeable gospel overtone, borrowing heavily from "Rock My Soul" in its chorus lyric (see also [502]; [741]). Boosted by the presence of Faith, Hope & Charity on backing vocals, the recording fuses traditional Afro-American songs of praise with the ongoing disco style almost seamlessly. As with his erstwhile partner's contemporary release, the track appealed mainly to R & B crowds without crossing over.


**TMG 1023a**
**THE MIRACLES**
**Night Life** (3:15)
(Moore—Griffin)
Produced by Freddie Perren
**Release Date**: 26 Mar 1976
**Position in Record Retailer Top 40**: -
**Equivalent US Release**: Tamla 54268 (May 1976)
**Position in Billboard Top 40 Pop**: -
**Position in Billboard Top 40 R & B**: -

Billy Griffin / Bobby Rogers / Warren 'Pete' Moore / Ronnie White

The Miracles' *City Of Angels* had appeared in the UK in November 1975 [1015], spawning the group's biggest hit recording of the 1970s. This glaring success aside, one of the more purposeful compositions on the set was used to close side 1, "Night Life" celebrating the city's vibrant party culture, characterised here by neon lights, cabaret, pool parties and of course 'the hippest chicks'. (The lyric also makes specific mention of Hollywood Boulevard, which prompted the album's cover art.) As with the rest of the album, "Night Life" is largely constructed on a dance foundation, with an enterprising chord sequence through its chorus. Benefiting from Scot Edwards' pounding bass guitar, the recording succeeds in capturing an appropriate sense of self-indulgence, yet with a palpable tension beneath its surface glamour. This double-edge can be understood in the context of Christine Yarian's ongoing account of the album's sequence: ostensibly the point at which the character

Michael is searching the party circuit for his Charlotte, his impatient unease lends an edginess to what might otherwise be a hedonistic nocturnal jaunt. (Whether the effect was pre-conceived is another matter.)

"Night Life", for all its celebratory elements, turned out to be a commercial disappointment after [1015] and would be the group's final single for Motown on either side of the Atlantic, followed by one further studio album in late 1976, *The Power Of Music* an unmitigated flop. Suddenly running out of steam, the act made a surprise shift to Columbia at the start of 1977, after which a couple of uneventful albums ensued, the group wrapping up in the early 1980s. With and without Smokey Robinson, The Miracles released at least one single during every calendar year the Tamla Motown label was running, their tally of 20 (excluding re-issues) making them one of the label's true stalwarts, their quiet departure a sorry conclusion to their illustrious tenure.

Producer Freddie Perren would shortly be gone too, scoring a notable triumph with Gloria Gaynor's "I Will Survive" which he co-wrote and produced with Dino Fekaris. The track topped the UK and US charts in 1979, and is regarded as a classic of the disco era.


## TMG 1023b
## THE MIRACLE WORKERS
**Overture** (3:10)
(Moore—Griffin)
Produced by Freddie Perren

Opting to couple "Night Life" with the parent album's "Overture" (The US edition had carried "Smog" as the flip), Tamla Motown had lined up an instrumental ill-suited for billing under the name The Miracles. The label were therefore compelled to list the B-side as by The Miracle Workers, the name given to the studio ensemble who recorded the set under direction of Freddie Perren. Thus, the billing follows a precedent set with [931b], citing the session musicians as an act in their own right and thereby worthy of particular mention here.

The recording itself commences with a slowly evocative prelude with angelic backing vocals from Carolyn Willis and Julia Tillman, before blossoming into a pleasant discotheque instrumental by the full band, whose cadenced ending gives way to ocean sound effects, illustrative of LA's seething beach life. The group itself was a fluid congregation, and the precise line-up on this particular track is not known. However the single most striking musical feature, a resounding orchestral kettle drum, is attributed to Paulinho Da Costa, a Brazilian percussionist who would become prolific as a session man, his CV including subsequent work on Michael Jackson's *Thriller*.[1]

Through the rest of their time as a performing outfit, The Miracles would routinely credit their backing group as The Miracle Workers, a happy pun which publicly acknowledges the importance of group musicianship, all too often regarded as dispensable next to the high profiles of star acts—Motown a pertinent historical case study in this respect.

*City Of Angels* as a whole cites the band as, John Barnes (keyboards), Scot Edwards (bass), Ed Greene and James Gadson (drums), Eddie 'Bongo' Brown and Paulinho (percussion), Victor Feldman (vibes) and Billy Griffin, Donald Griffin, Greg Poree and James Graydon (guitars). The album's producer Freddie Perren is credited with synthesiser and vibes.


**TMG 1024**
**DIANA ROSS**
**Love Hangover** (3:40)
(Sawyer—McLeod)
Produced by Hal Davis
**Release Date:** Apr 1976
**B-side:** Kiss Me Now
**Position in Record Retailer Top 40:** 10
**Equivalent US Release:** Motown 1392 (16 Mar 1976)
**Position in Billboard Top 40 Pop:** 1
**Position in Billboard Top 40 R & B:** 1


But for the title track of the *Mahogany* film [1010], Diana Ross' recording career had been in stasis for more than two years, during which time Tamla Motown had continued to exploit her popularity with a succession of singles, some of which were aging recordings, including most of *Diana & Marvin*. During the period, Ross' marriage to Bob Silberstein had become strained, a bright spot in her personal life arriving in November 1975 with the birth of her third daughter, Chudney Lane.¹ Yet the happy event brought no resolution for the parents and Silberstein left Ross once the baby was born, the latter promptly filing for divorce.

Against this backdrop, Ross the single mother-of-three set about compiling a new album for release in early 1976, which would be her first since *The Last Time I Saw Him* (see [893]). The consequent set found Ross asserting her new independence with the simple title *Diana Ross*, unfortunately repeating the name originally given to her solo debut from 1970.² Recorded at Motown's Hollywood studio with a variety of producers working under Berry Gordy's supervision, *Diana Ross* was to become a commercial success, helped by the inclusion of "Theme From Mahogany" [1010] as its opener.

This late exposure for Ross' late-1975 release helped finally push it into the UK charts, entering the top 40 on April 3 and climbing to number 5. Meantime, the US Motown label, as normal ahead of its UK counterpart, were sourcing a follow-up and had elected to pluck "I Thought It Took A Little Time (But Today I Fell In Love)" [1032] from the new LP, for a speculative February single. *Diana Ross*, though, had been drawing attention from several quarters and a decisive moment occurred when Motown learned that The Fifth Dimension had identified "Love Hangover" as a potential hit, and promptly announced the release of their own version on 45.

The timing was unfortunate. Realising they had missed out, Motown promptly issued an edited version of Ross' rendition which, owing to the recent release of "I Thought It Took A Little Time", made for two US singles in the space of a few weeks. In the UK the clash was equally problematic,

"Love Hangover" put out just as [1010] was finally breaking, and with which it would have to compete in the listings. Disgruntled by the incident, Ross went as far as to release a white label promotional edition of the track (as PSR 399) personally lambasting The Fifth Dimension for 'stealing' her song.[3] Yet however inconvenienced, Ross and Motown ought to have been grateful for the turn of events. Pressurised into the release, they watched "Love Hangover" top the US charts and go top 10 in Britain, poor timing not standing in the way of what became a highly popular hit single. ([1010] and [1024] were listed together in the UK top 40 for a run of five weeks.)

Penned by Pam Sawyer and Marilyn McLeod, "Love Hangover" was in effect two songs melded together. The first section, running to around 2:40, consists of a gently soulful love song, Ross close-miked and breathily sensuous. Viable in its own right, the track might have ended up as another straight ballad, and would undoubtedly have succeeded as such, were it not for Hal Davis' plan to turn it into a disco track. Thus the recording comes alive in its second half, an exaggerated coda which runs around for a further five minutes, recorded with flashing lights suspended in the studio. Ross' sense of enjoyment on this section is unmissable, her vocal play and laughter evidence that during the session, she and Davis were mildly drunk and revelling in a chance for some free expression at Motown's expense. Boosted by washy percussion and a driving bass riff from Eddie Watkins, the resultant instrumental spun the original conception joyfully off kilter, the editing of the two disparate sections into a gargantuan whole a matter of supreme judgement by the producer.

Notwithstanding the plaintive attraction of the song's orthodox first section, when the decision was made to release the track on 45 it was the front-end of the single which was largely excised, the lengthy 'disco' portion making the bulk of the mix. Why Motown elected to deploy the recording this way is a mystery; not only is Sawyer—McLeod's original composition attractive, the obvious solution of splitting the track across two halves in the manner of several recent precedents seems not to have been considered, despite the fact that it would have preserved the integrity of each element.

For Ross, the single's spectacular success came at an opportune moment, her viability as a recording star in question after a protracted time away from the studio. With a successful album and hit singles piling on one another, the early part of 1976 saw her career flourish again, the period remembered for a European tour in March and April which took in several UK dates and which was followed by a summer *Greatest Hits* package which climbed to number 2 on the UK album charts. Ross was back, almost accidentally re-invented as a disco performer, and achieving high acclaim for her period work.

"Love Hangover" is her pivotal recording of the mid 1970s, launching her into the second half of the decade with a vengeance. This popular track was put out by Tamla Motown again on 45 in 1985 [L070], and was re-mixed three years later by the then-massive PWL team for a blue label release (see Appendix 2).

[1] According to Taraborrelli (1989, p327) she was to be called Chutney, the registrar mis-spelling the name on her birth certificate.

[2] She was to make use of her personal stature repeatedly during her career. Besides the two different *Diana Ross* albums, she also released *Diana!* (1971), *Diana & Marvin* (1973), *Ross* (1978), *Diana* (1980) and *Ross* (1983).

³ As part of The Supremes, Ross had worked with and covered songs by The Fifth Dimension: see [607n] and [704].

**TMG 1025**
**YVONNE FAIR**
**It's Bad For Me To See You** (3:29)
(Sawyer—Jones)
Produced by Gloria Jones/Pam Sawyer
**Release Date**: 14 May 1976
**B-side**: Walk Out The Door If You Wanna
**Position in Record Retailer Top 40**: -
**Equivalent US Release**: Motown 1344 (17 Apr 1975)
**Position in Billboard Top 40 Pop**: -
**Position in Billboard Top 40 R & B**: -

Yvonne Fair's third and last Tamla Motown single was another lift from *The Bitch Is Black* [1013], which in keeping generally with her earlier singles was initially conceived for Gladys Knight & The Pips. Following the success of "If I Were Your Woman" [765], Gloria Jones and Pam Sawyer had come up with the notion of a concept album for Knight written largely around her earlier hit, on which "It's Bad For Me To See You" was to be included. However Knight was busy elsewhere and the two were unable to have her version released¹, leaving the song in the can for some years before the opportunity to work with Yvonne Fair presented itself.

Fair's version is a loaded matter, with a searing vocal in which one can almost hear her weeping, the lyrical subject apparent from the song's title. Similar in mood to "It Should Have Been Me" [1013], the recording is as emotionally intense—close to method acting—with an emphatic orchestral backing pushing the limits of her pain, in a dynamic mix with creative stereo panning. The most attractive of her three Tamla Motown singles, if only for the fact that it was new to public release, "It's Bad For Me To See You" locks in with her discography to date, and in the wake of its predecessor may have been a hit. Sadly it missed out, despite being coupled with a former US single cut, and has since been largely forgotten. Fair did not record again for Motown and is remembered in the UK primarily for "It Should Have Been Me" [1013]. (A comparable hit eluded her in the States.) She died in June 1994, aged 51.

¹ It has since surfaced on CD.

**TMG 1026**
**MARVIN GAYE**
**I Want You** (3:53)
(Ware—Ross)
Produced by Leon Ware/T-Boy Ross
**Release Date**: 30 Apr 1976
**B-side**: I Want You (Instrumental)

**Position in Record Retailer Top 40**: -
**Equivalent US Release**: Tamla 54264 (16 Mar 1976)
**Position in Billboard Top 40 Pop**: 15
**Position in Billboard Top 40 R & B**: 1

During 1975, Marvin Gaye elected to spend a small fortune on a luxury estate near Hollywood, which was to become home to him and his future wife Janis, their daughter Nona [923], and eventually a second baby, Frankie (known as Bubby) born on November 16. The palatial accommodation boasted stables, a swimming pool and a basketball court, plus parking for Gaye's ever-expanding fleet of high-class cars as the singer attempted to adopt a life of affluent domesticity. According to published accounts, Gaye was spending much of his time in the mid 1970s consuming copious quantities of cocaine and lounging in bed until midday, his sporadic recording work slotting into moments when he felt in the right mood and had nothing better to do.

Yet while this hedonistic existence on one level speaks of a man entirely fulfilled, as was often the case with Gaye, his life was racked with contradictions. Simultaneously pursed by his ex-partner Anna for child support, Gaye either claimed poverty or refused outright to co-operate, his failure to meet her demands landing him in court. Meantime he was continuing to display alarmingly unstable behaviour, exemplified by his sudden decision towards the end of 1975 to shave off all his body hair, including his beard, which he accounted for to associates as a 'protest' in support of Rubin Carter.[1]

In-between acrimonious meetings with his estranged wife, Gaye was able to find sanctuary in the studio, working extremely slowly on what was to become *I Want You*. The project at-hand, his long-awaited follow-up to *Let's Get It On* [868], came about as a result of Berry Gordy's determination to give Gaye a shove in the right direction. Stumbling across the track "I Want You", penned by Leon Ware [606] and Arthur 'T-Boy' Ross, brother of Diana, Gordy suggested Gaye tackle a version himself, and tapes were duly exchanged. Wildly enthused, Gaye promptly met with Ware to listen to more work-in-progress, and in no time agreed to record an entire album in collaboration, which was commenced at Motown's studios.

Work on the project was haphazard as weeks turned into months, Gaye and his cohorts too listless to get to grips with anything substantial. Lolling around Gaye's mansion was too great a temptation, and as the first-half of 1975 was spent, little got done. At some point during the year, Berry Gordy appears to have tried a spur, investing in a custom studio for Gaye which was located not far from the company's main facility on Sunset Boulevard. The move was calculated on Gordy's part; having seen Stevie Wonder come up with extraordinarily successful self-directed albums, and having been starved of substantial product from Gaye since *Let's Get It On*, he predicted that given equal freedom of expression, Gaye might just be able to focus himself on something new and comparable to his early 1970s output. Gaye also started his own production company called Right On, and although it appeared that he was preparing for serious work, his lackadaisical mood prevailed and the album was still not complete by the start of 1976.

Part of the problem was Gaye's self-management in which there was little day-to-day pressure on him. Almost inevitably the Marvin Gaye Studio became a sort of recreational centre, hangers-on taking advantage of the studio's plush interior in which Gaye had spent much of his time having a jacuzzi installed and designing a bedroom complete with water bed. Likened by David Ritz to a Playboy apartment[2], the facility was employed for the rest of the *I Want You* sessions, the assembled musicians effectively hanging-out there continuously for months on end, until the album was eventually wrapped-up in the new year.

How much effort Gaye was prepared to invest in the project can be glimpsed by his input. Apart from handling vocals, his principal contribution to the album was assistance with the lyrics to just four songs[3], Gaye not interested in directing his own work and content to resume the role of vocalist on someone else's material—something he had once fought against with determination. The fact was that Gaye, pampered through an almost endless stream of disposable income (most of which he succeeded in disposing of) and contented with his own past success, had little need to expend effort.[4] Nonetheless, Gaye was said to be proud of *I Need You* in 1976, citing it as amongst the best he had produced in the face of a comparatively cool critical reception. (In America, the album eventually charted two places higher than *What's Going On* had.)

The title track and first spin-off single testifies to the protracted manner in which recording was undertaken. Gaye's take of "I Want You" was commenced as a jam on 21 February 1975, re-visited on eight separate occasions over March, May and June, before being overdubbed on four further dates late in the year, accounting for roughly eight months from start-to-finish. Yet the resultant cut sounds as fresh as if it had been nailed in a single day, the fusion of guitars, vocals and throbbing percussion meshing into something with real direction, Coleridge Taylor Perkinson's arrangement capturing Gaye's patent sensualism and providing a semi-erotic, husky sound-world 'with overtones of Barry White'.[5]

But while the composition steers discreetly towards the harmonic shapes of "Mercy Mercy Me" [802], whose major 7th chords echo across the verses, the track had initially appealed to Gordy as a vehicle for Gaye because of its lyrical content. While in sound and form a continuation of Gaye's period approach, beneath the surface the track speaks of a deep insecurity, the singer engulfed in unrequited desire. And while hearing the single in the context of Gaye's mid 1970s work obscures the track's import, the lyric in fact shows a depth of expression absent from his recent singles which, coupled with the accomplishment of its recording, makes "I Want You" arguably his most affecting release since [802] itself.

Issued along with the "Intro Jam" from the *I Want You* album, billed here as an 'instrumental version', the single had obvious commercial potential and succeeded in scaling America's R & B listings in May. In Britain however, it followed the rest of Gaye's singles since 1970 [734] in failing to make a mark on the upper-reaches of the charts, although over the years it has earned some belated recognition: in 1991, Robert Palmer recorded a medley of "I Want You" and "Mercy Mercy Me" to score a UK top 10 hit, and subsequent readings by a host of other artists including both Madonna and, in 2007, Diana Ross, have kept the composition alive.

[1] Carter was a boxer convicted of murder, but widely regarded as having been framed. His case drew high public attention in 1975 after Bob Dylan recorded the track "Hurricane" in his defence.

[2] p273

[3] These being "Feel All My Love Inside" [1035b], "Since I Had You", "Soon I'll Be Loving You Again" and "After The Dance" [1035].

[4] His next album *Here My Dear* (1978) was driven by a requirement for financial payments to his former wife, which he sought to fund by settling the score with her on vinyl, and it would not be until 1981 when he next produced a straight self-composed album *(In Our Lifetime)*, his last ever studio-set for Motown. See [846n] for Gaye's own comments on his loss of impetus.

[5] Ritz, p271

## TMG 1027
## JUNIOR WALKER
**I'm So Glad** (3:18)
(Holland)
Produced by Brian Holland/Lawrence T. Horn
**Release Date**: 23 Apr 1976
**B-side**: Dancin' Like They Do On Soul Train
**Position in Record Retailer Top 40**: -
**Equivalent US Release**: Soul 35116 (5 Jan 1976)
**Position in Billboard Top 40 Pop**: -
**Position in Billboard Top 40 R & B**: -

Marking the start of Junior Walker's emergence as a solo artist, "I'm So Glad" was his first release not to bill The All Stars, despite the concurrent album *Hot Shot* being listed as a group effort.[1] In fact, this track was one of a number first cut by Brian Holland for a solo release on Invictus, leading the producer to return to his original band track and re-mix it with Walker's saxophone and vocals overlaid, thereby accounting for the absence of the group on the record's billing.[2]

A bristling R & B stomper, "I'm So Glad" is here updated for the disco market, in keeping with Motown's contemporary approach. Driving with its dance groove, Walker's vocals are at least equal in presence to Holland's accomplished original, but it is in the trademark instrumental passages that Walker surpasses his mentor. As presented here, "I'm So Glad" is a worthy addition to Walker's catalogue, sitting happily between his raw dynamic and the contemporary music scene in which he was attempting to rescue a flagging career. (Walker had seen nothing released in the UK in two years [894], his last studio album emerging a full three years previously.)

Not a hit single, "I'm So Glad" was an undeserved flop on both sides of the Atlantic. For Walker though, the release was the start of a new phase, *Hot Shot* to be followed by the solo *Sax Appeal* before the end of the year. Almost seeing out the 1970s with Motown, Walker departed for Whitfield Records in 1979 [1013], returning to Motown after the venture collapsed. Adored by Northern Soul fans, Walker was saluted with an all-too-brief slot at the *Motown 25* event in 1983, his death from cancer in 1995 finally silencing this prolific musician whose Motown output spanned three decades. Although generally overshadowed by Motown's more polished stars, Walker is recognised as one of the label's greats, his Tamla Motown catalogue of 20 singles including several genre classics such as "Shotgun" [509], "(I'm A) Road Runner" [559], "How Sweet It Is (To Be Loved By You)" [571] and "What Does It Take (To Win Your Love)" [712].

[1] In fact *Hot Shot* features none of the authentic All Stars, the band line-up consisting of Mike Wiggins, Marvin Crowell, Danny Saunders and Jackie Ivory. While The All Stars rarely appeared behind Walker on vinyl after 1969 [712n], the open billing of other session musicians, and the solo credit for Walker on the single, were significant.

[2] During the sessions Walker also tackled a rendition of "Why Can't We Be Lovers", which had given Lamont Dozier a surprise solo hit for Invictus in 1972.


**TMG 1028**
**EDWIN STARR**
**Time** (2:56)
**Re-issue of [725]**
**Release Date**: 30 Apr 1976
**Position in Record Retailer Top 40**: -


The last Tamla Motown re-issue in the label's main run appeared in the spring of 1976, Edwin Starr's 1970 release [725] put back on-sale with its original B-side unchanged. Several years since his only major hits [672]; [754], Starr's career had been on the slide for some time, and in 1975 he followed several of his colleagues (including his producer on "War") in leaving Motown, signing instead with the small Granite label for the tellingly titled *Free To Be Myself*. (His material was leased through Bradleys in the UK.)

Why Tamla Motown singled out "Time" in 1976 is not apparent. Possibly they sensed a resurgence of interest with his career on the move once again, but it would be some time before he had another commercial success on his hands. Following a switch to 20th Century in 1977, he scored with "Contact", number 6 in 1979 and "H.A.P.P.Y. Radio", number 9 that same year, and was adored by the UK's Northern Soul crowds throughout. Starr continued recording and performing during the remainder of his life, enjoying another minor UK hit in 1993 with a remake of "War". He died in 2003 following a heart attack at his Nottingham home.


**TMG 1029**
**THE SUPREMES**
**I'm Gonna Let My Heart Do The Walking** (3:33)
(Beatty—Holland—Holland)
Produced by Brian Holland
**Release Date**: 7 May 1976
**B-side**: Colour My World Blue
**Position in Record Retailer Top 40**: -
**Equivalent US Release**: Motown 1391 (16 Mar 1976)

| Susaye Greene / Scherrie Payne / Mary Wilson |
| --- |

Former Supreme Florence Ballard had suffered depressing poverty and emotional stress through the mid 1970s and was on prescription drugs for several ailments at the start of 1976. Discovered unconscious on the floor of her Detroit home on February 21, Ballard had suffered a cardiac arrest caused by a blood clot, and was duly rushed to hospital. The following morning it was announced that she had passed away, aged 32. Her funeral took place on February 27, with thousands of fans and mourners surrounding the New Bethel Baptist Church, Stevie Wonder and Diana Ross in attendance. That the singer, who had been an integral part of one of popular music's biggest acts, ended her life in such an ignominious way has been to Motown's eternal shame, her case frequently cited as evidence of the company's alleged lack of care for its performers.

News of her death reached Mary Wilson and the other Supremes at yet another crisis point for the group, not long after the debacle of their South African tour [1012]. Following the excitement of working with Brian and Eddie Holland again, The Supremes had convened to create what would become *High Energy*, a disco-oriented set with several creditable cuts. However as a performing act, The Supremes were flagging and, after a run of small and poorly attended gigs, a disenchanted Cindy Birdsong exited the camp for a second time.

Mary Wilson was determined to persevere with The Supremes and elected to pull in yet another singer who duly arrived in the form of Susaye Greene, a vocalist recently spotted by Wilson's husband/manager Pedro Ferrer. With *High Energy* in the can, The Supremes were faced with the prospect of releasing an album featuring a lead singer no longer in the act, Greene consolidating her arrival by overdubbing the album's title track, plus the first trailer single "I'm Gonna Let My Heart Do The Walking" which therefore features four Supremes. Released in April in America (and in the UK in May), *High Energy* was almost entirely written and produced by the Holland brothers with Harold Beatty and offered a lifeline to The Supremes whose position was, at least, recoverable.

An up-tempo dance cut, "I'm Gonna Let My Heart Do The Walking" was embraced by the disco movement as one of Motown's more successful ventures, although it could not stand its ground beside "Love Machine" [1015]. The production, arranged by James Carmichael, makes a feature of the pounding bass line, on which are superimposed Melvin Ragin's wah-wah guitar licks and, central to the sound, a relentless and hypnotic splash cymbal courtesy of James Gadson. Bang up to date, the single became a late success for The Supremes, scraping into the US top 40, a feat which the group had not managed since 1972 [821]. The single's popularity also drew attention to its parent album, *High Energy* considered one of the group's better post-Ross efforts.[1]

With this positive streak The Supremes were on a momentary high, and rapidly set about recording their first studio set with Greene, *Mary, Scherrie &*

*Susaye* emerging in October with Berry Gordy for once taking more than a passing interest. However a revival was not on the cards and Ferrer would shortly arrange for Mary Wilson, the only original Supreme in the act, to exit the group completely. Resigned to her fate, Wilson prepared psychologically for a solo career through 1977, during which she made her final appearance as a Supreme, pregnant and out of love with Ferrer.

The group's farewell concert was staged in England, The Supremes appearing at the Drury Lane Theatre in London on June 12, 1977. Broadcast by national radio, the gig was well-received, and saw the act return to their hit repertoire with songs such as "Love Child" [677] and "Someday We'll be Together" [721], on which none of the present line-up had originally featured, as well as a swathe of vintage HDH hits. Still unclear at this point where her future lay, Wilson surprisingly attempted to organise a South American Supremes tour in July but ended up running into opposition from her former band-mates, who had already said their public goodbyes. Consequently, she headed off for a series of shows billed as 'Mary Wilson Of The Supremes', performing with Debbie Sharpe and (again!) Cindy Birdsong.

The move merely drew out the group's demise, Wilson's solo career still in waiting and Motown unsure on whether The Supremes were officially on their books. In due course it became apparent that the act finally done and, despite endless rumours of reunions over the years and the emergence of an act known as Former Ladies of the Supremes (FLOS), the group who racked up 12 American number 1s, the most by anyone bar Elvis and The Beatles, was no more. They remain the most prolific act on Tamla Motown, with 33 standard singles on the label and a stack of re-releases taking their all-time tally towards 50.

[1] Ironically, "I'm Gonna Let My Heart Do The Walking" became better-known for its use by the American Heart Foundation as a promotion for public health and exercise.

## TMG 1030
## THE BOONES
**My Guy** (2:56)
(Robinson)
Produced by Mike Curb
**Release Date**: 9 Jul 1976
**B-side**: When The Lovelight Starts Shining Thru' His Eyes
**Position in Record Retailer Top 40**: -
**Equivalent US Release**: Motown 1389 (27 Feb 1976)
**Position in Billboard Top 40 Pop**: -
**Position in Billboard Top 40 R & B**: -

---

Debby Boone / Cherry Boone / Lindy Boone / Laurie Boone

---

This wholesome, all-American Christian outfit consisted of four sisters, Cherry, Lindy, Debby and Laurie, daughters of legendary rock and roller Pat Boone. With his recording career having dried up through the 1960s, Boone re-emerged in the early 1970s as an evangelical country performer, releasing albums such as *Songs For The Jesus Folks* before being recruited to Motown's Melodyland label in 1974. With him came his family group, who went variously by the names The Boone Family, The Boone Girls and The Boones and were assigned to the main Motown label in the US. In the UK, the outfit were diverted to Mo-West, releasing "Please Mr. Postman" and "When The Lovelight Starts Shining Thru' His Eyes" in 1974-75, both remakes of early Motown tracks ([E05]; [E34]: see Appendix 3). Tamla Motown picked up the act in the summer of 1976 for the release of another oldie, re-issuing on the B-side one of the group's former Mo-West singles.

"My Guy" is an innocently sweet remake of Mary Wells' famous original which but for some swooning strings does little to deviate from its template, bar a very brief 'country' guitar break. Arranged by Al Capps, the track is lightly delivered by Debbie Boone, her relaxed vocal contrasting with the relatively formal classicism of Wells'. As with the recent arrival and departure of star-in-waiting Stephanie Mills [1020a], Motown then let Debbie Boone in particular slip away without exploiting her potential. Come late 1977 she would be atop the US singles charts for a monumental ten weeks with "You Light Up My Life", recorded for Warners. Although the track didn't break the top 40 in Britain, it showed that in issuing [1030], Tamla Motown had recognised something vital in The Boones, a matter of judgement which defied their parent company's fading interest.


**TMG 1031**
**EDDIE KENDRICKS**
The Sweeter You Treat Her (4:50)
(Drayton—Turner—Akines—Bellmon)
Produced by Norman Harris
**Release Date**: 25 Jun 1976
**B-side**: Happy
**Position in Record Retailer Top 40**: -
**No Equivalent US Release**


Pulled from *He's A Friend* [1021], "The Sweeter You Treat Her" is the most obviously Philly-flavoured number released on Tamla Motown. Given the team behind the sessions this should come as no surprise, producer Norman Harris interpreting a track written by Jerry Akines, Johnnie Bellmon, Victor Drayton and Reginald Turner, who comprised Philadelphia soul outfit The Formations. (The group scored a belated 'Northern' hit with "At The Top Of The Stairs" shortly after metamorphosing into The Silent Majority, as whom they recorded for HDH's Hot Wax label in the early 1970s.)

Consequent of its background, "The Sweeter You Treat Her" is replete with recognisable Philadelphia ingredients, from the opening 'stepping gliss', reminiscent of the similar device on The Stylistics' recent "Can't Give You Anything (But My Love)" to its slow-footed wah-wah guitar. And with Kendricks' high-soaring vocal, the track comes through as a gentle hymn, bathed in soft-edged harmonies and smoothly ebbing strings. A serenely captured moment of musical poise, "The Sweeter You Treat Her" implores male listeners to value their women partners, the singer having learned his lesson the harsh way. (Whether by intent or chance, the writers here remind us that this is a Motown recording with the line 'My whole world ended', pointing back at Kendricks' former band-mate's [689].)

Coupled up by Tamla Motown with Caston—Wakefield's "Happy" taken from *The Hit Man* (and not to be confused with Michel Legrand's [848a]), this UK-only release would be Kendricks' final outing for the label. Although he continued recording for Motown for a couple more years, in 1978 he joined the ongoing exodus with a move to Arista followed by another to Atlantic. His 1980s work is best-remembered for a reunion with The Temptations and a joint album and several noted live shows with David Ruffin. Kendricks died in 1992, the year after his erstwhile colleague, a victim to lung cancer.


**TMG 1032**
**DIANA ROSS**
**I Thought It Took A Little Time (But Today I Fell In Love)** (3:18)
(Masser—Sawyer)
Produced by Michael Masser
**Release Date**: 25 Jun 1976
**B-side**: After You
**Position in Record Retailer Top 40**: 32
**Equivalent US Release**: Motown 1387 (20 Feb 1976)
**Position in Billboard Top 40 Pop**: -
**Position in Billboard Top 40 R & B**: -


With the US edition of "I Thought It Took A Little Time" having been forestalled earlier in the year (see [1024]), the number had yet to be effectively tested in the market, something Tamla Motown often relied on in advance of their own track selection. However they took a punt on the recording themselves in June, releasing the single coincident with Diana Ross' imminent UK tour. Having declared 'Diana Ross Month' in July, Motown re-pressed much of her back catalogue in a bid to push the singer's profile as much as possible, her healthy sales over the past year to a great extent keeping Tamla Motown in profit as the label's overall returns declined. And yet amid the concerts and publicity stunts, "I Thought It Took A Little Time" managed comparatively meagre returns, charting at a peak of 32, the last time Tamla Motown would place a standard release in the UK top 40. (The single appeared on chart on July 10, showing for the last time on August 7.)

The track itself however dates back to some point in 1975, penned by Michael Masser and Pam Sawyer and recorded for the then imminent *Mahogany* project [1010]. Taped by Ross in preparation for a full-scale soundtrack album, "I Thought It Took A Little Time" was shelved along with several others when it emerged that the material in the offing was insufficient to fill out a whole LP. Instead, the track was added to a small stockpile of recordings which appeared on *Diana Ross*, along with "After You", selected here as the B-side.[1]

Co-penned by Masser, the track maintains the power ballad style which to-date had made for most of Ross' major solo successes (including [1010]). Characteristically balancing its carefully premeditated musical shifts, the overall mood of the piece is 'classical', flowing through chiselled instrumental phrases and matching the changing moods of the narrative as it proceeds: commencing with a downcast statement of acute self-doubt, a momentum gradually gathers through the opening verse as the singer confesses a love that brings a metaphorical awakening until in its chorus the track comes into a positive bloom, reaching outwards rather than looking in. Never over-stretching itself, the song is ultimately restful, strings and woodwind gliding across the sky and serving the centred poise of the lyric, but only narrowly avoiding over-sweetness towards its finale.

Lacking the melodic colouring of [1010], the track is ultimately less memorable, perhaps doomed by the circumstances of its release which saw it follow-up the disco-oriented "Love Hangover" [1024]. This concluding piece in Diana Ross' Tamla Motown discography brought the curtain down discreetly, the singer having racked up 15 solo singles to date, all but "Good Morning Heartache" [849] going top 40. One of Motown's most popular assets in the 1970s, Ross would shortly perform a series of record-breaking Broadway shows, and in September appear at LA's Ahmanson Theater, as commemorated by the double LP *An Evening With Diana Ross*.

Divorced later in the year[2], Ross was heading into the late-1970s with a fresh impetus, her professional career on an all-time high. After appearing in Motown's *The Wiz* (1979), she resumed work with Ashford & Simpson for *The Boss*, and enjoyed several major hit singles and albums over the following decades. Ever-active, she continues to be a major attraction at the time of writing and, including her work with The Supremes, has placed at least one single in the UK charts on every calendar year between 1964 and 1996, a unique accomplishment.

[1] The other *Mahogany*-era recordings on Diana Ross are "To Love Again" and "Together", as well as the film's title track.

[2] She filed her application on the day [1032] was released.


**TMG 1033**
**G C CAMERON**
Me And My Life (3:39)
(Ross—Gibbs)
Produced by T. Boy Ross/Leon Ware
**Release Date**: 16 Jul 1976
**B-side**: Act Like A Shotgun
**Position in Record Retailer Top 40**: -
**No Equivalent US Release**

With The Spinners opting to depart in 1971 (see [766]), their lead vocalist found himself in an odd position, signed to Motown in his own right but with the rest of his group out of contract. The consequence was that when The Spinners signed to Atlantic, George Curtis Cameron stayed behind and embarked on a solo career which had been largely unintended. Commencing in August 1971, his US output to date ran to eight singles released initially on Mo-West and from 1973, on the US Motown label. While he failed to score a hit with any of these, he made a minor incursion into the R & B charts in late 1975 with "It's So Hard To Say Goodbye To Yesterday" (Motown 1364), which gained publicity from its inclusion in the contemporary film *Cooley High*, a comedy drama about two black students whose soundtrack was replete with 1960s Motown recordings.

Following the increase in public exposure which this brought, Cameron was afforded a second solo album[1], simply entitled *G C Cameron* and including in its contents the former movie hit and a version of "Include Me In Your Life" [890b], besides "Me And My Life" which would become a UK debut single. (Tamla Motown elected to couple the track with "Act Like A Shotgun", Cameron's US-debut release from 1971 on Mo-West.) A casually moving disco ballad, "Me And My Life" came through the same Ross—Ware stable as "I Want You" [1026], the connection with Diana Ross' brother possibly coming about as a result of Cameron's marriage to Berry Gordy's sister Gwen (formerly the wife of Harvey Fuqua) which embedded him in the Motown family. Pleasant but ultimately unspectacular, "Me And My Life" was not a hit, and would be Cameron's only UK single (barring a collaboration with Syreeta in 1979 (TMG 1094)).

Leaving Motown shortly thereafter, he continued to record for a number of labels (including MotorCity [683n]), and in 2000 re-united with The Spinners. He has since been recruited to a modern incarnation of The Temptations, but will always be remembered primarily for his vocal work on "It's A Shame" [755], easily his biggest professional success.

[1] His first was *Love Songs And Other Tragedies*, released in America only in November 1974.

**TMG 1034**
**THE COMMODORES**
**High On Sunshine** (3:09)
(Richie—McClary)
Produced by James Carmichael/The Commodores
**Release Date**: 27 Aug 1976
**B-side**: Thumpin' Music
**Position in Record Retailer Top 40**: -
**No Equivalent US Release**

---

Lionel Richie / Thomas McClary / Ronald LaPread / William King / Walter Orange / Milan Williams

---

Long-standing act The Commodores had been slow in breaking into the musical elite, but of late their albums and singles had started to sell particularly well, signalling to Motown that they in fact had a potentially major group on their hands. Yet to make a significant impact in Britain, The Commodores had enjoyed a first US top 10 single in February [1018] and seen their last two albums break into the American top 40. In June 1976, Motown released *Hot On The Tracks*, which contained another hit-in-waiting in the form of "Just To Be Close To You", which for reasons unclear was declined by Tamla Motown in favour of the album's "High On Sunshine". (Both discs shared the same choice of B-side.)

But in fact, "High On Sunshine" was a viable contender for the group's first big UK hit, a mid-tempo ballad with a hint of "Ain't No Mountain High Enough" [751] in its end-of-verse figures. A self-assured commentary on the joy of loafing, "High On Sunshine" celebrates the pleasures of a lazy afternoon, but with a hint of rebellion which serves as a reminder of the generational conflicts of the 1960s. The singer is 'stone free', hinting at cannabis indulgence with further period-cultural references to 'fancy colours' and 'rainbow shades'. And like the era it seems to reference, the carefree enjoyment is double-edged and comes with a knowing warning in its second verse, foretelling storms for the people unable to see right from wrong. Shifting to a pensive paroxysm against the futility of work for its middle-8, the track moves around its subject matter eventfully (if somewhat disjointedly), and with its radiant flush is the group's most engaging A-side to date.

That "High On Sunshine" failed to score was disappointing, but the group were on the verge of success with "Easy" which would deliver them a UK top 10 hit in 1977 (TMG 1073), with a couple of Tamla Motown-era tracks thrown onto the B-side [902]; [944]. From here, the future for The Commodores was bright, the act scoring several major hits over the next few years, including the number 1 "Three Times A Lady" in 1978 (TMG 1113), which consolidated their status as Motown's most important find since The Jackson 5 by becoming their biggest-selling UK single to date. Come 1981, Lionel Richie was ready to embark on a solo career which brought yet further success through the decade with two number 1 albums and, in "Hello", a chart-topping single which set another Motown-UK record with six weeks at the top in 1984 (TMG 1330). The biggest thing on Motown's hands for the next ten years, The Commodores and Lionel Richie almost kept the company's decline at bay for some time as the unforgiving 1980s gradually overtook the label.


**TMG 1035**
**MARVIN GAYE**
**After The Dance** (3:28)
(Gaye—Ware—Ross)
Produced by Leon Ware/T-Boy Ross
**Release Date**: 20 Aug 1976
**B-side**: Feel All My Love Inside
**Position in Record Retailer Top 40**: -
**Equivalent US Release**: Tamla 54273 (15 Jul 1976)
**Position in Billboard Top 40 Pop**: -
**Position in Billboard Top 40 R & B**: 14


The shady introduction to "After The Dance" announces this gently swaying love song with a sense of uncertainty, revealing the composition's guarded undercurrent. Finding his fantasy figure on the dance-floor, Gaye catches the woman of his dreams through half-glimpses, framed in coloured lights and moving evasively between the silhouettes of the surrounding throng. Singing as if through his mind's vision, Gaye begins with the declaration "I Want You" (referencing back to [1026]), before gradually closing in for the kill, his pervasive desires projected onto his lady. The track is vague as to whether his passion is requited: declaring that 'Morning came so soon', it is open as to whether the couple had spent the night together, or Gaye had merely marked the hours watching this semi-apparition from afar. In this context, the gently pattering drums can be heard as a ceaseless clock bringing the dance to a close as dawn rises, leaving the singer unfulfilled.

Recorded by Leon Ware for *I Want You*, the recording was made in at least seven separate sessions ranging between September 1975 and January 1976. (And as with his previous single [1026], the album also carries an independent instrumental version.) Released by Tamla Motown towards the end of August, the single neatly coincided with Gaye's European tour which arrived in the UK on September 27 for a show at the Royal Albert Hall.[1] Supported on the excursion by Rose Banks [1037], Gaye's last British tour until 1980 made for a parallel with Ross' current career [1030], a live album ensuing in 1977, capturing his opening night on vinyl. The set contains the only recording of "Jan", a homage to Gaye's long-term lover whom he would marry at the start of 1977.

Recording his ill-willed *Here My Dear* in order to raise funds to settle his former wife's alimony claims, Gaye whiled away the remainder of the 1970s before finding a new lease of life when he finally terminated his tense relationship with Motown, signing to Columbia in 1982 for a brief spurt of activity which generated the hit single "Sexual Healing" (released in the UK on CBS). Gaye would enter his final year temporarily back in the bosom of the 'family' for *Motown 25*, before a fight with his father resulted in his being shot and killed on the first day of April 1984, one day short of his 45th birthday.

[1] Famous for cancelling at the last minute, Gaye almost withdrew from the UK leg, citing concern over the demands he would make on Britain's temporarily rationed water supplies at the tail-end of a famously blazing summer.


**TMG 1036**
**DAVID RUFFIN**
**Discover Me** (4:03)
(McCoy)
Produced by Van McCoy
**Release Date**: 13 Aug 1976
**B-side**: Smiling Faces Sometimes
**Position in Record Retailer Top 40**: -
**No Equivalent US Release**

Following the successful New York sessions with Van McCoy which had spawned *Who I Am* [1017], Ruffin had returned to Media Sound with the same writer-producer, and backing group and Faith, Hope & Charity [1022] to record *Everything's Coming Up Love*. Released over the summer, the LP was almost all McCoy's work, Tamla Motown hoping to prise another hit single frm Ruffin as they had with "Walk Away From Love".

"Discover Me" is a curiously sorrowful matter if aimed at disco crowds; in Van McCoy's text, Ruffin is wearing a mask of happiness to screen the reality of emotional pain caused by loneliness. This theme, returned to time-and-again by songwriters, was employed on several occasions at Motown including [693] (The Isley Brothers) and [745] (The Miracles) and is re-stated here, on the opener to Ruffin's new album. Musically unadventurous and lyrically uninspired (Ruffin declares himself a 'lonely island'), the recording comes off for the textures of its production with Faith, Hope & Charity's flush backing harmonies, glistening with delicate bells, setting off Ruffin's dramatic rasp in which one can almost hear his larynx tear.

With one of Ruffin's most penetrating vocals, "Discover Me" was noted by Tamla Motown for this UK-only release, its title inadvertently hinting that the track was a plea for a hit. The recording was coupled with his version of "Smiling Faces Sometimes" [789]; [832] pulled from *Me 'N Rock 'N Roll Are Here To Stay* [936], the track better-known for an earlier recording by Ruffin's former band. Well-captured but not commercial enough to become a chart success, "Discover Me" marks the closure of Ruffin's Tamla Motown opus. Over the ensuing couple of years he would remain on the label before leaving for Warners in 1979.[1] Further success was to elude Ruffin, who found himself imprisoned for tax offences in the early 1980s, and he ended up reuniting with The Temptations in 1983 followed by a period of touring and recording with his old pal Eddie Kendricks under contract to RCA. Ruffin later also recorded for MotorCity, but was to die from a cocaine overdose on tour in 1991.

[1] His first album for the new label appeared around the same time that news was breaking that Van McCoy, his collaborator on "Discover Me", had died of a heart attack.

## TMG 1037
## ROSE BANKS
**Darling Baby** (3:34)
(Holland—Dozier—Holland)
Produced by Jeffrey Bowen
**Release Date**: 20 Aug 1976
**B-side**: Whole New Thing
**Position in Record Retailer Top 40**: -
**Equivalent US Release**: Motown 1404 (16 Sep 1976)
**Position in Billboard Top 40 Pop**: -
**Position in Billboard Top 40 R & B**: -

Born in March 1945, Motown's latest 'discovery' was a seasoned performer by the time she joined the company, happening to be born into a family which included brothers Sylvester and Frederick Stewart, who would go on to create and perform in Sly & The Family Stone (Sly being Sylvester's alias). Rose Stewart, or Rose Stone as she was better-known, was vocalist and keyboard-player for the group from 1968, and became noticed for pointedly donning a blonde wig on stage. While Sly & The Family Stone had been massively influential in the late 1960s and early 1970s (particularly, in Motown's case, on Norman Whitfield [707]), by the mid 1970s it seemed they had run their course and the group was more-or-less wound-up.

For Rose's part, she had married the group's volatile minder Hamp 'Bubba' Banks, who was instrumental in extracting her from the dissolving outfit and having her signed, as Rose Banks, to Motown in 1976. Offering a set of ready-made tracks for a proposed album, Bubba got the deal on condition that some Jobete copyrights were added in, which were duly recorded and credited to Bubba Productions Inc. The first product to emerge was the US single "Whole New Thing", a Motown original which appeared in America during April (Motown 1383). Next came the full album named simply *Rose* (the title presumably omitting 'Banks' in view of her changing surname) containing nine tracks, one of which was the old HDH number "Darling Baby" [551b], formerly used as the title of The Elgins' only Motown album. (Adapted from "Let's Talk It Over", a very early Lamont Dozier cut for Anna Records[1], this HDH re-working went high in the R & B charts in the hands of The Elgins but remained largely unknown in the UK where "Put Yourself In My Place" [551] was preferred.)

"Darling Baby" is a standardised doo-wop number, containing in its lyric the phrase of other Motown tracks, "It Should Have Been Me" [660] and "My World Is Empty Without You" [548]. Why it was selected by Banks is not obvious, although its archetypal 1950s chords set to a modern production clearly appealed to Tamla Motown in an era when Showaddywaddy were making a career out of such remakes.[2] In America, Motown were treading safer ground, selecting the Bubba Banks composition "Right's Alright" as the follow-up to "Whole New Thing" (Motown 1404), and utilising "Darling Baby" for a flip.

Ultimately a curiosity, [1037] failed to sell despite Rose Banks' profile being upped considerably in the UK thanks to her touring duties as support for Marvin Gaye [1035]. This would be her only UK single for Motown, although Banks stayed in the business as a backing vocalist, later working with Michael Jackson on his *Bad* album (1987).

[1] Anna 1125 was released in February 1961, Dozier going by the name Lamont Anthony.
[2] The group were in the midst of a run of major hits, which in 1977 included "You Got What It Takes", an early Motown-sourced hit for Marv Johnson co-written by Berry Gordy, which Showaddywaddy took to UK number 2.

## TMG 1038
## THE ORIGINALS
**Down To Love Town** (3:39)
(Daniels—Sutton—Wakefield)
Produced by Frank Wilson/Michael Sutton
**Release Date**: 17 Sep 1976
**B-side**: Just To Be Close To You

**Position in Record Retailer Top 40**: -
**Equivalent US Release**: Soul 35119 (15 Jul 1976)
**Position in Billboard Top 40 Pop**: -
**Position in Billboard Top 40 R & B**: -

---

Freddie Gorman / Walter Gaines / Ty Hunter / Henry "Hank" Dixon

---

By late summer 1976, it was apparent that Motown were about to re-brand, a move which would result in the creation in the UK of the blue Motown label and with it the termination of Tamla Motown. Seeing this coming, EMI gathered a carefully thought-out set of two dozen recordings spanning between "Dancing In The Street" [E54] and "You Are Everything" [890], and released them as a souvenir collection of 12 singles on September 3, resulting in a couple of last-minute chart incursions for the black label (see Chapter 6 for further details).

And as if to underline the poignancy of the moment, the next standard release belonged to The Originals, a group whose associations with Motown can be traced back to the very beginnings (see [592]). Having seen no UK singles put out in several years, The Originals had, like G C Cameron [1033], recorded prolifically through the early and mid 1970s with a good number of records issued at home. Tamla Motown by contrast had ignored everything after "God Bless Whoever Sent You" [822] until *California Sunset* in mid 1975 which they issued without pulling a trailer single.[1] And by the time they got around to issuing "Down To Love Town", The Originals may have well been a different act, this out-and-out disco dancer having little in common with the group's gentle early singles.

Written by Kathy Wakefield with Donald Daniels and Mike Sutton, "Down To Love Town" was originally included on the group's *Communiqué*, released in the US in May 1976, and in the UK contemporaneously with the single. A dance-floor smash, the recording rose up *Billboard's* short-lived disco charts to number 1, prompting the group to try for a second, even better version. Eventually appearing on an album of the same name, "Down To Love Town" in its new form became Motown's first American 12-inch single, backed with Jermaine Jackson's "Let's Be Young Tonight" [1040].[2]

From here, The Originals fell into abeyance and a UK single pencilled in as TMG 1066 was left unreleased. Come 1978 they had left Motown for the Fantasy label, C P Spencer welcomed back into the act after several years away [822]. Sadly Ty Hunter died in 1981, but the group would go on to record for MotorCity [683n], and have become an established touring stage-act despite the loss of other original members.

[1] The album was made in collaboration with Lamont Dozier at ABC, indirectly bringing him back into the fold just as his erstwhile colleagues the Holland brothers were making a similar move [946]. Dozier wrote and produced the set.

[2] The record appeared as M 00001 in November, over a year before the UK arm first utilized the 12-inch format. A British pressing later appeared as a 12-inch promo (PSLP 190), with the two versions of "Down To Love Town" on either side.

**TMG 1039**
**JERRY BUTLER**
**The Devil In Mrs Jones** (3:10)
(Smith)[1]
Produced by Mark Davis
**Release Date**: 24 Sep 1976
**B-side**: Don't Wanna Be Reminded
**Position in Record Retailer Top 40**: -
**Equivalent US Release**: Motown 1403 (19 Aug 1976)
**Position in Billboard Top 40 Pop**: -
**Position in Billboard Top 40 R & B**: -

Alongside new signing Rose Banks [1037], the recruitment of Jerry Butler brought to Motown an experienced performer with an accomplished history. Having moved from Mississippi to Chicago in his childhood, Butler had the fortune to meet Curtis Mayfield through his local church and in the 1950s the two formed the bedrock of a group going by the name The Roosters. Snapped up by Vee Jay, for whom Ewart Abner then worked, The Roosters were re-named The Impressions and, with Butler afforded top billing, released a couple of R & B hits including "For Your Love", which was certified gold.

For Butler though, the group was working against his desire to be a solo performer, and he left the act in 1958, embarking on an illustrious solo career which bagged him more than a dozen US top 40 hits in the 1960s, in parallel with the Curtis Mayfield-led Impressions who enjoyed similar success over the same period. (Butler's first solo release was on Ewart Abner's own Abner label, following which he returned to Vee Jay, later moving to Mercury.) During the period, Butler also briefly crossed paths with Motown, touring with Tammi Terrell when she was spotted by Harvey Fuqua [561] and later teaming-up with Gamble—Huff for *The Iceman Cometh* which included the top 10 hit "Only The Strong Survive", although in due course the pair would depart to form Philadelphia International [890], leaving Butler in limbo. Come 1975, Butler was out of contract, but old associate Ewart Abner picked him up and brought him to Motown, where he signed contracts on 28 April 1975.

Butler's first release for Motown was *Love's On The Menu*, a ten-track affair which included "I'm Goin' Left" [926] and appeared in June 1976. Lifted as a trailer-single was the coupling "The Devil In Mrs. Jones" / "Don't Wanna Be Reminded", Tamla Motown happy to follow their American counterparts in speculating on this well-known new arrival. Almost inevitably, though, the new material steered Butler towards the all-engulfing disco realm, "The Devil In Mrs. Jones" a punchy dancer built largely on a major 7th foundation. A prolonged joke about infatuation with an infernal lover, the track plays with rhymes and phrases liberally, glimpsing her 'ugly charms' and visiting a local gypsy for guidance. Fun from start to finish, "The Devil In Mrs. Jones" fits the disco idiom in its skewed way, a sort of demented cousin to Billy Paul's 1972 hit for Philadelphia International, "Me And Mrs Jones", although it is likely that the title is borrowed from an infamous 1973 porn movie directed by Gerard Damiano.[2]

This chancy release went nowhere on chart, and nothing further was lifted from the album. Motown continued to back the singer, however, and a couple more albums were recorded before he was teamed with Thelma Houston for a couple of sets of duets. With no substantial return on their investment, Motown let Butler go in 1978, and he signed to Philadelphia for a reunion with Gamble—Huff where he continued recording despite diversifying into local politics. Butler was inducted into the Rock And Roll Hall Of Fame along with the other Impressions in 1991.

[1] Elsewhere the track is credited to Smith—Ellis—McEastland, although the UK 45 cites Smith alone.

[2] The move is entitled *The Devil In Miss Jones*. The connotation is unfortunately compounded by the decision of 1980s porn actor Paul Siederman to adopt the professional name Jerry Butler after hearing the singer's "Only The Strong Survive" on the radio.

## TMG 1040
## JERMAINE JACKSON
Let's Be Young Tonight (3:48)
(Daniels—Smith)
Produced by Michael L Smith/Don Daniels
**Release Date**: 1 Oct 1976
**B-side**: Bass Odyssey
**Position in Record Retailer Top 40**: -
**Equivalent US Release**: Motown 1401 (5 Aug 1976)
**Position in Billboard Top 40 Pop**: -
**Position in Billboard Top 40 R & B**: 19

Just shy of release number 500[1], Tamla Motown closed its account with a new single from Jermaine Jackson, his first since 1973 [874]. His career resurrected after the rest of the Jackson brothers exited Motown a year earlier [1001], he had released the self-proclaiming *My Name Is Jermaine* over the summer, leading-off with "Let's Be Young Tonight", a slightly smarmy-sounding cabaret-disco track which made a minor dent on the R & B charts. As with the opening seconds of [501], the recording aptly fits its position in the release sequence, background chatter filtering through as the lights come up and car horns sound outside as if deliberately calling time on the Tamla Motown singles *œuvre*. With [1040] the party was finally over, and Tamla Motown was made a part of musical history.

It is fitting that the singles discography, which began with The Supremes and HDH, James Jamerson and Benny Benjamin jamming down at Hitsville, should terminate with a light disco number recorded in Hollywood, Los Angeles, the label having played itself out over the intervening 11 years. And it is apt too that it should sign off through an unpremeditated spin-off of the Jackson-Gordy union [874] which in itself tells the story of how Motown, and with it Tamla Motown, had metamorphosed in that time. Through the rest of the decade and into the 1980s, Motown would persevere and score several major hits albeit, in the eyes of many, as just another record company.

[1] Depending how they are counted, the number varies slightly. 495 TMG numbers were utilised in the main run but four were not put on general sale, and several others were re-released with their B-sides promoted. The actual number is best counted as the tally of TMG numbers made available to the public: 491. However If one were to add in the dozen issued in September 1976 as a commemorative box set (see [1038]), the count rises to 503 by the end of 1976, and has surpassed the 600-mark inclusive of those issued in the years since (see Chapter 6), totalling 610 at the point of writing.

## TIMELINE – 1976

Tamla Motown release 23 singles and 29 albums. (A further 3 singles and 2 albums are released in the UK on Rare Earth and Mo-West.)
Tamla Motown place just 2 new singles in UK top 40, its worst-ever tally. 1 makes top 10. (Two late-1975 releases also make top 10 in January and another in April)
Cindy Birdsong leaves Supremes for second time, replaced by Susaye Green

| | |
|---|---|
| **Jan 10** | Miracles: "Love Machine" enters UK top 50 (peak 3) |
| **Jan 15** | Michael Jackson gives evidence in lawsuit against Motown |
| **Jan 17** | David Ruffin: "Walk Away From Love" enters UK top 50 (peak 10) |
| **Jan 24** | Diana Ross: "Theme From Mahogany (Do You Know Where You're Going To)" number 1 in US (one week) |
| **Feb 22** | Ex-Supreme Florence Ballard dies in hospital from heart failure. Buried on Friday Feb 27 |
| **Mar 6** | Miracles: "Love Machine" number 1 in US (one week) |
| **Mar 14** | Diana Ross commences five-week European tour billed as 'An Evening With Diana Ross' |
| **Apr 3** | Diana Ross: "Theme From Mahogany (Do You Know Where You're Going To)" enters UK top 50 (peak 5) |
| **Apr 6** | Stevie Wonder re-signs at midnight in $13m deal |
| **Apr 23** | Junior Walker: "I'm So Glad" / "Dancin' Like They Do On Soul Train" first solo release, with Brian Holland |
| **Apr 24** | Diana Ross: "Love Hangover" enters UK top 50 (peak 10) |
| **May 29** | Diana Ross: "Love Hangover" number 1 in US (two weeks), is Motown's 39th single to top US charts. More follow in subsequent years |
| **Jun 25** | Diana Ross files for divorce from Robert Silberstein (aka Bob Ellis) |
| **Jul** | Mo-West label winds up |
| **Jul** | Motown declares 'Diana Ross Month' and re-releases numerous albums |
| **Sep 27** | Marvin Gaye embarks on first UK tour, seven dates, supported by Rose Banks |
| **Oct 1** | Final Tamla Motown single (bar re-issues), "Let's Be Young Tonight" by Jermaine Jackson. UK Motown label launched seven days later with TMG 1053, "Try Love From The Inside" by Táta Vega |

# Summary of era [839] to [1040]

The final four years of the Tamla Motown label cover the period in which Motown itself settled in the new surroundings of its Los Angeles base. Recording there off-and-on from the early 1960s, LA had gradually lured Berry Gordy, and in his wake went Diana Ross and, bit by bit, most of his empire. In the 1960s, Motown's LA sessions tended to take place at Armin Steiner's Hollywood studios [515], and in due course they made use of several other local facilities including The Sound Factory and Record Plant. Motown opened its own permanent studio off Santa Monica Boulevard in 1972, designed with input from Guy Costa and nicknamed Hitsville West.

Once the Detroit studios were abandoned, Motown did not attempt to revive the principle of a permanent house band, and most producers would book their own freelancers for recording projects. Sometimes sessions would involve various Funk Brothers who had migrated west, but frequently each producer would have his own circle of players, resulting in the dissipation of the company's once distinctive brand sound. To compound the issue, Hitsville West was relied on only partially, and in the era many notable recordings would take place elsewhere, Stevie Wonder and David Ruffin for example working extensively at Media Sound in New York [869]; [1017], Eddie Kendricks in Philadelphia [1021] and Marvin Gaye at his own facility [1026]. And inevitably the pool of musicians and backing vocalists broadened out, several writer-producers turning to established names for specific projects such as Jeff Beck [841], Faith, Hope & Charity [1022]; [1036], The Eddie Hazel Band [931b], Paulinho Da Costa [1023b] and so on, further diffusing the contemporary Motown sound, as did the occasional employment of non-Motown writer-producers, for example Jimmy Webb [859] or Burt Bacharach and Hal David [1020].

If the company had a brand identity at all in these years, it is perhaps most closely associated with California's local tradition, the 'laid-back' flavours which existed in the air an after-effect of LA's pivotal centre for the late-1960s flower-power movement. Motown though no longer had a fixed notion on how music should be made and emergent trends from Philadelphia and more generally disco, helped maintain diversity across the discography. For Tamla Motown's part, the tension between the excitement of the new and the endurance of the old continued to go unresolved, the label refusing a good many US releases in favour of an oldies re-issue policy which in the second half of 1974 dominated their singles output.[1]

A central factor in this process was a change in values at the LA base. The most fundamental shift to affect Motown was the new-found emphasis on albums. In the Detroit days, the 45 was the primary focus of interest, full LPs tending to latch onto one or more recent hits, fleshed out with hastily recorded session work (although there were exceptions). By the early 1970s however the situation had altered and in the wake of *What's Going On* in particular, the album came to be viewed as the principal format, Motown moving with the times and enjoying lucrative returns as a result. From here on, singles would tend to form part of ongoing bodies of work, issued on LP and then 'lifted' for individual release, Stevie Wonder's output in particular a case study in this respect.

But the relaxation of focus meant that on the singles front Motown, and therefore Tamla Motown, would begin to falter, the succession of hits slowing and, by 1976, almost drying up completely. The truth is that Motown had been caught up and overtaken by the disco boom and, whereas in the 1960s the company had blazed a trail all its own, by now it was lamely following fashions set elsewhere as star act after star act slipped through the company's fingers. It is impossible to determine what might have been, had events taken different turns, but it is noticeable that Motown, during this period of declining sales, failed to spot a staggering number of hit acts and material, which it let escape. An example is Johnny Bristol's mid 1974 hit "Love Me For A Reason" which topped the UK charts for three weeks, and could have gone to The Jackson 5. Similarly, Freddie Perren's UK/US chart-topper "I Will Survive" might have come Motown's way, while Gladys Knight & The Pips' "Midnight Train To Georgia" escaped, despite writers and recording act both being within Motown's grasp in 1973, shortly before the track topped the US charts on Buddah.

Post-Motown, Kiki Dee spent several weeks at number 1 on both sides of the Atlantic in 1976, while The Four Seasons did likewise the same year. Norman Whitfield's Rose Royce scaled the US charts in 1977, Deniece Williams topped the UK charts for a fortnight shortly afterwards, and Debbie Boone spent some ten weeks atop the US singles charts that same year. And in 1978, Frankie Valli enjoyed another US number 1 as part of a catalogue of successful recording stars Motown failed to keep, the list also including The Isley Brothers, The Spinners, Michael Jackson, Ashford & Simpson, and many more who achieved substantial commercial success after departing. And this is to say nothing of Meatloaf, who had stopped by Motown's door unknown in 1971, and by the end of the decade (as Meat Loaf) had released *Bat Out Of Hell*, just about the world's best-selling record at the time.

Coupled with this was the established roster's continued drift out the door which, apparent before 1972, became critical in the following few years. Diana Ross, while not retiring from recording, had been distracted to a great extent by her attempt to become a movie star, and The Jackson 5 had done their thing and were gone by 1976, their lead singer heading for mega-stardom. The Supremes meanwhile were virtually redundant by the mid 1970s and would never recover their standing. Losing touch with public tastes, Motown was trying to fathom ways of keeping pace, the quality of output remaining high but losing some intangible sense of vitality. The passion of the early days was exhausted as Motown's existing backbone of performers had simply matured dispersed and, in many cases, become excessively wealthy.

What remained in the void was a business plan to resurrect the brand name. The first substantial move was made in 1975, Gordy installing Barney Ales in place of Ewart Abner as president of the Records division, as Motown sought to re-define itself in the public eye. Although their first moves stalled (as evinced by the unplanned resumption of UK releases in September 1975 after the label had first been retired [1001]), a second attempt to revitalise was made near the end of 1976. In cancelling pre-existing agreements and opening Hitsville Distributors in Detroit, Berry Gordy sought to bring tighter control and profitability on the supply side of the company's product, mirrored by the creation of Motown International, the UK branch under the stewardship of Peter Prince. Thus, after 11-and-a-half years the UK Tamla Motown label was finally re-branded, giving way to the famous 'blue' Motown-EMI imprint which came into being on October 8 1976 with the release of Táta Vega's "Try Love From The Inside" / "Just As Long As There Is You" (TMG 1053).[2]

The blue label was promoted with the optimistic slogan 'The New Era', despite arriving at a time when Motown-UK was at an all-time low. (Given the widely perceived dip in quality from the mid 1970s onwards, the switch in UK labels serves to conveniently bisect Motown's output for aficionados and record collectors.) But while the futuristic new label and sleeve design signalled Motown's forward-looking ethic, the demise of Tamla Motown brought with it a sense that the glories of the golden years were irredeemably gone. And where did Motown-EMI stand in terms of its remaining talent base?

Besides The Commodores, Motown retained at the end of the 1970s a clutch of solo performers, all moulded by Berry Gordy long ago and striving through the passage of years to remain relevant. Marvin Gaye was on the books until the early 1980s, having re-invented himself as soul music's ultimate male sex symbol. Stevie Wonder, once the child prodigy, carved himself a niche in which he was, without question, the most powerful recording artist Motown had, and remains on the label at the time of writing, dozens of hit singles and albums later. Gordy's old partner Smokey Robinson also stuck around, occasionally turning out hit singles ("Being With You" (1981) incredibly out-sold even "The Tears Of A Clown" [745]) and Diana Ross stayed as well, despite upsetting many by signing to RCA for a short spell during the 1980s.

In the face of the seemingly insoluble tension between Motown's reliance on the old guard and need to pursue progressive new acts (which the LA-based operation conspicuously failed to do), the company's fortunes were nonetheless revived in the commercial sense. A survey of Motown's top-selling UK singles shows post-1976 releases occupying 6 of the top 7 slots, with the company reporting sales at an all-time high in 1980. Stevie Wonder's 1984 chart topper "I Just Called To Say I Love You" (TMG 1349) became Motown-UK's best-ever seller, edging ahead of Lionel Richie's "Hello" from the same year (TMG 1330) and The Commodores' "Three Times A Lady" from 1978 (TMG 1113).[3] Other major hits on the blue label included Billy Preston & Syreeta: "With You I'm Born Again" (TMG 1159); Diana Ross: "Upside Down" (TMG 1195); Stevie Wonder: "Masterblaster (Jammin')" (TMG 1204); Charlene: "I've Never Been To Me" (TMG 1260); Lionel Richie: "All Night Long (All Night)" (TMG 1319); DeBarge: "Rhythm Of The Night" (TMG 1376) and so on.

Motown was far from finished and over the passage of time their catalogue has gradually come to be regarded as one of the great strands of contemporary music. The heady days of Hitsville would never be recaptured, but the Motown legend lives on. Even as recently as 2007 members of The Funk Brothers were touring, their fame greater today than at any point in their original recording careers. Tamla Motown, this classic old British label which was responsible for bringing so much music to the UK public, holds a fond place in the hearts of music fans everywhere, and in Chapter 6 we look at how it has lived on in the hearts and minds of each generation since.

[1] See [899]; [903]; [905]; [907]; [909]; [911]; [915]; [918]; [922]; [923]; [925].

[2] Some discographies date Stevie Wonder's *Songs In The Key Of Life* to September 1976. It carried a free 7-inch EP also with the blue label, which would therefore have been its first appearance. The official release date though was October 8, the same day Táta Vega's single.

[3] This information comes from Abbott p249 who does not give original sources.

*"The funny thing is that we always had the idea it would never end, that it would go on and on—but as you see, it ended."*

**Earl Van Dyke**

# I GUESS I'LL ALWAYS LOVE YOU

## LOVE YOU

### *1976 and Beyond*

hapter 5 has taken us up to the official termination of the Tamla Motown label in October 1976. However this is not the end of the Tamla Motown story. Since that point the label has sporadically resurfaced, principally for re-issues of classic singles but also to host the odd archive recording. All-told, over 100 45s have been released on Tamla Motown in the three decades since the label was mothballed, a high proportion consisting of commemorative multi-single sets. These are detailed in this chapter and, in keeping with Chapter 1's early [E] numbers, each single is given an [L] number system, signifying a 'late' release.

**24 Top Hits** (3 Sep 1976)

In March 1976, EMI took the novel step of re-packaging the entire Beatles singles catalogue in a souvenir box edition. Also sold separately, the re-issues generated much interest and at one point in April the group had six titles back in the top 50. The idea undoubtedly inspired EMI's decision to mark the end of the Tamla Motown label with a similar collection issued both individually and in a box set edition, rounding up 12 couplings of former hits and accounting for the next available dozen TMG numbers. These singles were all issued in commemorative card sleeves, designed like the outgoing Tamla Motown paper bags on the front but with a colour pictorial listing of the series on the back. The selections do not adhere to any particular scheme, except in that they encompass the label's biggest hits over the foregoing 12 years, including all the number 1s. In doing so they sample the label's major acts, with three of the singles pairing tracks by different artists. Interestingly, each single in the set was pressed as a double A-side, a format the label had never pursued before. Two of the set charted as individual releases.

**Set Details:**

[L001] **TMG 1041**
**Diana Ross**: I'm Still Waiting [781] / Touch Me In The Morning [861] - *Reached number 41 in the UK charts*

[L002] **TMG 1042**
**Stevie Wonder**: Yester-me, Yester-you, Yesterday [717] / Uptight (Everything's Alright) [545]

[L003] **TMG 1043**
**The Temptations**: Just My Imagination (Running Away With Me) [773] / Get Ready [557]

[L004] **TMG 1044**
**Diana Ross & The Supremes**: Baby Love [E56] / Stop! In The Name Of Love [501]

[L005] **TMG 1045**
**Diana Ross & The Supremes & The Temptations**: I'm Gonna Make You Love Me [685] / **Marvin Gaye**: I Heard It Through The Grapevine [686] - *Featuring different acts on each side*

[L006] **TMG 1046**
**The Supremes**: Stoned Love [760] / Nathan Jones [782]

[L007] **TMG 1047**
**Diana Ross & Marvin Gaye**: You Are Everything [890] / **Marvin Gaye & Tammi Terrell**: The Onion Song [715] - *Featuring different Gaye duet partners on each side*

[L008] **TMG 1048**
**Smokey Robinson & The Miracles**: The Tears Of A Clown [745] / The Tracks Of My Tears [522] - *Reached number 36 in the UK charts*

[L009] **TMG 1049**
**Four Tops**: Reach Out I'll Be There [579] / Standing In The Shadows Of Love [589]

[L010] **TMG 1050**
**The Isley Brothers**: This Old Heart Of Mine (Is Weak For You) [555] / Behind A Painted Smile [693]

[L011] **TMG 1051**
**Martha Reeves & The Vandellas**: Dancing In The Street [E54] / Jimmy Mack [599]

[L012] **TMG 1052**
**Jimmy Ruffin**: What Becomes Of The Brokenhearted [577] / **Marv Johnson**: I'll Pick A Rose For My Rose [680] - *Featuring different acts on each side*

This retrospective collection appeared chronologically between [1037] and [1038], and was followed by the three final releases on Tamla Motown. Seemingly abandoned for good at that point, the Tamla Motown label did not surface again until 1979, when EMI began to employ it for intermittent re-issues of old hits. In the event, the policy was pursued then for several years, meaning that the fist half of the 1980s was particularly rich in 'new' Tamla Motown singles.

It is worth contextualising the policy by looking at the rest of the UK top 40 in the late 1970s and 1980s, and in particular the continuing

---

popularity of the Jobete catalogue in the hands of contemporary artists. From 1979, for a period of about ten years, a steady stream of top 10 covers manifested and three even made number 1. Hit re-makes included: The Flying Lizards: "Money (That's What I Want)" (no. 5, 1979); The Beat: "The Tears Of A Clown" (no. 6, 1979); Phil Collins: "You Can't Hurry Love" (no. 1, 1982); Bananarama: "He Was Really Saying Somethin'" (no. 5, 1982); Paul Young: "Wherever I Lay My Hat" (no. 1, 1983); Flying Pickets: "When You're Young And In Love" (no. 7, 1984); David Bowie & Mick Jagger: "Dancing In The Street" (no. 1, 1985); Kim Wilde: "You Keep Me Hangin' On" (no. 2, 1986); The Communards: "Never Can Say Goodbye" (no. 4, 1987) etc. Even Berry Gordy's early co-composition for Jackie Wilson, "Reet Petite", topped the listing in December 1986.[1]

Obviously there was ongoing hit potential in some of Motown's archive material and, in using the Tamla Motown brand, the nostalgia market was effectively tapped. Falling between such successes, the label would appear in Motown-EMI's normal sequence and each new release was simply assigned the next available TMG number, the lack of chronological sequencing accentuating their erratic numbering.

## Tamla Motown revived with seven new TMG numbers and an oddity

[L013] **TMG 1133** (2 Feb 1979)
**Barbara Randolph**: I Got A Feeling [628] / Can I Get A Witness / You Got Me Hurtin' All Over [628b]
Tamla Motown came back to life with TMG 1133, a second re-issue of Barbara Randolph's only Tamla Motown single, accompanied by its original B-side plus a bonus title: "Can I Get A Witness", a cover of a very early Marvin Gaye number [E31]. The extra track was previously released in 1968 as her second and last US single (Soul 35050), issued with the same B-side as her first, and was unavailable in the UK until this point. TMG 1133 is, therefore, her entire Motown discography on one disc yet, since Randolph never scored a hit single on either side of the Atlantic, its release in 1979 is surprising.

[L014] **TMG 1170** (9 Nov 1979)
**Frank Wilson**: Do I Love You (Indeed I Do) / Sweeter As The Days Go By
Originally known only to Northern Soul fanatics, Frank Wilson's step up to the microphone to demo a track which was considered as a launch for his proposed singing career has gone down in musical history. Considered to be the rarest single of the genre (although more correctly described as the most collectable) the two confirmed white label test pressings of "Do I Love You" on the Soul label are known to have changed hands for thousands of pounds, earning the disc legendary status among collectors.

With probably half a dozen copies initially pressed as tests, Wilson changed his career aspirations and the release on Soul was scrapped, no commercial copies ever manufactured or at least made publicly available. It was initially thought that none of the test pressings had survived, but in 1977 one was dug out of Motown's LA vaults and lent to Wigan Casino DJ Russ Winstanley who popularised the track despite making efforts to conceal its identity with fake labels, thereby preserving its obscurity. Sold on in 1978 and again in 1979 in a then staggering £350 deal, the single rapidly acquired fame amongst Northern Soul crowds, its reputation continually growing such that it changed hands once again in 1989 for a world-record £5,000. The following year a second authentic copy sensationally surfaced, causing widespread speculation that further stocks were in existence, but not deterring an extravagant £15,000 bid in 1996.

Tamla Motown delighted many Northern Soul fans by putting the first official edition out as TMG 1170, some 14 years after the recording was made. Such is the continuing interest in the track that this release is itself now one of the label's most collectable 1970s singles, especially in its ultra-scarce promo sleeve which carries a brief history of the record.[2] TMG 1170 has since been re-pressed twice by RCA before the track was re-issued afresh in the UK in 2004 (see [L111]). Bootlegs also exist showing the track on the Soul label, but with the UK catalogue number TMG 1170.

### [L015] **TMG 1176** (25 Jan 1980)
**Martha Reeves & The Vandellas**: Heatwave [E28] / Dancing In The Street [E54]
During 1979 and 1980, the mod movement was experiencing a revival in the UK, its main figureheads The Jam championing Northern Soul and including a cover of "Heatwave" on their 1979 album *Setting Sons* which was picked up in America and issued as the group's sixth single. The recording drew attention from a new generation of record-buyers, making Martha Reeves' original an obvious candidate for re-release, albeit poorly timed for the depths of a British winter. Motown also set about compiling *20 Mod Classics* to capitalise on the renewed interest, "Heatwave" trailering the set and appearing in a fashionable 'target' picture sleeve. (Volume II of the LP appeared in the spring of 1980, without a corresponding 45.)

### [L016] **TMG 1165** (15 Feb 1980)
**Michael Jackson**: Ben [834] / **Marvin Gaye**: Abraham, Martin And John [734]
An interesting coupling of two ballads by Michael Jackson and Marvin Gaye respectively, issued to promote Motown's *The Last Dance*, a collection of the label's more treacly love songs which topped the UK album charts for a fortnight in February, propelled by Valentine's Day sales. Perhaps missing the point, Tamla Motown's administrators paired a song inspired by a rat with a socio-political hymn to plug a collection of romantic numbers aimed at young lovers. (The degree to which Gaye's 'message' songs were correctly interpreted by latter-day listeners is uncertain, at least one reviewer calling "What's Going On" the 'sexiest' song in her collection.)

### [L017] **TMG 1180** (3 Apr 1980)
**Diana Ross & The Supremes**: Supremes Medley (Parts 1 & 2)
Prompted by the ubiquitous disco style, a US DJ elected to assemble a string of Supremes snippets set against a disco beat. The resultant medley

met with an enthusiastic reception from listeners, inspiring Motown to exactly duplicate the sequence and release it as an official 45. The mix comprised sections from the HDH years, [501]; [516]; [E65]; [560]; [E51] and [E56], and was split across two sides in the UK, although the original tracks were undoubtedly marred by the mechanical percussion which ran through the sequence. This single was one of a small number whose label retained the large A feature on commercial pressings, a detail normally restricted to demo copies. Its length, at almost eight minutes, naturally lent itself to the 12-inch format and a corresponding disc was duly released (see Appendix 1).

### [L018] **TMG 1189** (20 Jun 1980)
**The Detroit Spinners**: It's A Shame [755] / Sweet Thing [514]

With The Detroit Spinners suddenly in demand following their chart-topping "Working My Way Back To You" on the Atlantic label in March, Tamla Motown dusted off the biggest hit in the archives to run head-to-head with the group's forthcoming contemporary release, "Cupid". For a flip-side, The Spinners' first Tamla Motown single was selected, offering a rare chance for collectors to snap up a copy on 45. The single failed to chart, while Tamla Motown watched "Cupid" rise to number 4.

### [L019] **TMG 1100** (1980)
**Mary Wells**: My Guy [E42] / What's Easy For Two Is So Hard For One [E30b]

In the lull between 1976 and the revival of the Tamla Motown label in 1979, TMG 1100 was one of a number of re-issues which had emerged on the blue Motown label, originally released on 24 February 1978 (see Appendix 2 for details.) The date of this Tamla Motown edition is not clear, but copies in circulation are circa 1980, probably timed to capitalise on the 20th anniversary celebrations (see below). The disc coupled two early tracks by Wells for only her second Tamla Motown release after maxi-single [820], which carried the same A-side.

### [L020] **MW 3024** (1980)
**Frankie Valli & The Four Seasons**: The Night / When Morning Comes

Recorded in 1972, "The Night" was released as a UK single on Mo-West (see Appendix 3) and did little business. However while Valli and his group remained signed to the label in the States during a period of personal and professional frustrations, Britain's Northern Soul crowds had picked up on the track and elevated it to the status of a dance classic, with heavy endorsement from Russ Winstanley at the Wigan Casino. Alert to the Casino's knack for winkling out overlooked hits, the UK Mo-West label set about a second issue of "The Night", which appeared as MW 3024 in 1975, and climbed to number 7 on the UK charts.

By then however, Valli was gone from Motown, pursuing a successful recording career through the second part of the decade which saw him top the UK and US charts in 1976 with "December '63 (Oh What A Night)", followed by another major hit with "Grease". Motown-UK finally elected to cash in by re-pressing MW 3024 on collector-friendly Tamla Motown, for some reason neglecting to provide a new TMG number. This celebrated Northern anthem is worthy in its way of a place alongside the similarly lauded [L014].

## The Motown 20th Anniversary Singles Box (5 Sep 1980)[3]

Concentrating on the UK market, Motown celebrated its anniversary by sending a number of its top names to Britain to perform live, and in consequence the company enjoyed bumper sales throughout the year. Capturing a marketing opportunity, Tamla Motown began the task of issuing the 'missing' numbers in the TMG catalogue sequence left unused during 1975. Of the 45 vacant slots, 21 appeared here on a set of singles available as individual records or in a presentation 'collectors' box'. The package itself included a souvenir metal badge but confusingly the singles were slipped into a selection of sleeves, some in special purple Motown ones, with a specially designed "20th Anniversary" logo at the bottom, others in traditional style Tamla Motown sleeves, the rest plain black. (The Tamla Motown sleeves conform to the description in Appendix 4: olive sleeve, type 4.)

So far as the contents go, The Supremes, The Four Tops and The Jackson 5 are all particularly well represented, and the collection shows an overall bias towards male artists. The A-sides appear in chronological order, covering 1966 to 1972, all with approximately contemporary B-sides. (The coupling of "Bernadette" with the much later "It's All In The Game" can just about be excused by reference to its 1972 re-issue [803].)

There are two very interesting exceptions to the general theme. One is the welcome inclusion of (Little) Stevie Wonder's "Fingertips" [L031], making its first-ever appearance on Tamla Motown. But even more significantly, [L041] coupled two previously unreleased tracks by The Marvelettes and Kim Weston respectively, both dating to 1965 and making a considerable incentive for fans to buy the entire collection rather than just the individual singles they fancied. (This highly collectable tit-bit was only available in the box set and, as if to emphasise its regal status, was bestowed the prestigious catalogue number 1000.)

**Set Details:**

[L021] **TMG 956**
**Diana Ross & The Supremes**:You Can't Hurry Love [575] / The Happening [607]

[L022] **TMG 957**
**Smokey Robinson & The Miracles**: (Come 'Round Here) I'm The One You Need [584] / I Second That Emotion [631]

[L023] **TMG 958**
**Four Tops**: 7-Rooms Of Gloom [612] / If I Were A Carpenter [647]

[L024] **TMG 959**
**Stevie Wonder**: I Was Made To Love Her [613] / Never Had A Dream Come True [731]

[L025] **TMG 960**
**Diana Ross & The Supremes**: Reflections [616] / Love Child [677]

[L026] **TMG 961**
**Jimmy Ruffin**: I'll Say Forever My Love [649] / It's Wonderful (To Be Loved By You) [753]

[L027] **TMG 962**
**Junior Walker & The All Stars**:   What Does It Take (To Win Your Love) [712] / Take Me Girl, I'm Ready [840]

[L028] **TMG 963**
**Jackson 5**: I Want You Back [724] / The Love You Save [746]

[L029] **TMG 964**
**The Supremes**:  Up The Ladder To The Roof [735] / Automatically Sunshine [821]

[L030] **TMG 965**
**Four Tops**: It's All In The Game [736] / Bernadette [601]

[L031] **TMG 966**
**Stevie Wonder**: Signed, Sealed, Delivered, I'm Yours [744] / Fingertips (II) [E26] - *The first appearance of "Fingertips" on Tamla Motown*

[L032] **TMG 967**
**The Temptations**: Ball Of Confusion (That's What The World Is Today) [749] / Take A Look Around [808]

[L033] **TMG 968**
**Edwin Starr**:War [754] / **R. Dean Taylor**: Indiana Wants Me [763] - *Featuring different acts on each side*

[L034] **TMG 969**
**Jackson 5**: I'll Be There [758] / A B C [738]

[L035] **TMG 970**
**Diana Ross**: Remember Me [768] / Surrender [792]

[L036] **TMG 971**
**The Supremes & Four Tops**: River Deep, Mountain High [777] / You Gotta Have Love In Your Heart [793]

[L037] **TMG 972**
**Four Tops**: Simple Game [785] / Still Water (Love) [752]

[L038] **TMG 973**
**Michael Jackson**: Got To Be There [797] / **Marv Johnson**: I Miss You Baby (How I Miss You) [713] - *Featuring different acts on each side*

---

**592**                    *Tamla Motown - The stories behind the UK singles*

[L039] **TMG 974**
**The Supremes**: Floy Joy [804] / Bad Weather [847]
[L040] **TMG 975**
**The Jackson 5**: Lookin' Through The Windows [833] / Doctor My Eyes [842]
[L041] **TMG 1000**
**The Marvelettes**: Finders Keepers Losers Weepers / **Kim Weston**: Do Like I
Do - *Featuring different acts on each side. Both tracks previously unreleased*

**A pair by Michael Jackson**
[L042] **TMG 976** (Apr 1981)
**Michael Jackson**: One Day In Your Life [946] / Take Me Back
Having started the retrospective filling of missing catalogue numbers, it was
only natural that the process should continue with the next Tamla Motown
release, a re-mix of "One Day In Your Life". Originally released in April 1975
without much success, this spruced up recording was aimed at the US (released
there as Motown 1512), but the corresponding UK edition stole the limelight
by going to number 1, exploiting Jackson's popularity in the wake of his *Off
The Wall* album. By coincidence of timing, this single knocked Smokey
Robinson from top spot, the only time a TMG number has replaced another
at the top of the UK charts, the two discs receiving certification as gold and
silver respectively on 12 June with Robinson taking top prize. Appropriately,
the B-side is a recording of an early Miracles track and was sourced from the
same 1975 studio album, *Forever, Michael*. So successful was the single that
Motown-EMI assembled a compilation album of Jackson material named *One
Day In Your Life* and issued it over the summer.

[L043] **TMG 977** (Jul 1981)
**Michael Jackson**: We're Almost There / We've Got A Good Thing Going
Following the success of [L042], Tamla Motown pulled a track from the
current *One Day In Your Life* album for a trailer. The track is again sourced
originally from *Forever, Michael*, penned by Eddie and Brian Holland and
recorded during their first sessions back in the Motown hub after the failure of
their Invictus empire (see [946]). Although not a UK hit in 1975, "We're
Almost There" had been an R & B success in America (as Motown 1341) and
was later featured in the 1979 film *The Wiz*. This first UK edition was paired
with a flip-side taken from *Ben* (1972), although it is unclear whether the single
is a double A-side, the promotional picture sleeve listing the tracks as A and B,
the labels as A1 and A2. It reached a disappointing 46 despite also appearing
on a 12-inch edition. (Both TMG 976 and TMG 977 were black label Tamla
Motown releases, and yet for reasons unclear the demo copies appeared on
Motown-EMI's blue label.)

# RCA take the reins
Tamla Motown product was licensed to EMI as a result of deals first struck
in the early 1960s, but in mid 1981, Motown finally severed the 18-year
association, entering into a pressing and distribution contract with RCA
which reportedly resulted in the redundancy of several EMI staff. RCA did
not meddle with Motown's catalogue numbering for four years, so Motown

singles continued to appear in the sequential TMG sequence, Tamla Motown releases picking up whichever number was currently available. The first time RCA used the Tamla Motown label was in the spring of 1982 for a Four Tops single:

[L044] **TMG 978** (Apr 1982)
**Four Tops**: Baby I Need Your Loving [E53] / Yesterday's Dreams [665]
With "When She Was My Girl" reaching number 3 towards the end of 1981 on The Four Tops' current label Casablanca, the group were seen by Motown as viable for an opportunistic re-issue. The consequent disc consisted of an early classic in "Baby I Need Your Loving", which had previously appeared on Tamla Motown as the flip to [732], but had never yet been released as a Tamla Motown A-side. Backed with the poignant "Yesterday's Dreams", the release was again supported by a corresponding 12-inch.

**Motown Gold: The Classic Hits Series** [Set 1] (Feb 1983)

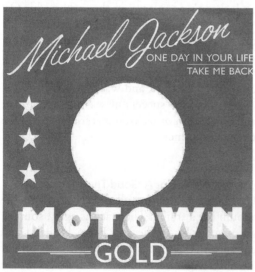

Ostensibly marking the 25th anniversary of Motown[4], a set of 20 singles was released in the first *Motown Gold* series. However only 18 were on Tamla Motown, the odd two, TMG 1113 and TMG 1159 retaining the blue labels the tracks had when first released. The bulk of the remainder consisted of straight re-pressings of previous Tamla Motown singles, but with the added interest of the set's special dark-brown sleeves which showed each artist and title at the top. The sleeves also had the full set listed on the back. As many were re-pressings from the existing TMG catalogue, they are not considered new releases, but for the record break down as follows: [599]; [705]; [841]; [868]; [896]; [L001]; [L003]; [L019]; [L021]; [L042]. (It will be noted that the latter were themselves only created as part of the post-1976 discography.)

But of the remaining discs, several carry brand new TMG numbers, which continue the process of filling in the sequential gaps, as follows:

[L045] **TMG 979**
**The Isley Brothers**: I Guess I'll Always Love You [572] / Take Some Time Out For Love [566]
[L046] **TMG 980**
**Smokey Robinson & The Miracles**: I Don't Blame You At All [774] / Ooo Baby Baby [503]
[L047] **TMG 981**
**Diana Ross & The Supremes**: Back In My Arms Again [516] / Love Is Here And Now You're Gone [597]
[L048] **TMG 982**
**The Temptations**: Cloud Nine [707] / Psychedelic Shack [741]
[L049] **TMG 983**
**Martha Reeves & The Vandellas**: I'm Ready For Love [582] / Forget Me Not [762]
[L050] **TMG 984**
**Marvin Gaye**: What's Going On [775] / God Is Love [775b] - *Re-issue of [775]*

Additionally, there were two re-pressings included which had previously existed only on the blue Motown label, these special editions therefore bringing them to Tamla Motown for the first time:
[L051] **TMG 1120**
**Four Tops**: I Can't Help Myself [515] / It's The Same Old Song [528] - *First released on the blue label on 29 Sep 1978*
[L052] **TMG 1124**
**The Velvelettes**: Needle In A Haystack [E61] / He Was Really Sayin' Somethin' [E71] - *First released on the blue label on 20 Oct 1978*

## Motown Gold: The Classic Hits Series [Set 2] (May 1983)

With healthy sales of the first series, a supplementary set of *Motown Gold* singles appeared in May, extending the collection by 10. As with the first run, most were re-pressings of pre-existing TMG numbers in the specially designed sleeves ([691]; [853]; [905]; [L004]; [L008]; [L010]; [L015] and [L034] and the blue label TMG 1240). However one new number was introduced, Eddie Kendricks' "Keep On Truckin'", re-issued with an updated catalogue number (for no obvious reason) to mark off one more of the vacant slots which now numbered just 14:

[L053] **TMG 985**
**Eddie Kendricks**: Keep On Truckin' [873] / Keep On Truckin' Part 2 [873b] - *Re-issue of [873]*
This second series had the same sleeve design as the first, but for a different listing on the back incorporating the additional titles.

## Five more releases, from the early 1980s
[L054] **TMG 986** (Jul 1983)
**Michael Jackson**: Happy (Love Theme From "Lady Sings The Blues") / We're Almost There
With *Thriller* in the process of outselling every album in history, and a slew of

major hit singles in the charts, Michael Jackson was by far the most popular artist on the scene in 1983. Little wonder that Motown were keen to capitalise by continuing to issue material from his back catalogue, in this instance a recording from his eponymous 1973 album, Michel Legrand's [848a] with the addition of Smokey Robinson's lyric. It was coupled with the recent minor hit, "We're Almost There" [L043] and issued in a picture sleeve which shared artwork with the contemporary 18 Greatest Hits, a number 1 album of Jackson's Motown material released on the Telstar subsidary. The single did respectable business, charting at 52, and was accompanied by a picture disc edition (TMGP 986), technically not part of the Tamla Motown catalogue.

[L055] **TMG 1320** (Oct 1983)
**The Temptations With Four Tops**: Medley / **The Temptations**: Papa Was A Rollin' Stone [839]
With Motown electing to celebrate its 25th birthday publicly in 1983, popular interest was on a high especially with the airing of Motown 25, a televised gala which brought together many of the company's biggest stars and ex-stars for a musical extravaganza. Besides Michael Jackson's famous 'Moonwalk', the highlight of the show, which featured live sets by Marvin Gaye and Stevie Wonder, was a scintillating duel between The Four Tops and The Temptations who swapped old hits across the stage, bringing the audience to its feet. Justifiably, Tamla Motown released the live recording for posterity, the full medley edited for 7-inch and carrying snatches of the following titles: [579]; [557]; [528]; [E67]; [722]; [515]; [587]. The choice of B-side was likely taken in respect of the planned 12-inch edition, there being a longer version also available.

[L056] **TMG 987** (Nov 1983)
**Marvin Gaye**: What's Going On [775] / I Heard It Through The Grapevine [686]
During his appearance at Motown 25, Marvin Gaye took centre-stage for a moving rendition of his anthem "What's Going On". As with the contemporary [L055] (above), the performance was noted by Tamla Motown who released the original studio recording, backed with "I Heard It Through The Grapevine", a particularly strong coupling which might have been a hit. The single appeared in support of Gaye's pending Greatest Hits, deliberately timed by Motown to clash with his new studio album on CBS, and came in a promotional picture sleeve reflecting the compilation's cover art. (Within months Gaye would be dead, "What's Going On" played at his funeral in April 1984.)

[L057] **TMG 988** (Jul 1984)
**Diana Ross**: Reach Out And Touch (Somebody's Hand) [743] / **The Supremes & Four Tops**: Reach Out And Touch (Somebody's Hand) [836]
Recording under independent contract to Motown's parent company RCA (releases in the UK appearing on Capitol), Diana Ross was still managing to turn out the occasional big hit, and with her Motown-sourced Portrait compilation also selling well, this trailer single was released, re-running her first solo 45. Interestingly, the selection was

backed with a recording of the same track by The Supremes & Four Tops (on which she did not appear) from 1972.

**[L058] TMG 1095** (1985?)
**Gladys Knight & The Pips**: Help Me Make It Through The Night [830] / Daddy Could Swear I Declare [876]

A re-pressing of a re-issue. Originally put out on the blue label on 11 November 1977, the rationale, and indeed timing, of this Tamla Motown edition are unclear. However the record's existence as a Tamla Motown single is consistent with RCA's general policy at the time, and indeed a similar situation surrounded the earlier [L019]. The typeface on the label is consistent with the *Motown Classics* set of April 1985 (see below), so it can be speculated that the release was more or less concurrent.

**Motown Classics Series** (Apr 1985)

Motown elected to issue another run of 20 singles in 1985, based on the same principles as the previous collections, avoiding duplication of titles (although not entirely) and again skewed in favour of male artists. By now the missing TMG numbers had been whittled down to 11 and all were finally issued here, closing the gap which had existed since 1975. The other nine singles in the set continued their numbering in sequence at TMG 1380, but all of these higher numbers bar three were on the blue label. Thus, so far as the Tamla Motown discography is concerned, we have 14 new singles here.

It is interesting to note that this collection materialised right at the end of the TMG catalogue series, which was about to be replaced by the European ZB system (as detailed below). The release therefore echoes EMI's parallel decision to mark the end of the standard Tamla Motown label in 1976 with a similar set. In fact the last catalogue number utilised in the *Motown Classic* set, TMG 1388, was followed by just one further release, in July 1985 (Alfie Silas' "Star").

Each title in this set was issued in a generic sleeve especially designed for the series, printed in dark blue and pink. Marked 'A Motown Classic Single', the sleeves also carried the set listing on the rear. Interestingly, [L071] had first appeared on a blue label as TMG 1069, but in a twist of policy was transferred to the black label here with an alternative B-side, the only case of a post-1976 recording earning black label A-side status. (The track in question, "Got To Give It Up (Part 1)" was the first half of a studio jam originally marketed as a live recording and pitched in the contemporary disco style, which had made the UK top 10 in 1977.) Also note-worthy was [L069], a coupling of two Supremes tracks not seen previously on UK singles the first of which had been an American hit in 1969. This and several others in the set are extremely difficult to find now and their scarcity has led to substantial rises in their re-sale value.

## Set Details:
[L059] **TMG 989**
**Stevie Wonder**: For Once In My Life [679] / I Was Made To Love Her [613]
[L060] **TMG 990**
**The Temptations**: Law Of The Land [866] / Beauty Is Only Skin Deep [578]
[L061] **TMG 991**
**Diana Ross & The Supremes & The Temptations**: I'm Gonna Make You Love Me [685] / I Second That Emotion [709]
[L062] **TMG 992**
**Diana Ross & The Supremes**: You Keep Me Hangin' On [585] / Come See About Me [E65] - *The first appearance of "Come See About Me" on Tamla Motown*
[L063] **TMG 993**
**Marvin Gaye & Tammi Terrell**: The Onion Song [715] / You Ain't Livin' Til You're Lovin' [681]
[L064] **TMG 994**
**Michael Jackson**: Got To Be There [797] / Rockin' Robin [816]
[L065] **TMG 995**
**Four Tops**: Bernadette [601] / If I Were A Carpenter [647]
[L066] **TMG 996**
**Jimmy Ruffin**: Gonna Give Her All The Love I've Got [603] / I've Passed This Way Before [593]
[L067] **TMG 997**
**The Temptations**: Ball Of Confusion (That's What The World Is Today) [749] / Ain't Too Proud To Beg [565]
[L068] **TMG 998**
**Diana Ross & Marvin Gaye**: You Are Everything [890] / Stop, Look, Listen (To Your Heart) [906]
[L069] **TMG 999**
**The Supremes**: The Composer / Take Me Where You Go - *The first appearance of both tracks on Tamla Motown*
[L070] **TMG 1380**
**Diana Ross**: Love Hangover [1024] / Remember Me [768]
[L071] **TMG 1381**
**Marvin Gaye**: Got To Give It Up (Part 1) / How Sweet It Is (To Be Loved By

You) [E60] - *"Got To Give It Up" previously released on the blue label only; "How Sweet It Is" making its first appearance on Tamla Motown*
[L072] **TMG 1388**
**Stevie Wonder**: He's Misstra Know-It-All [892] / Boogie On Reggae Woman [928]

[L067] was subsequently re-pressed as a promotional item for Budweiser beer in a purple Motown sleeve carrying Budweiser's logo, which is far more common than the original issue. The record itself is distinguishable from the first pressing in that it omits the 'in album' text on the label and the Tamla Motown logo has a single-lined box rather than the standard double-lined.

## The 'European' series begins

In May 1985, RCA inevitably abandoned the TMG system, supplanting it with the Europe-wide ZB prefix employed across-the-board for all of their labels. Since the system was thus used, Motown singles were not given consecutive ZB numbers, and the occasional Tamla Motown release, which continued to appear sporadically though 1986, are numbered erratically as a result. All 7-inch releases in the ZB scheme carried odd numbers, the intervening even numbers reserved for corresponding 12-inches. Many of the releases from here on had picture sleeves plugging the contemporary box set *150 Motown Hits Of Gold*, a nine-album round-up of Motown's history.

[L073] **ZB 40701** (Apr 1986)
**Marvin Gaye**: I Heard It Through The Grapevine [686] / Can I Get A Witness [E31]
The third time "Grapevine" had appeared since 1976 saw it re-enter the UK charts and climb to number 8 on the back of a campaign by Levi Strauss which used several vintage soul records as soundtracks for jeans advertisements. The single, with its classic Stateside-era B-side, comes in a picture sleeve.

[L074] **ZB 40709** (Apr 1986)
**Diana Ross & The Supremes**: You Keep Me Hangin' On [585] / Come See About Me [E65]
Released alongside [L073], in celebration of the group's 25th anniversary, the first stand-alone, post-1976 Supremes single was essentially a re-issue of [L062] from the *Motown Classics* series (see above), but with a new catalogue number. This edition came in an attractive 60s-style picture sleeve featuring a line-up of Ross and Wilson along with Cindy Birdsong, despite the fact that Flo Ballard was still in the group when both tracks were recorded and first released. (Although not numbered sequentially, this single and ZB 40701 were consecutive UK releases for Motown.)

[L075] **ZB 40743** (Jun 1986)
**The Temptations**: My Girl [E67] / Wherever I Lay My Hat (That's My Home)
The first appearance of The Temptations' classic "My Girl" as a Tamla

---

Motown A-side arrived with the group's previously unheard recording of the Marvin Gaye track "Wherever I Lay My Hat", recently popularised in Britain by Paul Young. (See also the 12-inch single TMGT 987 in Appendix 1). The release was a plug for Motown's group retrospective *25th Anniversary*, which included these titles and was prompted by the re-appearance on the live circuit of David Ruffin and Eddie Kendricks, playing with Hall & Oates in the wake of a successful appearance at the Live Aid charity event of 1985. The single failed to chart.

[L076] **ZB 40803** (Jul 1986)
**Diana Ross:** Ain't No Mountain High Enough [751] / It's My House
Having had her first UK number 1 since "I'm Still Waiting" [781] courtesy of the Bee Gees-penned "Chain Reaction", Motown gambled on a well-timed re-issue of Diana Ross' second solo single. The track was currently in use in a television advert for DHL Couriers, and had the benefit of coinciding with Motown's *The Very Best Of Diana Ross*. The B-side was an Ashford & Simpson-penned track first released on Motown's blue label as TMG 1169, a single which had struggled to number 32 in 1979.

**Motown Hits Of Gold – The Singles Collection** (Mar 1988)

After 1986, RCA abandoned the Tamla Motown imprint for good, with the sole exception of the records contained in this special set. The fourth collection of singles in seven years, the full list consisted of 19 Tamla Motown singles, and two blue label singles, one of which was a new re-mix of "I Want You Back" (ZB 41913). This time out the Tamla Motown singles featured a number of rare titles never previously re-issued, as well as three early titles making their first appearance on the label. All records in the set were pressed as double A-sides.

   The records came in card sleeves, with the artist's name and song titles plus the legend "Motown Hits Of Gold—The Singles Collection" on the front and the full set-listing on the rear. The singles were ordered roughly alphabetically by artist and, in keeping with the ZB numbering policy, skipped all the even numbers which were reserved for 12-inch singles (although none were issued in connection with these singles). Although the series stands on its own merits, it conceptually supplements the *150 Motown Hits Of Gold* box set of 1985 which it references on the sleeve credits as album sources for the applicable tracks.

## Set Details:
[L077] **ZB 41903**
**The Contours**: Do You Love Me [E10] / **Barrett Strong**: Money (That's What I Want) [E02]
- *Two very early releases by different acts. "Money" appears on Tamla Motown for the first time*
[L078] **ZB 41905**
**Four Tops**: 7-Rooms Of Gloom [612] / Loving You is Sweeter Than Ever [568]
[L079] **ZB 41907**
**Four Tops**: It's All In The Game [736] / Simple Game [785]
[L080] **ZB 41909**
**Marvin Gaye**: Ain't That Peculiar [539] / I'll Be Doggone [510]
[L081] **ZB 41911**
**Brenda Holloway**: Just Look What You've Done [608] / When I'm Gone [508]
[L082] **ZB 41915**
**Shorty Long**: Here Comes The Judge [663] / Function At The Junction [573]
[L083] **ZB 41917**
**The Marvelettes**: Too Many Fish In The Sea [E63] / Please Mr. Postman [E05]
- *Both tracks appearing on Tamla Motown for the first time*
[L084] **ZB 41919**
**The Miracles Featuring Billy Griffin**: Love Machine [1015] / **Edwin Starr**: 25 Miles [672]
- *Featuring different acts on each side. Miracles' billing amended to emphasise Griffin (now recording elsewhere as a solo act)*
[L085] **ZB 41921**
**Martha Reeves & The Vandellas**: Nowhere To Run [502] / Forget Me Not [762]
[L086] **ZB 41923**
**Diana Ross**: Reach Out And Touch (Somebody's Hand) [743] / Surrender [792]
[L087] **ZB 41925**
**Diana Ross & The Supremes**: Someday We'll Be Together [721] / My World Is Empty Without You [548]
[L088] **ZB 41927**
**David Ruffin**: Walk Away From Love [1017] / **Jimmy Ruffin**: I'll Say Forever My Love [649]
- *One side each from the Ruffin brothers*
[L089] **ZB 41929**
**The Detroit Spinners**: It's A Shame [755] / **Eddie Kendricks**: Keep On Truckin' (Part 1) [873]
- *Featuring different acts on each side*

[L090] **ZB 41931**
**The Supremes**: Up The Ladder To The Roof [735] / Floy Joy [804]
[L091] **ZB 41933**
**The Temptations**: I Can't Get Next To You [722] / (I Know) I'm Losing You [587]
[L092] **ZB 41935**
**Junior Walker & The All Stars**: How Sweet It Is (To Be Loved By You) [571] / What Does It Take (To Win Your Love) [712]
[L093] **ZB 41937**
**Stevie Wonder**: Fingertips (Part 2) [E26] / Blowin' In The Wind [570]
[L094] **ZB 41939**
**Stevie Wonder**: Never Had A Dream Come True [731] / Signed, Sealed, Delivered, I'm Yours [744]
[L095] **ZB 41941**
**Michael Jackson With The Jackson 5**: A B C [738] / The Love You Save [746]
- *Group name altered to emphasise Michael's presence*

Shortly after the set was produced, "Do You Love Me" was featured in the hit film *Dirty Dancing*. In consequence, Motown saw fit to re-press [L077] almost immediately, issuing it in a new picture sleeve featuring a still from the movie and taking the opportunity to plug the album *Motown Dance Party*, a big seller in May 1988. (An equivalent American release also appeared, the Yesteryear label re-issue emerging in a near identical sleeve, the track's new-found fame prompting The Contours to re-form after some 20 years.) A footnote to Dave Marsh's article in Abbott (p38) bemoans the emasculation of "Do You Love Me" for radio play, but it should be noted that the fake ending remains intact on both editions of [L077].

## End of the line?

The Contours' single looked like it would be the last ever to appear on Tamla Motown, some 26 years after it had first been released in the UK on Oriole American. The label, despite being in semi-retirement, had persevered through the 1980s with admirable defiance. Until mid 1988, some 95 'new' singles had appeared on Tamla Motown, several of which had charted and one of which had gone to number 1 [L042]. But 1988 was decisive not just for Tamla Motown but for the company itself as it became apparent that Berry Gordy was finally ready to sell after some years of speculation and negotiation. On June 29 Gordy finally accepted a joint bid from MCA and Boston Ventures for a little under $50m and henceforth, the three-decade-old Motown organisation ceased to be an independent.

So far as new releases were concerned from here on, the tail-off during the 1980s steepened and, although the company continued to produce into the following decade, success was increasingly scant and the artist roster generally wound-down as Motown depended ever more heavily on its back catalogue. The label's one big act, Stevie Wonder, was more or less a recluse and it seemed that, after three decades of brilliance, Motown, and its UK arm, was all but snuffed out for good. The Tamla Motown label was never revived in the 1990s, and few envisaged a re-appearance after such a sadly protracted demise.

After 16 years of obsolescence (a timescale longer than its original life-span), the Tamla Motown label was surprisingly revived in 2004 for a set of 20 double A-side singles, released in four instalments over the so-called 'Summer of Motown'. The occasion here was the 45th anniversary, which this time was chronologically correct for the organisation if not for Tamla Motown itself (which was, in point of fact, only 39 years old). By now, Motown was being distributed by Universal Music, whose catalogue numbering was used here. Each single had its own annotated sleeve based on the original design, in one of four different colours used.

To its detriment the set duplicated 13 titles from the *24 Top Hits* collection of 1976, and seven pairings which had already been matched for re-issues in the TMG series over the years, the five 'pink' releases of August including four of these. Despite this the series contained some particularly attractive double-siders and of particular interest to collectors was the 'star release' in the final 'green' set, consisting of a re-appearance of Frank Wilson's "Do I Love You (Indeed I Do)", carrying a different vocal take to the 1979 edition [L014], backed with another version of the track not previously issued.

### Set Details:

*26 Jul: Gold-brown sleeves*
**[L096] 9821 532**
**Jimmy Ruffin**: What Becomes Of The Brokenhearted [577] / Farewell Is A Lonely Sound [726]
**[L097] 9821 547**
**Smokey Robinson & The Miracles**: The Tears Of A Clown [745] / The Tracks Of My Tears [522]
*- This single repeats the coupling first seen on [L008]*
**[L098] 9821 549**
**Four Tops**: Reach Out I'll Be There [579] / Bernadette [601]

[L099] **9821 550**
**The Isley Brothers**: This Old Heart Of Mine (Is Weak For You) [555] / Behind A Painted Smile [693]
- *This single repeats the coupling first seen on [L010]*
[L100] **9821 606**
**The Temptations**: My Girl [E67] / Ain't Too Proud To Beg [565]

*2 Aug: Orange sleeves*
[L101] **9821 531**
**Martha Reeves & The Vandellas**: Dancing In The Street [E54] / Forget Me Not [762]
[L102] **9821 536**
**R. Dean Taylor**: There's A Ghost In My House [896] / Gotta See Jane [656]
[L103] **9821 546**
**Smokey Robinson & The Miracles**: Going To A Go-Go [547] / I Second That Emotion [631]
[L104] **9821 551**
**Diana Ross & The Supremes**: Baby Love [E56] / Where Did Our Love Go [E51]
[L105] **9821 631**
**Junior Walker & The All-Stars**: Shotgun [509] / (I'm A) Road Runner [559]
- *This single repeats the coupling first seen on [691]*

*16 Aug: Pink sleeves*
[L106] **9821 529**
**Diana Ross**: I'm Still Waiting [781] / Touch Me In The Morning [861]
- *This single repeats the coupling first seen on [L001]*
[L107] **9821 544**
**The Velvelettes**: Needle In A Haystack [E61] / He Was Really Sayin' Somethin' [E71]
- *This single repeats the coupling first seen on [595], and also on [L052]*
[L108] **9821 545**
**Marvin Gaye**: I Heard It Through The Grapevine [686] / What's Going On [775]
- *This single repeats the coupling first seen on [L056]*
[L109] **9821 628**
**Stevie Wonder**: Uptight (Everything's Alright) [545] / Yester-me, Yester-you, Yesterday [717]
- *This single repeats the coupling first seen on [L002]*
[L110] **9821 630**
**Edwin Starr**: War [754] / Stop The War Now [764]

*6 Sep: Green sleeves*
[L111] **9821 530**
**Frank Wilson**: Do I Love You (Indeed I Do) / **Chris Clark**: Do I Love You (Indeed I Do)
- *Being two versions of the same song, by different artists. Chris Clark's version was previously unreleased*

[L112] **9821 533**
**The Marvelettes**: Please Mr. Postman [E05] / When You're Young And In Love [609]
[L113] **9821 548**
**Four Tops**: I Can't Help Myself [515] / Walk Away Renee [634]
[L114] **9821 627**
**The Temptations**: Papa Was A Rollin' Stone [839] / Cloud Nine [707]
[L115] **9821 629**
**Michael Jackson & The Jackson 5**: I Want You Back [724] / Doctor My Eyes [842]
- *Group name altered to emphasise Michael's presence*

The compete collection was re-issued as a box set on 27 Sep.


# The label reborn
Although no Tamla Motown singles appeared between 1988 and 2004, Motown-UK had continued to market new product during the era. At one point they even re-launched the TMG number series at TMG 1401, but it was again out of use by 1995, the system reintroduced once more with TMG 1501 around the year 2000, primarily to accommodate releases by Motown's hottest new discovery, Denver-born singer India.Arie. The last of these was TMG 1509 in 2003, explaining the number used on Wonder's 2005 comeback single:

[L116] **TMG 1510** (16 May 2005)
**Stevie Wonder**: So What The Fuss / So What The Fuss Remix Feat. Q-Tip
Having released nothing of consequence for around a decade, Stevie Wonder chose to resume recording in 2005 with the new album *A Time 2 Love*, and a vinyl edition of the first associated single duly appeared, the recording featuring Prince on bass guitar. With the 2004 'Summer of Motown' releases gaining significant attention, the decision was made to use the old Tamla Motown label on the single, issued with a large play-hole, and a sleeve design almost exactly as-per the 20 singles of the previous summer. (Maintaining consistency, this too was billed as a double A-side.) Significantly, the use of a sequential TMG number marked the first entirely new Tamla Motown single for almost 30 years!

[L117] **9831 108** (4 Jul 2005)
**Diana Ross & The Supremes**: Honey Bee (Keep On Stinging Me)—Out On The Floor Mix / **Earl Van Dyke**: All Day All Night
Released in conjunction with the 42-track *A Cellarful Of Motown! Volume 2*, a compilation of previously unreleased archive material, Tamla Motown continued its revival of the traditional label with another 'new' single. Issued in a gloss-finish orange sleeve, the A-side was originally recorded on March 9 1968 for *Love Child* before being vetoed by Quality Control. Consequently it was re-done with more attack on May 21, this original version sitting in the can for 37 years. The B-side was an obscure 1965 track intended for Martha

Reeves & The Vandellas, and overdubbed by Van Dyke that October, in keeping with his practice of utilising 'hit' backing tracks for his own recording projects (see [506]). The Andantes can be heard performing backing vocals on what is essentially an instrumental (assuming it to be them, and not in fact The Vandellas). The single's sleeve makes mention of 'Motown Monday', recalling a series of 1966 concerts and broadcasts hosted by Scott Regen at Detroit's Roostertail theatre, but in fact plugging Motown's marketing initiative for 2005 which saw the release of a new CD on the first Monday of each month.

[L118] **TMG 1512** (28 Nov 2005)
**Stevie Wonder**: Positivity (UK Radio Edit) / If You Really Love Me [798]
The second single from *A Time 2 Love*, "Positivity" featured a guest appearance from Wonder's daughter Aisha, previously famed for her baby cries which were recorded and mixed onto "Isn't She Lovely" (1976).[5] With the album high in the charts, Motown capitalised on Wonder's rise in popularity by putting out a 'greatest hits' package—sales helped by a fairly recent collaboration with boy-band Blue on a remake of "Signed, Sealed, Delivered, I'm Yours" [744] which had introduced his earlier work to a new generation of fans in 2003. The time was therefore ripe to delve into the archives and exhume "If You Really Love Me" for use as the flip-side to his new single, the first true, non-set Tamla Motown re-issue in nearly two decades. (The concurrent CD edition dispensed with [798] in favour of a couple of later, post-1976 cuts from his back-catalogue.) The sleeve was of the same design as TMG 1510 and the single likewise had a large play-hole. Since TMG 1511 was passed over in the numbering sequence it is reasonable to assume that it had originally been allocated to The Supremes' July release before a Universal number was substituted.

[L119] **TMG 1513** (13 Feb 2006)
**Stevie Wonder**: From The Bottom Of My Heart / Every Time I See You I Go Wild [626b]
The third release from Wonder's 2005 album, "From The Bottom Of My Heart" appeared as TMG 1513, coupled up with "Every Time I See You I Go Wild", a 1966 recording previously released as the B-side to "I'm Wondering" in late 1967. In concocting the new song, Wonder shows a career-long interest in recycling phrases from earlier recordings, this quote from the lyric of "I Just Called To Say I Love You" (TMG 1349, 1984) following precedents such as [744]. At 5:16, the A-side clocks in at almost double the B-side, 2:25 and 40 years separating the recordings. The custom sleeve and large play-hole conform to the album's previous two trailer singles.

## Summary of post-1976 releases

It is difficult to meaningfully summarise the material released over these years, so diverse are the selections, ranging from re-runs of classic old hits through to brand-new recordings from the new millennium and a swathe of titles brought in form other labels. In fact, taking into account the late-1976 commemorative set, the records in Chapter 6 span three decades—more than twice the natural life-span of the label. Some releases are of interest because of the way the tracks have been coupled: for example there are two instances of singles with different versions of the same song on either sides, [L057] ("Reach Out And Touch") and [L111] ("Do I Love You"). Elsewhere we see 'themed' pairings such as Smokey Robinson's two 'tears' compositions [L008] or Edwin Starr's two 'war' hits [L110], and equally novel was a coupling of tracks by David and Jimmy Ruffin [L088].

The old Motown recordings which were previously available only on the pre-Tamla Motown labels are listed in the section "Statistics, Facts & Feats". And of those brought to Tamla Motown from the blue label, we have just Marvin Gaye's "Got To Give It Up" [L071], originally released in 1977 as TMG 1069 and Diana Ross' "It's My House" [L076b], originally released in 1979 as TMG 1169. Frankie Valli's "The Night" / "When The Morning Comes" was previously available on Mo-West, while The Supremes' "The Composer" [L069] plus Barbara Randolph's "Can I Get A Witness" [L013b] bring home titles hitherto available via the US singles discography.

But the main interest of the above releases lies in the previously unavailable material which Tamla Motown takes credit for issuing for the very first time. These selections warrant special mention, and number just eight, spread over five discs.

[L014] is Frank Wilson's classic "Do I Love You (Indeed I Do)", which was backed with the similarly obscure "Sweeter As The Days Go By". This 1979 disc has itself become part of the legend of its A-side, a track with a unique story in the history of Northern Soul. The following year [L041] was slipped onto a box set, coupling two buried gems in The Marvelettes' "Finders Keepers Losers Weepers" and Kim Weston's "Do Like I Do". The Temptations' reading of "Wherever I Lay My Hat (That's My Home)" [L075b] appeared during 1986, and when the post-2000 releases came along, we were treated to the previously unheard reading of "Do I Love You (Indeed I Do)" by Chris Clark [L111b] and a double-header in The Supremes' original recording of "Honey Bee (Keep On Stinging Me)" and Earl Van Dyke's "All Day All Night" [L117].

For those interested in collecting the singles, a note is warranted on the catalogue numbers available. With the back-filling of 'missing' TMG numbers completed in April 1985, a full collection of UK Tamla Motown 45s will comprise a core set running from TMG 501 through to TMG 1052 (less the four TMG numbers not released in their day). Additional TMG numbers on the black label are as follows, with the company responsible for the first Tamla Motown pressing given in brackets:

**TMG 1095 (RCA);**
**TMG 1100 (EMI);**
**TMG 1120 (RCA);**
**TMG 1124 (RCA);**
**TMG 1133 (EMI);**
**TMG 1165 (EMI);**
**TMG 1170 (EMI);**

**TMG 1176 (EMI);**
**TMG 1180 (EMI);**
**TMG 1189 (EMI);**
**TMG 1320 (RCA);**
**TMG 1380 (RCA);**
**TMG 1381 (RCA);**
**TMG 1388 (RCA);**
**TMG 1510 (Universal);**
**TMG 1512 (Universal);**
**TMG 1513 (Universal).**

There is also one odd Tamla Motown release with an MW number (see [L020]) and for those issued with the ZB prefix there are four from 1986, plus another 19 from a 1988 special set. Subsequently a set of 20 has appeared with Universal catalogue numbers, plus one similar 2005 Supremes' release, bringing the total number of different singles released on Tamla Motown since the end of the main run to 119 so far. The author suspects—indeed very much hopes—that this is not the end of the Tamla Motown label.

[1] Cliff Richard also took the non-Motown composition "Daddy's Home" [851] to number 2 in 1981.

[2] The slightly inaccurate text of which reads: "This is the record for which the North of England has been impatiently waiting nearly two years. Originally planned for release in America in December 1965 the single was withdrawn at the last minute. A handful of copies remained in circulation, one or two of which reached Britain, and in the last two years interest has grown to such a pitch that a copy recently changed hands for £500. Now the original tapes have been unearthed and brought to London. We were amazed. Unlike many Northern Soul obscurities whose appeal is limited to the clubs where they are played, this is a commercial hit single. Tamla Motown at its finest—available commercially for the first time."

[3] Motown's first release was in January 1959 (May 1959 in Britain [E01]). Thus, the true 20th anniversary would more sensibly have been celebrated in 1979. (The US Motown label itself commenced activity in 1960, but is an odd point of reference for a UK Tamla Motown anniversary set.) Tamla Motown were likely following the precedent set in 1970 when the '10th anniversary' was marked [732].

[4] As with the 20th anniversary releases, the celebrations were oddly timed, probably as a result of RCA's keenness. 25 years previously, Motown had yet to release anything, and the 25th 'anniversary' was, in any case, held less than two and a half years after the 20th. (Historical experts will point to the creation of Rayber in 1958, a pre-Motown label set up by Gordy. However the only release on Rayber, "I Can't Concentrate" / "Insane" by Wade Jones, did not appear until early 1959.)

[5] According to Sharon Davis (2006a, p115) the legend is false, the recording in fact being a different baby in the same hospital ward.

# ARTIST SUMMARIES

This index concentrates on the main discography, although post-1976 Tamla Motown releases are also included for label completeness. The names of all acts conform to a standard nomenclature, despite the fact that label credits can differ from release to release. For example all records released under the name 'Diana Ross & The Supremes' are found under 'Supremes', and 'Detroit Spinners' under 'Spinners'. Generally the chosen name is the one by which the artist made their main breakthrough. A handful of artists only ever appeared on Tamla Motown B-sides, but the decision was made to also list them since they contribute in a unique way to the discography.

Where a single entered the UK top 40, its highest position is given in parenthesis. Two singles ([555] and [599]) entered the top 40 when re-pressed and re-promoted some years after their first release, without being given a new catalogue number and these are therefore listed twice. Statistics are quoted against each act, and American data from the start of Motown up to November 1976 is also given for the sake of comparison.

### Gil ASKEY
Released 1 original single between 1965 and 1976. (US equivalent: 1 single.)
**[848b]** (1973)  Any Happy Home

### Rose BANKS
Released 1 original single between 1965 and 1976. (US equivalent: 2 singles.)
**[1037]** (1976)  Darling Baby

### J J BARNES
Released 1 original single between 1965 and 1976. (US equivalent: 0 singles.)
**[870]**   (1973)  Real Humdinger [Maxi-single]

### BLINKY & Edwin STARR
Released 1 original single between 1965 and 1976. (US equivalent: 1 single.) Also released 1 studio album on Tamla Motown.
**[720]**   (1969)  *Not released*: Oh How Happy
**[748]**   (1970)  Oh How Happy
(See also: Edwin STARR)

### The BOONES
Released 1 original single between 1965 and 1976. (US equivalent: 3 singles.) Also released 2 singles on Mo-West (one as The Boone Family).
**[1030]** (1976)  My Guy

### Dorsey BURNETTE
Released 1 original single between 1965 and 1976. (US equivalent: 4 singles.)
**[534]**   (1965)  Jimmy Brown

### Jerry BUTLER
Released 1 original single between 1965 and 1976. (US equivalent: 1 single.)
**[1039]** (1976)  The Devil In Mrs. Jones

## G C CAMERON
Released 1 original single between 1965 and 1976. (US equivalent: 10 singles.)
Also released 1 studio album on Tamla Motown.
**[1033]** (1976)  Me And My Life

## Choker CAMPBELL'S BIG BAND
Released 1 original single between 1965 and 1976. (US equivalent: 1 single.) Also
released 1 studio album on Tamla Motown.
**[517]**  (1965)  Mickey's Monkey

## CASTON & MAJORS
Released 3 original singles between 1965 and 1976. (US equivalent: 0 singles.)
Also released 1 studio album on Tamla Motown.
**[938]**  (1975)  Child Of Love
**[951]**  (1975)  Sing
**[1005]** (1975)  I'll Keep My Light In My Window

## Chris CLARK
Released 3 original singles between 1965 and 1976. (US equivalent: 6 singles.)
Also released 1 studio album on Tamla Motown.
**[591]**  (1967)  Love's Gone Bad
**[624]**  (1967)  From Head To Toe
**[638]**  (1968)  I Want To Go Back There Again
*Subsequent releases:*
[L111]  (2004)  Do I Love You (Indeed I Do)

## Tom CLAY
Released 1 original single between 1965 and 1976. (US equivalent: 2 singles; 1 top
40 hit.) Also released 1 single on Mo-West.
**[801]**  (1972)  What The World Needs Now Is Love—Abraham, Martin And John

## The COMMODORES
Released 8 original singles between 1965 and 1976, and scored 1 top 40 hit.
(US equivalent: 12 singles; 4 top 40 hits.) Also released 4 studio albums on
Tamla Motown.
**[902]**  (1974)  Machine Gun (20)
**[924]**  (1974)  The Zoo (The Human Zoo)
**[935]**  (1975)  Superman
**[944]**  (1975)  I Feel Sanctified
**[952]**  (1975)  Slippery When Wet
**[1007]** (1975)  Let's Do It Right
**[1018]** (1976)  Sweet Love
**[1034]** (1976)  High On Sunshine

## The CONTOURS
Released 5 UK singles prior to March 1965.
Released 6 original singles between 1965 and 1976, and scored 1 top 40 hit. (US
equivalent: 11 singles; 1 top 40 hit.) Also released 1 EP on Tamla Motown.

[531]   (1965)   First I Look At The Purse
[564]   (1966)   Determination
[605]   (1967)   It's So Hard Being A Loser
[723]   (1970)   Just A Little Misunderstanding (31)
*The Contours left Motown in 1972*
[886]   (1974)   Baby Hit And Run
[899]   (1974)   Do You Love Me
*Subsequent releases:*
[L077]   (1988)   Do You Love Me

## Kiki DEE
Released 1 original single between 1965 and 1976. (US equivalent: 2 singles.) Also released 1 studio album on Tamla Motown.
[739]   (1970)   The Day Will Come Between Sunday And Monday

## DETROIT SPINNERS: *See The SPINNERS*

## The DYNAMIC SUPERIORS
Released 2 original singles between 1965 and 1976. (US equivalent: 5 singles.) Also released 1 studio album on Tamla Motown.
[929]   (1975)   Shoe Shoe Shine
[1016]  (1975)   Deception

## Billy ECKSTINE
Released 1 original single between 1965 and 1976. (US equivalent: 7 singles.) Also released 3 studio albums on Tamla Motown.
[533]   (1965)   Had You Been Around

## The ELGINS
Released 3 original singles and 3 re-issues between 1965 and 1976, and scored 2 top 40 hits. (US equivalent: 4 singles; 0 top 40 hits.) Also released 1 studio album on Tamla Motown.
[551]   (1966)   Put Yourself In My Place
[583]   (1966)   Heaven Must Have Sent You
[615]   (1967)   It's Been A Long Long Time
*The Elgins left Motown in 1967*
[642]   (1968)   *Re-issue of [551]:* Put Yourself In My Place
[771]   (1971)   *Re-issue of [583]:* Heaven Must Have Sent You (3)
[787]   (1971)   *Re-issue of [551]:* Put Yourself In My Place (28)

## Yvonne FAIR
Released 3 original singles between 1965 and 1976, and scored 1 top 40 hit. (US equivalent: 6 singles; 0 top 40 hits.) Also released 1 studio album on Tamla Motown.
[913]   (1974)   Funky Music Sho' Nuff Turns Me On
[1013]  (1975)   It Should Have Been Me (5)
[1025]  (1976)   It's Bad For Me To See You

## The FANTASTIC FOUR

Released 1 original single between 1965 and 1976. (US equivalent: 4 singles.) Also released 1 studio album on Tamla Motown.

**[678]** (1968) I Love You Madly

**FOUR SEASONS**: See Frankie VALLI & The FOUR SEASONS

## FOUR TOPS

Released 2 UK singles prior to March 1965.
Released 25 original singles and 3 re-issues between 1965 and 1976, and scored 21 top 40 hits. (US equivalent: 29 singles; 17 top 40 hits.) Also released 10 studio albums and 2 EPs on Tamla Motown.

**[507]** (1965) Ask The Lonely
**[515]** (1965) I Can't Help Myself (23)
**[528]** (1965) It's The Same Old Song (34)
**[542]** (1965) Something About You
**[553]** (1966) Shake Me, Wake Me (When It's Over)
**[568]** (1966) Loving You Is Sweeter Than Ever (21)
**[579]** (1966) Reach Out I'll Be There (1)
**[589]** (1967) Standing In The Shadows Of Love (6)
**[601]** (1967) Bernadette (8)
**[612]** (1967) 7-Rooms Of Gloom (12)
**[623]** (1967) You Keep Running Away (26)
**[634]** (1967) Walk Away Renee (3)
**[647]** (1968) If I Were A Carpenter (7)
**[665]** (1968) Yesterday's Dreams (23)
**[675]** (1968) I'm In A Different World (27)
**[698]** (1969) What Is A Man (16)
**[710]** (1969) Do What You Gotta Do (11)
**[732]** (1970) *Re-issue of [515]*: I Can't Help Myself (10)
**[736]** (1970) It's All In The Game (5)
**[752]** (1970) Still Water (Love) (10)
**[770]** (1971) Just Seven Numbers (Can Straighten Out My Life) (36)
**[785]** (1971) Simple Game (3)
**[803]** (1972) *Re-issue of [601]*: Bernadette [Maxi-single] (23)
**[823]** (1972) Walk With Me, Talk With Me Darling (32)
*Four Tops left Motown in 1972*
**[829]** (1972) I'll Turn To Stone
**[850]** (1973) So Deep Within You
**[858]** (1973) I Can't Quit Your Love
**[1011]** (1975) *Re-issue of [634]*: Walk Away Renee
*Subsequent releases:*
[L009] (1976) Reach Out I'll Be There / Standing In The Shadows Of Love [AA-side]
[L023] (1980) 7-Rooms Of Gloom
[L030] (1980) It's All In The Game
[L037] (1980) Simple Game
[L044] (1982) Baby I Need Your Loving
[L051] (1983) I Can't Help Myself

---

[L065] (1985) Bernadette
[L078] (1988) 7-Rooms Of Gloom / Loving You is Sweeter Than Ever [AA-side]
[L079] (1988) It's All In The Game / Simple Game [AA-side]
[L098] (2004) Reach Out I'll Be There / Bernadette [AA-side]
[L113] (2004) I Can't Help Myself / Walk Away Renee [AA-side]
(See also: The SUPREMES & FOUR TOPS; The TEMPTATIONS with FOUR TOPS)

## Marvin GAYE
Released 6 UK singles prior to March 1965.
Released 22 original singles and 1 re-issue between 1965 and 1976, and scored 4 top 40 hits. (US equivalent: 38 singles; 26 top 40 hits.) Also released 11 studio albums and 2 EPs on Tamla Motown.

**[510]** (1965) I'll Be Doggone
**[524]** (1965) Pretty Little Baby
**[539]** (1965) Ain't That Peculiar
**[552]** (1966) One More Heartache
**[563]** (1966) Take This Heart Of Mine
**[574]** (1966) Little Darling (I Need You)
**[618]** (1967) Your Unchanging Love
**[640]** (1968) You
**[676]** (1968) Chained
**[686]** (1969) I Heard It Through The Grapevine (1)
**[705]** (1969) Too Busy Thinking About My Baby (5)
**[718]** (1969) That's The Way Love Is
**[734]** (1970) Abraham, Martin And John (9)
**[775]** (1971) What's Going On
**[796]** (1971) Save The Children
**[802]** (1972) Mercy Mercy Me (The Ecology)
**[817]** (1972) Inner City Blues (Make Me Wanna Holler)
**[846]** (1973) Trouble Man
**[868]** (1973) Let's Get It On (31)
**[882]** (1974) Come Get To This
**[923]** (1974) *Re-issue of [686]:* I Heard It Through The Grapevine
**[1026]** (1976) I Want You
**[1035]** (1976) After The Dance
*Subsequent releases:*
[L005] (1976) I Heard It Through The Grapevine
[L016b] (1980) Abraham, Martin And John
[L050] (1983) What's Going On
[L056] (1983) What's Going On
[L071] (1985) Got To Give It Up (Part 1)
[L073] (1986) I Heard It Through The Grapevine (8)
[L080] (1988) Ain't That Peculiar / I'll Be Doggone [AA-side]
[L108] (2004) I Heard It Through The Grapevine / What's Going On [AA-side]
(See also: Marvin GAYE & Kim WESTON; Marvin GAYE & Tammi TERRELL;
Diana ROSS & Marvin GAYE)

## Marvin GAYE & Kim WESTON
Released 1 UK single prior to March 1965.
Released 1 original single between 1965 and 1976, and scored 1 top 40 hit. (US equivalent: 2 singles; 1 top 40 hit.) Also released 1 studio album on Tamla Motown.
**[590]** (1967) It Takes Two (16)
(See also: Marvin GAYE; Kim WESTON)

## Marvin GAYE & Tammi TERRELL
Released 8 original singles between 1965 and 1976, and scored 5 top 40 hits. (US equivalent: 10 singles; 7 top 40 hits.) Also released 3 studio albums on Tamla Motown.
**[611]** (1967) Ain't No Mountain High Enough
**[625]** (1967) Your Precious Love
**[635]** (1967) If I Could Build My Whole World Around You
**[655]** (1968) Ain't Nothing Like The Real Thing (34)
**[668]** (1968) You're All I Need To Get By (19)
**[681]** (1968) You Ain't Livin' Til You're Lovin' (21)
**[697]** (1969) Good Lovin' Ain't Easy To Come By (26)
**[715]** (1969) The Onion Song (9)
*Subsequent releases:*
[L007] (1976) The Onion Song
[L063] (1985) The Onion Song
(See also: Marvin GAYE; Tammi TERRELL)

## The HIT PACK
Released 1 original single between 1965 and 1976. (US equivalent: 0 singles.)
**[513]** (1965) Never Say No To Your Baby

## Brenda HOLLOWAY
Released 1 UK single prior to March 1965.
Released 6 original singles and 1 re-issue between 1965 and 1976. (US equivalent: 11 singles; 3 top 40 hits.) Also released 1 studio album on Tamla Motown.
**[508]** (1965) When I'm Gone
**[519]** (1965) Operator
**[556]** (1966) Together Till The End Of Time
**[581]** (1966) Hurt A Little Every Day
**[608]** (1967) Just Look What You've Done
**[622]** (1967) You've Made Me So Very Happy
*Brenda Holloway left Motown in 1967*
**[700]** (1969) *Re-issue of [608]:* Just Look What You've Done
*Subsequent releases:*
[L081] (1988) Just Look What You've Done / When I'm Gone [AA-side]

## The HONEST MEN
Released 1 original single between 1965 and 1976. (US equivalent: 0 singles.)
**[706]** (1969) Cherie

## Thelma HOUSTON
Released 1 original single between 1965 and 1976. (US equivalent: 11 singles.)
Also released 2 singles and 1 album on Mo-West.
**[799]**   (1972)   I Want To Go Back There Again


## Willie HUTCH
Released 2 original singles between 1965 and 1976. (US equivalent: 10 singles.)
Also released 6 studio albums on Tamla Motown.
**[862]**   (1973)   Brother's Gonna Work It Out
**[885]**   (1974)   *Not released:* Tell Me Why Has Our Love Turned Cold
**[1008]** (1975)   Love Power


## The ISLEY BROTHERS
Released 8 original singles and 3 re-issues between 1965 and 1976, and scored 4
top 40 hits. (US equivalent: 8 singles; 1 top 40 hit.) Also released 3 studio albums
on Tamla Motown.
**[555]**   (1966)   This Old Heart Of Mine (Is Weak For You)
**[566]**   (1966)   Take Some Time Out For Love
**[572]**   (1966)   I Guess I'll Always Love You
**[606]**   (1967)   Got To Have You Back
**[652]**   (1968)   Take Me In Your Arms (Rock Me A Little While)
*The Isley Brothers left Motown in 1968*
**[555]**   (1968)   *Re-pressing of [555]:* This Old Heart Of Mine (Is Weak For You) (3)
**[683]**   (1969)   *Re-issue of [572]:* I Guess I'll Always Love You (11)
**[693]**   (1969)   Behind A Painted Smile (5)
**[708]**   (1969)   Put Yourself In My Place (13)
**[719]**   (1969)   *Re-issue of [566]:* Take Some Time Out For Love
**[877]**   (1973)   Tell Me It's Just A Rumour Baby
**[937]**   (1975)   *Re-issue of [555]:* This Old Heart Of Mine (Is Weak For You)
*Subsequent releases:*
[L010]   (1976)   This Old Heart Of Mine (Is Weak For You) / Behind A Painted
                          Smile [AA-side]
[L045]   (1983)   I Guess I'll Always Love You
[L099]   (2004)   This Old Heart Of Mine (Is Weak For You) / Behind A Painted
                          Smile [AA-side]


## Chuck JACKSON
Released 2 original singles between 1965 and 1976. (US equivalent: 8 singles.)
Also released 2 studio albums on Tamla Motown.
**[651]**   (1968)   Girls, Girls, Girls
**[729]**   (1970)   Honey Come Back


## Jermaine JACKSON
Released 4 original singles between 1965 and 1976. (US equivalent: 7 singles; 1
top 40 hit.) Also released 3 studio albums on Tamla Motown.
**[838]**   (1972)   That's How Love Goes
**[851]**   (1973)   Daddy's Home
**[874]**   (1973)   The Bigger You Love (The Harder You Fall)
**[1040]** (1976)   Let's Be Young Tonight

---

## Michael JACKSON

Released 8 original singles between 1965 and 1976, and scored 4 top 40 hits. (US equivalent: 8 singles; 5 top 40 hits.) Also released 4 studio albums on Tamla Motown.

**[797]** (1971)  Got To Be There (5)
**[816]** (1972)  Rockin' Robin (3)
**[826]** (1972)  Ain't No Sunshine (8)
**[834]** (1972)  Ben (7)
**[863]** (1973)  Morning Glow
**[900]** (1974)  Music And Me
**[946]** (1975)  One Day In Your Life
**[1006]** (1975)  Just A Little Bit Of You

*Subsequent releases:*
[L016]  (1980)  Ben
[L038]  (1980)  Got To Be There
[L042]  (1981)  One Day In Your Life (1)
[L043]  (1981)  We're Almost There
[L054]  (1983)  Happy (Love Theme From "Lady Sings The Blues")
[L064]  (1985)  Got To Be There

## The JACKSON 5

Released 19 original singles between 1965 and 1976, and scored 10 top 40 hits. (US equivalent: 20 singles; 16 top 40 hits.) Also released 10 studio albums on Tamla Motown.

**[724]** (1970)  I Want You Back (2)
**[738]** (1970)  A B C (8)
**[746]** (1970)  The Love You Save (7)
**[758]** (1970)  I'll Be There (4)
**[769]** (1971)  Mama's Pearl (25)
**[778]** (1971)  Never Can Say Goodbye (33)
**[809]** (1972)  Sugar Daddy
**[825]** (1972)  Little Bitty Pretty One
**[833]** (1972)  Lookin' Through The Windows (9)
**[837]** (1972)  Santa Claus Is Coming To Town [Maxi-single]
**[842]** (1973)  Doctor My Eyes (9)
**[856]** (1973)  Hallelujah Day (20)
**[865]** (1973)  Skywriter (25)
**[878]** (1973)  Get It Together
**[895]** (1974)  The Boogie Man
**[904]** (1974)  Dancing Machine
**[927]** (1974)  The Life Of The Party
**[942]** (1975)  I Am Love
**[1001]** (1975)  Forever Came Today

*Subsequent releases:*
[L028]  (1980)  I Want You Back
[L034]  (1980)  I'll Be There
[L040]  (1980)  Lookin' Through The Windows
[L095]  (1988)  A B C / The Love You Save [AA-side]
[L115]  (2004)  I Want You Back / Doctor My Eyes [AA-side]

## Marv JOHNSON
Released 1 UK single prior to March 1965.
Released 4 original singles between 1965 and 1976, and scored 2 top 40 hits. (US
equivalent: 4 singles; 0 top 40 hits.) Also released 1 studio album on Tamla Motown.
**[525]** (1965) Why Do You Want To Let Me Go
**[680]** (1968) I'll Pick A Rose For My Rose (10)
**[713]** (1969) I Miss You Baby (How I Miss You) (25)
**[737]** (1970) So Glad You Chose Me
*Subsequent releases:*
[L012] (1976) I'll Pick A Rose For My Rose
[L038b] (1980) I Miss You Baby (How I Miss You)

## Gloria JONES
Released 1 original single between 1965 and 1976. (US equivalent: 1 single.) Also
released 1 studio album on Tamla Motown.
**[910]** (1974) Tin Can People

## Eddie KENDRICKS
Released 9 original singles between 1965 and 1976, and scored 2 top 40 hits. (US
equivalent: 17 singles; 5 top 40 hits.) Also released 8 studio albums on Tamla Motown.
**[845]** (1973) If You Let Me
**[873]** (1973) Keep On Truckin' (18)
**[888]** (1974) Boogie Down (39)
**[901]** (1974) Son Of Sagittarius
**[916]** (1974) Girl You Need A Change Of Mind
**[947]** (1975) Shoeshine Boy
**[1003]** (1975) If Anyone Can
**[1021]** (1976) He's A Friend
**[1031]** (1976) The Sweeter You Treat Her
*Subsequent releases:*
[L053] (1983) Keep On Truckin' (Part 1)
[L089] (1988) Keep On Truckin' (Part 1)

## Gladys KNIGHT & The PIPS
Released 17 original singles and 5 re-issues between 1965 and 1976, and scored
5 top 40 hits. (US equivalent: 19 singles; 13 top 40 hits.) Also released 11 studio
albums on Tamla Motown.
**[576]** (1966) Just Walk In My Shoes
**[604]** (1967) Take Me In Your Arms And Love Me (13)
**[619]** (1967) Everybody Needs Love
**[629]** (1967) I Heard It Through The Grapevine
**[645]** (1968) The End Of Our Road
**[660]** (1968) It Should Have Been Me
**[674]** (1968) I Wish It Would Rain
**[714]** (1969) The Nitty Gritty
**[728]** (1970) Didn't You Know (You'd Have To Cry Sometime)
**[756]** (1970) Friendship Train
**[765]** (1971) If I Were Your Woman

**[805]** (1972) Make Me The Woman You Go Home To
**[813]** (1972) *Re-issue of [576]*: Just Walk In My Shoes (35)
**[830]** (1972) Help Me Make It Through The Night (11)
**[844]** (1973) The Look Of Love (21)
**[855]** (1973) Neither One Of Us (Wants To Be The First To Say Goodbye) (31)
**[864]** (1973) *Re-issue of [604]*: Take Me In Your Arms And Love Me
**[876]** (1973) Daddy Could Swear, I Declare
*Gladys Knight & The Pips left Motown in 1973*
**[903]** (1974) *Re-issue of [728]*: Didn't You Know (You'd Have To Cry Sometime)
**[945]** (1975) You've Lost That Loving Feeling
**[955]** (1975) *Re-issue of [765]*: If I Were Your Woman
**[1009]** (1975) *Re-issue of [855]*: Neither One Of Us (Wants To Be The First To Say Goodbye)
*Subsequent releases:*
[L058] (1985) Help Me Make It Through The Night

### Laura LEE
Released 1 original single between 1965 and 1976. (US equivalent: 0 singles.)
**[831]** (1972) To Win Your Heart

### Michel LEGRAND
Released 1 original single between 1965 and 1976. (US equivalent: 2 singles.)
**[848a]** (1973) Love Theme From "Lady Sings The Blues"

### The LEWIS SISTERS
Released 1 original single between 1965 and 1976. (US equivalent: 2 singles.)
**[536]** (1965) You Need Me

### Shorty LONG
Released 5 original singles between 1965 and 1976, and scored 1 top 40 hit. (US equivalent: 8 singles; 1 top 40 hit.) Also released 2 studio albums on Tamla Motown.
**[512]** (1965) Out To Get You
**[573]** (1966) Function At The Junction
**[600]** (1967) Chantilly Lace
**[644]** (1968) Night Fo' Last
**[663]** (1968) Here Comes The Judge (30)
*Subsequent releases:*
[L082] (1988) Here Comes The Judge / Function At The Junction [AA-side]

### MAGIC DISCO MACHINE
Released 1 original single between 1965 and 1976. (US equivalent: 2 singles.)
**[1004]** (1975) Control Tower

### MARTHA & The VANDELLAS
Released 8 UK singles prior to March 1965.
Released 13 original singles and 1 re-issue between 1965 and 1976, and scored 8 top 40 hits. (US equivalent: 26 singles; 12 top 40 hits.) Also released 8 studio albums and 2 EPs on Tamla Motown.

[502]   (1965)   Nowhere To Run (26)
[530]   (1965)   You've Been In Love Too Long
[549]   (1966)   My Baby Loves Me
[567]   (1966)   What Am I Going To Do Without Your Love
[582]   (1966)   I'm Ready For Love (29)
[599]   (1967)   Jimmy Mack (21)
[621]   (1967)   Love Bug Leave My Heart Alone
[636]   (1968)   Honey Chile (30)
[657]   (1968)   I Promise To Wait My Love
[669]   (1968)   I Can't Dance To That Music You're Playing
[684]   (1969)   Dancing In The Street (4)
[694]   (1969)   *Re-issue of [502]*: Nowhere To Run
[599]   (1970)   *Re-pressing of [599]*: Jimmy Mack (21)
[762]   (1971)   Forget Me Not (11)
[794]   (1971)   Bless You (33)
*Subsequent releases:*
[L011]   (1976)   Dancing In The Street / Jimmy Mack [AA-side]
[L015]   (1980)   Heatwave
[L049]   (1983)   I'm Ready For Love
[L085]   (1988)   Nowhere To Run / Forget Me Not [AA-side]
[L101]   (2004)   Dancing In The Street / Forget Me Not [AA-side]
(See also: Martha REEVES)

## Tony MARTIN
Released 1 UK single prior to March 1965.
Released 1 original single between 1965 and 1976. (US equivalent: 3 singles.)
[537]   (1965)   The Bigger Your Heart Is

## MARTIN & FINLEY
Released 0 original singles between 1965 and 1976. (US equivalent: 5 singles.)
[867]   (1973)   *Not released*: It's Another Sunday

## The MARVELETTES
Released 8 UK singles prior to March 1965.
Released 9 original singles and 2 re-issues between 1965 and 1976, and scored 1 top 40 hit. (US equivalent: 24 singles; 10 top 40 hits.) Also released 4 studio albums and 1 EP on Tamla Motown.
[518]   (1965)   I'll Keep Holding On
[535]   (1965)   Danger Heartbreak Dead Ahead
[546]   (1966)   Don't Mess With Bill
[562]   (1966)   You're The One
[594]   (1967)   The Hunter Gets Captured By The Game
[609]   (1967)   When You're Young And In Love (13)
[639]   (1968)   My Baby Must Be A Magician
[659]   (1968)   Here I Am Baby
[701]   (1969)   Reachin' For Something I Can't Have
*The Marvelettes left Motown in 1971*
[860]   (1973)   *Re-issue of [701]*: Reachin' For Something I Can't Have

**[939]** (1975) *Re-issue of [609]:* When You're Young And In Love
*Subsequent releases:*
[L041] (1980) Finders Keepers Losers Weepers
[L083] (1988) Too Many Fish In The Sea / Please Mr. Postman [AA-side]
[L112] (2004) Please Mr. Postman / When You're Young And In Love [AA-side]

## Barbara McNAIR
Released 1 original single between 1965 and 1976. (US equivalent: 6 singles.)
**[544]** (1966) You're Gonna Love My Baby

## Stephanie MILLS
Released 1 original single between 1965 and 1976. (US equivalent: 1 single.) Also
released 1 studio album on Tamla Motown.
**[1020]** (1976) This Empty Place

## The MIRACLES
Released 10 UK singles prior to March 1965.
Released 20 original singles and 4 re-issues between 1965 and 1976, and scored
6 top 40 hits. (US equivalent: 51 singles; 29 top 40 hits.) Also released 14 studio
albums on Tamla Motown.
**[503]** (1965) Ooo Baby Baby
**[522]** (1965) The Tracks Of My Tears
**[540]** (1965) My Girl Has Gone
**[547]** (1966) Going To A Go-Go
**[569]** (1966) Whole Lot Of Shaking In My Heart (Since I Met You Girl)
**[584]** (1966) (Come 'Round Here) I'm The One You Need
**[598]** (1967) The Love I Saw In You Was Just A Mirage
**[614]** (1967) More Love
**[631]** (1967) I Second That Emotion (27)
**[648]** (1968) If You Can Want
**[661]** (1968) Yester Love
**[673]** (1968) Special Occasion
**[687]** (1969) Baby, Baby Don't Cry
**[696]** (1969) *Re-issue of [522]:* The Tracks Of My Tears (9)
**[745]** (1970) The Tears Of A Clown (1)
**[761]** (1971) *Re-issue of [584]:* (Come 'Round Here) I'm The One You Need (13)
**[774]** (1971) I Don't Blame You At All (11)
**[811]** (1972) *Re-issue of [540]:* My Girl Has Gone
**[853]** (1973) *Re-issue of [547]:* Going To A Go-Go [Maxi-single]
**[891]** (1974) Don't Let It End ('Til You Let It Begin)
**[914]** (1974) Do It Baby
**[940]** (1975) Where Are You Going To My Love
**[1015]** (1975) Love Machine (3)
**[1023a]**(1976) Night Life
*Subsequent releases:*
[L008] (1976) The Tears Of A Clown / The Tracks Of My Tears [AA-side] (36)
[L022] (1980) (Come 'Round Here) I'm The One You Need
[L046] (1983) I Don't Blame You At All

[L084] (1988) Love Machine
[L097] (2004) The Tears Of A Clown / The Tracks Of My Tears [AA-side]
[L103] (2004) Going To A Go-Go / I Second That Emotion [AA-side]
(See also: The MIRACLE WORKERS)

## The MIRACLE WORKERS
Released 1 original single between 1965 and 1976. (US equivalent: 0 singles.)
**[1023b]** (1976) Overture
(See also: The MIRACLES)

**Motown Spinners**: See *The SPINNERS*

## The ORIGINALS
Released 5 original singles between 1965 and 1976. (US equivalent: 20 singles; 2 top 40 hits.) Also released 3 studio albums on Tamla Motown.
**[592]** (1967) Goodnight Irene
**[702]** (1969) Green Grow The Lilacs
**[733]** (1970) Baby I'm For Real
**[822]** (1972) God Bless Whoever Sent You [Maxi-single]
**[1038]** (1976) Down To Love Town

## Paul PETERSEN
Released 1 original single between 1965 and 1976. (US equivalent: 2 singles.)
**[670]** (1968) A Little Bit For Sandy

## Barbara RANDOLPH
Released 1 original single and 1 re-issue between 1965 and 1976. (US equivalent: 2 singles.)
**[628]** (1967) I Got A Feeling
*Barbara Randolph left Motown in 1968*
**[788]** (1971) *Re-issue of [628]:* I Got A Feeling
*Subsequent releases:*
[L013] (1979) I Got A Feeling [Maxi-single]

## RARE EARTH
Released 1 original single between 1965 and 1976. (US equivalent: 16 singles; 5 top 40 hits.) Also released 2 studio albums on Tamla Motown. Also released 5 singles and 6 albums on Rare Earth.
**[742]** (1970) Get Ready

## The REFLECTIONS
Released 1 original single between 1965 and 1976. (US equivalent: 0 singles.)
**[907]** (1974) (Just Like) Romeo And Juliet

## Martha REEVES
Released 1 original single between 1965 and 1976. (US equivalent: 1 single.)
**[843]** (1973) No One There
(See also: MARTHA & The VANDELLAS)

**Martha Reeves & The Vandellas**: See *MARTHA & The VANDELLAS*

## Smokey ROBINSON
Released 4 original singles between 1965 and 1976, and scored 1 top 40 hit. (US equivalent: 11 singles; 3 top 40 hits.) Also released 4 studio albums on Tamla Motown.
**[883]** (1974)  Just My Soul Responding (35)
**[898]** (1974)  A Silent Partner In A Three Way Affair
**[949]** (1975)  Baby That's Backatcha
**[1019]** (1976)  Quiet Storm

**Smokey Robinson & The Miracles**: See *The MIRACLES*

## Diana ROSS
Released 15 original singles between 1965 and 1976, and scored 14 top 40 hits. (US equivalent: 15 singles; 11 top 40 hits.) Also released 9 studio albums on Tamla Motown.
**[743]** (1970)  Reach Out And Touch (Somebody's Hand) (33)
**[751]** (1970)  Ain't No Mountain High Enough (6)
**[768]** (1971)  Remember Me (7)
**[781]** (1971)  I'm Still Waiting (1)
**[792]** (1971)  Surrender (10)
**[812]** (1972)  Doobedood'ndoobe, Doobedood'ndoobe, Doobedood'ndoo (12)
**[849]** (1973)  Good Morning Heartache
**[861]** (1973)  Touch Me In The Morning (9)
**[880]** (1973)  All Of My Life (9)
**[893]** (1974)  The Last Time I Saw Him (35)
**[917]** (1974)  Love Me (38)
**[941]** (1975)  Sorry Doesn't Always Make It Right (23)
**[1010]** (1975)  Theme From Mahogany (Do You Know Where You're Going To) (5)
**[1024]** (1976)  Love Hangover (10)
**[1032]** (1976)  I Thought It Took A Little Time (But Today I Fell In Love) (32)
*Subsequent releases:*
[L001] (1976)  I'm Still Waiting / Touch Me In The Morning [AA-side]
[L035] (1980)  Remember Me
[L057] (1984)  Reach Out And Touch (Somebody's Hand)
[L070] (1985)  Love Hangover
[L076] (1986)  Ain't No Mountain High Enough
[L086] (1988)  Reach Out And Touch (Somebody's Hand) / Surrender [AA-side]
[L104] (2004)  I'm Still Waiting / Touch Me In The Morning [AA-side]
(See also: Diana ROSS & The SUPREMES & The TEMPTATIONS; Diana ROSS & Marvin GAYE)

## Diana ROSS & Marvin GAYE
Released 5 original singles between 1965 and 1976, and scored 2 top 40 hits. (US equivalent: 3 singles; 2 top 40 hits.) Also released 1 studio album on Tamla Motown.
**[879]** (1973)  You're A Special Part Of Me
**[890]** (1974)  You Are Everything (5)
**[906]** (1974)  Stop, Look, Listen (To Your Heart) (25)

**[920]** (1974)  My Mistake (Was To Love You)
**[953]** (1975)  Don't Knock My Love
*Subsequent releases:*
[L007] (1976)  You Are Everything
[L068] (1985)  You Are Everything
(See also: Diana ROSS; Marvin GAYE)

**Diana Ross & The Supremes**: See *The SUPREMES*

## Diana ROSS & The SUPREMES & The TEMPTATIONS
Released 3 original singles between 1965 and 1976, and scored 3 top 40 hits. (US equivalent: 5 singles; 2 top 40 hits.) Also released 3 studio albums on Tamla Motown.
**[685]** (1969)  I'm Gonna Make You Love Me (3)
**[709]** (1969)  I Second That Emotion (18)
**[730]** (1970)  Why (Must We Fall In Love) (31)
*Subsequent releases:*
[L005] (1976)  I'm Gonna Make You Love Me
[L061] (1985)  I'm Gonna Make You Love Me
(See also: Diana Ross; The SUPREMES; The TEMPTATIONS)

## David RUFFIN
Released 6 original singles between 1965 and 1976, and scored 1 top 40 hit. (US equivalent: 15 singles; 2 top 40 hits.) Also released 6 studio albums on Tamla Motown.
**[689]** (1969)  My Whole World Ended (The Moment You Left Me)
**[711]** (1969)  I've Lost Everything I've Ever Loved
**[936]** (1975)  Take Me Clear From Here
**[1017]** (1975)  Walk Away From Love (10)
**[1022]** (1976)  Heavy Love
**[1036]** (1976)  Discover Me
*Subsequent releases:*
[L088] (1988)  Walk Away From Love

## Jimmy RUFFIN
Released 10 original singles and 5 re-issues between 1965 and 1976, and scored 9 top 40 hits. (US equivalent: 14 singles; 3 top 40 hits.) Also released 3 studio albums on Tamla Motown.
**[577]** (1966)  What Becomes Of The Brokenhearted (8)
**[593]** (1967)  I've Passed This Way Before (29)
**[603]** (1967)  Gonna Give Her All The Love I've Got (26)
**[617]** (1967)  Don't You Miss Me A Little Bit Baby
**[649]** (1968)  I'll Say Forever My Love
**[664]** (1968)  Don't Let Him Take Your Love From Me
**[703]** (1969)  *Re-issue of [593]*: I've Passed This Way Before (33)
**[726]** (1970)  Farewell Is A Lonely Sound (8)
**[740]** (1970)  *Re-issue of [649]*: I'll Say Forever My Love (7)
**[753]** (1970)  It's Wonderful (To Be Loved By You) (6)
**[767]** (1971)  Let's Say Goodbye Tomorrow
**[784]** (1971)  On The Way Out (On The Way In)

*Jimmy Ruffin left Motown in 1971*
**[911]**  (1974)  *Re-issue of [577]:* What Becomes Of The Brokenhearted (4)
**[922]**  (1974)  *Re-issue of [726]:* Farewell Is A Lonely Sound (30)
**[934]**  (1975)  *Re-issue of [593]:* I've Passed This Way Before
*Subsequent releases:*
[L012]  (1976)  What Becomes Of The Brokenhearted
[L026]  (1980)  I'll Say Forever My Love
[L066]  (1985)  Gonna Give Her All The Love I've Got
[L088]  (1988)  I'll Say Forever My Love
[L096]  (2004)  What Becomes Of The Brokenhearted / Farewell Is A Lonely
Sound [AA-side]

## The SAN REMO STRINGS
Released 2 original singles between 1965 and 1976, and scored 1 top 40 hit. (US
equivalent: 1 single; 0 top 40 hits.) Also released 1 studio album on Tamla Motown.
**[795]**  (1971)  Festival Time (39)
**[807]**  (1972)  Reach Out I'll Be There

## SISTERS LOVE
Released 2 original singles between 1965 and 1976. (US equivalent: 4 singles.)
Also released 1 single on Mo-West.
**[828]**  (1972)  Mr. Fix-it Man
**[1002]** (1975)  I'm Learning To Trust My Man

## The SPINNERS
Released 5 original singles and 1 re-issue between 1965 and 1976, and scored 1
top 40 hit. (US equivalent: 11 singles; 2 top 40 hits.) Also released 2 studio
albums on Tamla Motown.
**[514]**  (1965)  Sweet Thing
**[523]**  (1965)  I'll Always Love You
**[627]**  (1967)  For All We Know
**[755]**  (1970)  It's A Shame (20)
**[766]**  (1971)  Together We Can Make Such Sweet Music
*The Spinners left Motown in 1971*
**[871]**  (1973)  *Re-issue of [766]:* Together We Can Make Such Sweet Music
*Subsequent releases:*
[L018]  (1980)  It's A Shame
[L089]  (1988)  It's A Shame

## Edwin STARR
Released 13 original singles and 1 re-issues between 1965 and 1976, and scored
3 top 40 hits. (US equivalent: 17 singles; 3 top 40 hits.) Also released 5 studio
albums on Tamla Motown.
**[630]**  (1967)  I Want My Baby Back
**[646]**  (1968)  I Am The Man For You Baby
**[672]**  (1968)  25 Miles (36)
**[692]**  (1969)  Way Over There
**[725]**  (1970)  Time

[754]   (1970)   War (3)
[764]   (1971)   Stop The War Now (33)
[790]   (1971)   Agent Double O Soul
[810]   (1972)   Funky Music Sho' Nuff Turns Me On
[875]   (1973)   You've Got My Soul On Fire
[905]   (1974)   Stop Her On Sight (SOS)
[930]   (1974)   Who's Right Or Wrong
[1028]  (1976)   Re-issue of [725]: Time
*Subsequent releases:*
[L033]  (1980)   War
[L084]  (1988)   25 Miles
[L110]  (2004)   War / Stop The War Now [AA-side]
(See also: BLINKY & Edwin STARR)


**Barrett STRONG**
Released 1 UK single prior to March 1965.
Released 0 original singles between 1965 and 1976. (US equivalent: 6 singles; 1 top 40 hit.)
*Subsequent releases:*
[L077]  (1988)   Money (That's What I Want)


**The SUPREMES**
Released 4 UK singles prior to March 1965.
Released 33 original singles between 1965 and 1976, and scored 22 top 40 hits. (US equivalent: 40 singles; 30 top 40 hits.) Also released 20 studio albums and 2 EPs on Tamla Motown.
[501]   (1965)   Stop! In The Name Of Love (7)
[516]   (1965)   Back In My Arms Again (40)
[527]   (1965)   Nothing But Heartaches
[543]   (1965)   I Hear A Symphony (39)
[548]   (1966)   My World Is Empty Without You
[560]   (1966)   Love Is Like An Itching In My Heart
[575]   (1966)   You Can't Hurry Love (3)
[585]   (1966)   You Keep Me Hangin' On (8)
[597]   (1967)   Love Is Here And Now You're Gone (17)
[607]   (1967)   The Happening (6)
[616]   (1967)   Reflections (5)
[632]   (1967)   In And Out Of Love (13)
[650]   (1968)   Forever Came Today (28)
[662]   (1968)   Some Things You Never Get Used To (34)
[677]   (1968)   Love Child (15)
[695]   (1969)   I'm Living In Shame (14)
[704]   (1969)   No Matter What Sign You Are (37)
[721]   (1969)   Someday We'll Be Together (13)
[735]   (1970)   Up The Ladder To The Roof (6)
[747]   (1970)   Everybody's Got The Right To Love
[760]   (1971)   Stoned Love (3)
[782]   (1971)   Nathan Jones (5)

**[804]** (1972) Floy Joy (9)
**[821]** (1972) Automatically Sunshine (10)
**[835]** (1972) Your Wonderful Sweet, Sweet Love
**[847]** (1973) Bad Weather (37)
**[859]** (1973) Tossin' And Turnin'
**[884]** (1974) I Guess I'll Miss The Man
**[915]** (1974) Baby Love (12)
**[925]** (1974) Where Did Our Love Go
**[950]** (1975) He's My Man
**[1012]** (1975) Early Morning Love
**[1029]** (1976) I'm Gonna Let My Heart Do The Walking
*Subsequent releases:*
[L004] (1976) Baby Love / Stop! In The Name Of Love [AA-side]
[L006] (1976) Stoned Love / Nathan Jones [AA-side]
[L017] (1980) Supremes Medley (Part 1)
[L021] (1980) You Can't Hurry Love
[L025] (1980) Reflections
[L029] (1980) Up The Ladder To The Roof
[L039] (1980) Floy Joy
[L047] (1983) Back In My Arms Again
[L062] (1985) You Keep Me Hangin' On
[L069] (1985) The Composer
[L074] (1986) You Keep Me Hangin' On
[L087] (1988) Someday We'll Be Together / My World Is Empty Without You
         [AA-side]
[L090] (1988) Up The Ladder To The Roof / Floy Joy [AA-side]
[L104] (2004) Baby Love / Where Did Our Love Go [AA-side]
[L117] (2005) Honey Bee (Keep On Stinging Me)—Out On The Floor Mix
(See also: The SUPREMES & FOUR TOPS; Diana ROSS & The SUPREMES & The
TEMPTATIONS)

## The SUPREMES & FOUR TOPS
Released 4 original singles between 1965 and 1976, and scored 2 top 40 hits. (US
equivalent: 1 single; 1 top 40 hit.) Also released 3 studio albums on Tamla Motown.
**[777]** (1971) River Deep, Mountain High (11)
**[793]** (1971) You Gotta Have Love In Your Heart (25)
**[815]** (1972) Without The One You Love
**[836]** (1972) Reach Out And Touch (Somebody's Hand)
*Subsequent releases:*
[L036] (1980) River Deep, Mountain High
[L057b] (1984) Reach Out And Touch (Somebody's Hand)
(See also: The SUPREMES; The FOUR TOPS)

## SYREETA (aka Rita WRIGHT)
Released 5 original singles and 1 re-issue between 1965 and 1976, and scored 2
top 40 hits. (US equivalent: 7 singles; 0 top 40 hits.) Also released 1 studio album
on Tamla Motown. Also released 1 single and 1 album on Mo-West.
**[643]** (1968) I Can't Give Back The Love I Feel For You

---

[791]  (1971)  *Re-issue of [643]:* I Can't Give Back The Love I Feel For You
[912]  (1974)  Spinnin' And Spinnin'
[926]  (1974)  I'm Goin' Left
[933]  (1975)  Your Kiss Is Sweet (12)
[954]  (1975)  Harmour Love (32)

## Bobby TAYLOR & The VANCOUVERS

Released 1 original single between 1965 and 1976. (US equivalent: 3 singles; 1 top 40 hit.) Also released 1 studio album on Tamla Motown.
[654]  (1968)  Does Your Mama Know About Me

## R. Dean TAYLOR

Released 4 original singles and 1 re-issue between 1965 and 1976, and scored 3 top 40 hits. (US equivalent: 10 singles; 1 top 40 hit.) Also released 1 studio album on Tamla Motown. Also released 2 singles on Rare Earth.
[656]  (1968)  Gotta See Jane (17)
[763]  (1971)  Indiana Wants Me (2)
[786]  (1971)  *Not released:* Ain't It A Sad Thing
[896]  (1974)  There's A Ghost In My House (3)
[909]  (1974)  Don't Fool Around
[918]  (1974)  *Re-issue of [656]:* Gotta See Jane
*Subsequent releases:*
[L033b] (1980)  Indiana Wants Me
[L102]  (2004)  There's A Ghost In My House / Gotta See Jane [AA-side]

## The TEMPTATIONS

Released 4 UK singles prior to March 1965.
Released 30 original singles and 2 re-issues between 1965 and 1976, and scored 13 top 40 hits. (US equivalent: 50 singles; 35 top 40 hits.) Also released 19 studio albums and 2 EPs on Tamla Motown.
[504]  (1965)  It's Growing
[526]  (1965)  Since I Lost My Baby
[541]  (1965)  My Baby
[557]  (1966)  Get Ready
[565]  (1966)  Ain't Too Proud To Beg (21)
[578]  (1966)  Beauty Is Only Skin Deep (18)
[587]  (1966)  (I Know) I'm Losing You (19)
[610]  (1967)  All I Need
[620]  (1967)  You're My Everything (26)
[633]  (1967)  (Loneliness Made Me Realise) It's You That I Need
[641]  (1968)  I Wish It Would Rain
[658]  (1968)  I Could Never Love Another (After Loving You)
[671]  (1968)  Why Did You Leave Me Darling
[688]  (1969)  *Re-issue of [557]:* Get Ready (10)
[699]  (1969)  *Re-issue of [565]:* Ain't Too Proud To Beg
[707]  (1969)  Cloud Nine (15)
[716]  (1969)  Runaway Child, Running Wild
[722]  (1970)  I Can't Get Next To You (13)

**[741]** (1970) Psychedelic Shack (33)
**[749]** (1970) Ball Of Confusion (That's What The World Is Today) (7)
**[773]** (1971) Just My Imagination (Running Away With Me) (8)
**[783]** (1971) It's Summer
**[800]** (1972) Superstar (Remember How You Got Where You Are) (32)
**[808]** (1972) Take A Look Around (13)
**[832]** (1972) Smiling Faces Sometimes
**[839]** (1973) Papa Was A Rollin' Stone (14)
**[854]** (1973) Masterpiece
**[866]** (1973) Law Of The Land
**[887]** (1974) I Need You
**[931a]** (1975) Happy People
**[948]** (1975) Memories
*Subsequent releases:*
[L003] (1976) Just My Imagination (Running Away With Me) / Get Ready
[AA-side]
[L032] (1980) Ball Of Confusion (That's What The World Is Today)
[L048] (1983) Cloud Nine
[L055b] (1983) Papa Was A Rollin' Stone
[L060] (1985) Law Of The Land
[L067] (1985) Ball Of Confusion (That's What The World Is Today)
[L075] (1986) My Girl
[L091] (1988) I Can't Get Next To You / (I Know) I'm Losing You [AA-side]
[L100] (2004) My Girl / Ain't Too Proud To Beg [AA-side]
[L114] (2004) Papa Was A Rollin' Stone / Cloud Nine [AA-side]
(See also: Diana ROSS & The SUPREMES & The TEMPTATIONS; The
TEMPTATIONS BAND; The TEMPTATIONS with FOUR TOPS)

## The TEMPTATIONS BAND
Released 1 original single between 1965 and 1976. (US equivalent: 0 singles.)
**[931b]** (1975) Happy People
(See also: The TEMPTATIONS)

## The TEMPTATIONS with FOUR TOPS
Released 0 original singles between 1965 and 1976. (US equivalent: 0 singles.)
*Subsequent releases:*
[L055] (1983) Medley
(See also: FOUR TOPS; The TEMPTATIONS)

## Tammi TERRELL
Released 1 original single between 1965 and 1976. (US equivalent: 4 singles.) Also
released 1 studio album on Tamla Motown.
**[561]** (1966) Come On And See Me
(See also: Marvin GAYE & Tammi TERRELL)

## The UNDISPUTED TRUTH
Released 7 original singles between 1965 and 1976. (US equivalent: 15 singles; 1
top 40 hit.) Also released 6 studio albums on Tamla Motown.

[776]  (1971)  Save My Love For A Rainy Day
[789]  (1971)  Smiling Faces Sometimes
[818]  (1972)  Superstar (Remember How You Got Where You Are)
[897]  (1974)  Help Yourself
[919]  (1974)  I'm A Fool For You
[943]  (1975)  Law Of The Land
[1014] (1975)  Higher Than High

## Frankie VALLI & The FOUR SEASONS
Released 1 original single between 1965 and 1976. (US equivalent: 4 singles.) Also released 4 singles and 1 album on Mo-West.
[819]  (1972)  You're A Song (That I Can't Sing)
*Subsequent releases:*
[L020]  (1980)  The Night

## Earl VAN DYKE & The SOUL BROTHERS
Released 1 UK single prior to March 1965.
Released 3 original singles between 1965 and 1976. (US equivalent: 6 singles.) Also released 1 studio album on Tamla Motown.
[506]  (1965)  All For You
[759]  (1970)  6 By 6
[814]  (1972)  I Can't Help Myself
*Subsequent releases:*
[L117b] (2005)  All Day All Night

## The VELVELETTES
Released 2 UK singles prior to March 1965.
Released 4 original singles and 1 re-issues between 1965 and 1976, and scored 1 top 40 hit. (US equivalent: 7 singles; 0 top 40 hits.)
[521]  (1965)  Lonely Lonely Girl Am I
[580]  (1966)  These Things Will Keep Me Loving You
[595]  (1967)  He Was Really Saying Somethin'
*The Velvelettes left Motown in 1969*
[780]  (1971)  *Re-issue of [580]:* These Things Will Keep Me Loving You (34)
[806]  (1972)  Needle In A Haystack
*Subsequent releases:*
[L052]  (1983)  Needle In A Haystack
[L107]  (2004)  Needle In A Haystack / He Was Really Sayin' Somethin' [AA-side]

## Junior WALKER
Released 1 original single between 1965 and 1976. (US equivalent: 4 singles.) Also released 1 studio album on Tamla Motown.
[1027] (1976)  I'm So Glad
(See also: Junior WALKER & The ALL STARS)

## Junior WALKER & The ALL STARS
Released 20 original singles and 1 re-issue between 1965 and 1976, and scored 6 top 40 hits. (US equivalent: 27 singles; 12 top 40 hits.) Also released 11 studio

albums and 1 EP on Tamla Motown.

**[509]** (1965)  Shotgun
**[520]** (1965)  Do The Boomerang
**[529]** (1965)  Shake & Fingerpop
**[550]** (1966)  Cleo's Mood
**[559]** (1966)  (I'm A) Road Runner
**[571]** (1966)  How Sweet It Is (To Be Loved By You) (22)
**[586]** (1966)  Money (That's What I Want)
**[596]** (1967)  Pucker Up Buttercup
**[637]** (1968)  Come See About Me
**[667]** (1968)  Hip City (Part 2)
**[682]** (1969)  Home Cookin'
**[691]** (1969)  *Re-issue of [559]:* (I'm A) Road Runner (12)
**[712]** (1969)  What Does It Take (To Win Your Love) (13)
**[727]** (1970)  These Eyes
**[750]** (1970)  Do You See My Love (For You Growing)
**[824]** (1972)  Walk In The Night [Maxi-single] (16)
**[840]** (1973)  Take Me Girl, I'm Ready (16)
**[857]** (1973)  Way Back Home [Maxi-single] (35)
**[872]** (1973)  Holly Holy
**[889]** (1974)  Don't Blame The Children
**[894]** (1974)  Gotta Hold On To This Feeling
*Subsequent releases:*
[L027] (1980)  What Does It Take (To Win Your Love)
[L092] (1988)  How Sweet It Is (To Be Loved By You) / What Does It Take (To Win Your Love) [AA-side]
[L105] (2004)  Shotgun / (I'm A) Road Runner [AA-side]
(See also: Junior WALKER)

## Mary WELLS
Released 6 UK singles prior to March 1965.
Released 1 original single between 1965 and 1976, and scored 1 top 40 hit. (US equivalent: 12 singles; 8 top 40 hits.) Also released 1 studio album and 1 EP on Tamla Motown.
**[820]** (1972)  My Guy [Maxi-single] (14)
*Subsequent releases:*
[L019] (1980)  My Guy

## Kim WESTON
Released 1 UK single prior to March 1965.
Released 3 original singles between 1965 and 1976. (US equivalent: 9 singles.) Also released 2 EPs on Tamla Motown.
**[511]** (1965)  I'm Still Loving You
**[538]** (1965)  Take Me In Your Arms (Rock Me A Little While)
**[554]** (1966)  Helpless
*Subsequent releases:*
[L041b] (1980)  Do Like I Do
(See also: Marvin GAYE & Kim WESTON)

**Frank WILSON**
Released 0 original singles between 1965 and 1976. (US equivalent: 0 singles.)
*Subsequent releases:*
[L014]  (1979)  Do I Love You (Indeed I Do)
[L111]  (2004)  Do I Love You (Indeed I Do)


**Stevie WONDER**
Released 4 UK singles prior to March 1965.
Released 30 original singles between 1965 and 1976, and scored 20 top 40 hits.
(US equivalent: 41 singles; 29 top 40 hits.) Also released 12 studio albums and 1
EP on Tamla Motown.
**[505]**  (1965)  Kiss Me Baby
**[532]**  (1965)  High Heel Sneakers
**[545]**  (1966)  Uptight (Everything's Alright) (14)
**[558]**  (1966)  Nothing's Too Good For My Baby
**[570]**  (1966)  Blowin' In The Wind (36)
**[588]**  (1966)  A Place In The Sun (20)
**[602]**  (1967)  Travelin' Man
**[613]**  (1967)  I Was Made To Love Her (5)
**[626]**  (1967)  I'm Wondering (22)
**[653]**  (1968)  Shoo-Be-Doo-Be-Doo-Da-Day
**[666]**  (1968)  You Met Your Match
**[679]**  (1968)  For Once In My Life (3)
**[690a]** (1969)  I Don't Know Why (I Love You) (14)
**[690b]** (1969)  *Re-pressing with sides switched*: My Cherie Amour (4)
**[717]**  (1969)  Yester-me, Yester-you, Yesterday (2)
**[731]**  (1970)  Never Had A Dream Come True (6)
**[744]**  (1970)  Signed, Sealed, Delivered, I'm Yours (15)
**[757]**  (1970)  Heaven Help Us All (29)
**[772]**  (1971)  We Can Work It Out (27)
**[779]**  (1971)  Never Dreamed You'd Leave In Summer
**[798]**  (1972)  If You Really Love Me (20)
**[827]**  (1972)  Superwoman
**[841]**  (1973)  Superstition (11)
**[852]**  (1973)  You Are The Sunshine Of My Life (7)
**[869]**  (1973)  Higher Ground (29)
**[881]**  (1973)  Living For The City (15)
**[892]**  (1974)  He's Misstra Know-It-All (10)
**[908]**  (1974)  Don't You Worry 'Bout A Thing
**[921]**  (1974)  You Haven't Done Nothin' (30)
**[928]**  (1974)  Boogie On Reggae Woman (12)
*Subsequent releases:*
[L002]  (1976)  Yester-me, Yester-you, Yesterday / Uptight (Everything's Alright)
              [AA-side]
[L024]  (1980)  I Was Made To Love Her
[L031]  (1980)  Signed, Sealed, Delivered, I'm Yours
[L059]  (1985)  For Once In My Life
[L072]  (1985)  He's Misstra Know-It-All

[L093]   (1988)   Fingertips (Part 2) / Blowin' In The Wind [AA-side]
[L094]   (1988)   Never Had A Dream Come True / Signed, Sealed, Delivered, I'm Yours [AA-side]
[L109]   (2004)   Uptight (Everything's Alright) / Yester-me, Yester-you, Yesterday [AA-side]
[L116]   (2005)   So What The Fuss / So What The Fuss Remix Feat. Q-Tip [AA-side] (19)
[L118]   (2005)   Positivity (UK Radio Edit)
[L119]   (2006)   From The Bottom Of My Heart

**Rita Wright**: *See SYREETA*

**Popcorn WYLIE**
Released 1 original single between 1965 and 1976. (US equivalent: 1 single.)
**[932]**   (1975)   Funky Rubber Band

# STATISTICS, FACTS AND FEATS

## UK chart data

Despite Motown's constant presence in the upper reaches of the British charts only four Tamla Motown singles managed to reach number I between 1965 and 1976, even artists of the stature of The Supremes and Stevie Wonder missing out during the 140 months under examination. ("Baby Love" managed it on Stateside and another Tamla Motown single, TMG 946, topped the listings in 1981. See Chapter 6.)

**All Releases**: 491
**Top 40**: 184
**Top 10**: 71
**No. 1**: 4

The total number of singles released does not take account of the four scheduled but aborted releases which occupy TMG numbers, but the chart stats do count [599] and [690] twice each, as both enjoyed two separate runs in the UK listings. The all-inclusive count of 184 top 40 hits averages out to approximately one every 23 days for the entire period, and equates to a release-to-hit ratio of almost 40 percent—staggeringly high for the industry.

Given the defined limitations on the singles which qualifies for inclusion in these statistics, it is not viable to produce parallel information for US chart performance. Out of interest, however, from March 1965 until November 1976 Motown placed some 32 singles at number I in the US, and a staggering 66 at the summit of the R & B listings. (Many of these 94 successes account for The Funk Brothers' claim that they recorded more number Is than Elvis, The Beatles, The Rolling Stones and The Beach Boys combined. True—although, but for some early releases, none of these artists qualify for the R & B listings.) Motown's dominance of the R & B charts reached a peak with 11 number Is between October 1969 and December 1970 accounting for 45 of the 65 weeks, including an (unique) uninterrupted sequence of four chart-toppers for the company, spanning four continuous months.

### Annual top 40 placings

In the article reproduced in Abbott (p233), Peter Doggett talks of a 'Second Golden Era' for Tamla Motown, in (approximately) 1970-71. While few readily acknowledge it, the annual statistics presented here show a distinct peaking of popularity around then, with the label's most successful years, and 40 percent of its total top 40 hits arriving in the three years spanning the turn of the decade.

The label's early struggle to break through in the UK is graphically depicted, as is its sharp decline in 1975, leading to its eventual demise. Also notable is the distinct dip in success immediately following the departure of HDH in 1968, the only inconsistency in an otherwise smooth representation of the label's rise and fall. Singles are identified by year of release rather than point of chart entry, despite there being several issued prior to January I which only entered the listings after the new year.

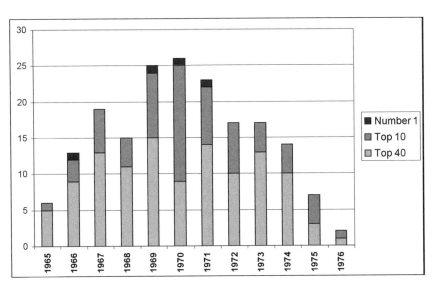

## Biggest hit year on year

A chronological view of Tamla Motown's most successful releases annually, with chart placing in parentheses.

1965: THE SUPREMES: Stop! In The Name Of Love [501] (7)
1966: FOUR TOPS: Reach Out I'll Be There [579] (1)
1967: FOUR TOPS: Walk Away Renee [634] (3)
1968: STEVIE WONDER: For Once In My Life [679] (3)
1969: MARVIN GAYE: I Heard It Through The Grapevine [686] (1)
1970: THE MIRACLES: The Tears Of A Clown [745] (1)
1971: DIANA ROSS: I'm Still Waiting [781] (1)
1972: MICHAEL JACKSON: Rockin' Robin [816] (3)
1973: STEVIE WONDER: You Are The Sunshine Of My Life [852] (7)
1974: R. DEAN TAYLOR: There's A Ghost In My House [896] (3)
1975: THE MIRACLES: Love Machine (Part 1) [1015] (3)
1976: DIANA ROSS: Theme From Mahogany [1010] (5)

## Most prolific artists

Ranked by number of full Tamla Motown singles, and ignoring re-issues.

1.  The SUPREMES (33)
2.  Stevie WONDER (29)
    The TEMPTATIONS (29)
4.  FOUR TOPS (25)
5.  Marvin GAYE (22)
6.  The MIRACLES (20)
    Junior WALKER & The ALL STARS (20)
8.  The JACKSON 5 (19)
9.  Gladys KNIGHT & The PIPS (17)
10. Diana ROSS (15)
11. MARTHA & The VANDELLAS (14)
12. Edwin STARR (12)

13. Jimmy RUFFIN (10)
14. The MARVELETTES (9)
    Eddie KENDRICKS (9)
16. The COMMODORES (8)
    Marvin GAYE & Tammi TERRELL (8)
    The ISLEY BROTHERS (8)
    Michael JACKSON (8)
20. The UNDISPUTED TRUTH (7)

Wonder's total counts "I Don't Know Why (I Love You)" and "My Cherie Amour" as one release rather than two, since the titles were either side of the same disc ([690]), despite both charting separately. If counted as two releases, Wonder would edge clear of The Temptations in second.

The Supremes released the most singles during the 1960s with 18, one more than closest rivals The Four Tops. The Jackson 5 are the most prolific of the 1970s, all 19 of their singles appearing in the decade. (Group members Jermaine and Michael released a further 12 between them as solo recording artists.) In all combinations, the most prolific individual is Diana Ross with 41 vocals, followed by Marvin Gaye with 36.

## Most popular recording artists in UK, based on top 40 hits

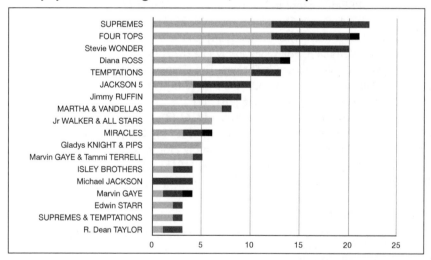

In the graph above, re-issues are included as hits in their own right, and individual tracks such as "Bernadette" [601] / [803] are therefore counted on two separate occasions. The graph makes interesting reading with Jimmy Ruffin comfortably out-performing 'bigger' artists such as Michael Jackson, Gladys Knight & The Pips and Marvin Gaye.

The Supremes' best tally of 22 does not take into account their hits prior to the creation of the label, which included the number 1 "Baby Love" on Stateside, although the track is counted for its number 12 showing on Tamla Motown in 1974. The group scored a further three with The Temptations and two in collaboration with The Four Tops (not shown), totalling 27. Of these, Diana Ross performed on 19 as well as a further 2 with Marvin Gaye, giving her a personal tally of 35, easily the best of any individual performer.

## Most consistent artists
Artists to have released a single in every calendar year the label was running.
The MIRACLES
The SUPREMES

The Supremes placed a record in the top 40 in each of the first 10 of the 12 calendar years; the Miracles released something every year between 1961 and 1976, and are the only outfit to have material issued on all four pre-Tamla Motown labels.

## One-single artists
At the other end of the spectrum, of the 84 acts to release singles on Tamla Motown, 31 can claim just one each. The following fall into that category, three of whom also feature in the pre-1965 catalogue as noted. The listing omits the handful of acts whose only appearance was on a B-side (eg The Temptations Band), and some individuals who have appeared on other singles under different act names (eg Martha Reeves, who also features with The Vandellas).

The HIT PACK [513]
Choker CAMPBELL'S BIG BAND [517]
Billy ECKSTINE [533]
Dorsey BURNETTE [534]
The LEWIS SISTERS [536]
Tony MARTIN [537] (released 1 pre-Tamla Motown single)
Barbara McNAIR [544]
Barbara RANDOLPH [628]
Bobby TAYLOR & The VANCOUVERS [654]
Paul PETERSEN [670]
The FANTASTIC FOUR [678]
The HONEST MEN [706]
Kiki DEE [739]
RARE EARTH [742]
BLINKY & Edwin STARR [748] (Starr released 12 singles as a solo artist)
Thelma HOUSTON [799]
Tom CLAY [801]
Frankie VALLI & The FOUR SEASONS [819]
Mary WELLS [820] (released 6 pre-Tamla Motown singles)
Laura LEE [831]
Michel LEGRAND [848a]
J J BARNES [870]
The REFLECTIONS [907]
Gloria JONES [910]
Popcorn WYLIE [932]
MAGIC DISCO MACHINE [1004]
Stephanie MILLS [1020]

The BOONES [1030]
G C CAMERON [1033]
Rose BANKS [1037]
Jerry BUTLER [1039]

**Biggest gap between releases**
Of these, only David Ruffin and The Originals maintained continuous, active
recording careers with Motown between the singles cited.
6 years, 6 months: SYREETA
[643] (Feb 1968) to [912] (Aug 1974)
5 years, 8 months: Earl VAN DYKE & The SOUL BROTHERS
[506] (Mar 1965) to [759] (Nov 1970)
5 years, 4 months: David RUFFIN
[711] (Sep 1969) to [936] (Jan 1975)
5 years, 1 month: The VELVELETTES
[595] (Feb 1967) to [806] (Mar 1972)
4 years, 3 months: The ORIGINALS
[822] (Jun 1972) to [1038] (Sep 1976)
4 years, 2 months: The ISLEY BROTHERS
[708] (Aug 1969) to [877] (Oct 1973)
4 years, 1 month: The CONTOURS
[723] (Jan 1970) to [886] (Feb 1974)

This list deals only with full Tamla Motown releases during the label's main
lifespan. Out of interest though, Chris Clark's final Tamla Motown single [638]
appeared in January 1968, her next appearance coming in September 2004
[L111], some 26 years and eight months later!

**Principal song-writing teams: Top 40 totals**

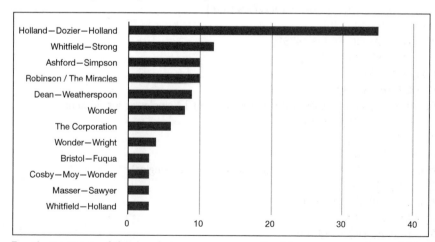

For the purpose of this graph, teams are generalized from a range of actual label
credits. The front-runners are overwhelming: HDH account for almost 20
percent of the label's hits, despite departing after just three years. Stevie Wonder
is the leading individual composer with 8. Smokey Robinson wrote 5 of his hits

alone but no other solo writer has achieved more than two.

Breaking the various teams into individuals (and therefore not all showing here), Eddie Holland appears most often, with 39 hits bearing his name. Stevie Wonder is credited more frequently than anyone outside the HDH team with a total of 20 in all set-ups. Norman Whitfield is next, with a personal tally of 18 in all guises.

## Selected writers covered by Motown artists

A full list of covers in the Motown annals would be immense, but of particular interest are the A-sides released in the UK, with material supplied by external composers. This is not a complete list and includes only the most noteworthy.

**Bob Dylan**: Needing no introduction, Dylan exerted a huge influence on the music of the day and had a subliminal effect on Motown, one of his songs appearing on 45 courtesy of Stevie Wonder [570].

**The Big Bopper**: Jiles Perry Richardson is better known as The Big Bopper, whose main hit "Chantilly Lace" was covered by Shorty Long [600].

**Van McCoy**: Later famed for his disco recordings (eg "The Hustle"), McCoy served his apprenticeship at New York's Brill Building under the tutelage of Leiber—Stoller. He wrote [609] and some years later came to Motown via David Ruffin ([1017]; [1022]; [1036]).

**Tim Hardin**: Folk singer Hardin wrote rock and roller and future Motown artist Bobby Darin's 1966 hit "If I Were A Carpenter" before The Four Tops picked it up the following year [647].

**Kenny Gamble**: Co-founder of the Philadelphia International label, Gamble is well-known for his compositions with Leon Huff. [685] was penned, prior to the creation of Philadelphia International, by Gamble and Jerry Ross.

**Lennon—McCartney**: The most successful songwriters of all time. Their influence is ubiquitous across the 1960s and 1970s, Stevie Wonder releasing their 1965 hit "We Can Work It Out" as [772].

**Phil Spector**: Maverick New Yorker Spector is best-known as a ground-breaking producer, but was listed with his Brill Building colleagues Barry—Greenwich on [777] and Mann—Weil on [945].

**Bacharach—David**: New Yorkers Burt Bacharach and Hal David wrote several standards in the 1960s, many of which were picked up by Motown including three which found their way onto singles: [801], [844] and [1020].

**Bill Withers**: His first hit single, the self-penned "Ain't No Sunshine" appeared in 1971 and within a year was remade by Michael Jackson [826].

**Kris Kristofferson**: Country writer and singer Kristofferson (remembered also for his acting career) supplied Sammi Smith with "Help Me Make It Through The Night" in 1971, which was remade by Gladys Knight & The Pips [830].

**Neil Diamond**: Singer Diamond wrote many of his own hits including the 1969 top-tenner "Holly Holy", which attracted a cover version courtesy of Junior Walker & The All Stars in 1970, belatedly put out on single [872].

**Bell—Creed**: In parallel with Gamble—Huff, Thom Bell and Linda Creed were part of the 1970s Philadelphia school, and wrote several hit tracks for The Stylistics. Two of the earliest were re-recorded by Diana Ross & Marvin Gaye for their collaborative album ([890]; [906]).

**Wilson Pickett**: Another notable duet between Diana Ross & Marvin Gaye was their recording of "Don't Knock My Love", a latter-day Wilson Picket hit co-written with Brad Shapiro [953].

**Gerry Goffin**: Another of the New York Brill Building set, Goffin became world-famous for his collaborations with Carole King in the early 1960s. He co-wrote "Theme From Mahogany (Do You Know Where You're Going To)" [1010] with Michael Masser, recorded by Diana Ross.

## Internal cover versions

On numerous occasions, Tamla Motown released singles which had already been recorded and released by other artists on the label. The following therefore appear as UK A-sides in versions by two different acts. (An even higher number occur via B-sides: see listing of song titles for examples.)

"I Can't Help Myself" [515] / [814]
"Take Me In Your Arms (Rock Me A Little While)" [538] / [652]
"Put Yourself In My Place" [551] / [708]
"Get Ready" [557] / [742]
"Reach Out I'll Be There" [579] / [807]
"Ain't No Mountain High Enough" [611] / [751]
"I Heard It Through The Grapevine" [629] / [686]
"I Second That Emotion" [631] / [709]
"I Want To Go Back There Again" [638] / [799]
"I Wish It Would Rain" [641] / [674]
"Forever Came Today" [650] / [1001]
"It Should Have Been Me" [660] / [1013]
"Reach Out And Touch (Somebody's Hand)" [743] / [836]
"Smiling Faces Sometimes" [789] / [832]
"Superstar (Remember How You Got Where You Are)" [800] / [818]
"Funky Music Sho' Nuff Turns Me On" [810] / [913]
"My Guy" [820] / [1030]
"Law Of The Land" [866] / [943]

## Standard Tamla Motown re-issues

Tamla Motown re-issued its own A-sides with new TMG numbers on 37 occasions prior to the closure of the label at the end of 1976. The singles in question are as follows:
**1968**: [642]
**1969**: [683]; [688]; [691]; [694]; [696]; [699]; [700]; [703]; [719]
**1970**: [732]; [740]
**1971**: [761]; [771]; [780]; [787]; [788]; [791]
**1972**: [803]; [811]; [813]
**1973**: [853]; [860]; [864]; [871]
**1974**: [903]; [911]; [918]; [922]; [923]
**1975**: [934]; [937]; [939]; [955]; [1009]; [1011]
**1976**: [1028]

Adding in the charting re-pressings of [555] and [599], and the double-hit [690] these exercises account for 18 top 40 entries, 8 of which went top 10.

**Most re-issues by artist**
The Elgins released just 3 standard singles on Tamla Motown, and also had 3 re-issues. Jimmy Ruffin released 10, and had 5 re-issues, the biggest tally proportionally for any artist amongst the 20 most prolific (as listed above). The most productive act, The Supremes, had no Tamla Motown re-issues at all during the label's reign, and neither did Stevie Wonder in joint second.
**5** Gladys KNIGHT & The PIPS
   Jimmy RUFFIN
**4** The MIRACLES
**3** The ELGINS
   FOUR TOPS
   The ISLEY BROTHERS
**2** The MARVELETTES
   The TEMPTATIONS

**Early numbers 're-released' on Tamla Motown**
Of the UK titles issued by the pre-1965 labels, 15 were revived by Tamla Motown during the period to 1976, 7 of which were used for A-sides. All bar the first two were from the Stateside discography:
[E10] Do You Love Me (The Contours): [899]
[E14] Two Lovers (Mary Wells): [820b]
[E30] You Lost The Sweetest Boy (Mary Wells): [820b]
[E32] Quicksand (Martha & The Vandellas): [684b]
[E42] My Guy (Mary Wells): [820]
[E51] Where Did Our Love Go (The Supremes): [925]
[E53] Baby I Need Your Loving (Four Tops): [732b]
[E54] Dancing In The Street (Martha & The Vandellas): [684]
[E56] Baby Love (The Supremes): [915]
[E56b] Ask Any Girl (The Supremes): [915b]
[E61] Needle In A Haystack (The Velvelettes): [595b] and [806]
[E66] Come On Do The Jerk (The Miracles): [696b]
[E67] My Girl (The Temptations): [688b]
[E68] Can You Jerk Like Me (The Contours): [886b]
[E71] He Was Really Sayin' Somethin' (The Velvelettes): [595]

The following nine titles have also appeared on Tamla Motown, in the post-1976 discography:
[E02] Money (That's What I Want) (Barrett Strong): [L077b]
[E05] Please Mr. Postman (The Marvelettes): [L083b] and [L112]
[E26] Fingertips (II) (Stevie Wonder): [L031b] and [L093]
[E28] Heat Wave (Martha & The Vandellas): [L015]
[E30b] What's Easy For Two (Is So Hard For One) (Mary Wells): [L019b]
[E31] Can I Get A Witness (Marvin Gaye): [L073b]
[E60] How Sweet It Is (To Be Loved By You) (Marvin Gaye): [L071b]
[E63] Too Many Fish In The Sea (The Marvelettes): [L083]
[E65] Come See About Me (The Supremes): [L062b] and [L074b]
(Yet more have been issued on Tamla Motown 12-inch singles: see Appendix 1.)

**Non-Motown titles 're-released' on Tamla Motown**

Motown purchased several local labels during the 1960s (Anna, Harvey, Tri-Phi, Golden World, Wingate, Ric Tic, Inferno, Stephanye, Maltese and Impact), and Tamla Motown re-pressed singles which had previously appeared on some of them:

*From Harvey:*
Junior WALKER: Cleo's Mood [550]
*From Ric Tic:*
The FANTASTIC FOUR: I Love You Madly [678]
Edwin STARR: Agent Double O Soul [790]
The SAN REMO STRINGS: Festival Time [795]
Laura LEE: To Win Your Heart [831]
J J BARNES: Real Humdinger [870]
Edwin STARR: Stop Her On Sight (SOS) [905]
*From Golden World:*
The REFLECTIONS: (Just Like) Romeo And Juliet [907]

**Different artists**

And lastly, a round-up of all Tamla Motown singles which show different acts on either side. Most, but not all, are post-1976:
[848] Michel Legrand / Gil Askey (1973)
[931] The Temptations / The Temptations Band (1975)
[1023] The Miracles / The Miracle Workers (1976)
[L005] Diana Ross & The Supremes & The Temptations / Marvin Gaye (1976)
[L007] Diana Ross & Marvin Gaye / Marvin Gaye & Tammi Terrell (1976)
[L012] Jimmy Ruffin / Marv Johnson (1976)
[L016] Michael Jackson / Marvin Gaye (1980)
[L033] Edwin Starr / R. Dean Taylor (1980)
[L038] Michael Jackson / Marv Johnson (1980)
[L041] The Marvelettes / Kim Weston (1980)
[L055] The Temptations With Four Tops / The Temptations (1983)
[L057] Diana Ross / The Supremes & Four Tops (1984)
[L077] The Contours / Barrett Strong (1988)
[L084] The Miracles / Edwin Starr (1988)
[L088] David Ruffin / Jimmy Ruffin (1988)
[L089] The Detroit Spinners / Eddie Kendricks (1988)
[L111] Frank Wilson / Chris Clark (2004)
[L117] Diana Ross & The Supremes / Earl Van Dyke (2005)

# INDEX OF TRACKS

This listing only contains titles released in the main run of Tamla Motown singles, as documented in chapters 2 to 5. A- and B-sides are both included. Ten of the titles feature in three different versions, only "Put Yourself In My Place" appearing four times.

**A B C** – The Jackson 5 [738a]
**Abraham, Martin And John** – Marvin Gaye [734a]
**Act Like A Shotgun** – G C Cameron [1033b]
**After The Dance** – Marvin Gaye [1035a]
**After You** – Diana Ross [1032b]
**Agent Double O Soul** – Edwin Starr [790a]
**Ain't It A Sad Thing** – R. Dean Taylor [786a]
**Ain't It Hell Up In Harlem** – Edwin Starr [930b]
**Ain't No Justice** – The Temptations [948b]
**Ain't No Mountain High Enough** – Marvin Gaye & Tammi Terrell [611a]
**Ain't No Mountain High Enough** – Diana Ross [751a]
**Ain't No Sun Since You've Been Gone** – The Undisputed Truth [818b]
**Ain't No Sunshine** – Michael Jackson [826a]
**Ain't Nothing Like The Real Thing** – Marvin Gaye & Tammi Terrell [655a]
**Ain't Nothing Like The Real Thing** – The Jackson 5 [865b]
**Ain't That Asking For Trouble** – Stevie Wonder [570b]
**Ain't That Peculiar** – Marvin Gaye [539a]
**Ain't Too Proud To Beg** – The Temptations [565a]; [699a]
**All For You** – Earl Van Dyke [506a]; [759b]
**All I Know About You** – The Supremes [607b]
**All I Need** – The Temptations [610a]
**All Of My Life** – Diana Ross [880a]
**All Of My Love** – Eddie Kendricks [1021b]
**All That's Good** – The Miracles [503b]
**All Turned On** – The San Remo Strings [795b]
**Angie Girl** – Stevie Wonder [679b]
**Any Happy Home** – Gil Askey [848b]
**Anything You Wanna Do** – The Marvelettes [546b]
**Anyway You Wanna** – Junior Walker & The All Stars [596b]
**Ask Any Girl** – The Supremes [915b]
**Ask The Lonely** – Four Tops [507a]
**Asleep On My Love** – Smokey Robinson [1019b]
**At Last (I Found A Love)** – Marvin Gaye [676b]
**Automatically Sunshine** – The Supremes [821a]

---

**Baby** – The Honest Men [706b]
**Baby, Baby Don't Cry** – The Miracles [687a]
**Baby Come Close** – Smokey Robinson [898b]
**Baby Don'tcha Worry** – Tammi Terrell [561b]
**Baby Hit And Run** – The Contours [886a]
**Baby I Need Your Loving** – Four Tops [732b]
**Baby I'm For Real** – The Originals [733a]; [822b]

---

**Baby It's Love** – Diana Ross [861b]
**Baby I've Got It** – Jimmy Ruffin [577b]
**Baby Love** – The Supremes [915a]
**Baby That's Backatcha** – Smokey Robinson [949a]
**Baby You Know You Ain't Right** – Junior Walker & The All Stars [550b]
**Back In My Arms Again** – The Supremes [516a]
**Back Street** – R. Dean Taylor [786b]
**Back Street** – Edwin Starr [790b]
**Bad Bad Weather (Till You Come Home)** – The Spinners [871b]
**Bad Girl** – Marv Johnson [713b]
**Bad Weather** – The Supremes [847a]
**Ball Of Confusion (That's What The World Is Today)** – The Temptations [749a]
**Bass Odyssey** – Jermaine Jackson [1040b]
**Beauty Is Only Skin Deep** – The Temptations [578a]
**Beginning Of The End** – Chris Clark [624b]
**Behind A Painted Smile** – The Isley Brothers [693a]
**Ben** – Michael Jackson [834a]
**Bernadette** – Four Tops [601a]; [803a]
**Best Friends** – Martin & Finley [867b]
**Better Never Than Forever** – The Commodores [1018b]
**Bigger You Love (The Harder You Fall), The** – Jermaine Jackson [874a]
**Bigger Your Heart Is (The Harder You Fall), The** – Tony Martin [537a]
**Bill, When Are You Coming Home** – The Supremes [735b]
**Black Maybe** – Syreeta [912b]
**Bless You** – Martha & The Vandellas [794a]
**Blood Donors Needed (Give All You Got)** – David Ruffin [936b]
**Blowin' In The Wind** – Stevie Wonder [570a]
**Boogie Down** – Eddie Kendricks [888a]
**Boogie Man, The** – The Jackson 5 [895a]
**Boogie On Reggae Woman** – Stevie Wonder [928a]
**Brainwasher** – Junior Walker & The All Stars [712b]
**Brother's Gonna Work It Out** – Willie Hutch [862a]
**Bump, The** – The Commodores [952b]
**But I Love You More** – The Supremes [747b]

---

**Call On Me** – Shorty Long [573b]
**Can You Jerk Like Me** – The Contours [886b]
**Candy Apple Red** – R. Dean Taylor [918b]
**Can't Give It Up No More** – Gladys Knight & The Pips [855b]
**Can't Help What I Am** – Eddie Kendricks [901b]
**Can't Seem To Get You Out Of My Mind** – Four Tops [710b]
**Can't Wait Until Tomorrow** – Diana Ross [751b]
**Can't You Tell By The Look In My Eyes** – The Reflections [907b]
**Chained** – Marvin Gaye [676a]; [923b]
**Change What You Can** – Marvin Gaye [640b]
**Chantilly Lace** – Shorty Long [600a]
**Cherie** – The Honest Men [706a]

---

**Child Of Love** – Caston & Majors [938a]
**Choosey Beggar** – The Miracles [547b]
**Christmas Won't Be The Same This Year** – The Jackson 5 [837b]
**Cleo's Back** – Junior Walker & The All Stars [529b]
**Cleo's Mood** – Junior Walker & The All Stars [550a]
**Cloud Nine** – The Temptations [707a]
**Cloud Nine** – Edwin Starr [810b]
**Cloud Nine** – Gladys Knight & The Pips [903b]
**Colour My World Blue** – The Supremes [1029b]
**Come Get To This** – Marvin Gaye [882a]
**Come On And See Me** – Tammi Terrell [561a]
**Come On Do The Jerk** – The Miracles [696b]
**(Come 'Round Here) I'm The One You Need** – The Miracles [584a]; [761a]
**Come See About Me** – Junior Walker & The All Stars [637a]
**Come Spy With Me** – The Miracles [614b]
**Control Tower** – The Magic Disco Machine [1004a]
**Country Boy** – Junior Walker & The All Stars [857b]
**Crazy About The La La La** – The Miracles [811b]

---

**Daddy Could Swear, I Declare** – Gladys Knight & The Pips [876a]
**Daddy's Home** – Jermaine Jackson [851a]
**Dancing In The Street** – Martha & The Vandellas [684a]
**Dancing Like They Do On Soul Train** – Junior Walker [1027b]
**Dancing Machine** – The Jackson 5 [904a]
**Danger Heartbreak Dead Ahead** – The Marvelettes [535a]
**Dark Side Of The World** – Diana Ross [743b]
**Darling Baby** – The Elgins [551b]; [642b]
**Darling Baby** – Rose Banks [1037a]
**Darling Dear** – The Jackson 5 [769b]
**Darling I Hum Our Song** – Four Tops [542b]
**Day Will Come Between Sunday And Monday, The** – Kiki Dee [739a]
**Day You Take One (You Have To Take The Other), The** – The
Marvelettes [609b]; [939b]
**Dear Michael** – Michael Jackson [1006b]
**Deception** – The Dynamic Superiors [1016a]
**Destination: Anywhere** – The Marvelettes [701b]
**Determination** – The Contours [564a]; [899b]
**Determination** – The Commodores [944b]
**Devil In Mrs Jones, The** – Jerry Butler [1039a]
**Didn't You Know (You'd Have To Cry Sometime)** – Gladys Knight & The
Pips [728a]; [903a]
**Discover Me** – David Ruffin [1036a]
**Distant Lover** – Marvin Gaye [882b]
**Do It Baby** – The Miracles [914a]
**Do The Boomerang** – Junior Walker & The All Stars [520a]
**Do What You Gotta Do** – Four Tops [710a]
**Do You Love Me** – The Contours [899a]

**Do You Love Me Just A Little, Honey** – Gladys Knight & The Pips [604b]
**Do You See My Love (For You Growing)** – Junior Walker & The All Stars [750a]
**Do Yourself A Favour** – Stevie Wonder [908b]
**Doctor My Eyes** – The Jackson 5 [842a]
**Does Your Mama Know About Me** – Bobby Taylor & The Vancouvers [654a]
**Don't Blame The Children** – Junior Walker & The All Stars [889a]
**Don't Bring Back These Memories** – Four Tops [698b]
**Don't Compare Me With Her** – Kim Weston [538b]
**Don't Fool Around** – R. Dean Taylor [656b]; [909a]
**Don't Knock My Love** – Diana Ross & Marvin Gaye [953a]
**Don't Let Her Take Your Love From Me** – Gladys Knight & The Pips [645b]
**Don't Let Him Take Your Love From Me** – Jimmy Ruffin [664a]
**Don't Let It End ('Til You Let It Begin)** – The Miracles [891a]
**Don't Let The Sun Catch You Crying** – The Jackson 5 [895b]
**Don't Look Back** – The Temptations [541b]
**Don't Mess With Bill** – The Marvelettes [546a]
**Don't Mess With Mr. T** – Marvin Gaye [846b]
**Don't Wanna Be Reminded** – Jerry Butler [1039b]
**Don't Wonder Why** – Stevie Wonder [772b]
**Don't You Miss Me A Little Bit Baby** – Jimmy Ruffin [617a]; [911b]
**Don't You Worry 'Bout A Thing** – Stevie Wonder [908a]
**Doobedood'ndoobe, Doobedood'ndoobe, Doobedood'ndoo** – Diana Ross [812a]
**Down To Earth** – Billy Eckstine [533b]
**Down To Love Town** – The Originals [1038a]

---

**Early Morning Love** – The Supremes [1012a]
**Eddie's Love** – Eddie Kendricks [888b]
**End Of Our Road, The** – Gladys Knight & The Pips [645a]
**Every Time I See You I Go Wild** – Stevie Wonder [626b]
**Everybody Needs Love** – Gladys Knight & The Pips [619a]; [1009b]
**Everybody Needs Love** – Jimmy Ruffin [649b]; [740b]
**Everybody's Angel** – Dorsey Burnette [534b]
**Everybody's Got The Right To Love** – The Supremes [747a]
**Everything Is Everything** – Diana Ross [893b]
**Everything Is Good About You** – The Supremes [548b]
**Evil** – Stevie Wonder [928b]

---

**Fading Away** – The Temptations [557b]; [699b]
**Fading Away** – Bobby Taylor & The Vancouvers [654b]
**Farewell Is A Lonely Sound** – Jimmy Ruffin [726a]; [922a]
**Feel All My Love Inside** – Marvin Gaye [1035b]
**Festival Time** – The San Remo Strings [795a]
**First I Look At The Purse** – The Contours [531a]; [723b]
**Floy Joy** – The Supremes [804a]

---

**For All We Know** – The Spinners [627a]
**For Once In My Life** – Four Tops [665b]
**For Once In My Life** – Stevie Wonder [679a]
**For Once In My Life** – Gladys Knight & The Pips [876b]
**Forever Came Today** – The Supremes [650a]
**Forever Came Today** – The Jackson 5 [1001a]
**Forget Me Not** – Martha & The Vandellas [657b]; [762a]
**Fork In The Road** – The Miracles [522b]
**Friendship Train** – Gladys Knight & The Pips [756a]
**From Head To Toe** – Chris Clark [624a]
**Function At The Junction** – Shorty Long [573a]
**Funky Music Sho' Nuff Turns Me On** – Edwin Starr [810a]
**Funky Music Sho' Nuff Turns Me On** – The Temptations [866b]
**Funky Music Sho' Nuff Turns Me On** – Yvonne Fair [913a]
**Funky Rubber Band (Instrumental)** – Popcorn Wylie [932b]
**Funky Rubber Band (Vocal)** – Popcorn Wylie [932a]

---

**Get It Together** – The Jackson 5 [878a]
**Get Ready** – The Temptations [557a]; [688a]
**Get Ready** – Rare Earth [742a]
**Get Ready For The Get Down** – Willie Hutch [1008b]
**Get The Cream Of The Crop** – Eddie Kendricks [1003b]
**Girl You Need A Change Of Mind (Part 1)** – Eddie Kendricks [916a]
**Girl You Need A Change Of Mind (Part 2)** – Eddie Kendricks [916b]
**Girls, Girls, Girls** – Chuck Jackson [651a]
**Give A Little Love** – Marvin Gaye & Tammi Terrell [611b]
**Give Her Up** – The Miracles [673b]
**Give Out But Don't Give Up** – The Supremes [950b]
**Go Ahead And Laugh** – Martha & The Vandellas [567b]
**God Bless The Child** – Diana Ross [849b]
**God Bless Whoever Sent You** – The Originals [822a]
**God Is Love** – Marvin Gaye [775b]
**Going Down For The Third Time** – The Supremes [616b]
**Going To A Go Go** – The Miracles [547a]; [853a]
**Gonna Give Her All The Love I Got** – Jimmy Ruffin [603a]
**Gonna Give Her All The Love I Got** – The Temptations [658b]
**Gonna Keep On Trying Till I Win Your Love** – Edwin Starr [630b]; [764b]
**Gonna Keep On Trying Till I Win Your Love** – Marvin Gaye [718b]
**Gonna Keep On Trying Till I Win Your Love** – The Temptations [800b]
**Good Lovin' Ain't Easy To Come By** – Marvin Gaye & Tammi Terrell [697a]
**Good Morning Heartache** – Diana Ross [849a]
**Goodnight Irene** – The Originals [592a]
**Got Myself A Good Man** – Gladys Knight & The Pips [714b]
**Got To Be There** – Michael Jackson [797a]
**Got To Find A Way To Get Maria Back** – Junior Walker & The All Stars [727b]
**Got To Have You Back** – The Isley Brothers [606a]

**Gotta Hold On To This Feeling** – Junior Walker & The All Stars [824b]; [894a]
**Gotta See Jane** – R. Dean Taylor [656a]; [918a]
**Green Grow The Lilacs** – The Originals [702a]
**Groove And Move** – Junior Walker & The All Stars [750b]

---

**Had You Been Around** – Billy Eckstine [533a]
**Hallelujah Day** – The Jackson 5 [856a]
**Happening, The** – The Supremes [607a]
**Happier Than The Morning Sun** – Stevie Wonder [921b]
**Happy** – Eddie Kendricks [1031b]
**Happy (Is A Bumpy Road)** – The Supremes [782b]
**Happy (Is A Bumpy Road)** – Four Tops [850b]
**Happy People** – The Temptations [931a]
**Happy People (Instrumental)** – The Temptations Band [931b]
**Harmour Love** – Syreeta [954a]
**He Doesn't Love Her Anymore** – Martha & The Vandellas [582b]
**He Holds His Own** – The Supremes [527b]
**He Was Really Saying Somethin'** – The Velvelettes [595a]
**He Who Picks A Rose** – Edwin Starr [754b]
**He's A Friend** – Eddie Kendricks [1021a]
**He's All I Got** – The Supremes [560b]
**He's Misstra Know-It-All** – Stevie Wonder [892a]
**He's My Man** – The Supremes [950a]
**He's My Sunny Boy** – The Supremes [721b]
**Headline News** – Edwin Starr [905b]
**Heaven Help Us All** – Stevie Wonder [757a]
**Heaven Must Have Sent You** – The Elgins [583a]; [771a]
**Heavy Day** – Syreeta [926b]
**Heavy Love** – David Ruffin [1022a]
**Help Me Make It Through The Night** – Gladys Knight & The Pips [830a]
**Help Yourself** – The Undisputed Truth [897a]
**Helpless** – Kim Weston [554a]
**Here Comes The Judge** – Shorty Long [663a]
**Here I Am Baby** – The Marvelettes [659a]; [860b]
**Hey Diddle Diddle** – Marvin Gaye [574b]
**Hey Girl (I Like Your Style)** – The Temptations [887b]
**Hey Love** – Stevie Wonder [602b]
**High Heel Sneakers** – Stevie Wonder [532a]
**High On Sunshine** – The Commodores [1034a]
**Higher Ground** – Stevie Wonder [869a]
**Higher Than High** – The Undisputed Truth [1014a]
**Hip City (Part 1)** – Junior Walker & The All Stars [667b]
**Hip City (Part 2)** – Junior Walker & The All Stars [667a]
**Hold Me** – Stevie Wonder [613b]
**Hold Me Oh My Darling** – Marvin Gaye & Tammi Terrell [625b]
**Holly Holy** – Junior Walker & The All Stars [872a]
**Home Cookin'** – Junior Walker & The All Stars [682a]

---

**Honey Chile** – Martha & The Vandellas [636a]
**Honey Come Back** – Chuck Jackson [729a]
**Honey Come Back** – Jimmy Ruffin [784b]
**Hooked On Your Love** – Eddie Kendricks [947b]
**Hope I Don't Get My Heart Broke** – Martha & The Vandellas [794b]
**Hot Cha** – Junior Walker & The All Stars [509b]
**How About You** – Diana Ross [768b]
**How Can I** – The Spinners [514b]
**How Can I Forget** – The Temptations [671b]
**How Can I Forget** – Marvin Gaye [734b]
**How Many Days** – Syreeta [933b]
**How Sweet It Is (To Be Loved By You)** – Junior Walker & The All Stars [571a]
**How Sweet It Is (To Be Loved By You)** – Earl Van Dyke & The Soul Brothers [814b]
**Hungry For Love** – The San Remo Strings [807b]
**Hunter Gets Captured By The Game, The** – The Marvelettes [594a]
**Hurt A Little Every Day** – Brenda Holloway [581a]

---

**I Ain't Going Nowhere** – Junior Walker & The All Stars [894b]
**I Ain't Gonna Do It** – J J Barnes [870b]
**I Am Love (Part 1)** – The Jackson 5 [942a]
**I Am Love (Part 2)** – The Jackson 5 [942b]
**I Am The Man For You Baby** – Edwin Starr [646a]
**I Am Your Man** – Four Tops [858b]
**I Can't Believe You Love Me** – Marvin Gaye & Tammi Terrell [715b]
**I Can't Dance To That Music You're Playing** – Martha & The Vandellas [669a]
**I Can't Get Next To You** – The Temptations [722a]
**I Can't Give Back The Love I Feel For You** – Syreeta [643a]; [791a]
**I Can't Help Myself** – Four Tops [515a]; [732a]
**I Can't Help Myself** – Earl Van Dyke & The Soul Brothers [814a]
**I Can't Quit Your Love** – Four Tops [858a]
**I Can't Quit Your Love** – The Jackson 5 [1001b]
**I Choose You** – Willie Hutch [862b]
**I Could Never Love Another (After Loving You)** – The Temptations [658a]
**I Don't Blame You At All** – The Miracles [774a]
**I Don't Know Why (I Love You)** – Stevie Wonder [690a]
**I Don't Want To Do Wrong** – Gladys Knight & The Pips [805b]
**I Don't Want To Do Wrong** – Junior Walker & The All Stars [840b]
**I Feel Sanctified** – The Commodores [944a]
**I Found That Girl** – The Jackson 5 [746b]
**I Got A Feeling** – Four Tops [601b]; [803b]
**I Got A Feeling** – Barbara Randolph [628a]; [788a]
**I Gotta Find Myself A Brand New Baby** – David Ruffin [689b]
**I Gotta Have A Song** – Stevie Wonder [757b]
**I Gotta Let You Go** – Martha & The Vandellas [762b]
**I Guess I'll Always Love You** – The Isley Brothers [572a]; [683a]
**I Guess I'll Always Love You** – The Supremes [632b]

---

**I Guess I'll Miss The Man** – The Supremes [884a]
**I Hear A Symphony** – The Supremes [543a]
**I Hear A Symphony** – The Isley Brothers [572b]
**I Heard It Through The Grapevine** – Gladys Knight & The Pips [629a]
**I Heard It Through The Grapevine** – Marvin Gaye [686a]; [923a]
**(I Know) I'm Losing You** – The Temptations [587a]
**(I Know) I'm Losing You** – Gladys Knight & The Pips [813b]
**I Like Everything About You** – Four Tops [568b]
**I Like Your Style** – The Originals [822b]
**I Lost My Love In The Big City** – Jermaine Jackson [838b]
**I Love You** – Chris Clark [638b]
**I Love You Madly (Instrumental)** – The Fantastic Four [678b]
**I Love You Madly (Vocal)** – The Fantastic Four [678a]
**I Miss You Baby (How I Miss You)** – Marv Johnson [713a]
**I Need Someone** – The Marvelettes [639b]
**I Need You** – The Temptations [887a]
**I Need Your Lovin'** – The Temptations [716b]
**I Promise To Wait My Love** – Martha & The Vandellas [657a]
**I Second That Emotion** – The Miracles [631a]
**I Second That Emotion** – Diana Ross & The Supremes & The
Temptations [709a]
**I Think I Can Change** – The Marvelettes [594b]
**I Thought It Took A Little Time (But Today I Fell In Love)** – Diana Ross [1032a]
**I Tried** – Martha & The Vandellas [669b]
**I Truly Truly Believe** – The Temptations [641b]
**I Understand My Man** – The Elgins [615b]
**I Wanna Be Where You Are** – Michael Jackson [826b]
**I Wanna Be With You** – The Miracles [891b]
**I Want A Love I Can See** – The Temptations [633b]
**I Want Her Love** – Jimmy Ruffin [617b]
**I Want My Baby Back** – Edwin Starr [630a]
**I Want To Go Back There Again** – Chris Clark [638a]
**I Want To Go Back There Again** – Thelma Houston [799a]
**I Want You** – Marvin Gaye [1026a]
**I Want You (Instrumental)** – Marvin Gaye [1026b]
**I Want You Back** – The Jackson 5 [724a]
**I Was Made To Love Her** – Stevie Wonder [613a]
**I Will Never Let You Get Away** – Jimmy Ruffin [922b]
**I Wish I Were Your Mirror** – Four Tops [770b]
**I Wish It Would Rain** – The Temptations [641a]
**I Wish It Would Rain** – Gladys Knight & The Pips [674a]; [1009b]
**I Wish It Would Rain** – Marvin Gaye [868b]
**I'd Be A Fool Right Now** – Stevie Wonder [717b]
**I'll Always Love You** – The Spinners [523a]; [627b]
**I'll Be Doggone** – Marvin Gaye [510a]
**I'll Be In Trouble** – Brenda Holloway [519b]
**I'll Be There** – The Jackson 5 [758a]
**I'll Keep Holding On** – The Marvelettes [518a]

**I'll Keep My Light In My Window** – Caston & Majors [1005a]
**I'll Pick A Rose For My Rose** – Marv Johnson [680a]
**I'll Say Forever My Love** – Jimmy Ruffin [649a]; [740a]
**I'll Take Good Care Of You** – Marvin Gaye [618b]
**I'll Turn To Stone** – Four Tops [612b]; [829a]
**I'm A Fool For You** – The Undisputed Truth [919a]
**(I'm A) Road Runner** – Junior Walker & The All Stars [559a]; [691a]
**I'm A Winner** – Diana Ross [792b]
**I'm Falling In Love With You** – Diana Ross & Marvin Gaye [879b]; [953b]
**I'm Glad About It** – The Supremes & Four Tops [793b]
**I'm Goin' Left** – Syreeta [926a]
**I'm Gonna Let My Heart Do The Walking** – The Supremes [1029a]
**I'm Gonna Make You Love Me** – Diana Ross & The Supremes & The Temptations [685a]
**I'm In A Different World** – Four Tops [675a]
**I'm In A Different World** – Jermaine Jackson [874b]
**I'm In Love Again** – The Supremes [501b]
**I'm Learning To Trust My Man** – Sisters Love [1002a]
**I'm Living In Shame** – The Supremes [695a]
**I'm Looking For A Love** – The Commodores [924b]
**I'm More Than Happy (I'm Satisfied)** – Stevie Wonder [744b]
**I'm Not A Plaything** – Marv Johnson [525b]; [737b]
**I'm Ready For Love** – Martha & The Vandellas [582a]
**I'm So Glad** – Junior Walker [1027a]
**I'm So Glad I Got Somebody (Like You Around)** – The Supremes [695b]
**I'm So Happy** – The Jackson 5 [809b]
**I'm Still Loving You** – Kim Weston [511a]
**I'm Still Waiting** – Diana Ross [781a]
**I'm The Exception To The Rule** – The Velvelettes [521b]; [806b]
**I'm Wondering** – Stevie Wonder [626a]
**I've Been Good To You** – Brenda Holloway [508b]
**I've Been Good To You** – The Temptations [620b]
**(I've Given You) The Best Years Of My Life** – Martha Reeves [843b]
**I've Got To Find It** – Brenda Holloway [622b]
**I've Lost Everything I've Ever Loved** – David Ruffin [711a]
**I've Passed This Way Before** – Jimmy Ruffin [593a]; [703a]; [934a]
**If Anyone Can** – Eddie Kendricks [1003a]
**If I Could Build My Whole World Around You** – Marvin Gaye & Tammi Terrell [635a]
**If I Were A Carpenter** – Four Tops [647a]
**If I Were Your Woman** – Gladys Knight & The Pips [765a]; [955a]
**If My Heart Could Tell The Story** – Edwin Starr [692b]
**If This World Were Mine** – Marvin Gaye & Tammi Terrell [635b]
**If You Can Learn How To Cry** – Stephanie Mills [1020b]
**If You Can Want** – The Miracles [648a]
**If You Don't Want My Love** – Four Tops [623b]
**If You Let Me** – Eddie Kendricks [845a]
**If You Really Love Me** – Stevie Wonder [779b]; [798a]

**If You Will Let Me, I Know I Can** – Jimmy Ruffin [726b]
**If You're Gonna Leave (Just Leave)** – Gladys Knight & The Pips [830b]
**In And Out Of Love** – The Supremes [632a]
**Include Me In Your Life** – Diana Ross & Marvin Gaye [890b]
**Indiana Wants Me** – R. Dean Taylor [763a]
**Inner City Blues (Make Me Wanna Holler)** – Marvin Gaye [817a]
**It Is As Good As You Make It** – The Commodores [935b]
**It Should Have Been Me** – Gladys Knight & The Pips [660a]
**It Should Have Been Me** – Yvonne Fair [1013a]
**It Takes Two** – Marvin Gaye & Kim Weston [590a]
**It's A Crying Shame** – Shorty Long [512b]
**It's A Shame** – The Spinners [755a]
**It's All In The Game** – Four Tops [736a]
**It's Another Sunday** – Martin & Finley [867a]
**It's Bad For Me To See You** – Yvonne Fair [1025a]
**It's Been A Long Long Time** – The Elgins [615a]
**It's Gonna Be Good Times** – The Elgins [787b]
**It's Got To Be A Miracle (This Thing Called Love)** – Marvin Gaye & Kim Weston [590b]
**It's Got To Be A Miracle (This Thing Called Love)** – The Supremes & Four Tops [777b]
**It's Growing** – The Temptations [504a]
**It's Out Of The Question** – The Isley Brothers [683b]
**It's So Hard Being A Loser** – The Contours [605a]
**It's So Hard For Me To Say Goodbye** – The Supremes [847b]
**It's Summer** – Gladys Knight & The Pips [674b]
**It's Summer** – The Temptations [749b]; [783a]
**It's The Same Old Song** – Four Tops [528a]; [803b]
**It's Time To Go Now** – Gladys Knight & The Pips [629b]
**It's Too Late To Change The Time** – The Jackson 5 [904b]
**It's Wonderful (To Be Loved By You)** – Jimmy Ruffin [753a]

---

**Jimmy Brown** – Dorsey Burnette [534a]
**Jimmy Mack** – Martha & The Vandellas [599a]
**Johnny Raven** – Michael Jackson [900b]
**Just A Little Bit Of You** – Michael Jackson [1006a]
**Just A Little Misunderstanding** – The Contours [564b]; [723a]
**Just Ain't Enough Love** – The Isley Brothers [606b]
**Just As Long As You Need Me** – Four Tops [553b]
**(Just Like) Romeo And Juliet** – The Reflections [907a]
**Just Look What You've Done** – Brenda Holloway [608a]; [700a]
**Just Loving You** – Kim Weston [511b]
**Just Memories** – Eddie Kendricks [845b]
**Just My Imagination (Running Away With Me)** – The Temptations [773a]
**Just My Soul Responding** – Smokey Robinson [883a]
**Just Passing Through** – Smokey Robinson [949b]
**Just Say, Just Say** – Diana Ross & Marvin Gaye [920b]

**Just Seven Numbers (Can Straighten Out My Life)** – Four Tops [770a]
**Just To Be Close To You** – The Originals [1038b]
**Just Walk In My Shoes** – Gladys Knight & The Pips [576a]; [813a]

---

**Keep An Eye** – Gladys Knight & The Pips [728b]
**Keep An Eye** – Diana Ross [812b]
**Keep Off, No Trespassing** – The Marvelettes [659b]
**Keep On Truckin' (Part 1)** – Eddie Kendricks [873a]
**Keep On Truckin' (Part 2)** – Eddie Kendricks [873b]
**Kiss Me Baby** – Stevie Wonder [505a]
**Kiss Me Now** – Diana Ross [1024b]

---

**L.A. (My Town)** – Four Tops [823b]
**Last Time I Saw Him, The** – Diana Ross [893a]
**Law Of The Land** – The Temptations [866a]
**Law Of The Land** – The Undisputed Truth [943a]
**Let Your Hair Down** – Yvonne Fair [913b]
**Let's Be Young Tonight** – Jermaine Jackson [1040a]
**Let's Dance** – The Hit Pack [513b]
**Let's Do It Right** – The Commodores [1007a]
**Let's Get It On** – Marvin Gaye [868a]
**Let's Go Somewhere** – R. Dean Taylor [896b]
**Let's Make Love Now** – The Supremes & Four Tops [815b]
**Let's Say Goodbye Tomorrow** – Jimmy Ruffin [767a]
**Life Of The Party, The** – The Jackson 5 [927a]
**Lil' Red Riding Hood** – The Undisputed Truth [943b]
**Little Bit For Sandy, A** – Paul Petersen [670a]
**Little Bitty Pretty One** – The Jackson 5 [825a]
**Little Darling (I Need You)** – Marvin Gaye [574a]; [796b]
**Little Miss Sweetness** – The Temptations [587b]
**Little Miss Sweetness** – The Isley Brothers [708b]
**Little Ole Boy, Little Ole Girl** – Marvin Gaye & Tammi Terrell [655b]
**Live Wire** – Martha & The Vandellas [694b]
**Living For The City** – Stevie Wonder [881a]
**Living In A World I Created For Myself** – Jimmy Ruffin [767b]
**(Loneliness Made Me Realise) It's You That I Need** – The Temptations [633a]
**Lonely Lonely Girl Am I** – The Velvelettes [521a]
**Lonely Lonely Man Am I** – Jimmy Ruffin [664b]
**Look Around** – Stevie Wonder [852b]
**Look Of Love, The** – Gladys Knight & The Pips [844a]
**Lookin' Through The Windows** – The Jackson 5 [833a]
**Love** – Martha & The Vandellas [530b]
**Love (The Lonely People's Prayer)** – Edwin Starr [875b]
**Love Bug Leave My Heart Alone** – Martha & The Vandellas [621a]
**Love Can Be Hazardous To Your Health** – David Ruffin [1017b]
**Love Child** – The Supremes [677a]

---

**Love Feels Like Fire** – Four Tops [829b]
**Love Hangover** – Diana Ross [1024a]
**Love I Saw In You Is Just A Mirage, The** – The Miracles [598a]
**Love Is Here And Now You're Gone** – The Supremes [597a]
**Love Is Here And Now You're Gone** – Michael Jackson [816b]
**Love Is Like An Itching In My Heart** – The Supremes [560a]
**Love Is The Answer** – Four Tops [736b]
**Love It Came To Me This Time** – The Supremes [835b]
**Love Like Yours (Don't Come Knocking Every Day), A** – Kim Weston [554b]
**Love Machine (Part 1)** – The Miracles [1015a]
**Love Machine (Part 2)** – The Miracles [1015b]
**Love Me** – Diana Ross [917a]
**Love Power** – Willie Hutch [1008a]
**Love Song** – The Jackson 5 [833b]
**Love Theme From "Lady Sings The Blues"** – Michel Legrand [848a]
**Love Twins** – Diana Ross & Marvin Gaye [906b]
**Love You Save, The** – The Jackson 5 [746a]
**Love's Gone Bad** – Chris Clark [591a]
**Love's Your Name** – R. Dean Taylor [763b]
**Loving You Is Sweeter Than Ever** – Four Tops [568a]

---

**Machine Gun** – The Commodores [902a]
**Magic Key** – Rare Earth [742b]
**Make Me The Woman That You Go Home To** – Gladys Knight & The Pips [805a]
**Mama I Got A Brand New Thing (Don't Say No)** – The Undisputed Truth [919b]
**Mama's Pearl** – The Jackson 5 [769a]
**Mame** – Four Tops [634b]
**Maria (You Were The Only One)** – Jimmy Ruffin [753b]
**Maria (You Were The Only One)** – Michael Jackson [797b]
**Masterpiece (Instrumental)** – The Temptations [854b]
**Masterpiece (Vocal)** – The Temptations [854a]
**Maybe Tomorrow** – The Jackson 5 [825b]
**Me And My Life** – G C Cameron [1033a]
**Memories** – The Temptations [948a]
**Mercy Mercy Me (The Ecology)** – Marvin Gaye [802a]
**Mickey's Monkey** – Choker Campbell's Big Band [517a]
**Mighty Good Lovin'** – Edwin Starr [672b]
**Moment Of Truth, The** – The Originals [733b]
**Money (That's What I Want) Part 1** – Junior Walker & The All Stars [586a]
**Money (That's What I Want) Part 2** – Junior Walker & The All Stars [586b]
**Moonlight On The Beach** – The Lewis Sisters [536b]
**More Love** – The Miracles [614a]
**Morning Glow** – Michael Jackson [863a]
**Mother Nature** – The Temptations [832b]
**Mother's Theme (Mama)** – Willie Hutch [885b]

**Motoring** – Martha & The Vandellas [502b]
**Mr. Fix-it Man** – Sisters Love [828a]
**Much Better Off** – The Miracles [661b]
**Music And Me** – Michael Jackson [900a]
**Music Talk** – Stevie Wonder [532b]
**Mutiny** – Junior Walker & The All Stars [682b]
**My Baby** – The Temptations [541a]
**My Baby Loves Me** – Martha & The Vandellas [549a]
**My Baby Must Be A Magician** – The Marvelettes [639a]
**My Cherie Amour** – Stevie Wonder [690b]
**My Girl** – Stevie Wonder [666b]
**My Girl** – The Temptations [688b]
**My Girl** – Michael Jackson [863b]
**My Girl Has Gone** – The Miracles [540a]; [811a]
**My Guy** – Mary Wells [820a]
**My Guy** – The Boones [1030a]
**My Little Baby** – The Jackson 5 [842b]
**My Mistake (Was To Love You)** – Diana Ross & Marvin Gaye [920a]
**My Weakness Is You** – Edwin Starr [646b]
**My Whole World Ended (The Moment You Left Me)** – David Ruffin [689a]
**My Whole World Ended (The Moment You Left Me)** – Kiki Dee [739b]
**My World Is Empty Without You** – The Supremes [548a]

---

**Nathan Jones** – The Supremes [782a]
**Need Somebody** – Marvin Gaye [686b]
**Need Your Lovin' (Want You Back)** – Marvin Gaye [563b]
**Need Your Lovin' (Want You Back)** – The Originals [592b]
**Needle In A Haystack** – The Velvelettes [595b]; [806a]
**Neither One Of Us (Wants To Be The First To Say Goodbye)** – Gladys Knight & The Pips [855a]; [1009a]
**Never Can Say Goodbye** – The Jackson 5 [778a]
**Never Dreamed You'd Leave In Summer** – Stevie Wonder [779a]
**Never Had A Dream Come True** – Stevie Wonder [731a]
**Never Leave Your Baby's Side** – Martha & The Vandellas [549b]
**Never Say No To Your Baby** – The Hit Pack [513a]
**Night Fo' Last (Instrumental)** – Shorty Long [644b]
**Night Fo' Last (Vocal)** – Shorty Long [644a]
**Night Life** – The Miracles [1023a]
**Nitty Gritty, The** – Gladys Knight & The Pips [714a]
**No Matter What Sign You Are** – The Supremes [704a]
**No One Could Love You More** – Gladys Knight & The Pips [864b]
**No One There** – Martha Reeves [843a]
**No One Will Know** – Caston & Majors [938b]
**No One's Gonna Be A Fool Forever** – Diana Ross [1010b]
**No Time For Tears** – The Marvelettes [518b]
**Nothing But Heartaches** – The Supremes [527a]; [925b]

**Nothing But Soul** – Junior Walker & The All Stars [571b]
**Nothing's Too Good For My Baby** – Stevie Wonder [558a]
**Now That You've Won Me** – Marvin Gaye [524b]
**Nowhere To Run** – Martha & The Vandellas [502a]; [694a]

---

**Oh Be My Love** – The Miracles [569b]
**Oh Be My Love** – The Supremes [859b]
**Oh How Happy** – Blinky & Edwin Starr [720a]; [748a]
**Oh How I'd Miss You** – Marvin Gaye & Tammi Terrell [681b]
**On The Way Out (On The Way In)** – Jimmy Ruffin [784a]
**One Day In Your Life** – Michael Jackson [946a]
**One More Chance** – The Jackson 5 [758b]
**One More Heartache** – Marvin Gaye [552a]
**One Nighter** – The Dynamic Superiors [1016b]
**One Too Many Heartaches** – The Isley Brothers [693b]
**One Way Out** – Martha & The Vandellas [621b]
**Onion Song, The** – Marvin Gaye & Tammi Terrell [715a]
**Only Time You Love Me Is When You're Losing Me, The** – Gladys Knight
& The Pips [955b]
**Ooo Baby Baby** – The Miracles [503a]
**Ooo Baby Baby** – Blinky & Edwin Starr [720b]; [748b]
**Operator** – Brenda Holloway [519a]
**Out To Get You** – Shorty Long [512a]
**Over And Over** – The Supremes [884b]
**Overture** – The Miracle Workers [1023b]

---

**Papa Was A Rollin' Stone (Instrumental)** – The Temptations [839b]
**Papa Was A Rollin' Stone (Vocal)** – The Temptations [839a]
**Paper Boy** – The Marvelettes [562b]
**Peace And Understanding Is Hard To Find** – Junior Walker & The All Stars [872b]
**Pick Of The Week** – Thelma Houston [799b]
**Place In The Sun, A** – Stevie Wonder [588a]
**Place In The Sun, A** – Diana Ross & The Supremes & The Temptations [685b]
**Please Let Me In** – J J Barnes [870b]
**Poor Girl** – R. Dean Taylor [909b]
**Precious Little Things** – The Supremes [821b]
**Pretty Little Baby** – Marvin Gaye [524a]
**Pride & Joy** – Choker Campbell's Big Band [517b]
**Psychedelic Shack** – The Temptations [741a]
**Pucker Up Buttercup** – Junior Walker & The All Stars [596a]
**Purple Raindrops** – Stevie Wonder [545b]
**Put Yourself In My Place** – The Elgins [551a]; [642a]; [787a]
**Put Yourself In My Place** – The Supremes [575b]
**Put Yourself In My Place** – Chris Clark [591b]
**Put Yourself In My Place** – The Isley Brothers [708a]

---

**Quicksand** – Martha & The Vandellas [684b]
**Quiet Storm** – Smokey Robinson [1019a]

---

**Reach Out And Touch (Somebody's Hand)** – Diana Ross [743a]
**Reach Out And Touch (Somebody's Hand)** – The Supremes & Four Tops [836a]
**Reach Out I'll Be There** – Four Tops [579a]
**Reach Out I'll Be There** – Diana Ross [781b]
**Reach Out I'll Be There** – The San Remo Strings [807a]
**Reachin' For Something I Can't Have** – The Marvelettes [701a]; [860a]
**Real Humdinger** – J J Barnes [870a]
**Reflections** – The Supremes [616a]
**Release Me** – The Dynamic Superiors [929b]
**Remember Me** – Diana Ross [768a]
**Remember When** – Four Tops [675b]
**Remove This Doubt** – The Supremes [585b]
**Right On Brothers And Sisters** – Junior Walker & The All Stars [824b]
**River Deep, Mountain High** – The Supremes & Four Tops [777a]
**Rock 'n' Roll (Are Here To Stay)** – David Ruffin [1022b]
**Rockin' Robin** – Michael Jackson [816a]
**Runaway Child, Running Wild** – The Temptations [716a]
**Running Away (Ain't Gonna Help You)** – The Temptations [722b]
**Running Back And Forth** – Edwin Starr [725b]; [1028b]

---

**Sad And Lonesome Feeling** – Jimmy Ruffin [934b]
**Sad Song** – Brenda Holloway [556b]
**Sad Souvenirs** – Four Tops [515b]
**Sad Tomorrows** – Marvin Gaye [802b]
**Santa Claus Is Coming To Town** – The Jackson 5 [837a]
**Satisfied Feeling** – Marvin Gaye & Tammi Terrell [697b]
**Save Me** – The Miracles [584b]
**Save Me From This Misery** – The Isley Brothers [877b]
**Save My Love For A Rainy Day** – The Undisputed Truth [776a]
**Save The Children** – Marvin Gaye [796a]
**Save The Children** – Diana Ross [917b]
**Say You Love Me True** – Caston & Majors [1005b]
**Scratchin'** – The Magic Disco Machine [1004b]
**Searching For A Girl** – The Contours [531b]
**Seems So Long** – Stevie Wonder [827b]
**7-Rooms Of Gloom** – Four Tops [612a]
**Shake & Fingerpop** – Junior Walker & The All Stars [529a]
**Shake Me, Wake Me (When It's Over)** – Four Tops [553a]
**She's Good** – The Jackson 5 [778b]
**She's Got To Be Real** – Marvin Gaye [539b]
**Shine On Me** – The Supremes [760b]
**Shoe Shoe Shine** – The Dynamic Superiors [929a]
**Shoeshine Boy** – Eddie Kendricks [947a]

**Shoo-Be-Doo-Be-Doo-Da-Day** – Stevie Wonder [653a]
**Shoot Your Shot** – Junior Walker & The All Stars [559b]
**Shotgun** – Junior Walker & The All Stars [509a]; [691b]
**Show Me The Way** – Martha & The Vandellas [636b]
**Signed, Sealed, Delivered, I'm Yours** – Stevie Wonder [744a]
**Silent Partner In A Three Way Love Affair, A** – Smokey Robinson [898a]
**Simple Game** – Four Tops [785a]
**Simple Thing Like Cry, A** – Diana Ross [880b]
**Since I Lost My Baby** – The Temptations [526a]
**Since I've Lost You** – Gladys Knight & The Pips [619b]
**Since I've Lost You** – The Undisputed Truth [776b]
**Since You Won My Heart** – The Miracles [540b]
**Since You've Been Gone** – Four Tops [589b]
**Since You've Been Loving Me** – The Velvelettes [580b]; [780b]
**Sing** – Caston & Majors [951a]
**Sing What You Wanna** – Shorty Long [663b]
**6 By 6** – Earl Van Dyke [759a]
**Skywriter** – The Jackson 5 [865a]
**Slippery When Wet** – The Commodores [952a]
**Smiling Faces Sometimes** – The Undisputed Truth [789a]
**Smiling Faces Sometimes** – The Temptations [832a]
**Smiling Faces Sometimes** – David Ruffin [1036b]
**Smooth Sailing From Now On** – The Temptations [808b]
**So Deep Within You** – Four Tops [850a]
**So Glad You Chose Me** – Marv Johnson [737a]
**So Tired (Of The Way You're Treating Our Love Baby)** – Gloria Jones [910b]
**So Will I** – Laura Lee [831b]
**Some Things You Never Get Used To** – The Supremes [662a]
**Somebody Knows, Somebody Cares** – Stevie Wonder [731b]
**Someday At Christmas** – The Jackson 5 [837b]
**Someday We'll Be Together** – The Supremes [721a]
**Something About You** – Four Tops [542a]
**Something On My Mind** – Syreeta [643b]; [791b]
**Son Of Sagittarius** – Eddie Kendricks [901a]
**Sorry Doesn't Always Make It Right** – Diana Ross [941a]
**Sorry Is A Sorry Word** – The Temptations [610b]
**Soul Clappin'** – Junior Walker & The All Stars [889b]
**Spaced Out** – The Undisputed Truth [1014b]
**Special Occasion** – The Miracles [673a]
**Spinnin' And Spinnin'** – Syreeta [912a]
**Standing In The Shadows Of Love** – Four Tops [589a]
**Starting The Hurt All Over Again** – Brenda Holloway [608b]
**Stay In My Lonely Arms** – The Elgins [583b]; [771b]
**Stepping Closer To Your Heart** – Gladys Knight & The Pips [576b]
**Still Water (Love)** – Four Tops [752a]
**Still Water (Peace)** – Four Tops [752b]
**Stoned Love** – The Supremes [760a]
**Stop Her On Sight (SOS)** – Edwin Starr [905a]

**Stop! In The Name Of Love** – The Supremes [501a]
**Stop, Look, Listen (To Your Heart)** – Diana Ross & Marvin Gaye [906a]
**Stop The War Now** – Edwin Starr [764a]
**Sugar Daddy** – The Jackson 5 [809a]
**Sun Country** – Frankie Valli & The Four Seasons [819b]
**Superman** – The Commodores [935a]
**Superstar (Remember How You Got Where You Are)** – The Temptations [800a]
**Superstar (Remember How You Got Where You Are)** – The Undisputed Truth [818a]
**Superstition** – Stevie Wonder [841a]
**Superwoman** – Stevie Wonder [827a]
**Surrender** – Diana Ross [792a]
**Sweet Harmony** – Smokey Robinson [883b]
**Sweet Love** – The Commodores [1018a]
**Sweet Soul** – Junior Walker & The All Stars [637b]
**Sweet Thing** – The Spinners [514a]; [755b]
**Sweeter You Treat Her, The** – Eddie Kendricks [1031a]
**Swept For You Baby** – The Miracles [598b]; [614b]
**Sylvia** – Stevie Wonder [588b]

---

**Take A Look Around** – The Temptations [808a]
**Take Me Clear From Here** – David Ruffin [936a]
**Take Me Girl, I'm Ready** – Junior Walker & The All Stars [840a]
**Take Me In Your Arms And Love Me** – Gladys Knight & The Pips [604a]; [864a]
**Take Me In Your Arms (Rock Me A Little While)** – Kim Weston [538a]
**Take Me In Your Arms (Rock Me A Little While)** – The Isley Brothers [652a]
**Take Me In Your Arms (Rock Me A Little While)** – Jermaine Jackson [851b]
**Take Some Time Out For Love** – The Isley Brothers [566a]; [719a]
**Take This Heart Of Mine** – Marvin Gaye [563a]
**Tears In Vain** – Stevie Wonder [505b]
**Tears Of A Clown, The** – The Miracles [745a]
**Tell Me It's Just A Rumour Baby** – The Isley Brothers [877a]
**Tell Me Why Has Our Love Turned Cold** – Willie Hutch [885a]
**That Girl** – The Miracles [774b]
**That's How Love Goes** – Jermaine Jackson [838a]
**That's The Way Love Is** – Marvin Gaye [718a]
**That's The Way Love Is** – The Temptations [741b]
**Theme From Mahogany (Do You Know Where You're Going To)** – Diana Ross [1010a]
**There's A Ghost In My House** – R. Dean Taylor [896a]
**There's A Song In My Heart** – The Commodores [902b]
**There's Fear** – Caston & Majors [951b]
**There's No Love Left** – The Isley Brothers [555b]; [937b]
**There's No Stopping Us Now** – The Supremes [597b]
**These Eyes** – Junior Walker & The All Stars [727a]
**These Things Will Keep Me Loving You** – The Velvelettes [580a]; [780a]
**Think Of Me As Your Soldier** – Stevie Wonder [798b]

**Third Finger, Left Hand** – Martha & The Vandellas [599b]
**This Child Needs Its Father** – Gladys Knight & The Pips [945b]
**This Empty Place** – Stephanie Mills [1020a]
**This Is The Story** – The Supremes [804b]
**This Is Your Life** – The Commodores [1007b]
**This Old Heart Of Mine (Is Weak For You)** – The Isley Brothers [555a]; [937a]
**Thumpin' Music** – The Commodores [1034b]
**Time** – Edwin Starr [725a]; [1028a]
**Time Changes Everything** – The Supremes [650b]
**Tin Can People** – Gloria Jones [910a]
**To Know** – The Jackson 5 [856b]
**To Win Your Heart** – Laura Lee [831a]
**Together** – Diana Ross [941b]
**Together 'Til The End Of Time** – Brenda Holloway [556a]
**Together We Can Make Such Sweet Music** – The Spinners [766a]; [871a]
**Tomorrow May Never Come** – The Spinners [523b]
**Tomorrow's Tears** – Jimmy Ruffin [593b]; [703b]
**Too Busy Thinking About My Baby** – Marvin Gaye [705a]
**Too High** – Stevie Wonder [869b]
**Too Many Fish In The Sea** – Earl Van Dyke & The Soul Brothers [506b]
**Tossin' And Turnin'** – The Supremes [859a]
**Touch** – The Jackson 5 [878b]
**Touch Me In The Morning** – Diana Ross [861a]
**Touch Of Time, The** – Barbara McNair [544b]
**Tracks Of My Tears, The** – The Miracles [522a]; [696a]
**Tracks Of My Tears, The** – Gladys Knight & The Pips [765b]
**Travelin' Man** – Stevie Wonder [602a]
**Trouble Man** – Marvin Gaye [846a]
**Truly Yours** – The Spinners [766b]
**Try It, You'll Like It** – Sisters Love [1002b]
**Tune Up** – Junior Walker & The All Stars [520b]
**25 Miles** – Edwin Starr [672a]
**Two Can Have A Party** – Marvin Gaye & Tammi Terrell [668b]
**Two Lovers** – Mary Wells [820b]
**Two Of Us, The** – Tony Martin [537b]

---

**Ungena Za Ulimwengu (Unite The World)** – The Temptations [783b]
**Until You Love Someone** – Four Tops [579b]
**Up Again** – The Miracles [940b]
**Up The Ladder To The Roof** – The Supremes [735a]
**Uptight (Everything's Alright)** – Stevie Wonder [545a]
**Uptight (Everything's Alright)** – Diana Ross & The Supremes & The Temptations [730b]

---

**Victors, The** – Tom Clay [801b]
**Visions** – Stevie Wonder [881b]

**Walk Away From Love** – David Ruffin [1017a]
**Walk Away Renee** – Four Tops [634a]; [1011a]
**Walk In The Night** – Junior Walker & The All Stars [824a]
**Walk Out The Door If You Wanna** – Yvonne Fair [1025b]
**Walk With Me, Talk With Me Darling** – Four Tops [823a]
**War** – Edwin Starr [754a]
**Way Back Home** – Junior Walker & The All Stars [857a]
**Way Over There** – Edwin Starr [692a]
**Way You Do The Things You Do, The** – Diana Ross & The Supremes & The Temptations [709b]
**We Can Make It We Can** – The Miracles [761b]
**We Can Work It Out** – Stevie Wonder [772a]
**We'll Have A Good Thing Going On** – David Ruffin [711b]
**What Am I Going To Do Without You?** – Chuck Jackson [729b]
**What Am I Going To Do Without Your Love** – Martha & The Vandellas [567a]
**What Becomes Of The Brokenhearted** – Jimmy Ruffin [577a]; [911a]
**What Does It Take (To Win Your Love)** – Junior Walker & The All Stars [712a]
**What Is A Man** – Four Tops [698a]
**What It Is** – The Undisputed Truth [897b]
**What Love Has Joined Together** – The Temptations [504b]
**What Love Has Joined Together** – Syreeta [954b]
**What The World Needs Now Is Love—Abraham, Martin And John** – Tom Clay [801a]
**Whatever You Got, I Want** – The Jackson 5 [927b]
**What's Going On** – Marvin Gaye [775a]
**When I Had Your Love** – Marvin Gaye [552b]
**When I'm Gone** – Brenda Holloway [508a]
**When The Lovelight Starts Shinning Thru' His Eyes** – The Boones [1030b]
**When The Words From Your Heart Get Caught Up** – The Miracles [648b]
**When You're Young And In Love** – The Marvelettes [609a]; [939a]
**Where Are You Going To My Love** – The Miracles [940a]
**Where Did Our Love Go** – The Supremes [925a]
**Where Did You Go** – Four Tops [507b]
**Where I Belong** – The Supremes [1012b]
**Where Were You** – Brenda Holloway [581b]
**Where Would I Be Without You Baby** – The Supremes & Four Tops [836b]
**Wherever I Lay My Hat** – Marvin Gaye [705b]
**Whisper You Love Me Boy** – The Supremes [516b]
**Who Could Ever Doubt My Love** – The Supremes [543b]
**Who Could Ever Doubt My Love** – The Isley Brothers [566b]; [719b]
**Whole Lot Of Shaking In My Heart (Since I Met You Girl)** – The Miracles [569a]; [853b]
**Whole New Thing** – Rose Banks [1037b]
**Wholly Holy** – Marvin Gaye [817b]
**Who's Gonna Take The Blame** – The Miracles [745b]
**Who's Loving You** – The Jackson 5 [724b]
**Who's Right Or Wrong** – Edwin Starr [930a]

**Why Did She Have To Leave Me (Why Did She Have To Go)** – The Temptations [707b]
**Why Did You Leave Me Darling** – The Temptations [671a]
**Why Do You Want To Let Me Go** – Marv Johnson [525a]
**Why Don't You Lead Me To Love** – Stevie Wonder [653b]
**Why (Must We Fall In Love)** – Diana Ross & The Supremes & The Temptations [730a]
**Why When The Love Is Gone** – The Isley Brothers [652b]
**Wigs And Lashes** – The Miracles [914b]
**Will This Be The Day** – The Supremes [677b]
**With A Child's Heart** – Stevie Wonder [558b]
**With A Child's Heart** – Michael Jackson [946b]
**Without The One You Love** – The Supremes & Four Tops [815a]
**World So Wide Nowhere To Hide (From Your Love)** – Jimmy Ruffin [603b]

---

**Yester Love** – The Miracles [661a]; [853b]
**Yesterday's Dreams** – Four Tops [665a]
**Yester-me, Yester-you, Yesterday** – Stevie Wonder [717a]
**You** – Marvin Gaye [640a]
**You Ain't Livin' Till You're Lovin'** – Marvin Gaye & Tammi Terrell [681a]
**You Are Everything** – Diana Ross & Marvin Gaye [890a]
**You Are The Sunshine Of My Life** – Stevie Wonder [852a]
**You Can Cry On My Shoulder** – Michael Jackson [834b]
**You Can't Hurry Love** – The Supremes [575a]
**You Can't Judge A Book By Its Cover** – Stevie Wonder [892b]
**You Can't Judge A Book By Its Cover** – Yvonne Fair [1013b]
**(You Can't Let The Boy Overpower) The Man In You** – Chuck Jackson [651b]
**You Don't Love Me No More** – Gladys Knight & The Pips [660b]
**You Got Me Hurting All Over** – Barbara Randolph [628b]; [788b]
**You Got The Love I Love** – Marv Johnson [680b]
**You Got The Love I Need** – The Undisputed Truth [789b]
**You Gotta Have Love In Your Heart** – The Supremes & Four Tops [793a]
**You Haven't Done Nothin'** – Stevie Wonder [921a]
**You Keep Me Hangin' On** – The Supremes [585a]
**You Keep Running Away** – Four Tops [623a]; [1011b]
**You Lost The Sweetest Boy** – Mary Wells [820b]
**You Make Your Own Heaven And Hell Right Here On Earth** – The Temptations [773b]
**You Met Your Match** – Stevie Wonder [666a]
**You Must Be Love** – The Miracles [631b]; [745b]
**You Need Love Like I Do (Don't You)** – Gladys Knight & The Pips [756b]
**You Need Me** – The Lewis Sisters [536a]
**You Stole My Love** – Four Tops [785b]
**You'll Lose A Precious Love** – The Temptations [565b]
**You're A Song (That I Can't Sing)** – Frankie Valli & The Four Seasons [819a]
**You're A Special Part Of Me** – Diana Ross & Marvin Gaye [879a]
**You're All I Need To Get By** – Marvin Gaye & Tammi Terrell [668a]

---

**You're Gonna Love My Baby** – Barbara McNair [544a]
**You're My Everything** – The Temptations [620a]
**You're My Everything** – Gladys Knight & The Pips [844b]
**You're Not An Ordinary Girl** – The Temptations [578b]
**You're The One** – The Marvelettes [562a]
**You're The One** – The Originals [702b]
**You've Been A Long Time Coming** – Marvin Gaye [510b]
**You've Been In Love Too Long** – Martha & The Vandellas [530a]
**You've Been So Wonderful To Me** – The Supremes [662b]
**You've Got It Bad Girl** – Stevie Wonder [841b]
**You've Got My Soul On Fire** – Edwin Starr [875a]
**You've Got To Earn It** – The Temptations [526b]
**You've Got To Make Your Choice** – Sisters Love [828b]
**You've Lost That Loving Feeling** – Gladys Knight & The Pips [945a]
**You've Made Me So Very Happy** – Brenda Holloway [622a]; [700b]
**Young Folks, The** – The Supremes [704b]
**Young Folks, The** – The Jackson 5 [738b]
**Your Changing Ways** – The Marvelettes [535b]
**Your Kiss Is Sweet** – Syreeta [933a]
**Your Love Grows Precious Every Day** – The Contours [605b]
**Your Love Is Amazing** – Four Tops [528b]
**Your Love Is Amazing** – Shorty Long [600b]
**Your Love Is Wonderful** – Four Tops [647b]
**Your Love's Got Me Burning Alive** – Paul Petersen [670b]
**Your Mother's Only Daughter** – The Miracles [687b]
**Your Precious Love** – Marvin Gaye & Tammi Terrell [625a]
**Your Unchanging Love** – Marvin Gaye [618a]
**Your Wonderful Sweet, Sweet Love** – The Supremes [835a]

---

**Zoo (The Human Zoo), The** – The Commodores [924a]

---

# Appendix I

# TAMLA MOTOWN EPS AND 12-INCH SINGLES

# EPs

In keeping with standard industry practise in the 1960s, Tamla Motown sought to market its UK product on three formats. Besides singles and albums, they issued a series of EPs, typically consisting of four-song collections on 7-inch disc running at 45 rpm. Since these are not classified as singles, they do not fall within the central part of this book, although the appeal to collectors of 45s is obvious. Most of Tamla Motown's were miniature compilations of earlier singles, which tend to dip into the pre-Tamla Motown catalogue for material but were nonetheless conceived on their own terms, and all wrapped in especially designed picture covers.

The EP format was not seriously pursued prior to 1965. Motown issued one UK EP via London American in 1961, a Miracles collection named after their first 45 "Shop Around" [E03], but the other licensees shunned the format until Stateside took the reins in 1963. Stateside issued five during the following 12 months, one dedicated to Little Stevie Wonder, the others consisting of four instalments of a series entitled *R & B Chartmakers*, sampling Motown's roster. All of these discs were generally intended to promote sales of the standard catalogue, and one, *Chartmakers No. 3*, included the rare and legendary "Too Hurt To Cry" by The Darnells (see [E33]), whose image was mysteriously missing from the cover.

When Tamla Motown began operations in March 1965, the inaugural singles were accompanied in the shops by a half-dozen new EPs, the first batch in a run of 19 releases over a two-year span. (These records have no American counterpart, the nearest equivalent being the 70-or-so juke-box singles pressed on the various American labels, but not put onto general sale.) As with the singles, chart positions are also provided, referring here to *Record Retailer's* EP listings, which commenced on 12 March 1960 and were discontinued after 2 December 1967. Tamla Motown had few successes in the listings, with the notable exception of the two Four Tops releases, which attained spectacular chart runs.

Many of the selected tracks below have also been released on single in the UK and where tracks have appeared in Tamla Motown's main sequence to 1976, reference numbers are supplied.

**TME 2001** (19 Mar 1965) **Various Artists**: *Hitsville USA No. 1*
Comprises: Marvin Gaye: Baby Don't You Do It / Brenda Holloway: I'll Always Love You // Carolyn Crawford: Devil In His Heart / Eddie Holland: Candy To Me
**Position in Record Retailer EP Chart**: -
Picking up where Stateside's Chartmakers series had left off, the Hitsville USA collection was planned to draw attention to some of Motown's numerous acts then vying for the UK market. As it turned out, there would never be a second instalment, the series ending as soon as it had begun. The track selection here included Gaye's minor American hit of the previous autumn (Tamla 54101), along with Holloway's early reading of [523], previously released in America (Tamla 54099). Particularly notable are the only recordings by Carolyn Crawford and Eddie Holland to be issued on 7-inch by Tamla Motown. Crawford's American B-side from 1963 (Motown 1050b) was written by Berry Gordy's brother Robert, and was not the same track as was recently covered

by The Beatles. Eddie Holland's American A-side (Motown 1063) was his last before his permanent back-room move.

**TME 2002** (19 Mar 1965) **The Contours**: *The Contours*
Comprises: Can You Jerk Like Me [E68] / That Day When She Needed Me [E68b] // Can You Do It [E43] / I'll Stand By You [E43b]
**Position in Record Retailer EP Chart**: -
Aside from the Hitsville disc, the initial batch of UK EPs were all themed by artist, each simply named after the featured act. The Contours' release rounds up each side of their previous two UK singles, which corresponded with the US Gordy label originals. The opening title was revived by Tamla Motown in 1974 as the flip to "Baby Hit And Run" [886b].

**TME 2003** (19 Mar 1965) **The Marvelettes**: *The Marvelettes*
Comprises: Too Many Fish In The Sea [E63] / He's A Good Guy, Yes He Is [E37] // You're My Remedy [E52] / Little Girl Blue [E33b]
**Position in Record Retailer EP Chart**: -
With the first of these tracks having made the US top 30 over Christmas, The Marvelettes seemed a promising bet for Tamla Motown who gathered their previous three Stateside singles here, together with "Little Girl Blue", an earlier B-side. Yet since the tracks were already included in their scant discography to date, fans of the group shunned the EP, accounting for its particular scarcity.

**TME 2004** (19 Mar 1965) **The Temptations**: *The Temptations*
Comprises: My Girl [E67] / I'll Be In Trouble [E47] // Why You Wanna Make Me Blue [E55] / The Girl's Alright With Me [E47b]
**Position in Record Retailer EP Chart**: 18
Kicking off with the classic "My Girl", this particularly strong set included two other early UK A-sides in "Why You Wanna Make Me Blue" and "I'll Be In Trouble", plus the B-side of the latter. The release was timed to make mileage from the success of "My Girl" which charted at 43 in the UK just as the EP appeared, The Temptations' first notable success here. This EP was Tamla Motown's first to chart.

**TME 2005** (19 Mar 1965) **Kim Weston**: *Kim Weston*
Comprises: A Little More Love [E59] / Another Train Coming // Looking For The Right Guy / Go Ahead And Laugh [E59b]
**Position in Record Retailer EP Chart**: -
Thus far, Weston had only one UK release, a single whose two sides book-end this EP. The other tracks were lifted from American singles (Tamla 54085b and Tamla 54100 respectively).

**TME 2006** (19 Mar 1965) **Stevie Wonder**: *Stevie Wonder*
Comprises: Fingertips [E26] / Happy Street // Hey Harmonica Man [E48] / The Square
**Position in Record Retailer EP Chart**: -
The last of Tamla Motown's initial batch of EPs featured four Stevie Wonder

cuts, including his two biggest American hits to date in "Fingertips" and "Hey Harmonica Man". "Happy Street" had also been an American 45 (Tamla 54103), while "The Square" was an album track and a somewhat obscure selection. (Wonder's other A-sides had already appeared on Stateside's earlier EP *I Call It Pretty Music*, accounting for the shortage of better-known titles. Nonetheless, "Castles In The Sand" [E41] had yet to be utilised and might have made a preferential choice.)

**TME 2007** (May 1965) **Mary Wells**: *Mary Wells*
Comprises: My Guy [E42] / Oh Little Boy (What Did You Do To Me?) [E42b] // What's Easy For Two Is So Hard For One [E30b] / You Lost The Sweetest Boy [E30]
**Position in Record Retailer EP Chart**: -
Two months after Tamla Motown's first releases, a second run of EPs was put together, the first of which featured "My Guy", Motown's inaugural UK top 10 hit a year earlier, plus its original B-side, "Oh Little Boy". Having just left the company Wells had no contemporary product out in the UK bar her *My Baby Just Cares For Me* album, and the EP was completed with either side of an earlier UK single. The first and last of the titles featured here were belatedly coupled up for a 1972 Tamla Motown 45 [820], her only single on the label until 1980 when [L019] appeared, a re-run of [820] switching the B-side for "What's Easy For Two Is So Hard For One", also featured on this EP.

**TME 2008** (May 1965) **The Supremes**: *Hits*
Comprises: Where Did Our Love Go [E51] / Baby Love [E56] // Come See About Me [E65] / When The Lovelight Starts Shining Thru' His Eyes [E34]
**Position in Record Retailer EP Chart**: -
The Supremes' two early smashes remained unreleased on Tamla Motown until into the 1970s, but appeared side-by-side as the opening half of this EP. They were complemented by the group's other Stateside A-sides, making for a neat résumé of their pre-Tamla Motown period.

**TME 2009** (May 1965) **Martha & The Vandellas**: *Martha & The Vandellas*
Comprises: Dancing In The Street [E54] / Live Wire [E36] // Wild One [E69] / In My Lonely Room [E44]
**Position in Record Retailer EP Chart**: -
As with The Supremes' EP above, this record collected together the A-sides of four Stateside singles, including the biggest attraction, "Dancing In The Street", the group's first UK top 30 hit the previous autumn.

**TME 2010** (Feb 1966) **The Temptations**: *It's The Temptations*
Comprises: My Baby [541] / Since I Lost My Baby [526] // It's Growing [504] / The Way You Do The Things You Do [E38]
**Position in Record Retailer EP Chart**: 8
Virtually a year into the label's run, Tamla Motown had enough material accumulated to start populating EPs with its own original singles. This particularly attractive short set featured The Temptations' previous three A-sides, plus the more aged "The Way You Do The Things You Do".

**TME 2011** (Feb 1966) **The Supremes**: *Shake*
Comprises: Chain Gang / Shake // Havin' A Party / (Ain't That) Good News
**Position in Record Retailer EP Chart**: -
Tamla Motown's hottest property The Supremes were experiencing a lull between the summers of 1965 and 1966, a situation not helped by the release of questionably themed albums which had frustrated their fans. These four titles were all sourced from *We Remember Sam Cooke*, released in Britain the previous July—confusingly so, since two further long-players had since appeared and contained better material. The group had performed the EP's title-song prior to that, on the *Ready Steady Go!* special which helped launch Tamla Motown in early 1965 (see Chapter 1).

**TME 2012** (Feb 1966) **Four Tops**: *The Four Tops*
Comprises: I Can't Help Myself [515] / Ask The Lonely [507] // Something About You [542] / It's The Same Old Song [528]
**Position in Record Retailer EP Chart**: 2
A compilation of the group's first four Tamla Motown singles, The Four Tops shows what might have been done for The Supremes instead of the disappointing *Shake*. That the tracks were already well-known did not bother the record-buying public, this EP becoming one of the label's biggest sellers, remaining on the EP charts for over a year.

**TME 2013** (Feb 1966) **Junior Walker & The All Stars**: *Shake And Fingerpop*
Comprises: Do The Boomerang [520] / Shake And Fingerpop [529] // Cleo's Back [529b] / Shotgun [509]
**Position in Record Retailer EP Chart**: -
Another appealing anthology of singles, Walker's only Tamla Motown EP supplemented the contemporary "Cleo's Mood", constituting his full A-side discography to date.

**TME 2014** (Apr 1966) **Various Artists**: *New Faces From Hitsville*
Comprises: Jimmy Ruffin: As Long As There Is Love / Chris Clark: Do Right Baby, Do Right // Tammi Terrell: I Can't Believe You Love Me / The Monitors: Say You
**Position in Record Retailer EP Chart**: -
Still struggling for consistent success in the UK market, Tamla Motown revived their 'various artists' formula for this, a sampling of some of the new talent on the books. At the time the EP was released, none of the four artists had put out a UK single (indeed The Monitors never would), a factor contributing to its moderate sales. Terrell's recording differs from that on 1969's *Irresistible*, and was subsequently re-engineered as a duet with Marvin Gaye [715b].

**TME 2015** (Apr 1966) **Kim Weston**: *Rock Me A Little While*
Comprises: Take Me In Your Arms (Rock Me A Little While) [538] / Don't Compare Me With Her [538b] // I'm Still Loving You [511] / Just Loving You [511b]
**Position in Record Retailer EP Chart**: -
Featuring either side of both of Weston's Tamla Motown 45s, this EP collects

her recordings together just as her tenure with Motown was coming to an end, and this would be her last solo release in Britain. This EP is valued above all the others including its scarce predecessor.

**TME 2016** (Apr 1966) **Marvin Gaye**: *Marvin Gaye*
Comprises: Ain't That Peculiar [539] / Pretty Little Baby [524] // I'll Be Doggone [510] / How Sweet It Is (To Be Loved By You) [E60]
**Position in Record Retailer EP Chart**: -
Gaye's first three Tamla Motown A-sides, bolstered by his Stateside-era "How Sweet It Is (To Be Loved By You)", which was being re-recorded by Junior Walker & The All Stars just as this EP appeared.

**TME 2017** (Oct 1966) **Martha & The Vandellas**: *Hittin'*
Comprises: What Am I Going To Do Without Your Love [567] / You've Been In Love Too Long [530] // Nowhere To Run [502] / Quicksand [E32]
**Position in Record Retailer EP Chart**: -
Compiled along the same lines as Marvin Gaye's April EP, Hittin' brings three A-sides together with an oldie, although the more logical fourth track would have been February's "My Baby Loves Me" [549], originally released chronologically between tracks 1 and 2.

**TME 2018** (Mar 1967) **Four Tops**: *Hits*
Comprises: Reach Out I'll Be There [579] / Loving You Is Sweeter Than Ever [568] // Standing In The Shadows Of Love [589] / Baby I Need Your Loving [E53]
**Position in Record Retailer EP Chart**: 1
Viewed alongside their previous Tamla Motown EP, Hits helps neatly survey the group's singles since the label started. The now obligatory oldie, in this case "Baby I Need Your Loving" completes the set, in lieu of the 'missing' A-side, "Shake Me Wake Me (When It's Over)" [553]. The collection was Tamla Motown's only number 1 in the EP charts, where it spent 22 weeks at the top, one week short of the all-time record, its residency there only terminated by the abolition of the listings on December 2. (The group's previous EP (TME 2012) had taken its time to appear on the chart but, having done so on 29 October 1966, featured for the next 58 weeks, also persisting until the chart's demise. The group were also experiencing considerable success on the album charts during 1967.)

**TME 2019** (Mar 1967) **Marvin Gaye**: *Originals From Marvin Gaye*
Comprises: Can I Get A Witness [E31] / Stubborn Kind Of Fellow [E16] / Baby Don't You Do It // You're A Wonderful One [E40] / Hitch Hike / Pride And Joy [E24]
**Position in Record Retailer EP Chart**: 3
Gaye's second Tamla Motown EP is unique in featuring six titles, whose combined running time stretched EMI's pressing technology to the limit; in fact the record is so out-of-line with established policy that it suggests Tamla Motown were aware it would be their last. All six titles pre-date the label (now two years old), and all bar "Stubborn Kind Of Fellow" had been hits in America. In effect the EP is a miniaturised retrospective, released just as Gaye

was finding a new career direction with Tammi Terrell. Moving full-circle, this final release included "Baby Don't You Do It", a track also included on the first such EP, in March 1965.

# Promo-only EPs

By 1967 the EP format was becoming obsolete in the face of popular recording artists' concentration on the developing album concept. *Record Retailer's* specialist EP listing was discontinued in December and losing interest, Tamla Motown would release no more, although a clutch of 3-track 'maxi-singles' appeared in the standard run in 1972-73 (see [803n]). However six years after releasing their final commercially available EP, Tamla Motown commenced the policy of occasionally releasing promo-only 4-track discs, publicising recent releases and sometimes introducing US-only singles to the British media and public. As time went on, Tamla Motown realised the benefit of these for album sales and began pressing an EP for disc jockeys each time one of the *Anthology* compilations was due on the market. All of the 12 discs which follow are regular vinyl records with labels as per the standard EPs (but for the final one which had a predominantly white label), and similarly all run at 45 rpm unless otherwise stated.

**PSR 352** (1973)  Comprises: The Detroit Spinners: We'll Have It Made / Al Kent: Ooo Pretty Lady // Eddie Kendricks: Girl You Need A Change Of Mind [916] / Willie Hutch: Slick

This promotional EP is the first of three which Tamla Motown sent to UK radio stations over 1973, speculatively plugging a clutch of Motown's album tracks and UK/US singles. PSR 352 is the only Tamla Motown 45 to feature Al Kent, a former Ric Tic singer and musician whose "Ooo Pretty Lady" had first appeared as a late-1967 single and resurfaced in the UK on *Ric Tic Relics* (Aug 1973). It was coupled on the A-side with "We'll Have It Made", a US single from January 1970 by The Detroit Spinners (VIP 25060), written and produced by Stevie Wonder. Despite making number 20 R & B, the track was only released in Britain on the album *Second Time Around* (Apr 1971) and was presumably included here because of the group's recent success on the Atlantic label, which saw "Could It Be I'm Falling In Love" make 11 on the UK charts in April 1973. The other two tracks appeared as US singles, "Girl You Need A Change Of Mind" (Tamla 54230) in January 1973, "Slick" (Motown 1252) in June, the latter also featuring in the movie *The Mack*.

**PSR 353** (1973)  Comprises: The Undisputed Truth: Mama I Got A Brand New Thing (Don't Say No) [919b] / Rare Earth: Big John Is My Name // Jermaine Jackson: The Bigger You Love (The Harder You Fall) [874] / Marvin Gaye: Let's Get It On [868]

Another selection of contemporary singles, all but "The Bigger You Love" appearing on 45 in the US. "Mama I Got A Brand New Thing" was released there in February 1973 (Gordy 7124), making the B-side of "I'm A Fool For You" in the UK the following year. "Big John Is My Name" was released in

October (Rare Earth 5056), while "Let's Get It On" appeared in June (Tamla 54234) and of course was released as a single in Britain two months later.

**PSR 357** (1973)   Comprises: The Miracles: What Is A Heart Good For / Eddie Kendricks: Darling Come Back Home // Four Tops: Standing In The Shadows Of Love [589] / The Supremes: Bad Weather [847]

The final sampler distributed to DJs contained a selection of recordings by well-known Tamla Motown artists including one vintage track in [589] and a recent UK hit from The Supremes [847]. Eddie Kendricks' "Darling Come Back Home" was a US-only single in April 1973 (Tamla 54236) but oddly The Miracles' track was a selection not released on 45 in America or the UK.

**SPSEP 209** (1973) **Tamla Triple Pack** (Comprises: The Jackson 5: Skywriter [865] / The Jackson 5: Hallelujah Day [856] / Gladys Knight & The Pips: Neither One Of Us (Wants To Be The First To Say Goodbye) [855] / Gladys Knight & The Pips: Don't It Make You Feel Guilty / The Temptations: Masterpiece [854] // The Temptations: Law Of The Land [866] / The Jackson Five: Skywriter [865] / Gladys Knight & The Pips: Daddy Could Swear, I Declare [876])

Issued in a picture sleeve, this widely distributed promotional EP ran at 33 rpm and featured edited extracts from the named tracks, which survey current albums from three acts (hence its title): *Skywriter* (The Jackson 5); *Masterpiece* (The Temptations); *Neither One Of Us* (Gladys Knight & The Pips). The title track from each LP appears amongst the selections. Narration is by Canadian-born Duncan Johnson, famous for his time as a UK-based pirate radio DJ before he accepted a job with EMI. It is interesting that Tamla Motown opted for the abbreviation 'Tamla' in the record's title, rather than the more popularly used 'Motown'. (None of the featured groups recorded for the Tamla label in America.)

**PSR 360** (Dec 1973) **The Temptations**: The Way You Do The Things You Do [E38] / Since I Lost My Baby [526] // Psychedelic Shack [741] / Superstar (Remember How You Got Where You Are) [800]

The principal artist-specific compilation format of the 1970s was the often extravagant and plushly packaged *Anthology* series, which encompassed most of Tamla Motown's biggest acts and ran irregularly from 1973 into the 1980s.[1] The first to appear was *The Temptations' Anthology: 10th Anniversary* [sic], released in December 1973. The album appeared in Britain on an American-style Motown label, this 4-track sampler carrying the standard Tamla Motown label.

**PSR 361** (Feb 1974) **Smokey Robinson & The Miracles**: I Gotta Dance To Keep From Crying [E35] / Come 'Round Here (I'm The One You Need) [584] // I Second That Emotion [631] / The Tears Of A Clown [745]

The second *Anthology* album was released in February 1974, and was dedicated to The Miracles. As with the previous *Anthology*-related promo, the disc's contents were ordered chronologically and included three well-known Tamla Motown A-sides along with an attractive oldie, in this case a 1964 Stateside single.

**674**                    *Tamla Motown - The stories behind the UK singles*

**PSR 362** (Mar 1974) **Gladys Knight & The Pips**: I Heard It Through The Grapevine [629] / Just Walk In My Shoes [576] // You Need Love Like I Do (Don't You) [756b] / If I Were Your Woman [765]

Switching the LP series to the orthodox Tamla Motown label, the new *Anthology* album was issued shortly after its predecessor. This promo EP carried three former A-sides by the group and an American-only single from 1970 which had appeared in the UK as [756b].

**PSR 364** (May 1974) **Marvin Gaye**: Can I Get A Witness [E31] / I'll Be Doggone [510] // Your Unchanging Love [618] / What's Going On [775]

Marvin Gaye's *Anthology* was released in May 1974, this promo following the established format by selecting four tracks in date order. The oldie, "Can I Get A Witness", was originally a November 1963 single on Stateside.

**PSR 365** (Jul 1974) **Diana Ross & The Supremes**: Baby Love [E56] / You Can't Hurry Love [575] // The Happening [607] / Love Child [677]

The Supremes' *Anthology* set made its first appearance on the American-style Motown label in July 1974. The promo 45 carried "Baby Love" as its opener, released simultaneously as a single [915], its first appearance on Tamla Motown. The other titles are all well-known hits from the golden years 1966-68.

**PSR 370** (Oct 1974) **Junior Walker & The All Stars**: What Does It Take (To Win Your Love) [712] / Do You See My Love (For You Is Growing) [750] // Take Me Girl, I'm Ready [840] / These Eyes [727]

The sixth *Anthology* album to appear within a year went to Junior Walker. This time the accompanying promo EP eschewed early material in favour of more contemporary hits, all four titles having appeared as A-sides between 1969 and 1973.

**PSR 371** (Oct 1974) **Four Tops**: I Can't Help Myself [515] / 7-Rooms Of Gloom [612] // Walk Away Renee [634] / It's All In The Game [736]

The Four Tops had seen their retrospective album issued as early as October 1973 under the title *The Four Tops Story: 1964-1972* and were not initially granted a release in the *Anthology* series. (An American edition was released in July, but didn't see light of day in the UK until 1982.) With the group having departed Motown, Tamla Motown had no new Four Tops singles to promote, and sought to belatedly promote *The Four Tops Story* with this round-up of former hits. This was the final such promo EP on Tamla Motown.

**PSR 378** (May 1975) **The Commodores**: The Bump [952b] / Wide Open // Slippery When Wet [952]

Accompanying the release of [952], this promotional disc went one-further than the contemporary single (and its standard A-label demo) by also including "Wide Open". Released in support of the album *Caught In The Act*, from which all three titles are sourced, the release is anomalous in that not only are the sides are switched as compared to the commercial single, but the usual Tamla Motown label is not used. Instead, the record has a white EMI demo label with the familiar Tamla Motown logo on a sticker placed over EMI's logo at the top of the label.

# Flexi-discs

There are two flexi-discs in existence which carry the Tamla Motown emblem, which for the sake of completeness are noted here:

**SFI 66** (Apr 1971) **Various Artists**: *Chartbusters Volume 5 Bonus Record*
Comprises: The Supremes: Together We Can Make Such Sweet Music / The Motown Spinners: (She's Gonna Love Me) At Sundown // The Jackson 5: Goin' Back To Indiana / Diana Ross: My Place / Four Tops: In These Changing Times
A 33 rpm disc included free with *Motown Chartbusters Volume 5* (see [599n]). The record contains a series of non-album tracks promoting titles from Tamla Motown's contemporary LP catalogue, 'presented by' DJ Noel Edmonds.

**Lyn 2639** (1974) **The Jackson 5**: *Talk And Sing Personally To* Valentine *Readers*
This 33 rpm record, manufactured by flexi-disc specialists Lyntone whose catalogue number it carries, was presented free with a 1974 edition of *Valentine*, a newsy magazine aimed at the female adolescent market. It contains a medley of the group's hits and spoken messages from each of the brothers, referencing their 'recent' UK tour. (In fact the group had not played the UK since 1972, their 1974 tour having been cancelled [904].)

# 12-inch Singles

The standardised issue of EPs fizzled out in the late 1960s and, despite the promotional discs above, Motown-UK abandoned them—but for a one-off 1976 release on the blue label, included as a freebie in Stevie Wonder's *Songs In The Key Of Life*. (Recalling where they had got to in the 1960s, they appropriately numbered it STME 2020.[2]) However industry innovation led to the advent of the 12-inch single in the late 1970s, with its more extravagant play time and better sound reproduction. 12-inch singles were almost always released as alternative format editions of concurrent 7-inch releases and thus, these records all have 7-inch equivalents as noted, which are more fully detailed in Chapter 6. Although record companies have tended to legitimise them on artistic grounds, in truth 12-inch singles were seen as a vehicle for selling essentially the same material to fans twice over. This is not to say they are without merit of course, and in Tamla Motown's case they are frequently of particular interest due to the extra tracks included, many of which did not appear on Tamla Motown singles elsewhere.

Motown-UK did not pursue the format in earnest until 1979 when some 20 were released on the blue label which amongst them included re-appearances of "Ain't No Mountain High Enough" [751] and "What's Going On" [775] as B-sides (see Appendix 2). And at the end of the year, with the Tamla Motown label now in intermittent use again, a promo-only 12-inch was put out in support of a Diana Ross album, which is effectively a latter-day equivalent of the old 7-inch promos listed above.

**PSLP 304** (Nov 1979) **Diana Ross**: Touch Me In The Morning [861] / Remember Me [768] // Love Hangover [1024] (Long Version)
This promotional record supports the 1979 release of Ross' *20 Golden Greats*,

heavily plugged on TV and issued with a (rarely-used) EMTV catalogue number. The album made number 2 on the UK charts and this selection of titles includes the long version of "Love Hangover" and the only appearance of "Touch Me In The Morning" on 12-inch. That the Tamla Motown label was chosen above the blue label is surprising, the company recognising perhaps that it had more credibility for DJs and serious music fans in the media.

**12TMG 1180** (3 Apr 1980) **Diana Ross & The Supremes**: Supremes Medley (Parts 1 & 2) / **Diana Ross**: Love Hangover [1024] (Long Version)
(7-inch equivalent: [L017])
With Motown-EMI having begun employing the format regularly through 1979, Tamla Motown's first commercially available 12-inch single arrived in support of [L017]. (For 12-inch catalogue numbers, the corresponding 7-inch TMG number would always be used either with the prefix 12 or the suffix T.) This release contained the full, uninterrupted medley and was appropriately referred to on the label as a 'Disco Mix', although the term would appear on the notation of all such 12-inch releases during the TMG era—usually without justification. As with the previous 12-inch, the track was backed with the long version of [1024] lifted from *Diana Ross* (1976), like the A-side, running close to eight minutes.

**12TMG 977** (Jul 1981) **Michael Jackson**: We're Almost There / We've Got A Good Thing Going
(7-inch equivalent: [L043])
Also labelled a 'Disco Mix', this two-track 12-inch had identical contents to the apparently non-disco 7-inch edition. The mixes and playing times are asper the original versions and have not been overdubbed.

**TMGT 978** (Apr 1982) **Four Tops**: Baby I Need Your Loving [E53] / Yesterday's Dreams [665] // Medley
(7-inch equivalent: [L044])
The first RCA-era 12-inch contained both sides of the 7-inch edition, backed with a medley of hits re-mixed in the style of the studio-sequenced Supremes release of 1980, likewise overdubbed with an automated percussion track. The samples in the medley consisted of five vintage HDH numbers, oddly supplemented with two later, and very different recordings: [515]; [553]; [589]; [579]; [601]; [858] and [752].

**TMGT 1320** (Oct 1983) **The Temptations With Four Tops**: Medley / **The Temptations**: Papa Was A Rollin' Stone [839] (Long Version)
(7-inch equivalent: [L055])
This 12-inch edition of the *Motown 25* commemorative release was backed by the original 'long' version of "Papa Was A Rollin' Stone" taken from *All Directions* (1973). Unlike previous 12-inch singles which had standard Motown sleeves, this came in a picture jacket. With the extra playing time afforded by the format, the full live medley was included, encompassing: [579]; [557]; [528]; [565]; [E53]; [E67]; [722]; [515]; [587]; [515]; [587]. An album of material from the show was also released.

**TMGT 987** (Nov 1983) **Marvin Gaye:** What's Going On [775] // I Heard It Through The Grapevine [686] (Extended Version) / Wherever I Lay My Hat (That's My Home) [705b]
(7-inch equivalent: [L056])
This 12-inch edition of "What's Going On" had on its B-side a new, extended mix of "I Heard It Through The Grapevine", running to 5:03. The extra needle-time was achieved by splicing the start of verse 2 just prior to the coda, which then played through again to the end. This edition also carried Gaye's early recording of [705b], selected in the wake of Paul Young's summer number 1 cover version.

**ZT 40702** (Apr 1986) **Marvin Gaye:** I Heard It Through The Grapevine [686] (Extended Version) / That's The Way Love Is [718] // Can I Get A Witness [E31] / You're A Wonderful One [E40]
(7-inch equivalent: [L073])
The start of the 'European' system (which employed only the even numbers for 12-inch singles) is marked by a second successive release of the extended "Grapevine" on 12-inch. Accompanied this time by "Can I Get A Witness" from the 7-inch edition, the release also carried additional oldies. "You're A Wonderful One" was, like "Witness", originally a Stateside single, the set neatly completed with Gaye's final 1969 A-side. As with the 7-inch edition, it was housed in a picture cover and appeared as both black and blue label editions.

**ZT 40710** (Apr 1986) **The Supremes:** You Keep Me Hangin' On [585] / Love Is Like An Itching In My Heart [560] // Come See About Me [E65] / I Hear A Symphony [543]
(7-inch equivalent: [L074])
As with the previous 12-inch single, this release delighted collectors with the inclusion of a pair of extra tracks unique to the format, in this case two of the group's slightly lesser-known, vintage Tamla Motown A-sides, [543] and [560]. The picture sleeve was identical to that on the 7-inch version.

**ZT 40744** (Jun 1986) **The Temptations:** My Girl [E67] / The Way You Do The Things You Do [E38] // Wherever I Lay My Hat (That's My Home) / My Baby [541]
(7-inch equivalent: [L075])
Maintaining recent policy, this 12-inch release contained an additional pair of classic recordings in the 1964 Stateside single "The Way You Do The Things You Do" and "My Baby" from 1965.

**ZT 40804** (Jul 1986) **Diana Ross:** Ain't No Mountain High Enough [751] (Extended Remix) / It's My House (Extended Remix) // The Boss (Extended Remix) / Remember Me [768]
(7-inch equivalent: [L076])
Both sides of the current 7-inch single were presented here as extended re-mixes and the additional material included a similar update to "The Boss", originally a 1979 blue label single (TMG 1150). In the case of "Ain't No

Mountain High Enough", the so-called 'remix' is in fact the original album cut from which the 7-inch version was distilled. In the other cases the re-mixing is confined to extending the play time, and the original instrumentation and arrangement is not interfered with. ("Remember Me" retains its original form.)

# The 'B Siders'...

Continuing to make the most of its back-catalogue during 1986-87, Motown occasionally supplemented 12-inch editions of newly recorded singles with vintage material. In each case, standard blue Motown labels are used as normal on the A-sides, Tamla Motown on the flips, despite the fact that most of the selections had not appeared on the label before. Four materialised until the policy was abandoned, all of which came in picture sleeves identical to t            h            e            i            r 7-inch editions. In each case the original single tracks are listed first in parentheses.

**ZT 40718** (Jun 1986) (Smokey Robinson: Sleepless Nights—Close Encounters Of The First Kind) **Smokey Robinson & The Miracles**: Mickey's Monkey [E27] / I Gotta Dance To Keep From Crying [E35]
The first B-side-only Tamla Motown record included two classic Miracles tracks, "Mickey's Monkey" dating back to 1963 when Oriole were the UK licensees, and "I Gotta Dance To Keep From Crying", a Stateside single from early 1964.

**ZT 40848** (Aug 1986) (Four Tops: Hot Nights / Again) **Four Tops**: Medley Of Hits
This 12-inch edition coupled the group's current single with the segued mix first heard on TMGT 978 in 1982 (see above). This new edit had the final two anomalous track selections removed and is therefore (arguably) new.

**ZT 40850** (Sep 1986) (The Temptations: Lady Soul / A Fine Mess)
**The Temptations**: Papa Was A Rollin' Stone [839] (Long Version)
Tamla Motown stalwarts The Temptations resumed recording for the label in the 1980s after a three-year absence, turning out contemporary material alongside other seminal artists such as Smokey Robinson and The Four Tops. This release re-ran the album version of [839], previously heard on TMGT 1320 (above) as backing for the trailer-single to *To Be Continued*.

**ZT 41148** (Mar 1987) (Smokey Robinson: Just To See Her / I'm Gonna Love You Like There's No Tomorrow) **Smokey Robinson & The Miracles**: You Really Got A Hold On Me [E13] / That's What Love Is Made Of [E57] / Ooo Baby Baby [503]
The final Tamla Motown 12-inch (at the time of writing) was the fourth to feature different labels on each side. "Just To See Her" was a minor UK hit in the spring (no. 52), and this supporting edition included the cherished "You Really Got A Hold On Me", a 1962-vintage track originally released on Oriole American, and shortly immortalised by The Beatles. "That's What Love Is Made Of" was a late-1964 single, and [503] completed perhaps the most attractive of the four 'B-siders'.

[1] The full *Anthology* series extends to cover 11 artists. Besides the seven noted above in connection with these promotional EPs, there also exist sets dedicated to: The Jackson 5 (Jan 1977); Martha Reeves & The Vandellas (Jun 1977) [single album]; Grover Washington Jr. (Sep 1982); Diana Ross (Oct 1983). The parallel US series included additional sets from The Marvelettes, The Commodores and Stevie Wonder (the last released in the UK with amended track listing, as *Essential Stevie Wonder* (Jul 1987)), and for some time US singles were housed in specially designed sleeves plugging the series.

[2] In 1983 Motown-EMI began issuing a series of cassette-only EPs, which also maintained the sequence, starting at CTME 2021. 16 appeared, another six were planned but scrapped, extending the numbering to 2042.

# MOTOWN'S BLUE LABEL

This book is not particularly concerned with Motown's blue label discography and readers may be relieved to learn that forests are not to be sacrificed for the sake of a full discography (for which, see Davis 1988, complete to the time of publication). However the study would be lacking if the Tamla Motown singles thusly re-issued were not mentioned, for the record.

The use of the blue label in this context falls into two main categories:
The 1976-79 gap, during which Tamla Motown was retired
The 1980s, when RCA were handling the label

# 1. 1976-79

Motown introduced its blue label, marking the supposed 'New Era', in October 1976. But it was not until February 1979 that Tamla Motown was revived and, in the interim, 11 7-inch singles were released with vintage material on one or both sides. The following were all issued on Motown's blue label:

**TMG 1070**
**Junior Walker & The All Stars**: What Does It Take (To Win Your Love) [712] / Take Me Girl, I'm Ready [840] (Double B-side to Junior Walker: "I Ain't Goin' Nowhere", 6 May 1977)
**TMG 1073**
**The Commodores**: Machine Gun [902] / I Feel Sanctified [944] (Double B-side to "Easy", 27 May 1977)
- Reached number 9 in the UK charts
**TMG 1078**
**David Ruffin**: My Whole World Ended (The Moment You Left Me) [689] (B-side to "I Can't Stop The Rain", 15 Jul 1977)
**TMG 1080**
**The Supremes**: Someday We'll Be Together [721] / You Keep Me Hangin' On [585] (26 Aug 1977)
**TMG 1081**
**The Jackson 5**: Skywriter [865] // I Want You Back [724] / The Love You Save [746] (26 Aug 1977)
**TMG 1095**
**Gladys Knight & The Pips**: Help Me Make It Through The Night [830] / Daddy Could Swear, I Declare [876] (11 Nov 1977)
- This single was re-pressed on Tamla Motown in 1985: See Chapter 6
**TMG 1100**
**Mary Wells**:
My Guy [E42] / What's Easy For Two Is So Hard For One [E30b] (24 Feb 1978)
- This single was re-pressed on Tamla Motown in 1980: See Chapter 6
**TMG 1118**
**Junior Walker & The All Stars**: Walk In The Night [824] (1 Sep 1978)

**TMG 1120**
**Four Tops**: I Can't Help Myself [515] / It's The Same Old Song [528] (29 Sep 1978)
*- This single was re-pressed on Tamla Motown in 1983: See Chapter 6*
**TMG 1124**
**The Velvelettes**: Needle In A Haystack [E61] / He Was Really Sayin' Somethin' [E71] (20 Oct 1978)
*- A re-issue of the pairing found on [595]. This single was re-pressed on Tamla Motown in 1983: See Chapter 6*
**TMG 1135**
**Diana Ross**: Ain't No Mountain High Enough [751] (B-side to "What You Gave Me", 16 Feb 1979)

Also in 1979, Motown-UK discovered the 12-inch format and decided to release 20! Amongst the titles are:
**12TMG 1135**
**Diana Ross**: Ain't No Mountain High Enough [751] (B-side to "What You Gave Me", 16 Feb 1979)
**12TMG 1168**
**Marvin Gaye**: What's Going On [775] (B-side to "Ego Tripping Out", Nov 1979)

# 2. 1980s
Once Tamla Motown was revived as a label, 'blue' re-issues were of course discontinued—at least in theory. As it happened, RCA arrived on the scene at the end of 1981, taking control of Motown-UK and opening their account with The Temptations' "Aiming At Your Heart" / "The Life Of A Cowboy" (TMG 1243). (TMG 1242 was also an RCA pressing, but appeared later.) The black label continued being used by RCA for vintage recordings, but the odd oldie managed to slip out on the blue label.
    The first with material of relevance emerged on both 7-inch and 12-inch formats:
**TMG 1248**
**Diana Ross & The Supremes**: Medley (B-side to Diana Ross: "Tenderness", Jan 1982)
*- This is a different medley to that featured on TMG 1180 (see Chapter 6). It is made up of sections from [585]; [548]; [575]; [677]; [616]; [543]; [597]; [721]*
**TMGT 1248**
**Diana Ross & The Supremes**: Medley - *12-inch edition of the above*

And pleased with their efforts, Motown cobbled a similar medley together from Miracles tracks, which also carried the 12-inch blue label:
**TMGT 1295**
**Smokey Robinson & The Miracles**: Greatest Hits Medley (B-side to the 12-inch edition of Smokey Robinson: "I've Made Love To You A Thousand Times", May 1983)

Another 12-inch single was issued just a year later as Motown exploited Michael Jackson's unheard other material. It included two other Tamla Motown titles:

**TMGT 1355**
**Michael Jackson**: Ben [834] / Ain't No Sunshine [826] (Double B-side to the 12-inch edition of "Girl You're So Together", Jul 1984)

These odd RCA releases represent exceptions to the general release policy, whereby the Tamla Motown label was used as appropriate. The policy was intact until 1986, although it is not altogether clear why RCA eventually ended it. (They did however use the Tamla Motown label on their 1988 commemorative set.) So from 1986, everything started to come out on the blue label again, by which time the TMG series had been shelved and the European catalogue was in play, with its ZB/ZT prefix. The following records were issued in the second part of the 1980s, and in every case there are 7-inch and 12-inch editions. Many of these were housed in picture sleeves and ZB 41373 came with a graphic from the film Platoon, in which the track had recently been included. Reflecting the label's continuing popularity, ZB 40701, ZB 41913 and ZB 41943 went top 10.

**ZB 40701**
**Marvin Gaye**: I Heard It Through The Grapevine [686] / Can I Get A Witness [E31] (Apr 1986)
- *Blue label pressing of [L073] in identical sleeve. Reached number 8 in the UK charts*
**ZT 40702**
12-inch edition of above
I Heard It Through The Grapevine (Extended Version) / That's The Way Love Is [718] // Can I Get A Witness / You're A Wonderful One [E40]
- *Also exists as a Tamla Motown 12-inch (see Appendix 1), in identical sleeve*
**ZB 41147**
**The Miracles**: The Tracks Of My Tears [522] (B-side to Smokey Robinson: "Just To See Her", Jun 1987)
- *This edition was a re-release of the blue label ZB 41147, but with the Miracles' track added on. The corresponding 12-inch was a 'B-sider'—see Appendix 1*
**ZB 41373**
**The Miracles**: The Tracks Of My Tears [522] / I Second That Emotion [631] (Jul 1987)
**ZT 41374**
12-inch edition of above
The Tracks Of My Tears / I Second That Emotion // Going To A Go Go [547] / Shop Around [E03]
**ZB 41431**
**The Temptations**: Papa Was A Rolling Stone [839] [Re-mix] / Ain't Too Proud To Beg [565] (Aug 1987)
- *Contemporary re-mix of A-side. Reached number 31 in the UK charts*

**ZT 41432**
12-inch edition of above
Papa Was A Rolling Stone (Vocal re-mix) // Ain't Too Proud To Beg / Papa Was A Rolling Stone (Dub)
**ZB 41655**
**Michael Jackson With The Jackson 5**: Santa Claus Is Coming To Town [837] (Track on 'The Christmas EP', Nov 1987)
**ZT 41656**
12-inch edition of above
**ZB 41793**
**The Commodores**: Machine Gun [902] / I Feel Sanctified [944] (Double B-side to "Easy", Jul 1988)
- *Re-issue of TMG 1073 (see above). Reached number 15 in the UK charts*
**ZT 41794**
12-inch edition of above
**ZB 41913**
**Michael Jackson With The Jackson 5**: I Want You Back '88 Re-mix [724] [Re-mix] / Never Can Say Goodbye [778] (Mar 1988)
- *Contemporary re-mix of A-side. This was an odd addition to the 1988 singles collection,* Motown Hits Of Gold *(see Chapter 6), occupying one of the catalogue numbers, and with its own sleeve design. Reached number 8 in the UK charts*
**ZT 41914**
12-inch edition of above
I Want You Back '88 Re-mix / I Want You Back [Original mix] // I Want You Back (You Know We Got Soul Dub Mix) / Never Can Say Goodbye
**ZB 41943**
**Four Tops**: Reach Out I'll Be There [579] [Re-mix] / Standing In The Shadows Of Love [589] (Jun 1988)
- *Contemporary re-mix of A-side. Reached number 9 in the UK charts*
**ZT 41944**
12-inch edition of above
Reach Out (12-inch Remix) / Reach Out (Original Version) // Reach Out (Re-mix Instrumental) / Standing In The Shadows Of Love
**ZB 41963**
**The Supremes**: Stop! In The Name Of Love [501] / Automatically Sunshine [821] (Jan 1989)
**ZT 41964**
12-inch edition of above
Stop! In The Name Of Love / Automatically Sunshine // Medley Of Hits [L017]
**ZB 41965**
**Edwin Starr**: 25 Miles (Single Version '89) [672] [Re-mix] / 25 Miles (Original Instrumental) (1989)
- *Contemporary re-mix of A-side*
**ZT 41966**
12-inch edition of above
25 Miles (12-inch Re-mix '89) / 25 Miles (Single Version '89) // 25 Miles (Instrumental) / 25 Miles (Dub '89)

**ZB 42307 Diana Ross:**
Love Hangover (PWL '88 Remix) [1024] [Re-mix] (Nov 1988)
- *Contemporary re-mix of A-side*
**ZT 42308** 12-inch edition of above
Love Hangover (Dance Mix) / Love Hangover (Extended Single Version) // Love Hangover (12-inch Version)
**ZB 43781 Diana Ross:**
I'm Still Waiting (Phil Chill Remix) [781] [Re-mix] / I'm Still Waiting (Original version) (Jun 1990)
- *Contemporary re-mix of A-side. Reached number 21 in the UK charts*
**ZT 43782** 12-inch edition of above
I'm Still Waiting (Phil Chill Remix - The Full Monty) // I'm Still Waiting (Funky In The Place 12-inch Remix) / I'm Still Waiting (Original Version)

Another series of releases emerged, probably in the late 1980s, although dating them has proved difficult. They consist of a run of some 43 12-inch singles, which some say are promotional items, although it seems likely they were available to the public in limited quantity. Many of them contained former Tamla Motown hits, and the series introduced a supplementary numbering system, TMGLTD. The series was structured such that particular artists were given a block of successive numbers, making it likely that all were issued at once, although this is not certain. All came in standard Motown 12-inch sleeves with "Motown Disco" printed in large, multi-coloured letters.

A few of the tracks are sourced from Stevie Wonder's 1987 album *Characters*, pinning the series to there or later. The following listing only includes the relevant discs with the relevant Tamla Motown tracks mentioned:
**TMGLTD 01**
**Stevie Wonder**: Don't You Worry 'Bout A Thing [908]
**TMGLTD 04**
**Stevie Wonder**: Superstition [841] / Too High [869b]
**TMGLTD 07**
**Stevie Wonder**: Living For The City [881]
**TMGLTD 10**
**Stevie Wonder**: Superwoman [827]
**TMGLTD 13**
**Stevie Wonder**: You Are The Sunshine Of My Life [852] / Higher Ground [869]
**TMGLTD 15**
**Diana Ross**: Love Hangover [1024]
**TMGLTD 16**
**Diana Ross**: Touch Me In The Morning [861] / Save The Children [917b]
**TMGLTD 26**
**Diana Ross**: Love Hangover [1024]
**TMGLTD 30**
**The Commodores**: Machine Gun [902]
**TMGLTD 32**
**Jackson 5**: The Love You Save [746] / I Want You Back [724] / The Life Of The Party [927]

**TMGLTD 33**
**Jackson 5:** A B C [738] / Lookin' Through The Windows [833]
**TMGLTD 34**
**Marvin Gaye:** What's Going On [775] / God Is Love [775b] / Mercy Mercy Me [802]
**TMGLTD 35**
**Marvin Gaye:** Inner City Blues [817] / Save The Children [796]
**TMGLTD 36**
**Marvin Gaye:** Trouble Man [846]
**TMGLTD 37**
**Marvin Gaye:** I Want You [1026]
**TMGLTD 38**
**Marvin Gaye:** After The Dance [1035]
**TMGLTD 40**
**Marvin Gaye:** Let's Get It On [868]
**TMGLTD 41**
**Marvin Gaye:** Distant Lover [882b]
**TMGLTD 42**
**Marvin Gaye (& Tammi Terrell):** I Heard It Through The Grapevine [686] / If I Could Build My Whole World Around You [635] / Ain't No Mountain High Enough [611] / Chained [676]
**TMGLTD 43**
**Marvin Gaye & Tammi Terrell:** You're All I Need To Get By [668]

The 1990s saw Motown significantly diminish its standing in the UK, as releases dried up and the company's profile generally shrank. In 1991 the blue label was scrapped for standard releases, replaced by the contemporary method of stamping the details directly onto the vinyl with a sort of paint, dispensing with paper labels completely.

Interestingly though, the old TMG system was re-introduced in 1991. When initially abandoned in 1985, it had left off at TMG 1390, and the new series commenced at TMG 1401, allocated to 18-year-old Shanice's Motown debut single, "I Love Your Smile", which climbed to number 2 in the UK. The new TMG series continued until the mid-1990s, hosting several singles for Motown's boy-band Boyz II Men, including the chart-topping "End Of The Road" (TMG 1411).

Of interest to us are two releases from Tamla Motown's back-catalogue:
**TMG 1418**
**Martha Reeves & The Vandellas:** Dancing In The Street [E54] / I Can't Dance To That Music You're Playing [669] (1993)
*- Issued in a picture sleeve, as a spin-off to a current Citroen advert which featured the A-side*
**TMG 1437**
**Stevie Wonder:** My Cherie Amour [690b] (B-side to his new release, "For Your Love", 1995)
*- Reached number 23 in the UK charts*

---

These are the only two of the 1400 series to contain vintage recordings. (Collectors should be wary of TMG 1405, which is The Temptations performing "Get Ready", but in a completely new version.) The series ran to about four dozen over four years, averaging a modest one single per month. It is perhaps significant that during this time, the biggest hit from Motown's catalogue was the number 2 showing of "My Girl" [E67] in early-1992, but it was not a Motown or Tamla Motown edition: the recording was licensed to Epic, and released on their label as a spin-off to a film of the same name. Such farming-out would have been unthinkable in the 1960s!

All-in, the blue label accounts for 24 7-inch and 36 12-inch singles with former Tamla Motown titles included.

# RARE EARTH, MO-WEST AND GAIEE

With Motown's UK releases always channelled onto a single label at any given time, the comings and goings of the various American imprints had little interest for the London office. Everything would invariably come out on Tamla Motown, or, prior to its creation, the UK outlets detailed in Chapter 1, and the UK arm made no attempt to create a parallel cluster of labels. Thus, when America launched first Rare Earth (1969) and then Mo-West (1971), recordings were shipped to London and issued on Tamla Motown as usual, [742]; [763]; [799]; [801] and [828] appearing in the main sequence.

However, it became apparent that both Rare Earth and Mo-West offered some form of viable alternative to mainstream Motown product, the former specialising loosely in rock-style material, the latter in West Coast product, mainly recorded by comparatively new signings. While the allocation of specific labels to specific styles was by no means a new strategy, other American imprints including the specialist Divinity (gospel), Workshop (jazz), Mel-o-dy (country), Black Forum (politics) etc., these two new imprints offered potentially commercial outlets in the pop-rock mainstream. And so in due course, Motown-UK elected to follow the American lead and initiated parallel labels for the UK, distributed through EMI, the idea being for the British equivalents to simply pass on American material directly. However it so happened that both US labels were wound up shortly after the UK brands got off the ground, forcing a revision in policy. If the UK labels were to survive, they would have to source their own releases and so both began scouting for talent around 1973. Each label recruited a modest number of UK-based acts onto the books, with management of this new enterprise undertaken by experienced Motowner John Marshall, and Trevor Churchill who once managed The Rolling Stones' label.

Although they are largely independent—notwithstanding a handful of recordings which were swapped between offices—the output of these two imprints is of obvious interest to Tamla Motown. It is fair to say that no major talent came the way of Motown as a result of this initiative, but the UK labels did have their own star acts and are worthy of note. Each is looked at below.

# Rare Earth

The UK arm of Rare Earth commenced operations in the autumn of 1970, the first outing a pressing of R. Dean Taylor's "Ain't It A Sad Thing" [786], snatched from Tamla Motown when on the point of release. Early on, the UK label ran in parallel to the US one, eight singles appearing in tandem on both sides of the Atlantic before Berry Gordy lost interest and releases gradually fizzled out. From mid 1972 onwards, the UK outlet began building its own roster, pulling on board several British acts, whose material was never exported back to the States.[1]

The discography has several releases of interest, including, through the US channel, an early single by Meatloaf (in collaboration with female singer Shaun 'Stoney' Murphy) backed with a cover of Smokey Robinson's "The Way You Do The Things You Do" [E38], and several tracks by Rare Earth, one of which is their acclaimed reading of "(I Know) I'm Losing You" [587] produced by

Norman Whitfield. In terms of British talent, Dan The Banjo Man was probably the most notable discovery, the act's hat trick of singles supplementing multi-instrumentalist and front man Phil Cordell's other work for Mo-West (see below). White rock group Slowbone & The Wonder Boys also made their mark with a UK recording of Neil Sedaka's "Happy Birthday Sweet Sixteen". Five other outfits recorded in the UK, including Wolfe, David Alexander, Sonny & The Sovereigns, The Rough Riders and Friendly Persuasion. The label was wound up in 1975.

The full singles listing is as follows:

**RES 101** (Sep 1971)
**R. Dean Taylor**: Ain't It A Sad Thing [786] / Back Street [786b]
*- Has its original TMG number in the run-out groove*
**RES 102** (Sep 1971)
**Rare Earth**: The Seed / I Just Want To Celebrate
**RES 103** (Oct 1971)
**Stoney & Meatloaf**: What You See Is What You Get / The Way You Do The Things You Do
**RES 104** (Jan 1972)
**Rare Earth**: Hey Big Brother / Under God's Light
**RES 105** (Apr 1972)
**Rare Earth**: Born To Wander / Here Comes The Night
**RES 106** (Jul 1972)
**R. Dean Taylor**: Taos New Mexico / Shadow
**RES 107** (Sep 1972)
**XIT**: I Was Raised / End
**RES 108** (Feb 1973)
**Wolfe**: Dancing In The Moonlight / Snarlin' Mama Lion - *A British recording*
**RES 109** (Aug 1973)
**Rare Earth**: Good Time Sally / Love Shines Down
**RES 110** (Aug 1973)
**Dan The Banjo Man**: Dan The Banjo Man / Everything Will Rhyme - *A British recording*
**RES 111** (Jan 1974)
**XIT**: Reservation Of Education / Young Warrior
**RES 112** (Mar 1974)
**David Alexander**: Love, Love, Love / Missy - *A British recording*
**RES 113** (Jun 1974)
**Dan The Banjo Man**: Black Magic / Londonderry - *A British recording*
**RES 114** (May 1974)
**Rare Earth**: (I Know) I'm Losing You / When Joannie Smiles
**RES 115** (May 1974)
**Michael Edward Campbell**: Roxanne (You Sure Got A Fine Design) / Roll It Over
**RES 116** (May 1974)
**Slowbone & The Wonder Boys**: Happy Birthday Sweet Sixteen / Tales Of A Crooked Man - *A British recording*
**RES 117** (Jul 1974)
**Sonny & The Sovereigns**: School Is Out / Warm Jetz - *A British recording*

**RES 118** (Sep 1974)
**The Rough Riders**: Hot California Beach / Do You See Me - *A British recording*
**RES 119** (Oct 1974)
**Slowbone**: Oh Man / Get What You're Given - *A British recording*
**RES 120** (Nov 1974)
**Friendly Persuasion**: Remember (Sha La La) / I'll Always Do The Best I Can - *A British recording*
**RES 121** (Jul 1975)
**Dan The Banjo Man**: Red River Valley / Theme Of Love - *A British recording*

# Mo-West

As with Rare Earth, the UK arm of Mo-West started out with the intent of passing on product from its equivalent American label. Mo-West-UK was launched with a party at Ronnie Scott's Jazz club in Soho, with Thelma Houston in attendance, and it was her "No One's Gonna Be A Fool Forever" which opened the label's catalogue. But by the late summer of 1972, the US label was already winding up, and in the process of transferring its more viable acts onto the main Motown label, the British arm therefore finding itself cut adrift almost from the start. However it eventually managed to issue an impressive 32 singles, two of which were later picked up by Tamla Motown and re-released, MW 3009 appearing as [1002], and MW 3025 as [1030b].

The UK discography includes imported recordings by both The Boones and Bobby Darin, neither of whom featured on Mo-West in America (although they did both have other material issued there on Motown).[2] Notable releases include a re-issue of "What The World Needs Now Is Love" [801] plus covers of "Please Mr. Postman" [E05], "When The Lovelight Starts Shining Thru His Eyes" [E34] and "I Can't Help Myself" [515], plus several recordings by Frankie Valli, both with and without The Four Seasons. (These include the Northern Soul classic "The Night", much later re-pressed on Tamla Motown [L020].)

British talent is more modestly represented, Hetherington, Phil Cordell and Riverhead putting out just over half a dozen singles between them. Phil Cordell was easily the most note-worthy, the ex-Tuesday's Children singer-songwriter reviving a career which had seen him record for both Pye and Mercury in the late-1960s. (Cordell's reading of Neil Sedaka's "Laughter In The Rain" in May 1974 appeared simultaneously with Slowbone & The Wonder Boys' version of the same writer's "Happy Birthday Sweet Sixteen" on Rare Earth.)

The 32 official releases ran until the summer of 1976 although to all intents and purposes the label was wound up almost a year sooner. The full singles discography is as follows:

**PSR 350** (Oct 1972)
**Tommy Vance** [narrator] Introducing Mo-West - *Exists as a promo only*
**MW 3001** (Oct 1972)
**Thelma Houston**: No One's Gonna Be A Fool Forever / What If

---

**MW 3002** (Oct 1972)
**Frankie Valli & The Four Seasons:** The Night / When The Morning Comes - *Re-issued in 1975 as MW 3024*
**MW 3003** (Mar 1973)
**Frankie Valli & The Four Seasons:** Walk On, Don't Look Back / Touch The Rainchild
**MW 3004 Thelma Houston:**
Black California / I'm Letting Go - *Single not released*
**MW 3005** (Oct 1973) **Thelma Houston:**
Piano Man / I'm Just A Part Of Yesterday
**MW 3006** (Jun 1973) **Syreeta:**
To Know You Is To Love You / Happiness
**MW 3007** (Jul 1973) **Hetherington:**
Teenage Love Song / That Girl's Alright - *A British recording*
**MW 3008** (Jul 1973) **Phil Cordell:**
Close To You / Londonderry - *A British recording*
**MW 3009** (Sep 1973) **The Sisters Love:**
I'm Learning To Trust My Man / Try It, You'll Like It - *Later re-issued on Tamla Motown [1002]*
**MW 3010** (Sep 1973) **The Devastating Affair:**
That's How It Was Right From The Start / It's So Sad
**MW 3011** (Sep 1973) **Phil Cordell:**
Roadie For The Band / Twistin' And Jivin' - *A British recording*
**MW 3012** (Nov 1973) **The Rockits:**
Livin' Without You / Love My Love
**MW 3013** (Dec 1973) **Tom Clay:**
What The World Needs Now Is Love—Abraham, Martin And John / The Victors - *Re-issue of 1972 Tamla Motown single [801]*
**MW 3014** (Apr 1974) **Bobby Darin:**
Blue Monday / Moritat (Mack The Knife)
**MW 3015** (May 1974) **Phil Cordell:**
Laughter In The Rain / If I Don't Get All The Luck - *A British recording*
**MW 3016** (Jul 1974) **The Rockits:**
I'm losing You / Gimme True Love
**MW 3017 Leo Bendix:**
Holdin' On You / Don't Take Your Love From A Clown - *Single not released*
**MW 3018** (Aug 1974) **Riverhead:**
I Can't Let Maggie Go / This Time Around - *A British recording*
**MW 3019** (Aug 1974) **Reuben Howell:**
Rings / I Believe (When I Fall In Love It Will Be Forever)
**MW 3020** (Sep 1974) **Severin Browne:**
Love Song / Snow Flakes
**MW 3021** (Sep 1974) **Phil Cordell:**
Cool Clear Water / Everywhere I Go - *A British recording*
**MW 3022** (Nov 1974) **Boone Family:**
Please Mr. Postman / Friends
**MW 3023** (Mar 1975) **Severin Browne:**
Romance / The Sweet Sound Of Your Song

**MW 3024** (Mar 1975) **Frankie Valli & The Four Seasons**:
The Night / When The Morning Comes - *Re-issue of MW 3002. This new edition polled number 7 on the UK singles chart. Later re-issued again on Tamla Motown [L020]*
**MW 3025** (Apr 1975) **The Boones**:
When The Lovelight Starts Shinning Thru' His Eyes / Friends - *The A-side was released on Tamla Motown in 1976 as [1030b]*
**MW 3026 Phil Cordell**:
Chevy Van / Strange Things - *A British recording. Single not released*
**MW 3027** (May 1975) **T G Sheppard**:
Trying To Beat The Morning Home / I'll Be Satisfied
**MW 3028** (Jun 1975) **Frankie Valli & The Four Seasons**:
Touch The Rainchild / Poor Fool
**MW 3029** (Jul 1975) **The Allens**:
High Tide / California Music
**MW 3030** (Aug 1975) **Frankie Valli**:
And I Will Love You / Sun Country
**MW 3031** (Oct 1975) **T G Sheppard**:
Another Woman / I Can't Help Myself
**MW 3032** (Oct 1975) **Jud Strunk**:
The Biggest Parakeets In Town / I Wasn't Wrong About You
**MW 3033** (Mar 1976) **T G Sheppard**:
Motels And Memories / Pigskin Charade
**MW 3034** (Jun 1976) **Frankie Valli**:
Life And Breath / Thank You
**MW 3035** (Jul 1976) **T G Sheppard**:
Solitary Man / Pigskin Charade

# Gaiee

Note should also be made of the very small Gaiee label, which was set up in New York in 1975 and released a lone single by Valentino with an overtly gay theme. Motown acquired distribution rights but possibly fearing controversy, utilised the Gaiee imprint rather than release it under their own banner. A UK counterpart label was also especially created for this one-off.

**GAE 101** (Jun 1975) **Valentino**:
I Was Born This Way / Liberation

These three labels were the only ones to run in parallel with Tamla Motown. After 1976 however Motown-UK became the primary outlet, and it so happened that a number of other smaller labels came and went from time-to-time in the years which followed. The American Gordy label was at one point introduced to the UK, and Morocco was also set up, both pressed into service intermittently for otherwise standard Motown releases and slotting into the same sequential TMG number system, and not therefore technically 'separate' so much as 'alternative' labels. However three further UK labels were also in use for a spell: Hitsville, to whom T G Sheppard transferred in 1977; MC, who released a brace of 45s in 1978; and Prodigal, Barney Ales' label which

Motown-US had acquired in 1975 along with its former owner. Rare Earth were eventually signed over to Prodigal and other acts to release material on the UK arm include Charlene and Phil Cordell. Between them these three labels put out 14 singles and as many albums in the late-1970s.

[1] The sole exception was Dan The Banjo Man's "Dan The Banjo Man" / "Londonderry", released in America as Motown 1293 in February 1974. The two titles were from separate UK singles.

[2] In the 1970s, Motown took an interest in several prominent figures from the rock and roll era besides Darin. Other notable names to appear include Pat Boone, Little Richard and Frankie Valli. (Duane Eddy has since also had material released via Motown.) Both sides of Darin's Mo-West single were taped live in LA. The US edition appeared on re-issue label Yesteryear, Mo-West no longer functioning there.

# Appendix 4

# INFORMATION FOR COLLECTORS

# PART 1: RECORD LABELS

While this book provides a complete discography of Tamla Motown's singles, it makes little reference to varieties of individual discs in circulation, which show minor differences in the label texts and layouts. This will be of interest to collectors since in some cases 45s were re-pressed and re-distributed some time after first release, with no statement to the effect on the label. Since Tamla Motown labels had a uniform design at any one time, and changes to the master layout occurred over the years, pressings can be dated by navigating the small print. In discussing successive label types, reference numbers for applicable releases constitute the lifespan each, and original pressings should conform to the description. Those which do not are, therefore, later re-pressings.

## EMI label: Type 1

The original EMI labels (Type 1) were in place for almost eight years, but fall into three distinct versions. The master design for Type 1 (see image) has 'MADE IN GT. BRITAIN" in capitals at the top, and 'E.M.I. RECORDS LIMITED' at the bottom, and this is the main distinguishing feature.

**EMI label Type I**

### Type 1, version A: [501] (Mar 1965) to [600] (Mar 1967)

The first version ran continuously from March 1965 March 1967, but thereafter was used only intermittently, until being dropped in early 1968. It conforms to the standard design, but is distinguished from the subsequent version B by the typeface used on the song titles and TMG number. Version A has 'tall, thin' lettering, whereas version B has 'short, fat' (see illustration). Note also that both versions include the text beginning, 'Sold in U.K...' in the central region of the disc.

*Tall, thin lettering*
*Sold in U.K. text*

### Type 1, version B: [601] (Mar 1967) to [703] (Jul 1969)

Introduced with [601], this amendment changed the typeface, but otherwise the label is unaltered. The old style was not phased out entirely, a number of discs after [601] (including [614], [622], [624], [627], [639] and possibly others) still appearing as 'tall, thin', and if a disc exists with both typefaces, these should be assumed the earlier pressings. It is not easy to differentiate the two without direct comparison, but the G in TMG shows the contrasting style quite clearly, being 'closed' in the early version and 'open in the later.

*Short, fat lettering*

*Sold in U.K. text*

**Top: version A typeface; bottom: version B typeface**

Type 1, version C: **[704]** (Jul 1969) to **[837]** (Dec 1972)
The design identified as Type 1, version B continued to be used, but it will be noted that the 'Sold in U.K...' text was discontinued in July 1969. All discs prior to the switch must, for legal reasons, have included it. The absence of such text therefore proves the disc was manufactured after July 1969.

*Short, fat lettering*

*No sold in U.K. text*

*(Collectors should be aware that some copies of [833] and [835] were manufactured in West Germany and have corresponding annotation at the top of the label (which names the country incorrectly as 'Germany'). These were nonetheless UK releases, and were shipped to Great Britain for sale.)*

# EMI label: Type 2

The general design template was overhauled in December 1972, and the layout of the perimeter text changed considerably. The lettering now ran in a continuous loop from '8 o'clock' over to '4 o'clock'. In addition, the words 'MADE IN GT BRITAIN' appear in small capitals at the very bottom.

**EMI label Type 2**

Type 2, version A: **[838]** (Dec 1972) to **[876]** (Oct 1973)

---

When the new text was introduced, the wording commenced 'THE GRAMOPHONE CO LTD', and this is the principal way to identify version A.

*Text begins 'THE GRAMOPHONE CO LTD…'*

*Labels have 'MADE IN GT BRITAIN' at the very bottom.*

**EMI label: Type 2, version A (detail)**

Type 2, version B: **[877]** (Oct 1973) to **[1040]** (Dec 1976, continued to 1980 (?)) In October 1973 the text was amended so that it now begins, 'EMI RECORDS LTD'. These remained in use through to the end of the label's main run, but for a brief spell in 1975 (see version C below).

*Text begins, 'EMI RECORDS LTD…'*

*Labels have 'MADE IN GT BRITAIN' at the very bottom.*

*([1010] used different fonts to the standard label, but the perimeter text was normal for its time.)*

**EMI label: Type 2, version B (detail)**

Type 2, version C: **[1001]** (Sep 1975) to **[1005]** (?) (Oct 1975) In use for just a brief spell, following the distribution confusions of 1975, these labels were essentially unchanged but omitted mention of EMI at the start of the wording. There are probably less than half-a-dozen in existence. The text commences, 'ALL RIGHTS OF THE MANUFACTURER'.

*Text begins, 'ALL RIGHTS OF THE MANUFACTURER'*

*Labels have 'MADE IN GT BRITAIN' at the very bottom.*

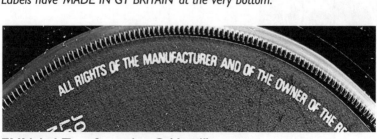

**EMI label: Type 2, version C (detail)**

Type 2, later versions: Version 2 continued to be used until around 1980 when the perimeter text was changed again, and 'MADE IN GT BRITAIN' was moved from the bottom of label (which was therefore now devoid of text completely) and tagged onto the end of the main perimeter text.

## RCA Labels:
In 1981 RCA replaced EMI as distributor of Tamla Motown, causing a temporary suspension of normal releases. From here-on perimeter texts mention RCA rather than EMI in the small print. They can be identified at-a-glance by the fact that the text runs in a continuous circle around the label's edge. RCA releases tended to be sporadic and there is no continuity in typeface, which varies quite considerably, the whole template being changed yet again when the TMG series was scrapped.

**Sample RCA label re-issue**

# PART 2: RECORD SLEEVES
Tamla Motown sleeves have never been fully researched and the following analysis is based on existing knowledge of EMI's manufacturing policy, and a certain degree of logical deduction. Tamla Motown generally used standardised sleeves which changed over time. Of necessity, the following acts as a guideline only and the dates given are approximate. However all generic Tamla Motown sleeves which do not conform to these types should be considered later copies, manufactured for record collectors.

### First-phase sleeves: Orange print
The first Tamla Motown sleeves were printed in bright orange, and all genuine ones are cut with a wavy top-edge. The sleeves were manufactured by gluing the flaps from the front panel over the outside of the back panel. The front of the sleeve shows a large-size Tamla Motown logo which almost touches the central hole. Orange sleeves with straight-cut tops are later reproductions, as are wavy-top ones with the flaps glued inside the back panel, and orange sleeves with LP records advertised on the rear.

**Front view of orange sleeve**

### Orange sleeve Type 1: Mar 1965

Following EMI's general design, the backs of these original sleeves carry advertisements for EMI products. The first batch advertised record tokens top-left, and the values shown include 6/-.

*Large Tamla Motown logo on front*
*Cut with wavy tops*
*Flaps folded outside the back panel along both sides*
*EMI record tokens show values "6/- to 50/-"*

**Back of orange sleeve Type 1**

### Orange sleeve Type 2: Jul 1967

The second batch of orange sleeves had the prices in the advert on the back altered to reflect the scrapping of 6/- record tokens, to now read "7/3 to 50/-".

*Large Tamla Motown logo on front*
*Cut with wavy tops*
*Flaps folded outside the back panel along both sides*
*EMI record tokens show values "7/3 to 50/-"*

Back of orange sleeve Type 2 (detail)

**Orange sleeve Type 3: Late 1967**

Another variety of orange sleeve came into use, as the manufacturing method changed. Whereas previously the sleeves had the front panel glued over the back panel along either side edge, now they were glued along the bottom and right-hand edge. Hand-in-hand with this was an enlargement in the print used on the back.

*Large Tamla Motown logo on front*
*Cut with wavy tops*
*Flaps folded outside the back panel along bottom and one side*
*EMI record tokens show values "7/3 to 50/-"*
*Typeface is enlarged on back*

Read the
**RECORD
MAIL**

A lively illustrated
Monthly Review of
the latest 'POPS'.
Full of pictures and
information about
your favourite artists.

Read the
**RECORD
MAIL**

A lively illus-
trated Monthly
Review of the
latest 'POPS'.
Full of pictures
and information
about your fav-
ourite artists.

**Larger lettering on orange sleeve Type 3 (right)**

**Full-colour sleeve: Dec 1967 (?)**

EMI printed three different full-colour sleeves in 1967, each showing a selection of concurrent EMI albums. The first two were most likely not used to house Tamla Motown singles, although the second, from around May, features amongst its images three Tamla Motown LPs on the front and a further three on the back, the most recent of which is Stevie Wonder's Down To Earth, released in April. Towards the end of 1967, Tamla Motown singles appeared in a third edition of the sleeve, which exclusively advertised Tamla Motown albums, 12 on the front and six on the back, with full-colour illustrations. The latest one featured was

---

Reach Out from November 1967, pictured second from top on the left-hand side of the front. (This also has record tokens cited as ranging from "5/- to 30/-".) It is not known to what extent Tamla Motown singles were actually sold in these sleeves, but clearly that is what they were manufactured for.

**Full-colour sleeve, Dec 1967**

### Second-phase sleeves: Olive-brown print

The olive-brown sleeves were introduced in February 1968 and caused grumbles of disapproval among the label's fans. The first set maintained the wavy-top design but it, and all subsequent editions, had the Tamla Motown logo reduced in size. Common opinion erroneously holds that these were introduced in mid-1967 but proof of their vintage can be found in the Tamla Motown LP adverts on the back. As time went on, the featured album covers would be swapped around and dating the sleeves is relatively simple because of this, although each update did not necessarily result in every illustration being replaced. These sleeves were in use for a substantial time and have come to be regarded as the standard company sleeve. As might be expected, there are a good number of reproduction sleeves in circulation, and any which do not agree with the following details are repros.

**Front view of olive-brown sleeve (note smaller badge)**

## Olive sleeve Type 1: Feb 1968

The first olive-brown sleeves maintained the manufacturing standard of the final orange sleeve—wavy tops and flaps glued over the back panel, bottom and right. However now, the backs advertised Tamla Motown LPs and in this earliest version include three titles released in January 1968, (STML 11063, STML 11061 and STML 11058) proving the sleeves were introduced thereafter. A quick way to identify specific types is through the lone LP cover featured bottom-right. This first version shows The Temptations: With A Lot Of Soul.

*Small Tamla Motown logo on front*
*Cut with wavy tops*
*Flaps folded outside the back panel, bottom and right*
*LP featured bottom-right: The Temptations: With A Lot Of Soul*

**Olive sleeve Type 1**

## Olive sleeve Type 2: Oct 1968

These sleeves, and all subsequent originals had straight-cut tops, with a long recess at the back to assist in removing the record. The initial batch which ran for another six months advertised The Temptations: Wish It Would Rain bottom-right.

*Small Tamla Motown logo on front*
*Cut with straight tops*
*Flaps folded outside the back panel, bottom and right*
*LP featured bottom-right: The Temptations: Wish It Would Rain*

**Olive sleeve Type 2**

---

*Tamla Motown - The stories behind the UK singles*

### Olive sleeve Type 3: Mar 1969

From now until the end of the label's normal run, EMI ceased amending the sleeve design. These are therefore by-far the most common, and advertise Edwin Starr: *Soul Master* bottom-right.

*Small Tamla Motown logo on front*
*Cut with straight tops*
*Flaps folded outside the back panel, bottom and right*
*LP featured bottom-right: Edwin Starr: Soul Master*

**Olive sleeve Type 3**

### Later olive sleeves

After Tamla Motown shut up shop in 1976, further singles continued to appear on the label from time-to-time. There are two sleeve types which can be considered genuine (ie not reproductions for collectors). These are of course for specific late issues, and it should be noted that several other sleeves have been used over the years since 1976, including picture sleeves and purple Motown sleeves, sometimes with additional badges and logos. These are not discussed here, but for the record, the official olive Tamla Motown sleeves are as follows:

### Olive sleeve Type 4: Post-1976 EMI sleeve:

Used in the late-1970s until the termination of EMI's distribution deal in 1981, these crop up for example on some of the singles in the commemorative set marking the label's 20th anniversary (October 1980). EMI are mentioned in the small print at the bottom, and it will be apparent that the records pictured have all been swapped. The Motown Gold compilation of 1975 can be seen top left.

*Small Tamla Motown logo on front*
*Cut with straight tops*
*Flaps folded outside the back panel, bottom and right*
*LP featured top-left: Motown Gold*

**Olive sleeve Type 4**

## Olive sleeve Type 5: RCA edition

With RCA having taken over the manufacture of Tamla Motown singles in late-1981, they also printed up their own Tamla Motown sleeves, and the LPs advertised were changed to illustrate a massive album re-issue campaign by the company. This sleeve is identified by the mention of RCA in the small print on the back, and the record cover top-left, The Supremes Sing Motown.

*Small Tamla Motown logo on front*

*Cut with straight tops*

*Flaps folded outside the back panel, bottom and right*

*RCA noted in small print*

*LP featured top-left: The Supremes Sing Motown*

**Olive sleeve Type 5**

As noted, there are many varieties of reproductions, some with wavy tops which should be straight-cut, some with the flaps glued inside the back cover, and some with the wrong details on the back. Those interested in housing their collection in the appropriate original sleeves should be highly diligent in identifying reproductions.

Special re-issue sets of singles generally had sleeves especially designed for the series in question (see Chapter 6). So far as the purple 'Motown' sleeves are concerned, these were introduced by EMI and varieties exist with EMI and RCA credits. Although specific usage has not been ascertained, some post-1976 Tamla Motown singles appeared in these sleeves, as well as the standard blue label releases.

No Tamla Motown singles appearing before the end of 1976 came housed in picture covers. However some had custom-designed sleeves for demo copies, including: "The Onion Song" [715]; "A B C" [738]; "Lookin' Through The Windows" [833]; "Love Theme From 'Lady Sings The Blues'" [848]; "Good Morning Heartache" [849]; "Skywriter" [865]; "Memories" [948]; "Theme From Mahogany" [1010]. From 1976 onwards however, picture sleeves were used on numerous standard and promotional editions.

# REFERENCES

Innumerable sources were consulted including record and CD sleeve notes, newspaper articles, interviews and websites. With this work several years in the making, it is not practical nor possible to list everything ever consulted, but thanks are accorded to everyone who has worked on researching and documenting Motown and the contemporary musical scene. The amount of literature pertaining to Motown is sizeable and new titles continue to appear with regularity. The following were cited in this book and used as primary sources of information on Motown's history.

The documentation of Motown as an entire musical entity has been attempted several times. The first serious study was by David Morse, whose concise volume remains one of the more penetrating, albeit limited in time due to its early publication. Peter Benjaminson offered an entertaining if generalised account several years later, followed by Don Waller's similarly pleasant text from 1985. That same year, Nelson George's *Where Did Our Love Go?* appeared, definitive for its day and setting a journalistic high for Motown. (It has been updated and re-printed in recent years.)

Three years later, a more epic narrative on the company arrived in the shape of Sharon Davis' *Motown: The History*, the most comprehensive documentation on Motown ever, detailing the label through to the late-1980s. Together with the simultaneous publication of David Bianco's volume, staggering in scope and detail, reader and researcher are afforded a comprehensive amount of factual information, if little by way of musical commentary. More recently, the anthology of articles edited by Kingsley Abbott has brought together a substantial number of pre-published pieces which map Motown's story, with a welcome (and rare) slant on the UK scene.

## BOOKS

Abbott, Kingsley (Ed.) (2001) *Calling Out Around The World: A Motown Reader* Helter Skelter, London

Ashford, Jack (2003) *Motown – The View From The Bottom* Bank House Books, New Romney

Bartlette, Reginald J (1991) *Off The Record: Motown By Master Number, 1959 – 1989 Volume 1: Singles* Popular Culture Ink, Michigan, USA

Benjaminson, Peter (1979) *The Story Of Motown* Evergreen, New York, USA

Bianco, David (1988) *Heat Wave: The Motown Fact Book* Popular Culture Ink, Michigan, USA

Brown, Ashley and Heatley, Michael (Eds.) (1985) *The Motown Story* Orbis, London

Coffey, Dennis (2002) *Guitars, Bars And Motown Superstars* Bee Cool Publishing, London

Dahl, Bill (2001) *Motown: The Golden Years* Krause Publications, Iola WI, USA

David, Sharon (1984) *Marvin Gaye* Proteus, London

Davis, Sharon (1988) *Motown: The History* Guinness, Middlesex

Davis, Sharon (2000) *Diana Ross: A Legend In Focus* Mainstream, London

Davis, Sharon (2006a) *Rhythms Of Wonder [2nd Edition]* Robson, London

Davis, Sharon (2006b) *Chinwaggin'* Bank House Books, New Romney

Dineen, Catherine (1993) *Michael Jackson In His Own Words* Omnibus, London

Edmonds, Ben (2001) *What's Going On?: Marvin Gaye And The Last Days Of The Motown Sound* Mojo Books, Edinburgh

Gambaccini, Paul *et al* (1990) *The Guinness Book Of British Hit Albums, [4th Edition]* Guinness, Middlesex

George, Nelson (1985) *Where Did Our Love Go?: The Rise And Fall Of The Motown Sound* Omnibus, London

Gordy, Berry (1984) *To Be Loved: The Music, The Magic, The Memories Of Motown* Headline, London

Gregory, Hugh (1991) *Soul Music A–Z* Blandford, London

Haskins, James with Benson, Kathleen (1979) *The Stevie Wonder Scrapbook* Cassell, London

Hirshey, Gerri (1984) *Nowhere To Run: The Story Of Soul Music* Pan, London

Howes, Paul (2001) *The Complete Dusty Springfield* Reynolds & Hearn, London

Jackson, Michael (1988) *Moon Walk* William Heinemann, London

Knight, Gladys (1977) *Between Each Line Of Pain And Glory: My Life Story* Hyperion, New York

Lodder, Steve (2005) *Stevie Wonder: A Musical Guide To The Classic Albums* Backbeat Books, London

Logan, Nick and Woffinden, Bob (1977) *The NME Book Of Rock 2* Star Books, London

MacDonald, Ian (1994) *Revolution In The Head: The Beatles' Records And The Sixties [Revised Edition]* Pimlico, London

MacDonald, Ian (2003) *The People's Music* Pimlico, London

Morse, David (1971) *Motown* November Books, London

Partridge, Marianne (Ed.) (1990) *The Motown Album: The Sound Of Young America – Three Decades Of Magic* Virgin Books, London

Posner, Gerald (2002) *Motown: Music, Money, Sex And Power [2nd Ed.]* Random House, New York, USA

Reeves, Martha (1994) *Dancing In The Street: Confessions of a Motown Diva* Hyperion, New York

Ritz, David (1985) *Divided Soul: The Life Of Marvin Gaye [2nd Edition]* Grafton, London

Roberts, David (Ed.) (2000) *British Hit Singles [13th Edition]* Guinness, London

Robinson, Smokey (1989) *Smokey: Inside My Life* Headline, London

Ross, Diana (1993) *Secrets Of A Sparrow: Memoirs* Headline, London

Rubin, Dave (2000) *Motown Bass Signature Licks*, Hal Leonard, Milwaukee, USA

Slutsky, Allen [as Dr. Licks] (1989) *Standing In The Shadows Of Motown: The Life And Music Of Legendary Bassist James Jamerson* Hal Leonard, Milwaukee, USA

Strong, Martin C. (1998) *The Great Rock Discography [4th Edition]* Canongate, Edinburgh

Taraborrelli, J. Randy (1986) *Motown: Hot Wax, City Cool And Solid Gold* Doubleday & Co., New York, USA

Taraborrelli, J. Randy (1989) *Call Her Miss Ross: The Unauthorized Biography Of Diana Ross* Birch Lane Press, New York, USA

Taraborrelli, J. Randy (1994) *Michael Jackson: The Magic And The Madness [Revised Edition]* Headline, London

Taraborrelli, J. Randy (2007) *Diana Ross: An Unauthorized Biography* Sidgwick & Jackson, London

Taylor, Harold Keith (2003) *The Motown Music Machine* Jadmeg, USA

Taylor, Rick (1985) *Stevie Wonder: The Illustrated Disco/Biography* Omnibus, London

Terrana, Ralph (2006) *The Road Through Motown* Bank House Books, New Romney

Turner, Steve (1998) *Trouble Man: The Life And Death Of Marvin Gaye* Michael Joseph, London

Waller, Don (1985) *The Motown Story* Charles Scribner's Sons, New York, USA

Whitburn, Joel (1983) *The Billboard Book Of US Top 40 Hits* Guinness, Middlesex

Whitburn, Joel (1987) *The Billboard Book Of USA Top 40 Albums* Guinness, Middlesex

Whitburn, Joel (2006) *The Billboard Book Of Top 40 R & B And Hip-Hop Hits* Billboard Books, New York, USA

Whithall, Susan (1998) *Women Of Motown: An Oral History* Avon Books, New York, USA

Williams, Otis (1988) *Temptations* Simon & Schuster, New York, USA

Wilson, Mary (1986) *Dreamgirl: My Life As A Supreme* Sidgwick & Jackson, London

Wilson, Mary (1990) *Supreme Faith: Someday We'll Be Together [2nd edition]* Cooper Square Press, New York, USA

Winstanley, Russ & Nowell, David (1996) *Soul Survivors: The Wigan Casino Story* Robson, London

## ARTICLES

"Blue Eyed Soul Sister' [interview with Chris Clark], by Lois Wilson, *Record Collector no. 313, Aug 2005*

"Diana Ross', by David Brown, *Record Collector no. 172, Dec 1993*

"Final Frontier', by Ben Edmonds, *Mojo, Aug 2003*

"Go Weston' [interview with Kim Weston], by Lois Wilson, *Record Collector no. 319, Jan 2006*

"Interview With The Ghost Of Studio A', by Dr. Licks, *Bass Player, Spring 1990*

"Motown Albums', by Richard Gardener and John Reed, *Record Collector no. 189, May 1995*

"Pure Smokey', by Peter Doggett, *Record Collector no. 266, Oct 2001*

"Rock Lives' [interview with Michael Jackson, 1977], by Timothy White, reprinted in *The Q Magazine/Omnibus Press Rock 'n' Roll Reader*, Issued free with *Q Magazine issue 91, March 1994*

"Standing In The Shadows Of Motown', by Lois Wilson, *Record Collector no. 308, Mar 2005*

"Tamla Motown British EPs', by David Sallis, *Record Collector no. 174, Feb 1994*

"Tamla Motown: UK Singles of the 60s', by Terry Wilson/Kingsley Abbott, *Record Collector no. 267, Nov 2001*

"The Northern Soul Story', by Stuart Maconie, *Q Magazine, Feb 1997*

* A major series of articles published by *Record Collector* in 1995 was also consulted. These are reproduced in Abbott, 2001 (see above).

**PRINCIPAL INTERNET SOURCES** (Web addresses correct at the time of publication)

Don't Forget The Motor City (Catalogue of Motown's Detroit recordings with substantive data): dftmc.info

Soulful Detroit (Includes forum and information centre of unparalleled scope and reliability): soulfuldetroit.com

Both Sides Now (Comprehensive US albums discography with track listings): bsnpubs.com/motown/motownstory.html

## ALSO AVAILABLE FROM CHERRY RED

**Indie Hits
1980-1989**

The Complete UK
Independent Chart
(Singles And
Albums)

**Compiled By
Barry Lazell**

Paper covers,
314 pages,
£14.99 in UK

**Cor Baby, That's
Really Me!**

(The New
Millennium
Hardback Edition)

**John Otway**

Hardback,
192 pages and 16
pages of
photographs
£11.99 in UK

**All The
Young Dudes,
Mott the Hoople
and Ian Hunter
The Biography**

**Campbell Devine**

Paper covers,
448 pages and 16
pages of
photographs
£14.99 in UK

**Embryo - A Pink
Floyd Chronology
1966-1971**

**Nick Hodges and
Ian Priston**

Paper covers,
302 pages and
photographs
throughout
£14.99 in UK

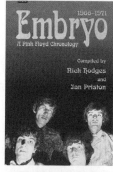

**Johnny Thunders
In Cold Blood**

**Nina Antonia**

Paper covers,
270 pages and
photographs
throughout
£14.99 in UK

**Songs In The
Key Of Z**

**The Curious
Universe of
Outsider music
Irwin Chusid**

Paper covers,
311 pages, fully
illustrated
£11.99 in UK

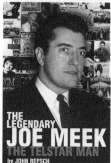

**The Legendary
Joe Meek
The Telstar Man**

**John Repsch**

Paper covers,
350 pages plus
photographs,
£14.99 in UK

**Random Precision
Recording the
Music of Syd
Barrett 1965-1974**

**David Parker**

Paper covers,
320 pages and
photographs
throughout
£14.99 in UK

www.cherryred.co.uk

## ALSO AVAILABLE FROM CHERRY RED

**Those Were The Days**

**Stefan Granados**

An Unofficial History of the Beatles' Apple Organization 1967-2002

Paper covers, 300 pages including photographs
£14.99 in UK

**The Rolling Stones: Complete Recording Sessions 1962-2002**

**Martin Elliott**

Paper covers, 576 pages plus 16 pages of photographs
£14.99 in UK

**Goodnight Jim Bob – On The Road With Carter The Unstoppable Sex Machine**

**Jim Bob**

Paper covers, 228 pages plus 16 pages of photographs
£12.99 in UK

**Our Music Is Red - With Purple Flashes: The Story Of The Creation**

**Sean Egan**

Paper covers, 378 pages plus 8 pages of photographs
£14.99 in UK

**Bittersweet: The Clifford T Ward Story**

**David Cartwright**

Paper covers, 352 pages plus 8 pages of photographs
£14.99 in UK

**The Secret Life of a Teenage Punk Rocker: The Andy Blade Chronicles**

**Andy Blade**

Paper covers, 224 pages and photographs throughout.
£12.99 in UK

**Burning Britain**

**Ian Glasper**

Paper covers, 410 pages and photographs throughout
£14.99 in UK

**Truth... Rod Stewart, Ron Wood And The Jeff Beck Group**

**Dave Thompson**

Paper covers, 208 pages plus four pages of photographs.
£14.99 in UK

www.cherryred.co.uk

## ALSO AVAILABLE FROM CHERRY RED

**Rockdetector
A-Z of THRASH
METAL**

**Garry Sharpe-Young**

Paper covers
460 pages
£14.99 in UK

ISBN 1-901447-09-X

**Rockdetector
A-Z of DOOM,
GOTHIC &
STONER METAL**

**Garry Sharpe-Young**

Paper covers
455 pages
£14.99 in UK

ISBN 1-901447-14-6

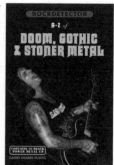

**Rockdetector
A-Z of '80s ROCK**

**Garry Sharpe-
Young
& Dave Reynolds**

Paper covers
752 pages,
£17.99 in UK

ISBN 1-901447-21-9

**Rockdetector
OZZY OSBOURNE
THE STORY OF
THE OZZY
OSBOURNE BAND
(AN UNOFFICIAL
PUBLICATION)**

**Garry Sharpe-Young**

Paper covers
368 pages
£14.99 in UK

ISBN 1-901447-08-1

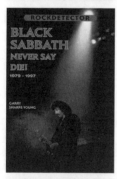

**Rockdetector
BLACK SABBATH
NEVER SAY DIE
1979-1997**

**Garry Sharpe-
Young**

Paper covers
448 pages
£14.99 in UK

ISBN 1-901447-16-2

**Rockdetector
A-Z of BLACK
METAL**

**Garry Sharpe-Young**

Paper covers
416 pages
£14.99 in UK

ISBN 1-901447-30-8

**Rockdetector
A-Z of DEATH
METAL**

**Garry Sharpe-
Young**

Paper covers
416 pages
£14.99 in UK

ISBN 1-901447-35-9

**Rockdetector
A-Z of POWER
METAL**

**Garry Sharpe-Young**

Paper covers
512 pages
£14.99 in UK

ISBN 1-901447-13-8

www.cherryred.co.uk

# ALL THE YOUNG DUDES

## Mott The Hoople
## & Ian Hunter

*Campbell Devine*

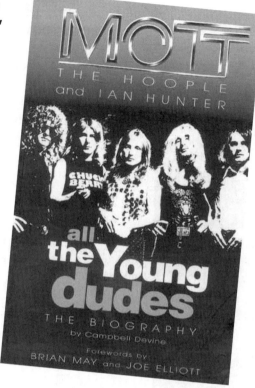

This, the official biography of Mott The Hoople, traces their formation and their inevitable rise to international stardom. Author Campbell Devine has successfully collaborated with Ian Hunter and members of 'Mott' to create a biography devoid of borrowed information and re- cycled press clippings but instead new, sensational and humorous inside stories, controversial quotes and an array of previously unpublished views from the band. With first hand input from members Hunter, Griffin, Watts, Allen and Ralphs, this book gives the complete insight into the legend of Mott The Hoople. Queen, The Clash, Kiss, Def Leppard, Primal Scream and Oasis have all cited Mott The Hoople as a major influence.

Queen's Brian May and Def Leppard's Joe Elliott have provided their own foreword to pay a long overdue tribute to a band who were simply one of rock's most treasured.

Already described as the 'definitive tome' on their careers, this unique and fascinating biography is by far the most scrupulously researched written work ever produced on Mott The Hoople. This book is welcomed by both the committed and casual rock reader as well as the ageing rocker and of course all the young dudes.

Relaunched in 2009 to coincide with the band's re-formation tour after more than 30 years.

# UPCOMING TITLES FROM CHERRY RED BOOKS:

**Number One Songs In Heaven**
The Sparks Story
*Dave Thompson*

**You're Wondering Now**
The Specials From Conception To Reunion
*Paul Williams*

**Death To Trad Rock!**
Celebrating the Discord - The Late Eighties UK Underground
*John Robb*

**Trapped In A Scene**
UK HardCore 1985-89
*Ian Glasper*

**The Doc's Devils Manchester United 1972-1977**
*Sean Egan*

**Independence Days**
The History Of UK Independent Record Labels
*Alex Ogg*

**101 Greatest Progressive Rock Albums**
*Mark Powell*

# CHERRY RED BOOKS

We are always looking for interesting books to publish.
They can be either new manuscripts or re-issues of
deleted books.
If you have any good ideas then please
get in touch with us.


**CHERRY RED BOOKS**
A division of Cherry Red Records Ltd.
Unit 3a,
Long Island House,
Warple Way,
London W3 0RG.

E-mail: iain@cherryred.co.uk
Web: www.cherryred.co.uk